Responsa 1991-2000:

The Committee on Jewish Law and Standards of the Conservative Movement

RESPONSA

1991-2000

The Committee on Jewish Law and Standards
of the Conservative Movement

Edited by Kassel Abelson and David J. Fine

 The Rabbinical Assembly · כנסת הרבנים
New York · 2002 · תשס"ב

Copyright © 2002 by The Rabbinical Assembly

All rights reserved

ISBN 0-916219-19-4 Hardcover

Printed in the United States of America

TABLE OF CONTENTS

Preface and Acknowledgments by Kassel Abelson and David J. Fine ix
Abbreviations xiii

RESPONSA RELATING TO ORAH HAYYIM   אורח חיים

הלכות ציצית / Tzitzit 3
   May Women Tie Tzitzit Knots? by Shoshana Gelfand 3

הלכות נשיאת כפיים / The Priestly Blessing 9
   Women Raise Your Hands by Mayer Rabinowitz 9
   Should N'siat Kapayim Include B'not Kohanim? by Stanley Bramnick
      and Judah Kogen 13

הלכות קריאת ספר תורה / Torah Reading 16
   May a Non-Kohen Be Called First to the Torah? by Herbert J. Mandl 16
   Joint Aliyot by Avram Israel Reisner 21
   Aliyot for Couples by Kassel Abelson 36
   Hazak, Hazak v'Nithazak by Nechama D. Goldberg 43

הלכות תפלות מנחה וערבית / Minhah and Maariv 50
   Late Minhah and Early Maariv by Gerald Skolnik 50

הלכות שבת / Shabbat 53
   Leasing for Shabbat by Joel Roth and Norman M. Krivosha 53
   *For Moshe It's Shabbat; For Chaim It's Shabbat; But For Chris It's Not
      Shabbat: An Analysis of Judge Krivosha's "Religious Lease" and an
      Alternate Proposal* by Ben Zion Bergman 58
   Jewish Businesses Open on Shabbat and Yom Tov: A Concurring Opinion
      by Elliot N. Dorff 64

הלכות פסח / Passover 71
   When Pesah Begins on Saturday Night by Kassel Abelson 71
   Canned Tuna Fish on Pesah by Mayer Rabinowitz 75
   Can Utensils Lined with Silverstone be Kashered? by Kassel Abelson 78

הלכות ראש השנה / **Rosh HaShanah** 81
   Omission of the Silent Amidah by Kassel Abelson 81

RESPONSA RELATING TO YOREH DE'AH   יורה דעה

הלכות שחיטה / **Kosher Slaughter** 91
   Is a K Kosher? by Kassel Abelson 91
   Shackling and Hoisting by Elliot N. Dorff and Joel Roth 93

הלכות בשר בחלב / **Meat and Milk** 98
   The Kashrut of Microbial Enzymes by Kassel Abelson 98
   Curiouser and Curiouser: The Kashrut of Genetically Engineered Foodstuffs
      by Avram Israel Reisner 101

הלכות מאכלי עובדי כוכבים / **Foreign Foods** 112
   On Mixing Fish and Meat by Paul Plotkin 112

הלכות חוקות עובדי כוכבים וכישוף / **Idolatry and Sorcery** 115
   Tattooing and Body Piercing by Alan B. Lucas 115

הלכות מילה / **Circumcision** 121
   Anesthesia and Brit Milah by Vernon H. Kurtz 121
   Induction Leading to Birth of a Baby on Shabbat and Brit Milah
      by Vernon H. Kurtz 125

הלכות גרים / **Conversion** 127
   The Case of the Unconverted Spouse by Ben Zion Bergman 127
   Conversion to Judaism Without Circumcision Due to Medical Complications
      by Herbert J. Mandl 132
   Maternal Identity and the Religious Status of Children Born to a Surrogate
      Mother by Aaron L. Mackler 137
   The Return of Second Generation Apostates by Gerald Zelizer 146

הלכות ספר תורה / **The Torah Scroll** 151
   Official Use of "God" by Kassel Abelson 151
   Display of a Pasul Torah in a Museum Case by Kassel Abelson 153

הלכות פדיון בכור / **Pidyon HaBen** 163
   Should There Be a Special Ceremony in Recognition of a First-Born Female?
      by Gerald Skolnik 163
   Delay of Pidyon HaBen by Vernon H. Kurtz 166
   Pidyon HaBen and Caesarean Sections by Howard Handler 171

הלכות ביקור חולים ורפואה / **Visiting the Sick and Medicine** 175
   Hesed or Hiuv: The Obligation to Preserve Life and the Question of
      Post-Mortem Organ Donations by Joseph H. Prouser 175
   Organ and Tissue Donation Card by Joseph H. Prouser 191
   Organ Donation: Parts I-IV by Joel Roth 194
   Responsibilities for the Provision of Health Care by Elliot N. Dorff
      and Aaron L. Mackler 319

Mental Retardation, Group Homes and the Rabbi by James S. Rosen 337
Peri- and Neo-Natology: The Matter of Limiting Treatment
    by Avram Israel Reisner 347

הלכות קריעה / Responding to a Death 357
Response to Miscarriage by Debra Reed Blank 357
Response to Miscarriage: A Dissent by Amy Eilberg 364
Jewish Ritual Practice Following a Stillbirth by Stephanie Dickstein 367
What's in a Name? A Concurrence and Dissent to the Responsum of Rabbi
    Dickstein on Ritual Practice Following a Stillbirth by Ben Zion Bergman ...377

הלכות אבילות / Mourning 379
Assisted Suicide by Elliot N. Dorff 379
Statement on Assisted Suicide by The Committee 398
Burial of Jews Practicing Christianity by Paul Plotkin 400
Bury Him, Yes, Bury Him: A Concurring Opinion to Paul Plotkin's "Burial
    of Jews Practicing Christianity" by Myron S. Geller 403
I Shall Sprinkle Pure Water Upon You and You Shall Be Purified: A Question
    of Taharah by Ben Zion Bergman 408
Exhuming the Dead by Myron S. Geller 413
A Matter of Grave Concern: A Question of Mixed Burial
    by Ben Zion Bergman 418
Peaceful Paths: Burial of Non-Jews in a Jewish Cemetery Following a
    Common Disaster by Myron S. Geller 426
Converts Mourning the Death of Close Relatives by Joel E. Rembaum 431
Jewish Ritual Practice Following the Death of an Infant Who Lives Less Than
    Thirty-One Days by Stephanie Dickstein 439
Kim Li: A Dissenting Concurrence by Avram Israel Reisner 450
Welcoming Mourners on Shabbat by Baruch Frydman-Kohl 452

RESPONSA RELATING TO EVEN HaEZER   אבן העזר

הלכות פריה ורביה / Marriage and Fertility 461
Artificial Insemination, Egg Donation and Adoption by Elliot N. Dorff 461
In Vitro Fertilization by Aaron L. Mackler 510
On the Use of Birth Surrogates by Aaron L. Mackler and Elie Kaplan Spitz 526
On the Use of Birth Surrogates by Elie Kaplan Spitz 529
Surrogate Parenting by Aaron L. Mackler 551
Mamzerut by Elie Kaplan Spitz 558
A Concurring Opinion Regarding Mamzerut by Daniel S. Nevins 587
Solemnizing the Marriage Between a Kohen and a Divorcee
    by Arnold M. Goodman 593
Solemnizing the Marriage Between a Kohen and a Convert
    by Arnold M. Goodman 599

הלכות אישות / Interpersonal Relations 602
The Role of the Non-Jewish Parent in Blessings for Bar/Bat Mitzvah
    by Jerome M. Epstein 602
Participation of Non-Jewish Parents or Grandparents in Home Religious
    Ceremonies by Jerome M. Epstein 605

*Issues Regarding Employment of an Intermarried Jew by a Synagogue or
   Solomon Schechter Day School* by Jerome M. Epstein 608
Consensus Statement on Homosexuality by The Committee 612
Homosexuality by Joel Roth 613
Homosexuality and the Policy Decisions of the CJLS by Reuven Kimelman 676
On Homosexuality by Mayer Rabinowitz 686
Jewish Norms for Sexual Behavior: A Responsum Embodying a Proposal
   by Elliot N. Dorff 691
The Status of Homosexuals in the Synagogue: A Concurring Opinion
   by Kassel Abelson 712
On Homosexuality and Biblical Imperatives: A Concurrence
   by Avram Israel Reisner 714
*In the Image of God: A Dissent in Favor of the Full Equality of Gay
   and Lesbian Jews Into the Community of Conservative Judaism*
   by Howard Handler 718
Placing Homosexual Rabbis in Congregations by Kassel Abelson 722
Placing Homosexual Rabbis in Congregations by Arnold M. Goodman 724
*A Concurring Opinion to Arnold M. Goodman's "Placing Homosexual
   Rabbis in Congregations"* by Aaron L. Mackler 726
The Gay Placement Question by Ben Zion Bergman 728

הלכות גיטין / **Divorce** 730
   *Mix and Match: The Use of Aramaic Phrases in Legal Documents Written
   in Hebrew* by Lionel E. Moses 730
   On Restoring the Shaliah l'Kabalah by Ben Zion Bergman 741
   Renewal of Marriage for Couples Without Get by Kassel Abelson
   and Mayer Rabinowitz 751
   Renewal of Marriage for Couples Without Get: A Dissenting Opinion
   by Judah Kogen 755

RESPONSA RELATING TO HOSHEN MISHPAT   חושן משפט

הלכות דיינים / **Jurisprudence** 759
   A Principled Defense of the Current Structure and Status of the CJLS
   by Gordon Tucker 759

הלכות חובל בחבירו / **Harming Others** 773
   Family Violence by Elliot N. Dorff 773

Contributors 817
Source Index 820
Subject Index 844

Preface and Acknowledgments

This volume is the continuation in a series devoted to publishing the complete papers of the Committee on Jewish Law and Standards of the Conservative Movement. But in many ways the publication of this volume stands as a landmark in the history of the development of halakhah in Conservative Judaism. We have here the complete collected papers covering ten years from 1991 to 2000. The sheer volume of papers and the diverse areas of concern to which they are addressed have never before been brought together in a single volume. We have also changed the title of the series from *Proceedings* to *Responsa* as we take note of the very traditional nature of this enterprise. This is essentially a book of שאלות ותשובות, a collection of responsa on the issues facing the Conservative rabbinate in the past ten years.

Classical Order of the Shulhan Arukh

The papers have been organized according to the classical order of the Shulhan Arukh, the medieval code of Jewish law. The "classification codes" are printed above each responsum as it appears in the volume. Such information is not provided in the Table of Contents so as not to overburden the reader. The classification codes consist of the Tur of the Shulhan Arukh (abbreviated as OH, YD, EH and HM for Orah Hayyim, Yoreh De'ah, Even HaEzer and Hoshen Misphat) the סימן and סעיף (at times no סעיף is provided) and then a period followed by the year that the Committee approved the paper. When there are multiple papers with the same classification code, then the year is followed by a lower case letter beginning with "a". The paper garnering the greatest number of votes is listed first, followed down the line. These are followed by concurrences and then dissenting opinions, which are each ordered alphabetically. This is the order by which the papers appear in this volume.

Through the Generations

The process of cataloguing the papers into a location in the Shulhan Arukh has been enlightening. Hundreds of years later we find that while so many of the questions and realities have changed, the basic rubric of halakhah retains its vitality for us, as we can schematize our concerns into the same chapters and subheadings that have been used through the generations. We know that generations from now our descendants will find no difficulty in finding what we had to say about a particular question. The issues change, and positions evolve, but what is constant through the ages is our devotion to the law. All responsa collections throughout Jewish history are but updates and new editions to the grand book of rabbinics.

Composition of the Committee on Jewish Law and Standards

The Committee on Jewish Law and Standards (often referred to as the CJLS or the Law Committee) is a committee of the Rabbinical Assembly offering halakhic guidance to the rabbis and organizations of the Conservative movement. The Committee consists of twenty five rabbis who are voting members, one hazzan representing the Cantors Assembly and five lay members representing the United Synagogue. The hazzan and five lay members participate in the discussions but do not vote. The twenty-five voting members are appointed by the Rabbinical Assembly, with five nominations from the Jewish Theological Seminary and five from the United Synagogue. A member is usually appointed to the Law Committee for five years. Great care is taken that the membership of the Law Committee represent the various concerns and perspectives found in the Conservative movement. The Law Committee includes some of the finest minds in the Movement, so that as a collective body the community of Conservative Judaism can expertly and meaningfully respond to the questions of the day.

The Process

When a שאלה comes before the Law Committee, it may be answered by the Chairperson citing past decisions of the Commitee. Or, the Chairperson can refer it to a subcommittee that is charged with responsibility for the subject. The Chairperson can also seek an individual to research the question. In either case, a responsum is written by a member of the Committee. The Committee then debates the paper, usually at two meetings, offering constructive criticism and give-and-take with the authors, so that the final products often reflect the collective wisdom of the Committee.

The Rules of Procedure

According to the rules of the Law Committee set by the Rabbinical Assembly, when a תשובה receives at least six votes it is considered an official opinion of the CJLS. Six votes represents twenty-five percent of the Committee, and as such represents a valid position within the Conservative rabbinate. There are times, then, when papers are approved with significant opposition and at times even with contrary positions that are also approved by at least six votes, making them also official opinions. Much of the time there is a consensus. And every effort is made when there are differing opinions to have a statement drawn up which clarifies both the points of agreement and difference. The voting records are provided in this volume at the beginning of each paper. Members of the Law Committee also have the right to contribute concurring or dissenting statements after a paper has been approved. These papers are included in this volume. However, since they were not voted upon, they are not official positions of the Committee.

Mara d'Atra

The Law Committee provides halakhic guidance to Conservative rabbis, but the individual rabbi is the מרא דאתרא, the teacher of Jewish law for the individual community. This is the case, for it is obvious that a decision of the Law Committee may not apply to a special situation, or a unique set of circumstances, in which case the rabbi might reach a different decision. Or the rabbi might disagree with a decision of the Law Committee, and base his or her decision on a different interpretation of the halakhic sources.

Rabbinic Standards

Decisions of the Law Committee serve to guide the Conservative rabbi in the decision making process, but members of the Rabbinical Assembly are required to follow Rabbinic Standards of Practice. Rabbinic Standards are positions approved by the CJLS and ratified by the Rabbinical Assembly at a Convention. They represent positions of crucial importance to the future of Judaism and the Jewish people. To date, there are three Rabbinic Standards, understood by the Rabbinical Assembly membership as:

> 1. No rabbi shall perform a marriage for a divorced man or woman unless such a person has obtained a גט or הפקעת קידושין.
>
> 2. A member of the Rabbinical Assembly or of the Cantors Assembly may not officiate or be present at the marriage of a Jew to an unconverted non-Jew nor may he or she officiate at a purely civil ceremony.
>
> 3. Ascription of Jewish lineage through a legal instrument or ceremonial act on the basis of anything other than matrilineal descent; or supervision of a conversion which omits טבילה in the case of females, or טבילה and ברית מילה in the case of males, shall continue to be regarded as violations of the halakhah of Conservative Judaism.
>
> They shall henceforth be violations of a Standard of Rabbinic Practice and be inconsistent with membership in the Rabbinical Assembly.

There have been no Standards of Practice proposed during the years covered by this volume.

For a fuller discussion of the nature of the Committee on Jewish Law and Standards, we direct the reader to Gordon Tucker's paper, "A Principled Defense of the Current Structure and Status of the CJLS" appearing in this volume on pp. 759-772.

A Note on Style

Except for commonly used terms, Hebrew phrases appear in Hebrew. For both rabbis and students, the use of Hebrew phrases in Hebrew is most efficient. While efforts have been made to create some level of standardization throughout the volume, the many authors employ different means of citation of rabbinic literature, and some of these various methods have been preserved in the individual papers.

Acknowledgments

The editors express their profound gratitude and appreciation to the members of the Committee on Jewish Law and Standards who have served throughout these years and offered their time and thought to these many responsa. We are especially grateful to the members who authored papers, mindful of the tremendous time and devotion that this entails, as well as the "ordeal" of presenting before the Committee. A list of contributors appears at the end of the volume, pp. 817-819.

We are grateful to Rabbi Joel Roth, who served as Chairman of the Committee on Jewish Law and Standards from 1984 to 1992. Rabbi Abelson has served as Chairman since 1992. We are appreciative of the work of our colleagues who have served as Secretary to the Committee: Rabbi Gail S. Labovitz (1990-1992), Rabbi Daniel S. Nevins (1992-1994), Rabbi Wesley Gardenswartz (1994-1996), and Rabbi Ellen S. Wolintz-Fields (1996-1999). Rabbi Fine has served as Secretary since 1999.

We also express our debt to those who were involved in the editing and publication process. Rabbi Kenneth Leitner was of tremendous service in devoting many hours painstakingly checking the references and accuracy of the notations. Rabbis Ben Zion Bergman, Paul Drazen, Robert E. Fine, Judah Kogen, Daniel S. Nevins, James S. Rosen, Joel Roth and Robert Scheinberg carefully read portions of the manuscript. We could not have prepared this volume for publication with the same efficiency and accuracy without the volunteer assistance of these rabbinic colleagues.

We are grateful to Annette Muffs Botnick for her many long hours in preparing the indices. We thank Tirza Covel and Ellen Miriam Brandwein, two JTS rabbinical students who each devoted a summer to work in the Rabbinical Assembly office converting these papers into clean standardized word processed documents in preparation for editing and publication. We extend our appreciation to Adam Blyweiss from Desperate Hours Productions and James Harris from G & H Soho for their patience and professionalism in handling the typesetting and printing, respectively. We are thankful for the kind assistance of the various members of the office staff at the Rabbinical Assembly, including Rabbi Jan Caryl Kaufman, Amy Gottlieb, Jennifer Klor, and Sara Gunther. We appreciate the enthusiasm and support for this project offered us by Rabbi Vernon H. Kurtz, President of the Rabbinical Assembly. And we are especially grateful for the care and attention devoted to our efforts by Rabbi Joel H. Meyers, Executive Vice President of the Rabbinical Assembly.

Finally, we are grateful to our spouses and loving partners, Joan Lipnick Abelson and Alla Fine, for their patience, understanding and support.

We offer this volume in the hope that it will serve as a guide, a teacher, a consultant, and a challenge, in the ongoing holy endeavor of the application of God's Torah to our lives.

Rabbi Kassel Abelson
Rabbi David J. Fine

ABBREVIATIONS

B.	Babylonian Talmud
CJLS	Committee on Jewish Law and Standards
E.H.	Even HaEzer
H.M.	Hoshen Mishpat
J.	Jerusalem Talmud
M.	Mishnah
M.T.	Mishneh Torah
O.H.	Orah Hayyim
PCJLS 27-70	*Proceedings of the Committee on Jewish Law and Standards of the Conservative Movement 1927-1970.* Edited by David Golinkin. 3 vols. Jerusalem: The Rabbinical Assembly and the Institute of Applied Halakhah, 1997.
PCJLS 80-85	*Proceedings of the Committee on Jewish Law and Standards of the Conservative Movement 1980-1985.* New York: The Rabbinical Assembly, 1988.
PCJLS 86-90	*Proceedings of the Committee on Jewish Law and Standards of the Conservative Movement 1986-1990.* New York: The Rabbinical Assembly, 2001.
PRA	*Proceedings of the Rabbinical Assembly*
S.A.	Shulhan Arukh
T.	Tosefta
Y.D.	Yoreh De'ah

Responsa Relating to Orah Hayyim
אורח חיים

הלכות ציצית	Tzitzit
הלכות נשיאת כפיים	The Priestly Blessing
הלכות קריאת ספר תורה	Torah Reading
הלכות תפלות מנחה וערבית	Minhah and Maariv
הלכות שבת	Shabbat
הלכות פסח	Passover
הלכות ראש השנה	Rosh HaShanah

OH 14:1.1997

MAY WOMEN TIE TZITZIT KNOTS?

Rabbi Shoshana Gelfand

This paper was approved on March 12, 1997, by a vote of twenty-one in favor (21-0-0). Voting in favor: Rabbis Kassel Abelson, Ben Zion Bergman, Elliot N. Dorff, Jerome M. Epstein, Samuel Fraint, Shoshana Gelfand, Nechama D. Goldberg, Arnold M. Goodman, Susan Grossman, Judah Kogen, Vernon H. Kurtz, Alan B. Lucas, Aaron L. Mackler, Lionel E. Moses, Paul Plotkin, Mayer Rabinowitz, Avram Israel Reisner, Joel E. Rembaum, James S. Rosen, Joel Roth, and Elie Kaplan Spitz.

The Committee on Jewish Law and Standards of the Rabbinical Assembly provides guidance in matters of halakhah for the Conservative movement. The individual rabbi, however, is the authority for the interpretation and application of all matters of halakhah.

שאלה

May women tie tzitzit knots?

תשובה

Traditional sources engage in much discussion and disagreement regarding whether women are permitted or forbidden to wear tzitzit (and perform other positive time-bound mitzvot). That, however, is not the question being addressed in this paper. This paper makes no assumptions regarding women wearing tzitzit, but rather deals only with the issue of women making tzitzit. The Committee on Jewish Law and Standards has other papers to deal with the broader issues of wearing talit, tefilin, etc.[1]

The Gemara does contain statements regarding who may make tzitzit and who may not. The focus, however, is not with women making them, but with non-Jews making them. For example, in Menahot 42a, we find a statement forbidding non-Jews to make tzitzit:[2]

אמר רב יהודה אמר רב, מנין לציצית בעובד כוכבים שהיא פסולה? שנאמר
"דבר אל בני ישראל ועשו להם ציצית" – בני ישראל יעשו ולא העובדי
כוכבים יעשו.

Rav Yehuda said in the name of Rav: From where is it derived that

---

[1] See, for a discussion of positive time-bound commandments and their relation to talit and tefilin: Joel Roth, "On the Ordination of Women as Rabbis" in Simon Greenberg, *The Ordination of Women as Rabbis* (New York: Jewish Theological Seminary, 1988), pp. 127-148.

[2] B. Menahot 42a. Note that on the following page [42b] there is a different version of this statement with the opposite meaning:

tzitzit [made] by a non-Jew are pasul? Because it is said, "Speak to the children of Israel and they shall make for themselves tzitzit"; the children of Israel shall make [tzitzit], and not the non-Jews.

This statement in the Gemara refers only to non-Jews. There is no discussion regarding the permissibility of women making tzitzit. Tosafot, however, is concerned with this question and extends the implications of the Gemara to apply to women.[3]

מנין לציצית בעובד כוכבים שהיא פסולה? משמע הא אשה כשירה....

From where is it derived that tzitzit made by non-Jews are pasul? It teaches that a woman is kosher. . . .

Tosafot focuses on Rav's method of reaching his conclusion in the Gemara. He could have argued logically, using the principle that non-Jews may not make tzitzit because "whoever does not wear, does not make" (אינו בלבישה אינו בעשייה). Were he to have used this line of reasoning, women as well as non-Jews would be forbidden to make tzitzit, for women (like non-Jews) do not wear them. Rav, however, chose not to use this reasoning. Rather, he used a verse to prove that non-Jews may not make tzitzit. This verse he interprets as specifically excluding non-Jews, but not necessarily women. Therefore, Tosafot concludes that women may indeed make tzitzit.

This is by no means a universal opinion, however. In Gittin 45b, we see that Tosafot maintains the position that women may tie tzitzit, but Rabbenu Tam is quoted as disagreeing. The argument here is placed within the context of the types of activities permissible for women (and people of other various statuses). The Gemara makes no actual mention here of tzitzit. It speaks only of writing a Torah scroll, tefilin or mezuzot. According to the Gemara, these scrolls are pasul if written by certain categories of people because of the verse, וקשרתם ... וכתבתם – "And you shall bind them. . .and you shall write them." The Gemara infers from this that those who are subject to "bind" may "write," but those who do not "bind" may not "write."

Based on this statement, Rabbenu Tam (as quoted by Tosafot) extends the argument to women being forbidden to tie a lulav or make tzitzit because they are not commanded to perform these mitzvot:[4]

כל שישנו בקשירה ישנו בכתיבה – מכאן אומר ר"ת דאין אשה אוגדת לולב ועושה ציצית כיון דלא מיפקדה....

"For all about whom it is taught regarding binding [i.e. tefilin], it is taught regarding writing [i.e. a Torah scroll, parchments for mezuzah or tefilin]" – from here Rabbenu Tam says that a woman may not tie a lulav or make tzitzit since she is not mentioned [regarding these mitzvot].

Tosafot, however, rejects Rabbenu Tam's ruling. Rather than extend the argument to mitzvot outside of the ones mentioned in the Gemara, Tosafot applies the restriction only to the mitzvot actually stated: writing a Torah scroll, tefilin or mezuzah:

R. Mordecai said to R. Ashi: You have had it reported so; but we had it reported thus: Rav Yehudah said in the name of Rav, From where do we know that the tzitzit made by a non-Jew is valid? Because it says, Speak to the children of Israel and they shall make them fringes; others may make [tzitzit] for them.

[3] Ibid., Tosafot s.v. מנין.

[4] B. Gittin 45b; Tosafot s.v. כל.

4

> ...ואין נראה דהא מדפסלינן בריש התכלת ציצית בעובד כוכבים דדריש בני
> ישראל ועשו ולא בעובדי כוכבים מכלל דאשה כשרה... ודוקא בס"ת
> וציצית ומזוזות דכתיב וקשרתם וכתבתם דרשינן הכי.

> But it does not appear that [Rabbenu Tam is correct that] we disqualify them [women], for at the beginning of פרק התכלת (Menahot 42a), we disqualify non-Jews based on the interpretation of a verse, (B'nei Yisrael make tzitzit, not non-Jews). From this, we can make a general rule that women are kosher [to make tzitzit]. . .and it is דווקה [limited] to a Sefer Torah and tefilin and mezuzot that we refer when we interpret "and you shall bind them and you shall write them."

In summary, the Gemara shows no concern regarding the question of women making tzitzit. It focuses instead on whether or not non-Jews may do so. The conclusion is that non-Jews may not make them because of the verse which has Moses telling "B'nei Yisrael" to make tzitzit. Tosafot then expands the discussion to question whether women should be permitted to make them. In Menahot 42a, Tosafot states that the Gemara didn't argue, "Anyone who doesn't wear, doesn't make." Rather, it argued from a verse. The Gemara's interpretation of the verse excludes only non-Jews. Therefore, women are permitted to make tzitzit. A second Tosafot agrees with the first, despite the fact that Rabbenu Tam raises an objection. Thus, Tosafot permits women to make tzitzit, although not all Rishonim agree with this decision.

The issue as expressed in the Gemara and Tosafot is restated in the codes by Rambam and the Hagahot Maimoniot. Like the Gemara, Rambam is concerned only with the case of the non-Jew, and does not mention the issue of women making tzitzit: ציצית שעשה אותו כותי פסול — tzitzit made by a non-Jew are pasul.[5]

While the Rambam does not mention how his statement might or might not apply to women, the Hagahot Maimoniot does extend the איסור to apply also to women, arguing that neither a non-Jew nor a woman fall into the category of "B'nei Yisrael." One must note, however, that while in the end the author rules against women making tzitzit, the contents of his statement show that he is clearly aware of cases למעשה where women are indeed making them.[6]

> מכאן פסק ר"י ורבינו יהודה שנשים יכולות לעשות ציצית מדאינו ממעט
> אלא עכו"ם וכן הודה רבינו יהודה לאשתו לעשות ציצית אבל בשם מורי
> שי' מצאתי דאין להם לעשות ציצית משום דכתיב "בני ישראל ועשו" אבל
> שאר תיקוני הטלית וטויית החוטים יכולות לעשות.

> From here [Rambam's ruling that non-Jews may not make tzitzit], the Ri and Rabbenu Yehuda ruled that women may make tzitzit, for this [statement of the Rambam's] excludes only non-Jews [and not women]. And so, Rabbenu Yehuda taught his wife to make tzitzit. But in the name of my teacher, I found that they [women] may not make tzitzit because it is written, "b'nei [translated as 'sons'] of Israel shall make." But the rest of the preparation of the talit and the spinning of the strings they [women] may do. . . .

---

[5] Rambam, M.T. Hilkhot Tzitzit 1:12.
[6] Ibid., Hagahot Maimaniot.

Thus, Hagahot Maimoniot makes it clear that there are two opinions regarding whether or not women may make tzitzit. He argues against it based on his interpretation of the verse in the Gemara, but he acknowledges that there are others who do permit it (including Rabbenu Yehuda who actually taught his wife how). In order to further bolster his argument against women making tzitzit, Hagahot Maimoniot quotes Rabbenu Tam's opinion from Tosafot Gittin 45b (despite the fact that in the context of Tosafot Gittin 45b, that ruling was rejected). Finally, the passage ends with the mention of several more actual cases of women who did tie tzitzit. (One of those cases was declared פסול by Rabbenu Tam, based on his ruling quoted in Tosafot Gittin 45b.)

> וכן היה מעשה בטרוי"ש באשה שהיתה רגילה לתקן ציצית להגדילם בטליתות ופסלם רבינו תם מההיא דפרק השולח כל שישנו בקשירה ושנו בכתיבה.
>
> And thus there was an actual case in Troyes where a woman used to prepare tzitzit to tie onto talitot. And Rabbenu Tam declared them to be pasul, according to the ruling in chapter "Ha-Sholeah" – "All about whom it is taught regarding binding, it is taught regarding writing" [Rabbenu Tam extends this principle to include tzitzit].

Thus, it is clear that the Hagahot Maimoniot does not approve of women tying tzitzit, despite the fact that there were actual cases of women doing it and of rabbis who approved of it (i.e. Rabbenu Yehuda).

Unlike the Gemara and the Rambam, the Shulhan Arukh is very clear about its opinion regarding women and tying tzitzit. It rules as follows:[8]

> ציצית שעשו גוי פסול, דכתיב "דבר אל בני ישראל" לאפוקי גוים. אשה כשרה לעשותן.
>
> Tzitzit that were made by a non-Jew are pasul as it is written in Num. 15:38, "Speak to the children of Israel" – this excludes non-Jews. A woman is kosher to make them.

Once again, we have the clear statement that non-Jews may not make tzitzit. The Shulhan Arukh is specific that the words "B'nei Yisrael" are intended to exclude *only* non-Jews from making tzitzit. But just in case there is any question remaining in the reader's mind, the text continues on to specifically state that women *may* indeed make tzitzit. There are absolutely no stipulations limiting their ability to do so.

Although this statement seems to be crystal clear, some of the commentaries try to temper it. The Rema, for example, does not openly disagree with the Shulhan Arukh. Rather, he qualifies the statement in order to discourage the practice, stating:[9]

> הגה: ויש מחמירים להצריך אנשים שיעשו אותו וטוב לעשות כן לכתחילה.
>
> There are those who are strict requiring that men make them; and it is good to do so לכתחילה.

According to the Rema, there are those who are strict regarding making tzitzit, and if asked whether or not a woman may make them, they will say no. But what if she has already

---

[7] Ibid.

[8] S.A. Orah Hayyim 14:1.

[9] Rema on S.A. Orah Hayyim 14:1.

made them? According to the Mishnah B'rurah's comment on this passage, we are told that after the fact, it is permitted – אסור לכתחילה, אבל בדיעבד מותר.[10]

In addition to these opinions, the codes preserve the most stringent view, that women are not permitted to make tzitzit under any circumstances (בדיעבד or לכתחילה). The Magen Avraham goes back to the reasoning offered by Rabbenu Tam in Tosafot Gittin 45b (despite the fact that Tosafot rejected this opinion), reasoning that one must be obligated by a mitzvah in order to make the objects involved:[11]

> ויש מחמירין – ולדידהו כל מצות שאין האשה מחויבת בהן כגון לולב וסוכה אינה רשאית לעשותן.
>
> There are those who are strict – And according to them, all mitzvot for which a woman is not obligated (for example, lulav and sukkah), she is not permitted to make them [the ritual objects required].

Reading between the lines of the text, however, it should be clear that if the Magen Avraham says יש מחמירים (that there are those who are strict in their ruling on this), it also implies that יש מקילים (that there must also be those who are *not* strict regarding women making tzitzit). (This also applies to the Rema's ruling above.) Thus, there seem to be a multitude of opinions on the matter. In the latter codes, only the stricter ones are recorded in order to restrict what the Shulhan Arukh clearly permits.

Summary

Historically, there has been halakhic disagreement regarding the permissibility of women making tzitzit. Neither the Gemara nor the Rambam make explicit statements regarding women. They concern themselves solely with the case of the non-Jew. The Shulhan Arukh explicitly permits women to make tzitzit. Other sources, such as the Magen Avraham, disagree with the Shulhan Arukh. In addition to the legal rulings, there are numerous stories which testify to the occurrence of this phenomenon, sometimes despite the objections of some of the commentators on the Mishneh Torah and Shulhan Arukh.

In light of the disagreement amongst commentators, and the clear התר given in the Shulhan Arukh, there is certainly plenty of room to permit women to engage in tying tzitzit. The only question is whether or not there is a compelling reason for them to do so.

While one could certainly argue that the Conservative movement's attitude toward egalitarianism gives a compelling enough reason to permit women to make tzitzit, there is an additional reason based on the needs of the day.

Many American Jews at the end of the twentieth century are searching for meaning in their lives. Rabbis in synagogues are constantly searching for ways to demonstrate to congregants that performing mitzvot can be a joyous and "spiritual" experience. In light of this, we should not only permit, but actively encourage, *both men and women* to make tzitzit and talitot. Educators know that successful teaching comes not only through the intellect, but also through tactile channels. It is our hope that an individual's personal involvement in this act of הידור מצוה will lead to greater participation in this mitzvah.

Many synagogues run highly successful bar and bat mitzvah programs in which parents and children together make talitot and learn about the mitzvah of tzitzit. Were we to forbid women from tying tzitzit, we would be discouraging these types of programs which are of

---

[10] Mishnah B'rurah, loc. cit.

[11] Magen Avraham, loc. cit.

great educational and spiritual value to men and women. Thus, there is clearly a compelling reason to permit women to tie tzitzit.

Conclusion

We should not only permit women to tie tzitzit, but we should encourage them to do so, and we should offer them (as well as men) every opportunity to learn how.

OH 128:2.1994a

WOMEN RAISE YOUR HANDS

Rabbi Mayer Rabinowitz

This paper was approved on December 14, 1994, by a vote of twelve in favor, seven opposed, and two abstaining (12-7-2). Voting in favor: Rabbis Kassel Abelson, Ben Zion Bergman, Elliot N. Dorff, Arnold M. Goodman, Susan Grossman, Jan Caryl Kaufman, Aaron L. Mackler, Mayer Rabinowitz, Joel E. Rembaum, Gerald Skolnik, Gordon Tucker, and Gerald Zelizer. Voting against: Rabbis Stanley Bramnick, Samuel Fraint, Judah Kogen, Alan B. Lucas, Paul Plotkin, Avram Israel Reisner, and Joel Roth. Abstaining: Rabbis Jerome M. Epstein and Vernon H. Kurtz.

The Committee on Jewish Law and Standards of the Rabbinical Assembly provides guidance in matters of halakhah for the Conservative movement. The individual rabbi, however, is the authority for the interpretation and application of all matters of halakhah.

שאלה

May a בת כהן participate in נשיאת כפים – the priestly blessing?

תשובה

For many years, the נשיאת כפים service was eliminated from services in most Conservative synagogues for a variety of reasons. Some felt it was too mystical, some did not want to continue a "caste system," and some did not want to continue a ritual of distinctions between kohanim and Israelites, when that ritual was so closely associated with the Temple Service. But there is a revival of the נשיאת כפים service in some of our synagogues, and בנות כהנים have asked about their participation in the service.

The source for the commandment for kohanim to bless the people Israel is found in the Torah.

> וידבר ה' אל משה לאמר. דבר אל אהרן ואל בניו לאמר כה תברכו את בני ישראל אמר להם. יברכך ה' וישמרך. יאר ה' פניו אליך ויחנך. ישא ה' פניו אליך וישם לך שלום. ושמו את שמי על בני ישראל ואני אברכם.
>
> The Lord spoke to Moses: Speak to Aaron and his sons – Thus shall you bless the people of Israel; say to them: The Lord bless you and keep you! The Lord deal kindly and graciously with you; the Lord bestow His favor upon you and grant you peace! Thus they shall link my Name with the people of Israel, and I will bless them.[1]

---

[1] Num. 6:22-27.

It is clear from these verses that this ritual is a מצות עשה מדאורייתא, a positive Biblical commandment for kohanim.[2] In fact, if a kohen is present during נשיאת כפים, and does not participate, he is guilty of transgressing three positive commandments.[3]

Because the verse states: אל אהרן ואל בניו, it would seem that only the male descendants of Aaron were to take part in the priestly blessing. In addition, the ritual originally took place in the Temple, where women did not participate in it. And after the destruction of the Temple, when the ritual was transferred to the synagogue, it continued to be conducted only by males. Kohanim were afforded special status based upon the biblical verse:

וקדשתו כי את לחם אלקיך הוא מקריב קדש יהיה לך כי קדוש אני ה' מקדשכם.

"And you must treat them as holy, *since they offer the food of your God,* They shall be holy to you, for I the Lord who sanctify you am holy."[4]

Later this special status provided for the kohen being granted the first aliyah and leading the ברכת המזון. Today, in addition to performing pidyon haben and נשיאת כפים, kohanim are granted the first aliyah to the Torah and are asked to lead ברכת המזון because of their special status.

Based on the above, it would seem that only males may participate in נשיאת כפים. However, a reexamination of the biblical texts and the development of the role of women in public ritual can provide us with a halakhic basis for including בנות כוהנים (the daughters of kohanim) to participate in נשיאת כפים.

The basis for permitting only males to participate in נשיאת כפים is the verse: דבר אל אהרן ואל בניו – "Speak unto Aaron and his sons."[5] However, we know that there are cases where the Torah uses the masculine form even though women are included, as is the case with pidyon haben. There are instances where the word בניו or variations of it refers to descendants, and not only to sons. In fact, the continuation of this verse is: כה תברכו את בני ישראל – "thus shall you bless the people of Israel," and it is clear that women are included.

Although there are many authorities who would not accept this point of view and would exclude women from this ritual,[6] nevertheless, in other cases where the masculine form is used, there are authorities who claim that בניו does include women. Based upon the verse in the Torah: ונתת הכסף לאהרן ולבניו – "And give the money to Aaron and his sons,"[7] Maimonides states וכן פדיון הבן לזכרי כהונה – "And similarly the redemption of the first born is for male priests."[8] But the Tosafot, Rashi and the Rosh state that a בת כהן may redeem a first born. Their decision in this case indicates their acceptance of lineal sanctity for the daughters of kohanim. As Rabbi Joel Roth points out: "Surely according to Tosafot and the Rosh in Rashi's name, pidyon haben is another indication of lineal sanctity for the daughters of Priests even if married. It is equally important to note that Maimonides' view does not either preclude or deny lineal sanctity to daughters of Priests.

---

[2] Rambam, Sefer HaMitzvot – positive commandment no. 26; M.T. Hilkhot T'fillah 15:6.

[3] B. Sotah 38b (מאמרו של רבי יהושע בן לוי – כה תברכו אמור להם ושמו את שמי); Rambam, M.T. Hilkhot T'fillah 15:12.

[4] Lev. 21:8.

[5] Num. 6:22.

[6] נשיאת כפים בי' והכהנים מן המנין – Rambam, M.T. Hilkhot T'fillah 15:1; S.A. Orah Hayyim 128:1.

[7] Num. 3:48.

[8] M.T. Hilkhot Bikurim 1:10.

This exclusion from the right to redeem is based on the biblical statement לאהרן ולבניו."[9]

There is, therefore, sufficient precedent for interpreting בניו as descendants, to allow the interpretation of the verse dealing with ברכת כוהנים to apply to both males and females. As in other cases, בניו can mean children, and indicates a lineal sanctity which applies to all children of kohanim.[10]

Another aspect of the ritual of נשיאת כפים concerns the role that the Priests played in transmitting a blessing to the people of Israel. If we look at this role, as described in the Torah, there are additional grounds for including women in this ritual today.

The commandment for the kohanim to bless the people ends with the words: ושמו את שמי על בני ישראל ואני אברכם – "Thus they shall link my Name with the people of Israel, and I will bless them." The Sifrei states: ואני אברכם שלא יהו ישראל אומרים ברכותינו תלויות בכהנים ת"ל ואני אברכם – "'And I will bless them.' Israel should not say that their blessings are dependent on the kohanim, for Scripture states: 'And I will bless them.' And the kohanim should not say we bless Israel, for Scripture states: 'And I will bless them.'"[11]

A similar statement is found in the Sifrei Zuta[12] indicating that the blessing is not dependent upon the will of the kohanim, but rather upon God's will because He is the one who will bless them.

And the Rashbam[13] explains the verses about נשיאת כפים as follows: "You shall not bless with the blessing of your words but you shall pray to Me that I will bless them." And later, the Rashbam adds: "When the kohanim bless Israel, it is in My name and not in theirs; I will bless Israel as the kohanim prayed for."

The verse and its interpretation indicate that the kohanim are not "blessing" the people but rather are a medium for conveying God's blessing. The Rashbam explains it as a prayer of the kohanim that the people of Israel be blessed by God. If this is the case, there is added reason to include the daughters of kohanim who have lineal sanctity, among those who can participate in this prayer, or serve as a medium for conveying God's blessing.

The history and development of נשיאת כפים and ברכת כהנים shows that it went through variations in both where it was performed and by whom. Originally, it was practiced in the Temple,[14] and outside the Temple as well. After the destruction of the Temple, the ritual of נשיאת כפים took place in the synagogue. At a certain point in time, additional phrases to be recited by the congregation were added. And, in the absence of the kohanim, the שליח צבור recited the blessing in place of the kohanim. So it is clear that the place, the words, and the individuals involved in the נשיאת כפים ritual varied based upon Rabbinic interpretation and the needs of the times. Until recently, only males were involved in synagogue rituals, and it is understandable that women did not participate in this as well as other rituals. But there is no reason why the history and development connected with this ritual should not continue.

For those whose objection to women's participation in this ritual is based upon the fact that it was a Temple ritual and the exclusive responsibility of males, it must be noted that

---

[9] Joel Roth, "The Status of Daughters of Kohanim and Leviyim for Aliyot," *PCJLS 86-90*, p. 429.

[10] Sifra, Shemini, Parshat א, commenting on the verse וישא אהרן את ידיו אל העם ויברכם connects מתנות כהונה ונשיאת כפים. Since it has been shown that lineal sanctity applies to daughters of priests, the same would be applicable for ברכת כהנים.

[11] Sifrei, Naso, piska 43 (Horvitz ed., p. 49).

[12] Sifrei Zuta, Naso 27 (Yaskowitz ed., p. 250).

[13] Num. 6:27.

[14] M. Tamid 8:2.

in the biblical verse there is absolutely no reference to the Temple or any other site for the recitation of the blessing. In fact, there is no mention of time or place for the performance of the ritual. The interpretation and codification that placed it in the Temple is Rabbinic and not Biblical. Therefore, to prohibit a בת כהן from participating in the ritual on the grounds that it is Biblically part of the Temple service (and therefore the exclusive responsibility of male kohanim) is not accurate. Were that the case, we would have been inclined to omit the recitation of the ברכת כהנים from the repetition of the Amidah whenever the hazzan was not a kohen.[15]

Although kohanim today are considered to be ספק כהנים,[16] in many circles they are still accorded special honors such as: the first aliyah, leading the ברכת המזון, pidyon haben and נשיאת כפים. In the first three cases, a בת כהן is permitted to receive these honors and participate in the ritual. This practice is based on lineal sanctity for daughters of kohanim or on different interpretations of Biblical or Rabbinic texts. There is no reason not to do the same for נשיאת כפים.

Conclusion

A בת כהן is permitted to participate in נשיאת כפים for the following reasons:

(1) בניו does not mean only sons but rather children;

(2) The role of the kohen is either to serve as the medium for God's blessing to Israel, or to pray for Israel to be blessed;

(3) There has been a steady development in the נשיאת כפים ritual, and there is no reason for that development to stop;

(4) We have permitted a בת כהן to participate in all other honors accorded to kohanim, and נשיאת כפים should not be an exception;

(5) The Torah gives no indication of a direct connection between this ritual and the Temple, where women were excluded from participating. Therefore, there is no Biblical basis for excluding them.

---

[15] An examination of discussions found in Menahot 18b and Taanit 26b-27a imply that there are grounds to permit daughters of kohanim to participate in ברכת כהנים. I thank my colleague Rabbi Avram Israel Reisner for bringing these sources to my attention.

[16] Rambam, M.T. Hilkhot Issurei Biah 20:13; Magen Avraham to Orah Hayyim 128:457. For a full discussion see David Novak, *Law and Theology in Judaism*, second series, (New York: Ktav, 1976), pp. 165-166.

OH 128:2.1994b

Should N'siat Kapayim Include B'not Kohanim?

Rabbis Stanley Bramnick and Judah Kogen

This paper was approved on December 14, 1994, by a vote of nine in favor, eleven opposed, and one abstaining (9-11-1). Voting in favor: Rabbis Stanley Bramnick, Jerome M. Epstein, Samuel Fraint, Judah Kogen, Vernon H. Kurtz, Alan B. Lucas, Paul Plotkin, Avram Israel Reisner, and Joel Roth. Voting against: Rabbis Kassel Abelson, Ben Zion Bergman, Elliot N. Dorff, Arnold M. Goodman, Susan Grossman, Jan Caryl Kaufman, Aaron L. Mackler, Joel E. Rembaum, Gerald Skolnik, Gordon Tucker, and Gerald Zelizer. Abstaining: Rabbi Mayer Rabinowitz.

The Committee on Jewish Law and Standards of the Rabbinical Assembly provides guidance in matters of halakhah for the Conservative movement. The individual rabbi, however, is the authority for the interpretation and application of all matters of halakhah.

שאלה

May a בת כהן participate in the ritual of נשיאת כפים (the Priestly Benediction)?

תשובה

The ceremony of נשיאת כפים in which the kohanim raise their hands and confer the Priestly Benediction upon the assembled Congregation began as part of the Temple worship and is prescribed in the Torah.[1] During the final days of the Temple, the practice had developed to conduct the Priestly Benediction at worship locations away from the Temple.[2] This provided the historical and theological bridge for including the Priestly Benediction in the revised prayer ritual which took the place of sacrifice after the destruction of the Temple.

In Israel, the Priestly Benediction was meant to be recited by kohanim every day of

---

[1] וידבר ה' אל משה לאמר. דבר אל אהרן ואל בניו לאמר כה תברכו את בני ישראל אמר להם. יברכך ה' וישמרך. יאר ה' פניו אליך ויחנך. ישא ה' פניו אליך וישם לך שלום. ושמו את שמי על בני ישראל ואני אברכם.

The Lord spoke to Moses: Speak to Aaron and his Sons – Thus shall you bless the people of Israel, Say to them: The Lord bless you and keep you! The Lord deal kindly and graciously with you! The Lord bestow His favor upon you and grant you peace! Thus shall they link My name with the people of Israel and I will bless them. (Num. 6:22-27)

[2] M. Tamid 7:2.

the year,³ although in many congregations outside Jerusalem, the practice is limited to Shabbat and major holidays. Outside Israel, it became customary to have kohanim invoke the Priestly Benediction only on major holidays.⁴ Whenever the kohanim do not recite the Priestly Benediction, it becomes a part of the final blessing recited by the Shaliach Tzibur in the repetition of the Amidah.

It should be noted as well that performing the Priestly Benediction is not optional — it is required by every kohen.⁵ Therefore, the question should not be "*May* a בת כהן participate," but rather "*Must* בנות כוהנים participate?" If male kohanim are *required* to participate, we may rule either that females of Priestly paternal descent are required to as well, or are not permitted to participate.

Historically, the kohen was elevated to a special level. The Torah uses the word וקדשתו "sanctify him" (Lev. 21:8), upon which the Talmud Bavli comments: "For all matters of holiness: To begin (reading the Torah) first, to have priority for leading the Grace after meals and to claim priority for a desirable portion.⁶ The Levush further comments: מצוה על אחרים לקדשו "It is a requirement that others sanctify him."⁷ There has been considerable discussion in recent years about the status of the בת כהן for purposes of being called to the Torah first like a male kohen.⁸ From the discussions, it should be clear that a בת כהן possesses the sanctity of כהונה like a male kohen and does not automatically lose her כהונה upon her marriage to a non-kohen. For example, if her first born is a male, there is no requirement of pidyon haben. If, following her divorce, she returns to her father's house, she resumes eating Terumah. By the same token, if she should go astray and become a harlot, she is subject to a special punishment (שרפה) for defiling her patrimony. It should also be clear that while the sanctity of a בת כהן extends to benefiting from the perquisites due to the descendants of Aaron, there is no indication that a בת כהן officiates in the manner of her male brethren in any ritual circumstance.

נשיאת כפים is arguably the only Temple ritual carried out today by kohanim in the manner prescribed by the Torah. While the primary source in Num. 6 does not necessary place נשיאת כפים in the Temple, another source does.⁹ If נשיאת כפים is to be regard-

---

³ The medieval codes treat the Priestly Benediction as a (perhaps theoretical) requirement of the *daily* service. See Maimonides M.T. Hilkhot, Tefilah chs. 14-15, Tur/S.A. Orah Hayyim 128-130. (The contrast between Eretz Yisrael and the Diaspora becomes evident in the comment of RMA to Orah Hayyim 128:44.) The earliest listing of the Priestly Benediction as following Shema and the Amidah in the daily service is in the Mishnah, itself composed in Eretz Yisrael (See, for example, Megillah ch. 3).

⁴ It has been incorrectly assumed in most Diaspora congregations that the exclusion of Shabbatot year-round encompassed festivals occurring on Shabbat as well. The first American rabbi to take issue with that assumption, to our knowledge, was Prof. Saul Lieberman in his capacity as Rabbi of the Synagogue of the Jewish Theological Seminary. In 1969, when several fall holidays occurred on Shabbat, he required the performance of the Priestly Benediction on Shabbat. His explanation was that a misunderstanding had grown up in the Diaspora around the principle that the Priestly Benediction was not to be recited on Shabbat. He noted that in Israel the ceremony routinely took place on Shabbat [personal communication between Judah Kogen and Prof. Lieberman ז״ל Sept. 1969]. Subsequent research, of course, bore him out. See RMA on Orah Hayyim 128:44 for his distinction between Festivals and "year-round" Shabbatot. Note the especially forceful repudiation centuries ago by the Taz (on the same passage, n. 38) of this still widespread mistake.

⁵ Orah Hayyim 128:39.

⁶ B. Moed Katan 28b.

⁷ *Levush*, op. cit.

⁸ See Joel Roth, "The Status of Daughters of Kohanim and Leviyim for Aliyot," *PCJLS 86-90*, pp. 419-434. Previously written papers are cited there and constitute a lengthy survey of the literature on the subject.

⁹ Lev. 19:22ff. Sotah 38a equates this passage with נשיאת כפים, while 38b describes it as part and parcel

ed as a continuation of a Temple ritual, it should be performed only by the descendants of Aaron who would have been eligible to perform it in the Temple.[10]

Conclusion

There is no support in Talmudic or post-Talmudic sources for the inclusion of a בת כהן in the ritual of נשיאת כפים. As a continuation of a Temple ritual, the Priestly Benediction should be performed by those who were authentically eligible to do so in the Temple. Women of Priestly descent may benefit from the perquisites of כהונה, but are excluded by the Torah from performing the rituals of kohanim in the Temple. Therefore, נשיאת כפים should be performed only by male kohanim.

---

of Temple ritual.

[10] Menahot 18b (and the parallel passage in Hullin 132b-133a) lists נשיאת כפים as one of fifteen rituals performed by the descendants of Aaron. While this text describes the Priestly Benediction as occurring both within the Temple and outside, it is performed by the *same* kohanim who carry out the other fourteen listed rituals.

OH 135:3.1991

May a Non-Kohen be Called First to the Torah in the Presence of a Kohen?

Rabbi Herbert J. Mandl

This paper was approved on May 29, 1991, by a vote of twelve in favor, two opposed and four abstaining (12-2-4). Voting in favor: Rabbis Elliot N. Dorff, Amy Eilberg, Richard L. Eisenberg, Dov Peretz Elkins, Jerome M. Epstein, Reuven Kimelman, Herbert Mandl, Avram Israel Reisner, Joel E. Rembaum, Seymour J. Rosenbloom, Joel Roth, and Morris M. Shapiro. Voting against: Rabbis Samuel Fraint and Mayer Rabinowitz. Abstaining: Rabbis Kassel Abelson, Ben Zion Bergman, Stanley Bramnick, and Gordon Tucker.

The Committee on Jewish Law and Standards of the Rabbinical Assembly provides guidance in matters of halakhah for the Conservative movement. The individual rabbi, however, is the authority for the interpretation and application of all matters of halakhah.

שאלה

At one of the recent meetings of the CJLS, the question was raised as to whether the first Torah aliyah may be given to a non-kohen[1] (especially on a weekday when there may be as few as one aliyah available should a kohen be called first to the Torah) without having to ask the kohen to leave the sanctuary or chapel within which services are being conducted.

תשובה

The halakhah itself in a number of settings presents a series of situations which help create the "problem" necessitating the "passing over" of the kohen for the first Torah aliyah. The halakhah and Jewish tradition speak of חיובים for an aliyah to the Torah, e.g. for a Bar-Mitzvah, בעל ברית (Sandek, Mohel, and father of a new born son are all called בעל ברית), groom on the day of his wedding, *Yahrzeit* — that day — for a parent, etc. Since obviously the vast majority of Jews are not kohanim and the calling of a kohen first to the Torah automatically restricts all Israelites to but one Torah aliyah on a normal Monday or

---

[1] This paper is written only according to the traditional halakhic view that a kohen normally must be called first to the Torah based on the Mishnah in Gittin and according to many authorities basing themselves as per the discussion in Gittin 59b that such a calling up of a kohen first is דאורייתא. The purpose of this paper is not to discuss or debate whether this practice is Toraitic or Rabbinic — that has been ably debated in other

Thursday morning or Saturday afternoon, it takes but two such חיובים (a highly common event in even a small congregation) to create a potential conflict among members truly deserving of a aliyah on any given weekday by the mere presence of a non-obligated kohen.

Traditionally, these kinds of circumstances have led our Rabbis to recommend that a kohen or kohanim "leave the synagogue" so that the Reader then can call an Israelite first to the Torah using the formula "There is no kohen present, therefore, let an Israelite ascend in the place of the kohen."

The Maharik (Rabbi Joseph Colon) writes that if the custom in any given community dictates that the first honor of the year for שבת בראשית is "auctioned" to the highest bidder, and that such funding is a major factor in the financial stability of the synagogue for the entire year, then the kohen "waives his honor" provided he leaves the synagogue. The Maharik stresses that this is a special case and not to be used as a *carte blanche* for ignoring the kohen's first aliyah in general.

Rabbi Joseph Colon (Resp. Shoresh 9) mentions two fifteenth-century traditions occurring apparently around the end of the Sukkot festival (שבת בראשית and Simhat Torah). The Jews of France and Germany would auction aliyot on those occasions in that century for synagogue capital funding for the year.

Apparently, even synagogue lighting was paid for by such aliyah auctions around that time of year. Such an honor was apparently seen as prestigious and lucky for the beginning of the new year. The Maharik states that if an Israelite purchases that first aliyah, the kohen waives his rights to the first honor. Should he not, he could be forcibly removed from the synagogue even by the non-Jewish authorities (an interesting note for anyone who may challenge the right of gabbaim, ritual committees or even the clergy to control who receives an aliyah).

As Rabbi David Novak recently pointed out in a responsum dealing with the broader issue of whether a kohen may be overlooked for the first aliyah in general, there is another side to the issue. There are authorities (Rabbi David Halevy, Turay Zahav on Orah Hayyim 135:3 sub 3) who base themselves on the Gaonim who rule that an Israelite, even if learned, may not be called up in the place of a kohen. Rav Huna was an exception in as much as the Talmud states that he was called first to the Torah though an Israelite, even on Shabbat and holidays (Gittin 59b). The Talmud, however, points out that Rav Huna's case was a special one since Rabbi Ami and Rabbi Asi, who were the most distinguished kohanim of that era, paid deference to him.

Rabbi Novak points out that even the stricter view of Rabbi David Halevy can only apply if there are kohanim present, so if they absent themselves from or at least leave the chapel or sanctuary, they do not violate this stricter view that they cannot waive their honor. This procedure is seen as similar to the Priestly Benediction when, if some kohanim absent themselves when ברכת כוהנים is called, they do not violate any of the three positive Torah commandments to bless the Jewish people (Rambam's Hilkhot B'rakhot 11:2 and Beur HaHalakhah Orah Hayyim 128:39).

A survey of the Aharonim yields the conclusion that most authorities seem to agree

---

papers as recently as this past season of the CJLS (see Mayer Rabinowitz, "Rishon or Kohen," *PCJLS 86-90*, pp. 437-443) – but rather to analyze and probe into traditionally acceptable halakhic alternatives to calling up a kohen first when such situations arise that mandate this variation (with the understanding that the above-stated premise of traditional halakhah always calling a kohen first to the Torah, is the underpinning of this paper). While the Mitzvah of honoring a kohen is Toraitic, this particular format, namely, Torah reading, is Rabbinic. Therefore, it would follow that according to those who feel that certain חיובים that are Rabbinic themselves can apply in the area of honoring a kohen during the Torah reading service, inasmuch as it itself is Rabbinically mandated.

that Toraitically a kohen may waive his honor even if present, but some of those poskim hold that the Rabbis forbade this practice as possibly creating conflict in the synagogue. The Responsa of the Maharsham (siman 214, section 1) seems to make a distinction between occasional instances of such waiving of priestly rights to the first Torah honor and a regular ongoing practice which would be forbidden.

The view of the Hatam Sofer (Responsum O.H. 25) forbids a permanent תקנה which would have seen the kohanim automatically leaving the synagogue *en masse* whenever asked to do so, regardless of the circumstances (in other words: for example, if it were on Shabbat or Yom Tov and there were adequate opportunities to afford as many aliyot as one wanted to everyone who needed or wanted one, why should the kohanim be forced to cede their first honor?!). He points out that the שבת בראשית case of Rabbi Joseph Colon was just a special exception to the rule.

The point is also made in the Mor Uktziyah (siman 135) that כבוד התורה still supersedes the honor of the kohen and, therefore, under certain circumstances it might be actually in the honor of the Torah for the kohen not to be called first.

The Maharam Schick (siman 59) even forbids selling aliyot to replace the kohen, again pointing out that the fifteenth-century case of the Maharik was an unusual one and occurred only once annually, where perhaps the whole synagogue annual budget was raised from that first honor to the Torah.

Getting closer to our issue at hand, there appears to be no reluctance to ask kohanim to leave the synagogue on *weekdays* when there is a non-kohen or several of them who have a חיוב.[2] Rabbi Zalman Druk of Jerusalem rules in one of his volumes, Mikdash M'at (Laws of Torah Reading), that it is appropriate for the kohen to waive his honor when there are numerous חיובים in the synagogue. Furthermore, in this fashion, such a waiver of one's "honor" would not lead to controversy as it is but occasionally and only for חיובים which is certainly understandable and justifiable and not just done for "some special individual."

The Kaf Hahayyim (Laws of Torah Reading, siman 135) writes that the Gaon Maharshak Kluger states that the Ashkenazim in Israel would call an Israelite in the place of a kohen (when there was need) and the hazzan would say אף על פי שיש כאן כהן especially because visitors (who needed to be recognized with an aliyah) were always present in the synagogue. The presumption was made that the kohanim would automatically want to waive the honor under these circumstances. (If there were not guests present, the kohanim automatically went up first.)[3]

Finally, Rabbi Aron Pichnik writes in *Shanah B'shanah*, a publication of Heichal Shlomo (1972-73 edition) that מחלת כהן מותר, but that the Talmud limits that principle to weekdays and Saturday afternoons only. He points out as well that the Rosh and the Tur agree with this principle and its limitations (vis-à-vis not on Shabbat or Yom Tov) as well. Rabbi Pichnik paraphrases the Shulchan Arukh by saying:

> גם משום פגמא שלא יחשדו שהכהן הוא פגום מפני זה קורים ישראל
> במקומו ועל כן מוכרח הוא לצאת מבית הכנסת אם רוצים לקרוא ישראל
> ראשון.

Rabbi Pichnik proposes that rather than "playing games" and having kohanim "step out" momentarily and possibly even be visible through a glass door entrance way to a synagogue, that if there be multiple חיובים, that one actually decreases the בזיון of the honor

---

[2] Hatam Sofer, Sha'arei HaT'fillah, Nisiat Kapayim V'Kriat HaTorah 19 in Sefer Da'at, Orah Hayyim 17.
[3] Hashmatot, Hilkhot Sefer Torah 8, p. 96.

of the kohanim by the reader or hazzan calling one of the two Israelite חיובים by saying simply ברשות הכוהנים as we do when an Israelite leads Grace after Meals in the presence of a kohen. However, Pichnik adds that this procedure would apply once again *only* on weekdays or Saturday afternoons but not on Shabbat or Yom Tov.

I would personally suggest that the phrase be replaced with במחילת הכהן, which is found in numerous places in our tradition regarding kohanim and does not really give more power to the kohanim then the tradition ever intended.

Hence, after surveying the sources, the presumption can be made that calling an Israelite who has a חיוב on a weekday in the presence of a kohen is acceptable without necessitating the kohen leaving the synagogue provided the phrase במחילת הכהן is utilized. With issues such as those referred to above, it is evident that various socio-historical evolutions and developments have clearly occurred within the halakhah or Tradition itself, especially with larger congregations where the necessity for additional congregants to receive aliyot exists and where fewer would be available. I would add that if possible, a word in advance explaining the procedure to the kohen present as to what was happening would be highly advisable.

An alternative procedure can be developed as a result of the writings of the great nineteenth-century German scholar, Rabbi David Hoffman, the head of the Rabbinical Seminary in Berlin, who quotes the following question (obviously posed to him from a smaller community):

> Until now our community had not had a kohen. We have now engaged a teacher who happens to be a kohen. Inasmuch as we do not have a levi, does he now need to be called to the Torah twice every time the Torah is read, and we do not even have the option of his leaving inasmuch as he is the Torah reader himself? By our having required him to take two Torah honors each time the Torah is read, funding in the synagogue is down because people normally pay contributions for their Torah honors. Our community is very small and we cannot afford this kind of loss. What shall we do?

Rabbi Hoffman responds that for many centuries the question of whether a kohen can waive his honor has been discussed by the great authorities of old. He responds that he cannot answer in depth to the question at the moment, but suggests that the writer consult with the ruling of the Maharam Shick in his Responsa, section Orah Hayyim, chapter 60, that a kohen is allowed to waive his honor, but that one should not cause the sanctity of the kohanim to disappear totally, but rather, that even if the kohen does waive his honor regularly, that on special occasions, maybe once a month, or on a special Shabbat, that the kohen should be called first to the Torah. Furthermore, in order to avoid any possible פגם or concern that there might be something invalidating the kohen, it should be said יעמוד... במחילת הכהן. Furthermore, in response to the possible objection that Maimonides appears to have in not permitting the kohen to waive his honor, Rabbi Hoffman refers the reader to the Responsa of Rabbi Yehuda Aszod, renowned Hungarian contemporary, who quiets the objections of Maimonides, and permits the kohanim to waive their honor, except for very special occasions.

Rabbi Aszod, in his Responsum No. 45 states that, "The honor of the Torah supersedes the honor of that due the kohen, and concludes that if the person who receives the honor is a great scholar, that יכול הכהן לחלוק לו כבוד אפילו בשבתות וימים טובים. Rabbi Aszod is trying to explain how the honor for the kohen can be a Toraitic Law and yet may be overridden. The question Aszod poses is: does the mitzvah of calling the kohen first derive from the expression וקדשתו, implying that the commandment is on every Jew, regardless of the desire of the kohen (meaning he cannot give up his honor) or rather, does it derive from later in that verse in Lev. 21:8 קדוש יהיה לך, an expression which had implied that the kohen can forego the honor due him? Aszod accepts the second possibility and, thereby, permits the kohen to forego his own honor by yielding that first aliyah, and yet, still stating that giving the kohen that first aliyah is a Toraitic command.

Actually, Rabbi Aszod discusses his question from the point of view of whether or not a kohen should be permitted to take a second consecutive honor should there be no levi in the congregation, inasmuch as it would lead to his saying the Torah blessings a second time and possibly, therefore, in vain. Rabbi Aszod concludes that it would be better to give the kohen the honor of taking out and returning of the Torah, and let him not receive a speaking honor during the Torah reading! This view, therefore, shows that a kohen can "step aside" for a variety of reasons.

Furthermore, the Ritva, commenting on Tractate Gittin 59a-b dealing with our subject states, "In a synagogue, one should not extend a kohen's honor to a levi or an Israelite if a kohen is in synagogue on Shabbat and Yom Tov, but on weekdays בשני וחמישי אם רצה לחלוק, חולק! If, however, the Israelite is a scholar of standing, then the kohen can step aside even on Shabbat and Yom Tov!" From this we learn that though the Ritva seems to qualify the calling of an Israelite in the place of a kohen on Shabbat and Yom Tov to the case of a scholar; nevertheless, that flexibility, in conjunction with Rabbi Aszod's view (that under necessary circumstances [such as the Torah reader who was a kohen in the small community], the practice of calling an Israelite in the place of a kohen on Shabbat or Yom Tov is permissible [provided it does not become a habitual practice Shabbat after Shabbat without at least reserving some special occasions and circumstances when a kohen will be honored]), enables us, I feel, to be flexible in terms of permissibility of calling an Israelite or a levi in the presence of a kohen every Shabbat or Yom Tov if and when needed.

Alternatively, one could utilize the stricter procedure recommended by the highly respected Rabbi Pichnik. One could thus honor the view of those concerned Talmudic and post Talmudic scholars to avoid any possible disgrace to kohanim by calling the kohen in his proper aliyah position on the Shabbat when there is a larger congregation present and the opportunity exists to easily add aliyot as needed. One could "halakhically skip over" the kohanim (in the above-described fashion only) when the need for those few aliyot so desperately exists — namely, on weekdays or Shabbat afternoons.

Conclusion

Where the kohen-levi system is used, an Israelite or a Levi may be called to the Torah for the first aliyah in the presence of a kohen on Shabbat and Yom Tov when needed. A stricter view would limit this to those who have a חיוב (for example, an *aufruf*) on weekdays and Shabbat afternoons. The words במחילת הכהן should be used in calling up the Israelite.

OH 136.1992

Joint Aliyot

Rabbi Avram Israel Reisner

This paper was approved on October 28, 1992, by a vote of eight in favor and six opposed (8-6-0). Voting in favor: Rabbis Jerome M. Epstein, Howard Handler, Reuven Kimelman, Judah Kogen, Lionel E. Moses, Avram Israel Reisner, Joel Roth, and Gerald Skolnik. Voting against: Rabbis Kassel Abelson, Ben Zion Bergman, Elliot N. Dorff, Ezra Finkelstein, Susan Grossman, and Gordon Tucker.

The Committee on Jewish Law and Standards of the Rabbinical Assembly provides guidance in matters of halakhah for the Conservative movement. The individual rabbi, however, is the authority for the interpretation and application of all matters of halakhah.

שאלה

May two (or more) people share an aliyah?

תשובה

The aliyah was always held to be an individual honor, and joint recitations of the blessings has been seen as a ברכה לבטלה (an unnecessary blessing) and running afoul of תרי קלי (the principle that two voices at once are not clearly heard). Therefore, it is preferable to grant single aliyot and resolve multiple demands through the use of a hierarchy of claims and the judicious use of additional aliyot. Where a couple has a joint שמחה (celebration) they may come up together but only one should be formally called and recite the blessings. Where congregations already call couples together, it is preferable if only one recites the blessing. Alternatively, splitting the blessings, fore and aft, is preferable to joint recitation.

Joint בני מצוה should receive separate aliyot (for evenhandedness, neither should be given the maftir aliyah, or, alternatively, the penultimate aliyah might be termed מפטיר ראשון), but only one person should recite the haftarah blessings. They may, however, split the reading of the haftarah or recite it together, since the congregation's attention to the doings of the בני מצוה is unusually rapt.

The question, as phrased, is general. "May two (or more) people share an aliyah?" The complications follow, like an avalanche. "Can they say the blessings together? One say the first and the other the second? One say the blessings with the other standing silently by? Relatives? Kohen? Levi?" What the question does not divulge is: What is the case? What drives the question? What problem seeks its solution? For it is evident that normative practice does not support joint aliyot, indeed the very notion of a "minyan" of seven suggests a head count, and normative practice has a commensurately normative claim upon us unless a case can be made for the need to diverge from it. Only with such a need in mind can the situation be fairly weighed. It will be necessary to speculate.

In the first instance, the joint aliyah that comes to mind is that of a couple. Why such an aliyah? In those synagogues that do not call women to aliyot, the perceived need to find appropriate methods to honor women within the service while holding the line on the traditional rules may be a dramatic need, indeed. In that case it would seem preferable that the male recite the blessings and the female stand silently. Alternatively, the couple's aliyah may be proposed for more balanced reasons. *Aufruf*, anniversary, baby naming. In these cases the demand for joint aliyot may cogently arise within egalitarian congregations, as well, and the joint recitation of the blessings would seem to be the preferred practice. The matter of the differing status of the partners would then become relevant. We should even consider, given the stricture against consecutive aliyot for first degree relatives, whether husband and wife may be called together at all. But another joker hides within this scenario. If an egalitarian synagogue is the venue, why create joint aliyot, a *novum*, when each partner can be given an independent aliyah? This question might very well intrigue feminist theoreticians. Would we consider joint aliyot for, let us say, the fathers of the bride and groom at an *aufruf*? If not, why should we do so for wives, subsuming women's identity once more within their marriage?

This last speculation points to yet another reason why joint aliyot might be required specifically in egalitarian congregations: too many חיובים (obligatory honors). Without women's aliyot, traditional congregations are often pressed by the weight of multiple celebrations into extra aliyot. If aliyot are to be given to women as well, the demand doubles, and surely the option of adding aliyot has some limit.[1] Here joint aliyot for the same gender would indeed make sense. But the natural grouping would recommend sending up, for instance, the uncles of bride A to one aliyah and the aunts of groom B to another, whereas the rules regarding separation of first degree relatives would force us to mix the parties (brother of bride and brother of groom, but not both of the bride's brothers together). Might we not be better being ruthless in limiting the number of חיובים (obligatory honors) we can honor?

It is with these speculations rampant that we approach the halakhot.

The Issues

There is a well-known dictum derived from the Gemara that appears on its face to argue against a shared aliyah: תרי קלי לא משתמעי – two voices simultaneously cannot be made out and therefore do not fulfill mitzvot of hearing. Although the Bavli reference, on Rosh Hashanah 27a, concerns a distant case and is unclear, the Bavli refers there to a tannaitic source for this principle, appearing on Megillah 21b and concerning the case of Torah reading which is before us.

> והא תניא: בתורה אחד קורא ואחד מתרגם. ובלבד שלא יהו שנים קורין ושנים מתרגמין.

> Is it not taught: In the Torah, one reads and one translates. Certainly, two may not read nor two translate.

---

[1] At the outset there is a technical limit set by the rules of verse division, as enunciated by Rabbi Eisenberg in his paper on a proper triennial cycle (unless we permit repetition of the reading as on Simhat Torah). That limit is more severe where reading the Torah on a triennial cycle. In either case, we really do not wish to test that limit. (See Richard Eisenberg, "A Complete Triennial System for Reading the Torah," *PCJLS 86-90*, p. 384.)

The text of that baraita is uncertain,[2] but the halakhah is not. On Megillah 21a the Mishnah states of Megillat Esther: "If two read it they have fulfilled their obligation," but the Gemara immediately appends (at the top of 21b): "It is taught: That is not so of the Torah." This conclusion holds, and is codified in Shulhan Arukh, Orah Hayyim 141:2.[3]

Now, originally the person called to an aliyah read that aliyah portion, in which case that prohibition would apply. Today, however, there is an appointed reader in lieu of the עולה, so that perhaps it would again be possible to have shared aliyot, as long as there were a single reader.[4]

In discussing the instant case in Yerushalmi Berakhot 5:3 the Gemara appears to suggest that this, too, is forbidden, for when the baraita is cited, Rabbi Zeira gives as the reason "on account of the blessing." If it is the dual blessing, and not the dual reading, which is at issue, then the modern situation changes nothing. The Talmud there rejects that reason, however, as follows:

והתני: לא יהו שנים מתרגמין ואחת קורא. אית לך מימר מפני הברכה? אלא משום שאין שני קולות נכנסין לתוך אוזן אחת.

> Is it not taught: Two should not translate and one read? Can you say that that is on account of the blessing? Rather (it is) because two voices do not enter a single ear.

The rejection of the reason of the blessing leaves open the possibility that two עולים sharing one blessing could be allowed. It should be noted, however, that the Talmud's rejection is based on the search for a single consistent reason for two clauses of the baraita. ברכה (blessing) is not such a reason. That does not imply that it would not be a sufficient reason for the first clause alone.[5]

---

[2] In addition to the two Bavli references cited, the baraita in question appears in J. Megillah 4:5 and Berakhot 5:3 and in T. Megillah 3:20 (Lieberman text, p. 359). See Prof. Lieberman's note in his long commentary, Tosefta Kifshuta, Megillah, p. 1194.

[3] In J. Berakhot 5:3, a competing baraita would permit dual readers. However, that baraita is never cited as a precedent להלכה.

[4] The commentators have difficulty with the very institution of the Torah reader, given this stricture against dual readers. For if the honoree is to say a blessing he surely must perform the function over which he recites a blessing, yet if the honoree recites alongside the reader, is this not a forbidden dual reading? (See Magen David no. 3 on S.A. Orah Hayyim 141). The law as codified by Karo is clearly in the nature of a compromise:

> לא יקראו שנים, אלא העולה קורא וש״ץ שותק, או ש״ץ קורא והעולה לא יקרא בקול רם. ומכל מקום צריך הוא לקרות עם הש״ץ כדי שלא תהא ברכה לבטלה. אלא שצריך לקרות בנחת שלא ישמיע לאזניו.

> Two persons may not read. Rather, the honoree reads and the cantor remains silent or the cantor reads and the honoree should not read aloud. But he does have to read with the cantor so that his blessing not be gratuitous. Rather he should read softly so that it not be audible.

This problem reaches even further, to the heart of contemporary custom. Relying on the Torah Reader, we are prepared to call anyone to the Torah, although the law as codified by Karo requires minimally a person who is able to read the Torah (Orah Hayyim 139:4). Relying, however, on a Yerushalmi text that rules that hearing alone suffices to fulfill the mitzvah, Maharil is reported in the Ashkenazic emendations to Karo, there, as ruling that we read for anyone, even a blind or ignorant (that is, Hebrew-illiterate) person and Magen David argues this case in Orah Hayyim 141. That being the case, the concern that the honoree mouth the words is a matter of preference and not of law.

[5] Indeed, the dictum of Rabbi Zeira is considered as a valid legal norm by Magen Avraham to Orah Hayyim 669, but is in doubt, there, because of another reason unrelated to the Yerushalmi's apparent rejection. The author of Sefer Haredim, in a commentary to this Yerushalmi passage, associates Rabbi Zeira's dictum with the verse גדלו לה׳ אתי ונרוממה שמו יחדו (Ps. 34:4: "Praise the Lord with me. Let us hallow His name together"). The speaker speaks in singular, not plural. That verse, along with the verse כי שם ה׳ אקרא הבו גדל לא-להינו (Deut. 32:3, "I will call upon the Lord's name. Exalt our God!"), serve as the supporting

If it could be established that a dual blessing is forbidden here, not just a dual reading, we would still wish to know if it is forbidden on account of תרי קלי (two voices) or ברכה לבטלה (a gratuitous blessing) such that two simultaneous blessings are forbidden, but splitting of the blessings fore and aft might be permitted, or if the unit nature of the aliyah is protected. The former would more likely be the case since the original requirement for blessings is only for the opening and closing blessings of the whole reading, and the intervening blessings are only said "as an enactment to address those who enter and those who leave" (Megillah 21a,b). No aliyah blessing unit had ever been proposed. Moreover, even that rule prohibiting simultaneous dual blessings could, perhaps, be waived for the intermediate aliyot since the median aliyot have their blessings only משום כבוד תורה (for the honor of the Torah). For those who would understand this prohibition of dual blessings as a type of gratuitous blessing, of course,[6] even the initial enactment establishing these median blessings is a problem. To compound this situation does not sit well. And this is not a workable solution, since permission will be taken as applicable to the first and last aliyah as well despite our words. Furthermore, such a ruling is contrary to the very enactment establishing these blessings. The Talmud's concern is that comers and goers not be misled as to the proper aliyah procedure. Those intermediate aliyot must represent that proper procedure. This argument, however, strengthens the possibility that we might permit shared aliyot with one עולה (honoree) reciting the first blessing and the other the second. This would mimic the original procedure wherein blessings were said by different people fore and aft.

Conflicting Rulings

This possibility appears to be foreclosed by the majority of halakhic decisors in a related case wherein they rule that if a person is stricken and unable to continue in the middle of an aliyah (assuming the honoree reads his own), the successor should begin that aliyah over again (S.A. Orah Hayyim 140). That rule applies, according to the Rema, even today, in the presence of a Torah Reader. The Tur, citing Talmud Yerushalmi (Megillah 4:5), gives the reason clearly,

> דאי תימא ממקום שפסק נמצא (הפסוקים) הראשונים נתברכו לפניהם ולא לאחריהם ואחרונים נתברכו לאחריהם ולא לפניהם.

> If you say [he picks up] where [the first honoree] stopped, it will follow that the first (verses) have a blessing before them but not after them, and the latter [verses] have a blessing after them but not before.

Rambam rules otherwise (Hilkhot Tefillah 12:6). If one may rely on the old order, then it would be unnecessary to repeat (save possibly the first aliyah) since one always calls many

---

texts for the responsive structure of public prayer (ברכו and זימון; Berakhot 45a and 21a, and see Yoma 37a), the latter specifically for the Torah blessings. This is an appealing construct and it would establish Rabbi Zeira's position, but nowhere are either of these verses expressly used to teach the prohibition of dual blessings. We are left with the sense that this was considered forbidden, but without solid proof.

[6] In a responsum (*Mi-ma-aynei Ha-yeshua* no. 32) in which he ultimately permits dual blessings, Rabbi Joshua Hirschhorn argues that the problem of dual blessings posed by Rabbi Zeira is a form of ברכה לבטלה or ברכה שאינה צריכה (gratuitous or unnecessary blessing), which concept he finds in an early Amoraic dictum by Resh Lakish on Yoma 70a and which is regularly used as a precedent להלכה. He is doubtless correct that that is, at heart, the issue. His lengthy *pilpul* on the parameters of that concept, however, fails. See below.

readers dependent on a prior blessing. (See BaH on this Tur). The ruling is that one may not so rely. Henceforth, if not before, we seem to have arrived at a requirement that each aliyah be an independent unit.

These extant rulings appear to side against shared aliyot. However, there continues to be some wiggling room. It might be possible to rule with Rambam. Alternatively, the BaH, in presenting the reasoning for decisively abandoning the old practice, relies on intentions and expectations. The stricken reader cannot have anticipated that another would need to rely on his blessing, therefore such reliance is impossible. But were such a procedure normative, it would be possible to rely on it. Or so it seems.

But even this is not clear. BaH bases his comments on the Rosh (Megillah 3:3) based on the aforementioned Yerushalmi text. Korban Netanel, there, no. 60, reports in the name of the RaN a differing assessment of that rule. By that assessment the issue is not intent, but rather an enactment which changed the grounds from requiring one broad Torah reading to requiring seven independent and complete reading units. Once that change was effected, and barring another enactment, blessings (by the same person) are required fore and aft of each aliyah. Korban Netanel offers this conclusion explicitly:

אם כן, אי אפשר ששני בני אדם זה יברך על תחילת הקריאה וזה יברך לאחריה.

> Therefore, it is not possible for two people to say the blessing, one before the reading and one after.

We are left in an odd position. The tendency of all this material appears to be to forbid shared aliyot. Yet loopholes abound. But none of those loopholes is particularly compelling. Is our need of this התר (permission) sufficient to override or manipulate the precedents that exist, such as they are?

Other Cases

It cannot be assumed that our forebears faced the demand for aliyot for couples. It is not unlikely, however, that they faced the pressure of conflicting חיובים (obligatory honors). Perhaps that situation can illuminate the issue before us.

Indeed, there are at least two laws, arguably three, that show rabbinic precedent in this regard. The first is known to all. I refer to the ruling that in the presence of two or more kohanim, but no levi'im, one kohen alone is called for both aliyot (S.A. Orah Hayyim 135:8). Why are both kohanim not called together? That would obviate any problem of preference and distribute the aliyot more fairly. It might be argued that Karo has available another solution to multiple kohanim, that of calling the many kohanim alternately with Israelites (S.A. Orah Hayyim 135:10) such that doubling up was unnecessary. However, Rema rules against that practice, and no one appears to propose aliyah sharing as a viable alternative solution. Indeed, where the Hafetz Hayyim considers the problem of two competing *aufruf* parties, he concedes that where necessary (במקום צורך) one can subdivide the parashah, calling one party with its one kohen in the first set of seven aliyot, then restart the series with the kohen from the second party (Mishnah B'rurah 36). This directly addresses the possibility of mixing the parties and sets some precedent against such a proposal. To our point, it fails to contemplate shared aliyot as a possibility, even though the proposed solution requires doing an injustice to the honor of a kohen.

The second precedent, though also a proof from omission, is stronger still. On Shabbat we are permitted to add to the statutory seven aliyot. Therefore, it is possible to expand the aliyah structure so as to resolve conflicts. That is not the case on Mondays and Thursdays and Shabbat afternoons when three and only three aliyot are permitted. If the first must go to a kohen and the second to that kohen or to a levi, what then do you do under pressure of your Israelite congregants and their lifecycle events? The voice is that of Rema (S.A. Orah Hayyim 135:1):

ואם היו שני חתנים בבית הכנסת והם ישראלים, מותר להוסיף לקרות ד׳ דלדידהו הוי כיו״ט שמותר להוסיף. נראה דהוא הדין לשני בעלי ברית...

If there were two grooms in the synagogue, and they are Israelites, it is permissible to add a fourth reading, for it is, for them, like a holiday wherein it is permissible to add. It would seem (also) that that is the case with regard to two circumcisions.

Again, the value of limiting aliyot to three is established by the Mishnah (Megillah 3:1). That law is authoritatively understood by the Gemara (Megillah 23a) as protecting workers' time. To neglect such a ruling should be troubling on its face. Furthermore, the proposed solution assumes a holiday which is clearly personal; what of the concerns of the workers? Yet Rema does not suggest doubling aliyot. Better to force a fourth. Indeed, Magen David, here, sides with those who would override this permission (as does Mishnah B'rurah):

ונראה לי דשפיר דלא נהגי כן.

It seems to me that they act more properly not doing so.

This effectively returns the original dilemma of two grooms. And the three aliyot stand. And nowhere is it recommended that there may be an alternative solution. As unsettled as are the grounds for rejecting dual aliyot, that clear was it to the **פוסקים** (halakhic decisors) that that was simply not an option. Indeed, the earliest and clearest ruling on this subject, in a responsum on the question of a dual haftarah with the joint recitation of blessings and text, is by Rabbi Isaac ben Sheshet Perfet (Rivash) in the fourteenth century, who rules:

א״כ ראוי למנוע אותם – וכ״ש שלא לברך שנים דאיכא משום ברכה לבטלה.

Therefore it is appropriate to prevent them — certainly two should not say the blessings since that would entail a gratuitous blessing.[7]

Simhat Torah

There is a situation, however, in which halakhists do, after all, address sharing aliyot. I believe it only goes to prove their unwillingness to do so, though the reverse might be argued: that it opens a door. The case is the unusual celebration associated with Simhat Torah. The well-known custom is to give everyone in synagogue an aliyah on that occasion, repeating the Torah portion as often as is necessary, and even giving a mass aliyah to the children (Rema, S.A. Orah Hayyim 669). Tellingly, he reports the unusual, but marginally acceptable practices of repeating the reading and giving the children aliyot (S.A. Orah Hayyim 282:2-3) but does not report mass aliyot save that of the children. Magen Avraham, however, attests the practice, on Simhat Torah, of doing so and wonders how this can be done in light of the dictum of Rabbi Zeira. Baer Heiteiv, there, cites opposition to

---

[7] Responsa of Rabbi Isaac ben Sheshet Perfet (Rivash), no. 36. Isserles, S.A. Orah Hayyim 284:5.

this practice, but Hafetz Hayyim (in Mishnah B'rurah 12) approves. Hafetz Hayyim is careful, however, to hem in his approval. He proposes that only one of the group should say the blessing, with the others simply listening. Or, that one, alone, should say the blessing before the reading and another, alone, say the blessing after (apparently relying on the interpretation of the Yerushalmi passage about the stricken reader which depends on intentionality). He advises that the mass children's aliyah should have a single adult who is the official recipient of the aliyah. In his Shaarei Ha-tziyyun, below the text of Mishnah B'rurah, he adds that, in any event, all these practices should be in the additional aliyot, after the statutory five aliyot of יום טוב have been called, "one by one."

One can see in the Hafetz Hayyim a support for the notion that intentionality may permit separating the former and latter ברכות and a willingness to accept dual aliyot, with or without this procedure, on Simhat Torah. Yet equally clear is the preference for a single voice of ברכה. Do we cite the preference or the acceptance as precedent? Moreover, all this is clearly part of the שמחה יתירה (exceptional festivity) which suffuses Simhat Torah and permits many aberrations.[8] Do we conclude from permissions given in this context that they may be applied in another, or do we not?

Arukh Hashulhan clearly understands that these permissions are not transferable. He rules, here, (669:2)

> וגם נהגו ששנים עולין ביחד ומברכין ואף שאינו נכון מכל מקום מפני שמחת סיומה עושין כן.
>
> There was also the custom that two come up together and say the blessings. Even though this is not proper, nevertheless, they do so on account of the joy of its (the Torah's) completion.

I think he is correct. In my synagogue, which does not give women aliyot, it was determined long before my tenure that women would receive aliyot after the men on Simhat Torah. It was popularly understood, even by those who have threatened to resign should women be given aliyot, that Simhat Torah is different and that the affirmative value of everyone sharing in the celebration of Torah was such as to permit what is otherwise forbidden. As a matter of legal fact, I believe that no more is evidenced here.

A Permission

One modern פוסק, alone, as far as I have been able to discover, found it correct to call two persons together to an aliyah, with both reciting the blessings. Rabbi Joshua Hirschhorn, chief rabbi of Montreal some thirty years ago, argued at length in a responsum that the

---

[8] See by Abraham Yaari's *Toldot Hag Simhat Torah*, pp. 91ff, especially pp. 96-97. Cited are numerous sources reporting Ashkenazi customs to call many at once to an aliyah on Simhat Torah. (Indeed, the *Levush* of Rabbi Mordecai Yaffe specifies,

> ונוהגין להרבות קרואים לספר תורה וכך הרבה לפרשה אחת ואין איסור ברכה לבטלה בדבר כדי לזכות כולם בקריאת התורה ביום סיומה.
>
> It is the custom to call many honorees to the Torah, even many to one portion. And this does not involve the prohibition against gratuitous blessings for it is intended to grant everyone the privilege of reading Torah on the day of its completion.

By implication, that concern would apply in other situations.)

Ephraim Zalman Margolioth (Ukraine, then Austria, early nineteenth century), in his work *Shaarei Ephraim* on the rules of the Torah Service (8:56, 9:8 and 9:30) rules as does the Hafetz Hayyim. Rabbi Joshua Hirschhorn appears to stand alone in understanding that those customs may be extended to the year. See below.

precedent of Simhat Torah may be generalized.⁹ He understands that the prohibition of dual blessings stated by Rabbi Zeira is a reflection of the general prohibition against unnecessary blessings (ברכה לבטלה). Since two are not needed for the aliyah, but only one, Rabbi Zeira prohibits the unnecessary second blessing. He understands, however, that the blessing is a personal performance blessing concerning the reading of the Torah, and that therefore, the blessing would be appropriate for each honoree, but that Rabbi Zeira rules that it is necessary to avoid incurring the need for excess blessings. This is not, however, the dominant rule, he argues, based on the later structure of blessings at each aliyah (which would not have been possible, he feels, were the blessing not justifiable) and from the permission to have additional aliyot, with blessings. These cases, as indeed the history of the medieval debate concerning whether personal performance blessings may be (or perhaps should be) said separately even though done together, or repeated after answering "Amen" to another, or whether one recitation of the blessing should suffice for all — a debate which is resolved by later Ashkenazi authorities in favor of private recitation — these lead him to conclude that Rabbi Zeira's dictum is null and that those sources which affirm it do not represent the final halakhah.

I do not know how Rabbi Hirschhorn would explain the extreme unwillingness of the tradition to consider joint aliyot if he is correct. More to the point, I do not believe he is correct that the Torah blessings are personal performance blessings. Indeed, the fact that the original enactment of Torah blessings assumed seven aliyot but blessings only at the beginning and end of the reading argues eloquently that the blessings were enacted for the public reading and not the personal performance of the honorees. Furthermore, personal performance blessings are typically recited before, not after, performance of a mitzvah. Indeed, the personal performance blessing with regard to Torah study is identical with the blessing before the reading of the Torah and is said in the preambles to Shaharit. There is, however, no blessing after. In fact, every honoree says a redundant blessing when called to the Torah משום כבוד תורה (to honor the Torah), which is the explanation offered for the enactment of the medial and additional blessings rather than Hirschhorn's proposed understanding. (This argues, too, against the BaH's view with regard to an interrupted reader who cannot continue. He argued that the honoree relies on the prior blessing, also seeing the blessings as the personal obligation of the honoree.) In the debate on multiple private vs. a single public blessing, private blessings won out with regard to personal performance. Not so with regard to a community obligation. With regard to public mitzvah blessings the etiquette is to prefer a single public blessing to many private ones, arguing ברוב עם הדרת מלך (the King is best honored in public assembly). It is self-evident to me that the aliyah structure is of that cloth.¹⁰

---

⁹ See n. 6 above.

¹⁰ On personal performance mitzvot, see S.A. Orah Hayyim 8:5 with Shaarei Teshuvah 8:7 and Arukh Hashulhan 8:11 and Mishnah B'rurah 8:13 thereon. The original preference of the classical texts for reciting a single mitzvah blessing for all is quashed over time, asserting itself only ברוב עם (in public), when the function is not personal but communal.

Hirschhorn spends interpretive time on the somewhat ambiguous source in Tosefta Berakhot 6:15. Its clauses can be variously interpreted (see Lieberman's Tosefta Kifshuta thereon, p. 117). He also cites J. Megillah 4:1, which is the same as Berakhot 7:1, (the continuation of the deliberation on the Mishnah wherein dual readers are discussed, now on to discuss the Mishnah's original ruling that blessings are to be said only before and after the Torah reading as a whole) which compares the Grace after Meals to the Torah blessing in order to derive blessings before and after the meal and before and after the reading of the Torah

Halakhic Conclusions

Given the unwillingness of our precedents to recognize dual or mass aliyot save on Simhat Torah, though subject to many of the same pressures that we face today, I believe that we should rule against dual aliyot. The forces that drive consideration of the issue are neither new nor overwhelming. Aliyot are conceived, correctly, as individual honors to the honorees, as well as honors to the Torah. If the latter, only, the procedure permitted on Simhat Torah should reign every time the Torah is read, and we have seen that it does not. Especially in

---

each from the other. This comparison is found in Mekhilta D'Rabbi Yishmael, Pas'ha (Bo) 16 and in Berakhot 21a and 48b. The Yerushalmi text continues with an illuminating inquiry:

ר' זעירא בעי: אילין ג' קרויות מה את עבד לון? כג' שאכלו כאחת או כג' שאכלו זה בפני עצמו וזה בפני עצמו? אין תעבדינון כג' שאכלו כאחת הראשון מברך ברכה ראשונה והאחרון מברך ברכה אחרונה והאמצעי אינו מברך כל עיקר אין תעבדינון כג' שאכלו זה בפני עצמו וזה בפני עצמו אפילו האמצעי מברך לפניה ולאחריה? אמר ר' שמואל בר אבודמא: [לא] למדו ברכת התורה מברכת המזון אלא לרבים. אם לרבים אפילו בינו לבין עצמו אינו מברך? א"ר אבא מרי אחוה דר' יוסי: עשאוה כשאר כל המצוות שבתורה. מה שאר כל המצוות טעונות ברכה אף זו טעונה ברכה.

Rabbi Zeira queried, "These three honorees, how do you treat them? Are they like three who have eaten together or like three who ate separately? If you treat them like three who ate together, the first recites the first blessing and the last recites the final blessing and the middle one does not say a blessing at all. (But) if you treat them as three who ate separately, even the middle one should recite both the blessings before and after." Said Rabbi Samuel bar Avudma, "They did (not) derive a Torah blessing from the Grace after Meals except for the public." If they are (derived) only for the public, does he say no blessings alone? Said Rabbi Abba Mari, brother of Rabbi Yose, "They made it (Torah blessings) like all other mitzvot in the Torah. Just as all other mitzvot require a blessing, so this one requires a blessing."

Hirschhorn, here, considers the possibility that the Torah blessings in their original formulation were public. He assumes, however, that Zeira is functioning before the change in practice to median blessings and wonders, that being the case, how Zeira can ask this question of proper practice when the Mishnah is explicit and fits the public nature of the event. He concludes that Zeira wondered, given the analogy to Grace after Meals, whether these blessings have both public and private dimensions and that his question concerned the possible interplay of those two dimensions, to wit whether the middle honorees have a personal obligation to say the blessing should they have been late, for instance, and missed the opening blessing. The answer of Abba Mari is, then, that these blessings are treated as personal performance blessings.

While this interpretation is impressively clever, it is not necessary. It is probably better to assume that Zeira's inquiry is part of the discussions which underlay the shift to median blessings. Zeira assumes that these blessings are personal performance blessings and questions the Mishnah's ruling on that basis and through the analogy to Grace after Meals. Shmuel bar Avudma answers that Torah blessing is a public event, with blessing required of the event not the personal performance. That position is questioned: Does that mean (private) Torah study has no blessing at all? And Abba Mari answers: Of course it does; in that regard it is like all other mitzvot, with a blessing required of every individual. It is unclear if he means to suggest that a blessing before, alone, is required, or whether he intends thereby to extend the requirement of both blessings to the median aliyot as the Bavli does. I believe the former is the case. In any event, the Yerushalmi proceeds to speculate with another story, from an earlier Amoraic generation (Zeira and company are fifth generation, the story is second or third generation), set apparently in the private study domain, in which people are urged to remember that a blessing is necessary when reading from the Torah:

א"ר שמואל בר נחמן: ר' יונתן הוה עבר סידרא שמע קלון קרויי ולא מברכין. אמר לון: עד מתי אתם עושין את התורה קרחות קרחות?

Said Rabbi Samuel bar Nahmani: Rabbi Yonatan was passing by the study session and heard voices reading Torah and not reciting a blessing. Said he to them, "For how long will you leave the Torah bald?"

Though the Talmud, there, does not ever clearly rule that median blessings should be required, as the Bavli does, the germs of the sensitivity to reading without blessings is evident. The Bavli does not, however, rule (as Hirschhorn understands in light of the Yerushalmi) that the rabbinic enactment was to make median blessings fore and aft a personal-performance requirement. Rather, as all subsequent commentary has understood, the Talmud's enactment on account of those coming and going (Megillah 21a) was established to honor the Torah during its public reading: משום כבוד התורה נתקנה כשקורא בתורה.

our age of heightened sensitivity to the radical dignity of the individual, to begin a custom which treats individuals as corporate entities is, I believe, incorrect. Rather, I would recommend the following.

(1) Egalitarian synagogues can utilize standard הוספות (additional aliyot) to gain sufficient aliyot to cover their חיובים (obligatory honors). Non-egalitarian synagogues will not be as severely pressed. An order of חיובים (obligatory honors) such as was practiced with regard to mourner's kaddish when it was being said individually[11] should be available to the gabbai so as to assure evenhandedness and to limit strife. I propose the following:

> *First round*   Principals: Bar or Bat Mitvzah, Aufruf, baby-naming, שלושים (if it is the first aliyah since shivah), Yahrzeit
>
> *Second round*   Parents: Bar or Bat Mitzvah, Aufruf, baby-naming (grandparents)
> Principals: anniversary
>
> *Third round*   Other first degree relatives: Bar or Bat Mitzvah, Aufruf, baby-naming, anniversary
> Principals: שלושים (if it is not the first aliyah since shivah), guest
>
> *Fourth round*   Other relatives, friends (simhah order as above)

Obviously, where conflicts can be avoided through careful scheduling, that is to be preferred.

(2) When aliyot for couples are appropriate to an occasion, such as an anniversary, aufruf or baby naming, so that calling the couple is not counterindicated by respect for the individual, one may be called with the spouse attending (יעמוד/תעמוד... עם אשתו/בעלה...) and only the first party reciting the ברכות. In this case the second is clearly not the honoree, but an attendant. Thus none of the restrictions against dual aliyot apply.[12] However, where the synagogue permits women aliyot, the honoree may not be the husband as a matter of course. Rather, the birthing mother should take precedence in receipt of the aliyah at a baby-naming, and the home-based party – bride or groom – at an aufruf. Where neither has precedence, as on an anniversary, or when both bride and groom are congregants, the choice should be made by the couple. The kohen/levi/yisrael status of the attendant, in such a case, is immaterial since only the official honoree is in receipt of the aliyah.

(3) There are many congregations that have already begun assigning shared aliyot. To those congregations I would advise that that custom should preferably be rolled back as soon as possible. Where it does not appear possible to roll back the extant custom, it is possible to defend that custom as מנהג המקום (local practice), where the custom is for the couple to split the blessings, one fore and one aft, relying on the BaH's interpretation that the bar to such blessings is a matter of intention which is resolved in this case, or, where the blessings are chanted jointly, relying on the rejection of Rabbi Zeira's dictum by the Yerushalmi. Both cases rely on the precedent of Simhat Torah. It bears

---

[11] See S.A. Orah Hayyim 666:4 with commentaries, and J.D. Eisenstein, *Otzar Dinim Uminhagim* p. 359b.

[12] Rabbi Martin Berman informs me in a correspondence of a custom he has seen among the Sephardim for the family of the honoree to stand during his aliyah. This bears some similarity to the notion advanced of attending the honoree. Rabbi Gerald Skolnik asks where these rulings leave a custom of his synagogue, upon installation of officers, to call all incoming or outgoing officers to a group aliyah. Here the special nature of the communal occasion recommends to me that it would be possible to draw a limited extension of the Simhat Torah rules to permit this. One should be appointed to say the blessing for all if at all possible, however.

repeating that it is to be strongly preferred that aliyot be given to only one. A silent partner is preferable where a couple shares an aliyah. Failing that, splitting the blessings is probably preferable to joint blessings.[13]

(These congregations, if they have not eliminated the custom of specifying aliyot for kohen and levi, as permitted by CJLS in 1990,[14] are faced with the need to determine the place of a mixed lineage couple. The husband's status, of course, is that of his father. The wife's status is itself more problematic. In a CJLS responsum in 1989, entitled "The Status of Daughters of Kohanim and Levi'im for Aliyot," Rabbi Joel Roth establishes that a lineal sanctity adheres in כוהנות on the basis of their fathers, and that that lineal sanctity suffices for receipt of the first aliyah.[15] Faced with two potentially conflicting statuses we must

---

[13] This preference, in light of ancient practice. Note that Margolioth and Mishnah B'rurah seem to prefer that, as well. Rabbi Hirshhorn's reasoning, however, tends to the reverse.

[14] Mayer Rabinowitz, "Rishon or Kohen," *PCJLS 86-90*, pp. 437-443.

[15] Joel Roth, "The Status of Daughters of Kohanim and Leviyim, for Aliyot," *PCJLS 86-90*, pp. 419-434. Rabbi Roth, in fact, discusses two forms of female priestly sanctity: lineal sanctity and associative sanctity. It is the latter form of sanctity which controls the laws concerning the eating of תרומה (the priest's food). There, the daughter of a kohen eats of תרומה when in her father's house before marriage to an Israelite or again subsequent to a divorce; conversely, the daughter of an Israelite may eat תרומה when married to a kohen, but not upon divorce. Permission to eat תרומה comes from association with the house of a kohen and is not based upon her own lineage. Lineal sanctity, however, appears to control the other perquisites mentioned.

Rabbi Roth supports giving aliyot as כהנות to women who have lineal sanctity. He refuses, however, to rule on whether it would be proper to give such aliyot to women without lineal sanctity who are married to kohanim. For our immediate purposes the issue is moot, since such a woman has a kohen husband, by definition. Since we rule that the kohen aliyah follows upon the presence of one kohen, her status does not matter. However, there will be times when that wife of a kohen will appear in synagogue without her husband. Is she then to be treated as a כוהנת by association or as a ישראלית by lineage?

It is necessary to determine whether the rules of תרומה or those of מתנות כהונה (priestly perquisites) apply to aliyot; it is clear to me that both should not. This does not so much stem from precedent as from our need for clarity. Indeed, the precedent of the priest's perquisites seems to argue that the two can function together, for an Israelite wife of a kohen surely could receive the priest's perquisites for her husband as an Israelite man can receive them for his wife the כוהנת. And she has no lineal sanctity. But the example is misleading. It is precisely not on account of her associative sanctity that she may receive the priest's perquisites. The husband of a כוהנת has no such associative sanctity. Rather, a stranger (זר) may receive these, if only said stranger is associated with a kohen or כוהנת. It is as a stranger that the wife of a kohen is qualified here, unlike תרומה. Associative sanctity and lineal sanctity function in separate spheres.

While it might be possible to argue that any association with priesthood should suffice to merit an honor, such a position raises anomalies that argue forcefully against our taking such a position. We do not wish to cast our women as appendages of their husbands. Furthermore, the call to strip a recognized כוהנת of long standing of her customary honor upon divorce is objectionable in its own right. All the more so since only associative כוהנות would lose their privilege upon divorce. Lineal כוהנות who marry kohanim would not.

Lineal sanctity fits the model of independent women which we now share, by and large. Associative sanctity is suspect in an age of working women. The matter of תרומה is as received, but it is not necessary to extend that category. Rabbi Roth has established precedent to recognize aliyot for lineal כוהנות, like other perquisites of priesthood and unlike תרומה. Let it be so exclusively.

One more problem does arise out of applying the precedent of priestly perquisites to aliyot. This is a corollary of the problem of independence versus association that we found with the concept of associative sanctity. Ruling that couples may receive a shared kohen aliyah based on the status of one of them and the example of priestly perquisites is straightforward enough, but shares the problems of association. Should the Israelite partner now be given the kohen aliyah in the absence of their kohen spouse? The precedent permits just such a transferred honor. Again, upon divorce such an honor would have to be removed. This structure may be more egalitarian than the former one (being true of husband or wife), but is no less jarring. For that reason alone we should rule, and I propose that we do so rule, that the association of a זר or זרה to a כוהנת or kohen for the purpose of aliyot be applied only in the presence of the kohen spouse. Absent the spouse, the individual should be called to the Torah in accord with his or her own lineage. This is a חומרה (a stringency)

determine which aliyah to give. Here, Rabbi Roth's sources are determinative. Rabbi Roth learns the lineal sanctity of women from the cases of priestly perquisites (מתנות כהונה) and redemption of the first born. In both cases there is not only precedent of women receiving these perquisites, but also of their non-kohen husbands receiving them in their absence. Clearly, then, having ruled that an aliyah is deemed equivalent to these perquisites, it follows that said honor inheres as well in the couple, who should be called (exclusively) to the kohen aliyah.[16])

בני מצוה

One large item remains, and that is the problem of multiple בני מצוה on one Shabbat morning. While each might be given a separate aliyah, the contest for the haftarah is bound to be great. It would be preferable to have the בני מצוה doing separate pieces of the service. For instance, one could recite the haftarah and the other could read Torah or lead Musaf. When that is not acceptable to the community or to the families, however, we need to determine the proper procedure.

Although the maftir itself is clearly defined as a separate and superfluous reading (kaddish and repetition), the halakhah codifies the same restrictions in S.A. Orah Hayyim 284 with regard to the maftir and haftarah as with regard to the Torah. As noted previously, the first clear prohibition on dual aliyot was formulated and codified on this basis precisely with regard to the haftarah. Nevertheless, these restrictions are all based on a simple analogy to the rules regarding Torah reading, and it is not clear that that must be so.[17]

---

with regard to the precedents of priestly perquisites, and well within our jurisdiction. I believe that this will be instantly recognizable to the congregation, who would understand the linked kohen aliyah as such and the individual aliyah as such.

Lastly, it must be pointed out that some of this discussion is moot if no dual aliyot are given, and *that* is the ruling of this paper. It is nonetheless necessary to decide the status, with regard to the kohen aliyah, of the spouse of a kohen. The problems of association remain and this ruling is unaffected.

[16] The permission to rely on the status of the kohen in a shared aliyah follows, here, squarely from the association of husband and wife. This would not be true of a shared aliyah of unrelated individuals given because of the large number of חיובים (obligatory honors). In that case the kohen and levi aliyot should be given only to those who qualify individually. Similarly, the rest of the statutory aliyot should include no kohanim or levi'im so as to cast no aspersions on their status. If it is necessary to have a joint aliyah including mixed status individuals that aliyah should be reserved for a הוספה (an additional aliyah).

[17] S.A. Orah Hayyim 282 and 284. There is an alternative baraita and subsequent statement by Ulla in Yerushalmi Berakhot 5:3:

תני שנים קוראין בתורה ואין שנים מפטירין בנביא. אמר עולא: קרויות בתורה ואין קרויות בנביא.

It is taught: Two people read from the Torah but two do not add from the prophet. Ulla says: There are 'calls' with regard to the Torah, but not with regard to the prophet.

This might have import here. As understood by Pnei Moshe, the subject is dual reading and Ulla's comment interprets the baraita. The tannaitic source is non-normative (it would permit dual reading of Torah which we expressly do not). Ulla explains that the requirement to read Torah is more substantial than the requirement to read from the prophets, wherefore people attend less well to the haftarah than to the Torah reading. This reading would support the notion that where attention patterns differ the ruling might follow. Indeed, Baer Heiteiv no. 1 understands that the original requirement of reading a passage from the prophets came as a result of the banning of the proper Torah reading. If so, when the Torah reading is in place attention to the haftarah is clearly of less moment.

Rabbi Solomon Sirillo, however, proposes a different reading of that Gemara, one that I believe to be correct. He understands Ulla's comment as independent of the baraita. קרויות (calls) refers to what we would call aliyot. "There are (separate persons) called up within the Torah reading, but not within the haftarah reading." This reading is supported by the use of the term קרויות with this meaning in Massekhet Sofrim, chapter 13,

The Torah reading rules, as we have seen, appear to be based on three principles: תרי קלי (two voices), ברכה לבטלה (gratuitous blessing) and the unit nature of the aliyah, with blessings fore and aft. With regard to the former there is strong reason to doubt whether it applies to a bar mitzvah. The base ruling of תרי קלי prohibits such reading for Torah but does not do so for the Megillah. If the issue is, as stated, that many voices are difficult to hear, this too should be prohibited. The Gemara (Megillah 21b) explains that with regard to Megillah and Hallel even ten may read because these texts are especially beloved and people will therefore pay special attention. Some recommend this as the justification for permitting shared aliyot on Simhat Torah only.[18] In celebration of the Torah people will pay special attention. In my experience that does not correspond to people's Simhat Torah practice. It does, however, correspond highly with people's behavior with respect to בני מצוה. It is perfectly clear that where בני מצוה are involved the attention accorded the haftarah far exceeds that accorded the Torah reading. Insofar as the reading alone is concerned, then, we might be correct to permit dual reading of the haftarah (and even the maftir) because people are clearly focused on the doings of the בני מצוה.

On the matter of the blessings, however, it is at once more and less clear. Whereas the blessings of the Torah were originally applied only around multiple honorees, it appears that that was never the case for the haftarah. If the analogy to the Torah blessings is to their original format, it might be possible to split the haftarah blessings. If it is to the Torah blessings as practiced, and we understand that as does Korban Netanel rather than the BaH, then it would appear improper for two בני מצוה to split a haftarah and its blessings. Then again, if the issue is ברכה לבטלה, blessings are required fore and aft no less than for the Torah blessings.

As with the Torah blessings, whereas I cannot prove it absolutely, I sense in this material that split and joint aliyot run counter to the intent and practice of the tradition. That understanding is stated clearly by Korban Netanel and Arukh Hashulhan about Torah blessings and by Rivash about the blessings of the haftarah. And I believe it to be the intention behind Ulla's words in Yerushalmi B'rakhot (5:3), that the aliyah was designed as a unitary honor.[19] I think we are well advised, given our own assumptions concerning the radical respect due the individual, that that form be maintained.

The best format, then, for two בני מצוה who must share a haftarah would be to assign separate aliyot to the בני מצוה (for evenhandedness it is better that neither receive the maftir aliyah or, alternatively, the penultimate aliyah might be termed מפטיר ראשון either as a standard הוספה or as an additional repetitive reading after kaddish) and that they then split the reading of the haftarah as two successive readers for the maftir, who should recite the blessings around the haftarah alone. The concept of a Torah reader for the haftarah is not very familiar, but there have been communities wherein the prophet was read from a

---

and elsewhere in Yerushalmi Berakhot 7:1 (= Megillah 4:1). Ulla's dictum, taken thus, is a clear statement of the unit nature of the haftarah with its blessings fore and aft. (See *Encyclopedia Talmudit*, vol. 10, p. 5, and Gedalia Felder, Yesodei Yeshurun, vol. 4, p. 417.)

Ephraim Zalman Margolioth rules simply, אין לקרות שני אנשים לעלות יחד לתורה ואפילו למפטיר יש למנוע. "One may not call two people simultaneously to the Torah. Even for the maftir one should prevent this." His language suggests less certainty on his part with regard to the haftarah, probably due to the general sense that it is of less moment than the Torah reading, like the Pnei Moshe understanding of Ulla's comments. But his language simply reflects the language of Rivash, and there is no uncertainty there. Whereas I initially leaned toward this leniency, I have increasingly come to see it as insubstantial and Sirillo as correct concerning Ulla.

[18] Eliyahu Rabbah no. 12 to S.A. Orah Hayyim 669.

[19] See n. 17 above.

scroll, in which case the Torah reader read the haftarah for the honoree as he did the Torah.[20] The integrity of the aliyah and of the blessings around the haftarah is thus maintained. If it is strongly preferred that the בני מצוה chant the haftarah together, they should nonetheless not recite the maftir and haftarah blessings together, nor one after the other. Rather, one should be called to maftir and recite the Torah blessings and the other recite the haftarah blessings (though they might stand together), and they may then chant the haftarah together.[21] The key to these arrangements is to let it be known that the בני מצוה are not a joint entity, but separate בני מצוה (especially important when they are twins), and that they are sharing leadership in the service but are not two sides of one coin. I believe that to be psychologically proper, as it is halakhically so.[22]

Obiter Dicta

On the matter of first degree relatives and their proximity at aliyot and whether that should apply to spouses as well: there is no halakhic bar to proximate aliyot for first degree relatives (S.A. Orah Hayyim 141:6), but only one of custom due to עין הרע (the evil eye). We do not hold such superstitions. Orhot Hayyim proposes an alternative reason related to the prohibition of first degree relatives in the matter of testimony,[23] which would apply to spouses, but his is not the regnant reasoning. While "tradition" may be sufficient reason to continue the practice of not assigning proximate aliyot to first degree relatives, we need not expand the category to include a new class of persons unmentioned in the literature.

It should be clear that we may not grant any pulpit privileges to the spouses of Jews who are intermarried. Congregations which grant such aliyot to the Jewish partner should not see the status of the silent partner as an attendant to the proper honoree as an opportunity to honor the family. On the contrary, we are always to be careful not to recognize intermarried couples as such.

---

[20] Mishnah B'rurah to S.A. Orah Hayyim 284:8. Gedaliah Felder, *Yesodei Yeshurun* 4, p. 413. Successive readers are uncommon for a single honoree to the Torah since the portions are short. It is not at all unusual within the full reading, nor for longer texts such as the Megillot. Here, not length but the demands of the בני מצוה control. But there does not appear to be any stricture in theory against such a successive reading.

Ephraim Zalman Margolioth posits such a stricture for a whole parashah (*Shaarei Ephraim* 3:6), but offers no support for it. Given the original practice wherein each honoree read his own aliyah this seems unreasonable. Even he concedes that if the Torah reader is late and an unprepared reader had begun, it would be appropriate to switch in midstream, though only between aliyot.

[21] Surprisingly, although it is not recommended, some precedent exists for separating the reader of the haftarah from the recipient of the maftir aliyah as long as some tie of haftarah to maftir is maintained. That precedent (in a wholly different context) might be applied here, allowing the bar mitzvah who was not maftir to say the haftarah blessings since the bar mitzvah who had maftir reads the haftarah with him. (See S.A. Orah Hayyim 284:4, Isserles and Magen Avraham no. 3 there and Mishnah B'rurah nos. 7-8 thereon. But see Mishnah B'rurah no. 10, as well. The Hafetz Hayyim is not fully consistent here, citing different and opposing sources. The key seems to be the difference that, with regard to one unable to continue, the haftarah was already begun by the maftir.)

[22] For a different suggestion on the problem of two בני מצוה competing for the same maftir, see Moshe Feinstein (*Iggrot Moshe* 1, Orah Hayyim 102), who proposes holding a minyan in reserve for the second bar mitzvah during the first maftir and repeating the maftir and haftarah for that minyan that had been absent for the first. This appears to be the preferred mode of modern Orthodox writers. See Gedaliah Felder, *Yesodei Yeshurun* IV, pp. 416ff., and Eliezer Waldenberg, at length, *Tzitz Eliezer* 6, no. 36.

[23] Gedalia Felder, *Yesodei Yeshurun* 2, p. 238.

Conclusion

The aliyah was always held to be an individual honor, and joint recitations of the blessings has been seen as a ברכה לבטלה (an unnecessary blessing) and running afoul of תרי קלי (the principle that two voices at once are not clearly heard). Therefore, it is preferable to grant single aliyot and resolve multiple demands through the use of a hierarchy of claims and the judicious use of additional aliyot. Where a couple has a joint שמחה (celebration) they may come up together but only one should be formally called and recite the blessings. Where congregations already call couples together, it is preferable if only one recites the blessing. Alternatively, splitting the blessings, fore and aft, is preferable to joint recitation.

Joint בני מצוה should receive separate aliyot (for evenhandedness, neither should be given the maftir aliyah, or, alternatively, the penultimate aliyah might be termed מפטיר ראשון), but only one person should recite the haftarah blessings. They may, however, split the reading of the haftarah or recite it together, since the congregation's attention to the doings of the בני מצוה is unusually rapt.

OH 136:1993

Aliyot for Couples

Rabbi Kassel Abelson

This paper was approved by the CJLS on February 17, 1993, by a vote of eleven in favor, seven opposed, and three abstaining (11-7-3). Voting in favor: Rabbis Kassel Abelson, Ben Zion Bergman, Elliot N. Dorff, Ezra Finkelstein, Arnold M. Goodman, Jan Caryl Kaufman, Reuven Kimelman, Aaron L. Mackler, Mayer Rabinowitz, Joel E. Rembaum, and Gordon Tucker. Voting against: Rabbis Samuel Fraint, Howard Handler, Judah Kogen, Lionel E. Moses, Avram Israel Reisner, Chaim Rogoff, and Joel Roth. Abstaining: Rabbis Stanley Bramnick, Jerome M. Epstein, and Gerald Skolnik.

The Committee on Jewish Law and Standards of the Rabbinical Assembly provides guidance in matters of halakhah for the Conservative movement. The individual rabbi, however, is the authority for the interpretation and application of all matters of halakhah.

שאלה

Many Conservative congregations have instituted the practice of calling couples to the Torah for an *aufruf*, for baby namings, and to celebrate anniversaries. In other congregations the practice has developed of calling the parents of the bar/bat mitzvah or of the bride and groom to the Torah for an aliyah. Are these acceptable Conservative practices?

תשובה

The Torah reading is the focal point of the service. It functions not only as an opportunity to hear the Torah read, and to study, but it also serves as a community bulletin board keeping the members of the congregation informed about what is happening in the lives of their fellow members. And it provides the congregation with the opportunity to reinforce values it holds to be important. The Torah reading has had a long and revealing history, and understanding that history will help us to answer the שאלה, the question.

Origins of the Torah Service

The origins of the Torah service are traced by tradition to Moses and to Ezra. The Rambam summarizes the tradition in the Mishneh Torah.

> משה רבינו תיקן להם לישראל שיהו קורין ברבים בשבת ובשני ובחמישי
> בשחרית כדי שלא ישהו שלשה ימים בלא שמיעת תורה. ועזרא תיקן שיהו
> קורים כן במנחה בכל שבת משום יושבי קרנות. וגם הוא תיקן שיהו קורין
> בשני ובחמישי שלשה בני אדם. ולא יקראו פחות מעשרה פסוקים.

Moses our teacher decreed that Israel should read the Torah publicly on Shabbat and on Monday and Thursday mornings so that three days should not pass without the Torah being heard. And Ezra decreed that the Torah should be read every Shabbat at Minhah for the sake of the idlers. He also decreed that on Mondays and Thursdays three people were to be called to the Torah, and that not less than ten sentences were to be read.[1]

Additional Blessings

Originally the person who received the first aliyah recited the opening blessing over the Torah and the one who received the last aliyah recited the concluding blessing.

הפותח והחותם מברך לפניה ולאחריה.

> He that begins and he who concludes the reading from the Torah recite a blessing, one at the beginning and the other after it.[2]

Each recipient of an עליה thus read a section from the Torah, but only the first and the last readers recited benedictions. But conditions changed, and in Amoraic times it was decreed that the same person recite the blessings before and after each עליה. Why the change? The reason given in the Talmud is:

גזירה משום הנכנסים ומשום היוצאין.

> It is a decree so that those arriving [during the Torah reading] and those leaving [before its conclusion could hear both blessings].[3]

It would seem then, that the Rabbis made a great effort to accommodate congregants who were tardy or who were impatient to leave services before the Torah reading was over. They instituted the blessings over the intermediate aliyot even though it seemed to contradict the basic principle of ברכה לבטלה, not reciting an unnecessary blessing. Since the only required blessings were the ones to be recited at the beginning of the Torah reading and at the end, the in-between blessings are not necessary. Nonetheless, the rabbis found reasons to allow blessings to be recited by each עולה, so as not to mislead those casual worshippers whose brief stay at services might lead them to think that only one blessing was required. This practice was also presumably meant to give honor to the Torah (משום כבוד התורה).

The Torah Reader

As already indicated, the ancient practice was to have the portion read by members of the congregation who would divide the portion to be read that day and would read it without any assistance. In some congregations, however, there may not have been seven people who knew how to read the Torah properly. This would probably be the case in small communities, or in communities outside of Eretz Yisrael, where most people were not fluent in Hebrew.

והעליות לא נהגו כן. אלא אחד קורא את כל הפרשה.

---

[1] M.T. Hilkhot T'fillah 12:1.

[2] M. Megillah 4:2.

[3] B. Megillah 21 a-b.

> [In such cases] it was not customary to have individual aliyot.
> Rather, one person would be assigned to read the entire portion.[4]

The realities of congregational life forced the development of a new stage in the Torah reading. In those congregations where there were few skilled Torah readers an expert Torah reader would be assigned to assist those who had trouble reading the portion assigned to them. This is probably reflected in the Talmudic debate as to whether two persons may read together from the Torah. One baraita holds that it is forbidden for two persons to read together:

> מפני שאין שני קולות נכנסין באזן אחת.

Two voices together cannot be heard distinctly.[5]

Another baraita however holds:

> שנים קוראין בתורה. ואין שנים קוראין בנביא.

Two can read together from the Torah, but two cannot read together from the Prophets.[6]

One skilled person could read the haftorah, but among the seven readers of the Torah portion, there would be some who required an expert to assist them — hence two voices. This baraita from the Yerushalmi is a key teaching, for it gives Talmudic support to those who believe that joint aliyot are permissible. A further development is recorded in the Shulhan Arukh:

> לא יקראו שנים. אלא העולה קורא וש"ץ שותק, או ש"ץ קורא והעולה לא יקרא בקול רם ומכל מקום צריך הוא לקרות עם הש"ץ כדי שלא תהא ברכתו לבטלה. אלא שצריך בנחת שלא ישמיע לאזניו.

Two do not read together. If the עולה [person called to the Torah] reads then the ש"ץ [official reader] keeps quiet, but if the ש"ץ reads then the עולה does not read aloud. But he is required to read with the official reader so that his blessing will not be a ברכה לבטלה [a redundant blessing]. But he must read quietly, so it will not be heard.[7]

There are two issues which are interconnected. The first issue is that of two voices reading together, and the second is that of the ברכה לבטלה [unnecessary blessing]. The practice of having the עולה mouth the reading was recommended, as a way to avoid the problem "of two voices together," while technically conforming to the Jewish practice of having the person who says the blessing perform the act. Here the blessing and the act are done by two different people. The עולה recites the blessing, but the ש"ץ does the reading. The practice of having the ש"ץ assist an inexpert reader soon became our present practice of having the ש"ץ read for every עולה so that no one called to the Torah would be embarrassed by being unable himself to read the Torah. The law as it later developed ignores the question of ברכה לבטלה [a redundant blessing], separates blessing from deed, and no longer even requires the עולה to mouth the reading.

---

[4] J. Megillah 4, 75a.
[5] J. Megillah 4:1, 77d.
[6] Ibid., 4:1, 77d.
[7] S.A. Orah Hayyim 141.

Additional Aliyot

The number of aliyot is fixed by the Mishnah:

> זה הכלל: כל שיש בו מוסף ואינו יום טוב קוראין ארבעה, ביום טוב חמשה, ביום הכפורים ששה, בשבת שבעה, אין פוחתין מהן אבל מוסיפין עליהם, ומפטירין בנביא.
>
> This is the general principle: any day where there is musaf [additional service] but is not a Yom Tov, four read; on a Yom Tov, five; on Yom Kippur, six; on the Sabbath, seven. They must not reduce the number but they may increase it, and they conclude with a reading from the prophets.[8]

The Mishnah gives permission on Shabbat to add aliyot to accommodate those congregants who have חיובים (entitlements) by giving them an aliyah. And this seems to have been the method used by congregations to solve the problem of there being more people who were entitled to aliyot on the Sabbath then there were statutory aliyot. The Mishnah, however, rules differently for weekday mornings:

> בשני ובחמישי ובשבת במנחה קורין שלשה, אין פוחתין ואין מוסיפין עליהם, ואין מפטירין בנביא.
>
> On Monday and on Thursday, and on Shabbat at the Minhah [afternoon] service three persons read; they must not reduce the number nor add to it; nor do they conclude with a haftorah [reading from the prophets].[9]

The reason given for this stringent limitation is that there were people present at weekday mornings services who had to get to work.[10] But when there was a pressing need for additional aliyot, a way was found to evade the limitation and meet the need:

> ואם היו שני חתנים בבית הכנסת והם ישראלים, מותר להוסיף לקרות ד' דלדידהו הוי כיו"ט שמותר להוסיף, ונראה שהוא הדין לשני בעלי ברית.
>
> If there were two grooms in the synagogue and they were Israelites, [and could not receive the kohen or levi aliyah] it is permitted to add a fourth reader, because it is like a Yom Tov [holiday] when it is permitted to add, and apparently the same ruling would apply if there are two בעלי ברית [celebrants of a Brit] present.[11]

The element of שמחה (celebration) was sufficient reason to change the rules governing aliyot, a suggestive precursor of what follows.

Simhat Torah

The extreme flexibility of the developing Halakhah of the Torah service was utilized by one modern posek to justify calling two people for one aliyah and having them recite the blessings together. Rabbi Joshua Hirschhorn was Chief Rabbi of Montreal several decades ago.

---

[8] M. Megillah 4:2.
[9] M. Megillah 4:1.
[10] B. Megillah 23a.
[11] Rema, Orah Hayyim 135.

A תשובה in his book *Mi-ma'aynei Ha-yeshua* [no. 32], deals with the question of two בני מצוה on the same Shabbat.

Rabbi Hirschhorn begins by citing the widespread practice of calling a number of men to the Torah at Simhat Torah for the same aliyah. They recite the ברכות together, and the ש"ץ (Torah reader) reads the פרשה (Torah portion). He reasons that this custom is not a violation of ברכה לבטלה (redundant blessing), or of תרי קלי (two voices cannot be heard distinctly), because a violation of the Torah would not have been permitted on Simhat Torah, which is the celebration of Torah. And he tries to prove his claim with a carefully reasoned argument in which he cites early authorities in support of his case. Rabbi Hirschhorn's reasoning leads him to affirm that since group aliyot are permitted on Simhat Torah, it is permissible to have group aliyot during the rest of the year. And in the case of the two בני מצוה:

> אם יש שני בר מצוה בביהכ"נ ורוצים ששניהם יברכו אם אי אפשר בענין אחד אין להכביד עליהם ויש להתיר להם לברך שנים על התורה. והחזן יקרא או שאפילו אחד הנערים יקרא והשני ישמע קריאתו ויוכלו לברך שניהם ברכה שניה. כי יש בזה לסמוך על הראשונים הסוברים דאין בזה משום ברכה שאינה צריכה.

> If there are two bar mitzvahs in the synagogue and it is desired that both of them say the blessing, and no other way is possible, we can permit both to say the blessing together over the Torah, and the hazzan [cantor] will read, or even one of the boys will read and the other will hear his reading, then both can recite together the second blessing. For this we can rely on those Rishonim [early authorities] who hold that this would not be an unnecessary blessing.[12]

Joint Aliyot

Until the development in the Middle Ages of Simhat Torah, the rabbis seemed to consider single aliyot as normative. Rabbi Avram Reisner, in his responsum entitled "Joint Aliyot," maintains that the normative tradition, through the years, has not endorsed joint aliyot, and there is no compelling reason that we should permit them. He writes that,

> Given the unwillingness of our precedents to recognize dual or mass aliyot save on Simhat Torah, though subject to many of the same pressures that we face today, I believe that we should rule against dual aliyot. The forces that drive consideration of the issue are neither new nor overwhelming. Aliyot are conceived, correctly, as individual honors to the honorees, as well as honors to the Torah. If the latter, only, the procedure permitted on Simhat Torah should reign every time the Torah is read, and we have seen that it does not. Especially in our age of heightened sensitivity to the radical dignity of the individual, to begin a custom which treats individuals as corporate entities is, I believe, incorrect.[13]

---

[12] *Mi-ma'aynei Ha-yeshua*, p. 114.
[13] Rabbi Avram Israel Reisner, "Joint Aliyot," above, pp. 29-30.

Rabbi Reisner goes on to discuss congregations that have already instituted shared aliyot:

> To those congregations I would advise that that custom should preferably be rolled back as soon as possible. Where it does not appear possible to roll back the extant custom, it is possible to defend that custom as מנהג המקום (local custom), where the custom is for the couple to split the blessings, one fore and one aft, relying on the BaH's interpretation that the bar to such blessings is a matter of intention which is resolved in this case, or where the blessings are shared jointly, relying on the rejection of R. Zeira's dictum by the Yerushalmi. Both cases rely on the precedent of Simhat Torah.[14]

Looking Back

From the days of Moses and Ezra there has been a continuing evolution of the Torah service in response to the changing needs of the congregation. Originally each recipient of an aliyah read a section from the Torah but only the first and last readers recited benedictions. In Amoraic times it was decreed that the עולה recite blessings before and after each aliyah read. And a reason was found for this change. The reason given was, "not to mislead those casual worshippers whose brief stay at services might lead them to think that only one blessing was required." To accomplish this the principle of ברכה לבטלה (redundant blessings) was ignored. When an expert Torah reader was introduced to enable those who were not skilled Torah readers to have an aliyah, the tradition of having the same person who says the blessing perform the act was overlooked, for the עולה recited the blessing while the ש"ץ read the Torah. And the Yerushalmi quotes a baraita which affirmed that "two can read together from the Torah," which gives Talmudic support to those who believe that joint aliyot are possible. The Mishnah affirms that additional aliyot are permissible on Shabbat, but not on weekdays. But the Rema declared a weekday Shaharit to be a Yom Tov to enable two חתנים (who were neither Kohanim nor Levi'im) to both have aliyot. And, when it seemed desirable that joint aliyot be instituted, they were introduced. On Simhat Torah the custom developed of calling groups to the Torah and all together reciting the Torah blessings, rather than repeating the Torah reading and lengthening the service, or breaking up the congregation into smaller units and reading from several Torahs. Both "two voices" and "redundant blessings" were ignored in this development. When the number of בני מצוה increased in the congregation, Rabbi Hirschhorn, Chief Rabbi of Montreal, found adequate precedent in the words of the Rishonim and in the precedent of Simhat Torah to permit two בני מצוה to recite the Torah blessings together on a Shabbat.

Rabbi Avram Reisner, though he disapproves of dual aliyot, finds in his responsum "Joint Aliyot," that it is possible to defend the practice of those congregations that have introduced dual aliyot on the grounds of מנהג המקום (local custom). To sum up, when the need arose, previous precedents were found to be flexible enough to permit radical innovations in the Torah service. The question is then, "Are the needs of our congregations such as to make family and group aliyot a desirable development?"

---

[14] Ibid., p. 30.

In Our Congregations

In our congregations the Torah reading serves as a means of reinforcing the values of the congregation, and of keeping the congregation informed and involved in what is happening in the lives of the families of the congregation. A basic value of Judaism, which needs reinforcing in our generation, is the marriage tie. In an age that stresses the "radical dignity of the individual," and in a society where individual happiness and self-fulfillment often are given priority over responsibilities to others, it is important to emphasize and celebrate the relationship of husband and wife, and appropriate to do so in the context of the Torah reading. Many of our congregations have already instituted joint aliyot for couples entering a marriage, observing an anniversary, naming a child, or celebrating a bar mitzvah. An important subliminal message is being conveyed to the congregation when a couple says the blessings together, figuratively "speaks with one voice," as they enter a marriage, name a child, celebrate an anniversary or a bar or bat mitzvah. Even when there is a divorce in a family, if the parents of a bar or bat mitzvah have a joint aliyah, a statement is being made to the extended family and to the congregation that the parents continue to share responsibility for the raising of the child. In any event, the מרא דאתרא has the opportunity to discuss the situation with the parents, to talk about the issue of joint responsibility for the child's welfare, and to work through a mutually satisfactory solution to the question of whether the parents' aliyah is to be handled jointly or individually.

In cases where one of the couple is a kohen or a levi our congregations make a choice. Some may follow the approach of Rabbi Mayer Rabinowitz in his responsum, "Rishon or Kohen" and call the couple any place in the course of the Torah reading.[15] Others follow the approach of Rabbi Joel Roth who rules that lineal sanctity for the כהונה (priesthood) adheres both to men and women, and that in the case of a mixed couple associative sanctity would apply.[16] Hence the couple would be called either to the kohen or levi aliyah or among the הוספות (aliyot added to the customary seven on Shabbat).

Conclusion

The answer to Rabbi Reisner's question — Are the needs of our congregations such as to make family and group aliyot a desirable development? — is a resounding "yes." The instituting of aliyot for couples by Conservative congregations to mark family events can be seen as a response to the compelling need to recognize the community importance of marriage ties and to jointly celebrate family events.

Aliyot for couples can be justified halakhically by recognizing the readiness of the rabbis of past generations to find good reasons to meet the needs of their changing congregations, by the baraita found in the Yerushalmi permitting two to read together from the Torah, by the precedent of group aliyot on Simhat Torah, by the contemporary responsum permitting joint aliyot for בני מצוה, and by the מנהג (custom) in many of our congregations of giving couples joint aliyot. Hence though aliyot for individuals remains the norm, the practice in many of our Conservative congregations of giving aliyot to couples is acceptable.

Group aliyot for other members of a family or for communal occasions such as the installation of the officers of the congregation, honoring Hebrew school teachers, Volunteers for Israel etc., may be desirable, but each instance will have to be carefully examined and individually justified, utilizing an approach similar to the one used for joint aliyot for couples.

---

[15] Mayer Rabinowitz, "Rishon or Kohen," *PCJLS 86-90*, pp. 437-443.
[16] Joel Roth, "The Status of Daughters of Kohanim and Levi'im for Aliyot," *PCJLS 86-90*, pp. 419-434.

OH 139:11.2000

Hazak, Hazak, v'Nithazak

Rabbi Nechama D. Goldberg

This paper was approved on March 8, 2000, by a vote of twenty in favor and one opposed (20-1-0). Voting in favor: Rabbis Kassel Abelson, Ben Zion Bergman, Paul Drazen, Jerome M. Epstein, Nechama D. Goldberg, Arnold M. Goodman, Susan Grossman, Judah Kogen, Vernon H. Kurtz, Alan B. Lucas, Aaron L. Mackler, Daniel S. Nevins, Paul Plotkin, Mayer Rabinowitz, Avram Israel Reisner, Joel E. Rembaum, James S. Rosen, Joel Roth, Elie Kaplan Spitz, and Gordon Tucker. Voting against: Rabbi Samuel Fraint.

The Committee on Jewish Law and Standards of the Rabbinical Assembly provides guidance in matters of halakhah for the Conservative movement. The individual rabbi, however, is the authority for the interpretation and application of all matters of halakhah.

שאלה

When doing the triennial Torah cycle, is it permissible to pronounce חזק חזק ונתחזק for each of the five books every year (even though only one-third of each would have been read that year), or must one wait until the three-year cycle is completed?[1]

תשובה

The earliest reference to the custom of saying חזק to one who reads from the Torah is found in *HaManhig*, written by Abraham ben Nathan ha-Yarhi who wrote at the end of the twelfth and beginning of the thirteenth centuries regarding the customs of Jews of France, Germany and Spain. He writes:

> מה שנהגו בצרפת ובפרובינצא לכל הקוראים בתורה כשסיימין שאומר להם
> החזן בקול רם חזק, מצאתי סמך לדבר בבראשית רבה לא ימוש ספר התורה
> הזה מפיך, אין אומרים הזה אלא למי שתולה החפץ בידו, מלמד שהיה ספר
> תורה בחיקו שליהושע, ואומר לו הקב"ה חזק ואמץ מכאן למסיים בתורה
> אומרים לו חזק. אב"ן.[2]

As was the custom in France and Provence that all who read from the Torah, as they concluded, the hazzan would say to them in a loud voice, חזק, I have found support for this in Bereshit Rabbah, "Let not this Book of Teaching cease from your lips." The word הזה

---

[1] For a comprehensive analysis of the recitation of חזק, see Yaakov S. Speigel, "אמירת חזק ויישר כח" ספר השנה למדעי היהדות והרוח 26 and 27 (5755): 343-370.

[2] Hilkhot Shabbat 56, ed. Rafael, p. 182.

is used only to the one who holds the object in his hand, from which we learn that the Sefer Torah was in Joshuah's lap. And God said to him, "Be strong and resolute." From here, to the one who concludes the Torah reading we say to him, חזק.

According to the custom, חזק was recited to each person who read from the Torah. At that time, Torah reading customs were in flux. It was customary for each person who was called to the Torah to read for himself. As fewer people were able to read the Torah, especially with the appropriate trope, a designated reader replaced the congregant. The blessing of חזק was addressed to the reader. (*HaManhig* refers only to the reader and does not distinguish a separate individual receiving an aliyah.)

The citation from Bereshit Rabbah is used as prooftext that the person reading from the Torah (or reciting the blessings) should be holding on to the Torah. By inference, since God said חזק to Joshua while he was holding the Torah, we should also say חזק to one who holds the Torah:

> אמר ר' שמעון בן יוחאי ספר משנה תורה היה סיגנם ליהושע, בשעה שנגלה עליו הקב"ה מצאו יושב וספר משנה תורה בידו, אמר לו חזק יהושע אמץ יהושע לא ימוש ספר התורה הזה וגו' (יהושע א:ח), נטלו והראה לו גלגל חמה, אמר לו כשם שלא דממתי מזה כך אתה דום מלפני מיד וידם השמש וגו'.[3]

> R. Shimon b. Yohai said: The Book of Deuteronomy was an ensign for Joshua. When the Holy One, blessed be He, revealed Himself to him, He found him sitting with the Book of Deuteronomy in his hand. Said He to him, "Be strong, Joshua, be of good courage, Joshua; This book of the law shall not depart out of thy mouth," (Josh. 1:8). Thereupon he took it and showed it to the orb of the sun which he apostrophised thus: "Even as I have not stood still from (studying) this, so do thou stand still before me!" Straightaway, "And the sun stood still," etc.

The next source to report on this custom is *Orhot Hayyim* by Aaron ben Jacob HaKohen of southern France writing in the beginning of the fourteenth century:

> ובב"ר לא ימוש ספר תורה הזה מפיך מלמד שהיה ספר התורה בידו של יהושע שאין אומרים הזה אלא שמי שתופס החפץ בידו. וכשסיים אומרים לו חזק ואמץ. ומכאן יצא המנהג לומר למסיים לקרות בתורה חזק וכך המנהג בצרפת ובפרובינצה אבל בספרד אין אומרים אותו אלא בסיום התורה בלבד והכל הולך אחר המנהג.[4]

> In Bereshit Rabbah, "This book of the law shall not depart out of thy mouth," teaches that the Sefer Torah was in Joshua's hand since one only uses הזה when one is holding the object in his hand. And when he concludes, we say to him, חזק ואמץ. From here the custom derives to say to the one who concludes his reading in the Torah, חזק, and thus is the custom in France and Provence. But in Spain, we only say this at the conclusion of the Torah exclusively, and each behaves according to his custom.

---

[3] Genesis Rabbah 6:18, ed. Theodor-Albeck, pp. 49-50.
[4] *Orhot Hayyim*, Halakhot 2 and 5, 19.

Orhot Hayyim reiterates what was stated in *HaManhig*, but adds a conflicting custom from Spain. The custom in Spain is to recite חזק only at the completion of the Torah as opposed to reciting it after each reader.

David ben Joseph of 14th century Spain, in his *Abudraham*, cites *HaManhig* in his opinion, although his attribution of the Spanish custom is not to be found in *HaManhig*. He explains the Spanish custom a little further:

ובספרד לא נהגו לאמרה אלא כשסיימים כל ספר וספר מחומשי התורה ואולי סוברים למסיים בתורה מן הספר ממש קאמר.[5]

> In Spain, they are only in the habit of saying it [חזק] when they conclude each book of the five books of the Torah and perhaps they believed that it referred to the one who concludes a book of the Torah explicitly.

We see here the custom of reciting חזק at the conclusion of each book of the Torah, although it is addressed to the person who reads and not the event of the conclusion.

The interpretation of the word למסיים contributes to variations in custom. It may refer to each person called to the Torah who concludes his own reading, or to the one who concludes the reading at the end of the book.

The matter of reciting חזק is first mentioned in the codes in the Bet Yosef (1522-1542) on the Tur. Here he quotes from *Orhot Hayyim*:

בבראשית רבה (סוף פרשה ו) לא ימוש ספר התורה הזה מפיך (יהושע א:ח) מלמד שהיה ס"ת בידו של יהושע שאין לומר הזה אלא למי שתופס החפץ וכשסיים אומרים לו חזק ואמץ מכאן יצא המנהג לומר למסיים לקרות התורה בכל פעם חזק עכ"ל.[6]

> In Bereshit Rabbah, "This book of the law shall not depart out of thy mouth" teaches that the Sefer Torah was in Joshua's hand since one only uses הזה when one is holding the object. And when he concludes, we say to him, חזק ואמץ. From here the custom derives to say to the one who concludes his reading in the Torah each time, חזק.

The Bet Yosef cites the custom of France and Provence and stops short of mentioning the alternative custom of Spain. When codifying law in the Shulhan Arukh, Joseph Karo does not mention the matter of חזק. Moses Isserles, in his gloss to the Shulhan Arukh, inserts the custom from the Bet Yosef:

הקורא בתורה צריך לאחוז בספר תורה בשעת ברכה. הגה: וסמכו מנהג זה על מה שנאמר ביהושע לא ימוש ספר התורה הזה מפיך חזק ואמץ (יהושע א:ח-ט) ומזה נהגו לומר למסיים לקרות בתורה בכל פעם חזק (ב"י בשם ארחות חיים).[7]

> The one who reads from the Torah must hold the Sefer Torah at the time of the blessing. Gloss: This custom is based upon what is said in Joshua, "This book of law shall not depart out of thy mouth...be resolute and of good courage." From here we have the custom to say to the one who concludes the reading of the Torah each time, חזק.

---

[5] *Abudraham*, Shaharit for Shabbat, p. 171.
[6] Bet Yosef on Orah Hayyim 179:11, s.v. כתב בעל.
[7] S.A. Orah Hayyim 139:11.

The inclusion of this gloss would lead us to believe that this was a prevalent Ashkenazic custom. Rabbi Jacob Moses Toledano, the Chief Sephardi Rabbi of Tel Aviv, expressed his surprise in an article in *Bet HaKnesset* in 1947:

> וזה פלא, שבימנו רואים אנו שבארצות המזרח נוהגים לומר לעולה המסיים לקרות בתורה "חזק", או "חזק וברוך" ובסיום התורה לא נוהגים לומר כך, כ"א במקומות אחדים, ואצל האשכנזים נהגו לומר בסיום התורה "חזק, חזק", ולעולה לתורה אומרים ברוב המקומות "יישר כח" ולא "חזק", ואם כי, מובן אחד לשניהם, רואים אנו כבר מימי הרמ"א ועד כה, שינוי במנהג.[8]

> And this is surprising, since in our day we see that in eastern countries they are accustomed to saying to the one who concludes the reading of the Torah, חזק, or חזק וברוך and at the completion of the Torah they are not accustomed to saying that, and so it is in several places. And among the Ashkenazim they are accustomed to saying at the completion of the Torah, חזק, חזק, and to the person called up to the Torah they say in most places, יישר כח and not חזק. And although, the understanding is the same for both of them, we see already in the days of the Rema until now a change of custom.

Rabbi Toledano cites several other eastern sources who record the custom of saying חזק. He concludes that the multiple expulsions of the Jews in Europe contributed to the varying customs and the changes within the communities.

The words one uses and to whom it is said can change depending upon the purpose one sees to saying those words. Rabbi Moses ben Isaac Mintz in his שאלות ותשובות of the fifteenth century reasoned:

> וכמו שאומרים הדרן עלך בסיום מסכתא כי יחזור שלא ישכחם, כך אומרים כאן חזק שסיימת החומש ויישר כחך ועוד בפעם תתחיל.[9]

> And just as we say הדרן עלך at the conclusion of a massekhet, that we will return so that we not forget, so too we say here חזק that you finished the Humash and יישר כח that you will start once again.

This focuses on the accomplishment of an event and not specifically on the individual.

The Peri Hadash, Hezekiah ben David Da Silva, in late seventeenth-century Jerusalem, in his commentary on the Shulhan Arukh, comments on the Rema's gloss:

> בכל פעם חזק אולי יצא מנהג זה משום שהתורה נקראת תושיה שמתשת כוחו של אדם ועוד דאמרינן פרק אין עומדים ד' דברים צריכין חיזוק ואלו הן תורה ומ"ט וכו' שנאמר חזק ואמץ חזק בתורה ואמץ במ"ט.

> Each time חזק: Perhaps this custom developed because the Torah is called a support that weakens the strength of man. Also it says in the chapter אין עומדים, there are four things that need strengthening and these are them: Torah and good deeds, etc. As it is said, חזק ואמץ – חזק in Torah, ואמץ in good deeds.

The force of this is to focus the blessing on the individual, to gird up his strength.

---

[8] *Bet HaKnesset* 3 (5708): 24.

[9] Rabbi Moses ben Isaac Mintz, *She'elot u-Teshuvot*, 85.

The custom of reciting חזק on Simhat Torah varies widely according to community in practice and in reasoning. The phraseology and the number of times one says חזק varies as well. The origins of reciting חזק, חזק, ונתחזק are unknown, but the phrase is mentioned in the writings of Hatam Sofer (who lived in the late eighteenth and early nineteenth centuries in Hungary) and in Arukh HaShulhan, Orah Hayyim, written 1903-1907 by Jehiel Michal ben Aaron Isaac HaLevi Epstein in Belorussia:

> צריך לאחוז בעמודי הספר תורה בשעת ברכה ובשעת קריאתה יסמכו זה על
> מה שנאמר ביהושע לא ימוש ספר התורה הזה מפיך דמשמע שתופסה
> בידו.... ודע דבקרא דלא ימוש כתיב חזק ואמץ ומזה נהגו לומר למסיים
> ספר חזק חזק ונתחזק ויש רוצים שיאמרו חזק ג' פעמים שהם מספר משה
> ונכון הוא.[10]

> One must hold the handles of the Torah at the time of the blessing and at the time of its reading and this is based upon what is written in Joshua, "Let not this book of teaching cease from your lips," which means to hold it in one's hand. . . .And know that in Scripture where it is written לא ימוש it is also written חזק ואמץ and from this we are accustomed to saying to the one who concludes the book חזק, חזק, ונתחזק. And there are those who wish to say חזק three times because that is the number for Moses (in gematria) and this is correct.

Not only are the origins of this phrasing unknown, but few commentaries try to explain the reason for the addition of נתחזק.

In an analysis of the blessing of חזק, Israel M. Ta-Shma in an article in *Tarbiz*, 1987, states that a midrash in Bereshit Rabbah requires those standing near the one reciting the blessings over the Torah to strengthen him with the blessing of their mouths by saying חזק out loud just as God did for Joshua. Our custom of saying חזק at the end of the חומש and יישר כח after each aliyah are remnants of the earlier custom. Ta-Shma speculates that the reason for saying חזק to each individual who came to the Torah was that as each individual held on to the Torah, they were actually supporting it so that it would not fall – as in "perez Uzzah" in 2 Samuel. As those who actually read (and held onto) the Torah changed, those to whom the blessing was addressed and the purpose for the blessing changed.

The custom of reciting חזק has changed over the centuries from place to place. One can only speculate as to the original or true purpose of this blessing. What is its purpose today and is it used uniformly in all places that recite חזק? If it has come to signify the conclusion of each of the five books of the Torah, and is universally understood and accepted that way, then the recitation of חזק should occur only on those occasions. If it is detached from that specific event, for which there is precedent, and viewed more broadly as a blessing associated with the reading of the Torah, it may be recited more frequently.

In his paper, "A Complete Triennial System for Reading the Torah" – which conforms to the system of triennial reading approved by the Law Committee in the paper by Rabbi Elliot N. Dorff, "Annual and Triennial Reading Systems for Reading the Torah" – Rabbi Richard Eisenberg addresses the question of reciting חזק: "Since no skipping is allowed on the same day, the concluding verses of each book are read only during year three. Therefore, חזק should only be recited during that year and not during the first two years of the cycle. This is indeed the only logical solution, since the Books are completed only in the third

---

[10] Arukh HaShulhan, Orah Hayyim 139:15.

year; it is not desirable to proclaim their completion before that point."[11] The question remains whether the purpose of reciting חזק is to proclaim their completion. Must it be attached only to those last verses?

We may take some guidance from our observance of Simhat Torah for those who read Torah on a triennial basis. Rabbi Lionel Moses, in his תשובה, "Is There an Authentic Triennial Cycle of Torah Readings?" quotes some observations of Benjamin of Tudela:

> "Four days from thence [i.e. Fayum] brings us to Mizraim, or Memphis, commonly called Old Cairo. This large city stands on the banks of the Nile, called Al-Nil, and contains about two thousand Jews. Here are two synagogues, one of the congregation of Palestine, called the Syrian, and the other of the Babylonian Jews, or those of Iraq. They follow different customs regarding the division of the Pentateuch into parshioth and sedarim. The Babylonians read one parashah every week, as is the custom throughout Spain, and finish the whole of the Pentateuch every year, whereas the Syrians have the custom of dividing every parashah into three sedarim, concluding the lecture of the whole once in three years. They keep, however, the long-established custom of assembling both congregations to perform public service together, as well as on the day of the joy of the law [i.e. Simhat Torah] as on that of the dispensation of the law [i.e. Shavuot]."[12]

Without commenting on the precision of this information from Benjamin of Tudela, it is interesting to note that the Jews of the Palestinian congregation joined those of the Babylonian congregation for the annual celebration of Simhat Torah. Rabbi Moses further quotes from a source called *Hahillukim Shebein Anshei Mizrah Uvnei Eretz Yisrael* which states that the people of the east celebrate Simhat Torah every year while those of Eretz Yisrael celebrate every three and a half years. This would place the celebration of Simhat Torah not on the last day of Sukkot as was the custom for those who follow the annual cycle, but on whatever Shabbat the cycle of readings was completed.

It is the general practice of congregations reading on a triennial cycle to celebrate Simhat Torah annually on the day following Shemini Atzeret (יום טוב שני של גלויות). Technically, the Torah is read in its entirety only once in three years. We have broadened the interpretation of Simhat Torah so that we may celebrate with Klal Yisrael on an annual basis, even when we have completed only one third of the reading in a given year.

Summary

Our present custom of reciting חזק, חזק ונתחזק at the conclusion of each book of the Five Books of Moses has taken many various forms for a great variety of reasons since its first notation in the late twelfth century. There was not a single standardized custom among Ashkenazim nor among Sephardim. The custom among any particular group frequently shifted as historical circumstances dictated. The recitation of חזק is parallel in purpose to the recitation of יישר כח as can be witnessed by the Sephardic custom to say חזק וברוך

---

[11] Richard Eisenberg, "A Complete Triennial System for Reading the Torah," *PCJLS 86-90*, p. 385.

[12] See Lionel Moses, "Is There an Authentic Triennial Cycle of Torah Readings?" *PCJLS 86-90*, p. 335. See p. 369, n. 8.

while Ashkenazim say יישר כח to one who has just received an aliyah to the Torah. The greeting is one of congratulations, a girding of strength and a wish for continued study.

Conclusion

The variety of interpretations of the meaning and purpose of reciting חזק, and the ample precedent of variations in practice allow for reexamination of current day practice. It is not mandatory that one recite חזק each year, but it is permissible.

OH 233:1.1994

Two Questions on the Timing of Prayer Services: How Late May One Recite Minhah and How Early May One Recite Maariv?

Rabbi Gerald Skolnik

This paper was approved on May 25, 1994, by a vote of ten in favor, one opposed and six abstaining (10-1-6). Voting in favor: Rabbis Elliot N. Dorff, Jan Caryl Kaufman, Judah Kogen, Vernon H. Kurtz, Paul Plotkin, Mayer Rabinowitz, Avram Israel Reisner, Joel Roth, Gerald Skolnik, and Gordon Tucker. Voting against: Rabbi Kassel Abelson. Abstaining: Rabbis Ben Zion Bergman, Myron S. Geller, Arnold M. Goodman, Aaron L. Mackler, Lionel E. Moses, and Joel E. Rembaum.

The Committee on Jewish Law and Standards of the Rabbinical Assembly provides guidance in matters of halakhah for the Conservative movement. The individual rabbi, however, is the authority for the interpretation and application of all matters of halakhah.

שאלה

With regard to the timing of weekday afternoon and evening services, two questions have been addressed to our Committee.
(1) May the מנחה service be recited after sundown?
(2) May the מעריב service be recited before sundown?

תשובה

Regarding these questions, two equally valid options have been endorsed by the Shulhan Arukh and subsequent פוסקים:

ואסיקנא דעביד כמר עביד ודעביד כמר עביד.

> And it has been decided, that one who practices according to the one sage, let his practice be that way; and if another practices according to the other sage's opinion, then his practice is also legitimate.[1]

Both of these opinions are grounded in the original mention and subsequent discussion of this issue in Mishnah Brakhot 4:1 and Massekhet Brakhot 27a.

---

[1] S.A. Orah Hayyim 233:1.

The first option, that of Rabbi Yehuda, is predicated on a system of שעות זמניות ("seasonally correct hours" calculated by totaling the number of minutes from sunrise to sunset and dividing by twelve). Rabbi Yehudah holds that, although one who davens the מנחה service from six and one-half שעות זמניות onward has fulfilled his obligation – during what is commonly referred to as the time of מנחה גדולה – the truly appropriate time for the recitation of מנחה is from nine and one-half שעות זמניות until פלג המנחה (half the time between this nine and one-half hour starting point and sunset). This relatively narrow window of time, commonly referred to as מנחה קטנה, would allow the recitation of מנחה until ten and three-quarter שעות זמניות. פלג המנחה is therefore, by definition, one and one-quarter שעות זמניות before sunset, but Rabbi Yehudah would nonetheless allow for the immediate subsequent recitation of מעריב:

> דזהו דבר פשוט דכשכלה זמן תפילת מנחה מתחיל זמן תפילת ערבית כן הסכימו רבותינו התוספות הרא"ש וכל הפוסקים.

> It is a simple and obvious matter that once the time for reciting מנחה has passed, the time for reciting מעריב has begun. On this matter, the Tosafot, the Rosh and all of the פוסקים agree.[2]

The only stipulation for this early recitation of מעריב is that after צאת הכוכבים (the visible appearance of three stars in the sky) one should repeat the recitation of the שמע (all three paragraphs) without any of the accompanying blessings. This owes to the fact that the true time for reciting the evening שמע is after three stars have been seen in the sky.[3]

The second option sanctioned by the Shulhan Arukh is that of the חכמים. Like Rabbi Yehudah, the חכמים also maintain that, although the truest beginning time for מנחה is nine and one-half שעות זמניות, one who recites מנחה from six and one-half שעות זמניות onward has fulfilled his obligation. (This earlier time is when the afternoon *tamid* sacrifice was offered in cases when Erev Pesah fell on Shabbat.)[4] Unlike Rabbi Yehudah, however, the חכמים hold that מנחה may be recited until שקיעה (sunset), and מעריב immediately thereafter. If מעריב is recited between sunset and the appearance of three stars, then the שמע would still have to be repeated at a later hour, after dark. One could, however, obviate that need by reciting מנחה up to the time of sunset and then waiting until the appearance of three stars to recite מעריב.

With regard to both of these opinions, the sources are clear that either one is a valid option (a precedent for more than one valid option which long predates our own Committee!). The only caveat offered by the Shulhan Arukh is that consistency is called for (והוא שיעשה לעולם כחד מינייהו.): "But one should practice always according to *one* of them"). That is to say, one should adopt either the position of Rabbi Yehudah or that of the חכמים and practice it consistently, so as to avoid reciting מנחה after פלג המנחה and מעריב before sundown on the same day. However, both the Shulhan Arukh and the gloss of the Remah make it clear that, either בשעת הדחק – in an emergency – or בדיעבד (once one has already done so), such inconsistency does not render the prayer invalid. The Arukh Hashulhan, quoting the Magen Avraham, also makes reference to the existing practice of davening מנחה after פלג המנחה and מעריב before sundown because of the difficulty in gathering a minyan together a second time.[5]

---

[2] Arukh Hashulhan, Orah Hayyim 233:1.

[3] Ibid., Orah Hayyim 235:8.

[4] See Rambam, M.T. Hilkhot T'fillah 3:1.

[5] Arukh Hashulhan, Orah Hayyim 233:10.

Conclusion

The two options available to us are, therefore, clear: דעביד כמר עביד ודעביד כמר עביד. Though the natural tendency is to seek one opinion to follow, in this particular instance, one can follow either Rabbi Yehudah or the חכמים, and the appropriate hours for מנחה and מעריב will vary accordingly, as I have outlined. It is fair to say as well that, although it is certainly preferable to follow either opinion consistently, there is ample precedent for a synthetic approach, davening מנחה after פלג המנחה according to the חכמים and מעריב immediately thereafter according to Rabbi Yehuda. If such a synthesis enhances the possibility of assembling a minyan, it would be far better than davening without benefit of a minyan. Someone needing to recite Kaddish might well claim that such a circumstance constitutes a legitimate שעת דחק. (Obviously, the option of davening מעריב after פלג המנחה but before sundown applies only to weekdays, and not to שבתות and חגים). There is not, however, any halakhic ground on which to base davening מנחה after sundown, or מעריב before פלג המנחה. Those living in Arctic latitudes, where at certain times of year there is no darkness for months, must simply select and adopt a time frame consistent with a given community in the lower latitudes and follow it.[6]

One cannot help but assume that the reason for these questions having reached the CJLS is an effort to stretch the parameters of acceptable times for evening prayers, so as to more easily accommodate the realities of our congregants' schedules — particularly as regards the issue of reciting מנחה after dark. It is, without doubt, easier to secure an evening minyan later in the day than earlier. During the winter months, this virtually assures that the minyan will be taking place when it is already dark out. Are we allowed to wait until people get home from work and eat, and then do a מנחה/מעריב service because that is when we can get a minyan? The answer to that question must be no, as the sources are clear, and there is no overwhelming reason to call such a clear ruling into question.

A final thought: If the rationale behind the question of a late מנחה is to accommodate the Kaddish need of mourners, then whether or not מנחה is recited, it is important to remember that the *yahrzeit* which fell on the preceding Jewish date has already concluded once darkness has descended. In that context, the Kaddish which would be recited after מנחה would at any rate be inappropriate. If, however, the questions to our Committee are motivated by a desire is to add as many קדישים as possible to a service so as to elevate the soul of the departed closer to ultimate reunification with the Source of all spirit, according to the mystical understanding of Kaddish, then in lieu of forcing מנחה into an inappropriately late slot, a better idea comes to mind. A דבר תורה or לימוד session would facilitate the recitation of a קדיש דרבנן. Let that לימוד and Kaddish precede מעריב, and the problem has been at least slightly ameliorated. It has also been suggested in this regard that, from a spiritual perspective, Torah study dedicated to a person's memory on his or her *yahrzeit* is as efficacious in elevating the soul of the departed as is the recitation of Kaddish. In the absence of a minyan at the appropriate time, this affords another option.

---

[6] See Shaarei Teshuvah, S.A. Orah Hayyim 344.

OH 242.1995a

Shabbat Lease Agreement

Rabbi Joel Roth and Judge Norman M. Krivosha

This paper was approved by the CJLS on June 14, 1995, by a vote of fourteen in favor, one opposed, and five abstaining (14-1-5). Voting in favor: Rabbis Kassel Abelson, Stephanie Dickstein, Jerome M. Epstein, Samuel Fraint, Arnold M. Goodman, Judah Kogen, Aaron L. Mackler, Lionel E. Moses, Paul Plotkin, Mayer Rabinowitz, Avram Israel Reisner, Joel Roth, Gordon Tucker, and Gerald Zelizer. Voting against: Rabbi Ben Zion Bergman. Abstaining: Rabbis Elliot N. Dorff, Myron S. Geller, Susan Grossman, Alan B. Lucas, and Joel E. Rembaum.

The Committee on Jewish Law and Standards of the Rabbinical Assembly provides guidance in matters of halakhah for the Conservative movement. The individual rabbi, however, is the authority for the interpretation and application of all matters of halakhah.

Leasing for Shabbat
Rabbi Joel Roth

שאלה

May a lease arrangement be utilized in the agreement between a Jew and a non-Jew for Shabbat?

תשובה

This paper is occasioned by an objection raised in the Committee's deliberations on the lease submitted by Judge Norman Krivosha. The purpose of this paper is very limited. It will be restricted to demonstrating that leasing is an acceptable avenue for a Shabbat arrangement.

It is relatively common for the Hafetz Hayyim to preface his comments on a specific סימן with an introductory comment on the contents of the entire passage. That is the case with סימן 243 of Orah Hayyim, which is entitled: דין המשכיר שדה ומרחץ לאינו יהודי – law of one who rents a field or a bath-house to a non-Jew. Here are the comments of the Mishnah B'rurah:

> Be aware that there are three categories [involved in the subject matter of this passage]. The first category is profit-sharing (אריסות) in which one hires a non-Jew to work in the field or the bath-house, with the profits or the crops shared. The second category is leasing (or, rental) (שכירות) in which the non-Jew gives the Jew a fixed amount for his field or bath-house for the entire year. These two

categories are completely permissible with regard to a field, and technically legal with regard to a bath-house, [the reason being] that the non-Jew is working on his own behalf. The sages forbade these two categories with regard to a bath-house because of the appearance of impropriety (מראית העין), namely, that since the bath-house is known as the bath-house of the Jew, people will suspect that the non-Jew is working as the agent of the Jew.

The third category is job contracting (קבלנות) in which all of the profits belong to the Jew who pays the non-Jew a fixed amount each year for his labor. This is surely forbidden by law with regard to a bath-house since the non-Jew is the agent of the Jew, and the Jew benefits from the Sabbath labors of the non-Jew since the Jew would lose the profits of any day on which the non-Jew did not work.

Thus, if it is customary for most of the local residents to lease or to give in a profit-sharing manner (i.e., and the problem of מראית העין would no longer apply since everyone would know that the Jew had leased out his bath-house to a non-Jew), the status of the bath-house becomes identical in law with the status of the field. That is, categories one and two are permissible and category three is forbidden.

And the permissive types of leasing must be done in the context of an overall lease (הבלעה) which includes weekdays as well. It would be forbidden to lease even a field for Shabbat alone, even where the arrangement is generally well known.

The basis of the permissibility of the leasing arrangement is that the non-Jew is working for himself even if the Jew is also profiting. The proviso added by the Hafetz Hayyim is that the lease should be done בהבלעה, lest the non-Jew be considered an agent of the Jew hired for Shabbat alone, and working on behalf of the Jew.

It is interesting to note that the Mishnah B'rurah justifies a partnership arrangement on the basis of its comparability to a profit-sharing management. In comment 10 to סימן 245 the Hafetz Hayyim explains that a non-Jewish partner may keep the profits of Shabbat because he is like the אריס who is working on his own behalf.

In the Talmudic Encyclopedia, volume 8 entry הבלעה, column 131, the author says: "אחרונים have written that if one hires a Jewish guard to guard for him on Shabbat he should stipulate that he should also guard a few hours before Shabbat and a few hours at the conclusion of Shabbat. In this way the Shabbat wages are paid בהבלעה." Thus, it follows that if the lease with a non-Jew is written to become effective several hours before Shabbat and to terminate several hours after the onset of work on the first workday following Shabbat (or Yom Tov), the non-Jew's Shabbat or Yom Tov profits will have been earned בהבלעה.

Conclusion

A lease arrangement is an appropriate mechanism for an agreement between a Jew and a non-Jew for a Shabbat contract. The contract should take effect several hours before Shabbat or Yom Tov and should terminate several hours after the onset of business on the next business day.

Religious Lease
Judge Norman M. Krivosha

This Lease made and entered into this _____ day of _____, _____, by and between _____ hereinafter referred to as ("Landlord"), and _____ hereinafter referred to as ("Tenant").

WITNESSETH:

WHEREAS, Landlord is currently the owner of a certain _____ business known as _____ and operating in the location(s) as described on Exhibit A; and

WHEREAS, Landlord desires to observe the Halakhah concerning the prohibition against a Jew engaging in gainful employment on the Sabbath or certain holidays; and

WHEREAS, Tenant is willing to assist Landlord in fulfilling the prohibition concerning working on the Sabbath and certain holidays by leasing from Landlord the above described business on those days, and running said business and paying to Landlord for such lease the rental agreed to herein; and

WHEREAS, each of the parties hereto recognize and agree that the sole and only purpose for entering into this Lease agreement is to permit Landlord to observe the Halakhah;

Now THEREFORE, it is hereby agreed by and between the parties as follows:

1. *Leased Premises.* Landlord hereby leases to Tenant and Tenant hereby takes from Landlord the business situated in the location(s) as more particularly set out and described in Exhibit A, attached hereto and made a part hereof as fully as though set out herein verbatim; together with all of the inventory equipment, fixtures, furnishings, goods, wares, design, decor, decorations, installations, appurtenances and personal property located therein and used in connection with the operation of the described business; it being however specifically understood and agreed that said Lease does not include any bank accounts of any kind, nature, or description belonging to Landlord and used in connection with said business during the remainder of the time that said business is not otherwise operated by Tenant as lessee.

2. *Commencement and Term.* The term of this Lease shall commence on the date of the execution hereof and shall be effective as follows: to wit,
    A. Beginning one-half hour before sundown on each and every Friday, during the term of this Lease and ending one-and-a-half hours after sundown on Saturday of each and every week; plus beginning one-half hour before sundown of the dates shown on Exhibit B as "Beginning Day", and ending one-and-a-half hours after sundown on such days as shown on Exhibit B as "Ending Day". It being the purpose and intention of this Lease that Landlord shall lease to Tenant said business and premises one-half hour before the beginning of the Sabbath and ending one-and-a-half hours after the end of the Sabbath, or such additional days as are designated as religious holidays and set out on Exhibit B. Said Lease arrangement shall continue each week for such time as the parties may mutually agree, it being fully understood and agreed that such lease shall automatically ter-

minate in accordance with paragraph (12) following, or either party may terminate such lease upon giving the other written notice of such termination, not less than 24 hours prior to the beginning of any day on which Tenant is to exercise Tenant's Leasehold rights and operate said business.

3. *Rental.* Tenant shall pay to Landlord as rental for such Lease, a sum equal to _____% of the gross receipts earned by Tenant during the day or days Tenant shall be exercising rights over the Leased premises and operating said business. The remainder of such gross receipts shall be the sole and absolute property of Tenant. Payment by Tenant to Landlord shall be accomplished by making appropriate accounting entries and Landlord shall remit to Tenant the payment due, if any, within _____ day(s) after the same has been earned by Tenant.

4. *Use of Premises.* Tenant shall use said premises only for conducting the business established by Landlord in accordance with all of the procedures and processes previously established by Landlord for the operation of said business and Tenant shall make no changes either with regard to the manner in which the business is conducted, nor the prices for goods sold or services rendered, nor the salary or wages of any employee. Moreover, Tenant shall make no structural changes to said premises and shall exercise such care to see that no waste shall be committed upon said Leased premises while Tenant is operating said business.

5. *Subletting.* Tenant shall have no right to sublet either the business or the premises, or any part thereof, nor shall Tenant be permitted in any manner to encumber or burden said Lease or the Leased premises.

6. *Services.* Landlord shall at its sole and own expense provide all services necessary to operate said business including but not limited to heat, water, air conditioning, electricity and garbage disposal at Landlord's sole and own expense and Tenant shall be under no obligation to provide any such services. The cost for such services shall be included in the rental paid by Tenant to Landlord as described in paragraph 3 above.

7. *Indemnity Liability Insurance.* Save and except for acts of willful or gross negligence committed by Tenant, Tenant shall assume no liability for the operation of said business or said premises and Landlord shall indemnify and protect Tenant from any and all liability of any kind, nature, or description, unless such liability is occasioned by acts of the Tenant, which constitutes willful or gross negligence; and Landlord shall be responsible at Landlord's sole and own expense to provide all necessary insurance to protect against either liability or loss of any nature.

8. *Operation of Business.* During the day or days that the Tenant shall be actually operating said business, under the terms of this Lease, Landlord shall exercise no management rights, nor shall in any manner engage in the operation of said business, provided however that Tenant shall conduct said business in full accord with the terms of this lease, including Article 4. above.

9. *Notices.* Any notice, demand, request, or other communication given hereunder or made by either party to the other shall be in writing and mailed by Certified Mail in a post-paid envelope addressed as follows:
   A. If to Tenant: as shown on Exhibit C.
   B. If to Landlord: as shown on Exhibit C.

10. *Access to premises.* Landlord may enter the Lease premises at any reasonable time, on reasonable notice to Tenant, for purpose of inspection and to show the premises to prospective mortgagees or purchasers.
11. *No representations.* Neither party has made any representations or promises except as contained in this Lease.
12. *Automatic Termination.* Each of the parties recognize and agree as to the true purpose of this Lease and the personal nature thereof. Should either party die or if married, file for any form of divorce or separation, this Lease shall automatically terminate. Furthermore, should either party be adjudicated a bankrupt, make a general assignment for the benefit of creditors or take the benefit of insolvency act, have a judgment lien entered in favor of another and against either party to this agreement or in any manner become indebted for the payment of any taxes of any kind, nature or description, this Lease shall automatically terminate at once.
13. *Entire agreement.* This Lease supersedes all agreements previously made between the parties relating to its subject matter. There are no other understandings or agreements between them.

Dated this _____ day of _____, _____.

_____

Landlord

_____

Tenant

OH 242.1995b

For Moshe It's Shabbat; For Chaim It's Shabbat; But For Chris It's Not Shabbat: An Analysis of Judge Krivosha's "Religious Lease" and an Alternate Proposal

Rabbi Ben Zion Bergman

This paper was approved by the CJLS on June 14, 1995, by a vote of eleven in favor, one opposed, and eight abstentions (11-1-8). Voting in favor: Rabbis Kassel Abelson, Ben Zion Bergman, Stephanie Dickstein, Elliot N. Dorff, Arnold M. Goodman, Susan Grossman, Aaron L. Mackler, Lionel E. Moses, Mayer Rabinowitz, Gordon Tucker, and Gerald Zelizer. Voting against: Rabbi Judah Kogen. Abstaining: Rabbis Jerome M. Epstein, Samuel Fraint, Myron S. Geller, Alan B. Lucas, Paul Plotkin, Avram Israel Reisner, Joel E. Rembaum, and Joel Roth.

The Committee on Jewish Law and Standards of the Rabbinical Assembly provides guidance in matters of halakhah for the Conservative movement. The individual rabbi, however, is the authority for the interpretation and application of all matters of halakhah.

שאלה

There are many businesses which find it necessary to remain open on Shabbat and Yom Tov. Certain manufacturing operations, for example, that utilize intense foundry-like furnaces, if fires would have to be banked on Shabbat, would require an inordinate amount of time to fire up again to the required temperature. The loss of available working time would then be considerable with resultant economic consequences that would make it virtually impossible for that business to survive in a competitive market. Many retail establishments, as well, would find it hard to survive in a competitive market place if forced to remain closed on Shabbat, the day on which most retail consumers find it most convenient to shop for their major needs.

Is there a way in which a Jewish-owned business may remain open on Shabbat and Yom Tov with the Jewish owner not being in violation of the halakhah?

תשובה

This question has a history. Several years ago, Rabbi David Lincoln, then a member of the CJLS, responded to this question. That תשובה was based primarily on two תשובות of Rabbi

Moshe Feinstein. The solution was the creation of a partnership between the Jewish owner and a non-Jew, in which the non-Jewish partner operates the business on Shabbat and Yom Tov with the Jewish owner absent. The partnership agreement also stipulated that the profits or losses accruing on Shabbat and Yom Tov would belong exclusively to the non-Jew, with the Jewish partner receiving the profits or losses of an equal number of weekdays immediately subsequent to the Jewish holy days.

When Rabbi Lincoln presented his תשובה to the CJLS, Judge Krivosha pointed out that certain adverse consequences could arise in a partnership arrangement. Specifically, if the non-Jew is a partner, upon his death his partnership interest would become a part of the assets of his estate and would devolve to his heirs, who might not, and probably could not, serve as the managing partner on Shabbat and Yom Tov. Similarly, if the non-Jew becomes divorced, his partnership interest could become part of the marital assets subject to distribution between husband and wife. In either of these events, the Jewish owner would have lost some portion of his/her business and is back at "square one" vis-à-vis the problem of operation on Shabbat and Yom Tov. Judge Krivosha then suggested that he would attempt to solve the problem through a rental agreement rather than a partnership. He has submitted the attached document entitled "Religious Lease".

Analysis

There are a number of questions that arise in connection with Judge Krivosha's proposal:

(1) Basic to the proposal is the question whether one can rent a business. One can rent premises, equipment, or any other physical asset. But among the assets of a business are such abstractions as good-will. Can one rent another's good-will, itself the product of another abstraction, i.e. reputation? Even more basic to the question itself is the fact that a business, as an entity, is an abstraction that transcends its assets. A business is an entity created to enter into transactions with other entities with the purpose of (hopefully) generating profits. As such, most crucial to the operation of a business is the instrument and vehicle through which funds flow. Without it, a business is not a business. In Judge Krivosha's proposal, however, the bank accounts of the business are specifically excluded from the rental agreement. The basic question, then, is what is being rented and leased? (Additionally, if the business *qua* business is not in its entirety under the dominion of the tenant, then the tenant is, in reality, only a worker operating it for the Jewish landlord.)

(2) A question ancillary to the one above is: How does one rent consumable and expendable inventory? In a normal rental agreement, the lessee agrees to return the leasehold to the lessor, at the termination of the lease, in reasonably the same condition as at the commencement of the lease. If the business deals with "widgets", this might be possible. But many, if not most, businesses may deal with unique merchandise and/or materials which cannot be replaced exactly, and certainly not within the period of the lease, which is usually only a little over twenty-four hours.

Even if, *arguendo*, a business is leasable, I run into a problem of consideration that operates on two different levels:

> A. In the proposed agreement, there is no possibility of loss to the tenant. Since the rental is specified at x% of gross revenues, the tenant is retaining 100-x% for him/herself. In essence, since the gross revenues (merchandise sold, etc.) are the result of the landlord's investment, the landlord is only getting his/her principal back with a possible overage that might serve to cover utilities, taxes, and

other overhead expenses. But the tenant has no possibility of out-of-pocket loss. Furthermore, if the percentage accruing to the landlord is more than these overhead costs, then the Jewish landlord is specifically profiting from work done on the Sabbath, which is precisely what we are trying to avoid.

B. The only consideration that we can consider as the non-Jewish tenant giving for the leasehold is his work. But the way in which the agreement specifies the rental payment, viz. x% of the gross receipts, is tantamount to the non-Jew working on commission. The purpose of the arrangement with the non-Jew is to create a situation where he/she is working for him/herself. While the agreement is worded as a lease establishing a tenant-landlord relationship, that may in truth be illusory.

(3) As Rabbi Lincoln has indicated, one of the halakhic issues that must be dealt with is אמירא לנוכרי (instructing the non-Jew to do work on the Sabbath). While one may on a weekday, by indirection (a hint of some sort), indicate to a non-Jew the work you wish to have performed on the Sabbath, one may not instruct the non-Jew directly. Article 8 of the rental agreement specifies that "Landlord shall exercise no management rights." However, it includes, by reference, Article 4 which specifically binds the tenant to the rules, procedures, prices set, etc., previously determined by the landlord. Such rules of operation, etc., being conveyed to the tenant could be considered as violative of אמירא לנוכרי.

(4) Another problem with the rental agreement is its failure to deal with the problem of carry-over of work begun by the landlord on a weekday that has to be continued on Saturday or work begun by tenant on Saturday that has to be continued into the weekdays. These problems certainly exist in manufacturing operations but can occur also in a retail establishment.

The תשובה of R. Moshe Feinstein and its corresponding partnership agreement stresses the obligation of the Jew to continue the work begun by the non-Jew but must give the non-Jew the option to refuse to continue the work begun by the Jew. The issue again is אמירא לנוכרי. If the non-Jew elects to do so, in a partnership situation, he/she is compensated in proportion to the contribution to the finished product.[1]

It should be pointed out that what is being sought is not a fictitious designation of the status of the business on Shabbat and Yom Tov a la מכירת חמץ (the selling of the hametz). The two situations are not analogous. In hametz, the issue is the ownership status of the חמץ which can be designated in many ways. One can change the ownership of property by sale, gift, bequest, etc. All it requires is some legal formality and the status then remains static until further change. Nobody touches the hametz. In our case, the problem is to change the ongoing business operations (not a static condition) which require acts performed by a non-Jew which are forbidden to the Jew on the Sabbath. The means must be found to have these acts performed by a non-Jew on his/her own behalf and אדעתא דנפשיה (at his or her own option).

In the partnership scenario, the non-Jew is a bona-fide partner and not a fictitious one. (Indeed R. Moshe Feinstein makes a point of distinguishing this from מכירת חמץ, saying the use of a similar sales agreement, which may have been used for fields and flour mills in Europe, is not to be used for this purpose.[2]) The non-Jew is a partner on Wednesday as

---

[1] See אגרות משה, ד׳, ס״י, צ׳.

[2] See end of אגרות משה, ד׳, ס״י, צ׳.

well as on Shabbat. The only unusual wrinkle in the partnership agreement is the manner in which the profit/losses are allocated.

Proposed Solution

Fully cognizant of the problems raised by Judge Krivosha regarding the partnership agreement, I believe those problems are obviated in the following proposal which is halakhically valid.

Instead of a partnership agreement, the business should be incorporated as a closed corporation. The non-Jew is then sold shares in proportion to the total shares, equivalent to the proportion of holy days to the days of the year. (I'm not sure how R. Moshe Feinstein arrived at twenty-five percent, unless he also included חול המועד plus a brief time before sundown on Friday and holiday eves plus brief time after sundown on Saturday and holidays.) The shares are paid for by a promissory note held by the Jewish owner. In the sales agreement (and possibly in the Articles of Incorporation) it is stipulated that the shares are not transferable or assignable and in the event that the minority shareholder is incapacitated, divorced, dies, or does anything that would affect the status of his shares, the shares must be tendered to the corporation for cancellation of the debt. In a separate agreement, the Jewish major shareholder and the non-Jewish shareholder agree to the terms specified in Rabbi Feinstein's agreement, including the allocation of profits and losses and distribution of dividends as the distribution to the non-Jew representing the profits of the Jewish holy days and the dividends distributed to the Jewish shareholder representing the profits of the other days.

Incidentally, one can make a case that such a method of distribution exists constructively. If I own shares of GM (which I do not) or Boeing (which I do), I am one of the owners of that corporation, infinitesimal as my percentage of ownership may be. Now these corporations operate on Shabbat and Yom Tov and consequently my share of profits (dividends) represent and include the profit of work done on holy days. I know of no פוסק (recognized halachic decisor) who has forbidden Jews to own stock in publicly held companies. Therefore, there must be a constructive stipulation operative in Jewish Law that profits accruing to Jewish shareholders are the profits generated on days other than the Jewish holy days.

This arrangement has several advantages. In any given situation, the non-Jew would be a trusted employee who is in the major management cadre. He/she therefore knows the business and its methods of operation and does not have to be told. Furthermore, he/she is motivated to exert best efforts since he/she shares in the profits. Also some of the profits of the non-Jew can revert to the Jew as interest on the note. Another advantage is that although it would be possible, it would be onerous to calculate the specific profits/losses attributable to specific days. In that case, distributions can be apportioned by הבלעה (proportionately).

Conclusion

To enable a Jewish-owned business to remain in operation on Shabbat and Yom Tov without the Jewish owner being in violation of Shabbat or Yom Tov, the business should be incorporated as a closed corporation. A trusted non-Jewish employee who knows the business should be sold a number of shares proportionate to the total number of shares in the same ratio as the Jewish holy days to the days of the year. These shares would be paid for by a promissory note. The shares are not transferable and in the event of incapacity, divorce or death of the minority shareholder (the non-Jew), the shares revert to the corporation for cancellation of the debt evidenced by the promissory note which would be reconveyed. In a supplementary agreement, the minority shareholder and the majority shareholder would agree to the attribution of profits/losses and distribution of dividends as accruing to the minority shareholder for work done on the Jewish holy days and the remainder attributable to the Jewish majority shareholder for efforts expended on the other days of the year.

Addendum (submitted June 14, 1995)

The issue of the halakhic validity of the "Shabbat Lease" proposed by Judge Krivosha vis-à-vis my proposed corporation was debated over several meetings of the CJLS with no vote taken, awaiting a formal תשובה to be presented by Rabbi Joel Roth, giving a halakhic rationale for the validity of Judge Krivosha's proposed lease.

During the course of the discussions, I continued to maintain that, in addition to certain problematic terms and conditions in Judge Krivosha's proposal, a lease by its very nature is an invalid instrument with which to effectuate the desired result. The problem with a lease is that title does not transfer to the lessee. Therefore, if the business under consideration is a retail or wholesale establishment, any sale by the lessee of the business inventory is either commission of a theft, or is valid only if the lessee is acting on behalf of the Jewish lessor, since the lessee does not own the property. And since שלוחו של אדם כמותו, the Jewish lessor has engaged in a sale on Shabbat, which he is not allowed to do. If the business is engaged in the manufacture or fabrication of merchandise in which the non-Jewish lessor would be converting the raw material or altering the product in some way, as a lessee, he has no right to make changes in the property of the lessor, unless he is doing so at the instruction and behest of the Jewish lessor, in which case, the Jewish owner has, through an agent, committed a Sabbath violation.

Judge Krivosha has attempted to justify the sale by the non-Jew of the lessor's inventory by analogy to merchandise on consignment. The example he used was that of a dairy consigning milk to a grocery, in which the grocer has the right to sell the milk, with the dairy receiving its payment for the milk sold and taking back the unsold milk. But this really does not change the issue in regard to the sale on Shabbat. Merchandise delivered on consignment does not become the property of the consignee. Its legal status is that of a "bailment for sale" (in reference to Sachs, D.C. Md., 31 F2nd, 799,800.). The consignee (the grocer in this example) is then a bailee. In Jewish law, his status would be that of a שומר חינם. (The fact that he makes money by selling the milk at a price higher than that which he has to pay the dairy, does not make him a שומר שכר, since he is not being compensated for his guardianship of the milk.) And in Jewish Law, a שומר חינם does not have the right to sell or alter the פיקדון. Even in the case where the bailment is in danger of depredation, there is a מחלוקת as to whether the שומר may sell in order to salvage some value for the bailor. (See Bava Metzia 38a *et seq*.) Therefore, the sale by the non-Jewish lessee, even if the merchandise is considered to be on consignment, is a sale in which the consignee (the non-Jewish lessee) is acting as the agent of the Jewish lessor.

During the discussion, Rabbi Roth attempted to counter the argument by making the statement that there is no איסור for someone doing something for a Jew on Shabbat. This is surprising since, in addition to ignoring the whole issue of אמירא לנוכרי, it also ignores a basic halakhic principle, alluded to supra, that שלוחו של אדם כמותו. What is even more surprising is that if that were indeed true, there would be no need for R. Moshe Feinstein's partnership agreement; no need for my solution by means of a corporation; nor need for Judge Krivosha's attempted (albeit unsuccessful) solution by means of a lease. All that would be necessary would be to hire non-Jews exclusively for Shabbat. Yet there is no authority who proposes that as a valid means by which a Jewish business can continue to operate on Shabbat.

It must be borne in mind that the issue is the validity of the leasing of a business *qua* business. There is no problem with the lease of premises or equipment. But premises and equipment are assets of a business; they do not constitute the business *per se*. As I point out in the body of my paper, the business is an entity that transcends its assets. In that connection, it must be pointed out that Rabbi Roth's citation from the Mishnah B'rurah is not on point. The Hafetz Hayyim is dealing with the lease of a bathhouse and not a business. The Hafetz Hayyim's bathhouse is analogous to R. Moshe Feinstein's mill which R. Feinstein goes out of his way to point out is not to be used as an example. In those cases, the non-Jew is operating his own business. He is not operating the Goldberg Milling Co. or the Finkelstein Spa Co. on Shabbat. He is not milling Jewish grain nor bathing persons on behalf of the Jewish owner. He is only renting the facilities in which he is conducting his own commercial enterprise. Furthermore, the citation is not on point since it is specifically dealing with a lease for the entire year. Indeed, the last statement in the citation states specifically: "And the permissive types of leasing must be done in the context of an overall lease (הבלעה) which includes the weekdays as well. It would be forbidden to lease even a field for Shabbat alone, even where the arrangement is generally well known." It is therefore difficult to understand how Rabbi Roth arrives at the conclusion that a lease is an appropriate mechanism for a Shabbat contract between a Jew and a non-Jew.

I therefore must conclude that the only way in which a Jewish business can operate on Shabbat is either through a Partnership Agreement as proposed by R. Moses Feinstein or by creation of a Closed Corporation as I have suggested. Rabbi Feinstein's proposal is subject to the problems which Judge Krivosha brought to the attention of the Law Committee. My proposal avoids those problems. It must be admitted, however, that the "corporate" solution also has a price. As a corporation, there would be double taxation. The corporation would be taxed on its profits and then the individuals receiving the dividends distributed from those profits would also be taxed. But that is a price that an observant Jew must be willing to sustain. The alternative is to operate in violation of Shabbat or go out of business.

OH 242.1995c

JEWISH BUSINESSES OPEN ON SHABBAT AND YOM TOV: A CONCURRING OPINION

Rabbi Elliot N. Dorff

This paper was submitted as a concurrence to both "Shabbat Lease Arrangement," by Rabbi Joel Roth and Justice Norman Krivosha and "Shabbat Corporation Agreement," by Rabbi Ben Zion Bergman. Concurring and dissenting opinions are not official positions of the Committee on Jewish Law and Standards.

The Committee on Jewish Law and Standards of the Rabbinical Assembly provides guidance in matters of halakhah for the Conservative movement. The individual rabbi, however, is the authority for the interpretation and application of all matters of halakhah.

The Issue

The problem with which we are faced is to find a way in which a Jewish owner of a business might formalize the transfer of the business to a non-Jewish employee on Shabbat and Yom Tov so that the Jew would not be violating the laws of those days by having the business open then. Presumably, the Jew either cannot close then (e.g., if the business is a factory that involves machines which cannot be easily turned off and on) or, more likely, does not want to close the business and lose the profits. This latter motivation is especially understandable in North America, where people often do not work on Saturday and use it for shopping and other personal errands, thus making Saturday the busiest day of the week for many retail establishments.

Judge Norman Krivosha and Rabbi Ben Zion Bergman have presented us with two (really three) alternate proposals on this subject — namely, a lease, a partnership, or a closed corporation. The assumption behind them all — and also behind the one I am about to make — is that the Jewish owner is not him or herself working on Shabbat or Yom Tov. Indeed, the whole purpose of these proposals is to enable the Jew not to work on those days so that he or she is free to observe them according to Jewish law. The cases we are all addressing, then, are those in which the business would be operated by a non-Jew on those days.

It is also assumed that the Jew and non-Jew have not already created a partnership in American law for business reasons. If they had established a formal agreement of partnership, then, presumably, they can stipulate in (or amend) their agreement such that the two of them will divide the profits and losses equally even though there will be days in which one of the partners will not be present. Such days would include Shabbat and Yom Tov, but they would also include, for example, the times in which each partner is on vacation or is ill. From the point of view of Jewish law, then, the business could legitimately remain open, and the Jew would share in the profits and losses through הבלעה (literally, the "swallowing" of the profits on Shabbat and Yom Tov into the overall profits and losses of the business throughout the week).[1]

In our case, then, there is no such partnership agreement, but rather the non-Jew is an employee of the Jew whom the Jew trusts to manage the business on Shabbat and Yom Tov in his or her absence. The non-Jew, however, does not own any part of the business.

The Current Proposals and their Problems

In the discussions of the Committee on Jewish Law and Standards in March and June, 1995, I, for one, have been convinced by both Judge Krivosha and by Rabbi Bergman, but on different points. On the one hand, I agree with Rabbi Bergman that Judge Krivosha's tenancy arrangement poses problems from the point of view of Jewish law, and, on the other, Rabbi Bergman's proposal, as Judge Krivosha points out, seems unworkable from the point of view of American law.

To take Rabbi Bergman's points first, if the employee is construed as a tenant, as Judge Krivosha suggests, and if the landlord gives the tenant the right to sell some of the inventory of the Jew's business on Shabbat or Yom Tov (which, after all, is the whole point of the Jew's interest in doing this in the first place), the non-Jew is, without doubt, acting not as a tenant but as the Jew's agent. In that case, at least as a matter of rabbinic enactment (שבות), it would be forbidden for the Jew to gain from the non-Jew's sales on those days, for the Jew would be illegitimately instructing the non-Jew to sell inventory for him on Shabbat and Yom Tov in a public way (אמירה לנכרי שבות).[2] It is even worse if the Jew bought the inventory on consignment, such that it does not really transfer from the supplier to the Jew until it is bought by someone else, for then the non-Jew would effectively be buying the inventory sold on Shabbat or Yom Tov for the Jew each time he or she sells something. In that case, the non-Jew would not only be selling for the Jew, but buying as well, and, in my view, in doing either of those activities the non-Jew would be illegitimately acting as the Jew's agent, not his or her tenant. Ultimately, as Rabbi Bergman says, when I rent a car, I have fair use of that car during the lease, but I do not have the right to sell the car or any part of it. Indeed, I must buy the gasoline myself; far from being enabled by the rental to sell some of the inventory, I must replenish whatever inventory I use. Thus the arrangement between the non-Jewish employee and the Jew is not fairly construed as a rental but is, in all honesty, a form of agency. Since, in Jewish law, "the agent of a person is like him or her,"[3] Judge Krivosha's lease, in my view, will not do the trick — that is, it will not enable the Jewish owner to have business done for him or her on Shabbat and Yom Tov in a way that distances him or her sufficiently from the transaction to free him or her from liability for transgressing the laws of Shabbat or Yom Tov.

On the other hand, if we were to create a partnership or closed corporation, as Rabbi Bergman suggests, that might engender immense tax and inheritance problems in American law, so much so that anyone would be well advised to avoid such arrangements. Aside from the sheer burden of drawing up such documents, Judge Krivosha points out

---

[1] B. Nedarim 37a; B. Bava Mezia 58a; Rosh, Avodah Zarah, ch. 1, par. 25; Tur, Orah Hayyim 243, see Bet Yosef there, s.v. בהבלעה: Mishnah B'rurah on S.A. Orah Hayyim 243:1. In general, on this, see הבלעה in Encyclopedia Talmudit 8:130ff., esp. p. 133.

[2] Cf. S.A. Orah Hayyim 244:1 and 252:3 for this public/private distinction.

[3] M. Berakhot 5:5; B. Haggigah 10b; B. Kiddushin 41b, 43a; B. Bava Mezia 96a; etc.

that these arrangements are inadvisable for strictly business reasons. If, as we are supposing, the Jew and non-Jew have not, for business reasons, established a partnership, doing so to enable the Jew to observe Shabbat and Yom Tov would *ipso facto* give the non-Jew and his or her heirs title to a share of the business, an implication that the Jew certainly does not intend or desire. Rabbi Bergman's other suggestion, namely, forming a closed corporation, would subject the business to double taxation, and that is also a result which the Jewish owner would clearly wish to avoid.

We are left, then, with none of the three proposals — tenancy, partnership, or closed corporation — doing everything that we want them to do. The first of those is not a fair representation of what indeed is happening and, in any case, fails from the point of view of Jewish law. The second and third of the proposals may work in Jewish law but causes major problems in American law.

My Proposal: Create a Document in Jewish Law Alone

American Jews live under two legal systems, American law and Jewish law. We suffer from this in divorce law, where Jewish couples must be divorced in each legal system separately, for neither recognizes the divorce proceedings of the other. In the cases before us, I would propose that we take advantage of the First Amendment's separation of church and state by creating a document that announces at its inception in the clearest possible terms that the following document is meant exclusively as a religious document for the sole purpose of enabling the Jew named in it to follow the requirements of his or her religious tradition in observing specific sacred days within the Jewish religion. Within American law, it is not meant for any commercial or secular purpose whatsoever. It seems to me that if we were to append such notice to the top of the document we create, separately signed or initialed by both parties, any American court would see it as it is intended — namely, as a document with an exclusively religious purpose which, therefore, should not be treated by American courts at all.

I discussed this possibility with Professor Arthur Rosett, with whom I team-teach a course in Jewish law at UCLA School of Law. His fields of expertise are contract law and international law; indeed, he wrote the books that are used in many law schools on those subjects. He was not happy about the whole prospect of circumventing the Torah's command that we not work on the Sabbath, nor our "manservant or maidservant" (Exod. 20:10), but I pointed out to him that the Torah was talking about a slave who could not choose to do other than his or her master's bidding and who, if forced to work on Shabbat, would thus effectively be an extension of the master engaging in forbidden work on those days. We, on the other hand, are talking about free non-Jews who are not obligated to observe Jewish law and who might choose to work on specific days to earn some money.

Once assured that we were not trying to violate the spirit of the law through a legalistic interpretation of its letter (a good thing for laypeople to warn rabbis about from time to time!), he concurred that, from the point of view of American law, we could indeed create a document solely for religious purposes that would be held as such by American courts. We must be very clear that the parties do not want this document to have some ramifications in American law but not others; that would undermine the document's solely religious character and would therefore void its protection from review by American courts. To avoid any hint of that, the wording he suggested to me was the following:

> THE PARTIES INTEND THAT THIS DOCUMENT SHALL HAVE NO EFFECT ON THEIR LEGAL RIGHTS AND OBLIGATIONS UNDER ANY LAW OTHER THAN

Jewish religious law. The parties specifically disclaim that this document shall create any obligations enforceable in the courts of any state or in any arbitral tribunal.

That language should appear in capital letters at the top of the document and be separately initialed by both parties. He also provided me with some materials from American law that describe the basis for the procedure I am suggesting. I am attaching those materials as an Appendix.

Once we are freed from Judge Krivosha's worries about the effects of what we do in American law, we are able, it seems to me, to create a document that will best suit the purposes of Jewish law. For the reasons advanced by Rabbi Bergman and described above, that is not a tenancy agreement. Since closed corporations of the type that exist in American law do not, as far as I know, exist in Jewish law, the best option, as far as I can tell, would be to draw up a partnership agreement in Jewish law exclusively. It should state at the outset the language that Professor Rosett has provided for us. The document should be as short and as simple as possible so that observant Jews will not be impeded from completing it by its sheer size or by worry of any fine print in it.

In part of our discussion, several members of the Committee on Jewish Law and Standards suggested that we might use Judge Krivosha's tenancy agreement but construe it, for purposes of Jewish law, under the laws of קבלנות (subcontracting for piecework). The purest case of such קבלנות occurs when the Jew hires the non-Jew to do a task that the non-Jew chooses to do on Shabbat or Yom Tov but which he or she could do on other days; since the non-Jew is not obligated to observe Shabbat or Yom Tov, he or she may freely choose to work on those days, and since he or she chooses to do that of his or her own free will and could do otherwise, the Jew does not violate Jewish law even if he or she benefits from the non-Jew's work on those days.[4] A non-Jewish manager of a business who works for the owner during the week with or without the owner present might be construed, it was suggested, in the same way – namely, as choosing to work on Shabbat or Yom Tov in order to earn a salary for those days. While that will justify the employee doing work on the Sabbath, it will not provide legal cover for the transfer of property that is involved in buying and selling, for the non-Jewish manager or salesperson buys or sells as the Jewish owner's agent and therefore it is as if the owner him or herself did the buying or selling. Therefore, a partnership agreement with part of the non-Jew's salary for work on our sacred days subsumed into his or her salary for all of the days of the week is the right way to go, for it legitimizes Jewish owners profiting from sales on the Sabbath or Festival through making those profits part of the general profits of the business (הבלעה), a well-established institution in Jewish Sabbath laws.

I have therefore voted affirmatively only on Rabbi Bergman's proposal because I think that it is the only one that satisfies the demands of Jewish law on this issue. I would agree with both Rabbi Bergman and Judge Krivosha that whatever document is used must carry a disclaimer at the very top that Jews who use it must check its legal status with their lawyer to make sure that it does not run afoul of the laws of the particular state or province in which it is being executed and that, under the laws of that

---

[4] On the definition of קבלנות (hiring someone to do a specific job, however long or short it takes) and its differentiation from hiring an employee on the basis of the time he or she will work: B. Bava Mezia 77b (and Rashi on 77a, s.v., "sh'anei lei," 112a); M.T. Hilkhot Sekhirah 9:4; S.A. Hoshen Mishpat 333:5. On the implications of that distinction for hiring a non-Jew to do work on Shabbat: S.A. Orah Hayyim 244:5; 252:2. On the whole institution of hiring a non-Jew to do that which is forbidden for a Jew to do on the Sabbath, see Jacob Katz, *The "Shabbes Goy": A Study in Halakhic Flexibility* (Philadelphia: Jewish Publication Society, 1989).

state or province, the Jewish owner does not incur any liability that he or she does not intend to incur.

In concurring with Rabbi Bergman here, then, I am making another suggestion to both the Jewish owner and his or her attorney – namely, that one investigate, as per Professor Arthur Rosett, the possibility within the laws of one's region of "punting" out of civil legal concerns entirely by announcing at the beginning of the document that it is intended solely for religious purposes. In this way, I seek to respond to Judge Krivosha's important concerns about making sure that any document we recommend, on Jewish grounds, does not have untoward consequences in American law. (I have not investigated whether this is possible in Canada.)

In the discussion of the Committee on June 14, 1995, Rabbi Joel Roth objected to my proposal, stated at that time only orally, on the grounds that this is even more of a subterfuge (הארמה) than any of the other proposals. I think not. On the contrary, it seems to me that this is the most honest and straightforward of all of the proposals because it spells out at the very beginning exactly what the intentions of the parties are so that not only the parties, but any judge in either American or Jewish law will understand exactly what the parties intend and what they do not intend. In fact, the document I am proposing is even less ambiguous than the wedding contracts (כתובות) that we all use, for those never say that they are for religious purposes only and, as a result, American courts have interpreted them in a variety of ways, from a pre-nuptial agreement to be given legal effect in American law to a religious document that should not be given such effect.[5] The document which I am proposing for Jewish businesses which are to be open on Shabbat and Yom Tov, in contrast, says candidly and clearly exactly what legal effects it is to have by identifying the legal system in which it is to be operative and that in which it is not to be. In Jewish law, of course, there is a kind of double-reverse here, for the document establishes a partnership while stating also (or at least understanding by implication) that the secular law which governs such matters is not to pay attention to this partnership. In other words, this is a partnership in Jewish law, but Jewish law itself defers to secular law to define and govern partnerships ("the law of the land is the law" – at least in commercial matters).[6] The tenancy proposal, though, involves even more of a subterfuge because it pretends that the non-Jewish worker is a tenant rather than the agent that he or she really is. Truth to tell, the very nature of what we are trying to do here requires a legal fiction of some sort, one that we are clearly prepared to accept, and the legal fiction involved in my proposal, I think, is more clearly announced and therefore less dishonest than the tenancy arrangement. Moreover, as I stated above, I also think that it is, from the point of view of Jewish law, the only legally effective way to proceed, for it "calls a spade a spade" in acknowledging that the non-Jew is indeed going to be transferring property in ways that will benefit the Jew on Shabbat and Yom Tov.

---

[5] *Wener v. Wener*, 59 Misc. 2d 959, 301 N.Y. Supp. 2d 237 (Sup. Ct. 1969); 33 App. Div. 2d 50, 312 N.Y. Supp. 2d 815 (2d Dept. 1970); *In re Estate of Armin H. White*, 78 Misc. 2d 157 (1974); *Brett v. Brett*, (1969) 1 All. E.R. 1007 (Ct. App.); *Margulies v. Margulies*, 42 App. Div. 2d 517, 344 N.Y. Supp. 2d 482 (1st Dept. 1973); *Matter of "Rubin" v. "Rubin"*, 75 Misc. 2d 776, 348 N.Y. Supp. 2d 61 (Family Ct. 1973); *Pal v. Pal*, 45 App. Div. 738, 356 N.Y. Supp. 2d 672 (2d Dept. 1974); and *Avitzur v. Avitzur*, N.Y. Court of Appeals, 58 N.Y. 2d 108, 459 N.Y. 2d 572 (1983). For a discussion on how civil courts have handled the conflict of laws involved in Jewish divorce, see Rabbi Elliot N. Dorff and Arthur Rosett, *A Living Tree: The Roots and Growth of Jewish Law* (Albany: State University of New York Press, 1988), ch. 15; for a discussion of how Jewish sources have handled it, see ibid., ch. 14.

[6] B. Nedarim 28a; B. Gittin 10b; B. Bava Kamma 113a; B. Bava Batra 54b-55a; and see Dorff and Rosett, *A Living Tree*, pp. 515-23.

With this proposal added to Rabbi Bergman's responsum for the consideration of the Jewish owner and his or her attorney then, I leave it to Rabbi Bergman or anyone else on the Committee who, like him, knows this area of the law better than I do, to draw up such a partnership agreement.

Appendix

E.A. Farnsworth, *Contracts*, 2d ed. (Boston: Little, Brown, 1990), pp. 122-3:

3.7. INTENTION NOT TO BE BOUND. Parties to agreements, especially routine ones, often fail to consider the legal consequences of the actions by which they manifest their assent. The fact that one gives the matter no thought does not impair the effectiveness of one's assent, for there is no requirement that one intend or even understand the legal consequences of one's actions. For example, one who signs a writing may be bound by it, even though one neither reads it nor considers the legal consequence of signing it. This rule, making a party's intention to be legally bound irrelevant, has the salutary effects of generally relieving each party to a dispute of the burden of showing the other's state of mind in that regard and of helping to uphold routine agreements.

A different rule applies, however, in those unusual instances in which one *intends* that one's assent have no legal consequences. Under the objective theory, a court will honor that intention if the other party has reason to know it. And it will honor it if the other party actually knows it.

The easiest way for a party to make clear an intention not to be legally bound is to say so. In a number of commercial contexts, parties enter into "gentlemen's agreements" that state that they are not legally binding, and it is beyond question that the parties can in this way turn an otherwise enforceable agreement into an unenforceable one. The same result has been reached even though a written agreement is made as a sham, for the purpose of deceiving others, with an oral understanding that it will not be enforced.

Circumstances, rather than words, may also indicate a party's intention not to be bound.

American Law Institute, Restatement of the Law, Second, Contracts

CHAPTER 3, SECTION 21: INTENTION TO BE LEGALLY BOUND. Neither real nor apparent intention that a promise be legally binding is essential to the formation of a contract, but a manifestation of intention that a promise shall not affect legal relations may prevent the formation of a contract.

COMMENT B.: AGREEMENT NOT TO BE LEGALLY BOUND. Parties to what would otherwise be a bargain and a contract sometimes agree that their legal relations are not to be affected. In the absence of any invalidating cause, such a term is respected by the law like any other term, but such an agreement may present difficult questions of interpretation: it may mean that no bargain has been reached, or that a particular manifestation of intention is not a promise: it may reserve a power to revoke or terminate a promise under certain circumstances but not others. In a written document prepared by one party it may raise a question of misrepresentation or mistake or overreaching; to avoid such questions it may be read against the party who prepared it.

The parties to such an agreement may intend to deny legal effect to their subsequent acts. But where a bargain has been fully or partly performed on one side, a failure to perform on the other side may result in unjust enrichment, and the term may then be unenforceable as a provision for a penalty or forfeiture.... In other cases the term may be unenforceable as against public policy because it unreasonably limits recourse to the courts or as unconscionably limiting the remedies for breach of contract.

REPORTER'S NOTE ON COMMENT B. . . . As Comment B. indicates, most of the arguments against enforcing a "not binding" clause are based on unfairness to one party. . . .

J. Calaman and J. Perillo, *The Law of Contracts*, 3d ed. (West Publishing Company, 1987), pp. 28-9.

2-4. MUST THE PARTIES INTEND TO BE BOUND OR INTEND LEGAL CONSEQUENCES?

As asked, the question in the caption must be answered in the negative because it is well settled that the parties need not manifest an intent to be bound or consciously advert to legal consequence that might arise upon breach. . . . This rule is consistent with the rule that mistake as to a rule of law does not necessarily deprive an agreement of parties of legal effect. The same result can be reached by employing the reasonable man test because "a normally constituted person" would know, however dimly, that legal sanctions exist.

However, if, from the statements or conduct of the parties or the surrounding circumstances, it appears that the parties do not intend to be bound or do not intend legal consequences, then under the great majority of the cases there will be no contract. Two types of cases arise in this area. In one, the parties expressly agree that they do not intend to be bound. In the other, the parties do not expressly so agree but the conclusion is reached from the surrounding circumstances.

Under the majority rule, when the parties expressly state that they do not intend to be bound by their agreement or do not intend legal consequences — the so-called gentlemen's agreement — the courts conclude that a contract does not arise. The type of case envisaged is one where the parties enter into agreements regulating commercial relations but further agree that the agreement is to create no legal obligation. In such a case, as stated above, the general rule is that the agreement is not binding. There is, however, a strong minority current which hold that, when the parties have acted under the agreement and it is unfair not to enforce the agreement, it should be enforced. Such cases have been explained as instances where "the principle of reimbursing reliance is regarded as overriding the principle of private autonomy." Failure by one party to perform may also result in his unjust enrichment, presenting an additional ground for enforcement in contract or quasi contract. Many of the minority cases have involved pension plans upon which employers could reasonably expect employees to rely and which in fact did induce reliance. In addition, the minority view has been used in bonus and employee death benefit cases. Under the majority rule no protection is available to an employee where the agreement explicitly stated that it was non-contractual. This is one of the abuses the Pension Reform Act of 1974 was designed to curtail.

As indicated above, the intent not to be bound or to intend legal consequences need not be stated in so many words: it may be inferred from the circumstances of the case.

OH 444.1993

WHEN PASSOVER BEGINS ON SATURDAY NIGHT

Rabbi Kassel Abelson

This paper was approved by the CJLS on December 9, 1993, by a vote of twenty-one in favor (21-0-0). Voting in favor: Rabbis Kassel Abelson, Ben Zion Bergman, Elliot N. Dorff, Jerome M. Epstein, Ezra Finkelstein, Samuel Fraint, Arnold M. Goodman, Susan Grossman, Jan Caryl Kaufman, Reuven Kimmelman, Judah Kogen, Aaron L. Mackler, Herbert Mandl, Lionel E. Moses, Paul Plotkin, Mayer Rabinowitz, Avram Israel Reisner, Joel E. Rembaum, Chaim Rogoff, Joel Roth, and Gordon Tucker.

The Committee on Jewish Law and Standards of the Rabbinical Assembly provides guidance in matters of halakhah for the Conservative movement. The individual rabbi, however, is the authority for the interpretation and application of all matters of halakhah.

שאלה

What practices are to be followed when the first night of Passover falls on a Saturday night?

תשובה

Many of the practices that are usually performed on the night or the day before the seder are moved back to Thursday or Friday. This is done to assure the proper observance of Shabbat.[1]

סיום בכורים – *Thursday Morning*

A first born (whether of the mother or of the father) should fast on the day before Passover. In commemoration of the deliverance from Egypt.[2] It is the custom for synagogues to make סיום (a public completion of the study of a tractate of the Talmud) on the morning before Passover. Since the סיום is followed by a סעודת מצוה (a festive meal which follows the performance of certain mitzvot), a first born who is present may eat, and having eaten, need not fast that day. Since a fast for the firstborn cannot take place on Shabbat or be moved to Friday, the סיום and the סעודת מצוה are held on Thursday morning.

---

[1] Acknowledgments: This responsum is based on "A Statement on Pesah Observance," issued by the CJLS on 6 Feb. 1974. Thanks to Rabbi Noah Golinkin for his thoughtful paper, "When the First Seder Occurs on Saturday Night," which I consulted when writing this responsum.

[2] S.A. Orah Hayyim 470:1.

בדיקת חמץ – *Thursday Evening*

בדיקת חמץ (search for leaven) is customarily done on the night before Passover immediately after sunset.[3] When Passover begins on Saturday night, the בדיקת חמץ is done on Thursday night. The blessing for בדיקת חמץ is recited. One may elect to keep enough חמץ for the Sabbath meals. If so, the כל חמירא ("All the *hametz*. . .") formula for nullifying unseen *hametz*) should not be recited at this time, since one does not want to nullify the *hametz* reserved for Shabbat. However, if the intention is to use מצה עשירה, then the כל חמירא is recited Thursday evening.

ביעור חמץ – *Friday Morning*

This day should be treated as an ordinary erev Pesah in regard to ביעור חמץ (removal of *hametz*). The burning of the *hametz* should be completed by the fifth hour after sunrise. The stove should be kashered for Pesah. All cooking should be done in Pesah pots and only Pesah utensils should be used. Food required for Shabbat as well as for the first seder should be cooked at this time.

Shabbat Meals

There are two traditional practices that present complications when the first seder is held on a Saturday night:

1. It is customary to refrain from eating matzah on the day before Pesah, so that one will eat the matzah with appetite at the seder.
2. It is customary to eat three meals on Shabbat. At least two of these meals should include food over which Hamotzi is recited.

There are two acceptable ways of dealing with these complications:

(A) Set aside enough *hametz* for the Sabbath meals. A *hametz* dish should be provided for the challot. Care should be taken to prevent any crumbs from coming into contact with the other dishes. To avoid such a problem it is recommended that plastic or paper plates and cutlery be used at both the Friday night and Shabbat morning meals.

No *hametz* may be eaten on erev Shabbat beyond a time approximately four hours past sunrise. Hence on Shabbat morning, the Shabbat services should be completed early enough to allow for the סעודת שבת, including challah, to be eaten in time. After the meal, the residue of the *hametz* should be flushed away or otherwise disposed of since, of course, nothing can be burned on Shabbat. The tablecloth should be carefully removed from the table, shaken outside of the house, and then stored with the other *hametz*. The כל חמירא formula should now be recited.

Synagogues that do not have a congregational seder or serve kiddushim during the Pesah holiday may have services early on Shabbat morning, and if they choose, serve a *hametz* meal, have non-Jewish staff dispose of the *hametz* and keep the kitchen locked during the holiday. The כל חמירא formula may be recited by the assemblage, or individually at home.

(B) Have full Pesah meals both on Friday evening and Saturday morning. This is possible because one may use מצה עשירה (enriched matzah, that is to say egg matzah) for

---

[3] S.A. Orah Hayyim 431:1.

המוציא. Though מצה עשירה may not be used for the seder, it is not *hametz*. It is produced under strict rabbinical supervision and may be used during Passover. It may not be used for the seder, for it is עשירה (rich) and what is required for the seder is לחמא עניא (the bread of poverty and affliction). And precisely because egg matzah may not be eaten at the seder, it may be eaten the day of the seder both at the Friday night meal and at the Shabbat lunch.

Rabbi Moshe Feinstein in the *Iggrot Moshe*[4] recommends that those who prefer to remove all *hametz* before Shabbat use מצה עשירה for המוציא and that Birkat Hamazon (grace after meals) be recited following the meal.

> ולכן טוב לאלו שאין רוצים להניח חמץ על יום השבת משום שחוששים למכשולים שאפשר לבא מזה יקיימו מצוות שתי הסעודות במצה עשירה שכיון שקובע עלייהו סעודות השבת יצטרך לברך המוציא ובהמ"ז.

> Therefore, it is preferable for those who do not want to have *hametz* on Shabbat because they are concerned about all the complications that can flow (from having *hametz* in a *Pesahdige* house), to use מצה עשירה for the two meals. Since it is the staple of the meal, Hamotzi must be said and Birkat Hamazon recited.

Rabbi Feinstein maintains that the Rabbis did not require the removal of all *hametz* before Shabbat and the use of מצה עשירה because they did not want to put a burden on those who would find it difficult to do so. However,

> לאלו הרוצים ואפשר להם להטריח ולאפות מצה עשירה לשתי הסעודות הוא עדיף.

> Those who want to, and it is possible for them to take the trouble to bake מצה עשירה, it is preferable for them to do so.

In regard to those who might object and say that a פת (bread or regular matzah) is needed to say Hamotzi and Birkat Hamazon, Rabbi Feinstein reasons,

> דכיון שאוכל אותם לסעודות שבת המחוייבית בפת אין לך קביעות גדולה מזה.

> Since one eats them for the Sabbath meals where a פת is required, there is not greater designation as the staple than this.

And he proceeds to buttress his argument with numerous citations.

Egg matzah is easy to obtain nowadays. It would therefore seem preferable to avoid the complications of using *hametz* in an otherwise *Pesahdige* home, to use מצה עשירה (egg matzah) and not challah for the Sabbath meals.

Rabbi Feinstein does, however, impose a restriction to be in accord with those who hold a different view on the use of מצה עשירה.

> אלא יאכלו שתי הסעודות במצה עשירה ולאוכלם רק בזמן היתר אכילת חמץ.

> They should eat the two meals only during the hours when it would be permitted to eat *hametz* [until the fifth hour after sunrise].

However, since we hold that מצה עשירה may be used during Passover (except at the seder), we can use egg matzah until a later hour, until מנחה קטנה (approximately 2½ halakhic

---

[4] *Iggrot Moshe*, Orah Hayyim pt. 1, p. 274.

hours before sunset). Thus the second Shabbat meal may be eaten at the regular hour, and Shabbat services need not end especially early.

If the option of using מצה עשירה is used, then the כל חמירא formula is recited Shabbat morning before going to the synagogue. There are some congregations that recite the כל חמירה together in the course of the services.

סעודה שלישית

Whether one follows the practice of eating *hametz* on Shabbat or of making the house *Pesahdige* and using מצה עשירה, the סעודה שלישית should not include either *hametz* or מצה עשירה. It should consist of a snack of fruit, fish or eggs. The meal should be completed by the time of מנחה קטנה (approximately 2½ halakhic hours before sunset).

Conclusion

The practices relating to Pesah that begins on Saturday night are as outlined above. The option of making the house *Pesahdige* on Friday and using מצה עשירה is preferable. There is less chance of making mistakes, and it will provide a day of Shabbat relaxation before the seder. However, having *hametz* for the first two סעודות on Shabbat, and following the procedure as described, is an alternative possibility.

OH 447:5.1995

Canned Tuna Fish on Pesah

Rabbi Mayer Rabinowitz

This paper was approved by the CJLS on December 13, 1995, by a vote of twenty in favor and one abstaining (20-0-1). Voting in favor: Rabbis Kassel Abelson, Ben Zion Bergman, Stephanie Dickstein, Elliot N. Dorff, Jerome M. Epstein, Shoshana Gelfand, Myron S. Geller, Susan Grossman, Judah Kogen, Vernon H. Kurtz, Alan B. Lucas, Aaron L. Mackler, Paul Plotkin, Mayer Rabinowitz, Avram Israel Reisner, Joel E. Rembaum, Gerald Skolnik, Elie Kaplan Spitz, Gordon Tucker, and Gerald Zelizer. Abstaining: Rabbi Baruch Frydman-Kohl.

The Committee on Jewish Law and Standards of the Rabbinical Assembly provides guidance in matters of halakhah for the Conservative movement. The individual rabbi, however, is the authority for the interpretation and application of all matters of halakhah.

שאלה

May tuna fish packed in water without השגחה for Pesah be used on Pesah? If so, are there any restrictions or requirements?

In order to answer the question of tuna on Pesah, one must consider the following issues: the processing of tuna fish; the regulations concerning the processing and labeling of tuna fish; and the כשרות concerns which apply to Pesah.

תשובה

Processing Tuna Fish

Tuna boats, which are at sea for months at a time, usually freeze their catch in brine to transport to the cannery. At the cannery the fish is thawed, cleaned, and partly cooked. Then it is boned, trimmed of skin and scales, and sent through automatic equipment for shaping, cutting, and canning. The cans are then vacuum sealed and heated, to complete the cooking process. The FDA calls this process retorting, also known as autoclaving.

FDA Regulations[1]

The Food and Drug Administration's HHAS provides the regulations concerning the processing of tuna fish in "Part 113 – Thermally Processed Low-Acid Foods Packaged

---

[1] I want to thank Mr. Lou Blecher for his help in obtaining and explaining the regulations concerning the processing of tuna fish.

in Hermetically Sealed Containers," with some additional information appearing in Section 161.1900 of that document.

Included in these regulations are: the types of fish that can be labelled as tuna [Section 161.190 A(2)]; the types of seasoning or flavoring that may be added to the tuna [Section 6]; and the fact that canned tuna may be packed in water [Section A(5)].

According to the regulations, if the packing medium is water, the label must read "in water." If seasoning is added, the label must specify "seasoned with x," and the name or names of the ingredient or ingredients used must be listed.

In order to inhibit the development of struvite crystals, sodium acid pyrophosphate may be added not in excess of 0.5% by weight of the finished food. Where added, this ingredient must also appear on the label.

Kashrut Concerns for Pesah

In studying the regulations concerning the use of tuna fish on Pesah, the concerns revolve around the additions to tuna fish which is packed in water — usually, but not limited to, salt. There is also the concern that additives, oil, or seasoning may have inadvertently been added during the processing of the fish.

This responsum applies only to tuna packed in water, to which only sodium acid pyrophosphate has been added. (This information will appear on the label.)

Food prepared under rabbinical supervision for Pesah is devoid of any חמץ (leaven), and can be bought and used during Pesah. Processed food that does not contain חמץ and does not have rabbinical supervision for Pesah, may not be purchased during Pesah. However, these foods may be purchased prior to Pesah, and can then be used during Pesah. One example of this type of food is frozen vegetables (non-legumes) which are washed, peeled, and in some cases salted, and then frozen. Since the ingredients are not חמץ, the product may be purchased before Pesah and used during the holiday.

During the seven/eight days of Pesah, חמץ does not lose its identity in an admixture, no matter how small a proportion of חמץ may be involved. Therefore, the minutest amount of חמץ renders the whole admixture חמץ, and its use is prohibited on Pesah. However, during the rest of the year, חמץ follows the normal rules of admixtures (i.e. it loses its identity in an admixture of one part חמץ to sixty parts non-חמץ [בטל בשישים]).[2] This affords us the opportunity to differentiate between foods purchased before Pesah and foods purchased during Pesah.

In order to prevent the deliberate use of this rule to prepare admixtures that are prohibited, like meat and milk, the Rabbis decreed that אין מבטלין איסור לכתחילה:[3] the deliberate nullification of a prohibited item before the fact, is prohibited. But in the inadvertent mixing of milk and meat, where done accidentally, the admixture is permissible.

In the case of tuna packed in water, even if some ingredient inadvertently fell into the mixture, it would be extremely difficult to argue that the processors deliberately added חמץ in the proper amount in order to nullify it. Therefore, any inadvertent admixture, if it occurred, would be permissible. When tuna in water, without any other additives, is purchased before Pesah, any additional ingredient (vegetable oil, seasoning, etc.) that may have inadvertently found its way into the can, would be nullified. Therefore, if the can of tuna in water is purchased before Pesah, it is not considered an admixture according to halakhah, and may be used during Pesah.

---

[2] Yoreh De'ah 98:1.
[3] Yoreh De'ah 99:5.

The only remaining concern is the use of sodium acid pyrophosphate. Sodium acid pyrophosphate is a chemical that is not derived from grain or alcohol, and is itself not חמץ. It therefore does not pose a problem in water-packed tuna which is purchased before Pesah.

Conclusion

Tuna fish packed in water may not contain any additives without those additives appearing on the label of the can. If salt is added to the fish, the label must indicate that ingredient. Therefore, one can assume that no additional ingredient has been added to the fish if the label does not list it.

Inadvertant mixtures follow the rule of בטל בשישים throughout the year, except during Pesah itself. Before Pesah, any inadvertently added ingredient would lose its identity, and would be nullified. Therefore, even without Passover השגחה tuna packed in water without any additives, or with only salt added, may be used during Pesah if purchased prior to the holiday. However, it may not be purchased during the holiday itself.

Most cans of tuna packed in water do have additional ingredients in them. Therefore, one must look at the label carefully, before purchasing. *This responsum applies only to tuna fish packed in water (with or without salt), but with no other additives.*

OH 451:3.1991

CAN UTENSILS LINED WITH TEFLON OR SILVERSTONE BE KASHERED?

Rabbi Kassel Abelson

This paper was approved by the CJLS on May 29, 1991, by a vote of seventeen in favor (17-0-0). Voting in favor: Rabbis Kassel Abelson, Ben Zion Bergman, Stanley Bramnick, Elliot N. Dorff, Amy Eilberg, Richard L. Eisenberg, Dov Peretz Elkins, Jerome M. Epstein, Samuel Fraint, Reuven Kimelman, Herbert Mandl, Avram Israel Reisner, Joel E. Rembaum, Seymour J. Rosenbloom, Joel Roth, Morris M. Shapiro, and Gordon Tucker.

The Committee on Jewish Law and Standards of the Rabbinical Assembly provides guidance in matters of halakhah for the Conservative movement. The individual rabbi, however, is the authority for the interpretation and application of all matters of halakhah.

שאלה

Can utensils lined with Teflon or Silverstone be Kashered?

תשובה

Teflon is manufactured by the Dupont Company. Teflon is the name of an entire family of non-stick coatings. Teflon is a synthetic fluorine-carbon compound. Silverstone is a member of the Teflon family, more exactly Polytetrafluoroethylene PTFE. It is used for the coating of pots. Teflon is chemically inert, non-absorbing and remains unchanged at full cooking temperatures (up to 600°F/316°C). When Teflon/Silverstone is used to coat non-stick metal cookware, it is applied in a very thin film, the average thickness of the coating being less than 2 mils (1 mil = 1/1000 inch). Some manufacturers recommend using only plastic utensils for mixing or stirring and not metal ones, since Teflon/Silverstone may scratch. If Teflon/Silverstone is scratched, the coating is so thin that the scratch will go down to the underlying metal.

Though Teflon was first manufactured in 1938, there were forerunners, coatings applied to metal pots to make them better cooking vessels than plain metal. Questions about kashering such pots were directed to previous generations of rabbis. The problem that disturbed the authorities of past generations was the nature of the coating. The composition of the coating was a carefully guarded trade secret held closely by the craftsmen who made the cookware. There are authorities who held that in the absence of definitive information, the coating should be considered as earthenware. Consequently, they did not permit such cookware to be kashered by boiling water if it inadvertently became טריף. The Hatam Sofer evidently believed that it was חרס, and he required that the metal of the pot be kashered only with burning coals regardless of the damage done to the coating of the cooking vessel:

> והעקר נ"ל דלא ליעבד להו הגעדה כמש"ל אבל למלאות גחלים ש"ד
> דמסתמא לא ניחוש דפקעו ואי פקעו הרי קמן כ"ח שהרי פקע ע"י
> האש ואמנם אי לא פקעי לא נימא דלא אסיק להן שפיר משום דחייס עליי׳
> דכיון דאינו אלא שוע בעלמא וגם ספק אם הוא חרס.[1]

The Maharam Shick has doubts, even though a "modern rabbi" investigated the chemical composition of the coating and determined that it is not חרס, and consequently permitted kashering it if it became טריף by הגעלה, though not for use on Passover. The Maharam is reluctant to trust the testimony of non-Jewish craftsmen, that the coating is not made of חרס. Nonetheless the Maharam concludes that if it is shown definitely that it is not made of חרס, then there are grounds to permit it to be kashered, not only for year around use, but for Passover use as well:

> ולכך אין להתיר הקדירות האלו המצופין מבפנים בהיתוך שהוא ספק חרס
> בהגעלה אלא א"כ יתברר לן שאינו חרס ומ"מ מי שרוצה להתיר אין גוערין
> בו כיון שיש צדדים הנ"ל מיהו דווקא מאיסור להיתר אבל מחמן לפסח כל
> זמן שלא יתברר בעדות ברור שאין הציפוי של חרס בוודאי לא שייך כל
> התירים הנ"ל דבפסח הוא במשהו.[2]

The Arukh Hashulkhan deals with the same issues and provides us with a useful approach to the question. He also describes metal cooking ware lined with white coating whose composition is doubtful — since the manufacturers keep the formula secret. If such cookware inadvertently becomes טריף, kashering it by ליבון (heating it until it glows) requires considerable expertise to avoid irreparable damage. In these cases where it is uncertain whether the coating is of metal or חרס, and the pot itself is metal, then to avoid considerable material loss, kashering by הגעלה (boiling water) is permitted. And if it can be demonstrated that it is not חרס, it is certainly kasherable by boiling water. And since there is some indication that the coating is not חרס, it is reasonable to consider it like metal and permit it to be kashered by הגעלה:

> מ"מ בספק ציפוי חרס או מתכות, ועצם הקידרה הוא ודאי של מתכות
> פשיטא שיש להקל בדין ברור כזה ולחוס על ממונם של ישראל וקצת ראיה
> יש שהציפוי הוא של מתכת ולא של חרס.[3]

Rabbi Isaac Klein concludes his investigation of the nature of Teflon as follows: "Today we know that the lining is not made of a porous substance, nor of a substance that would be damaged by boiling. Hence kashering should be permitted."[4]

Conclusion

The composition of Teflon (Silverstone) is well known and easily verifiable. It is a fluorocarbon compound and not חרס (earthenware). When it is used to line metal cookware, it does not absorb food nor the taste of food that is cooked in it. It is chemically inert and is

---

[1] Responsa of the Hatam Sofer, Part 2, 113.
[2] Responsa of Maharam Schick, Orah Hayyim 238.
[3] Arukh Hashulhan, Yoreh De'ah 121:27.
[4] Rabbi Isaac Klein, *A Guide to Jewish Religious Practice* (New York: Jewish Theological Seminary, 1979), p. 113.

not affected by cooking, even at high temperatures. If the coating is scratched, then the food will touch the metal of the pot. Hence, if such cookware becomes טריף, it may be kashered by הגעלה, by careful cleansing and by boiling water. The same would apply to kashering for Pesah. In the case of Pesah the cooking pot should be kashered only after 24 hours of non-use, and the kashering should be complete by 10:00 A.M. ערב פסח. Baking pans may not be kashered. In general, it is recommended that, where feasible, separate cookware be purchased for Passover use.

OH 582.1995

Omission of the Silent Amidah

Rabbi Kassel Abelson

This paper was approved on June 4, 1995, by a vote of eighteen in favor, two opposed and one abstention (18-2-1). Voting in favor: Rabbis Kassel Abelson, Ben Zion Bergman, Stephanie Dickstein, Elliot N. Dorff, Jerome M. Epstein, Myron S. Geller, Susan Grossman, Judah Kogen, Alan B. Lucas, Aaron L. Mackler, Lionel E. Moses, Paul Plotkin, Mayer Rabinowitz, Avram Israel Reisner, Joel E. Rembaum, Joel Roth, Gerald Skolnik, and Gerald Zelizer. Voting against: Rabbis Samuel Fraint and Arnold Goodman. Abstaining: Rabbi Gordon Tucker.

The Committee on Jewish Law and Standards of the Rabbinical Assembly provides guidance in matters of halakhah for the Conservative movement. The individual rabbi, however, is the authority for the interpretation and application of all matters of halakhah.

שאלה

During the High Holidays the services are very lengthy. The congregation includes many worshippers who are not regular attendants, and who tend to get restless, to talk among themselves, and to go in and out of the synagogue. In order to shorten the service and to increase participation, the synagogue ritual committee is considering several innovations. They want to know: "Is it permissible to omit the silent Amidah and to have the שליח ציבור (the congregational reader) recite the Amidah aloud?"

תשובה

The Amidah is, next to the Shema, the most essential part of the prescribed daily services. It is comprised of a series of benedictions expressing praise, thanksgiving, confession and petition. Because of its importance, the Talmud often refers to it simply as התפילה, that is, "the prayer" *par excellence*. It is recited silently, three times daily, and it receives its name from the position in which it is recited (the word Amidah means standing).

There are various forms of the Amidah designated for different occasions. On weekdays, the Amidah originally had eighteen benedictions, later increased to nineteen. On fast days another benediction is added in the course of the repetition by the reader. On Sabbaths and Festivals there are only seven benedictions. On Rosh Hashanah there are nine in the Musaf (and seven in the Shaharit).[1]

---

[1] Raphael Posner, *Jewish Liturgy* (Jerusalem: Keter Publishing House, 1975) p. 80.

Repetition of the Amidah

The Talmud holds that the recitation of the Amidah is obligatory for every member of the congregation, but there is a difference of opinion as to the reason the repetition of the Amidah was introduced:

כשם ששליח צבור חייב כך כל יחיד ויחיד חייב. רבן גמליאל אומר שליח צבור מוציא את הרבים ידי חובתן. תניא: אמרו לו לרבן גמליאל לדבריך למה צבור מתפללין? אמר להם כדי להסדיר שליח צבור תפלתו. אמר להם רבן גמליאל, לדבריכם למה שליח צבור יורד לפני התיבה? אמרו לו כדי להוציא את שאינן בקי. אמר להם כשם שמוציא את שאינן בקי, כך מוציא את הבקי.

> Just as the congregational reader is under obligation, so every individual is under obligation. Rabban Gamaliel says: The congregational reader exempts the congregation from its obligation. It has been taught: "They said to Rabban Gamaliel: Accepting your view [that the reader may recite on behalf of the congregation] why do the congregation [first] say the [עמידה] prayer? He replied, So as to give the reader time to prepare his prayer [in those days the prayers were recited from memory]. Rabban Gamaliel then said to them: Accepting your view [that each individual must pray for himself], why does the reader go down [and stand] before the ark? They replied: So as to clear from his obligation one who is not familiar [with the prayers]. He said to them: Just as he clears one who is not familiar [with the prayers], so he clears one who is familiar [with the prayers].[2]

The introduction of the repetition of the Amidah was at a time when there were no prayerbooks, for prayerbooks were first introduced in the eighth century, and it was not until the fifteenth century that ordinary congregants had prayerbooks.[3] Many people did not know the Amidah by heart and needed help. They waited until the more learned congregants recited the Amidah silently, thereby fulfilling their obligation. The ש"ץ (congregational reader) then repeated the prayer aloud for the sake of the less learned, who, by listening and repeating "Amen," fulfilled their obligation. Rabban Gamaliel held a different view. He said the purpose of the initial silent prayer was to give the ש"ץ (who also did not have a siddur) time to rehearse in his mind the prayer, and to prepare himself to say it aloud. And, Rabban Gamaliel added, listening to the repetition and responding "Amen," was effective in clearing both the learned and the less learned of their obligation.

Repetition Can Cause Problems

Even though the introduction of the repetition of the Amidah into the service was done for worthy reasons, the results were not always desirable. This is apparent in a responsum of the Rambam in which he deals with the question of the repetition of the Amidah.[4]

---

[2] B. Rosh Hashanah 34b.

[3] Isaac Klein, *A Guide to Jewish Religious Practice* (New York: The Jewish Theological Seminary of America, 1979), p. 24

[4] Israel Friedlander, "A New Responsum of Maimonides Concerning the Repetition of the Shemonah Esreh," *Jewish Quarterly Review*, n.s., 5 (1914-15), 1ff. A very similar responsum is found in Teshuvot HaRambam, pp. 482-484.

Maimonides was asked whether there was any merit to the suggestion of a scholar who had come from a Christian country "that the hazzan should recite the Amidah but once, and this with a loud voice," thus dispensing altogether with the silent recitation. Maimonides replied that the Talmud requires a double recitation of the Amidah. The first, a silent one, so that all who can read, including the hazzan, can fulfill their duty. And the second recitation to be said aloud by the hazzan, to enable all those who cannot read to recite the prayers after him. Nonetheless, the practice of omitting the silent recitation is a good one, but not for the reasons cited by the questioner. The silent prayer ought to be abolished because of the indecorous behavior of the congregation. And he explains:

> שכך ראוי בזמננו מפני סבה שאבארה והיא שכשיחזור ש"ץ להתפלל בקול רם כל מי שהתפלל ויצא ידי חובתו, יהפוך פניו לספר עם חברו או לשיחה בטלה ויחזור פניו מהמזרח וירוק ויסור כיחו וניעו. וכשיראה זה חבירו שאינו בקי יעשה גם הוא כן בלי ספק ויחשוב שזה שאומר ש"ץ אין לסמוך עליו, ואם כן יצא כל מי שאינו בקי, והוא לא יצא ידי חובתו. ותתבטל הכונה אשר בעבורה חוזר ש"ץ התפלה, שהוא להוציא את שאינו בקי.

> It is appropriate in our time, for a reason that I will explain, for when the ש"ץ repeats aloud, one who has already said the prayer and fulfilled his duty, turns to a friend to talk or to gossip, and turns from facing east and spits out phlegm. When his fellow congregant who is less expert in the prayers sees this and infers from the behavior of the learned that the loud repetition is of no importance, he behaves likewise and may even go out [of the synagogue], thereby defeating the purpose for which the repetition was instituted, to enable the uneducated to repeat the prayers after the hazzan.

And the Rambam proceeds to point out the benefits of omitting the silent prayer:

> ואמנם כשלא יתפללו הקהל בלחש כלל, אלא יתפללו הכל אחר ש"ץ תפלה אחת בקדושה. כל מי שיודע להתפלל יתפלל עמו בלחש והבלתי בקיאים ישמעו ויכרעו כולם עם ש"ץ ופני כל העם אל ההיכל בכונה ויצאו כולם ידי חובתם ויהיה הדבר הולך על נכון ויושר ותמנע אריכות החזרה ויוסר חלול השם שנתפשט בין הנכרים שהיהודים זה תמיד. וזה היותר נכון אצלי באלו הזמנים מצד הסבות שזכרתי. וכתב משה.

> When the congregation does not say the silent prayer at all, but says, after the ש"ץ, one prayer with the Kedushah, all who know how to pray will say it quietly with him, and the uneducated will listen and prostrate themselves [say "Amen"] with the ש"ץ. Then the entire congregation will pray devotedly directed to the Temple. All will have fulfilled their duty and everything will be as it should be. There will be a saving of time, and it will remove the Hillul Hashem which arises when non-Jews [the Moslems whose prayers are brief and characterized by almost military precision] make fun of the Jews who spit, hawk, and talk during their prayers.[5]

The Rambam concludes, "The abolition of the silent prayer is therefore necessitated by the particular conditions of the time."

---

[5] Ibid., Friedlander, pp. 10–11.

The Mishneh Torah

Though the Rambam, in his responsum, identifies the reason for the abolition of the silent Amidah as "necessitated by the particular conditions of the time," in the Mishneh Torah he implies that it could be halakhah, at least for the High Holidays:

> שליח צבור מוציא את הרבים ידי חובתן. כיצד? בשעה שהוא מתפלל והן שומעין ועונין אמן אחר כל ברכה וברכה הרי הן כמתפללין. במה דברים אמורים: במי שאינו יודע להתפלל. אבל היודע אינו יוצא ידי חובתו אלא בתפלת עצמו. במה דברים אמורים: בשאר הימים חוץ מראש השנה ויום הכפורים של יובל. אבל בשני ימים אלו שליח צבור מוציא את היודע. כשם שמוציא את שאינו יודע. מפני שהן ברכות ארוכות, ואין רוב היודעין אותן יכולין לכוון דעתן בהן כשליח צבור. לפיכך אם רצה היודע בשני ימים אלו לסמוך על תפלת שליח צבור להוציא חובתו ידי הרשות בידו.

> The reader discharges the obligation of the congregation. How so? When he recites the prayers and they respond with the utterance of "Amen" after every blessing, they are regarded as praying. This only applies to one who does not know the liturgy. One who is proficient does not discharge his obligation unless he recites the prayers for himself.

> The foregoing rule holds good for all days of the year except New Year's day and the Day of Atonement in a Jubilee Year. On those two days the Reader discharges the obligations of the proficient as of the non-proficient, on the ground that the prayers recited on those days are lengthy and the majority of those acquainted with them cannot concentrate their minds as the Reader can. Hence, if one who is proficient wishes on those days to rely on the Reader's recital of the prayers, he may do so.[6]

A Challenge

Though the Rambam permitted the omission of the silent Amidah in the conditions of his day, the question continued to arise. Rabbi David ibn Zimra (1480-1573), known as the Radbaz, dealt with the issue. A dispute had broken out in the community about the practice instituted by the Rambam 200 years earlier to have only one Amidah said aloud by the ש"ץ.

There were complaints by Sephardic congregations that a Moroccan congregation followed the practice of Egyptian congregations and omitted the recitation of the silent Amidah, which was against the ruling of the Gemara (Talmud), the poskim (Rabbinic authorities), and the Kabbalah (mystical books). Other communities, it was stated, had followed that practice, but had changed and returned to the earlier Talmudic tradition. And so should this congregation.

The Radbaz's response focused on the role of a תקנה (a legislative revision of an existing rule) in Jewish communal life. The Rambam had won the concurrence of the Rabbinic leaders of his generation to his תקנה omitting the silent Amidah, and having the ש"ץ recite

---

[6] M.T. Hilkhot T'fillah 8:9-10.

the Amidah aloud. However it was never universally accepted. It seemed to have been limited to Egypt and its environs. The Rambam's תקנה was limited in time and to the people and the conditions that called for correction. Moreover, he maintained the תקנה did not accomplish its goal. Even in those congregations which recite only one Amidah aloud, the congregation begins to talk in the middle of the recitation of the Amidah by the ש"ץ:

> אני מעיד מה שראיתי בעיני שהשליח צבור לא הגיע לחצי התפלה וכבר
> השלימו רוב הקהל וחזרו לדבר זה עם זה והדרן קושיין לדוכתא ונמצינו
> עוברין על דברי הגמרא והפוסקים ובעלי הקבלה ולא הועלנו כלום
> בתקנתנן.

> I testify that I saw that the ש"ץ had not even finished saying half
> of the T'fillah [Amidah], when most of the congregation who
> had already finished saying [the Amidah] turned to one another
> and began talking.[7]

The Radbaz claimed that if the Rambam had seen the ineffectiveness of his תקנה he would return to the previous practice of repeating the Amidah in accordance with the Talmud, the Poskim and the Kabbalah, for it is important to maintain the traditional practice of the Talmud. Hence, the Radbaz advises that the matter be discussed with the congregation following the Rambam's תקנה. However:

> אם אפשר להחזירם לדין הגמרא שיתפללו שתי תפלות בלא מחלקת כן ראוי
> לעשות אבל אם אי אפשר לבטלת אלא ע"י מחלקת שב ואל תעשה.

> If it is possible to have them return to the earlier Talmudic practice of
> saying the T'fillah twice without causing controversy then it is worth
> doing so. But if it is impossible to avoid controversy, then do nothing.[8]

The Radbaz bases his call to return to the Talmudic practice on the limited nature of the Rambam's תקנה and its ineffectiveness rather than a challenge to the right of the Rambam to institute such a change in Talmudic practice. And his conclusion that avoiding controversy over the practice is essential would seem to imply that those congregations that followed the practice of omitting the repetition of the Amidah had a right to do so.

Other Precedents

The Talmudic practice of repeating the Amidah prevailed, because to do so was the established custom. According to the Shulhan Arukh:

> קהל שהתפללו וכולם בקיאים בתפלה אף אל פי כן ירד שליח צבור וחוזר
> להתפלל כדי לקיים תקנת חכמים.

> A congregation that has prayed, even where all are knowledgeable
> in the prayers, the ש"ץ nonetheless repeats the Amidah to sustain
> the תקנה of the Rabbis.[9]

Nonetheless, there remained a flexibility of practice that reasserted itself when there was a need to do so:

---

[7] Teshuvot HaRadbaz, Responsum 1165.

[8] Ibid.

[9] S.A. Orah Hayyim 124:2.

> שיעבור זמן התפלה יוכל להתפלל מיד בקול רם והצבור מתפללין עמו מלה
> במלה בלחש עד לאחר האל הקודש.

If the time prescribed for prayer would pass [if both Amidot were recited] it is permissible for the ש"ץ to begin praying aloud immediately and the congregation says quietly together with the ש"ץ, word for word until after האל הקודש (the remaining blessings are recited silently).[10]

In many Conservative congregations this practice (known as the הכי קדושה) is often followed to keep the service shorter, not only at weekday Minhah services, but also on Sabbath and festivals. The practice developed in Sephardic congregations of having the ש"ץ recite aloud, together with the congregation, the first three benedictions, the intermediate blessings are recited silently, and the last three benedictions are recited aloud by the ש"ץ.[11]

These developments seem to indicate that with the availability of סידורים (prayerbooks) there was less concern about those who were not knowledgeable about the prayers. The reasoning may have been, that in days when there were no prayerbooks, even less knowledgeable people knew the prayers almost by heart. Because of their familiarity with the prayers, the recitation by the ש"ץ was all that was necessary to remind them. Hearing the prayers then fulfilled their responsibility. However once סידורים became widely available, it could be assumed that a person who could not pray from a סידור would not be familiar with the prayers and hearing it repeated would be of little help. No longer feeling the need to repeat the Amidah for the sake of the less informed, other practices took root, and were not discouraged on the grounds that they contradicted the תקנה of the Rabbis.

There is also the curious case of the late-arriving ש"ץ who enters the synagogue after the congregation has finished reciting the silent Amidah. In such a case the ש"ץ does not have to recite the Amidah quietly, but may immediately begin reciting the Amidah aloud.[12]

The fact that the ש"ץ need not say the silent Amidah, where it may inconvenience the congregation, seems in direct contradiction to the opinion of Rabban Gamaliel who says that the recitation of the silent Amidah was to provide an opportunity for the ש"ץ to prepare the prayer. This, too, can probably be traced to the availability of סידורים, which made it unnecessary for the ש"ץ to mentally review the Amidah. He could now read it. Whatever the reason, it is evident that טרחא דצבורא (congregational discomfort) was also deemed a sufficient reason for the ש"ץ to omit the silent Amidah and to proceed directly to the repetition of the Amidah.

As is obvious from the brief history outlined above there have been several attempts to deal with problems that may arise from the lengthening the service by repeating the Amidah. What may have been effective in one era and area may not have worked well in other times and places. Hence, before we institute any changes in the way the Amidah is recited, we should look carefully at our congregations, our congregants, their needs, and our educational and spiritual objectives.

The Silent Amidah Today

The common availability of מחזורים with good English translations makes it possible for all attending the High Holiday services to fulfill their obligation to recite the

---

[10] *Mapah* on Orah Hayyim 124:2.

[11] *Be'er Heiteiv* on Orah Hayyim 4.

[12] S.A. Orah Hayyim 124:2.

Amidah.[13] It is evident from the fact that so many stand quietly looking into the מחזור, that most of the congregation does use the time allocated for the silent prayer either to read the Amidah, to recite their own prayers, or simply to meditate. Thus to eliminate the silent Amidah today, despite historical precedents, would result in losing an opportunity for spiritual expression and transform many in the congregation from participants to auditors during this section of the service.

In addition there are practical halakhic problems. It is difficult for the congregation to remain standing in place for the entire recitation of the single Amidah. If everyone remained in their places there would be no one who could move to open the Ark, sound the shofar, announce pages, lead English readings, etc.[14]

The elimination of the silent Amidah does not appear to be either a desirable or a practical way to shorten the lengthy High Holiday services. However, there are other possibilities which the rabbi and the ritual committee of the synagogue should explore.

Shortening High Holiday Services

Our congregations have seen an increase in the numbers of congregants that attend Shabbat services regularly. Nonetheless, there are large numbers of people who are in the synagogue only on the High Holidays. If the services are too lengthy they tend to get restless, and as the Rambam noted, in his congregation, restlessness in a portion of the congregation tends to affect the כונה (spiritual intensity) of the entire congregation. Hence, alternative methods of shortening the service should also be considered.

(A) פיוטים (poetic prayers) are introduced into the service at different times to give meaning to contemporary events and to enhance the spiritual experience of worshippers in terms meaningful to their generation. These additions were retained in the מחזור, even though succeeding generations may no longer have understood their relevance or even their meaning. The High Holiday services, therefore, continued to grow longer in succeeding generations.

The RA *Mahzor* recognized this process and began to reverse it by omitting many פיוטים. However, there are still פיוטים in the מחזור which are recited, sometimes at length, and which could be omitted, saving time and allowing for the introduction of contemporary פיוטים, readings and religious poetry, which could enhance the meaning and spirituality of the service for our contemporaries.

(B) Musical elaborations of the prayers add beauty to the service, but also, cumulatively, add a great deal of time. Strict limits on repetition of words and careful selectivity of musical compositions could shorten the service and the introduction of brief congregational melodies would encourage more participation.

(C) Rabbinic comments provide an understanding of the meaning of the service and give relevance to the themes of the Holy Days. However, they too add to the length of the service, and should be limited in time and number.

(D) The shortening of the פסוקי דזמרה is also a possibility and presents no halakhic difficulty.

(E) Sermons are still the prime method of reaching the mass of our congregants and teaching them how to live, think and feel as Jews. However, lengthening sermons, in the age of sound bites, do not make them more persuasive.

---

[13] Rosh Hashanah 34b. The fact that the Amidah can be said in English is an advantage for those who are not Hebraically literate.

[14] I am grateful to Rabbi Judah Kogen for pointing out these problems in a letter to me.

(F) It is possible to use the הכי קדושה mode of reciting the Amidah for Shaharit thereby retaining the Silent Prayer, while shortening the time. It is not practical to do so in the Musaf, because of the need to blow shofar and the emotional importance of the recitation with the congregation of prayers such as the *Unetaneh Tokef*.

Summary

The Talmud instituted the repetition of the Amidah for one of two reasons: either to help those not knowledgeable in the prayers to fulfill their obligation to recite the prayer, or to provide an opportunity for the Reader to review the prayer while the congregation recited it silently. With the introduction of סידורים and מחזורים these reasons no longer seem convincing.

Even before prayerbooks were widely available, the Rambam found that the recitation of both the silent Amidah and the repetition of the Amidah led to a loss of decorum at the services which resulted in a חילול השם (desecration of God's name). The Rambam therefore instituted the practice of having the ש"ץ recite the Amidah aloud only once and the congregation repeating word for word or, for the less knowledgeable, responding "Amen" after each blessing. The Rambam stated in the Mishneh Torah that on Rosh Hashanah and Yom Kippur that, because of the length of the service and the unfamiliarity of the prayers, the Reader fulfilled the obligation of even the knowledgeable by his recital of the prayers (thereby making the repetition of the Amidah unnecessary).

The Radbaz declared that the תקנה of the Rambam was limited to a specific time, place and people, and did not accomplish its goal, and therefore should no longer be followed. He called for a return to the Talmudic practice of a silent Amidah and a repetition of the Amidah. The תקנה of the Rabbis should be respected.

The development of the הכי קדושה to save time by so many congregations, and the Sephardic variant point to the conclusion that "respect for the תקנה of the Rabbis" was not sufficient to discourage innovations whose goal it was to shorten the services when needed.

The congregation on the High Holidays includes many worshippers who do not attend regularly during the rest of the year, and while they seem to be better behaved than was the congregation of Maimonides, they do get restless, begin to talk and to go in and out of the synagogue when the service gets lengthy. It is, therefore, praiseworthy to find ways to shorten the services and to increase participation so that those attending services will not feel burdened and will feel part of a worshipping congregation. There are numerous alternatives that provide opportunities to shorten services without infringing on halakhic precedents, and they should be explored by the מרא דאתרא and the ritual committee.

Conclusion

The silent Amidah is an important part of congregational worship and should not be omitted. It is permissible, in order to save time and to improve decorum, to find ways of shortening the High Holiday Services. The מרא דאתרא and the synagogue religious committee should examine alternative ways to accomplish this goal.

Responsa Relating to Yoreh De'ah
יורה דעה

הלכות שחיטה	Kosher Slaughter
הלכות בשר וחלב	Meat and Milk
הלכות מאכלי עובדי כוכבים	Foreign Foods
הלכות חוקות עובדי כוכבים וכישוף	Idolatry and Sorcery
הלכות מילה	Circumcision
הלכות גרים	Conversion
הלכות ספר תורה	The Torah Scroll
הלכות פדיון בכור	Pidyon HaBen
הלכות ביקור חולים ורפואה	Visiting the Sick and Medicine
הלכות קריעה	Responding to a Death
הלכות אבילות	Mourning

YD 1:1.1993

Is a *K* Kosher?

Rabbi Kassel Abelson

This paper was approved by the CJLS on October 27, 1993, by a vote of twenty-three in favor (23-0-0). Voting in favor: Rabbis Kassel Abelson, Ben Zion Bergman, Stanley Bramnick, Elliot N. Dorff, Jerome M. Epstein, Ezra Finkelstein, Samuel Fraint, Myron S. Geller, Arnold M. Goodman, Susan Grossman, Jan Caryl Kaufman, Reuven Kimelman, Judah Kogen, Vernon H. Kurtz, Aaron L. Mackler, Herbert Mandl, Lionel E. Moses, Paul Plotkin, Mayer Rabinowitz, Avram Israel Reisner, Joel Roth, Gerald Skolnik, and Gordon Tucker.

The Committee on Jewish Law and Standards of the Rabbinical Assembly provides guidance in matters of halakhah for the Conservative movement. The individual rabbi, however, is the authority for the interpretation and application of all matters of halakhah.

שאלה

Questions have been raised about a *K* symbol on food products. Does a *K* on a food container signify that a rabbinic authority has granted the product in that container a certification of compliance with the laws of kashrut? Can one be sure that a food producer/packager cannot print a *K* on the container without such authority? Does the Rabbinical Assembly have a list of acceptable products bearing a *K*?

תשובה

A *K*, which is often found on food packages, is not the symbol of a particular rabbi or kashrut organization. It is a letter of the alphabet, and under American law a letter may not be trademarked. There are over fifty rabbis (including Conservative rabbis) or agencies that use a *K* to signify that a product is kosher. The standards of kashrut will vary, depending on the particular rabbi or agency and the rabbinic פוסק (authority) followed. Even where there is a state law that governs kashrut, the state will not get involved in a dispute in the religious Jewish community as to which פוסק determines whether a food is kosher. And this applies equally to all kosher symbols.

The State of New York requires that any kashrut symbol, including a *K*, must be backed by a supervising rabbi or agency and be registered with the New York State Department of Agriculture. Hence most food products that are distributed nationally would also be distributed in New York State and would have kashrut supervision. It is, however, conceivable that a manufacturer might put a *K* on the package without having proper kashrut supervision. This could be the case in California, where no rabbinical supervision is necessary for a food supplier to put *K* on a food product. However, the consumer fraud laws would be invoked against a food producer who marked a food product with a *K* knowing that it was not kosher (See letter from Herschel T. Elkins, Senior Assistant Attorney General of the State of California, dated June 25, 1993, and memo from Rabbi Elliot N. Dorff dated June 30, 1993).

The Rabbinical Assembly does not presently maintain a list of food products that are certified to be kosher, whether bearing a *K*, the O-U, or any other kashrut symbol.

Conclusion

The presence of a *K* on a food product does not necessarily mean that the food is kosher. It is important to check to see whether a particular food product bearing a *K* has been rabbinically certified. In most cases a copy of the הכשר will be sent together with the name of the supervising rabbi. If desired, additional information can be obtained from the rabbi about the standards used in supervising the food product.

YD 6.2000

SHACKLING AND HOISTING

Rabbis Elliot N. Dorff and Joel Roth

This paper was approved by the CJLS on September 20, 2000, by a vote of twenty-one in favor (21-0-0). Voting in favor: Rabbis Kassel Abelson, Ben Zion Bergman, Elliot N. Dorff, Paul Drazen, Baruch Frydman-Kohl, Nechama D. Goldberg, Arnold M. Goodman, Susan Grossman, Judah Kogen, Aaron L. Mackler, Daniel S. Nevins, Hillel Norry, Stanley Platek, Paul Plotkin, Mayer Rabinowitz, Avram Israel Reisner, Joel E. Rembaum, James S. Rosen, Joel Roth, Elie Kaplan Spitz, and Gordon Tucker.

The Committee on Jewish Law and Standards of the Rabbinical Assembly provides guidance in matters of halakhah for the Conservative movement. The individual rabbi, however, is the authority for the interpretation and application of all matters of halakhah.

שאלה

Is shackling and hoisting animals in the process of slaughtering them a violation of Jewish laws prohibiting inflicting pain to animals (צער בעלי חיים)?

תשובה

We would first like to thank Mr. Aaron Frank and Rabbi Adam Frank for raising this issue and for providing us with some important information regarding this method of slaughter. We would also like to thank Dr. Temple Grandin, whose research and writing[1] has been primarily responsible for bringing this entire issue to the attention of the Jewish community and who graciously presented this material to rabbinical students at the University of Judaism in spring, 1999, and at the Jewish Theological Seminary in fall, 1999.

We shall begin by quoting a few paragraphs from a letter that Rabbi Adam Frank and Mr. Aaron Frank circulated to the Committee on Jewish Law and Standards:

---

[1] Among her writings on this subject, see "High Speed Double Rail Restrainer for Stunning or Ritual Slaughter," *Proceedings of the 33rd International Congress of Meat Science and Technology* in Ghent, Belgium, 1:101 (1987); "Humane Restraint Equipment for Kosher Slaughter," *Kashrus Magazine* (June 1991): 18-21; "Religious Slaughter and Animal Welfare: A Discussion for Meat Scientists," *Meat Focus International* 3 (Mar. 1994): 115-123 (with Joe M. Regenstein); "Animal Welfare in Slaughter Plants," *Proceedings of the American Association of Bovine Practitioners* (1996), pp. 22-26; "Objective Scoring of Animal Handling and Stunning Procedures in Slaughter Plants," *Journal of the American Veterinary Medicine Association* 212 (1998): 36-39, as well as her book, *Thinking in Pictures* (New York: Vintage, 1996), pp. 40-42, 153-154, 204-206. See also C.S. Dunn, "Stress Reactions of Cattle Undergoing Ritual Slaughter Using Two Methods of Restraint," *Veterinary Record* 126 (1990): pp. 522-525; and Phyllis Klasky Karas, "Is Kosher Slaughter Inhumane?" *Moment* (Feb. 1991): 40-45 and 54. We would like to thank Mr. Aaron Frank for supplying us with some of these articles, and we call the reader's attention to Dr. Grandin's website, *www.grandin.com*.

Shackling and hoisting is a method of slaughter restraint in which a fully conscious animal is shackled with a chain around its back leg and hoisted into the air. The animal hangs upside down, often for minutes, prior to slaughter. Often, nose tongs are used to pull the head back to allow for the throat to be cut.

Shackling and hoisting came into widespread practice when the U.S. Pure Food and Drug Act of 1906 stipulated that, for sanitary reasons, an animal cannot be slaughtered on the ground falling into the blood of another animal. At that time, shackling and hoisting was implemented as the primary method of both kosher and non-kosher slaughter. Ironically, due to the cruel nature of this method, the regulations were once strongly resisted by the Jewish community.

Shackling and hoisting of conscious animals was later outlawed as inhumane in the United States by the Humane Slaughter Act of 1958. This legislation required that all cattle be instantaneously rendered unconscious before being hoisted from the ground. Kosher slaughter was specifically exempted from this ban because, at the time, no alternative existed in order to comply with both the halakhic requirement of the animal being conscious and the sanitary requirement of the federal government.

By 1963 alternative methods of kosher slaughter existed which kept cattle upright and relatively calm during שחיטה. Today, state-of-the-art methods are being used by major slaughter facilities which allow for efficient and economical upright kosher slaughter. Nevertheless, shackling and hoisting are still practiced in kosher slaughter today. . . .

Today about 10% of large cattle are being shackled and hoisted. However, 50% of veal calves and 100% of sheep and lamb are still being shackled and hoisted. Furthermore, inverted kosher slaughter is the primary method used for most countries outside of the United States.

It is important to note, as Dr. Joe Regenstein pointed out to us, that Congress recognized and affirmed that Jewish ritual slaughter (שחיטה) itself is humane. Congress granted exemptions to the Jewish community only for pre-slaughter handling of the animals. The exemption Congress afforded us does not entitle us to engage in cruel slaughter. Still, as we shall develop below, we have major reservations in continuing to take advantage of that exemption now that another alternative is available that saves the cattle from the pain and anguish of being shackled and hoisted before slaughter.

Second, we should point out that shackling and hoisting animals is neither a requirement of, nor a violation of, the laws of kosher slaughter. It was a method that was, from 1906 to 1958, a requirement of American law to insure sanitary conditions, but with the invention of the upright pens to restrain the animals, shackling and hoisting was no longer necessary to assure proper sanitation. In fact, shackling and hoisting conscious animals was banned by American law as inhumane in 1958. The method that was then substituted, stunning the cow before slaughter, was taken to violate the laws of kosher slaughter,² and so Congress enacted a specific exemption to allow cattle destined for kosher slaughter to be shackled and hoisted while conscious. Shackling and hoisting, though, are not required for kosher slaughter; these were simply the only methods available at the time to produce kosher meat while fulfilling the U.S. government's requirements for sanitation. Conversely, to the best of our knowledge, no פוסק has maintained that the use of the new pen violates Jewish laws of slaughter, at least if the pen holds the cow's neck extended to enable bleeding, as the modern ones do. Thus meat from cattle that have been shackled and hoisted while they were conscious is still kosher in the sense that the technical procedures required by the laws of kosher slaughter can be fulfilled even if the cattle are shackled and hoisted, but shackling and hoisting violate the laws prohibiting undue pain to animals in doing so. We therefore maintain that now that both sanitation and Jewish ritual fitness (כשרות) can be assured through the use of upright pens without shackling and hoisting, the latter procedures should no longer be used so as not to violate the prohibition of causing undue pain to animals.

We have good evidence that shackling and hoisting animals while still conscious causes immense pain to the animals themselves. This is especially true for large animals like cows; Dr. Grandin herself has fewer concerns with shackling and hoisting small animals. With regard to cows, though, the evidence is clear, as Dr. Grandin has demonstrated in many of her writings. In their letter to the CJLS, Mr. Aaron Frank and Rabbi Adam Frank summarize her findings and those of other researchers on this matter:

> Hanging a 1,000 to 1,200-pound animal upside down by one leg unquestionably causes tremendous suffering. It is common that this method causes bruising, torn flesh, and even broken bones. Furthermore, stress levels can be measured empirically through stress hormone (cortisol) levels. Stress levels for inverted slaughter with devices known as the Weinberg pen (which are less stressful than shackling and hoisting) have yielded the highest average stress ratings ever published (almost 300% higher than cattle killed in upright pens).

Even worse, in some procedures the animals are not only shackled and hoisted before slaughter, but then moved on a conveyer belt in that position to where the slaughterer is; this compounds the pain and cruelty even more. Especially since a much less painful alternative is available for kosher slaughter, shackling and hoisting them unquestionably constitutes a violation of Jewish laws that forbid us to cause undue pain to animals (צער בעלי חיים).³

For that matter, some of the pens now being used also violate those laws. As Dr. Regenstein has pointed out in an e-mail to us, the technology of some pens requires that the animal be turned upside down. "The Facoima pen is at best marginal — and is used by at least one major OU facility in the US — although they have now gone from 180 degrees of rotation to 135 degrees. . . .The UK has moved to [require] upright kill. The Weinberg

---

² A paper by Rabbi Rabinowitz currently before the CJLS argues for the acceptability of stunning animals before slaughter. The impact of the possible adoption of that paper on the subject of this one should be treated in a separate paper. In any case, it is unlikely that all kosher slaughter will include stunning, and so this תשובה will continue to be relevant. [Editors' Note: "A Stunning Matter: Stunning and Bolting After Shehitah" by Rabbi Mayer Rabinowitz was adopted by the CJLS on 13 Mar. 2001.]

³ For the general principle and some of its applications in classical Jewish law, see B. Shabbat 128b; B. Bava Metzia 32a-32b; M.T. Laws of Murder and Guarding Life 13:13; S.A. Hoshen Mishpat 272:9 (gloss). See also "Animals, Cruelty to," *Encyclopaedia Judaica* 3:5-7.

pen, which is not as well designed as the Facoima pen and also moves the animal upside-down, is unacceptable." To be clear, then, in this ruling we intend not only to ban shackling and hoisting animals, but also those pens that turn the animals upside down before slaughtering them. Only moving and killing the animals in an upright pen satisfies the requirements of Jewish law forbidding cruel treatment of animals.

Furthermore, people who slaughter conscious animals that have been shackled and hoisted are themselves in danger because the large animals sometimes kick the slaughterer. Those who work in slaughterhouses routinely wear helmets, but they are still at risk of considerable injury and even death from hoisted animals that are scared and violent. It is precisely to avoid this risk and the Workmen's Compensation costs that injuries or death would entail that the largest slaughterhouses have reformed their process of slaughter to use restraining pens rather than shackling and hoisting the animals. Especially since kosher slaughter can now be accomplished much more safely through the use of the restraining pens, there is no longer any excuse for exposing workers to these dangers.

Clearly there are halakhically acceptable methods to convey animals to slaughter, for some 90% of cattle slaughtered in the United States are already restrained in upright pens. The most common argument for maintaining shackling and hoisting in the remainder of kosher slaughter, then, is the economic one that plants now using this method would incur financial expenses in transforming their operations to the upright pens.

While the economic costs are real, several points should be made about them. First, secular society required all non-kosher plants to abandon the shackling and hoisting of conscious animals in 1958, demanding instead that all animals be stunned before being subjected to such treatment. Since stunning was understood at the time to violate Jewish dietary laws, and since pens that would keep the animals standing before slaughter and would yet fulfill the government's sanitary requirements were not yet available then, the Jewish community had to argue for an exemption from this rule. Now that there is a humane alternative, we no longer need that exemption. Moreover, while slaughter-houses that cater to the non-kosher trade can still legally stun animals and then shackle and hoist them, most have voluntarily changed over to the new pens. That is, most have spent what is necessary to transform their slaughtering to the new pens, and so it must be possible to stay in business and yet adopt the new pens.

Second, we have good reason to discontinue using the exemption, for we definitely should not do anything to suggest to non-Jews that the Jewish religion requires a lower standard of morality and humane slaughter than is now commonly accepted by the rest of society and, indeed, enacted as law. Acting in any way that suggests that we abide by lower moral standards than the rest of society is a clear violation of our duty to avoid a desecration of God's name (חילול השם). Moreover, the danger of this particular desecration becoming public is both great and imminent: all that has to happen is that any of a number of animal rights groups discovers that the more humane alternative of the pens could satisfy our religious needs and yet we continue to insist on being allowed to use the painful shackling and hoisting method.

Third, the cost itself will vary with the equipment used and the size of the operation. Based on their research, Rabbi Adam and Mr. Aaron Frank estimate that, for a small plant, installing one such pen would cost $2,000, and for a larger plant to convert their kosher slaughter now using shackling and hoisting to the pens would cost something like $15,000. Dr. Regenstein pointed out to us that the cost may be considerably more than that, that while Dr. Grandin has designed efficient, low cost equipment, the serious meat plant needs expensive equipment. Line speeds are another issue that must be addressed as they strongly effect the economic issues. Blood splash is another issue. Equipment and handling must be carefully designed to minimize this problem. The fact that the rabbis take a large amount of the slaughter off-shore is partly because most plants cannot routinely do mainstream kosher slaughter and survive economically. It is important to recognize that the kosher plant needs to meet all the U.S. regulatory requirements of non-kosher slaughter (and therefore has incurred most of the same costs) while it still needs to incur the special costs and equipment needs of kosher slaughter. The only state mandate not being met is the need for stunning — and this is not the most expensive operation when done in the non-kosher mode.

We are concerned about the cost, for kosher slaughter must be economically viable if it is to occur in the United States. We are also concerned that the practice of using abattoirs outside the United States to provide kosher meat removes the protections of U.S. law for both sanitation and humane slaughter. Still, we Jews must not be seen as impervious to the moral demands of humane slaughter. Kosher slaughterhouses certainly have the right to earn money, but shackling and hoisting is an impermissible method of doing that now that the demands of kosher slaughter can be met in a much more humane way. In that context, to continue shackling and hoisting animals violates Jewish laws demanding humane treatment of animals and safety for human beings.

Conclusion

Now that kosher, humane slaughter using upright pens is both possible and widespread, we find shackling and hoisting to be a violation of Jewish laws forbidding cruelty to animals (צער בעלי חיים) and requiring that we avoid unnecessary dangers to human life. As the CJLS, then, we rule that shackling and hoisting should be stopped.

YD 87:10.1994

THE KASHRUT OF
MICROBIAL ENZYMES

Rabbi Kassel Abelson

This paper was approved by the CJLS on December 14, 1994, by a vote of sixteen in favor and three abstaining (16-0-3). Voting in favor: Rabbis Kassel Abelson, Ben Zion Bergman, Stanley Bramnick, Elliot N. Dorff, Samuel Fraint, Jan Caryl Kaufman, Judah Kogen, Vernon H. Kurtz, Alan B. Lucas, Paul Plotkin, Avram Israel Reisner, Joel E. Rembaum, Joel Roth, Gerald Skolnik, Gordon Tucker, and Gerald Zelizer. Abstaining: Rabbis Jerome M. Epstein, Susan Grossman, and Aaron L. Mackler.

The Committee on Jewish Law and Standards of the Rabbinical Assembly provides guidance in matters of halakhah for the Conservative movement. The individual rabbi, however, is the authority for the interpretation and application of all matters of halakhah.

שאלה

Are cheeses made with microbial milk-clotting enzymes (sometimes referred to as rennin or rennet) kosher?

תשובה

Rabbi Isaac Klein, of blessed memory, in a responsum adopted unanimously by the CJLS on January 20, 1972, affirmed, "It is our considered opinion that cheeses, all cheeses, including those in which rennet, any rennet, is used as the curdling agent should be permitted." And he explains:

> The rennet used today cannot be considered forbidden because, first of all, most of it is derived from dried up skins that have become like a piece of wood. In addition, the extraction is brought about by the use of strong chemicals and acids which removes the substance from the status of a food fit even for a dog. And third, the rennet goes through a number of chemical changes that transform it into a new substance. Finally, the rennet is not put into the milk in a pure form but is diluted with other substances so that it is בטל בשישים, annulled in sixty times its bulk.[1]

---

[1] Isaac Klein, "Kashrut," in *Responsa and Halachic Studies* (New York: Ktav Publishing House, 1975), p. 57, and "The Kashrut of Cheese," *Conservative Judaism* 28 (winter 1972): 46.

The question is still relevant, however, for those among us who do not accept the conclusions of the Klein Teshuvah.

Enzymes In Cheese Making

Cheese is manufactured by adding a starter culture, which can consist of any of a number of different microbes depending on the type of cheese to be produced, to a vat of milk. At a specific pH designated by the cheesemaker clotting enzymes are added to the milk. The milk clots, forming curds and whey. The curds are separated from the whey and then blocked in a press to form the cheese which is aged until the desired flavors and texture result.[2]

Chymosin (also known as rennin), is one of several natural enzymes which coagulate milk. It is found in the stomachs of all ruminant animals. For centuries, extracts of ruminant stomachs containing chymosin have been used to clot milk for cheese manufacture. Calf rennet, extracted from the stomachs of calves has long been recognized as the premier source of the milk coagulant chymosin, and is widely used in the industrial manufacture of cheese. The supply of calf rennet is limited, and fluctuates in cost depending on the availability of calves. In the late 1800s research scientists began to try to standardize and supply reproducible sources of calf chymosin extracts. One major way, increasingly used in the cheese industry is the production of microbial rennin and the use of other milk-clotting enzymes.[3]

Microbial Rennin

Microbial rennin is an enzyme that is produced by a pure culture of microorganisms. Bacteria, molds and yeasts are single celled vegetative microorganisms. The appropriate microorganisms are isolated from the environment, or from calf chymosin, or may even be the product of genetic engineering. They are cultured by a process of fermentation in huge vats. The enzymes are harvested from the growing medium or broth by filtering the broth and isolating the enzyme from the filtrate by suitable purification treatment. All materials used in the process of production are food grade and are typically carbohydrates, such as glucose and starch, proteins from vegetable sources such as soy meal, and vitamin extracts, as well as inorganic phosphates and salts. The use of carbohydrates may present a problem for Passover use. However a number of kashrut certifying agencies are certifying cheeses made with microbial rennin for use during Passover.

The milk-clotting enzyme is concentrated, purified and standardized to uniform milk-clotting activity, specific gravity, pH and preservative levels. There are several stages in the process when chemicals are used in concentrations which would be harmful if the broth were eaten. Thus the broth would lose the status of food (נפסל מאכילת כלב), thereby solving possible kashrut and Passover problems. The final product is of high purity and less variable than the traditional extract from calf stomachs.

Microbial enzymes are competitive cost-wise with calf's rennet. A very significant portion of the cheese made in the United States is made with microbial rennin or other microbial milk-clotting enzymes.[4] It should be noted that the term microbial rennet is not technically correct. The term microbial milk-clotting enzymes is the proper term.

---

[2] Z. Berk, *The Biochemistry of Foods*, p. 68.
[3] Letter from Morris H. Katz. Mr. Katz has been extremely helpful in supplying information and in reviewing and correcting the technical details.
[4] Letter from H. Heinson.

Microbial Enzymes Are The Product Of Vegetative Cells

Rabbi Klein, in his responsa on the kashrut of gelatin (1969) and the kashrut of cheese (1972), analyzes a number of principles that have wide application to the questions arising from modern methods of food production.[5] These principles are amplified and applied in the responsum on mono- and diglycerides and in the responsum on the definition of a דבר חדש.[6] These papers are valuable in dealing with chemical changes, and the creation, from substances that may have been originally non-kosher, of food additives that are neutral.

However the essential principle used in the above papers, דבר חדש פנים חדשות, need not be utilized in the case of microbial rennin. The enzyme chymosin and other milk-clotting enzymes are not derived from animal sources. They are derived from microorganisms which are living vegetative cells, namely, yeasts, bacteria and molds and pose no problem in so far as the dietary laws are concerned. This also seems to be the conclusion reached by many of the kosher supervising agencies. *Kashrus Magazine*, in a brief report on biotechnology, states:

> The FDA has recently published a formal ruling that products produced by biotechnology, i.e., by transferring a gene (a small amount of genetic material) from one organism to another, does not have to be labeled. Although the press and groups opposed to this policy have cited the concern of religious groups, it seems that most most kosher supervising agencies are accepting these products as coming from the organism, i.e., the bacteria, yeast, or plant that actually makes the protein. For example, chymosin [rennet] from calves is now being made by bacteria and has received kosher acceptance as being a bacterial enzyme. We also believe that the kosher supervising agencies will accept porcine lipase (an enzyme from pigs) once it becomes available from a bacterial source.[7]

Conclusion

Pure microbial milk coagulating enzymes or so-called "microbial rennets" are kosher, and cheese manufactured with these products may be eaten. Those concerned about use during Passover may want to restrict themselves to cheeses that have Passover certification.

---

[5] Isaac Klein, "Kashrut," pp. 43-57, and "The Kashrut of Gelatin," pp. 59-74, in *Responsa and Halachic Studies*.

[6] Kassel Abelson, "The Kashrut of Mono- and Di-Glycerides," *PCJLS 80-85*, pp. 181-185; Kassel Abelson and Mayer Rabinowitz, "Definition of a Davar Hadash," *PCJLS 80-85*, pp. 187-90.

[7] Dr. Joe and Carrie Regenstein, "Looking In," *Kashrus Magazine* (Feb. 1993): 40. Both the Orthodox Union (O-U) and the "circle-K" supervise the manufacture of microbial milk-clotting enzymes.

YD 87:10.1997

CURIOUSER AND CURIOUSER: THE KASHRUT OF GENETICALLY ENGINEERED FOODSTUFFS

Rabbi Avram Israel Reisner

This paper was approved by the CJLS on December 10, 1997, by a vote of sixteen in favor (16-0-0). Voting in favor: Rabbis Kassel Abelson, Ben Zion Bergman, Elliot N. Dorff, Shoshana Gelfand, Susan Grossman, Judah Kogen, Vernon H. Kurtz, Alan B. Lucas, Aaron L. Mackler, Paul Plotkin, Mayer Rabinowitz, Avram Israel Reisner, Joel E. Rembaum, James S. Rosen, Joel Roth, and Gerald Zelizer.

The Committee on Jewish Law and Standards of the Rabbinical Assembly provides guidance in matters of halakhah for the Conservative movement. The individual rabbi, however, is the authority for the interpretation and application of all matters of halakhah.

שאלה

Modern science has succeeded in circumventing the natural process of sexual reproduction by learning how to manipulate and engineer the DNA which is at the heart of all biological cells — that which is formally known as recombinant DNA technology. Increasingly, the market seeks to introduce genetically altered strains of common food items. If a genetic sequence is adapted from a non-kosher species and implanted in a new strain of a kosher foodstuff — for example, if a gene for swine growth hormone is introduced into a potato to induce larger growth, or if a gene from an insect is introduced into a tomato plant in order to give it unusual qualities of pest resistance — is that new strain rendered non-kosher?

תשובה

At the outset it is desirable to indicate what I *do not* deal with in this responsum. Much good might be derived medically from this ability to alter flawed genes to eliminate malformations and overcome disease. There is little question that that should be permitted under our broad conception of healing — but this responsum does not concern such human genetic engineering. Even the bio-engineering of plants and animals can be turned to medical uses. Thus, the ability to create transgenic animals who bear or lack traits that mimic human diseases has enormous potential for research.[1] Since the products are not for consumption,

---

[1] B. Davis, *The Genetic Revolution* (American Academy of Arts and Sciences, 1991), pp. 122-123. S. Donnelley, C.R. McCarthy and R. Singleton Jr., "The Brave New World of Animal Biotechnology," *The Hastings Report* Special Supplement (Jan.-Feb. 1994).

however, these are not the subject of this responsum. Or again, research has been undertaken with an eye toward developing products in plants and animals by genetic alteration, which products will then be available to treat human disease. Thus pigs have been altered to produce proteins that are active in humans and such pigs can be used as a resource for large scale production of medically necessary proteins that are in short supply. Similar uses as factories for the production of pharmaceuticals have been proposed for plants.[2] Here human consumption is precisely the intent behind the genetic alteration. In all these cases, however, Judaism's emphasis on healing individuals who are sick is likely to override any combination of concerns that might otherwise impact the technique. Whereas some consideration of the above cases is in order, these are not properly my concern here.

The concern here is that, absent health considerations, many genetic alterations are proposed for purely commercial reasons. Thus the majority of tests for specific traits of transgenic crops in industrialized countries prior to 1992 were for resistance to herbicides, so that it might be possible to treat a field with a substance to kill other growth and leave the crop plant unaffected. Similarly, most of the other traits tested were for insect and disease resistance, altered ripening qualities and other such matters important to the farmer and marketer, but morally neutral.[3] It is in such cases that the question of the kashrut of the resulting hybrid is relevant.

The Kashrut Issue

Superficially, the primary potential problem with such a hybrid is the problem of the admixture of a non-kosher product with a kosher product. With regard to admixtures the primary rule is that they are forbidden בנותן טעם – when they impart a flavor to the resultant product. This is estimated, as a matter of law, at one part in sixty, such that a lesser admixture is permitted, a greater admixture forbidden. Several caveats are affixed to this basic ruling. First, the ruling is taken as applicable only in accidental admixtures. Thus intentionally mixing less than one part in sixty of a non-kosher product in one's preparation bars use of the resultant product altogether. Here there is an open debate as to whether an admixture of a non-kosher product prepared intentionally by a non-Jew is to be treated at law as an intentional admixture, hence non-kosher, or as an unintentional admixture, since the non-Jew was permitted to prepare the food in that way, and the Jew first addresses the question only after it already was completed, as he does with an accidental admixture. Further, an exception is made for non-kosher ingredients that serve as stabilizers and flavoring agents which are deemed to have a perceptible effect even in tiny proportions, thereby rendering the final product non-kosher.[4]

Were it the case that the rules of admixture should, in fact, be applied here, then it would be appropriate to consider whether a genetic alteration using a gene from a non-

---

[2] Donnelley, McCarthy and Singleton, ibid. J. Rissler and M. Mellon, "Perils Amidst the Promise," *The Union of Concerned Scientists*, (Dec. 1993): 6.

[3] Rissler and Mellon, ibid., p. 9. On the matter of the moral neutrality of these considerations, see below.

[4] Joseph Karo, S.A. Yoreh De'ah 98ff.

On the matter of non-Jewish commercial preparations manufactured intentionally for public (non-Jewish) use, the CJLS has gone on record with the more stringent ruling in its 1985 responsum by Rabbi Elliot N. Dorff on "The Use of All Wines" (*PCJLS 86-90*, pp. 203-226). But many of the national kashrut agencies apparently rely on the lenient opinion, see *Kashrut Magazine* 44 (Mar.-Apr. 1989): 54-56. Indeed that position was cited by R. Max Arzt in his 1940 responsum on eating fish out. It is cited as the normative position by R. Eliezer Wolff in his book, *Keeping Kosher in a Non-Kosher World*, no. 100.

kosher source, always much less than one part in sixty,[5] but intentionally administered, albeit largely by non-Jews, having a perceptible effect, for it changes the attributes of the animal or vegetable in some way, otherwise it would not be desirable, but most often an invisible effect — whether such an alteration renders the resultant product non-kosher or whether it does not. However, these common sense criteria prove to be altogether immaterial. And the reason is contained within the essential nature of these very criteria.

Halakhah had to distinguish between that which is counted and that which is nullified, that which is perceptible and that which is not. In the matter of stabilizers and flavoring agents it needed to determine in every case whether the standard rules of nullification or the specialized rules for "perceptible substances" should apply. In so doing, Jewish law in the modern period has settled on the rule of thumb that microscopic items, not visible to the naked eye, are discounted altogether is determining Jewish law. This ruling was made by R. Yehiel Michel Epstein in his work Arukh Hashulhan, Yoreh De'ah 84:36, published in the 1890s, and is generally accepted. As he rightly points out, were we to consider microscopic life forms we would be unable to drink the water or breathe the air.[6] It is for this reason among others that the major kashrut agencies have permitted the use of genetically engineered chymosin (microbial rennet) in the production of cheese, wherein a microbe is induced to produce an enzyme generally found only in animal stomachs and that enzyme is then used to curdle milk. Similarly, here, genetic transfer happens at a submicroscopic level which the halakhah is hard-pressed to consider.[7]

Several other considerations similarly conspire to nullify any kashrut concerns here. Transfer of material from a non-kosher animal at the genetic level would not constitute prohibited "eating" under the laws of foods. It has already been determined that eating must include "oral stimulation," and that absent that no blessings are required. Similarly, most authorities rule gastric tube feeding would not constitute a transgression of the restrictions of Yom Kippur. This insight serves as the basis variously for permitting transfusion, though the eating of blood is prohibited, and of permitting the use in a Jewish patient of a porcine heart valve. Indeed, all Jewish law on transplantation begins with the assumption that to receive a transplant is not, at heart, a prohibited act of cannibalism. Rather, the principle is clearly enunciated by R. Isser Yehudah Unterman, the late chief rabbi of Israel, in his responsum which opened the path to all subsequent considerations of transplantation in Jewish law, that an organ that is implanted in a body and flourishes by connection to that body's functions becomes a part of the host in all respects.[8] Thus the rules of kashrut, the

---

[5] In natural cross-breeding, if one of the animals were non-kosher the offspring would be non-kosher, see S.A. 297:5. However, in such a case 50% of the DNA would be from the non-kosher animal. Not so, here.

[6] A similar response by R. Moshe Feinstein, Iggrot Moshe, Yoreh De'ah 3, 120:5 with regard to measurement considers that the law cannot possibly demand microscopic exactness, since microscopes were not available to our ancestors. Reference to this standard without attribution, among other points, is made, as well, by the late twentieth century Jerusalem sage R. Shlomo Zalman Auerbach in his responsa, Minhat Shlomo, p. 87 about transient sparks which may be invisible to the naked eye. Dr. Fred Rosner makes reference to this ruling, without source, in "Genetic Engineering and Judaism," Jewish Bioethics, p. 417. This nullification of microscopic agents is true only of those agents that are by their nature invisible to the naked eye, and not to ingredients which are visible in the form in which they are used, but become imperceptible to the consumer, being dissolved or integrated in the final product.

[7] See M.M. Chaudry and J.M. Regenstein, "Implications of Biotechnology and Genetic Engineering for Kosher and Halal Foods," Trends in Food Science & Technology, May 1994, pp. 165-168.

[8] See Sha'arei T'shuvah to S.A. Orah Hayyim 197:8 and R. Eliezer Waldenberg, Tzitz Eliezer 10:25:21.

R. Isser Yehudah Unterman's famous responsum is in his volume Shevet Mi Y'hudah (vol. 1, 1.21). See also the interesting example provided by R. Judah Greenwald, cited in Fred Rosner, Jewish Bioethics, p. 363.

rules of admixtures, simply fail to address the nature of transgenic creations. Absent a reason to declare the new product non-kosher, it would appear to be fit for consumption.

The כלאים Question

The more relevant question is that of כלאים, or Biblically prohibited mixing across species lines. Are transgenic creations to be prohibited as extensions of the Biblical rule of כלאים? The question is somewhat vexing, because the Biblical laws of כלאים are unclear as to their reason and scope. Several different forms of כלאים are recorded. It is prohibited to mix seed of different agricultural species, called כלאי זרעים (Lev. 19:19); it is also prohibited to plant different species adjacent to one another in the same field, called כלאי הכרם (Deut. 22:9). It is prohibited to cross-breed animals or to graft plants, together the class of הרכבה (Lev. 19:19); or simply to yoke an ox and donkey, or any other two species, together to the plow (Deut. 22:10). It is even prohibited to interweave specifically wool and linen, known as שעטנז (Lev. 19:19 and Deut. 22:11). But at no time is any reason presented. The tradition faced a problem in analyzing these rules precisely because it needed first to give them a context and an explanation.

A context is, in fact, suggested by the text of Lev. 19:19. In full, the verse reads:

> את חקתי תשמרו: בהמתך לא תרביע כלאים, שדך לא תזרע כלאים, ובגד כלאים שעטנז לא יעלה עליך.

> You shall observe my laws. You shall not mate your cattle with a different kind; you shall not sow your field with two kinds of seed; you shall not put on cloth from a mixture of two kinds of material.

The introductory phrase begs an explanation. One is offered by Samuel in reflecting on the (minority!) Tannaitic opinion that כלאים (cross-breeding but not interweaving) is among the laws applicable to gentiles (מצות בני נח):

> מנא הני מילי? אמר שמואל – דאמר קרא: "את חקתי תשמרו" – חוקים שחקקתי לך כבר: "בהמתך לא תרביע כלאים," ו"שדך לא תזרע כלאים."
> מה בהמתך בהרבעה אף שדך בהרכבה....

> Whence this assertion? Said Samuel – Scripture says: "You shall observe my laws" – the laws I have already enacted for you. "You shall not mate your cattle with a different kind" and "you shall not sow your field with two kinds of seed." Just as this refers to cross-breeding of your cattle, so it refers to hybridization of your field (i.e. your produce).[9]

Mr. Steven Drucker of the Alliance for Bio-Integrity argues that since a genetic transfer, unlike an admixture, is dynamic, it will grow over time and become significant, wherefore it should not be nullified, as a gelling agent (מעמיד) is not null. The concept is itself significant, for some halakhists do argue that, despite earlier nullification (ביטול), if more of the original forbidden substance was added, bringing the total volume of the forbidden substance over the one-in-sixty limit, that the previously nullified material is rekindled (חוזר וניעור) and is no longer null. This position is clearly taken by Moses Isserles, Yoreh De'ah 99:6 and, while opinions to the contrary are brought by Shabtai Hakohen, Shakh 21, ibid., he concludes, "My (more lenient) view is nullified against theirs." Counter to this argument is precisely the understanding that once a gene is incorporated in an organism, its products are not foreign products at all, thus adding mass to the alien, forbidden matter, but they are to be treated as a part of that organism itself.

[9] The Tannaitic position is recorded in a ברייתא on Sanhedrin 56a-b. Samuel's commentary is there, on 60a. This and many other rabbinic texts cited here were first called to my attention by the introduction to Yehuda Feliks' work on the first chapter of Mishnah כלאים, "Mixed Sowing, Breeding and Grafting" (Hebrew).

This position appears to be that of the Sifra, Kedoshim 4:17 cited in Yerushalmi Kilayim 1:7:

מנין שאין מרכיבין... ת"ל: "את חקותי תשמרו."

Whence [the ruling] that we do not hybridize? . . .The teaching is: "You shall observe my laws."

as it is interpreted by R. Yonah and R. 'Lezer in the name of Rav Kahana to apply even to Adam. In that light, an elaboration of this reason is offered, there, "Why? Because 'of every kind' [Gen. 1:21] is written about them." But R. Yosi interprets this text from Sifra, in the name of R. Hila, in line with the majority opinion which holds that כלאים is only prohibited to Jews as of Sinai. Either way, transgenic creations might be prohibited as כלאים, a fundamental rebellion against the species created by God in the beginning.

Ramban (Nahmanides) takes that tack in his commentary on כלאים on the relevant passages in Kedoshim (Leviticus 19). "The reason for כלאים is that God created species in the world. . .and gave them the ability to procreate in order that said species should continue forever, [that is] for as long as God wishes for the world to continue. . . .Whoever intermingles two species changes and denies the Creation, as if he thought that God did not complete the work of His world as much as necessary, and he wishes to aid in the creation of the world, to add creatures to it." And he adds, as well, another observation, that in nature "the species of animals do not cross-breed, and even [with regard to] close relatives in nature, those that may be born to them. . .are infertile. We see that, as far as this is concerned, the act of cross-breeding species is a repugnant and futile act." Indeed, in the modern day, Mary Douglas has seconded Ramban's appreciation, arguing that the very rules of kashrut are intended to reflect a pure speciation of the universe, with natural creatures that cross the lines of the classes that the Torah perceives being declared non-kosher thereby.[10] Thus in the growing secular debate about transgenic plants and animals, Ramban is prominently quoted by an organization called "The Alliance for Bio-Integrity" which seeks to form an interfaith lobby against transgenic foods or for their labeling. They write, "Genetic engineering rejects the idea that man must defer to a higher power, and its underlying theology has no room for a purposeful Creator whose plan must be respected."[11] To repeat the question: Are transgenic creations to be prohibited as extensions of the Biblical rule of כלאים? This reasoning would appear to argue strongly that they should be.

The above is based, as we said, on a particular interpretation of the reasons behind the commandment of כלאים which are nowhere stated explicitly. There is another way to explain the leading words at the beginning of the cited verse in Leviticus. It is possible to understand that the rules of כלאים as stated are without cognitive reason. That the acceptance of the divine commandment, in this case, is to be taken on faith. Indeed, the very word חוקה (law) which appears prominently in that verse, is taken to refer to divine decrees without stated reason.[12] In this light Rashi's comment to this verse takes on legal significance. To wit:

---

[10] Mary Douglas, *Purity and Danger* (London: Ark, 1984), pp. 53-57.

[11] The Alliance for Bio-Integrity, P.O. Box 2927, Iowa City, IA 52244, www.bio-integrity.org.

[12] The classic example of a חוקה – a decree without reason – is the red heifer. The Torah begins its description of the red heifer with the words זאת חקת התורה, "These are the laws of the Torah" (Num. 19:2). The Midrash notes that this rule appears internally contradictory, for in performing the very purification rite, the priest becomes impure. It sees the very unreasonableness of the rite as an occasion for doubts. It responds unambiguously: אמר הקדוש ברוך הוא: חקה חקקתי, גזרה גזרתי. אי אתה רשאי לעבר על גזרתי, "Said the Holy One [praised be He]: I have enacted a rule, decreed a decree. You may not transgress my decree!" (Bamidbar Rabbah 19:1 and 5). It relates the well known story in which a gentile asks Rabban Yohanan ben Zakkai if the red heifer ceremony isn't just hocus-pocus. Rabban Yohanan ben Zakkai answers that it is just like an exor-

> את חקתי תשמרו – ואלו הן: בהמתך לא תרביע כלאים וגו'. חקים אלו
> גזרות מלך שאין טעם לדבר.
>
> "You shall observe my laws" – and these are they: "You shall not
> mate your cattle with a different kind," etc. These laws are decrees
> of the sovereign which have no reason.

Such a classification has clear and clearly relevant ramifications. That which is taken as a decree of the written word is taken to be specific and precise, limited exactly as written. As Rashi notes on the second Mishnah on Menahot 27a, reflecting the reasoning of the gemara, there: "כתיב 'חוקה'... ו'חוקה' 'עיכובא' – The Torah writes 'decree' – and a 'decree' is limiting." Throughout Rabbinic literature, a חידוש – an unprecedented turn in the Torah's decrees, may not be extended, for to extend it would be hubris when the very intent and meaning is unclear. By this interpretation, then, only the specific examples in the Biblical text are prohibited as כלאים, that is, cross-breeding and hybridization through natural means, and any extension we seek to take to transgenic species arrived at through means unimaginable to the Bible may not be valid.[13]

The Law of כלאים

An assessment of the settled law of כלאים as codified, leads me to conclude that the Rabbis chose the more lenient approach with regard to the laws of כלאים. In the first instance, the midrash חוקים שחקקתי לך כבר, "The laws I have already enacted for you," is tailor made for the conclusion at which Ramban arrives about the laws of כלאים, that כלאים is in contravention of God's creation, wherefore כלאים should be forbidden to humankind. Indeed, it was brought with regard to a minority position that the law of כלאים applies to Adam. But the majority rules that only Israel is prohibited כלאים, and offers the barely modified version of the midrash חוקים שחקקתי בעולמי, "The laws I have enacted in my world," as referring to the laws given at Sinai to Israel alone.[14] Only if we favor Rashi's interpretation does it make any sense to permit כלאים to gentiles while forbidding it to Israelites.[15] This leniency is suggested in Shulhan Arukh, Yoreh De'ah 297:4, by the prohibition of allow-

---

cism, which answer satisfies the gentile but perplexes his students. They seek a better answer, and he tells them: חייכם! לא המת מטמא ולא המים מטהרין! "By your life! A corpse does not cause impurity and water does not purify!" He then cites the above (Bamidbar Rabbah 19:8). Indeed, the term חוקה is specifically used to mean 'without reason' in 19:6: "The Holy One [praised be He] said to Moses: I will reveal the reason for the [red] heifer to you. But to others – it is a חוקה – a decree."

[13] R. Abraham Karelitz writes, in Hilkhot Kilayim 1: אי לאו דומיא דבהמתך, אין לנו לבדות מעצמנו איסור הרכבה – "If it is not similar to [cross-breeding] your cattle, we may not create on our own a prohibition of hybridization." Maimonides, in the *Guide for the Perplexed* 3:49, presents a different reason altogether for the prohibition of כלאים. He understands the laws against animal cross-breeding as a function of the rules against aberrant sexual relations and the laws against hybridization as a function of the rules against idolatry and idolatrous fertility rites. Maimonides' positions in this regard are not normative, as the *Guide* is not a halakhic work, and at any rate, his positions are also subject to some of the comments which will follow.

[14] See B. Menahot 60a and J. Kilayim cited and Tosafot and Ritba ad locum. Despite its familiarity, the rule of the seven Noahide commandments does not appear in Shulhan Arukh. It can be found in Maimonides, *Hilkhot Melachim*, ch. 9. Having codified the seven, Rambam writes in 10:6 that these are also traditionally prohibited for non-Jews. See the comments of *Kesef Mishneh* and *Lehem Mishneh* ad locum. *Mishnah LaMelech* satisfies himself by pointing out that in Hilkhot כלאים 1.6, Maimonides himself seems to accept that a gentile may cross-breed his own livestock; that position is accepted without question by both Kesef Mishneh and Radbaz. This is the dominant ruling, see Shach to Yoreh De'ah 297:3. See also S. Lieberman, *Tosefta Kifshuta*, Kilayim, p. 619.

[15] Indeed, particularly if Ramban is correct that speciation is inherent in the very acts of Creation, then Rashi would be correct, as well, that such a dichotomy is logically untenable. It is a dichotomy which can occasion

ing non-Jews to cross-breed an animal owned by a Jew, implying, of course, that to do so with his own animal would be permitted.

But the law is more liberal still. In his comments to Rambam, Hilkhot Kilayim 1:6, Radbaz offers the following:

ומותר לומר לנכרי להרביע בהמתו של הנכרי ולהרכיב אילנו של הנכרי
אע"ג דאומר לו אני אקנה אח"כ.

It is permissible to tell a gentile to cross-breed the cattle of the gentile or to hybridize the tree of the gentile, even though he says to him that he will buy [the product] subsequently.

No attempt is made or suggested to reduce the incidence of Jews suborning כלאים.

In a third point the law's leniency is also evident. Shulhan Arukh, Yoreh De'ah 297:5 reads as follows:

מי שעבר והרכיב בהמתו כלאים, הרי הנולד מהם מותר בהנאה, ואם מין
טהורה עם מין טהורה מותר באכילה.

If one transgressed and cross-bred one's animal, the offspring is permissible for use, and if the species were both pure (kosher), it is permissible to eat it.

A similar rule is enunciated concerning hybridization of plants in 295:7:

אסור לקיים המורכב כלאים, אבל פרי היוצא ממנו מותר ואפילו לזה שעבר
והרכיבו. ומותר ליקח ענף מהמורכב ולנטעו במקום אחר.

It is forbidden to maintain כלאים but the fruit produced thereby is permitted even to him who transgressed and produced the hybrid. It is permitted to take a branch from the hybrid and plant it elsewhere.[16]

Elsewhere in Jewish tradition a monetary fine is levied against willful transgressors to prevent them from disregarding the law.[17] The principle of אין חוטא נשכר — that the transgressor should not be rewarded, is well established. But here, no such defensive fine is contemplated. On the contrary, use of the product of the hybridization is affirmatively permitted. In fact, many hybrids are presently on the market, both hybrids of different strains of the same type of plant, which would not be כלאים, and those of separate species, which would be considered כלאים, the product of agricultural and animal husbandry techniques honed before the advent of genetic engineering. No such product is banned. Indeed, this is not even a modern leniency, having its earliest source in the Tosefta.[18]

In the most direct application to our issue, the great twentieth century sage R. Avraham Karelitz, known as the Hazon Ish, reports the ruling that כלאים is to be for-

---

doubts, and if we hold it nonetheless, that is because we hold it to be a decree without reason, whose limits are opaque to us, therefore a decree which we cannot extend.

[16] S.A. Orah Hayyim 318:1 and 307:20. See also Rambam, *Hilkhot Kilayim* 1:7 and Radbaz, ibid.

[17] The classic case concerns items cooked illicitly on Shabbat. In T. Shabbat 2:15, as reported widely, R. Meir, R. Yehudah and R. Yohanan haSandlar all agree that one who intentionally cooks on Shabbat is forbidden to eat that food on Shabbat. They differ about whether it is permissible to eat it after Shabbat or not and whether it is permitted for another to eat it or not. Much diversity attends the proper interpretation, but all agree that a fine is called for. Even were one only to transgress the Rabbinic prohibition by instructing a gentile to transgress the Sabbath for you, one may not benefit until enough time has elapsed after Shabbat that it could have been prepared afterward. A closer case, that of castration, sees a similar fine. R. Joshua Falk tries to justify that distinction, see Drisha to Tur, Yoreh De'ah 297, the latter half beginning וכתב ז"ל הנולד מכלאים on the last line of p. 243a.

[18] T. Kilayim 2:15 and S. Lieberman, *Tosefta Kifshuta*, ibid.

bidden exclusively where there is genital contact, but that "there is no prohibition against placing the seed of one species into another."[19] If artificial insemination does not cross the boundaries of כלאים even though it introduces the entire genome of one species into another, certainly the transfer of a few genes by genetic engineering techniques far removed from natural sexual contact cannot be seen as prohibited.

A Caveat

The Union of Concerned Scientists, the Alliance for Bio-Integrity and others raise some serious concerns of potential damage to the earth's ecosystems through genetic engineering run amok.[20] They raise concerns that a damaging genetically engineered strain will be unleashed into the world's ecosystems and prove unstoppable. This type of concern animated the Michael Crichton thriller, *The Andromeda Strain*, and its successors. The scientific community has always responded that such a scenario is unlikely, that its track record is exemplary, and that they had put in place careful research protocols to lessen the likelihood of any such mishap. But candor requires admitting that no safeguards are foolproof and that not all potential damage will prove predictable. A case in point was reported by the *New York Times* on August 16, 1997. Under the headline, "A Delicate Pacific Seaweed is Now A Monster Of The Deep," Marlise Simons reports that a strain of seaweed, engineered two decades ago in Germany for its looks, was widely distributed to various aquariums. In a renovation, the Oceanographic Museum in Monaco emptied its tanks some 15 years ago. Now, that strain of seaweed is propagating out of control in sections of the Mediterranean, crowding out and killing most other plants and animals in the regions it controls. Moreover, it is resistant to all attempts that have been made to kill it or halt its advance.

Potentially, this concern is of halakhic import. There are clear rulings which prohibit experimental medical procedures under the rubric of ונשמרתם מאד לנפשותיכם, "You shall be exceedingly careful" (Deut. 4:15). But there are equally clear permissions granted where the danger is remote and the benefit great.[21] Some would prohibit smoking,[22] but the majority clearly do not. Skiing and bungee jumping could both be prohibited on this basis. Clearly we permit risk taking when the danger has not risen to the level of our concern. The relevant question is whether concern here is in order. Thus it could reasonably be argued that the current AIDS epidemic was facilitated by the ease of international air travel, but we would not consider the distant concern of some unknown virus sufficient to prohibit air travel. Despite the current case of the rampant seaweed, where potential strategies of control are also being discussed, the harm proposed appears to me to be too fanciful

---

[19] R. Avraham Karelitz, *Hazon Ish*, Kilayim 2:16.

[20] J. Rissler and M. Mellon, *Perils Amidst the Promise: Ecological Risks of Transgenic Crops in a Global Market*, Union of Concerned Scientists, Dec. 1993; *Genetically Engineered Food: Why It Is Wrong*, the Alliance for Bio-Integrity; "Views Differ Sharply Over Benefits, Risks of Agricultural Biotechnology," *Chemical and Engineering News*, 21 Aug. 1995.

[21] This issue comes up, inter alia, in R. David Bleich's discussion of plastic surgery, *Contemporary Halakhic Problems I (CHP I)*, pp. 119-123, and Hazardous Medical Procedures, *CHP II*, pp. 80-84. A section is dedicated to the question in Dr. Fred Rosner's *Jewish Bioethics*, pp. 377-397.

[22] Such was the position of R. Seymour Siegel in a responsum, "Smoking: A Jewish Perspective," *PCJLS 86-90*, pp. 7-11. A similar position has been reported, of late, in the name of former Israeli Sephardic Chief Rabbi Ovadiah Yosef.

and unspecific to elicit our halakhic prohibition of any and all genetic engineering. Specific cases, should they come to our attention, may merit further consideration. At the very least, our secular legislatures must consider any potential risk to human health and establish appropriate regulations as a matter of public policy.

Thus, the Alliance further argues, in the alternative, for clear labeling laws that will require producers to indicate if a product has been genetically engineered. While implementation of such rules is not required by this responsum, and while the technical difficulties in enforcing such a standard are significant, there is sufficient minority warrant for a halakhic position which would prohibit said products as כלאים. Labeling rules would permit those who seek to follow the חומרא (the added restriction) to do so.[23]

Beyond my concern for these matters, there is a point at which, it seems to me, the חומרא (the added restriction) might be cogent and the pull of Ramban's concern for Creation's integrity may yet require our consideration. While we have permitted genetic engineering to produce desirable traits within the foods we consume, there is a point at which the product of genetic engineering is less like a hybrid and more like a differing creature. Imagine, if you will, producing a small winged lamb that does, indeed, fly. The aerodynamic problem, of course, is primary, but heavier-than-air craft can fly, and even this is not beyond our imaginings. Is such a creature to be treated as permitted? Can such genetic mixing be allowed?

The arguments, herein, present a prima facie case to answer these questions in the affirmative. But my heart wishes to answer in the negative. Why? There seems to be a qualitative difference between traits that, while they may be tested for, are expressed invisibly within an apparently unchanged creature and those gross characteristics that make up our traditional taxonomic observations. Thus, for instance, the Torah's very kashrut criteria are of gross features such as split hooves, scales, or number of legs (Leviticus 11). Rambam seeks to codify just such a distinction when he writes, in Hilkhot Kilayim 3:5: אין הולכים בכלאים אלא אחר מראית העין, "With regard to [the laws of] כלאים, one follows appearances." This dovetails rather well with the concept that we discovered concerning kashrut that halakhah disregards the microscopic, that which is invisible. Yet small genetic changes can effect large scale, visible results. Among the early experiments with genetic engineering was an experiment transplanting the illuminating mechanism of a firefly into a plant, producing a luminescent plant. Is that to be treated as permissible, a human-induced mutation not unlike the mutations which occur naturally, or has the species line been crossed? The burden of this paper is להקל and would permit even such a genetically engineered plant. Still, when we are able to change not a single trait, but much of the genome of a creature, to create, as it were, a creature of our own devising, then we must ask, is that the point at which we must stop?

There is an odd Tannaitic text which reflects both sides of this question. On Pesahim 54a we find the following:

ר' יוסי אומר: שני דברים עלו במחשבה ליבראות בערב שבת ולא נבראו עד מוצאי שבת, ובמוצאי שבת נתן הקב"ה דיעה באדם הראשון מעין דוגמא של מעלה והביא שני אבנים וטחנן זו בזו ויצא מהן אור והביא שתי בהמות והרכיב זו בזו ויצא מהן פרד. רבן שמעון בן גמליאל אומר: פרד בימי ענה היה.... דורשי חמורות היו אומרים: ענה פסול היה לפיכך הביא פסול לעולם.

---

[23] This concern has recently had significant support in the lead article in the current issue of *The Hastings Center Report*, Paul B. Thompson, "Food Biotechnology's Challenge to Cultural Integrity and Individual Consent" (July-Aug. 1997).

> R. Yosi says: Two things were planned for creation on Friday but were not created until Saturday night. On Saturday night the Holy One (praised be He) granted Adam wisdom similar to that in heaven and he took two stones and ground them against each other and created fire, and he took two animals and mated them and created a mule. Rabban Shimon ben Gamaliel says: The mule was [created] in the days of Ana. . . .The allegorical interpreters would say: Ana was impure, so he created an impurity.

Rabban Shimon ben Gamaliel and the allegorical interpreters clearly understood that כלאים was an aberration. R. Yosi, however, argued that כלאים was a piece of divine wisdom.[24] Yet כלאים, shown by God to Adam, was nevertheless forbidden to Jews. Are we ready to challenge this, "the wisdom of heaven?"

Josephus, not a halakhic authority, to be sure, but an early interpreter of Rabbinic traditions, was aware of the potential of cross-breeding to denigrate the respect in which we hold Creation, and ultimately humankind. In Antiquities 4.8.20 he speculated on the ultimate reason behind the prohibition. He wrote:

> Nature does not rejoice in the union of things that are not in their own nature alike. You are not to permit beasts of different kinds together, for there is reason to fear that this unnatural abuse may extend from beasts of different kinds to men. . .by imitation whereof any degree of subversion may creep into the constitution.

It is excessive to place barriers against manipulation of the human species at the point of genetic manipulation of protein expression. It may not be excessive to place such barriers at manipulation of the very characteristics by which species are identified. I reserve final judgment in this area.

Conclusion

The kashrut laws of prohibited admixtures do not apply to the submicroscopic manipulation of genetic material. The laws of כלאים, which might apply, show an extraordinary tendency toward leniency. "Natural" כלא products, though the fruit of an illicit operation of כלאים, have nonetheless been permitted as early as the Tosefta and the rationale tying the laws of כלאים to the Creation, while often tempting exegetes, has not become the dominant law. Of genetically engineered foodstuffs it should be minimally said that even if genetic engineering is to be prohibited, the products thereof are permissible.

Of the process of genetic engineering itself, moreover, I think there is ample reason to permit it even to the Jew. (1) The process of genetic engineering bears only a very minimal resemblance to the sexual and grafting processes that the Torah bans. If, indeed, we are enjoined to treat the Torah's ban as a חוקה – a ukase – and not to expand its parameters beyond the parameters given, then it seems that no extension to

---

[24] The medieval sage Maharal MiPrague (Judah Loew ben Bezalel) is cited by R. Michael Broyde in the *Journal of Halacha and Contemporary Society* 34, p. 64 (Be'er HaGolah [Jerusalem 5731], pp. 38-39), thus: "The creativity of people is greater than nature. When God created in the six days of creation the laws of nature, the simple and the complex, and finished creating the world, there remained additional power to create anew, just like people can create new animal species through interspecies breeding. . . .People bring to fruition things that are not found in nature; nonetheless, since these are activities that occur through nature, it is as if it entered the world to be created. . . ."

genetic techniques is warranted. (2) Although the question was formulated to focus on commercial use of genetic engineering, a fuller review of those very commercial considerations would find that most commercial considerations have a ramification which could be life-saving. Thus, for instance, increased pest resistance, though useful to the food conglomerates in terms of their efficiency, will also prove useful in the endeavor to feed the world's starving population. Already such reports are mixed in among the early results of genetic engineering.[25] Nothing appears more crassly commercial than engineering for greater shelf-life, but this, too, can facilitate distribution of foodstuffs to the needy. Given the law's tendency to limit the scope of the prohibition of כלאים, this would appear to be sufficient reason to permit genetic engineering to continue. (3) On the matter of gross changes in the characteristics by which species are recognized it remains necessary to engage in further study and consideration.

---

[25] "Higher Content of Essential Amino Acids May Aid in Fight Against Malnutrition," reports the Weizmann Institute in their newsletter. Clipping without date, 1994.

YD 116:2.1998

ON MIXING FISH AND MEAT

Rabbi Paul Plotkin

This paper was approved by the CJLS on September 9, 1998, by a vote of nineteen in favor (19-0-0). Voting in favor: Rabbis Kassel Abelson, Elliot N. Dorff, Jerome M. Epstein, Baruch Frydman-Kohl, Myron S. Geller, Nechama D. Goldberg, Arnold M. Goodman, Judah Kogen, Vernon H. Kurtz, Lionel E. Moses, Paul Plotkin, Mayer Rabinowitz, Avram Israel Reisner, Joel E. Rembaum, James S. Rosen, Joel Roth, Elie Kaplan Spitz, Gordon Tucker, and Gerald Zelizer.

The Committee on Jewish Law and Standards of the Rabbinical Assembly provides guidance in matters of halakhah for the Conservative movement. The individual rabbi, however, is the authority for the interpretation and application of all matters of halakhah.

שאלה

Is it permissible to eat fish and meat on the same dish?

תשובה

In the Shulhan Arukh, Yoreh De'ah 116, we find a series of prohibitions, all related to the issue of סכנה, danger to your health. In paragraph 2, we have the specific prohibition to be careful not to eat meat and fish together because it states שקשה לצרעת which I understand to mean either that it causes difficulty to one who has leprosy or it causes difficulty that could lead to leprosy.[1] That this is a prohibition specifically to prevent us from physical danger, as opposed to a biblically prohibited food pairing, is clear from the context of the entire סימן. It deals with many cases of סכנה; including taking caution from the danger of other people's body sweat, not putting coins in your mouth, not carrying bread under your arms or drinking from various beverages that had remained uncovered. There is another list of prohibitions on the grounds of סכנה found in Hoshen Mishpat 427:9, which, in addition to listing more prohibitions, specifically refers back to Yoreh De'ah 116, as a list of סכנות.

Issues of סכנה are rabbinic and are derived from the then understood science, and medicine, and it was not something to be trifled with. Indeed, in Hullin 10a, we read חמירא סכנתא מאיסורא, "danger to one's health is more serious than an actual form of prohibition." Here we are warned by Isserles, Yoreh De'ah 116:5, that we are to be more concerned with

---

[1] The uncertainty of the phrase קשה ל... can be seen in the translation of the Soncino on Pesahim 76b where it translates the phrase דקשיא לריחא ולדבר אחר as "because it is harmful to [one's] smell and in respect of 'something else.'" The term "in respect of" is a generalization to cover the options I mentioned above. The footnote explains the "something else" to be leprosy.

a ספק of סכנה than we are with a ספק of actual איסור. Nevertheless, I believe that the application of the principle of סכנה to a specific case could always be amended as either the physical reality or our scientific understanding changed to give us more accurate information. This can be seen in the very same chapter of Shulhan Arukh, Yoreh De'ah 116:1, where it says that, "exposed beverages were forbidden by the rabbis because they feared that snakes would have drunk from them, and left behind venom." And then it goes on to say, "but now when snakes are not found amongst us, it is permitted." This is a clear indication that the prohibitions based on סכנה can be lifted when the danger is no longer present.[2]

Furthermore, I can find no reference in the Bavli to any general prohibition of eating fish and meat.[3] Rambam is silent on the subject as well. Thus it would appear to be a statement reflecting the best understood science in the time of the Shulhan Arukh.

As to the issue of changing a ruling of the great rabbis of the past who legislated with wisdom for our well being, the Mateh Yehonaton on Yoreh De'ah 116:1, deals with the issue. When an established number (מנין) of rabbis have decreed a prohibition, it can only be overturned by an equal מנין of rabbis in the future, but this is only in cases where the rabbis forbade and stated no defining or limiting conditions (תנאי). In the cases of rabbinic prohibitions where a תנאי was necessary to cause the prohibition – and when that condition is absent – he argues that the prohibition can be overturned without מנין. Thus when snakes are deemed to be the danger for uncovered beverages not to be consumed and when there are no more snakes in the community, the ruling for the סכנה can be overturned.

The prohibition for the reason of סכנה of consuming meat and fish together was based on the danger that was perceived from the consumption of eating the two simultaneously. The danger of eating them consecutively is already a matter of conjecture and though Rabbi Karo requires washing one's hands between the two and eating some bread as a cleansing of the mouth, Isserles (Yoreh De'ah 116:3) tells us that we do not have to worry about that, rather only when they are cooked together and *then* eaten is there a concern. Furthermore, we see that it is permissible to cook fish in a clean meat pot; even in paragraph 2, where the prohibition of eating together is stated, Isserles prohibits roasting fish and meat together at the same time because of concerns of ריחא (flavor imparted one to the other in the cooking process). But even there he admits that – after the fact – it would not be prohibited. Furthermore, fish can be served on meat dishes (Taz and Hokhmat Adam 68:1). So it becomes clear that the prohibition based on health considerations is really about consumption of meat and fish together and that any other

---

[2] This argument is further strengthened by the position of the Magen Avraham. The Magen Avraham on Orah Hayyim 173:2 – dealing with a ruling that one is required to wash one's hands between meat and fish because it is harmful to דבר אחר – says that: "perhaps in this time there is no סכנה of any consequence, for we see a number of things mentioned in the Gemara that are סכנה too – bad moods and other things – but today are not harmful because nature has changed, and also we go according to the nature of a particular country."

[3] There is a passage in Pesahim 76b, which talks about the imparting of flavor through the smells transferred by being baked in the same oven at the same time. "[A] fish was roasted together with meat, [whereupon] Raba of Parzikia forbade it to be eaten with *Kutcha*." Mar b. R. Ashi said, 'Even with salt too it is forbidden, because it is harmful to [one's] smell and in respect of 'something else.'" It appears that Raba of Parzikia has no problem with the fish being eaten. His objection is only with *Kutcha* which is dairy and the fish has now absorbed meat flavor and cannot be eaten with dairy. Mar b. R. Ashi forbids it as being harmful, yet if this was the true source for the prohibition, it is difficult to imagine that the Rama would add specifically (Yoreh De'ah 116:2) that roasting meat and fish is forbidden because of the ריחא and then say that בדיעבד it is not forbidden. If it was accepted that roasting together led to specific health dangers, it would be prohibited at all times.

secondary prohibitions are precautionary at best. Therefore, the only reason to prohibit putting fish and meat on the same plate would be our fear that, invariably, we would co-mingle some of the fish and meat if they were that close together, and that would lead to eating something which would be a סכנה.

Today, there is no scientific medical reason to prohibit the consumption of meat and fish together. We may argue that either the physical world has changed from the time of the rabbis and their experience, or our science has progressed to give us a greater insight showing us that there is no medical danger to consuming meat and fish.[4] As such, the prohibition of meat and fish should be abolished much the same as the prohibition of exposed beverages was canceled when a concern of snake cantamination was not part of the physical world of the rabbis.

Conclusion

The prohibition of fish and meat is based on a specific סכנה. Historically when the סכנה ceased to exist, the rabbis had the power to end the prohibition. Today we know that there is no סכנה affecting צרעת by eating fish and meat together. Therefore, we would permit not only putting fish and meat on the same plate, but would allow them to be consumed together.

---

[4] Doctors and nutritionists approached could find nothing in the literature to even hint at a danger of fish and meat for any disease, let alone צרעת.

YD 180.1997

Tattooing and Body Piercing

Rabbi Alan B. Lucas

This paper was adopted by the CJLS on March 11, 1997, by a vote of seventeen in favor and four abstaining (17-0-4). Voting in favor: Rabbis Kassel Abelson, Ben Zion Bergman, Elliot N. Dorff, Samuel Fraint, Baruch Frydman-Kohl, Myron S. Geller, Nechama D. Goldberg, Susan Grossman, Judah Kogen, Alan B. Lucas, Aaron L. Mackler, Paul Plotkin, Mayer Rabinowitz, James S. Rosen, Joel Roth, Elie Kaplan Spitz, and Gordon Tucker. Abstaining: Rabbis Jerome M. Epstein, Lionel E. Moses, Avram Israel Reisner, and Gerald Zelizer.

The Committee on Jewish Law and Standards of the Rabbinical Assembly provides guidance in matters of halakhah for the Conservative movement. The individual rabbi, however, is the authority for the interpretation and application of all matters of halakhah.

שאלה

Is body piercing (nose, navel, etc.) and tattooing permitted? Does it preclude taking part in synagogue rituals or being buried in a Jewish cemetery?

תשובה

This question deals with two separate issues: body piercing and tattooing. It also deals with three different implications of these two issues: (1) the question of permissibility; (2) participation in synagogue rituals; and (3), burial in a Jewish cemetery.

Tattooing

The prohibition of tattooing is found in the Torah:

ושרט לנפש לא תתנו בבשרכם וכתבת קעקע לא תתנו בכם אני ה'.

> You shall not make gashes in your flesh for the dead, nor incise any marks on yourselves: I am the Lord.[1]

It is the second part of this verse from which we derive the general prohibition against tattooing.

From the outset there is disagreement about what precisely makes tattooing a prohibited act. The anonymous author of a mishnah states that it is the lasting and permanent nature of tattooing which makes it a culpable act:

---

[1] Lev. 19:28.

> הכותב כתבת קעקע... אינו חיב עד שיכתב קעקע בדיו ובכחול ובכל דבר שהוא רשום.

> If a man wrote [on his skin] pricked-in writing [he is culpable]... but only if he writes it and pricks it in with ink or eye-paint or anything that leaves a lasting mark.[2]

But Rabbi Simeon b. Judah disagrees and says that it is the inclusion of God's name which makes it a culpable act:

> ר' שמעון בן יהודה משום ר' שמעון אומר אינו חיב עד שיכתוב שם השם שנאמר: וכתבת קעקע לא תתנו בכם אני ה'.

> Rabbi Simeon b. Judah says in the name of Rabbi Simeon: He is not culpable unless he writes there the name [of a god], for it is written, *"Or incise any marks on yourselves: I am the Lord."*[3]

The Gemara goes on to debate whether it is the inclusion of God's name or a pagan deity that makes it a culpable act.

The Rambam clearly sees the origin of this prohibition as an act of idolatry. He includes it in his section concerning idolatry and then explicitly states:

> וזה היה מנהג העכו"ם שרושמין עצמן לעבודת כוכבים.

> This was a custom among the pagans who marked themselves for idolatry.[4]

But, the Rambam concludes that regardless of intent, the act of tattooing is prohibited.[5]

Aaron Demsky of Bar Ilan University in an article in the Encyclopaedia Judaica[6] goes even further to suggest that non-idolatrous tattooing may have been permitted in Biblical times. He cites the following Biblical references:

> זה יאמר לה' אני וזה יקרא בשם יעקב וזה יכתב ידו לה' ובשם ישראל יכנה.

> One shall say, "I am the Lord's," another shall use the name of "Jacob," another shall mark his arm "of the Lord's" and adopt the name of "Israel."[7]

> הן על כפים חקתיך.

> See, I have engraved you on the palms of My hands.[8]

> ביד כל אדם יחתום לדעת כל אנשי מעשהו.

> Is a sign on every man's hand that all men may know His doings.[9]

While these verses may be purely metaphoric, Demsky suggests they could be taken liter-

---

[2] M. Makkot 3:6.

[3] Ibid. Emphasis added.

[4] Maimonides, M.T. Hilkhot Avodat Kokhavim 12:11.

[5] Ibid.

[6] *Encyclopaedia Judaica*, (Jerusalem: Keter Publishing, 1972), vol. 16, p. 663ff., s.v. "Writing".

[7] Isa. 44:5.

[8] Isa. 49:16.

[9] Job 37:7.

ally as instances of tattooing that was acceptable in Biblical times. He goes on to add that A. Cowley showed that in Elephantine, slaves of Jews were marked with the name of their owners as was the general practice.[10]

Regardless of the exact limits of this prohibition, over time, the Rabbis clearly extended the prohibition to include all tattooing.[11]

In our day, the prohibition against all forms of tattooing regardless of their intent, should be maintained. In addition to the fact that Judaism has a long history of distaste for tattoos, tattooing becomes even more distasteful when confronted with a contemporary secular society that is constantly challenging the Jewish concept that we are created בצלם אלוקים, "In the Image of God," and that our bodies are to be viewed as a precious gift on loan from God, to be entrusted into our care and not our personal property to do with as we choose. Voluntary tattooing even if not done for idolatrous purposes expresses a negation of this fundamental Jewish perspective.

As tattoos become more popular in contemporary society, there is a need to reenforce the prohibition against tattooing in our communities and counterbalance it with education regarding the traditional concept that we are created בצלם אלוקים, "In the Image of God." But, however distasteful we may find the practice there is no basis for restricting burial to a Jew who violates this prohibition or even limiting their participation in synagogue ritual. The fact that someone may have violated the laws of kashrut at some point in their life or violated the laws of Shabbat would not merit such sanctions, the prohibition against tattooing is certainly no worse. It is only because of the permanent nature of the tattoo that the transgression is still visible.

New laser technology has raised the possibility of removing what was once irremovable. To date, this procedure is painful, long, and very expensive. However, it will probably not be long before the process is refined to the point where it will not be painful, overly involved or very expensive. At such time it might be appropriate for the Law Committee to consider whether removal of tattoos should become a requirement of תשובה, conversion or burial.

The prohibition of tattooing throughout the halakhic literature deals only with personal, voluntary tattooing. With respect to the reprehensible practice of the Nazis who marked the arms of Jews with tattooed numbers and letters during the Shoah, the Shulhan Arukh makes it clear that those who bear these tattoos are blameless:

אם עושה כן על בשר חבירו אותו שנעשה לו פטור.

If it [the tattoo] was done in the flesh of another, the one to whom
it was done is blameless.[12]

Tattoos which are used in cancer treatment or any similar medical procedure, to permanently mark the body for necessary life saving treatment are also not included in the prohibition against tattooing.[13]

The prohibition against tattoos applies only to permanent marks to the skin. Therefore hand stamps or other popular children's decorations which mimic tattoos and paint the skin in a nonpermanent manner cannot be included under the prohibition of tattooing. However, לשם חינוך, for the purpose of education it might be appropriate for parents to

---

[10] A. Cowley, *Aramaic Papyri of the Fifth Century B.C.* (1923) 28:2-6.

[11] Tosafot on B. Gittin 20b, s.v. בכתובת קעקע.

[12] S.A. Yoreh De'ah 180:2.

[13] Ibid., 180:3. The *Siftei Kohen* clearly states that since the purpose is for medical purposes it is permitted.

make the distinction clear to their children. These also present an excellent opportunity to introduce young children to the concept that we are created בצלם אלוקים, "In God's Image," and the implications of that concept.

Body Piercing

The issue of body piercing is also presenting no small challenge to many a contemporary parent. For what has long been an issue of only "ear piercing" and limited to women, has now been extended to men and to almost every imaginable part of the body capable of being pierced.[14]

While many of us may not understand why anyone would want to pierce some of the parts of the body, the question before us asks if such acts render one unfit for ritual inclusion or burial.

Ear-piercing is mentioned in the Bible in several contexts. The most familiar is with reference to a Hebrew slave who was to be freed in the seventh year of servitude and in declaring his love for his master he might refuse to go free:

> והגישו אדניו אל האלוקים והגישו אל הדלת או אל המזוזה ורצע אדניו את אזנו במרצע ועבדו לעלם.
>
> His master shall take him before God. He shall be brought to the door or the doorpost, and his master shall pierce his ear with an awl; and he shall then remain his slave for life.[15]

There is some disagreement in the Gemara as to how permanent this piercing of the slave's ear was supposed to be.[16] But our piercing is clearly of a non-permanent nature and its intent is purely decorative. This type of piercing was also known in the Bible:

> ואשאל אתה ואמר בת מי את.... ואשם הנזם על אפה והצמידים על ידיה.
>
> I inquired of her, "Whose daughter are you?" . . . And I put the ring on her nose and the bands on her arm.[17]

> ויאמר אליהם אהרן פרקו נזמי הזהב אשר באזני נשיכם.
>
> Aaron said to them, "Take of the gold rings that are on the ears of your wives. . . ."[18]

> ואעדך עדי.... ואתן נזם על אפך ועגילים על אזניך.
>
> I decked you out in finery. . . . I put a ring in your nose, and earrings in your ears.[19]

This is also well documented in Rabbinic times:

---

[14] And some you didn't even think were capable of being pierced. In an article downloaded from the Internet, instructions were readily available on how to pierce the nostril, septum, eyebrow, Nieburh or Erle (the tissue between the eyes), the lip, cheek, tongue, navel, nipples, handweb, outer labia, inner labia, clitoral hood, clitoral triangle, clitoris, princess albertina, frenum, prince albert, ampallang, apadravya, dydoe, foreskin, and scrotum.

[15] Exod. 21:6.

[16] B. Kiddushin 21b.

[17] Gen. 24:47.

[18] Exod. 32:2.

[19] Ezek. 16:11. See also Exod. 35:22, Num. 31:50, Judg. 8:24, and Isa. 3:21.

> הבנות יוצאות בחוטין ואפילו בקיסמין שבאזניהן.

> Small girls may go out [on Shabbat] with threads or even chips in their ears.[20]

It also appears that there may be references to male ear piercing in the Talmud as well. In a discussion regarding the wearing of jewelry on Shabbat, the Gemara states:

> לא יצא החייט במחטו התחובה לו בבגו ולא נגר בקיסם שבאזנו.

> A tailor must not go out with a needle stuck in his garment, nor a carpenter with a chip in his ear.[21]

Rashi refers to a custom in his day for men to wear earrings that were signs of their respective trades.[22] While Rashi seems to understand this chip as being tucked behind the ear, Jacob Lauterbach understands it as an example of piercing.[23] The same expression, בקיסם שבאזנו, is found in the above cited mishnah of Shabbat and clearly refers to piercing.[24] It was also an established custom in European countries well into the Middle Ages for tradesmen to wear pierced earrings of the symbol of their trade.

The surgical process of piercing both the ear and the nose seems to be well documented in the Bible and the Talmud. While there are many today who would find the Biblical custom of nose piercing unacceptable, there are apparently many young people today who find it attractive. And while some are uncomfortable with men having their ears pierced, even this has a precedent in traditional literature. The only issue that seems to direct this matter is the fashions of the day. It is hard to argue from a halakhic perspective that there is a substantive difference between the nonpermanent piercing of the ear for fashion purposes and the non-permanent piercing of the eyebrow, navel or even nipple. The lack of aesthetic appeal to many of us is hardly a halakhic consideration.

There are some legitimate concerns which could and should be raised. There is a concern that an inappropriate procedure or lack of proper hygiene involved in the piercing of a clitoris, nipple, or scrotum, for example, could lead to an infection with significant consequences. Piercing should only be done by those medically qualified to address these concerns.

In addition there is the issue of בצלם אלוקים, "In God's Image," and צניעות, modesty. With respect to the traditional Jewish value of צניעות, one has to wonder if "private" parts of the body are being pierced for fashion purposes, if the intent is to keep that private part private. While there may be no prohibition against such body piercings, they must be placed in the larger context of צניעות, which remains an important Jewish value.

And, while ear piercing seems to be a fairly benign practice, there comes some point at which multiple piercings of the body, however fashionable, begin to challenge our concept of בצלם אלוקים, that we are created in God's image. It seems to me that Jews sufficiently educated and sensitive to the concepts of צניעות, modesty, and בצלם אלוקים, being created in God's image, will limit themselves appropriately regarding body piercing. I am

---

[20] M. Shabbat 6:6.

[21] B. Shabbat 11b.

[22] Rashi on B. Shabbat 11b, s.v. בקיסם שבאזנו. Rashi explains that it was the custom of tradesmen to wear signs of their trade in the form of earrings so that when they walked in the marketplace people would know their particular trade and could hire them.

[23] Responsa on Pierced Ears, Sept. 1983, *CCAR Yearbook*.

[24] M. Shabbat 6:6. And in a discussion of what causes a permanent blemish, the Talmud, in Bekhorot 37a, gives piercing of the ear as an example.

reminded of a דבר תורה Rabbi David Weiss Halivni once gave at the Seminary regarding the permissibility of animal hunting for pleasure by Jews. He quoted a תשובה by Rabbi Ezekiel ben Judah Landau.[25] After taking some time to explain why it was indeed permitted by the Torah he concluded by saying, "Yes, it is permitted, but what kind of a Jew would want to hunt for pleasure?" While not nearly as serious an issue as hunting, one can only wonder what questions about body piercing and tattooing tell us about our contemporary community.

Ultimately this seems to be a matter of fashion which will pass with time. But until then, we should strengthen the sense of צניעות, modesty, which should guide our fashion choices and underscore our belief that we are created בצלם אלוקים, "In God's Image" in an attempt to balance contemporary pressures. But I see no basis for any sanctions against those who engage in such fashions, certainly not of the magnitude of refusing burial in a Jewish cemetery or refraining from including them in any synagogue practices.

Conclusion

Tattooing is an explicit prohibition from the Torah. However, those who violate this prohibition may be buried in a Jewish cemetery and participate fully in all synagogue ritual. While no sanctions are imposed, the practice should continue to be discouraged as a violation of the Torah. Body piercing is not prohibited, although legitimate concerns regarding צניעות, modesty, and other other traditional Jewish values should be taken into consideration and guide one's choices. At all times a Jew should remember that we are created בצלם אלוקים, "In God's Image." We are called upon to incorporate this understanding in all our decisions.

---

[25] *Noda B'yehudah* to Yoreh De'ah 10, s.v. המתחיל ואומנם מאד.

YD 264:3.1998

Anesthesia and B'rit Milah

Rabbi Vernon H. Kurtz

This paper was approved by the CJLS on March 25, 1998, by a vote of sixteen in favor (16-0-0). Voting in favor: Rabbis Kassel Abelson, Ben Zion Bergman, Elliot N. Dorff, Samuel Fraint, Myron S. Geller, Nechama D. Goldberg, Judah Kogen, Vernon H. Kurtz, Alan B. Lucas, Aaron L. Mackler, Paul Plotkin, Avram Israel Reisner, Joel E. Rembaum, Joel Roth, Gordon Tucker, and Gerald Zelizer.

The Committee on Jewish Law and Standards of the Rabbinical Assembly provides guidance in matters of halakhah for the Conservative movement. The individual rabbi, however, is the authority for the interpretation and application of all matters of halakhah.

שאלה

May anesthesia be used during a ברית מילה?

תשובה

The mitzvah of ברית מילה is one of the most important and long standing of all Jewish traditions. Periodically throughout history there have been attacks against the ritual. The enemies of the people of Israel have seen it as a barbaric rite and members of the Jewish people who have serious concerns about the ritual and its practice have raised significant issues.

Recently questions have been raised concerning the pain experienced during circumcision. Most circumcisions are performed on eight-day-old male babies, and therefore it is very difficult to evaluate the nature of the pain that may be present at that time. However, circumcisions can also be performed on males who are older than eight days. These can occur when a male converts to Judaism and is not circumcised or when a Jewish male has not, for some reason, undergone the halakhic procedure at the proper time. Examples of this latter omission may include the population that was born during the Holocaust when a ברית מילה was a death sentence; Jews who have joined the Jewish people from Eastern Europe and the former Soviet Union where circumcision was not practiced among the general population; and even some Jews born in the lands of freedom whose parents did not wish them to undergo the procedure.

The question has arisen whether it is possible to use anesthesia for the person undergoing a ברית מילה. This question has been raised not only by those who are affiliated with the Conservative movement but by those of other movements as well. Rabbi Michael

Herzbrun raises the issue of pain during the circumcision.[1] Rabbi Ovadiah Yosef also raises the question.[2] But perhaps Lisa Braver Moss offers the most serious challenge.[3] She is a freelance writer whose two sons underwent the ברית procedure. Having witnessed her two sons crying during the procedure, she now wonders whether the procedure should be reexamined. Her concerns are probably those of many parents who contemplate the procedure, and since their lives are not totally enveloped within the halakhic framework, they therefore look for opportunities not to perform a ברית מילה.

She writes, "We must also address the reality that Jewish parents are questioning circumcision more than ever before. Some find the pain and risks problematic. . . . This reality is far from bleak: Each of these concerns reflects a deep regard for Jewish values. Jews are questioning circumcision for Jewish reasons. In my own case, questioning the rite has only deepened my love for Judaism and strengthened by Jewish identity." Thus it behooves us to reexamine the issue of pain during the circumcision and possible solution which might be available both from a medical and a halakhic point of view.

In the case of an adult, there is no doubt that pain is present during this surgical procedure. Is pain a necessary requirement for a proper ברית מילה to take place? Rabbi Meir ben Aaron Judah Arik (1885-1926) in his work, *Imrei Yosher*,[4] contends that pain should accompany the circumcision ritual. He bases his proof on Abraham, the first person to be circumcised. He suggests that the patriarch received a double reward from heaven for enduring the pain of the procedure. He also bases his argument on an element of omission. Since the rabbis knew of and accepted pain-reducing medication during medical procedures, the fact that they never wrote about them in the context of circumcision suggested to him that they should not be used.

His view has been severely criticized by two recent scholars. Rabbi A.L. Baron suggests that in the matter of enduring pain during circumcision we do not follow the example of Abraham our Patriarch. "We follow the commandment of Moses, our Rabbi, from Sinai and there we did not learn that one must endure pain during circumcision." It is his contention that, "pain during circumcision is not a necessary requirement of the commandment."[5] Rabbi Ovadiah Yosef[6] agrees with this opinion since, "there is no obligation to be in pain during circumcision," and the fact that the Rabbis did not mention the use of pain-reducing medication is not proof whatsoever to disallow it.

In fact, most halakhic authorities agree that in the case of an adult male, local or a general anesthesia is permitted. For example, Ephraim Oshri was asked the question whether it was permitted to administer an anesthetic to a ten-year-old child.[7] A group of boys had been hidden during the Holocaust, and the parents had deliberately avoided circumcising them so that they could pass unnoticed among the gentiles. One ten-year-old boy refused to be circumcised unless it could be promised to him that he would not suffer pain. Rabbi Oshri allows the anesthetic to be administered

---

[1] Michael B. Herzbrun, *CCAR Journal* 38 (fall 1991).

[2] Rabbi Ovadiah Yosef, *Sheelot u'Teshuvot Yabea Omer*, helek 5, siman 22.

[3] Lisa Braver Moss, *Tikkun* 5, (Sept./Oct. 1990) no. 5; *Midstream* 38 (Jan. 1992), no. 1.

[4] Rabbi Meir ben Aaron Judah Arik, *Imrei Yosher*, vol. 2, siman 140, ot 3.

[5] Rabbi A.L. Baron, "In the matter regarding whether it is permissible to circumcise by means of spreading anesthetic on the member prior to circumcision so as not to feel the pain of circumcision." (Hebrew) *HaDarom*, 1989, pp. 13-22.

[6] Rabbi Ovadiah Yosef, *Noam* 12 (Hebrew): 1-10.

[7] Ephraim Oshri, *Sheelot U'Teshuvot Mimama'akim* 2, no. 1.

since the halakhah does not mandate pain as part of the circumcision ritual.

The second question that needs to be answered is does the נמול, the individual being circumcised, need כוונה – intentionality? Rabbi Jehiel Jacob Weinberg[8] believes that, "if we induce a general anesthetic then he will be as an inanimate stone and we do not establish a covenant with a stone." However, his view seems to be definitely in the minority. Rabbi Ovadiah Yosef, as but one example, does not see this as a problem. First of all, the person upon whom the ברית is performed does not need כוונה, as evidenced from the ברית of an infant who cannot have כוונה and, secondly, even if it were an issue, one can appoint another to perform the ברית before the anesthetic has been administered.[9]

Since these scholars have permitted the use of anesthetics on an adult during the circumcision, what should our opinion be with regard to an eight-day-old child? The issue of כוונה, even if it is a category that must be present, does not apply since any anesthetic that might be administered will be a local one. In fact, if כוונה is an issue, it is important to recognize that the mitzvah of מילה is incumbent on the father, and he can either do the ברית מילה himself or appoint a מוהל to do it.

The major issue left to answer is that concerning the issue of pain. While it is difficult to judge the pain element in such a young baby, many medical researchers do believe the baby does endure some pain. While this pain may be inconsequential, researchers do believe that infants do experience pain with at least short-term significant sequelae.[10] If indeed some pain is present in the circumcision procedure, then a study reported in the Journal of the American Medical Association, that newborns that received an anesthetic had significantly less pain, could be used to our advantage.[11] Even if this is the case, it should make no difference whether the person being circumcised is eight days old or older; we should be able to use the same reasoning to allow the use of anesthetic medication in the circumcision procedure. While this will not alleviate the concern of all parents with regard to the procedure on their young children, having it available will at least allow the מוהל to use it and calm their concerns. We can, therefore, respond positively to the concerns of parents such as Lisa Braver Moss who wish to follow Jewish tradition but have reservations about the procedure.

As to what type of anesthetic application should be used, I leave that to medical professionals. There are some that perform the procedure who are also physicians and who use either a dorsal penile nerve block or a ring block through an injection.[12] Recently a new topical cream, EMLA, has appeared on the market. There are some מוהלים who find it very useful and still others who are not sold on its use.[13] However, all agree that these methods can be used during the procedure for an eight-day-old child. As for a person who is older, either a local or a general anesthetic can be used.[14]

---

[8] Rabbi Jehiel Jacob Weinberg, *Sridei Eish* 3:6.

[9] Rabbi Ovadiah Yosef, ibid.

[10] Franca Benini, C. Celeste Johnston, Daniel Faucher, and J.V. Aranda, "Topical Anesthesia During Circumcision in Newborn Infants," *JAMA*, (Aug. 1993): 2.

[11] Janice Lander, Barbara Brady-Fryer, James B. Metcalfe, Shemin Nazarali, and Sarha Muttit, "Comparison of Ring Block, Dorsal Nerve Block, and Topical Anesthesia for Neonatal Circumcision," *JAMA* 278 (24) (24-31 Dec. 1997).

[12] Discussion with Dr. Larry Veltman, graduate of ברית קודש Program.

[13] See Dorothy Greenbaum, "In Pursuit of the Painless Bris," *Berit Mila Newsletter* of the National Organization of American Mohalim/ot (Reform); Rabbi Eric Silver, private communications with Rabbi Andy Sacks (Conservative); Rabbi Moshe Tendler, Discussion and Lecture before ברית מילה Board of New York, 1993 (Orthodox).

[14] Rabbi Isaac Klein, *Responsa and Halachic Studies*, p. 125.

Conclusion

It is permissible to use either a general or a local anesthetic during the procedure of ברית מילה whether the person is a baby or an adult. I would leave up to the individual מוהל the decision as to what type of anesthetic may be used. However, if its use alleviates some of the concerns of the parents as to whether they wish to have a ברית מילה for their child, the מוהל should seriously consider using a form of anesthetics which is acceptable to him or her.

YD 266:2.1996

Induction Leading to Birth of a Baby on Shabbat and B'rit Milah

Rabbi Vernon H. Kurtz

This paper was approved by the CJLS on December 18, 1996, by a vote of twenty in favor (20-0-0). Voting in favor: Rabbis Kassel Abelson, Ben Zion Bergman, Jerome M. Epstein, Samuel Fraint, Baruch Frydman-Kohl, Myron S. Geller, Nechama D. Goldberg, Arnold M. Goodman, Judah Kogen, Vernon H. Kurtz, Alan B. Lucas, Aaron L. Mackler, Lionel E. Moses, Paul Plotkin, Mayer Rabinowitz, Avram Israel Reisner, Joel E. Rembaum, James S. Rosen, Joel Roth, and Elie Kaplan Spitz.

The Committee on Jewish Law and Standards of the Rabbinical Assembly provides guidance in matters of halakhah for the Conservative movement. The individual rabbi, however, is the authority for the interpretation and application of all matters of halakhah.

שאלה

When labor is induced so that a baby is born on Shabbat, does the ברית מילה occur on the following Shabbat?

תשובה

In checking with obstetrician gynecologists, I learned that there are two reasons that labor may be induced. One reason is for medical issues, the other is for convenience.

If a doctor recognizes that there is a danger in the pregnancy, either for the mother or the baby, the doctor may induce the mother to give birth sooner rather than later. This may occur where there is evidence of fetal distress; problems caused by an elevation in blood pressure; diabetes or other medical problems; or in a case where the mother's waters may have broken but labor itself is not proceeding on course. If a baby is judged late, there may not necessarily be a need to induce the mother unless danger signals are present.

There are times when labor is induced due to the schedules of the parents, doctors or hospital. In this case it may be an elective decision. This should strongly be discouraged since the desecration of Shabbat will no doubt occur, and we should minimize that occurrence under all circumstances.

If induction occurs either on Friday or on Shabbat itself and the baby is born on Shabbat, the question has been asked whether a ברית מילה should take place on the following Shabbat or not. The answer revolves around the question of whether induction itself is considered artificial and, thus, should not lead to a ברית מילה on Shabbat, or is it the birth itself that is determinative?

The Talmud in Shabbat 135a states:

> Rabbi Assi said: He whose mother is defiled through confinement (טמאה לידה) must be circumcised at eight days, but he whose mother is not defiled through confinement is not circumcised on the eighth day because "when a woman at childbirth bears a male, she shall be unclean seven days. . .on the eighth day the flesh of his foreskin shall be circumcised." (Lev. 12:2-3)

Rashi suggests that a woman who is not confined is one who gives birth by Caesarean section. However, one who has a male child through vaginal birth is considered to be טמאה לידה. The mother, in this circumstance, becomes ritually unclean because of delivery, and according to the Talmudic text, the circumcision takes place eight days later. This view is codified by the S.A. Yoreh De'ah 266:10.

Thus, the act of induction itself is not determinative but the manner of birth is. If a child is born by Caesarean section then a Shabbat brit is not permitted. It will be held on Sunday. However, if the child is born by vaginal birth, a Shabbat ברית מילה should be performed. The rules governing a ברית מילה on Shabbat have already been discussed by the Rabbinical Assembly Committee on Jewish Law and Standards in a תשובה written by Rabbi Arnold M. Goodman and approved by the CJLS in March, 1988.[1]

Conclusion

If induction for any reason takes place so that a woman gives birth on Shabbat, arrangements should be made for a Shabbat ברית מילה to take place.

---

[1] Arnold M. Goodman, "Shabbat and Brit Milah," *PCJLS 86-90*, pp. 311-315.

YD 268.1993

THE CASE OF THE UNCONVERTED SPOUSE

Rabbi Ben Zion Bergman

This paper was approved by the CJLS on February 17, 1993, by a vote of eight in favor, eleven opposed, and four abstaining (8-11-4). Voting in favor: Rabbis Kassel Abelson, Ben Zion Bergman, Elliot N. Dorff, Ezra Finkelstein, Arnold M. Goodman, Howard Handler, Joel E. Rembaum, and Gordon Tucker. Voting against: Rabbis Stanley Bramnick, Jerome M. Epstein, David Feldman, Samuel Fraint, Judah Kogen, Herbert Mandl, Lionel E. Moses, Avram Israel Reisner, Chaim Rogoff, Joel Roth, and Gerald Skolnik. Abstaining: Rabbis Jan Caryl Kaufman, Reuven Kimelman, Aaron L. Mackler, and Mayer Rabinowitz.

The Committee on Jewish Law and Standards of the Rabbinical Assembly provides guidance in matters of halakhah for the Conservative movement. The individual rabbi, however, is the authority for the interpretation and application of all matters of halakhah.

שאלה

May one convert a married gentile who intends to remain married to the unconverted gentile spouse even after completion of the conversion?

תשובה

This is not a case of first impression for the CJLS. The CJLS minutes of March 13, 1956, record that this question was posed and the Committee's decision was in the affirmative. Subsequent correspondence of the CJLS similarly reflects that the question was asked a number of times by individual rabbis and in each case the Secretary of the CJLS answered that the position of the CJLS was to approve such a conversion. In 1985, Rabbi Joel Roth presented a paper to the CJLS in which he proposed that such a conversion should not be undertaken. His paper failed to garner the six votes required to make it an acceptable option for members of the Rabbinical Assembly. The present status of the issue, therefore, is that it is permitted to convert a married gentile who will continue to live with the unconverted gentile spouse. I see no reason to change the status quo.

Introduction

The 1956 decision recorded in the CJLS minutes is not accompanied by a rationale or even a record of any discussion pro and con. We therefore do not know the basis of their decision.

Rabbi Roth, in his paper, argued that to convert a married gentile who will continue a marital relationship with an unconverted gentile spouse is tantamount to creating an intermarriage and therefore should be forbidden.

Rabbi Roth, in his paper, is correct that the classical sources are silent on the question. The silence is not surprising since the question would never arise in a social context where Jewish and gentile communities were strictly separated and the situation would represent an anomaly. Indeed, what we consider an intermarriage was anomalous in previous times since any union between a Jew and a non-Jew would have required the conversion of one to the faith of the other. It is precisely in our open society, where intermarriage is possible with both spouses adhering to their individual religious affiliation, that the question becomes actual.

One therefore has to consider this question in the total context of our position on intermarriage, the reasons for our refusal to perform intermarriages, and the decisions we have made vis-à-vis intermarried couples within our congregations. The issue, therefore, has to be considered both from the aspect of halakhah and public policy.

The Halakhic Issue

The contention that such a conversion by a Conservative rabbi results in the rabbi virtually creating an intermarriage may not necessarily render the conversion forbidden.

One can argue that to transgress the Biblical injunction: ולא תתחתן בם, "You shall not intermarry with them" (Deut. 7:3), requires a positive act of marriage, as the verse itself continues: בתך לא תתן לבנו ובתו לא תקח לבנך, "Do not give your daughters to their sons or take their daughters for your sons." In the present situation, there is no *act* of intermarriage. If the conversion results in an intermarried status, the intermarried status ממילא קאתי has come about indirectly.

The issue as to whether a permitted act is forbidden if it will result in an undesired consequence, which consequence itself would be forbidden if undertaken purposely, is a classic dispute between R. Simeon and R. Judah found in various places in the Talmud. The primary source is the following baraita:

> תניא ר׳ שמעון אומר גורר אדם כסא מטה וספסל ובלבד שלא יתכוון לעשות חריץ. ר׳ יהודה אומר אין הכל נגררין בשבת חוץ מן העגלה שהיא כובשת.
>
> Rabbi Simeon says: One may drag a chair, bed, or bench [on the Sabbath] as long as there is no intention to make a rut. Rabbi Judah says: Nothing may be dragged on the Sabbath except a wagon because it presses (i.e. merely presses the earth down and does not dig it out) (Betzah 23b, also Shabbat 22a, Menahot 41b).

In the discussion, *ad locum*, the Talmud extrapolates the jurisprudential principles held by the disputants as R. Simeon holding that דבר שאין מתכון מותר, when the forbidden consequence is unintentional, the act which creates it is permitted, and R. Judah holding that דבר שאין מתכון אסור, the act is forbidden *ab initio* when a prohibited consequence might result.[1]

---

[1] See also Shabbat 29b where it appears that R. Judah would go so far as to forbid dragging in circumstances where a rut was impossible, such as on a stone floor, since in most other circumstances the surface would not be a hard one. See also Shabbat 41b and Ketubot 5b with its attendant Tosafot s.v. דם מיפקד פקיד או דם חיבורי מיחבר.

In the Amoraic discussion of this issue, there is a dispute between Rav and Samuel, with Rav maintaining that אין הלכה כר׳ שמעון בגרירה, regarding "dragging" the law does not follow R. Simeon, and Samuel holding הלכה כר׳ שמעון בגרירה, the law follows R. Simeon in dragging. However, the later Amoraic consensus clearly comes down that הלכה כר׳ שמעון, the law follows R. Simeon, since Abaye reported that his teacher, Rabbah, would always follow the view of Rav over that of Samuel, except in three issues in which he followed the view of Samuel. One of the three is the case of dragging on the Sabbath (Shabbat 22a, also Pesahim 101a).

The issue is not confined to Sabbath violations. In Nazir 42a the Mishnah which reads נזיר חופף ומפספס אבל לא סורק, a Nazirite may rub or scratch his hair but may not comb it — is explained in the Gemara as being the view of R. Simeon, that it is permitted because any removal of hair by rubbing or scratching is unintentional, while the combing referred to is explained as combing with the intention of removing knotted clumps. Similarly, in Kilaim 9:5:

> מוכרי כסות מוכרין כדרכן ובלבד שלא יתכוונו בחמה מפני החמה ובגשמים מפני הגשמים.
>
> Clothing merchants may sell [garments made from forbidden mixtures and may hang them for display] in the usual manner, provided they do not intend them on sunny days as protection from the sun or as protection from the rain when it is raining.

Therefore, since דבר שאין מתכון מותר, the act is permissible despite its leading to an unintended consequence which would be forbidden were it intentional, in our case, the conversion would be permitted, since the intermarried status is an unintended consequence.

One might counter that R. Simeon's position would not hold where the unintended consequence is a certainty to occur:

> אביי ורבא דאמרי תרוויהו מודה ר״ש בפסיק רישא ולא ימות.
>
> Abaye and Rava both maintain that R. Simeon would agree that the act is forbidden when the consequence is an inevitability (Shabbat 75a, 111b, Ketubot 6a et al.).

Nevertheless, as long as it is not an *absolute* inevitability, it is permitted, as is indicated in Ketubot 6b where the issue is whether the first marital intercourse with the virgin bride may be consummated on the Sabbath, since in the process a wound is created. And even though this could be an unintentional consequence, Abaye questions the identification of those who would permit it as being the view of R. Simeon, since even R. Simeon would not permit an act whose forbidden consequence is inevitable. Rava counters this by saying, לא כהללו בבליים שאין בקיאין בהטייה אלא יש בקיאין בהטייה, "Not like those Babylonians who are not expert in turning aside (i.e. able to engage in intercourse without causing bleeding) but some are expert at this." Thus as long as it is not an absolute inevitability, it is permitted even for the one who is not expert in the maneuver.

One can argue that in the case of the converting spouse the intermarried status is not an *absolute* inevitability, since (A) there may be instances where divorce would ensue, or (B) in the process, the other spouse may be inspired by the example and decide to convert as well. Therefore, even when the stated intention is to remain married to an unconverted spouse, since it is not always an absolute inevitability, the dictum would hold that דבר שאין מתכון מותר, the unintended consequence does not prohibit the act that might cause it.

Thus, there is ample room to argue that converting someone who intends to remain married to the unconverted gentile spouse is not violative of the halakhah.

Policy Issues

Over and above the halakhic argument, I feel even more strongly that forbidding such a conversion would be detrimental to the interests of the Jewish people, inconsistent with other CJLS decisions, and would reflect failure to respond reasonably to the sociological reality.

The inconsistency with our position vis-à-vis intermarried couples within the synagogal organization would be patent. We have taken the position that, while the non-Jewish spouse may not be a member, the Jewish partner in the intermarriage may be a member of the congregation.[2] Now between the Jew who actively, consciously, and purposely violated the law by intermarrying, and the convert who becomes a partner to an intermarriage by indirection, clearly the former is the more egregious. Yet to forbid the latter from entering into and participating in the Jewish religious community, while permitting the former, is to treat the innocent more severely than the sinner. Even if our position on the intermarried Jew were to deny him/her membership in the congregation, one could make a case that such denial should not extend to a convert. If congregational membership is open to the intermarried Jew, קל וחומר, *a fortiori*, it must be extended to the convert whatever his/her marital status.

To phrase it in the converse — if conversion is denied because it would indirectly result in an intermarriage, then we are saying that an intermarried person, even if the intermarried status was not the result of a positive act in violation of Jewish law and standards, may not be a member of the Jewish community. Then קל וחומר, *a fortiori*, the person who consciously and directly violated Jewish law by contracting a marriage with a non-Jew should not be allowed membership in the Jewish community.

Since we are anxious to hold on to the allegiance of all Jews — even the sinners among us — and to retain their sense of identity with the Jewish people, we try not to alienate the intermarried Jew. Logical consistency then requires that we permit all to convert, with the resultant indirect intermarried status not a deterrent.

The same consideration also prompts us to maintain that denial of conversion in these circumstances is detrimental to the best interests of the Jewish people. In light of our decreasing numbers, we have consciously embraced a policy of קירוב — of encouraging conversion to Judaism. To deny this conversion sends a contrary signal. In addition, it is expressly counter-productive.

In our desire to encourage conversion, we have permitted conversion in cases where the major — sometimes the sole — motivation is to enable the non-Jew to marry a Jew. As some have said: "Out of a desire to embrace a Jew rather than to embrace Judaism." Traditionally, where the sole purpose of the conversion was to facilitate a marriage, conversion would be denied because of the ulterior motive. Nevertheless, we do accept converts whose motivation is marriage to a Jew. In our case, it is clear that the conversion is not motivated by any such ulterior motive. There can possibly be no clearer indication of a conversion that is out of sincere conviction. To deny it is counter-productive to the best interests of the Jewish people since we would possibly be refusing the best and most sincere convert who could be the greatest asset and a source of strength to the Jewish community.

---

[2] See *PCJLS 27-70*, 3:1027-1037; *PCJLS 80-85*, pp. 129-173 [– EDS.].

The same considerations lead to the conclusion that permitting this conversion is the proper response to the sociological reality. We oppose intermarriage because, in addition to the halakhic reasons, historically — and in most instances today as well --- intermarriage resulted in a loss to the Jewish people. Not only the loss of those who intermarry, but also of זרעיותיו עד סוף העולם, their descendants until the end of time. In the present circumstance, however, despite the ancillary intermarriage, the conversion results in a gain — of the convert and possible numerous descendants. One could characterize this as a "reverse intermarriage" which results in benefit to the Jewish people.

Under the present conditions, the only proper response to the sociological pressures that militate against Jewish identity and Jewish survival is to welcome all sources of additional Jewish strength and vitality.

Caveat

This is not to deny the fact that conversion under the stated conditions presents its own inherent problems. This convert, though sincerity and motivation are beyond question, does have a greater difficulty in fulfilling Jewish responsibility and achieving a Jewish lifestyle.

The rabbi and bet din who supervise and carry out the conversion have the responsibility to make sure that the non-converting spouse (and other non-Jewish members of the household) are supportive of the convert and will cooperate with the convert in maintaining standards of kashrut, Shabbat and holiday observance, etc. This will require extensive consultation and counseling with the convert and the convert's family. Only when the bet din is convinced that this support and cooperation are forthcoming should the conversion be completed.

Conclusion

A married gentile may convert to Judaism even though the convert intends to remain married to the unconverted gentile spouse. Such conversion should take place, however, only after proper counseling and consultation assuring that the convert will be able to practice the Jewish religion without interference by the non-Jewish members of the family. Under those conditions, those who seek לחסות תחת כנפי השכינה – to shelter under the wings of the Shekhinah – ירבו כמותם בישראל – may their numbers increase in Israel – ותבוא עליהם ברכה – and may blessings be bestowed upon them.

YD 268:1.1994

CONVERSION TO JUDAISM WITHOUT CIRCUMCISION DUE TO MEDICAL COMPLICATIONS

Rabbi Herbert J. Mandl

This paper was approved by the CJLS on October 5, 1994, by a vote of fifteen in favor, three opposed, and five abstaining (15-3-5). Voting in favor: Rabbis Stanley Bramnick, Jerome M. Epstein, Samuel Fraint, Jan Caryl Kaufman, Judah Kogen, Vernon H. Kurtz, Alan B. Lucas, Lionel E. Moses, Paul Plotkin, Mayer Rabinowitz, Avram Israel Reisner, Joel E. Rembaum, Chaim Rogoff, Joel Roth, and Israel Silverman. Voting against: Rabbis Myron S. Geller, Gordon Tucker, and Gerald Zelizer. Abstaining: Rabbis Kassel Abelson, Ben Zion Bergman, Elliot N. Dorff, Arnold M. Goodman, and Susan Grossman.

The Committee on Jewish Law and Standards of the Rabbinical Assembly provides guidance in matters of halakhah for the Conservative movement. The individual rabbi, however, is the authority for the interpretation and application of all matters of halakhah.

שאלה

May a male non-Jew convert to Judaism without ברית מילה and only טבילה, ritual immersion, if serious, possibly life threatening medical conditions prohibit circumcision?

תשובה

The great nineteenth century German פוסק, Rabbi David Zvi Hoffmann, who very often (for an Orthodox rabbi of his era) tended to be lenient in his views (as a matter of fact, specifically so in a number of areas of conversion law and for which he was criticized by many of his Orthodox colleagues for those views), states succinctly in his (מלמד להועיל (חלק ב, יו״ד ס׳ פ״ו) in one terse sentence that such a conversion cannot take place under those circumstances (where circumcision is impossible).

The late nineteenth and early twentieth century halakhic authority, Rabbi Isaac Jacob Rabinovitch (known as the Ponivicher Iluy) in his work זכר יצחק discusses this issue philosophically as well as practically. The basis for the requirement of a potential male proselyte needing both ritual circumcision *and* ritual immersion, in that order, is the following statement, in Yevamot 46a:

> Our Rabbis taught if a proselyte was circumcised, but had not performed the prescribed ritual immersion, Rabbi Eliezer says "Behold he is a proper proselyte – for we so find that our forefathers were cir-

cumcised and had not performed ritual immersion." If one performed the prescribed immersion, but had *not* been circumcised, Rabbi Joshua says, "Behold he *is* a proper proselyte for so we find that the mothers of the Jewish people (the matriarchs) have performed ritual immersion but had not been circumcised." However, the Sages, of blessed memory, say, "Whether he has performed immersion but has not been circumcised, or whether he had been circumcised but had not performed the prescribed ritual immersion, he is *not* a proper convert unless he had been circumcised *and* has also performed the prescribed immersion," *in that order!* [All emphases added.]

Nevertheless, the Talmud continues (Yevamot 46b) "all agree that ritual immersion without circumcision is effective, and they only differ regarding circumcision without immersion!" אלא בטבל ולא מל כולי עלמא לא פליגי דמהני כי פליגי במל ולא טבל.

The question that is raised in the Talmud in Yevamot 46a-b, is whether this fact (that a convert could immerse and not be circumcised) can be learned from the matriarchs or women of Israel, when only immersion took place and obviously no circumcision is involved. The objection is made that one is, thereby, trying to learn the possible (our case involving a man) from the impossible (women being physically unable to be circumcised under any circumstances) and therefore, learning about male circumcision from women (and thus an inappropriate derivation).

The responsum of Rabbi Rabinovitch then returns to the issue of a non-Jew who has lost his membrum, where circumcision *would* be impossible, and that our case should be considered similar to women converts whose "purification" takes place with just one of these requirements, namely immersion, only.

A challenge is raised, however, that the case of someone who could not be circumcised because of life-threatening conditions stated above is not comparable to our case, since the term "impossible to circumcise" would apply, for example, if one did not have a sexual organ or it had been cut off. However, in our case we are dealing with a situation where a potential convert cannot be circumcised *now*, and possibly *now only*, rather than dealing with the situation where there was no physical organ to circumcise at all. Therefore, one could draw the conclusion that with a potential convert who is ill, who could possibly be healed in the future, conversion, without circumcision at the present time would, therefore, be forbidden by Jewish law and postponed until the possible improvement of the medical condition.

The Tosafot in Yevamot 47b (ד"ה מטבילין) as well as הריטב"א and הנמוק"י all write that if a pregnant woman converts and has a male embryo in utero at the time, that son is born as a Jewish male convert and does *not require* ritual immersion (and only normal circumcision). Normally circumcision precedes immersion for a convert. This case is different, however, inasmuch as this embryo was immersed with its mother in utero and the child was not fit for a circumcision (as if it were a woman) since it was in utero. From this case we have learned that since it was impossible *now* to circumcise this child, the immersion alone satisfied the needs of conversion *without* circumcision at the time the embryo was in utero, inasmuch as *at that moment* the child was unable to be circumcised as it was in the mother's womb. That case would be somewhat similar to our question where the potential convert could not be circumcised *now* because of *present* medical conditions, or theoretically could be circumcised at a later time. That logic can lead one to think that a potential convert who could not be circumcised *now* could possibly be converted without circumcision and immersion alone would suffice.

The Talmud, however, then states in the name of Rabbi Hiyya ben Abba in the name of Rabbi Jochanan, that a man can *never* become a proselyte unless he has been *both* circumcised and also performed the prescribed ritual of immersion. It goes on to explain that this is a matter of dispute between an individual rabbi and a majority, with the halakhah following the majority (with the majority holding that both circumcision and immersion are required). The Talmud then clarifies that the majority is the view of Rabbi Jose. Before it was thought "if a convert came on his own and stated 'I have been circumcised but have not performed ritual immersion,' he is permitted to perform ritual immersion and the proper performance of the previous circumcision does not matter and is not investigated!" This is a view of Rabbi Judah. Rabbi Jose said "he is not allowed immersion" (because *both* circumcision and immersion are required). If the validity of the circumcision is in doubt in this case, the latter must not be allowed immersion unless some act of circumcision, even a token circumcision is done again, but carried out specifically for the purpose of ברית מילה (and not medical reasons) and prior to ritual immersion.

It is, therefore, assumed that Rabbi Jose's view as followed by a majority of the Rabbis, is that circumcision forms a principal and necessary part of the conversion, in addition to immersion.

Rabbah stated that it once occurred at the court of Rabbi Hiyya, that there came before them a convert who had been circumcised but had not performed ritual immersion. The rabbi told him "wait here until tomorrow and we shall arrange for your immersion." From this incident three rulings may be deduced: It may be deduced that the initiation of a convert requires the presence of three men (a בית דין), and that a man is not a proper proselyte unless he has been circumcised *and* has also performed the prescribed immersion! Finally, it may also be deduced that the immersion of a convert may not take place during the night time hours (inasmuch as he had to wait until the next day)!

The responsum of Rabbi Isaac Jacob Rabinovitch views the debate as revolving around the question as to whether or not circumcision acts as a type of "purification ceremony," or if it is the prohibition of permitting an *uncircumcised person* to "enter the Jewish people" that mandates circumcision. If the issue is one of purification, then theoretically under certain extenuating circumstances, circumcision could even be done at a later time, such as after immersion since one could always become "purified" at some later point (as per the רמב"ן). If the issue is one of not permitting someone to join the Jewish people who is uncircumcised, then someone who could not be medically circumcised could never enter the Jewish people!

> והתוספות והרא"ה ס"ל דמלבד דין הטהרה ע"י מעשה המילה דין הערלות
> בעצמה מעכבת להיעשותו לנכנס תחת כנפי השכינה ולזה כתבו (בריטב"א
> שם יבמות מב:) "דהוי כטובל ושרץ בידו!" וא"כ כמו שערל אסור בפסח
> כן נמי אי אפשר לו להיות ישראל כל שיש עליו ערלה, לזה בעי מילה
> תחילה!

The שרידי אש (Rabbi Yechiel Yaakov Weinberg) in שו"ת חלק ב' סי' ק"ב, deals with this issue in response to a question posed to him. He states that he found that very little had been written in the sources, specifically, about a case of one unable to be circumcised for conversion to Judaism because of medical dangers. He immediately rejects from a long list of sources any similarity to a case where a man may already be circumcised and only require הטפת דם, or a case where a man has lost his private membrum — in both of those cases ritual immersion would suffice, since a full circumcision could not physically be done under any circumstances! He feels that the discussion revolving around the issue of an injured individual in the sense of lacking a penis, and not revolving around the issue of illness, points to the fact that the Rabbis of old did not compare the two circumstances or conditions. He further points out that according to the Yerushalmi (יבמות פ׳ מערל) that if a person immerses oneself first *before* circumcision, the immersion *does not count* as if he were "someone who immersed himself with an unclean object in his hands," thus exiting the מקוה still unclean. In such a case one would have to go to the מקוה again. Even according to the view of the Ramban where בדיעבד he accepts immersion before circumcision; nevertheless, he also states that it is impossible to become Jewish as a male with immersion only. The שרידי אש concurs with the Ramban that circumcision is a non-negotiable requirement in becoming Jewish!

The sources make clear reference to the fact that someone born Jewish who is unable to be circumcised for medical reasons, nevertheless is part of the Jewish people and is "part and parcel" of the Jewish folk and fold. Here, in our case, the *very act of becoming Jewish is precluded* for medical reasons!

The שרידי אש concludes that a potential convert should not be converted where circumcision is impossible for medical reasons. Furthermore, he states that if the potential convert wishes to "take the chance" to undergo circumcision against medical advice, one should not accept him because there is a defaming of God's name if one were to die under circumstances such as these due to circumcision:

> ובהא סליקנא, שאין להתיר בשו״א גירות בטבילה לחוד במי שהמילה סכנה היא לו. ולא עוד, אלא אפילו אם יתרצה להכניס את עצמו לסכנה ולמול, אין לקבלו, לפי שיש בזה חילול השם וסכנה לכלל ישראל אם ח״ו ימות מחמת מילה. ואף שמרן הגאון חתם סופר בתשובותיו יור״ד סי, רמ״ה כתב, שמי שמתו אחיו מחמת מילה רוצה לימול את עצמו רשאי לסכן בנפשו – זה דווקא בישראל. שיש מצוה במילתו ו,שומר מצוה לא ידע דבר רע׳. אבל נכרי, שאין מצוה כלל במילתו, שהרי אינו מחוייב להתגייר, ודאי שאסור לסכנו במילה.

The end of the matter is: one should not permit in any fashion whatsoever, conversion with immersion alone in the case of one where circumcision is a danger to him! Furthermore, even if the individual wishes to possibly endanger himself and undergo this circumcision, one should not accept him as a convert because there is a desecration of God's name in this matter, and a danger to all of Israel should he die because of the circumcision. Even though our master and teacher, the Hatam Sofer, wrote in his responsum section Yoreh De'ah, ch. 245, that one whose brothers died because of circumcision, who wishes to be circumcised is permitted to do so and endanger himself that ruling applied only to a Jew [wanting to be circumcised], in which case it is a mitzvah to circumcise him, since "a person who observes a commandment should know no evil" (Eccles. 8:5); however, in the case of a non-Jew where there is no mitzvah whatsoever in his circumcision in that he is not obligated to convert, it is definitely forbidden to endanger him through circumcision.

Rabbi Kook, of blessed memory, in his work דעת כהן states that one cannot become Jewish without ברית מילה, and the advice given to the potential convert should be to keep the seven Noahide Laws and be counted among the חסידי אומות העולם.

The words of Rabbi Kook are clear:

> וקם דינא דאינו גר עד שימול ויטבול, ודוקא מילה ואחר כך טבילה.... וכל זה שלא מל אי אפשר כלל לטפל בדבר להחשיבו כגר, להשיאו בת ישראל...

הא פשיטא לן שאין לנו לקבלו, ולהשיאו בת ישראל, עד שיכנס לקדושת ישראל כדברי תורה ככל גירי הצדק, במילה וטבילה וקבלת מצוות.

The law is that one does not become a convert until he has been both circumcised and immersed — specifically with circumcision preceding immersion.... As long as he is not circumcised, it is impossible to consider him a convert, or to marry a Jewish woman, until he enters the Jewish people according to the laws of the Torah, like all converts with ritual circumcision, rtual immersion, the acceptance of the mitzvot.

Conclusions

1. Under normal circumstances Jewish law mandates for men who convert to Judaism both circumcision (or הטפת דם ברית if already medically circumcised) and ritual immersion in a proper מקוה, in that order.

2. Secondly, if a man had a serious medical threat to life or health which could possibly be resolved at a later time in one's life, or after some type of treatment, then the conversion is postponed for him until that time or circumstance is reached.

Parenthetically, I would add, that based on the views of stringency of Rabbi Hoffman and the חכמים (the majority) in the Talmud, Rabbi Kook, the שרידי אש as well as a statement conveyed to me by our late professor of codes and rabbinics, Rabbi Dr. Boaz Cohen, of blessed memory, of the Jewish Theological Seminary, in a public lecture on ברית מילה given in 1968 that "one cannot convert without circumcision" and the fact that the Ponivicher does not decide the issue of whether מילה for a גר is טהרה (and one should be מיקל) or איסור ערלה (and one should be מחמיר) that such a conversion must be postponed it until possible resolution of the medical problems at hand.[1]

3. If a man has a serious medical threat to life or health which cannot later be resolved in his life, than he should be advised that acceptance into the Jewish faith through Halakhic conversion is impossible for him, and that he be encouraged to follow the seven Noahide Laws and be considered among the "righteous gentiles" of the world.

---

[1] I recently found the following article in the *Jerusalem Post* Overseas Edition:

"A new technique for removing the foreskin using a laser has prompted a debate on whether it is halakhically permissible for use in circumcisions on babies suffering from hemophilia.

"A doctor and rabbi discuss this issue in a recent issue of *Harefuah*, the journal of the Israel Medical Association. The authors note that according to the Sages, the ברית מילה should not be performed if it could endanger life, as in families suffering from blood-clotting disorders.

"A 12-year-old boy who was diagnosed in Russia with hemophilia arrived in Israel with his parents, who asked that he undergo the procedure using its new ND-Yag laser. Laser surgery involves very little bleeding.

"The authors queried rabbinical arbiters, who hesitated over the problem because the use of lasers as a bloodless alternative to customary circumcision devices could create public pressure for using it on healthy babies.

"The authors concluded that 'apparently, Jewish law allows the use of lasers for circumcision in special cases in which conventional techniques would endanger life. . .[b]ut its use on a daily, ordinary basis remains an open question.'"

It is evident to me that this new laser ברית מילה may in the near future, at least partially change the conclusion of this paper for those individuals unable to undergo a regular circumcision for medical reasons, but able to undergo a laser circumcision. The conclusions reached above remain the same for those unable to undergo laser circumcision should that eventually be fully acceptable in Jewish law.

YD 268:6.1997

Maternal Identity and the Religious Status of Children Born to a Surrogate Mother

Rabbi Aaron L. Mackler

This paper was approved by the CJLS on September 17, 1997, by a vote of fourteen in favor and five abstaining (14-0-5). Voting in favor: Rabbis Kassel Abelson, Ben Zion Bergman, Elliot N. Dorff, Jerome M. Epstein, Samuel Fraint, Baruch Frydman-Kohl, Nechama D. Goldberg, Vernon H. Kurtz, Aaron L. Mackler, Lionel E. Moses, Avram Israel Reisner, Joel E. Rembaum, James S. Rosen, Gordon Tucker, and Gerald Zelizer. Abstaining: Rabbis Shoshana Gelfand, Judah Kogen, Paul Plotkin, Joel Roth, and Elie Kaplan Spitz.

The Committee on Jewish Law and Standards of the Rabbinical Assembly provides guidance in matters of halakhah for the Conservative movement. The individual rabbi, however, is the authority for the interpretation and application of all matters of halakhah.

שאלה

How do we determine maternal identity and religious status for a child born to a surrogate mother?

תשובה

I argue elsewhere that surrogacy cannot be halakhically recommended, and in at least most cases would be forbidden by Jewish law and ethics. Nonetheless, the issue of the status of a child born to a surrogate mother must be addressed for cases where surrogacy does occur. These cases might represent exceptional circumstances that I do not preclude, or people following a more lenient ruling such as that of Rabbi Elie Spitz, or people simply proceeding with surrogacy without necessarily having sought halakhic guidance.[1]

When the surrogate mother is artificially inseminated by the contracting/intended father, it is clear that she is the child's mother in the eyes of halakhah. Her ovum is fertilized in her body, she gestates the child, and she gives birth. I am aware of no halakhic source that claims otherwise. Accordingly, the child's religious status follows that of the (surrogate) mother.

---

[1] See Aaron L. Mackler, "Surrogate Parenting," below, pp. 529-535; Elie Kaplan Spitz, "On The Use of Birth Surrogates," below, pp. 536-557.

Things become more complicated in the case of a gestational surrogate. Here, one woman provides an ovum which is fertilized in vitro and could be seen as the genetic mother. Another woman gestates and gives birth to the child and could be seen as gestational/birth mother. While I will conclude that in such cases (as in all others) halakhah recognizes the birth mother as mother, more of an argument is required.

Intuitions on Maternity

People's gut feelings or intuitions on maternal identity are not halakhically decisive.[2] Still, these can affect the extent to which people are receptive to and convinced by more formal halakhic considerations. More generally, gestation and birth represent powerful experiences of intimacy and nurturing that have great significance. Parents' feelings of attachment at the birth of their children reflect not only awareness of genetic linkage, but also the lived experience of months of physical changes, observations, and care-giving, as well as the intense and miraculous event of birth. The mother's experience has included unique connections of biology, combined with the conscious acceptance of risks and burdens, and emotional and intellectual responses of often surprising power. Perhaps for this reason the Hebrew word for intense and other-regarding love, רחמים, is linked to the word for womb, רחם.

Such acknowledgment of the importance of gestation and birth has been reflected by non-Jewish as well as Jewish writers. Lawyer George Annas, for example, argues that in cases of dispute the relationship of the gestational mother to the child should be recognized as primary, in part because of the extent of her biological and psychological investment in the child.[3] Rosemarie Tong notes a feminist objection to surrogacy, that "such arrangements privilege a possible relationship over an actual one, an abstract intention over concrete experience." Concerns are also expressed with treating persons and relationships as commodities.[4] As Rabbi Spitz notes, not all feminists agree in rejecting surrogacy, but Tong's feminist claims focusing on relationships and responsibilities resonate importantly with general Jewish values. While some thinkers have speculated that a woman's role of gestation and birth might be replaced by an artificial womb, others have speculated that with developments in genetic engineering the role of sperm and eggs in conveying genetic information might be replaced, strengthening the claims of gestation as primary. Both sets of claims are speculative; the important point is to avoid an unwarranted assumption that genetics are somehow essential and gestation and birth somehow accidental to parental identity.[5]

---

[2] Some material in this section may be found as well in my companion paper on "Surrogate Parenting."

[3] George J. Annas, "Death Without Dignity for Commercial Surrogacy: The Case of Baby M," *Hastings Center Report* 18, no. 2 (1988): 23-24.

[4] Rosemarie Tong, "The Overdue Death of a Feminist Chameleon: Taking a Stand on Surrogacy Arrangements," Kenneth D. Alpern, ed., *The Ethics of Reproductive Technology* (New York: Oxford University Press, 1992), pp. 291, 285, 289.

[5] Intuitively it might seem to some that gestation is a relatively straightforward process that science will likely develop ways to replace artificially, while the genetic material of the human genome is hopelessly complex and will elude scientists. On the other hand, the understanding of human genetics and the ability to synthesize genetic material have been progressing rapidly and at accelerating rates, while the capacity to nurture the developing human are only very slowly, if at all, moving later than the first week of embryonic development in vitro, and earlier than about week 23-24 of development for extremely premature infants (New York State Task Force on Life and the Law, *Fetal Extrauterine Survivability* [New York: New York State Task Force on Life and the Law, 1988]). More generally, speculation on future scientific progress is uncertain at best. Writing in 1957, Isaac Asimov was able to envision a world of interstellar space travel and human-like robots, in which most of the process of gestation and human development could be managed artificially, but in vitro fertilization remained elusive and fertilization itself could only take place in the body (*The Naked Sun* [New

The Precedent of a Woman who Converts while Pregnant

A number of halakhic authorities have addressed the issue of maternal identity in cases in which one woman gestates and gives birth to a child deriving in part from the ovum of another. Many of these statements have been summarized in a review article by Rabbi J. David Bleich. These sources suggest that maternal identity is to be determined primarily by gestation and birth.[6]

A central precedent in the discussion is the case of a pregnant woman who converts: even if conception is by a non-Jew, even from an ovum of a non-Jew; and even if the fetus is gestated by a non-Jew and then by a Jew; and a woman who is Jewish gives birth. Halakhah is clear that the child is Jewish. As stated by the Shulhan Arukh (Yoreh De'ah 268:6):

כותית שנתגיירה והיא מעוברת בנה אין צריך טבילה.

> If a non-Jewish woman converts when she is pregnant, her child does not require immersion.

The rationale for this ruling is less clear. For some later authorities, such as Rabbi Isaac Klein, this is simply because the woman's status at the time of birth determines the child's identity. "If a woman converts while pregnant, the child does not require conversion, even if it was conceived before conversion, because at the time of its birth its mother was already Jewish."[7] For Rabbi Yehezkel Landau (*Dagul Merevavah*), however, the reason is that the woman's own immersion in a mikveh at her conversion serves as the immersion required for the child's conversion.[8]

Some support for Landau's interpretation is found in the Talmudic source of the Shulhan Arukh's ruling, Yevamot 78a, where at least one opinion holds that the reason the child's immersion is not required is that the woman's body does not constitute a barrier to the immersion of the fetus. This interpretation becomes less plausible however, in light of another passage, Yevamot 97b, that discusses the status of twins born to a woman who converts while pregnant. (This position was later codified in the Shulhan Arukh, Y.D. 269:4.)

ת"ש שני אחים תאומים גרים וכן משוחררים לא חולצין ולא מייבמין ואין חייבין משום אשת אח. היתה הורתן שלא בקדושה ולידתן בקדושה לא חולצין ולא מייבמין אבל חייבין משום אשת אח. היתה הורתן ולידתן בקדושה הרי הן כישראלים לכל דבריהן.

> Come and hear: twin brothers who are converts, and similarly if they are emancipated slaves, they do not participate in חליצה or ייבום (levirate marriage), and they are not liable for the prohibition

---

York: Doubleday, 1957]). Within a few decades, this apparently elusive element had in fact been achieved, while other developments remained distant.

[6] J. David Bleich, "In Vitro Fertilization: Maternal Identity and Conversion," *Contemporary Halakhic Problems IV* (New York: Ktav, 1995), pp. 237-272; a revised version of an article that appeared in *Tradition* 25, no. 4 (1991): 82-102. As Bleich notes, a few writers have articulated minority positions according to which the child in such cases has no mother, or the genetic mother is primary. As I indicate in the body of the paper, I believe that stronger justification supports the view that has been advocated by most authorities who have addressed these issues, that maternal identity is to be determined primarily by gestation and birth.

[7] Isaac Klein, *A Guide to Jewish Religious Practice* (New York: Jewish Theological Seminary of America, 1979), p. 446. This would seem to be the view of R. Boaz Cohen as well. In a letter dated 5 Dec. 1955 (CJLS Archives) he wrote: "If the woman is converted while she is still pregnant, her children will be born Jewish, otherwise they will need conversion."

[8] *Dagul Merevavah*, on Shulhan Arukh, Y.D. 268:6. Accordingly, Landau suggests that if the בית דין at her conversion did not know that she was pregnant, another immersion might be required.

of marrying a brother's wife. If they were conceived when the woman was not Jewish (lit., "not in holiness") but were born when she was Jewish, they do not participate in חליצה or ייבום, but they are liable for the prohibition of not marrying a brother's wife. If they were conceived and born when the woman was Jewish, they have the status as Jews in all regards.

The first clause reflects the Talmud's understanding that when an individual converts to Judaism, their familial relations are understood to start from a blank slate for purposes of Jewish law; they are considered to be as newly born (תינוק שנולד). But, according to the second clause, the twin brothers born to a woman who converted while pregnant are in a different category. They must be brothers, and Jews, from the moment of birth.[9] Hence, they must be recognized as having the status of Jews simply because of their mother's status at the time of birth. Indeed, Rashi gives this rationale explicitly in his commentary. He explains that the twins do not participate in חליצה or ייבום because these practices apply to brothers with the same father, and their biological father is not technically recognized as their father for these purposes:

אבל חייבין כרת משום אשת אח מן האם שהרי היא כישראלית שילדה בנים.

"But they are liable": for the penalty of excision (כרת) for the prohibition of not marrying a brother's wife, because they are brothers who share the same mother, because she was Jewish when she gave birth.

Klein's rationale for the Jewish status of a child born to a woman who converted while pregnant is supported by, and is virtually a paraphrase of, this explanation.

As surveyed by Bleich, a number of Orthodox authorities have suggested varied understandings of these sources and of the status of children gestated by and born to one woman but deriving in part from the genetic material of another. Among the most significant views:

Rabbi Avraham Yitzhak Halevi Kilav argues that in general the birth mother is decisive for the child's identity. However, there is a difference between "national" relations and "familial" relations. A child's status as Jewish depends on the woman in whose body conception and early development takes place, but if the child is Jewish, the birth mother is decisive for all other purposes. While this provides an ingenious reconciliation of the Talmudic sources, it seems excessively speculative and far-fetched. Kilav does not explicitly address the issue of a genetic mother who provided an ovum that was fertilized in vitro. He might be interpreted to offer some support for the genetic mother's religious status determining that of the child, though the genetic mother would not be considered to be the child's mother for any other purposes. (On the other hand, his discussion of the importance of gestation in accounting for differences between maternal and paternal identity suggests that he might not extend his argument to the case of in vitro fertilization). Kilav specifies that his discussion is only for purposes of theoretical discussion and *pilpul*, and is not intended to offer halakhic guidance.[10]

---

[9] Further casting doubt upon Landau's view, if the brothers are seen as undergoing conversion, either they are not officially Jewish until their circumcision eight days after birth, or one would have to postulate that it is possible for a male to convert to Judaism without circumcision. See Zalman Nehemiah Goldberg, יחוס אמהות בהשתלת עובר ברחם של אחרת, *Tehumin* 5 (5744): 255.

[10] Kilav, מי היא אמו של ילוד, ההורה או היולדת, *Tehumin* 5 (5744): 260-274.

For Rabbi Moshe Sternbuch, the birth mother simply is the mother, for all halakhic purposes. In fact, the child could marry children of the woman who provided the ovum, for they would in no way be considered siblings. Rabbi Sternbuch understands the discussion of immersion not to involve conversion to become Jewish, but rather a purification process to remove what he perceives as "impurity of gentileness" (טומאת עכו"ם). According to this view, a child born to a non-Jewish gestational mother would not be Jewish. Since Conservative Jewish authorities (and many others) reject his understanding of "impurity of gentileness," the child's status would simply follow that of the birth mother in all cases.[11]

Rabbi Moses Soloveitchik discusses a number of views, including positions that the mother is the woman who gestated the fetus on its fortieth day of development, or the first woman to gestate the fetus on or after the fortieth day without another maternal relationship having been already established. For cases such as gestational surrogacy where fertilization occurs in vitro, the birth mother's status would be decisive, the genetic mother's irrelevant. Similarly, in the case of ovum donation the birth mother would be recognized as mother.[12]

For Rabbi Zalman Nehemiah Goldberg, the maternal relationship is determined by the mother who gives birth. Another woman in whose body fertilization and early gestation took place would not have halakhic status as mother. All the more so, a woman who provides an ovum that is fertilized in vitro would not have halakhic status as mother. If conception takes place in the body of a non-Jew from her ovum, and a Jewish woman then gestates the fetus and gives birth, the child would be Jewish according to the view that the fetus's status is subservient to the mother's (עובר ירך עמו). For those who hold the view that the fetus's status is not subservient, conversion should take place, but the child would then be regarded as the child of the birth mother in all regards. According to this view, a child born to a non-Jewish gestational surrogate would not be Jewish. In the case of ovum donation from a non-Jew to a Jew, the birth mother would be recognized as mother. Conversion would not be required for those agreeing that עובר ירך עמו, but should occur for those disagreeing with this view.[13]

The Talmudic sources and ensuing halakhic discussion are thus rather complicated. Virtually all authorities would agree, however, that birth (or gestation) represents the prime determinant of maternal status and that a child born to a non-Jewish gestational surrogate would require conversion to Judaism. In my judgment, Klein's position, while not addressing all of the questions raised by the Talmudic sources, makes the most sense for deriving a conclusion for practical halakhah. The Talmudic sources may well simply reflect differing views among Talmudic authorities, which contributed to differing views among halakhic authorities. Klein's view certainly represents the most authoritative statement on this issue by a Conservative authority to this point.

Additional Considerations

Halakhah recognizes the gestational/birth mother as mother in all regards. The above discussion of cases involving a woman who converts while pregnant provides the key halakhic evidence. At the same time, a number of additional considerations provide further support

---

[11] Sternbuch, תינוק מבחנה, *Bishvilei Harefuah* 8 (5747/1986): pp. 29-37. See Elliot N. Dorff, "Artificial Insemination, Egg Donation, and Adoption," below, pp. 496-497.

[12] Joseph B. Soloveitchik, בדין התינוק המבחנה, *Or Hamizrah* (1980/5741): 122-128.

[13] Goldberg, pp. 245-259.

for this position. While I do not claim that each of these by itself would be decisive, together I believe they are compelling.

1. Halakhah views the status of a fetus as subservient to that of the woman. As the Talmudic phrase עובר ירך עמו, (Hullin 58a) is explicated by Rabbi David Feldman: "The fetus is deemed a 'part of the mother' rather than an independent entity." While this is not the unanimous view of all halakhic authorities, it seems to be the most common. This has been the position of all Conservative authorities who have addressed the issue and has helped to shape Conservative positions on abortion.[14] Accordingly, the status of the gestating woman determines the status of the fetus, and the status of the birth mother determines the status of the child.

2. The above argument is strengthened by the fact that embryo transfer takes place well within the first forty days of development, and in fact within the first few days of embryonic development, when the Talmudic designation of the embryo/fetus as "mere fluid" (מיא בעלמא, Yevamot 69b) most clearly applies. The embryo at this stage consists of only a few cells, without any specialization of cells or embryonic structure.[15]

3. The halakhic identification of a firstborn son as one who "opens the womb" offers some additional support for defining the birth mother as the child's mother.[16]

4. Some have suggested that one reason for basing Jewish identity on matrilineal descent is that the child's mother can always be identified. This consideration would support determining the child's status on the basis of the birth mother.[17]

5. Some (non-Jewish) thinkers have advocated identifying the birth mother as mother on policy grounds, in order to best assure the welfare of newborns. As George Annas argues, the birth mother "will of necessity be present at birth and immediately thereafter to care for the child."[18] These considerations would be important to halakhah under the rubric of הטוב והישר (Deut. 6:18), the injunction to do "the right and the good."

6. Targum Yonatan (Gen. 30:21) and Rabbi Samuel Edels (Maharsha, commenting on Niddah 31a) relate that, prior to the birth of Joseph and Dinah, Leah was pregnant with a male, and Rachel with a female. Leah prayed that Rachel would give birth to the male, and God switched the embryos. Dinah, conceived by Rachel but born to Leah, is considered Leah's child; Joseph, conceived by Leah but born to Rachel, is considered Rachel's child. Abstracting from the issue of the historical accuracy of this account, it does reflect rabbinic understandings and assumptions regarding maternity. This offers some support for the view that the status of the birth mother determines the child's identity.[19]

Accordingly, the woman who gestates and gives birth to the child is to be treated as the child's mother for purposes of Jewish law, including the determination of Jewish iden-

---

[14] David M. Feldman, "Abortion: The Jewish View," in *PCJLS 80-85*, p. 11. The phrase is also cited in the תשובות of R. Robert Gordis, "Abortion: Major Wrong or Basic Right," ibid., p. 22; and R. Isaac Klein, "A Teshuvah on Abortion," ibid., p. 33.

[15] See David M. Feldman, *Birth Control in Jewish Law*, 3d ed. (Jerusalem: n.p., 1995), p. 266.

[16] See Exodus 13, and Dorff, below, p. 497. It should be noted that this argument serves only in a secondary, supportive role in this paper. If a child were born by Caesarean section, for which halakhah would not apply the category of opening the womb (פטר רחם), this would in no way affect the recognition of the birth mother as the child's mother.

[17] See, e.g., Walter Jacob, ed., *Contemporary American Reform Responsa* (New York: Central Conference of American Rabbis, 1987), p. 63; and Shaye J.D. Cohen, "The Origins of the Matrilineal Principle in Rabbinic Law," *AJS Review* 10 (1985): 40-41, who reports but argues against this view.

[18] Annas, pp. 23-24.

[19] See Bleich, pp. 247-48; Dorff, below, pp. 496-497.

tity. If a Jewish woman gives birth to a child, that child should be considered Jewish, whether the egg came from a Jewish or non-Jewish woman. If a non-Jewish woman gives birth to a child, that child would not be Jewish (and so would require conversion in order to be recognized as a Jew), whether the egg came from a Jewish or non-Jewish woman.

A less satisfactory alternative position to identifying the birth mother as mother, which might also be compatible with halakhic precedent, would be to recognize both the genetic and birth mothers as having maternal status: even if birth is the primary determinant of maternal identity, the genetic mother would be treated as mother because of doubt, or in order to follow a more stringent position. For the case of surrogacy, this would lead to little practical difference. As I argue elsewhere, in a paper approved by the Committee on Jewish Law and Standards (CJLS), this would prove far less satisfactory for the much more common practice of ovum donation and in vitro fertilization (IVF). The alternative is in some ways attractive at the theoretical level, for it would formally recognize the contributions of both women to the child's birth. At the practical level, however, it would impose unnecessary complications for the use of donated ova. If an anonymously donated egg were used, the presumption (outside of Israel) would be that the donor is not Jewish; accordingly, the child (born to a Jewish mother) would require conversion in order to be fully Jewish. Moreover, the child would have obligations of honoring her or his (genetic) mother (כיבוד אב ואם) that likely would be unfulfilled. Furthermore, recognizing only the birth mother and not additionally the genetic mother as mother for purposes of halakhah enables Jews to donate eggs and embryos, an important consideration in light of Jewish ethics and the halakhic mandate of דרכי שלום.[20]

While the genetic mother should not be viewed as mother halakhically, genetic siblings should not marry (or engage in sexual relations with) one another (as opposed to the opinion of Moshe Sternbuch). The most basic reason for this prohibition is that offspring of a consanguineous union face a high risk of genetically-based disease; this concern alone would suffice to support a rabbinic prohibition. Combining this ruling with those found in R. Dorff's paper, one comes to the unsurprising conclusion that one should not marry (or engage in sexual relations with) children of one's genetic, gestational, or social parents. Technically, the prohibition would be Toraitic with regard to children of one's genetic father and birth mother, and would reflect the category of secondary relations (שניות) for children of other parents.[21]

Intentions as Determinative?

Rabbi Elie Kaplan Spitz has argued that intentions can be determinative for maternal identity. He has done so both in an academic paper, and in a thoughtful paper prepared for the CJLS but subsequently withdrawn from consideration.[22] In these papers, Rabbi Spitz agrees that a child born to an "ovum-surrogate," who provides genetic material as

---

[20] See Mackler, "In Vitro Fertilization," below, pp. 524-526. Reporting on procedures conducted in 1993, the Society for Assisted Reproductive Technology notes 2,766 IVF procedures using donated eggs, leading to 716 deliveries, and an additional 625 procedures using donated embryos, leading to 108 deliveries. The paper also reports 246 procedures involving gestational surrogacy, resulting in 78 deliveries (Society for Assisted Reproductive Technology, American Society for Reproductive Medicine, "Assisted Reproductive Technology in the United States and Canada: 1993 Results Generated from The Society for Reproductive Medicine/Society for Assisted Reproductive Technology Registry," *Fertility and Sterility* 64 [1995]: 13-21).

[21] See Dorff, below, pp. 476-477; S.A. Even HaEzer 15.

[22] "The Religious Identity of Offspring Born to a Surrogate," submitted to the CJLS but withdrawn, 1997; "'Through Her I Too Shall Bear a Child': Birth Surrogates in Jewish Law," *Journal of Religious Ethics* 24 (1996): 89-91.

well as gestation and birth, follows the status of that mother. He argues, however, that in the case of a gestational mother, the child's status should follow that of the genetic/intended social mother instead of that of the gestational/birth mother. In advancing this position he relies on an argument of David Kraemer, that parents' feelings about their fetus/child-to-be can affect its status in thinking about abortion.[23]

In my best judgment, halakhah cannot support such an exception. First, the precedents supporting the status of the gestational/birth mother in determining identity are powerful. As well, Kraemer's arguments for the importance of feelings in thinking about abortion do not translate easily to determining halakhic status. Kraemer presents his paper on abortion as exemplifying an approach to Jewish ethics that is sharply distinguished from halakhah; he seeks "to do ethics with traditional sources without accepting the ways of Halacha." On the specific issue of the status of the fetus, Kraemer argues that this should depend on the parents' feelings; the status "may change as a function of our emotional connections to it."[24] His claim that decisions about abortion hinge in large part on subjective feelings, known fully only to the individual and to God, is plausible and thought-provoking. To base the religious status of a child on such factors is more troubling. The problems are clearest in cases of ambivalence or dispute. For example, what if a gestational surrogate becomes subjectively convinced at some point in pregnancy that the child is really hers and should be raised by her, and gives birth with this subjective intentionality in mind? We would have a situation in which factors indicating the child's status would be evenly divided. Things would be further complicated if the genetic/social mother's feelings were ambivalent. In real life, subjective feelings and emotional connections are likely to vary widely. That is one reason why such factors generally are not and should not be decisive in determining parental identity and status.

An alternative position, which I do not believe Rabbi Spitz advocates, would determine religious status on the basis of contract. In U.S. contract law, "intent" can be understood in a technical sense, as expressed in the wording of contracts rather than the thoughts and feelings of the persons involved. Kraemer's example of giving a gift to one's fetus, however, argues against such contractual intent being decisive. One generally cannot give a gift to a fetus, whatever language is used, unless these emotional and subjective feelings are present. More general halakhic grounds argue against defining parenthood and status on the basis of contract. One cannot buy or sell, or achieve by intent and formal agreement, the status of parent, child, kohen, Jew, etc. Such attribution of status would diverge more strongly from traditional precedent than does the Reform movement's acceptance of patrilineal descent. It also unacceptably treats relations as commodities.

Other practical difficulties can be anticipated as well. Imagine the case of two women (perhaps a lesbian couple) who decide to have children together by having the ova from one fertilized in vitro and gestated by the other. They plan for one of them to assume primary custody for the first child born, and the other to assume custody for the next. One woman is Jewish, and the other is not. According to the proposal (once) advocated by Rabbi Spitz, this could result in the birth of twins, one of which was Jewish from birth, the other of which was not Jewish. I do not believe that such a result would be an acceptable development for halakhah.[25]

---

[23] David Kraemer, "Jewish Ethics and Abortion," *Tikkun* 8, no. 1 (1993): 55-58 and 77.

[24] Ibid., pp. 55 and 58.

[25] I am grateful to Rabbi Avram Israel Reisner for raising this issue.

In addition, the reasons given in Rabbi Spitz's paper for this dramatic change in halakhah do not seem compelling. He argues that requiring conversion for a child born to a non-Jewish gestational mother would offend the genetic/social parents. The conversion of infants, and ritual circumcision performed in this context, are common: for example, in cases involving adoption, or children born to a Jewish husband and non-Jewish wife who are raised as Jews. These ceremonies are joyful, welcoming, and affirming, especially when guided by rabbis with thoughtfulness and sensitivity. These children are really the couple's children, as Rabbi Elliot Dorff argues in his discussion of adoption.[26]

Finally, Rabbi Spitz argues that to follow the birth mother in determining status would make Judaism seem "behind the times" to parents who live in states where the genetic/social parents are recognized as sole parents. Such states remain in the minority.[27] It could be argued that to disregard the status of the gestational/birth mother in states where this is legally important would make Judaism seem less respectful of women's experience of gestation and birth (or of Jewish tradition) than secular authorities. Determining Jewish status using different criteria in different states of the U.S., not to mention other countries, is clearly unacceptable. Most basically, however, halakhah cannot follow דינא דמלכותא דינא (deference to civil law) in determining the religious status of children.

Conclusion

Halakhah recognizes the woman who gestates and gives birth to a child as the child's mother. Accordingly, the religious status of a child follows that of the gestational/birth mother, in cases involving surrogacy as in all other cases. Children born to a non-Jewish surrogate would require conversion to be halakhically recognized as Jewish. Rabbis should display personal and pastoral sensitivity in such cases.[28]

---

[26] Dorff, below, pp. 501-504; Avram Israel Reisner, "On the Conversion of Adopted and Patrilineal Children," *PCJLS 86-90*, pp. 157-183.

[27] Furthermore, states currently recognizing the genetic mother as mother in cases of gestational surrogacy could well change. In California, the minority report of a legislative committee, supported by six of its members, recommended identifying the genetic mother as mother in such cases; but the majority report, supported by twelve members, argued that the birth mother should be recognized as mother irrebuttably ("Commercial and Noncommercial Surrogate Parenting," a report to the California Legislature from the Joint Legislative Committee on Surrogate Parenting, 1990).

[28] For their suggestions and thoughtful insights which have contributed greatly to this paper, I would like to thank Lorraine Newman Mackler, and members of the Committee on Jewish Law and Standards, including my fellow members of the Subcommittee on Biomedical Ethics: Rabbis Kassel Abelson, Elliot N. Dorff, Shoshana Gelfand, Avram Israel Reisner, Joel Roth and Elie Kaplan Spitz.

YD 268:12.1995

THE RETURN OF SECOND GENERATION APOSTATES

Rabbi Gerald L. Zelizer

This paper was approved by the CJLS on June 14, 1995, by a vote of thirteen in favor and five opposed (13-5-0). Voting in favor: Rabbis Kassel Abelson, Ben Zion Bergman, Stephanie Dickstein, Elliot N. Dorff, Myron S. Geller, Arnold M. Goodman, Susan Grossman, Judah Kogen, Alan B. Lucas, Aaron L. Mackler, Lionel E. Moses, Gordon Tucker, and Gerald Zelizer. Voting against: Rabbis Samuel Fraint, Mayer Rabinowitz, Avram Israel Reisner, Joel E. Rembaum, and Joel Roth.

The Committee on Jewish Law and Standards of the Rabbinical Assembly provides guidance in matters of halakhah for the Conservative movement. The individual rabbi, however, is the authority for the interpretation and application of all matters of halakhah.

שאלה

May a member of the Rabbinical Assembly officiate at the marriage of a person born of a Jewish mother who was raised in the church but who now disavows that affiliation?

תשובה

This question should be seen in the context of halakhic literature treating the general matter of rabbinic officiation at the marriage of an apostate who disavows the apostasy and proceed by inference to the child of an apostate. The first issue has already been dealt with both in the classic halakhic literature and by the CJLS.

Background

The sources consider the קידושין of a Jew who committed apostasy, notwithstanding that act of apostasy, to be valid:

> ישראל מומר שקידש קדושיו קדושין גמורים, וצריכה ממנו גט. ואפילו זרעו שהוליד משהמיר אם קידש אותו זרע ישראלית, קדושיו קדושין.

> An Israelite who committed apostasy and then married, his marriage is valid and necessitates a גט when divorcing; and even when his offspring, born after his apostasy, marries a Jewish woman, his marriage is valid.[1]

---

[1] E.H. 44:9.

This halakhah is based on discussion in the Gemara of Yevamot 47b and B'horot 30b the conclusion of which was subsequently summarized in a responsum of Rashi that:

המשומד הרי הוא כישראל חשוד לכל דבר שאמר. חטא ישראל אע"פ
שחטא, ישראל הוא – ואין לחלקי מידת ישראל.

> An apostate is regarded as a suspect Israelite in all matters, because it is said that "[a]n Israelite who has sinned is regarded as an Israelite, and we do not separate him from the religion of Israel, [and his marriage is valid]."[2]

It is noteworthy how Rashi changed his understanding and explanation of the phrase, "An Israelite who has sinned is regarded as an Israelite." The phrase originated in the Talmudic statement: אמר רבי אבא בר זבדא: אע"פ שחטא ישראל הוא – "Rabbi Abba Bar Zabda said, even though he sins, he remains an Israelite."[3] Rashi *ad locum* quotes the Biblical proof text: Since it does not say that in Joshua, chapter 7, "the people sinned," but rather, "the people committed a trespass (וימעלו), concerning the sacred thing," קדושה still is applied to the people of Israel. Rashi's commentary in Sanhedrin therefore explains the classic phrase as applying to the *collectivity* of Israel and not to *individual* Israelites.

Jacob Katz posits that the change in interpretation from the collective to the individual occurred because by the time of Rashi, apostasy had generally become compulsory.[4] In order to ease the readmission of those forced to apostatize to Christianity, Rashi shifted his own understanding of the original source. In contrast to the earlier Gaonic tradition, Rashi began to emphasize the power of תשובה for the errant Jew: "An *individual* Israelite who has sinned is nevertheless regarded as an Israelite."[5]

Application of Halakhic Sources to the Apostate

If Katz's general thesis is correct, then we have a case when the original reason for the law may no longer be valid and thus we are free to alter the halakhah, when compelling new circumstances warrant.

Jews who apostatize today are no longer coerced, but do so willingly. The reasoning of Rashi which stimulated lenient treatment of apostates is no longer a basis to regard the קידושין of a contemporary apostate as automatically valid, or for a rabbi to "solemnize" that marriage by officiating.

What should be done with such a person who wished to marry back into the Jewish community? The Shulhan Arukh explains:

ואפילו חזר ועבד עבודת כוכבים, הרי הוא כישראל מומר שקידושיו
קידושין.

> And even when he reverted and worshipped idols he is to be

---

[2] Responsa of Rashi: no. 173.
[3] B. Sanhedrin 44a: ישראל אף על פי שחטא.
[4] *Gershom G. Scholem Jubilee Volume* (Jerusalem: Hebrew University, 1958), pp. 77-91 (in Hebrew).
[5] Emphasis mine. This reversal even went so far as: "An apostate kohen who did teshuvah shall participate in dukhanen and shall be called first to the Torah, for if you rule that he shall not participate in dukhanen and not be called first to the Torah, you are weakening the hands of the repentant and it is not correct to do this." Jacob Katz, quoting the Teshuvot of Rabbenu Gershom M'Or Hagolah as followed by Rashi, cited in ישראל אף על פי שחטא in *Scholem Jubilee Volume*, p. 87.

regarded as a suspect Israelite for all matters and his marriage is valid.[6]

To which the Rama adds:

ישראל מומר שעשה תשובה אינו צריך לטבל רק מדרבנן יש לו לטבול. ולקבל עליו דבר בפני שלשה.

When an apostate Israelite repents of his or her apostasy, there is no need to require טבילה, but מדרבנן he should immerse himself and accept upon himself his statement of sincerity before a bet din.

Clearly, a formal ceremony of readmission is a Rabbinic, not a Toraitic stricture. But in our time, because the circumstances prompting Rashi's leniency are no longer valid, we should adhere to the rabbinic חומרה and insist on טבילה and bet din (and circumcision or הטפת דם ברית if it was not done at birth or at a previous conversion) prior to the marriage of such a person to another Jew.

Perhaps it was these considerations which prompted Rabbi Boaz Cohen to write in 1949:

> A repentant apostate must first undergo immersion in a מקווה, and then make a solemn declaration affirming his sincere desire to return to his original faith and to abide by the precepts of Judaism. This avowal must be made in the presence of a bet din consisting of the rabbi and two prominent laymen of the congregation. This טבילה is done without the ברכה.[7]

The Child of an Apostate Raised With Full Commitment and Socialization in a Church

On the other hand, the circumstance of the child of an apostate, raised in the Christian Church is different. A distinction should be made between two categories; the child who, in the judgment of the מרא דאתרא has been raised in the church with full commitment — i.e. in most cases, including baptism and/or Christian education.[8] On the other hand, there are children of apostates who, in the judgment of the מרא דאתרא, have accompanied their parents to a church but have not experienced full and formal socialization into the church. In the former case, since they have formally passed into another religion, a formal ceremony of readmission into Judaism would be required. This would include מקווה, and bet din, for a female. For a male who was uncircumcised, both מקווה and ברית מילה, which have been declared a Standard of Rabbinic Practice in the case of conversion, are required.[9] In the

---

[6] Y.D. 268:12.

[7] Committee on Jewish Law and Standards, 1949, with Digest of Answers (circular to Rabbinical Assembly membership, CJLS archives).

[8] It should be understood that various churches designate different stages at which the "unchurched" becomes "churched" and accepted into the particular Christian community. In one church acceptance depends on baptism in childhood; whereas in another on baptism as an adult; whereas still a third church may require an additional educational component. Because this threshold varies, this teshuvah uses the generalized wording, "full and formal socialization into a church," which will differ according to denomination and should be gauged by the מרא דאתרא. In addition, even though the teshuvah addresses apostasy into the Christian church, its arguments and conclusions also apply to apostasy into any sect within Christianity or for that matter, any religion or sect other than Judaism.

[9] Joel Roth and Akiba Lubow, "A Standard of Rabbinic Practice Regarding Determination of Jewish Identity," *PCJLS 80-85*, p. 178.

instance when there has been only an earlier medical circumcision, then the male should undergo הטפת דם ברית. On the other hand, in cases where the male had ברית מילה as a child prior to the apostasy, then only מקווה and bet din are necessary for readmission.

A reality in our society is that some of these children of apostates who have been socialized into the church, may have already married Jewish spouses. In spite of the requirement of halakhic reentry requirements, their marriages to Jews, בדיעבד, should be considered as תופסין and a גט is necessary in the instance of divorce from that spouse. Also, after the reentry of the Jewish partner, the couple should also be encouraged to have a proper marriage, כדת וכדין.

The Child of an Apostate Raised Without Full Commitment and Socialization in a Church

In contrast, when a child has not experienced full and formal socialization into the church, a procedure of readmission, although necessary, need not be so halakhically stringent.

Since with apostasy itself, the requirement of טבילה and bet din is מדרבנן, there is no reason to be as demanding with the child of a Jewish mother who is an apostate. This child should be regarded in the halakhic category of: תינוק שנשבה בין הגויים – "a child who is in captivity against his or her will among the gentiles." There is ample precedent in Jewish law to be more lenient in this situation than with someone who knowingly and intentionally violates Jewish law and tradition.

Thus, the Mishnah states that one who knows the commandment of Shabbat and violates it with multiple transgressions must bring a קרבן חטאת, a sin offering for each and every Shabbat violation. On the other hand: כל השוכח עיקר שבת ועשה מלאכות הרבה בשבתות הרבה אינו חייב אלא חטאת אחת – "A person who is unaware of the essence of Shabbat, and violates it with many individual violations, is liable for only one (general) sin offering."[10]

In the subsequent discussion in the Gemara, Rav and Shmuel contend that the transgressor in the latter case is responsible for only one sin offering because he or she is as a תינוק שנשבה בין הגויים. A more lenient opinion of Rabbi Yohanan and Resh Lakish contends that: דוקא הכיר ולבסוף שכח אבל תינוק שנשבה בין הנכרים וגר שנתגייר לבין הנכרים פטור. "The requirement of one sin offering applies only when one knew of Shabbat and forgot, but a child who is captive among the gentiles, or a proselyte who became converted in the midst of gentiles (so that they never knew of Shabbat) is exempt."[11] The halakhah follows Rav and Shmuel, but according to both opinions the principle is that the child of an apostate is treated with greater leniency than one who is aware of the structure of Shabbat and violates it.

This leniency is codified in Rambam who states that such a person: אינו חייב אלא חטאת אחת שהכל שגגה אחת – "He is liable for only one sin offering since all individuall transgressions result from one inadvertent error."[12]

One who was born of a Jewish mother, but subsequently raised within a church without full commitment and socialization to that church, should be regarded as תינוק שנשבה בין הגויים. If that person disavows the church affiliation, and wished to marry a Jew, he or she should be allowed to do so without the totality of ceremonial encumbrance required of an apostate. It is important that the מרא דאתרא designate some formal tran-

---

[10] B. Shabbat 67b.

[11] B. Shabbat 68b.

[12] M.T. Hilkhot Sh'gagot 7:2.

sition back into Judaism. מקווה is preferable. However, since מקווה is not required מדאורייתא, it may be substituted by other affirming acts, such as an educational program, similar to that of a convert; a letter of renunciation of the former religion and accompanying affirmation of faith in Judaism, and/or the recitation of the שמע before the ארון קודש. In our Movement we are aggressive in seeking to convert to Judaism those who are sincere and eligible for conversion. Simultaneously, we are attempting to recoup those born of Jewish ancestry whose parents have led them astray. Since those children of apostates are still technically Jewish, they should undergo symbolic acts of reentry into Judaism, but the מרא דאתרא may be flexible and creative in the specific nature of those acts. Of course, in the case of a male, he must undergo the essential ברית מילה or הטפת דם ברית, if not previously done.

Conclusion

The CJLS has already ruled that an apostate seeking readmission into Judaism should undergo טבילה, מקווה and bet din (and ברית מילה or הטפת דם ברית when male, when not previously done). The child of an apostate who in the judgement of the מרא דאתרא has been formally committed to a church should undergo the same halakhic procedure when seeking readmission to Judaism and marriage to a Jew. The child of an apostate who, in the judgement of the מרא דאתרא was not formally committed to the Christian church should be resocialized into Judaism through any one or a combination of reentry mechanisms, preferably מקווה. Alternative possibilities which are acceptable are, a letter renouncing the former faith and affirming Judaism, the reading of the שמע before the ארון קודש, and an educational program such as we utilize with prospective converts. When this child is male, he must undergo ברית מילה or הטפת דם ברית, if not previously done. Once these requirements are fulfilled, the returnee is eligible for all obligations and rights of Judaism and the rabbi may officiate at the marriage of that person to a Jew. Of course, the child of a male apostate and a gentile woman who was raised in another religion, must undergo conversion through our standard procedure before the rabbi may solemnize his or her marriage to a Jew.

YD 268:12.1995

Official Use of "God"

Rabbi Kassel Abelson

This paper was approved by the CJLS on May 19, 1993, by a vote of twenty-four in favor (24-0-0). Voting in favor: Rabbis Kassel Abelson, Ben Zion Bergman, Stanley Bramnick, Elliot N. Dorff, Jerome M. Epstein, Ezra Finkelstein, Samuel Fraint, Myron S. Geller, Arnold M. Goodman, Susan Grossman, Jan Caryl Kaufman, Reuven Kimelman, Judah Kogen, Vernon H. Kurtz, Aaron L. Mackler, Lionel E. Moses, Paul Plotkin, Mayer Rabinowitz, Avram Israel Reisner, Joel E. Rembaum, Chaim Rogoff, Joel Roth, Gerald Skolnik, and Gordon Tucker.

The Committee on Jewish Law and Standards of the Rabbinical Assembly provides guidance in matters of halakhah for the Conservative movement. The individual rabbi, however, is the authority for the interpretation and application of all matters of halakhah.

שאלה

Should the different branches of the Conservative movement write out the full word "God," or employ the hyphenation "G-d" in their publications?

תשובה

The Rabbis, basing themselves on Deut. 12:3-4, deduced that it is forbidden to erase the name of God from a written document. Since any paper upon which God's name was written might be discarded and thus "erased," the Rabbis forbade explicitly writing the name of God, except in holy books. And provisions were made for the proper disposal of such books. However, it is clear from the Talmud (Shevuot 35a-b) that the prohibition applies only to seven Biblical names of God and not to other names or attributes of God which may be freely written. The prohibition was later codified by Maimonides (see M.T. Yesodei HaTorah 6:1-2).

Shabbetai b. Meir Hakohen states that the prohibition of erasure of the Divine names applies only to the names in Hebrew but not in the vernacular (see Siftei Kohen to Shulhan Arukh, Y.D. 179:8, and see also Avraham Tzvi Hirsch Eisenstadt in his Pithei Teshuvah to Y.D. 276:9). However Jehiel Michael Epstein in his Arukh Hashulhan (H.M. 27:3) opposes the practice of writing the Divine name even in the vernacular in correspondence. As a result, the custom has grown among some ritually strict Jews not to write the word God or any other name of God in full, even in the vernacular. The practice of using circumlocutions or hyphenations in the vernacular is not universal even among the most observant Jews.

Conclusion

The practice of writing the full word "God" and other names of God in the vernacular has clear precedent and justification in the halakhah. It is therefore permissible, for our national Conservative organizations, to follow this practice.

YD 282.1997

DISPLAY OF A PASUL TORAH IN A MUSEUM CASE

Rabbi Kassel Abelson

This paper was approved by the CJLS on June 4, 1997, by a vote of nineteen in favor and one abstaining (19-0-1). Voting in favor: Rabbis Kassel Abelson, Ben Zion Bergman, Elliot N. Dorff, Samuel Fraint, Shoshana Gelfand, Myron S. Geller, Nechama D. Goldberg, Arnold M. Goodman, Susan Grossman, Judah Kogen, Vernon H. Kurtz, Alan B. Lucas, Aaron L. Mackler, Paul Plotkin, Avram Israel Reisner, James S. Rosen, Joel Roth, Elie Kaplan Spitz, and Gerald Zelizer. Abstaining: Rabbi Joel E. Rembaum.

The Committee on Jewish Law and Standards of the Rabbinical Assembly provides guidance in matters of halakhah for the Conservative movement. The individual rabbi, however, is the authority for the interpretation and application of all matters of halakhah.

שאלה

Is it permitted to display a pasul Sefer Torah in a museum case in a place of honor and dignity as a reminder of the Holocaust?

תשובה

All Hebrew books have a measure of holiness if they contain the name of God. However, the Sefer Torah is considered especially sacred because it not only contains the name of God, it is considered to be the word of God, and it plays a central role in the Jewish worship service.

The Sefer Torah in the Synagogue

The writing of a Sefer Torah is carefully prescribed to assure both sanctity and accuracy.[1] The כבוד, the honor and dignity, of the Sefer Torah is of great concern.[2] Its כבוד is assured by keeping it in a special container, the ארון הקודש (Holy Ark), except when it is in active use. Care is taken not to drop the Torah. Should it be dropped, the person who dropped the Torah is required to fast. According to some traditions, those who see a Torah fall are also required to fast.[3] The fasting serves to impress the congregation with the sacredness of the Sefer Torah.

---

[1] Rambam, M.T. Hilkhot Sefer Torah, ch. 7-10. See also Y.D. 270-278.

[2] An entire chapter of the Yoreh De'ah, Y.D. 282, describes in detail different ways in which the Sefer Torah must be shown honor and its dignity preserved. I have chosen to describe only a few of the more common ways.

[3] Isaac Klein, *A Guide to Jewish Religious Practice* (New York: Jewish Theological Seminary, 1979), p. 253. Rabbi Klein cites the Kitsur Shulhan Arukh 28:12; Magen Avraham to O.H. 44, n. 5.

Keeping a congregation conscious of the sacredness of the Sefer Torah was a constant challenge, as witness the condemnation of people talking, leaving the synagogue in the middle of the Torah reading,[4] or failing to close the Sefer Torah upon departure. It should be noted that the struggle to assure the reverent attention of the congregation during the Torah reading continues in our day.

The Sefer Torah Elsewhere

A possible detriment to the כבוד (dignity) of the Sefer Torah would arise if it were casually moved from place to place. Custom permits the moving of a Torah for services but sets limits:

1. An appropriate Ark, closet, or other storage must be prepared in advance.

2. The Torah must be read, at the new location, at least three times before it is returned. Hence, if it is to be read at a *shivah* מנין in a home, the practice has arisen of having מנחה services on Shabbat at the home of the mourner so as to use the Torah three times.[5]

Individuals may own a Sefer Torah. However, if a Sefer Torah is not kept in the synagogue, but in a home or elsewhere, it may not be kept in a bedroom (where conjugal relations take place). It must be stored in an appropriate container which will assure its honor and dignity.[6]

A פסול *Sefer Torah*

The Rambam makes note of twenty factors which would disqualify a Sefer Torah from being read at a service, such as: written on skin of a non-כשר animal, an untanned skin, skin that had been tanned without the express purpose of being used as a Sefer Torah, or even if a single letter was omitted, or a single letter was so marred that it cannot be read, etc.

Such scrolls need not be put into a גניזה (hidden). The Rambam holds that such פסול Torahs still have a purpose. They can be used for educational purposes. However it must be noted they do not possess, and never had, the sanctity of a Sefer Torah.

> עשרים דברים הן שכל אחד מהן פוסל את ספר תורה. ואם נעשה בו אחד
> מהן הרי הוא כחומש מן החומשים שמלמדים בהן התינוקות ואין בו קדושת
> ספר תורה, ואין קורין בו ברבים.

> There are twenty factors, any one of which disqualifies a scroll of the law. If any of these occurs, the scroll is like one of the books of the Pentateuch out of which children are taught. It does not possess the sanctity of a scroll of the law, and is not used for public reading.[7]

A Sefer Torah that once had been כשר but is found to be פסול (defective) can no longer be read in the synagogue service. It must be repaired as soon as possible. If it is so worn or torn that it can no longer be repaired, it is not casually discarded.

---

[4] B. Berakhot 8a.

[5] J. David Bleich, *Contemporary Halakhic Problems* (New York: Ktav and Yeshiva University Press, 1977), pp. 67-69. Rabbi Bleich discusses the moving of a Sefer Torah for services. I only cite moving a Sefer Torah to a house of mourning because it is the most common reason for moving a Torah in our congregations.

[6] *Pesikta deRav Kahana*, 14, and B. Megillah 22a. See also the interesting note in *Talmud El Am Berakhot*, p. 148, entitled "The Torah Scroll."

[7] M.T. Hilkhot Sefer Torah 10:1.

It is disposed of in a way that will assure that it not desecrated.[8] In some communities it is buried in a cemetery, near the grave of a scholar if possible. The Shulhan Arukh states:

ספר תורה שבלה מניחין אותו בכלי חרס וגונזין אותו בקבר תלמיד חכם.

A worn-out Sefer Torah is placed in a clay vessel and buried near the grave of a scholar.[9]

In other communities they are placed in a גניזה (a designated storage room) in the synagogue. The גניזה in the synagogue in Cairo, found by Solomon Schechter, had several centuries of worn Hebrew books and documents and serves as a rich source of information for scholars. The common practice in our communities is to bury worn-out scrolls and other ספרי קודש (holy books) in our cemeteries.

Torahs of the Holocaust

The Nazis collected Sifrei Torah from despoiled, burning or water soaked synagogues. The Nazis did not destroy them but stored them near Prague. The reason, some say, was to establish a museum after the war, which would record the culture of an extinct race, destroyed by the Nazis.

Some 1,100 Sifrei Torah have been recovered, many of them in various stages of disrepair, some seriously damaged. Those that could be repaired, were repaired and given to synagogues to be used for services. The question arose as to what should be done with those Sifrei Torah that were so damaged that they could no longer be repaired and consequently were not fit for public reading in a synagogue.

The Sifrei Torah had been transferred to the Westminster Synagogue in London. The synagogue catalogued them, and noted their origins as best they could. In this task of identifying the Torahs, they were aided by the German practice of tattooing numbers on the Torahs, much as concentration camp inmates were tattooed.[10]

The question now arose, "What is to be done with these פסול Torahs?" Should they be put into a גניזה (hidden away or buried), or can they still have a use? It was decided that they could continue to serve an important educational purpose. They could serve as a memorial to the victims of the Holocaust, a silent witness to the determined efforts of Hitler and the Nazis to destroy the Jews and Judaism and of the indifference or passivity of so many Europeans in the face of such evil.

The Memorial Scrolls Trust

An organization to accomplish this purpose was set up and named the Memorial Scrolls Trust. A notice was sent to synagogues, museums, colleges and similar institutions throughout the world offering such a scroll on condition that they be kept on perpetual display as a reminder of the Holocaust. Over four hundred synagogues, museums, colleges, etc., have

---

[8] B. Megillah 26b, Shulhan Arukh, Y.D. 282:10; O.H. 154:5.
[9] S.A. Orah Hayyim 154:5. There is a later discussion as to whether the burial receptacle is restricted to a clay vessel, or whether other receptacles may be used, e.g. a wooden box or even nylon wrapping. See Rabbi Hayyim David HaLevi, *Mekor Hayyim*, pt. 3, p. 96.
[10] This practice is the basis of the book for children, Marvell Ginsburg et al., *The Tattooed Torah* (New York: Union of American Hebrew Congregations, 1983).

received such Torahs and keep them on display as a reminder of the Holocaust.[11]

In essence, the purpose of the Memorial Scrolls Trust was to establish another category of Sifrei Torah which parallels the category described by the Rambam of Torahs which are פסול and cannot be used in the synagogue but which have educational uses. The vital difference between the categories is that the category described by the Rambam had never been כשר, while the Holocaust Torahs had once been כשר and still had residual sanctity. Usually they would have been put in a גניזה.

גניזה

The question must now be asked, "Is the term גניזה limited to burial or to storage in a special room, or are there other acceptable forms of גניזה?" To answer this question, we turn to the rules governing a Sefer Torah in which an error is found. It is forbidden to use such a Sefer for Torah reading. However the Sefer does not lose its sanctity. It may be kept in the ארון קודש until it is corrected, but must be tied or wrapped in a distinctive manner, so that it will not be taken out by mistake and read. It is our practice to put the Torah binder on the outside of the Torah mantle as a reminder not to use that Torah for public reading.

How long may a Torah which is פסול (disqualified) stay in the ארון קודש? The Yoreh De'ah limits it to thirty days, and the Rama adds that this applies to all ספרים (holy books):

> ספר תורה שאינו מוגה אסור להשהותו יותר משלשים יום אלא יתקן או יגנז. (והוא הדין לשאר ספרים.)

> It is forbidden to leave a Sefer Torah, which has not been corrected, more than thirty days (in the ארון קודש or elsewhere). One must either correct it or "hide" it. (The Mapa adds: And that is the law for all other holy books.)[12]

---

[11] I am grateful to Rabbi Bernard Raskas for supplying information on the Holocaust Torahs. A brief pamphlet describing the work of the Czech Memorial Scrolls Committee between the years 1964 and 1988 has been published. What follow are brief excerpts describing the procedure followed by the Committee:

> ...A system of cataloguing was devised; and in accordance therewith, each scroll was gone through by an expert, and a record made, so far as was possible, of the origin and age of the scroll, the physical condition of its components and, most important, the state of the writing and the defects therein. On the basis of this study, the scrolls classified into grades, from best to unusable. The middle grades were such as could be made usable by a little or a greater amount of labour, and such as had some parts which were or could be made usable. Of the remainder, most were destined to serve as sacred memorials.

> ...In the allocation of scrolls during the past 20 years, priority has been given to Synagogues needing a scroll for use in services....Practically all the scrolls which can be made kosher have been distributed, and the remainder are being allocated to those congregations who wish to have a memorial to the martyred communities.

> Some scrolls, not necessarily fit for use in synagogue but appropriate as solemn memorials, have been assigned for display in religious and educational centres,...One went to Westminster Abbey, where it was a feature in the exhibition arranged by the Council of Christians and Jews in connection with the Abbey's 900th Anniversary Commemoration, and is now permanently in the library of the Council of Christians and Jews. Others have gone to the Royal Library at Windsor; Brandeis University,...Northwestern University,...University of Rochester,...University of York and York Cathedral and Yad Vashem.

It is apparent, from the list of educational and religious institutions, that Memorial Scrolls were distributed to both secular and religious institutions including Christian cathedrals despite the presence of Christian symbols. This subject requires further study in another תשובה.

[12] Y.D. 279:1.

The Arukh HaShulhan concurs and explains that the Rabbinic authorities say that if it remains in the ארון it may lead to the sin of the vain recitation of blessings (if the Torah is read by mistake):

> אמרו חז"ל בכתובות (יט, ב') דספר תורה שאינו מוגה אסור להשהות יותר משלשים יום ואחר זמן זה מחוייב לתקנו, ולאו דווקא ספר תורה. וחז"ל אמרו ספר סתם, אלא שהפוסקים אמרו ספר תורה, מפני שבה יש קלקול גדול שמברכים ברכות לבטלות, אבל איסור יש בכל הספרים, בין ספרי תנ"ך ובין תלמוד ופוסקים, כי על פי טעות ביכולת לבוא לידי מכשול הוראה.

> Hazal said in Ketubot 19b that it is forbidden to leave a Sefer Torah that has not been corrected (in an Ark) for more than thirty days, and after this period of time one must correct it. And not necessarily a Sefer Torah, but any ספר (holy book). However the poskim (rabbinic authorities) were especially concerned about a Sefer Torah for it can result in a great sin, the recitation of "vain blessings." But the prohibition applies to all ספרים (holy books), whether it be other books of the Bible, the Talmud, or the Poskim (rabbinic authorities), for textual errors can lead to mistaken teachings.[13]

Both the Shulhan Arukh and the Arukh HaShulhan agree that the need for גניזה applies to all holy books that need correction or are so worn that they are no longer usable. The stringency for the Sefer Torah was to avoid the possibility of it being mistakenly read at a service leading to the recitation of ברכה לבטלה (a blessing recited in vain). One might therefore conclude that if proper precautions are taken to avoid mistakenly reading the Torah, that the same rules for גניזה that apply to all ספרים would apply equally to a Sefer Torah.

גניזה *is Not Limited to "Hiding Away"*

Are there forms of גניזה other than "hiding away" that would be permitted? The Nodah b'Yehudah deals with the issue in a responsum answering the question, "Is it permitted to leave defective ספרים, which can not be repaired, in an ארון (Ark) used for kosher ספרים?"

He points to congregational practice and uses halakhic reasoning to answer the question:

> אם הלכה זו רופפת בידך פוק חזי מה עמא דבר. ומעשים בכל יום כשמוצאים טעות בשבת בשעת קריאה מחזירין ספר זה לארון ומוציאים אחרת, הרי שאף שספר זה נמצא פסול לשעתו, אפילו הכי מחזירין לארון הקודש המיוחד לספרים הכשרים.

> If you are uncertain about the halakhah, "Go check the practice of the people." It is common practice that when an error is found on Shabbat during the Torah reading that this Torah is returned to the Ark and another Torah is taken out. Thus a פסול Torah is put into an Ark specially designated for kosher Torahs.

He reasons that a defective Torah retains its קדושה and the difference between a Sefer Torah that can be corrected and one that cannot is only a matter of economics. It is cheaper, in cases of extensive wear or damage, to write a new Torah than to repair

---

[13] Yehiel Epstein, Arukh HaShulhan, Y.D. 279:1.

the defective Torah. And he concludes:

> ואם כן כשם שמחזירין בשבת ספר שנמצא בו פסול לארון כן אין אסור
> להניח ספרים הללו בארון הקודש.

> Since it is permissible to return a Sefer Torah in which a defect is found, while reading the Torah on Shabbat, to the Ark, so it is *not* forbidden to leave פסול (disqualified) Torahs in the Ark.[14]

The Nodah b'Yehudah adds that the reason for the 30 day restriction is to assure that the Torah will be quickly repaired and thereby avoid the possibility of mistakenly taking the defective Sefer Torah from the Ark and reading it at a Service.

One could therefore conclude that it would be permissible to mark a Sefer (e.g. by putting the binder outside the mantle) and thereby avoid the possibility of making a mistake, and leave it indefinitely in the ארון. Or, alternatively, put the Sefer in a special receptacle in the ארון or outside of it, where it could not be taken out by mistake and read at a Service.

Rabbi Jacob Ettinger, in his book of Responsa entitled *Binyan Tzion*, expands on this thesis. He says that the practice of burying worn out or defective Sifrei Torah near the grave of a scholar is advice to be followed:

> זה דוקא אם אין לו מקום להניחו וצריך לגנזו קמל"ן היאך יגנזו. אבל אם
> רצה להניחו בארון הקדש במקום מיוחד, זהו גניזתו.

> Only if he has no place to put it and he has to "hide" it, then this is the proper way to do it. However, if he wants to put it in a special place in the ארון הקודש he may do so, and this is its גניזה – "hiding."[15]

Rabbi Ettinger differs with the Nodah b'Yehudah in the reason for the thirty day limitation on keeping a defective Torah in the ארון קודש, holding that the reason is not the likelihood of mistakenly reading the Torah, but that it is a sin not to correct a Torah that can be corrected. However, regarding a Torah which is so defective that it cannot be corrected and there is no intention of ever reading from it, there is no sin involved in leaving it in a special place in the ארון קודש. And this place is to be considered an appropriate גניזה.[16]

And Rabbi Ettinger makes a very pragmatic observation:

> ולכן מה שנוהגים בהרבה קהלות שאינם גונזים ספרי תורה שבלו רק
> מניחים אותם בארון הקדש במקום מיוחד ומוצאים אותם בשמחת תורה
> להרבות ההקפה.

> Therefore the practice in many congregations is not to "hide" the worn out Sifrei Torah, but to place them in a special place in the ארון קודש and to take them out on שמחת תורה for use during the הקפות (Torah circuits).[17]

It is therefore clear that the useful life of a Sefer Torah need not end when it can no longer be read in a service. And he cites the practice in many congregations as prece-

---

[14] Yehezkel Landau, *Nodah b'Yehudah*, O.H. siman 9. Emphasis added. I am grateful to Rabbi Joel Roth for suggesting this source, as well as the following source, from the *Responsa of the Binyan Tzion*.

[15] *Binyan Tzion*, O.H. siman 97.

[16] Op. cit.

[17] Op. cit.

dent for using such פסול Torahs for another purpose, the הקפות at שמחת תורה. And we can add still another use — to be held by a congregant during the Kol Nidre service.

Museums

This leads to another question, that must now be considered. The additional use of the defective Sefer Torah seems to be related to a synagogue service. Would it be permissible to place a Sefer Torah in a museum and use it as an educational exhibit?

There is no clear prohibition, only limitations on the reasons that one may sell a Sefer Torah. Nonetheless, Jewish sentiment may be opposed to turning over a Torah for the purposes of public exhibition. However, an example from the early history of the State of Israel in which the Seminary played a role provides a precedent.

President Chaim Weizmann came from Israel to the United States to see President Harry Truman. He wanted to present President Truman with a meaningful gift that would show appreciation for having helped Israel win recognition as an independent state. He consulted with Dr. Louis Finkelstein, then the chancellor of the Jewish Theological Seminary, and decided to give President Truman the gift of a Torah which belonged personally to Dr. Finkelstein. Rabbi Bernard Lipnick, then a student, was the שליח who brought the Torah from Dr. Finkelstein to President Weizmann. President Weizmann then presented the Torah to President Truman.

The Torah was put into a suitable museum case, and was exhibited at the White House for several years. The Torah was then transferred to the Truman Library, where it still is on public exhibition.[18]

When we decide halakhah, we do not only turn to literary precedents, but also to the precedents set by halakhic personalities. Dr. Finkelstein was a great authority in halakhic literature, and well aware that he was a role model, at least for Conservative rabbis. Dr. Finkelstein was aware of the implications of the gift, and he would not have done anything that was contrary to Jewish law, as he understood it.

When Dr. Finkelstein turned the Torah over to President Weizmann, he was aware of the possibility that it would be publicly exhibited, as were so many other gifts to presidents. And even when he sought to have President Truman donate the Torah to the Jewish Theological Seminary, it still was for the purpose of exhibiting it at the Seminary or at the Jewish Museum, as an historical object.[19] Hence, it is fair to conclude that

---

[18] In the process of preparing this paper, I discovered this family tradition about my brother-in-law, Rabbi Bernard Lipnick, of which I was not aware. In response to an inquiry from Rabbi Lipnick about the present whereabouts of the Sefer Torah, President Truman wrote,

> February 12, 1953
>
> Dear Rabbi Lipnick:
>
> The Torah to which you refer was presented by President Weizmann. The ark to contain it was presented by the people of Israel. The Torah is in the Ark and is now on exhibition in the Smithsonian. When the Truman Library is constructed that is where it will be placed.
>
> Sincerely yours,
>
> Harry Truman

[19] The proposition that Dr. Finkelstein was agreeable to having this Torah publicly displayed is not mere speculation. Rabbi Judah Kogen related to me that Dr. Finkelstein told him that when President Truman visited the Seminary after leaving office, Dr. Finkelstein asked the former president's permission to exhibit this Torah scroll at the Jewish Museum. President Truman decided instead to exhibit the Torah scroll at the Truman Library where it would be viewed by many more people. The Torah has been on display at the Truman Library ever since and Dr. Finkelstein was pleased with the outcome.

there is no halakhic objection to exhibiting a Sefer Torah in a public place, or a museum, even if the museum is not under Jewish auspices. And a museum case in which the Torah can be properly exhibited and viewed, could be considered an appropriate receptacle.

The Torah given by Dr. Finkelstein was a כשר Torah (which can be used at synagogue services), and the שאלה (question) we are dealing with concerns a פסול Torah (which can not be read in the synagogue). Using the logic of the Talmud (a קל וחומר) we can say that if a כשר Torah can be exhibited publicly, how much more so a פסול Torah.

In addition, there have been, to my knowledge, no objections to displaying ancient Hebrew manuscripts in museums as, for example, the Isaiah scroll in the Jerusalem Shrine of the Book. Since all פסול sefarim are on a par when there is no opportunity to mistakenly read such a Sefer Torah at a service, this is another precedent for the permissibility of exhibiting a פסול Sefer Torah in a museum.

An Open or Shut Case

This, however, does not answer the question, "May a פסול Torah be exhibited partially unrolled, or must it be rolled and covered?" We are conditioned to showing כבוד to the Torah by keeping it rolled or covered, except when it is actually being read at services (and on occasion to acquaint the Torah Reader in advance with the כתב of the scroll). This also serves to protect the ink from fading because of too much exposure to the light, and prolonging its use as a כשר Torah.

But, what would constitute כבוד for a Holocaust Torah? The purpose of the Holocaust was to close the chapter on the Jewish people in the history of Europe. A closed Sefer Torah would seem to be a symbolic confirmation of the success of the Nazi endeavors. An open Sefer Torah sends the message, "The Jewish people live, and its history is open-ended." Hence, כבוד for a Holocaust Torah can be found in leaving it open and, if it is possible, at a place which conveys a meaningful message — e.g., "Remember what Amalek did. . . ," or the Ten Commandments, or the שמע ישראל.

The "Practice of the People"

If there are still doubts as to what the halakhah should be, then פוק חזי מה עמא דבר, "Go check the practice of the people." The Jewish museums and the synagogues that I have visited exhibit the Holocaust Torahs with a column or two unrolled. I remember vividly a "leather jacket" made from the קלף (parchment) of a Torah scroll that was exhibited in a Holocaust exhibit on Mt. Zion. When the Shrine of the Book exhibited the original Isaiah scroll, it too was unrolled.

The Meaning of עמא

When I use the term עמא, I use it to mean serious individuals who are concerned about tradition and devoted to the Jewish people, not Jews who may be indifferent to Jewish tradition. Those who are in charge of these exhibits, in synagogues or in Jewish museums, both here and in Israel, are serious and responsible Jews. They seem to have decided that the message of the open scroll is the correct message for our day. The sight of such open scrolls has not evoked protest from the countless Jews who have viewed these exhibits. Hence, the practice of the עמא can be a reliable guide in helping decide what the halakhah should be.

In The Synagogue

Museums are generally quiet places where people behave with decorum. Where synagogues have special museums, separated from the foyers, this is the preferred location for a Holocaust Torah. If, as in most synagogues, the Holocaust Torah is exhibited in the foyer of the synagogue, then some precautions are advisable to assure the כבוד of the Torah.

The foyer is a multipurpose area used for social purposes, for Purim carnivals, for youth activities, as well as for entering and leaving the synagogue building. At times the behavior of people may not be decorous. If possible, the museum case should be built with a curtain which can be drawn, or a screen placed in front of the case, or a cover put on the museum case when a lack of decorum is anticipated.[20]

The exhibit case, whether in the synagogue or a museum should have a label which explains the significance of the Torah as a "witness" to the Holocaust. It should also refer to the fact that the sefer is פסול, so damaged that it can no longer be used at a synagogue service.

Summary

The Sefer Torah is venerated by Jews and every effort is made to assure that it will be treated with כבוד, honor and respect. When it can no longer serve the sacred purpose of being read publicly in the synagogue, it is disposed of by a process called גניזה. גניזה may mean burial, placing in a special chamber for worn out ספרים (holy books), marking it (so that it will not be mistaken for a valid Torah) and leaving it in the ארון קודש (Holy Ark), placing it in a special place in the Ark, or elsewhere in a suitable receptacle. A clearly marked פסול Torah may be used for purposes other than reading in the synagogue service, i.e. הקפות at Simhat Torah, or as an educational exhibit in a synagogue or museum.

The Torahs that have survived the Holocaust were not and should not be buried or hidden away. Just as the Rambam spoke of a category for educational purposes, these Sifrei Torah also constitute a special category; one not envisioned in the past. This is a category of scrolls that may no longer be used in the synagogue service, in which the previous sanctity still adheres, and to which history has added a significant dimension. For, even in their damaged condition they still have a purpose and can function in the spirit of their original intent — to educate.

They can continue to serve as silent witnesses to the vitality of Jewish life before the Holocaust, to the murder of six million Jews, helping to educate coming generations about the evils that the Nazis perpetrated, and to serve as a warning that "it can happen again" unless people are ready to oppose evil. The common practice of exhibiting the scroll (where possible) unrolled to a relevant passage can teach that the Jewish people live and Judaism has a message for the world.

Conclusion

It is permitted to utilize a Sefer Torah that is פסול (invalid) as a Holocaust display. Every effort should be made to assure the honor of the Torah scroll. It should be displayed in a museum case that would be appropriate to the sacred nature of the scroll. Since the pur-

---

[20] See Walter Jacob, *Questions and Reform Jewish Answers* (New York: Central Conference of American Rabbis, 1992), pp. 218-220, for a Reform responsum on the question of Holocaust Torahs.

pose is to educate the viewer, and not to be read at a service, the Sefer Torah may be left open to an appropriate place. The museum case should stand in a room or corridor where people behave with dignity and reverence, and have a cover or screen that can be used if less than decorous behavior is anticipated. The case should have a plaque explaining the history of the Torah, its significance as a witness to the Holocaust, and pointing out that it was so damaged that it cannot be used for reading at services.

It should be emphasized that this responsum applies only to a פסול Sefer Torah. The display of a כשר Sefer Torah in a museum case requires further study, and a separate תשובה.

YD 305:1.1993

SHOULD THERE BE A SPECIAL CEREMONY IN RECOGNITION OF A FIRST-BORN FEMALE CHILD?

Rabbi Gerald Skolnik

This paper was approved by the CJLS on May 19, 1993, by a vote of seventeen in favor and six abstaining (17-0-6). Voting in favor: Rabbis Kassel Abelson, Stanley Bramnick, Elliot N. Dorff, Jerome M. Epstein, Samuel Fraint, Arnold M. Goodman, Reuven Kimelman, Judah Kogen, Vernon H. Kurtz, Lionel E. Moses, Paul Plotkin, Mayer Rabinowitz, Avram Israel Reisner, Joel E. Rembaum, Chaim Rogoff, Joel Roth, and Gerald Skolnik. Abstaining: Rabbis Ben Zion Bergman, Myron S. Geller, Susan Grossman, Jan Caryl Kaufman, Aaron L. Mackler, and Gordon Tucker.

The Committee on Jewish Law and Standards of the Rabbinical Assembly provides guidance in matters of halakhah for the Conservative movement. The individual rabbi, however, is the authority for the interpretation and application of all matters of halakhah.

שאלה

Should there be a special ceremony in recognition of a first-born female child?

תשובה

While the desire to enhance the sense of worth and value to the Jewish community of a female child is understandable and laudable, it would be preferable to include the element of בת בכורה as a component of a שמחת בת ceremony, rather than create a new ceremony which few would be likely to utilize and which would have no true halakhic integrity.

The general question of whether or not a פדיון הבן ceremony might properly be performed for a female first-born child is answered clearly and unequivocally in the Torah. The mandated practice of redeeming the first-born son from his special religious obligations via the agency of the levi'im (or today their descendants, the kohanim; see Exod. 13:1-2, and Num. 3:11-13 and 18:15-16) clearly holds only with regard to male first-born children, and not female. No matter what the motivation, one cannot change history and retroactively project this obligation onto a female child.

In our own time, a number of factors have conspired to cause the practice of פדיון הבן to fall into widespread disuse. In addition to the general unfamiliarity of our laity with its origins and significance, large numbers of adoptions in the Jewish community, the tremendous number of women who have had previous abortions or miscarriages, or whose first-born sons were delivered by Caesarean section, have contributed to this situation even more. All are practices or states of being which render a פדיון הבן unnecessary. While it might be something of an exaggeration to call a פדיון הבן a rare occurrence, it certainly does not occur with the frequency of a ברית מילה or a שמחת בת. Moreover, those instances when a פדיון הבן does occur are, as often as not, more excuses for food to be served and friends and relatives to be gathered together than they are religious events of any real significance.

None of this in any way renders null and void the Torah's command with regard to the redemption of the first born son. Certainly, the ignorance of the laity on this matter cannot be the determining factor, nor can the relative rarity of the event. These ceremonies should be taking place when they are supposed to.

Yet the fact that the Torah clearly restricts the practice of פדיון הבן to male first-born children only serves to reinforce the sense of distress experienced by some men and women regarding gender-related status issues in the Jewish community. Is a first-born female child less precious to God in our eyes than a male one? The exclusive obligations and privileges of a first-born male Jewish child in ancient Israel certainly do, to many, suggest that. And for those who feel that way, the absence of a parallel ritual today for first-born female Jewish children only serves to exacerbate the sense of historic inequity.

It was to address this situation that the Chairman of the Committee on Jewish Law and Standards suggested that perhaps someone would be interested in drafting a ceremony to take note of the special status — in our eyes, today — of the first-born female Jewish child. I volunteered believing at the time that such a ritual might alleviate the aforementioned inequity perceived by some, without doing harm to the halakhic issues involved in פדיון הבן.

Although it is somewhat uncomfortable to say so, I have, after a good deal of consideration, come to the conclusion that the development of such a ceremony is unnecessary and perhaps even ill-advised. I would rather withdraw from my original position than compose some sort of service that I myself would probably never utilize.

The reasoning behind my decision is as follows. To a great degree, the development and increasing prevalence of שמחת בת ceremonies has effectively served the purpose of providing a meaningful and parallel yet unique vehicle for welcoming a female child into the covenant between Israel and God. The task before me, therefore, was not to create some sort of ritual expressing the covenant idea. And, though the true thematic rationale for the ceremony would be redemption, it also increasingly seemed to be a mistake to create a ceremony which would assume that women needed to be redeemed from obligations which they never had in the first place.

What remained, therefore, was to create a ritual vehicle for expressing the special spiritual and familial status of the first-born Jewish female child, much as a first-born male child would enjoy in today's family. Ultimately, I came to the conclusion that it would be better to incorporate the aspect of "first-born-ness" into the שמחת בת ceremony than to create an entirely different ceremony which relatively few people would ever utilize.

In a very brief span of time as Jewish law goes, the שמחת בת ceremony has become widely accepted and utilized, even outside the Conservative community. To the degree that we can reinforce the importance of welcoming a female child into the covenant with the same sense of enthusiasm that we do a male child, הרי זה משובח. The absence of a halakhic time-mandate for a שמחת בת affords parents the opportunity to hold the ceremony at their convenience. Unless they are specifically wedded to the parallelism of a ברית בת ceremony on the eighth day after birth, there is no reason why the שמחת בת ceremony for a first-born female child could not be held on the day when a פדיון הבן would have been held for a male first-born child — i.e., ופדויו מבן חדש תפדה (Num. 18:16).

For an idea as to how to thematically and appropriately bring the notion of the פדיון ceremony into the שמחת בת, I am grateful for the creative suggestion of my friend and colleague Rabbi Laurence Sebert. The juxtaposition of the command to redeem the first-born Israelite child in Exodus 13 with the account of the plague of the slaying of the Egyptian first-born in Exodus 12 has, to some commentators, suggested an association between the two. In that light, the well-known text from Sh'mot Rabbah 1:12 seems particularly appropriate:

> דרש רבי עקיבא בשכר נשים צדקניות שבאותו הדור נגאלו אבותינו ממצרים.
>
> Rabbi Akiva interpreted: By virtue of the reward due the righteous women of the generation of the Exodus were our forefathers redeemed from Egypt.

What better or more appropriate connecting text could there be?

Conclusion

For all of the above reasons, I have therefore concluded that the Biblically mandated practice of פדיון הבן is restricted to male first-born children, and should not be expanded to include first-born female children. However, all gatherings which serve the purpose of enhancing the sense of blessing and specialness associated with the birth of a first-born female child are to be encouraged.

YD 305:11.1995

Delay of Pidyon HaBen

Rabbi Vernon H. Kurtz

This paper was approved by the CJLS on March 21, 1995, by a vote of twenty in favor (20-0-0). Voting in favor: Rabbis Kassel Abelson, Ben Zion Bergman, Stephanie Dickstein, Elliot N. Dorff, Jerome M. Epstein, Myron S. Geller, Arnold M. Goodman, Susan Grossman, Judah Kogen, Vernon H. Kurtz, Alan B. Lucas, Aaron L. Mackler, Lionel E. Moses, Paul Plotkin, Mayer Rabinowitz, Avram Israel Reisner, Joel E. Rembaum, Joel Roth, Gerald Skolnik, and Gerald Zelizer.

The Committee on Jewish Law and Standards of the Rabbinical Assembly provides guidance in matters of halakhah for the Conservative movement. The individual rabbi, however, is the authority for the interpretation and application of all matters of halakhah.

שאלה

May פדיון הבן be postponed beyond the thirty-first day?

תשובה

One of my tasks in my current congregation is to teach a life cycle class to students of בר/בת מצוה age and their parents. One of the topics discussed is פדיון הבן, the redemption of the first-born son. Most students and many parents are unfamiliar with the concept and the ritual.

Over the course of six years teaching the class, two families have approached me and recognized that their son should have been redeemed, but was not. In each case, since the מצוה remained the responsibility of the parents until their son became a בר מצוה, we arranged for the ritual to take place. Thus, I could say to the congregation on their בר מצוה day that though my tenure at the congregation was not of such a lengthy duration, I had participated at both the פדיון הבן and בר מצוה of these two boys.

Though many Conservative Jews are not familiar with the ritual, it is clearly a mitzvah from the Torah. The Torah states: "All first-born of man and animals shall be yours (the כהן). But the first born of man must be redeemed. . .from the age of one month. The redemption price is the value of five sanctuary shekels (of silver), each weighing twenty *gerah*" (Num. 18:15-16).

According to the text, פדיון הבן takes place after one month of life. This coincides with the child being a בר קיימא, a viable human being. There is a discussion in the sources whether the month should be seen as מעת לעת, exactly a month by astronomical time, or not. The Shulhan Arukh in Yoreh De'ah 305:11 states:

> אין הבכור ראוי לפדיון עד שיעברו עליו שלשים יום, ואחד שלשים יום יפדנו מיד שלא ישהה המצוה.

> The first-born can only be redeemed after he has passed thirty days of life. After the thirtieth day he should be redeemed immediately so as not to delay the mitzvah.

Though there is a disagreement among some of the sources as to what exactly constitutes thirty days and whether a full month can be seen as approximately 29½ days, the prevailing custom has been that the first-born is redeemed on the thirty-first day.

In fact, Asher Anshel Grunwald in *Zocher HaBrit* (page 179:14) states:

> רבים נוהגים לעשות הפדיון אחר הצהרים סמוך למנחה. ואולי חששו דלפעמים יארע שנולד סמוך לחשכה ולא שלמו לו כ"ט ימים.

> Many are accustomed to do the פדיון late in the day so that they can be sure that the full time period has elapsed.

Grunwald does not agree with this custom and suggests לא נכון לבטל מצות זריזים – "It is better to fulfill the custom of being zealous in doing the mitzvot and not wait until late afternoon."

The question has been raised whether פדיון הבן can be held later than the thirty-first day. Yechiel Michael Epstein in the Arukh Hashulhan writes in Yoreh De'ah 305:44:

> כשיעברו שלושים יום מצוה לפדותו מיד ביום שלושים ואחד שלא להשהות את המצוה ויש להסתפק אם עובר בעשה בכל יום כשאינו פודיהו כמו במילה לאחר שמונה אם לאו.

> When thirty days are completed it is a mitzvah to perform the redemption immediately on the thirty-first day so as not to delay the performance of the mitzvah. Should one not do so I am uncertain whether they transgress the mitzvah each day that the child is not redeemed (like ברית מילה after eight days) or not.

The Arukh Hashulhan thus raises the issue whether performing the פדיון הבן on the thirty-first day is a necessity, and thus, one transgresses the Biblical commandment if one does not do so, or whether it is not necessarily a requirement. On this issue there seems to be a divergence of opinions among the sources. The Rosh (end of Bekhorot) writes:

> כמו שאמרו חכמים ז"ל "ושמרתם את המצות" קרי ביה "ושמרתם את המצוות" אם באת מצוה לידך אל תחמיצנה.

> Our Rabbis taught that based on the Biblical verse (Exod. 12:17) "And you shall observe the Feast of Unleavened Bread" (*HaMatzot*) read: "You shall observe the commandments (*HaMitzvot*)." One should not be slow to perform a religious duty.

One should therefore do the mitzvah as soon as one is physically able. However, what if that is impossible?

פדיון הבן does not take place on Shabbat or Yom Tov, unlike ברית מילה, because it is considered "a business arrangement" (מקח וממכר). However, it does take place on Hol HaMoed (Shulhan Arukh, Orah Hayyim 546). The *Zocher HaBrit* quotes two possibilities as to what should occur if Shabbat or Yom Tov are the thirty-first day. The Shulhan Arukh (Y.D. 305:11) states:

> ואם חל יום שלושים ואחד בשבת אין פודין אותו בשבת אלא ימתין עד יום ראשון.

If the thirty-first day occurs on Shabbat the פדיון does not take place on that day. Rather, one waits until Sunday to perform it.

Karo believes that one should wait until Sunday since presumably he believes that the ceremony should take place during the day. However, the *Zocher HaBrit* also quotes another source, Responsa of Rav Yehuda Asad, Yoreh De'ah 265:

יש אומרים דאם חל פדיון הבן בשבת יעשה הפדיון והסעודה במוצאי שבת.

There are some who hold that if the פדיון is to take place on Shabbat, he should perform the ceremony and have the festive meal on Saturday night.

This view holds that since the ceremony can take place in the evening, it should be done as soon as possible after the conclusion of the Shabbat so as not to delay the פדיון more than is absolutely necessary.

These two views, I believe, are based upon the question whether one sees the thirty-first day as essential to the performance of the mitzvah or a stated goal. In the book *Pidyon HaBen KeHilchato*, the author, Gedalya ben Yehiel Oberlander, quotes the sources for these two conflicting points of view (page 144-145). He states that while the Rosh believes, מצוה הבאת לידך אל תחמיצנה – "One should not delay the performance of a mitzvah," this is only אין זה דין מיוחד בפדיון הבן שמבטל המצוה אם (to expedite the mitzvah) and זריזות לא קיימה בזמנה – "This is not a special requirement for פדיון הבן so that the mitzvah would not be fulfilled if it is not accomplished at its proper time." However, others disagree and suggest that after the thirty-first day: עובר בכל יום בעשה – "He transgressess the commandment each day that it is not performed" (See Oberlander, p. 142:17).

Both Oberlander and Grunwald disagree with this latter view and accept the opinion of the Shulhan Arukh and the majority of poskim (including R. Ovadia Yosef)[1] that המאחר הפדיון אינו עובר בעשה – "One who delays the פדיון does not transgress the commandment."

Once the פדיון הבן has been postponed, is it possible to delay it further? Most authorities suggest that it should be done as soon as possible. However, the Magen Avraham to Orah Hayyim 568:10 states:

מילה אף על פי שעבר זמנה כל שעתא ושעתא זמנה הוא דאסור לעמוד ערל אבל פדיון הבן כיון שעבר זמנה יכולין לדחותו יותר.

With regard to ברית מילה, each moment (after the eighth day) is an appropriate time for the ceremony since one should not remain uncircumcised. However, once the time of פדיון הבן has passed, it is possible to delay it even further.

The Magen Avraham holds that since it has already been postponed, it may be accomplished whenever it is feasible. According to Rabbi Eugene J. Cohen, in his *Guide to Ritual Circumcision and Redemption of the First Born*, "This view stresses that the Torah states 'after' the child is a month old, and the word 'after' has no limit in time."

Finally Rabbi Moshe Feinstein in his *Iggrot Moshe* (Y.D. vol. 2, siman 118, p. 191) responds to a question concerning the delay of the פדיון הבן:

פדיון הבן שחל יום שלושים ואחד באמצע השבוע ואבי הבן רוצה לדחות ליום ראשון כדי שתהיה סעודה גדולה ודאי אסור לדחותה מזמנה כדי

---

[1] See R. Ovadia Yosef, *Yabia Omer*, Y.D. vol. 2, siman 25, Letter 2 for an analysis of the various opinions.

> שלא ישהה המצוה. ואף שבאמצע השבוע לא יבואו אנשים הרבה להסעודה אין לשהות המצוה שתהא הסעודה יותר גדולה... לכן יש לעשות הפדיון בזמנה אף שתהיה הסעודה קטנה.

> In a case of פדיון הבן where the thirty-first day occurs during the middle of the week and the father wants to delay the ceremony until Sunday so that he can hold a more elaborate celebratory meal, it is clear that one should not do so, so as not to delay the mitzvah. Even though during the week there will not be many people who will attend, one should not delay it so more can be present. . . .Therefore it is proper to make the ceremony at its proper time even if the attendance is small.

Here Rabbi Feinstein clearly seems to be of the opinion that one should not delay the פדיון in order to allow friends relatives and the wider community to be present. However, then he adds:

> ואם האב אינו רוצה בשום אופן לעשותו קודם יום ראשון, צריך לעשותו ביום הראשון, והמצוה יקיים ממש כמו בזמנה... פדיון הבן (בזמנה) הוא רק מצד שלא משהינן ולא עבר אעשה.

> However, if the father refuses to do the ceremony before Sunday, it can be held on that date and the mitzvah will have been accomplished just as if it were held at its proper time. פדיון הבן (at its proper time) is important so as not to delay the mitzvah but one does not transgress the commandment (if it is delayed).

Rabbi Feinstein thus seems to allow a delay in the ceremony at the insistence of the father for what seems to be not very compelling reasons.

Conclusion

Based on these sources I therefore conclude:

1. The mitzvah of פדיון הבן should be encouraged among Conservative Jews.[2]

2. We should strongly encourage פדיון הבן at its appointed time, בזמנה, on the thirty-first day. We accept the desired goal of זריזים מקדימים למצוות, "the zealous perform mitzvot as soon as they are able to do so." If we do not do so, we are unfair to the tradition's response to the timeliness of mitzvot and the need to adapt our lives to "Jewish time."

3. Should the thirty-first day occur on a Shabbat or Yom Tov, the פדיון הבן should occur during the daylight hours on the next possible date (Sunday or after the Second Day of the Festival).

4. If these dates are not agreed to by the parents then it is possible to hold the ceremony during the evening hours.[3]

---

[2] I commend the work of the Federation of Jewish Men's Clubs in this matter. The guide to the ritual, the explanatory essays and the certificates are well done and should be made readily available to members of our community. Dr. Neil Gillman offers an interesting homiletical explanation: "The פדיון הבן ceremony serves as a constant reminder that we have little ultimate control over our possessions. This lesson in humility is part of the touching message of the פדיון הבן ritual" (*A Guide to the Pidyon HaBen Ceremony* [New York: Federation of Jewish Men's Clubs, 1993], p. 4).

[3] Oberlander in *Pidyon HaBen KeHilchato* writes: פדיון הבן מותר לפדות בלילה אך נוהגים לפדות ביום. ומנהג הספרדים לפדות בליל שלשים ואחד – "It is permissible to have the פדיון in the evening but it is customary to hold it during the day. The Sephardic custom is to perform it on the evening of the thirty-first." Allowing people to use

5. If the parents persist and for their own reasons want the ceremony to take place on a date later than on the thirty-first day then we may allow it on the authority of the *Iggrot Moshe* and the fact that most authorities do not believe that one עובר בעשה בכל יום, "transgresses the positive commandment each day."

Perhaps our opinion is best expressed by the *Sefer HaHinukh* mitzvah 392:

> אף על פי שאין למצוה זו זמן קבוע דבכל שעתא ושעתא אחר שלשים יום זמנה היא, אעפ״כ חכם לב יקח מצוות ויקדים ויעשה אותן מיד שאפשר לו.

> Even though this mitzvah does not have a fixed time, since anytime after the thirtieth day is possible for פדיון הבן, even so the pious will do the mitzvah as soon as one is able to accomplish it.

---

the evening hours for the ceremony may permit them to have family and friends present and perhaps alleviate the need to postpone the ceremony indefinitely.

YD 305:24.1991

Pidyon HaBen and Caesarean Sections

Rabbi Howard Handler

This paper was approved by the CJLS on October 16, 1991, by a vote of seventeen in favor, two opposed and two abstaining (17-2-2). Voting in favor: Rabbis Ben Zion Bergman, Stanley Bramnick, Jerome M. Epstein, David M. Feldman, Ezra Finkelstein, Samuel Fraint, Howard Handler, Jan Caryl Kaufman, Reuven Kimelman, Aaron L. Mackler, Herbert Mandl, Lionel E. Moses, Avram Israel Reisner, Joel E. Rembaum, Chaim A. Rogoff, Joel Roth, and Gerald Skolnik. Voting against: Rabbis Richard L. Eisenberg and Mayer Rabinowitz. Abstaining: Rabbis Elliot N. Dorff and Arnold M. Goodman.

The Committee on Jewish Law and Standards of the Rabbinical Assembly provides guidance in matters of halakhah for the Conservative movement. The individual rabbi, however, is the authority for the interpretation and application of all matters of halakhah.

שאלה

May a first-born male child born by Caesarean section have a פדיון הבן?

תשובה

In very ancient times, the first-born son in every Israelite family was vested with special responsibilities. From the day of his birth he was consecrated to the vocation of assisting the priests in the conduct of worship.

Later when a Tabernacle was built in the wilderness this vocation of the first-born was transferred to the Levites, a priestly tribe. The Torah then decreed that every father release his firstborn son from the duties incumbent upon all firstborn sons by redeeming him from a Kohen. The ancient obligations of the firstborn son thus continues to be recalled.[1]

Rabbi Gary Atkins of Temple Beth El in Lancaster, Pennsylvania has asked whether a first-born male child born by Caesarean section may have a פדיון הבן. His opinion is that in Talmudic times Caesarean sections were a rare event whereas today they constitute thirty percent of all births. The sources are as follows:

---

[1] J. Harlow, *A Rabbi's Manual* (New York: Rabbinical Assembly, 1965), p. 14.

1. אי זהו בכור לנחלה ולכהן המפלת שפיר מלא מים מלא דם מלא גנינן המפלת כמין דגים וחגבים, שקצים ורמשים והמפלת ליום ארבעים הבא אחריהם בכור לנחלה ולכהן. יוצא דופן והבא אחריו שניהן בכור לא לנחלה ולא לכהן. ר׳ שמעון אומר: הראשון לנחלה והשני לחמש סלעים.

Which is a first born both [in respect] of inheritance and of redemption from a priest? If [a woman] discharges a sac full of water or full of blood or an abortion consisting of a bag full of a many-colored substance. If [a woman] discharges something like fish or locusts or reptiles, or creeping things or if she discharges on the fortieth day [of conception]. [The infant] which follows after [these discharges] is a first-born [in respect] of inheritance and redemption from a priest. Neither a fetus extracted by means of the Caesarean section nor the infant which follows is either a first-born for inheritance or a first-born to be redeemed from a priest. R. Shimeon however says: the first is a first-born of inheritance and the second is a first-born as regards the redemption with five selas (Mishnah Bekhorot 8:2).

2. ראשון לנחלה לא, "וילדו לו" [דברים כא:טו]. בעינן לחמש סלעים נמי לא, "פטר רחם" [שמות יג:ב]. בעינן שני לנחלה לא, "ראשית אונו" [דברים כא:יז]. בעינן לחמש סלעים נמי לא, קסבר בכור לדבר אחד לא הוי בכור. ר׳ שמעון אומר: הראשון לנחלה והשני לחמש סלעים ר, שמעון לטעמיה² דאמר "תלד" [ויקרא יב:ה] לרבות יוצא דופן והשני לחמש סלעים, קסבר בכור לדבר אחד הוי בכור.

The first is not a first-born of inheritance because the condition required by Scripture is: *and they have borne him*. It is also not a first-born [as regards redemption] with five selas because the condition required [by Scripture] is: *openeth the womb*. The second offspring is not a first-born of inheritance because the condition required [by Scripture] is: *the first-fruits of his strength*. He is also not a first-born as regards redemption with five selas because [the Tanna in the Mishnah] holds: A first-born in one respect only [i.e. as regards the womb alone] is not considered a [legal] first-born. "R. Simeon however says: the first is a first-born for inheritance and the second is a first-born as regards redemption with five selas." R. Simeon here follows his line of reasoning elsewhere when he said: [Scripture says], *but if she bear*, intimating the inclusion of a fetus extracted by means of the Caesarean section. And the second is a first-born as regards redemption with five selas because he holds: A first-born in one respect only is considered a [legal] first-born (B. Bekhorot 47b).

3. וידבר ה׳ אל משה וגו׳ קדש לי כל בכור זו אחת משלש עשרה מדות

---

² רש״י: לטעמיה דאמר במס׳ נדה פ׳ יוצא דופן [דף מ.] ואם נקבה תלד לרבות תלד יוצא דופן דהוי לידה מעליא ויושבת עליו ימי טומאה וטהרה הלכך גבי וילדו לו נמי לידה מעליא חשיב ליה דגמרינן מהתם.

שהתורה נדרשת בהם מכלל שהוא צריך לפרטו ופרט שהוא צריך לכללו קדש לי כל בכור פטר כל רחם וגו' כלל אחד זכרים ואחד נקבות במשמע כל הבכור אשר יולד וגו' פרט יצאי נקבות ממשמע אני אקרא את הכלל מה ת"ל את הפרט שאם אני קורא את הכלל אבל לא את הפרט שומע אני כל שיולד ראשון בין זכר בין נקבה יהיה בכור ת"ל כל הבכור וגו' הזכר זכרים אבל לא נקבות אני אקר' את הפרט מה ת"ל את הכלל אם קורא אני את הפרט ולא את הכלל שומע אני כל זכר שיולד בין שהוא פותח רחם ובין שאינו פותח רחם יהיה בכור ת"ל קדש לי כל בכור עד שיהא זכר ופותח רחם לקיים מה שנא' כל פטר רחם לי וכל מקנך תזכר (מכילתא בא פ' ט"ז).

"And the Lord spoke unto Moses," etc. "Sanctify unto Me all the first-born." This is one of the rules for interpreting the Torah. There are instances in which not only does the general term need its specific term, but the specific term also needs its general term. "Sanctify unto Me all the first-born, whatsoever openeth the womb," etc., is the general term, including in its meaning both males and females. "All the firstling males that are born of thy herd and of thy flock thou shalt sanctify unto the Lord thy God" (Deut. 15:19), is a specific term, the meaning of which excludes females. Now, once I read the general statement, what need is there of making the specific statement? Because if I read merely the general statement without the specific, I might understand it to mean that whatsoever is born first, whether male or female, is to be considered a "first-born." Scripture therefore says: "All the firstling males that are born of thy herd and of thy flock," etc. – males but not females. Then, let me read only the specific statement. What need is there of making the general statement? Because if I read only the specific statement without the general statement, I might understand it to mean that as long as it is the first male offspring whether it is the one that first opened the womb or not, it is to be considered a "first-born." Therefore, Scripture says: "Sanctify unto Me all the first-born, whatsoever openeth the womb" – it must be both a male and first to open the womb. This confirms what has been said: "All that openeth the womb is Mine; and every firstling among thy cattle, whether ox or sheep, that is male" (Ex. 34:19).[3]

4. יוצא דופן והבא אחריו שניהן אינן בכורים הראשון לפי שלא נולד ונאמר "וילדו לו בנים" והשני שהרי קדמו אחר.

Neither the child that emerged from the mother's side nor the child that came after such a child is a first-born – the former because he was not *born*, and it is written *And they have borne him children* (Deut. 21:15), and the latter, because he was preceded by another child (M.T. Laws of Inheritance 2:11).

---

[3] Mekilta de-Rabbi Ishmael [Masekhet d'Pisha, Bo 17], Jacob Z. Lauterbach, trans. (Philadelphia: Jewish Publication Society, 1933), pp. 128-129.

5. יוצא דופן והנולד אחריו כדרכו שניהם פטורין הראשון מפני שלא יצא
מהרחם ושני מפני שקדמו אחר (שלחן ערוך יורה דעה סימן ש"ה סעיף
כד).

One born by Caesarean section and one born in the normal fashion afterwards are both exempt; the first because it did not exit the womb, the second because it was preceded by another (Shulhan Arukh Y.D. 305:24).

Conclusion

In light of the above mentioned sources, it is clear that פדיון הבן is a limited institution. It applies specifically to an obligation that falls upon first-born male children born through the birth canal only. The traditional ritual for פדיון הבן would not be appropriate for any other child because the blessing involved can only be recited where there is an obligation to redeem. In this case לא זזה משנה ממקומה.[4]

---

[4] The conclusion of this paper neither mandates nor precludes the development of an alternative ceremony for first born boys by Caesarean section.

YD 336.1995

HESED OR HIYUV? THE OBLIGATION TO PRESERVE LIFE AND THE QUESTION OF POST-MORTEM ORGAN DONATION

Rabbi Joseph H. Prouser

This paper was approved by the CJLS on December 13, 1995, by a vote of fourteen in favor and seven opposed (14-7-0). Voting in favor: Rabbis Kassel Abelson, Ben Zion Bergman, Stephanie Dickstein, Elliot N. Dorff, Jerome M. Epstein, Baruch Frydman-Kohl, Susan Grossman, Judah Kogen, Alan B. Lucas, Aaron L. Mackler, Mayer Rabinowitz, Avram Israel Reisner, Joel E. Rembaum, and Elie Kaplan Spitz. Voting against: Rabbis Shoshana Gelfand, Myron S. Geller, Vernon S. Kurtz, Paul Plotkin, Gerald Skolnik, Gordon Tucker and Gerald Zelizer.

The Committee on Jewish Law and Standards of the Rabbinical Assembly provides guidance in matters of halakhah for the Conservative movement. The individual rabbi, however, is the authority for the interpretation and application of all matters of halakhah.

שאלה

What is the halakhic status of post-mortem organ and tissue donation?

תשובה

I. Preservation of Human Life as Obligatory

The inestimable value of human life is a cardinal principle of Jewish Law. As Rabbi David Bleich writes:

> Human life is not a good to be preserved as a condition of other values but an absolute, basic, and precious good in its own right. The obligation to preserve life is commensurately all-encompassing.[1]

This obligation includes not only self-preservation, but the duty to save the life of one's fellow human being, should he or she be in mortal danger. The Torah's commandment, לא תעמוד על דם רעך – "You shall not stand idly by the blood of your neighbor"[2] – provides the halakhic basis for this obligation.

---

[1] Rabbi J. David Bleich, *Contemporary Halakhic Problems* (New York: Ktav, 1977), p. 93.
[2] Lev. 19:16.

In addition, the Talmud[3] reformulates this prohibition (מצוה לא תעשה) into a positive, prescriptive obligation (מצות עשה), by relating the duty to intervene in life-threatening situations to the commandment[4] regarding restoration of lost property — השבת אבידה. "Every individual, insofar as he is able, is obligated to restore the health of a fellow man no less than he is obligated to restore his property."[5]

II. Who is Obligated?

In codifying this mitzvah, Maimonides emphasizes how broadly its obligation devolves: כל היכול להציל ולא הציל עובר על לא תעמוד על דם רעך — "Anyone who is able to save a life, but fails to do so, violates 'You shall not stand idly by the blood of your neighbor.'"[6] In describing the analogous duty to save the life of one being pursued by an assailant (רודף), Maimonides leaves no room for exemption: כל ישראל מצווין להציל — "All Israel are commanded to take life-saving action."[7]

Indeed, not even the inability personally to save the life in peril relieves one of this obligation:

> לא תעמוד על דם רעך לא תעמוד על עצמך משמע אלא חזור על כל צדדין שלא יאבד דם רעך.
>
> "You shall not stand idly by the blood of your neighbor," means "You shall not rely on yourself, alone." Rather, you must turn to all available resources so that your neighbor's blood will not be lost.[8]

III. Precedence of the Obligation

It is abundantly clear that the mandate to preserve life — פקוח נפש — takes precedence over other religious obligations and considerations. (The prohibitions against murder, sexual immorality, and idolatry are, under normal circumstances,[9] the only exceptions — יהרג ואל יעבור, "let him die and not transgress".)[10] Former British Chief Rabbi Immanuel Jakobovits articulates this principle in no uncertain terms:

> It is obligatory to disregard laws conflicting with the immediate claims of life, and...it is sinful to observe laws which are in suspense on account of danger to life or health....[I]t is not only permitted but imperative to disregard laws in conflict with life or health.[11]

Thus, the seriously ill are required to eat on Yom Kippur. Similarly, it is forbidden to circumcise a sick or weakened infant if this would further compromise his health. The circumcision must be delayed, for אין לך דבר שעומד בפני פקוח נפש — "preservation of life

---

[3] B. Sanhedrin 73a.

[4] Deut. 22:1.

[5] Bleich, p. 95.

[6] Maimonides, Hilkhot Rotzeah u'Shmirat Nefesh 1:14.

[7] Ibid., 1:6.

[8] B. Sanhedrin 73a, Rashi ad loc.

[9] During a period of religious persecution, however, the law is more stringent, extending the requirement of martyrdom even to minor religious practices. See Yoreh De'ah 157:1.

[10] B. Sanhedrin 74a; Yoma 82a.

[11] Rabbi Immanuel Jakobovits, *Jewish Medical Ethics* (New York: Bloch, 1975), p. 50.

overrides all other considerations."[12] This principle has many applications in regard to the laws of Shabbat. The requirement to preserve life at the expense of Sabbath observance is unambiguous indeed:

> מי שיש לו חולי שיש לו סכנה מצוה לחלל עליו את השבת והזריז הרי זה משובח והשואל הרי זה שופך דמים.

> It is commanded that we violate the Sabbath for anyone dangerously ill. One who is zealous (and eagerly violates the Sabbath in such a case) is praiseworthy; one who (delays in order to) ask (questions about the law) is guilty of shedding blood.[13]

A noteworthy expression of this zeal is the recommendation (directed at Israeli society) in ספר שמירת שבת כהלכתה that when it becomes necessary to drive an ambulance on the Sabbath, it is preferable that Sabbath-observant Jews do the driving.[14]

IV. Primary Objections to Post-Mortem Procedures

To be sure, post-mortem donation of human tissue is not without halakhic difficulties. The halakhic objections to this practice include the prohibitions against ניוול המת (disgracing the dead body, as by disfigurement), הנאה מן המת (deriving benefit from a dead body), and הלנת המת (delaying burial).[15]

All three of these concerns, collectively termed כבוד המת (the dignity of the dead), are addressed in a responsum by former Israeli Chief Rabbi Isser Yehuda Unterman. As to the first two issues, Rabbi Unterman rules succinctly:

> השאלה היא אם מותר מצד הדין לעשות נתוח בבשר אדם מת ולהעביר ממנו בשר... שיתקשר אח"כ באופן אורגני כחלק מן החי... ופשוט בעיני הדבר שיש בהם משום פקוח נפש לא קמבעי לן שאיסורי-תורה חמורים נדחים מפני פקוח נפש, ולכן הנתוחים שעושים להצלת נפש ודאי מותרים.

> Regarding the question of whether the law permits surgical removal of tissue from a dead body. . .subsequently to be transplanted as an organic part of the living. . .I find the matter to be simple. Since these procedures constitute preservation of life there is no difficulty. After all, weighty Torah prohibitions are set aside for the preservation of life. Hence, such surgical procedures conducted to save a life are absolutely permitted.[16]

Rabbi Efrayim Oshry rules with similar clarity: היכא דשייך ענין של פקוח נפש לא חיישינן לניוול המת – "Where saving a life is involved, we are not concerned with the desecration of the dead."[17] So too, Rabbi Theodore Friedman: פקוח נפש גדול מכבוד המת –

---

[12] B. Yoma 82a. Similarly, סכנת נפשות דוחה את הכל, Yoreh De'ah 263:1.

[13] Orah Hayyim, 328:2.

[14] Rabbi J.I. Neuwirth, *Shmirat Shabbat K'hilchatah* (Hebrew), p. 541.

[15] See Rabbi Isaac Klein, "Autopsy," in *Responsa and Halachic Studies* (New York: Ktav, 1975), p. 40.

[16] Rabbi I.Y. Unterman, *Shevet Mi-Yehuda*, (Mosad Harav Kook 1983 ed.), p. 54. See also p. 368 for an identical ruling based on *Noda B'Yehuda* and *Maharam Shik* rulings on autopsies.

[17] Rabbi Efrayim Oshry, *She'eilot u'Teshuvot mi-Ma'amakim*, 2:10. English translation from *Responsa From the Holocaust*, p. 72, "Performing a Caesarean Section on a Dead Woman." Rabbi Oshry authorized a Caesarean section on a woman whose murder he witnessed, even though it was uncertain the baby was still alive.

"Greater is saving a life than the dignity of the dead (*kevod ha-met*)."[18]

As to the question of burial, Rabbi Unterman discusses only the particular organs or tissue being transplanted. In this regard, he considers transplanted tissue to be restored to life and thus not requiring burial with the donor's remains. The question of whether the donor's transplanted tissue will eventually be buried together with the recipient is not compelling, just as the requirement that blood be buried poses no obstacle to blood donation.[19]

Rabbi Unterman does not discuss the issue of delaying burial to facilitate post-mortem procedures. Since, however, such delay is neither typical nor necessary, we should not consider it an impediment.[20] In those few, rare cases where burial is delayed, we should rely on Rabbi Unterman's general approach: preservation of life takes precedence, and the prohibition of הלנת המת (delaying burial) is likewise suspended. אין לך דבר שעומד בפני פקוח נפש – "Preservation of life overrides all other considerations."

While organ and tissue transplantation is a relatively new halakhic quandary, the related question of autopsy has a longer general and halakhic history.[21] "Many medical practitioners," writes Russell Scott, "regard autopsy as essential to maintaining high standards of medical knowledge, hospital care, and community health."[22] The trend toward permitting autopsy under the rubric of פקוח נפש, however, has generally been conditioned by the stipulation that a specific beneficiary of information gained through the procedure be identified (חולה נמצא לפנינו).[23] That is, theoretical medical knowledge alone does not constitute פקוח נפש. A demonstrable need for information required to avert immediate danger to a specific human life is necessary to render autopsy permissible. In the absence of such a need, autopsy remains prohibited. Indeed, Rabbi Unterman suggests organ donation as a desirable recourse when civil authorities mandate autopsies which would otherwise be halakhically objectionable:

היכי שחתכוהו בלאו הכי עפ"י דרישת החוק לצורך חקירה משפטית וכדומה אפשר שאין זה ניוול אם נשתמשו בחלק מחותך לרפואה.

---

[18] *PRA* 17 (1953): 44.

[19] On the requirement that blood be buried, see "A Guide for the Chevra Kadisha" in Rabbi Maurice Lamm, *The Jewish Way in Death and Mourning* (New York: Jonathan David, 1969), p. 244.

[20] "The Circle of Life: Organ and Tissue Donation," American Council on Transplantation.

[21] In *The Body as Property* (New York: Viking Press, 1981), Russell Scott calls autopsies "the oldest medical activities that use bodies" (p. 29). Skilled dissection of human bodies can be traced to antiquity, as discriminating removal of organs was necessary for embalming, which was commonplace in ancient Egypt (see Gen. 50:2-3,26). Western civil regulation of autopsies can be traced at least to 1504, when the Town Council of Edinburgh granted a charter for post-mortem procedures to the British Guild of Surgeons and Barbers (Scott, p. 5).

[22] Scott, p. 15.

[23] This principle was recognized as early as the Talmudic Period. B. Hullin 11b discusses the permissibility of an autopsy to determine whether a murder victim was a טריפה – already suffering from a fatal wound or condition, in which case no death penalty was imposed. The prohibition of ניוול המת was suspended, as the findings of the autopsy might save the life of the convicted murderer! The earliest clear application of this principle in the responsa literature is in Rabbi Yechezkiel Landau's *Noda B'Yehuda* (Mahadura Tinyana, Yoreh De'ah no. 310), in which he stipulates that an autopsy is permissible only if a patient in the same hospital is suffering from the same condition and there would thus be an immediate, life-saving benefit from the procedure. Rishon L'Tzion Benzion Meir Chai Uziel ruled more leniently, extending the principle of פקוח נפש to general advances in medical knowledge. The Knesset passed the Law of Anatomy and Pathology in 1953, based on an agreement with the Chief Rabbinate, although there were later attempts to restore the more stringent guidelines of the *Noda B'Yehuda*. Rabbi Isaac Klein concludes his responsum on the question of autopsy thus: "If medical science claims that these may save lives. . .it is not only permitted, but it is actually a mitzvah."

In cases where an autopsy (one otherwise not in conformity with Jewish law) is performed in accordance with the demands of civil law, as part of a criminal investigation or the like, it may no longer be considered a desecration (ניוול) if excised tissue is used for healing.[24]

So long as highly sophisticated, computerized, international organ registration networks readily identify prospective organ recipients, the requirement of חולה נמצא לפנינו is, in the case of organ donation, ipso facto satisfied. So immediate and specific is the need for organs that a prospective recipient typically "wears a pocket pager, waiting for a call saying that a new heart is available."[25] (As Rabbi Unterman indicates, however, fulfillment of this condition remains considerably more difficult to establish in regard to autopsy, the benefits of which are generally far less direct and immediate. Autopsy thus remains prohibited unless it is deemed necessary for saving the life of a חולה נמצא לפנינו.)

V. Dimensions of the Need

The halakhic mandate to preserve life by consenting to post-mortem tissue donation takes on compelling urgency by virtue of the massive need for tissue transplants. As of April, 1995, 39,735 people were on the waiting list of the United Network for Organ Sharing.[26] "Every thirty minutes, someone is added to this national waiting list. More than 500 patients on the national waiting list are children."[27] Due directly to the shortage of willing donors, "thousands continue to die each year because of a shortage of donated organs and tissues."[28] According to one estimate, seven people die each day for lack of available organs.[29]

The life-saving impact of organ donation reaches far beyond the sizable number of potential recipients. "Faced with a dire lack of organs from cadavers, transplant surgeons are looking with increasing interest at living donors,"[30] in particular, close relatives of recipients. A recent, unsuccessful transplant attempt dramatizes this dangerous, emerging trend:

> In a desperate attempt to save the life of a 9-year-old Minnesota girl whose lungs had failed, doctors first transplanted part of her father's lung and, when that was not enough, tried to transplant part of her mother's lung....While still on the operating table, the girl, Alyssa Plum, died.[31]

Prospective living donors, as well as recipients, are thus needlessly placed at mortal risk by the shortage of cadaver organs. "Parents want to donate even when doctors are unwilling to do the operation because they think it would be futile or that there is too much risk for the donor."[32] This unacceptable risk led Dr. Thomas Starzl, the renowned

---

[24] Unterman, p. 60.
[25] Calvin Stiller, M.D., *Lifegifts: The Real Story of Organ Transplants* (Toronto: Stoddart Publishing, 1990), p. 57.
[26] UNOS Newsletter, Apr. 1995. UNOS manages the National Organ Procurement and Transplant Network (OPTN). For updated figures on the data related in this paragraph, see below, p. 191.
[27] "30 Facts About Organ Donation and Transplantation," The National Kidney Foundation, p. 2.
[28] "History of Transplantation and Organ Donation," Hartford Transplant Center, p. 4.
[29] Susan Reed, "Toward Remedying the Organ Shortage," *Technology Review* (Jan. 1994): 38.
[30] Gina Kolata, "Lungs from Parents Fail to Save Girl, 9, and Doctors Assess Ethics," *New York Times*, 20 May 1991, p. A-11.
[31] Ibid.
[32] Ibid., quoting pediatrician/ethicist Dr. John Lantos.

surgeon who pioneered liver transplants,[33] to announce that he would no longer perform transplants from living donors. In 1987 he explained his decision:

> The death of a single well-motivated and completely healthy living donor almost stops the clock world-wide. The most compelling argument against living donation is that it is not completely safe for the donor.[34]

Nevertheless, medical reliance on living donors continues to mount. In August of 1995, *The New England Journal of Medicine* reported "increasing numbers of persons donating kidneys to their spouses."[35] Citing evidence that "the survival rates of these kidneys are higher than those of cadaveric kidneys," the article concludes that "spouses are an important source of living-donor kidney grafts." Such a trend in the field of transplantation places tremendous pressure on relatives of prospective organ recipients to imperil themselves by serving as donors. In 1994 alone, 2,980 kidney transplants were performed using living donors.[36]

The *N.E.J.M.* article provides separate statistical data for kidney donation by husbands to wives based on whether the wife had ever been pregnant. The success rate for transplantation into women who had previously been pregnant is 76%, as opposed to 87% for women who had never been pregnant.[37] It must be assumed that among the former are a significant number of mothers with young children. Spousal donation in such cases means that both parents (donor and recipient) — and, therefore, their children's well-being — are placed at mortal risk. Yet an accompanying editorial asserts that there is "no ethical objection to using emotionally related (that is, spousal) donors(!)."[38]

Even a minute risk to the living is a significant halakhic datum. Rabbi Jakobovits thus rules that "while the gift of blood constitutes a religious obligation, it cannot be enforced, since it may entail some risk for the donor."[39] Similarly, he views higher-risk living donation of organs "as acts of supreme charity but not as an obligation."[40] Risk to life, statistically insignificant or profound, constitutes a mitigating factor which renders living donation commendable but optional. This risk is, by definition, completely absent in post-mortem donation. With the absence of risk as a mitigating factor, post-mortem organ donation is, logically, rendered obligatory.

Indeed, the risk to prospective living donors makes the need for cadaver organs — and the halakhic mandate for donation — all the more urgent. It should be noted that, in addition to altruistic relatives acting as living donors, the shortage of cadaver organs has also

---

[33] Scott, p. 20.

[34] Christine Gorman, "Matchmaker, Find Me a Match," *Time*, 7 June 1991: 61.

[35] Paul Terasaki et al., "High Survival Rates of Kidney Transplants from Spousal and Living Unrelated Donors," *New England Journal of Medicine* 333 (10 Aug. 1995): 333-336.

[36] UNOS Newsletter, Apr. 1995.

[37] Terasaki et al.

[38] Jean-Paul Soulillou, M.D., "Kidney Transplantation from Spousal Donors," *New England Journal of Medicine* 333 (10 Aug. 1995): 379-380.

[39] Jakobovits, p. 285.

[40] Ibid., p. 291. Rabbi Jakobovits here draws a distinction between מצוה and חובה. His allusion to "charity" is instructive: charity is a religious "obligation" which "cannot be enforced" at every juncture. One may, to a great extent, determine those occasions on which one will and will not give charity. In the same manner, according to Rabbi Jakobovits' argument, one may elect whether or not to preserve another's life at one's own risk. Every such act of פקוח נפש is a מצוה (fulfillment of a "religious obligation"); not every such opportunity for פקוח נפש, however, is a חובה (mandatory).

led to "a recognized market in human body parts."[41] That is, individuals are hired to donate organs which are redundant (a kidney), "non-essential" (corneas), or regenerative (sections of liver).[42] While almost universally illegal, trade in human organs, like the "long-shot" attempts of relatives to save the lives of loved ones through living donation, demonstrates the desperate situation caused by the lack of available cadaver organs, and the personal desperation of prospective recipients.

VI. Who Can Donate?

It should be stressed that mandating consent for post-mortem organ donation does not mean that all, or even most compliant individuals will actually serve as donors. However, any individual donor may well be uniquely qualified to save the life of a prospective recipient. About two million deaths are recorded annually in the United States. "Primary donors are between ages 15 and 65. They are in good health but have died suddenly, possibly through accidents and are declared brain dead. . . .An estimated 20,000 to 25,000 brain deaths occur in the United States each year."[43] This select group of potential donors is further narrowed, as any particular organ transplant requires compatible tissue obtained from a "good genetic match" to minimize chances of natural organ rejection. Six pairs of genes are examined to determine matching human lymphocyte antigens (HLA proteins). The closer the match, the higher the prospects for a successful transplant.[44] Only an identical twin guarantees a perfect match. The smaller the pool of donors, the less likely it is to find a suitable cadaver organ for transplantation.

VII. Secondary Objections to Obligation

An objection raised by some authorities posits that while פקוח נפש may indeed be a privilege for the dead, it cannot properly be ruled an obligation.[45] The dead are not bound by Jewish law (חפשי מכל המצוות)![46] This suggestion is mere semantics. The consent required for organ donation is given prior to one's death, or by surviving, responsible relatives. The deceased is the means by which פקוח נפש is achieved. The act of consent while alive (or the consent of survivors) constitutes the fulfillment of the mitzvah itself.

It is curious indeed, with the consistent historical penchant for unambivalent zeal in matters of פקוח נפש, that the mandatory status of post-mortem organ donation has not previously been widely asserted. Various reasons for this apparent pattern of omission can be discerned. The first is that the technology of transplantation is still quite young. In the early 1940s "Sir Peter Medawar (Oxford, England) described the rejection phenomenon, for which he won the Nobel Prize. This discovery laid the foundation for the modern era of transplantation."[47] This era came into fruition[48] only in the late 1940s, precisely the time Rabbi Unterman was composing his responsum on this topic. The first successful kidney

---

[41] Scott, p. 3.

[42] See Scott, Chapter 1.

[43] "30 Facts About Organ Donation and Transplantation," The National Kidney Foundation.

[44] See Paul Terasaki, "Getting the Most Mileage from Donated Hearts," *Annals of Thoracic Surgery* 49 (Feb. 1990): 177-178; Verdi J. DiSesa, M.D. et al., "HLA Histocompatibility Affects Cardiac Transplant Rejection and May Provide One Basis for Donor Allocation," ibid., pp. 220-224.

[45] See, for example, Rabbi Yekutiel Greenwald, *Kol Bo al Avelut* (Jerusalem: Feldheim, 1997), p. 46.

[46] See, for example, B. Shabbat 151b, Nidda 61b.

[47] "History," p. 3. See above, n. 28.

[48] Historical synopsis based on Scott, p. 19ff.

transplant did not take place until 1954, two years after publication of Rabbi Unterman's שבט מיהודה. Liver and lung transplants were first performed in 1963, and then only with limited success. The first recipient of a liver died within three weeks. The first successful heart transplant was performed in South Africa by Dr. Christiaan Barnard in 1967, and provoked years of debate and controversy. Successful lung transplants are an extremely recent achievement.

Thus, those responsa and rabbinic pronouncements issued early in the still short history of transplantation could not assert with confidence that the procedures were in fact life-saving.[49] The first attempts at each new procedure met with only limited success. Immuno-suppressive therapy — the technology whereby natural rejection of "foreign" organs is medically and chemically combated — is still being perfected. However, this developing technology already accounts for "a near doubling in the numbers of heart, kidney and liver transplants performed. These advances also have increased the survival rates of kidney transplant recipients over age sixty by as much as ten percent."[50]

Only with time and experience do transplant operations become sufficiently dependable to constitute clear פקוח נפש.[51] Kidney transplants currently enjoy an eighty to ninety percent success rate; heart transplants a success rate of eighty to ninety percent, liver transplants sixty-five to seventy percent. Combined heart-lung transplants have a success rate of approximately seventy percent.[52] Success implies restoration of the recipient's quality of life and normal life expectancy. "Post-mortem donor kidney transplantation function of more than 20 years is well-documented."[53]

Similarly, before the advent of sophisticated, coordinated and computerized national and international organ registries, mandating donation would have been premature. Recipients were more difficult to locate and identify. The requirement of חולה נמצא לפנינו (a specific recipient) could not always be fulfilled early on in transplant history. This, as discussed above, is no longer commonly the case. The United Network for Organ Sharing (UNOS), a government sanctioned organ registry, has replaced the less efficient methods for identifying recipients of earlier decades.

VIII. Determination of Death

Finally, there was a greater reluctance in the early years of the transplant era to mandate (indeed, to allow) donation due to fears regarding determination of the donor's death. Using brain-death as a medical, much less halakhic, determinant of death dates only to the twenty-second World Medical Assembly held in 1968.[54] Brain-death is defined as "permanent functional death of the centers in the brain that control the breathing, pupillary, and other vital reflexes."[55] Rabbinic proponents of such a definition of death, that is, the total

---

[49] See Rabbi Moshe Tendler, in *Jewish Medical Ethics*, 5th ed. (New York: Federation of Jewish Philanthropies, 1975), p. 50.

[50] "30 Facts," p. 3.

[51] In fact, confidence of long-term success should not be a prerequisite to mandating organ donation; see Orah Hayyim 329:4. See also *Shmirat Shabbat K'hilchatah*, p. 430, par. 2. However, organ transplants were, early in their history, considered a calculated risk which might actually result in shortening the life of the recipient. At such a juncture, the permissibility of such procedures would still be at issue; mandating donation would certainly have been premature.

[52] "Questions About Organ Donation" and "Fact Sheet, Organ/Tissue Donation and Transplantation," Hartford Transplant Center.

[53] "30 Facts," p. 3.

[54] Scott, pp. 158-159.

[55] *The Bantam Medical Dictionary* (New York: Bantam Books, 1990), p. 112, s.v. "Death."

cessation of brain and brain-stem activity, as indicated (among other diagnostic methods) by an isoelectric or "flat" electroencephalogram (EEG), include Rabbis Seymour Siegel ז"ל,[56] Elliot N. Dorff,[57] Avram Israel Reisner,[58] and David Golinkin[59] (all of the Rabbinical Assembly), Rabbi Moshe Tendler,[60] a preeminent Orthodox authority on Jewish medical ethics, as well as the Chief Rabbinate of Israel. As Tendler writes:

> All rabbinic authorities agree that the classic definition of death in Judaism is the absence of spontaneous respiration in a patient with no other signs of life. . . .Brain death is a criterion for confirming death in a patient who already has irreversible absence of spontaneous respiration.[61]

It should be noted that the determination of brain-death is often made while the deceased appears to be breathing and to have a pulse, due to the use of a mechanical respirator. Where brain-death is determined, these misleading data in no way constitute life. Quite to the contrary, "it might be forbidden to continue artificial means of 'life' in these conditions, since it would, in fact, be הלנת המת, a delay in burying a dead person."[62]

Writing in 1975, Rabbi Jakobovits pointedly discusses the implications of this issue:

> The question of defining the moment of death with precision has . . .been rendered both more difficult and more critically acute by . . .the demand for viable cadaver organs for transplant purposes. The lapse of only a few minutes may spell the difference between success and failure in such operations; on the other hand, the premature removal of organs from the dying may hasten death and constitute murder.[63]

Greater familiarity with the practice of transplantation, as well as a broader medical and rabbinic literature on determination of death and brain-death, have largely eliminated this concern. Prevalent pre-modern fears of "false death" are no longer compelling. The final moments of the donor's life are safeguarded by requirements that two physicians certify death, and that these physicians not be involved in the transplant procedure.[64]

IX. כבוד המת: The Dignity of the Dead

Perhaps the most decisive factor in rabbinic reluctance to mandate post-mortem organ donation, however, has simply been "the widespread aversion to any interference with the

---

[56] "Updating the Criteria of Death," *Conservative Judaism* 30 (winter 1976).

[57] Elliot N. Dorff, "A Jewish Approach to End-Stage Medical Care," *PCJLS 86-90*, pp. 65-126. Rabbi Dorff writes of brain-death: "If the patient meets the criteria for neurological death, we can, on good authority, consider the person dead within the terms of Jewish law."

[58] Avram Israel Reisner, "A Halakhic Ethic of Care for the Terminally Ill," *PCJLS 86-90*, pp. 13-64.

[59] *Responsa of the Va'ad Halakhah of the Rabbinical Assembly of Israel*, vol. 5, pp. 119-124 (Hebrew).

[60] See, for example, "Communications," *Tradition* 28 (spring 1994): 94-96. In this letter, written together with ethicist Dr. Fred Rosner, Rabbi Tendler also asserts acceptance of the brain-death criterion by his late father-in-law, Rabbi Moshe Feinstein, until his death the "dean" of American Orthodox halakhic decisors (poskim).

[61] Ibid., p. 96. For the primary source on cessation of spontaneous respiration as determinant of death, see Yoma 85a.

[62] Siegel, p. 28, citing Rabbi David Novak.

[63] Jakobovits, p. 277.

[64] See, for example, Connecticut Anatomical Gift Act, Section 7(b).

dead among most Jews."⁶⁵ In general, this "aversion" reflects entirely appropriate devotion to a venerable religious principle, and should be commended. As Rabbi Lamm writes:

> Man is created in the image of God, and thus possesses dignity and value. . . .An indignity inflicted on man is a profanation of the name of God. The body that housed the soul is sanctified by Judaism. . . .Sanctity adheres to the body even after the soul has left. The care and consideration and respect that are bestowed upon the living must be accorded the dead as they are attended, prepared and escorted to their final abode on earth.⁶⁶

כבוד המת – the dignity of the dead – is a weighty and cherished religious imperative. This is indicated by the designation given those charged with these religious tasks: חברה קדישא, the "Holy Society." As Rabbi Dorff writes:

> If the body is honored to the extent that it is in Judaism, even in death. . .one can easily understand how many Jews would hesitate to mutilate it – or allow one's own body to be mutilated – even when it is for the noble purpose of helping to save someone else's life.⁶⁷

It is precisely a sensitivity to such well-intentioned sentiments which characterizes Rabbi Unterman's call "to influence relatives and to persuade them to consent" (להשפיע על הקרובים ולשדלם שיסכימו) to organ and tissue donation.⁶⁸ Framing this teaching in terms of persuasion rather than coercion does not imply that this life-saving action is elective. Are not rabbis frequently engaged in educational endeavors and persuasive techniques aimed at generating compliance with clear halakhic obligations? Persuading a Jew, for example, to comply with the laws of Shabbat does not suggest that this observance is optional. Indeed, Rabbi Unterman's call for persuasive outreach reflects his recognition of the obligatory nature of פקוח נפש. So, too, Rabbi David Golinkin:

> לא זו בלבד שמותר ליהודי לצוות את איבריו להשתלה לאחר מותו אלא מצוה עליו לעשות כן כדי להציל נפש אחת או נפשות רבות.
>
> It is not merely permissible for a Jew to bequeath his organs for transplantation following his death, it is a mitzvah for him to do so, in order to save one life, or several lives.⁶⁹

Rabbi Tendler similarly states that "if one is in the position to donate an organ to save another's life, it's obligatory to do so."⁷⁰ The most sacred institutions and practices of Judaism may – indeed, must – be suspended for the purpose of saving lives. Does it not stand to reason that understandable but strictly subjective aversions and aesthetic objections to post-mortem organ donation likewise must be set aside?

---

⁶⁵ Jakobovitz, p. 279.

⁶⁶ Rabbi Maurice Lamm, "A Guide for the Chevra Kadisha," in his *The Jewish Way in Death and Mourning*.

⁶⁷ Rabbi Elliot Dorff, "Choosing Life: Aspects of Judaism Affecting Organ Transplantation," in Stuart J. Younger, Renée C. Fox, and Laurence J. O'Connel, eds., *Organ Transplantation: Meanings and Realities* (Madison: University of Wisconsin Press, 1996), pp. 168-193.

⁶⁸ Unterman, p. 368.

⁶⁹ See note 59. Rabbi Golinkin's responsum carries the unanimous assent of the Va'ad Halakhah. The English precis in the same volume renders this passage as follows: "It is a mitzvah to donate organs after death."

⁷⁰ Quoted in "Religious Views on Organ Donation and Transplantation," in *American Council on Transplantation Promotional Kit* (Alexandria, Va.: 1989), p. 21. Rabbi Tendler adds: "It is given that the donor must be brain dead."

As to the similar conflict between personal rights and the halakhic obligation to preserve life, the general observation of renowned Israeli jurist Haim Cohn is instructive:

> Jewish law, as a system of law, knows no explicit rights. . . .It is no accident that Jewish law concentrates on duties and has no room for rights. It is the performance of duties by which God is served.[71]

Rabbi Unterman similarly considers individual liberties, to the extent they have any halakhic status, to be included among those values set aside for פקוח נפש.[72] We affirm that אין לך דבר שעומד בפני פקוח נפש – Preservation of life overrides all other considerations. We ought not, as our final act, glorify personal preference at the expense of other human beings' lives.

X. Emotional and Psychological Considerations

Rabbi Unterman's early call for educational outreach in regard to fulfilling the mitzvah of פקוח נפש through organ donation was predicated not only on halakhic principle, but on the spiritual significance of such an act. His metaphysical speculation also reflects a concern with the emotional impact of organ donation on the bereaved. Rabbi Unterman thus offers reassurance to donors' families:

> זכות גדולה לו וקורת רוח לנשמתו שנעשית מצוה גדולה כזו בגופו, ואין לזלזל בחשבון כזה.
>
> It is a great merit to the deceased, and gratifying to his soul, that so great a mitzvah is fulfilled with his body. One must not underestimate this consideration.[73]

It is essential that one undertaking the persuasive outreach advocated by Rabbi Unterman follow his example in sensitively placing organ donation into a constructive context. Referring to life-saving transplant procedures as the "harvesting" of organs, for example, evokes a sense of violence and disregard for the deceased, as indicated by a grieving father:

> I'm a farmer and I know what harvest means. When we harvest corn, we tear the corn from the stalk – it just gets trampled under the tires and then thrown away. Nobody is going to harvest my boy.[74]

"Recover" or "retrieve" are more appropriate terms to describe the donation process. It is similarly imperative that a ventilator not be referred to as "life support," as this implies that the patient is not yet dead. (The ventilator is used following brain death to maintain circulation of oxygenated blood to viable organs.) Referring to the deceased by name (rather than as "the donor") "shows respect and sensitivity for the family's grief over the loss of their loved one."[75]

---

[71] Justice Haim Cohn, "The Right to Die in Jewish Law," lecture delivered at the Jewish Theological Seminary, 10 Apr. 1984. For a more extensive treatment of this subject, see Cohn's *Human Rights in Jewish Law* (New York: Ktav, 1984), pp. 17-19.

[72] Unterman, p. 61. Rabbi Bleich, citing Rabbi Tucazinsky, states: "It is an established verity that, from the point of view of Judaism, man has no proprietary rights to his body," (See Bleich, p. 126). See also Rabbi Moshe Feinstein, *Iggrot Moshe*, Yoreh De'ah, pt. 3, no. 140; and Abraham S. Abraham, M.D., "Euthanasia," in Fred Rosner, M.D., ed., *Medicine and Jewish Law*, p. 124.

[73] Unterman, p. 60.

[74] Stiller, p. 56.

[75] Franki Chabalewski, RN, and M.K. Gaedeke Norris, RN, "The Gift of Life: Talking to Families About Organ and Tissue Donation," *American Journal of Nursing* (June 1994): 28-30.

Dr. Calvin Stiller, Chief of the Multi-Organ Transplant Service at University Hospital in London, Ontario, provides an inviting perspective on the transplant procedure:

> When the decision to transplant is made, the donor and the recipient are taken to the operating room. The donor's body is treated with profound respect, because we are watching one of the most extraordinary acts that a human being can accomplish. The surgical theatre is hushed and reverence for life prevails as the donor organ is removed and taken carefully to the sick, partially destroyed body of the recipient. The sick organ is removed to make way for the new healthy organ. We watch in silence as the retrieval of life from the donor occurs and the restoration of life in the recipient begins. We watch as the skin begins to clear, the body chemistry begins to improve and the brain gradually quickens as the new organ functions and restores life.[76]

Those contemplating organ donation should also be made aware that "studies have found that donation of the organs and/or tissue of a loved one who has died helps to shorten the time needed by members of a bereaved family to recover from their loss."[77] Serving as an organ donor thus not only saves lives, but also provides comfort and healing to one's own loved ones, "a blessedness made more remarkable and unexpected precisely because of its association with an experience of such abysmal despair and suffering. . . .It doesn't remove the pain or loss, but it allows something good to be salvaged from an otherwise horrible occurrence."[78] The emotionally therapeutic impact of organ donation is illustrated by the experience of a family who mourned the death of an 18-year old, killed in a motorcycle accident:

> We were so proud of Walter. Even in death his quiet, unassuming generosity was still alive. On the day of the funeral, a friend of ours on the police force called to let us know that the heart recipient was doing very well, and was setting records for recovery. This gave our whole family a lot of faith for getting through that day.[79]

In addition to the "redemptive comfort"[80] inherent in the act of giving, donor families identify further emotional benefits of organ donation. These include the sense that donors "will never be forgotten" by those whose lives they save. Relatives of donors also report a sense of "extended family" and "community" with other donors and recipients: "The giving and receiving of life is the peculiar essence of family, and the gift of life that is tissue and organ donation has extended my family in a very real sense."[81]

The adverse affect on the bereaved who are denied the opportunity to facilitate lifesaving organ donations can also be profound. Donation may be precluded if the cause of

---

[76] Stiller, pp. 57-58.

[77] "30 Facts," p. 5.

[78] Peter G. Sandstrom, MD, "What Helps When it Hurts: It is More Blessed to Give Than to Receive," in *For Those Who Give and Grieve* (spring 1995): 3-8. This publication is a quarterly newsletter for donor families published by the National Kidney Foundation. Dr. Sandstrom's wife of twenty-six years served as an organ donor, having been declared brain-dead following a cerebral hemorrhage.

[79] Bonnie Langeveld, quoted in Stiller, *Lifegifts*, p. 94.

[80] Sandstrom, "What Helps When it Hurts."

[81] Ibid.

death is unknown. Potential donors may also be disqualified for various medical reasons: malignancies, transmissible disease, hemophilia, auto-immune diseases, rheumatoid arthritis, etc.[82] Often, however, missed opportunities are due to the timidity of hospital personnel in approaching families for consent. One Canadian woman, whose husband suffered a fatal brain aneurysm, anticipated the opportunity to facilitate organ donation with a measure of solace. Her husband had, on principle, registered as an organ donor. By the time she was informed of his death, however — some ninety minutes thereafter — his organs were no longer viable:

> A wave of grief swept over her. Grief exceeding that of loss. It was now laced with anger. Her husband had been denied an opportunity to carry out his last wish. Judy left the hospital filled with rage. She, too, had been denied. The grieving process was now doubly bitter for her.[83]

Jewish mourners, called upon to grant consent for the use of a loved one's organs in a transplant procedure are, by definition, אוננים. This stage of mourning, אנינות, comprises the period between death and burial. As Rabbi Joseph Soloveitchik explains:

> *Aninut* represents the spontaneous human reaction to death. . . . Man responds to his defeat at the hands of death with total resignation and with all-consuming, masochistic, self-devastating black despair.[84]

It is little wonder that many individuals at this stage of grief are not naturally inclined to seek out opportunities for organ donation. Understandably, an אונן is emotionally ill-equipped to act selflessly and magnanimously for the preservation of human life. It is precisely the אונן who is least prepared to "carry the human-moral load"[85] by opting for organ donation. For this reason, many bereaved families tragically miss a unique opportunity for an act of religious significance and personal therapeutic value. Such was the case of a mother mourning her twelve-year-old son:

> Anguish and grief at a time like that is such that all rational acts and thoughts are cast to the side. . . .Time eventually restores you to reality and thoughts of what you could have done before and after the tragic loss. . . .I wish that some or all of Jason's organs and eyes could have been used to help people less fortunate than himself. . . .If only I could look at another human and know that my son lives on in them and that they have had another chance at life because of Jason.[86]

Consenting to organ donation provides an effective source of comfort and emotional healing. Mandating organ donation thus doubly exemplifies human sensitivity. It brings physical healing to the deathly ill. It also brings emotional healing to the bereaved, while relieving them of an emotional burden they are temporarily unable to bear.

---

[82] "Guidelines for Tissue Donation," Northeast Organ Procurement Organization and Tissue Bank.

[83] Ibid., p. 91.

[84] Rabbi J.B. Soloveitchik, quoted by Rabbi Jack Reimer, *Jewish Reflections on Death* (New York: Schocken, 1975), p. 76.

[85] Ibid.

[86] Stiller, p. 14.

XI. Specific Procedures

A. Vital Organs and Corneas

Procedures which replace vital organs are the most obviously life-saving in nature. These include transplantation of the heart, lung, liver, pancreas, kidney, as well as the rarer joint heart/lung transplant.[87] A single cadaveric donor can facilitate transplants in multiple recipients, saving several lives simultaneously.

As early as 1953, Rabbi Theodore Friedman, "with the approval of a majority of the [R.A. Law] committee," ruled corneal transplants permissible, stating that "it should readily be granted that blindness should be deemed a case of פקוח נפש:"[88]

> The use of eyes removed from the dead, including their bequest for eye-banks, for corneal transplants has also generally been permitted. In the view of the majority the restoration or preservation of eye-sight is to be regarded as a life-saving act.[89]

While one might infer from the existence of "eye banks" that the requirement of חולה נמצא לפנינו is not satisfied, this is not the case. Transplantation is performed within three to seven days after donation.[90] Furthermore, over ninety percent of all such procedures successfully restore the recipient's vision.[91] With 43,743 corneal transplants in 1994, this represents both the most common and most successful transplant procedure being practiced,[92] "despite a continual shortage of donors."[93] To the extent that restoration of eye-sight can be construed as preservation of life, corneas may thus be accorded the halakhic status of vital organs for the purpose of post-mortem donation.

As with other anatomical gifts, one should specify that consent is given for transplantation only. As Rabbi Jakobovits stresses, "the disused part of the eye after the cornea has been removed should not be disposed of except by burial."[94]

B. Skin

The use of tissue from cadaveric donors for skin grafting, however, presents a different set of considerations. According to Dr. Richard Kagan[95] of the Shriner's Burn Institute of Cincinnati, and chairman of the American Association of Tissue Banks' Skin Council, the most urgent need for skin-grafting is in the treatment of severe burn victims. While some surgeons prefer to use skin within three days of death, this is not always possible. Skin is frozen in a cryostat, and retained by skin banks until a need arises. Due to the nature of their injuries, unlike other transplant recipients, there can

---

[87] According to UNOS, sixty-nine such procedures were performed in 1994, as compared to 11,108 kidney transplants.

[88] *PRA* 17 (1953): 42.

[89] Jakobovits, p. 285.

[90] "Questions and Answers About Eye Donation and Corneal Transplantation," Eye Bank Association of America.

[91] Ibid.

[92] Ibid.

[93] "Transplant Gives Gift of Sight," *ConnSight* (Newsletter of The Connecticut Eye Bank & Visual Research Foundation), (Jan. 1995): 1.

[94] Jakobovits, p. 286.

[95] This characterization of skin grafting and skin banks, as well as all otherwise unattributed quotations in this section, are based on a telephone interview with Dr. Kagan, 18 Dec. 1995.

be no waiting list for burn victims. The need is sudden and immediate.

The preferred method in treating burn victims is "auto-graft," the transfer of healthy tissue from elsewhere on the victim's own body. In cases of extensive burning, a "homograft," the transfer of skin from a human donor can be used only as a temporary measure. Skin is typically retrieved from relatively flat surfaces such as the back, thighs, and hips: not from the neck or face. "The grafted skin greatly enhances the surgeon's ability to handle a burn wound and to prevent infection," but must be considered "life-enhancing, not life-saving." Skin used in a homo-graft eventually falls off the wound "like a scab." Where auto-graft is impossible, homo-graft is "the tool of first choice." Synthetic "skin" can serve the same purpose, but represents "a very distant second choice."

Cadaveric skin thus represents a preferred mode of treatment, not an indispensable or vital medical resource. Skin homo-grafts cannot properly be classified as transplantation, due to the temporary nature of such procedures. Thanks to the availability of other treatment options, any shortage of donor skin cannot accurately be described as life-threatening. Indeed, death of severe burn victims is increasingly linked not to burns, but to pneumonia resulting from smoke inhalation. Donated skin, while frozen, has a limited "shelf-life." Although the donor can specify that skin not be used for research, tissue which exceeds this period can simply not be used for grafting.

In light of these considerations, no obligation to make an anatomical gift of skin can be inferred from the prohibition of לא תעמוד על דם רעך. Such donations, however, should, if used for healing, be considered entirely permissible[96] acts of profound charity and kindness: חסד.

XII. Conclusion

Given the increasing sophistication and success of transplant technology, and the increased confidence regarding determination of death,[97] the post-mortem donation of vital organs and tissue incontrovertibly constitutes פקוח נפש, which overrides all other considerations. The demand for organs far outweighs the supply, creating thousands of desperate, specific, life-threatening situations.

We must therefore conclude that consent must be granted when requested by doctors or hospitals for use in lifesaving transplantation procedures.[98] This obligation can also be fulfilled by personally registering as a donor by, for example, properly completing a donor card to be carried on one's person,[99] and by informing family members of one's intention in this matter. It is most advisable to provide family members with written documentation of one's donor status, possibly as part of a more general "living will."[100]

---

[96] See, for example, Rabbi David Golinkin, *Responsa of the Va'ad Halakhah of the Rabbinical Assembly of Israel*, vol. 5, p. 122 (Hebrew); Rabbi Grunvald asserts that the prohibition of הנאה מן המת does not apply to skin grafts (*Kol Bo Al Aveilut*, p. 45f (Hebrew)).

[97] While the medical and ethical issues relating to determination of death are increasingly complex, the former rabbinic concern regarding "false death" is no longer compelling.

[98] According to the National Kidney Foundation, "most states have passed 'required request' laws, which make it mandatory for the hospital to offer the family the option of donating their deceased loved one's organs and tissues" ("Understanding the Organ Procurement Process").

[99] Connecticut's 1988 Anatomic Gift Act ruled that "an anatomical gift not revoked by the donor before death is irrevocable and shall not require consent or concurrence of any person after the death of the donor," (Section 2(h)).

[100] See the Rabbinical Assembly's "Jewish Medical Directives for Health Care," edited by Rabbi Aaron Mackler and based on responsa of Rabbis Elliot N. Dorff and Avram Israel Reisner. Through this document one can indicate the "desire that when I die any or all of my vital organs and other body parts be donated for the purpose of transplantation. The rest of my remains should then be buried in a Jewish cemetery in accor-

The preservation of human life is obligatory, not optional. Since all conflicting halakhic duties are suspended, and specific, readily identifiable human lives are at stake, withholding consent for post-mortem organ and tissue donation when needed for lifesaving transplant procedures is prohibited by Jewish law. It violates the Torah's prohibition of לא תעמוד על דם רעך, as well as the prescriptive obligation to preserve human life.[101] This applies to the individual in anticipation of his or her own death, as well as to health care proxies or "next of kin"[102] whenever they are legally empowered to make such decisions[103] on behalf of the deceased. The identity, and certainly the religious status, of the recipient are irrelevant. Life-saving action is obligatory, "even if the donor never knows who the beneficiary will be."[104]

"The act of saving the life of another by donating an organ after death, seems to me the best and most practical demonstration of faith."[105] A bereaved family member who grants consent for organ donation acts as an agent and partner of the deceased in observance of the mitzvah of פקוח נפש. By so doing he or she renders only profound and genuine honor to the deceased, while simultaneously bringing comfort to those who mourn. "There is no greater כבוד המת than to bring healing to the living."[106]

והשואל שופך דמים – One who delays is guilty of shedding blood.[107] When needed for life-saving transplantation, withholding consent for post-mortem tissue donation must be considered forbidden.

כי נר מצוה ותורה אור ודרך חיים תוכחות מוסר

---

dance with Jewish law and custom." The document is distributed by United Synagogue Book Service, 155 Fifth Ave., New York, NY 10010, and appears in *PCJLS 86-90*, pp. 137-153.

[101] See notes 3 and 4.

[102] A typical system of precedence, as in Connecticut's Anatomical Gift Act: spouse, adult son or daughter, parent, adult sibling, grandparent, guardian (Section 3(a)).

[103] Civil law limits the right of a family member to consent to donation, as when "the person proposing to make an anatomical gift knows of a refusal or contrary indications by the decedent." So, too, medical facilities are restricted from accepting organ and/or tissue donations "if the donee knows of the decedent's refusal or contrary indications." (Connecticut Anatomical Gift Act, Sections 3[a] and 6[c], 1988; based on Uniform Anatomical Gift Act [UAGA], U.S. 1987; see Stiller, Appendix E. According to UNOS and the Department of Health and Human Services, Division of Organ Transplantation, similar provisions have been in force in all 50 states since 1968. For a state by state analysis of variations and revisions to the UAGA, see D. Sipes and L.J. McGaw, "UNOS & Uniform Anatomical Gift Act Revisions," *Nephrology News and Issues*, June 1989.) So, too, the Human Tissue Gift Act of 1986 (Ontario, Canada; Similar legislation has been adopted in all Canadian provinces and territories): "No person shall act upon a consent given under this section if he has reason to believe that it was subsequently withdrawn...[or] if he has reason to believe that the person who died or whose death is imminent would have objected thereto" (Stiller, Appendix D). Such refusal, however, is itself in violation of Jewish law. Under ordinary circumstances, an instruction to violate Jewish law, even by a parent, must be disregarded (see Lev. 19:3, Rashi ad loc., citing B. Baba Metzia 32a; Yoreh De'ah 240:15). Since such disregard would violate the law of the land, one is, rather, duty-bound to urge revocation of such refusal prior to death, explaining both the extent of the need and the religious imperative. It should be noted, however, that mere "failure to make an anatomical gift...is not an objection to the making of an anatomical gift" (Section 3[e]). Similarly, "A gift to give (or a refusal to give) certain particular parts is not to be taken as a refusal to give other parts. Thus the next of kin may feel free to give additional anatomical gifts," (see Sipes/McGaw, p. 21; citing Revised UAGA, sections 2[j] and 2[k]).

[104] Rabbi Moshe Tendler. See n. 70.

[105] Stiller, pp. 166-167.

[106] Rabbi Isaac Klein, *A Guide to Jewish Religious Practice* (New York: Jewish Theological Seminary, 1979), p. 275.

[107] It is likewise incumbent upon individual rabbis and rabbinic organizations to educate the Jewish community as to the seriousness of this religious obligation. (See, for example, "Resolution on Organ and Tissue Donation," *PRA* 52 (1990): 279.

והנשאל הרי זה מגונה שהיה עליו לדרוש ברבים – "A rabbi whose spiritual charges delay life-saving action out of ignorance of the law is disgraced, for he has been remiss in not addressing the matter publicly" (Orah Hayyim 328:2, Magen Avraham ad loc.).

YD 336.1996

ORGAN AND TISSUE DONATION CARD

Rabbi Joseph H. Prouser

This pamphlet was developed and then subsequently approved by the CJLS on June 12, 1996, by a vote of seventeen in favor and one abstention (17-0-1). Voting in favor: Rabbis Kassel Abelson, Ben Zion Bergman, Stephanie Dickstein, Elliot N. Dorff, Arnold M. Goodman, Susan Grossman, Judah Kogen, Vernon H. Kurtz, Alan B. Lucas, Aaron L. Mackler, Lionel E. Moses, Paul Plotkin, Avram Israel Reisner, Joel E. Rembaum, Elie Kaplan Spitz, Gordon Tucker and Gerald Zelizer. Abstaining: Rabbi Myron S. Geller.

The Committee on Jewish Law and Standards of the Rabbinical Assembly provides guidance in matters of halakhah for the Conservative movement. The individual rabbi, however, is the authority for the interpretation and application of all matters of halakhah.

Summary

The Rabbinical Assembly Committee on Jewish Law and Standards has ruled that one is obligated to permit postmortem transplantation of his or her organs in lifesaving medical procedures and that withholding consent for such organ donation is contrary to Jewish law.

"*There is no greater K'vod ha-Met (honor to the deceased) than to bring healing to the living.*" (Rabbi Isaac Klein)

The Need

- Over 68,000 people are waiting for organ transplants.
- Of this number, over 2,100 are children.
- Many thousands more need donated tissues.
- Every 16 minutes a new name is added to the list.
- Typically, 13 patients each day (5,000 each year) die while waiting for their life-saving organ transplant.

The Success

- Most organ transplants are very successful, either saving lives or greatly improving the quality of life for the recipients.
- One-year success rates range from 70% for livers and lungs, to over 90% for kidneys.

- Many of these recipients have had functioning transplants for over 25 years.
- Success rates continually improve as better methods to control rejection are identified.

The Process

1. Collect information about donation and transplantation.
2. Familiarize yourself with the Jewish obligation to preserve life.
3. Talk to your family about your decision.
4. Sign the attached donor card in the presence of two witnesses.
5. Carry the signed card in your purse or wallet with your identification. Include your donor status in any more comprehensive advance medical directives.

Other Information to Help You Decide

- The body of an organ and/or tissue donor is always treated with care and respect.
- There is no charge to the donor or to his or her family for donation.
- Organ and tissue donation will not delay funeral arrangements.
- Studies show that organ donation helps to shorten the time needed by members of a bereaved family to recover from their loss.
- The traditional Jewish belief in resurrection in no way precludes organ donation.

"You shall not stand idly by the blood of your neighbor." (Lev. 19:166)

"Anyone who is able to save a life but fails to do so violates this Mitzvah." (Maimonides)

"It is not merely permissible for a Jew to bequeath his organs for transplantation following his death, it is a Mitzvah for him to do so, in order to save one life, or several lives." (Rabbi David Golinkin, Law Committee Chairman, Rabbinical Assembly of Israel; Dean, Seminary of Jewish Studies, Jerusalem)

"The overriding principles of honoring the dead (K'vod ha-Met) and saving lives (Pikuah Nefesh) work in tandem. That is, saving a person's life is so sacred a value in Judaism that if a person's organ can be used to save someone else's life, it is actually an honor to the deceased." (Rabbi Elliot N. Dorff, Rector, University of Judaism)

"The preservation of human life is obligatory, not optional. Since all conflicting halakhic duties are suspended and human lives are at stake. . .consent must be granted for postmortem organ donation when requested by doctors or hospitals for use in lifesaving transplantation procedures. . . .This applies to the individual in anticipation of his or her own death, as well as to health care proxies or next of kin whenever they are legally empowered to make such decisions on behalf of the deceased." (Rabbi Joseph H. Prouser, "The Obligation to Preserve Life and the Question of Post-Mortem Organ Donation," Responsum adopted by the Rabbinical Assembly Committee on Jewish Law and Standards)

The Donor Card

Please detach and give this portion of the card to your family. You may wish to provide copies of this document to various family members:

"This is to inform you that I want to be an organ and tissue donor if the occasion ever arises. Please see that my wishes are carried out by informing attending medical personnel that I am a donor. In so doing, you will be acting as my partner and agent in the Mitzvah of *Pikuah Nefesh*, saving lives.

"In keeping with the Jewish belief that the human body is God's creation, and is thus to be accorded sanctity even after death, please see that all appropriate steps are taken on my behalf to maintain *K'vod ha-Met* (honor to the deceased). As soon as needed organs or tissues are retrieved in accordance with my instructions, see that the rest of my remains are buried in a Jewish cemetery, in accordance with Jewish law and custom."

Thank you.

Signature: _____ Date: _____

- -

In keeping with the moral and religious teaching of Jewish law, and in an effort to help others, I hereby make this anatomical gift, if medically acceptable, to take effect upon my death. For Purposes of Transplantation Only, I donate:

_____ a) Any needed organs or tissues
_____ b) Only the following organs or tissues: _____

Limitations or special wishes, if any: _____

Signature of donor: _____ Birthdate: _____

City and State where signed: _____ Date: _____

Witness: _____

Witness: _____

Must be signed by donor and two witnesses in the presence of each other.

YD 336.1999-

Organ Donation: Parts I-IV

Rabbi Joel Roth

Preface

I shall forego an extensive excursus on the history of organ transplantation, as interesting as it would be. I do so because the reality of transplantation is so clear that the historical discussion would add little of substance to our halakhic deliberation. Similarly, I shall also not include an extensive description of the scientific background. Whenever such material is required to comprehend the halakhic discussion, I shall include it within the body of the halakhic discussion.[1]

Part I: Artificial Limbs

This paper was approved by the CJLS on March 16, 1999, by a vote of eighteen in favor (18-0-0). Voting in favor: Rabbis Kassel Abelson, Ben Zion Bergman, Elliot N. Dorff, Jerome M. Epstein, Baruch Frydman-Kohl, Myron S. Geller, Nechama D. Goldberg, Arnold M. Goodman, Susan Grossman, Judah Kogen, Vernon H. Kurtz, Alan B. Lucas, Aaron L. Mackler, Lionel E. Moses, James S. Rosen, Joel Roth, Elie Kaplan Spitz, and Gordon Tucker.

The Committee on Jewish Law and Standards of the Rabbinical Assembly provides guidance in matters of halakhah for the Conservative movement. The individual rabbi, however, is the authority for the interpretation and application of all matters of halakhah.

שאלה

Is the use of artificial limbs and organs permissible in Jewish law? Are any limbs more problematic halakhically than others? If permissible, are there any restrictions in general or in particular?

---

[1] A good summary of that material can be found in Abraham Steinberg, ed., אינציקלופדיה הלכתית רפואית (Jerusalem: The Dr. Falk Schlesinger Institute, 1991), pp. 191-210.

תשובה

In general, the use of artificial organs and limbs for transplantation is the least problematic halakhic area. So long as the chances for successful implantation and use are greater than the danger involved to the patient from the procedure or its possible after effects, it is difficult to see what the halakhic objections might be. Indeed, for precisely this reason, there is very little in the halakhic literature on the use of artificial limbs and organs, with the exception of the case of the artificial heart. Thus, it is clear that the use of artificial heart valves,[2] bone replacements, joints, and skin is acceptable without any reservations.

We should, in fact, include dialysis in this category of deliberation,[3] since dialysis is a type of mechanical replacement for insufficiently functioning kidneys. The cleansing of toxins from the blood can be accomplished artificially either by hemodialysis or by peritoneal dialysis. The former requires the patient to be hooked up to a machine, usually several times a week for several hours each. It causes a significant loss of mobility to the patient, who must always be near his or her appropriate place of treatment. Peritoneal dialysis, in which the removal of toxins is accomplished via a stoma in the abdomen, is much more convenient for the patient as far as restrictions on normal life activities is concerned. It does, however, entail greater medical risks than hemodialysis. The greatest risk is the risk of infection – peritonitis. However, since kidney failure results in death, it is clear that the risk and/or inconvenience of either of these methods is far outweighed by their benefit, and, when medically indicated, there can be no halakhic objection to dialysis.

One more artificial "organ" should be included in the category of the clearly permissible. The heart-lung machines used during open heart surgery are, of course, artificial organs. Obviously, however, they are not used except in cases when open heart surgery is required, and we must assume that the surgery is being performed because there is greater risk or danger to the patient without it than with it. Under those circumstances, it is clear that there is no halakhic objection to the use of the artificial heart-lung machine during the surgery.

The single artificial organ to which significant attention has been paid in the halakhic literature is the artificial heart. At present, of course, there is not much of a success rate in the use of an artificial heart, and work on it must be considered still experimental. On the one hand, therefore, it might be possible to claim that its use is currently forbidden in Jewish law. Since the likelihood of success is so minimal, the patient should not agree to its implantation, and the halakhically committed doctor should also not agree to perform the operation. That is precisely the contention of Abraham Sofer-Abraham, who wrote in his medical commentary to Shulhan Arukh entitled *Nishmat Avraham*:[4] במצב היום שהדבר הוא אך ורק בגדר הנסיוני, מסתבר שיהיה אסור לחולה להסכים לניתוח כזה ולרופא לבצע זאת. – "In today's situation where [artificial heart surgery] is entirely experimental, it seems probable that it is forbidden for the patient to agree to such surgery, and for the doctor to perform it."

On the other hand, even that is not so clear. After all, the most famous case of artificial heart surgery was that of Dr. Barney Clark, in 1983. Dr. Clark lived for 112 days after implantation of his artificial heart. And, his surgery was pushed up one day earlier than originally scheduled because his doctors were convinced that he would not live out the

---

[2] This includes even porcine parts. See below, pp. 208ff.

[3] I recognize, of course, that dialysis machines and heart-lung machines (which will be mentioned in the next paragraph) are not actually artificial organs. Organs are permanently affixed or implanted and these are not. Nonetheless, this is the appropriate place for their mention.

[4] *נשמת אברהם* (ירושלים: מכון שלזינגר, תשנ"ג), הלכות עבודת כוכבים, סימן קנ"ה, אות ב (1), עמוד מ"ה.

night if surgery were not performed immediately.[5] So, for Dr. Clark, even the very experimental procedure served to prolong his life, the dangers of the procedure and its uncertainty notwithstanding. The halakhic dilemma, of course, lies in the fact that the judgment of the likelihood of prolonged life with an experimental procedure can only be made with relative precision after the fact. Nonetheless, it is sufficient to note that an absolute prohibition against the use of an admittedly experimental procedure is unwarranted. We should remember that initiating a highly experimental treatment is likely only when all else has failed, and the condition of the patient leaves no other option, short of allowing the patient to die. Under those conditions, it is not self-evidently clear that use of an artificial heart must be considered halakhically forbidden, even today.

Since the matter of agreeing to experimental treatment is not the subject of this paper, we shall suffice with a brief statement. We quote the following from Dr. Avraham Steinberg:[6]

> חולה שצפוי למות בזמן קרוב, וכבר קיבל כל הטיפולים הידועים והמקובלים עד כה, וכעת רוצים לנסות עליו תרופה חדשה, או טיפול ניסיוני אחר, אשר מצד אחד יתכן שיאריך את חייו, אך מאידך עלול לקרב את מיתתו... מסקנת הפוסקים היא שמותר לעשות כן אם הסיכוי להצלה הוא גדול יותר מהסיכון למות.

> [In the case of a] sick person whose death is expected soon, and who has already received all of the known and customary treatments, and now they want to try some new drug, or other experimental procedure on him, which, on the one hand, might prolong his life, but, on the other hand might hasten his death...the conclusion of the poskim is that it is permissible to do so, if the likelihood of saving is greater than the danger of dying.

One of the central issues in the literature regarding cadaver heart transplants has been the question of the harvesting of the donor heart, and whether or not that very act constitutes an act of homicide. When we deal with heart transplants of that nature, we will address that question. In the matter of artificial hearts, however, the issue is moot, since there is no donor. In that regard, then, the use of artificial hearts is less problematic halakhically than the use of cadaver hearts because one side of the equation — the donor side — has no halakhic problem whatsoever, since there is no donor.

Of course, even in the use of artificial hearts there is a recipient, just as there is in cadaver heart transplantation. We shall focus now, therefore, on the halakhic issues as they involve the recipient of a heart, either cadaver or artificial. If the issues can be resolved permissively, we shall have reached the conclusion that artificial heart transplantation is permissible (and that cadaver heart transplantation is permissible from the perspective of the recipient).

In the earliest discussions of the halakhic status of heart transplant surgery, the questions regarding the recipient focused on two issues: (1) Does the removal of the diseased heart itself constitute an act of homicide?[7] (2) If it is an act of homicide, what is the legal status of the heart recipient following a successful heart implantation?

---

[5] See the *New York Times*, 24 Mar.1983, p.1.

[6] אנצקלופדיה הלכתית רפואית (ירושלים: המבון ע"ש ד"ר פלק שלזינגר, 1994), כרך ד', ערך "נסויים רפואיים בבני אדם," עמ. 489-490. Dr. Steinberg provides a bibliography there, in n. 90. See especially *Iggrot Moshe*, Yoreh De'ah, pt. 1, no. 36.

[7] The question of the halakhic acceptability of brain death is irrelevant to this issue since heart transplants are not performed on brain dead recipients.

The major sources brought to bear on the first question reflected a dispute between Rabbi Zevi Ashkenazi (Hakham Zevi, 1660-1718) and Rabbi Yonatan Eybeschuetz (1690-1754). In three teshuvot,[8] the Hakham Zevi dealt with the case of a woman who was preparing a chicken to be soaked and salted and claimed that she could find no heart in it. The Hakham Zevi affirmed that the chicken was to be considered kosher because no creature can live for even an instant without a heart.[9] Therefore, he concluded, the cat which had been nearby waiting to eat must have managed to take away the heart without the woman's noticing. The chicken, however, is kosher! What's more, even if there are witnesses who claim that they saw the whole process from beginning to end and who testify that there was no heart, the chicken is still considered kosher because they must be lying.

Eybeschuetz took issue with the decision of the Hakham Zevi, at least in the instance when there are witnesses.[10] He claimed that the witnesses are to be believed because we have no real grounds to make them into false witnesses by our mere assertion that they must be. The reality must have been that there was no normal heart (hence the testimony of the witnesses), but rather, יש לתלות... דיש דבר אחר דלמראית עין אין מראהו דומה ללב כלל... שהיה משמש במקום הלב – "It should be assumed that there was some organ (tissue) which did not at all have the appearance of a heart, but which fulfilled the function of the heart."[11]

Among the earliest poskim who dealt with the issue of heart transplants, the views of the Hakham Zevi and the *Kereti u'Feleti* played a significant role. Rabbi Judah Gershuni wrote:[12]

> אם מותר להוציא הלב מהחולה מסוכן כדי לשתול לב חדש, דאם נאמר דתיכף כשמוציאין את הלב הוא נחשב כמת וע"י הוצאת הלב הורגין בן אדם... אם כן אפשר דאסור לעשות כן... ואף שהיה מקודם בבחינת טריפה על פי קביעות הרופאים, בכל זאת אסור לכתחילה להרוג טריפה ויש כאן איסור לאו דלא תרצח... ומה ששותלין אח"כ לב חדש הוה כבריה חדשה.

> Regarding whether it is permissible to remove the heart from a dangerously ill person in order to implant a new heart, for if we say that immediately upon removal of the heart he is considered dead and that murder is committed by removing the heart...[i]f so, it may be forbidden to do so...[a]nd even though the person was already in the category of a *terefah* by determination of the doctors, it is nonetheless forbidden before the fact to kill a *terefah* and involves a violation of the negative commandment "Thou shalt not murder"...[a]nd the subsequent implantation of a new heart constitutes the person as a new being.

The source for Gershuni's initial premise is the Hakham Zevi, as he himself says in a part of the responsum not quoted. Note, too, how Gershuni moves from the first of the two issues (is it murder?) to the second (what is the status of the patient after receiving the

---

[8] שו"ת חכם צבי, סי' ע"ד, ע"ו, ע"ז.

[9] And any body motion that exists must be considered merely convulsive (פרכוס), and not indicative of life.

[10] See כרתי ופלתי (על יו"ד), סי' מ' סע' ה', ס"ק ד' בכרתי.

[11] Interestingly, the כרתי ופלתי did not declare the chicken kosher. He declared it *terefah* on the grounds that it didn't have a normal heart. The Hazon Ish (Rabbi Abraham Karelitz, 1878-1953), Yoreh De'ah 4:14, took exception to the decision of the כרתי ופלתי, at least according to Eybeschuetz's own reasoning, for it is the absence of a heart that makes an animal *terefah*, not the normalcy of the appearance of the heart.

[12] אור המזרח, vol. 18, no. 3 (issue 64), Nisan 5729, p. 138, reprinted in the collection of his responsa, ספר קול צופיך, Jerusalem 5740, p. 378b.

heart?). The fact that the person is now alive does not necessarily imply that the act of removing his heart was anything but murder. No matter what the positive result, the doctor has committed murder.[13]

Rabbi Menahem M. Kasher also dealt at length with the views of the Hakham Zevi and Eybeschuetz.[14] After quoting from the responsum of the Hakham Zevi, Kasher wrote:[15]

> הרי מפורש יוצא מדבריו לפי שיטתו, שבעת שנוטלין ממנו הלב, לא רק
> שאין לו חזקת חיים, אלא שיש לו דין מת ממש, ובוודאי לשיטתו אם בא
> לשאול, אם לעשות נתוח כזה, יש לפסוק לו שאסור לישראל לכתחילה
> לעשות נתוח כזה, שהרי הוא ממית עצמו בכך. ואף שהרופאים אומרים
> שעל ידי הנתוח אפשר שיחיה תקופה יותר ארוכה מאשר אם לא יעשה נתוח
> כזה, מ"מ מכלל ספק לא יצא. והנה לשיטת החכ"צ אין ספק חיים יותר
> ארוכים בעתיד מתירים מיתה ודאית לחיים שהם ברגע זה חיים ודאים,
> ואפילו אפשר שאינם אלא חיי שעה.

> It clearly follows from his words that according to his (the Hakham Zevi's) view, when his heart is removed from him, he has not only lost the presumption of life, he has the legal status of a dead person. And surely according to his view, if one comes to ask whether to undergo such surgery, one must decide for him that it is forbidden for a Jew to undergo such surgery, *a priori*. In doing so he commits suicide. And even though the doctors claim that the surgery may enable him to live longer than he would without the surgery, [their claim] is still in the category of "doubtful." And, according to the Hakham Zevi, "doubtful" longer future life does not permit "certain" death for life which is "certain" at this moment, even if it is possible that [his current life] is only temporary.

And, like Rabbi Gershuni, Kasher also links the second issue with the first. Near the end of his teshuvah Kasher wrote:[16] על מה שכתבתי לעיל שלדברי החכ"צ אם הוציאו הלב מן האדם יש לו דין מת... נמצא שיש בחידוש השתלת הלב מעין תחיית המתים. "Regarding my earlier claim that according to the view of the Hakham Zevi one has the legal status of a dead person if his heart has been removed. . .it follows that the renewal [of life] by the heart implantation is a type of revival of the dead."

Furthermore, Kasher makes an important observation regarding the relationship of the views of the Hakham Zevi and Eybeschuetz. He wrote:[17]

> ובכן המו"מ בין הגדולים הנזכרים נוגע רק בנקודה זו, שלפעמים נוצרה
> אפשרות באבר אחר למלא התפקידים של הלב, אבל כשהלב הנורמלי נעקר
> הרי אז בוודאי שאין בגוף חיות עצמית עד שהמחדש נקלט כראוי ומפעיל את
> כל הגורמים להחיות את כל חלקי הגוף כקדם.

> And so, the debate between the two sages whom I have mentioned regards only this point: that perhaps a condition can exist

---

[13] Gershuni does not reach a definitive conclusion. Indeed, the section of the responsum from which the quotation in the paper comes ends with ועוד צריך עיון גדול בזה ללבן ההלכה.

[14] See *Noam*, vol. 13, 5730, pp. 10-20, printed as well in דברי מנחם, חלק ג', חשן משפט, סי' כ"ז, pp. 240-245.

[15] *Noam*, p. 12, דברי מנחם, p. 241a.

[16] *Noam*, p. 20, דברי מנחם, p. 244b.

[17] *Noam*, p. 11, דברי מנחם, p. 240b.

where some organ (tissue) can fulfill the function of the heart. But when the normal heart is removed [and there is no such other tissue present], surely [both agree] that the body has no independent vitality until the new heart is appropriately implanted and controls the functions necessary to revitalize all the parts of the body as prior.

Rabbi Kasher makes very clear that, in his opinion, the dispute between the Hakham Zevi and the *Kereti u'Teleti* does not have any real significance regarding the matter of the permissibility of removing the heart from the potential recipient of a transplanted heart. Even according to Eybeschuetz, when the damaged heart is removed the person is considered dead because there is no basis to claim that there was some other tissue perfoming the functions of the heart at the time of the removal of heart.[18]

Rabbi J. David Bleich has also written an extensive article on the subject of the artificial heart.[19] He, too, concurs that the dispute between the two sages of the eighteenth century may not indicate any difference between them with regard to the removal of the diseased heart. He wrote:[20]

> It has been argued that, since according to the Hakham Tsevi it is impossible for any creature to survive without a heart, removal of a diseased heart *ipso facto* causes the death of the patient and hence constitutes an act of homicide. Reanimation by means of subsequent implantation of a cadaver heart would thus be viewed either as a form of *pirkus* (convulsive movement) or as the generation of a new life.
>
> Actually, the selfsame argument can be formulated in a manner which is entirely consistent with the position of the *Kereti upeleti*. As already noted, this authority accepts the basic premise that, absent a heart, a living creature cannot survive. *Kereti upeleti* merely posits the possibility that cardiac functions may be assumed by an organ which does not at all resemble a normal heart. Hence *Kereti upeleti* might well concede that removal of the heart from a living creature would lead to its immediate demise.

Before we deal with the question of whether or not the removal of the diseased heart is itself an act of murder, let us deal first with the matter of the status of the recipient subsequent to the implantation of the new heart, *even if we assume that the removal of the diseased heart was an act of murder.*

We saw above that Gershuni, Kasher, and Bleich refer to the person as a type of new person, an instance of revival of the dead — at least according to their understanding of the view of the Hakham Zevi. So, let us pose a question that will seem absurd at first blush. If a person is killed and then revived, is his halakhic identity the same after his revival as it

---

[18] Kasher also does not reach a definitive conclusion in his earlier version. His responsum, in *Noam*, ends with והדבר צריך עיון גדול. In דברי מנחם, however, there is an additional small section which does affirm that the removal of a heart from one live person for implantation in another constitutes murder, and while that statement was made about the donor, there is no halakhic difference between removing the heart of a still-living donor and removing the heart of a still-living recipient.

[19] The article appears in Hebrew in תורה שבעל פה 25 (5744): 151-163, and in English, A.M. Fuss, ed., *Jewish Law Association Studies III* (Atlanta: Scholars Press, 1987), pp. 109-145.

[20] In the English version, p. 121, and in the Hebrew article (in slightly different wording), p. 155.

was before his death? If the answer is affirmative, his wife would still be his wife, his children would not have automatically inherited his estate, his family would not have been required to sit shivah and begin the recitation of kaddish. If the answer is negative, his wife would be free to remarry without a *get*, mourning rites should have begun, and his estate would have been passed already to the heirs. These questions may be fascinating (though absurd) to raise, but the answer to them is of interest to us for only one reason. If the person remains the same person halakhically, and if a doctor is confident that he will be able to resurrect the person he kills by implanting an artificial heart, there *may* be grounds to conclude that the act of removing the heart would not itself be an act of homicide. Such a possibility is untenable if the person becomes somebody new as a result of the implantation. The "earlier" person is dead, the "revived" person is an entirely new entity.

It is quite clear that the literature cannot be full of prior precedents on this matter. There seem to be two approaches to this issue in the literature. One of them is reflected well and succinctly in an article by Rabbi Moshe Hershler, who wrote:[21]

> האם יש לדון שעם השתקתו של הלב הטבעי נעשה האדם בגדר "מת," והשתלתו של הלב המלאכותי הוא מעין "תחיית המתים" מחודשת. יסוד גדול חייבים תמיד להזכיר בזה, כי להחיות אדם מת אינו בכוח של האדם והמדע. מפתח תחיית המתים נמסר ביד הקב"ה[22]... וכל שאנו רואים שאדם קם לתחייה אחר שנחשב כמת, הוכיח סופו על תחילתו שמעולם לא מת הלז... משום כך אין לשאול כאן ולהסתפק דמיד כשהוציאו והשתיקו את הלב, ונשאר זה נטול לב, נמצא כאילו האדם מת ואינו חי, ורק עם השתלת הלב החדש קם זה לתחייה.

> Ought we to consider that with the stopping of the natural heart the person becomes categorized as "dead," and that the implantation of the artificial heart constitutes a type of new "resurrection of the dead?" We are duty bound to mention in this context an important axiom: that resurrecting the dead is not within the power of humans or science. The key to resurrection is entrusted only to God[23]...and whenever we see a person resurrected after being considered dead, the end proves about the beginning that the person was never really dead....Therefore, there is no reason to ask in our case and to wonder whether upon removing and stopping the heart, leaving the person without a heart, it is as though the person has ceased living and died, and only upon implantation of the new heart been resurrected.

Hershler's approach is more theological than halakhic. True resurrection of the dead is only within the capability of God. If humans perceive something as death followed by resurrection through human agency, it could not have been death. If that is the way it appeared to us, we must change our definition of death. Thus, there is no halakhic impediment to the removal of the diseased heart. It cannot be murder since the subsequent rean-

---

[21] "הלב המלאכותי בהלכה" in *הלכה רפואה* 4 (5745): 84-90. The quotation comes from p. 87. An earlier version of this article appeared in תורה שבעל פה, 5743, pp. 99-103. The quotation does not appear in the תורה שבעל פה version.

[22] He adds: וכל התופעות שאנו מוצאים כמעשה אליהו ואלישע ושאר צדיקי עולם, תופעות ניסיות הם למעלה מן הטבעיות והישג אדם.

[23] He adds: And all of the instances which we do find, like the acts of Elijah and Elisha and other righteous of the world, are miraculous occurrences, beyond nature and human ability.

imation of the person demonstrates that death had not really occurred. For Hershler, then, the status of the "reanimated" person is clear. It is the same person as before, because there was no death.

Not surprisingly, Hershler's approach is not shared by Bleich, who seeks more classical halakhic evidence to answer the question. He starts with the premise that, with the removal of the heart, the person is, in fact, dead, at least according to the Hakham Zevi and Eybeschuetz. Assuming that, what is the person's status following reanimation? The Gemara records:[24]

> רבה ורבי זירא עבדו סעודת פורים בהדי הדדי. איבסום. קם רבה שחטיה לרבי זירא. למחר בעי רחמי ואחייה. לשנה אמר ליה ניתי מר ונעביד סעודת פורים בהדדי. אמר ליה, לא בכל שעתא ושעתא מתרחיש ניסא.

> Rabbah and Rabbi Zeira made their Purim meal together. They became drunk, and Rabbah arose and slaughtered Rabbi Zeira. The next day he prayed on his behalf and restored him to life. The next year he said to him: "Let the master come and we will have a Purim meal together." He responded: "A miracle does not occur every moment."

In commenting on this episode recorded in the Gemara, Rabbi Hayyim Joseph David Azulai (Hida, 1724-1806) wrote the following:[25]

> ויש להסתפק, אשת ר' זירא כי נשחט בעלה ומת ודאי פקעי קדושיהו והותרה לשוק, וכי חיה למחר ר' זירא היה צריך לקדש לאשתו קידושין חדשים דפנויה היא, ודמי למחזיר גרושתו דבעי קידושין חדשים דקידושי קמאי נדדו הלכו בגט ופנים חדשות באו לכאן, והוא הדין בזו שמת בעלה הנה מיתתו מתירה אף מפקיעה קידושין דידיה, וכי הדר חי, מילתא חדתא היא. או דילמא הא דהאשה קונה עצמה במיתת הבעל היינו דווקא כאשר מת ונשאר מת, אך כשלא נקבר וחי ע"י נביא או חסיד, אגלאי מילתא דאותה מיתה לא היתה מיתה כמות כל האדם, ולא פקעי קידושי קמאי, ואשת איש, ולא תפס בה קידושי דאיניש דעלמא, ובעלה כאשר חי מותר בה מיד כאשר היה לפני מותו.

> The following is in doubt: When Rabbi Zeira was slaughtered and clearly dead, was the marriage between him and his wife absolutely dissolved with her becoming marriageable to others, such that when he was resurrected the next day he had to betrothe her anew because she was unmarried? [Is this case] comparable to one who remarries a woman whom he has divorced, which requires a new betrothal because the first marriage is gone, terminated by divorce, and a new situation is now present; such that similarly in the case where her husband has died, his death makes her permitted to others and terminates his marriage to her and when he is subsequently revitalized it is a new matter? Or perhaps, the premise that a woman acquires the right to marry others upon the death of her husband applies only when the man has died and remained dead, but if he were never buried and was resurrected

---

[24] Megillah 7b.

[25] ברכי יוסף, אבן העזר, י"ז: א.

by some prophet or righteous figure it becomes clear that his death was not a normal death, and his original marriage is not terminated, his wife remains married to him and any betrothal contracted by her with another is null and void, and when her husband is revitalized he may resume marital relations with her immediately, as it was before his death?

The Hida raises the question of the halakhic status of a person who has died and been resurrected. He couches it in the clearest of all categories, a man's marriage to his wife. Death terminates a marriage. If the resurrected man is halakhically a new creature, that new creature was never married to the woman who was the wife of the person who has died. If, however, the legal status of the revived man is the same as it was prior to his death, he is not a new creature, and remains married to his wife. This is the question that the Hida has raised. He turns to the Yerushalmi to find the answer.

The Mishnah reads:[26] הרי זה גיטך מעכשיו אם לא באתי מכאן ועד י"ב חדש ומת בתוך י"ב גט — חדש הרי זה גט "[If a man says:] 'Let this be your divorce from now if I do not return within the twelve months,' and he dies within twelve months, it is a valid *get*." On this the Yerushalmi comments:[27] מהו שתהא מותרת לינשא? ר' חגיי אתר מותרת לינשא, רבי יוסי אמר אסורה לינשא, אני אומר נעשו לו נסים וחיה — "What is the law regarding her right to be married [immediately upon learning of the death]? Rabbi Haggai said: 'She is permitted to marry [immediately].' Rabbi Yosi said: 'She is forbidden to marry [immediately]. For I say that perhaps miracles were performed for him and he was resurrected.'"[28] Obviously, if the classical codes include the view of Rabbi Yosi as law, the answer to the question of the status of the resurrected man would be clear. He would be the same person after revival as he was before death. However, that is not the case. When Maimonides recorded the consequences of the Mishnah he wrote:[29] הרי זה גיטך מעכשיו אם לא באתי מכאן ועד י"ב חדש... מת בתוך י"ב חדש אע"פ שאי אפשר שיבוא והרי היא מגורשת לא תנשא במקום יבם עד אחר י"ב חדש כשיתקיים התנאי — "[If one says to his wife:] 'This is your divorce from now if I don't return within twelve months'...and he died within the twelve months, even though it is impossible for him to come and she is divorced, she should not get married in a case when the levirate law would apply until after twelve months have passed and the condition has been fulfilled." In other words, Maimonides' concern is whether her remarriage would be permitted because she is a widow or because she is a divorcee. If the former, she must comply with the levirate laws if they apply; if the latter, the levirate laws are inapplicable by definition and she may marry whoever she wishes. So, he mandates that she wait until she definitely becomes a divorcee, making the levirate laws inapplicable. Maimonides is obviously *not* concerned with the possibility that the husband *himself* might return after being miraculously revived.

The question for the Hida then becomes the following: Does the failure of the poskim to take account of the view of Rabbi Yosi indicate that he is mistaken? If the view of Rabbi

---

[26] Gittin 7:8, 76b.

[27] Gittin 7:3, 48d (40a).

[28] That is, had the man been resurrected and returned home within the twelve months, he would not be divorced from his wife. And if we would permit her to remarry immediately upon hearing of the death of her husband, we do not take account of this possibility, and the result might be that she would be married adulterously to a second husband because her original husband has been miraculously resurrected and returned home within the time frame of his condition.

[29] M.T. Hilkhot Gerushin 9:11, and cf. S.A. Even HaEzer, 144:3.

Yosi is mistaken, then a person who was miraculously revived would be legally a different person from the one who died. And if Rabbi Yosi is not mistaken, why do the poskim ignore his view? The Hida wrote:[30]

> אף שהפוסקים לא חיישי כלל לשמא נעשו לו נסים וחיה, היינו מפני שזה לא שכיח כלל, ואפי' ר"מ דחייש למיעוטא[31] מ"מ למיעוטא דמיעוטא לא חייש, כ"ש דלא חייש להא דלא שכיח כלל. מ"מ מוכח מהירושלמי דאם אחר שמת נעשו לו נסים וחי אכתי אגידא ביה אשתו זאת, ולא מהניא לה מה שמת ודאי, דלבסוף חי. ובהא אית לן למימר גדם תלמודא דידן מודה, דאי אתרמי כי האי, המיתה שמת כמאן דליתה.

> Even though the poskim do not concern themselves at all with the possibility that he was revived by miracles performed on his behalf, the reason [for the lack of concern] is because it is a very uncommon occurrence. And even Rabbi Meir who is concerned about infrequent occurrences,[32] is not concerned with very infrequent occurrences, and surely is not concerned with this possibility which is *utterly* infrequent. Nonetheless, it is clearly demonstrated from the Yerushalmi that if one is miraculously revived after he has died, he remains married to his wife. Even the fact that he was definitely dead is irrelevant since, in the end, he lived. And regarding this even our [Babylonian] Talmud would agree, that if something like this happened, the death would be as though it didn't happen.

The Hida makes several important points. First, the silence of the poskim does not mean that Rabbi Yosi is incorrect. They ignore his view because the law simply does not mandate required behaviors on the basis of infrequent occurrences, and certainly not on the basis of utterly infrequent occurrences. Second, even though the Bavli's analysis of the Mishnah in Gittin ignores Rabbi Yosi's view altogether, that should not be misunderstood. The Bavli ignores Rabbi Yosi because what he posits is so unlikely, not because he would be wrong if it actually occurred.[33] Third, the person may, in fact, have died. The death, however, is rendered null and void by the subsequent resurrection. The Hakham Zevi and Rabbi Yonatan Eybeschuetz can be correct that the removal of the heart entails certain death. What the Yerushalmi proves is that the death is superseded by the subsequent revival, without any legal change in the status of the person who died.

As applied to the question under discussion, Bleich puts it well:[34]

> According to *Birke Yosef*'s analysis, it necessarily follows that removal of a diseased heart followed by implantation of either a cadaver organ or an artificial heart does not constitute an act of

---

[30] See above, n. 25.

[31] יבמות קי"ט, א, ומובא בהרבה מקומות.

[32] Yevamot 119a, and referred to in many places.

[33] This point is very important for the Hida. If the interest of the Bavli in the levirate issue must be understood to imply that it is the only possible issue, the Bavli would have rejected the view of Rabbi Yosi, not simply ignored it. If the Bavli rejects a view of the Yerushalmi, it is the Bavli which prevails in the determination of the law. Rabbi Yosi would be deemed incorrect, and were any person to be resurrected he would have to be considered a new person, legally speaking.

[34] English article, p. 117; Hebrew version (not quite identical with the English version), p. 153.

homicide since, in his view, death is retroactively nullified by virtue of subsequent animation.

To this point, therefore, we conclude that the status of the recipient of an artificial heart is the same after the implanation as it was prior to the removal of his heart. According to Hershler this is so because he cannot have been considered dead, since resurrection is only possible for God, not for doctors. According to the Hida, it is so because the subsequent resurrection nullifies the death and the view of Rabbi Yosi in the Yerushalmi proves that the status of the individual is unchanged after his revival from what it was before his revival.

It is a little surprising that Bleich did not refer to a source even earlier than the Hida. Rabbi Hayyim Benveniste (1603-1673) refers, as well, to the same issue, though from the perspective of the death of the woman. He wrote:[35]

וסבור אני דאם מתה אשה תחת בעלה מיתה ודאית ושוב חיתה על ידי נביא כמו אליהו לבן הצרפתית[36] ואלישע לבן השונמית[37] דלא פקעה זיקת הבעל מעליה ואינה יכולה להנשא לאחר, ויש סעד מעובדא דאשת ר' חנינא בן חכינאי.[38]

And it seems to me that if a woman died, unmistakably, while married, and was then revived by a prophet, like Elijah with the son of the Zarephatit[39] or Elisha and the son of the Shunamit,[40] her marital relation has not been terminated, and she may not marry another. And there is support [for this contention] from the precedent of the wife of Rabbi Hanina ben Hakhinai.[41]

The case of the wife of Rabbi Hanina records the miraculous resurrection by Rabbi Hanina of his wife, whom he surprised by returning from the academy after a twelve-year absence from home. Upon seeing him, she died. Rabbi Hanina cried out to God: "Is this her reward [for faithfulness during my long absence]?" He prayed on her behalf, and she was resurrected. This incident is taken as support for the claim of Benveniste because there seems to be no indication that there was any need for a new act of betrothal by Rabbi Hanina.

Rabbi Eliezer Waldenberg deals with the question of the need for a new betrothal following the stoppage of the natural heart for open heart surgery in a thorough responsum. He writes there:[42]

העלה הבעל כנסת הגדולה בפשיטות דלא פקעה זיקת הבעל מעליה ואינה יכולה להנשא לאחר, וא"כ דין מינה במכל שכן על כגון נידוננו דלא מת ממש וחיותו של הבעל נמשכת במציאות כל הזמן דבודאי ובודאי דעל ידי הוצאת הלב לזמן מה לא נפקע על ידי כך כלל זיקתו של הבעל, והרי היא נידונית בכל העת ההיא כאשת איש גמורה, וממילא כשמחזירים לו הלב וחוזר לחיות חיי משפחה אינה זקוקה כלל לקדושין מחדש.

---

[35] כנסת הגדולה, אבן העזר סי' י"ז, הגהות הטור אות ב'.

[36] 1 Kings 17.

[37] 2 Kings 4.

[38] Ketubot 62b.

[39] 1 Kings 17.

[40] 2 Kings 4.

[41] Ketubbot 62b.

[42] שו"ת ציץ אליעזר, חלק ט"ז, סי' כ"ד. The quotation in the paper comes from p. 52, letter *heh*.

The author of the *Keneset ha-Gedolah* concluded definitively that the marital relationship was not terminated, and that the woman could not marry another. If so, deduce from that by an argument of "surely so" regarding our case (of open heart surgery) in which the man does not actually die, and his vitality continues in reality throughout. It is absolutely clear that the act of removing the heart temporarily does not terminate the marital status. His wife is considered throughout to be married, and certainly when his heart is restored and he resumes normal family life she requires no new act of betrothal.

Thus, it is clear to Waldenberg that the person remains after the surgery exactly the same person as before the surgery. And, in a later responsum,[43] he makes very clear that there would be no difference in this regard between a case in which the heart is physically removed from the body and a case in which the heart is merely stopped, but not physically removed.

There is one more direction for our discussion of this issue to take. We quoted Bleich above[44] to the effect that the *Kereti u'Feleti* may not disagree with the Hakham Zevi. Bleich also argues in the opposite direction, and his argument is convincing. The argument between the Hakham Zevi and Eybeschuetz is most probably over the probability that the chicken had some other organ that took over the functions of the heart. The Hakham Zevi considered that so unlikely a prospect that he was compelled to consider false the testimony that there was no heart present. But what would the Hakham Zevi say if he had incontrovertible evidence that some other organ had *in fact* assumed the functions of the heart? Surely it is not the physical presence of an actual heart that determines for him whether there is life present. When people die, the heart remains physically present, but the people are dead. Why should the opposite case be any different? If some other organ were *clearly and incontrovertibly* fulfilling the functions of the heart would there be any reason for the Hakham Zevi to disagree with the *Kereti u'Feleti*? Logic would dictate a negative answer. What must matter for both of them is whether there is something causing the blood to flow through the circulatory system. If there is, the person is alive; if there is not, and it cannot be quickly restored, the person is dead. It is a functioning heart or heart replacement that is determinative for both. Death is not caused by the stoppage of the heart, but by the irreversible cessation of cardiac activity. Were that not the case, every instance of open heart surgery would also be an act of homicide, for the pulsation of the heart is stopped on purpose[45] and the functions of the heart taken over by a heart-lung machine. No halakhic decisor has even raised this issue, let alone determined that open heart surgery is forbidden because it constitutes homicide. The reason must be obvious. It is cardiac function that is critical, not whether that function is being carried out by one's heart.

Bleich is not the only, or even the first, to make this claim. It appears before him, too. The earliest claim to this effect, as far as I have been able to find, was made by Rabbi Aryeh Leib Grossnass, who wrote:[46] ואף שהחח״צ כתב דבלי לב הוי כמת, אבל בעניננו שהמכונה עושה כל תפקידי הלב ולא נפסק זרם מרוצת הדם בגוף אף לרגע ואח״כ כששתלו בו הלב היה חי א״כ בודאי לא היה מת מעולם — "And even though the Hakham Zevi wrote that without a heart one is considered dead, surely in our case we must consider that the person was never dead since

---

[43] Ibid., no. 64.

[44] Above, p. 199.

[45] In order to prevent movement of the organ being operated upon.

[46] שו״ת ליב אריה (London: 5733), vol. 2, 36, p. 120b.

a machine fulfilled all the functions of the heart and the flow of blood through the body did not stop even for a minute, and after the implantation of the heart the person was alive." Hershler also made a similar claim.[47]

A fine synopsis of the issues and the directions we should go in on this issue can be found in נשמת אברהם:[48]

> במרוצת הזמן אי"ה והידע הרפואי יתקדם עד שיהיו סיכויים טובים וברורים להצלחת הניתוח ולהארכת ימי החולה, יתכן שאז יהיה מותר לחולה שימיו ספורים, וככל ניתוח לב פתוח. והסכים אתי בענין זה הגאון רש"ז אויערבאך שליט"א [זצ"ל]. ואמנם ראיתי שדנו בזה לאיסור משום רציחת החולה בעצם הוצאת הלב מגופו. אך צריך עיון, הלא בכל ניתוח לב פתוח היום׳ אמנם אין מוציאים את הלב מגופו של החולה, אך משקיטין אותו לחלוטין על ידי תרופות וכל תפקידו של הזרמת דם לכל חלקי הגוף נעשה ע"י מכונה (לב מלאכותי) העומד מחוץ לחולה ובו הוא קשור, ולא שמעתי על מי שמפקפק בניתוח לב פתוח משום רציחת החולה... ובמיוחד כאן שתפקוד הלב, דהיינו הזרמת דם לכל חלקי הגוף, נעשה ע"י מכונה.

> With the passage of time, God willing, and the advancement of medical knowledge, [this matter of artificial hearts] will progress to the point that the chances for successful surgery and the prolonging of the life of the patient will be good and clear. It is probable that at that time it [implanting an artificial heart] will be permissible for a terminal patient, just as any open heart surgery. And Rabbi Shlomo Zalman Auerbach agreed with me on this matter. Indeed, I have seen that some have judged this forbidden on the grounds of the murder of the patient by the very removal of the patient's heart. But the argument requires investigation because in every open heart surgery today, while it is true that the heart is not removed from the patient's body, drugs are administered to stop the heart completely, and the function of causing the blood to flow through the entire body is carried out by a machine (artificial heart) which is external to the patient and to which he is attached, and I have not heard of anyone who harbors reservations about open heart surgery on grounds of murdering the patient. . .and especially in this case where the functioning of the heart, i.e., causing the flow of blood throughout the body, is fulfilled by a machine.

We have thus supported logically, theologically, and by formal halakhic argumentation our intuitive feeling that artificial hearts must be halakhically acceptable, provided they are medically feasible.

There are two final postscripts to add to this section of the paper. First, we have been dealing with the long term use of an artificial heart as a permanent replacement for one's natural heart. It is in this area that the success rate is thus far not very great, though improving. Artificial organs are also being used with greater success as temporary replacements, pending finding a natural organ for implantation. Since the success rates are reasonable, there is little halakhic objection to attaching a patient to an artificial heart

---

[47] See above, n. 21. In the תורה שבעל פה article, see p. 101, and in the הלכה ורפואה article, see p. 87.
[48] See above, n. 4.

replacement while waiting for the availability of a heart for implantation. The wrinkle in this is that the longer one is attached, the more medical problems are likely to develop, particularly infection and internal bleeding, and with these developments, the patient becomes an increasingly less likely candidate for a transplant. Thus, careful attention must be paid to the likely time until the replacement heart becomes available.

Second, when the time arrives that use of artificial hearts becomes common, it will probably be possible in some instances to utilize parts of the diseased heart which are still functional for implantation in others. There should be no halakhic objection to such use, provided the decision to implant an artificial heart is made independent of the need of a potential recipient for heart parts.[49]

Conclusions

1. The use of artificial heart valves, bones, joints and skin is permissible.

2. Both hemodialysis and peritoneal dialysis are permissible.

3. The use of a heart-lung machine during open heart surgery is permissible, as is its use as a temporary measure awaiting the availability of a heart for transplantation. In the latter case, consideration of the likely time span before receiving the heart for transplantation should be a factor in deciding whether or not to use it, since prolonged use may create complications that will make successful transplantation less likely.

4. Use of an artificial heart as a long term matter is fraught today with dangers, and is very experimental. Agreeing to such surgery should be discouraged so long as there is any other alternative whatsoever. However, if there is no other alternative available and the prospect for prolonged life is greater with an artificial heart than without it, it is permissible to implant an artificial heart even today.[50]

5. When the success rate for artificial hearts becomes such that the likelihood of successful implantation and use are greater than the danger to the patient from the procedure or its possible after effects, the routine use of artificial hearts will be permissible. Indeed, it will be preferable because it will eliminate the need to wait until a donor heart becomes available, and it will obviate the need to fix the moment of the death of the donor. The act of removal of the diseased heart is not an act of murder, and there is no change in the halakhic status of the patient after implantation than before removal of the diseased heart.[51]

---

[49] See the end of Hershler's article, referred to above, n. 21.

[50] Compare below, n. 68.

[51] This claim is an interesting correlative to the case of conversion. There we claim halakhically and psychically that the convert is "reborn" after conversion even though he or she is the same person physically. Here, the person remains the same person legally and psychically even though he or she has been "reborn" physically.

Part II: Use of Animal Organs

This paper was approved by the CJLS on March 16, 1999, by a vote of eighteen in favor (18-0-0). Voting in favor: Rabbis Kassel Abelson, Ben Zion Bergman, Elliot N. Dorff, Jerome M. Epstein, Baruch Frydman-Kohl, Myron S. Geller, Nechama D. Goldberg, Susan Grossman, Judah Kogen, Vernon H. Kurtz, Alan B. Lucas, Aaron L. Mackler, Lionel E. Moses, Mayer Rabinowitz, James S. Rosen, Joel Roth, Elie Kaplan Spitz, and Gordon Tucker.

The Committee on Jewish Law and Standards of the Rabbinical Assembly provides guidance in matters of halakhah for the Conservative movement. The individual rabbi, however, is the authority for the interpretation and application of all matters of halakhah.

שאלה

Is the use of animal tissues or organs for transplantation in humans permissible in Jewish law? If permissible, are there any restrictions?

תשובה

The use of animal organs for human transplantation is no less experimental than the use of an artificial heart.[52] In a certain sense, the success rate for such experiments is even more disappointing than the rate for artificial hearts. Attempts have been made, though not in any great numbers, since 1964. Thus far, all attempts at the transplantation of animal organs into human beings have failed to prolong the lives of the recipients significantly.[53] Even in the most successful case thus far, the Baby Fae case of 1984, in which the heart of a baboon was implanted into the chest of an infant, the infant continued to live for only twenty days.[54] Thus, it is clear that all of the cautionary comments made in the previous section with regard to the experimental nature of artificial heart implantation will apply to this issue as well.[55]

If and when animal organ transplantation becomes a medical feasibility, it will go without saying that halakhah will demand that the animal organs be taken from the animals with all due consideration to the issue of צער בעלי חיים. It will be equally true, however, that the primacy of human life over animal life will also be an halakhic given.

This is not the place to engage in a lengthy discourse on the issue of צער בעלי חיים. We shall suffice with brief proof that the primacy of human life over animal life will be an halakhic given. The Bible itself hints that animals are to be used by humans for their needs. Gen. 1:28 gives humans dominion over the animals, and Gen. 9:2 ff. intimate the right of humans to utilize animals for their needs. Nahmanides also makes it very clear in his commentary to Gen. 1:26 that the term וירדו implies dominion and rule.

The idea that humans have the right to use animals for their own purposes, and that that was the intent of creation, is implied in the baraita quoted at the very end of Kiddushin (82b):

---

[52] See above, p. 195 for our brief comments on experimental treatment.

[53] A summary of attempts at such implantation can be found in W.E. Parks et al., *Surgical Clinics of North America* 66:663, 1986.

[54] See L.L. Bailey et al., *JAMA* 254:3321, 1985.

[55] In regards to both artificial hearts and animal organs, I have been speaking only of the permissibility of their use. I can as yet conceive of no circumstances in which it would be halakhically mandatory to agree to either type of medical experimentation.

> ר' שמעון בן אלעזר אומר: מימי לא ראיתי צבי קייץ וארי סבל ושועל
> חנווני, והם מתפרנסים שלא בצער, והם לא נבראו אלא לשמשני....

> Rabbi Simon the son of Elazar says: I never saw a deer tending crops, or a lion bearing a burden, or a fox operating a store, and they sustain themselves without suffering, *and they were created only to serve me*. . . .

The earliest responsum that deals specifically with the applicability of צער בעלי חיים to uses of animals by human beings is by Rabbi Israel Isserlein (1390-1460)[56] who affirmed that pulling feathers out of a live goose was not forbidden on grounds of צער בעלי חיים, so long as one was doing it for one's need and use, since all creatures were created for the use of human beings. His student, Rabbi Jonah (Ashkenazi),[57] subsequently wrote[58] in the name of Tosafot Avodah Zarah[59] that even though the prohibition against צער בעלי חיים is דאורייתא, if there is some purpose behind the act, it is permissible. To this Rabbi Jonah adds that the "some purpose" means "some medical purpose," even for one who is not dangerously ill. Finally, for our purposes now, this view is codified by Rabbi Moses Isserles:[60]

> כל דבר הצריך לרפואה או לשאר דברים, לית ביה משום איסור צער בעלי
> חיים.

> The prohibition against cruelty to animals does not apply to anything which is needed for purposes of healing, or other matters.[61]

When that time comes, and it becomes clearer exactly what issues of צער בעלי חיים may be involved, it will be critical to have a paper dealing with that subject. That paper will have to discuss even the ultimate question, namely, whether considerations of צער בעלי חיים can ever outweigh the use of an animal organ to save or to prolong a human life. The focus of our discussion at the moment, however, is on the permissiblity in halakhah of having an animal organ implanted into a human at all.

While the issue of צער בעלי חיים is what makes animal organ transplantation more halakhically complicated than artificial organ transplantation, animal organ transplantation is not a difficult halakhic issue. Given the axiomatic premise that human life takes precedence over animal life, there could be no halakhic objection to the use of animal organs to save the lives of humans. Even now it is not at all uncommon for valves from the hearts of pigs to be utilized in heart valve replacement surgery of human beings.[62] Of course, if artificial and animal organs were both equally feasible and equally effective, whatever issues of צער בעלי חיים might exist would make it preferable to utilize an artificial organ. Obviously, though, if both were available, but the animal organ would be more effective, it would be preferable to an artificial organ.

---

[56] תרומת הדשן, פסקים וכתבים, סי' ק"ה.

[57] See below, n. 230.

[58] ספר איסור והיתר, כלל נ"ט, דין ל"ו.

[59] Probably 11a, ד"ה עוקרין, even though the wording is not exactly as quoted by the ספר איסור והיתר.

[60] אבן העזר סי' ה', סע' י"ד.

[61] For other responsa which also affirm that צער בעלי חיים does not apply when there is medical need, see שו"ת שבות יעקב ח"ב, סי' ע"א, שו"ת בנין ציון ח"א, סי' ק"ח, שו"ת חלקת יעקב ח"א, סי' ל', שו"ת שרידי אש ח"ג, סי' ד', שו"ת ציץ אליעזר חי"ד, סי' ס"ח.

[62] It is interesting to point out that the Gemara in Ta'anit 21b also posits the similarity of swine internal organs to human internal organs. On that basis it mandates that a pestilence among swine is grounds for declaring a fast for humans. See Orah Hayyim 576:3.

After the Baby Fae case, Rabbi Shlomo Goren wrote an article in the Mizrahi – Po'al ha-Mizrahi newspaper הצופה[63] in which he wrote:

אין כל סבה לחשוש מהשתלת לב בבון או אפי' של חיה באדם משום שמשוכנעים אנו שהלב שיושתל, במידה שההשתלה תצליח, לא יהווה יותר מאשר משאבה להספקת דם מחומצן למוח ללא כל השפעה אינטלקטואלית או פסיכולוגית על האדם.... יוצא איפוא למסקנה שכל שיתברר שמבחינה רפואית יוכל הלב של בבון וכיוצא בו למלא את תפקידו הפונקציונלי של הלב הטבעי של האדם, לא תתעורר שום בעיה של שינוי זהות באדם שבחזהו הושתל לבו של הבבון, וממילא אין שום הסתייגות הלכתית או אתית יהודית מהשתלת לב חיה או של קוף בחזהו של אדם, בתנאי שיעלו הסיכויים להאריך חייו של האדם מעבר לימים ספורים, כפי המצב עד כה, כדי שלא לסכן לשוא את חיי השעה של החולה בנסיון כירורגי–רפואי.

> There is no reason to be concerned about implanting the heart of a baboon, or even a beast, in a human being. For we are convinced that the transplanted heart, insofar as the transplant succeeds, will be nothing more than a pump for the provision of oxygenated blood to the brain, with no influence whatsoever on the human, intellectually or psychologically. . . .It follows as a conclusion, therefore, that whenever it becomes clear that medically speaking the heart of a baboon, or similar animal, can fulfill the functional purpose of the natural heart of a person, there will arise no problem of changed identity of the person into whose chest the baboon's heart has been transplanted. As a result, there should be no halakhic or Jewish ethical reservation regarding the transplantation of the heart of an animal or monkey into the chest of a human being. [This permission] is conditional upon an increased probability that the life will be increased by more than a few days, as is now the case, otherwise we should not endanger in vain even the temporary (terminal) life of one who is sick, for a surgical-medical experiment.

Some of the wording of Rabbi Goren's conclusions will make better sense when it is understood that he devoted a large part of his article to proving that it is not the heart alone which determines and controls humanness and human characteristics and attributes. One can even understand the issue on a theoretical level. After all, the Midrash counts and lists fifty-eight characteristics which emanate and are controlled by the heart.[64] Perhaps, then, metaphysically speaking, if one were to implant an animal heart in a human being, that human being might acquire the characteristics of the animal that its heart controlled, and lose those characteristics of his own human personality that were controlled by his now-removed human heart. Once Rabbi Goren was able to dismiss that concern, there remained for him no other real halakhic concerns. Nor do there remain any such concerns for us.

Lest there be any ambiguity whatsoever, we should make clear that if and when such transplants become frequent, there will also be no restriction whatsoever on the animals

---

[63] 6 Kislev 5745 (30 Nov. 1984), p. 5, with conclusion on p. 8.
[64] Kohelet Rabbah 1:38. Biblical proofs are adduced for all 58.

which can be used. Yehudah ha-Levi said it well enough in the *Kuzari*:[65] קשה בעיני הקראי ההנאה מן החזיר, אפילו לשם רפואה, אם כי על צד האמת אין זאת כי אם אחת העבירות הקלות שאדם חייב עליהן מלקות – "It bothers the Karaite to derive any benefit from a pig, even for purposes of healing. In fact use of a pig [by eating it] would be no more than a minor infraction for which a person would be liable for lashes [and not liable at all when used for medical reasons]."[66]

It is highly premature to attempt anything but a brief comment about the latest experimental technology called xenografts or xenotransplantation. The technology attempts to utilize organs of animals for transplantation into humans (usually pig organs, which resemble human organs both in infancy and adulthood). Obviously, if such a technology were to become scientifically feasible, many problems could be solved, particularly the problem of the shortage of available organs for transplantation. The major problem to be met, scientifically, is the matter of rejection by the body of the "foreign" implant. One of the avenues being tested includes some genetic engineering of the pigs to include some human genes, in order to minimize that problem.

There are, also, scientific concerns that have to be resolved, including the danger of transferring disease from animals to human beings, which is probably what happened with HIV.

This is a very new field, and it is in its infancy. Halakhically, however, there would be no objection to the utilization of such organs for transplantation.[67]

Conclusions

1. When medically feasible, the use of animal tissue or organs for transplantation into humans will be entirely permissible.

2. At that time, there will be no restrictions on the animals that may be utilized as donors.

3. Animal transplants are currently experimental, with little probability of extending the life of the recipient significantly (if at all). Under these circumstances, agreeing to such a procedure should be weighed very carefully against its risks.[68]

---

[65] Kuzari 3:49, in the Dvir Publishing ed. of 5733, p. 134.

[66] I admit that the wording of the *Kuzari* is a little cryptic. It seems to me unthinkable, however, that Yehudah ha-Levi is claiming that deriving benefit from pig meat for purposes of healing would be punishable in Jewish law. That might be possible only if one were talking of someone not seriously sick. More likely, the phrase אפילו לשם רפואה is parenthetical, and אם כי על צד is the direct continuation of הנאה מן החזיר. This is the way I have translated it.

[67] I offer Web site URLs for several articles about xenografts. The first of them ends with a link to a bibliography:

www.onysd.ednet.edu/~g98s46/library/xenografts.html

www.the-scientist.library.upenn.edu/yr1995/august/ . . .

www.dukenews.duke.edu/med/xenobkgd.htm

www.cdc.gov/ncidod/EID/vol2no1/michler.htm

[68] I am very aware of the difficulty implied by the fact that I am discouraging Jews from allowing themselves to be used as experiments, and allowing them to derive the benefits of others doing just that. Nonetheless, I remain convinced that this difficulty does not override the halakhic mandate to preserve even חיי שעה when tampering with it is not likely to produce positive benefits to the patient. The wording of the conclusion avoids positing an absolute prohibition, however. I can imagine circumstances similar to those of the Dr. Barney Clark case in which it would be halakhically permitted to allow oneself to undergo a transplant from an animal donor, even knowing the experimental nature of the operation and the slim chance for prolonged benefit.

Part III: Live Donors — Blood and Bone Marrow

This paper was approved by the CJLS on March 7, 2000, by a vote of fifteen in favor, one opposed, and five abstaining (15-1-5). Voting in favor: Rabbis Kassel Abelson, Elliot N. Dorff, Paul Drazen, Samuel Fraint, Nechama D. Goldberg, Arnold Goodman, Judah Kogen, Vernon H. Kurtz, Alan B. Lucas, Aaron L. Mackler, Daniel Nevins, Paul Plotkin, James S. Rosen, Joel Roth, and Gordon Tucker. Voting against: Rabbi Elie Kaplan Spitz. Abstaining: Rabbis Ben Zion Bergman, Susan Grossman, Mayer Rabinowitz, Avram Israel Reisner, and Joel E. Rembaum.

The Committee on Jewish Law and Standards of the Rabbinical Assembly provides guidance in matters of halakhah for the Conservative movement. The individual rabbi, however, is the authority for the interpretation and application of all matters of halakhah.

שאלה

Is it halakhically permissible to donate blood or bone marrow for one who needs them now? If so, is it ever halakhically required to do so? If so, when? May one donate blood for deposit in a blood bank? For storage for one's own later use? May one donate blood or bone marrow for compensation? Under what circumstance, if any, may blood or bone marrow be donated on Shabbat?

תשובה

At the present time, there are only four transplants from live donors: blood, bone marrow, liver parts, and kidneys.[69] The first, blood, is often not even popularly thought of as a transplant, though technically, of course, it is. There would be a certain logic to treating all four of these together. However, there are also good reasons to treat blood and bone marrow together, and kidneys[70] separately. The two things that distinguish blood and bone marrow from kidneys are that the former two replenish themselves after being removed from the donor, while the removed kidney does not; and, in general, there is very little danger to the donor from the extraction of the blood or the bone marrow, while there is some danger in the removal of the kidney, both immediate and potentially in the future. Because these differences are so important, this paper will treat kidneys separately in the next section. The drawback to this approach is that in those few areas of real halakhic concern regarding blood and bone marrow, the issues become the same as those involved in kidney transplants, and it is our intention to leave detailed discussion of those issues to the next section. Hopefully, this will not be too difficult a problem.

We shall take no time in proving both the need and usefulness of blood and bone marrow in the critical medical treatment of patients, both being exceptionally clear.

As a general and guiding principle it would seem logical to posit that the utilization of organs, limbs, or tissues from live donors would be least difficult to justify halakhically when: (A) the extraction or removal of the organ does not produce any significant medical danger to the donor; (B) the life of the donor subsequent to the removal of the organ

---

[69] Ovary implantation and sperm donation would be other instances of live donor transplantation, with their own set of complicated halakhic issues. Since these matters are the subject of a separate paper before the CJLS (see below, pp. 461-509), this paper will not treat them at all.

[70] Whatever conclusions will apply to kidneys will apply, in principle, to liver parts, as well. Thus, we will not treat them separately. However, see below, pp. 308-309.

is basically unaffected by the fact that it has been removed; (c) the donor does not require special treatments or extensive medical follow-up; and (D) the implantation of the organ, limb, or tissue extracted from the donor is the most beneficial treatment for the recipient and has a good medical chance of working.[71] The first three of the points above most surely apply to blood and bone marrow donation. In the case of blood, the discomfort is usually no more than the initial discomfort of the insertion of the needle, and the follow up "medical treatment" is basically limited to drinking more than usual for a brief period of time, and restricting the giving of a subsequent donation for a period of six to eight weeks. (None of this is to deny that some people get very nervous and/or faint prior to donation, during it, or subsequent to it; feel weak after donation and must lie down for some brief period; and generally find the experience unpleasant and would rather avoid it entirely.) In the case of bone marrow donation, the amount of marrow removed is usually between three and five percent of the marrow of the donor, and it takes between two and three weeks for the marrow to be replenished. The discomfort of donation is greater than that of giving blood, as absolutely evidenced by the fact that bone marrow aspiration is carried out under general anesthetic, that the donor is kept in the hospital for observation for a day or two, and that there is often soreness around the pelvis which is the primary site of the aspiration.[72] The fact of the use of general anesthetic also increases the medical dangers to the donor.

But, when all is said and done, neither procedure is particularly complicated, nor are the inherent dangers very great. The follow up is relatively simple. And the beneficial and life saving or prolonging effect of the donation cannot be gainsaid. Even the issue of the danger of the general anesthesia must be kept in perspective. At the current time, the mortality rate from general anesthesia is about 1 in 10,000, and appears to be even lower for young people, those in good health, and those who are anesthetized for only brief periods.[73] It seems inescapable, therefore, to conclude that blood and bone marrow donations are halakhically permissible, at least sometimes.

We have couched the first question of this section of the paper in terms of blood and bone marrow donations to "one who needs them now," because that is the simplest of the issues. We shall discuss some of the more complicated issues in a subsequent section, where we will deal thoroughly with the primary sources which allow these types of activities only under the circumstance – כשהחולה לפנינו, and particularly the responsum of the *Noda B'Yehudah*.[74] What is clear now, however, is that when there is "one who needs them now," blood and bone marrow donations are permissible.

The question to which we move now, then, is whether one can be halakhically compelled to donate either blood or bone marrow for the life saving benefit of a חולה לפנינו. The *Nishmat Avraham* states the following with the apparent agreement of Rabbi Shlomo Zalman Auerbach:[75]

---

[71] In adopting these criteria, I agree with Dr. Abraham Steinberg, who lists them in the entry השתלת איברים in the אנציקלופדיה הלכתית רפואית, p. 213.

[72] The greater pain involved in bone marrow donation carries with it some halakhic complications. See below, n. 249.

[73] See Alan F. Ross and John H. Tinker, "Anesthetic Risk," in Robert Miller, ed., *Anesthesia*, 3d ed. (New York, 1990), vol. 1, pp. 712ff.; and J. David Bleich, *Contemporary Halakhic Problems*, vol. 4 (New York: Ktav Publishing House, Inc. and Yeshiva University Press, 1995), pp. 286f., and especially n. 29.

[74] נודע ביהודה תנינא, חלק יורה דעה, סי' ר"י.

[75] נשמת אברהם, הלכות אבלות, סי' שמ"ט, ס"ק ג(2).

> מוח עצם – כאן אין כל סכנת ניתוח מבחינת התורם אך יש סכנה של מיעוט
> דמיעוטא עקב ההרדמה כללית בזמן לקיחת מוח העצם ממנו.... כאן
> לכאורה לכל הדעות יהיה מותר, ומצוה לקרוב משפחה לנדב את עצמו
> לעת הצורך כדי להציל נפש מישראל, והסכים אתי הגרש"ז אויערבאך.

> Bone marrow — Regarding this there is no surgical danger for the donor, even though there is a very small degree of danger as a result of the general anesthesia. . . .In this case it is likely that according to all opinions it is permissible, and it is a mitzvah for familial relations to volunteer at the time of need in order to save a Jewish life. And Rabbi Shlomo Zalman Auerbach agreed with me in this matter.

The essence of the claim is that the only argument which might be presented against some type of mandatory donation of bone marrow is the argument that it poses danger to the donor. Since those arguments are inapplicable to bone marrow donation, there could be no grounds for a prohibition. Thus, it is surely permissible. It looks, though, that the choice of the word mitzvah is not accidental, and that it implies an act of goodness and piety — a good deed — but not a legal obligation that could be compelled in the case of refusal. It is also unclear why the donation would be a mitzvah for family members, but not for others.[76] Though Sofer-Abraham gives a hint of something beyond mere permission, it is difficult to deduce a legal obligation from his words. Finally, it would follow from this statement of the *Nishmat Avraham* about bone marrow, that it would apply קל וחמר to blood, at least so far as the mitzvah status of donation at time of need is concerned. It is not clear whether the *Nishmat Avraham* would mandate an actual obligation for blood donation.

It is possible that his very carefully worded statement is an attempt to take into account the opinion of Rabbi Eliezer Waldenberg, to whom Sofer-Abraham addressed a question in 5736. The *Nishmat Avraham* had published an article in *Noam* about medical experimentation on human beings.[77] Rabbi Waldenberg sent him some comments, which he subsequently published in *Ziz Eliezer*.[78] There he wrote:

> ועל כן דעתי להלכה היא דנהי דאם הרופאים קובעים שאין כל סכנה
> בניסים כאלה שמציעים שאז מותר לו לאדם למסור את עצמו לעריכת
> ניסים שכאלה בגופו לטובת חולה אחר, וכן לתרום מדמו וכדומה, וגם
> מקיים מצוה בכך, אבל לחייב אותו עבור כן על פי דין תורה, זה אי אפשר
> בשום פנים.

> Therefore my legal opinion is that if the doctors determine that there is no danger in the experiments which they suggest, it is permissible for a person to allow himself to be experimented upon for the benefit of another ill person, and similarly, to donate blood and such things. Indeed, he perfoms a mitzvah thereby. But it is absolutely impossible to obligate him for such things by law of Torah.

---

[76] But see our discussion below, p. 315.

[77] *Noam* (Jerusalem: מכון תורה שלמה, 5734), vol. 17, pp. 160-163.

[78] Vol. 13, no. 101. The quoted selection is from par. 6.

There is also a later responsum in which Rabbi Waldenberg reaffirms his view. It is important to note that responsum, since one might otherwise be misled by it. In 5743, the *Ziz Eliezer* was asked if there is an obligation for a sickly and squeamish (חלוש ורך מזג) person to donate blood for a dangerously sick person who requires his blood type, which is rare and unavailable for purchase from the blood bank, when donating will weaken the donor and make him bedridden, even though it will not make him seriously ill. Since the question is couched in terms of a sickly individual who would become bedridden as a result of donating blood, it might be possible to understand the answer as restricted to such people. That would be a misreading.

It seems clear, therefore, that the term mitzvah, as used both by the *Nishmat Avraham* and the *Ziz Eliezer* refers to a permissible, desirable, admirable and laudable, but *not mandatory* act. That, too, is what the term will mean throughout this section, unless otherwise indicated in the section itself.

One basis of Waldenberg's responsum[79] is the claim that nobody could ever be obligated to donate a quantity of blood equal to or greater than the amount on which life might depend. And, since the Gemara defines a quarter of a *log* as the minimum definition of נפש,[80] a very small amount indeed, it follows that nobody could be required to donate more than a רביעית. The prohibition cannot be restricted to the sickly, because even the healthy would be potentially endangered by giving more than what the Gemara considers שעור חיות. Thus, even though the question is about a sickly person, the answer is not restricted in any way. It applies to all. And this is what Rabbi Waldenberg concludes:

> ועל כן אין חיוב על האדם לתת רביעית ויותר מדמו לשם הצלת אחר אפילו שיש בו סכנה ולא משיגים סוג דם זה במקום אחר. ורק מי שחפץ ברצון עצמו לתרום מדמו ומרגיש שלא יוזק מזה, מדת חסידות יש בזה, ואשרי חלקו מי שיוכל לעמוד בזה.
>
> Therefore there is no obligation on any person to give a quarter of a *log* or more of his blood, even in order to save someone who is endangered and whose blood type cannot be acquired elsewhere. One who wishes, of his own desire, to donate his blood, and feels that he will not be hurt by that, perfoms an act of piety. Blessed is the lot of one who can do so.

Bleich[81] rejects the reasoning on the *Ziz Eliezer* as "fanciful." The Gemara, after all, views bloodletting as therapeutic,[82] and surely more than a רביעית was removed. Bleich may well be correct about that, but Waldenberg's conclusion should not be rejected so quickly. First of all, this is not his only proof, and we shall get to his other proof shortly. Furthermore, later in his responsum he claims that if it were legally mandatory to donate blood in times of such need, the most devoted advocates of such a mandate would seek the incorporation of the mandate in civil legislation, which has not happened, says the *Ziz*

---

[79] הלכה ורפואה, כרך ד', תשמ"ה, עמ' קמ"ג published also in שו"ת ציץ אליעזר, חלק ט"ז, סי' כ"ג.

[80] See Hulin 72a, Nazir 38a. Although translating rabbinic measures into modern terms is very difficult, a *log* seems to be about 0.3 liters, and a רביעית one quarter of that. One liter = 0.264 gallons. Thus, 0.3 liter would equal 0.079 gallons, and one quarter of that would be 0.019 gallons. That amount translates to approximately 0.16 pint. That is, the Gemara's definition of the amount of blood on which the נפש depends is about 16 percent of the amount of blood taken from blood donors at a blood bank. And, in fact, in times of emergency it is possible to remove more than a pint of blood from a donor without very great danger.

[81] See reference above, n. 73, Bleich, p. 285, n. 28.

[82] Shabbat 128a.

Eliezer. Indeed, to the best of my knowledge, there has been no such suggestion made in the United States or in Israel, ever. Even the medical profession has not made such a recommendation. In both the United States and Israel, furthermore, blood donation cannot be compelled even from members of the military, even when on duty. They may be given inducements to donate, and disinducements if they do not volunteer to donate, but by law they cannot be compelled to donate, and their refusal to donate is not actionable by the American or the Israeli army. Furthermore, if it were halakhically mandated, one should be able to coerce people and remove their blood from them when there is a need, even against their will. Yet, nobody entertains such an idea. Even those whom we shall soon refer to who consider blood donation mandatory do not make this claim.

The basic source for the claim that people can be coerced to perform mitzvot that they do not wish to perform is found in the following statement of the Gemara:[83]

תנינא במה דברים אמורים במצות לא תעשה אבל במצות עשה כגון שאומרין לו עשה סוכה ואינו עושה, לולב ואינו עושה, מכין אותו עד שתצא נפשו.

> We have learned: To what does this apply [Rashi in Ketubbot: that one is given forty lashes]? To negative commandments, but regarding positive commandments, for example, they [i.e., the court] tell him to make a sukkah and he does not do so, to prepare a lulav and he does not do so, we beat him until he dies.

The quotation above might be understood to imply that there can be coercion only regarding positive commandments. That is, for negative commandments one could receive only after-the-fact whipping, but one could not be whipped in order to make one comply with the negative commandment. We shall quote several authorities, however, whose words make quite clear that coercion is also possible for negative commandments (like, for example, the negative commandment לא תעמוד). We must, of course, refer only to negative commandments where the coercion would come in time to prevent the violation of the negative commandment, otherwise, we would apply the first clause of the baraita, namely, that the person who had already violated the commandment would receive the regular, court administered lashes as punishment, but not as preventive coercion.

The Ran wrote the following:[84]

אם היה בפסח והיה אוכל חמץ מלקינן ליה אם לא רצה לעמוד מלאכול חמץ אף דמצות לא תעשה היא מחינן ליה או עד שיאמר רוצה אני או עד שתצא נפשו.

> If it was Passover, and one was eating hametz, we beat him if he doesn't agree to stop eating hametz. Even though it is a negative commandment, we smite him either until he says, "I'll stop," or until he dies.

There is really no ambiguity in these words of the Ran. What they clearly mean is that if coercion can prevent further, on-going violation of the negative norm, we do not satisfy ourselves with the claim that the court will administer the accustomed lashes for violation of that norm; rather, we hit the person who is violating the norm in order to prevent that person from further violation. And, it is absolutely clear from the last words of the Ran, "or

---

[83] Ketubbot 86a, and cf. Hulin 132b, especially Rashi's differing explanations of the first clause.
[84] *Hiddushei ha-Ran* to Hulin 132b.

until he dies," that he is referring to the same type of hitting as the baraita which is the focus of our current discussion. It follows from this claim of the Ran, that if one were violating לא תעמוד by refusing to give blood for someone who needs it, we should be mandated to "twist his arm," quite literally, until he agrees to do so.

Now, one might argue that there is a difference between the case of the Ran and the case we are discussing. In the Ran's case, the person is actually *doing something*. The "something" that he is doing is an act which is legally a negative commandment ("Thou shalt not eat any hametz"), but the person is not simply sitting and doing nothing. In our case, though, the person is not *doing anything*. He is just standing there and refusing to do what לא תעמוד would mandate that he do. Maybe the Ran's claim does not cover such a case. If one wishes to argue thus, it must be pointed out that our case would have to be considered as one of לאו הניתק לעשה, that is, a negative command which is rectified by a subsequent act.[85] That is, if one has eaten a forbidden food, there is no act which can be done to rectify what has already taken place; but if one has refused to give blood, and the person is still alive and in need of the blood, there is an act which can be done to rectify what has taken place (i.e., the refusal) – give blood now. That is precisely what a לאו הניתק לעשה is. If one were to raise this objection to applying the Ran to our case, a quote from Rabbi Zevi Ashkenazi (1660-1718) would indicate that, in fact, coercion should be possible even in such a case:[86] אף בלאו הניתק לעשה אם הוא דבר שאפשר לתקן, ודאי ב״ד כופין אותו, שלא יעבור הלאו מכאן ולהבא – Even in the case of a לאו הניתק לעשה, if it is a matter which can be corrected, surely the court should compel him, in order that he not violate the negative prohibition from now on.

What the Hakham Zevi is saying is that though one does not usually get lashes for a לאו הניתק לעשה, if one is violating that לאו, and can be coerced into not violating it before it is too late, we should coerce the person not to violate it. The result, of course, will be that the person will have learned his lesson, and will not violate it in the future. That is directly applicable to our case. If we truly believe that refusing to give blood is a violation of לא תעמוד, most cases will be such that the coercion could bring about the non-violation of the commandment in the first place, and would surely teach the one coerced that he ought not to violate the commandment in the future.

One might, however, object even to the application of the Hakham Zevi to our case on the grounds that it was our logic that provided the עשה, when, in fact, there really is no biblical *aseh* which serves as the rectification of the לאו of לא תעמוד.[87] To respond to this we refer to the claim of the Gemara[88] that Rava coerced Rav Nathan bar Ami, and took four hundred *zuz* from him for charity. The Tosafot[89] question how Rava could have coerced him, when that seems to violate the dictate of the Gemara[90] according to which no court may compel compliance for any mitzvah for which the Torah itself stipulates a reward, and the Torah stipulates a reward for charity in Deut. 15:10 – "For in return [for giving charity] the Lord your God will bless you in all your efforts and in all your under-

---

[85] For example, the Torah commands in Lev. 19:13 that, "Thou shalt not rob." In Lev. 5:23-24, however, the Torah mandates a positive act which rectifies the offense, namely, restoring the stolen article, plus a twenty percent penalty.

[86] *Hakham Zevi*, no. 105.

[87] It is for precisely that reason that we said above: "would have to be considered as."

[88] Ketubbot 49b.

[89] Ibid., s.v. אכפייה.

[90] Hulin 110b.

takings." Not all of the answers of the Tosafot are relevant to our discussion, but one of them is particularly relevant. In their final line, the Tosafot contend that the reason Rava coerced Rav Nathan bar Ami is because there are two negative commandments about charity: לא תאמץ and לא תקפץ – "Do not harden your heart and do not shut your hand against your needy kinsman."[91] The actual commandments in the Torah concerning charity include two negative commandments. That is why Rava felt it justified to compel the donation from Rav Nathan, say the Tosafot. On this claim of the Tosafot Rabbi Pinhas ben Zevi Hersch ha-Levi Horowitz (1730-1805), teacher of the Hatam Sofer, makes the following observation:[92]

> משמע דפסיקא להו דהיכא דאיכא לאו כופין אותו שלא יעבור, והא דאמרינן לקמן דף פ"ו במה דברים אמורים במצות לא תעשה אבל במצות עשה וכו' צריך לומר דלא מיירי התם קודם שיעבור בלא תעשה דודאי כופין אותו דלא תעשה חמור מעשה כדאיתא דריש פרק האשה רבה אם לא רצה דפנו וכו', אלא מיירי התם במלקות לאחר שעבר הלאו.

> Implied [by the claim of Tosafot] is that it is established law for them that where there is a negative commandment, we may coerce someone in order to prevent them from violating it. Thus, when we say later on, on page 86: "To what does this apply? To negative commandments, but regarding positive commandments," etc., we must say that the Gemara there is not dealing with [what is appropriate] *prior* to violating the negative commandment, for surely under those circumstances we would coerce him, for negative commandments are more stringent than positive ones, as it says at the beginning of Chapter *ha-Ishah Rabbah*, "If he refuses, compel him." Rather, [therefore, we must say] that there the Gemara is dealing with lashes after the לאו has been violated.

We must understand what the claim of the *Sefer Hafla'ah* is. The fact is, he claims, that the Tosafot argue that an act of coercion was legitimate on the basis of the fact that there are two negative commandments regarding the matter about which the coercion took place. That argument would be useless and irrelevant if it were not clear to Tosafot that coercion for negative commandments is mandatory, or, at least, permissible. Thus, the clearest proof that we can coerce for compliance with negative commandments comes directly from Tosafot. Of course, if that is the case, we must understand the first part of the baraita[93] to refer only to lashes *after* the negative commandment has been violated, and not to imply that there would be no lashes for negative commandments prior to the commandments being violated. Regarding lashes prior to the violation of the commandment, negative commandments are no different than positive commandments. For both, coercion to bring about compliance is acceptable. And, it is not only acceptable, it is logical. Why? Because there is a greater stringency regarding negative commandments than positive commandments, and if it is permissible to coerce the observance of positive commandments, surely it is permissible to coerce observance of negative commandments. And how do we know that there is a greater stringency to negative commandments than to positive ones? We know it because the Gemara in

---

[91] Deut. 15:7.

[92] *Sefer Hafla'ah*, to Ketubbot 49b, concerning Tosafot s.v., אכפייה.

[93] See above, p. 216.

Yevamot[94] quotes a baraita which indicates that we must force a priest to refrain from forbidden marriages, and those prohibitions are negative commandments. Yet, we find no instance in which we are told to compel priests regarding positive priestly commandments.

The claims of the Ran, the Hakham Zevi, and the *Sefer Hafla'ah* are logical and compelling. In most instances, violating a negative commandment means that one is doing an act which is forbidden. It is like קום ועשה. Violating a positive commandment means that one is refraining from doing what one is commanded to do, that is, like שב ואל תעשה. If one has violated a negative commandment by doing the forbidden act, coercion is unwarranted because there is nothing one can do about it. But if the negative commandment is such that its violation is an on-going matter (as in the eating hametz case), or that violating it means *not* doing something that is required of one (for example, *not* throwing a drowning person a rope violates לא תעמוד), there is something one can do about it that would result in compliance with what is required, and that is to compel the person not to violate the negative commandment by doing what it is that that commandment demands (i.e., stopping eating hametz or throwing the drowning person a rope). These types of negative commandments are more like a positive one, and just as coercion for positive commandments is normative, so, too, is coercion for negative commandments which are similar to them.

What follows from what we have been discussing for the last several pages is that the compulsion issue which was raised by the *Ziz Eliezer* is not so easily ignored, even if his thesis about the amount of blood which constitutes "life blood" is "fanciful." If one considers failure to donate blood to be a violation of לא תעמוד, there must be serious discussion of the compulsion issue. There has been no such serious discussion, either in halakhic circles or in non-halakhic circles. That can only be because nobody really considers compelling blood donation, literally, to be a viable option. If so, there is no way to call it a violation of לא תעמוד, and that is the category that most of the literature discussing the question seeks to apply to it.

As much as we may wish to encourage and laud those who willingly undertake to donate blood to those in need, Rabbi Waldenberg correctly urges caution against drawing the conclusion that such a donation falls under a person's mandatory halakhic obligation. It is a cautionary note that must be taken to heart, for we would not wish to stipulate a halakhic requirement which we could not really insist upon. We would have to be honest with ourselves about the implications of donation as an halakhic requirement. It is one thing to call an honorable and laudatory act a mitzvah; it is quite another to call it mandatory, with all of the legal implications implied by such an decision.[95] Furthermore, as we shall see below,[96] Waldenberg's thesis is not dependent entirely on this element of the argument.

The above, however, does not mean that no poskim have decided that donation of blood under such conditions is a requirement. Rabbi Samuel ha-Levi Woszner of B'nei Berak is one. He was asked whether a person who has a rare type of blood and refused to donate it for a critically sick individual stands in violation of the prohibition of לא תעמוד על דם רעך – Do not stand idly by the blood of thy neighbor[97] – even if the donor is physically weak, or does not wish to be bothered, or is afraid of donating blood.

---

[94] 88b, referring to Lev. 21:8, and cf. Sifra, *ad locum*.

[95] Others who have taken the same stand include Rabbi Moshe Dov Welner in התורה והמדינה, VII-VIII, 5716-17, pp. 307ff, and, apparently, the Brisker Rav, as indicated in a letter to *Assia*, vol. 14, no. 1-2, p. 208, written by Rabbi Avigdor Nebenzahl.

[96] See below, pp. 220ff.

[97] Lev. 19:16. The responsum appears in שבט הלוי, חלק ה׳, חו״מ סי׳ רי״ט and was reprinted in הלכה ורפואה, כרך ד׳, תשמ״ה, עמ. קל״ט-קמ״ב. We shall deal with the issue of לא תעמוד על דם רעך in the next section of this paper, beginning from the start of the section and dealing with it in all its complexities.

The answer of the *Shevet ha-Levi* is unequivocal. He states: אם לקחת רק מנת דם בשיעור לא גדול... דלא נקרא מכניס עצמו לספק סכנה... בכה"ג בודאי מחויב ליתן – "If one takes a reasonable quantity of blood…which does not put the donor even in the category of 'doubtful danger,'…then surely under those conditions he is obligated to give." At the end of the responsum Woszner makes very clear that his answer applies even if donating the blood will put the donor in the category of חולה שאין בו סכנה, someone who does not feel well, but is in no medical danger.[98]

A similar position had also been adopted by Rabbi Moshe Ze'ev Zorger in his responsa when he wrote:[99]

> פשוט שמחוייב לתת מדמו לצורך ישראל דאע"ג דאינו מחויב להכניס עצמו בספק סכנה להציל חבירו מודאי סכנה, שאני בהא שמעשים בכל יום שעושים כן ואין בזה שום חשש סכנה, ואין להכחיש חוש הראות.

It is obvious that one is obligated to give his blood for another Jew's need. Even though there is no obligation to put oneself into "doubtful danger" to save one's fellow from certain danger, this case is different for it has become a regular occurrence to do so without entailing any danger at all. One should not deny the evidence of the senses.

Others who have adopted this view include Rabbi Moshe Meiselman,[100] and Rabbi J. David Bleich.[101] Rabbi Avraham Steinberg also wrote:[102] ברור שיש במצב זה דין של לא תעמוד על דם רעך, שכן הסיכון הוא מינימלי וחייב – "It is clear that the prohibition 'Do not stand idly by the blood of your fellow' applies to this situation. Since the danger is minimal, one is obligated." Obviously, too, any whom we shall find in the next section of this paper would obligate one to donate a kidney would also have to affirm that one must donate blood and bone marrow.

Even though we have intimated above[103] that our discussion of לא תעמוד will be in the next section, we should look back to the Gemara which discusses the prohibition of לא תעמוד, before we reach any tentative conclusion about the issue of compelling blood and bone marrow donations. There,[104] the Gemara requires two verses – לא תעמוד) Lev. 19:16 על דם רעך) and Deut. 22:2 (והשבותו לו) – to deduce that one is required to attempt to save the life of another both בנפשיה and מטרח ומיגר אגורי. That is, one must save the life of the other by one's own actual action, and one must be willing to expend one's own money and take the trouble to hire others if one cannot do it oneself. Maimonides writes[105] that the obligation of a doctor to heal נכלל בפי' מה שאמר הפסוק "והשבותו לו" לרפאות את גופו שהוא כשרואה שהוא מסוכן ויכול להצילו או בגופו או בממונו או

---

[98] Though I am convinced that this is the correct reading of his responsum, one thing does give me pause. At the end he writes: ולענין עיקר שאלתו בנתינת דם פשוטה ודאי בגדר מצוה היא – "Regarding the basic question about normal blood donation, it is certainly in the category of a *mitzvah*." Nonetheless, the wording and the tone of the rest of the responsum convinces me that he really means "obligation" in his use of the word "mitzvah."

[99] וישב משה (Jerusalem, 1989), vol. 1, no. 84, p. 246.

[100] הלכה ורפואה (Jerusalem: מכון רגנשברג, 5741), vol. 2, p. 118.

[101] See reference above, n. 73, Bleich, p. 284f.

[102] See reference above, n. 71, אנציקלופדיה הלכתית רפואית, p. 218, n. 62.

[103] See above, n. 97.

[104] Sanhedrin 73a.

[105] Commentary to M. Nedarim 4:4 (41b).

בחכמתו — is included in the explanation of the verse "And you should restore it to him," namely, to heal his body. That is, when he sees that he is in danger and he can save him either with his own actions or his money or his wisdom [he must do so].

It seems quite clear that Maimonides' בגופו is the same as the Gemara's בנפשיה. In both it seems very clear that the intent is "through one's bodily action." This is clearly the meaning of the Gemara itself which is speaking about one who is drowning or being mauled by an animal. If I can save that person myself, I must do so. If it is necessary for me to hire help, I must do so. The meaning of both the Gemara and Maimonides is, to quote the *Ziz Eliezer*:[106]

> פשוט דכוונתו על פעולה פיזית בגופו, אבל לא לתת לשם כך ממה שבעצמיות גופו וממבנה חייו העצמיים.

> Clearly that their intent is to some physical bodily action [on the part of the one who is saving], but not to giving him something of the very essence of his own body and the very structure of his own life.

Rabbi Shaul Yisraeli shares the understanding of the Gemara which we have given above in the name of the *Ziz Eliezer*. But since his words will take us on another excursus, we shall quote him in full, even though a major part of the quotation deals with kidney donation, which is the subject of the next section of this paper. Rabbi Yisraeli wrote:[107]

> עוד נלמד מאותן דוגמאות שהבאנו, שאין חיוב ההצלה, רק במה שכרוך *בטרחה* של המציל, ואף אם זו דורשת *מאמץ גופני*, ואף סיכון במדת מה. אולם *אין חיוב* לתרום מגופו הוא, אבר או רקמה דוגמת כליה וכיוצא בזה, שאינו עומד להתחדש בגוף התורם, ואף על פי שהסיכון הוא, כאמור, לא רב. אם כי "מדת חסידות" יש גם בזה בכדי להציל חבירו ממות "ואשרי חלקו מי שיוכל לעמוד בזה." ואם הנדרש להצלת חיים הוא תרומת דם, או מוח עצמות וכיוצא בזה, דברים שהגוף עומד לחדש ולהחזיר למצב הקודם, נראה שגם בזה אין חויב, ומכל מקום יש *להמליץ* על זה בתור מעשה, שהוא מגדר לפנים משורת הדין (האותיות העבות במקור).

> It can further be deduced from the examples which we have brought that the requirement to save applies only to what involves the *trouble* of the saver, and even if it demands *physical effort*, and even some small amount of danger. However, *there is no obligation* to donate from one's own body either an organ or tissues, like a kidney, or similar things, which will not regenerate in the body of the donor, even if the danger is, as we have said, not great. There is מדת חסידות in such an act, in order to save the life of one's fellow, "and fortunate is he who can do it." And if what is required to save a life is a blood donation or bone marrow, or such things, which the body will regenerate and restore to the status

---

[106] See above, n. 78.

[107] *Assia*, issue 57-58, Kislev 5757, vol. 15: 1-2, pp. 5-8. This article by Rabbi Yisraeli, a senior member of the Chief Rabbinate Council, also appeared in English in, M. Haperin and D. Fink, eds., *The Proceedings of the First International Colloquium on Medicine, Ethics & Jewish Law* (Jerusalem: Schlesinger Institute for Medical-Halakhic Research, 1996), pp. 231-237. See also a related article by the same author in *Assia*, issue 59-60, Iyyar 5757, vol. 15: 3-4, pp. 105-107. Our discussion of the kidney related matters which Rabbi Yisraeli raises begins below, p. 313.

quo ante, it nonetheless seems that even here there is no obligation. In any event, one should *urge* these as an act which can be defined as לפנים משורת הדין. [Emphasis in original.]

First and foremost for our current deliberation, Rabbi Yisraeli clearly understands the Gemara exactly as we have understood it above, and as the *Ziz Eliezer* has understood it. That understanding makes it impossible to view blood or bone marrow donation as an obligation stemming from לא תעמוד. What he adds to our discussion, however, is the association of the donation of blood or bone marrow to the category of לפנים משורת הדין, "inside the line of the law," "beyond the line of strict justice," "beyond the requirements of the law." What we shall undertake now, therefore, is an analysis of this category of לפנים משורת הדין, with particular attention to the degree of its mandatoriness, and the right to coerce its observance.

An Excursus: לפנים משורת הדין

Let us quote first several of the passages of the Gemara which involve the category of לפנים משורת הדין and which are relevant to our deliberation. We shall omit those which invoke the principle, but are irrelevant to our discussion.[108] A passage in Ketubbot reads:[109]

> איבעיא להו: זבין [מישהוא קרקע ואנו יודעים שמכר כי רצה לקנות משהו] ולא איצטרכו ליה זוזי [כי בעל החפץ שרצה לקנות חזר בו מכוונתו למכור], הדרי זביני או לא הדרי זביני? ת"ש דההוא גברא דזבין ארעא לרב פפא דאיצטריכו ליה זוזי למיזבן תורי, לסוף לא איצטריכו ליה ואהדריה ניהליה רב פפא לארעיה. רב פפא לפנים משורת הדין דעבד.

> A question was raised: [If someone] sold [land, and we know that he sold it because he wanted to buy something specific with the money, and, it turned out] that he did not need the money [because the owner of the item he wanted to buy changed his mind about selling], is the sale reversed or not? Come and hear: There was a case of a man who sold land to Rav Papa because he needed to money to buy oxen. In the end he did not need the money, and Rav Papa returned his land to him. Rav Papa acted beyond the requirements of the law.

Taken as it appears, there is no way to understand this passage except to imply that Rav Papa acted in a way that the law did not require him to act. His act was one of righteousness, not legal mandate. Furthermore, there is no clue in this passage to the possibility that Rav Papa might have been able to be forced to act in this way, even though the law did not require it. Rav Papa did the moral thing, but not all moral things are legal mandates, and they cannot be compelled, even though they are moral.

A second passage reads:[110]

> ההיא איתתא דאחזיא דינר לר' חייא. אמר לה מעליא הוא. למחר אתאי לקמיה ואמרה ליה אחזיתיה ואמרו לי בישא הוא ולא קא נפיק לי. אמר

---

[108] These include Berakhot 7a, which refers to God's own prayer that He act לפנים משורת הדין in His dealing with Israel, and Berakhot 45b, which deals with two people stopping their eating to join one in zimmun.

[109] 97a.

[110] Bava Kamma 99b.

ליה לרב זיל חלפיה ניהלה וכתוב אפנקסי דין עסק ביש.... ר' חייא לפנים משורת הדין הוא דעבד.

A certain woman showed a *dinar* to Rabbi Hiyya. He told her it was good. The next day she came back to him and said: "I showed it to [others] and they told me that it was no good. And, indeed, I could not use it." He told Rav: "Go exchange it for her, and write in my ledger, 'This was bad business....'" Rabbi Hiyya acted beyond the requirement of the law.

First let us understand the story. Rabbi Hiyya was a prosperous and wealthy man, and an expert in money. According to the law, experts in money are not liable for a mistaken identification of a coin as good. Rabbi Hiyya gave such a mistaken identification to a woman, and when she came back to complain, Rabbi Hiyya instructed his nephew Rav to give her a refund in apparent compensation for his error. Ultimately, however, the Gemara affirms that Rabbi Hiyya was not, in fact, obligated to exchange the *dinar* for the woman. He did so beyond the requirements of the law. In this passage, too, there is not a hint of any type of legal obligation to have acted לפנים משורת הדין, nor of any ability to coerce one to act that way.

A third passage reads:[111]

ר' ישמעאל ברבי יוסי הוה קאזיל באורחא פגע ביה ההוא גברא הוה דרי פתכא דאופי. אותבינהו וקא מתיפח. א"ל דלי לי. אמר ליה כמה שוין? א"ל פלגא זוזא. יהיב ליה פלגא זוזא ואפקרה. הדר זכה בהו, הדר יהיב ליה פלגא דזוזא ואפקרה. חזייה דהוה קא בעי למיהדר למזכייה בהו, א"ל לכולי עלמא אפקרנהו ולך לא אפקרנהו.... והא ר' ישמעאל בר' יוסי זקן ואינו לפי כבודו! ר' ישמעאל בר' יוסי לפנים משורת הדין הוא דעבד.

Rabbi Yishmael the son of Rabbi Yosi was walking along the road, when he chanced upon a man who was carrying a bundle of wood. He put it down, and was resting. The man said to him: "Help me lift them." Rabbi Yishmael asked: "How much are they worth?" He answered: "A half *zuz*." He gave him a half *zuz* and declared the wood ownerless. The man took possession of the wood [and asked again that Rabbi Yishmael help him lift it], so Rabbi Yishmael gave him another half *zuz* and declared it ownerless. He saw that the man was about to take possession again, so he said to him: "To the whole world I declare it ownerless, except to you." ...But was not Rabbi Yishmael the son of Rabbi Yosi an elder, and one for whom the act of helping to lift the wood was not commensurate with his stature? Rabbi Yishmael the son of Rabbi Yosi was acting beyond the requirement of the law.

In this passage we find Rabbi Yishmael offering to buy the wood from the man, so as not to have to help him lift the bundle. The man takes advantage of Rabbi Yishmael by accepting the money and then repossessing the wood, and asking for help again. Rabbi Yishmael pays him a second time. Only when he is about to be taken advantage of again, does he cut the man off by claiming that the wood is no longer "ownerless" for the man. The Gemara wonders why Rabbi Yishmael had to do any of this. After all, elders and people of

---

[111] Bava Metzia 30b.

stature are exempt from having to help others load and unload.[112] So, Rabbi Yishmael could have ignored the fellow right from the start. The Gemara answers that Rabbi Yishmael was acting לפנים משורת הדין, beyond the requirement of the law. In this passage, too, there is no clue to either mandatory behavior or coercion. Quite the contrary, the simple meaning of the Gemara's question implies that the Gemara perceives no type of obligation whatsoever on the part of Rabbi Yishmael to act as he did. His behavior is unexpected, and can be accounted for only as an act beyond the requirements of the law.[113]

We look to another talmudic text, which reads:[114]

> רב יהודה הוה שקיל ואזיל בתריה דמר שמואל בשוקא דבי דיסא. א"ל מצא כאן ארנקי מהו? א"ל הרי אלו שלו! בא ישראל ונתן בה סימן מהו? א"ל חייב להחזיר. תרתי? אמר ליה, לפנים משורת הדין, כי הא דאבוה דשמואל אשכח הנך חמרי במדברא ואהדרינהו למרייהו לבתר תריסר ירחי שתא לפנים משורת הדין.

Rav Yehudah was holding up the cloak of Mar Samuel and walking with him in the market of ground grains. He (i.e., Rav Yehudah) asked him: "What would be the law if someone found a purse here?" He answered: "The money would belong to him." [He asked:] "And if a Jew came and identified it [as his] on the basis of a clear identifying mark, what would be the law?" He answered: "He would be obligated to return it." [He asked:] "Is that not a contradiction?" He answered: לפנים משורת הדין. Just as in the case of the father of Samuel who found donkeys in the desert and [yet] returned them to their owners after an entire year because of לפנים משורת הדין.

First let us understand what the facts of the case are. By law, if one lost an article in a public place frequented by both Jews and non-Jews, the finder is entitled to keep the lost article, on the presumption that the loser would give up ever recovering it since it was likely to have been found by a non-Jew, who would not return it. The market of the ground grains was just such a place, and, therefore, the answer which Mar Samuel gave to the first question of Rav Yehudah is not at all surprising. But when Rav Yehudah posed his second question, and was told that the finder would be obligated to return it, if it were subsequently identified by a Jew, the Gemara finds it baffling. Does that answer not contradict the first answer, which seemed to assume that the item belonged to the finder, whether the loser was Jewish or not? Samuel's answer is that the grounding of the answer to the second question is not the law, but the principle of לפנים משורת הדין, and is consistent with the behavior of Samuel's father in returning the donkeys. What the two cases have in common is that the law does not require that the lost item(s) be returned, but they should be returned because of לפנים משורת הדין.

Unlike the first three examples we have looked at, this one does carry an element of obligation. Samuel uses the word חייב in his answer to the second question of Rav Yehudah. That is a word associated with obligation. Nonetheless, the word cannot here imply "legal

---

[112] See the baraita on Bava Metzia 30a.

[113] That seems to be the understanding of Maimonides, too, who records (M.T. Hilkhot Roze'ah u-she-mirat Nefesh 13:4): This is the rule: In any case when if it were one's own animal he would load or unload, one must help his fellow load or unload. And if one were a חסיד, and acts beyond the requirement of the law, then, even if he were the great Patriarch and saw his fellow's animal bent under the weight of his burden of straw or wood, or similar things, he should load or unload with him.

[114] Bava Metzia 24b.

obligation," because that would contradict the final answer. Thus, this passage seems to imply a type of obligation associated with לפנים משורת הדין. Of course, it is possible to claim that Samuel's use of the term חייב was not intended to imply actual obligation, and that he used it as a literary parallel to the answer to the first question. That is, both answers come from the language of the Mishnah in the second chapter of Bava Metzia, and the distinction drawn in the Mishnah is always between "the item would belong to him" and "the finder would be obligated to return it." Once the final answer of לפנים משורת הדין is given, it becomes retroactively clear that the term חייב did not really imply obligation. That seems to be the way Maimonides understood this Gemara. For in recording this law, he wrote:[115]

> הרי המציאה שלו ואפי׳ בא ישראל ונתן סימניה, שהרי נתייאש ממנה כשנפלה מפני שהוא אומר עכו"ם מצאה. אע"פ שהיא שלו, הרוצה לילך בדרך הטוב והישר ועושה לפנים משורת הדין מחזיר את האבידה לישראל כשיתן את סימניה.

> The lost article belongs to him [i.e., the finder] even if a Jew comes and offers identifying marks, for the loser had given up hope of recovering it when [he discovered that] it fell because he assumed that a non-Jew had found it. Even though it is his, one who wishes to walk in the path of the good and the right, and acts beyond the requirements of the law, will return it to a Jew who identifies it as his.

There is no way that Maimonides could have codified his legal conclusion from the passage we are discussing this way if he had taken the term חייב to imply obligation. He must have understood it in a less literal way. Clearly, the implication of this decision of Maimonides is that לפנים משורת הדין is beyond the realm of the enforceable, and within the realm of the moral, but not legally mandated. We shall look at several other primary passages before we look to those who understand the implications of this passage differently from Maimonides.

Another talmudic passage reads as follows:[116]

> רבה בר בר חנה תברו ליה הנהו שקולאי חביתא דחמרא. שקל לגלימייהו. אתו אמרו לרב. אמר ליה הב להו גלימייהו. אמר ליה דינא הכי. אמר ליה אין "למען תלך בדרך טובים" (משלי ב:כ). יהיב להו גלימייהו. אמרו ליה עניי אנן וטרחינן כולא יומא וכפינן ולית לן מידי. אמר ליה זיל הב אגרייהו. א"ל דינא הכי. אמר ליה אין "וארחות צדיקים תשמור" (משלי ב:כ).

> Some porters broke a cask of wine of Rabbah bar bar Hannah. He took their cloaks. They came and told Rav. He said to him: "Return their cloaks." He asked: "Is that the law?" Rav answered: "Yes, 'In order that you tread in the path of the good' (Proverbs 2:20)." He returned their cloaks. The porters said to Rav: "We are poor, and have labored all day long and are hungry, and we have nothing." Rav said to Rabbah bar bar Hannah: "Pay them their wages." He asked: "Is that the law?" Rav answered: "Yes, 'And you should observe the paths of the righteous.'"

The term לפנים משורת הדין does not actually appear in this passage, but it is the way Rashi explains what Rav meant by quoting the verse from Proverbs. We accept the notion that

---

[115] M.T. Hilkhot Gezeilah va-Aveidah 11:7.

[116] Bava Metzia 83a.

this passage reflects an instance of לפנים משורת הדין. There is simply no way that Rav's answers to Rabbah bar bar Hannah could be understood to imply actual legal mandate since the porters had broken his wine cask through negligence and he was entitled to take their cloaks, and he did not owe them for their labor.

Surely, though, this passage also intimates an obligatory nature to לפנים משורת הדין. When Rav answers "Yes" to Rabbah bar bar Hannah's question, "Is that the law?," twice, what else could he possibly mean but that the latter was obligated to take the actions that Rav had commanded? But, it is interesting and important to note that Rav quotes a verse from Proverbs as his support for the obligation of Rabbah bar bar Hannah. Rav Yosef taught[117] that לפנים משורת הדין was derived from the Torah itself, from Exod. 18:20 – אשר יעשון. The Tosafot[118] explain that Rav utilized the verse from Proverbs, rather than the verse from Exodus, on the grounds that לפנים משורת הדין would not have been sufficient grounds to obligate Rabbah bar bar Hannah to comply with what Rav had ordered, because the porters had caused him so great a loss. Clearly implied by Tosafot is that לפנים משורת הדין is not a catch-all. Nonetheless, this passage does imply some type of obligation to a moral decision, which is not mandatory law.

The very passage in which the Exodus verse is used to deduce the category of לפנים משורת הדין is important to quote:[119]

> "אשר יעשון", זו לפנים משורת הדין, דאמר ר' יוחנן לא חרבה ירושלים אלא על שדנו בה דין תורה. אלא דיני דמגיזתא לדיינו? אלא אימא שהעמידו דיניהם על דין תורה ולא עבדו לפנים משורת הדין.

> "Which they should do" – this refers to לפנים משורת הדין, as Rabbi Yohanan said: "Jerusalem was destroyed only because they judged Torah judgment therein." And should they judge arbitrarily!? Say rather, "[It was destroyed only] because they insisted on acting according to Torah judgment, and did not behave beyond the requirements of the law."

The very words of the verse imply that one should act on לפנים משורת הדין, and the very forceful statement of Rabbi Yohanan indicates that sometimes the moral thing to do may be different from the requirements of the law. On the other hand, his very statement implies that there is no ability to coerce behaving לפנים משורת הדין, because if it were possible, his court should have made people behave that way and avert the destruction of Jerusalem. So, Rabbi Yohanan lauds לפנים משורת הדין greatly, and makes clear that failure to act on it may have disastrous consequences, but he does not really claim that acting on it is mandatory or enforceable.

There is yet one further passage that comes up in the discussion of the commentators as relevant to our deliberation, even though the phrase לפנים משורת הדין does not appear in it at all. That passage reads:[120]

> אמר ר' חייא בר אבא אמר ר' יוחנן האומר לחבירו מנה לי בידך והלה אומר איני יודע, חייב בבא לצאת ידי שמים.

> Rabbi Hiyya bar Abba said in the name of Rabbi Yohanan: "If one

---

[117] Bava Metzia 30b.
[118] Bava Metzia 24b, s.v. לפנים.
[119] Bava Metzia 30b.
[120] Bava Kamma 118a.

says to his fellow, 'You owe me a *maneh*,' and the other answers, 'I don't know,' the other is obligated [to pay him], if he wishes to discharge his duty toward Heaven."

It is pretty clear why this passage comes up in the context of our discussion. The phrase "to discharge his duty toward Heaven" means, essentially, to act beyond what the law requires. Note, then, that if we equate these two, this passage also indicates an obligation to act לפנים משורת הדין, though it seems not to imply any way to enforce that requirement.

We have looked briefly at seven talmudic passages. Of those seven, four do not imply any obligation to act לפנים משורת הדין, though they clearly recognize that the moral thing to do may be other than what the law requires. Three of the passages intimate an obligation to לפנים משורת הדין, two by using the term חייב and one by answering "yes" to the question "is that the law?" If we assume that what is obligatory can be enforced or coerced, then these passages also indicate some type of enforceability.[121]

Our next step, then, is to see what became of these passages in the process of halakhic evolution. A critical comment appears in both the Mordecai[122] and the *Hagahot Maimoniyot*.[123] We quote from the latter:

מצא כאן ארנקי... חייב להחזיר א"ל לפנים משורת הדין.... ואשכחן נמי בהגזול בתרא חייב בבא לצאת ידי שמים, וכיון דחזינא דהוו כייפין להו להכי כדאיתא פ' האומר (צ"ל האומנין) גם אנן כייפינן למיעבד לפנים משורת הדין אם היכולת בידו לעשות דתני רב יוסף והודעתם להם וכו' ואמר ר' יוחנן לא חרבה ירושלים אלא מפני שהעמידו דבריהם על דין תורה ולא עשו לפנים משורת הדין. וכן פריש רבינו מקינון דכייפינן ליה לעשות לפנים משורת הדין עכ"ל הראבי"ה.

"If he found a purse here. . .he is obligated to return it. He said to him: לפנים משורת הדין. . . ." And we also find in the latter *ha-Gozel*: "He is obligated if he wishes to discharge his obligation to Heaven." And since we see that they used to compel people, as is demonstrated in *ha-Omer* (must be: *ha-Umanim*), we, too, compel a person to act לפנים משורת הדין, if he is able to do so, for Rav Yosef taught [on the basis of the verse in Exod. 18:20 which begins] "And you should inform them" etc. [including אשר יעשון as a source for לפנים משורת הדין], and Rabbi Yohanan said that Jerusalem was destroyed only because they insisted on acting according to Torah judgment, and did not act לפנים משורת הדין. And so explained our Master from Chinon[124] that we compel one to act לפנים משורת הדין. This is the language of the Ra'avia.[125]

---

[121] We shall ignore in all following deliberation of this issue the possibility that these passages make לפנים משורת הדין different for scholars than for others. It should not go unnoted, however, that *Responsa Heshiv Moshe* 48 (Rabbi Moses Teitelbaum) makes just that point. He goes as far as to say that for an אדם חשוב an act which is for others in the category of לפנים משורת הדין is for him דין גמור.

[122] Bava Metzia, ch. 2, siman 257.

[123] Hilkhot Gezeilah va-Aveidah, ch. 11, letter gimel.

[124] The reference is probably to Rabbi Mattathias of Chinon, who was one of the teachers of the Ra'avia.

[125] I am not able to find this passage in *Sefer Ra'avia*. Of course, that book contains almost nothing on sedarim Nashim and Nezikin. Ra'avia's comments on these were probably included in his book *Avi-asaf*, which is known to us only from quotations of it.

The *Hagahot Maimoniyot* begins by quoting the passage we have quoted above, page 224, which includes the claim of obligation to return the lost article. He then refers to the passage which did not include the phrase לפנים משורת הדין, but spoke of "discharging one's obligation to Heaven," above, page 226. Then he refers to the passage in which Rav made Rabbah bar bar Hannah return the cloaks of the porters and pay them for their labor (above, page 225). He concludes from these passages, that there is both an obligation and enforceability to לפנים משורת הדין, and since the consequences of not acting לפנים משורת הדין can be so catastrophic (as evidenced by what Rabbi Yohanan had to say, above, page 226), we, too, compel behavior on the basis of לפנים משורת הדין. The *Hagahot*, however, includes the words "if he is able to do so," and we shall have to see what those words are understood to mean. It is not at all clear who the "he" is, and what his ability has to do with the matter. Note, however, at least, that the cases to which the *Hagahot* applies coercion seem to be restricted to lost articles and loans which the borrower cannot remember.

Rabbi Joseph Karo, in the Beit Yosef, has this to say:[126]

כתב ר' ירוחם בשם הרא"ש אין כופין על לפנים משורת הדין, ופשוט הוא בעיני. ותמהני על מה שכתב המרדכי בפ"ב דמציעא דכייפינן למעבד לפנים משורת הדין, מהנך עובדי דמייתי ראיה מינייהו לא נזכר בהם כפיה.

> Rabbenu Yeruham wrote in the name of the Rosh that there is no coercion for לפנים משורת הדין, and that seems simple in my view. I am amazed at what the Mordecai wrote in the second chapter of [Bava] Metzia, that we do compel compliance with לפנים משורת הדין. In those examples which he brings as proof compulsion is not mentioned.

Karo quotes the claim of the Rosh,[127] quoted by Rabbenu Yeruham, according to which there is no coercion for לפנים משורת הדין. But more than merely quoting it, he expresses agreement with it, claiming it to be virtually self-evident that coercion for לפנים משורת הדין is impossible, almost by definition. As far as the cases cited by the Mordecai and the *Hagahot Maimoniyot* are concerned, they prove nothing, since none of them mentions coercion at all. The Beit Yosef is correct that none of them mentions coercion directly. We had deduced coercion from the use of words like חייב and "yes" in answer to "is it the law." Remember, though, that we have already referred to Maimonides' codification of the law for one of those passages, and it did not intimate any obligation or enforceability whatsoever, even though the word חייב appeared in the talmudic passage.[128] It is very likely that Karo understands the obligatory nature of these passages exactly as Maimonides does. Indeed, there is great logic to that understanding, since it is difficult to understand why it would be called לפנים משורת הדין, if it were enforceable. It is probably the *peshat* of the term that led Karo to assert that it was virtually self-evident to him that לפנים משורת הדין was not enforceable. Very clear expression of this view can be found in the work of Rabbi Samuel David Munk, who wrote:[129]

---

[126] Tur, Hoshen Mishpat 12, Beit Yosef s.v. רבינו ירוחם.

[127] See Rosh to Bava Metzia 2:7.

[128] The talmudic passage appears above, p. 224, and the comment of Maimonides, above, p. 225. Note, too, that the term לפנים משורת הדין appears in legal contexts in Maimonides only there and in Hilkhot Gezeilah va-Aveidah 11:17, and in Hilkhot Roze'ah u-Shemirat Nefesh 13:4 (see above, n. 113). In none of these is there any intimation of coercion. He also uses the term in Hilkhot Yesodei ha-Torah 5:11, and in Hilkhot De'ot 1:5, but there the context is not legal.

[129] *Pe'at Sadekha* (Jerusalem: M. Safra, 5735), siman 155.

והרא"ש דחי לה בלא ראיה כלל דסברא פשוטה היא בעיניו שלא נתנה תורה רשות לב"ד לכוף אלא על הדין ואין מרחמין בדין... וסברא זו פשוטה היא כל כך עד שכדאי לדחוק בלשון חייב להחזיר דחיובא בעלמא קאמר, אבל אין כופין על כך. ונר' שזהו טעמו של הרב ב"י שכתב על דברי רבינו ירוחם בשם הרא"ש ופשוט הוא בעיני ותמיהני על המרדכי ולא פירש טעם תמיהתו.

And the Rosh rejected that idea [i.e., that one could coerce for לפנים משורת הדין] without any proofs whatsoever, on the grounds that it is a simple premise in his eyes: that the Torah does not grant permission to a court to coerce except for legal judgment, in which no mercy has a part [i.e., as it surely does in לפנים משורת הדין] . . .and this idea is so self-evident that it becomes preferable to force the meaning of the phrase, "he is obligated to return it," to mean a mere obligation, which is not enforceable. And it seems that this is the reasoning also of the Beit Yosef who wrote concerning the view of Rabbenu Yeruham, which he had quoted from the Rosh, "and that seems simple in my eyes, and I am amazed at what the Mordecai wrote," without ever explaining the source of his amazement.

The thesis which cannot easily accept forcing the meaning of the word חייב is best expressed by the BaH, who wrote as follows:[130]

איתא בסוף האומנין בעובדא דרבה בר בר חנא דתברו ליה הני שקולאי... משמע דרב הוה כייף ליה לרבה בר בר חנא, דאם לא כן מאי קאמר ליה דינא הכי אם לא בא לכופו.... וכן במצא ארנקי בשוק בפרק אלו מציאות דקאמר חייב להחזיר משום לפנים משורת הדין, לפחות משמע חייב להחזיר בבא לצאת ידי שמים כדאמר פרק הגוזל בתרא... דאם לא כן, מאי "חייב." ולכן פסק המרדכי דכייפינן ליה למיעבד לפנים משורת הדין אם יכולת בידו לעשות, שהוא עשיר... וכן פסק ראב"ן וראבי"ה דכייפינן להחזיר היכא דהמוצא עשיר. מיהו ב"י הביא דברי הר"ר ירוחם בשם הרא"ש דאין כופין על לפנים משורת הדין... ולית', אלא הנהו עובדא מיירי בכפייה כדפרישית וכן נוהגין בכל ב"ד בישראל לכוף לעשיר בדבר ראוי ונכון ואף על פי שאין הדין כך.

At the end of Chapter *ha-Umanin*, regarding the case in which the porters broke casks of Rabbah bar bar Hannah. . .it is implied that Rav would have compelled Rabbah bar bar Hannah, for otherwise what did he mean by telling him that the law was thus. . . .Similarly in the case of one who found a purse in the market, in chapter *Eilu Mezi'ot*, where he said that he is obligated to return it because of לפנים משורת הדין, at least that implies that he must return it if he wishes to discharge his obligation to Heaven, as it says in the latter chapter *ha-Gozel*. . .for if not, what is the meaning of "must." . . .Therefore the Mordecai decided that we do compel obedience for לפנים משורת הדין, where he is able, that is, when he is wealthy. . . .And thus did

---

[130] BaH, Hoshen Mishpat 12, s.v. וכל דיין.

Ra'avan[131] and Ra'avia decide, that we compel one to return it when the finder is wealthy.[132] Nonetheless, the Beit Yosef quoted the words of Rabbenu Yeruham in the name of the Rosh, that we do not compel for לפנים משורת הדין...but that is not correct. Rather, all of these instances refer to cases of coercion, as I have explained. And it is the custom of all Jewish courts to compel a wealthy person in an appropriate and just matter, even though that might not be the law.

The BaH quotes the three passages which intimate coercion, which we have already seen above. What else could those "intimating" words mean if not some type of coercion? This is the opposite of the view of Munk, explaining the Rosh and the Beit Yosef. The *peshat* of words like חייב implies coercion, so, even if it seems that the *peshat* of לפנים משורת הדין does not, that must be mistaken. And that is precisely what the decision of the Mordecai (and the *Hagahot Maimoniyot*) makes clear.

The question to ask, however, is where did the BaH get the claim "where the finder is wealthy?" Obviously, he quotes it in the name of early Ashkenazic authorities, so the tradition does not originate with him. It seems most likely that it is the BaH's explanation of the phrase in the Mordecai and *Hagahot Maimoniyot* which reads: אם היכולת בידו, and about which we said earlier[133] that we would have to come back to it. The phrase, as it appears in the *Hagahot Maimoniyot* is cryptic, to say the least. It means, according to the BaH, that if the *finder* is able, that is, if returning the lost article will not cause him financial problems, then we would coerce him to return it. Of course, there is nothing in the words of the Mordecai and the *Hagahot Maimoniyot* that actually states that the finder must be wealthy. What's more, the talmudic passage which seems to be the essential source for this derivation gives no clue that a wealthy person is necessarily being spoken about.[134] In that passage[135] Mar Samuel answers a question posed to him by Rav Yehudah, and there is no hint that his answer is restricted to a wealthy finder!

Nonetheless, the BaH is a decisor of considerable influence, and, in any event, the view is reflected in early Ashkenazic authorities. It is not surprising, therefore, that this view of what type of coercion takes place, and in what types of cases, finds echoes from then on, either just as stated, or with modifications which attempt to bring conflicting posi-

---

[131] I am not able to find exactly this statement anywhere in *Sefer Ra'avan*. However, in his comments to Bava Metzia 24b (p. 197, end of b, in the Grossman Publishing ed., with commentary *Even Shelemah*), the Ra'avan does say: "...therefore, it is right (דינא) that Simon should act לפנים משורת הדין and return the purse to Reuven." And in his comments to Ketubbot 49b (page 260c in that ed.), he does mention wealth as a factor in determining whether we compel a father to support his children. If the father is wealthy, we compel him; if he is not, we request, but do not compel.

[132] Their view is also quoted by the *Sefer ha-Agudah* (Elazar Brazil ed., Jerusalem: 5730), Bava Metzia, p. 20, par. 34, which says about returning a lost article לפנים משורת הדין: "And it is our custom to return it, and so did Ra'avia and Ra'avan decide that we coerce to return it if the finder is rich." But see previous note.

[133] Above, p. 227.

[134] It is interesting to note that in S.A. Hoshen Mishpat 259:5 Rabbi Joseph Karo writes: "Even though by law one is not obligated to return an object lost in a place where the majority are not Jews, even if a Jew indicates a definite identifying mark, it is good and just to act לפנים משורת הדין and to return it to the Jew who identified it." This comment of Karo makes no distinctions based on wealth, and seems to imply this behavior as desirable for anyone. Also, there is no clue here to any type of coercion. At the end of this paragraph the Rema adds the following comment: "And if he (i.e., the finder) is poor, and the owner of the article is rich, it is not necessary to act לפנים משורת הדין." While the Rema does make the distinction between rich and poor, this passage makes no statement about coercion. However, see below, pp. 233-234.

[135] Above, p. 224.

tions closer together. Let us look at an example from Rabbi Menahem Mendel Krochmal of Nickolsburg (1600-1661), the *Zemah Zedek*, who wrote:[136]

מ"מ נר' אם זה שמצא הארנקי אינו עני צריך להחזיר... משום לפנים
משורת הדין וכייפינן אלפנים משורת הדין דהכי כתב המרדכי אהא
דאמר בפרק אלה מציאות... וכן פסק ראב"ן ואבי העזרי דכייפינן להו
לעשות לפנים משורת הדין. ותו התם במרדכי אהא דרבא הוה שקיל
ואזיל בתריה דרב נחמן בשוקא דגלדאי וכו' אמר ליה מצא כאן ארנקי
מהו אמר ליה הרי אלו שלו ומסק נעשה כצווח על ביתו שנפל כתב
המרדכי וז"ל נר' לראבי"ה מא דלא כייפינן התם לעשות לפנים משורת
הדין אפשר שהמוצא היה עני ובעל האבידה היה עשיר עכ"ל הרי מבואר
דכייפינן על לפנים משורת הדין. ואע"ג דהרא"ש כתב הך דרב יהודה הוה
שקיל ואזיל בתריה דמר שמואל... וז"ל לאו דכייפי ליה דאין כופין
לעשות לפנים משורת הדין עכ"ל נראה לי [דלא] כתב כן אלא דאין כופין
בשוטין אבל בהורדת נכסים מודה דכייפינן כיון דנקט לשון חייב
להחזיר... ודאי דכייפינן עליה אלא דאין כופין בשוטין אבל בהורדת
נכסים כייפינן.

Nonetheless it seems that if the one who found the purse is not poor, he must return it. . .on grounds of לפנים משורת הדין. We coerce for לפנים משורת הדין because that is what the Mordecai wrote regarding what is taught in chapter *Eilu Mezi'ot*. . .and thus decided Ra'avan and Ra'avia that we coerce people to comply with לפנים משורת הדין. Furthermore, there in the Mordecai, regarding the case of Rava who was holding the cloak and following after Rav Nahman in the market of leather workers etc., he said to him: "If one found a purse here what would be the law?" He answered: "It would belong to him." And the conclusion there is that the loser of the purse would be as one who is yelling about his collapsed house. On that passage the Mordecai wrote[137] as follows: "It seems to Ra'avia that the reason that we don't compel in that case to act in accordance with לפנים משורת הדין could be because the finder was poor and the loser was rich." Thus it is clear that we coerce for לפנים משורת הדין. And even though the Rosh wrote concerning the case of Rav Yehudah who was holding the cloak of Mar Samuel and following after him. . .as follows: "Not that we compel him, for we do not compel for לפנים משורת הדין," it seems to me that he meant only that we do not coerce with physical force, but he admits that we could coerce by taking away possessions. Since [the Gemara] uses the expression חייב להחזיר. . . surely we can coerce him, but not by physical force, only by removing possessions.

The other talmudic case to which this passage from the *Zemah Zedek* refers, appears in the Gemara immediately following the Rav Yehudah and Mar Samuel incident.[138] The new incident is identical with the earlier one, except that it takes place in the market of

---

[136] *Zemah Zedek*, 89.

[137] Mordecai, Bava Metzia, ch. 2, 257.

[138] Bava Metzia 24b.

the leather workers. The characters are Rav Nahman and Rava. Rav Nahman gives the same answer as Mar Samuel to the first question. But when Rava asks what the law would be if a Jew came and offered an identifying mark, Rav Nahman answered that the finder could still keep the purse. Rava asks: "But he is standing there yelling and claiming his purse, with identifying marks." To this Rav Nahman answers: "His screaming and yelling is just like one who yells about the fact that his house has collapsed or his ship has sunk." That is, his yelling is ineffective to bring about the return of the lost item.

The responsum of the *Zemah Zedek* was, in fact, about a case very similar to the case of the Gemara. He asserts that if the finder is not poor,[139] he must return the item. He gives as his proofs all of those we have seen referred to already. Then he adds an additional proof based on another statement of the Mordecai, deduced by the Ra'avia from the Rav Nahman and Rava incident. That incident seems to be identical with the Rav Yehudah and Mar Samuel incident, yet Mar Samuel and Rav Nahman give two different answers. The Ra'avia explains that, in fact, there is no contradiction between the two incidents. In the latter, the finder must have been poor and the man who lost the item was rich. That is why Rav Nahman did not insist on action לפנים משורת הדין. Had the finder been wealthy, even Rav Nahman would have insisted.

Thus far, then, we see how the *Zemah Zedek* accepts the claim of the Mordecai and *Hagahot Maimoniyot* positing wealth as the determining factor in whether לפנים משורת הדין would be coerced. He even offers a further proof which we have seen in his words for the first time. However, he cannot ignore the Rosh, and he attempts to close the gap between the Rosh and the Mordecai. For the Rosh, too, the Gemara uses the phrase חייב להחזיר, and it is virtually inconceivable to the *Zemah Zedek* that the Rosh would simply ignore the implication of the words. Thus, he says, the Rosh, too, agrees that if the finder were wealthy we could compel him to return the item. The difference between the Rosh and the Mordecai is entirely in the manner of coercion. Here, however, the *Zemah Zedek* gets a little unclear, at least as far as the view of the Rosh is concerned. For the Mordecai, all is clear. We could force the finder to return the item, even to the point of physical coercion. For the Rosh, we can force the finder to return the item (that is what הורדת נכסים must mean in this discussion), but we cannot have recourse to physical coercion. He does not seem to answer how we accomplish this if the finder simply refuses. In any case, though, he has reduced the gap between the two views by positing that the Rosh, too, allows for some type of coercion for לפנים משורת הדין.

We shall quote only one more passage which directly reflects the view of the BaH. The Rabbinic Court Decisions of the State of Israel has the following:[140]

> והנה בשו"ע חו"מ סי' יב סע' ב' כתב הרמ"א שתי דעות אם כופין לפנים משורת הדין, והב"ח הכריע להלכה כדעה שכופין לפנים משורת הדין אם יכולת בידו לעשות כגון כאשר הוא עשיר. וכן נוהגין בכל בי"ד בישראל לכוף לעשיר בדבר הראוי והנכון ואע"פ שמן הדין אינו חייב בזה.

In the Shulhan Arukh, Hoshen Mishpat, siman 12, paragraph 2, the Rema wrote two views about coercion for לפנים משורת הדין. The BaH tipped the balance in law in favor of the view that we do coerce for לפנים משורת הדין, if he is able, for example, when he is

---

[139] Clearly he is changing the quality of the finder from "wealthy" to "not poor." Nonetheless, the intent is the same, and it is useless for us to spend time on this distinction.

[140] *Piskei Din Rabbaniyim*, vol. 11, p. 262.

wealthy. And that is the custom of all Jewish courts to compel a wealthy person in an appropriate and just matter, even though that might not be the law.

We have already noted that we have seen references to compelling compliance with לפנים משורת הדין only concerning the return of a lost article or money. This leads to an interesting question concerning what we have been discussing: Even if there is coercion for לפנים משורת הדין, does it apply to categories that do not involve the return of money or lost articles? A quotation from the *Minhat Yitzhak* is the only passage this author has found that deals with the subject at all.[141] Rabbi Isaac Jacob Weiss wrote:[142]

> וצ"ע אם לומר כן גם במקום אחר, בתובע ונתבע בשאר ענינים, היכא דשייך לפנים משורת הדין, וי"ל דדוקא באבידה אמרינן כן, דסוף כל סוף אינו מחזיר רק ממון מחבירו, משא"כ בשאר מקומו'.

> And it requires investigation whether to say so even in other instances, with a plaintiff and defendant in other matters to which לפנים משורת הדין applies. And it is reasonable to say that we claim thus specifically in the matter of a lost item, in which, in the final analysis he is returning money which originated with the other person. That would not be the case in other matters.

Rabbi Weiss' contention is logical and compelling. If there is going to be any coercion at all for לפנים משורת הדין, it is reasonable that it should occur in an instance in which we are returning to a person what came from him anyway. So, for example, if one dropped a purse in a location frequented by Jews and non-Jews, even though one might relinquish ownership because one suspects that the purse could well be picked up by a non-Jew, it is nonetheless logical that if a Jew picked it up it should be returned to the original owner who identifies it, even though he has really relinquished ownership of it. It may not be legally required, since the owner has relinquished ownership, but one could claim that it is right and just to return what was his originally. That is a far cry from claiming that one who is exempt from a certain act because of his stature or status should be compelled to do the act which falls under the category of לפנים משורת הדין. The person may choose to do it, but his act does not merely return to another what was his to begin with.

As was noted in the decision of the Rabbinical court, Karo makes no statement in the Shulhan Arukh on the matter of coercion for לפנים משורת הדין,[143] but Moses Isserles does. He wrote:[144]

> ואין בית דין יכולין לכוף ליכנס לפנים משורת הדין, אף על פי שנר' להם מן הראוי (ב"י בשם ר"י ובשם הרא"ש), ויש חולקים (מרדכי פ"ב דמציעא).

> The court may not coerce someone to act beyond the requirements of the law, even though it might seem appropriate to them

---

[141] I have also not succeeded in finding any source which speaks of compelling compliance with לפנים משורת הדין in a non-financial matter.

[142] *Minhat Yitzhak*, vol. 5, 121.

[143] But see above, n. 134, for a comment by Karo on לפנים משורת הדין, with no comment on coercion, and the reaction of the Rema.

[144] Hoshen Mishpat, siman 12, par. 2.

(Beit Yosef in the name of Rabbenu Yeruham and the Rosh), but some disagree (Mordecai, chapter two of [Bava] Metzia).

The Rema dutifully records both of the views we have already seen. By the generally accepted principles of decision making in the Rema, his view coincides with the first view, and not with the יש חולקים. That, of course, does not prove that those who came after him must agree with his decision. But, for the moment, note that both Karo and Isserles agree that there is no coercion for לפנים משורת הדין.

Since the ויש חולקים of the Rema is clearly the Mordecai, and since we have noted earlier that the phrase אם היכולת בידו which appears there is problematic, we shall now turn our attention to a different strand of interpretation of the Mordecai.

Rabbi Yonatan Eybeschuetz (1690-1714) wrote the following:[145]

"ויש חולקים" – דעה זו היא בהמרדכי ובכל ראיה שמביא המרדכי שם אין בו ראיה מכרעת שיש כח ביד ב"ד לכוף ליכנס לפנים משורת הדין. ועוד יש לדקדק בלשון המרדכי דכתב דאנן כייפינן לפנים משורת הדין אם יש יכולת בידינו עכ"ל ולכאורה זה שתלה הדבר ביכולת או אינו יכולת בלתי מובן, דמה ענין זה לפשר, אף בגוף הדין אם אין יכולת בידינו מה לעשות, ובעוונותינו הרבים מיום שגברו בעלי זרוע תש כח ידי ב"ד ואם יכולת ביד ב"ד לכוף לדין א"כ לשיטתו אף לפשר נכוף. מאי שנא פשר מדין? והב"ח פי' יכולת שהוא עשיר, והמעיין במרדכי יראה דהך חילוק בין עשיר לעני לא נאמר אחר כך במרדכי, ולא אמרה מקודם כנר' מלשונו שם. ולכן נראה ברור כי מכל הראי' שהביא מרדכי הוא רק שנאמר בו לשון חייב והוא מורה על כפיה, והיינו כפייה במילי כמו שיש דיעות ביבמות וכתובות גבי כופין אותו להוציא ואומרים לו חייב אתה לעשות כן ואם אינך שומע אתה עברייין אבל לא נכוף אותו בשוטים ונדוי וכדומה כיון דאין דאין שורת הדין כן, עיין כתו' דף נ' גבי עשיתינהו ע"ש בתוס'.... ולכך קאמר המרדכי אם היכולת בידינו לעשות הרצון שהוא גברא דציתנא ושומע בקול ב"ד של ישראל מבלי לעבור על דבריהם, אבל אם אין יכולת, דמשמעותו ודברי ב"ד כדאמרינן בדברים לא יוסר עבד, אין לכוף אותו בשוטים ונדוי משא"כ בדין כופין בכל מיני כפיות ואתי שפיר. ועתה יש לומר דגם הרא"ש מודה לזה, ואין כאן מחלוקת כלל.

"And some disagree" – This view appears in the Mordecai. But none of the proofs which he offers there is conclusive evidence that the court has the authority to compel people to behave לפנים משורת הדין. Furthermore, one can make a deduction based on a careful reading of the language of the Mordecai, who wrote: "We compel for לפנים משורת הדין if we are able." Now the fact that he made the matter dependent upon our ability or lack thereof is not comprehensible, for what does this have to do with compromise. Even in actual law, what can be done if we do not have the ability. And because of our many sins, the authority of the court has diminished since the powerful ones have ascended. But if the court has the ability to compel for law, then, according to his view, it should compel for compromise too. Why should compromise be any different than law?

---

[145] *Urim ve-Tumim*, Tumim to Hoshen Mishpat, siman 12, subpar. 4.

And the BaH explained "ability" to mean that the person is wealthy. If one looks in the Mordecai he will see that the distinction between a rich person and a poor person is said only later by the Mordecai, and he did not intend it earlier, as is apparent from his language there. It therefore seems clear to me that the only proof that the Mordecai has from all the cases he quoted is the fact that they say חייב, and that seems to indicate coercion. But that means coercion by words, as there are views in Yevamot and Ketubbot regarding the cases where we coerce him to divorce. And we say to him: "You must do as we say. If you do not obey, you are considered a sinner." But we do not coerce him physically or with excommunication, or similar things, since the strict law does not require what we require of him. Look at Ketubbot 50, in the context of עשיתינהו, looking there at Tosafot. . . .Therefore the Mordecai says: "If we are able" to do what is desirable, that is, if he is an obedient person who listens to what a Jewish court says, and does not violate their dictate. But if there is no ability, for he is not obedient, and the words of the court are as we say:[146] "A slave is not chastised by words," we may not coerce him physically or with excommunication. All of this is not the case with a matter of law, where we coerce with all manners of coercion. It all works well. And now we can even say that the Rosh, too, admits to this, and there is no dispute at all.

This has been a lengthy quotation, and it includes other passages that we will have to look at in order to see what the *Urim ve-Tumim* was talking about. He begins, though, by quoting the final two words of the comment of the Rema's gloss in the Shulhan Arukh. He correctly identifies the source of the Rema's comment, but asserts that none of the proofs of the Mordecai is conclusive. Quite the contrary, he argues, a careful look at the language of the Mordecai will lead to a very different conclusion. After all, the Mordecai says that we coerce for לפנים משורת הדין if we are able (אם יכולת בידנו),[147] making the last clause appear to be part of the theory of coercion, and not just a statement of actual ability of the court to enforce its decision. As part of the theory it makes no sense, says Eybeschuetz. Even in actual law, if the court does not have the ability to enforce its decision, nothing can be done. But we do not make the court's ability to enforce part of the theory of coercion. When we state a law in the abstract, we would simply say that we may compel obedience. So, here, too, according to the theory of the Mordecai that coercion is permissible for לפנים משורת הדין, there should have been no reason for him to include the "reality" matter, "if we are able." Thus, Eybeschuetz's claim to this point is that the language of the Mordecai does not support the conclusion that real coercion is permissible, since if that is what he was arguing, he would never have included the phrase "if we are able" as part of the theoretical statement. At this point, therefore, the *Tumim* remains without an explanation for why the Mordecai included that cryptic clause.

---

[146] The reference is to Prov. 29:19, as understood by the gemara in Ketubbot 77a to imply that physical coercion is likely to be far more effective than verbal coercion since "A slave is not chastised by words."

[147] This is not the reading of the printed version of the Mordecai. There the reading is as quoted by the *Hagahot Maimoniyot*, אם יכולת בידו. That is the phrase which we said above was cryptic. Now it is clear that Rabbi Eybeschuetz has a different version in that statement.

Then Eybeschuetz refers us to the explanation of the BaH, according to which that clause refers not to the court's ability, but to the ability of the finder to tolerate the loss of the article which is legally his because he is wealthy. Eybeschuetz rejects this interpretation of the clause in the Mordecai on the grounds that the distinction between wealthy and poor is utilized by the Mordecai only in the passage which follows the one in which the cryptic clause appears. Had the Mordecai intended that interpretation to apply to his previous passage, he would have introduced it there. Indeed, we had noted above, page 234, that there was nothing in the words of the Mordecai to indicate a distinction between wealthy and poor. That distinction only appears in the next comment of the Mordecai.[148]

Having rejected the possibility that the passages referred to by the Mordecai themselves imply actual coercion, and having rejected the explanation of the BaH as to what the Mordecai was the talking about when he used the phrase "if we (he) are (is) able," Eybeschuetz contends that the only basis on which the view of the Mordecai can be based is the fact that the passages contain words like חייב, which indicate some type of coercion. But, says the *Tumim*, getting to his own explanation of what the Mordecai meant, that refers to verbal coercion, similar to the views of some commentators in passages in Yevamot and Ketubbot where the Mishnah says, "We compel him to divorce," by saying to him: "You are duty bound to do thus, and if you do not obey you are a sinner." But, we do not compel him physically or with excommunication, or such things, for this is not the strict line of the law.

There are some mishnayot in both Yevamot and Ketubbot that record a requirement that a man divorce his wife, under certain circumstances. The requirement is sometimes phrased, יוציא ויתן כתובה (he should divorce her and pay her marriage contract), and sometimes כופין אותו להוציא (we compel him to divorce).[149] Eybeschuetz refers us to the commentators on those passages who claim that when the passage in the Talmud says כופין, that refers to actual physical coercion; but when it says יוציא, it means oral persuasion, but not physical persuasion. He actually refers us to a single Tosafot in Ketubbot, to which we will come in due course. We will not start there, however, since it is not from a passage in which any of our key words of obligation actually appears. The words that Eybeschuetz says we say to the person we are trying to persuade appear first in the Tosafot[150] in the name of Rabbenu Hananel. They wrote:

ורבינו חננאל הביא מירושלמי דכל הנך יוציא דמתניתין אין כופין והכי איתא התם אמר שמואל אין מעשין אלא לפסולות... ופסק ר"ח משם שמע מינה שאין כופין אלא היכא שמפרש בהדיא כופין אבל היכא דאמור רבנן יוציא אומרים לו כבר חייבוך חכמים להוציא ואם לא תוציא מותר לקרותך עבריינא, אבל לכפותו לא.

And Rabbenu Hananel deduced from the Yerushalmi that in all the cases of יוציא in the Mishnah we do not coerce. And this is what it says there:[151] "Samuel said: 'We do not compel except for those who are disqualified.'" . . . On that basis Rabbenu Hananel

---

[148] Bava Metzia, ch. 2, 257.

[149] See the mishnayot of the seventh chapter of Ketubbot for both. In Yevamot, see ch. 4:2, 9, and 12; 14:1, 8, and 9 for יוציא, and 9:3 and 13:12, 13 for כופין.

[150] Ketubbot 70a, s.v. יוציא.

[151] J. Yevamot 9:4, 10b, and other places. In addition to the quote in the passage in the text, Samuel is quoted there as saying: "We do not compel except for the likes of a high priest to a widow, or a priest to a divorcee." That is, we compel for biblical prohibitions, but not for rabbinic dictates. Whether this second statement of Samuel is really his, or is the Talmud's in explanation of his statement is irrelevant to our discussion.

decided: "We do not compel except in those cases where the Talmud states explicitly that we compel. But where the sages said that he should divorce, we say to him: 'the sages have already obligated you to divorce, and if you do not divorce, it is permissible to call you a sinner.'" But to compel him, no.

While it may be that the *Tumim* refers us directly only to one Tosafot, it is not unlikely that this other Tosafot, quoting the RaH, was one of the commentators to Yevamot and Ketubbot to which he referred,[152] especially since the words that he quotes that we say to the sinner are almost identical with the words quoted by Rah. Where does this leave us? Since יוציא means "he is obligated to divorce her," it follows that an expression of obligation does not necessarily imply the right to coerce physically. It may refer to verbal inducement or exhortation only, but exclude physical force.

Since the Mordecai has been critical in these deliberations, it is important to note that he, too, agrees with the claim of the Rah in at least two places. We shall quote one of them:[153]

אין כופין אלא היכא דקתני בפירוש כופין, אבל היכא דאמור רבנן יוציא אמרינן ליה חיובך להוציא ואם לא הוציא שרי למקרייה עבריינא, אבל לכפותו בשוטים לא.

We do not compel except where the Mishnah explicitly teaches כופין. But where the sages said that he should divorce, we say to him: "It is your obligation to divorce, and if you do not divorce, it is permissible to call you a sinner." But, to compel him physically, no.

The wording of the Mordecai is almost identical with the wording of the Rah. Surely his conclusion is the same. How likely is it that the Mordecai would be so explicit about the restricted admissibility of physical coercion in this case, yet intend such latitude for coercion in the לפנים משורת הדין? It simply is not likely, claims Eybeschuetz. It cannot be that the Mordecai would present two such dissimilar positions.

Now let us look at the Tosafot to which the *Tumim* himself refers us. It is based on a Gemara which reads as follows:[154]

אמר ר' אילעא אמר ריש לקיש באושא התקינו הכותב נכסיו לבניו הוא ואשתו ניזונין מהם.... איבעיא להו הלכתא כוותיה או אין הלכתא כוותיה? ת"ש דר' חנינא ור' יוחנן הוו קיימי אתא ההוא גברא גחין ונשקיה לר' יוחנן אכרעיה. אמר ליה ר' חנינא מאי מאי? א"ל כותב נכסיו לבניו הוא ועשיתינהו לזניה. אי אמרת בשלמא לאו דינא, משום הכי עשייניה, אלא אי אמרת דינא עשינהו בעי.

Rabbi Ila'a said in the name of Resh Lakish: "In Usha they ordained that one who assigns all of his possessions to his sons must be sustained together with his wife from the estate." . . . A question was raised: Is the law in accordance with this edict or not? Come and hear: Once Rabbi Hanina and Rabbi Yohanan

---

[152] Note that in the Tosafot referenced above, n. 150, the view of Ri is also quoted. He holds the position that we do compel for the cases in which the mishnah says יוציא. For the purposes of our argument, however, even that would not be conclusive proof that Ri would believe that compulsion is also called for for לפנים משורת הדין, which is not even in the category of rabbinic prescriptions.

[153] Mordecai, Ketubbot, 194. The other is also in Ketubbot, 204. Both of these appear in the seventh chapter of Ketubbot, which is the one in which כופין and יוציא appear.

[154] Ketubbot 49b.

were standing when a man came over, bent down and kissed the feet of Rabbi Yohanan. Rabbi Hanina said to him: "What is that all about?" He answered: "He had assigned all of his possessions to his sons, and I compelled them to sustain him." Now if you say that the law does not follow the edict, that is why he compelled them. But if you say that the law does follow the edict, he was duty bound to compel them.

The meaning of the story is fairly easy to follow, until the conclusion. The fact that the man kissed Rabbi Yohanan's feet indicated great gratitude. That is, Rabbi Yohanan had done something kind for the man, beyond the requirements of the law, and he was so grateful that he kissed his feet. From this the Gemara deduces that the law does not follow the *takkanat Usha* in this matter. If that is correct, it is clear why the man kissed Rabbi Yohanan's feet. But, if the law does follow the *takkanah*, the man's behavior is not very explicable. According to Rashi it means: If the law follows the *takkanah*, what Rabbi Yohanan did for the man was to force compliance with the law, as he ought to have. And, therefore, Rabbi Yohanan didn't do any favor for the man. So, why did the man kiss his feet? Rashi's explanation of the *sugya* would not be of any use to Eybeschuetz, because it would be impossible to prove that the *piel* of the root עשה means verbal coercion. The way Rashi understands the *sugya*, Rabbi Yohanan may have coerced the sons physically to sustain their father. The man shows gratitude for this coercion of לפנים משורת הדין by kissing his feet. If it were the law, however, he would not have kissed his feet, because the physical coercion would not have been beyond the requirements of the law.

Nonetheless, the use of that root for coercion is somewhat strange. The root חייב would be the more common verb to use even for physical coercion to comply with the mandate of the law. Therefore, the *Tumim* refers us to the Tosafot,[155] who have a very different explanation:[156]

> האי עשתינהו צריך לומר דהיינו בדברים... והשתא אתי שפיר דאמר עשיתינהו בעי דאם מן הדין היה מה היה לו לעשותם בדברים היה לו להלקותם ולכופם עד שיזונו אותו, פירש רבינו תם.
>
> This "I coerced them" must mean verbally.... And now [the *sugya*] flows smoothly. For it says: "Ought he have coerced them verbally?" If the sons were obligated to feed their father by law, why would he have sought to compel them verbally? He should have lashed them and compelled them to feed him. And thus did Rabbenu Tam understand.

The view of the Tosafot, probably motivated by the question we have just raised, is very different from that of Rashi. Here is the way they understand the *sugya*. The verbs in the sugya from the root עשה mean to coerce verbally, but not physically. If the law does not follow the *takkanat Usha*, then it is easy to understand why the man kissed the feet of Rabbi Yohanan, since he had verbally coerced the sons to behave beyond the requirements of the law. But, if the law follows the *takkanah*, "should he have coerced him verbally?" Tosafot read those two words of the text as a question, as opposed to Rashi who reads them as declarative.

---

[155] Ketubbot 50a, s.v. עשיתינהו.

[156] See, too, Rashba, Ritba, and Shita Mekubbezet, *ad locum*.

Now we can follow the thrust of the argument of the *Tumim*. The only real proof of coercion for לפנים משורת הדין that the Mordecai has is expressions like חייב which imply coercion. But that coercion is not physical, but verbal, similar to the type of coercion implied, according to many commentators, by the passages in Yevamot and Ketubbot, where at least claims that יוציא means by verbal coercion, and the threat of being called a sinner, but not physical coercion. And the same is implied by the understanding of Tosafot of the *sugya* in Ketubbot which we have just analyzed. And, in that *sugya*, the gratitude of the man toward Rabbi Yohanan was because he had coerced his sons verbally to act לפנים משורת הדין.

Having proved that the only possible coercion for לפנים משורת הדין is verbal, the *Tumim* goes back to the cryptic clause in the Mordecai, which had been explained by the BaH to refer to wealth. He says: When the Mordecai wrote אם היכולת בידינו he meant, "If we are able to bring about compliance with לפנים משורת הדין on the basis of our verbal coercion, because the man is obedient to Jewish courts and obeys what they tell him, fine and good. But if the man is not inclined to be obedient, we cannot force him physically or with excommunication. And all of this is the opposite of actual law, where we would compel obedience by whatever means were necessary." Now, for the *Tumim*, the clause in the Mordecai is, in fact, part of the theory of coercion for לפנים משורת הדין, and not just a statement of some reality. Our ability to be persuasive in our verbal coercion determines whether there is coercion even in theory, not just because Jewish courts may no longer have the power they once did. Even if that same power still existed in Jewish courts, they could still compel obedience to לפנים משורת הדין only because of their persuasive powers, not their enforcement powers.[157]

Having gotten to this point, Rabbi Eybeschuetz can now add the frosting to the cake. When the Rosh (and, we might add, the Beit Yosef) reject out of hand the possibility of coercion for לפנים משורת הדין, they refer only to physical coercion. But, even they would agree that the court should engage in verbal coercion for לפנים משורת הדין, and that those who do not comply could be called sinners. So, in the final analysis, says the *Tumim*, there is no dispute at all. The Rosh and the Mordecai agree with each other. Each was talking about a different matter.

Just as the view of the BaH had a following in later authorities, so, too, does the view of the *Tumim*, either with or without crediting him. For example, Rabbi Jacob Reicher (c.1670-1733) wrote:[158]

> לפנים משורת הדין הא מבואר בש"ע סי' י"ב שני דעות... דעת המרדכי פ' אלו מציאות דכופין על לפנים משורת הדין, והרא"ש ורבינו ירוחם הובא בב"י סי' זה דאין כופין. והב"ח מסיק עיקר להלכה דכופין... ויותר תמוה לי על הב"י ותשובת צ"צ שנעלם מהם סוגיא דש"ס דכתובות פרק נערה דף נ' ע"א גבי כותב נכסיו לבניו ועשתינהו לזניה יע"ש בפי' רש"י ותוס' לשם דכופין על לפנים משורת הדין היינו בדברים בעלמא, והמרדכי פ' המדיר כתב בשם ר"ת כגון לגזור עליו שלא לישא וליתן עמו וכה"ג, אבל לא על ידי מלקות ושמת'.

Two views are explained concerning לפנים משורת הדין in the Shulhan Arukh, [Hoshen Mishpat,] section 12. . .the view of the Mordecai in chapter *Eilu Mezi'ot* that coercion is possible for לפנים

---

[157] Understanding the Mordecai to refer only to verbal persuasion eliminates the contradiction between our previous understanding of the Mordecai's intent and the passage of his we quoted above, p. 237.

[158] *Responsa Shevut Ya'akov*, pt. 1, 168.

משורת הדין, and the Rosh and Rabben Yeruham, quoted by the Beit Yosef in the same section, that coercion is not possible. And the BaH concluded the law in accordance with the view that we do coerce...[b]ut I am most surprised at the Beit Yosef and the *Zemah Zedek* who seemed to have ignored the *sugya* in Ketubbot, chapter *Na'arah*, page 50a, concerning the case of one who had assigned his possessions to his sons, and they were forced to support him. Look there in the commentaries of Rashi and the Tosafot [for evidence that] coercion for לפנים משורת הדין refers only to verbal coercion. And the Mordecai wrote in Chapter *ha-Maddir*[159] in the name of Rabbenu Tam, that it means, for example, making a declaration that nobody should do business with him, and similar things, but not [to coerce him] with whipping or excommunication.

Rabbi Reicher lays out the range of views, which we have already seen. He then expresses surprise at both the Beit Yosef and the *Zemah Zedek* for having paid no attention to the *sugya* we analyzed in our discussion of the *Tumim*. For the Beit Yosef, the surprise is that he did not refer to it as evidence that physical coercion is forbidden,[160] and for the *Zemah Zedek* the surprise is that he did not see that it belies the possibility of physical coercion. For Rabbi Reicher, too, the statement of the Mordecai in Ketubbot that rejects physical coercion seems to undermine the reading of his statement in Bava Metzia to imply physical coercion, and the two can be reconciled by understanding the Bava Metzia statement to refer exclusively to verbal coercion.

We quoted above, page 229, the words of Rabbi Samuel David Munk in explanation of why the view of the Rosh and the Beit Yosef was so logical that it did not even require proof. Munk himself agrees with them, and concludes:[161]

ולכן נלענ"ד הלכה למעשה כדברי האומרים כופין בדברים, ואם הוא דבר שנאמר בפוסקים חייב כופין אף בדברים קשים.

So, it seems to me that the law is in accordance with those who say that the coercion is with words, and if it is a matter where the poskim have used the word חייב, then the words can be harsh.

Rabbi Munk finds the logic of his defense of the view of the Rosh and the Beit Yosef so convincing and compelling that it persuades him that the law must reflect that logic. Therefore, the only type of coercion that could be possible for לפנים משורת הדין is verbal coercion. His concession to the strength of the word חייב is that in those instances where the poskim have used that word, as in the instance of returning a lost article found where many non-Jews are but identified by a Jew, the words used to coerce can be harsh.

There is one more avenue to go down before we finish this excursus on לפנים משורת הדין. One of the talmudic passages, above, page 226, that we have been considering as one speaking of לפנים משורת הדין did not, in fact, use the term. It used instead the phrase חייב בבא לצאת ידי שמים, he is obligated, if he wishes to discharge his duty towards Heaven. We assume this comment to be the equivalent of חייב בדיני שמים. What we must do now is see whether the matter of coercion is any different for חייב בדיני שמים than for לפנים משורת הדין.

---

[159] I.e., Mordecai, Ketubbot, 204.

[160] It is possible that his surprise at the Beit Yosef is over why he did not raise the *sugya* as a rebuttal of the proofs brought by the Mordecai.

[161] See reference above, n. 129.

The greatest concentration of items for which there is חיוב בדיני שמים can be found in Bava Kamma.[162] We need concern ourselves with only one of them. A baraita lists four matters for which one is exempt by law, but obligated by דיני שמים. One of the items is: הכופף קמתו של חבירו בפני הדליקה, one who bends the standing crops of his fellow toward a fire. In explaining the specifics of this case, the Gemara offers two explanations. First, it asks, if the crops were bent toward the flame in such a way that the fire would reach them even with a normal wind (ברוח מצויה) the perpetrator should be liable even by law, so, it must be that he bent the crops in such a way that they could not be burnt by a normal wind, but could be by an abnormal one (רוח שאינה מצויה). For such damage the perpetrator is exempt by law, but liable to Heaven. Rav Ashi says that the baraita refers to a case in which someone covered over the standing crops of his fellow as the flame was approaching. This is the case in which he is not liable at law, but liable to Heaven. Why is he not liable at law? Because it is not he who set the fire. Why is he liable to Heaven? Because his act resulted in the crops being in the category of "hidden," for which the Sages exempt from legal liability.[163] Thus, if he had not covered the crops, whoever lit the fire would have been liable for the damages to the crops caused by the fire. Now, however, that the crops are "hidden," he is no longer liable, and, thus, the act of covering the crops resulted in a loss to the owner of the crops that will now go uncompensated. This is his liablility toward Heaven.

The Gemara proceeds to explain why the author of the baraita had to list the four he did, when those four do not exhaust the list of items for which one would be liable toward Heaven. For each of the four, the Gemara claims, there might have been an argument that would have led one to believe that the person would not even have been liable toward Heaven, and the baraita had to teach that one does not argue thus. Regarding our case, the Gemara gives the following explanations, one for each of the opinions as to its specifics:[164]

> הכופף קמתו של חבירו נמי מהו דתימא? לימא, מי הוה ידענא דאתיא רוח שאינה מצויה ובדיני שמים נמי לא ליחייב, קמ"ל. ולרב אשי דאמר נמי טמון איתמר מהו דתימא אנא כסויי כסיתיה ניהלך, ובדיני שמים נמי לא ליחייב, קמ"ל.

> In the case of one who bends his fellow's crops, too, what might you have said? [He could contend:] "How could I have known that an unusual wind would blow," and, if so, he should not even be considered liable to Heaven. Its inclusion in the baraita comes to teach us that we do not make that claim. And according to Rav Ashi who said that the case is one of "hidden," what might you have said? [He could contend:] "I covered your crop for your benefit," and, if so, he should not even be considered liable to Heaven. Its inclusion in the baraita comes to teach us that we do not make that claim.

The reason for the inclusion of our case, according to the first explanation of its specifics, is to indicate that a person should think about the possibility of unusual occurrences, at least as far as liability toward Heaven is concerned. A human court may not be able to consider such a person liable, but that person should pay for the damages caused if he wishes to fulfill his obligation to Heaven. According to Rav Ashi's view of the specifics

---

[162] Beginning of ch. 6, 55a-56a.

[163] See M. Bava Kamma 6:5, 61b.

[164] Bava Kamma 56a.

of our case, it is included in the baraita in order to indicate that even if a person were to claim that he had covered the crops in order to impede the flame, and without any intention to cause harm to the owner of the crop, that would not be sufficient to exempt him from liability toward Heaven.

The Tosafot[165] wonder why the theoretical claim according to Rav Ashi is not, in fact, sufficient to exempt the man from liability even to Heaven, since God knows whether he is telling the truth or lying, and if he is telling the truth, he should be exempt even in God's eyes. Their answer is that even if his intention was completely pure, it was his responsibility to be extremely careful and consider the possibility that the act which he was doing from pure motivation might still cause damage to the very one he was trying to protect. Since he obviously didn't do that in our case, he stands obligated toward Heaven.

Rabbi Solomon Luria (c. 1510-1574) has a comment which refers to this *sugya*, and deals directly with coercion for חיוב בדיני שמים. He wrote:[166]

> ומצאתי כתוב בתשובה וז"ל נ"ל היכא דאיתמר חייב בדיני שמים אע"ג דאין לב"ד לכופו לשלם, מ"מ בדברים בלי כפיה יש לדוחקו, דאם לא כן איך קאמר בפרק הכונס גבי הטמין קמה של חבירו לפני הדליקה כו' מהו דתימא מצא אמר אנא כסייא כסתיה ובדיני שמים נמי לא לחייב קמ"ל. ולא מאי קאמר והא היודע מחשבות הוא יודע דעתו אלא כדפי' עכ"ל. ולא נהירא לי מדלא תירצו התוס' כך ש"מ דלא ס"ל כלל. גם לישנא דדיני שמים לא משמע להיות חיובא אפי' במקצת דיני אדם, אלא לעניין יוצא ידי שמים לחוד קאמר. וכן מצאתי בצפנת פענח וז"ל כל מקום שאמרו חייב בדיני שמים, אם בא צריך להודיעו "אין אנו יכולין לחייב אותך אבל צריך אתה לצאת ידי שמים כי דינך מסור לו," כדי שיתן אל לבו וירצה את חבירו ויצא ידי שמים.

I found a responsum in which the following was written: "It seems to me that wherever it says 'he is liable before Heaven,' even though the court cannot coerce him to pay, nonetheless, it may push him to do so verbally, without [physical] coercion. If this is not so, how does the Gemara say in Chapter *ha-Kones*, in the context of one who "hid" the crop of his fellow before the fire: 'What might you say? He could say, "I covered it," and not be liable even before Heaven, so the baraita comes to teach that we do not say that.' And what kind of an argument is that, since He who knows the thoughts of all, knows what his intent was. Rather, [it must be] as I have explained." But this claim is not acceptable to me. Since the Tosafot did not explain that way, it implies that they did not agree with that view at all. Furthermore, the expression "laws of Heaven" does not imply any liability whatsoever according to "laws of man," but rather [is restricted] exclusively to fulfilling an obligation toward Heaven. And thus did I find in *Zofenat Pa'ane'ah*:[167] Wherever they said, חייב בדיני שמים, if one comes he must be informed thus: "We are not able to make you liable, but you are

---

[165] *Ad locum*, s.v. כסויי.

[166] *Yam Shel Shlomo*, Bava Kamma 6:6.

[167] *Zofenat Pa'ane'ah* is a name by which *Sefer Ra'avan* is sometimes called. The passage quoted by Luria appears there (see above, n. 131, for ed. information), p. 190a.

duty bound to fulfill your obligation toward Heaven, for your case is handed over to It," in order that he will take the matter to heart, appease his fellow, and fulfill his obligation to Heaven.

The *Yam Shel Shelomo* begins by quoting an anonymous responsum, according to which verbal coercion for חיוב בדיני שמים is permissible, even though other coercion is not. How does the author of the responsum deduce this? He deduces it from the answer of the Gemara, according to the position of Rav Ashi, to the theoretical argument one might have raised against considering the one who "hid" the standing crop of his fellow liable בדיני שמים. The author's claim is this: In fact, that claim, namely, that he had acted with the best intention of the crop owner in mind, *should* exempt him from דיני שמים. Why does it not? Because since only God knows whether he is telling the truth or not, Rav Ashi believes that the man can be verbally pressured to pay. While we have no idea of what that wording would be, the juxtaposition of this part of Luria's quote with the next, leads one to believe that the wording would be something like: "God who knows the thoughts of all knows whether you are telling the truth. Are you absolutely positive that your motivation was entirely pure? If you are not, you will spend the rest of you life obligated in the eyes of Heaven to the man whose crop you caused damage to. Would you not be smarter to fulfill your possible obligation to Heaven, and pay the man for the damage you caused him?"

We should summarize the argument of the anonymous author of the responsum quoted by Luria this way: The Gemara clearly implies that in all matters of חיוב בדיני שמים there can be verbal, though not physical, coercion. Why is that the implication? Because the Gemara should really *accept* the argument which Rav Ashi says we *do not* accept in the case of the man who "hid" his fellow's crops. Now if we should accept it, but we do not accept it, that can only be because in matters of דיני שמים we can engage in verbal coercion under all circumstances, so the fact that the person has a claim which might be valid (if he is telling the truth) is irrelevant (since he might also be lying). This seems to be the way the anonymous author understands the Gemara. Note, that the author accepts the problem of the Tosafot, but does not offer their answer.

Luria expresses disagreement with the author of the responsum on two grounds. The first is that the Tosafot raise the same problem as he does, but do not give the same answer. They give an answer which makes the man liable even if it is assumed that he is telling the truth. They make no claim that we deduce anything about coercion, verbal or otherwise, from this *sugya*. Therefore, claims Luria, they must reject that possibility. And why do they reject it? Because according to them, there can be no coercion whatsoever, even merely verbal for חיוב בדיני שמים.

The second grounds for rejection are based on the expression itself. What else, asks Luria, could an expression like "liable in the sight of Heaven" mean if not, "We, the human court, can do nothing about this case; but you, the person involved are liable in the sight of Heaven"? "By the laws of Heaven" is clearly intended to be contrasted with "By the laws of man." It is only about the latter that human courts can do anything. About the former they are absolutely powerless to do anything but inform the person that they have an obligation toward Heaven.

Where does this leave us regarding coercion for חיוב בדיני שמים? At the maximum, if we accept the claim of the anonymous responsum, there can be verbal coercion for חיוב בדיני שמים, but nothing more. If that is the case, this type of obligation is identical in terms of coercion with the view of the *Tumim*, and others, regarding coercion for לפנים משורת הדין. For both categories the most that a court could do would be to exercise verbal persuasion. If we reject the view of the anonymous responsum, either on the grounds that

Luria did or on other grounds, we are left with the view of Luria himself. According to him, there can be no verbal coercion for חיוב בדיני שמים whatsoever. The most there could be would be verbal informing.

Luria sees a difference between verbal informing and verbal coercion. We have tried to make that difference clear in preceding paragraphs. It is possible to argue, however, that what Luria quotes as verbal informing in the name of Ra'avan is precisely what we have meant all along by verbal coercion. If we say the former, then חיוב בדיני שמים has even less enforceability than לפנים משורת הדין. If we say the latter, the two are equal, at least as the *Tumim* understood coercion for לפנים משורת הדין.

We have been on a lengthy excursus, initiated because Rabbi Shaul Yisraeli linked blood and bone marrow donation with לפנים משורת הדין.[168] The time has come to summarize the route we have taken, and where it has led us. We began with the presentation of the actual talmudic passages that deal with relevant instances of לפנים משורת הדין. Of the seven passages, four carried no implication whatsoever of obligation for לפנים משורת הדין and surely no implication of coercion; three, by using such words as "obligated" and answering "yes" to the question "Is that the law?" seemed to imply obligation. That, in turn, led us to discuss whether obligation should be understood in these contexts to imply the right to compel obedience with the dictate of לפנים משורת הדין. We quoted Maimonides, whose view is clearly that it does not. Then we quoted the words of the Mordecai (corresponding to the view of the *Hagahot Maimoniyot*) which clearly say that we compel for לפנים משורת הדין, but appends the words אם היכולת בידו (or: בידנו). In tracing what happens to this Mordecai in legal history, we noted that the Beit Yosef, taking his cue from the Rosh and Rabbenu Yeruham, rejects it entirely, saying that it is clear to him that there is no coercion for לפנים משורת הדין, and expressing surprise at what the Mordecai had said. We found the explanation of the certainty of the Beit Yosef most compelling as offered by Rabbi Samuel David Munk, namely, that "Torah does not grant permission to a court to coerce except for legal judgment."

The BaH, however, defended and explained the Mordecai. He understood the key phrase אם יכולת בידו to refer to the finder of the lost article which should be returned because of לפנים משורת הדין. He explained it, probably on the basis of some early Ashkenazic authorities, though not really implied by the Gemara itself, to mean that the finder was wealthy. Under those circumstances there is an obligation for the finder to return it, and the court can compel obedience. We then traced the support for the view of the BaH through the *Zemah Zedek* and the Rabbinic Court Decisions of the Religious Courts of Israel. We concluded our tracing of the BaH's position with a reference to the *Minhat Yitzhak* who asserts that the coercion issue refers only to instances of returning to one what was his in the first place, as evidenced by the fact that it applies to the wealthy who are compelled to return to losers who are poor what was theirs originally. To other matters, however, coercion would not apply.

Consistent with his view in the Beit Yosef, Karo makes no statement about the admissibility of coercion in the Shulhan Arukh. The Rema also states that coercion is not permitted, but notes that some disagree. The "some disagree," of course, is the Mordecai. In his comments to the Shulhan Arukh, Rabbi Yonatan Eybeschuetz, the *Urim ve-Tumim*, rejects the view that the Mordecai means physical coercion at all, and the contention that a wealthy person is being spoken of. What the Mordecai means is verbal coercion, and nothing more. Eybeschuetz's evidence is based on two things: his version in the Mordecai,

---

[168] See above, pp. 221-222.

which reads אם היכולת בידנו, and passages in Ketubbot and Yevamot. The former, according to this explanation, refers to the persuasive power of the court to convince the person to act לפנים משורת הדין, and makes no reference to physical coercion. The latter lead Rabbenu Hananel to conclude that, as a matter of law, physical coercion is utilized only in contexts where the law includes the term כופין. That, of course, would exclude all instances of לפנים משורת הדין.

We then saw further quotations from the Mordecai that indicate agreement with the Rah, thereby lending support to the thesis of the *Tumim* concerning the original quotation from the Mordecai, rather than lending support to the understanding of the BaH. Then we returned to the *Tumim* and saw his further proof from the Tosafot's explanation of the *piel* of the root עשה to indicate only verbal persuasion. Subsequently, we traced the followers of the *Tumim* through Rabbi Jacob Reicher and Rabbi Samuel David Munk.

In a postscript to our extensive treatment of לפנים משורת הדין, we engaged in a brief discussion of the admissibility of coercion in matters of חיוב בדיני שמים. Our discussion was based primarily on a passage of Rabbi Solomon Luria, quoting an anonymous responsum and a Tosafot in Bava Kamma. Our conclusion was that the only type of coercion possible in such matters would be verbal, at most.

If we were forced to take an unequivocal stand from all of the views we have quoted and explained, it would have to be in favor of the view of the Rambam, the Beit Yosef, the Rosh, and the preferred position of the Rema. It simply stretches the language too far to think that there could be a humanly enforced coercive element in matters that are "beyond the requirements of the law," or "to discharge one's obligation to Heaven." But even if we do not make that absolute judgment, the weight of precedent from the middle ages on seems to favor either restricting coercion to wealthy people returning objects to their original owners or to verbal persuasion and coercion. And, if we adopt the later position, it is uncontested. That is, everybody agrees that the court should attempt to convince a person to behave לפנים משורת הדין. It is the moral thing to do, and there can be no objection to attempting to convince a person to behave accordingly. That, however, is a far cry from claiming that there is a legal right to compel obedience.

None of this is meant to deny that the view that coercion for לפנים משורת הדין exists, if one relies on the early Ashkenazic sources of the Mordecai without considering the legal history of those sources' claims. That, however, would be irresponsible law.

Rabbi Yisraeli was the only one who attributed the status of לפנים משורת הדין to blood and bone marrow donation. All the others treated it in terms of לא תעמוד. We have now demonstrated that by either standard there is not a legal obligation to donate either blood or bone marrow. Given the relative ease of these procedures, however, we affirm that it is the moral thing to do. Yisraeli equates a moral act with לפנים משורת הדין, and states very beautifully:[169] "A moral obligation (לפנים משורת הדין, which is the opposite of *midat sedom*) is more than a mere praiseworthy action (*midat chasidut*). In the latter case, a volunteer should be encouraged; in the former, one should be encouraged to volunteer." Yisraeli was silent about his views on coercion for לפנים משורת הדין in his article. But this quotation makes it very clear. "One should be encouraged to volunteer" is a statement of verbal persuasion and encouragement. The most one could possibly call it is verbal coercion.

The motivation of those who would make blood donation and bone marrow donation mandatory is both understandable and laudable. However, it is probably not implied by the Gemara either as לא תעמוד or as לפנים משורת הדין, and takes a step that creates unen-

---

[169] See n. 13 in the English version of the article referenced above, n. 107.

forceable and bad law. Of course we must encourage people to donate blood and bone marrow, especially to those in critical need. We must admonish them to overcome common tendencies to claim that one cannot do so for a host of reasons. We must stress what a great mitzvah they will be performing by becoming donors, and how great the reward of saving another's life will be. But, we would be ill advised to posit either blood donation or bone marrow donation as a legal requirement which any halakhically observant Jew *must* agree to when needed. To mandate them as halakhic requirements implies the right to compel halakhic Jews to donate. We would be better off to take the lesser step, which is more defensible. To refuse to donate violates ועשית הישר והטוב and perhaps לפנים משורת הדין, which cannot be coerced, but does not violate לא תעמוד על דם רעך.

There is an obvious difference between donating blood for deposit in a blood bank, either for the use of someone else or for one's own use, and donating blood for a חולה שלפנינו. In the latter case, the person in need of the blood is present and waiting, while in the former case, the ultimate recipient is not yet in need of the blood. The question, then, is whether that fact makes any difference in terms of the halakhic permissibility to donate blood under such circumstances. In addition, we shall see that this issue is tied to the question of the permissibility of donating blood for compensation.

Let us begin with the primary halakhic sources that impinge on our question. The Mishnah reads:[170]

> מעשה באחד שפרע ראש האשה בשוק. באת לפני ר' עקיבא וחייבו ליתן לה ארבע מאות זוז. אמר לו: רבי, תן לי זמן. ונתן לו זמן. שמרה עומדת על פתח חצרה ושבר את הכד בפניה ובו כאיסר שמן. גלתה את ראשה והיתה מטפחת ומנחת ידה על ראשה. העמיד עליה עדים ובא לפני רבי עקיבא. אמר לו: לזו אני נותן ד' מאות זוז? אמר לו: לא אמרת כלום, החובל בעצמו אף על פי שאינו רשאי פטור, אחרים שחבלו בו חייבים.

> There was a case of a man who removed the head covering of a woman in the market place. She came before Rabbi Akiva who declared the man liable to pay her four hundred *zuz*. He said to him: "Rabbi, give me some time." He granted him time. [During that time,] he waited until she was standing by the door of her courtyard. He broke a pitcher in her presence that contained about an *issar*'s worth of oil. She removed her head covering and began patting the oil [into her palm] and putting it on her head. The man had brought witnesses to her act. He came before Rabbi Akiva and said: "Am I to pay four hundred *zuz* to such a one?" He answered: "Your claim is irrelevant. For, even though one should not damage oneself, if one did, one is exempt; but, if others cause the damage, they are liable."

Even though the woman had also caused herself some type of disgrace (damage), the claim of the man that this exonerated him from liability fell on deaf ears. There is a difference, says Rabbi Akiva, between one who inflicts damage on oneself and one who inflicts damage upon another. Both have done something wrong, but the former is not legally liable, while the latter is.

In its discussion of the Mishnah, the Gemara[171] quotes a baraita in which Rabbi Akiva is quoted as saying: צללת במים אדירים והעלית חרס בידך, אדם רשאי לחבול בעצמו — "You have

---

[170] Bava Kamma 8:6 (90b).
[171] Bava Kamma 91a.

dived into turbulent waters but brought up only sherds. A person is entitled to inflict damage upon himself." The view of Rabbi Akiva in this baraita is that it is permissible to inflict injury upon oneself. In the Mishnah he claimed it was forbidden, though one who did so was not liable at law. In its further discussion, the Gemara[172] affirms that the view of Rabbi Akiva expressed in the Mishnah is his view as understood by Rabbi Elazar ha-Kappar. But, at a minimum, we see that there are two opinions about whether it is permissible to inflict injury or damage upon oneself.

Maimonides records the law in accordance with the view of Rabbi Akiva of the Mishnah. He wrote:[173] אסור לאדם לחבול בין בעצמו בין בחברו – "It is forbidden for one to inflict damage either upon oneself or upon one's fellow."[174] This, too, seems to be the view of the Rif and the Rosh, since both quote the wording of the Mishnah without any indication of the contrary view of the baraita.[175] The Tur also affirms that it is forbidden to inflict injury upon oneself, but then adds:[176] כתב הרמ"ה שאינה הלכה אלא האדם רשאי לחבול בעצמו – "Rabbi Meir ha-Levi Abulafia wrote that this is not the law. Rather, a person is entitled to inflict injury upon himself."[177] Finally, the Shulhan Arukh[178] records the law precisely in the language of the Mishnah.

It seems clear, therefore, that the classical poskim have taken the view that inflicting injury upon oneself is forbidden. Only according to the Ramah is that not the case. Obviously, if one adopts the position of the Ramah, there can be no halakhic objection to blood donation, even without the presence of one who is awaiting the blood right now.[179] However, adopting that view would leave one in the position of ignoring the weight of precedent, which favors the view that self-injury is forbidden. The question, then, becomes whether blood donation is permissible or forbidden according to the view of the majority of the poskim.

One factor which is relevant to that question is whether the status of the prohibition against self-injury is דאורייתא or דרבנן. If it is the former, we would be inclined to be strict in a matter of doubt, based on the principle ספיקא דאורייתא לחומרא; and if it is the latter, we would be inclined to be lenient in a matter of doubt, based on the principle ספיקא דרבנן לקולא.

An apparently straightforward answer is offered by the Meiri in his comments to Bava Kamma, where he wrote:[180] זה שבארנו במשנה שאין אדם רשאי לחבול בעצמו מן התורה הוא –

---

[172] Bava Kamma 91b.

[173] M.T. Hovel u'Mazik 5:1.

[174] He intimates the same in Hilkhot Shevuot 5:17, where he states: נשבע להרע לעצמו כגון שנשבע שיחבול בעצמו, אע"פ שאינו רשאי, שבועה חלה עליו – If one swears to do evil to himself, as, for example, he swears to inflict injury upon himself, the oath is effective even though he is not permitted to do so.

[175] See Rif, 32a, and Rosh 8: 13.

[176] Hoshen Mishpat 420.

[177] The Beit Yosef (בד"ה ומ"ש בשם הרמ"ה) explains the reasoning of the Ramah based on the fact that the Gemara attributes the view of Rabbi Akiva in the Mishnah to Rabbi Elazar ha-Kappar, and the law never follows him. Thus, the law must be in accordance with Rabbi Akiva of the baraita. The BaH (בד"ה החובל) refers to the Gemara in Shevuot 8a as proving that the sages disagree with the view of Rabbi Elazar ha-Kappar from which support for the view of Rabbi Akiva in the Mishnah was adduced. Since the sages disagree with him, the systemic principle יחיד ורבים הלכה כרבים – in a dispute between one sage and the majority, the law follows the majority- impels us to reject the view of Rabbi Elazar ha-Kappar, and if it is that view which supports the Rabbi Akiva version of the Mishnah, it, too, must be rejected in favor of the Rabbi Akiva version of the baraita.

[178] Hoshen Mishpat 420:31.

[179] Though see below, p. 248, for the view of Rabbi Menashe Klein, even according to the Ramah.

[180] בית הבחירה לבבא קמא, Kalman Schlesinger ed. (Jerusalem, 1963), p. 266.

"What we have explained in the Mishnah, that it is forbidden for one to injure oneself, is from the Torah." What complicates this apparently straightforward answer is that a few lines later the Meiri writes: אע"פ שאמרו אין אדם רשאי לחבול בעצמו, אם נשבע שיחבול [ב] עצמו, שבועה חלה עליו... שאין זו מצוה גמורה אלא דברי סופרים... וכבר בארנו שכל שהוא איסור סופרים מדרבנן — שבועת ביטוי חלה עליו "Even though the sages said that a person is not entitled to injure himself, if one swore that he would do so, the oath takes effect...for this [prohibition against self-injury] is not a complete mitzvah, but rather based on the words of Soferim (i.e., is דרבנן)...and we have already explained...that all such rabbinic prohibitions are subject to fulfillment in the case of oaths."

At first blush, there seems to be a conflict within the Meiri's words. He calls the prohibition against self-injury דאורייתא, and then claims that an oath to injure oneself applies because the prohibition against self-injury is דרבנן. The resolution to the problem is found in the Ran. In his comments to the Rif on Shevuot[181] he wrote: אע"ג דבפרק החובל אמרינן דאין אדם רשאי לחבול בעצמו מדרשא אתיא לן, (ו)כל דליתא מן התורה מפורש לא מיקרי מושבע ועומד לענין שלא תחול שביעה עליו — "Even though we say in *Perek ha-Hovel* that a biblical midrash serves as the source for the claim that a person is not entitled to injure himself, nothing that is not explicit in the Torah falls in the category of 'already under oath,' such that oaths not apply to it." The Ran affirms that the prohibition against self-injury is דאורייתא. One would, however, still be obliged to fulfill an oath to inflict such injury upon oneself because one is exempt from such fulfillment only in the case of מושבע ועומד, and that applies only to explicit prohibitions of the Torah. The distinction is made even more clearly by the Ran in his comment to Nedarim[182] where he wrote: כל מידי דאתא מדרשא אע"פ שהוא מן התורה, כיון דליתיה מפורש בקרא בהדיא שבועה חלה עליו — "Even though anything deduced by midrash has the status of דאורייתא, oaths apply to such matters since they are not explicit in the Torah." Indeed, the same distinction as is drawn by the Ran is the most reasonable solution to the apparent contradiction in the words of the Meiri. From both of them, then, it follows that the prohibition against self-injury is דאורייתא.

Based on precisely these sources, Rabbi Menashe Klein draws the apparently inevitable conclusion, in his monumental work משנה הלכות:[183]

> שמעינן מיהו דדעת המאירי והר"ן ז"ל ושאר הראשונים דאיסור דחבול בעצמו דאורייתא היא ומעתה ודאי אזלינן בזה לחומרא.... וממילא שמעינן נמי לפשוט שאילתא דידן דודאי אסור לישראל ליתן מדמו לבלאט באנ"ק דהרי כשנותן דם לבאנק הרי חובל בעצמו הוא, והעיקר חבלה הוא כל שהוציא דם, וכיון דקיי"ל אין אדם רשאי לחבול בעצמו א"כ אסור ליתן דם מעצמו שהרי בזה חובל בעצמו ואע"פ שרוצה אינו רשאי, והוא באיסור תורה.

We learn, at any rate, that the view of the Meiri and the Ran, of blessed memory, and the other Rishonim is that the prohibition against self-injury is דאורייתא. Thus, surely, we are strict concerning it.... And from this we can also deduce the answer to our question, namely, that it is certainly forbidden for a Jew to donate his blood to a blood bank. For when one donates to a bank one inflicts injury upon oneself, the essence of which being the actual removal of the blood. And since we have established that a person is not

---

[181] P. 11a, ד"ה אביא נשבע.

[182] P. 8a, ד"ה הא קמ"ל.

[183] Menashe Klein, *Mishneh Halakhot* (Brooklyn: 5747), vol. 4, no. 245, p. 380.

entitled to inflict injury upon himself, it follows that it is forbidden to donate blood since that constitutes self-injury. And it is forbidden דאורייתא even if one wishes to donate.

Rabbi Klein adds one more important point that pertains even to the position of the Ramah, who holds that it is permissible to inflict injury upon oneself. Based on a claim of Rabbi Shelomo Luria[184] that אפילו לפירוש הרמ"ה אינו מותר אלא לצורך דאי לא לצורך לכ"ע אסור אפילו להזיק בגדים – "Even according to the understanding of Abulafia, it is permissible only for need, for without need all agree that it is even forbidden to damage clothing" – Klein concludes[185] that it would be forbidden to donate to a blood bank even according to the Ramah, since some possible future need of the donor for blood (which would not even be the blood he donated) does not constitute "need."

If the Ramah permits only for need, it must follow that those who forbid must forbid even for need, otherwise there is no dispute between the Ramah and the others. Indeed, the Tosafot[186] make precisely this point: ואור"י... שאסור לחבול אפי' לצורך – "And Ri says...that it is forbidden to injure even for need."

The responsum of Rabbi Klein was written on January 9, 1964 (though not published until about twenty-three years later). Klein often takes note of responsa of Rabbi Moses Feinstein, though in this instance he does not. Feinstein had written a responsum on the question of the permissibility of donating blood for compensation on October 26, 1962.[187] It is, of course, very possible that Klein did not know of it at all. Feinstein begins with the premise that it should be forbidden, since the view of Maimonides is that self-injury is forbidden, and the Ri has made it clear that the prohibition applies even when there is "need." Earning money is "need," but would still be prohibited according to this. At the end of the responsum, however, the following appears:

> אבל בחבלה זו להוציא דם על פי השגחת הרופאים יש טעם גדול שלא לאסור, דהא מצינו שבדורות הקודמים היו נוהגין להקיז דם אף רק לאקולי כמפורש בשבת דף קכ"ט (ע"ב).... ולכן אף שנשתנה אח"כ... מ"מ ודאי גם עתה איכא גם רפואה בזה דלא יהיה שינוי גדול כ"כ וגם היום מוציאין הרופאים כמעט בלא צער, ולכן אפשר אין לאסור בחבלה זו דהקזת דם. והרוצה להקל אין למחות בו כיון שהוא סברא גדולה.

But there is a compelling reason not to forbid this injury of removing blood under medical supervision, for we find that in earlier generations it was customary to let blood even for palliative purposes, as is explained in Shabbat 129(b)....So even though matters [concerning bloodletting changed] afterwards...nonetheless there must be some therapeutic value even now because such a great change is improbable. And furthermore, doctors today are able to take the blood with almost no pain. Therefore, it is possible that one should not forbid this injury of bloodletting. One who wishes [to donate] should not be prevented, since this is compelling logic.

---

[184] ים של שלמה, בבא קמא, פרק ח" סי' נ"ט.
[185] Ibid., p. 381.
[186] Bava Kamma 91b, ד"ה אלא האי.
[187] שאלות ותשובות אגרות משה, חשן משפט, חלק א' סי' ק"ג.

Feinstein seems to be making two points. First, if the taking of blood were in the category of self-injury, it would have been permissible to let blood in the talmudic period only for therapeutic reasons, but not for mere palliative ones. After all, self inflicted injury is forbidden, as stipulated by Ri, even for "need." Yet, the evidence of the Gemara is that it was done even for merely palliative reasons. Hence, if the Gemara did not prohibit it for the palliative need, we should not prohibit it for the financial need of the donor who is giving for compensation. The reason the Gemara did not forbid blood letting for palliative purposes is that there must always also have been some medical benefit to the person. Thus, even though attitudes toward blood letting have changed over time, it is unlikely that the changed reality could be so great that there is no medical benefit to the removal of blood. Furthermore, the very grounding of the prohibition may no longer be applicable. Giving blood should be forbidden only if it constitutes self-injury. Today the medical personnel are able to take it without any pain or injury to the individual at all. Hence, the sole defensible justification for the prohibition is no longer applicable, and the prohibition no longer obtains.

Feinstein is clearly trying very hard to find a היתר, but his grounds are both weak, and we would be disinclined to rely upon them. While it may have been difficult for Rabbi Feinstein to admit the possibility that חז"ל may have been entirely mistaken in believing that there are medical benefits to blood letting, we do not find such a premise so impossible. Therefore, any היתר to donate blood which is based on the premise that the removal of the blood benefits the donor medically would be untenable. Furthermore, enough donors have black and blue marks on their arms after donation to make the claim that all blood donation is painless and without injury unacceptable as a grounding for halakhic decision making.

There is another avenue, however, which seems to be more halakhically sound. The passage in Maimonides from which the prohibition against self-injury is deduced reads in its entirety:[188]

> אסור לאדם לחבול בין בעצמו בין בחברו. ולא החובל בלבד, אלא כל המכה אדם כשר מישראל בין קטן בין גדול בין איש בין אשה דרך נציון, הרי זה עובר בלא תעשה, שנא': לא יוסיף להכותו (דב' כה:ג), אם הזהירה תורה מלהוסיף בהכאת החוטא, קל וכמר למכה את הצדיק.

> It is forbidden for one to injure either himself or someone else. [And the prohibition applies] not only to inflicting actual injury, but rather even anyone who strikes another Jew, whether a minor or an adult, whether a man or a woman, in a manner of strife,[189] violates a negative commandment. Scripture says: "He should not add to his lashes." If the Torah warns against adding lashes in the whipping of the sinner, *kal va'homer* regarding one who is not a sinner.[190]

We quote from the words of Rabbi Abraham Sofer Abraham, who gives a reasonable explanation of the conclusion that should be drawn from the careful wording of the Rambam. The *Nishmat Avraham* wrote:[191]

---

[188] M.T. Hilkhot Hovel u'Mazik 5:1.

[189] Based on Exod. 21:22 – וכי ינצו אנשים. Most editions of Maimonides have a marginal gloss suggesting the reading בזיון instead of נציון. For the purposes of the argument soon to be made, either reading would lead to the same result.

[190] The actual scriptural derivation is not relevant to our deliberation. See, however, Sifre Devarim, 286: לא יוסיף, אם היה מוסיף עובר על לא תעשה, and Rashi to Ketubbot 33a, ד"ה ופרכינן חובל, and Sanhedrin 85a.

[191] *Nishmat Avraham*, Hilkhot Aveilut, siman 349:2, letter ג, p. 265; appearing also in המעין, Nisan 5745, p. 27.

וממה שכתב "דרך נציון" משמע דוקא דרך נציון, דהיינו ריב (או דרך בזיון), אבל אם עשה זאת לא לשם ריב (או בזיון) אלא לתועלת, ולא מיבעיא לתועלת של ריפוי אלא אפילו לתועלת של ממון, מותר.

> And one can deduce from the fact that he wrote "in a manner of strife," that the implication is that it applies only when done in a manner of strife (or a degrading manner). But if one did it (i.e., inflict injury) not for the purpose of strife (or degradation), but for some positive purpose, not restricted to medical positive purpose but even financial positive purpose, it is permissible.

The wording of Maimonides does not imply an absolute prohibition against inflicting injury. The prohibition is not independent of the intent when inflicting the injury. Only when the intent is to injure or degrade, as opposed to injury or degradation being an unavoidable result of the act, does the act fall under the prohibition of חובל. Surely that is not the case with blood donation. It is not the intent of either the donor or the technician to inflict injury. The intent of both is merely to extract blood, not to engage in strife or degradation. Thus, the prohibition against self-injury is simply inapplicable to the question at hand, and since there is no other conceivably applicable prohibition, there is no prohibition whatsoever.[192]

A different approach is also indicated by Rabbi Joseph Babad in his *Minhat Hinukh* when he wrote:[193]

ונלע"ד דזה שחייבה התורה בהכה אביו ואמו או בחבירו היינו דוקא בלא רשות, אבל אם אביו ואמו אומרים לו שיכם או יקללם, או חבירו, אינו בלאו הזה, ואינו חייב מלקות ולא מיתה.

> It seems to me that when the Torah makes one liable for hitting one's father or mother, or one's fellow, it does so specifically in the case where one did so without permission. But, if one's father or mother ask to be hit or cursed, or [similarly] one's fellow, this negative commandment (i.e., the prohibition against being חובל) does not apply, and one is not liable either for lashing or death.

In the case of blood donation the injury is being inflicted with permission from the donor. Surely the claim of Babad exonerates the technicians from any liability. It is reasonable, as well, to affirm that if the actual inflicter of the injury is exonerated by the grant of permission by the injured party, that party must have had permission to forego his own prohibition against self-injury.[194]

---

[192] Two comments: First, it is a little surprising that Feinstein himself did not have recourse to this argument, since he himself makes the same deduction from Maimonides in a different context. In אגרות משה, חשן משפט, חלק א', סי' ג' Feinstein wrote: משמע דאם אינו דרך נציון לא הוי בכלל הלאו כלל. Second, in fairness to Rabbi Menashe Klein, he might interpret Maimonides' clause דרך נציון to refer only to the case of hitting someone without causing any injury. If one hits someone in that way, in the manner of strife, one violates a negative mitzvah even though there is no injury. If there is no injury and no manner of strife, no mitzvah is violated. If, however, one actually causes injury, the negative mitzvah is violated even if not in a manner of strife.

[193] מנחת חנוך, מצוה מ"ח, אות ב', דף ע' ע"א (ירושלים: הוצאת פרדס, תשי"ט).

[194] The claim of the מנחת חנוך is surely not self evidently true. There is no clear statement in the Talmud that permits one to supersede the prohibition against self-injury. One could even make the opposite case fairly strongly. The clearest statement of the opposite view can be found in the שלחן ערוך הרב, ח"ה, הלכות נזקי גוף ונפש, סע' ד' where בעל התניא wrote: אסור להכות את חברו אפילו הוא נותן לו רשות להכותו כי אין לאדם רשות על גופו כלל להכותו. A fascinating analysis of the issue can be found in Shlomo Yosef Zevin, לאור ההלכה: בעיות ובירורים in the chapter entitled משפט שיילוק לפי ההלכה, pp. 181-196, esp. pp. 188-189. (ירושלים: מוסד הרב קוק, תש"ו).

Finally, Abraham Sofer Abraham[195] claims that Rabbi Shlomo Zalman Auerbach permitted blood donation to a bank because the act is ultimately one intended for saving a life, even if the primary motivation of the donor may have been monetary. That is, the prohibition against חבלה is inapplicable because it is superseded by the mandate of הצלת נפש.[196]

We claimed above[197] that the majority of poskim, who disagree with the Ramah, forbid self-injury, even for need. Rabbi Moshe Zorger refers[198] to an incident with Abba Hilkiah in order to draw a helpful distinction. On his way home from the fields one day, several sages saw Abba Hilkiah lift up his clothing as he approached a field of thorns and brambles. Obviously, his intention was to prevent tears in his clothing that would be caused by the thorns. When the sages had a chance to discuss this, and other elements of his behavior, with him, they expressed surprise that he lifted his clothing, but allowed himself to be pricked by the thorns. Abba Hilkiah answered: זה מעלה ארוכה וזה אינה מעלה ארוכה — "The skin will heal itself, but the clothes will not."

If the prohibition against inflicting self-injury applies even to cases of need, without any distinctions, the behavior of Abba Hilkiah is difficult to understand. Based on this, Zorger concludes:

> הרי שכדי שלא להפסיד בגדיו התיר לעבור במקום קוצים לחבול בעצמו משום שגופו מעלה ארוכה. להכי נראה לדינא שכל חבלה שאינו מעלה ארוכה, כגון לקטוע ידו ורגלו וכדומה אסור לצורך ממון, אבל לחבול להוציא דם וכה"ג מותר לצורך ממון.

> It seems that he (Abba Hilkiah) permitted passing through thorns and injuring himself in order to protect his clothing since his body would heal itself. Thus it seems reasonable to conclude legally that an injury which will not heal itself, for example, amputating a hand, a foot, or something similar, would be forbidden even for monetary need. But to inflict self-injury in order to remove blood, and similar matters, would be permissible for monetary need.

The distinction which Rabbi Zorger draws does not appear in the work of other poskim, at least as far as I have been able to find. Nonetheless, it seems to be a reasonable and even compelling distinction. It leaves the laws of self-injury as follows: (1) all self-injury which will not heal itself is forbidden, even for cause (other than medical necessity); (2) self-injury which will heal itself is nonetheless forbidden in the absence of cause; and, (3) self-injury which will heal itself is permissible for cause.

In the case of blood donation, the cause which permits might be the financial need of the donor who is donating for money, or the ongoing protection of one and one's family in the event that blood is needed by them in the future, or (in an extension of Rabbi Auerbach's claim above) the saving of the life or health even of a stranger or one whose identity is as yet unknown because his need of blood is not yet present.

Though many of the poskim restrict their permission to donate blood to those who have a rare blood type, which is often unavailable for purchase, or which might cost a great

---

[195] See above, n. 191.

[196] I shall forego the "pleasure" of a lengthy discourse at this time on the subject of whether this would apply if the chances were significant that the recipient might be non-Jewish. Rabbi Moshe Ze'ev Zorger addresses this issue in וישב משה (ירושלים 1989), סי', צ"ד.

[197] P. 249.

[198] וישב משה, סי' צ"ג, אות ב', דף רמ"ב ע"א, referring to the Gemara in Tan'anit 23b.

deal because it is so rare, there is no reason to be so restrictive. While it is true that there are sometimes acute shortages of rare blood types, hospitals and blood banks are always in need of all types of blood. There never seems to be a glut in the blood market of even the most common types of blood. If there is never enough blood, there is always a need.

Our deliberation thus far has made mention of the donation of blood for compensation. But, the essence of our discussion was about the laws of self-injury and their applicability to blood donation. Now, though, we will turn our attention specifically to the question of the permissibility of donation for compensation.[199] Obviously, there is a relationship between one's view on the issue of self-injury, and one's view on the permissibility of donating blood for compensation. If one forbids self-injury even for need, as does Rabbi Menashe Klein, it must be forbidden to donate blood for compensation even when in financial need. Indeed, Klein says so explicitly at the end of his responsum.[200] According to the views above that exempt blood donation from the laws of self-injury either on the grounds that there is medical benefit to the donor, or that there is no injury, or that the prohibition against self-injury does not apply when the donor gives permission for the injury to be inflicted, or because the category of הצלת נפשות supersedes the prohibition, or because the prohibition against self-injury does not apply to injuries inflicted for cause and which heal themselves — there can be no objection to donation for compensation based on the prohibition of חבלה. Indeed, that is the thrust of Rabbi Feinstein's responsum,[201] the comment of Rabbi Auerbach quoted by Abraham Sofer Abraham,[202] and the responsum of Rabbi Zorger.[203]

The question that needs yet to be addressed, however, is whether there are other grounds on which receiving compensation for blood donation should be considered halakhically prohibited. The issue that might be raised is that the blood donation and the bone marrow donation are in the category of a mitzvah, and perhaps the performance of a mitzvah for compensation is itself forbidden. Without going into the history of the acceptance of pay by those who perform mitzvot — like teachers, doctors, *mohalim,* and *shohatim* — it is now an accepted practice. Indeed, the Radbaz makes an interesting comment about those who might practice מילה without pay. He wrote concerning one who had taken an oath not to derive any benefit from the inhabitants of a city, whose services were then needed, and about whom Maimonides codified that his oath should be annulled:[204] דאפ׳ אם רוצה לעשות בחנם מתירין לו, דאסיא במגן מגן שויא[205] וכיון שאינו נוטל שכר לא יעשה המצוה כתקנה — "That even if he wishes to perform the services without cost,[206] the oath should be annulled, because 'a doctor who treats for nothing is worth nothing,'[207] and since he would be taking no wage, he would not be fastidious in performing the mitzvah correctly."

---

[199] There is clear evidence of some types of sale. In the Mishnah (Nedarim 9:5, 65b), Rabbi Akiva insists that a man pay the full amount of his wife's ketubbah, even if he has to sell his own hair to eat! It seems, too, that Rabbi Akiva was drawing on his own family experience, for the Yerushalmi (Shabbat 6:1, 7d) records that his wife used to sell her hair in order to support him at the academy.

[200] See above, n. 183.

[201] See above, n. 187.

[202] See above, p. 252.

[203] See above, p. 252.

[204] M.T. Hilkhot Shevuot 6:9.

[205] בבא קמא פ״ה ע״א.

[206] Thereby avoiding the need to annul the oath since he would not be deriving any benefit from the inhabitants of the city since he would be acting without charge.

[207] Bava Kamma 85a.

We must be realistic in this matter. If we declare compensation for blood donation (or blood platelets, or bone marrow) to be halakhically forbidden because the donation is a mitzvah, we will succeed mainly in reducing the supply of available blood. Donors, after all, have the right to refuse to donate. If receiving fair and reasonable compensation for their time and pain can serve as an inducement to donate, we should not seek to impose a level of "piety" upon them that will do nothing more than reduce the available supply.

We might wish to make a theological claim similar to that made by Rabbi Moshe Sternbuch:[208]

> אם תורם מדמו למצוה לשם שמים, הלוא זוכה למצוה גדולה של הצלת נפש מישראל שאין כמוה ואם לוקח על זה כסף לא נוכל למנוע אותו ולהורות שצריך בחנם דוקא, אבל ודאי ששכרו מן השמים פחות.

> If one donates his blood as an act of מצוה לשם שמים, he merits the great and incomparable mitzvah of saving a life. But if he takes compensation for this, we should not prevent him from doing so by issuing a decision that the donation must be free. Surely, though, his heavenly reward will be less.

We would even wish to add the admonition of Rabbi Moshe Ze'ev Zorger[209] that

> אם אינו נותן דמו רק בשביל כסף ועושה מזה איזה מסחר, הגם דנראה דלפי מה שפירשתי אין לאסור מדינא דהא חבלה מותר לצורך פרנסה אם הוא מעלה ארוכה, מכל מקום מכוער הדבר.

> If one does not give his blood except for compensation, making a type of business of it, even though it follows from what I have explained that it is not forbidden by law since self-injury is permissible for purposes of a livelihood when the body heals itself, it is nonetheless unseemly.

But, we would be ill advised to prohibit compensation for the donation of blood or bone marrow.

We shall have to return to this issue later, as well. Suffice it for now to affirm that the distinction drawn by Rabbi Zorger between מעלה ארוכה and not מעלה ארוכה may, but also may not, allow us to distinguish between compensation for blood or bone marrow, on the one hand, and the creation of markets for the sale of other organs (like kidneys, for example), on the other.

We can deal with the question of Shabbat blood donation with some brevity, since two quotations epitomize what our view of the subject should be. Rabbi Moshe Ze'ev Zorger wrote the following:[210]

> והנה זה ברור לדינא שבשבת אסור לתרום דאפשר לתרום בחול. ומ"מ יתכן שאם הוא עת מלחמה ואין להם זמן אחר להקיז וליקח תרומות דם רק בשבת, כגון שפרצה מלחמה פתאום ואין די דם מהמוכן עד שיוכלו להמתין עד יום ראשון או שקשה מאוד ליקח ביום ראשון דם.... לא ידעתי מקום לאסור ליתן דם.

---

[208] תשובות והנהגות, מהדורה חדשה (ירושלים תשנ"ב), חלק א', סי' תתצ"ח, עמ' תקפ"ג.

[209] See p. 246a of Zorger's responsum detailed above, n. 198.

[210] וישב משה (ירושלים, 1989)' סי' צ"ד, דף רמ"ו ע"א.

The following is clear legally, that it is forbidden to give blood on Shabbat since it is possible to donate during the week. Nonetheless, it is likely that if it is war time, and there is no other time to take the donations than Shabbat, as, for example, if the war broke out suddenly and there is insufficient available blood to allow waiting until Sunday to take donations, or if it will be very difficult to take the donations on Sunday.... [Under such conditions,] I know no reason to forbid blood donations [on Shabbat].

In a similar vein, but expanded beyond the eventuality of war, Rabbi Joshua Isaiah Neubirt wrote:[211]

> כשיש צורך בעירוי דם לחולה ואי אפשר להשיג דם מן המוכן בבנק הדם, מותר לבריא לתרום דם בשבת, ואף מותר, בעת הצורך להשתמש ברכב להבאת התורמים או ציוד ההתרמה, ומותר לעשות גם אם התרומה מותנית ברישום שם התורם.

> When a blood transfusion for a sick patient is needed, and it is impossible to obtain blood from the available supply in the blood bank, it is permissible for a healthy person to donate blood on Shabbat. It is even permissible, when necessary, to use automobiles to transport the donors or the donation equipment. And it is permissible [to carry out the donations] even when they are contingent upon recording the names of the donors.

Under normal circumstances, blood donation on Shabbat is inappropriate, and entails prohibited acts. It should be avoided whenever possible. Blood donation on Shabbat is permissible, however, in circumstances that can be defined as פקוח נפש. When it would be permissible to desecrate the Sabbath in other ways, it is also permissible to desecrate it through blood donation. When Shabbat blood donation is permissible, one should seek to avoid ancillary Sabbath desecrations, but when they are unavoidable, they do not render the donation forbidden. Rather, the ancillary desecrations should be violated, and the blood donated and collected.

Conclusions

1. There is no halakhic impediment to the donation of either blood or bone marrow for the use of an identifiable individual. Indeed, under such circumstances donation is a great mitzvah and should be greatly encouraged and lauded. It should be spoken of in terms of moral imperative, reflected in the halakhic categories of ועשית הישר והטוב and, possibly, לפנים משורת הדין. Those in positions of authority or influence should couch their encouragement to donate in the strongest possible religious and theological terms, stressing the obligation of Jews to behave morally and ethically. Refusal to donate is not, however, a violation of the negative commandment לא תעמוד על דם רעך, for which physical coercion would be halakhically justified.

2. It is permissible, indeed, desirable and praiseworthy, to donate blood to a blood bank for later use either by oneself or by someone else. Such donation does not put the donor in violation of the prohibition against self-injury.

---

[211] שמירת שבת כהלכתה, מהדורה חדשה (ירושלים: בית מדרש הלכה – מוריה, תשל"ט), פרק מ', סע' כ"ה in the name of Rabbi Moshe Wasserman, שאילת משה, סי' נ'.

3. Though it should be discouraged as unseemly, donation of blood or bone marrow for compensation is not halakhically forbidden. Of course, if civil law forbids accepting compensation, it becomes forbidden under the category of דינא דמלכותא דינא.

4. Blood donation on Shabbat is forbidden except under circumstances of פקוח נפש. Under such circumstances, even prohibitions which are ancillary to the actual donation process become permissible, when unavoidable.

Part IV: Live Donors – Kidneys

This paper was approved by the CJLS on March 16, 1999, by a vote of fifteen in favor and one abstaining (15-0-1). Voting in favor: Rabbis Kassel Abelson, Ben Zion Bergman, Elliot N. Dorff, Baruch Frydman-Kohl, Myron S. Geller, Nechama D. Goldberg, Arnold M. Goodman, Judah Kogen, Vernon H. Kurtz, Lionel E. Moses, Mayer Rabinowitz, James S. Rosen, Joel Roth, Elie Kaplan Spitz, and Gordon Tucker. Abstaining: Rabbi Susan Grossman.

The Committee on Jewish Law and Standards of the Rabbinical Assembly provides guidance in matters of halakhah for the Conservative movement. The individual rabbi, however, is the authority for the interpretation and application of all matters of halakhah.

שאלה

Is it permissible to donate a kidney? If so, is it ever halakhically required? If so, when? May one donate a kidney for compensation? Are there instances in which donation would be forbidden even if the potential donor wishes to donate?

תשובה

The essential issue which must be discussed thoroughly before any answers can be offered to the שאלות of this section is the question of putting oneself in danger for the benefit of another. The issue, as we shall see, has many subissues, and is a matter of considerable disagreement among poskim. We shall be best served by presenting the central primary texts first, and following them through the deliberations of poskim.

Maimonides records the following:[212]

> כל היכול להציל ולא הציל עובר על לא תעמוד על דם רעך. וכן הרואה את חבירו טובע בים או ליסטים באים עליו או חיה רעה באה עליו ויכול להצילו הוא בעצמו או שישכור אחרים להצילו ולא הציל, או ששמע גוים או מוסרים מחשבים עליו רעה או טומנין לו פח ולא גלה אוזן חבירו והודיעו, או שידע בגוי או באנס שהוא קובל על חבירו ויכול לפייסו בגלל חבירו ולהסיר מה שבלבו ולא פייסו, וכל כיוצא בדברים אלו, העושה אותם עובר על לא תעמוד על דם רעך.

> Anyone who is able to save one in danger and who does not do so violates the negative commandment, "Do not stand idly by the blood of your fellow." And similarly, if one sees one's fellow drowning in the sea, or being attacked by bandits or by a dangerous ani-

---

[212] M.T. Hilkhot Rozeah 1:14.

mal, and is able to save him either by himself or by hiring others to save him, and does not do so; or, if one heard either non-Jews or informers plotting evil against someone, or laying a trap for him, and did not inform the person; or, if one knew about a non-Jew or some violent person who was lodging a complaint about his fellow, and he could appease that person on behalf of his fellow and did not do so; and all such similar matters, whoever does these things violates, "Do not stand idly by the blood of your fellow."

For the moment, we shall suffice with the following brief observations about this quotation from Maimonides. First, the obvious talmudic source which serves as Maimonides' basis is the Gemara in Sanhedrin 73a. Second, while the baraita quoted there by the Gemara uses the phrase חייב להצילו — "He is obligated to save him" — Maimonides does not.

In commenting on this passage, Joseph Karo writes:[213] וכתב הגהות מיימון... בירושלמי מסיק אפילו להכניס עצמו בספק סכנה חייב עכ"ל. ונר' שהטעם מפני שהלה ודאי והוא ספק — "The *Hagahot Maimon[iyot]* wrote... 'The Yerushalmi concludes that one is even obligated to put oneself in uncertain danger.' The reasoning of the Yerushalmi seems to be that the endangered person is a case of 'certainty,' while the potential saver is a case of 'doubt.'"[214] At face value, Karo understands the *Hagahot* to imply that the certainty of the death of the endangered person supersedes the uncertain danger of the potential saver, and compels him to attempt to save, even though he is himself potentially jeopardized thereby.

The Tur[215] basically quotes the Rambam. Karo, in the Beit Yosef, refers again to the comment of the *Hagahot*, using almost exactly the same language as he did in the *Kesef Mishneh*, but adding וכל המקיים נפש אחת מישראל כאילו קיים עולם מלא — "And anyone who preserves one life of Israel is as though he preserved the entire world." Note, though, that neither the Rambam nor the Tur state explicitly that one must put oneself in jeopardy in order to save the life of another. It is, apparently, precisely because they do not say so that Karo adds the comment to each. Additionally, and perhaps surprisingly considering his comments on Maimonides and the Tur, the Shulhan Arukh itself also contains no statement obligating one to put oneself in jeopardy in order to save another. Neither the Rosh nor the Rif has such a comment either.

None of the sources that refer to the Yerushalmi clarify where the passage appears in the Yerushalmi. Among the few who adopt the view clearly, Rabbi Ya'ir Haim Bacharach seeks to buttress support for the unidentified Yerushalmi from the Bavli. He wrote:[216]

כתב בכסף משנה ספ"א דהלכות רוצח ושמירת נפש בשם הירושלמי שמחויב לכנוס לספק נפשו להציל נפש חבירו וש"ס דידן ב"מ ד' ס"ב [ע"א] נמי הכי משמע התם שאם ישתו שניהם ימותו ודאי מה שאין כן בספק יש לומר ישתו שניהם ולא ישתה הוא לבדו וימות חבירו ודאי, וא"כ מחויב לכנוס לספק נפשות אפי' בספק הצלה.

The *Kesef Mishneh* wrote in the name of the Yerushalmi at the end of chapter one of *Hilkhot Rozeah* that one is obligated to put one-

---

[213] Kesef Mishnah, *ad locum*.

[214] The comment attributed by Maimonides to the *Hagahot Maimoniyot* does not appear in our editions of the Mishneh Torah. It does, however, appear in the Constantinople printing of 1509, and reads: בירושלמי מסיק אפילו להכניס עצמו בספק סכנה.

[215] Hoshen Mishpat 426.

[216] שאלות ותשובות חות יאיר, סי' קמ"ו.

self in jeopardy in order to save the life of another. And our Talmud, in Bava Metzia 62[a] also implies the same thing by referring to a case in which if both drink they will surely die, but implying that were it doubtful whether both would die if they both drank, perhaps both should drink rather than he alone drinking and bringing about the certain death of the other. Thus, [the Bavli also implies that one is] obligated to jeopardize himself, even when the ultimate saving is also in doubt.

The *Havat Ya'ir* refers to the passage which contains the dispute between ben Petura and Rabbi Akiva concerning the case of two who were in the desert, but had only a small amount of water. About this case the Gemara claims: אם שותין שניהם מתים, ואם שותה אחד מהם מגיע לישוב – "If they both drink, they will die; but if only one drinks, he will be able to arrive at a populated area [and get more water]." Ben Petura affirms that they should share the water, even if both die, rather than that one should see the death of the other. Rabbi Akiva claims that the verse וחי אחיך עמך – "That your fellow might live with you"[217] – implies that חייך קודמין לחיי חברך – "Your life takes precedence over the life of your fellow."

Bacharach understands this passage to intimate agreement between the Bavli and Yerushalmi that one must jeopardize oneself in attempting to save another. He deduces this by affirming that the dispute between ben Petura and Rabbi Akiva refers to a case where it is absolutely certain that both will die if they share the water. In that case ben Petura says they should share, while Rabbi Akiva – whose view is normative – says that one should drink. Implied, however, is that in a case where it is not certain that both will die if they both share, even Rabbi Akiva would agreee that they should share. Since the law follows the view of Rabbi Akiva, it would follow that one is obligated to put oneself in potential danger in order to attempt to save the life of another.[218] If the analysis of the *Havat Ya'ir* is uncontestable, the combined support of the Bavli and the Yerushalmi for the position it espouses would make it a potent argument.[219]

The view of the *Havat Ya'ir* was taken on directly by Rabbi Eliyahu ben Samuel of Lublin.[220] He claimed that the dispute between ben Petura and Rabbi Akiva is in a case of doubt. That is, though the chances are that they both will die if they share the water, it is not absolutely certain that they will. In this case ben Petura says they should share, and Rabbi Akiva says that only one should drink, to insure that one survives even if that also insures that the other dies. Since the view of Rabbi Akiva is normative, it follows from the *Yad Eliyahu* that the passage in Bava Metzia does not support the claim of the

---

[217] Lev. 25:36.

[218] Our major focus, at the moment, is on the question of putting oneself in potential jeopardy. However, we should not overlook the other important implication of this statement of Bacharach. He claims that one must put oneself in potential jeopardy even if it is uncertain that one's efforts to save the other will be successful. One could have held that it is obligatory to put oneself in danger for the benefit of another only when it is certain that one's efforts will succeed, even if one dies in the process.

[219] Bacharach ends his analysis with the claim וצ"ע. He does not exactly explain what requires further investigation. Perhaps he is wondering why, if the Bavli supports the view of the Yerushalmi, the poskim seem to ignore them.

[220] He lived in the second half of the 17th century and the first part of the 18th century, serving communities in Poland, Lituania and Moravia. He died in Hebron in 1735. His responsa, שו"ת יד אליהו, were published in Amsterdam in 1712. The responsum in which he deals with our subject of discussion is no. 43, pp. 48a-50b of the book.

Yerushalmi, because Rabbi Akiva mandates that one *not* put oneself even in doubtful jeopardy for the benefit of another.[221] Indeed, the passage from the Bavli contradicts the view of the Yerushalmi.[222]

The *Yad Eliyahu* is not the only one to reject the explanation of this passage given by the *Havat Ya'ir*. Rabbi Naftali Zevi Berlin, the Netziv, also understands that passage differently from Bacharach. The passage itself appears not only in the Bavli, but also in the Sifra.[223] There it is clear that both ben Petura and Rabbi Akiva base their views on the verse וחי אחיך עמך. Ben Petura requires both to drink because he understands the verse to mean: "Your brother must live together with you." Ostensibly, the implication seems also to be that if your brother cannot live together with you, you, too, should not live. Rabbi Akiva understands: "Your brother should live with you," but you come first. If he can live "with you," fine; if he cannot live "with you," you take precedence.

The Netziv understands the dispute as does the *Yad Eliyahu*, but comes at it by logic. He wrote:[224]

> ולכאורה דעת בן פטורי תמוה, וכי בשביל שאי אפשר לקיים וחי אחיך מחוייב הוא להמית את עצמו, חס וחלילה, ואיזו תועלת תהיה מה שיתן גם לחבירו. אלא הענין דאם ישתו שניהם על כל פנים יחיו יום או יומיים גם שניהם, שלא יגיעו לישוב, ואולי עד כה יזדמן להם מים, מה שאין כן אם לא יתן לחבירו הרי ימות בודאי בצמא, ובא ר' עקיבא ודרש וחי אחיך עמך חייך קודמין.

> It seems that the view of ben Petura is astonishing. Is it reasonable that just because one cannot fulfill "Your brother shall live," that he should be obligated to kill himself, God forbid? And what will it help to share the water with his fellow [since they will both die for sure anyway]? Rather, the issue is that if they both drink, they will both live for another day or two. And even though they will not reach a populated area, perhaps they will find some water during that period [and both live]. But that would not be the case if he did not share with his fellow, for his fellow would then die of thirst with certainty. [Thus, ben Petura insists that they share in the hope of ultimately fulfilling "Your brother shall live *together with you*]. But Rabbi Akiva came along and explained the verse to mean: "Though your brother should live together with you," your life comes first.

For Berlin it is so illogical that two should certainly die when one could certainly live, that he affirms that ben Petura could not have meant that. He must have been referring to

---

[221] We shall not deal at length with the textual evidence for and against the views of Bacharach and Eliyahu of Lublin. Suffice it to say, however, that the phrase אם שותים שניהם מתים seems to support the *Havat Ya'ir*, implying that if both drink they will surely both die. On the other hand, the phrase ואל יראה אחד מהם במיתת חברו is problematic for him, because surely one will still see the death of the other (it being highly unlikely that both will die at exactly the same instant). For the *Yad Eliyahu*, on the other hand, that phrase is less problematic. He understands it to mean: Both should drink when it is not clear that both will die, rather than one of them drinking and surely seeing the death of the other because *he causes that certain death by withholding water from him*. For the Yad Eliyahu, though, the phrase אם שותים שניהם מתים is not so smooth.

[222] We shall return to this point, and its possible implications on our subject, below.

[223] Parashat Behar, Parashah 5, Mishnah 3, to Lev. 25:36, Weiss ed., p. 109c.

[224] *She'eltot*, no. 147, *Ha'amek She'elah*, near the end of par. 4, p. 212.

a case when two might die because they share, but they might also both live. It is precisely the element of doubt that justifies ben Petura's view. The normative view, however, is that of Rabbi Akiva for whom the certain life of the one takes precedence over the doubtful life of both. Hence, for Berlin, too, this passage implies that one ought not put oneself in even potential jeopardy for the benefit of another.

What's more, the Netziv finds support for his understanding from elsewhere in the Gemara, as well. The Talmud[225] proves the principle that life endangerment supersedes the Sabbath by quoting a variety of biblical proofs offered by a variety of sages. The last verse quoted as proof, by Samuel, is וחי בהם – "And live by them."[226] Samuel says: וחי בהם ולא שימות בהם – "You should live by them, not die because of them." When the Gemara proceeds to ask how we know that even a case of potential life endangerment supersedes the Sabbath, it rejects all of the verses quoted by the sages other than Samuel. None of those verses necessarily applies to ספק פקוח נפש, but Samuel's does. Thus, וחי בהם is applied by the Talmud itself to ספק פקוח נפש, implying that even potential life endangerment supersedes the other mitzvot of the Torah. Thus, the mitzvah to save the life of another is also superseded in the face of potential life endangerment to the saver.

In the final analysis, then, the Netziv and the *Yad Eliyahu* agree that the passage quoted by the *Havat Ya'ir* to support the position of the Yerushalmi not only does not support the Yerushalmi, it contradicts it.

Rabbi Haim Heller[227] also rejects the explanation of the *Havat Ya'ir*. Bacharach had deduced from אם ישתו שניהם ימותו that the case was about inevitable death to both, and that ben Petura and Rabbi Akiva were discussing the same case. Thus, it is only in the case of inevitable death to both that Rabbi Akiva allows one to drink without sharing, whereas if it were doubtful that both would die, even Rabbi Akiva would demand sharing. Heller claims that the phrase אם ישתו שניהם ימותו was correctly understood by the *Havat Ya'ir* to imply certain death for both. But, Bacharach is mistaken, says Heller, in thinking that ben Petura and Rabbi Akiva must both be referring to exactly the same case. The words of ben Petura are a רבותא, applying only to ben Petura. That is, he indeed does require that both drink, even if the death of both is certain. Rabbi Akiva's disagreement with him, though, is not restricted to that case. Rabbi Akiva believes that even if the death of both is not certain, the water should not be shared, but drunk by one of them.[228]

It is not only moderns who assume that the dispute between ben Petura and Rabbi Akiva is about ספק נפשות. The יחוסי תנאים ואמוראים also makes the same claim:[229] ונראה – "[The essence of the dispute] seems to be linked to the fact that they are walking on the way and are both in potential danger, since water is not readily available in the desert."

---

[225] Yoma 85a and b.

[226] Lev. 18:5.

[227] In his edition of the *Sefer ha-Mitzvot* of Maimonides, negative commandments, no. 297, n. 9, pp. 175.

[228] What seems to lead Rabbi Heller to this explanation is that if Bacharach is correct, one must jeopardize oneself to save another even when it is not certain that the saving will actually be effective (see above, n. 218). That claim, says Heller, seems to go beyond the demand of the Yerushalmi which לא אמר אלא שמחוייב להציל את חבירו ואפ' אם כניס את עצמו לספק נפשות והיינו היכא שבודאי יצילנו, אבל משום ספק הצלה לא מצינו – "Demands only that one put oneself in potential jeopardy in order to save another, but only when the saving is certain, but there is no demand [to put oneself in potential jeopardy] when the saving is doubtful." Heller feels that the conclusion to which Bacharach is drawn by his understanding of the passage is so unlikely that it calls the entire understanding into question, and forces its rejection.

[229] Judah Leib Maimon ed. (Jerusalem: Mosad ha-Rav Kook, 5723), p. 33.

We were led to the discussion of the past few pages by the fact that Bacharach affirmed the position of the Yerushalmi, as stipulated by the *Hagahot Maimoniyot*, and contended that the position was supported by the Bavli. We have been analyzing whether his understanding of the Bavli is compelling. We have quoted the opinions of the *Yad Eliyahu*, the *Ha-amek She'elah*, Rabbi Haim Heller, and the יחוסי תנאים ואמוראים, all of whom find that understanding wanting. Given the understanding of these four, the very passage adduced by Bacharach as support, contradicts his claim and indicates a disagreement between the Bavli and the Yerushalmi. Of course, of the four, only the Netziv sought support for his understanding of the passage from elsewhere in the Bavli. For three of the four, at least, the matter boils down to a difference of opinion on the meaning of the *sugya*, but their interpretations do not disprove Bacharach's.

As the *Havat Ya'ir* took a clear stand in favor of the view of the Yerushalmi, there is a chain of others who took a clear stand against the view of the Yerushalmi. We shall quote a couple of them. The ספר איסור והיתר wrote:[230]

> הרואה את חבירו טובע בנהר או חיה רעה או ליסטים באין עליו ויכול להצילו ואינו מציל נחשב כאילו הרגו.... ומיהו אם בודאי היה גם כן הוא מסוכן עמו אין לו לסכן גופו מאחר שהוא חוץ מן הסכנה, אע"פ שרואה במיתת חבירו כדדרשינן וחי אחיך עמך ולא מצינו חילוק בין סכנה למיתה ודאית.

> If one who sees his fellow drowning in the river or attacked by an animal or robbers and is able to save him but does not, he is considered as though he had killed him.... Nonetheless, if he would also become endangered together with him, he should not endanger himself, since he is currently not in danger, even if that results in the death of the other. For thus have we understood "And your fellow should live together with you," and there is no distinction between endangerment and certain death.

Similarly, the *Sema* (Rabbi Joshua Falk, 1555-1614) wrote:[231]

> ובהג"מ כתבו דבירושלמי מסיק דצריך אפי' להכניס עצמו לספק סכנה.... גם זה השמיטו המחבר ומור"ם ז"ל, ובזה יש לומר כיון שהפוסקים הרי"ף והרמב"ם והרא"ש והטור לא הביאו בפסקיהם משום הכי השמיטוהו גם כן.

> The *Hagahot Maimoniyot* wrote that the Yerushalmi concludes that one must even put oneself into potential danger....This, too, is omitted by Karo and Isserles, of blessed memory. It is reasonable to claim that they omitted this because neither the Rif, the Rambam, the Rosh, or the Tur included it in their Codes.

The *Eliya Rabbah*[232] quotes the *Issur ve-Heter* as his decision in the matter. And Rabbi Hayyim Benveniste (1603-1673) agrees, writing:[233] אבל אם הבא להציל יש שיסתכן בהצלתו אין לו להצילו וליכנס עצמו בספק סכנה — "But if the one who attempts to save would

---

[230] Kelal 59:38. The book is often attributed to Rabbi Jonah Gerondi, but was most probably written by a Rabbi Jonah who was a student of Rabbi Israel Isserlein.

[231] S.A. Hoshen Mishpat 426, *Sema*, par. 2.

[232] Orah Hayyim 329:8. The Eliya Rabbah was written by Rabbi Eliyahu Shapira, 1660-1712.

[233] *Kenesset ha-Gedolah*, Hoshen Mishpat 425:10.

endanger himself in the act of saving, he ought not to save him by putting himself in potential danger." Rabbi Shneur Zalman of Lyady (1745-1813) is also very clear, sounding much like the *Issur ve-Heter*. He wrote:[234]

> ומ"מ אם יש סכנה אין לו לסכן עצמו כדי להציל את חבירו מאחר שהוא חוץ מן הסכנה, ואף שרואה את מיתת חבירו, ואע"פ שהוא ספק וחבירו ודאי מ"מ הרי נאמר וחי בהם ולא שיבא לידי ספק מיתה ע"י שיקיים מה שנאמר לא תעמוד על דם רעך.

> Nonetheless, if there is danger, one should not endanger himself in order to save his fellow, since he is currently not in danger, even if that results in the death of his fellow. And even though his death is "doubtful," while his fellow's is "certain," nonetheless, it says: "And live by them," and not that he should put himself in potential danger by virtue of fulfilling the verse, "Do not stand idly by the blood of your fellow."

Rabbi Shnuer Zalman is equally clear in another place as well.[235] ואפי' ליכנס בספק – סכנה י"א שצריך כדי להציל את חבירו ממיתה ודאית ויש חולקים בזה, וספק נפשות להקל "And even regarding putting oneself in danger there are some who say that one must do so in order to save one's fellow from certain death, while others disagree. And [we apply the principle that] we rule leniently in matters of doubt where life may be involved." The קולא, obviously, is that we do not require one to endanger oneself, even if that will result in the death of another.

At some point it seems reasonable to seek the source in the Yerushalmi which is referred to by so many, but not defined. The earliest identification of the source that this author is able to find is by the *Yad Eliyahu*. Though admitting near the beginning of his responsum that he is not certain that the *Hagahot Maimoniyot* referred to the same Yerushalmi he would later explain, the *Yad Eliyahu* refers to a passage of Yerushalmi as a potential source for deducing that one must put oneself in potential danger in order to attempt to save the life of another. His doubts notwithstanding, everyone else who attempts to define where the source in the Yerushalmi is, accepts the identification of the *Yad Eliyahu* as accurate. Let us look at the source:[236]

> רבי אימי איתצד בסיפסיפה. אמר ר' יונתן יכרך המת בסדינו. אמר ר' שמעון בן לקיש עד דאנא קטיל אנא מיתקטיל אנא איזיל ומשיזיב לי' בחיילא. אזול ופייסון ויהבוניה ליה.

> Rabbi Ami was trapped in a place of great danger. Rabbi Yonatan said: "Let the dead be wrapped in his shroud." Rabbi Shimon ben Lakish said: "Either I shall kill or I shall be killed, but I am going to save him by force." He went and appeased them, and they handed him over to him.

The translation above reflects the understanding of the P'nei Moshe on this passage. Assuming it to be the passage to which the *Hagahot Maimoniyot* referred, it must be understood as follows: Rabbi Yonatan and Resh Lakish disagree over the appropriate response to the plight of Rabbi Ami. Rabbi Yonatan considers it forbidden. Rabbi Ami

---

[234] *Shulhan Arukh ha-Rav*, Orah Hayyim 329:8.

[235] Ibid., Hoshen Mishpat, *Hilkhot nizkei guf va-nefesh*, par. 7.

[236] J. Terumot 8:4, 32b (46b).

should prepare to die. Resh Lakish, however, disagrees and affirms that though he will put himself in potential danger, he will go attempt to save Rabbi Ami. The *Hagahot* understands their dispute to be over whether or not one is obligated to endanger oneself for the benefit of another. Rabbi Yonatan says no, and Resh Lakish says yes. The *Hagahot* feels that the thrust of the Yerushalmi favors the view of Resh Lakish, whose act should be viewed as a מעשה רב. Hence, "the Yerushalmi concludes that one is even obligated to put oneself in danger."

In his response to this passage, the *Yad Eliyahu* says: אפשר לומר דר' יונתן דאמר יכרוך המת בסדינו רוצה לומר דאינו מחוייבים להסתכן, אך ריש לקיש עביד ממדת חסידות ולא מצד דין – "It is possible to say that Rabbi Yonatan meant to imply by his statement, 'Let the dead be wrapped in his shroud,' that there is no [legal] obligation to endanger oneself. But Resh Lakish acted out of piety, but not law." In other words, the fact that Resh Lakish took the risk does not mean that one must take a risk. It is permissible, as an act of piety, to endanger oneself for another, but it is not mandatory. The same position is affirmed by the Netziv:[237] מכל מקום, הרוצה להחמיר רשאי והיינו עובדא דרבי שמעון [בן לקיש] בירו' דתרומות, ולא פליג על ר' יונתן בדינא, אלא החמיר על עצמו – "In any event, one who wishes to be strict upon himself is allowed, and that is the case of Rabbi Shimon [ben Lakish] in the Yerushalmi Terumot; and not that he disagrees with Rabbi Yonatan about the law, but that he was strict for himself."

Rabbi Haim Heller[238] also questions whether the Yerushalmi implies what the *Hagahot* affirms:

ואמנם בעיקר הדין שמביא הגהות מיימוניות מירוש' והוא כמו שהביאו כולם מירושל' תרומות (ספ"ח)... ומכאן המקור לכל הדין. ולענ"ד שהראשונים פירשו פי' אחר בירושל' שמוכח היפך הדין הזה וה"ק רשב"ל עד דאנא קטל פי' אם אלחם אתם וטרם שאהרגם אנא מתקטל יוכל להיות שיהרגוני ולזה אינו מחוייב כלל אנא איזיל ומשיזיב ליה בחיילא מוטב לי שאפדנו בממון וכך עשה אזל ופייסון ומעתה כמובן לא קשיא מידי על הא דהשמיטו הפוסקים דין זה.

Indeed, regarding the law quoted by the *Hagahot Maimoniyot* on the basis of the Yerushalmi, it is, as all have said, based on Yerushalmi Terumot (end of chapter eight). . .which serves as the basis for the decision. And it seems to me that the Rishonim [must have] explained it differently, such that it yields the opposite of this law [as understood by the *Hagahot*], to wit: This is what Resh Lakish meant: עד דאנא קטל – "If I fight them, and before I kill them" – אנא מתקטל – "It could be that they will kill me" – for which he is not at all obligated. אנא איזיל ומשיזיב ליה בחיילא – "I am better off ransoming him with money" – which is what he did, אזל ופייסון ("He went and appeased them"). And now it is completely comprehensible why the poskim omitted this law [of the *Hagahot*].

In essence, all of the commentators are trying to figure out why the classical codifiers seem to ignore the view of the *Hagahot*. Heller's answer is that they all ignored it because they understood the Yerushalmi very differently from the way the *Hagahot* understood it. The Yerushalmi, they understood, rejects the claim that one must put one-

---

[237] *She'eltot*, no. 129, *Ha'amek She'elah*, letter four, p. 76; cf. no. 147, *Ha'amek She'elah*, letter four, p. 212.
[238] See above, n. 227.

self in potential danger for the benefit of another. Even Resh Lakish who says: "Why should I take the chance of getting myself killed before I can kill enough of them to save Rabbi Ami. I am under no legal obligation to do so, thereby endangering my life. I'll take ransom money and go to buy his freedom," does not believe that he is legally obligated to endanger himself. Why did the poskim ignore the view of the *Hagahot*? They ignored it because they disagreed with the way he understood the Yerushalmi on which his decision was based![239] An explanation of the Yerushalmi very similar to Heller's was also given by Rabbi Ovadiah Yosef.[240]

Rabbi J. David Bleich[241] rejects Yosef's explanation as not being in accordance with the plain meaning of the text; and Heller's explanation as strained. It is worth noting, however, at least in passing, that the reading of the Venice printing and the Leiden manuscript has עד דאנא קטיל ואנא מתקטיל which would lend support to the meaning, "Rather than that I should go and kill while being killed." What's more, the ending of the story – אזל ופייסון ויהבוניה ליה – "He went and appeased them, and they gave him to him" – seems also to support the view that force was not the method used by Resh Lakish.

We have now been analyzing the only Yerushalmi reference which is quoted as being the source of the claim of the *Hagahot Maimoniyot*. We have raised several explanations for why the poskim may have ignored this decision of the *Hagahot*. The first is that there is a dispute in the Yeruashalmi passage, and no incontrovertible evidence that the view of Resh Lakish is normative. Perhaps it is the view of Rabbi Yonatan which is normative. Second, perhaps there is no real dispute between Resh Lakish and Rabbi Yonatan at all. Both agree that one is under no obligation to endanger oneself for the benefit of another. The behavior of Resh Lakish, then, is to be understood either as his having acted out of piety,[242] but not intimating an obligation to endanger oneself; or, that even Resh Lakish did not endanger himself, because he went to ransom rather than to force or because he went with a large contingent that could easily have overpowered those holding Rabbi Ami, without endangering them.

There is one further comment on the Yerushalmi to be made before we move on. One author, Rabbi Yehiel Ya'akov Weinberg,[243] believes that the Yerushalmi can be understood to imply that even Rabbi Yonatan agrees that one must endanger oneself for the benefit of another. According to him, Rabbi Yonatan would agree that one must endanger oneself for the benefit of another, but only when it is clear that the effort, if carried out, will result in saving the person in danger. In the case of Rabbi Ami, Rabbi Yonatan thought it was probably a lost cause. There would probably be no success in saving him. That is what he meant by יכרך המת בסדינו. But were saving Rabbi Ami certain, even Rabbi Yonatan would agree that one must endanger oneself. According to his explanation, one must say that Resh Lakish was certain that his efforts would succeed, and that is why he undertook the mis-

---

[239] Rabbi Menashe Klein, משנה הלכות, vol. 6, no. 324, p. 394, finds this thesis problematic because קשה לפרש כן נגד כל הראשונים והאחרונים ז"ל שלא פירשו כן – "It is difficult to explain thus against all the Rishonim and Aharonim who did not explain thus." I do not understand Klein's objection. After all, we don't have explanations of Rishonim on this passage in the Yerushalmi. All we have is their continued quotation of the *Hagahot* that such a deduction can be made from the Yerushalmi.

[240] See his thorough article in דיני ישראל, vol. 7, pp. 27-43. This point is on p. 28. The only significant difference between him and Heller is that Rabbi Yosef takes חיילא to mean "large force," rather than "money," as Heller does.

[241] *Contemporary Halakhic Problems* (New York: Ktav and Yeshiva University Press, 1995), vol. 4, p. 275, n. 6.

[242] These two explanations are also offered by the *Ziz Eliezer*, vol. 9, no. 45, letter ה, p. 181a.

[243] *Moriah* 4, issues 3-4 (Nisan-Iyyar 5732): p. 64, as part of an entire article, pp. 62-67.

sion. Only that would justify Resh Lakish's putting himself in potential danger. According to this, the lesson of the Yerushalmi must be refined to mean that one is obligated to put oneself in danger for the benefit of another only when it is certain that the efforts will be marked by success. That is, when it is certain that the person being saved will, in fact, be saved if the person doing the saving survives the attempt, the attempt should be made.

It is well known that for poskim, the Bavli has primacy over the Yerushalmi. One turns to Yerushalmi for guidance on issues where there is no guidance in Bavli, but only very rarely would one decide according to the Yerushalmi when it disagrees with the Bavli. It would not be surprising, then, to expect decisors and commentators to seek evidence elsewhere in the Bavli to prove that the Bavli disagrees with what the *Hagahot* says the Yerushalmi says. If one can find such evidence, it would surely account for why the poskim ignored the *Hagahot*. The *Hagahot* must be mistaken, as a matter of actual law, because the Bavli disagrees. It is to such evidence among the poskim that we now turn.

Both the *Yad Eliyahu* and the *Agudat Ezov*[244] refer to the following story of the Gemara:[245]

> הנהו בני גלילאה דנפק עלייהו קלא דקטול נפשא אתו לקמיה דרבי טרפון אמרו ליה לטמרינן מר אמר להו היכי נעביד אי לא אטמרינכו חזו יתייכו אטמרינכו הא אמור רבנן האי לישנא בישא אע"ג דלקבולי לא מבעי מיחש ליה מבעי זילו אתון טמרו נפשייכו.

> There were certain Galileans about whom there was a report that they had killed someone. They came to Rabbi Tarfon and said to him: "Let the master hide us." He answered: "What should I do? If I do not hide you, they will find you. If I do hide you, the Sages have said that though one should not listen to rumors, one must be concerned about them. Go and hide yourselves."

Rabbi Tarfon refused to hide the suspects, though they were clearly in danger, and certain danger, at that. Rabbi Tarfon, however, seems not to have been in certain danger, but only potential danger. After all, perhaps they would never be found, and even if they were, he might not be identified as the one who hid them, or he might well be able to convince the authorities that he was unaware of their crime. Also, maybe the rumor was just that, and they were innocent of any wrongdoing and would be exonerated at trial. Thus, Rabbi Tarfon's refusal to hide the suspects clearly indicates that the Bavli does not believe that one must jeopardize oneself for the benefit of another.

This understanding of the passage is predicated on the assumption that what Rabbi Tarfon was worried about concerning himself was that he might be endangered if he were discovered to be harboring fugitives. That is exactly the understanding of the Tosafot, who explain in the name of the *She'eltot*:[246] אם אטמין אתכם חייבתם ראשי למלך – "If I hide you, you make me liable for execution." Rashi, on the other hand, does not understand the Gemara that way. He understands that Rabbi Tarfon is concerned about hiding the men because שמא הרגתם ואסור להטמין אתכם – "Perhaps you did commit the murder, and it is forbidden to hide you." For Rashi, then, the passage is irrelevant to our discussion because Rabbi Tarfon's concern is not for his safety, but for the halakhic legitimacy of hiding the men since they might be guilty. The passage is understood by the *Yad Eliyahu* and the *Agudat Ezov* according to Tosafot, and they see it as confirm-

---

[244] Rabbi Moshe Ze'ev Ya'avetz, in the דרושים section of the book, p. 3c, and later there, p. 38b.
[245] Niddah 61a.
[246] Ibid., ד"ה אטמרינכו, referring to *She'eltot* no. 129, p. 76 in the *Ha'amek She'elah* ed.

ing that one need not put oneself in jeopardy for the benefit of another.

But even if we understand the passage according to Tosafot, it is not conclusive proof. It may be only partial proof. That is, it is clear from the passage that Rabbi Tarfon was concerned that the fugitives might be found and the purpose of their hiding thwarted. Thus, hiding them was not certain to save them, but only potentially saving. Thus, the point of the passage is that one need not endanger oneself for doubtful saving. Perhaps, though, both Rabbi Tarfon and the Yerushalmi agree that one must endanger oneself for certain saving.[247] Furthermore, there is another difference between the Rabbi Tarfon instance and the Rabbi Ami instance of the Yerushalmi. Rabbi Ami was completely guiltless while the fugitives in the Rabbi Tarfon case were, at least, the subject of a government search because of some accusation against them. Perhaps the degree of requirement to jeopardize oneself is greater when the one who needs to be saved is a total innocent.

This last claim leads us to comment on an interesting fact. Tosafot refer to the *She'eltot*, as we have already indicated. In the *She'eltot*, the end of Rabbi Tarfon's comment reads as follows: למיחש ליה מיבעי דילמא איתא למילתא ולא מסתייעא מילתייכו וגרמיתון צערא לדילי נמי אזילו אתון אטמירו נפשייכו – "One must be concerned lest the rumor is true and the matter of hiding you not work out, and you will cause pain to me, too. Therefore, go and hide youselves." Ignore, for the moment, the words "and you will cause pain. . . ." The Netziv comments on the Rabbi Tarfon case as follows:[248]

> ולפי זה יש להוכיח (עוד) מדקאמר ר' טרפון דילמא איתא למילתא, הא אם היה ברור לר' טרפון שאינו אלא עלילת שקר היה מזדקק לטמורינו אע"ג שאי לא מסתייע מילתא היה מסתכן בעצמו ומחייב ראשו והיינו כמש"כ בהג"מ... בשם הירושלמי.... ולכאורה הכי דעת התוס' ורא"ש בשמו של רבינו.

> From this one can demonstrate that since Rabbi Tarfon [justified not hiding them on the grounds that] "maybe the rumor is true," it would follow that if it were clear to Rabbi Tarfon that the accusation was entirely false, he would have been required to hide them even though he himself might have been endangered and even become liable for execution if the hiding was not effective. And that would be exactly as is written in the *Hagahot Maimoniyot*. . . in the name of the Yerushalmi. . . .And it appears that this is precisely the view of the Tosafot and the Rosh in the name of our Master [i.e., the *She'eltot*].

What is fascinating is that the very passage in Niddah which was used by the *Yad Eliyahu* and the *Agudat Ezov* to prove that the Bavli *disagrees* with the Yerushalmi, is understood by the Netziv to prove that the Bavli *agrees* with the Yerushalmi. Rabbi Tarfon could refuse to hide the persons involved only because the rumor about them might be true. If it were clear to him that the rumor was false, he would have to hide them, even if his own life were jeopardized thereby. That, says the Netziv, is how the Tosafot must have understood, since they say that Rabbi Tarfon was worried that ראשי למלך – "You will make me liable for execution."

---

[247] The proof from Niddah is rejected in precisely this way by Rabbi Yehiel Heller in שו"ת עמודי אור, no. 96, sec. 3, p. 80a. See Ovadiah Yosef's article in *Dinei Yisrael*, vol. 7, p. 29, and cf. the explanation of the Yerushalmi given above (p. 264) by Rabbi Ya'akov Weinberg.

[248] See the passage referred to above, n. 237, letter ד in the Netziv.

But, continues the Netziv, our version of the *She'eltot* does not support this conclusion.

> אבל לפנינו ליתא כל זה בדברי רבינו אלא וגרמיתון צערא כו' והא ודאי
> דמחויב לקבל כל צער שבעולם להצלת נפש... אבל ספק סכנת נפשות
> עדיין לא שמענו.... ורבינו פוסק שאין להכניס עצמו בספק סכנה בשביל
> חבירו.... והנראה דדעת התו' והרא"ש ג"כ אין מוכרח להלכה דדינא הכי
> אלא מדת חסידות היא.

> But our version of the *She'eltot* does not have any such thing [i.e., that "You will make me liable for execution"], but rather "You will cause me pain, etc." And surely it is the case that one must endure significant pain in order to save the life of another. . .[b]ut there is no proof that one must jeopardize his very life. . . .And it is the view of our Master that one need not jeopardize one's life for one's fellow. . . .And it seems that even the view of Tosafot and the Rosh is not to be taken as a definite legal requirement, but rather as an act of piety.

In the final analysis, the Netziv denies that the Niddah passage supports the Yerushalmi, according to his version of the *She'eltot*. The Niddah passage requires one to endure pain in order to save the life of another,[249] but does not require one to jeopardize one's own life. And even according to Tosafot, the implication of the Niddah passage need not be that one *must* jeopardize one's life. One is permitted to jeopardize one's life as an act of piety, but one is not required to do so.

We have now analyzed a passage in Niddah which has been utilized to prove both that the Bavli disagrees with the Yerushalmi and that the Bavli agrees with the Yerushalmi. We do not deny that the passage can be defensibly understood in either of those ways. We affirm, however, that neither understanding is so compelling as to force us to conclude either that the Bavli agrees or disagrees with the Yerushalmi. Thus, the Niddah passage can become supportive, but not determinative.

The next Bavli passage which is quoted both by the *Yad Eliyahu* and the *Agudat Ezov* as proving the Bavli's disagreement with the Yerushalmi is from Sanhedrin 73a. There the Gemara quotes a baraita which deduces the obligation to save a person who is drowning or being chased by an animal or bandits from the verse לא תעמוד על דם רעך. Whereupon the Gemara asks:

> והא מהכא נפקא מהתם נפקא אבדת גופו מניין ת"ל והשבותו לו אי מהתם
> הוה אמינא הני מילי בנפשיה אבל מיטרח ומיגר אגורי אימא לא קמ"ל.

> Is it true that we deduce [the obligation to save] from here? Do we not deduce it from the following: "From where do we know that one is obligated to return the body of someone to him (i.e., save him)? The Torah says: 'Return it to him (Deut. 22:2)'? If we were to deduce exclusively from there, I would claim that the obligation applies only when the person doing the saving can do so alone. But I would think that there is no obligation if it would be necess-

---

[249] Even this is not certain. See, for example, the comment of Rabbi Jacob Emden in מגדל עוז, אבן בחן, א:פ' ג, who wrote: "One need not – גם יסורים קשים ומרים נר' שאין צריך לסבול בשביל הצלת חבירו דגנידא קשי ממותא endure great pain and torture in order to save another, for whipping is worse than death." On the last clause, cf. Ber. 55a, חלמא בישא קשה מנגדא – "A nightmare is worse than a beating." The view of Emden has serious implications for the question of bone marrow donation, as well, since there is more than a little pain involved. See *Nishmat Avraham*, Hilkhot Avodah Zarah, 157:5, p. 66; and, in his מהדורה תנינא, Even HaEzer, Hilkhot Ketubbot, 80:1, pp. 193-194.

sary for him to bestir himself and go hire help [to save the person]. The verse "Do not stand idly by" teaches us [that he must even hire help].

At face value, this passage indicates that two verses are needed in order to know both that one must save another by his own efforts and that he must also take the trouble to go out and hire help in order to accomplish the act. We shall quote from the *Yad Eliyahu* his proof that this passage contradicts the claim of the Yerushalmi, but the same deduction is made by the *Agudat Ezov*. The *Yad Eliyahu* wrote:

> הרי לפניך דאינו חייב רק למיטרח ולמיגר ולחזור על כל הצדדין שלא יאבד דם רעהו ואי הוי ס"ד דצריך אפילו לסכן עצמו מאי בעי קרא על טרחתו למיגר אגורי ועוד טפי הוה ליה למימר דקרא דלא תעמוד אתא דצריך אפילו לסכן עצמו דלא הוה ידעינן מקרא דוהשבת לו.

> This clearly demonstrates that one is obligated only to exert himself and hire help in seeking every way to insure that the blood of his fellow not be lost. And if the Gemara felt that one is required even to jeopardize himself, why would a verse be needed to prove that one must hire help. Furthermore, [if one really were obligated even to jeopardize himself,] it would have been much more likely for the Gemara to claim that the verse "Don't stand idly by" comes to teach that one must endanger himself, for we would not know that fact from "And you shall restore it to him."

The *Yad Eliyahu* makes the following claim: The argument of the Gemara proves that one need not endanger oneself for the benefit of another. The Gemara deduces from לא תעמוד that one must hire help to save. That would be self-evidently true if one were also obligated to endanger oneself. It would be so self-evident that there would be no need of a verse to prove it. Thus, the fact that we do need the verse to prove it demonstrates that the obligation to endanger oneself must not exist. Furthermore, if there were such an obligation, it would have been most logical for the Gemara to deduce it from לא תעמוד, since it cannot be deduced from והשבותו לו, which is needed to deduce the obligation to save in the first place, and could not be used to deduce that one must also endanger oneself. Hence, the passage in Sanhedrin proves that according to the Bavli there is no obligation to jeopardize oneself in order to save another. Finally, in the absence of any convincing evidence to the contrary one would have to say that the obligation to jeopardize oneself does not exist even if it is only potential jeopardization of the saving party and certain death for the party to be saved.

That this sugya proves that the Bavli disagrees with the Yerushalmi has met with wide agreement. Rabbi Moses Schick (1807-1879) affirms it.[250] Rabbi Jacob Ettlinger affirms it.[251] It may well be the basis on which those who were quoted at the beginning of this section

---

[250] See שו"ת מהר"ם שיק, חלק יו"ד, סי' קנ"ה: ואי כירושלמי אפי' בספק נפשות לא פריך הגמרא וע"כ דהש"ס דידן לא סבירא ליה כן – "And if the law were according to the Yerushalmi that [one must endanger oneself] even for a case of doubtful saving, the Gemara would not argue [about the need for לא תעמוד]. Therefore, perforce, our Gemara must not agree." It is interesting to note that in the continuation of the responsum, Schick equates the Rabbi Akiva and ben Petura dispute with the Bavli-Yerushalmi dispute. Rabbi Akiva agrees with the Bavli view and ben Petura with the Yerushalmi view. Of course, in order to make that equation, Schick must assert that the case is one in which it is not certain that the one who does not drink will die, but rather that he will put himself in potential jeopardy.

[251] See *Arukh La-ner*, Sanhedrin, 73a, s.v. והא מהכא.

were so certain that the requirement of the Yerushalmi is not normative. Rabbi Menashe Klein accepts it.[252] The Ziz Eliezer says about it:[253] הראיה היסודית של הגאון בעל אגודת אזוב — מההיא דסנהדרין דאין חיוב להכנס לספק סכנה חזקה היא — "The basic proof of the author of *Agudat Ezov* from Sanhedrin that one need not enter a state of potential danger is strong."

And the support comes not only from Aharonim. Here are the straightforward words of the Meiri:[254]

> בהצלתו, ולא סוף מי שראה חברו טובע בנהר או חיה גוררתו או לסטים באים עליו חייב להשתדל דבר בעצמו אם הוא יכול בלא סכנה.

> If one sees his fellow drowning in the river, or being dragged by a beast, or attacked by bandits, he is duty bound to attempt to save him, and not only by himself if he can do so without danger.

And here is what the Sefer Hasidim has to say, based on this passage in Sanhedrin:[255]

> כתיב לא תעמוד על דם רעך אבל אם הרבה מתלחמים עליו אל ישליך עצמו בסכנה ואל יעשה פשיעה בגופו ואם אדם טובע בנהר והוא כבד אל יעזור לו פן יטבע עמו.

> Scripture says: "Do not stand idly by the blood of your fellow," but if he is under mass attack, he should not put himself in danger and should not commit an offense toward his body. And if a person is drowning, and he is corpulent, he should not help him, lest he himself drown.

Even though Joseph Karo does not include the requirement of the Yerushalmi in the Shulhan Arukh, the very fact of his mentioning it both in the *Kesef Mishneh* and the Bet Yosef makes it highly desirable to find some method to defend it. In this instance, then, that would require finding some explanation of the Sanhedrin passage that does not put it in direct conflict with the Yerushalmi. The direction that takes is based upon the comments of the Ran to the passage in Sanhedrin.

In order to understand them completely, we must note that the primary focus in the *sugya* is really about the case of the רודף — one who can be summarily killed in order to save the life of another. The classical case is of one who is running after another with the intent to kill him. A third party is entitled to kill the pursuer in order to save the pursued. It is not critical to understand the details of the Talmud's proof of the legitimacy of such behavior, but we should understand the overall picture. The right to kill a pursuer is deduced either by קל וחמר or by הקש from the case of similar permission to kill one who is pursuing a woman for purposes of rape. Once deduced, the permission to kill the pursuer who is intent on killing is itself considered as proved from Scripture.

Both Tosafot and the Ran ask:[256]

> ואם תאמר וכיון שמצווה הוא להרוג הרודף כדי שיציל הנרדף למה לי קרא דלא תעמוד על דם רעך פשיטא דהוא מצווה לטרוח בהצלתו כגון טובע בנהר או ליסטים באים עליו. י״ל דמקרא דניתן להצילו בנפשו לא שמעינן

---

[252] See משנה הלכות, חלק ו׳, מדור התשובות סי׳ שכ״ד, עמ׳ קצ״ז ע״ב.

[253] שו״ת ציץ אליעזר, חלק ט׳, סי׳ מ״ה, אות ט׳, עמ׳ קפ״ג ע״א.

[254] *Beit ha-Behirah*, Sanhedrin, Abraham Schreiber ed., p. 272.

[255] *Sefer Hasidim*, Reuven Margoliolh, ed. (Jerusalem: Mossad Harav Kook, 1964 [5724]), sec. 674, p. 428.

[256] Tosafot, Sanhedrin 73a, s.v. להצילו, and ע״ג ע״א חידושי הר״ן, סנהדרין, Jerusalem, 5718 ed., p. 138. We quote from the text in the Ran, whose answer is different from the answer of Tosafot.

אלא במי שברור לו כשמש שהוא רוצה להרגו ובכי האי גוונא במי שברור
לו כשמש שיטבע בנהר אם לא יצילוהו הוא דמחייב להצילו אבל על ספק
לא שמעינן מידי משום הכי אתא קרא דלא תעמוד על דם רעך לומר שהוא
מצווה לטרוח אף על הספק.

And if you ask: Since one is already commanded to kill the pursuer in order to save the pursued, what purpose does "Do not stand idly by the blood of your fellow" serve? Obviously one is commanded to bestir himself to save one who is drowning or who is being attacked by bandits [since it is even mandatory to kill someone in order to prevent the death of the pursued]. One might answer: From the scriptural proof that one may kill the pursuer for the benefit of the pursued one would assume that [the obligation to save] applies only to a case in which it is absolutely clear that the pursuer is intent on killing, or, similarly, that it is absolutely clear that the person will drown if he does not save them. Only in such cases of certainty is one obligated to save him. But, in cases of doubt we would have no evidence one way or the other. It is precisely for that purpose that the verse "Do not stand idly by the blood of your fellow" comes, to teach that one is commanded to bestir oneself [to save] even in cases of doubt.

We must first understand the Ran on his own terms. Then we will apply his explanation to our subject of discussion, viz., does the Bavli disagree with the Yerushalmi. As an explanation of the *sugya* itself, the Ran says that לא תעמוד (which the Gemara said proves that one must bestir himself and hire aid) refers to a specific category of cases, and not to the overall category of all people in danger. It refers to the category of people whose danger is uncertain, doubtful. לא תעמוד demonstrates that even for them one must bestir himself and go out and hire help to assist them, even though it is not certain that they are in danger. לא תעמוד could not possibly be telling us that we must bestir ourselves for the benefit of those who are in certain danger. We already know that from the fact that if we are sometimes duty bound even to kill for the benefit of one in certain danger, surely we are duty bound to bestir ourselves and hire aid for those in certain danger. We might have thought, however, that when one cannot himself save one in doubtful danger, he is under no obligation to do anything further. It is to negate such a thought that לא תעמוד comes, according to the Ran.

Now let us apply this to our issue. For the Ran, the לא תעמוד verse deals with cases of doubtful danger to the person who requires saving. It cannot be referring to a case in which the saver would also be in doubtful danger together with the person needing saving, and mandating that the saver nonetheless attempt himself to save him. Why not? Because if both were in the same category, namely, doubtful danger, what would be the grounds for mandating action on the part of the saver? To the contrary, we would say מי יימר דדמא דחבריה סומק טפי דילמא דמא דידיה סומק טפי — "Who says the blood of one's fellow is sweeter? Perhaps his own blood is sweeter."[257] There would be no reason to mandate the precedence of the life of the one who needed saving over the life of the saver. Quite the contrary, if both were in the same degree of danger, we should apply

---

[257] Cf. Sanhedrin 84a where the opposite claim is made to prove that one cannot save one's own life at the cost of another's life. Here, the Ran would assert that if both parties are in doubtful danger, the party requiring saving has no greater claim on being saved than the saver has on not endangering himself.

חייך קודמין לחיי אחיך. Thus, what does לא תעמוד teach us? It teaches that even in the case where one would not be required to attempt himself to save the other, he would still be obligated to seek his saving through bestirring himself to get aid. But, if the case were one in which the person requiring saving were in certain danger, while the saver was in doubtful danger, the Ran might well affirm that the sugya in the Bavli does require him to attempt to save the other. At a minimum, we can say that the Bavli does not reject that claim, and there is, therefore, no proof of a contradiction between the Bavli and the Yerushalmi.

This approach to proving that even the passage in Sanhedrin does not necessarily contradict the thesis of the Yerushalmi is adopted by Rabbi Ovadiah Yosef[258] and by Rabbi Haim Heller.[259] One must admit, though, that this application of the Ran to our issue is a little forced. Why, after all, would the Ran need a special verse to prove that one should bestir himself to save even when the danger to the person in need of saving was doubtful? Is it not well known and clear that even ספק פקוח נפש supersedes the Sabbath? If one may violate a capital offense for a ספק, is there any real doubt that one should bestir oneself to help save someone, even if the danger is only a ספק?[260]

Rabbi Meir Slutz[261] attempts to go even further, and to demonstrate that the Bavli actually agrees with the Yerushalmi. He contends that the sugya shows that there are three sources for derivation of laws on the subject: (1) the הקש or קל וחמר, (2) the verse והשבותו לו, and (3) the verse לא תעמוד. He claims that the three can be used to deduce (1) the essential requirement for one to save another himself, (2) the requirement to bestir oneself and hire help when needed, and (3) the requirement even to put oneself in some danger in order to effectuate the certain saving of the other.[262] Once going that far, though, Rabbi Slutz must account for why the *Hagahot Maimoniyot* bases his claim on the Yerushalmi rather than on the Bavli. He answers that the Yerushalmi was the preferable basis because the norm is explicit there in the behavior of Resh Lakish, while in the Bavli it is only implicit.

The attempts of Rabbi Ovadiah Yosef, Rabbi Haim Heller, and Rabbi Meir Slutz are valiant, but, though possible, are less than entirely convincing. For the former two, the Bavli is basically silent about the subject of self-endangerment, and for the latter the most far reaching conclusion is left to be entirely inferred. Neither is likely.

Furthermore, some affirm that the very wording of the law as it appears in Maimonides argues against the thesis that the *sugya* implies or is silent about a requirement to endanger oneself. Let us look once more at Maimonides' wording:

> כל היכול להציל ולא הציל עובר על לא תעמוד על דם רעך. וכן הרואה את
> חבירו טובע בים או ליסטים באים עליו או חיה רעה באה עליו ויכול להצילו
> הוא בעצמו או שישכור אחרים להצילו ולא הציל, או ששמע גוים או
> מוסרים מחשבים עליו רעה או טומנין לו פח ולא גלה אוזן חבירו והודיעו,
> או שידע בגוי או באנס שהוא קובל על חבירו ויכול לפייסו בגלל חבירו

---

[258] *Dinei Yisrael*, vol. 7, p. 32.

[259] See above, n. 227.

[260] See the article by Rabbi Meir Slutz, *Halakhah u'Refu'ah*, vol. 3 (Jerusalem, 5743), pp. 158-163, and especially p. 162 for this point. Slutz attempts to resolve the issue by claiming that the fact that ספק supersedes the Sabbath does not necessarily imply an obligation to act, but only permission to act. Thus, we would still need the second verse. What he says is possible, but also seems quite forced.

[261] See previous note.

[262] Slutz agrees with the Ran and the *Arukh la-Ner* that there is no necessary link between the words of the verses and the derivations from them. The derivations are based on יתורים. The Ran phrases the same claim thus: מיתורא דקראי הוא דמרתינן גופי' וממוניה הכי כתיבי תרי קראי.

ולהסיר מה שבלבו ולא פייסו, וכל כיוצא בדברים אלו, העושה אותם עובר על לא תעמוד על דם רעך.

Anyone who is able to save one in danger and who does not do so violates the negative commandment "Do not stand idly by the blood of your fellow." And similarly, if one sees one's fellow drowning in the sea, or being attacked by bandits or by a dangerous animal, and is able to save him either by himself or by hiring others to save him, and does not do so; or, if one heard either non-Jews or informers plotting evil against someone, or laying a trap for him, and did not inform the person; or, if one knew about a non-Jew or some other violent person who was lodging a complaint about his fellow, and he could appease that person on behalf of his fellow and did not do so; and all such similar matters, whoever does these things violates "Do not stand idly by the blood of your fellow."

In commenting on this wording of Maimonides, quoted by the Tur, the BaH wrote:[263]

נראה דלפי דמלשון הברייתא משמע דחייב להצילו אפי׳ אינו ברור לו שיוכל להצילו חייב להכניס עצמו בספק סכנה להצילו אבל הרמב״ם כתב "יכול להצילו" דמשמע דדוקא בדאין ספק שיכול להצילו אבל אינו חייב להכניס עצמו בספק סכנה להצלת חברו.

It seems that the language of the baraita implies that one is obligated to save another even when it is not certain that he will be able to save him. He is duty bound to place himself in danger in order to save him. But the Rambam wrote, "And he is able to save him," which specifically implies that there be no doubt that he can save him, but that he is not obligated to put himself in potential jeopardy in order to save his fellow.

The BaH notes the difference between the language of the baraita and the language of Maimonides. The baraita says שהוא חייב להצילו – "He is obligated to save him" – while Maimonides uses the phrase ויכול להצילו – "And he is able to save him." After having quoted the language of the baraita, the Tur quotes the language of the Rambam. The BaH is explaining this apparent redundancy by clarifying that the Tur quotes the Rambam as well as the baraita in order to make certain that we understand that the baraita is to be understood as the Rambam understood it, and not as we might mistakenly have understood it, namely, to imply an obligation to put oneself in danger.[264]

The claim of the BaH on the basis of the language of Maimonides affirms that the Rambam understood the Bavli to disagree with the Yerushalmi. Thus, Maimonides must be numbered among those who reject the view of the Yerushalmi because it is contradicted by the Bavli. This inference from the language of Maimonides is affirmed by

---

[263] BaH to Tur, Hoshen Mishpat, 426.

[264] It is virtually impossible that the wording of the Rambam implies a disagreement between the Rambam and the baraita. Since the baraita is uncontested in the Gemara, there is just no way that the Rambam would reject it in his code. In this, Rabbi Isaac Jacob Weiss (מנחת יצחק, חלק ה׳, סי׳ ד׳ אות י״ג, עמ כ״ט ע״א) is absolutely correct when he wrote: הטור רצה לשלול שלא תטעה בלשון הברייתא, אבל באמת גם הברייתא ס״ל כן, דבודאי הרמב״ם לא יחלוק על הברייתא – "The Tur wants to make sure that we not misunderstand the language of the baraita. But, in fact, [what Maimonides says] is the view of the baraita too, since surely Maimonides would not disagree with the baraita."

Rabbi Isaac Jacob Weiss,[265] by Rabbi Eliezer Waldenberg,[266] Rabbi Hayyim David ha-Levi,[267] and Rabbi Pinehas Barukh Toledano.[268] Admittedly, the final three also raise objections to this derivation and claim that the proof is not definitive.

By far the most interesting objection to this derivation from the language of the Rambam is offered by Rabbi Yehiel Ya'akov Weinberg.[269] It is well known that before each collection of laws Maimonides lists the positive and negative commandments which the laws reflect. If one looks at that list for *Hilkhot Roze'ah* it will become clear that Maimonides does not list a positive commandment to save a person who is in danger. He lists only a negative commandment against standing idly by such a person's blood. Of course, the existence of the negative commandment implies some positive action, but the purpose of the action, legally speaking, is to avoid violation of the negative commandment. Thus, Weinberg claims, the language of Maimonides reflects nothing at all about whether the Bavli disagrees with the Yerushalmi. Rather, it reflects a wording which allows Maimonides to couch the failure to save as a violation of a negative commandment. Obviously, if one literally cannot save another one does not violate the negative commandment. So the only way for Maimonides to word the law so as to make clear that failure to save is a violation of a negative commandment, and yet make it clear that not all failures to save constitute such a violation, is to phrase the law thus: "If you are able to save and do not do so, you violate a negative commandment against standing idly by the blood of your fellow." The wording intimates *nothing, one way or the other,* about whether or not one should endanger oneself in order to save one's fellow.

There is a benefit to finding some way to account for Maimonides' wording that does not imply that one ought not jeopardize oneself for the benefit of another. If the wording *did* imply that, it would be difficult to understand why Karo, in the *Kesef Mishneh*, would refer to the Yerushalmi position without at least noting that it was rejected by Maimonides. It would not be problematic, however, if the wording of Maimonides were silent on the subject.

Whether or not the language of Maimonides proves his understanding of the passage in Bavli Sanhedrin can be a matter of disagreement. There is no disagreement, however, with the affirmation that the Rambam does not clearly insist that self-endangerment for the benefit of another is a requirement of the law.

At this point, then, we have analyzed another Bavli passage which is understood by some to prove that the Bavli disagrees with the Yerushalmi. We have affirmed that the evidence is strong, though not absolutely conclusive. As a postscript, we have also discussed whether the language of Maimonides' codified position based on this passage implies that *he* understood the passage to reject the Yerushalmi view. We have claimed that his language can certainly be understood that way, and that some have understood it precisely that way. It is not, however, the only way to understand the language of Maimonides.

There are other Bavli passages which we must address. But, having referred to the language of Maimonides as evidence of Bavli disagreement with the Yerushalmi, we turn to another example of the same phenomenon. The Mishnah records[270] that one who has

---

[265] See preceeding note.

[266] *Ziz Eliezer*, vol. 10, no. 25, ch. 7, letters א and ב, pp. 124-125.

[267] *Sefer Asia* (Jerusalem: Reuben Mass, 5743), vol. 4, p. 255.

[268] *Barkai* 3 (fall 5746): 24. Rabbi Toledano is head of the Sefardic court in London. *Barkai* is a journal of the Mizrahi — ha-Po'el ha-Mizrahi, and was under the editorship of Rabbi Saul Yisraeli.

[269] *Moriah* 4, issue 1-2 (Nisan-Iyyar 5732): 63.

[270] Makkot 2:7 (11b).

committed manslaughter and gone into exile into one of the cities of refuge may not leave it. He may not leave it ואפי׳ ישראל צריכים לו ואפילו שר צבא ישראל כיואב בן צרויה אינו יוצא – "Even if the people of Israel need his aid, and even a general of Israel like Yoav ben Zeruiah, he may not leave." When Maimonides records this norm[271] he adds a phrase not found in the mishnah: ואם יצא התיר עצמו למיתה – "And if he does leave, he surrenders himself to be killed."

In explaining the purpose for this addition, the content of which seems quite self-evident, Rabbi Meir Simha of Dvinsk, the *Or Sameah*, writes:

> הוסיף רבינו טעם למה אינו יוצא הלא פקוח נפש דוחה כל מצות שבתורה ומכל שכן פקוח נפש דכל ישראל ואסתר תוכיח.... וכיון שהותר דמו לגואל הדם אין לו להכניס עצמו בספק סכנה עבור הצלת חבירו מסכנה ודאית, כן נראה. ומוכח מזה דלא כהגמ״י בשם ירושלמי דתרומות.... ומירושלמי גופיה אינו מוכח למעיין היטב בו.

> Our master [i.e., Maimonides] added a reason to explain why he should not leave since saving another, and surely saving all of Israel, should supersede all mitzvot of the Torah [including the commandment not to leave the city of refuge], as the case of Esther proves.[272] ...But since [the act of leaving] makes him eligible to be killed by the blood avengers, he ought not put himself in a positon of potential life endangerment even to save another from certain life endangerment. This seems [to be the implication of Maimonides' having added the clause]. And this proves that the view of the *Hagahot Maimoniyot* in the name of Yerushalmi Terumot is incorrect....And a careful look at the Yerushalmi itself will demonstrate that it need not be understood [as the *Hagahot*].

Before we deal with the essence of the claim of the *Or Sameah*, let us comment briefly about his final sentence. Rabbi Meir Simha *must* affirm that the Yerushalmi need not mean what the *Hagahot* says. Indeed, it probably cannot mean that! Maimonides is explaining the law of the Mishnah, and he understands it to imply that one ought not jeopardize oneself for another. Since the Yerushalmi has the same Mishnah as the Bavli, it is highly unlikely that Maimonides would understand the Mishnah contrary to the Yerushalmi without absolutely firm basis to believe that the Bavli disagrees with the Yerushalmi. Since there is no such basis in this case, it must be that the Yerushalmi need not be understood to imply what the Rambam rejects.

As to the substance of the claim of the *Or Sameah*, he contends that there could be only one reason for Maimonides to add the apparently superfluous clause to his codification of the law. It adds an explanation which clarifies an otherwise inexplicable law. Since all commandments are superseded in order to save the life of another, there should be no distinction between the commandment to remain in the city of refuge and any other commandment.[273] Yet, according to Maimonides' codification, there is. Though a manslaughterer can violate any

---

[271] M.T. Hilkhot Roze'ah 7:8.

[272] Though the *Or Sameah* does not stipulate exactly what about Esther proves the point, he apparently means that Esther's consorting with a pagan king was justified because it was needed to save Israel, even though such relationships are otherwise forbidden. The discussion in Sanhedrin 74b is an attempt to explain why Esther was not obligated to allow herself to be killed rather than violate one of the cardinal sins which are not superseded by פקוח נפש.

[273] See *Tiferet Yisrael*, Makkot 2:8, *Bo'az*, letter ב.

other commandment in order to save a life, he cannot violate the commandment to remain in the city. Why? Because the mitzvot are superseded in order to save lives only when the life of the saver is not thereby endangered. When the saver's life is endangered, even potentially, the mitzvot are not superseded. In the case of a manslaughterer there is potential endangerment if he leaves the city, because he becomes fair game for the blood avenger. Thus, he should not leave the city even to save others because by doing so "he surrenders himself to be killed."[274]

If the *Or Sameah* is correct, the Mishnah itself proves that one ought not to jeopardize himself for the benefit of another, and the *Hagahot Maimoniyot* must surely be mistaken, and that is why the view was ignored as a matter of actual law by all of the classical poskim. What's more, the implications of Maimonides are very far-reaching. They imply that a single individual may not jeopardize himself, even potentially, even for the benefit of all of Israel. It is no wonder, then, that others have rushed to reject this claim of Rabbi Meir Simha.

The most direct attack can be found in *Klei Hemdah*, by Rabbi Meir Dan Plotzki (1867-1928), who wrote:[275]

> במחילת כבוד תורתו לא דיבר נכונה שהדבר ברור שחובה להכניס עצמו בסכנה להצלת ישראל. ובדין רוצח אין הפירוש בדברי הרמב"ם כמ"ש האור שמח שמפני זה לא יצא אפי' במקום פקוח נפש, אלא נהפוך הוא, שמאחר שגזרת הכתוב שלא יצא משם לעולם אפי' לצורך פוק"נ של כל ישראל.... אבל חס וחלילה לומר כמ"ש הראו שמח שאין להכניס עצמו בספק סכנה להציל כלל ישראל מסכנה, והאור שמח עצמו הוכיח מאסתר להיפך, ואף פנחס סיכן עצמו בהריגת זמרי להצלת כלל ישראל, זה ברור.

> With all due deference, he is simply mistaken. For it is clear that one is obligated to put oneself in danger in order to save Israel. And the law of the manslaughterer in Maimonides should not be understood as the *Or Sameah* did to imply that one ought not endanger oneself even in a case of פקוח נפש, but just the opposite. [The manslaughterer case] contains a biblical decree that he should not leave [the city of refuge] ever, even for the פקוח נפש need of all of Israel. . . .But God forbid that we should say as the *Or Sameah* that [in general] one should not jeopardize oneself even potentially even in order to save Klal Yisrael from danger. And even the *Or Sameah* himself proves the opposite [by referring to] Esther. And so too did Pinehas endanger himself by killing Zimri in order to save Israel. And this is clear.

The essential claim of the *Klei Hemdah* is that the manslaughterer case is exceptional, a גזרת הכתוב.[276] It cannot be a paradigm for other cases. Thus, Maimonides is correct in his statement of the law, but the deduction of Rabbi Meir Simha is erroneous. Note, though,

---

[274] Rabbi Meir Simha makes the same claim in his Torah commentary, *Meshekh Hokhmah*, to Ex. 4:19. There God tells Moses to return to Egypt כי מתו כל האנשים המבקשים את נפשך. The *Or Sameah* affirms that God had to tell Moses that his enemies had died because otherwise Moses would have been obligated to violate God's command to return because fulfilling it would have put Moses in potential jeopardy.

[275] Beginning of Parashat Pinhas.

[276] It is clear that the restriction of the manslaughterer to the city of refuge is not exclusively for his protection against the blood avenger. See, for example, the statement of Abbaye (Makkot 11b) that even if the manslaughterer dies immediately after conviction, his bones must be taken there. Besides that, those who die in the city of refuge are buried there, even though they are no longer in any danger from the blood avenger. One must admit, though, that this argument is not overly persuasive as a way of accounting for the language of Maimonides, ואם יצא התיר עצמו למיתה.

that Rabbi Plotzki restricts his rejection of Rabbi Meir Simha to the case of general endangerment of Klal Yisrael.[277] He makes no claim that one must endanger oneself for the benefit of a single other. There may, in fact, be no such obligation, but that cannot be proved as the uncontestable view of the Mishnah, based on the language of Maimonides.[278]

We return, then, to our analysis of Bavli passages which have been understood to imply that the Bavli disagrees with the Yerushalmi. The Gemara in Nedarim[279] quotes a baraita which reads:

> מעיין של בני העיר, חייהן וחיי אחרים חייהן קודמין לחיי אחרים, בהמתם ובהמת אחרים בהמתם קודמת לבהמת אחרים כביסתן וכביסת אחרים כביסתן קודמת לכביסת אחרים חיי אחרים וכביסתן חיי אחרים קודמין לכביסתן רבי יוסי אומר כביסתן קודמת לחיי אחרים.

> Regarding a spring which belongs to one city [but which other surroundings cities which have no spring also use: if the amount of water available is such that it creates a conflict between] their lives and the lives of the others, their lives take precedence over the lives of the others; their cattle and the cattle of the others, their cattle take precedence over the cattle of the others; their laundry and the laundry of the others, their laundry takes precedence over the laundry of the others; the lives of others and their laundry, the lives of the others take precedence over their laundry. Rabbi Yosi says that their laundry takes precedence over the lives of the others.

The contents of the baraita produce no surprise until the last line, the view of Rabbi Yosi. On the surface, it seems counterintuitive. In explaining the importance which Rabbi Yosi attributes to cleaning clothes, the Gemara continues:[280]

> כביסה אלימא לר' יוסי דאמר שמואל האי ערבוביתא דרישא מתיא לידי עוירא ערבוביתא דמאני מתיא לידי שעמומיתא ערבוביתא דגופא מתיא לידי שיחני וכיבי.

> Laundry is so critical for Rabbi Yosi because of what Samuel said: "The skin disease resulting from insufficient attention to the cleanliness of the head leads to blindness, that resulting from insufficient attention to the cleanliness of clothing leads to madness, and that resulting from insufficient attention to cleanliness of the body leads to boils and scabs.

Finally, the *sugya* seeks the biblical grounding for the view of Rabbi Yosi, and says:

> קרא מנלן... דכתיב[281] ומגרשיהם יהיו לבהמתם ולרכושם ולכל חיתם מאי חיתם אילימא חיה והלא חיה בכלל בהמה היא אלא מאי חייתם חיותא ממש פשיטא אלא לאו כביסה דהא איכא צערא דערבוביתא.

---

[277] It is very difficult to understand how the *Or Sameah* seems to have ignored the fact that Esther put herself in potential danger by appearing in the king's anteroom without having been beckoned.

[278] Similar arguments to those of the *Klei Hemdah* are also offered by Rabbis Slutz and Toledano in the articles referred to earlier, and by Rabbi Shlemo Zevin in לאור ההלכה (Jerusalem: Mosad haRav Kook, 5706), p. 8f. See, too, Abraham Sofer Abraham in המעין, Nisan 5742, pp. 35-36.

[279] 80b. See also T. Bava Metzia 11: 33-37, Lieberman ed., p. 127f.

[280] Nedarim 81a.

[281] במדבר לה:ג.

What is the scriptural verse. . .as it is written:[282] "And the surrounding fields should be for their cattle and their possessions and all חיתם." What is the meaning of חיתם? If we say it means "beasts," beasts are included in "cattle." Rather, perhaps, חיתם means their sustenance, literally. [No, because] that is obvious. It is, rather, [that חיתם] means "laundry," because there is the pain of the resultant skin disease [for insufficient attention to it].

Taken at face value, without embellishment, the Gemara seems to be claiming that for Rabbi Yosi, understood on the basis of Samuel's dictum, refraining from laundering presents real danger, and, therefore, the laundry of the community on whose territory the spring is found takes precedence over the thirst needs of the other community. The *tanna kamma* obviously disagrees, but it is not clear on what basis. Does he hold that the thirst needs predominate even if the real danger from not laundering materializes? Does he disagree with the premise that there are serious consequences to not laundering?

The earliest decision we have regarding the dispute of Rabbi Yosi and the *tanna kamma* comes in the *She'eltot*:[283]

אלא מאי היא [וחייתם שבפסוק]? כביסה, וקרי ליה רחמנא חייתם. וטעמא מאי? משום דשמואל דאמר ערבוביתא דמנא אתיא לידי שעמום, והילכך כביסה הוויא חיותא, וחייהן וחיי אחרים חייהן קודמת לחיי אחרים וכן הילכתא.

Rather what is [חייתם of the verse]? It is laundry, which is called חייתם ("their life") by Torah. And why [is laundry equated with life]? [It is equated] because of Samuel who said: "The skin disease resulting from insufficient attention to laundering leads to madness." And therefore, laundry is equated with life, and their lives take precedence over the lives of others. And that is the law.

The Geonic decision recorded in the *She'eltot*, therefore, determines the law in accordance with Rabbi Yosi. The Netziv[284] notes that the *She'eltot* seems to be deciding in favor of Rabbi Yosi because Samuel agrees with him, and because a verse is quoted to support his position. He objects, however, by reminding us that Samuel's statement was not made as an explanation of Rabbi Yosi's statement. It is an independent *and uncontested* statement. There is no hint that the *tanna kamma* disagrees with Samuel. What's more, it is highly unlikely, says the Netziv, that the argument between the *tanna kamma* and Rabbi Yosi is over whether certain things are dangerous, since such matters are "objective." Thus, the Netziv explains:

במאי קמיפלגי? ונראה דודאי אינה דומה סכנת צמא לסכנת בהמתן וכביסתן, דסכנת צמא ברור שימותו בצמא מה שאין כן בהמתן וכביסתן אפשר שיבואו לידי סכנה, אבל... כמה בני אדם אינם באים לידי שעמום בהעדר הכביסה אלא דמכל מקום ספק סכנת מפשות הוא, וס"ל לת"ק דחייב להכנס בספק סכנת נפשות בשביל ודאי פקוח נפש של חבירו כמו שכתב הב"י חשן משפט סי' תכ"ו בשם הגהות מיימוניות ור' יוסי פליג על זה, ופסק רבינו כר"י ולא משום דשמואל קאי כוותיה אלא כיון דהכי

---

[282] Num. 35:3.
[283] Parashat Re'eh, no. 147, p. 212 in the *Ha'amek She'elah* ed.
[284] *Ha'amek She'elah*, letter ד.

קאמר שמואל דיש בזה ספק סכנת נפשות, ממילא הלכה כר"י דאין להכנס
בספק סכנת נפשות בשביל ודאי פקוח נפש של חבירו.... והפסק הוא על
פי הירושלמי תרומות... דר"ל עביד הכי במדת חסידות אבל הכא במילתא
דבני העיר לא שייך להתחסד ולסכן טפלי דלאו בני מחילה נינהו אם אין
הדין הכי.

About what do they differ? It seems [that they differ about the following:] That surely the danger of thirst is not exactly comparable to the danger of their cattle[285] and their laundry. The danger of thirst will certainly result in death, while regarding their cattle and laundry it is [merely] possible that they will result in endangerment, since . . .some people do not go mad because of the absence of laundry. Nonetheless, [not laundering] constitutes a potential life endangerment. The *tanna kamma* holds that one must put oneself in potential danger for the certain saving of another, as the Bet Yosef wrote in Hoshen Mishpat, no. 426, quoting the *Hagahot Maimoniyot*. And Rabbi Yosi disagrees. Our Master [the *She'eltot*] decided in favor of Rabbi Yosi. [He did so] not because Samuel agreed with him, but because it was Samuel who informed us that there was potential danger in this. From this it follows that the law is according to Rabbi Yosi, that one should not put oneself in potential life endangerment even for the certain saving of another. . . .And the decision is based on the Yerushalmi Terumot. . .where Resh Lakish acted out of piety. But in our case about the city dwellers [whose water supply is not sufficient to share], it is inappropriate to behave with such piety and endanger the lives of children, if the law is not that way, since they (the children) are not entitled to forego their legal rights.

The Netziv, remember, is explaining the decision of the *She'eltot*, who decided in favor of Rabbi Yosi. Rabbi Berlin claims that the dispute between Rabbi Yosi and the *tanna kamma* parallels the dispute in the Yerushalmi concerning the need to put oneself in potential life endangerment for the certain saving of another. The *tanna kamma* holds that one should, and Rabbi Yosi holds that one need not. The *She'eltot* decides in favor of Rabbi Yosi because, as the Netziv understands the Yerushalmi,[286] Resh Lakish acted from מדת חסידות, not from legal requirement. Hence, since there is no attested legal requirement to endanger oneself, the law in the Nedarim passage under discussion must follow Rabbi Yosi. This is the way the Netziv can explain the view of the *She'eltot*, which, on the surface ignores the majority view (*tanna kamma*) in favor of a דעת יחיד. Hence, assuming that the Netziv is correct, this passage reflects that for the *She'eltot* the Bavli disagrees with the Yerushalmi, as understood by the *Hagahot Maimoniyot*.

It seems, though, that one can raise serious objections against the *She'eltot*, as

---

[285] The baraita in the Bavli has no disagreement between Rabbi Yosi and *tanna kamma* about cattle. The Netziv, however, quotes a clause from the Tosefta (Bava Metzia 11:33) in which there is such a disagreement: אחרים ובהמתן חיי אחרים הן קודמים לבהמתן ר' יוסי אומר בהמתן קודמת לחיי אחרים. The Netziv explains that the view of Rabbi Yosi is based on the statement of the Mekhilta (Beshalah, Vayasa, Parashah 6, Horovitz-Rabin ed., p. 174) that בהמתו של אדם הוא חייו של אדם המהלך בדרך אם אין בהמתו עמו מסתגף הוא. Thus, both בהמה and laundry are potentially life threatening. For the purposes of our discussion, we can ignore the בהמה clause.

[286] See above, p. 263.

explained by the Netziv. Since the Yerushalmi is ambiguous, why not claim that this very passage of Bavli proves that Resh Lakish acted from legal obligation, not piety? After all, if the majority view in our passage is that of *tanna kamma*, should not the *She'eltot* have decided in favor of the majority, and clarified thereby that both the Bavli and the Yerushalmi require one to jeopardize oneself for the benefit of another?

While it is impossible to prove, it seems reasonable that it was precisely such an objection that prompted others to seek a different reason for the decision of the *She'eltot*. Rabbi Menashe Klein[287] thinks that when the *She'eltot* adopted the view of Rabbi Yosi on the basis of Samuel, he meant "on the basis of Samuel's view concerning ספק פקוח נפש in which the law follows him." We have already referred[288] to the *sugya* in Yoma 85a and b, from which the Talmud deduces that even ספק פקוח נפש supersedes the Sabbath. Only the proof of Samuel from the verse וחי בהם is affirmed as an uncontestable proof. Thus, claims Rabbi Klein, when the *She'eltot* refers to Samuel it is not only because it was he who taught that failure to launder can lead to problems, but because it was he who taught the uncontestable law that ספק סכנת נפשות must be avoided, even at the cost of Sabbath desecration. It must follow, therefore, that since failure to launder sufficiently can lead to ספק סכנת נפשות, and since Samuel has proved conclusively that we should avoid such things, the law in the dispute between Rabbi Yosi and the *tanna kamma* must follow the view of Rabbi Yosi. Thus, it is the internal consistency of the Bavli that leads the *She'eltot* to conclude as he does, and that very consistency proves that the Bavli disagrees with the Yerushalmi on the basis of the passage in Nedarim.

There could be another explanation of why the *She'eltot* decided in favor of Rabbi Yosi. This explanation, too, does not require an *a priori* understanding of what Resh Lakish meant in the Yerushalmi. The Gemara in Eruvin[289] asserts that הלכה כר' יוסי מחבריו – "The law follows Rabbi Yosi even when he disagrees with more than one other sage." There is considerable uncertainty about whether the correct version is as we have just quoted, or whether it ought to read הלכה כר' יוסי מחברו – "The law follows Rabbi Yosi when he disagrees with one other sage [but not when he disagrees with more than one other sage]."[290] Nonetheless, there are many[291] who have the first reading, and it could well be that the *She'eltot* decided in favor of Rabbi Yosi because of that mandate of the Gemara itself. Furthermore, the opinions of Rabbi Yosi are defined several times by the Gemara itself by the phrase ר' יוסי נימוקו עמו – "Rabbi Yosi's reasoning is cogent."[292] Thus, there could be more than one reason that might have prompted the *She'eltot* to decide in favor of Rabbi Yosi, and those reasons are independent of the Yerushalmi. The argument of the Netziv that the dispute between Rabbi Yosi and the *tanna kamma* reflects the issue of whether one should endanger oneself for the benefit of another has merit, and the decision of the *She'eltot* in favor of Rabbi Yosi lends support to the claim that the Bavli disagrees with the Yerushalmi.

A proof that one need not endanger oneself for the benefit of another, based on our

---

[287] Mishneh Halakhot, vol. 6, no. 324, p.396.

[288] See above, p. 260.

[289] 46b.

[290] See Tosafot, *ad locum*, ד"ה כרבי יוסי and Eruvin 83b, Tosafot s.v. שבעת, and *Dikdukei Soferim* to Eruvin 46b.

[291] See Ta'anit 28a, Tosafot s.v. ר"מ אי; *Semag*, positive commandment no. 74 (46d) who claims that this was the version of Ri and Rambam; *Sefer Ra'avia*, Megillah, siman 579 (Aptowitzer ed., vol. 2, p. 306). See Rabbi Ovadiah Yosef's article in *Dinei Yisrael*, vol. 7, p. 34.

[292] See Eruvin 14b and 51a, Gittin 67a, and Bava Kamma 24a.

passage in Nedarim, is also brought by Rabbi Abraham Braun in his comments to the *Sefer Issur ve-hetter*.[293] He wrote:

> ויש להביא ראיה (דאינו חייב להכנס לספק סכנה) מנדרים ד"פ ע"ב דפליגי ר יוסי ורבנן, לר"י אמר כביסתן קודמת לחיי אחרים דכיון דבמניעת כביסה איכא צערא טובא חיי נפש הוא.... הרי דאף שאין זה ברור כל כך סכנתו וסכנתם ברורה ומ"מ אין להם ליכנס בספק סכנה עבור חביריהם. וגם חכמים לא פליגי רק משום דס"ל דכיבוס אין בהם חיי נפש כ"כ.

> One can bring proof (that there is no obligation to enter even into doubtful danger) from Nedarim 80b, where Rabbi Yosi and the sages disagree. Rabbi Yosi holds that the laundry of the city takes precedence over the lives of the others because in refraining from laundering there is great anguish, actual life endangerment. . . . From this it follows that even though their danger is not so certain and the danger of the others is certain, nonetheless they need not put themselves in potential danger for the benefit of their friends. And the sages disagree only because they feel that there is no significant danger in refraining from laundering.

The comment of the *Zer Zahav* differs from what we have seen already seen in one important way. For him, the disagreement between the Bavli and the Yerushalmi, as evidenced by this passage from Nedarim, is not at all contingent on whether the law follows the sages or Rabbi Yosi. Both agree that one need not endanger oneself for the benefit of another. Their dispute is over a question of *realia*, viz., does refraining from laundering have such potentially dire consequences. The very matter that the Netziv found unlikely to be the source of their disagreement becomes for the *Zer Zahav* the very essence of their dispute.

The relevance of our passage to our discussion also comes up in the context of the comments of commentators on the Shulhan Arukh. Karo wrote:[294]

> פסקו לה מזונות הראוים לה והרי היא מתאוה לאכול יותר או לאכול מאכלות אחרים, יש מי שאומר שאין הבעל יכול לעכב מפני סכנת הולד שצער גופה קודם ויש מי שאומר שיכול לעכב.

> If they had ordained for her (a nursing mother) an appropriate amount of food, but she craves eating more or eating other foods, some claim that the husband may not prevent her on the grounds of the danger to the child because her bodily discomfort takes precedence, while some claim that he may stop her.

The first view alluded to is none other than the Rambam. He is very clear on the subject, saying:[295] הרי זו אוכלת... כל מה שתרצה ואין הבעל יכול לעכב ולומר[נש]ימות הולד מפני שצער גופה קודם – "She may eat. . .whatever she wants, and her husband may not stop her by claiming that the child will die, because her physical discomfort takes precedence." There is no ambiguity in the Rambam's wording either. The passage implies a conflct

---

[293] *Zer Zahav*, Comment 21, to Kelal 59, no. 38. See above, p. 261, where we have already quoted the passage from the *Sefer Issur ve-Hetter*.

[294] Even HaEzer 80:12.

[295] M.T. Hilkhot Ishut 21:11.

between the death of the infant and the bodily discomfort of the mother,[296] and the stance of Maimonides does not seem unclear. Its clarity, of course, does not eliminate surprise. In the comments of the *Bet Shmuel* (Rabbi Samuel Phoebus, mid-seventeenth century) to the quotation above from *Even HaEzer*, Phoebus quotes the *Helkat Mehokek* (Rabbi Moses Lima, 1605-1658) and then offers his own reflection. The *Bet Shmuel* wrote:[297]

"שצער גופה קודם" – כן כתב הרמב"ם. וכתב בחלקת מחוקק: 'אם מגיע מזה לולד ספק סכנה ולה אין סכנה אלא צער, מהי תיתי דמכח צער תסכן הילד, ואם גם לה סכנה לא ידעתי מי שיחלוק על זה דחייה קודמין בוודאי, ואפשר לומר אע"ג דמגיע לולד ספק סכנה מ"מ מותרת לאכול כמה דאיתא בש"ס נדרים דף פ' בכיסתה וחיי אחרים כביסתה קודם אע"ג דאינו אלא צער. מיהו שם ר' יוסי סבירה ליה כן ורבנן פליגי על זה וסבירא להו חיי אחרים קודם, ומנא ליה לרמב"ם לפסוק כר"י.

"For her physical discomfort takes precedence" – thus wrote the Rambam. And the *Helkat Mehokek* wrote: "If [her eating] results in potential danger to the child, and she experiences discomfort but not danger, from where could one deduce that the child should be endangered on account of her discomfort? And if she, too, is endangered, I do not know of anyone who would disagree that under those circumstances her life would surely take precedence." And it is possible to say that even though the child is potentially endangered, nonetheless it is permissible for her to eat, as we find in the Talmud, Nedarim 80, that the laundry of a city takes precedence over the lives of another city, even though [refraining from laundering] causes only discomfort. However, it is Rabbi Yosi who holds this view there, while the sages disagree with him and affirm that the lives of the others take precedence. And on what basis did the Rambam decide according to Rabbi Yosi.

The Shulhan Arukh had given two views, one permitting and the other forbidding the mother from eating more than had been stipulated as her need. That, of course, implies a dispute. The *Helkat Mehokek* is in a quandry because he cannot understand the grounds of any dispute. If the child is potentially endangered and the mother suffers only discomfort, surely the child should take precedence, and there should be no dispute. If both the child and the mother are potentially endangered, the mother should take precedence, and there should be no dispute.

The *Bet Shmuel*, without having to say so, surely agrees with the final point of the *Helkat Mehokek*. He offers, as well, an answer to the first claim of the *Helkat Mehokek*. The *sugya* in Nedarim contains an example of the discomfort of one potentially superseding the life of another, if one adopts the view of Rabbi Yosi. That, says the *Bet Shmuel*, is what Maimonides seems to have done. The problem he has with this is his inability to see what basis the Rambam would have for such a move.

The *sugya* we are analyzing is cited as the source for the Rambam's view, provided that Maimonides decides according to Rabbi Yosi. That is what Maimonides did, and that is the

---

[296] We will not go into a long digression on whether pain and discomfort ever supersede the life of another. Surely, though, it would follow by קל וחמר that for anyone who would allow pain to supersede the life of another, ספק סכנת נפשות surely would. We have already made passing reference to the question of pain, above p. 267, and n. 249. See, too, in Rabbi Ovadiah Yosef's article, p. 34.

[297] Even HaEzer, sec. 80, par. 15.

underpinning of that view in the Shulhan Arukh. Even if the *Bet Shmuel* can find no justification for Maimonides' doing so, we have seen several justifications above. So, here again, our *sugya* becomes the evidence that the Bavli disagrees with the Yerushalmi. If we can say that Maimonides was motivated in his decision regarding the nursing mother by any of the proofs offered above as to why the view of Rabbi Yosi should predominate over the view of the sages, we can understand well why Maimonides makes no mention in his code of a requirement potentially to endanger oneself for the benefit of another.

There are some, however, for whom this view in the name of Maimonides is so astounding, that they must find some other explanation of the Nedarim passage which does not leave Maimonides claiming that the personal discomfort of one supersedes the life of another. If one could find such an approach, and if one continues to affirm that what is true of discomfort is also true of ספק פקוח נפש, our *sugya* might no longer be evidence of a disagreement between the Bavli and the Yerushalmi.

One such approach redefines the way we have understood חיי אחרים – the lives of the others – until now. Thus far, we have taken the words literally, and understood Rabbi Yosi to be allowing their lives to be forfeit, while the sages have affirmed that their lives take precedence. The author of יחוסי תנאים ואמוראים[298] understands that אפשר להו על ידי טורח להסתפק ממעיין אחר או ילכו למקום אחר – "It is possible for them, with effort, to use another spring or to go elsewhere." Under such conditions, Rabbi Yosi allows the convenience of the original city to override the convenience of the other city, even though for one it is a convenience relating to their laundry while for the other it is a convience relating to their drinking water. Similarly, Rabbi Pinhas ha-Levi Horowitz wrote:[299] נר׳ דהתם לא מיירי ביש סכנה להעיר האחרת אלא שיכולים להביא מים מעיר אחרת או שילכו משם – "It seems that there they are not dealing with a case in which there is real [life threatening] danger to the other city because they can bring water from some other city or leave there." Also, Rabbi Moses Feinstein wrote:[300]

> הא לא איירי שם באופן פקוח נפש דלא יפלוג ר׳ יוסי לומר שכביסתן קודמת לחיי אחרים כשאיכא פק"נ.... וגם אם היה בכביסה פקוח נפש, איך פליגי רבנן דמאי שנא פקוח נפש דשתייה מפקוח נפש דכביסה.
>
> We are not dealing there with a case of real life endangerment, for Rabbi Yosi would never say that their laundry would take precedence over the lives of others when there is real life endangerment. . . .What's more, if there were real life endangerment in laundry, how could the sages disagree [with Rabbi Yosi,] because there is no difference between life endangerment resulting from [absence of water for] drinking and life endangerment resulting from [not doing the] laundry.

Finally, Professor Saul Lieberman wrote[301] פשיטא שאין מדברים בסכנת נפשות ממש – "It goes without saying that we are not speaking about real life endangerment."

For all of the above, the dilemma presented by the view of Rabbi Yosi is ameliorated. One must admit, however, that the language of the text of the Talmud does not so easily lend itself to that meaning. But, assuming this understanding, our passage in Nedarim is

---

[298] Judah Leib Maimon ed., p. 34.

[299] קונטרס אחרון (Warsaw, 1861), ספר כתובה הוא חוק אחד מן ספר הפלאה, עם קונטרס אחרון in the קונטרס אחרון, sec. 80, no. 12.

[300] *Iggrot Moshe*, Yoreh De'ah, pt. 1, no. 145, p. 288a.

[301] T. Bava Metzia 11:33, p. 127 in the פרוש הקצר to line 112. See, too, the באור הארוך in *Tosefta Ki-feshuta*, p. 326.

silent on the issue under our discussion, namely, whether one must put oneself in jeopardy for the benefit of another.

There is another small group that reacts to the decision of Maimonides in the nursing mother case in a way that rejects his having deduced his decision from the Nedarim *sugya*. This approach posits that the nursing mother might endanger herself if she does not satisfy her craving. If so, her potential self endangerment takes precedence over the potential endangerment of the child, and that is why Maimonides says that the husband cannot stop her. Rabbi David Oppenheim is one who adopts this view. He wrote:[302] גם צערא דתאוות מאכל אתיא לידי סכנה כדאיתא עובדא טובא בש״ס דכתובות (דף ס״א ע״א וב׳)....וכן ע״כ צ״ל לדעת הרמב״ם שכתב דצער גופה קודמת — "Even the discomfort of food craving can lead to [real] danger, as the examples in Ketubbot 61a and b[303] show. . . .And, perforce, that must be the view of the Rambam when he wrote that her bodily discomfort takes precedence." The same view is espoused by Rabbi Pinehas Toledano[304] אם לא נמלא את רצונה בזה... "חולי" זה עלול להביאה לידי — "ספק סכנה" — "If we do not fulfill her craving. . .this 'disease' is likely to result in 'potential danger.'" This explanation would surely explain why Maimonides decided as he did. It is also not an entirely untenable (though not entirely smooth, either) reading of his words. It does leave very difficult to understand why the Shulhan Arukh would record a dispute about the matter, however. And finally, according to this explantion, there is no relationship at all between Maimonides' decision in the nursing mother case and the *sugya* in Nedarim.

In the final analysis, then, we have again made a reasonably strong, but not decisive, case that the Nedarim passage, at least as understood by the *She'eltot* and possibly understood by Maimonides, demonstrates that the Bavli rejects the view of the Yerushalmi that one must endanger oneself for the benefit of another.

Thus far, then, we have seen and analyzed four *sugyot* from the Bavli, and several decisions of the Rambam. Each of the four was understood initially to imply that the Bavli disagreed with the Yerushalmi. For each, that argument was clearly defensible. However, each of the four, some more strongly than others, could be understood differently. At a minimum, they could be understood in such a way that there was no conflict between the Bavli and the Yerushalmi, because the Bavli was silent on the matter; and two of them were understood by some to imply even that the Bavli agreed with the Yerushalmi. Of the four, the *sugya* from Sanhedrin 73a seemed to provide the most convincing proof of a disagreement between the Bavli and Yerushalmi, but even it is not absolutely conclusive. Additionally, it is good to remind ourselves that even the Yerushalmi itself is not so clear. Though the *Hagahot* understands it to imply an obligation to jeopardize oneself, it may be that others disagree with that explanation, seeing the behavior of Resh Lakish not as a reflection of mandatory behavior, but as an act of piety.

There is one final *sugya* which we shall deal with. Unlike those we have already seen, however, this one is quoted originally to prove that the Bavli agrees with the

---

[302] שו״ת נשאל דוד, חלק אבן העזר, סי׳ ו׳ (Jerusalem: Machon Hatam Sofer, 5735), p. 13b.

[303] That very *sugya*, in which Rav Ashi apparently puts himself at risk by sticking his finger in the king's food for the benefit of Mar Zutra, is raised by Rabbi Ovadiah Yosef (p. 40) as perhaps indicating at least that one is entitled, if not obligated, to jeopardize himself for the benefit of another. Rabbi Yosef himself rejects the claim that this *sugya* really proves that. First of all, the *sugya* makes clear that Rav Ashi saw that something was wrong with the food, and thus was probably not endangering himself. Secondly, Rav Ashi was known to be a friend of the king, and his act would not have endangered him. Rabbi Chaim Heller also mentions this passage as a possible proof, but concludes his reference with ויש לדחות. He does not, however, actually provide the דחיה.

[304] See reference above, n. 268. This point is made there on p. 27.

Yerushalmi. Rabbi Baruch ha-Levi Epstein, the *Torah Temimah*, wrote the following regarding Lev. 19:16 – לא תעמוד על דם רעך:[305]

> ועי' בחו"מ סי' תכ"ו... ובב"י ובאחרונים שם חקרו אם מחויב אדם להכניס עצמו בספק סכנה כדי להציל את חבירו מודאי סכנה, ואפשר להביא קצת ראיה דמחויב בזה מאגדה דברכות ל"ג א': מעשה בערוד שהיה מזיק את הבריות, באו והודיעו לר' חנינא בן דוסא, אמר להו הראו לי את חורו, נתן עקבו על פי החור, יצא ונשכו ומת הערוד.... והנה בפ"ג דתענית כ"ד ב' ובכמה מקומות באגדות אמרו על ר' חנינא בן דוסא שהיה מלומד בנסים, נמצא דלפני רחב"ד היתה העמידה על חורו של הערוד ספק סכנה כיון שרגיל בנסים, ולפני אחרים היה הערוד ודאי סכנה, והרי מבואר דמחויב אדם להכניס עצמו בספק סכנה כדי להציל חבירו מודאי סכנה. ופשוט דלא שייך בזה לומר אין למדין מן האגדות אחרי שזה מעשה שהיה.

> See Hoshen Mishpat, no. 426. . .and in the Bet Yosef and other Aharonim there is investigation of whether one is obligated to put oneself in potential danger in order to save one's fellow from certain danger. And some proof of such an obligation can be brought from the aggadah of Berakhot 33a: It happened once with a lizard that was injuring people, that they came and told Rabbi Hanina ben Dosa. He asked them to show him the lizard's hole. He put his foot on the hole. The lizard came out and bit him and the lizard died. . . .Now in the third chapter of Ta'anit, 24b, and in several other aggadic passages, it is said about Rabbi Hanina ben Dosa that he was experienced with miracles. Therefore, standing on the hole of the lizard was [only] potential danger for him since he was accustomed to miracles, while for others it would be certain danger. Thus this tale proves that one must put oneself in potential danger in order to save another from certain danger. And it goes without saying that one may not object to deducing something from this passage on the grounds that one ought not deduce matters of legal behavior from aggadah, since this incident actually happened.

At the end of this passage, the *Torah Temimah* rejects the potential objection that might be raised at its use in the first place, namely, that it is an aggadic statement which cannot serve as a legal source. He rejects that claim because the passage is a record of a real event. The essence of the proof is that since Rabbi Hanina ben Dosa was no stranger to miracles, putting his foot on the hole was only a potential danger for him, and his action provides evidence that one is obligated to do so for the benefit of others who are in certain danger.

The proof of the *Torah Temimah* is rejected both by the *Ziz Eliezer*[306] and Rabbi Ovadiah Yosef,[307] on the grounds that for Rabbi Hanina ben Dosa there was no danger at all because he was accustomed to miracles.[308] Rabbi Waldenberg makes an interesting addi-

---

[305] *Torah Temimah* to Lev. 19:16, no. 110.

[306] Vol. 9, no. 45, par. 6, p. 181b.

[307] P. 41.

[308] This could also account for other acts of sages that seem to rely on the miraculous. See Ta'anit 20b, 21a, 25a, and Kiddushin 29b.

tional comment to the effect that this claim must be correct, or else we must consider the danger to Rabbi Hanina to be certain, not just potential. Supernatural factors can never be used to change the status of real dangers from certain to doubtful. If one is not certain that he merits a miracle being worked for him, he must refrain from any danger which in the natural world would be considered a certain danger. Reliance on the supernatural is acceptable only when one is certain of one's merit.

We end this set of analyses inconclusively. We cannot prove definitively one way or the other regarding the view of the Bavli, though we incline to believe that it seems to disagree with the Yerushalmi. We note, however, that none of the passages dealt directly with the issue, but only by implication. We turn our attention, then, to the one posek whose direct words on this subject become the focus of attention of almost all subsequent poskim, the Radbaz (Rabbi David Ibn Abi Zimra, 1479-1573). First, the question that was addressed to him:[309]

> שאלת ממני אודיעך דעתי על מה שראית כתוב אם אמר השלטון לישראל הנח לי לקצץ אבר אחד שאינך מת ממנו או אמית ישראל חברך, יש אומרים שחייב להניח לקצץ מאבר הואיל ואינו מת, והראיה מדאמרינן בע"ז (כ"ח ע"ב) חש בעיניו מותר לכוחלה בשבת ומפרש טעמא משום דשורייני דעינא בלבא תליא. משמע הא אבר אחר לא. והשתא יבוא הנדון מק"ו: ומה שבת החמורה שאין אבר אחד דוחה אותה היא נדחית מפני פקוח נפש, אבר אחד שנדחית מפני השבת אינו דין שתדחה מפני פקוח נפש? ורצית לדעת אם יש לסמוך על טעם זה.

> You asked me to express my view concerning what you found written, viz., that if the ruling power said to a Jew: "Let me cut off one limb, from which you will not die; or I will kill your fellow Jew," that some say that he is obligated to allow the limb to be cut off, since he will not die. And the proof [for that view] comes from what is said in Avodah Zarah (28b), that one who experiences eye pain on Shabbat is allowed to apply salve. [And that permission] is explained on the basis of the fact that the eye muscles are connected to the heart [and would endanger one if he did not take care of the eye]. The implication [of the reason for the permission] is that for some other limb it would not be permissible [to violate the Sabbath]. And now our case can be answered by קל וחמר: If the Sabbath, which is strict insofar as it is not superseded by other limbs, is superseded by [a limb which, if not tended to would cause] life endangerment; surely other limbs, which are superseded by the Sabbath, should also be superseded by life endangerment. And you wish to know if one should rely on this reasoning.

The opinion which the Radbaz's questioner cites comes almost verbatim from the late thirteenth-early fourteenth century Italian kabbalist and halakhist, Rabbi Menahem Recanati.[310] He mandates that one must allow a limb to be cut off in order to save the life of another, provided it is not a limb whose removal will result in certain death. Recanati reaches that conclusion on the basis of a קל וחמר, based on the Gemara in Avodah Zarah. From the Gemara it follows that one may tend to his eye problem on Shabbat *only because failure to do so*

---

[309] שו"ת הרדב"ז, חלק ג', סי' תרכ"ז (אלף נב).

[310] See פיסקי ריקאנטי, סי' ת"ע.

would endanger him. If failure to tend to some other limb would not endanger him, he may not desecrate the Sabbath for that limb, even though he might lose it. Surely, then, it follows that one must forfeit such a limb for the benefit of another, since saving the life of another supersedes even the Sabbath, even though saving that limb would not. It is to this argument that the Radbaz is asked to react by his questioner.

Almost every line of the response of the Radbaz is important. We shall quote the entire responsum, in sections. We shall number the sections in the English translations.

> תשובה: זו מדת חסידות אבל לדין יש תשובה. מה לסכנת אבר דשבת שכן אונס דאתי משמיא ולפיכך אין סכנת אבר דוחה שבת, אבל שיביא הוא האונס עליו מפני חבירו לא שמענו.

> I. Response: This is an act of piety, but as a matter of law, there is a rebuttal. What distinguishes the case of the endangerment of a limb on the Sabbath is that the danger came from Heaven, and therefore, the endangerment of that limb does not supersede the Sabbath; but we have never heard of a requirement to bring such a danger on himself for the benefit of his fellow.

First, the Radbaz defines the act of sacrificing the limb in order to save the life of the threatened person an act of piety. There can be no question that the term מדת חסידות intimates both approval and praise. However, the קל וחמר which led Recanati to posit the sacrifice of the limb as mandatory is flawed. The essence of the argument of Recananti was based on a comparison to a person's obligation to forfeit a limb, the loss of which would not kill him, in deference to the Sabbath. Radbaz's answer is that in the Sabbath case the obligation to forfeit the limb stems from the fact that God Himself has endangered it. The person himself had nothing to do with it. It would be erroneous to conclude that because one must forfeit a limb in a case where the danger is already existent one must also "chose" to forfeit a limb in a case where the danger to it is not already there, not from Heaven. From this statement of the Radbaz it would follow that the halakhic evidence which proves that one must sometimes submit to danger not of his own making is insufficient to compel the halakhic conclusion that one must ever bring danger upon oneself. Allowing one's limb to be cut off in order to save another is a laudable act, a pious act, but not a required act.

> ותו, דילמא על ידי חתיכת אבר אע"פ שאין הנשמה תלויה בו שמא יצא ממנו דם הרבה וימות, ומאי חזית דדם חבירו סומק טפי, דילמא דמא דידיה סומק טפי. ואני ראיתי אחד שמת על ידי שסרטו את אזנו שריטות דקות להוציא מהם דם ויצא כל כך עד שמת. והרי אין לך באדם אבר קל כאוזן, וכ"ש אם יחתכו אותו.

> II. Furthermore, perhaps the act of cutting off a limb the loss of which does not entail death will result in sufficient blood loss to cause death; and on what basis would one conclude that the blood of the other person is sweeter, perhaps his own blood is sweeter. Indeed, I have witnessed the case of one on whose ear were made thin lacerations in order to remove blood, which resulted in such profuse bleeding that he died. And there is no thinner organ on a human [and yet we see that even it can result in death], and surely [such danger] would exist if one were to cut off the ear.

Beyond the fact that the קל וחמר does not work, the very premise that the limb can be removed without putting the person in potentially life threatening danger is questionable.

Even the simplest surgery can result in uncontrolled bleeding and cause death. And if that can happen even when one is not intending actually to remove the limb, how much more can it happen when that is one's intention. Surely one might have to take such risks for one's own health, but there is no halakhic basis to a claim that another's life is more important than mine. Thus, I could be under no obligation to put myself at risk, even potential risk, that could result in my death.

> ותו דמה לשבת שכן הוא ואיבריו חייבין לשמור את השבת, ואי לאו דאמר קרא "וחי בהם" – ולא שימות בהם" הוה אמינא אפילו על חולי שיש בו סכנה אין מחללין את השבת, תאמר בחבירו שאינו מחוייב למסור עצמו על הצלתו אע"ג דחייב להצילו בממונו, אבל לא בסכנת איבריו.

III. Furthermore, what distinguishes the Sabbath case is that one is duty bound to observe it with all of his limbs. And were it not for the derivation from "And live by them — rather than die for them," one would have held that one should refrain from desecrating the Sabbath even for a dangerous disease. Could one possibly make the same claim regarding one's fellow, for whose benefit one is not obligated to forfeit one's own life? And even though one is obligated to forfeit one's money to save him, one is not obligated to put one's limbs in danger.

It would probably have been better to have part III after part I, since it, too, offers a rebuttal to the קל וחמר of Recanati. The argument of part III is as follows: It is not self-evident that the Sabbath should be desecrated in life-threatening situations. Indeed, were it not for the midrash on the verse "And live by them," which interprets the verse to mean, "Don't die by them," there would be no grounds to make such an assumption. In other words, we need the Torah itself to teach us that the maintenance of our lives takes precedence over the commandments of the Torah. But, unlike the case of forfeiting one's life for God, it would never occur to anyone to think that there is an obligation to forfeit one's life for another, since one's own blood may be sweeter than his. Indeed, we need a special scriptural derivation even to learn that one must sacrifice one's wealth to save the life of another. Surely, then, there could be no argument to compel one to sacrifice one's limbs for the benefit of another.

> ותו דאין עונשין מדין ק"ו ואין לך עונש גדול מזה שאתה אומר שיחתוך אחד מאיבריו מדין ק"ו, והשתא ומה מלקות אין עונשין מדין ק"ו, כל שכן חתיכת אבר.

IV. Furthermore, one may not impose punishment on the basis of an argument by קל וחמר.[311] And there could be no greater "punishment" than cutting off one's limb on the basis of a קל וחמר. Now if one cannot even impose lashes on such a basis, how much more so the cutting off of a limb.

Even if the קל וחמר offered by Recanati were solid and irrefutable, it could not become the basis for an actual decision that involves removing somebody's limb. Removal of a limb falls into the category of עונש, and cannot become mandated by a קל וחמר argument.

> ותו דהתורה אמרה פצע תחת פצע כויה תחת כויה, ואפי' הכי חששו שמא ע"י הכוייה ימות, והתורה אמרה עין תחת עין ולא נפש ועין תחת עין, ולכך

---

[311] See Sanhedrin 54a, 73a, 74a.

> אמרו שמשלם ממון. והדבר ברור שיותר רחוק הוא שימות מן הכויה יותר
> מעל ידי חתיכת אבר ואפי׳ הכי חיישינן לה, כל שכן בנידון דידן. תדע
> דסכנת אבר חמירא דהא התירו לחלל עליה את השבת בכל מלאכות
> שהם מדבריהם, אפי׳ על ידי ישראל.

> v. Furthermore, the Torah says:[312] "A wound for a wound, a burn for a burn," and even so the sages were concerned that an actual burn might result in death. And since the Torah said: "An eye for an eye," and not "An eye and a life for an eye," the sages mandated that [the law is fulfilled by] monetary compensation.[313] And it is clear that the danger of death from a burn is far less likely than from cutting off a limb, and still the sages were concerned about it. Surely, then, it is so in our case. And know how serious a limb is [to the sages], for they permitted the violation of all rabbinic prohibitions on the Sabbath, even by the Jew himself, in order to save it.[314]

This section of the Radbaz's argument provides additional proof of the lengths to which the law goes to protect even limbs which would not automatically result in loss of life if lost. The demand of the Torah is, "An eye for an eye, a wound for a wound, a burn for a burn." When the sages stipulated that monetary compensation replace the literal fulfillment of the Torah's mandate, the motivation was to protect against possible life endangerment. Even though the inflicting of a wound or a burn on a person is not likely to result in that person's death, surely less likely to do so than the removal of a limb, the law is concerned even for the unlikely. Compensation replaces literal fulfillment of the law in order to prevent accidental and unintended loss of the limb. Limbs are very important, even to the extent that rabbinic violations of the Sabbath are ignored in order to protect them. Surely, then, there can be no requirement to sacrifice a limb for the benefit of another, since, even though perhaps unlikely, such an act could lead to the endangerment of one's own life.

> ותו דכתיב דרכיה דרכי נעם וצריך שמשפטי תורתינו יהיו מסכימים אל
> השכל והסברא. ואיך יעלה על דעתנו שיניח אדם לסמא את עינו או
> לחתוך את ידו או רגלו כדי שלא ימיתו את חבירו. הלכך איני רואה טעם
> לדין זה אלא מדת חסידות, ואשרי מי שיוכל לעמוד בזה. ואם יש ספק
> סכנת נפשות הרי זה חסיד שוטה דספיקא דידיה עדיף מוודאי דחבריה.
> והנראה לע״ד כתבתי.

> vi. Furthermore, it is written:[315] "Its ways are ways of pleasantness." That implies that the laws of our Torah must agree with common sense and logic. And is it logical to think that a person would allow another to blind his eye or cut off his hand or foot in order to prevent the killing of his fellow? Therefore, I see no justification for this as law, but only as an act of piety. Happy is he who can fulfill it. But if there is any danger of a life threatening type, such a person would be a "foolish saint," for his

---

[312] Exod. 21:25.

[313] Bava Kamma 84a.

[314] On this complicated subject, see Orah Hayyim 328:17.

[315] Prov. 3:17.

doubtful danger supersedes the certain danger of his fellow. This is my opinion.

Finally, the Radbaz argues that positing such a requirement is counterintuitve, and violates the premise that the laws of the Torah must be reasonable and logical. It is simply not reasonable to demand that one allow the cutting off of a limb of his even in order to save the life of another. It is not a demand that most people will find acceptable and reasonable. A pious individual might be able to accept this, and blessed would be such a person. Then, as almost a post script, the Radbaz adds that if by doing so one puts oneself in the position of even doubtful life threatening danger, he would be a "foolish saint" for doing it.

The following conclusions would seem to follow from the responsum of the Radbaz:

1. There is no halakhic obligation to allow the amputation or removal of a limb, even to save another from certain death.
2. It is permissible to allow it, even though it puts a person in סכנת אבר, and that one who does allow it is praiseworthy, acting from מדת חסידות.
3. A person who allows it is a "foolish saint" if the act engenders ספק סכנת נפשות.

Clearly, somehow the Radbaz is distinguishing between סכנת אבר and סכנת נפש. Two things, however, complicate a clear understanding of the view of the Radbaz. First, does labeling a person as a חסיד שוטה imply that the act is forbidden; or does it remain a permissible act, intimating only that the person is a fool for having done it? Second, how can we really distinguish between סכנת אבר and סכנת נפש in any reasonable way when the Radbaz himself, in parts II and V, makes the claim that even the most ostensibly "safe" actions might involve life endangerment?

Surely the Mishnah is not too fond of a חסיד שוטה, listing it among those who destroy the world.[316] When the Bavli gives an example of such a "foolish saint," it is embodied in the case of man who refuses to save a drowning woman because it is improper to look upon her.[317] The Yerushalmi gives as its example one who refuses to jump in the water to save a drowning child without first removing his tefillin, fearing that the water will erase the parchments, while the child drowns in the meanwhile.[318] The Radbaz himself uses the term elsewhere to define one who refuses to desecrate the Sabbath in a case of פקוח נפשות.[319] In these cases, it seems quite clear that we would define acting as a "foolish saint" to be forbidden. If we apply this to our case, it would follow that for the Radbaz it is permissible to donate an organ when the act does not endanger the life of the donor, and forbidden to do so when the act does endanger the donor.

Having said that, the relevance of the second complication raised above becomes all the more critical. The *Ziz Eliezer* addresses the issue:[320]

---

[316] Sotah 3:4 (20a), and reading מכלי עולם rather than as appears in the Mishnah in the Bavli, מבלי עולם. Of course, even the latter reading is anything but favorable.

[317] Sotah 21b.

[318] J. Sotah 3:4, 19a. Quoted by the Tosafot, Sotah 21b, s.v. היכי.

[319] שו"ת רדב"ז, חלק ד', סי' אלף קלט (סז).

[320] Vol. 9, no. 45, par. 11. See, too, vol. 10, no. 25, ch. 7, par. 5, p. 127a, b. I admit that I am ignoring a distinction that Rabbi Waldenberg makes between internal and external organs. Nonetheless, his basic distinction stands.

ובאמת יש לעיין מתי יצויר הדבר שנאמר שזאת מדת חסידות ולא נקרא
חסיד שוטה, הא הרדב"ז שם מאריך בדבריו לבאר שכל הפסדת אבר
מאדם כרוך בספק סכנה.... וצריך לומר שסבר הרדב"ז שאעפ"י כשיבואו
לשאול לנו נגדיר הכל בגדר ספק סכנה, מ"מ לא נדקדק על כך למי
שרוצה לנדב מרצון לבו כל אבר שאין הנשמה תלויה בו... ונאמר לו שלא
יקרא ע"כ חסיד שוטה כי אם זוהי דרגא גדולה של מדת חסידות.... [ו]אם
יקבעו שיש בזה ספק סכנת נפשות הרי זה חסיד שוטה דספיקא דידיה
עדיף מודאי דחבריה.

> In truth, some thought is required to determine when it should be considered an act of piety and not the act of a foolish saint, since the Radbaz went to some length to explain that all limb removal entails danger to a person. . . .So one must say that the view of the Radbaz is that if one comes to ask, we must define all limb removals as entailing potential danger. However, we should not be overly zealous [to discourage or forbid] with one who wishes, of his own free will, to donate an organ the loss of which will not cause certain death. . .and we should say to such a person that the act is not one of a foolish saint, but rather constitutes the highest level of acts of piety. . . .But if [experts] determine that the act entails significant potential danger, [the donor] would be a pious fool, since his case of doubtful danger supersedes even the certain danger of the other.

Rabbi Waldenberg treads a fine line. But he is forced to do so by the responsum of the Radbaz. The term חסיד שוטה seems to have a fairly clear meaning, and implies more than simply discouraging one from taking an act. And the Radbaz does go to lengths to make clear how potentially life threatening all organ removals can be. Yet, he also does define the act of the donor of a limb for the benefit of another as an act of piety. Since it is reasonable to assume that the Radbaz is not contradicting himself within a single responsum, the solution of Rabbi Waldenberg is not unreasonable. There is always the possibility that a life threatening situation could arise, even in the "safest" of procedures. One who is worried about that possibility may rest assured that the law does not require him to donate an organ, even to save the life of another. However, when that possibility is more remote than real, the act of donation is a highly praiseworthy act of piety. When that possibility is more real than remote, a person would be a foolish saint to put himself in that position, and should even be instructed not to do so, since being a חסיד שוטה is actually forbidden, no matter how pure the motivation.[321]

Rabbi Menashe Klein[322] even raises the possibility that there is no conflict between

---

[321] Rabbi J. David Bleich, *Contemporary Halakhic Problems*, vol. 4, p. 279, n. 20, has a different approach. He prefers to understand that חסיד שוטה in the context of the responsum of the Radbaz means foolhardy, but discretionary and not forbidden. He reaches this possibility by contending that the claim מי יימר דדמא דידיה סומק טפי, דלמא דמא דידך סומק טפי becomes an imperative only when "the danger to one's own life is greater or equal to the danger to the person in need of rescue." If there is real danger to the donor, but it is not greater than the danger to the one in need of rescue, the donation may be foolhardy, but it is permissible. Rabbi Bleich offers no proof to this claim. Furthermore, the Radbaz raises the דלמא דמא דידך סומק טפי argument in section II, where the ostensible danger to the donor was far less than the danger to the person needing rescue. Bleich would have to say that there the claim merely allows one to refuse to donate, but does not intimate even that the act was foolhardy. But I can see no place in the Radbaz's teshuvah where the degree of danger to the donor versus the degree of danger to the one in need of rescue is raised or hinted at as a factor.

[322] משנה הלכות, חלק ו', סי' שכ"ד, דף קצט, ע"ב.

this responsum of the Radbaz and the Yerushalmi. The latter mandates jeopardizing oneself for the benefit of another only when the saving party reverts, upon successful completion of his mission, to a state of no longer being in danger. But in the case of organ donation, the danger into which the donor enters remains forever, since the organ will be forever gone. In such a case, even Resh Lakesh would not insist that one is duty bound to endanger oneself.

Rabbi Moses Feinstein also expounds upon the responsum of the Radbaz.[323] On July 15, 1968, he reacts to it as part of a responsum on heart transplants. Rabbi Feinstein did not have the actual responsum of the Radbaz before him, and referred to it through the *Pithei Teshuvah*.[324] While the actual teshuvah of the Radbaz is directed at answering the position of Recanati, Rabbi Feinstein provides a theoretical basis for the Radbaz's thinking. The reason one is not obligated to donate one's limb is that the prohibition of לא תעמוד is not different from all other prohibitions. About all other negative commandments the law mandates that one must expend one's fortune in order to avoid violating it, but there is nowhere indicated that one must go beyond that. Surely one need not give up one's life in order to avoid violating the prohibition. One might wonder whether losing a non-life threatening limb is in the category of life or money. The Shakh[325] contends that one need not give up a limb in order to prevent violation of a לאו. Thus, the logic of the Radbaz is that since it is permissible to violate a לאו rather than lose a limb over it, it is possible to violate the commandment of לא תעמוד rather than lose a limb over it.

Even without having the actual responsum of the Radbaz in front of him, Feinstein also raises the possibility that the law requiring forfeiting a limb rather than violating the Sabbath might seem to belie his claim. And he gives exactly the same explanation of the difference between the two as does the Radbaz himself, in section I. So, concludes the *Iggrot Moshe*:

> סובר הרדב"ז מאחר שלא מצינו שעל לאו דלא תעמוד על דם רעך יהיה חמור מכל לאוין שבתורה שיהיה מחוייב גם לחתוך אברו להציל חברו שאינו מחוייב דבלא ראיה להחמירו משאר לאוין אין לנו לומר חדוש כזה, ולכן אינו מחוייב לחתוך אבר בשביל הצלת חברו.

> The Radbaz holds that since we find no indication that the negative commandment, "Do not stand idly by the blood of your fellow," is any more strict with regard to being obligated to cut off a limb in order not to violate it than any other negative commandment in the Torah, [it follows] that it is not mandatory. For we cannot apply such a novelty to this commandment against all others without evidence. Thus, one is not obligated to sever a limb in order to save another.

The argument of Rabbi Feinstein is quite substantive. There is no indication that לא תעמוד is different from other לאוין, so why should this mitzvah demand a measure of sacrifice that no other negative mitzvah demands, or gets. The problem which Feinstein's analysis leaves him with is that it could push him to claim that not only is it not required, it is forbidden. After all, we do not usually permit one to sacrifice a limb in order to pre-

---

[323] שו"ת אגרות משה, יורה דעה, חלק ב', סי' קע"ד, ענף ד', עמ' רצ"ב ואילך. An answer very similar to the one which Rabbi Feinstein gives is also given by Rabbi Aryeh Leib Grossnass, שו"ת לב אריה, חלק ב, סי' ל"ח, דף קכ"ב ע"א.
[324] Yoreh De'ah 157:15.
[325] Ibid., par. 3.

vent the violation of other negative commandments. We tell them to violate the commandment instead. He avoids that conclusion by assertion that להציל נפש חברו אף שג"כ הוא רק באיסור לאו יהיה מותר להכניס עצמו בספק מוכר דעכ"פ יוצל נפש מישראל – "To save the life of one's fellow, even though [that obligation stems] from a negative commandment, it would be permissible to put oneself in potential danger, since the life of another Jew will be saved."[326]

Rabbi Isaac Jacob Weiss also affirms that the right to donate exists, and that the dispute between the *Hagahot Maimoniyot* and the poskim who disagree with him is only about אם צריך או לא, אבל מותר אם רוצה [ו]כל זה דוקא אם יכניס עצמו לספק סכנה יציל את חבירו ברור – "Whether it is mandatory or not. But it is permissible. And all of this concerns a case in which it is certain that the other will be saved if the donor puts himself in potential danger."[327]

We have been analyzing a responsum of the Radbaz which seems to state very clearly that there is no obligation to donate a limb, even if failure to do so will certainly cause the death of another. While there is no obligation, it is an act of great kindness and piety to do so, provided the donation does not put the donor in a situation of ספק סכנת נפשות. If it does put him in such a situation, he would be a חסיד שוטה to donate.

There is, however, another responsum of the Radbaz which considerably complicates our ability to understand him. Indeed, on some level, this second responsum of his seems to contradict the teshuvah we have been dealing with until now. Therefore, we must look at the second responsum of the Radbaz.[328]

מה שכתב הרב ז"ל[329] "כל היכול להציל [ולא הציל עובר על לא תעמוד על דם רעך]" איירי במי שיכול להציל להדיא בלא שיסתכן המציל כלל, כגון שהיה ישן תחת כותל רעוע שהיה יכול להעירו משנתו ולא העירו או כגון שיודע לו עדות להצילו, עבר על לא תעמוד על דם רעך.

1. When the Master [Maimonides] wrote:[330] "Whoever can save [but does not save violates "Do not stand idly by the blood of your fellow,"] it refers to one who is clearly able to save without endangering himself at all; for example, if one was sleeping at the foot of a rickety wall and it was possible to wake him from his sleep, but he did not do so; or, for example, that one knew exculpatory testimony [concerning the other, but did not offer it], these constitute violations of "Do not stand idly by the blood of your fellow."

Maimonides wrote that כל היכול להציל ולא הציל עובר על לא תעמוד על דם רעך – "Whoever is able to save and does not do so violates 'Do not stand idly by the blood of your fellow.'" The Radbaz offers a straightforward explanation of this clause. It applies to cases in which saving is certain and there is no danger whatsoever to the saving party, as, for example, warning people to move from a dangerous location.

---

[326] Rabbi Feinstein restricts this permission to certain saving of the person in need, when accompanied by only potential danger to the saving party. He does not permit one to sacrifice his life, even if that sacrifice would surely save another. That one may not do, even if the one who will be saved is a sage or a saint.

[327] שו"ת מנחת יצחק (ירושלים, תשל"ו), חלק ו', סי' ק"ג.

[328] שו"ת הרדב"ז, חלק ה', ללשונות הרמב"ם, סי' אלף תקפ"ב (רי"ח). All of part v of the Responsa of the Radbaz is devoted to explanations of questions arising from the Rambam and the *Hasagot* of the Ravad, two hundred and thirty-four such questions in all.

[329] רמב"ם, הלכות רוצח ושמירת נפש, פרק א', הל' י"ד.

[330] M.T. Hilkhot Rozeah u'Shemirat Nefesh 1:14.

After this clause, Maimonides paraphrases the end result of the passage in Sanhedrin,[331] mandating saving one from drowning or attack by animals or bandits, both by one's own efforts and by hiring help, if needed. He then adds a couple of other examples which do not come from the Talmud, including them in the prohibition against standing idly by. The Radbaz continues:

> ולא זו בלבד אלא אפילו יש בו קצת ספק סכנה, כגון ראה אותו טובע בים או לסטים באים עליו או חיה רעה שיש בכל אלו ספק סכנה, אפילו הכי חייב להציל, ואפילו שלא היה יכול להציל בגופו לא נפטר בשביל כך אלא חייב להציל בממונו ולא זו בלבד דברי היזיקה אלא אפילו שמע עכו"ם [או מוסרים מחשבים עליו רעה או טומנין לו פח ולא גלה אוזן חבירו והודיעו או שידע בגוי או באנס שהוא קובל על חבירו ויכול לפייסו בגלל חבירו ולהסיר מה שבלבו ולא פייסו וכל כיוצא בדברים אלו], דלא ברי היזיקה כולי האי דדילמא ממלכי ולא עבדי, אפילו הכי חייב להציל ואם לא הציל עבר על לא תעמוד על דם רעך.

II. And not only in the cases already mentioned [is one duty bound to save], but even in cases where there is some small potential danger; for example, if he saw somebody drowning or attacked by bandits or an animal — in all of which there is some potential danger — nonetheless he is duty bound to save. And he is not exempt from this responsibility even if he cannot save him alone. Rather, he must save him with his money. And not only in such cases where the danger to the one in trouble is clear and certain, but even if he heard pagans [or informers plotting evil against him, or setting a trap for him, and he did not reveal the information to his fellow and tell him; or if he knew about some gentile or property confiscator who was registering a complaint against his fellow, and he could assuage him on behalf of his fellow to alter his intention, and he did not do so; and such similar things, even in these cases where] the danger is not as clear and certain, for perhaps they would rethink their intentions and would not carry them out, nonetheless one is obligated to save them, and if he did not do so, he is in violation of "Do not stand idly by the blood of your fellow."

One is obligated, says the Radbaz, to save another even when there is some small potential danger to oneself. Normally, one can save a drowning person by throwing him a rope. Usually, the danger to the saver is minimal. But, it could happen that he might fall into the water, or be pulled in by the drowning person, and be endangered. Nonetheless, he must take that risk. Furthermore, the obligation to save extends even beyond the cases of immediate and clear danger to the person needing saving, like drowning or being under attack. The obligation encompasses even cases in which one is privy to information about plans which, if acted upon by those plotting them, would endanger one's fellow.

Note that nothing in the first responsum of the Radbaz contradicts part II of this responsum. The contents of this section are based on the Gemara in Sanhedrin. It already anticipates the possibility of minimal potential danger to the saving party, and already includes failure to act under those circumstances in the לא תעמוד prohibition. The first responsum may seem to be unaware of the Yerushalmi, but it cannot be unaware of the

---

[331] 73a.

Bavli. It is inconceivable that the intent of the Radbaz in the first responsum was to exclude the obligation to attempt to save another who was drowning on the grounds that one might be pulled into the water, because such an exclusion would contradict the Bavli. Thus, in this responsum, the Radbaz makes clear that the obligation to save extends to these circumstances.

But, the Radbaz concludes:

> הוי יודע שיש בכלל לאו זה שלא יעמוד על הפסד ממון חבירו אלא שאינו חייב להכניס עצמו לספק סכנה בשביל ממונו. אבל להציל נפש חבירו... אפילו במקום דאיכא ספק סכנה חייב להציל, והכי איתא בירושלמי. ומכל מקום, אם הספק נוטה אל הודאי אינו חייב למסור עצמו להציל את חבירו, ואפי' בספק מוכרע אינו חייב למסור עצמו דמאי חזית דדמא דידך סומק טפי דילמא דמא דידיה סומק טפי.[332] אבל אם הספק אינו מוכרע אלא נוטה אל ההצלה והוא לא יסתכן ולא הציל עבר על לא תעמוד על דם רעך. הנראה לעניות דעתי כתבתי.

> III. Be aware that refraining from saving the wealth of one's fellow is included in the prohibition, though one is not duty bound to put himself in potential danger for another's wealth. But one is obligated to save the life of another, even when it entails potential danger, and that is what the Yerushalmi says. However, if the potential danger leans toward certainty, he is not obligated to put himself in such a position for another's benefit. And even if the potential is fifty-fifty, he is not obligated, for why would it be certain that your blood is sweeter, perhaps his blood is sweeter.[333] But if the danger is not even fifty-fifty, but leans toward saving without his being endangered, one violates "Do not stand idly by the blood of your fellow" if one does not save him. So it seems in my opinion.

Part III of this responsum goes considerably further than part II. It obligates one to save another even when there is some danger to himself, greater than the minimal danger indicated in part II. The Radbaz distinguishes between levels of danger. He seems to be saying that one violates לא תעמוד if he fails to attempt to save his fellow when the chances are fifty percent or less that attempting to save him will result in actual danger to himself. One does not violate לא תעמוד if the chances of actual danger to oneself are greater than fifty percent, and, as a result, one does not attempt to save the person in danger.

Surely there appears to be a conflict between this responsum and the first. In part II of the first the Radbaz makes the case that even the most minor surgery can result in life threatening danger. His example of bleeding to death as a result of a laceration on the earlobe surely must be one where such a chance was less than fifty percent. And in part V of the first responsum, where he talks about why restitution is made rather than literal fulfillment of פצע תחת פצע כויה תחת כויה, it is also clear that the chances were less than fifty percent that literal fulfillment of the verse would result in death. Yet, these arguments led him to conclude that there is no obligation to endanger oneself at all, and that doing so would be an act of מדת חסידות. Surely, though, if one did not do so he would not be guilty of violating לא תעמוד, even though he would not be a חסיד.

---

[332] ברור שצריך להיות: דמאי חזית דדמא דידיה סומק טפי, דילמא דמא דידך סומק טפי.

[333] This must clearly be read: "Why is it certain that his blood is sweeter; perhaps your blood is sweeter."

One might wish to argue that in the second responsum the Radbaz is explicating the view of Maimonides, while it is in the first responsum that his own view is expressed. That is highly unlikely, however. First of all, there does not seem to be anything in the language of Maimonides that implies what the Radbaz says in part III of the second responsum. Furthermore, many poskim reject the view of the *Hagahot* precisely because they thought the Rambam, the Rosh and the Tur decided against it by ignoring it. Additionally, the Radbaz does not link anything in part III of the second responsum with the language of Maimonides himself, while he does do that in parts I and II. Finally, the Radbaz actually says that part III of the second responsum is based on the Yerushalmi. So, we must reasonably conclude that the contents of the second resposum reflect the opinion of the Radbaz himself,[334] creating a contradiction between the two responsa.

There exists the theoretical possibility that one of the responsa is intended to be a retraction of the other. There is no hint to that, however. Besides, we could probably never tell which responsum is the retraction!

Another possibility is simply to concede that the two contradict each other, and decide which we would choose to follow on the basis of which we think the more compellingly argued. This approach would leave part III of the second responsum at a great disadvantage, since it is not *argued* at all, but merely *asserted*. What's more, the Radbaz does not identify the Yerushalmi which ostensibly is the basis for the essential claim of part III. We would have no choice but to identify it as we have assumed all along. And, in that Yerushalmi passage there is no evidence whatsoever what percentage chance of endangerment Resh Lakish accepted in deciding to go after Rabbi Ami.

A significant number of poskim who refer to the Radbaz as the source of their decisions on our question do not refer to the second responsum at all. They appear totally unaware of it. This is true, for example, of Rabbi Feinstein, Rabbi Isaac Jacob Weiss, Rabbi Aryeh Leib Grossnass, Rabbi Pinchas Toledano, and Rabbi Menashe Klein. In his responsum in volume 9 of the *Ziz Eliezer*, Rabbi Eliezer Waldenberg also makes no mention of the second responsum of the Radbaz. There are others, however, who are aware of the second responsum of the Radbaz, including Rabbi Waldenberg in volume 10, and it is to them that we turn our attention now. Not surprisingly, of course, the premise which they all try to substantiate is that there is no contradiction between the two teshuvot of the Radbaz. The reconciliations take two different directions, and we shall focus first upon the direction taken by the *Ziz Eliezer*.

After spelling out the apparent contradiction between the two teshuvot, and quoting the last part of section III of the second responsum in which the Radbaz distinguishes between various percentages of potential danger, Rabbi Waldenberg wrote:[335]

> הרי בהדיא שהרדב"ז ז"ל חזר והבהיר את דעתו וגם הטה לכך כוונת הירושלמי, שרק בספק שאינו מוכרע אלא נוטה אל ההצלה אזי מחויב גם ליכנס לכך כדי להציל את חבירו אבל כל שהספק לכך מוכרע אזי איננו מחויב כבר למסור נפשו ואמרי' להיפך דילמא דמא דידיה סומק טפי. ולפי זה אין יותר סתירות בדברי הרדב"ז.

The Radbaz explicitly clarifies his opinion, and even intimates that it is the intent of the Yerushalmi. Only if the danger is less than 50%, inclining toward saving, is one obligated to put one-

---

[334] It does seem reasonable to claim that the Radbaz saw no contradiction between Maimonides and what he says in part III of the second responsum. I do admit that it is difficult to see how he reaches that conclusion.

[335] *Ziz Eliezer*, vol. 10, no. 25, ch. 28.

self in danger in order to save his fellow. But whenever the danger is 50% [or greater], one is no longer obligated to put himself at risk. Indeed, we say the opposite: "Perhaps his own blood is sweeter." In this way, there are no contradictions in the words of the Radbaz.

The solution of the *Ziz Eliezer* to the contradiction between the teshuvot of the Radbaz is to claim that the two complement and clarify each other, rather than contradict each other. That solution is also adopted by several others: Rabbi Abraham Sofer Abraham,[336] Rabbi Ovadiah Yosef,[337] and Rabbi Moshe Hershler.[338] And the idea that this distinction is also implicit in the Yerushalmi also appears earlier than the Ziz Eliezer. Rabbi Haim Benveniste wrote in כנסת הגדולה[339]: ואפילו לסברת ההגהות אם הספק נוטה אל הודאי ואפי ספק – מוכרח אינו חייב.... אלא דוקא בספק שאינו מוכרח נוטה אל ההצלה "Even according to the *Hagahot*, one is not duty bound if the potential danger inclines toward certain or is even. . . .[He is obligated] only when the danger is less than even, inclining toward saving." And Rabbi Moses Schick wrote:[340] נ"ל דגם הירושלמי לא קאמר בחשש סכנה ממש וספק השקול אלא דאיכא חשש עפ"י המיעוט אבל עפ"י הרוב ליכא ספק נפשות – "It is my opinion that even the Yerushalmi does not refer to a significant danger or an even danger; but only to a case in which there is usually only slight danger, but usually not significant danger."

The motivation of these poskim to wish to reconcile the teshuvot of the Radbaz is both understandable and commendable. It is eminently reasonable to assume that the Radbaz would not contradict himself so blatantly. And if that is reasonable, there must be some way to reconcile his teshuvot. The test of the reconciliation, however, lies in the ability to apply it to the teshuvot in question. In our case, the distinction made by the Radbaz in the second responsum is presumed to apply also to the first responsum. We would then have to say that the חסיד שוטה of the first responsum is one who donates a limb even when that endangers him more than fifty percent. But to which level of danger can the category of מדת חסידות be applied? Since it is clear that מדת חסידות refers to an act of piety, rather than a dictate of law, it cannot be applied to a case of less than fifty percent risk on the part of the donor, because according to the second responsum that donation should be mandatory and not merely an act of piety. What's more, as we have said above,[341] in the first responsum the Radbaz uses cases where the danger is less than fifty percent to prove that there is no obligation to donate, while in the second responsum those very cases should be obligatory. Thus, the reconciliation proposed by the *Ziz Eliezer*, and the others, works well enough to help us define a חסיד שוטה, but not well enough to help us distinguish between an obligatory act and an act of piety which is not obligatory.

It is perhaps just such considerations that moved other poskim toward a different solution to the contradictions in the Radbaz. This direction differentiates the two teshuvot in such a way that they are dealing with entirely different subjects and ought not be compared at all. This approach is formulated by Rabbi Moshe Hershler as follows:[342]

---

[336] See נשמת אברהם, הלכות אבילות, סי' שמ"ט, p. 34, and המעין, ניסן תשמ"ב, pp. 25-26, and cf. המעין, ניסן תשמ"ה, עמ' רס"ד.

[337] See דיני ישראל ז', עמ' כ"ז–כ"ח, and his article in יחוה דעת, חלק ג', סי' פ"ד, עמ' רפ"ד.

[338] See הלכה ורפואה, כרך ב', תשמ"א, עמ' קכ"ג–קכ"ד.

[339] Hoshen Mishpat no. 426, comments on Beit Yosef, no. 1.

[340] ספר מהר"ם שיק על תרי"ג מצוות (מונקאטש, תרנ"ח), מצוה רל"ח.

[341] P. 294.

[342] See above, n. 338.

בתשובת הרדב"ז... כתב עוד הבדל יסודי... והוא שכל עקירת אבר פנימי יש סיכון ואסור לו (לו)[מ]ספק להכנס לסכנת נפשות, ומדבריו משמע דלגבי חתיכת אבר אין תלוי בגודל הסיכון, וגם אין מקום לומר שיש הבדל אם זה ספק שקרוב להצלה או קרוב לספק השקול, אלא כל אבר שהנשמה תלויה בו כל העושה זאת הרי הוא תמיד שוטה ואסור לו להכנס לספק סכנת נפשות.... [ו]אם רצה להציל חברו בזה כיון שאין בזה סכנת נפשות מותר והרי זה מדת חסידות בעלמא.

> In the responsum of the Radbaz [i.e., the first responsum]. . .he indicates a fundamental distinction. . .[namely,] that any removal of an internal organ is dangerous, and it is forbidden for one to enter into a situation of potential life endangerment. And his words imply that the removal of limbs is not at all contingent upon level of danger, even the case where the danger is not significant or the danger is even. Rather, nobody may put himself in potential danger regarding an organ on which life depends, and is always considered a "fool" [if he does]. . . . But if he wishes to save his fellow through [limb donation of a limb on which life does not depend], it is permissible as an act of piety since it does not entail life endangerment.

Hershler's assertion is that the responsa run on different tracks. The second responsum, which distinguishes between levels of danger and posits a requirement even to endanger oneself at times, refers to a danger which passes entirely when the saving is done. When the saving party is done saving, he is no longer in danger and has reverted to his former state. When one pulls another from the water, the danger to both ceases when the act is completed, and both are as they were before the event occurred. Even in such cases there is no requirement to endanger oneself if the chances are greater than fifty-fifty that the saving party will be endangered. The first responsum, on the other hand, does not indicate any such distinctions precisely because they are inapplicable. Sacrificing a limb is different because it is permanent, and because it always is potentially dangerous, even when it seems to be not very dangerous. Nobody is ever obligated to donate an organ. Indeed, if he donates one the loss of which is likely to cause his death, he is a "foolish saint." If he wishes to donate one the loss of which is not likely to cause his death, he may, as an act of piety.

The same view is expressed by Rabbi Moshe Meiselman, who wrote:[343] ומה שכתב הרדב"ז דכשנוטה להצלה חייב, כל זה דוקא במקום דליכא הפסד אבר אבל במקום דיש הפסד אבר הרדב"ז עצמו כתב בתשובה אחרת דאין כאן חיוב — "And when the Radbaz wrote [in the second responsum] that there is an obligation [to endanger oneself] when saving is almost certain, that applies only when no loss of limb is entailed. But when there is loss of limb, the Radbaz himself wrote in another responsum that there is no obligation."

Rabbi Shaul Yisraeli also distinguishes between the two responsa.[344] He contends that the first responsum considers the act as מדת חסידות alone because there is no obligation under לא תעמוד when the saving would entail either pain or suffering or the invasion of the body in any way. The second responsum, however, would be included under לא תעמוד, because it refers to physical activity, effort, and difficulty, but not physical invasion or bodily pain and suffering.

---

[343] הלכה ורפואה (ירושלים: מכון רגנשברג, תשמ"א), כרך ב', עמ' קי"ח.

[344] We have quoted from this responsum above, p. 221. The way he distinguishes between the two responsa of the Radbaz is made clear in n. 8 of that article.

There is more to be said in favor of this direction for resolving the apparent conflict than there is in favor of the first direction. Assuming that the Radbaz is not just simply contradicting himself is reasonable. After all, these two teshuvot, if seen as contradictory, are fundamentally different from each other. It is simply unlikely that the Radbaz would have changed his mind so radically, and left unstated that he had changed his mind. One of the two should tell us it is a retraction of the other. Furthermore, the first responsum never leaves the issue of limbs. It never distinguishes between percentage chances of saving or endangerment. It never says that the absence of obligation regarding limbs does not extend to other types of dangers. It simply ignores other types of dangers. And the second responsum never mentions limbs or organs. Indeed, if the distinctions within it applied to limbs as well, the Radbaz had a wonderful chance to make that clear in his conclusion, which is where he introduces the factor of percentage of danger. It is possible that the responsa are connected, but it is not probable.

Additionally, there is a common sense distinction to be drawn between subjecting oneself to danger which passes and leaves one unchanged, and a danger which may pass, but leaves one permanently changed; or, between a requirement to extend oneself physically for the benefit of another, and a requirement to allow the invasion of one's body for the benefit of another. It does not seem implausible that the Radbaz meant just such distinctions when he claimed that the demands of the law must seem reasonable and logical to average people. It is reasonable that the law might demand of one to put himself in some minimal amount of temporary danger in the anticipation that the danger will not materialize and the person will return to his prior state. It is less reasonable to think that the law would demand of one to subject himself to a similarly minimal amount of temporary danger from which, even if the danger does not materialize, he will not return to his previous state of being. It is precisely because the latter is unreasonable to demand of average people that the Radbaz affirms that acting in such a manner is an act of admirable piety, worthy of praise, but impossible to impose.

We have been discussing two teshuvot the Radbaz at length. They have been the focus of our discussion because they were the focus of discussion of so many of the poskim. At the point we began this discussion, we had concluded that the talmudic passages raised as relevant to the issue of endangering oneself for the benefit of another were inconclusive, though some made quite strong cases that the Bavli did not require self endangerment. Now we see that the first of the responsa of the Radbaz is exceptionally clear, and cogently argues against a requirement of self endangerment. It calls one who risks endangerment for the sake of another a pious person, provided the risk does not pose a significant danger to his life. If it does, and the person yet undertakes it, the Radbaz calls that person a חסיד שוטה – "a foolish saint." The second responsum seems to contradict the first by requiring self endangerment if the chances of its actualization are less than fifty percent. We have argued, however, that it is improbable that the two responsa, so widely different on the surface, really contradict each other. It is precisely because they are so widely different that it is unlikely that the same decisor would have contradicted himself thus. One possibility we entertained was that the second responsum fills in detail not clear from the first. That is, that the two complement each other. That possibility seemed far less likely, however, than the possibility that the two deal with different issues. Thus, at this point we would say that the view of the Radbaz about self endangerment resulting from organ removal or donation is as summarized earlier in this paragraph.

There is one other approach to the question of self endangerment for the benefit of another that we should look at. It is espoused by Rabbi Eliyahu ben Samuel of

Lublin, the *Yad Eliyahu*.[345] What is quite remarkable is that the *Yad Eliyahu* makes no mention of the Radbaz whatsoever. He actually puts his conclusion right at the beginning of the responsum:

אך לעניות דעתי עיקרא דהאי דינא הכי: אם שניהם שוים במעלה, כגון שניהם תלמידי חכמים או עמי הארץ, ומכ״ש אם המציל ת״ח והניצל ע״ה, דאינם רשאים להכניס עצמם אפילו בספק בהצלה ודאי, ולא איכפת לן בספק או בודאי בזה.... אך אם המציל אינו ת״ח כמו הניצל אז נלע״ד דמותר להכניס עצמו אבל אינו מחויב אם לא ממדת חסידות אם ירצה.

> In my opinion, the basic law in this matter is thus: If the two are of equal standing, for example, if they are both scholars or both uneducated, and surely if the potential saver is a scholar while the party in need of saving is uneducated, one is not permitted to endanger oneself. [And this is so] even if the endangerment is merely potential while the saving is certain. In these circumstances the categories of "doubt" and "certainty" are irrelevant. . . .But if the saving party is less of a scholar than the party to be saved, it seems to me that it is permissible as an act of piety, without legal obligation, to put oneself in danger if one wishes.

Later in the responsum he adds that regarding one's own teacher it is not only permissible to put oneself in danger, but מצוה נמי בשביל רבו... ממדת חסידות, אע״פ שאינו מחויב – "There is even a mitzvah to do so for one's teacher. . .as an act of piety, even though one is not obligated." Putting the two together we can summarize the view of the *Yad Eliyahu* as having three parts: (1) Persons of equal standing should not endanger themselves for each other. (2) One may endanger oneself for a person of higher standing as an act of piety, though there is no obligation to do so. (3) Though there is no legal obligation to do so, it is a mitzvah to endanger oneself for one's teacher as an act of piety.

The evidence of the *Yad Eliyahu* that there are different statuses which have legal implications is very clear. The mishnayot at the end of Horayot[346] list the order of precedence for saving, and end with the claim that the stipulated order applies only when the persons in question are of equal wisdom, but if among two people in need of saving one is an עם הארץ high priest and the other a sage ממזר, the latter takes precedence over the former – ממזר תלמיד חכם קודם לכהן גדול עם הארץ.[347]

It is also clear that if one is himself among those in need of saving, as in the case of multiple captives, he takes precedence over everyone else. There is a clear baraita to this effect in Horayot[348] which states: היה הוא ואביו ורבו בשבי הוא קודם – "If he, his father and his teacher were captives, he takes precedence."[349] If he himself takes precedence when they are already captive, surely it follows that he is under no obligation to endanger himself even for the benefit of his teacher when he himself is not in danger. And you should not think that he himself takes precedence only when he and others are in equal

---

[345] No. 43. See above, pp. 262ff., where we have dealt with parts of the responsum already.

[346] 3:7-8.

[347] See M.T. Hilkhot Matanot Aniyim 8:15-18; Yoreh De'ah 251:9, 252:8, and the comment of the Rema in 248:15.

[348] 13a.

[349] The baraita itself includes the claim that one's mother takes precedence over all three for redemption. The Shakh, Yoreh De'ah 252:10, affirms that this is so only when none is in danger of death. If they are in danger of death, חייו קודמין אפי׳ לשל אמו.

danger, but if his danger is only "doubtful" and his ability to save is certain, he ought to endanger himself for the benefit of another (even his equal, not only his superior). There is no such distinction drawn in any authoritative source. Indeed, the very silence of the mishnayot about the matter of "doubtful" versus "certain" seems to imply that the distinction is irrelevant. Had it been relevant, either the Mishnah itself, or at least the Gemara, would have told us that the list of precedence applies only when the people in danger are in equal degrees of danger. If the danger of one lower on the list, however, was greater than the danger of one higher on the list, the one lower on the list should be saved first. Neither the Mishnah nor the Gemara say anything of the sort and, therefore, they imply that it is not true. Thus, there is no grounds to distinguish between "doubtful" and "certain." What matters is status. But, one's own danger, certain or doubtful, takes precedence over the danger of even one's superiors. Thus it follows, at a minimum, that one need not endanger oneself, even "doubtful" danger, for the benefit of another.

The basis of the claim that one's own redemption from captivity takes precedence over even that of one's father and teacher is that the obligation to save a life is linked to the obligation to save the property of another. After all, the context of the verse והשבתו לו,[350] from which the obligation to save the life of another is deduced,[351] is returning lost articles, i.e., saving the money of another. So it is logical that as one's lost article takes precedence over those of all others,[352] so too should one's own life take precedence over the lives of all others.

Yet, the Gemara makes quite clear that one ought not be so much a stickler on the precedence of his own money over that of others that he never is prepared to risk his own money for the benefit of others. As Rav put it:[353] כל המקיים בעצמו כך סוף בא לידי כך – "Anyone who is too fastidious [in observing the verse 'Be careful not to impoverish yourself' (Deut. 15:4)] ultimately becomes what he sought to avoid." Rashi explains: "Even though Scripture does not impose it upon him, a person should act beyond the requirement of the law. He should not always say to himself, 'Mine comes first.' He should say that only when significant loss is likely. And if he is overly fastidious, he ignores the obligation for גמילות חסדים and charity, and will ultimately himself need the aid of others."

Finally, the *Yad Eliyahu* puts together all of the relevant verses and concludes:

> אי כתב קרא דוהשבתו לו, הוי אמינא דלא מיטרח ומיגר, כתב לא תעמוד. ואי כתב לא תעמוד הוי אמינא דצריך אפי׳ לסכן עצמו.... ועל כן כתב רחמנא והשבתו לו כמו אבידת ממונו דשלך קודם לשל כל אדם. אך עדיין הוי אמינא דהרשות בידו לסכן עצמו בשביל כל אדם כמו באבידת ממון דהרשות בידו אע"פ שאינו מחויב בדבר, כתב רחמנא דרשה דחייך קודמין, דאינך רשאי לסכן עצמך. ואי כתב הני תרתי ולא קראי דוהשבתו ה"א דאינו רשאי לסכן עצמו אפי׳ בשביל רבו ומי שגדול הימנו, כתב רחמנא קרא דוהשבתו לו דגבי אבידה על כל פנים רשאי ומצוה נמי בשביל רבו כמו שכתבתי לעיל ממדת חסידות אף על פי שאינו מחויב.

If Scripture had written only והשבתו לו, I would have believed that there is no obligation to expend money to save another. So, Scripture included לא תעמוד [to teach that one must do so.] And

---

[350] Deut. 22:2.
[351] Sanhedrin 73a.
[352] M. Bava Metzia 2:11, 33a.
[353] Bava Metzia 33a.

if Scripture had written only לא תעמוד, I would have believed that one must put oneself in danger [for the benefit of another]. . . . Therefore Scripture wrote והשבתו לו, [in order to make the obligation to save a life] comparable to saving the possessions of another, in which one's own takes precedence over those of all others. Yet, even so I would have believed that one is allowed, though not obligated, to endanger oneself for the benefit of another as one is allowed with one's money. Therefore, Scripture indicates through midrash that your life takes precedence, namely, that you are not allowed to endanger yourself. And if only these two [i.e., לא תעמוד and חייך קודמין] had been written, but not והשבתו לו, I would have believed that one is not allowed to endanger oneself even for one's teacher or one greater than oneself. Therefore Scripture wrote והשבתו לו in the context of lost articles, from which I have demonstrated above that one is allowed, though not obligated, to endanger oneself, and for one's teacher it is a mitzvah.

The *Yad Eliyahu* constructs a צריכותא, utilizing והשבתו לו, לא תעמוד (including its contextual juxtaposition with monetary possessions), and חייך קודמין to prove the three points he began with: one may not endanger oneself for someone of identical or lesser status, may for anyone of higher status, and may – with an element of true piety verging on mitzvah – for one's teacher. And, *mirabile dictu*, one of the passages he quotes to demonstrate that one is entitled, though not obligated, to endanger oneself for the benefit of another of identical status is the Yerushalmi to which we have been referring all along. In that passage, the *Yad Eliyahu* views the act of Resh Lakish not only as one of מדת חסידות as opposed to legal obligation, but also one in which Resh Lakish and Rabbi Ami are not just "any men," but both sages.

The *Yad Eliyahu* may present the most complete argumentational defense for the position he espouses, but he is not the only one, or even the first one, to advocate it. Rabbi Judah he-Hasid had already written in the twelfth century:[354]

> שנים שיושבים ובקשו אויבים להרוג אחד מהם, אם אחד תלמיד חכם והשני הדיוט מצוה להדיוט לומר הרגוני ולא חבירי כר' ראובן בן איצטרובלי שבקש שיהרגוהו ולא לר' עקיבא כי רבים היו צריכים לר' עקיבא.

> If enemies demanded to kill one from among two who were sitting, and one of the two was a sage while the other was a commoner, it is a mitzvah for the commoner to say: "Kill me, not my fellow." And this is what Rabbi Reuven ben Strobilus did when he requested that they kill him rather than Rabbi Akiva, since the many needed Rabbi Akiva.

This passage could, on the one hand, be understood as a great support for the position of the *Yad Eliyahu*. We quoted another position of the *Sefer Hasidim*[355] in which he had decided clearly that one should not endanger oneself for the sake of another, even if that meant certain death for the other. Yet, here, Rabbi Judah he-Hasid affirms that it is at

---

[354] *Sefer Hasidim*, Reuven Margolioth ed. (Jerusalem: Mossad haRav Kook, 5734), no. 698, p. 436.

[355] Above, p. 269, taken from *Sefer Hasidim*, no. 674, p. 428.

least very praiseworthy, even if not exactly mandatory, to actually sacrifice oneself for the benefit of another, provided the other is a sage. Indeed, that is exactly the way Rabbi Menashe Klein understands the relationship between the two passages. He wrote:[356]

ומיהו לא קשיא מידי דהכא מיירי בשניהם שוים אבל באחד גדול מותר אפילו למסור נפשו וכמו שכתב לעיל וזה ראיה גדולה להיד אליהו.

> In reality, there is no conflict between the two passages of the *Sefer Hasidim*. For there [i.e., in the passage from section 674] the case deals with two people of identical status. But, in a case where one is a great person, it is permissible even to sacrifice one's life, as he [Rabbi Judah he-Hasid] wrote above [i.e., in section 698]. And this constitutes a great proof for the view of the *Yad Eliyahu*.

On the other hand, the proof is not necessarily so compelling, as the *Ziz Eliezer* realized.[357] First of all, the beginning of the passage can be understood to mean that the initial demand was to kill one of them, with no stipulation as to which to kill. In which case, the claim of the *Sefer Hasidim* would be somewhat more restricted. It would mandate a mitzvah for the commoner to sacrifice himself only under those circumstances. There would be no mitzvah on the commoner, however, to offer himself instead of the sage who had been stipulated as the victim. One must admit, though, that the end of the passage argues against this understanding of its beginning. The end of the passage does seem to indicate that Rabbi Akiva had been stipulated as the victim, and even so Rabbi Reuven ben Strobilus offered himself instead. But even if we understand this way, the incident does not necessarily support the *Yad Eliyahu* because the clause כי רבים היו צריכים לר' עקיבא – "Since the many needed Rabbi Akiva" – could intimate that Rabbi Reuven's action was motivated by a desire to help the many, not a single individual.[358]

Even more, the incident of Rabbi Reuven ben Strobilus has no talmudic source. There does seem to have been an ancient tradition concerning Rabbi Reuven's desire to sacrifice himself, but it cannot be traced to the Talmud itself.[359] It would be risky, claims the *Ziz Eliezer*, to base a legal claim that it is a mitzvah to sacrifice oneself upon the *Sefer Hasidim* alone.[360]

Rabbi Yehudah he-Hasid is the earliest to espouse the view subsequently adopted by the Rabbi Eliyahu ben Samuel (d. 1735 in Hebron). But a younger contemporary of

---

[356] משנה הלכות, חלק ו', סי, שכ"ד, עמ' 396 ע"ב.

[357] Vol. 10, no. 25, ch. 7, p. 128a and b.

[358] שיירי כנסת הגדולה, יורה דעה סי' קנ"ז, הגהות בית יוסף It is interesting to note that Rabbi Hayyim Benveniste, in אות ל"ה quotes only the first part of the *Sefer Hasidim*. According to him, therefore, it would follow that the reference to Rabbi Reuven ben Strobilus in the *Sefer Hasidim*, and the fact that Rabbi Akiva was needed by the many, are incidental. The behavior of Rabbi Reuven ben Strobilus indicates the desired, though not mandatory, behavior of any single individual toward another single individual of higher status. All of this also assumes that Rabbi Akiva was clearly of higher status than Rabbi Reuven, who was as a commoner vis-a-vis Rabbi Akiva. That claim, too, is debatable since Rabbi Reuven was also a *tanna*.

[359] In the ספר סדר הדורות, חלק ב' (סדר תנאים ואמוראים), אות ר', Rabbi Yehiel ben Solomon Heilprin (1660-1746) makes brief reference to the same tradition, but there רצה שיהרגהו במקום ר' יהודה בן בבא – "[Rabbi Reuven] wanted to be killed in lieu of Rabbi Yehudah ben Baba." The version of the עשרה הרוגי מלכות published by Dr. Aaron Jellinek in בית מדרש (Jerusalem: Bamberger & Wahrmann, 1938), vol. 6, p. 35, also records the incident. There, too, the two involved are Rabbi Reuven and Rabbi Yehudah ben Baba. In that version, Rabbi Reuven asks of Rabbi Yehudah: רצונך שאמות אני תחתיך ותנצל אתה – "Do you wish that I should die instead of you, and you be saved?"

[360] Of course, the *Yad Eliyahu* barely mentions the *Sefer Hasidim*, and it would be an error to conclude that this claim of the *Ziz Eliezer* constitutes any direct refutation of him.

his also espoused the same view, carrying it even further than does the *Yad Eliyahu*. Rabbi Jacob Emden (1697-1776) also quotes[361] as law the passage from *Sefer Hasidim* which affirms the mitzvah of sacrificing oneself for another of greater status. Even more stunning, however, is the extrapolation from it made by Emden. He wrote:[362]

גם נראה פשוט שאין אדם רשאי למסור עצמו להריגה להציל חברו מרצון פשוט ומאהבה שאינה תלויה בדבר, אם אינו ברור שחברו תלמיד חכם כשר וצדיק יותר ממנו או בשביל אביו ורבו דאי לא הכי ודאי אמרינן מאי חזית דדמא דידיה סומק מדידך. ולפיכך אפי' בנו יחידו אשר אהב אינו יכול להציל באופן זה אם לא שהאב זקן שאי אפשר לו לקיים עוד מצות פרו ורבו, בזה נרא' להקל כשהבן אדם כשר לפחות, אפי' אינו גדול כמותו ולא ממלא את מקומו, או שהוא ילד שעדיין לא התנכר במעלליו, ועדיין צריך עיון.

> It is very clear that one is not allowed to sacrifice himself out of pure good will and selfless love in order to save the life of another, except if it is certain that the other is a scholar who is more worthy and righteous than he, or for one's father or teacher. Except for such cases, we claim, "Why do you think his blood is sweeter than yours." Therefore, one cannot sacrifice himself thus even for his dearly beloved son, except if the father is old and no longer capable of fulfilling the commandment to procreate. In that case one can be lenient, provided the son is at least worthy, even if not as great as he himself is and not his replacement; or, if the son is yet young, not yet having established alienating behaviors. Still, the matter requires investigation.

Emden extrapolates from the principle of the *Sefer Hasidim* in a way that no one else had. Not only may one sacrifice himself for an actual scholar, one may do so also for one who is owed honor by him, namely, his father. One may not do so for his son, however, except if one has reached the stage of his life that it seems clear that the life of his son will be "more useful and productive" than his own. Even then he may do it only if the son is at least minimally worthy. Finally, he may sacrifice himself for his son who is so young that judgments of his character and worthiness cannot yet be made. Having made the extrapolations, Emden ends with a cautionary note. That note is sufficient for the *Ziz Eliezer* to claim that one should not act on the view of the מגדל עוז. In the absence of support from other poskim, and in light of Emden's own doubts, his words should not be implemented למעשה, lest one find himself in violation of the biblical prohibition ונשמרתם מאד לנפשותיכם because he has acted in accordance with an unsupported view.

Finally, the *Ziz Eliezer* objects to the conclusions of the *Yad Eliyahu* because he believes that he never saw the words of the Radbaz. Had Rabbi Eliyahu ben Samuel seen the words of the Radbaz, who so clearly and compellingly argued against any obligation to endanger oneself for the benefit of another without any mention whatsoever of distinctions between statuses as a factor, he surely would not have decided as he did. The most use that one should make of the view of the *Yad Eliyahu* is as support in cir-

---

[361] ספר בירת מגדל עוז, אבן בוחן, פנה א', אות ע"ח. Remember, too, that it was Emden to whom we referred above in n. 249, who claimed that one need not even endure extreme pain for the benefit of another. That makes it all the more striking that he allows the actual sacrifice of one's life for a sage.

[362] Ibid., אות פ"ה.

cumstances when the doctors are convinced anyway that the level of danger to the donor is very minimal.

At the other end of the spectrum, Rabbi Menashe Klein finds the argument of the *Yad Eliyahu* very convincing. As he puts it:[363] ע"ש באריכות גדולה מה שהקיף העניינים מכל הצדדים ולא השאיר מה שראוי להתגדר בו כלל – "See [how the *Yad Eliyahu*] dealt at length with all the pertinent matters from every angle, and left no stone unturned and requiring further comment." What's more, Rabbi Klein immediately proceeds to refer to the Radbaz, seeing no inherent conflict between the two.

Finally, Prof. Abraham Sofer Abraham quotes a private communication to him from Rabbi Joshua Isaiah Neubirt:[364] היום אנו נוהגים כהרדב"ז גם כשהמציל והניצל שוים – "Today we follow the view of the Radbaz even when the potential saver and the one in need of saving are equal." That is, we are not concerned with matters of status in terms of permissibility or prohibition to donate.

We began this section with the assertion that we must undertake an analysis of the issue of self-endangerment in halakhah. We have been engaged in that enterprise until now. We have now reached the end of our analysis of texts – talmudic, medieval, and modern – that impinge on the subject. Though we have provided summaries periodically throughout, it is appropriate to summarize once again now that we have reached the end.

None of the authoritative codes contains a clear requirement to put oneself in danger, even potential, for the sake of another. There are, however, references in commentators to the codes to a passage of Yerushalmi which does require it. We undertook discussion of a responsum of Rabbi Ya'ir Bacharach which sought basis for the Yerushalmi view in Bavli Bava Metzia 82a. Our analysis, during the course of which we first made mention of the *Yad Eliyahu*, led us to conclude that Bacharach's understanding of the passage, though possible, was hardly conclusive. Indeed, we quoted others who used the very same passage to prove the opposite, namely, that Bava Metzia proves that the Bavli disagrees with the Yerushalmi. At a minimum, the passage remains inconclusive.

Thereafter, we analyzed passages from Yoma 85a and b, the Yerushalmi at the end of chapter eight of Terumot, Niddah 61a, Sanhedrin 73a, Nedarim 80b and 81a, Berakhot 33a, and several codified statements of Maimonides. These passages were quoted principally because they have been used by various poskim to prove that the Bavli disagreed (or agreed) with the Yerushalmi. In the course of analysis we affirmed that none of the passages was conclusive, one way or the other. The passage from Sanhedrin did seem to be very strong evidence that the Bavli disagreed with the Yerushalmi, though even it was not conclusive. We noted that the Yerushalmi itself goes unidentified by the early authorities, and that its identification by the *Yad Eliyahu* seems to be universally accepted thereafter as the source of the reference of the early authorities. The Yerushalmi itself was inconclusive upon analysis, and could cogently be argued to affirm that self-endangerment was not a legal requirement, but an act of piety. It could be that those codifiers who actually knew the Yerushalmi passage may have decided that it did not mandate such a requirement, and that is why they did not codify such a view. For whatever reason, the vast majority of poskim do not include any requirement to put oneself in danger for the sake of another, and many include specific statements contending that one ought not to do so. We conclude that it is impossible to find sufficient talmudic evidence for such a far reaching requirement that would warrant positing it as an halakhic requirement.

---

[363] See above, n. 356.

[364] המעין, ניסן תשמ"ה, p. 25.

Our analysis then turned to two responsa of the Radbaz, with which we dealt at length. His first responsum was a reaction to a decision of Rabbi Menahem Recanati which mandated that one must allow the removal of a non-life-threatening limb in order to save the life of another. The Radbaz presented strong arguments against Recanati's claim, and concluded with a three-tiered answer to our question: (1) There is no legal requirement to sacrifice a limb for the benefit of another. (2) Sacrificing such a limb would be an act of great piety and highly praiseworthy, if its severance did not confront one with significant threat to life. (3) If the removal of the limb would endanger one significantly, agreeing to have it removed would be the act of a "foolish saint," and forbidden.

The second responsum of the Radbaz, which makes reference to the Yerushalmi, posits that it is mandatory to put oneself in jeopardy for the benefit of another, provided that the chances are less than fifty percent that the potential danger will be actualized. We rejected the claim that the second responsum merely explains the view of Maimonides, but not of the Radbaz himself, and the claim that one or the other of the responsa retracts the Radbaz's earlier view. We entertained the view that the second responsum clarifies the first. That view allowed us a fairly clear definition of when one would be considered a חסיד שוטה, but left us in a real quandry over how to define the act as מדת חסידות. If the fifty percent level is the divide between mandatory and "foolish piety," where is the domain of מדת חסידות? Ultimately, therefore, we preferred the view that the two responsa run on parallel tracks. The first, dealing with the sacrifice of limbs, is as we have summarized. The second mandates self-endangerment when the risk is lower than fifty percent in cases where the risk to the saver does not involve threat to his limbs, and is not permanent and continuing, but passes when the act of saving is over. This resolution to the contradiction between the teshuvot allows us a fairly clear definition of מדת חסידות and חסיד שוטה in the first responsum: one's act is one of piety when, under usual conditions, one endures סכנת אבר but not ספק סכנת נפשות; and one's act is that of a חסיד שוטה when, under usual conditions, one endures significant ספק סכנת נפשות.

Finally, we turned again to the *Yad Eliyahu* who also posits a three-tiered view: (1) that if persons are of equal status, or if the potential saver is of higher status than the person to be saved, it is forbidden to endanger oneself for the benefit of the other, and the categories of "doubtful" and "certain" are irrelevant; (2) that if the saver is of lower status than the person to be saved, it is permissible to endanger oneself as an act of piety, but not mandatory; and (3), if the person to be saved is the parent or teacher of the saving party, the act of piety is in the category of mitzvah, though still not obligatory. We noted that his view is not without talmudic basis, and that it finds echoes in the decisions of others, both earlier than he and later than he. We affirmed that some of these other views, as, for example, the *Sefer Hasidim*, need not be understood to imply the same position as the *Yad Eliyahu*. We quoted an *obiter dictum* of Rabbi Joshua Isaiah Neubirt to the effect that today we follow the Radbaz, even in cases where the parties are of equal status. Beyond that, it should be noted that far more poskim affirm the position of the Radbaz than affirm the view of the *Yad Eliyahu*. We, therefore, reject the stringencies of the *Yad Eliyahu*, and posit that donation is an act of piety under the situations stipulated by the Radbaz no matter what the status of the two parties; and accept the leniencies of the *Yad Eliyahu* in defining as a mitzvah certain acts of donation to one's parent, teacher, or child (following the extrapolation of Rabbi Jacob Emden).[365]

---

[365] It must be as clear as possible that we accept only that such donation would be a mitzvah. We do not intend to intimate that one may literally cause his or her own death through donation to parent, teacher or child. Even if we were inclined (and we are not so inclined) to go that far, no physician could currently perform such surgery without becoming liable for prosecution for murder.

We turn our attention now from the theoretical to the practical. Just what danger is involved in the donation of a kidney from a live donor? It is important for us to deal with this issue in order to determine whether such donations should be considered piety or foolishness, and to guide us in determining the extent to which we should encourage or discourage those who come to us for consultation on this matter.

Kidney transplantation is not particularly new, as far as transplantations are concerned. There were Russian experiments as early as 1936, French in the 1940s, and American beginning in the 1950s. At the present time, kidney transplantation from live donors is considered virtually medically routine. In 1988 there were 8,831 kidney transplants reported to UNOS (United Network for Organ Sharing), and 10,204 reported in 1996. The increased number derives mainly from the increase in donations from live donors, from 1,812 to 3,149 during the same period.

The most current statistics on one-year survival and projected ten-year survival reveal the following: when the donor is an HLA-identical[366] living sibling, the one-year survival rate is 96%, and the projected ten-year survival rate is 73%; when the donor is an HLA-mismatched living donor, those figures become 91% and 56%. Compare these figures to those for cadaver donors. In that category, when the cadaver donors were HLA-matched, the percentages were 89 and 55, comparable to those for *HLA-mismatched living* donors. For cadaver donors that were not HLA-matched, the figures drop to 82% and 39%.[367] The differences remain striking even at the three-year survival rate which, for recipients of live kidney donations is 90%, while for cadaver kidney recipients is 80%.[368] All studies show that survival rates for kidney donation from live related donors is higher than for dialysis and cadaver donations, and related donors are still preferred over unrelated donors.[369]

In terms of the danger and risks undertaken by the donor, we note the following. Immediate post-operative (usually called now "perioperative") mortality rates for the donor are very low, under 0.03%.[370] Immediate medical complications following removal of the live donor kidney fluctuate between 15% and 47%, mainly mild and passing, with 2.5% being serious.[371] In the study referred to in footnote 370, which is based on the 920 kidney transplants performed at the University of Minnesota between January 1, 1988, and December 31, 1995, from live donors, the overall complication rate was 8.2%, with only 0.2% considered to be serious. In that study, most donors were discharged from the hospital in fewer than five days, and only 4% of the donors expressed dissatisfaction and regret at having been a donor. Long term medical complications are always more difficult to measure, and there are not yet as many studies. One study did show that 10% to 20% of donors develop mild hypertension, and about 33% develop proteinuria (loss of protein in the urine). Some believe that these findings are directly related to the earlier kidney donation which causes some type of long term damage to the remaining kidney.[372] Others dis-

---

[366] The abbreviation stands for Human Leukocyte Antigens, and refers to a test of tissues for genetic compatibility.

[367] See J. Michael Cecka and Paul I. Terasaki, eds., *Clinical Transplants 1997* (Los Angeles: UCLA Tissue Typing Laboratory, 1998), ch. 1, pp. 1-2, 13-14.

[368] J. Krakauer et al., *New England Journal of Medicine* 308:1558, 1983.

[369] Greater success is being achieved in recent years with unrelated live donors when the patient preparation includes blood transfusions from the donor. See A.S. Levey et al., *New England Journal of Medicine* 314:914, 1986, and M. Evans, *Medical Ethics* 15:17, 1989.

[370] See ch. 22 of Cecka and Terasaki, above n. 367, p. 231. Note, however, that in the specific study from which the data of that chapter were drawn, the morbidity rate was zero.

[371] See A. Spital et al., *Archives of Internal Medicine* 146:1993, 1986.

[372] See R.M. Hakim, *Kidney International* 25:930, 1984.

pute that interpretation and believe that these after effects are a natural result of the aging process of the donor and have no relationship to the kidney donation.[373]

An additional factor which should be mentioned stems from the desirability of related donors as the best matches for kidney transplants. If the transplant is necessitated by a genetic or hereditary problem, the statistical probability is increased that the donor will himself develop the same problem at some later stage in his life. Rabbi Moshe Meiselman reports[374] having been asked about such a case in which the hereditary nature of the disease made it likely that donation of the kidney was likely to shorten the life of the donor by ten years.

The final potential additional danger, logically speaking, is the possibility that the kidney donor's remaining kidney will suffer a trauma or disease. Bleich reports[375] the Connecticut case of *Hart v. Brown*, in which the court accepted medical testimony to the effect that such danger is minimal, and that life insurance companies do not even rate such individuals higher than those with two kidneys. Bleich himself adds the phrase, "Perhaps overly optimistic," in his reporting of the medical testimony.

The facts and figures now presented make it clear that almost all kidney donations have a statistically high chance of prolonging the life of the recipient significantly. The dangers and risks to the donor, however, are neither negligible nor overwhelming, and include unknowns about which judgment is virtually impossible. Even according to the most demanding interpretation of the Radbaz — not the interpretation we have recommended — it is highly unlikely that kidney donation could be considered halakhically mandatory. The thrust of his second responsum seems to have mandated jeopardizing oneself for the benefit of another when the risk to the donor was less than fifty percent only in cases when the effectiveness of the intervention to save the person in need was certain. In the case of kidney donations, particularly to unrelated persons, the effectiveness is high, but certainly not certain.

It should be clear, therefore, that all common and usual kidney donations would surely be in the category of מדת חסידות, and should be encouraged and praised as the laudatory act they are. We must, however, walk the fine line between the just praise we lavish on those who are able and willing to undertake kidney donation, and couching that praise in a way that induces great guilt in those who are unwilling. It would be appropriate to utilize the view of the *Yad Eliyahu* and the extrapolations of Rabbi Jacob Emden especially when we discuss the possibility of donation from a relative.

Though we have argued the position that the donation cannot be compelled and that it does put one in potential jeopardy, סכנת אבר, and even ספק סכנת נפשות, we end this part of this section with the wise and sage counsel of Rabbi Moshe Ze'ev Ya'avetz, the *Agudat Ezov*, who wrote:[376]

> ומ"מ צריך לשקול העניין היטב אם יש בו ספק סכנה או לא, ולא לדקדק ביותר שמא יש סכנה, וכמ"ש (בב"מ לג ע"ש) כל המדקדק ומקיים בעצמו כך, סוף בא לידי כך.
>
> Nonetheless, it is mandatory to evaluate the matter with great care to determine whether or not there really is danger, and not to be

---

[373] See A. Spital, above, n. 371.

[374] הלכה ורפואה (ירושלים: מכון רגנשברג, תשמ"א), כרך ב', עמ' קי"ט.

[375] *Contemporary Halakhic Problems*, vol. 4, p. 291, and nn. 53, 109.

[376] P. 38b. See above, n. 244.

overly cautious [to decide in almost every case that] maybe there is danger. And that is what the Talmud (Bava Metzia 33a) cautions against when it says that one who is overly punctilious in fulfilling [the law that one's own money takes precedence over the money of others] is destined to end up in the state of need.

The same idea was also expressed by Rabbi Yehiel Epstein, with an ending more in tune with modern sensibilities:[377]

> בש"ס שלנו מוכח שאינו חייב להכניס את עצמו [לספק סכנה], ומיהו הכל לפי הענין, ויש לשקול הענין בפלס ולא לשמור את עצמו יותר מדאי ובזה נאמר[378] "ושם [דרך] אראנו בישע אלקים," זהו ששם אורחותיו, וכל המקיים נפש אחד מישראל כאלו קיים קיים עולם מלא.

> It is clear from the Bavli that one is not obligated to put himself in potential danger. Nonetheless, everything depends on circumstances. It is essential to weigh each situation carefully, and not to be overly cautious. And about such matters is it said:[379] "To one who appraises [his path], I will show the salvation of the Lord." And this [careful, but not over zealous weighing] is the meaning of "appraising one's path." And one who saves a Jewish life is as though he had saved an entire world.

We affirmed above[380] that whatever conclusion would apply to kidney donation would also apply to the donation of liver parts. It should be pointed out, however, the donation of liver parts is much newer medically and there have not been nearly as many attempts as there have been for kidney donations. The need for the development of this technology is clear: as of July 1999, there were 13,519 people awaiting liver transplants in the United States. In 1998, only 4,450 liver transplants were performed, and more than 1,125 people died waiting for a liver. So, if it were possible to receive one of the lobes of the liver of a live donor, rather than having to wait for the death of a donor, and if the miraculous ability of the liver to regenerate itself continues unabated, the problem of the shortage of available livers could be virtually eliminated. Nonetheless, clear caution is to be advised. Surgeons report that the operation is technically difficult, because blood vessels and bile ducts must be carefully divided between the donor and the recipient. This same issue does not exist in kidney donation, and its existence puts the liver part donor at considerably higher risk than the kidney donor. Even more, until recently almost all such donations were from an adult to a child, because such an operation would only require removal of about fifteen to twenty percent of the adult's liver. In adult-adult donation, however, it may be necessary to remove as much as sixty percent of the donor's liver, the entire right lobe, for the operation to be effective for the recipient. The medical world, as yet, has little experience with this, and that makes the dangers to the donor greater.

Regrettably, there are not yet, at least to the best of my knowledge, enough data on this matter to allow us to determine whether agreeing to donate would be an act of מדת חסידות, or the act of a חסיד שוטה. This practical caveat is therefore included in this

---

[377] Arukh ha-Shulhan, H.M. 426:4.

[378] תהילים נ:כ"ג, על פי מועד קטן ה סע"א, על סמך משחק מלים בין "ושם" (בנקודה בצד שמאל) ו"שם" (נקודה בצד ימין).

[379] Ps. 50:23, as understood by Mo'ed Katan 5a, with a play on words between *ve-sam* and *ve-sham*.

[380] Above, p. 212.

section, even though the halakhic issues involved in liver part donation are the same as in kidney donation.[381]

We have dealt above[382] with the question of blood and bone marrow donation for compensation, and need not repeat all of the discussion again. Suffice it to say that even those who would forbid donation of blood to a bank because of חבלה, would have to permit חבלה for the donation of a kidney, since kidneys are not removed from live donors except for an actual recipient – חולה לפנינו – and, thus, fall under the category of פקוח נפש. Once we accept the premise that kidney donation is not entirely forbidden on grounds of self-endangerment, we must confront head on the question of whether donation for compensation changes our view of the permissibility of the donation.

(N.B. – It is our intent to deal with compensation for organ donation from a live donor from a halakhic perspective. There is always the theoretical possibility that halakhah may permit what דינא דמלכותא may forbid. Obviously, Jews do not have the legal right to violate a prohibition of civil law because Jewish law permits the act forbidden by civil law. On the other hand, if Jewish law forbids what דינא דמלכותא permits, Jews have no halakhic right to violate the halakhic prohibition on the grounds that civil law permits it.)

I do not have statistics on this matter, but am prepared to assume that the issue of compensation for donation is very uncommon when the case is of donation from related donors. However, with the increased success in transplants from live, unrelated donors, the problem will be more acute. That is particularly true considering the intense shortage of kidneys available for transplantation. People in dire financial straits, convinced that the donation will not place them in significant danger, may consider donation entirely unobjectioable, and perhaps even a mitzvah. People in need of a kidney, knowing that they are likely to die without a transplant, may consider it unobjectionable to offer money for a kidney, particularly when the party to whom the money would accrue is in financial need.

Rabbi Isaac Zilberstein, of B'nei Berak, wrote the following simple sentence in the context of a more complicated issue that he was discussing:[383] ישנם המציעים לחולי כליות את כליתם למכירה, ונראה שאין בזה איסור חבלה והדבר מותר – "There are those who offer their kidney for sale to someone with renal disease. It seems that this does not fall under the prohibition of self-injury, and is permissible." In the previous sentence he had made clear that he was speaking of people in dire financial straits, who saw no way to extricate themselves from their financial problems except through sale of their organs.

Professor Abraham Sofer Abraham writes at greater length:[384]

> מה יהיה הדין לגבי אדם שמוכן, מתוך בריאות שלמה, לתרום כליה אחת לחולה הזקוק להשתלת כליה, אך דורש עבור הכליה סכום כסף. ישנה אפשרות שהוא מנהל משא ומתן ישירות עם החולה או עם סוכן שמטפל בענין. האם הדבר מותר או אסור כשיוצאים מהנחה שתרומת כליה לא מהוה אלא סכנה קטנה... ו[ו]אדם שעושה את זה כדי להציל נפש קרובו ולשם שמים חסיד יקרא, אך כמובן אין לחייב אותו מן הדין לעשות את זאת.

---

[381] Much of the information for these paragraphs about liver part donation came from an article in the 3 Aug. 1999 edition of the *International Herald Tribune*, based on an article by Denise Grady of the *New York Times* Service.

[382] Pp. 253-254.

[383] זכרון ישעיהו: ורפא ירפא – לדמותו של רופא חרדי, לזכרו של הר"ר ד"ר ישעיהו לוי זצ"ל, 1989, p. 32.

[384] נשמת אברהם (ירושלים: המכון ע"ש ד"ר פלק שלזינגר, תשנ"ג, הדפסה שניה מתוקנת), כרך ד', חשן משפט סי' ת"כ, ס"ק א', עמ' רי"א-רי"ב.

What would be the law regarding a completely healthy person who is prepared to donate a kidney to a sick person in need of a kidney transplant, but who demands compensation for the kidney? This can occur either through direct negotiation between him and the sick person, or via a middleman who handles such matters. Is it permissible or forbidden, presuming that the donation is only minimally dangerous...and that a person who did the same for the benefit of a sick relative, and acting for the sake of heaven, would be considered pious, though there is no obligation on his part to donate.

Here is the issue, in all of its initial complexity. The act in question is identical to an act about which we have already made a praiseworthy judgment. We have decided that the medical risks do not prohibit the act, while we affirm that the halakhah also does not demand the act. The only difference between the two acts is that one is carried out on behalf of the relative of the donor, and without compensation; and the other is carried out for a stranger, and with compensation. Does that difference change the halakhah?

Prof. Sofer Abraham continues:

ואין לומר שהתורם הזה, במקום לעשות מצוה גדולה עד מאד של הצלת נפש מישראל עושה אדרבה דבר מגונה. כי אם אמנם אין עליו שום חיוב לתרום כליתו להציל את הזולת, אם בכל זאת הוא עושה את זה, מצוה גדולה יחשב לו. ויש לעיין אם עושה את זה רק משום בצע כסף, האם יש כאן שום מעשה מצוה או אדרבה, מכיון שאינו מכוין למצוה יש לדון אם אין כאן איסור משום חבלה.... אך אם הוא עצמו זקוק לכסף כדי להציל את קרובו הנמצא במצב של פקוח נפש (וזקוק לטיפול מסויים הכרוך בהוצאות כספיות), יתכן שעושה מצוה כפולה, ומותר לו לתרום את כליתו עבור תשלום, כי מאי נפקא מינה אם הוא תורם את כליתו ורק מציל חולה באופן ישיר, או גם מציל חולה עם הכסף שהוא מקבל כתשלום עבור כליתו.

One cannot claim that this donor, instead of performing a very great mitzvah of saving the life of another Jew, is, to the contrary, guilty of an unseemly act. For if, in fact, he is under no obligation to donate his kidney to save another, and he does so nonetheless, it must be considered a great mitzvah for him. What needs to be investigated is whether one who does the same from pure avarice is also considered to have performed a mitzvah; or whether, to the contrary, he is in violation of the prohibition against self-injury because there was no intention on his part to perform a mitzvah....But if the donor needs money in order to pay for the medical treatment of a dangerously ill relative of his [who needs a certain expensive treatment], it is probable that his act of donation constitutes a double mitzvah, and it is permissible for him to donate his kidney for compensation. For what difference could it make [legally] if he donates his kidney for the exclusive purpose of directly saving another, or he also saves yet another party with the money he receives in compensation for his kidney.

Professor Sofer Abraham begins his answer: Since there is no legal obligation to donate, a donation must be considered an act of kindness. Even if the donor demands payment for his kidney, part of his desire is to save the life of another. That cannot be considered an unworthy or blameworthy act.[385] Indeed, one can posit a situation in which demanding payment for a kidney may constitute a double mitzvah. If one donates for pay in order to use the proceeds for the medical expenses of one's relative, one saves two lives. His act is no less praiseworthy for having received the compensation than if he had donated exclusively to save the life of the kidney recipient.

Prof. Sofer Abraham continues:

> וכתב לי הגרש"ז אויערבאך שליט"א: בנדון זה שלפנינו נראה שגם אם התורם הוא עני או שרוצה בכך לפרוע חובותיו, אך הואיל ויודע שמציל בכך נפש מישראל ודאי קעביד מצוה אע"ג שבשביל הצלה בלבד לא היה תורם, עכ"ל.... ולגבי הסרסור שמתווך, תמורת אחוזים, בין החולה הזקוק להשתלה ובין התורם, אמר לי הגרש"ז אויערבאך שליט"א שגם מותר לכתחילה ואין בזה שום מעשה מגונה או עבירה, כי את כספו הוא מקבל עבור המאמץ והטרחה למצוא ולתאם בין התורם ובין המקבל האבר, עכ"ד. ולכאורה אין הבדל בין זה לבין מרכז או משרד שישולח רופא תורן, בכל שעות היממה, לבית החולה כדי להצילו ומקבל תשלום עבור השרות.

> And Rabbi Shlomo Zalman Auerbach wrote to me: "In the matter before us it seems that even if the donor is a poor person or wants to pay off his debts, he has still performed a mitzvah since he knows that his act of donation will save a life, even though he would not have donated for that reason exclusively."...And regarding the broker who serves as a middleman between the sick person in need of a transplant and the donor, in exchange for a percentage, Rabbi Auerbach told me that his deeds are permissible *ab initio*, and entail no transgression or unseemly act, since he receives his payment in exchange for his efforts and labor to find and co-ordinate between the donor and the recipient. [This is what he told me.] And there seems to be no difference between this [brokering] and a center or office which provides and sends on-duty physicians on house calls at any hour of the day to provide medical services, and receives a fee for this service.

Relying on communications from Rabbi Shlomo Zalman Auerbach, Prof. Sofer Abraham completes his answer. Whatever the motivation of the donor, he knows that his donation will be used to save a life. That knowledge cannot be separated off from any assessment of the donor's act. Even if his exclusive motivations were personal financial ones, the act of donation for compensation is not illegal or even blameworthy. Even the broker is not guilty of any illegal or immoral act. He is providing a service for a fee, just as many others provide such services. He is not compelling the donor to donate, but rather serving as a go-between to co-ordinate between the two parties.

There is both logic and reason to the line of reasoning offered by Sofer Abraham/Auerbach. If the level of danger in kidney donation is low enough to make it permissible in the first place, why should motivations short of pure and selfless altruism on the part of the donor impel us to forbid him from putting himself in an acceptable level of danger? It is hard to have it both ways. We cannot easily justify the danger as acceptable when, in our opinion, the motivation of the donor is also acceptable; and judge the danger as unacceptable when, in our opinion, the motivation of the donor is unacceptable. By what logic do

---

[385] See, however, the comments of Rabbis Sternbuch and Zorger, quoted above, p. 254.

we reach the conclusion that one's desire to free oneself from terrible financial burdens is less defensible a justification to enter into acceptable ranges of danger that result in saving the life of another than is the pure desire to save the life of another? Perhaps Rabbi Sternbuch is correct that the Divine reward for the selfless act is greater, but that alone does not constitute grounds for forbidding the act itself.[386]

Earlier on,[387] we quoted from Rabbi Moshe Ze'ev Zorger a distinction between injuries which are מעלה ארוכה – "heal themselves" – and those which are not. Rabbi Zorger permitted injury to self healing organs for money, but not to organs which do not heal themselves. His own examples of organs which do not heal themselves were the amputation of an arm or a leg. Obviously, therefore, he could not have meant that the open wound remains forever open, because there is some closing of the wound after the removal of an arm or leg. What he appears to mean is that it is forbidden to remove an organ which is not self replacing, if the motivation to remove it is financial. Thus, one could receive compensation for blood and bone marrow because they replenish themselves; but one could not receive compensation for a kidney because it does not grow back, and one is not allowed to remove it for financial reasons.

If we adopt the view of Rabbi Zorger, it appears to allow us grudgingly to permit compensation for blood and bone marrow donation, but to forbid it for kidney donation. Of course, we must remember that Rabbi Zorger was not talking about kidneys in his responsum, and it is our responsibility to judge whether he would have included them with arms and legs, or with blood and bone marrow.

There is, medically speaking, a vast difference between removing an arm or leg, and removing a kidney. The removal of the former affects the person from then on. One may learn to compensate for the absence of an arm or leg, but one does not function identically with one arm or leg as one would with two. There will always remain things that one could do when he had both arms or legs that one cannot do now. On some level, his functioning is adversely affected by the removal of the arm or leg. This is not the case with the removal of a kidney. The claim of the doctors is that one will not notice its absence at all. No function of the body will be adversely affected. The kidney will not replace itself, but its absence will be irrelevant, so long as the patient does not suffer any of the immediate or possible long term after effects of the surgery, and so long as the remaining kidney remains healthy. In truth, then, even for Rabbi Zorger, the removal of the kidney should be considered more comparable to the removal of blood and bone marrow than to the removal of an arm or leg.

This conclusion, then, leaves us where we were before we reintroduced Rabbi Zorger's distinction between מעלה ארוכה and not מעלה ארוכה. It leaves us with the conclusion that there is no halakhic reason to forbid kidney donation for compensation, no matter how much our hearts may incline us otherwise.[388] That, too, was the conclusion

---

[386] The conclusion of Prof. Sofer Abraham's position is not relevant to our analysis, but worthy of being quoted: "What needs to be looked into is a community that permits a person to reach such a low level in terms of his debts, and certainly in terms of his inability to pay for needed, though costly, medical treatment, that he finds no alternative solution to his problem than to sell an organ in order to earn enough money for livelihood or medical care."

[387] P. 252.

[388] Rabbi Mordecai Halperin in an article in *Assia* 45-46 (Tevet 5749): pp. 54-55, attempts to make two further halakhic arguments to prohibit donation of kidneys for compensation. He contends that the financial pressure and need which ultimately motivate donors for compensation prevent complete informed consent and willingness (גמירות דעת). It is risky, to say the least, to begin to posit that actions done out of financial need can be invalidated in halakhah, because they lack these ingredients. Halperin is forced to untenable considerations such as these because he believes that there is no longer authority to make תקנות and גזרות which will be universally authoritative among Jews. Even by his reasoning, though, each מרא דאתרא still

drawn by Rabbi Shaul Israeli[389] and Rabbi Israel Meir Lau.[390]

The question is, why do our hearts incline us otherwise? If kidneys are like blood and bone marrow halakhically, why do we accept compensation for blood donation with relative equanimity, yet recoil from the idea of compensation for kidney donation? We quote, in translation, from the words of Rabbi Abraham Steinberg:[391]

> The matter of commerce in organs is a very difficult question. There are numerous possibilities for receiving compensation for the donation of organs: (1) receipt of compensation from another living person, when the transplant is intended to be carried out in the life of both of them; (2) receipt of compensation by one person from another, when the transfer of the organ will be done after the death of the organ owner; (3) receipt of compensation by members of the family of a deceased person in exchange for their agreement to transfer the organ;[392] (4) receipt of compensation by the organ owner during his life, or by his family after his death, from an organization or state, in exchange for their agreement to donate the organs; and, (5) the purchase of organs by people in need of transplants in order to push them to the head of the line.
>
> Most ethicists and doctors who perform transplants oppose all commerce in organs in exchange for compensation, other benefits, political pressure, etc., and prefer that all selection be made on a purely medical basis of preference. [They prefer this] since there is a real danger that there might be created a medicine that is not even-handed, such that the rich will receive preferential treatment in receiving organs; and the poor will not only not receive organs, they will become a source for the acquiring of organs as a result of financial pressure. Indeed, this very thing has happened in reality in poor countries, like India and states in South America, where living people have offered to donate their organs [on which life depends] in exchange for money. Beyond that, there are medical centers which suggest transplants for citizens of other countries in exchange for compensation, or which export organs to citizens of other countries in exchange for money, thus giving citizens of other countries preference over their own citizens.

---

possesses the authority to make such enactments for his community. Thus, even if he were correct that we cannot make a גזרה, it would be better to suggest that each מרא דאתרא make the necessary enactment than to argue on the basis of informed consent and גמירות דעת.

[389] See *Assia*, vol. 15:3-4, nos. 57-58 (Kislev 5757): p. 8.

[390] See *Tehumin* (Alon Shevut: Tzomet, 5758), vol. 18, pp. 125-138.

[391] אנציקלופדיה הלכתית רפואית (ירושלים: המכון ע"ש פלק שלזינגר, 1991), כרך ב', עמ' 239–240.

[392] This was forbidden by Rabbi Shlomo Zalman Auerbach because the receipt of money by the family would constitute הנאה מן המת. He allowed it when the money received would be used for payment of medical treatment by another family member (see his notes to *Nishmat Avraham*, vol. 4, Hoshen Mishpat 420:2). It was also forbidden by Rabbi Eliahu Bakshi-Doron, on the grounds that the family of the deceased has only an obligation to bury, but have no proprietary rights to organs or limbs of the deceased relative (see *Torah she-be-al Peh*, vol. 38, 5752). Rabbi Eliezer Waldenberg, however, permitted it on the grounds that it is not הנאה מן המת, relying on the view of the *Imrei Yosher* (Rabbi Mordecai Arik), pt. 2, no. 22, that when one performs a mitzvah with something that would otherwise be אסור בהנאה, one is not liable for profiting from איסורי הנאה.

Many recoil at the idea of compensation for organs because it conjures up images of the exploitation of the underprivileged,[393] of a reversal of whatever small progress has been made toward universal medical rights and treatment. Compensation for organ donation would be a step backward in its potential consequences. We have become too civilized to tolerate the use of one's body parts as an economic commodity. Such use diminishes the צלם אלקים of humans. All of this is true! Commerce in body parts could throw us back to earlier standards of ethics that we believe we have long outgrown, and the return of which we could not tolerate.

Let us be clear and honest with ourselves. We oppose organ donations for compensation because we cannot devise a reasonable and enforceable method to allow it in a controlled and acceptable way, even if we think there could even be a controlled and acceptable way.[394] We fear, and not without reason, that the slightest breach in the wall will bring a flood of uncontrollable activities that will make humans into mere commodities, restoring a medieval standard of conduct in which the value of human life will be diminished because it will become an economic commodity to be bought and sold on the open (and not so open) market.

In halakhic terms and categories, we need to make a גזרה that forbids the permissible. We would forbid all commerce in organs by halakhic decree, in order to put up a protective fence against human abuse of the limits of what might be acceptable. We should do this, but with full knowledge of what we are doing. We, who are so eager always to remember that "Whoever saves one life is as though he saved the entire world," will make a decree that will make that impossible in certain circumstances when there would be no technical halakhic objection. We must at least acknowledge that we will allow people to die when they might live, in order to prevent abuses that we will not be able to control. And we should not delude ourselves into thinking that this will be an infrequent occurrence. As the medical potential for successful transplantation of kidneys from unrelated donors increases, the impetus to purchase such a kidney from a donor willing to sell will be very great. We are making the difficult judgment that the צלם אלקים of the potential donor is safeguarded more by refusing to allow him to benefit from the money which he might earn, than by allowing him to improve his life through the sale of an organ, the loss of which is not likely to cause him any long term debilitation of any kind. Our imposition of this judgment not only leaves the potential donor in no less financial need than he was before, it probably will often condemn the intended recipient to death.

We ought to take the step of making such a גזרה with full knowledge of its consequences, both positive and negative. And though we make it, we should not be too quick to judge the contrary view as totally indefensible and unreasonable.

Once we have affirmed that kidney donation is permissible as an act of piety, but not as a mandatory act, there are conflicts of values and interests that can arise. It is not our intention to deal with these at length, but to make a few comments.

---

[393] It is fascinating to note that Rabbi Judah HaHasid used the same thesis to explain the Torah's prohibition against remarrying one's divorced wife if she has been married subsequently. In his remarks to the end of Parashat Ki Teze (יצחק שמשון לנגה, טעמי מסורת המקרא לר' יהודה החסיד [ירושלים, תשמ"א]) he says that "if it were permissible, the rich would hire the poor to divorce their own wives so that the rich could marry them for their pleasure, and when they were sated, they would divorce them and they would return to their original husbands."

[394] Rabbi Lau, in the article referred to above, n. 390, precisely makes the point that we should not mandate a prohibition against what is in fact lawful. We should, rather, make laws to prevent our worst fears from coming to pass.

It is clear that the objection of one's spouse or parents to one's fulfillment of a legal obligation is null and void, legally. The obligations of the law supersede the objections of spouses and parents. But what is the status of such objections regarding positive and praiseworthy acts which are not mandatory, but acts of מדת חסידות?

We referred above[395] to a comment by Rabbi Isaac Zilberstein, taken from the context of a more complex discussion. The subject of that discussion was our current question. The actual respondent in Rabbi Zilberstein's article was Rabbi Moshe Sternbuch, to whom the questions had been sent, after having been raised.

Regarding a conflict between the husband's desire to donate a kidney and his wife's opposition, Rabbi Sternbuch was inclined to allow the wife to have veto power. His considerations included, among others, that since there was some danger in the donation, both immediate and long term, especially the fear that something might happen to his one remaining kidney, the wife could claim that his act infringed on her rights. And since the act was one of piety but not obligation, her rights should predominate. After having formulated his response, Rabbi Sternbuch writes:[396]

> הצעתי את הדברים לפני מורי וחמי הגאון ר' יוסף שלום אלישיב שליט"א ולא הסכים להם: הוא סובר שאם תרומת הכליה תפגע בחיובי "עונה" אין הבעל רשאי להיות חסיד על חשבון אשתו ולקפח זכויותיה. כמו כן אם יפגע בפריה ורביה.... אבל כאשר מצות עונה ופריה ורביה לא יפגעו, אין די משקל בהתנגדות האשה מול הערך העליון של הצלת נפש.

> I presented my position to my master and father-in-law, Rabbi Yosef Shalom Elyashev, and he did not agree with my view: He claimed that if the donation of the kidney would interfere with the fulfillment of the obligation for conjugal relations, the husband would have no right to be a pious one at his wife's expense, infringing on her rights. And similarly if it would interfere with procreation. . . .But when these would not be affected, his wife's objection is insufficient to out-balance the supreme value of saving a life.

Rabbi Elyashev's remarks were accepted by Rabbi Sternbuch, who retracted his own view in favor of his father-in-laws's view. Indeed, Rabbi Elyashev's view seems completely on the mark. There is a potential conflict between the husband's desire to donate and his wife's rights. If there is a significant risk that those rights will be infringed upon, the act of piety is no longer so pious. Indeed, Rabbi Elyashev called it גזל – "robbery." But, in the kidney case, the evidence is great that the donation will not result in any infringement of the rights of his wife. It is not that her concerns are without any basis, but rather that her fears are not likely consequences of his act of donation. In such circumstances, his desire predominates, and his donation is permissible as an act of מדת חסידות. Since Rabbi Elyashev's reasoning is ultimately based on whether the rights of the wife would likely be infringed, that would clearly be the basic concern if the situation were reversed, too. Thus, it seems clear, that if it were the wife who wished to donate, and the husband who objected, his objection would not be sufficient to forbid her donation, since she would be able to fulfill all of her obligations after donation, and there would be no infringement of his rights.

The same type of conflict could arise between the desire of a child to donate and the wish of the child's parents that he or she not donate. The added wrinkle here is a

---

[395] N. 383.

[396] P. 32 in Rabbi Zilberstein's article.

specific commandment incumbent upon children to honor their parents. It is not simply a matter of infringement of their rights, as in the spouse case. In the parent case there is a specific duty of children to be obey their parents, so long as they do not order them to violate the law.

In dealing with this issue, Rabbi Sternbuch refers to a statement of the *Sefer Hasidim*[397] which forbids a child from continuing to observe voluntary fasts, because his parents object.[398] He refers, as well, to the claim of Rabbi Moshe Greenvald[399] that a son whose parents have ordered him not to immerse himself in any mikveh which is unheated must convince them to withdraw their objection, or else he may not violate their order.

But Rabbi Sternbuch's conclusion makes an important distinction:[400]

> מסתבר שאין להתחשב בהורים, כי רק מצוה שהיא ממדת חסידות אין לעבור על כבוד אב ואם לעשותה, מה שאין כן בעניננו שתרומת כליה מצוה גדולה מאד היא שכל המציל נפש אחת מישראל כאילו קיים עולם ומלואו, אלא שהחיוב הוא רק ממדת חסידות, כי אינו חייב לאבד אבר להצלת חברו, ודאי שמצוה גדולה זו דוחה כיבוד אב ואם.

> However, it stands to reason that the objection of the parents can be ignored [in the kidney case]. The only time the wishes of the parents cannot be ignored is when the mitzvah itself is only ממדת חסידות. But that is not the case in the matter of the kidney donation because it itself is a very great mitzvah, since whoever saves a Jewish life is considered as though he had saved an entire world. Only the obligation to donate the kidney is an act of piety, since nobody is legally obligated to forfeit a limb for the benefit of his fellow. In such circumstances, surely this great mitzvah supersedes the honor of parents.

The voluntary fasts of which the *Sefer Hasidim* spoke, and the immersion in the mikveh of which the ערוגת הבושם spoke, are very different from kidney donation. In the former two cases, the entire mitzvah is completely voluntary. There is no obligation of any kind to undertake voluntary fasts. There is no obligation of any kind for men to immerse themselves in the way that pious men often do, as a regular or daily act of sanctification. The fasting and the immersion are themselves "acts of piety," with no element of law whatsoever. The kidney case is very different. There is an actual legal obligation to save the life of another. That commandment is not an act of piety, but a legal mandate. There are limits, however, to how far one must go in fulfilling that commandment. An obligation to forfeit an organ is beyond the limit of requirement, and is permissible only as an act of piety. The underlying commandment which this act of piety fulfills, however, is not itself merely an act of piety, but a real commandment. Thus, concludes Rabbi Sternbuch, if one is motivated to act piously in the fulfillment of the mitzvah to save another person by donating a kidney, one's parents cannot prevent him from fulfilling the mitzvah because they object to his willingness to go further than the law requires.

---

[397] Margolioth ed., no. 340, p. 256.

[398] To show to what extent the mitzvah to honor parents goes, consider that in the case described by the *Sefer Hasidim* the child is undertaking these voluntary fasts as a method of convincing his parents to stop their own punishing voluntary fasts, which the child fears are too difficult on them. Nonetheless, the child is obligated to cease his own fasts because of parental objection, even though his desirable goal will remain unaccomplished.

[399] ערוגת הבושם, או"ח סי' י"ט.

[400] Zilberstein article, pp. 32-33.

The principles adduced by Rabbis Elyashev and Sternbuch seem very sound. They can serve us well as preliminary guidance in resolving conflicts that might arise between potential kidney donors and their spouses, parents, and children. And, since other relatives have even less of a claim against the potential donor, their objection, too, would be insufficient to forbid the donor from donating.

There is one further issue to be dealt with briefly. Since there are countries that are reported to be taking organs from prisoners against their will, our position should be clear and unambiguous. Prisoners are no less created in the image of God than anybody else, and their bodies and organs belong to the government no more than those of anyone else. Organs may not be taken from prisoners against their will.

What about suggesting kidney donation to a prisoner with either an explicit or implied promise that the donation will benefit the prisoner somehow? The following quotation, written about the same question regarding a suggestion to prisoners that they allow themselves to be used for medical experiments, speaks exactly to the issue:[101]

> העולה הן האמור עד כה הוא כי מותר לאסיר להתנדב לעריכת ניסויים ומחקרים רפואיים על גופו אך אסור לכפותו.... לכאורה מדובר באסיר הפועל בהתנדבות, אך עם זאת יתכן שהוא פועל מתוך אוירת לחץ ובמיוחד כשנאמר לו במפורש או ברמז שאם יסכים לעריכת הניסוי יזכה לשיפור בתנאיו, כגון סיכוי לשחרור מוקדם, ניכוי שליש ממאסרו כו'. היש בכך כפיה?... נר' כי רצוי להתרחק מכפיה, ולא להשיג הסכמת האסיר לעריכת ניסויים בגופו ובנפשו על ידי איום מפורש או נרמז כגון שחרור מוקדם וכדומה. יש להציג בפניו את חשיבות הניסויים על הסיכונים שבהם ולא לקשור אותם להקלות אחרות בתנאי המאסר. הוא, האסיר, יעשה את החשבון לעצמו, ואם בין היתר יחשוב שהדבר משתלם לו, אין בכך משום כפיה. ככל שהסיכון גדול יותר... יש להדגיש יותר את חומרת הסיכון.

> What follows from what we have said so far is that it is permissible for a prisoner to volunteer to be a subject of a medical experiment or research, but it is forbidden to compel him....Ostensibly, we are speaking of a prisoner who acts [completely] voluntarily. But, it is probable that[, in fact,] he is acting from an atmosphere of pressure, especially if he has been told either explicitly or implicitly that if he agrees to the experiment he will benefit from improved conditions, for example, a chance to be freed early, a one-third reduction in his term, etc. Does this constitute "compulsion?"...It is clear that it is desirable to refrain from [all] compulsion, and not to obtain the agreement of the prisoner for the experiments on his body or soul by means of either an explicit or implicit promise (like early freedom, etc.). We must present before him how important the experiments are, together with the dangers that might be involved, but make no connection to any other leniencies in the conditions of his imprisonment. He, the prisoner, will make his own calculation, and if, among other things, he thinks it might pay for him, that does not constitute "compulsion." The greater the danger...the more one must stress the seriousness of the danger.

---

[101] *Tehumin* (Alon Shevut: Tzomet, 5740), vol. 1, pp. 533-36. The author is listed as "the editor." The beginning of the volume lists only one editor, Dr. Itamar Warhaftig.

Prisoners may be treated no differently than any other person. Just as we would not remove the kidney from a living donor without the donor's consent, so, too, we may not remove a kidney from a prisoner without his or her consent. What's more, we have already made clear that we will refuse to allow any compensation for the donation of the kidney, and that refusal must apply to the prisoner as well as to everyone else.

The added wrinkle in the prisoner case is the possibility of subtle coercion. The reaction of the author above, whom we assume to be Dr. Itamar Warhaftig, seems to be exactly correct. Any type of subtle coercion which we can recognize as probably putting pressure on the prisoner to agree, is unacceptable. On the other hand, we do not wish to create a situation that would make it totally impossible for prisoners to be kidney donors, since we do not prohibit others from donating. A prisoner might well be motivated by exactly the same altruistic motives that we hope others will be motivated by. Prisoners, in fact, may have the additional motivation of a type of teshuvah for some earlier act. We may not link donation to any other benefit which we might have to offer, and we must give prisoners exactly the same honest evaluation of the risks involved in the procedure as we do all others, but once we have taken care to do these things, there is every reason to allow prisoners to become live kidney donors.

Conclusions

1. It is permissible for a live donor to donate a kidney, and under general circumstances the act is highly laudable. Indeed, it is considered by some to be even more than merely laudable when the donation is made to a parent, teacher, or child (in some instances), based on the view of the *Yad Eliyahu* and Jacob Emden.[402] Except for the possible exceptions intimated above, however, the act of donation is one of piety and not of legal obligation.

2. We affirm our commitment to a גזרה forbidding donation for compensation under all circumstances, even as we affirm that there is no compelling technical halakhic objection to such donation.

3. An objection to donation by the spouse, parents, or children of the potential donor is insufficient to forbid it.

4. Prisoners may be considered voluntary kidney donors when they have agreed to donate, have been given no explicit or implicit promise of improved conditions, are not being compensated, and have been apprised of the possible dangers and risks of the procedure.

---

[402] See above, pp. 301-303.

YD 336:1.1998

Responsibilities for the Provision of Health Care

Rabbis Elliot N. Dorff and Aaron L. Mackler

This paper was approved by the CJLS on September 9, 1998. The introduction and Part I were approved by a vote of sixteen in favor and four abstaining (16-0-4). Voting in favor: Rabbis Kassel Abelson, Elliot N. Dorff, Baruch Frydman-Kohl, Myron S. Geller, Nechama D. Goldberg, Arnold M. Goodman, Judah Kogen, Vernon H. Kurtz, Aaron L. Mackler, Lionel E. Moses, Mayer Rabinowitz, Avram Israel Reisner, Joel E. Rembaum, James S. Rosen, Elie Kaplan Spitz, and Gordon Tucker. Abstaining: Rabbis Jerome M. Epstein, Paul Plotkin, Joel Roth, and Gerald Zelizer.

Part II was passed by a vote of fourteen in favor and six abstaining (14-0-6). Voting in favor: Rabbis Kassel Abelson, Elliot N. Dorff, Myron S. Geller, Nechama D. Goldberg, Arnold M. Goodman, Judah Kogen, Vernon H. Kurtz, Aaron L. Mackler, Lionel E. Moses, Avram Israel Reisner, Joel E. Rembaum, James S. Rosen, Elie Kaplan Spitz, and Gordon Tucker. Abstaining: Rabbis Jerome M. Epstein, Baruch Frydman-Kohl, Paul Plotkin, Mayer Rabinowitz, Joel Roth, and Gerald Zelizer.

Part III was passed by a vote of twelve in favor, one opposed and seven abstaining (12-1-7). Voting in favor: Rabbis Kassel Abelson, Elliot N. Dorff, Jerome M. Epstein, Nechama D. Goldberg, Arnold M. Goodman, Judah Kogen, Vernon H. Kurtz, Aaron L. Mackler, Avram Israel Reisner, Joel E. Rembaum, James S. Rosen, and Elie Kaplan Spitz. Voting against: Rabbi Myron S. Geller. Abstaining: Rabbis Baruch Frydman-Kohl, Lionel E. Moses, Paul Plotkin, Mayer Rabinowitz, Joel Roth, Gordon Tucker, and Gerald Zelizer.

The Committee on Jewish Law and Standards of the Rabbinical Assembly provides guidance in matters of halakhah for the Conservative movement. The individual rabbi, however, is the authority for the interpretation and application of all matters of halakhah.

Introduction

Providing health care in modern nations is a great and growing challenge. While health care in centuries past was both largely ineffective and inexpensive, in our time medicine can do remarkable things to save and enhance our lives, but all at a considerable cost. How shall we apportion that cost, and how should societies decide what to provide each citizen in the first place?

The provision of health care touches on values and responsibilities that are central to the Jewish tradition. Moreover, in the Jewish understanding, health care involves issues of justice and communal obligation relevant to all societies. While classical Jewish sources presume a context in which medicine was less expensive and less complicated than it is now, the Jewish tradition nevertheless offers important guidance for individual patients, family members, and health care providers in our day.

While traditional sources less directly address the responsibilities of societies in the provision of health care, halakhic guidance on these issues is needed as well. The Jewish tradition understands the provision of needed health care to involve issues of justice and communal obligation that are relevant for all societies. Jews who are citizens of democracies accordingly have at least some degree of responsibility to concern themselves with the justice and well-being of these national societies, including the just and beneficent distribution of health care.

This paper presents three related תשובות on the responsibilities of individuals, health care providers, and communities for the provision of health care. These are preceded by an overview of Jewish understandings of medical care and human needs that will be relied on by each תשובה. The תשובות will provide limited but important guidance from our halakhic tradition. One limit relates to the need for prudential judgment, as well as compassion, in applying these guidelines to complex real life situations. Another limit reflects the scope of the paper. Additional questions that might profitably be addressed in future papers (by us or others) include: more specific guidelines for when better care should be chosen (by patients, health care providers, or society) despite increased cost, the role of rabbis as patient advocates in settings such as managed care, asset shifting to family members to become eligible for Medicaid, the right of physicians to strike, the priority to be accorded to research relative to current patient care, triage and the allocation of limited resources (such as organs for transplantation), and the selling of organs. Additional issues continue to develop. Despite these limitations, guidance from the tradition is both possible and important.

Traditional Views on Health Care and Human Needs

A. The Duty to Provide Medical Care

1. The theological and legal bases for medical intervention

Until the discovery of penicillin in 1938, physicians could do little to cure disease. Preventive medicine was better developed, although not uniformly practiced, but curative medicine was largely ineffective. When physicians could not do much to heal a sick patient, their services were easily attainable and relatively cheap. When the Talmud says, "The best of physicians should go to hell,"[1] it reflects the fact that patients seldom were cured by physicians, even though doctors held out that hope.

With the advent of antibiotics, other new drug therapies, and new diagnostic and surgical techniques, however, there has been an immense increase in the demand for medical care precisely as it has become much more expensive. This raises not only the "micro" questions of how physicians and patients should treat a given person's disease, but also the "macro" questions of how we, as a society, should arrange for the medical care to be dis-

---

[1] M. Kiddushin 4:14 (82b). Exactly why "the best of physicians are destined for hell" is disputed. Rashi suggests several reasons: (1) Being unafraid of illness, they do not appropriately adjust the diet of the sick and feed them instead food for healthy people; (2) Again, because they do not fear illness and sometimes cure it, they are haughty before the Almighty; (3) Their treatment is sometimes fatal; and, finally, (4) On the other hand, by refusing treatment to the poor, they may indirectly cause their death. Hanokh Albeck, in his commentary to the Mishnah ([Tel Aviv: Dvir, 1958], vol. 3, p. 330), suggests that it is because they are not careful in their craft and thus cause sick people to die (similar to Rashi's first and third explanations combined). Philip Blackman suggests in his commentary to the Mishnah ([New York: Judaica Press, 1963], vol. 3, p. 484, n. 27) that the subject of this curse is not doctors *per se*, but, "one who pretends to be a specialist and in consequence brings disaster to his patients." The Soncino translation and commentary to the Talmud ([London: Soncino, 1936], Nashim, vol. 4, p. 423, n. 9, citing the *Jewish Chronicle* of 3 January 1935), says that "it is probable that it is not directed against healing as such, but against the 'advanced' views held by physicians in those days."

tributed. On both levels, the ultimate question is the Kantian one: nobody has a duty to do that which humanly cannot be done, but once we gain the ability to do X, the moral question arises as to whether we should. On the macro level, this becomes the question of how much medical care should be provided to everyone in society as part of our collective duty to care for each other.

According to Jewish law, we have the clear duty to try to heal, and this duty devolves upon both the physician and the society. This, theologically, is somewhat surprising. After all, since God announces in the Bible that He will inflict illness for sin and, conversely, that He is our healer,[2] one might think that medicine is an improper human intervention in God's decision to inflict illness.

The Rabbis were aware of this line of reasoning, but they counteracted it by pointing out that God Himself authorizes us to heal. In fact, they maintain, God requires us to heal. They found that authorization and that imperative in various Biblical verses, including Exod. 21:19-20, according to which an assailant must insure that his victim is "thoroughly healed," and Deut. 22:2, "And you shall restore the lost property to him." The Talmud understands the Exodus verse as giving "permission for the physician to cure." On the basis of an extra letter in the Hebrew text of the Deuteronomy passage, the Talmud declares that that verse includes the obligation to restore another person's body as well as his or her property, and hence there is an obligation to come to the aid of someone in a life-threatening situation. On the basis of Lev. 19:16, "Nor shall you stand idly by the blood of your fellow," the Talmud expands the obligation to provide medical aid to encompass expenditure of financial resources for this purpose.[3]

In addition to these halakhic grounds for providing health care, there is an important theological underpinning. God is to be our model Whom we are to imitate. As the Talmud (Sotah 14a) teaches:

> "Follow the Lord your God," (Deut. 13:5). What does that this mean? Is it possible for a mortal to follow God's presence? The verse means to teach us that we should follow the attributes of the Holy One, praised be He. As He clothes the naked, you should clothe the naked. The Bible teaches that the Holy One visited the sick; you should visit the sick.

We praise God in the Amidah: "You support the falling, heal the ailing, free the fettered."[4] Accordingly, we are called upon to help others and provide health care to those in need.

While each Jew must come to the aid of a person in distress, and while the assailant has the direct duty to cure his victim, Jewish law recognized the expertise involved in medical care and thus here, as in other similar cases, the layman may hire the expert to carry out his obligations. Experts, in turn, have special obligations because of their expertise. Thus Joseph Karo (1488-1575) says:

> The Torah gave permission to the physician to heal; moreover, this is a religious precept and is included in the category of sav-

---

[2] God inflicts illness for sin: Lev. 26:16; Deut. 28:22, 59-60. God as our healer: e.g., Exod. 15:26; Deut. 32:39; Isa. 19:22; 57:18-19; Jer. 30:17; 33:6; Hos. 6:1; Ps. 103:2-3; 107:20; Job 5:18.

[3] B. Bava Kamma 85a; B. Sanhedrin 73a.

[4] Translations from *Siddur Sim Shalom*, ed. Jules Harlow (New York: Rabbinical Assembly and United Synagogue, 1985), pp. 19, 107.

ing life, and if the physician withholds his services, it is considered as shedding blood.[5]

That the community shares in this responsibility together with the physician becomes clear from several sources. The Talmud, for example, describes ten services that a city must provide to make it fit for a Jewish scholar to live there, and the service of a physician is one of them:

> A scholar (of Torah) should not reside in a city where (any of) the following ten things is missing: 1. A court of justice that (has the power to) impose flagellation and decree monetary penalties; 2. A צדקה fund collected by (at least) two people and distributed by (at least) three; 3. A synagogue; 4. Public baths; 5. A privy; 6. One who performs circumcisions (a מוהל); 7. A physician; 8. A scribe (who also functions as a notary); 9. A (kosher) butcher; 10. And a schoolmaster. Rabbi Akiba is quoted as including also several kinds of fruit (in the list) because they are beneficial to one's eyesight.[6]

Since each Jewish community needed a rabbi to interpret Jewish law and to teach the tradition, this list of requirements for having a rabbi effectively makes it every Jewish community's responsibility to furnish medical services. In the Middle Ages, Nahmanides (1194-1270) offers an additional rationale for this communal duty, basing it on the commandment in the Torah, "You shall love your neighbor as yourself," and reasoning that just as you would want medical care when you need it, so you need to provide it for others when they need it.[7]

2. Prevention in preference to cure

Illness is debilitating. In addition to any physical pain involved, sickness brings with it the frustration of not being able to pursue our normal tasks in life. We feel shaken in our sense of physical and psychological integrity, our sense of safety and security, and, indeed, in our sense of ourselves.

Illness is also degrading. When sick, we feel diminished as human beings. As much as we need to divorce ourselves from a common American evaluation of people in terms of their skills and accomplishments, recognizing instead the inherent value in every human being, when sick we inevitably feel that the divine aspect of power has been reduced in us. It also can be humiliating to have to be dependent on others for help in doing the everyday tasks of living. One feels like an infant.

These characteristics of illness make it preferable to prevent it in the first place than to cure it once it strikes. There are, of course, pragmatic considerations as well. It is still true today that "an ounce of prevention is worth a pound of cure," and sometimes, as is currently the case with regard to AIDS, we cannot cure a disease at all but we can prevent it. Historically, that was true for most diseases; for doctors were not able to cure very much, but their knowledge of preventive techniques was, in some ways, quite sophisticated. The fact that in practice we can prevent disease more easily and more economically than we can cure it, though, is not the whole of the story; we must prefer prevention to cure also in order to ward off the debilitating and degrading aspects of disease.

---

[5] Joseph Karo, S.A. Yoreh De'ah 336:1.

[6] B. Sanhedrin 17b.

[7] Nahmanides, *Kitvei Haramban*, ed. Bernard Chavel (Jerusalem: Mosad Harav Kook, 1963), vol. 2, p. 43 (Hebrew). The verse from the Torah: Lev. 19:18.

B. Precedents and Analogies for the Provision of Health Care: Poverty and the Redemption of Captives

Halakhic sources are clear that members of the community are obligated to perform the mitzvah of בקור חולים, visiting the sick. Even if our ancestors did not have many medications at hand to cure diseases, they knew better than we that cure depends crucially on the patient's will to live. Disease is inherently isolating and degrading. Those who visit the sick and engage them in adult conversations therefore contribute immeasurably to their recovery. This is especially crucial in our own time, when patients with serious illnesses are often treated not in the familiar surroundings of home, but rather in the strange, antiseptic environment of the hospital. Our communal responsibility for health care demands our time and caring. In addition to conversation and prayer, attending to spiritual needs of the sick individual, visitors are expected to care for the tangible needs of the patient as well.[8]

Some authorities also articulate a general expectation that the community as a whole will contribute to the healing of ill individuals.[9] Traditional sources, though, have relatively little discussion of the extent of this responsibility. This is not surprising, as both the effectiveness and costs of medical treatments were much more limited in past centuries than they are today. Traditional sources, however, have more extensive discussion of the extent of the community's responsibility to provide for individuals in other contexts, of which two are especially relevant to health care: צדקה, support for the poor; and פדיון שבויים, redeeming captives.[10]

1. Poverty Legislation (צדקה)

Halakhah understands the responsibility of צדקה, literally meaning "justice," to entail enforceable obligations for the community and its members. Codifying traditions going back to the Talmud, the Shulhan Arukh states that "each individual is obligated to give צדקה.... If one gives less than is appropriate, the courts may administer lashes until he gives according to the assessment, and the courts may go to his property in his presence and take the amount that it is appropriate for him to give."[11]

Halakhic authorities seek to specify the minimum levels of support required by צדקה from the perspectives of both giver and recipient. The general rule is that one pay a tenth of one's income (including acquired capital) for צדקה. Giving one fifth represents "choice" fulfillment of the obligation, and one should give, "according to the needs of the poor," even above one fifth of one's income, if one can afford to do so. Many authorities add that one must give at least one fifth when one can afford to do so without difficulty and there is pressing need, and one must give whatever is required in cases immediately involving the saving of life. In other cases, giving more than one fifth is generally seen as commendable, but not obligatory.[12]

---

[8] S.A. Yoreh De'ah 335; Immanuel Jakobovits, *Jewish Medical Ethics*, 2d ed. (New York: Bloch,1975), pp. 106-109. In addition, the Shulhan Arukh (Yoreh De'ah 249:16) indicates that the financial needs of the sick have at least equal claim on communal resources as other requirements of צדקה, and may have special priority.

[9] See n. 7.

[10] These issues are further discussed in Aaron L. Mackler, "Judaism, Justice, and Access to Health Care," *Kennedy Institute of Ethics Journal* 1 (1991): 143-161; and in Elliot N. Dorff, *Matters of Life and Death* (Philadelphia: Jewish Publication Society, 1998), ch. 12.

[11] S.A. Yoreh De'ah 248:1. The obligation of צדקה in Judaism is binding, analogous to the duty to pay income taxes in the United States.

[12] S.A. Yoreh De'ah 249:1. See Cyril Domb, *Maaser Kesafim* (Jerusalem: Feldheim/Association of Orthodox Jewish Scientists, 1980), pp. 34-38.

The limits on the redistribution of resources required by צדקה depend most importantly on the needs of the poor. The exact determination of needs is debatable, but a broad consensus does emerge from the tradition, centered on the idea of lack, or that which is missing. The Talmud sets parameters in its exegesis of the verse in Deuteronomy (15:8), "You shall surely open your hand to him, and shall surely lend him sufficient for his need/lack, according as he needs/lacks," (די מחסרו אשר יחסר לו). The Talmud cites an earlier baraita: "'Sufficient for his lack' — you are commanded to support him, and you are not commanded to enrich him; 'according as he lacks' — even a horse on which to ride, and a servant to run in front of him."[13] As Maimonides paraphrases the guideline, "according to that which is lacking for the poor person, you are commanded to give him. . . .You are commanded to fill in for his lack, but you are not commanded to enrich him."[14] Note that צדקה, and by implication the distribution of health care, only requires meeting the needs of all members of society, not providing anything that would be of benefit. At the same time, as the second half of the baraita suggests, we must be prepared to construe these needs broadly.

The general standard against which lacks are evaluated is largely implicit. Traditional sources, though, do provide a list of paradigmatic cases:

> If it is appropriate to give him bread, they give him bread; if dough, they give him dough. . .if to feed him, they feed him. If he is not married and wants to take a wife, they enable him to marry; they rent a house for him, and provide a bed and furnishings.[15]

A woman who wishes to be married is similarly provided with a dowry. Clothing and other basic needs are implicit. Moses Isserles notes that the provision of such needs is primarily the responsibility of the community.[16] The basic requirement of צדקה is thus to provide food, clothing and shelter, and with these, the opportunity for family life.[17] Yet even the meeting of other needs may be obligatory, as the baraita's discussion of providing a horse at least rhetorically reminds us.[18]

Extrapolating from these general requirements would require the provision of a "decent minimum" of health care, sufficient to meet the needs of each member of the community. Such needs could generally be interpreted in a fairly basic and objective way, though special needs of individuals may in some cases be considered as well.

2. Redemption from Captivity (פדיון שבויים)

The redemption of captives, those captured by slave traders or unjustly held prisoner, provides a precedent even more closely analogous to at least some types of medical care. This category of acute needs is seen to take precedence even over general obligations of צדקה. Funds collected or allocated for any other purpose may be diverted to securing the release

---

[13] B. Ketubbot 67b.

[14] Moses Maimonides, M.T. Laws of Gifts to the Poor 7:3.

[15] S.A. Yoreh De'ah 250:1.

[16] Ibid.

[17] The provision of universal education is a separate communal obligation. See S.A. Yoreh De'ah 245:7, 249:16; Encyclopaedia Judaica, s.v. "Education."

[18] The Talmud, and subsequently codes, understand the "lack" of a horse as relative to the previous condition of a once-wealthy recipient. Following this paradigm, special needs might be understood in terms of the previous status of an individual, current psychological needs, or expectations or felt needs. While this paper follows a relatively conservative interpretation of focusing on objective needs and a basic level of support, the provision of a horse serves as a rhetorical injunction to be sensitive to special needs of individuals, at least in exceptional cases.

of captives when necessary. Maimonides, for example, states that "the redemption of captives takes precedence over the support of the poor, and there is no greater obligatory precept than the redemption of captives." He offers the explanation that, "a captive falls in the category of the hungry and the thirsty and the naked, and stands in danger of his life."[19] Health care shares these characteristics that justify the priority accorded to פדיון שבויים: both concern individuals who are suffering and may be in immediate danger. Further, both categories entail special needs that vary greatly among individuals. Jewish law and ethics understand the community to have a fundamental obligation to save lives whenever possible, diverting funds from other projects as required.[20]

Part I: The Responsibility of Patients and Their Families

שאלה

To what extent are individual patients and their family members responsible for providing health care?

תשובה

Individuals bear some of the responsibility for maintaining their health. This begins with taking steps to prevent illness in the first place. While curative medicine in past centuries was not well developed, our ancestors knew a great deal about preventive medicine. Thus Maimonides (Mishneh Torah, Deot, 4:1ff.), for example, asserts a positive obligation "to avoid anything that is injurious to the body, and to conduct oneself in ways that promote health." He already states the importance of proper diet, exercise, hygiene, and sleep. Conversely, he repeats the Talmud's prohibition of abusing our bodies through unhealthy habits. In carrying out our primary duty to provide for our own health care, then, we in our time need to pay heed to those ancient prescriptions for keeping ourselves healthy so that we can carry out our God-given mission to help others and to fix the world.

When one needs the aid of health care professionals, the individual must bear at least some of the financial burden. Thus the Shulhan Arukh rules as follows:

> If someone is taken captive and he has property but does not want to redeem himself, we redeem him (with the money that his property will bring) against his will.[21]

While this source speaks of redemption from captivity and not health care, the duty to redeem captives is based on the danger to their lives in captivity. As argued above, this rule about financing a person's freedom is thus a reasonable source for determining whether an individual has a financial responsibility for his or her own health care as well, and the ruling makes it clear that one does.

In traditional Jewish sources, these requirements are described as the duties of a man toward his own health care, but a man's responsibility to pay for the health care of his wife

---

[19] M.T. Laws of Gifts to the Poor 8:10. See also S.A. Yoreh De'ah, 252:1.

[20] S.A. Yoreh De'ah 252:4; Talmud Bavli Gittin 45a. The standard case in the tradition is that in which payments for the captive's release are necessary and will be effective in securing the captive's freedom. Accordingly, the analogy would apply to medical care that is both necessary and effective.

[21] S.A. Yoreh De'ah 252:11.

is even clearer, for among the obligations that a man assumes in marriage is the medical care of his wife.[22] Similarly, for her redemption the Shulhan Arukh rules:

> If a man and his wife are in captivity, his wife takes precedence over him. The court invades his property to redeem her. Even if he stands and shouts, "Do not redeem her from my property!" we do not listen to him.[23]

Thus a man has a clear duty to provide medical care for his wife, especially, but not exclusively, when her life is threatened in captivity or, presumably, in some other way.

He has the same duty vis-à-vis his children and other relatives if they cannot care for themselves. Once again, the precedent for this comes from the laws of redemption from captivity:

> A father must redeem his son if the father has money but the son does not. Gloss: And the same is true for one relative redeeming another, the closer relative comes first, for all of them may not enrich themselves and thrust [the redemption of] their relatives on the community.[24]

In our own, more egalitarian society, these sources would presumably mean that spouses of either gender have responsibility for the health care of each other and of their children. In carrying out that responsibility, one may not preserve the family fortune and make the Jewish community or government pay for one's own health care or that of one's spouse or children, except to the extent that the government itself makes provision for all sick, elderly citizens in programs like Medicare without restrictions as to a person's income or estate. Absent such provisions in the law, one must provide for one's own health care and for that of one's relatives. One might do that by using one's own assets or through buying a health insurance policy, either privately or through one's employment. One may only, according to these sources, call on public aid when and if one qualifies for aid to the poor through programs like Medicaid.[25]

---

[22] M. Ketubbot 4:9; S.A. Even HaEzer 79.

[23] S.A. Yoreh De'ah 252:10, Even HaEzer 78. This is ultimately based on the Mishnah's insistence that a man redeem his wife from captivity before being able to divorce her; cf. M. Ketubbot 4:9.

[24] S.A. Yoreh De'ah 252:12.

[25] The individual also has a duty to contribute to the medical care of others. Although this generally is not spelled out in just those words, it is a clear implication of the understanding of the community's obligations seen above. Traditional sources obligate individuals to contribute to the needs of others through צדקה and פדיון שבויים. Moreover, the Rabbis, as we have seen, see the absence of health care as shedding blood. Since the physician alone cannot be expected to bear the costs of health care for those who cannot afford it, this duty devolves upon the community, and the costs of health care for the poor become part of the צדקה one must give, a strict and enforceable obligation. See the discussion above in section I; M.T. Laws of Gifts to the Poor 7:10; S.A. Yoreh De'ah 248:2. At the same time, there are limits on this obligation. The Shulhan Arukh and the Jewish tradition in general, acknowledge limits on the obligation to provide for the needs of others, at least in exceptional cases. In the most extreme case, one does not have to endanger one's own life in order to save the life of another. As seen above, each individual is generally not obligated to pay more than ten or twenty per cent of income toward the provision of the needs of the poor. While the obligation to provide all resources necessary to save lives generally supersedes all such limits, halakhic sources can envision cases in which not all lives can be saved, and offer various sets of priorities to consider in such extreme cases. S.A. Yoreh De'ah 252:5-12; see Shlomo Dichowsky, "Rescue and Treatment: Halakhic Scales of Priority" (Hebrew), *Dine Israel* 7 (1976): 45-66; Martin Golding, "Preventive vs. Curative Medicine," *Journal of Medicine and Philosophy* 8 (1983): 276-279; Fred Rosner, *Modern Medicine and Jewish Ethics*, 2d ed. (Hoboken, N.J.: Ktav, and New York: Yeshiva University Press, 1991), pp. 375-390.

Patients who have no resources to pay for health care may accept public assistance to procure it. In fact, they must do so, for to refuse needed care is to endanger their lives which is, for Jewish law, tantamount to committing suicide. Still, the Shulhan Arukh strongly condemns those who use public funds for their health care when they do not need to do so, and it appreciates those who postpone calling upon the public purse for as long as possible:

> Anyone who does not need to take from the צדקה fund and deceives the community and takes money will not die until he does indeed need צדקה from others. And whoever needs to take such that he cannot live unless he takes, for example, an elderly person or a sick person or a suffering person, but he forces himself not to take is like one who sheds blood (namely, his own) and he is liable for his own life, and his pain is only the product of sin and transgression. But anyone who needs to take (צדקה) but puts himself instead into a position of pain and pushes off the time (when he takes צדקה) and lives a life of pain so that he will not burden the community will not die until he sustains others, and about him Scripture says, "Blessed is the man who trusts in God."[26]

Conversely, unless a given drug or medical procedure is so scarce that the government has put limits on who may obtain it even with their own money, individual patients who have the money to afford something that the government or their private plan does not provide may decide to use it to pay for the drug or procedure privately. Thus, the Shulhan Arukh, following earlier formulations of Jewish law, puts a limit on the amount of money a community may spend on redeeming any given captive in order to depress the market in captives and ultimately to deter kidnapping altogether, but even though that is a distinct social good, a given individual is free to spend as much of his own funds as he wishes to redeem himself or his relative:

> We do not redeem captives for more than their worth out of considerations of fixing the world, so that the enemies will not dedicate themselves to take them captive. An individual, however, may redeem himself for as much as he would like.[27]

This is unfair in one sense, but it is only the unfairness built into any capitalistic system, and Jewish sources do not require that Jews use socialism as their form of government or their rule for distributing and charging goods. In the provision of health care as in other areas, the Jewish tradition does not enforce a ceiling of the resources one may spend for one's own benefit, but rather seeks to establish a floor that, at a minimum, assures at least the basic needs for all.

Conclusion

Individuals and family members have the responsibility to care for their own health, and the primary responsibility to pay (directly or through insurance) for health care needed by themselves or by family members. When they cannot do so, they may and should avail themselves of publicly funded programs to acquire the health care they need. In any case, one should seek to prevent illness rather than wait to cure an illness that has already occurred.

---

[26] S.A. Yoreh De'ah 255:2.
[27] S.A. Yoreh De'ah 252:4.

Part II: The Responsibility of Physicians and Other Health Care Professionals

שאלה

To what extent are physicians and other health care providers responsible for providing health care?

תשובה

The same general principles would apply to the societal obligation for provision of health care. To begin with the physician, halakhic sources, as noted above, discuss in general terms the mandate for the individual physician to heal and for the individual patient to seek healing.[28] While physicians have very definite obligations towards their patients, they generally may expect to receive appropriate fees.

Nonetheless, Jewish medical writers through the ages have urged physicians to treat the poor without charge. The Talmud commends as an ideal the practice of Abba the therapeutic blood letter. He had his patients deposit their payments in a box so that those who could afford to pay could pay, while those who could not afford to do so could receive treatment without embarrassment. In some cases he would give a needy patient money for sustenance during recuperation.[29] In the nineteenth century, Rabbi Eleazar Flekeles ruled that free care of the poor was not only a virtue to be expected from a benevolent physician, but a halakhic obligation enforceable by a (religious) court.[30] While there are limits on the extent of such obligation in contemporary societies, as discussed below, the strong expectation that physicians will provide health care that is needed is clear.

While traditional sources focus on the responsibility of providing health care for the needy, in our own day these questions no longer affect the poor alone. Most people simply cannot pay for some of the new procedures, no matter how much money they have or can borrow. The size of the problem makes even conscientious and morally sensitive physicians think that any individual effort on their part to resolve this issue is useless. Moreover, the costs that they themselves assumed in gaining a modern medical education must somehow be repaid — to say nothing of malpractice insurance, overhead for their offices and for the hospitals in which they practice, staff, and the like. The question of paying for medical care in our society therefore becomes a critical issue.

Traditional Jewish communities that expected physicians to treat those in need without pay customarily offered tax benefits and other privileges in return. In some cases, the community would directly hire physicians to provide for the treatment of the poor and others. While unpaid treatment of the poor was the norm, the Portuguese-Jewish community in Hamburg in 1666 declined the offer of a physician to treat the poor with no charge, on grounds that "it is not fitting to engage someone without salary; for the payment will force the doctor to be [o]n time when called in by a patient."[31] Along the same lines, the Talmud asserts that a physician who heals for nothing is worth nothing.[32]

---

[28] See above, section I; S.A. Yoreh De'ah 336; Rosner, 5-19; J. David Bleich, "The Obligation to Heal in the Judaic Tradition: A Comparative Analysis," in *Jewish Bioethics*, eds. Fred Rosner and J. David Bleich (New York: Sanhedrin Press, 1979), pp. 1-44.

[29] B. Ta'anit 21b.

[30] Eleazar Flekeles, *Teshuvah Me'Ahavah* (Prague, 1820), p. 70, on S.A. Yoreh De'ah 336.

[31] Jakobovits, pp. 224-228.

[32] B. Bava Kamma 85a.

Still, the example of Abba, the bleeder, and the stipulation in the Shulhan Arukh that withholding medical care is akin to murdering someone both establish that in Jewish law physicians have a primary duty to provide medical care. This would make systems of managing care that discourage doctors from providing needed and effective care Jewishly illegitimate, or at least suspect. Capitation, for instance, gives doctors a sum of money for each patient per year regardless of the amount of care they provide; that makes it economically disadvantageous to doctors personally to treat patients extensively, for the more time they spend with a patient, the less they earn per patient. Such a system can only be reconciled with the fundamental Jewish duty of physicians to care for their patients if there is some way to offset this economic pressure that mitigates against treatment so as to guarantee that doctors will nevertheless provide good care. Modifications of the physicians' professional code of ethics or government regulation may be part of what is needed to spell out accepted standards of care, and, however the standards are established and announced, capitation would inevitably require more frequent peer review than now occurs. If such measures proved unsuccessful in counterbalancing the economic pressures of capitation so as to guarantee a reasonable level of care, Jewish principles would forbid capitation as a violation of the duty to provide needed medical care.[33]

In addition, the underlying duty of physicians to provide care means that they bear at least some responsibility for making health care available to those who cannot afford their normal fees. This would impose on doctors the obligation to do some work at reduced rates or for free. Like other people, though, they have a right to earn a living, and so the community and the individual patient must also share a portion of the financial burden.

In times past, all medical procedures were administered by two types of personnel: the physician and the surgeon. It is only in recent times that other health care professions have arisen as separate entities. Thus classical Jewish sources do not speak about nurses, physician assistants, health care technicians, social workers concentrating in health care, etc. One would expect, though, that the sources discussed above governing physicians would apply, *mutatis mutandis*, to other health care personnel as well. That is, such personnel, on this analysis, would have the positive obligation to provide some *pro bono* and emergency services, but that obligation would be limited so that they can earn a fair living. The remainder of the cost must be provided by the community and individual patient.

---

[33] In the United States, a number of states have passed laws restricting financial incentives to physicians. For example, Texas prohibits financial incentives that serve as inducements to limit medically necessary care (Tracy E. Miller, "Managed Care Regulation: In the Laboratory of the States," *Journal of the American Medical Association* 278 [1997]: 1104). According to the Council on Ethical and Judicial Affairs of the American Medical Association, "financial incentives are permissible only if they promote the cost-effective delivery of health care and not the withholding of medically necessary care." Furthermore, "regardless of any allocation guidelines or gatekeeper directives, physicians must advocate for any care they believe will materially benefit their patients," ("Ethics in Managed Care," *Journal of the American Medical Association* 273 (1995): 334-335). Before affiliating with a managed care plan, an individual physician has the responsibility to ascertain the implications for his or her being able to provide appropriate patient care (as Haavi Morreim, a secular ethicist who is generally sympathetic to managed care, notes [*Balancing Act: The New Medical Ethics of Medicine's New Economics* (Washington: Georgetown University Press, 1995), pp. 121-23]). A physician should be willing to make at least some degree of financial sacrifice in order to better care for patients. In some cases, some degree of compromise from the ideal might be required in order for a physician to be able to practice in a given area. Precise resolution of such dilemmas is beyond the scope of this paper. Note, though, that for the Council on Ethical and Judicial Affairs of the American Medical Association, "physicians should not participate in any plan that encourages or requires care at or below minimum professional standards" ("Ethics in Managed Care," pp. 334-35).

Conclusion

Physicians and other health care professionals must treat patients in case of emergency, and they have some responsibility more generally to make health care available to those who cannot afford their normal fees. At the same time, health care professionals legitimately may expect compensation for their efforts and expenses, and should be able to earn a living.

Part III: The Responsibility of the Community

שאלה

What is the extent of the community's responsibilities to provide health care? In contemporary countries such as the United States and Canada, to what extent are these responsibilities of the Jewish community? Of the general society?

תשובה

A. Responsibilities

As communities have grown larger and the provision of health care more expensive, the role of the community in assuring provision of needed care has become more central.[34] While accepting Flekeles's nineteenth-century ruling on the individual physician's obligation to provide care, the contemporary authority Rabbi Eliezer Yehudah Waldenberg notes problems in enforcement even within a traditional Jewish community today. The logical basis for the ruling, he observes, is that when an individual cannot afford to pay for medical care, the court, on behalf of the community, acquires the obligation for that person's healing. Because the court has responsibility for the health care of that individual, it has the power to force the physician to treat the individual. The community's responsibility for the care of that person logically falls on the physician more than anyone else, because of the physician's special knowledge and ability.[35]

Waldenberg asserts that while a virtuous physician is expected to provide charitable free care for the poor, this can only be enforced as a legal responsibility in a community that has just one physician. In contemporary communities with more than one physician, possibilities for meeting the community's obligation to assure provision of health care include appropriating money from the general welfare (צדקה) fund, conducting a special financial appeal, and equitably apportioning cases to all physicians for treatment on a *pro bono* basis. The most praiseworthy option, however, is to establish a special fund for the payment of physician fees for treatment of the poor.[36]

The central point of Waldenberg's analysis is consistent with the tradition's understanding of the importance of health care, and the general guidance provided by discussion of צדקה and פדיון שבויים. If an individual cannot afford to pay for needed health care, the obligation to provide for that care devolves on the community as a whole. The community may legitimately choose any of a variety of ways to meet this responsibility, so long as the responsibility is met in every case of need. While it is commendable for a physician to treat the poor with-

---

[34] Indeed, by the sixteenth century Isserles noted that the central locus for the provision of צדקה had shifted from individuals to the community (S.A. Yoreh De'ah 250:1).

[35] Eliezer Yehudah Waldenberg, *Ramat Rachel* (printed with vol. 5 of *Tzitz Eliezer*) (Jerusalem, 1985), responsum no. 24, p. 31.

[36] Ibid., pp. 31-32.

out charge, and while a virtuous physician will do so routinely as part of his or her practice and always when an emergency arises, such treatment represents a halakhic obligation and requirement of justice only when the community has fairly designated the physician as responsible for fulfilling the community's obligation. Preferred ways to meet this communal responsibility for the care of the poor include a societal health payment program, perhaps analogous to Medicare or national health insurance, or direct government provision of medical care.

The standard for the amount of care to be assured is that of need. Patients are not entitled to, and society not obligated to provide, all care that is desired, all care that might offer some benefit, or all care that anyone else in the society receives. The community is obligated, however, to assure access to all care that is needed by a patient to lead a reasonably full life.[37] While identifying "needed" treatments will change with developing medical practice and vary among individual cases, in general it would be treatment that would be effective in sustaining life, curing disease, restoring health, or improving function.[38]

Two areas of health care require special mention. First, in distribution of health care as in other areas, halakhah would understand health and health care to include mental as well as physical health.[39]

Second, the community's responsibilities to provide health care are not limited to curative care; they include preventive care as well.[40] In the societies of times past, the preventive medical care that was available was relatively limited in cost, and so the need to allocate significant resources for such care does not seem to have arisen. Nevertheless, in our own time the provision of some preventive care, such as vaccination and prenatal care, is mandatory on two grounds. First, since prevention is often less expensive than cure, and since society is ultimately obligated to provide all curative care needed, communities should provide significant preventive care as a cost-effective way to meet that duty.[41]

---

[37] Traditional Jewish sources find concepts analogous to "need" relatively unproblematic, and devote little attention to specifying the levels of food, shelter, or medical care required by justice. The generally implicit standard of the codes at least roughly corresponds with the concept of "natural function" or "species-typical functioning," developed by Christopher Boorse and utilized by Norman Daniels in discussing allocation of health care (Daniels, *Just Health Care* [New York: Cambridge University Press, 1985], esp. pp. 26-32).

[38] Possible limits on the degree to which a particular society can afford to provide such care as balanced against its other obligations are discussed below.

[39] Rabbi Elliot N. Dorff, "The Jewish Tradition," in *Caring and Curing: Health and Medicine in the Western Religious Traditions*, eds. Ronald L. Numbers and Darrel W. Amundsen (New York: Macmillan, 1986), pp. 23-25; David M. Feldman, *Health and Medicine in the Jewish Tradition* (New York: Crossroad, 1986), p. 49; citing: B. Yoma 82a; Nahmanides, *Torat HaAdam*; Israel Meir Mizrahi, *Responsa Pri HaAretz*, Yoreh De'ah no. 2; Mordekhai Winkler, *Responsa Levushei Mordekhai*, Hoshen Mishpat no. 39; *Responsa Minhat Yitzhak*, vol. 1, no. 115; *Responsa Iggrot Moshe*, Even HaEzer no. 65.

[40] See Martin Golding, "Preventive vs. Curative Medicine," *Journal of Medicine and Philosophy* 8 (1983): 269-86.

[41] Louise Russell and others, however, note that the relative cost effectiveness of preventive and curative care varies greatly, and that many preventive measures cannot be justified solely on the basis of cost effectiveness. While preventing one person's disease is generally less expensive than curing disease that has occurred, large numbers of patients may need to be screened and treated for each case of disease prevented. Studies have found that screening for cervical cancer among low-income elderly women who had not been screened in many years can save money, for example, but that routinely screening women every year instead of every two years costs $1.8 million for each year of life saved, far more than many curative interventions (Louise B. Russell, "The Role of Prevention in Health Reform," *New England Journal of Medicine* 329 [1993]: 352-354). See also Russell's "Some of the Tough Decisions Required by a National Health Plan," *Science* 246 (1989): 892-896; *Is Prevention Better Than Cure?* (Washington, DC: Brookings Institution, 1986), p. 110; David M. Eddy, "Cost-effectiveness Analysis: Is It Up to the Task?" *Journal of the American Medical Association* 267 (1992): 3346-3347. The extent of preventive care that should be considered appropriate or "needed" is an issue of ongoing debate in bioethics and health policy. Paul Menzel (*Medical Costs, Moral*

Moreover, since prevention avoids the degradation of illness, communities must provide preventive care for that theological and humanitarian consideration as well.

B. Limits

At the same time, there are some limits. The responsibility to provide for the redemption of captives may also be limited when the captive is responsible for his own predicament, though only in the most extreme cases. The Shulhan Arukh considers the case of one who sells himself into captivity, or is held prisoner as a result of defaulting on a loan. The community must pay to free the captive if this is the first or second time that he has brought about his own captivity, but the community need not make such payments after the third such occurrence. In case of immediate threat to the captive's life, though, even the captive responsible for his own captivity must be rescued.[42] By analogy, those who make choices (in lifestyle or health care) that turn out to be unfortunate or irresponsible thereby attenuate their claims to the community's support, but do not forfeit all such claims. Individuals who do not purchase health insurance when they are able to do so fail to live up to their responsibilities. Still, they remain persons of infinite value, created in God's image. The community must continue to provide some care even for those responsible for their own misfortune, in this or other ways, especially in cases involving threats to life. Formulating an equitable public policy within these parameters is a complex challenge. Possible alternatives include universal national health insurance, and requirements for individuals to purchase catastrophic health insurance coverage.

A more general limitation is noted on the financial extent of the obligation to redeem captives. "One does not redeem captives for more than their monetary worth" as slaves. This provision dates back to the Mishnah, and the Talmud debates whether such a limit could be justified as protecting the community from onerous burdens or as "improving the world" (תיקון עולם) by avoiding incentives for future hostage taking. The Shulhan Arukh, following Maimonides and other codifiers, accepts only the latter justification.[43] Resources to help an individual with exceptional needs may be limited to generally accepted levels when this limitation is necessary to avoid endangering others. By analogy, it could be argued that a community's paying for extremely expensive experimental treatments, such as an artificial heart, might significantly weaken the health care system as a whole, thereby depriving future patients of needed care. In such cases, a community may be justified in limiting expenditures to the range reasonably expected by most patients.

Moreover, the community must use its resources wisely. The Talmud lists ten services that a community must provide, and in our own day, there are undoubtedly others which the non-Jewish government took care of in Talmudic and medieval times but which are vital to any society — services like defense, civil peace, and roads and bridges. The community must balance its commitments to health care against its responsibility to provide other services, whether those on the Talmud's list of ten or others that arise and are deemed necessary, and it must ensure that those who get public assistance for their health care deserve it.

Choices [New Haven: Yale University Press, 1983], p. 83), for example, argues that even granting that "people need to avoid suffering or dying does not mean that they need all the things which reduce the chances of suffering or dying." At the same time, even preventive measures that increase health care expenses may be warranted because they prevent suffering and support human dignity, as discussed in the text.

[42] S.A. Yoreh De'ah 252:6.

[43] B. Gittin 45a; S.A. Yoreh De'ah 252:4.

Such limits should not be invoked too quickly, however. Very few interventions require such extraordinary expenditures that their provision would not only be burdensome for society, but would endanger the health care system. More basically, possible limits to intervention must always be weighed against the value of human life and healing, and the injunction that a physician who fails to provide needed care is considered as one who sheds blood. In the case of redemption of captives (פדיון שבויים), some authorities state that even excessive ransoms may (or must) be paid in cases of immediate danger to a hostage, despite the importance of saving future lives.[44]

Similarly, while the Talmudic consideration of a limit on payments for the redemption of captives in order to avoid an onerous burden on the community has been accorded little weight by halakhic authorities, it might be argued that modern medical technology has revived the need for consideration of such limits on societal obligations, at least in extreme cases involving very expensive and questionably effective procedures. The relevance of such limits to contemporary nations such as the United States requires further consideration and empirical research. Given the relative affluence of such countries, though, much more could be done for the poorest and most disadvantaged without approaching the above limits on minimal obligations. In particular, these societies do not face the absolute poverty that would force them to allow otherwise preventable deaths by failing to provide adequate health care (or by failing to provide adequate food, clothing, or shelter). While there is some room for consideration of limits on expenditures, the strong presumption of the Jewish tradition is for provision of the resources necessary to preserve and save life.[45]

C. Responsibilities of the Jewish and General Communities

The community has a responsibility to provide needed health care to all of its members. But what counts as a community — the United States as a whole, a synagogue, a metropolitan area's general or Jewish population? And, however we define "community," what are the obligations to those outside the community?

Jewish sources do not provide an unambiguous position. Our own best reading of them is that all members of the community, and in fact all humans, have equal intrinsic value before God.[46] From this point of view, I relate to each human person as a being of value whom I must respect. Yet I additionally stand in a variety of special relationships with some persons, such as family members and fellow citizens. These special relationships of care and commitment entail particular responsibilities in varying degrees. To take a contemporary example, it may be appropriate for United States citizens to accord some degree of priority to fellow citizens over the needy in other nations or even over those living here illegally.

Consistent with this view, halakhic sources picture the individual's responsibilities as radiating in concentric circles, with responsibility most acute for those to whom one stands in closest relation. Accordingly, if an individual's resources to meet the needs of others are limited, priority should be given to members of his or her household before others, and to inhabitants of one's own city before those of other cities. While greatest

---

[44] See above, and S.A. Yoreh De'ah 252:4; 336.

[45] While full evaluation of arguments for rationing is beyond the scope of this paper, rationing that denies needed health care is a last resort, and at best premature given the lack of serious efforts to provide needed health care or to limit that which is unneeded.

[46] See Louis Finkelstein, "Human Equality in the Jewish Tradition," in *Aspects of Human Equality*, ed. Lyman Bryson et al. (New York: Harper and Brothers, 1956), pp. 179-205. Finkelstein argues that all humans are equal in that they may serve and have obligations to God, and that all may have a share in the world to come.

resources should be devoted to those with whom one stands in closest relationship, however, one must offer some degree of support to those who are more distant as well.[47]

Some degree of responsibility would extend to those beyond the community. Throughout most of Jewish history, Jews have formed independent or semi-autonomous communities; only in recent centuries have Jews been equal citizens in societies of nation-states. For most classical sources, then, the "community" refers to the Jewish community. Even from this vantage point, classical sources call on Jews to support the needy outside the Jewish community along with needy Jews, "for the sake of the paths of peace."[48]

In our own day, Jewish federation councils coordinate the fund-raising activities of the Jewish community, and so the federation may be seen as the communal agency that, according to the sources, should be responsible for providing for health care. Federations, however, do not have the taxing or police powers of pre-Enlightenment Jewish communities, and so federations are not completely parallel to the communal authorities of the past. In any case, the cost of health care today is far beyond the resources of federations to supply. Such costs are more appropriately borne by insurance companies and governments, as is indeed the case.

The real question, then, is whether federations should provide some support for Jewish hospitals as an expression of the Jewish communal duty to provide health care. Jewish communities in the early decades of the twentieth century sponsored hospitals in order to provide places where Jewish doctors could work, given that they were barred from practicing in many non-Jewish hospitals. When that form of anti-Semitism diminished in mid-century, Jewish federations continued to sponsor hospitals in order to provide kosher food and other Jewish amenities to Jewish patients, and also as the Jewish contribution to the general community's health care. In our day, the cost of health care is far beyond the resources of the Jewish community, and there are many other important claims on the Jewish community's resources in the areas of Jewish education and social services. Individual federations will need to judge whether any of the former grounds for Jewish support of hospitals still hold or whether there are new reasons for the Jewish community to support health care and, if so, how those resources should be balanced against the other needs of the community. In any case, because the federation is not the full equivalent of the communal governing authorities of the past, and because unmet health care costs far exceed those of the past, Jewish law would not require federations to support hospitals or other forms of health care, leaving it rather to the judgment of the federation to balance this communal activity against the others that would benefit the community. Ultimate responsibility for the meeting of health care needs is that of the nation's government and health care system as a whole.

According to the Jewish model of צדקה and its application to the distribution of health care, the community has concrete responsibilities to provide all needed health care to all within the community. Responsibilities to those outside the community are less strictly enforceable, but still significant. By implication, national communities would have an obligation to provide all needed health care to those within the community: to all citizens without question, probably to all residing legally in the country, and perhaps even to those here

---

[47] This priority may be found in M.T. Laws of Gifts to the Poor 7:13; S.A. Yoreh De'ah 251:3. While these texts are unclear about whether there are exceptions to this order, R. Yehiel Michal Halevi Epstein argues that this order of priority is not absolute (Arukh Hashulhan, Yoreh De'ah 251:4).

[48] M. Gittin 5:8; B. Gittin 61a; M.T. Laws of Idolatry 10:5, Laws of Gifts to the Poor 7:7. The tradition sees Jews as having special responsibilities to support those within the community, but these responsibilities extend to others in the broader human community as well, albeit to a lesser degree.

illegally. After all, as Rabbi Eugene Borowitz observes, the Bible's creation story, depicting all of humanity as descendants of a common ancestor, suggests that "all human beings have familial obligations to one another."[49]

One basic issue in current discussions of allocation of health care resources is whether contemporary nations are the types of communities that have obligations towards their members. Especially in the United States, the distribution of health care is often debated as if providing access to health care were a matter of charity and benevolence. Even on these grounds, it would seem that enlightened self-interest would provide a compelling reason for affording universal access to needed health care. A vision of the nation as a community would make a stronger claim. The Jewish position developed above would make a claim yet stronger, based upon our duty to pursue justice, and to love and care for our neighbor and, indeed, the stranger.

Specific claims of halakhah are not binding on secular nations, of course. Jewish understandings of justice should not (and could not) be imposed monolithically, but should contribute to a national dialogue in which diverse philosophical, religious, and other views would be represented. In the Jewish understanding developed in this paper, securing access to all health care that is needed represents a matter of foundational justice. And whatever the differences between traditional Jewish societies and contemporary countries such as the United States and Canada, all societies are appropriately responsible for the achievement of foundational justice. Jews who are citizens of democratic societies have at least some degree of responsibility to support general institutions that will assure the provision of needed care, through lobbying, social action, and other means.

From the time of the Bible, Judaism has understood social justice as both morally obligatory and crucial to national security. And since that time, Jews have been urged to seek the peace and well-being (shalom) of the nations in which they live.[50] If such counsel was given even for the Babylonia of Jeremiah's time, the responsibility of Jewish citizens of contemporary nations, in which Jews are full and free citizens, to lobby for sufficient health care for all citizens (and possibly all residents) is much stronger.[51]

Conclusions

Jewish law requires that people be provided with needed health care, at least a "decent minimum" that preserves life and meets other basic needs, including some amount of preventive care. The responsibility to assure this provision is shared among individuals and families, physicians and other health care providers, and the community.

The community bears ultimate responsibility to assure provision of needed health care for individuals who cannot afford it, as a matter of justice as well as a specific halakhic obligation. The "community" that bears that responsibility in our day is the national society, through its government, health care institutions, insurance companies, and private enterprise. Jewish citizens should support (by lobbying and other means) general societal

---

[49] Eugene B. Borowitz, *Exploring Jewish Ethics* (Detroit: Wayne State University Press, 1990), p. 99. See also M. Sanhedrin 4:5; Simon Greenberg, *A Jewish Philosophy and Pattern of Life* (New York: Jewish Theological Seminary of America, 1981), esp. pp. 219-221.

[50] Jer. 29:7.

[51] As Abraham Joshua Heschel wrote in another context: "In regard to the cruelties committed in the name of a free society, some are guilty, while all are responsible. I did not feel guilty as an individual American. . .but I feel deeply responsible. 'Thou shalt not stand idly by the blood of thy neighbor' (Lev. 19:15). This is not a recommendation but an imperative, a supreme commandment" (*Moral Grandeur and Spiritual Audacity*, ed. Susannah Heschel [New York: Farrar, Straus and Giroux, 1996], p. 225).

institutions that will fulfill this responsibility. The Jewish community, though its federations, synagogues, and other institutions, must assess whether and to what extent it should support hospitals and other forms of health care. It should balance that purpose against its commitment to other important Jewish needs, such as Jewish education and social services, in light of contemporary patterns of funding health care.

The guarantee of provision of needed health care does not extend to all treatment that is desired, or even all that might provide some benefit. Even needed treatment might be limited when it is so extraordinarily expensive that its provision would deprive other patients of needed care. Still, possible limits to interventions must be weighed against the value of human life and healing, and the injunction that a physician who fails to provide needed health care is considered as one who sheds blood.

Summary of Conclusions

1. Jewish law requires that people be provided with needed health care, at least a "decent minimum" that preserves life and meets other basic needs, including some amount of preventive care. The responsibility to assure this provision is shared among individuals and families, physicians and other health care providers, and the community.

2. Individuals have the responsibility to care for their own health, and the primary responsibility to pay (directly or through insurance) for health care needed by themselves or by family members. When they cannot do so, they may and should avail themselves of publicly funded programs to acquire the health care they need. In any case, one should seek to prevent illness rather than wait to cure an illness that has already occurred.

3. Physicians and other health care professionals must treat patients in case of emergency, and they have some responsibility more generally to make health care available to those who cannot afford their normal fees. At the same time, health care professionals legitimately may expect compensation for their efforts and expenses, and should be able to earn a living.

4. The community bears ultimate responsibility to assure provision of needed health care for individuals who cannot afford it, as a matter of justice as well as a specific halakhic obligation. The "community" that bears that responsibility in our day is the national society, through its government, health care institutions, insurance companies, and private enterprise. Jewish citizens should support (by lobbying and other means) general societal institutions that will fulfill this responsibility. The Jewish community, though its federations, synagogues, and other institutions, must assess whether and to what extent it should support hospitals and other forms of health care. It should balance that purpose against its commitment to other important Jewish needs, such as Jewish education and social services, in light of contemporary patterns of funding health care.

5. The guarantee of provision of needed health care does not extend to all treatment that is desired, or even all that might provide some benefit. Even needed treatment might be limited when it is so extraordinarily expensive that its provision would deprive other patients of needed care. Still, possible limits to interventions must be weighed against the value of human life and healing, and the injunction that a physician who fails to provide needed health care is considered as one who sheds blood.

YD 336:1.2000

Mental Retardation, Group Homes and the Rabbi

Rabbi James S. Rosen

This paper was approved by the CJLS on March 7, 2000, by a vote of seventeen in favor, three opposed, and two abstaining (17-3-2). Voting in favor: Rabbis Kassel Abelson, Ben Zion Bergman, Elliot N. Dorff, Paul Drazen, Jerome M. Epstein, Nechama D. Goldberg, Arnold M. Goodman, Judah Kogen, Vernon H. Kurtz, Alan B. Lucas, Aaron L. Mackler, Daniel S. Nevins, Mayer Rabinowitz, Avram Israel Reisner, Joel E. Rembaum, James S. Rosen, and Joel Roth. Voting against: Rabbis Samuel Fraint, Baruch Frydman-Kohl, and Paul Plotkin. Abstaining: Rabbis Myron S. Geller and Elie Kaplan Spitz.

The Committee on Jewish Law and Standards of the Rabbinical Assembly provides guidance in matters of halakhah for the Conservative movement. The individual rabbi, however, is the authority for the interpretation and application of all matters of halakhah.

שאלה

From a halakhic perspective, must one support a group home for the "developmentally challenged" in one's back yard? Does one have the halakhic right to be opposed to the placement of such a group home in his or her neighborhood? Is a rabbi to speak for or against this issue?

תשובה

In the United States, there are an estimated 7.5 million people with mental retardation. This constitutes between 2.5 and 3 percent of the U.S. population. As such, mental retardation is fifteen times more prevalent than cerebral palsy, thirty times more prevalent than neural tube defects such as spina bifida, and thirty-six times more prevalent than total blindness. It is also fifty times more prevalent than total deafness.[1] Worldwide, approximately 156 million people, or 3 percent of the world population, have mental retardation.[2]

Though several hundred causes for mental retardation have been discovered, the three major sources are Down's syndrome, fetal alcohol syndrome and fragile X syndrome. In addition to genetic conditions, primary causes can include problems during pregnancy such as rubella, toxicity, malnutrition, RH incompatibility, radiation, pre-

---

[1] "What is Mental Retardation?" at *www.paso.org/about/whatismr.html*, quoting the American Association on Mental Retardation (AAMR). See also *Diagnostic and Statistical Manual of Mental Disorders (DSM IV)* (Washington, DC: The American Psychiatric Association, 1994), pp. 40-46.

[2] "What is Mental Health?", ibid., quoting the World Health Organization.

maturity or birth injury. Environmental issues are sometimes factors as well, including physical accident, fever, malnutrition, lead poisoning, poor parental care, sensory deprivation and educational deprivation.[3]

Mental retardation is most often divided into three categories:

Mild: This category encompasses those with an IQ range between fifty-five and seventy. Individuals in this range are often physically indistinguishable from the typical population. They are capable of learning academic skills to approximately an eighth grade level. They can usually acquire vocational and social skills necessary for independent living. Of all individuals with mental retardation, eighty-nine percent are mildly retarded.

Moderate: Those with an IQ range between forty and fifty-five. Within this range, individuals have significant impairment in achieving academic success. However, they can learn self-care, social and vocational skills. The language is generally functional and partial independence is achievable.

Severe: Those with an IQ range between twenty-five and forty. (Sometimes combined with *Profound*, where IQ scores fall below twenty-five.) In this category, individuals are less capable, but with special instruction, can achieve a significant degree of self-care and independence in highly structured settings. Individuals in this category have some language but understand more than they can express. Only 3.5% of all persons with mental retardation have severe or profound retardation.[4]

In the 1970s, a wholesale move towards de-institutionalization took place. Most large institutions are now gone. Intermediate care facilities (ICFs) and group homes have replaced them. The hope was that, in this way, individuals with retardation could more closely integrate into the community. The Americans with Disabilities Act (1990) mandates that individuals with disabilities be provided with the least restrictive environment for the services they receive.[5] As such, group homes help developmentally delayed people live in the community while providing the care they need.

Commonly, one finds a range of individuals who reside in group homes. However, those with lesser skills benefit greatly from the safety of these environments. Medications and safety can be more carefully monitored in such facilities. Physical accommodation is more readily supervised when necessary. In general, it is considered the safest setting for those with greater support needs.[6]

Typically, four to six individuals live in a group home along with supervisory staff. Residents typically receive other services provided by private agencies or the government such as vocational training, social outings, etc.

Homes are organized by individuals, private agencies and, in some cases, by state agencies for the retarded. Housing sources include Supplemental Security Income (SSI), states' SSI supplements, Social Security Disability Insurance, Section 8 vouchers, housing subsidies and private sources including family trusts, housing associations, community land trusts, community loan funds, Habitat for Humanity, etc.

Currently, most people with mental retardation live with their families. However, as parents age, other living arrangements are sought. Over 87,000 individuals nationwide liv-

---

[3] "Mental Retardation," ARC (The Association of Retarded Citizens) at *www.main.org/arc/mr.html*.

[4] Ibid. See also AAMR report.

[5] ADA Technical Assistance Manual General Requirements III-3.1000. ADA Regulations 28CFR36.201-36.213 and 36.203-Integrated Settings.

[6] "Consumer Control of Housing," University of Missouri at Kansas City Developmental Disabilities Resource Center at *www.moddrc.com/info/cch.htm*.

ing with families are waiting for other arrangements. The waiting time for individuals hoping to enter group homes can be as long as twelve years. Most states prioritize their lists allowing emergency cases such as homeless children and those who suffer the death of parents to move more immediately into group home settings.[7]

All group homes are licensed by the state and must meet zoning, health, fire and general safety regulations. Many homes can cost up to half a million dollars per year to administer.[8]

N.I.M.B.Y.

The "not in my back yard" phenomenon is a common concern in twentieth-century America. Frequently, neighborhood residents have banded together to protest the building of prisons, waste dumps and other unsightly institutions within proximity to their neighborhoods. At times, there have been ugly expressions of protest against the purchase of a home designed for group living of the developmentally disabled. Among concerns cited are the possibility of residents wandering at odd times throughout the neighborhood, declining property values and "a slippery slope" leading to criminal halfway houses. While such concerns are exaggerated, it is fair to raise a potential concern that may be voiced by neighbors to group homes. In order to provide services, many homes have frequent visitors who arrive to provide transportation, therapies and other medical services to residents. Some home might appear to be a virtual agency within a residential neighborhood. It is likely that there would be a more frequent parade of visitors than one might find in a typical residential neighborhood.

Of late, protests have centered far more on the establishment of actual halfway houses. The Federal Fair Housing Act[9] prohibits discrimination in sale or rental of housing on the basis of race, religion, color, national origin or sex. In 1988, amendments to that act extended to people with disabilities and families with children. Disability is defined as including physical or mental impairment. Furthermore, the U.S. Supreme Court has ruled that communities cannot utilize single-family zoning to bar group homes for the disabled by enforcing occupancy limits in a discriminatory way. Thus, group homes for the developmentally disabled, provided they meet state licensing requirements, are protected under American law.[10]

Indeed, many advocates for retarded citizens have noted the relative decline of overt protests against the establishment of group homes for those with developmental delay. Group home leaders take great pains to introduce residents to neighbors, open their homes to visitation and do everything possible to demonstrate their intention to be good neighbors.[11] While this improvement can be partially traced to a greater receptivity of handicapped individuals, pockets of opposition are sure to remain.

There is a significant volume of halakhah governing the roles of neighbors and the physical construction of homes and property in order to provide privacy and security. For example, we read in the Mishnah, Bava Batra 2:4:

---

[7] Dennis Geary, Director, Jewish Association for Communal Living (JCL), Hartford, Connecticut. (Personal conversation.)

[8] Ibid.

[9] U.S. code, Title 42, Chapter 45.

[10] *http://www.bazelon.org/cpha/n/c95pap.html*. Also see *lectlaw.com*, *New York Times* Services, 16 May 1995.

[11] Dennis Geary. (Personal conversation.) See also D.A. Arens, "What Do the Neighbors Think Now? Community Residences on Long Island," Community Mental Health Health Journal 29(3): 235-245, 1993.

If one has a wall running alongside his neighbor's wall, he should not bring another wall alongside unless he keeps it (at least) four cubits away. If there are windows (in the neighbor's wall), he must leave a clear space of four cubits whether above or below or opposite.

The Gemara there[12] elaborates that allowing such a space is a means of avoiding one from "peeping" into another's room.

Some might argue that there is a potential for group home residents to constitute a disturbance because of their "unusual appearance." Some might even assert that the placement of a group home in proximity to neighbors potentially constitutes a form of חזק ראיה, a kind of damage in halakhah that emerges from unseemly sights in a neighbor's property.

We shall see below all other considerations supercede this potential. Moreover, the Gemara reflects debate whether or not חזק ראיה is genuine damage or not.[13] Also, the scenario in the Mishnah cited above is entirely mutual. The laws governing the construction of walls and the placement of windows protects both parties.

Mental Retardation and Halakhah

The most relevant halakhic categories to mental retardation are the שוטה and the פתי. Concerning the שוטה, the Talmud in Haggigah 3b states the following:

איזהו שוטה? היוצא יחידי בלילה והלן בבית הקברות והמקרע את כסותו.

Who is named a שוטה? One that goes out alone at night and he that spends the night in a cemetery and he that tears his garments.

A שוטה is typically translated as "idiot," "imbecile," "mentally impaired," or "incompetent." It is an ambiguous category to delineate.

In the Gemara, Rav Huna states that one is not considered a שוטה unless he manifests each of the three forms of bizarre conduct described herein.[14] Rav Yochanan holds that if one manifests any of the three forms of erratic conduct depicted, one is deemed a שוטה. In general, the חרש – deaf mute – שוטה and minors are not required to fulfill the mitzvot and not subjected to the penalties for which adults would normally be culpable. שוטים are legally classed as minors in this regard.[15]

The שוטה, as presented in the Gemara, displays the kind of behavior typically associated with emotional disturbance such as psychoses, bizarre or stereotypic actions characterized by self-abuse and inappropriateness of orientation. Certainly, not all individuals with mental retardation would fit this description. Those with mild or moderate expressions of retardation are intellectually immature but rarely display such inappropriate behaviors.

Maimonides introduces a new element regarding שטות in discussion of עדות. In the Mishneh Torah we read:

הפתאים ביותר שאין מכירין דברים שסותרין זה את זה ולא יבינו עניני הדבר כדרך שמבינין שאר עם הארץ, וכן המבהלים והנחפזים בדעתם והמשתגעים ביותר–הרי אלו בכלל השוטים.

---

[12] Bava Batra 22b. See also the discussion in the *Encyclopedia Talmudit* (Jerusalem: Encyclopedia Publishers Ltd., 1980), vol. 8, pp. 759, 786-788, s.v. חזק ראיה.

[13] Bava Batra 2b.

[14] See also Tosefta Terumot 1:3.

[15] Rashi, Haggigah 3b, s.v. איזהו שוטה.

> The extremely simple-minded who do not recognize things which contradict one another and who do not comprehend the particulars of a situation as do the rest of the masses; and so also those whose thought processes show confusion and disinhibition, as well as those who are extremely bewildered are included among the שוטים (M.T. Hilkhot Edut 9:10).

This would indicate that with respect to עדות, where requirements are particularly stringent, the Gemara's categories are merely representative of a consistent pattern that would disqualify one from serving as a witness. Any consistent confusion or bizarreness of thought would also classify one as a שוטה.[16]

Maimonides believes that some forms of שטות are temporary:

> He who is sometimes a שוטה and sometimes normal, as is the case with epileptics, his actions are like any other individuals when he is normal. . .and witnesses are needed to determine whether he may have committed his action either at the beginning or end of his abnormal episode (M.T. Hilkhot Mehira 29:5).[17]

Clearly, for Maimonides, the issue of דעת, a capacity to function intellectually with consistent clarity, is central in defining clear qualifications for עדות. However, halakhah recognizes gradations in the שוטה's capacity to function. We read in the Shulhan Arukh in Orah Hayyim 199:10 (Rama) that, a חרש or a שוטה can be included in the זימון for ברכת המזון if they can concentrate and comprehend even though the חרש does not hear the blessing. The Mishnah Brurah there states that the שוטה referred to is not a complete שוטה since such a total שוטה could not be part of the quorum. This individual is simply not as intelligent as others, and the masses regard him as a שוטה. Again, though popularly considered a שוטה, a lack of intellectual capability alone would not make one fit this categorization. There is no disoriented behavior involved.[18]

The second category is that of the פתי. As quoted above, Maimonides defines the פתיים as a sub-class of שוטים whose members display impaired intellectual ability. Reuven Hammer, in a תשובה concerning the permissibility of conducting a Bar/Bat Mitzvah for children with mental retardation, asserts that the Rambam's inclusion of the פתי as a שוטה is only to exclude both שוטים and פתיים from serving as witnesses. He draws a sharp

---

[16] See also Kesef Mishnah on עדות 9:9.

[17] This is particularly relevant for marriage and divorce. A גט could be authorized by a husband when in a period of lucidity. See S.A. Even HaEzer 121:3.

[18] Two more recent responsa addressed the question of placing a child with retardation in a setting where non-kosher food would be given. The Hatam Sofer (Rabbi Moses Sofer) denied permission to have a seven year-old boy placed in an institution though his bizarre behavior and weak intelligence made him a candidate for such an environment. The Hatam Sofer rules that because this particular boy was considered educable and "curable," his placement in this institution would improve his mental status and make him responsible to fulfill the mitzvot upon reaching adulthood. However, feeding him non-kosher food in his childhood would prejudice him against a life of mitzvot.

In a תשובה by Moshe Feinstein, a contradictory conclusion is reached. Feinstein rules that there is no problem in placing an eleven year-old girl whose retardation was ascribed to brain injury in a setting where non-kosher food would be served. Her condition is considered incurable and, hence, she will forever be free from observing all of the mitzvot. Feinstein also states that the case of the Hatam Sofer refers to a situation where there is a possibility that the individual was not a שוטה at all but that his intelligence was weak and that in such a setting, that his real status as פתי would emerge. As such, a פתי is required to observe the commandments and feeding him non-kosher food would be clearly wrong. See *Teshuvot Hatam Sofer* Orah Hayyim no. 83 and *Iggrot Moshe* Orah Hayyim, vol. 2, no. 88.

distinction between the שוטה who displays clear mental illness and the פתי who has reduced cognitive capacity.[19]

While such distinctions are important for discerning the status of halakhic obligation to observe the mitzvot, they are less relevant in our matter. There may be a biological difference but little practical distinction between an individual suffering from an acute psychotic episode and a profoundly retarded adult who cannot understand proper social behavior in a given setting. In any event, such a person needs a safe home in which to live.

Clearly, the שוטה is a highly subjective category requiring individual assessment. Some people with mental retardation at the severe or profound levels may, indeed, display some of the classic disoriented behavior of the שוטה. Others will be best viewed as פתיים, those of significantly diminished intelligence. Both are at a societal disadvantage and require concerted efforts to attain integration into the culture at large.

Disability in the Torah

There are sources in the Torah that indicate that disabilities were considered a sign of disgrace. When, for example, the Philistines discover the secret of Samson's strength, they seize him and put out his eyes as an act of humiliation (Judg. 16:21). When Nebuchadnezzar defeats Jerusalem during the reign of King Zedekiah, the King attempts to flee, but he and his sons are captured and brought before Nebuchadnezzar. We read: "They captured the King and brought him before the King of Babylon at Riblah, and they put him on trial. They slaughtered Zedekiah's sons before his eyes; they put out Zedekiah's eyes, bound him in bronze fetters and brought him to Babylon" (2 Kings 25:6-7). Here, too, the theme of humiliation is linked to a created disability.

The Book of Leviticus provides for us a long list of physical attributes that disqualify the Kohen from service:

> Speak to Aaron and say: not man of your offspring throughout the ages who has a defect shall be qualified to offer the food of his God; no one at all who has a defect shall be qualified, no man who is blind, or lame, or has a limb too short or too long; no man who has a broken leg or a broken arm; or who has a hunchback or is a dwarf, whoever has a growth in his eye or who has a boil, scar or scurvy, or crushed testes. No man among the offspring of Aaron the Priest who has a defect shall be qualified to offer the Lord's offerings by fire; having a defect he shall not be qualified to offer the food of his God (Lev. 21:17-21).

Maimonides comments: "For the multitude does not estimate man by his true form but by the perfection of his bodily limbs and the beauty of his garments, and the Temple was to be held in great reverence by all."[20]

At the same time, many Biblical characters though physically blemished are still deemed heroic. The patriarch Isaac has dim eyes (Gen. 27:1); Moses protests his allotted mission due to a speech defect (Exod. 4:10). The Divine response is: "Who gives man

---

[19] תשובות ועד ההלכה של כנסת הרבנים בישראל, כרך ד' תש"ן-תשנ"ב עמ' 11–14.

[20] Moses Maimonides, *The Guide for the Perplexed*, trans. Moses Friedlander (New York: Dover Publications, 1956), 3:45, p. 357.

speech? Who makes him dumb or deaf, seeing or blind? Is it not I, the Lord? Now go, and I will be with you as you speak and instruct you what to say" (Exod. 4:11-12).

There is, of course, the admonishment from Leviticus:

לא תקלל חרש ולפני עור לא תתן מכשל.

> You shall not insult the deaf nor place a stumbling block before the blind (Lev. 19:14).

This passage has often been utilized as a basis for avoiding the deception of the unknowing or vulnerable in general. Indeed, Nahmanides asks the question:

אין לי אלא חרש, מנין לרבות כל אדם.

> The Torah speaks only of the חרש. How do we know that this applies to all people?[21]

The implication is not only must those with disabilities be treated justly, there are instances when all are in a sense "disabled" by ignorance, circumstances, etc. Thus, all deserve proper treatment.

Rabbinic literature outlines a variety of specific disabilities. Among them: the סומא (the blind person), the נכפה (one who has epilepsy), the טומטום and אנדרוגינוס (one who is sexually neuter and a hermaphrodite), the סריס ואילונית (one who is sterile), the אלם (one who is mute) and, of course the חרש and שוטה. A ברכה is ordained where one sees an individual possessing such conditions. The text, משנה הבריות, simply notes the variety of divine creations. The blessing makes no mention of divine justice but simply celebrates the various forms of God's creations.

The Inviolability of Human Life

The Torah makes no distinction between fully competent and challenged individuals in declaring that all humans are created in God's image. Any act that compromises the intrinsic worth of a handicapped person is prohibited by the Torah. We are forbidden to defame the character of such an individual nor place him or her in any situation where physical or psychological harm might take place.[22]

The inviolability of human life is expressed in a variety of other ways. For example, we read in the Biur Halakhah that slaying a handicapped person is no different than slaying a non-handicapped person, and we violate Shabbat in cases of פקוח נפש for a challenged person as well."[23] Furthermore:

היה הבן ממזר או חרש שוטה וקטן קיים המצוה.

> If one has fathered a ממזר or חרש or a שוטה, one has fulfilled the commandment (of "be fruitful and multiply").[24]

Also, with respect to criminal penalties, the offender is culpable for damages against the שוטה.[25]

---

[21] Nahmanides, ad loc.
[22] See the discussion in Edwin Kaminetzky, *Studies in Torah-Sins of Omission-The Neglected Children* (New York: Yeshiva University Press, 1977), p. 90.
[23] Mishnah Berurah, Biur Halakhah on S.A. Orah Hayyim 329:4.
[24] See the Beit Yosef and M. Isserles on S.A. Even HaEzer 1:6.
[25] S.A. Hoshen Mishpat 424:8.

The Halakhic Requirement to Support Group Homes

The fundamental goal of establishing group homes is to provide a safe living environment for people coping with retardation. Their mental status certainly makes them among society's most vulnerable members. Individuals with autism, for example, often display not only significant mental impairment but also unusual repetitive or self-abusive behavior, and, as such, need supervised settings. Those with a greater capacity to function (the פתיים) often do well in less supervised apartment settings. Thus, to support group homes is to assist the most disadvantaged among the disadvantaged in many cases.

It is crucial to remember that many individuals with mental retardation suffer from a variety of physical ailments. In addition to concerns for self injury, it is common to find cardiac, neurological and other impairments in the population of the developmentally disabled. The physical needs can be very great.

Moreover, mental retardation is a form of mental illness. It is so classified in the *DSM IV*. Though in certain contexts we might de-emphasize this diagnostic aspect lest such individuals be stigmatized, it is important here to note that these conditions, whatever their etiologies, are permanent, debilitating, and, in more extreme cases, even life-threatening.

Group homes provide not only shelter, but also food, and attentiveness to medical problems. It is not unusual to find within them residents who have difficulty in picking up a pill and swallowing it, much less understanding its purpose. As such, the most significant argument on behalf of group homes in one's neighborhood is that such places fall under the rubric of caring for the ill.

Recent תשובות of the Committee on Jewish Law and Standards have addressed the central necessity of preserving life. A responsum of Rabbi Joseph H. Prouser[26] argues that Organ Donation is a halakhic obligation in light of פקוח נפש – the saving of life.

As Maimonides states:

כל שיכול להציל ולא הציל – עובר על: "לא תעמד על דם רעך" (ויקרא י"ט:ט"ז).

> Anyone who is able to save a life but fails to do so violates "You shall not stand idly by the blood of your neighbor" (Lev. 19:16).[27]

Rabbis Elliot N. Dorff and Aaron L. Mackler, in a series of three related תשובות, have argued that individuals, physicians and the community must provide a decent minimum for health care. These תשובות have also been adopted by the Committee on Jewish Law and Standards.[28]

Among their salient points: To visit and care for the sick is a fundamental expression of *Imitatio Dei* as the aggadah in Sotah 14a states. They also cite the source from Sanhedrin (17b) which states that a Torah scholar should not reside in a city where a physician is absent. This effectively makes it every Jewish community's responsibility to furnish needed medical services.[29]

---

[26] Rabbi Joseph H. Prouser, "Hesed or Hiyuv? The Obligation to Preserve Life and the Question of Post-Mortem Organ Donation," above, pp. 175-190.

[27] Hilkhot Rotzeach v'Shmirat Nefesh 1:14.

[28] Rabbis Elliot N. Dorff and Aaron L. Mackler, "Responsibilities for the Provision of Health Care," above, pp. 319-336.

[29] Ibid. p. 322.

Drawing from the analogy of צדקה on behalf of the poor, they state that we provide for those in need according to their needs (די מחסרו אשר יחסר לו).[30] In the paradigmatic cases there quoted from Shulhan Arukh Yoreh De'ah 250:1, we find that one must rent a house for one in need. All the more so is this a need for many who have mental retardation.

In the תשובה that specifically relates to the community's responsibility, they state, "In distribution of health care as in other areas, halakhah would understand health and health care to include mental as well as physical health."[31] This is supported by traditional sources including Yoma 82a and the *Iggrot Moshe* E.H. no. 65 of R. Moshe Feinstein. Moreover, we might add that in a contemporary, diverse society we would make no distinction between Jews and non-Jews regarding support for a group home. As Maimonides states: "We bury the dead of heathens, comfort their mourners and visit their sick as this is the way of peace."[32]

A group home serves as an element of a "decent minimum" of care for those of the mentally retarded population who need it the most. It is a clear expression of social justice reflected in Lev. 19:16, "Nor shall you stand idly by the blood of your fellow." At the same time, there is another verse from Leviticus that gives us an added imperative to support group homes in our midst. We read:

> וכי ימוך אחיך ומטה ידו עמך והחזקת בו גר ותושב וחי עמך. אל תקח
> מאתו נשך ותרבית ויראת מאלהיך וחי אחיך עמך.
>
> If your kinsman being in straits comes under your authority and you hold him as though a resident alien, let him live by your side; do not exact from him advance or accrued interest, but fear your God. Let him live by your side as your kinsman (Lev. 25:35-36).

While individuals with mental retardation may or may not be in personal financial straits at any one point in time, their vulnerability is clear. Moreover, the goal of group homes extends beyond a mere shelter and security. A second important goal of group homes is to integrate people with developmental delay into the general community. These homes provide an opportunity to fulfill the imperative of וחי אחיך עמך.

The principle of וחי אחיך עמך has a noble history with respect to people with disabilities in the Conservative movement. The Tikvah programs at Camp Ramah wherein children with a variety of learning and mental challenges participate in a full camping program at the Ramah camps serve as a fine example of this principle in action.

The support of the establishment and maintenance of a group home is a fundamental act of גמילות חסדים, a form of צדקה, which is a mitzvah unto itself.[33] To do so in one's own neighborhood provides rabbis with a powerful opportunity to advocate for the insistence by halakhah on caring for the ill and recognizing the uniqueness of all human life as created בצלם אלוקים.

---

[30] Ibid. p. 324.

[31] Ibid. p. 331.

[32] Mishneh Torah, Hilkhot Avel 14:12.

[33] T. Peah, ch. 4; Bavli Sukkah 49b, J. Peah, ch. 1:5.

Conclusion

Group homes provide genuine physical and emotional shelter to the people with developmental disabilities who live in them. They are places of care for those who culp with the illness and challenge of mental disability. Such homes are frequently the only proper placement, given de-institutionalization and other societal trends.

The tradition's concern for caring for the ill and the well being of those with handicapping conditions, as well as the inviolability of human life, requires that we support independent living conditions for them especially in our neighborhoods.

YD 339.1995

Peri- and Neo-Natology: The Matter of Limiting Treatment

Rabbi Avram Israel Reisner

This paper was approved by the CJLS on September 13, 1995, by a vote of eighteen in favor (18-0-0). Voting in favor: Rabbis Kassel Abelson, Ben Zion Bergman, Stephanie Dickstein, Elliot N. Dorff, Shoshana Gelfand, Myron S. Geller, Arnold Goodman, Susan Grossman, Judah Kogen, Vernon H. Kurtz, Aaron L. Mackler, Paul Plotkin, Mayer Rabinowitz, Avram Israel Reisner, Joel Rembaum, Gerald Skolnik, Elie Kaplan Spitz, and Gerald Zelizer.

The Committee on Jewish Law and Standards of the Rabbinical Assembly provides guidance in matters of halakhah for the Conservative movement. The individual rabbi, however, is the authority for the interpretation and application of all matters of halakhah.

שאלה

When are we justified, if ever, to allow a malformed newborn to die without applying maximum technological efforts to save that child or to extend its life?

תשובה

Developments in the field of peri- and neo-natology are coming apace and nothing written today can hope to digest developments on the morrow. This said, there are certain general judgments that can be made.

First some terminological matters. For some time, the field of treating high risk babies was known as neonatology and consisted of the treatment of damaged, pre-mature and low birth weight infants. In the last decade, however, the fields of genetic testing, intrauterine diagnosis and microsurgery have all expanded dramatically, offering the possibility of diagnosing fetal flaws in the womb and intervening in that environment to correct them.[1] Consequently a new term has entered the field to describe treatment of

---

[1] A particularly striking example is at the heart of the popular book, *The Baby Doctors*, by Gina Kolata (New York: Delacorte, 1990), reporting on some of the pioneering attempts at fetal surgery. Many newborns were dying, with little hope of successful intervention, due to respiratory insufficiency. No respirator or incubator therapy could replace the lung maturity that was absent. Stunningly, a significant subset of these children were found to be suffering from diaphragmatic hernias, wherein the diaphragm had failed to close properly in early fetal development and the intestinal organs had migrated up through the hole, effectively preventing the later developing lungs from forming in the cavity they now filled. By learning to operate in utero to draw down the migrating intestines and close the hole in the diaphragm, the perinatal surgeons were able to forge room for the lungs to develop and the children would be born healthy. Effectively, a small mechanical problem was killing large numbers of babies

an infant both before and after birth, that term, perinatology, has been added to the older term in the literature.[2] As a result, it is necessary today to speak of treatment of the fetus as well as of the newborn.

The Status of the Fetus

As David Feldman sets out in his magnificent *Birth Control in Jewish Law*,[3] the unborn child is not seen as a separate and full life under Jewish law. It is protected, however, as potential life and may be aborted only for maternal causes. Concern for potential pain and burden on the unborn child cannot be a reason to choose abortion; not because that would be murder, but because to do so would be to meddle in God's domain, whereas treatment of the mother is in ours. Nevertheless, any and all acts that we might undertake to heal or strengthen the potential life of the fetus are in order. As with human life, we are enjoined to heal. That is part of the divine mandate.

Often, however, the mother's interests intervene in any calculations regarding the fetus. Unlike the potential life of the fetus, the mother's life is established. As such it takes clear precedence under Jewish law. The Mishnah in Ohalot (7:6) clearly permits abortion, even at a very late date, to save the mother's life. No calculation of viability is material here: only birth. With this as the primary precedent, Jewish legal sources included the health and even the mental well-being of the mother as potential reason to permit abortion. Some have argued that these precedents may be stretched to include the child's own disabilities where they would severely and negatively impact the mother's mental composure, her family situation, or even the economics thereof.[4] The upshot of this literature is to permit abortion for cause, but not simply by unsupported choice. What constitutes sufficient cause is a decision to be made on a case by case basis by the parents and their rabbi. This position is stated clearly in the definitive rulings by the CJLS on this subject on August 23, 1983.[5]

---

and a comparatively simple procedure could be devised to save them (although nothing is truly simple in intrauterine surgery due to the size and speed of growth of the fetus).

[2] The *Random House College Dictionary* (1982), p. 892, defines neonatology as, "the branch of medicine that specializes in care of newborn children, especially those that are premature," and a neonate as, "a newborn child, or one in its first 28 days." (Note the similarities to Rabban Gamaliel's thirty-day measure in Tosefta Shabbat 15:7.) That dictionary does not yet attest "perinatology," although it is clearly built on the Greek root "peri" meaning "around." Thus the new term "perinatology" connotes treatment around birth, before, as well as after.

The introduction to the first chapter of *Behrman's Neonatal-Perinatal Medicine* (St. Louis: Mosby, 1983) defines the field as follows: "The term 'perinatal' is used to designate the period from the twelfth week of gestation through the twenty-eighth day after birth." The "neonatal period" is defined as "the first four weeks of life and is the period of the greatest mortality in childhood." In practice, an active neonatologist offers this definition: "The perinatal period extends from the beginning of the third trimester until the end of the first postnatal week. The neonatal period begins immediately after birth and extends until the end of the fourth postnatal week. A perinatologist is an obstetrician with added subspecialty training who cares for the mother and fetus. A neonatologist is a pediatrician with added subspecialty training who cares for high risk newborns" (personal letter from Dr. Charles Paley to R. Stephanie Dickstein, 6 Sept. 1995).

[3] For the details of this position, see David M. Feldman, *Birth Control in Jewish Law* (New York: NYU Press, 1968), chs. 14 and 15, and infra. Schocken published a paperback reprint in 1987 under the new (and more accurate) title *Marital Relations, Birth Control and Abortion in Jewish Law*.

[4] See R. Eliezer Waldenberg, *Tzitz Eliezer*, 2d ed. (Jerusalem, 1985), vol. 9, no. 51.3; vol. 13, no. 102; vol. 15, no. 43. His positions are summarized in A. Steinberg, *Hilkhot Rofeim uRefuah* (Jerusalem: Mossad HaRav Kook, 1978), pp. 30-46. See also Feldman, n. 3, above.

[5] *PCJLS 80-85*, pp. 1-37.

Much more can be done for the fetus in utero today, however, than in the past, and even more will be possible in the future. Are we required to offer medical assistance to this fetus even when we do not recognize the fetus as a fully vested life and could conceivably abort it? The upshot of these permissive (but not pro-choice) rulings is that where aiding the fetus could have negative ramifications for the mother, any and all medical assistance for the fetus may be foregone. Any manipulation of the fetus, whether surgical or medicinal, would, in fact, entail some risk to the mother. Whereas the results are uncertain and the risks are real it is appropriate to forgo endeavors to aid the fetus.

But forgoing medical treatment of the fetus in utero, while permissible, is not required. The mother's desire to undertake some risk for her child and the true extent of that risk must be considered in every case. We would, without much hesitation, permit a kidney donation to a relative, although life with only one kidney is clearly more precarious than with two. We would encourage sea rescues, despite the risk of drowning, because we understand the risk is small when measured against what may be gained. The desire to aid the fetus is very real and should be considered. Action to save a life, even a potential one, is meritorious, and proceeds even at the cost of Shabbat transgressions.[6] But fetal life is just that, potential life not yet actualized, not, as the tradition claims, within the category of נפש אדם, a human life. Efforts to aid are subject to that inequality between the mother's status and the fetus'. It should be noted that even when other human lives are at stake, there is a point when rescuers are restrained from reentering a burning building, although they had done so before, because, assessing the situation, we determine that the risk has grown too great. All the more so here.

There is a second issue which enters here, the issue of viability.[7] It appears to me that a viability standard at the end of the seventh month (31-32 weeks)[8] when survival approaches 85%, must be extended to the fetus if we speak of the presumption of life potential for medical purposes. That correlates well with the abilities of peri-natology today. This is not to say that a late term fetus has attained the status of a full life, but that greater concern for the potential life of the fetus is in order. Rabbi Waldenberg, at least, seems to hint at such

---

[6] This conclusion is based, primarily on the notion: חלל עליו שבת אחת כדי שישמור שבתות הרבה – One should transgress this one Shabbat in order that he may observe many (Shabbat 151b). This would apply well to a fetus, even though the fetus is not yet alive. See Feldman, p. 264 and Waldenberg, vol. 13, no. 102, section 3.

[7] On 3 June 1992 the CJLS approved a paper by Rabbi Stephanie Dickstein on "Jewish Ritual Practice Following the Death of an Infant Who Lives Less Than Thirty-One Days," below, pp. 439-449. The CJLS approved an alteration of the law of mourning from the cautious view of Rabban Simeon ben Gamaliel that mourning is not required of an infant that dies in those first thirty days (Shabbat 135b), in favor of the more subjective measure of the Mishnah in Niddah 5:3,

תינוק בן יום אחד... הרי הוא לאביו ולאמו ולכל קרוביו כחתן שלם.

[Even] a day-old infant is considered by his father and mother and all its relatives as a full bridegroom.

In "Kim Li: A Dissenting Concurrence," below, pp. 450-451, I argued that the measure was incorrect. If we seek to measure the subjective considerations of the parents, it is more realistic to try to measure their expectations than their hopes. Not all children, born, are, in fact, expected to live, even by their parents. In fact, a likelihood that the child would live is not established by a 50-50 chance but by some significant preponderance of the chances that the child would live.

I proposed a 31-32 week threshold, corresponding to the end of the seventh month by obstetrical count. I remain convinced of that position.

[8] The vagueness inherent in establishing a 31-32 week threshold rather than a date certain is intended to convey that obstetrical count is itself notoriously fallible (although with ultrasound measurements it is much firmer than it has historically been), and that we always are bound to the best judgment of the physician. Said flexibility should be permitted to push the date back as far as the beginning of the third trimester (27-28 weeks) where the doctor feels that his neonatal unit reaches eighty-five percent viability that early.

a standard when he writes of abortion on account of Tay-Sachs disease:

יש לדעתי להתיר הפסקת הריון כזה לפחות עד שבעה חודשים.

> It appears to me that such an abortion may be permitted at least through the seventh month.[9]

Surgical and medical treatment of the fetus in utero, at this late date, should be encouraged if there is a good chance of curing the fetus and little risk to the mother.

This is not in conflict with the permission we have granted abortion for cause. Thirty-one to thirty-two weeks is the end of the seventh month by obstetrical count, or well into the third trimester. Abortion at that late date is exceedingly rare and will not be performed except where the mother's health is endangered, or in cases of rape or incest where the mother's mental well-being is at issue, or where there are genetic indications which occasion it (where again we would permit abortion readily based on the mother's well-being). Indeed, the law of the land supports such a distinction, ruling in *Roe vs. Wade* that states may not prohibit abortion in the first two trimesters, but that they may do so in the third.

Nor do we prohibit abortion even in the eighth and ninth month. But it is correct that the claim on life of the fetus should grow closer to that of its mother in those latter days, and treatment questions as well as abortion questions should be weighed in that light.[10]

The Status of the Newborn

Birth is the defining moment with regard to the status of the infant. Nevertheless, there are substantial misgivings in the halakhic literature concerning even the viability of newborns. The Talmud accepts as a given that a seven or nine month child may live, but that an eight month child will not. Thus, Shabbat circumcision is required of a seven and nine month child, but prohibited for an eight month child or for one about whom we hold a significant question. The same would not be true of a doubtful eight month birth with regard to medical treatment, wherein health needs override Shabbat regulations even in the event of uncertainty. But it would be true, according to the classical halakhah, that even medical treatment could not be given on Shabbat to a verified eight month baby, of whom the Tosefta writes:

הרי הוא כאבן. ואין מטלטלין אותו, אבל אמו שוחה עליו ומניקתו.

> He is like a stone. One does not move him [on Shabbat], but his mother may bend over him to suckle him.

(The commentators are quick to add: מפני צער החלב שמצערה – "due to her pain of engorgement,"[11] not due to our concern for that infant's life.)

Indeed, Rabban Simeon ben Gamaliel's dictum that a child is not considered to be viable until the thirty-first day after birth is itself apparently predicated on this uncertainty.[12]

The notion that an eight month baby cannot live and therefore does not merit our attention is profoundly disturbing (yet it is indicative of our options to withhold care from

---

[9] Waldenberg, vol. 13, no. 102, sect. 5, and see sect. 1.

[10] Dr. Charles Paley, in his correspondence with R. Stephanie Dickstein, notes that this is largely a theoretical permission of abortion. In reality, he notes, a fetus of this age would have a substantial potential for survival. Consequently, most crises related to the mother's ability to proceed with the pregnancy would be resolved not by abortion but by Caesarean section.

[11] Tosefta Shabbat 15.5-7, B. Shabbat 135a, J. Yevamot 4.2, S.A. Orah Hayyim 330.5ff. See also the lengthy pilpul in this regard by R. Yitzhak Yaakov Weiss, *Minhat Yitzhak*, vol. 4, no. 123.

[12] Shabbat 135b. See above, n. 7.

hopeless cases, to which we will return in a moment). It is disturbing because it does not correlate with our best science and would ask us to withhold critical care from those infants we might save. Furthermore, the eight month infant in question is in his ninth month by obstetrical count, since this is a count of months *completed*.[13] Yet viability in the ninth month, today, approaches 100%!

Candor would have us simply state that the Talmud's eight month rule cannot stand in light of current understanding. Indeed, the well respected sage, Avraham Karelitz, known as Hazon Ish, argued tentatively:

כמדומה דעכשיו נשתנה הטבע וכפי בחינת הרופאים.

It seems that now nature has changed and we follow the discernment of the doctors.

While this opinion was not yet current in the early literature,[14] it seems to have gained current assent.[15] Concerning the laws of mourning, the Committee on Jewish Law and Standards has opted to waive Rabban Simeon ben Gamaliel's argument in

---

[13] That the count is of *completed* months is clear from the Tosefta's definition (15.7):

איזהו בן שמונה? כל שלא יצאו לו חדשיו.

Which is an eight month infant? One who has not completed his months.

and by the Talmud's use, on Shabbat 136a, of:

קים לי ביה שכלו לו חדשיו.

I am certain that he has completed his months.

as a synonym for a viable, full term baby. Otherwise he would need assert only that the baby had reached the ninth month. Many modern halakhic writings refer to the eighth month by obstetrical convention and assume the non-viability of the eight month child to refer to that. (See, for instance, R. Neria Gutal, "haPagut l'Or haHalakha," *Assia*, no. 44 (vol. 11, no. 4), pp. 5-30 and in notes 1 and 2 to his second installment of that article, *Assia*, no. 45-6 (vol. 12, no. 1-2), p. 97. This appears to me to be insupportable. But Dr. Steinberg, ever reasonable, understands the count to be of completed months and thus cites the Talmud, "A baby born *after* [my emphasis] eight months of gestation is non-viable" (Dr. Abraham Steinberg, "The Defective Newborn – Halachic Considerations" in Dr. Fred Rosner, *Medicine and Jewish Law II* [Northvale, NJ: Jason Aronson, 1993], p. 125).

It is further the case that obstetric and Jewish count are discrepant month by month. Obstetrical count assumes a beginning at the last menses and an extent of 40 weeks or 280 days. These amount to 9 months and one week of the secular calendar's 30-31 day months (To wit: every three months is, on average, 91 days. $3 \times 91 + 7 = 280$).

The Rabbinic count begins at conception, roughly two weeks later than the obstetrical count, and is just 271 days. This extent is determined by the Talmud, Niddah 38b, on the basis of the numerical value of the word הריון (pregnancy). Months, however, are lunar, set for this purpose at 30 days each. Nine months equals 270 days, with the birth presumed to be on the following day. The ninth month thus differs a bit accordingly.

(This is the traditional Rabbinic count. I prefer to believe that the rabbis, who knew quite well that the lunar month approximates 29.5, not 30, days, and who consequently alternated months of 29 and 30 days on their calendar, knew 9 months to be somewhat shorter (to wit: $9 \times 29.5 = 265.5$), which would better match the obstetrical count of 280 days which begins 14 days earlier. That they allowed 271 days to stand, I think, was in light of the gematria and their certain knowledge that any number, here, is a gross approximation of a number quite variable, in fact.)

[14] Thus Magen Avraham, S.A., O.H. 330.16, represents those who obviated the Talmud's ruling by finding all but the most certain of cases to be uncertain, therefore to be treated even on Shabbat. Indeed, even in a case similar to the one he finds certain, it would be possible to adjudge the infant of uncertain gestational age, (A) because it is possible that the infant was formed in order to be born after seven months and he tarried (see Lieberman *Tosefta Kifshuta*, Shabbat, p. 249) or (B) because she might have been mysteriously impregnated (נתעברה באמבטי – see Hagiga 15a).

[15] Hazon Ish, Yoreh De'ah 155.4. I have not seen the original, but have seen Hazon Ish cited in *Sefer Assia* 4, p. 44 and in *Assia*, no. 45-6 (vol. 12, no. 1-2), p. 108, n. 37, and again in *Bishvilei haRefuah* 9 (Tevet 5749): 84. See also Steinberg, p. 125, n. 7, and the other citations cited there.

favor of the more subjective standard of אביו ואמו. With regard to medical treatment we should waive it as well, in order to correspond to the reality which greets us.[16]

Medical treatment of a viable newborn (see next) should therefore proceed as strenuously as it would for an adult. Those treatments that would be appropriate for an adult must be provided a newborn (save where the medical requirements of a newborn dictate otherwise). Where it is appropriate to withhold or withdraw treatment from an adult, it would be appropriate also to do so for a newborn.[17]

Genetic Abnormalities

With regard to the fetus, we have already said that abortion is permitted for cause. Clearly, genetic factors affecting that fetus can and will have an effect on the mother's emotional well-being and will factor into any abortion decision that may be made. It is when a child is born with unexpected genetic deficiencies or is severely premature that we are faced with the awful choice of whether and to what extent to extend treatment. May we consider the viability of that child in making treatment decisions and forgo treatments where they are considered unlikely to promote the child's long-term survival? Both Rabbi Waldenberg and Dr. Jakobovitz, writing on this precise question, assume the newborn should be treated exactly as would be any patient.[18] Yet in light of the Talmud's treatment of the eight-month birth and in light of the extended discussion in the gemara of the third chapter of Niddah concerning the status of varying types of concepti, there might be room to consider the basic nature of the infants in question. In the words of the Mishnah:

חכמים אומרים: כל שאין בו מצורת האדם אינו ולד.

The sages say: Whatever does not have the aspect of a human being is not [considered] a birth.[19]

---

[16] Rabban Simeon ben Gamaliel's opinion is not so easily dismissed. What differentiates a newborn from an older child, he claims, is that חזקת חיים, a presumption of life, does not yet inhere in a newborn. But the Mishnah of abortion, in Ohalot 7:6, which forbids abortion the moment the head or majority of the body has exited the birth canal, is explicit in arguing that the presumption of life does apply immediately upon birth, "and we do not set aside one life for another."

Certain other areas of halakhah stand to be impacted by our desire to waive Rabban Simeon ben Gamaliel's ruling were we to do so across the board as the realia dictate that we do. These are discussed by R. Yitzhak Zilberstein in "פגים ונפלים ביחידה לטיפול נמרץ," *Sefer Assia* 6, pp. 42-45. Regarding יבום and חליצה (levirate marriage and its ceremonial rejection), waiving the thirty day rule would be salutary, as it would exempt more women from these requirements. Regarding פדיון הבן (Redemption of the First Born), however, it might require redemption of the parents of an infant who died prior to thirty days (if not in our most extreme category) whereas present regulations exempt. One could, however, rule with Tosafot that the thirty day limit regarding redemption is established by Scripture independent of viability and thereby hold on to the simple ruling of exemption if any infant dies prior to thirty days. In any case, the exemption of further births is not dependent on the viability of that first infant, for any infant, even a stillbirth, would exempt future children from redemption. Nor would it affect inheritance. See Zilberstein for further detail.

[17] See R. Avram Reisner, "A Halakhic Ethic of Care for the Terminally Ill," *PCJLS 86-90*, pp. 13-64, and see also R. Elliot Dorff, "A Jewish Approach to End-Stage Medical Care," *PCJLS 86-90*, pp. 65-126.

It is, of course, impossible to speak of the patient's autonomous will in the case of newborn infants. Family and physicians function under the constraints of unappointed surrogates, seeking the best course of treatment.

That a dying newborn whose situation is futile would be treated as would an adult in a similarly futile state is stated clearly, most recently, in the article by Dr. Steinberg, in Rosner, p. 123.

[18] R. Eliezer Waldenberg, Tzitz Eliezer, vol. 13, no. 88. Dr. Yoel Jakobovits, *Tradition*, vol. 22, no. 3 (Fall 1986): 13-30.

[19] Mishnah Niddah 3:2.

On its face this would appear to exclude "monstrosities," as delineated by the Mishnah, this would include "fish-like creatures," "insect-like creatures," "animal-like creatures," etc. and exclude apparently normal children. But Baraitot and amoraic dicta in the gemara extend this category to include one whose "forehead, eyebrows, eyes, cheeks and chin (or jaw?) are not of a piece," and establish a further extension which rests on non-viability.[20] Thus, a woman who miscarries an infant whose esophagus is sealed (but not where it is simply perforated), whose (lower?) body is closed,[21] whose skull is malformed,[22] or whose face is crushed, is considered not to have given birth to a child. These extensions, it seems to me, permit the question, is there some level of non-viability at which the defective newborn should be permitted to expire?

The problem before us in relying upon this Talmudic material is the generic problem of scientific knowledge. We do not know precisely what situations the Talmud sought to describe, nor the extent of their medical discernment. To say that of the Talmud is, of course, not generally allowed. But the commentators and decisors were not at all unwilling to say that of themselves. Thus, this material does not appear in codified law, not because it is inappropriate to include it, but because the decisors did not feel they could draw practical conclusions therefrom. In the relevant section of Shulhan Arukh (Yoreh De'ah 194:3), we read:

עכשיו שאין אנו בקיאין בצורות חוששת לולד.

Now, when we are not expert in the formation [of the fetus], [the birthing mother] must consider these births.

But to be fair to the extraordinary advances of medicine in our day, it might precisely be said that today, as never before, we *are* expert in this area.

With much trepidation, I conclude that there are, in fact, such situations. Anyone who works in the field of neonatology can confirm episodes where, in the judgment of the medical team, an infant was too severely malformed to attempt any rescue.[23] Similarly, in the case of anencephaly, a neural tube defect by which the conceptus is born without a developed brain in which case the infants do not have a life expectancy beyond one month, the child should be considered akin to the Talmud's conceptus with the malformed skull. In such a case there seems to me to be no requirement on the part of the physician to engage in attempts to save the child. Similarly, the major chromosomal

---

[20] Niddah 23b-24a:

אמר רבא... ושטו אטום אמו טהורה. ת"ר: המפלת גוף אטום אין אמו טמאה לידה. ואיזהו גוף אטום? רבי אומר: כדי שינטל מן החי וימות. וכן אמר רב גידל אמר רבי יוחנן: המפלת את שגולגלתו אטומה אמו טהורה.

Rava says: If his esophagus is sealed, his mother is pure [i.e., it is not considered a birth]. The Rabbis taught: She who miscarries a sealed [lower?] body, its mother is not impure the impurity of birth. Which is a "sealed body"? Such that were [that portion] taken from the living, he would die. Thus does Rav Gidal say in the name of R. Yohanan: She who miscarries one whose skull is sealed, its mother is pure.

[21] Maimonides, Mishneh Torah, Issurei Biah 10:11. (He includes this full gemara passage in that chapter.) Precisely what these conditions refer to is debated by the Amoraim there. This appears to refer to an improperly developed gastrointestinal tract. As to why the other codes do not include this material, see ahead.

[22] The word translated here as "malformed" is אטום in the Hebrew, the same word as is used with regard to the closing of the esophagus and, if I am correct, the intestinal tract. Rashi here, however, translates "missing" under the influence of the prior gemara, and I suspect, his inability to imagine the situation being described. That the reference is to a "collapsed" skull, rather than a missing one, seems to me more likely. See above, n. 20.

[23] This area has occasioned much debate. See the excellent popular study, *Playing God in the Nursery* by Jeff Lyon (New York: W.W. Norton, 1985), particularly the chapter, "Sanctity of Life vs. Quality of Life" and the report of the President's Commission for the Study of Ethical Problems in Medicine and Biochemical and Behavioral Research.

abnormalities of trisomy 13, wherein the infant suffers severe abnormalities of brain and facial features and most often cannot support breathing on its own, and of trisomy 18, wherein the infants almost always succumb to respiratory difficulties within the first year, may be seen as indications of the non-viability of the infant. Although, fully supported, such children may live a year,[24] upon diagnosis within the first days after birth, it is correct to class these infants as non-viable and end their support. I am unwilling, however, to follow the logic of these Talmudic positions to the extreme conclusion that such children are altogether not considered live births. Were we to do so, there would be no impediment to treating such infants as donors while yet alive. If only due to our humility, but even more so due to our extreme reverence for life, it is unacceptable to do so. Rather we should classify such newborn infants as born dying, and allow the latitude of non-treatment that we would consider appropriate at the end of life.[25] Given the reality of scientific advance, I believe this ruling grants the needed flexibility.

---

[24] Presentation by Dr. Alan Fleischman, Director of the Division of Neonatology at Weiller Hospital of Albert Einstein College, to the Subcommittee on Biomedical Ethics of the CJLS, 13 Sept. 1989. See also, in detail, D.W. Smith, *Recognizable Patterns of Human Malformation* (vol. 7 in W.B. Saunders, *Major Problems in Clinical Pediatrics*, 3d ed.). Another such case would be chromosomal triploidy, a very rare occurrence in which there is no survival (indeed, most such births miscarry).

As our intervention in the womb grows we must anticipate larger numbers of malformed concepti which were destined to miscarry early in their gestation but which we shall reach alive. While abortion of such flawed concepti is permitted for maternal causes, it is not permitted to abort a fetus due to considerations of its own infirmities or suffering. Whereas, once born, we would countenance withholding of mechanical life support, the fetus' life support in utero is within the natural realm. It cannot be aborted but by an aggressive act on our part which is permissible only in the context of saving another. But see above, n. 5 and n. 6.

[25] See above, n. 17.

Thus use of a respirator or heart-lung machine, or extensive use of dialysis beyond immediate hope of repair of the kidneys or holding toward transplant would be counterindicated. An incubator should be required however, as the function of an incubator is to enhance the biological functioning of the newborn and not to replace those functions mechanically.

It goes without saying that once brain death has been declared such an infant may serve as an organ donor, as may any adult. The same criteria of brain death apply.

This responsum runs counter to the one direct early precedent known to me in this matter. R. Eleazar Fleckeles, in his responsum *Teshuvah MeAhavah* no. 53 (Prague, 1800), is asked about leaving monstrous newborns unattended, even to permit them to starve to death. The questioner, R. David Ber Cohen, effectively sets out the case based on these Talmud texts that monstrous newborns should not be considered human, for which reason, יש כאן צד היתר לסבב המיתה. R. Fleckeles dismisses this opinion out of hand, arguing that the gemara deals in matters of impurity, not life and death, and that none of the sub-human monsters included could possibly survive to birth. Furthermore, we do not consider ourselves capable of making this determination. And even if we could make that determination, that conceptus would be classed a טרפה or a גוסס, neither of whom may be put to death, or, at very least, the equivalent of an animal who may also not be caused gratuitous pain.

Were we to cite this responsum as the controlling precedent, as does Pithei Teshuvah to Shulhan Arukh, Y.D. 194, no. 5, or as do R.J. David Bleich in his *Contemporary Halakhic Problems*, vol. 1, p. 366 and R. Immanuel Jakobovitz, *Tradition* 5 (spring 1963): 268, then we would be bound by precedent to rule more restrictively. But a case-by-case consideration of his arguments yields a different result.

As I have said, the extent of our expertise has risen considerably in the two centuries since R. Fleckeles wrote, and he himself was suitably tentative about an opinion offered without substantial support. More important, however, the questioner seeks to rule that said defective newborns are sub-human and to permit their death by starvation on that basis. We have been more cautious. If the Talmud's presentation, in theory, posits sub-human defectives then out of uncertainty we will certainly not entertain actively killing same, but only class these as dying and apply those rules to them. We only allow that categorization may color our thinking on treatment decisions. In every case we do not draw ultimate conclusions from somewhat strained halakhic argumentation, but only allow it to move us a notch along the spectrum. This is, I believe, a thoroughly traditional model of halakhic decision making. In the instant case, it resolves the rest of R. Fleckeles' concerns, for it does not permit the killing of a טרפה nor the equivalent of cruelty to animals but only a measured response to the situation as we understand it.

With regard to severely premature newborns, the medical ground is shifting particularly fast. Lung development now seems to determine the earliest possible survivability, but opinion differs as to whether that is a real boundary or whether it might be overcome by increasing medical innovations.[26] Experimentation with a pseudo-womb environment continues. Therefore, it is prudent to leave the assessment of severely premature newborns to the medical experts. Where a child is found to be so severely premature as to preclude any realistic chance of survival, they may be classed with defective newborns and aggressive efforts to save the life of the child may be forgone. But where a realistic chance of survival exists, all efforts to achieve that result should proceed.[27]

Other abnormalities, including trisomy 21 (Down's syndrome), do not effect the newborn as severely, and the infant should be treated as are all other newborns.[28] As it is impossible to categorize every neonatal possibility, it remains for the doctors and the family's rabbi to determine the appropriate category for the case before them.[29]

In a recent issue of *B'Or HaTorah* (no. 8 English 1993, p. 10), R. Yitzhak Zilberstein also cites this source and adds two other very contemporary views which, like R. Fleckeles, prohibit euthanizing said creatures but do not seem to address clearly this more cautious approach.

In a related matter, R. Zilberstein himself, in a responsum in *Bishvilei HaRefuah* vol. 9 (Dec. 1988), pp. 81ff. (citing R. Eliezer Waldenberg for support) cannot find a true prohibition against leaving untreated extremely premature newborns, but nevertheless recommends their treatment. He defines extreme prematurity as prior to 24 weeks, viz. the end of the sixth month, understanding the "seven month infant" of the Talmud as "in the seventh month" (see n. 13). Similarly, we treat the extremely premature infant as a subset of all patients, believing it appropriate to give even the littlest ones the best chance we can. Uncertainty (ספק) is not sufficient ground for retreating. When uncertainty is replaced by futility then we would back off. But that is true of any patient, if, perhaps, more likely true of the extremely premature newborn.

Most recently, Dr. Abraham Steinberg in "The Defective Newborn – Halachic Considerations," in Dr. Fred Rosner's *Medicine and Jewish Law II*, p. 125, seems to follow along a similar track, citing Talmudic rulings that are not in effect to justify present day leniencies. Though he cites "recent rabbinic decisors" as holding that the Talmudic ruling of eight month babies is inapplicable, he goes on to state, "The determining factor in the decision as to whether to treat or not to treat a defective newborn depends on its chances of viability, in accordance with the scientific knowledge and technical capabilities at the time. From the pure halakhic standpoint, it might be forbidden to desecrate the Sabbath nowadays for any severely handicapped newborn who is expected to die within a few days. An anencephalic newborn falls into this category, since such a baby has the same halakhic status as a baby born after eight months of gestation as described in the Talmud." I have preferred to extrapolate from a ruling that was not applied explicitly due to lack of expertise rather than from a ruling voided due to "changed nature." In either case, however, what has really changed is precisely our medical expertise.

[26] New York State Task Force on Life and the Law, Report of the Committee on Fetal Extrauterine Survival, p. 9.

[27] What constitutes "realistic" remains the province of the rabbi to determine. No percentage can be substituted for a judgmental ruling here. As Dr. Steinberg notes (Rosner, p. 131), "There are uncertainties as to the extent of morbidity and its severity. Moreover, there are still very few early prognostic markers for survival and for significant morbidity in individual babies... .Even the definition of futility is variable. Therefore, in Jewish Law, an individual baby who has a chance for survival should be treated as vigorously as needed."

It may be asked why our viability measure does not come into play here. The answer, however, is apparent. Concerning a fetus we need a preponderant chance for that fetus to rise near the level of a presumption of life. But a newborn has, in fact, gained a חזקת חיים, a presumption of life, by virtue of having been born. Henceforth we would need more than even a preponderant likelihood that the child would die to declare further ministrations futile. See above, n. 16.

[28] Even a "closed" intestinal tract, specified in the Talmud as a non-viable birth (see above, n. 20), might, today, be susceptible to surgical correctives which should therefore be undertaken where possible.

[29] Many cases will not fall clearly into one category or another. In cases of microcephaly, encephalocele and many other genetic abnormalities which may range in their severity, a medical judgment must be made concerning the extent of disability and the rabbi must judge if the weight of the non-viable category is met. See conclusion 6.

Conclusions

1. Abortion of the fetus is permitted throughout pregnancy for cause.
2. The claim of the potential life of the fetus to our ministrations is greater upon attaining viability, that is after seven months (31-32 weeks by obstetrical count).
3. Ordinarily, newborns must be cared for as we would care for any adult.
4. Severely deformed and compromised newborns are classed as born dying and treatments aimed at their survival may be discontinued. Severe deformity refers to anencephaly, trisomies 13 and 18 or other similar large scale genetic deformities. Jewish law does not insist on aggressive treatment in such cases. The term does not apply to lesser deformities, such as trisomy 21 (Down's syndrome).
5. Prematurity is generally to be considered part of the category of lesser deformities. In cases of severe prematurity the rabbi, in consultation with the family and physician, may conclude that the infant should be classed as unable to survive.
6. In fact, everything said here is said as guidance to the rabbi who must carefully assess the case in consultation with the family and physicians in order to determine the proper course in the instant case.

Addendum Concerning Mourning Practices

The following is not within the purview of this paper, nevertheless I would suggest:

1. A defective newborn who dies within Rabban Simeon ben Gamaliel's thirty day period should not require mourning since the parent did not reasonably expect that child to live. If the parents wish to observe mourning voluntarily they may do so, just as one may voluntarily observe mourning for an in-law.
2. Full mourning should be accepted as a voluntary observance for stillborn children and late term miscarriages (eighth and ninth month).

YD 340:30.1991a

RESPONSE TO MISCARRIAGE

Rabbi Debra Reed Blank

This paper was approved on March 6, 1991, by a vote of seventeen in favor, one opposed and three abstaining (17-1-3). Voting in favor: Rabbis Kassel Abelson, Stanley Bramnick, Elliot N. Dorff, Richard L. Eisenberg, David M. Feldman, Samuel Fraint, Arnold M. Goodman, Howard Handler, Herbert Mandl, Lionel E. Moses, Mayer Rabinowitz, Joel E. Rembaum, Chaim A. Rogoff, Seymour J. Rosenbloom, Joel Roth, Morris M. Shapiro, and Gordon Tucker. Voting against: Rabbi Ben Zion Bergman. Abstaining: Rabbis Dov Peretz Elkins, Jerome M. Epstein and Avram Israel Reisner.

The Committee on Jewish Law and Standards of the Rabbinical Assembly provides guidance in matters of halakhah for the Conservative movement. The individual rabbi, however, is the authority for the interpretation and application of all matters of halakhah.

שאלה

What should the Jewish response be to miscarriage?

תשובה

The question of what constitutes an appropriate response to miscarriage has been placed on the agenda of the Committee on Jewish Law and Standards. The assumption underlying this question is that the tendency to ignore in ritual the emotional impact and physical trauma of miscarriage is probably erroneous. The Jewish mindset, dominated by halakhah and its formulated responses to virtually every activity and event in one's life, is stymied when confronted by a miscarriage, a traumatic event for which there is no formulated response. So we must ask: What should the Jewish response be to miscarriage?

A paper on this question that was submitted to the CJLS and subsequently withdrawn built on the idea of miscarriage as constituting a death[1] (which, indeed, it does – the death of a fetus, the death of the hopes and dreams of the parents), and applied to miscarriage the classical categories of אנינות and אבלות. That paper allowed for varying responses to miscarriage, and proposed that the individual rabbi, after speaking with the parents, would decide upon the level of אנינות and אבלות appropriate for the specific case.

That opinion, it seems to me, has two significant weaknesses. First, it is problematic that individual rabbis would determine varying level of אנינות and אבלות: parents may not express their full degree of mourning until long after the event; there is the risk of seem-

---

[1] That paper also addressed the issues of response to neonatal and perinatal death. I do not discuss those matters herein.

ing to offer preferential treatment when one couple but not another is urged to observe full אנינות and אבלות; and a community may be reluctant to fulfill its responsibilities (e.g., daily minyan, shivah visits, etc.) during a period of אבלות in the case of miscarriage.

The other weakness, in my opinion, is the application of אנינות and אבלות to the death of a fetus. Our tradition has always been careful to make a distinction between a fetus and a person, holding that "personhood" comes only with birth. While the advances of fetal medicine have served to highlight the ambiguities, a fetus, no matter how viable, is not yet a person. Therefore, to apply אנינות and אבלות – ritualized behaviors in response to a dead person – to miscarriage is to obliterate the distinction between fetus and person to the point where the question of abortion, on which Judaism has held a relatively tolerant view, would have to be reexamined with all of the problematic ramifications.

Thus, it is my opinion that אנינות and אבלות, even in varying degrees, are inappropriate responses to the event of miscarriage from halakhic, emotional and logical points of view. This is not, however, to downplay the emotional impact which a miscarriage may have on the parents. The emotional effects of a miscarriage can be devastating and long-lasting. Even in a case where it is statistically probable that soon the woman will conceive again (i.e., in a situation of relative youth, good health, and an absence of fertility problems), she, as well as her husband, may grieve deeply for *this* pregnancy, for *this* child. But in addition to feelings of loss, frustration, anger, and even sexual inadequacy, issues of aging, infertility, sexual dysfunction or family discord are apt to complicate and prolong the grief.

The present lack of a ritual response to miscarriage is a glaring gap, especially for people whose lives are in every other way governed by Jewish law. There must be a formulated response to miscarriage which addresses the emotional impact and the physical trauma; a response which enables the parents to channel and express their emotions, and which enables the community to acknowledge their loss. So if אנינות and אבלות are not the appropriate responses, what is?[2] In this paper, I will propose guidelines for response to miscarriage, both on the couple's part and on the community's. Throughout I shall be dealing with patterns which have always, in fact, been permissible. In that sense, my paper is not a halakhic innovation. However, it is necessary to say these things in writing, because there has been a widespread misperception that Jewish law proscribed these behaviors in the case of miscarriage.

We begin by defining the term "miscarriage" for our purposes. While the medical world defines miscarriage as occurring up to the fetal age of twenty weeks,[3] even fetal loss after this point may be described as a "miscarriage" by the couple.[4] While for the purpose of this paper I have had in mind fetal loss up to twenty weeks, the suggestions made herein could be followed as well by a couple whose loss occurred at a later stage – assuming that they felt more comfortable with these guidelines rather than others which might be presented to them. Thus, "miscarriage" should be understood as having happened where the couple themselves use this term.[5]

---

[2] An effort to begin addressing this question can be found in Robert H. Loewy, "A Rabbi Confronts Miscarriage, Stillbirth, and Infant Death," in *Journal of Reform Judaism* 35 (spring 1988): 1-6.

[3] See, for example, *Stedman's Medical Dictionary*, 23rd ed., s.v. "miscarriage."

[4] See, for example, the imprecise use of the term "miscarriage" in the *New York Times*, 14 Mar. 1991, p. A22.

[5] While elected, therapeutic abortion is not a miscarriage, neither in medical parlance nor in lay, the grief attending such a tragedy is certainly not unlike that of a miscarriage. I would argue that the suggested responses to miscarriage presented in this paper could also be applied to such a case of elected abortion, should the couple agree to its appropriateness.

The proposal of this paper is that the category of חולה and the mitzvah of ביקור חולים can provide us with a framework in which to respond to miscarriage.

The first question we must ask is whether or not the category of חולה is applicable. In other words, is a woman who has just miscarried technically a חולה? Moreover, can her husband be technically considered a חולה? And are they therefore entitled to, and in need of, the benefits due a חולה?

A חולה is "a person who is stricken with an illness which depletes the strength of his or her entire body...such that he or she is not able to walk in the market and has taken to bed."[6] A woman who has just miscarried may feel very weak throughout her entire body, be unable to walk more than a step or two (if that), and be in need of bedrest. The physical trauma of miscarriage should not be underestimated, for a problematic miscarriage may not only be protracted and physically taxing, but complications may threaten the woman's life. Thus, for the woman there is no question that she qualifies as a חולה, on the physical evidence alone.

But what about the father who endures no physical trauma? The assumption of the question at hand is that miscarriage can be emotionally traumatic not only for the mother but for the father as well. So we must ask: Does mental distress qualify one as a חולה? With reference to the aforementioned definition, we observe that mental distress *can* make one feel enervated, and one might take to his or her bed — but one also *might* not. In fact, the husband of one who has just miscarried, despite his mental distress, is very likely to be physically active, attending to the needs of his wife and his household. So can he be considered a חולה?

While, to my knowledge, this specific question does not appear in the responsa literature, comments by poskim in matters of mental health suggest that we can consider the father a חולה. For example, "Mental health is equal to physical health as a halakhic concern."[7] A sentiment expressed again and again in the literature is that "ביקור חולים is for the body and the soul."[8] Admittedly, "the soul" is interpreted as referring to that of the one who is physically sick, i.e., his or her emotional, psychological and spiritual needs should be addressed as well as the physical. But since the literature recognizes the interdependence of physical and mental health,[9] it seems reasonable to assert that mental distress, by virtue of the potential effect it may have on the physical well-being, can also require ביקור חולים. Therefore, I suggest that we can assume that the father too, because of his mental distress, can be considered a חולה.

Since one of the main purposes of ביקור חולים is to attend to the person's needs,[10] we can test our argument that the woman who has just miscarried and her husband are חולים by asking whether or not they are in need of such attention.

---

[6] *Encyclopedia Talmudit*, vol. 13, col. 233. See this description used also in S.A. Hoshen Mishpat 250:5. I alone am responsible for the translation of this phrase, as well as for all other translations occurring in this paper.

I call to attention to the fact that a יולדת is considered a חולה (col. 325, which cites Rashi, Shabbat 129a, כל צורכי). Since the physical trauma of miscarriage can be like that of labor, an analogy can be made from the יולדת to the one who has miscarried. However, even without this helpful analogy, the main body of this paper proves that the basic definition for חולה can be applied to one who has miscarried.

[7] David M. Feldman, *Health and Medicine in the Jewish Tradition* (New York: Crossroad, 1986), p. 49.

[8] See, for example, Jehiel Tucatzinsky, *Gesher HaHayyim* (Jerusalem, 1960), p. 27.

[9] See, for example, Feldman, *Health and Medicine*, p. 31.

[10] *Gesher HaHayyim*, p. 27; Rambam, *Torat Ha-Adam*, in *Kitvei Rambam*, ed. Charles B. Chavel (Jerusalem, 1963), vol. 2, p. 17. See also Rashi, Nedarim 40a, "...מפני שבני אדם"; the other primary purpose is to say a prayer on behalf of the חולה.

In the case of miscarriage an adult member of the household is indisposed for at least a few days. This inconvenience is compounded by trips to the doctor or by hospitalization. Added to the disruptions of traumatic physical illness is the mental distress, which magnifies the inconvenience. Because of her physical condition alone, the woman is unable to attend to errands, household responsibilities and childcare. Because of her husband's attention to the care of his wife, along with his distress, he may well have difficulty attending to them adequately. There is no question that in such a situation there is need for the physical benefits of ביקור חולים, and certainly the couple is entitled to them.

Now that I have argued that the category of חולה and the mitzvah of ביקור חולים apply to a miscarriage, what are the specifics of their application?

In order for a community to fulfill its responsibilities for ביקור חולים, the חולה has to notify his or her rabbi and/or friend(s) so that word of this loss can be spread. Thus, the workings of ביקור חולים are dependent upon the חולה's willingness to make his or her illness public knowledge. This is a handicap of this proposed response to miscarriage, an event which some people feel reluctant to make public knowledge. If the woman and/or her husband seem reluctant to tell people, a friend or rabbi can gently encourage the couple to share with their community the news of their loss and can help the couple identify those friends and family members who can be told. The rabbi, while explaining the מי שברך, הגומל and מקוה visit (all discussed further on), can assure the couple of possibilities for discretion, should that be their concern.

Immediately after the event, the husband may wish to make or arrange for a מי שברך at synagogue for his wife,[11] with as much consideration for the request for רפואת הנפש as for הגוף. In light of his status as חולה, he may ask that one be made for him as well. After the woman has recovered physically, she can recite הגומל.[12] In doing so, she marks her own return to physical strength and independence.[13]

Both of these prayers are ways in which the couple can publicly, yet discreetly, remark on their recent experience. Concerned community members will note these prayers and perhaps inquire as to their reason: On both occasions the answer can be as vague or as specific as the person wishes. But the mere statement of the prayers, as responses to and markers of a physically and emotionally traumatic event, will have been therapeutic for the couple.

Finally, it should be noted that a מקוה visit is required in the aftermath of a miscarriage. In those cases where the couple is not accustomed to observing הילכות טהרת משפחה, the rabbi might suggest to the woman a מקוה visit at an appropriate time.[14] The

---

[11] On the therapeutic importance of this prayer see Feldman, *Health and Medicine*, pp. 30-31.

[12] Regarding the appropriateness of a woman who has recently miscarried reciting הגומל, I have relied upon Karo's opinion that anyone "who was sick and who has recovered" should recite it (Shulhan Arukh, Orah Hayyim 219:1), "even if [the illness] was not life-threatening" (219:8). I have chosen to disregard Isserles' note that the Ashkenazic practice is to limit הגומל to life-threatening illnesses (ad loc.). The comments of Magen David and Sha'arei T'shuvah (ad loc.) suggest to me that the concern is that one should not be reciting הגומל for insignificant, transitory illnesses (e.g., a headache). While one may hesitate to describe miscarriage as life-threatening (i.e., to the woman; although see my qualification above), one could hardly describe it as insignificant and transitory. Therefore, I do not think it an abuse of הגומל for a woman who has recently miscarried to recite it.

[13] Here again, a comparison can be drawn to a יולדת. Even where a birth has not been marked by the woman's physical trauma or an actual threat to her health, she recites הגומל. Even in the tragic case of neonatal death, she recites הגומל as a יולדת. So too in the case of miscarriage, where the woman may be occupied by her feelings of grief, she is encouraged to pause a moment and give thanks for her return to health and, one hopes, to renewed possibilities for conception.

[14] See S.A. Yoreh De'ah 194:2 and the commentaries thereon for the guidelines in determining the appropriate time for the visit.

rabbi can take special care in describing the symbolic merits of such a visit, with emphasis upon its serving as a marker for a new beginning.

The prayers and מקווה visit help to serve as ritual responses to the emotional and physical trauma of miscarriage, and will also help the couple to begin channeling and expressing their emotions. But they are not entirely sufficient: In the first place, they do not provide for the comfort and support which the couple need during those few days following the miscarriage. In the second place, they do not address the feelings of grief which the couple might be experiencing.

It is with regard to the first point that the community's responsibility enters into the picture via ביקור חולים. As mentioned above, when the rabbi or friend is first told the news, his or her response should be: "Whom shall I call? Whom would you like to be told?" And, if the person is unable, due to distraction, to provide names, the rabbi or friend can make suggestions of whom he or she might telephone. With the couple's consent, the rabbi can also make a discreet announcement in synagogue (depending upon the synagogue's ambiance and customs; for example, "Plonit has been suddenly ill this week and came home from the hospital yesterday. Friends are welcome to stop by."). Once people have been informed, the laws of ביקור חולים should be followed and are most appropriate under the circumstances:[15] close friends and relatives should come immediately; more casual friends, for example a couple in the community who has recently had a miscarriage and who is willing to provide an empathic ear and make suggestions for helpful reading or activities, can visit a few days later. (The rabbi might be particularly helpful in making this connection.)

People should take care that their visit does not become a burden: Do not come at an inappropriately early or late hour, do not stay overlong, do not come with advice on medicines and doctors, and do not regal the couple with one's own history of miscarriage.[16]

Aside from ascertaining and attending to needs which the couple may have (shopping, cooking, cleaning), the visitor is also responsible to offer a prayer for their recovery, physical and emotional, from this loss.[17] The formulated prayer given in the Shulhan Arukh[18] is appropriate: המקום ירחם [עליכם] בתוך חולי ישראל.

Finally, ביקור חולים offers us a model for behavior if the couple feels uncomfortable with visitors: One can still check whether a particular need — an errand, shopping, childcare, etc. — could be met.[19]

But what about the second point raised above, that of addressing the grief which the couple may be experiencing? The recitations of the מי שברך and הגומל, along with the visit to the מקווה, may still not fully address the poignant loss which the miscarriage represents for the couple.

---

[15] Here I have been guided by S.A. Yoreh De'ah 335; *Gesher HaHayyim*, p. 27f.; Rambam, Hilkhot Avel, 14.

[16] On these latter two points especially see *Gesher HaHayyim*, p. 27.

[17] See above, n. 10.

[18] Yoreh De'ah 335:6. See also 335:4-5 for the requirement of this statement and the permissibility of its recitation in any language.

[19] Yoreh De'ah 335:8. It should be noted that this passage describes someone inquiring whether specific errands need to be done — e.g., "Does the laundry need to be done? Does the house need to be cleaned?" Too often people couch their offers to help in general, non-committal language ("Is there anything I can do?"). Consequently these offers are viewed as courteous formalities and declined. Karo's language is instructive for it prods us to make our offers very pointed ("I'm on my way to the grocery. What do you need?" "I can take your kid off your hands for you tomorrow — what time would be good?" "I'd like to make you dinner for Friday night: Is broiled chicken okay?").

As a direct response to these feelings, the rabbi should explain that the מי שברך is not only an acknowledgement of the woman's physical trauma, but also her mental distress; likewise הגומל, which can be delayed until the women is feeling "back on her feet" emotionally as well as physically. The מקוה visit can serve as a powerful symbol that, in spite of fetal loss, the life-cycle does continue.

Additionally, the rabbi and/or a חברת ביקור חולים can provide the couple with תהילים and/or prayers composed specifically for the occasion of miscarriage, along with suggestions for when and how these might be read (e.g., silently before the מי שברך and הגומל; together every evening and morning for the following week; at the מקוה).

The couple's grief can be further addressed by their feeling that their loss has been acknowledged by their community and by their having the opportunity to verbalize their grief. ביקור חולים will bring caring people to the couple's side and afford them the possibility of speaking about their grief. As with a shivah visit, a ביקור חולים visit can serve as an acknowledgement of the couple's grief, even a sharing in it.

A visit of ביקור חולים can be just as much an expression of grief as it is a wish for health: When visiting a dying friend, one's visit is much more a grieving for the loss soon to come than it is a futile wish for health. So too with miscarriage: While the ostensible reason one visits is to make an offer of assistance and wish the couple their health, the visit also serves as an acknowledgment of their loss and as an opportunity to share in their grief.

It can be argued that these responses, in part or in total, while not without benefit, still do not adequately address the feeling of grief and loss which a miscarriage may cause. But no ritual, no behavior, no prayer, can remove feelings of loss. An analogy can be made to the death of a parent and the attendant rituals and behaviors. Shivah, shloshim, kaddish, yizkor and yahrzeit do not, in and of themselves, ease the complex of emotions which one feels. But they provide ritual frameworks for one to verbalize and act out his or her loss, and also provide a framework in which others can acknowledge this loss. So too with the rituals and frameworks suggested here as responses to miscarriage.

Before its applicability to miscarriage can be made, everyone's individual responsibility for ביקור חולים must be underscored: ביקור חולים מצוה על הכל.[20] Too often this responsibility is overlooked in our communities, due in part to women in the work-force, but also due to over-reliance upon the telephone, the pastoral role of our rabbis and designated committees to perform certain deeds. While a phone call, or a card, or a sympathetic remark made later are not without merit, none is equal to the physical presence of someone who is willing to listen, offer words of support and attend to specific needs during those days of illness and crisis.

We are all guilty of having forgotten our responsibilities for ביקור חולים. They are not responsibilities which can be left solely to the rabbi of a community, in part because no rabbi can bear that burden, but also because during illness one needs one's friends around as well as one's rabbi. Nor should ביקור חולים be left entirely to a חברה, which may offer some excellent support but cannot offer the sympathetic ear which only a friend can.[21]

---

[20] Rambam, Hilkhot Avel 14:4.

[21] See J. David Bleich, *Judaism and Healing: Halakhic Perspectives* (New York: Ktav, 1981), pp. 43-44, who emphasizes that a חברת ביקור חולים does not "exempt others" from their responsibilities.

Aside from direct care, such as babysitting, food preparation, etc., a חברה could prepare a pamphlet which explains the protocol of ביקור חולים and how it can be applied to miscarriage. Such a pamphlet could also contain prayers composed specifically for the event of miscarriage.

A telephone call is not a substitute for ביקור חולים.[22] One can phone ahead to see when the best time to visit might be, but the call does not constitute a visit. One may call to see what food items are needed in the house or if an errand needs running, but a call does not substitute for the presence of a caring, sympathetic ear.[23]

Nor should ביקור חולים be left for only those instances of extremely serious and terminal illness: One should not have to contract cancer or heart disease to merit the visits of friends and the offers of assistance. Even allowing for concerns that ביקור חולים not be abused (e.g., one should not expect nor demand it when afflicted by hay fever), there are nevertheless many illnesses which, while perhaps not life-threatening, are traumatic, painful and enervating — for the חולה as well as for her/his family; and these illnesses, miscarriage among them, merit ביקור חולים.

The eclipse of the importance of ביקור חולים has contributed to a loss of the sense of community within our communities as well as to the loss of interest in synagogue (i.e., community) involvement. ביקור חולים is like an insurance policy: The more one contributes to it, the more one will get out of it. So even if the considerations of mitzvah and social responsibility do not compel one, self-interest should! Because they know they may need it tomorrow, people have learned to take shivah minyans seriously. The same could be said of ביקור חולים. But, education is an important factor: People have been educated to the need for and the workings of shivah minyans. So too they must be educated to the need for and the workings of ביקור חולים.

Conclusion

The category of חולה and the mitzvah of ביקור חולים, along with מקוה, provide us with guidelines for an appropriate and sufficient response to miscarriage, both on the couple's part and on the community's, without any stretching of the halakhic limits. These frameworks provide us with rituals which help to acknowledge the emotional impact and physical trauma of miscarriage. They also provide ways for the couple to channel emotions and for the community to acknowledge the loss. If the suggestions made herein were followed, then no one experiencing a miscarriage would need to feel overwhelmed by day-to-day responsibilities in a time of great stress, or want for sympathetic ears, or sense their loss unacknowledged by either their community or their religion.

---

[22] On this question, see Moshe Feinstein, *Iggrot Moshe*, Yoreh De'ah vol. 1, n. 223, p. 450. Feinstein also emphasizes the importance of attending to the needs of the חולה.

[23] For a summary of the importance of the visit, see Feldman, *Health and Medicine*, pp. 32-33.

YD 340:30.1991b

Response to Miscarriage: A Dissent

Rabbi Amy Eilberg

This paper was submitted as a dissent to "Response to Miscarriage" by Rabbi Debra Reed Blank. Dissenting and concurring opinions are not official positions of the Committee on Jewish Law and Standards.

The Committee on Jewish Law and Standards of the Rabbinical Assembly provides guidance in matters of halakhah for the Conservative movement. The individual rabbi, however, is the authority for the interpretation and application of all matters of halakhah.

I rejoice that the Law Committee has affirmed a paper on the subject of miscarriage, a profound event in the lives of families, one which hitherto had received very little response from the traditional halakhic system. I also have a great deal of enthusiasm for much of the material presented in Rabbi Blank's paper. Her paper serves as a valuable tool for all of us involved in educating Jews about the mitzvah of ביקור חולים. I was especially delighted to hear some of her specific observations on more and less helpful ways to observe the mitzvah, her emphasis on the personal visit rather than ביקור חולים by answering machine, her wonderful suggestions about specificity ("Is chicken okay for dinner tonight?" rather than "Is there anything I can do?"), and about the broad applicability of the mitzvah to all illness, not just life-threatening diseases. However, it is my belief that her use of the category of ביקור חולים in response to miscarriage is an unhelpful application of the mitzvah, because it distorts and denies the essence of the experience of miscarriage.

A mother, and a father, who have lost a fetus by miscarriage, are not sick. They are grieving. This is not a disease, not illness; their experience has nothing to do with pathology — either physical or mental. What they have suffered is a loss, and what they need most of all is acknowledgment of the reality and profundity of that loss, and support in their grieving process.

This flaw in Rabbi Blank's approach becomes apparent in the paper, in my opinion, when she attempts to explain why the mitzvah of ביקור חולים should be applied to the fetus' father as well as the mother. After all, he is obviously not sick. Rabbi Blank must apply considerable rhetorical energy to this question: how, in her approach, can we include the father as one of the people needing care in this situation, when he is obviously suffering no physical illness? She concludes that he is suffering from "mental distress," thus making his experience into a pathological psychological process.

This whole section of the paper highlights what is, for me, its central flaw. Miscarriage is not illness. The father is not sick, but then neither is the mother. Yes, she may be exhausted, sore, weak; she may even have some minor medical complications following the miscarriage. She is, almost always, less sick than a woman with the flu.

Even still, it would not hurt the bereaved parent to receive the benefits of ביקור חולים, especially as Rabbi Blank envisions it, including meals, child care for older children, sensitive offers of support. But the message that accompanies the care for these "sick" people is that when "illness" passes, very soon, they will no longer be sick. Thus, the well-meaning visitors of the "sick" carry with them two implicit messages: (1) the central problem these people are struggling with is "illness," or even the vague and judgmental "mental stress," rather than the truth-they are experiencing bereavement; and (2) that this "illness" is a one-time event that will heal quickly, with appropriate medical care, and then be over.

In short, to apply the model of ביקור חולים to miscarriage is to convey to the bereaved parents two highly dysfunctional messages about pregnancy loss: their primary problem, loss, is denied and distorted, and they are encouraged to think in highly unrealistic terms about the grieving process. Grieving, unlike illness, takes time — a lot of it. This is not because grieving is "sick;" it is not. But healthy grieving takes time, far more than the few days these parents could imagine themselves to be חולים. Bereavement professionals agree that grieving a pregnancy loss quite normally may take a full year.

I will never forget a nurse I worked with some years ago. She was a mature woman, self-aware and psychologically healthy. In the course of a brief conversation about her children, I stopped and asked, "How many children do you have?" Instantaneously, she responded, "Four. Well, that includes the one I lost by miscarriage." It emerged that this had been a first-trimester miscarriage suffered fifteen years earlier. Still, fifteen years later, in the course of casual conversation this woman still counted the lost fetus as one of her children. I carry this experience with me as I work with parents who have suffered miscarriage. These people know that, while the loss may be different from other losses, it is a loss nonetheless, and one that desperately needs to be acknowledged.

Surely the loss of a fetus is significantly different from the loss of a grown person, even of a child who lived long enough to have developed a relationship with his or her loved ones. For that matter, each loss is unique and requires its own unique bereavement process: the loss of a child is different from the loss of a parent; the loss of one's first parent is different from the loss of one's last parent; a sudden loss is different from an anticipated one; a loss from natural causes is different from a traumatic loss. Many would argue that the loss of a fetus is fundamentally different, because the fetus never became a person — halakhically or philosophically. But grief is not a philosophical category; it is an emotional experience, something which the Rabbis understood with exquisite sensitivity. Women, and their partners, who experience miscarriage, know that the loss of a fetus, the loss of their hopes and dreams for this child, is a significant loss. They know, too, that many of their loved ones deny this loss, with misguided if not insensitive approaches like, "You can always have another one" or "At least you never had the chance to know him or her and love him or her."

There is now a voluminous literature on the psycho-social dynamics of pregnancy loss. The insights of this literature have filtered down throughout the medical and mental health community. In hospitals around the country, nurses, doctors, social workers and chaplains work with newly bereaved parents to help them acknowledge and grieve the loss of their fetus. The parents are encouraged to give the baby a name, to hold him or her one last time if possible, to save whatever hair or blankets or hospital gear may have accompanied the baby, to plan a memorial service, to keep a memory book. In short, medical and mental health professionals around this country are now highly sensitized to the need for bereavement ritual around this particular loss.

No, this fetus is not a baby — halakhically, philosophically, or legally — nor need these new insights affect in any way the national debate on abortion. This fetus is not a baby by any objective standard. But walk into any maternity unit, and you will hear nurses and parents alike talking about the fetus as "baby." This language is used because it matches the emotional experience of parents. They may have already chosen a name, connected this baby-to-be with a deceased, beloved relative, they may have felt it move within the mother's body, they may have made all kinds of changes in their lives to prepare to accommodate a new member of their family. This fetus, whom they have never met, who was philosophically not a person, was emotionally very real. Thankfully, hospital personnel are increasingly willing to support the family in their emotional reality: this being was very real in their lives, and needs to be grieved before they can be open to moving on. To refuse Jewish parents the essential comfort of hearing their rabbi and community acknowledge the reality and pain of their loss — because of the philosophical consideration that our use of the word "baby" may affect the Supreme Court debate — is, I believe, to communicate to the parents something very sad. Your doctor understands what happened to you, your nurse understood, the social worker at the hospital understood. Your rabbi is not willing to call this loss by its right name. In short, your Jewish community is not here for you.

What saddens me about Rabbi Blank's approach is the failure to use the available option which would provide so much help to these parents. After all, Jewish law has a superbly developed approach to bereavement — a set of rituals and perspectives that affirm the essence of grief: it needs to be acknowledged and ritualized immediately after the loss, and it takes time and support and ongoing acknowledgment to resolve healthfully. We have precisely such a system, and we are not using it.

In a paper that I prepared for the Law Committee on the same subject, I suggested that for some bereaved parents, full halakhic bereavement rituals might be appropriate and helpful. The committee rejected this approach. Perhaps instead there needs to be a modification of the practices of אבלות for the occasion of pregnancy loss, acknowledging that this particular loss is different from the death of a living person. But Jewish bereaved parents need so desperately to hear and feel that their community, and the halakhah itself, is capable of responding to what really hurts them — and what really hurts here is grief. I would advocate some modification of halakhic bereavement rituals: קריעה, a modified burial service, a סעודת הבראה with perhaps a small circle of family and friends, and modified אבלות — at least one day of private shivah, including those family and friends whom the parents can trust to be appropriately supportive, and kaddish for thirty days. Such a ritual response would distinguish this loss from the death of a living person, but would communicate powerfully to the family that this loss was real, and that the Jewish community understands and wants to provide support as the bereavement process gradually unfolds.

Finally, I am grateful that this issue has come to the attention of the Conservative movement. Any new halakhic response to pregnancy loss is a step forward, in demonstrating to members of our movement that halakhah does respond to the most profound events in their lives. It is my profound belief that an approach which has the courage to call this particular loss by its right name is the one which ultimately brings most honor to Torah in our day.

YD 340:30.1996a

Jewish Ritual Practice Following a Stillbirth

Rabbi Stephanie Dickstein

This paper was approved on March 13, 1996, by a vote of twelve in favor and four abstentions (12-0-4). Voting in favor: Rabbis Kassel Abelson, Stephanie Dickstein, Elliot N. Dorff, Shoshana Gelfand, Myron S. Geller, Arnold M. Goodman, Susan Grossman, Judah Kogen, Vernon H. Kurtz, Aaron L. Mackler, Lionel E. Moses, and Gordon Tucker. Abstaining: Rabbis Ben Zion Bergman, Mayer Rabinowitz, Gerald Skolnik, and Elie Kaplan Spitz.

The Committee on Jewish Law and Standards of the Rabbinical Assembly provides guidance in matters of halakhah for the Conservative movement. The individual rabbi, however, is the authority for the interpretation and application of all matters of halakhah.

שאלה

What should Jewish ritual practice be following a stillbirth?

תשובה

Background

The body of halakhah associated with death and mourning is one of the richest and most admired areas of all Jewish law. Halakhah defines a wealth of ritual responses which teach us how to treat the body with respect, how the mourners should behave, and it specifies the critical role of the community. Until recently, however, those who face the loss of a pregnancy or a stillbirth, which is closely related to death, or the death of a newborn, have not had a Jewish way of actively responding to the tragedy which they confront. In fact, one of the books on mourning which is most used by laypeople states, "A life duration of more than thirty days establishes a human being as a viable person. If a child dies before that time, he is considered not to have lived at all. And no mourning practices are observed."[1] In traditional practice, there is only the burial of the body in an unmarked grave in a special section of the cemetery. While this is, in fact, not the only response to the death of a newborn found in halakhic literature, the idea that Judaism says "nothing happened" is what all Jews "know" as Jewish law. Anonymous burial has also been the only ritual act in the case of a miscarriage after

---

[1] Maurice Lamm, *The Jewish Way in Death and Mourning* (New York: Jonathan David Publishers, 1969), p. 83.

the fifth month of pregnancy and in the case of a stillbirth, there has been no ritual response to an earlier miscarriage.

During the past two decades, there has been an increasing interest in developing Jewish rituals for dealing with pregnancy loss and infant death. This is most likely a result of changing expectations of and attitudes towards pregnancy, as well as one of the areas of Jewish life which has opened up as women have become more involved in the process of Jewish law. Traditional rituals are being applied to these losses, and new rituals are being created.

The Committee on Jewish Law and Standards has undertaken a process of developing the halakhah in this area. In 1991, the CJLS approved a תשובה by Rabbi Debra Reed Blank on a ritual response to miscarriage. That paper advocates considering a miscarriage in the category of illness, with both parents treated as we would someone who is ill, with some additional practices related directly to the loss of an incomplete pregnancy. In 1992, the CJLS accepted a תשובה by Rabbi Stephanie Dickstein, "Jewish Ritual Practice Following the Death of an Infant Who Lives Less Than Thirty-One Days." That paper obligated parents and the community for both a burial service and full mourning rituals.

Neither of those papers provides a satisfactory response to stillbirth. In 1987 the CJLS approved a תשובה by Rabbi Isidoro Aizenberg, "Treatment of the Loss of a Fetus through Miscarriage." Rabbi Aizenberg's paper restates the traditional halakhah which requires burial of a fetus after the fifth month of gestation. He advises rabbis to respond sensitively to the pain of the parents and permits the rabbi to accompany parents to the burial and to offer words of comfort. I believe that while Rabbi Aizenberg's תשובה was an important first step in the area of stillbirth, it is not a sufficient response, particularly because it lacks any communal component.

This paper presents an alternative halakhic response to stillbirth. It takes into account the experiences of rabbis and bereaved parents with whom I have shared this work since I became involved with it a decade ago. This paper should be read in the context of the תשובות referred to above, which contain full discussions of the halakhic material related to pregnancy loss and neo-natal death. For the purposes of this תשובה, stillbirth will be defined as the death of the fetus in utero after the point of viability, or during delivery before the emergence of the head or the majority of the body. The issue of viability will be discussed later in the paper.

Much of the halakhic material discussed below is in the category of רשות – permitted – rather than חובה – required. The ritual response to stillbirth is still in the process of developing. The current status is the widespread belief among lay and professional Jews alike that there is no ritual response to stillbirth, and that, in fact, anything resembling mourning, or even the emotion of grieving, is forbidden by Jewish law. Therefore, the first purpose of this תשובה is to educate the community that there are Jewish rituals related to both the burial of a stillborn infant, and comforting the mourners and that the Jewish community should be involved. A second purpose is to suggest and recommend specific rituals. It is anticipated that this this תשובה becomes more widely known, and rabbis engage families and their communities in these rituals, some or all of these rituals will become standard practice. At that time, we may reconsider the strength and flexibility of the legal language which is used in this תשובה.

From the point of view of Jewish law, a fetus or a stillbirth is a נפל, and is neither a baby nor an infant. Nevertheless, it is common practice to use the term "baby" in discussing the unborn fetus or the result of a stillbirth. As a legal paper, this תשובה will generally use the term "fetus" or "stillborn" when referring to the נפל both in utero and if it is stillborn. However, at times, when discussing the subjective experience of the family, the fetus will be referred to as a "baby."

The Need for a Specific Response to Stillbirth

Why does this loss, stillbirth, require a response which is different from either miscarriage or neo-natal death? From the vantage of traditional halakhah, a fetus is a נפל, not a human being, until its head or the majority of its body emerges from its mother's body. At the moment it is mostly emerged, it is considered a legal person. Prior to that moment, halakhah would make no distinction with regard to appropriate mourning practices between a fetus which dies after the onset of labor and an embryo. There are a very few halakhic distinctions among fetuses based on gestational age. The embryo that miscarries or is aborted less than forty days after conception has no halakhic consequences for the priestly status of any future children of its mother (פדיון הבן would still be required for the firstborn son). A more mature fetus must be buried.

The halakhic reality of the "equality" of all fetuses is critical to our position on the permissibility of abortion. Until the moment that the baby emerges from its mother's body, its potential life never takes priority over the mother's life and health. Nothing in this paper should be read as challenging that position.[2] It is unlikely that in its halakhic development, the lack of mourning rituals in the event of a stillbirth had any relation to rabbinic concern for the permissibility of abortion. Today, however, this has become a serious issue. There is a concern that if we permit rituals resembling mourning for a stillborn fetus, we will be implying something about the human status of that fetus vis-à-vis the current American political debate on abortion. While we must be politically astute, we must also not allow our religious practice to be defined by those politics. A late term fetus is not considered by Jewish law to be a human being, yet it is a potential human being, with a degree of holiness associated with its human form and potentiality. At this late point in the pregnancy, Jewish law would only permit an abortion due to a serious threat to the mother, or a condition which dooms the fetus. When a mother has continued her pregnancy into the third trimester, and if the fetus must be aborted, there is a need for a ritual response. This issue will be discussed further at the end of the תשובה.

It is clear that contemporary rabbis and halakhic bodies cannot continue to treat a stillbirth as non-event, identical to the miscarriage of an embryo or a non-viable fetus. Rabbi Blank limits the applicability of her תשובה to twenty weeks, or some point shortly after that. Much of the medical/therapeutic literature dealing with pregnancy loss does not make a significant distinction between a stillbirth and the death of a newborn. In that literature, both losses are treated as the death of a baby. By the third trimester, the physical condition of the mother and the emotional state of the parents is similar in both cases. The mother whose infant is stillborn must still go through the exertion of labor and delivery. Afterwards, her body does not discern that the baby she delivered was not alive. She experiences the same hormonal changes and physical discomforts as her body returns to its non-pregnant state.

Psychologically, once a pregnancy reaches the third trimester, the parents assume that they will have a live baby. Even if the baby is born prematurely, and requires medical intervention, the expectation is that their child will come home. Today, medical technology enables the father and the mother to "see" their baby through ultrasound imagery (many carry around a "picture" of the fetus in utero), to hear the fetus' heart beat and to monitor its movements. Although the father's connection to the fetus is obviously quite different from the mother's, he, too, quite frequently "knows" and "interacts" with his baby.

By the third trimester, the community is also involved in the pregnancy, and awaits the arrival of the new baby. This involvement ranges from the intimate connection of grand-

---

[2] Papers on abortion which have been approved by the CJLS are found in *PCJLS 80-85*, pp. 3-40.

parents, aunts and uncles and siblings, and the plans for a ברית מילה or שמחת בת made with the rabbi, to the concerned interest of friends and co-workers, to the comments of mail carriers and dry cleaners. If the fetus dies, no new baby enters this community. This is not a private or secret happening. This is a public loss, one which parents and the community need to confront.

Stillbirth Requires a Ritual Response Related to אבלות

Underlying both the תשובה approved by the CJLS requiring full mounting for a baby which dies within a month following birth, and this תשובה on stillbirth, is that there has been a change in the halakhic presumption of infant viability. The traditional מקיל (lenient) position, which does not require engaging in the obligations of אבלות (formal mourning) for an infant, is based on the presumption that a significant number of even full term infants will not survive their first month. אבלות is considered to be דרבנן, (of Rabbinic authority). In cases of ספק (doubt) in matters which are דרבנן, we are מקיל. Given the high incidence of infant mortality in the past, the viability of a baby was doubtful until it survived for one month. Therefore, it became the custom not to require the rituals of mourning for an infant who died before the thirty-first day of life. The rituals of אבלות are a serious imposition on the life of the mourners. It is likely that in not obligating the parents of a dead infant to engage in אבלות, the rabbis were being compassionate. In times of high infant mortality, parents might otherwise be excessively burdened by repeatedly becoming אבלים. In contrast, burial is considered to be דאורייתא (of Biblical authority). In cases which are דאורייתא, when we deal with a situation which is ספק, we take the מחמיר (strict) position. The body of a fetus has a human form and was a potential life. Therefore, burial has been required for the body of a dead newborn infant or for a stillbirth. Today, due to improvements in medical technology, our presumption is that the vast majority of full term infants and a significant majority of premature infants born alive are viable and will survive past their first month. Therefore, the viability of an infant born alive is not a ספק, and we cannot be מקיל in אבלות when a baby dies. Given the rarity and shock of stillbirth, or infant death, today it is cruel, rather than compassionate, not to permit parents to behave as אבלים.

Part of the debate surrounding the 1992 תשובה requiring mourning in the event of neonatal death concerned the question of whether it was appropriately applied to all infants born alive, who survive even the shortest time, no matter how premature the baby was. In a Dissenting Concurrence to my תשובה on neo-natal death, Rabbi Avram Reisner suggests that a gestational age of thirty/thirty-one weeks which is a time of more certain viability should mark the time at which אבלות becomes a חיוב (obligatory).[3]

From a logical point of view, some would claim that a stillbirth is, by definition, not a viable fetus, and discussions of the duration of a pregnancy and viability seem irrelevant. However, it is also possible to argue that up until the moment of its death in utero, the third trimester fetus is potentially viable. Recently, the CJLS approved a תשובה, "Peri and Neo-Natology: The Matter of Limiting Treatment" by Rabbi Avram Reisner.[4] If, for some reason, that third trimester fetus had been delivered prior to its death, we would be obligated to treat it as we would any other human being, in accordance with Rabbi Reisner's paper.

Significant and relevant to this discussion is the section of his תשובה on peri-natal treatment in which Rabbi Reisner states that, "surgical and medical treatment of the fetus in utero at this late date after 31-32 weeks) should be encouraged." While such sur-

---

[3] Rabbi Avram Israel Reisner, "Kim Li: A Dissenting Concurrence," below, pp. 450-451.

[4] Rabbi Avram Israel Reisner, "Peri- and Neo-Natology: The Matter of Limiting Treatment," above, pp. 347-356.

gery is not required, due to the even minimal risk to the mother, it is permitted, despite the possible risk to the mother. "This is not to say that a late term fetus has attained the status of a full life, but that greater concern for the potential life of a fetus is in order." In his conclusion, Rabbi Reisner states that, "The claim of the potential life of the fetus to our ministrations is greater upon attaining viability, that is after seven months (31-32 weeks by obstetrical count)." The issue of the viability of a fetus is a legitimate one in the eyes of the CJLS.

The issue of the presumption of viability is one which is critical to the discussion of stillbirth and neo-natal death. The other is the emotional connection of the parents to their child. The halakhic statement underlying my תשובה on neo-natal death is that of Mishnah Niddah 5:3.

תינוק בן יום אחד, הרי הוא לאביו ולאמו כחתן שלם.

A one-day-old infant, if it dies, is considered to its father and mother like a full bridegroom.

The Talmud Yerushalmi in Kiddushin 4:11 extends this to the infant who dies after its head and the majority of its body emerges, and includes the relatives other than the parents among those who grieve. These statements recognize the emotional connection of the family with even the newest of newborns and the appropriateness of applying the strictures of אבלות to the family of a newborn who dies.

The case for a ritual response modeled on אבלות when parents and community are confronted with a stillbirth is a strong one. It is based on three considerations: (1) the recognition of the emotional connection that exists even with a fetus or very short-lived baby; (2) the appreciation of a fetus as a potential life (as it has always been in Jewish law); and, (3) the assumption of viability of the third trimester fetus due to current medical technology.

The Point at Which We Invoke Rituals to Mourn a Stillbirth

We have a halakhic system which prefers absolute to approximate times in deciding whether or not a particular halakhic obligation applies. The exact duration of a pregnancy which would define viability in relation to the rituals of mourning for a stillbirth remains problematic. Viability may depend as much on the technology available in a particular hospital as on the size or objective health of a particular baby or its mother's health during pregnancy or delivery. Rabbi Reisner argues strongly, both in his תשובה on the limits of peri-natal and neo-natal treatment, and in his concurring dissent to the neo-natal mourning תשובה, that after thirty-one weeks by obstetrical count, we are dealing with more certain viability. In fact, as we had anticipated, the time of more certain viability has been moving earlier. Currently, there is an eighty-five percent survival rate for babies delivered at twenty-eight weeks gestation.[5] However, there are still eight to ten weeks between the limits of Rabbi Blank's תשובה on miscarriage and the thirty-one weeks Rabbi Reisner suggests or the most current expectations of viability. As much as I recognize the halakhic discomfort with leaving the decision of how to treat the loss of a fetus after twenty weeks but before 28-31 weeks up to an individual rabbi and family, I do not see a reasonable alternative. Both the responses to miscarriage and to stillbirth should be available during this gray area. Some families will want to avail themselves of the

---

[5] Letter from Charles Paley, M.D., who is a Neonatologist and Attending Physician at St. Luke's-Roosevelt Medical Center and on the faculty at Columbia University. 6 Sept. 1995. Dr. Paley informs me that in the medical literature, the term "viability" is used to indicate the time at which survival is first possible, currently at twenty-three weeks.

more public, mourning-like rituals for stillbirth. Others will prefer the model with more private ritual and with ביקור חולים as the communal response. Rabbis and the community must respond to the particular situation of each family. Certainly in the later period of this gray area, burial is required, whichever ritual model the parents choose.

Ritual Responses to Stillbirth

It is the loss of a potential human life and the significant effect on the parents and their community which makes stillbirth a religious issue and requires a religious response. How can Judaism respond in a way which is sensitive and halakhically appropriate? We can find appropriate ways of responding to a stillbirth by applying rituals from the treatment of the חולה (a sick person), the treatment of a dead body, the treatment of an אבל (person mourning one of seven immediate relatives), and by using liturgy creatively and sensitively.

Since stillbirth is related to miscarriage, many of the recommendations from Rabbi Blank's paper apply here as well. The mother is a חולה in body and soul and the father is חולה in soul. A מי שברך for their recovery should be recited. At some point, when the mother has recovered physically from the pregnancy and delivery, and possibly surgery, she should recite ברכת הגומל (thanksgiving for deliverance from danger). As tragic as the loss of the baby is, she must still acknowledge that she faced physical danger and survived. The community must respond by fulfilling its obligation for ביקור חולים (visiting the sick), as described in Rabbi Blank's paper. The family should be visited by close friends, meals can be provided and other services offered by the broader community. In addition, at the proper time, a visit to the מקוה is recommended as Rabbi Blank comments, "In a case where the couple is not accustomed to observing הלכות טהרת המשפחה. . .the rabbi can take special care in describing the symbolic merits of such a visit." Some beautiful תחינות have been written for the occasion.[6]

The above recommendations from Rabbi Blank's תשובה apply to miscarriages. However, a stillbirth is an event which is significantly different from the much more common early miscarriage. Despite the fact that in Jewish law, the fetus never lived as a human being, our language refers to it in words of life, stillbirth and its death in utero. There is a need to mark and mourn this potential life that came so close to being, and to respond to the loss and grief of the expectant parents and their community. As discussed above, the issue of the viability of the third trimester fetus is a significant factor. For a full response to stillbirth, we turn to the rituals associated with burial and mourning.

Burial/Funeral Service

In fact, traditional halakhah does already note the quasi-human status of this potential life. It does so by requiring burial of the body of a formed fetus from the end of the fifth month on. The body should be wrapped in a clean white sheet and placed in a kosher coffin. Some authorities require circumcision while others do not mention it. Circumcision need not be done, but it may be done during the preparation of the body if it would be of comfort to the parents. No ברכה is recited. טהרה need not be done. Burial should be in a Jewish cemetery. Often, cemeteries have a special section for the graves of stillborns and infants. The stillborn may also be buried in a family plot. Many funeral homes and cemeteries reduce or do not charge a fee to bury a stillborn.

Traditional halakhah does not require any special liturgy or service. It is, however around the burial of the body that we have the opportunity to provide an important ritual

---

[6] Rabbi Diane Cohen, "Smikhat Horim: Providing Support for Parents Suffering a Miscarriage," unpublished paper.

response in the face of a tragedy and a way to begin the healing. If at all possible, parents and other relatives and friends should attend the burial. In conversations with women of all ages who had had a stillbirth, I found that there was a universal sense of distress that they had not been a participant in the burial of their child, and they regretted not knowing the exact spot of the grave. It has been the experience of rabbis who have done funerals for stillborns that attendance at the burial is larger than expected. This indicates that family and friends want to respond to the loss in a Jewish way and that attending a funeral is a natural way of confronting tragedy and a first step in comforting the parents.

The funeral should be held as soon as possible. However, to enable the mother to attend, the burial may certainly be delayed until she recovers enough physical strength to be present at the cemetery. The service would consist of prayers, psalms and other readings. A liturgy for the funeral of a stillborn, or infant of any age, is in the proposed new Rabbinical Assembly Rabbi's Manual. In addition, there are moving liturgies in many of the new books which contain sections on Jewish women's life cycle.[7] The burial service for a stillborn should not include צידוק הדין. There will be no eulogy. But the rabbi should speak words of comfort to the family. קריעה may be done, as is the usual custom, either on a piece of clothing or the black ribbon.

Kaddish may or may not be recited, at the discretion of the rabbi. Some rabbis prefer to limit kaddish to very specific situations related to those who are obligated to recite it. That does not include this family, since there was no death of a living person. Other rabbis permit the recitation of kaddish in many situations and feel that this loss is close enough to death to make kaddish an appropriate part of the funeral liturgy.

The baby should be given a Hebrew name and that name should be included in the service. The name might be the one which the parents had intended to use for their child. Alternatively, they might choose a name like Menachem or Nechama, indicating a desire for comfort. Jewish folk tradition recommends giving the child a name so that the parents will be able to find their child when they arrive in גן עדן. Contemporary therapeutic thought is that giving the stillborn a name aids the parents in the healing process and helps to distinguish that child from any other children of that couple.

At the conclusion of the service, the parents should walk between two lines of comforters, and the traditional statement of comfort should be said to them.

At some later time the grave should be marked with a stone that includes the name chosen by the parents for their child.

Mourning Practices Following the Burial

A meal of concern should be provided by the community on the return of the family from the cemetery. The family might also light a 24-hour yahrzeit candle or even a Shabbat candle. When contrasted with the traditional seven day candle, this more quickly extinguished candle symbolizes that the potential life of the baby did not come to fruition.

The strict position on burial — requiring burial and the strong recommendation of a funeral service — does not extend to all other practices of אבלות following burial. In particular, this paper does not recommend shivah. It is clear that in the case of a stillbirth, in contrast to a neo-natal death, we do not have a halakhic mandate for shivah. In

---

[7] See, for example, liturgies by Rabbi Sandy Eisenberg Sasso and Rabbi Amy Eilberg in *Life Cycles: Jewish Women on Life Passages and Personal Milestones*, ed. Rabbi Debra Orenstein (Woodstock, Vt.: Jewish Lights Publishing, 1994), pp. 45-46, 48-51.

addition, rabbis who have adapted the תשובה on neo-natal death to deal with stillbirths have told me that parents of stillbirths prefer a "one-day shivah."

In recognition of the fact that we are dealing with a loss that is not identical with, but is close to, death, we recommend a one day יום ניחום, a Day of Comfort, to be observed by both the parents and the community. The parents should remain at home. The community should be present and should offer comfort. The יום ניחום could include a minyan at the parents' home the evening following the funeral. The parents may recite kaddish or some other prayer or psalm. The rabbi should speak words acknowledging the loss of the expected baby and instructing the community in how to treat the parents.[8]

After this one day יום ניחום, the community obligation would revert to the ביקור חולים model. However, the unique nature of the illness/loss would have been publicly acknowledged. The parents should not be prohibited from observing some of the private practices associated with shivah during the remainder of the week following burial, or from reciting kaddish in a minyan. Despite the fact that we are not obligating or even calling the mourning time shivah, there is a connection between the seven days of shivah and the seven days following birth, after which the ברית מילה or שמחת בת would have been held.

The usefulness of the model based on אבלות as a response to stillbirth is especially important for the father. Husbands and wives do have different experiences of pregnancy and will experience the loss of the expected baby in different ways. However, the father's loss is no less real than the mother's for all that its manifestations may be less physical or obvious. When the father is treated as an אבל equal to the mother, he is relieved of the burden of "being strong." He has a specific set of ritual tasks to do and a specific role, through which he can confront his loss. In addition, family and friends have a responsibility to be present and to care for him as well as for the mother. Pregnancy loss and infant death is associated with an increased risk of divorce. This is often related to the inability of the parents to share their grief with each other or with others. Through these rituals, Judaism provides a structure for the parents to be supported and protected from the isolation associated with stillbirth.

Although the stillborn's grandparents will not have the status of אבלים, the public nature of these funeral and יום ניחום rituals is also very important for them. They, too, need permission to grieve, as well as specific rituals through which they can help their bereaved children.

As with any death/loss, it is important to remember that the family is not healed and does not recover after one day or a week or a month. The family has been irrevocably changed. The community needs to continue to express its concern and offer support, as it should for all mourners.

Yahrzeit

The final recommendation is that parents may observe the yahrzeit of their lost baby. Some have expressed discomfort with marking the loss, which was not exactly a death, with the rituals associated with death. Nevertheless, this anniversary will be noted in any event (most often by a minor depression or some other type of crisis).[9] Reciting kaddish, giving

---

[8] There are an increasing number of books and pamphlets about dealing with pregnancy loss which will be useful to families, friends and rabbis. A particularly helpful book, which is based on work with families in a pregnancy loss support group sponsored by the National Council of Jewish Women, is Ingrid Kohn and Perry Lynn Moffitt, *A Silent Sorrow* (New York: Delta/Dell/Bantum, 1992).

[9] Sandra Blakeslee, "New Groups Aim to Help Parents Face Grief when a Newborn Dies," *New York Times*, 8 Sept. 1988, p. B13.

צדקה and/or lighting a yahrzeit or Shabbat candle provides a ritual outlet for remembering a tragic event in the family's past.

When would the yahrzeit of a stillbirth be observed? In most cases, the exact time of the fetus' death is unknown, and delivery will be at a later time. When the exact date of death is unknown, one custom is to observe the date of the funeral as the yahrzeit. Another option, when it is impossible to determine the date of death, is for the relative to choose a day on which to observe the yahrzeit.[10] This seems to be be most reasonable solution. Some parents might choose to observe the day when they learned that the fetus would be stillborn; others might choose the day when the body was delivered; still others might choose the day of burial.

Since there is no חיוב associated with this yahrzeit observance, the parents, and even siblings who were alive and old enough at the of the stillbirth, may mark the anniversary for only the first year, or for as many years as it is meaningful to them. It is not morbidity or an inability to close a sad chapter which suggests continuing to mark yahrzeit after the first year, but rather a ritualized acknowledgement of a fact in the history of that family.

Death of a Premature or Compromised Infant

Following the adoption of the תשובה on neonatal death, Rabbi Reisner wrote "Kim Li: A Dissenting Concurrence," referred to above, expressing his difficulty with requiring full mourning for an infant born alive prior to the thirty-first week; that is prior to a point of more certain viability. Also noted above, twenty-eight weeks is now the time of 85% survival. I feel that the practices I have recommended in this תשובה for a stillbirth would also be an appropriate alternative halakhic response, as well as one which is psychologically sound, in dealing with the death of a premature infant born alive prior to twenty-eight weeks, who survives only minutes or hours.

In addition, the practices recommended in this תשובה on stillbirth could also apply in the case of a severely deformed and compromised newborn classified as dying in Rabbi Reisner's תשובה on limiting treatment for peri- and neo-natology. The presumption that this baby would die might make the full mourning normally recommended for a baby born alive a less compassionate response. On the other hand, it is likely that the parents and family would still have developed a relationship with such a baby in the days or weeks before its death and would want to engage in full mourning.

Third Trimester Abortion

These rituals should also be available to parents in the tragic and rare situation in which an almost full-term pregnancy must be terminated due to danger to the life or health of the mother, or to her mental inability to carry to term a non-viable fetus. Our understanding of the halakhah would still require burial of the body in this event, based on fetal age. In most cases today, medical practice at this late point in the pregnancy when the mother's life is in danger, is to attempt to deliver and then treat a viable, albeit premature, baby.[11] Such a late-term abortion is more likely in a situation where tests indicate that the fetus is already doomed. Some suggest that treating the aborted fetus as almost human would increase the parents' guilt over the abortion. However, I believe that it is possible to acknowledge and mourn the loss of the potential life while still

---

[10] Rabbi Aaron Felder, *Yesodei Smochos* (New York, 1976), p. 134.

[11] Dr. Charles Paley, op. cit.

asserting that the mother's life and health took priority. These rituals can provide an important opportunity to mourn and to comfort parents whose isolation from God and from their community is extreme.

Theology

A particular concern of many bereaved parents is what happens to the soul of their never-to-be-born baby. The question of ensoulment (when a soul enters a particular body) is not an area of set dogma in Jewish theology. There are numerous sources suggesting a variety of different entry times for the soul, from conception, to birth to even later. I would suggest that the rabbi be extremely sensitive to the parents' need to to know that God has not abandoned them or their never-to-be-born baby. Whatever the rabbi's personal theology on ensoulment, this is a time to share with the parents that there is a Jewish view that the fetus had a unique soul and that God is caring for it.[12]

Conclusion

In the event of a stillbirth, burial at a Jewish cemetery is required. We strongly recommend a funeral service at the time of burial attended by family and others. The stillborn may be named and circumcision can, but need not, be done. The grave should later be marked.

Following the burial, we recommend a one day יום ניחום (Day of Comfort) which may include a minyan at which the parents may recite kaddish or some other prayer. After the first day, the parents may observe the practices associated with שבעה בצניעות (private observances which do not involve the community). After the יום ניחום, the community should treat the parents as if they were in the category of חולים (those who are ill), visiting them if it is desired and providing for their physical needs. The parents may observe yahrzeit.

---

[12] For a collection of some Talmudic material in English on the issue of the soul, see A. Cohen, *Everyman's Talmud* (New York: Schocken Books, 1949/1975), pp. 76-78. Note in particular the discussion between Rabbi Judah and Antoninus in Sanhedrin 91b.

YD 340:30.1996b

WHAT'S IN A NAME? A CONCURRENCE AND DISSENT TO THE RESPONSUM OF RABBI DICKSTEIN ON RITUAL PRACTICE FOLLOWING A STILLBIRTH

Rabbi Ben Zion Bergman

This paper was submitted as a concurrence and dissent to "Jewish Ritual Practice Following a Stillbirth," by Rabbi Stephanie Dickstein. Concurring and dissenting opinions are not official positions of the Committee on Jewish Law and Standards.

The Committee on Jewish Law and Standards of the Rabbinical Assembly provides guidance in matters of halakhah for the Conservative movement. The individual rabbi, however, is the authority for the interpretation and application of all matters of halakhah.

Rabbi Dickstein has presented a sensitive and sympathetic response to the anguish of a family that has suffered the tragedy of a stillbirth. No one can, or will, dispute the fact that such an event can be devastatingly traumatic. Nor would anyone dispute the concept that appropriate ritual or rituals could be extremely beneficial in helping the stricken couple confront their tragedy. Furthermore, it is especially important that such ritual have its roots in traditional Jewish practices so that (1) the tradition is not silent but rather made relevant to the couple in their hour of need, and (2) the Jewish community is involved, thus strengthening the couple's ties to the community, and preventing what could otherwise be felt as abandonment.

I therefore basically concur with Rabbi Dickstein's responsum. However, there is one element in particular in her proposal which prevented me from voting in favor of her paper and led to my abstaining in the vote.

Rabbi Dickstein writes: "The baby should be given a Hebrew name, and that name should be included in the [burial] service. . . . At some later time the grave should be marked with a stone that includes the name chosen by the parents for their child." It is with this element in the responsum that I find myself in serious disagreement.

My disagreement is prompted by two considerations – one practical but less compelling, and the other more theoretical but, to my mind, most compelling. First the practical consideration:

Most couples on the verge of parenthood begin quite early to think of possible names for the prospective child. Today, since the sex of the child can be ascertained in utero, and many avail themselves of that knowledge, only one name or set of names has to be chosen. Many then, in anticipation, begin to refer to the fetus by the name they have chosen to be bestowed when it is born. I even know of couples who, even before it was medically possible to ascertain the sex of the child, were so set in their minds that it was going to be of a certain gender, that they began to use the name they had chosen for that eventuality. (Often they were surprised.) Now, among Ashkenazic Jews it is customary to name a child after a deceased relative. This is considered an honor to the memory of the deceased. If a name is going to be bestowed upon the stillborn, the name would almost certainly be the one which had been chosen in anticipation and which the parents had used in speaking of their prospective child.

I hasten to point out that it is no honor to a deceased relative to have a נפל (a stillborn) named after one. Additionally, that effectively preempts the use of that name for future children to be born in the extended family. My brother's name is Leibel, and I have a whole pack of cousins named Leonard, or Louis, or Libby, or Lillian, etc., all of whom were named after my paternal grandfather, Leib Yitzchak. Had the birth of these been preceded by a stillbirth upon whom the name had been bestowed, my grandfather's name would never have been carried by a living descendant. Superstitious though it might be, it would certainly have been considered inappropriate to give a living child the same name as one who had never lived. And for Sephardim who bestow honor upon living relatives by naming children after them, it is similarly no great honor to have a נפל named after one's self, and might similarly result in the loss of the use of that name for children born subsequently.

The other consideration, as noted above, is theoretical albeit more compelling. Rabbi Dickstein, quite correctly, makes the point that nothing in her paper should be construed as inimical to our position on the permissibility of abortion. Yet that could be a result of creating a practice of officially bestowing a name upon a stillborn.

A child when born is at first only a living mass of protoplasm arranged in the form of a human child, not vastly different from other newborns. Unique "personhood" develops. The first element of "personhood" by which we distinguish this blue-eyed or brown-eyed, blonde, brunette, or bald child from others similarly endowed, is by bestowing a name. Before that, the baby is only a baby. A name makes him or her a person.

Now, the so-called "pro-life" forces have attempted to invoke the Fourteenth Amendment in support of their position against abortion. The Fourteenth Amendment states: "Nor shall any State deprive any *person* of *life,* liberty or property, without due process of law; nor deny to any *person* within its jurisdiction the equal protection of the laws" [emphases added]. The crux of their position is whether the fetus can be defined as a person. If the fetus is considered a person, its "right to life" is protected by the Fourteenth Amendment, and an abortion could be performed only after "due process of Law" in each case. Legal commentators have refuted the position on the basis that neither legally nor philosophically can the unborn fetus that has never lived be termed a person. The problems inherent in defining the fetus as a person and therefore entitled to Fourteenth Amendment protection were already noted in *Roe v. Wade*, 410 US. 113, 93 S. Ct. 705 (1973) fn. 54.

Since a name begins to invest a child with "personhood," bestowing a name upon a stillborn is equivalent to considering the stillborn as a "person," which, in light of the above, would give substantiation to the claim of the anti-abortion forces. Hence, by making the giving of a name a standard part of the Jewish ritual practice following a stillbirth, we serve to vitiate our position regarding abortion.

I therefore find myself in fundamental disagreement with that element in Rabbi Dickstein's proposal and would vigorously urge that it be deleted from any ritual practice prescribed by the CJLS in the case of a stillbirth.

YD 345.1997a

Assisted Suicide

Rabbi Elliot N. Dorff

This paper was approved by the CJLS on March 11, 1997, by a vote of twenty-one in favor, two opposing and one abstaining (21-2-1). Voting in favor: Rabbis Kassel Abelson, Ben Zion Bergman, Elliot N. Dorff, Jerome M. Epstein, Samuel Fraint, Baruch Frydman-Kohl, Nechama D. Goldberg, Arnold M. Goodman, Susan Grossman, Judah Kogen, Vernon H. Kurtz, Alan B. Lucas, Aaron L. Mackler, Lionel E. Moses, Paul Plotkin, Mayer Rabinowitz, Avram Israel Reisner, James Rosen, Joel Roth, Elie Kaplan Spitz, and Gerald Zelizer. Voting against: Rabbis Myron S. Geller and Gordon Tucker. Abstaining: Rabbi Shoshana Gelfand.

The Committee on Jewish Law and Standards of the Rabbinical Assembly provides guidance in matters of halakhah for the Conservative movement. The individual rabbi, however, is the authority for the interpretation and application of all matters of halakhah.

שאלה

May Jews assist others in committing suicide or request that others assist them in their own suicides?

תשובה

The Medical and Legal Contexts for This Question

Killing oneself and murdering others have always been technically possible but forbidden in Jewish law. In our time, though, the matter has taken on new dimensions. On the one hand, while people in the past had no choice but to endure the pain of dying, with minimal medication available to ease their suffering, now we have sophisticated ways to diagnose levels of pain and to calibrate pain medication to need. We also have developed hospice care, where the patient is supported physically, psychologically, and socially by a whole team of people, including family and friends. These factors should diminish the number of people who seek to take their lives.

On the other hand, though, we can now sustain bodily functions almost indefinitely, and so dying people may live through a long period of disability. Moreover, the drive to save money in health care has limited medical services for the dying, and in the future even less money will be spent on the care of each dying person as more and more of the baby boomers call upon whatever resources exist and as the need to contain health care costs becomes even more critical. This is especially problematic in our age of protracted life spans, where people generally die of chronic rather than acute illnesses.

Moreover, we can now predict the course of a disease with greater accuracy, and so people have less room for unrealistic hope. We now also have the means to bring about a quick, virtually painless death. These latter factors have prompted some people faced with an incurable disease to take their own lives, sometimes asking others to assist them.

Those who commit suicide and those who aid others in doing so act out of a plethora of motives. Some of them are less than noble, involving, for example, children's desires for Mom or Dad to die with dispatch so as not to squander their inheritance on "futile" health care, or the desire of insurance companies to spend as little money as possible on the terminally ill.[1] The morally hard cases, though, are those where the primary intention is the benign desire to stop the pain of a dying patient. Indeed, some have claimed that mercy killing is the only moral path, that keeping a person alive under excruciating and/or hopeless circumstances is itself immoral.

The Ninth Circuit Court of Appeals and the Second Circuit Court of Appeals have both recently affirmed that under the Fourteenth Amendment it is an American's right to commit suicide and to request others to assist in that process. The Ninth Circuit based its argument on the Amendment's clause that forbids states from depriving liberty to any person without due process of law. The Second Circuit, noting that people with terminal illnesses can legally request to be disconnected from life support systems but other people are denied aid in dying, based its argument on the Amendment's clause forbidding states from denying any person the equal protection of the laws.[2] As of this writing, the United States Supreme Court has taken both of those cases on appeal. [NOTE: The U.S. Supreme Court subsequently rejected these Constitutional grounds for permitting assisted suicide, returning the matter to the discretion of each state. *Washington v. Glucksberg* 117 S.Ct. 2258 (1997); *Quill v. Vacco* 117 S.Ct. 2293 (1997).]

These new medical and legal realities, then, require us to reexamine and reevaluate Judaism's stance on suicide and assisted suicide so that contemporary North American Jews will know their tradition's views of these issues and the reasons for those views.

Jewish Theological and Legal Grounds for Opposing Suicide and Assisted Suicide

A. Suicide

Judaism's stance on suicide and assisted suicide is rooted in its understanding of the body as God's possession. God, in fact, created and owns everything in the universe.[3] God has granted us the normal use of our bodies during our lifetimes, and that inevitably

---

[1] As we shall discuss below, though, the economic realities behind these arguments are real, but they argue not for assisted suicide, but for much greater utilization of hospice care.

[2] *Compassion in Dying v. State of Washington* 79 F.3d 790 (9th Cir. 1996); *Quill v. Vacco* 80 F.3d 716 (2d Cir. 1996). (A subsequent petition for the Ninth Circuit to rehear the case *en banc* was denied: 85 F.3d 1440 [9th Cir. 1996].) The Ninth Circuit also invoked the Supreme Court's past decisions on abortion in interpreting the Fourteenth Amendment's liberty clause to protect a person's right to make his or her own health care decisions. Thus Judge Stephen Reinhardt, writing for an 8-3 majority, stated that, "By permitting the individual to exercise the right to choose, we are following the constitutional mandate to take such decisions out of the hands of government, both state and federal, and to put them where they rightly belong, in the hands of the people."

[3] See, for example, Exod. 19:5; Deut. 10:14; Ps. 24:1. See also Gen. 14:19, 22 (where the Hebrew word for "Creator," קנה, also means "Possessor," and where "heaven and earth" is a merism for those and everything in between) and Ps. 104:24, where the same word is used with the same meaning. The following verses have the same theme, although not quite as explicitly or as expansively: Exod. 20:11; Lev. 25:23, 42, 55; Deut. 4:35, 39; 32:6.

involves some dangers and risks; but God, as Owner, imposes specific requirements and prohibitions intended to preserve our life and health as much as possible.[4]

One such provision relevant to our topic is that Jews may not even injure themselves, let alone kill themselves.[5] To do either one of those things would be to harm or destroy what belongs to God. Since we do not own our bodies, we do not have the right to expose ourselves to injury or death beyond the requirements of normal living and must instead seek to preserve our lives and health. The only three times, in fact, when a Jew is supposed to prefer death to violating the law — namely, where the choice is death or being forced to commit murder, idolatry, or adultery/incest[6] — are all choices of death for the sake of God, not for oneself.

When the Romans burned Rabbi Hananyah ben Teradiyon at the stake for teaching Torah, he refused to inhale the flames to bring about his death more quickly, saying "Better that God who gave life should take it; a person may not injure himself or herself." The Romans, though, had attached tufts of woof soaked with water to his chest to make his dying slower and more painful, and Rabbi Hananyah allowed his students to bribe the executioner to detach them. From this and other sources, later Jewish authorities deduced that one may remove impediments to the natural process of dying but not actively cause one's own death, much less someone else's.[7] Indeed, based on the biblical story of Ahitofel's suicide, medieval sources maintain that "he who commits suicide while of sound mind has no share in the World to Come" and is to be buried outside the Jewish cemetery or at its edge.[8]

Saul's suicide (1 Sam. 31:3-5), though, is recorded in the Bible without objection, and the Talmud, apparently approvingly, records the case of children who take their lives to avoid being sexually violated.[9] These cases undoubtedly served as the backdrop for Jewish law's justification of suicide when done as an act of martyrdom in

---

[4] Bathing, for example, is a commandment according to Hillel: Leviticus Rabbah 34:3. Maimonides summarizes and codifies the rules requiring proper care of the body in M.T. Laws of Ethics (De'ot), chs. 3-5. He spells out there in remarkable clarity that the purpose of the positive duties to maintain health is not to feel good and live a long life, but rather to have a healthy body so that one can then serve God.

[5] The prohibition against injuring oneself is stated in M. Bava Kamma 8:6 (90b); cf. M.T. Laws of Injury and Damage 5:1. Tannaitic sources recorded in the Talmud (B. Bava Kamma 91b) state divided opinions as to whether individuals may inflict non-fatal wounds on themselves. The later sources generally agree that people are not allowed to injure themselves, although some restrict the prohibition against self-injury to cases where wounds are produced (*Hemdat Yisrael*, commandment 310), and some think that the prohibition is not a violation of Gen. 9:5 or Deut. 4:9 (interpreted as a command to maintain one's health) but is rather rabbinic (Lehem Mishneh on M.T. Hilkhot De'ot 3:1). In any case, people who injure themselves are not punished specifically for doing that, but they may be punished at the hands of Heaven (Tosefta Bava Kamma 9:11), and rabbinic courts may inflict disciplinary flogging (מכת מרדות) for injuring oneself (M.T. Hilkhot Rotzeah 11:5; S.A. Hoshen Mishpat 420:31; 427:10) — understandable, but more than a bit ironic! See "Hovel," *Encyclopedia Talmudit* 12:681f. (Hebrew).

The prohibition against suicide is not recorded in the Talmud itself. The post-talmudic tractate, Semahot (Evel Rabbati) 2:1-5 serves as the basis for most of later Jewish law on suicide, together with Genesis Rabbah 34:13, which bases the prohibition on Gen. 9:5. Cf. M.T. Hilkhot Rotzeah 2:3; Hilkhot Sanhedrin 18:6; S.A. Yoreh De'ah 345:1ff. See "Suicide," *Encyclopaedia Judaica* 15:489-491.

[6] B. Sanhedrin 74a.

[7] B. Avodah Zarah 18a; S.A. Yoreh De'ah 339:1 (with gloss).

[8] 2 Sam. 17:23. See Irving J. Rosenbaum, *The Holocaust and Halakhah* (New York: Ktav, 1976), p. 36 and p. 162, n. 21, for a discussion of the origins of this maxim. Burying suicides outside the cemetery: M.T. Hilkhot Aveilut 1:11; S.A. Yoreh De'ah 345:1 — or at its edge: Responsum no. 763 of Rabbi Solomon ben Abraham Adret (the "Rashba," c. 1235-c. 1310).

[9] B. Gittin 57b.

defense of Judaism[10] or as a way of avoiding the temptation to convert under torture.[11] Later Jewish law has taken this yet further: by narrowing the definition of a suicide to those who took their lives with competence of mind and freedom of will, modern authorities have maintained that those who suffered, or could be presumed to have suffered, from temporary insanity do not fall into the category of willfully committing suicide and are therefore permitted a normal Jewish burial.[12]

This distinction between the status of suicide itself and what one does with the body of a suicide *post facto* has important implications for assisted suicide. As our colleague on the Committee on Jewish Law and Standards, Mr. Frederick Lawrence, has pointed out, one must distinguish *justification* from *excuse*. If suicide is permissible, as it is in American law, a person who committed suicide would be justified in doing so, and an accomplice might or might not share in that justification. Hence the current debate over assisted suicide in the American courts and in state referenda.

In Jewish law, though, suicide is a criminal act except for the specific situations mentioned above. It is only in those exceptional cases that a justification for suicide exists; in all others the principal can at best have an excuse that does not render the act permissible but may mitigate punishment. The accomplice may suffer too. The aide's duress, however, is separate and apart from the principal's suffering, and so the aide's excuse to mitigate punishment must be judged independently. Indeed, while sometimes that excuse may be compelling, as in cases where the aide acted at the patient's express request to end his or her own suffering despite having the advantages of full medical and social support, in cases at the other end of the spectrum the aide may have acted to stop the medical bills and the need to care for the patient, perhaps even contrary to the desires of the patient. In no case, though, does the accomplice have a *justification* for assisting in the suicide. Even if the principal had a valid justification for committing suicide, the aide does not share in that justification and is therefore fully liable for the violations committed by assisting the suicide.

Suicide itself, then, remains forbidden by Jewish law except in the dire circumstances of martyrdom. Even then, a poignant ruling from the Holocaust indicates that suicide is to be avoided if at all possible. Rabbi Ephraim Oshry permitted a man who was to be tortured by the Nazis to force him to identify the whereabouts of other Jews to commit suicide lest he betray those other Jews, but Rabbi Oshry did not permit this ruling to be published for fear that it would undermine the commitment to life of the other Jews of the Kovno ghetto, and, other authors, both during and after the Holocaust, have taken pride in the small number of Eastern European Jews who committed suicide in the midst of the Nazi terror.[13] Moreover, Rabbi Oshry was ruling in a case where the person, were he not to commit suicide, faced the prospect of endanger-

---

[10] B. Sanhedrin 74a-74b. Cf. M.T. Hilkhot Yesodei Torah, ch. 5; S.A. Yoreh De'ah 157:1.

[11] E.g., Tosafot on B. Avodah Zarah 18a, s.v. ואל; Tosafot on B. Gittin 57b, s.v. קפצו.

[12] *Kol Bo 'al Aveilut*, p. 319, sec. 50; Yehiel M. Tuchinski, *Gesher HaHayyim* (Jerusalem: Solomon, 1960), 1:271-273; Isaac Klein, *A Guide to Jewish Religious Practice* (New York: Jewish Theological Seminary of America, 1979), pp. 282-283 (but note the mistake in citing the passage from *Gesher HaHayyim*: it should be 1:271-273, as noted above, not 1:71-73, as printed there). This may be based on an earlier source – namely, B'samim Rosh no. 345 – claiming to be the opinion of the much-respected Rabbenu Asher (the "Rosh," c. 1250-1327), who there permits full Jewish burial of people who commit "suicide because of a multiplicity of troubles, worries, pain, or utter poverty." That source, even if accepted as authentically the opinion of Rabbenu Asher, does *not* permit committing suicide in the first place, and neither do the later Jewish authorities cited above; they only permit normal Jewish burial after the fact.

[13] See Rosenbaum, *The Holocaust and Halakhah*, pp. 35-40.

ing the lives of others; those are not the circumstances in the vast majority of cases in which the contemporary question is being raised.[14]

In sum, then, the tradition prohibits suicide except as an act of martyrdom. Contemporary medical cases that raise the question anew clearly do not fit into that exception: the people involved ask to die in response to the excruciating pain of their illness, not in fear of being tortured by interrogators or forced to convert to another religion. Their suicide, then, would not be justified, even if people who violate this law would retroactively be permitted a traditional Jewish burial.

B. Assisted Suicide

Since suicide itself is prohibited, aiding a suicide is also forbidden. The grounds for that prohibition depend upon how the assistance is administered.

Sometimes the aide provides the means for the patient to commit suicide but is not involved in any other way. In some typical cases, the assistant hands an overdose of pills to the patient or sets up a machine so that the patient can administer a lethal substance intravenously. Once supplied the means to commit suicide, the patient acts completely on his or her own.

In such cases, the helper minimally violates Lev. 19:14, "Do not put a stumbling block before the blind," for the Rabbis interpreted that verse to prohibit moral stumbling blocks as well as physical ones.[15] The aide is guilty at least of misleading the patient to think that a forbidden act is permissible, of placing a stumbling block before a patient who is morally blinded by his or her medical condition to be able to see the authority and importance of the Jewish norm prohibiting suicide.[16]

Worse, the aide in such circumstances makes it possible for the patient to do what is forbidden. In talmudic terminology, the aide is "strengthening those who commit a sin" or "aiding those who commit a sin," both of which are forbidden.[17] Such a person is even more culpable than the one who simply misleads a person into thinking that the

---

[14] While it is distinctly uncomfortable to second-guess a rabbi ruling in those dire circumstances, one must also note, as Rabbi Aaron Mackler has pointed out to me, that Rabbi Oshry's decision is, in the end, one rabbi's ruling, and since it extends permission to commit suicide to cases beyond the well-established exceptions of martyrdom, it may simply be an erroneous ruling. I would prefer to deny its relevance as a precedent on the basis of the important distinctions between his case and ours — namely, that the man in his case faced the prospect of endangering the lives of others through no fault of his own, while the cases we are discussing include no such factor.

[15] The prohibition of putting a stumbling block before the blind: Lev. 19:14. The rabbinic extension of that prohibition to apply not only to the physically blind, but to the morally blind as well: B. Pesahim 22b; B. Moed Katan 5a, 17a; B. Bava Mezia 75b; etc. (The principle is also applied to prohibit intentionally giving bad advice to people [see Sifra on this verse] and to those who are theologically blind in that they might be tempted to worship idols [B. Nedarim 42b].)

[16] If the aide additionally convinced the person to commit suicide, the aide may be considered an "inciter" (מסית). One who incites another person to worship idols is subject to death by stoning (Deut. 13:7; M. Sanhedrin 7:4, 10). In the case of other sins, though, the defendant can invoke the talmudic principle (B. Bava Kamma 56a), דברי הרב ודברי התלמיד מי שומעין? "When the words of the Master and the words of the student [conflict], to whom does one listen?" — the Master here being God and the student a human being. According to the Talmud (B. Sanhedrin 29a), however, those who incite other Jews to engage in idolatry cannot avail themselves of this defense because with regard to that offense the Torah (Deut. 13:9) specifically says, "Show him no pity or compassion, and do not shield him." Thus while inducing someone to commit any other sin — like suicide — is certainly not laudable behavior, it is not culpable in law because each of us is responsible for knowing right from wrong and for resisting lures to do the wrong.

[17] "Strengthening one to commit a sin": B. Nedarim 22a; B. Gittin 61a. "Helping one to commit a sin": B. Avodah Zarah 55b. I would like to thank Rabbi Ben Zion Bergman for alerting me to this point.

act is permissible because the culprit in this case actively makes it possible for a person to commit the sin.

The aide in such cases might also be construed to be liable for injuring the patient indirectly (גרמה). One who does that is retroactively free of monetary liability for any harm done, but *ab initio* nobody may deliberately cause harm to another, even indirectly.[18]

Furthermore, one who harms another indirectly, while free of liability in human courts, is culpable in the judgments of Heaven. In fact, one specific case that the Talmud includes in this category concerns a person who placed deadly poison before the animal of a neighbor; if divine retribution is to meted out to a person who threatens the life of an animal in that way, God would undoubtedly be even more upset with someone who puts the life of a human being at risk in that way.[19]

If the assistant not only provides the patient with the means to kill himself or herself, but also participates in the process, the liability of the assistant depends upon how the help is given. If the aide directly causes the wound that eventuates in the patient's death, then she or he violates Jewish laws prohibiting the deliberate injury of another. Even if the victim asks to be injured, others may not do that, and they are fully liable for the injury.[20] This would be true even if the patient willingly took part in the act. So, for example, if a physician compromises the life of a patient by administering a given dose of medication or poison intravenously but leaves it to the patient to push a lever to insert the rest of the dose necessary to bring about death, the physician is liable both for misleading the patient morally and for injuring him or her.

Finally, some forms of assisted suicide amount to murder. So, for example, if the aide shoots the victim with a gun or knowingly administers a lethal dose of a medication or poison with the intent of bringing about the person's death, such acts clearly constitute murder, even though the motive was, by hypothesis, benign.

Note that these Jewish arguments against suicide and assisted suicide differ radically from the reasons invoked by many Christian opponents of euthanasia. Some Christians base their opposition on the redemptive character of suffering. Euthanasia is unwarranted, the argument goes, because pain is itself salvational, symbolized most graphically by the crucifixion of Jesus. Other Christian voices oppose any medical intervention, including those intended to reduce pain, as an improper human intrusion onto God's prerogatives of deciding when to inflict illness and when to bring healing.[21]

Judaism's opposition to euthanasia cannot be grounded in either of these lines of argument. For Judaism, the pain of disease is not in and of itself a good thing to be sustained for its own sake. *Retroactively*, when trying to explain how God could be just and yet innocent people suffer, the Rabbis suggested, among other approaches, that the pain of the innocent may be "afflictions of love" (יסורין של אהבה) designed by God either to teach the person virtues of patience and faith or to punish the person in this life for his or her small number of sins so as to make his or her reward in the next life pure and all

---

[18] See B. Bava Batra 22a, and see Tosafot there.

[19] B. Bava Kamma 56a, which refers, among other such cases, to the one in B. Bava Kamma 47b concerning the person who places poison before a neighbor's animal.

[20] M. Bava Kamma 8:7 (92a); M.T. Laws of the Injury and Damage 5:11; S.A. Hoshen Mishpat 421:12.

[21] For a sampling of varying religious approaches to assisted death, including my own more extensive treatment of Jewish perspectives on this issue, see *Must We Suffer Our Way to Death? Cultural and Theological Perspectives on Death by Choice*, eds. Ronald P. Hamel and Edwin R. Dubose (Dallas: Southern Methodist University Press, 1996).

the greater,[22] but that doctrine was never used before the fact to justify withholding pain medication from the suffering. On the contrary, the Talmud records that Rabbi Hiyya bar Abba, Rabbi Yohanan, and Rabbi Eleazar all say that neither their sufferings nor the reward promised in the World to Come for enduring them are welcome — that is, they would rather live without both the suffering and the anticipated reward.[23] Moreover, from its earliest sources, Judaism has both permitted and required us to act as God's agents in bringing healing or, failing that, in reducing pain.

I sympathize enormously with patients going through an agonizing process of dying, and in cases of irreversible, terminal illness, I have taken a very liberal stance on withholding or withdrawing life-support systems, including artificial nutrition and hydration, to enable nature to take its course. I would also permit the use of any amount of medication necessary to relieve pain, even if that is the same amount that will hasten a person's death, as long as the intention is to alleviate pain.[24] The Committee on Jewish Law and Standards has validated that stance as well as that of Rabbi Avram Reisner, who permits withdrawing machines and medications from the patient but not withholding or withdrawing artificial nutrition and hydration, and who permits using large doses of morphine to relieve pain up to, but not including, the amount that poses a risk to the patient's life.[25]

The Jewish tradition takes mental illness seriously as illness,[26] and so some might ask: What is the difference between administering a large dose of morphine for reducing physical pain and using that same dosage in response to a person saying, "I want to end this"? In other words, why is it the case that physical pain counts as sufficient ground to justify doses of morphine that may risk death while mental distress does not?

---

[22] M. Avot 2:16; B. Berakhot 4a; B. Eruvin 19a; B. Ta'anit 11a; B. Kiddushin 39b; Genesis Rabbah 33:1; Yalkut Shimoni to Ecclesiastes, 978. Among later Jewish philosophers, Saadia is the first to affirm this doctrine (*Book of Opinions and Beliefs*, books 4 and 5), while Maimonides rejects it (*Guide for the Perplexed*, pt. 3, chs. 16-23).

[23] B. Berakhot 5b. I would like to thank Rabbi Baruch Frydman-Kohl for suggesting the use of this source here.

[24] See Rabbi Elliot N. Dorff, "A Jewish Approach to End-Stage Medical Care," *PCJLS 86-90*, pp. 65-126.

[25] Rabbi Avram Israel Reisner, "A Halakhic Ethic of Care for the Terminally Ill," *PCJLS 86-90*, pp. 13-64; and, especially, Avram Israel Reisner, "Mai Beinaihu?" *PCJLS 86-90*, pp. 127-129.

In Rabbi Reisner's view, I would imagine, if the physician knowingly administers enough morphine to kill a person, the physician would be liable for murder, even though his or her primary intent was to reduce pain. For me, in contrast, the primary intent of the physician to reduce pain makes such a case not one of injury at all, little less murder, but rather one of permissible benefit. Therefore the physician would not be liable for violating even the prohibition against indirect injury but would rather be carrying out his or her mandate to heal.

This case must be distinguished from acquiescing to a patient's request to die, even when the death is requested for the express reason of relieving pain. To kill oneself, or to ask others to help in doing so, is forbidden in Jewish law, and so if that is the intent, it is illegitimate. In practice, this difference in motive may translate into the amount of medication administered. Specifically, in light of the fact that within a given range of dosages of morphine doctors never know whether a given patient will die or not, these cases never fall into the talmudic category of פסיק רישיה ואל ימות ("Can you cut off the chicken's head and it will not die?" [B. Shabbat 75a; see Rashi on this principle on B. Sukkah 33b]), for within that range the result is never inevitable. Therefore doctors' attempt to relieve pain is legitimate, in my view, even if they fear that the amount they need to use in the last stages of life may be crossing the line into a fatal dosage for a given patient, for they are still within the range where they do not know that for certain. On the other hand, to administer a dosage that beyond all reasonable doubt will kill the person is to commit murder, even when the stated intent of the physician is to relieve pain and even if the patient requests it. (I want to thank Rabbi Gordon Tucker for calling my attention to the need to make this distinction clearly.)

[26] See, for example, Moshe Halevi Spero, *Judaism and Psychology: Halakhic Perspectives* (New York: Ktav, 1980). I would like to thank Rabbi Mayer Rabinowitz for raising the question discussed in this paragraph.

The answer is that in these cases physical pain occurs against the will of the patient and the morphine is therefore a therapeutic response sanctioned by Jewish law and theology, while "I want to end this" is an expression of the individual's will, a desire that it is illegitimate to fulfill according to Jewish law and theology. We do indeed need to respond to the patient's mental distress, but our response must be in the form of supplying sufficient pain medication, treating clinical depression if that is present, and, most importantly, providing the personal and social support that patients in these circumstances direly need.

Even though Jewish law, then, goes quite far in permitting terminally ill patients to die with whatever palliative care they need and without any further medical interference, it does not permit suicide or assisted suicide. The tradition bids us instead to maintain a firm line separating permissible withholding and withdrawal of medical efforts, on the one hand, and illegitimately helping a person actively to take his or her own life, on the other. To fail to do that would be to violate Jewish law and to destroy creatures belonging to God.

The Contemporary Factors that Sully Arguments for Euthanasia

We have expounded express Jewish law on the issues involved in assisted suicide. Sometimes contemporary circumstances or values argue for changing the stated law as it has come down to us, and we in the Conservative movement are open to considering such challenges. In this case, though, several aspects of the current situation instead present additional arguments for retaining the traditional position prohibiting assisted suicide. All of these factors invoke parts of Jewish law or the broader Jewish tradition. These, then, are not simply general concerns, but Jewish ones, and hence they are part of what should be our understanding and articulation of Jewish law on this issue:

Theological

First and foremost, as already indicated above, theological concerns underlie the Jewish legal position forbidding assisted suicide. The entire discussion of assisted suicide in American courts, in fact, calls into play two of the sharpest differences between American secular perspectives and Jewish views.

America's ideology, as expressed in its economic system, its philosophy (especially the distinctly American school of pragmatism), in the media (where it is almost always the young and the able-bodied that are pictured), and even in contemporary reforms in American welfare legislation, would have us think of ourselves in utilitarian terms, where our worth is a function of what we can do for ourselves and others. American attitudes and laws thus permit suicide, especially when a person can no longer do anything useful for herself or himself or others. Judaism, in contrast, requires us to evaluate our lives in light of the ultimate value inherent in us because we were created in God's image. Jewish ideology and law therefore strongly oppose committing suicide or assisting others in doing so, for life is sacred regardless of its quality or usefulness.

Second, in American law and ideology, as expressed in the Declaration of Independence and in American constitutional law and court rulings, we each own our own bodies and, short of harming someone else, we all inherit the liberty to do with our bodies what we will. This tenet, according to the interpretation of the Ninth Circuit Court of Appeals, has made it part of every American's liberty to determine the course of his or her medical care, even to the point of committing suicide and asking others to assist them in doing so. Suicide itself is a legal act in all fifty states.[27]

In sharp contrast, according to Judaism God created and therefore owns the entire universe,[28] including each person's body, and we therefore each have a fiduciary responsibility to God to preserve our life and health. We certainly do not have the right unnecessarily to destroy or damage God's property, including even God's vegetation and inanimate property.[29] This makes suicide an act of theft from God, a violation of God's prerogatives, and, indeed, a trespass of the proper boundaries between God and human beings.[30] Rabbi Yehiel M. Tuchinski, in his restatement of the laws of death and mourning entitled *Gesher HaHayyim (Bridge of Life)*, puts these points starkly:

> The sin of one who murders himself is greater than that of one who murders someone else for several reasons: First, through this murder he has left no possibility for any remorse and repentance. Second, death (according to Talmud Bavli Yoma 86, etc.) is the greatest form of repentance, but he, on the contrary, has committed through his death the greatest sin, namely, murder. Third, through his act he has made clear his repudiation of his Creator's ownership of his life, his body, and his soul: he has denied the simple idea that he did not participate in his creation at all, but [thinks] rather [that] his entire identity is exclusively within his power to sustain, to reproduce his existence or to destroy it. He is like one who actively [and intentionally] burns a scroll of the Torah, for our Sages, may their memory be blessed, compared the creation of the soul to a scroll of the Torah that [now] has been burned and he must therefore face judgment in the future for this as well.
>
> He is also among the unequivocal deniers of the continued existence of the soul and of the existence of the Creator, may His name be blessed, and of the future judgment after the departure of the soul [from the body].[31]

---

[27] As Rabbi Aaron L. Mackler has pointed out to me, the fact that American states do not criminalize suicide may be a function of the medicalization of suicide in our time rather than recognition of a legal right. That is, instead of putting those who attempt suicide in prison, we sedate them, treat them for depression, and restrain them if necessary. That does not mean, though, that suicide is a legal right, for if it were, we would not try to prevent people from taking their lives. The Ninth Circuit, though, has interpreted suicide, and therefore also assisting in suicide, as a legal privilege embedded in the Fourteenth Amendment's guarantee of liberty. Presumably, then, the only reason for trying to prevent people from committing suicide is that we doubt that they have the mental competence required by law to make that decision.

[28] See note 3 above.

[29] This includes even inanimate property that "belongs" to us, for God is the ultimate owner. This is the law of בל תשחית, the prohibition of destroying the world when human need does not require that. Cf. Deut. 20:19-20; B. Bava Kamma 8:6, 7; B. Bava Kamma 92a, 93a; M.T. Laws of Murder 1:4, where Maimonides specifically invokes this theological basis for the law against suicide; M.T. Laws of Injury and Damage 5:5; Sefer Ha-Hinnukh, Commandment 529; S.A. Hoshen Mishpat 420:1, 31. See Earl Schwartz and Barry D. Cytron, *When Life is in the Balance* (New York: United Synagogue, 1993).

[30] As Rabbi Myron Geller pointed out to me, one could conclude the exact opposite – namely, that since God inflicted the patient's illness, aiding the person in committing suicide would be just assisting God in bringing about what is presumably God's intended goal. While that is certainly logical, it is not the line of reasoning that the Jewish tradition has followed. On the contrary, Jewish law, as noted above, has consistently denied people the right to commit suicide or assist others in that path.

[31] Yehiel M. Tuchinski, *Gesher HaHayyim* (Jerusalem: Solomon, 1947, 1960), pp. 269-270 [Hebrew; this is my translation]. He adds there that the person who commits suicide "is like one who flees to a place where the

Contemporary Jews may not share all of Rabbi Tuchinsky's traditional beliefs about life after death enumerated here, but even a comparatively liberal view of Judaism must, in order to remain recognizably Jewish, begin with the tenet that the body belongs to God.[32]

The American and Jewish traditions, then, begin with radically disparate assumptions about the worth and ownership of our bodies. These variances sometimes lead the two traditions to different prescriptions for the care of the dying. Even when the two traditions agree on a given course of action, they often arrive at their respective positions using different arguments with different burdens of proof.

Specifically, since the American tradition of pragmatism and hedonism leads us, as Americans, to value life only if we can do things and enjoy life, a physically or mentally compromised life is not considered worth living. Moreover, each person has the right to determine the fate of his or her body. It is this perspective that undergirds requests for suicide in America, the legal grounding for those requests as expressions of autonomy and liberty, and the sense of compassion that those who assist in a suicide feel.

The Jewish tradition, in contrast, calls upon us to evaluate life from God's perspective. That means that the value of life does not depend on the level of one's abilities; it derives from the image of God embedded in us. The tradition thus strongly affirms the divine quality of the life of disabled people, even though everyone would undoubtedly prefer not to be disabled. Indeed, our tradition demands that, upon seeing a disabled person, we bless God for making people different, thus boldly reasserting the divine quality of such lives.[33] We certainly must do everything in our power to dissuade anyone thinking of committing suicide because of disability from doing so. Embedded in the arguments for assisted suicide, though, is an assumption frighteningly close to an assertion of the worthlessness of disabled people, for the terminally ill are also disabled. In line with its view of the disabled, then, the Jewish tradition requires that we recognize the divine quality of people in the last stages of life, regardless of the quality of their lives.

Moreover, even when life is not ideal and we question its divine dignity and its character as a gift, we lack the authority to destroy it because the body belongs to God, who alone has the right to terminate it. In other words, in the American setting arguments for permitting assisted suicide on the basis of autonomy have been taken very seriously, and in its worst forms these arguments are based on a culture of selfishness that diminishes human life by valuing only those who can be productive and enjoy it fully. The clear stance of Judaism, on the other hand, sets strict limits to the autonomy we have in this arena, given that we are God's creatures and agents, and it strongly affirms the value of human life regardless of its usefulness or quality. We might ask why a compassionate God would deny us the authority to take our lives when we can no longer function. Moreover, according to Maimonides, we must keep our bodies in good

---

hand of the government will catch him and can bring him back to this place with additional punishment also for his escape" – an understandable metaphor in his theology, but one that unfortunately makes life a prison sentence!

[32] I say this even though one Reform writer has maintained the contrary, claiming that contemporary Jews overwhelmingly believe that their body is their own and thus refuse to abide by medical directives based on God's ownership of our bodies. See Matthew (Menachem) Maibaum, "A 'Progressive' Jewish Medical Ethics: Notes for an Agenda," *Journal of Reform Judaism* 33:3 (summer 1986): 27-33.

[33] B. Berakhot 58b; M.T. Laws of Blessings 10:12. For an excellent account of these laws and the theology and practice surrounding them, see Carl Astor, "...*Who Makes People Different*": *Jewish Perspectives on the Disabled* (New York: United Synagogue, 1985).

health so that we may serve God,[34] and if we cannot do that any longer, it would seem that God should allow us to curtail our lives. While we can certainly challenge God in either of these ways, the tradition is unanimous in asserting that God does not give us that authority, that even when people are incapacitated by, say, a stroke, God forbids us to commit suicide or to assist in one.[35]

In Judaism's perspective, then, it is not a compassionate act at all to assist a person in taking his or her own life because doing that would make both oneself and the person committing suicide violators of some of the most fundamental values and laws of Judaism, namely, those insisting that we not murder and that, on the contrary, we set aside virtually all of Jewish law in order to save lives.[36] We all sin, of course, but these are the most serious sorts of sin, ones that it is anything but compassionate to help someone do.

Social/Economic

Several aspects of the current social and economic contexts make the prospect of permitting assisted suicide all the more troubling than it is inherently. One element lurking in the background of this discussion is the history of condoned assisted suicide in Holland, where there has been a wide range of rationales that have prompted physicians to help people end their lives. In the United States, Dr. Jack Kevorkian has similarly assisted people in all sorts of physical conditions to commit suicide, most recently in response to a person's chronic fatigue syndrome. He has admittedly sensationalized the whole subject, and it is not wise or fair to judge the issue on the basis of his actions alone. Moreover, I am not usually convinced by slippery slope arguments, for the essence of moral discernment is that we learn to distinguish cases.[37] Nevertheless, the experience in Holland and Dr. Kevorkian's cases have both clearly demonstrated just how slippery this particular slope is. Even though there are undoubtedly some situations where the case for assisting a suicide may seem compelling, we must prohibit assisted suicide altogether in order to prevent diminishing the value of life in the public eye and in public policy.

Another current factor that makes any opening to assisted suicide dangerous is the push to save money in health care. Motivated largely by how that economic agenda will

---

[34] M.T. Laws of Ethics (Hilkhot De'ot) 3:3; see also 4:1.

[35] The argument that assisting a suicide would be to further God's purpose in making the person sick in the first place is specifically rejected by Rashi and by Tosafot. Commenting on the Talmud's statement (B. Bava Kamma 85a) that Exod. 21:19 (ורפא ירפא) serves as permission for physicians to heal, Rashi (s.v., נתנה רשות לרופאים לרפאות) says, "And we do *not* say that the Merciful One struck [the patient] and he [the physician illegitimately] heals." Tosafot there (s.v. שניתנה) points out that one can derive authorization for the physician to heal from just the first of the words in the phrase in Exod. 21:19, ורפא ירפא, and so why does the Torah state the verb "to heal" in two different forms? Because if it were only stated once, Tosafot suggests, one might think that the physician may heal only those maladies inflicted by human beings but not those inflicted by God; the double presence of the verb in the biblical verse indicates that the physician has permission to heal even illnesses inflicted by God.

[36] This is the law of פקוח נפש, saving a life, whether one's own or someone else's; see B. Sanhedrin 74a and B. Yoma 85b, and see notes 3-6 above and the text for those notes. In American law, by contrast, until recently when "Good Samaritan laws" were passed by many states, you could actually be sued if you tried to save a person in good faith and some injury resulted, and to this day no American law requires that you go out of your way to save a life. This is, in my view, American individualism at its worst.

Along the same lines, while aiding a suicide is against the law in most states, committing suicide itself is not a violation of the law, another manifestation of American individualism. (Most life insurance policies, though, become null and void if the insured commits suicide.)

[37] See my short essay, "Moral Distinctions," *Sh'ma: A Journal of Jewish Responsibility*, 21/401 (16 Nov. 1990): 6-8.

affect care at the end of life, the American Medical Association, in briefs to the Supreme Court, strongly opposed legalizing assisted suicide. They were justifiably worried about what such action would do to both the patient and the physician, for, especially under conditions of managed care, *permission* to take one's own life and to enlist the aid of others in doing so will quickly become all but an *obligation* to end the lives of those who have no reasonable hope for cure. Doctors, in the worst scenario, will be pressured by hospitals or health insurance companies to convince their patients that suicide is the best option, not only because it will end the patient's pain and thus serve the best interests of the patient, but also (and maybe primarily) because it will save the hospital or insurer money. The role of the physician as the patient's advocate thus becomes severely compromised.

The same considerations apply to the patient's family members. If assisted suicide becomes a guaranteed constitutional right in American law, patients will feel all the more pressed by their families to end their lives rather than drain the family's finances in keeping them alive. If Jewish law is also interpreted to permit assisted suicide, both the social and the religious setting in which American Jews will be making these decisions will argue for the legitimacy of such pressure, to the point that patients or family members who resist the suicide option will eventually feel that *they* are being unreasonably obstinate, that "normal" people would just end their lives once they cannot be cured. Indeed, in the context of such changed social expectations, even when family members do not want the patient to commit suicide and say that as clearly as they can, patients may feel that their families want them to end their life; my relatives, the patient may think, are just trying to be nice, but they really want me to end my own agony and theirs. Legitimating assisted suicide thus dangerously shifts the burden of proof: currently those who want to take a life must justify that course of action, but if assisted suicide becomes legal, those who refuse it will need to show why.

The economic arguments in support of assisted suicide are not completely frivolous. In the United States people spend more on their health care in the last six months of life than they do throughout the rest of their lives. About 2.5 million Americans die each year, and more than fifty percent of those deaths occur in an acute care hospital.[38] Surely the money could be better spent, the argument goes, if people were given the choice and aid to die.

While the economic factor is real, assisted suicide is not the appropriate response. Hospice care is. In "hospice" care, all concerned recognize that the patient's disease is incurable, and the course of medical care is therefore not directed to aggressively and invasively trying to prolong life, but rather to the goal of providing comfort and pain relief. In hospice care, patients spend most of their last months of life at home, with some outpatient visits along the way. That form of care is not only more medically realistic and inexpensive, but more humane. Hospital care, after all, puts the patient in a strange, antiseptic setting where she or he is subjected to the hospital schedule, to repeated and possibly painful medical procedures, and to the loneliness of having the company of only occasional visitors. Hospice care, by contrast, puts the patient at home amidst family and friends, where pain medication can be administered when and how the patient feels most comfortable.

Hospice care should therefore be suggested to most people afflicted with terminal, irreversible illnesses. Moreover, contrary to current practice, patients need not first endure initial stays in intensive care units where improbably successful or knowingly futile aggres-

---

[38] See Terrence Monmaney, "How We Die May Be Behind Assisted Suicide Debate," *Los Angeles Times*, 8 Jan. 1997, pp. A1, A9.

sive care is attempted; they should rather be provided hospice care as soon as it becomes clear that the odds of curing the patient are slim to nil.

Along with hospice care for the patient, respite care can and should be provided for family caregivers. The bill for hospice and respite care combined will pale by comparison to what we are spending for people's last weeks and months now, and the patient will gain in dignity and comfort in the bargain.

Medical

Possibly the most common and compelling ground suggested for justifying assisted suicide is to relieve a patient of racking pain. This would be both understandable and compassionate if there were no other alternative, but doctors today have ample means for controlling almost all physical pain. A very small number of patients (perhaps one in 10,000) need dosages of morphine that will make them unconscious, and in those cases patients may have to choose between some amount of pain with consciousness or losing consciousness as all pain is quelled. That is a legitimate choice that should be offered to patients.

American physicians, though, often do not offer or employ sufficient pain medication. Reasons for this vary. Sometimes doctors honestly do not know how much morphine to administer, for people differ in size and in their thresholds of pain. That is an understandable reason for failing to employ enough pain medication.

Some doctors, though, say they minimize pain medication for fear of inducing drug addiction. That is a proper concern in general, but a truly bizarre one in the case of terminally ill patients. Other doctors have a "John Wayne attitude" toward pain, claiming that good, morally worthy patients grin and bear their pain rather than complaining about it and requesting medication to quell it. Even worse, some of this is socio-economic: centers that treat primarily white patients provide pain relief more adequately than those treating minority patients, producing, on a percentage basis, many more requests for assisted suicide among the latter.

Perhaps the most pervasive root of this refusal to control pain is the American culture of medicine itself. American medicine, far more than medicine in other Western countries, is based on technological cures,[39] and when those do not work, doctors consciously or subconsciously avoid the patient who symbolizes the failure of their methods. They do not bother to administer pain relief either, for that is either not part of their goals in the first place (the "John Wayne attitude") or a secondary goal to be invoked only when they have failed to cure. Whatever the basis for this pattern of supplying insufficient pain medication, physicians should certainly seek to control pain rather than acquiesce to a request to die.[40]

Requests for aid in committing suicide stem from another medical phenomenon as well: far too many people with irreversible, terminal illnesses are subjected to futile, aggressive treatment. As indicated earlier, about 2.5 million Americans die each year, and fifty percent of those deaths occur in an acute care hospital. That high level of "hospitalized death," researchers say, suggests that too few terminally ill patients are taking advantage of hospice care.

---

[39] For a fascinating comparative study of how the same diseases are treated differently in the United States, Great Britain, France, and Germany as a reflection of their national cultures, see Lynn Payer, *Medicine and Culture* (New York: Henry Holt, 1988).

[40] On the other hand, in cases where patients are not seeking to die and choose to endure some pain in order to be able to remain conscious, that request must be honored. It is *permissible*, in my view, to use whatever amount of medication is necessary to alleviate pain, but it is *not required* to relieve pain at the cost of consciousness if the patient chooses instead to remain conscious with some degree of pain.

Moreover, as an editorial in the *Annals of Internal Medicine* maintained, far too many people are finding that their express desire for life support to be withheld or withdrawn, as stated in their living wills, is being ignored by "physicians who are so preoccupied with the preservation of life that they can no longer see the broader human context of their work." Similarly, the largest study to address the human context of dying, known by the acronym SUPPORT, involves more than 10,000 seriously ill people at five medical centers in five cities. A chief finding of that study was that about half of all patients spent the end of life in what the researchers termed "an undesirable state," including a week or so in an intensive care unit, having a physician who was unaware of wishes not to be resuscitated, or being in serious, insufficiently treated pain. "I believe the enthusiasm for physician-assisted suicide is driven, in part, by the fear that we will receive overly aggressive care at the end of life and that our suffering may be prolonged," said Dr. William Knaus, an internal medicine specialist at the University of Virginia Medical School and a coordinator of SUPPORT.[41] Clearly, if that is what is prompting a request for assistance in suicide, the appropriate response is for physicians conscientiously to make themselves aware of their patients' advance directives and then to adhere to a patient's desire to remove impediments to the natural process of dying.

Psychological

While some requests for assistance in dying are based on the patient's excruciating pain, others are rooted in the hopelessness of the situation. We are, after all, mortal, and some diseases cannot be cured. When afflicted with such a disease, patients cannot realistically hope to return to the life they knew. They instead face the prospect of continued suffering and debilitation until death, and some would prefer to end things quickly to avoid the suffering and degradation of the last stages of their illness.

Such cases are precisely the ones that have produced the term "mercy killing" to describe active euthanasia, and, indeed, the hopelessness embedded in the medical situation of such people often makes their requests for assistance in dying emotionally compelling. Nevertheless, we should respond to such cases by doing things other than assisting people to commit suicide.

Physicians or others asked to assist in dying should recognize that people contemplating suicide are often alone, without anyone who takes an interest in their continued living. Rather than assist the patient in dying, the proper response to such circumstances is to provide the patient with a group of people who clearly and repeatedly reaffirm their interest in the patient's continued life.

My mother once had a roommate in a nursing home who was literally visited by nobody. She had one son who lived on the other side of the country and who called from time to time, but she had no other family or friends. Worse, some clothes her son sent her as a birthday gift were stolen by the night staff. Under such conditions of abandonment (and, in this case, violation), one can understand why people would wonder why they should continue to fight to live – indeed, why they should get up in the morning at all.

Requests to die, then, must be evaluated in terms of the degree of social support the patient has, for such requests are often withdrawn as soon as someone shows an interest in the patient staying alive. In this age of individualism and broken and scattered families, and in the antiseptic environment of hospitals where dying people usually find themselves,

---

[41] This paragraph is based on the article, "How We Die May Be Behind Assisted Suicide Debate," by Terrence Monmaney, *Los Angeles Times*, 8 Jan. 1997, pp. A1, A9.

the mitzvah of visiting the sick (ביקור חולים) becomes all the more crucial in sustaining the will to live, for, as the tradition recognized, visitors aid the person psychologically, physically, and religiously. Thus the Talmud says this:

> Rabbi Abba son of Rabbi Hanina said: He who visits an invalid takes away a sixtieth of his pain [or, in another version, a sixtieth of his illness]. . . .
>
> When Rabbi Dimi came [from Palestine], he said: He who visits the sick causes him to live, while he who does not causes him to die. How does he cause this? . . .He who visits the sick prays that he may live, . . .[while] he who does not visit the sick prays neither that he may live nor die.[42]

The Talmud here is asserting two aspects of the spiritual elements of coping with illness. On a social plane, those who visit the sick help to shift the patient's focus from the pain and degradation of the illness to the joy of the company of friends and family. They thus take away a sixtieth of the pain of the illness. Visitors also reassure the patient that family and friends are keenly interested in his or her recovery or, if that is impossible, in his or her comfort. They also remind the patient of life outside the sick room and thereby re-enforce the patient's determination to live on. Visitors are thus instrumental in motivating the patient to follow a medical regimen of healing or palliation, however tedious or painful it may be, and so, in the Talmud's alternate reading, they effectively take away a sixtieth of the patient's illness itself.

As discussed above, hospice care, endorsed by both Rabbi Reisner and me, recommends itself for economic and medical reasons. It is perhaps best, though, in responding to the psychological pressures of the dying process. Much of the loneliness inherent in being confined to a hospital is eliminated when the patient instead is cared for at home. Family members cannot be expected to shoulder all of this burden; ביקור חולים remains an important imperative for friends, even when the patient is living at home. The very familiarity of the home setting, though, together with the increased chances it offers of providing the companionship of family and friends, makes hospice care clearly preferable to hospitalization when doctors cannot realistically expect to cure.

Visitors can affect the physical quality of patients' lives not only by buoying up their will to live, but also by attending to their physical needs. Thus the Talmud tells the following story:

> Rabbi Helbo fell ill. Rabbi Kahana then went [to the house of study] and proclaimed, "Rabbi Helbo is ill." Nobody, however, visited him. Rabbi Kahana rebuked them [the disciples], saying, "Did it ever happen that one of Rabbi Akiba's students fell ill, and the [rest of the] disciples did not visit him?" So Rabbi Akiba himself entered [Rabbi Helbo's house] to visit him, and because they swept and sprinkled the ground before him [that is, cleaned the house and put it in order], Rabbi Helbo recovered. Rabbi Akiba then went forth and lectured: He who does not visit the sick is like one who sheds blood.[43]

---

[42] B. Nedarim 39b-40a.

[43] Ibid.

Taking physical care of the sick can include not only cleaning house, but shopping for groceries, doing laundry, taking over carpool duties, and seeing to the other needs of the patient's children. Depending upon the circumstances, it can also include more direct physical interventions like taking the patient for a ride in a wheelchair (if medically permitted), feeding the patient (if necessary), and attending to the patient's other physical needs.

Visitors affect the patient on a more religious plane as well. By praying for and with the patient, and by indicating that prayers are being offered in the synagogue on his or her behalf, visitors invoke the aid of God, the ultimate Healer. Jewish prayer is traditionally done in community, in part because Jewish sources maintain that communal prayer convinces God to grant a request more effectively than private prayer does.[44] Praying with the patient at bedside and for the patient in the synagogue thus throws the weight of the entire community behind the patient's own plea to God for recovery or, failing that, for comfort.

The medical hopelessness of people with a terminal, irreversible illness remains, and it violates our duty to tell the truth to try to deceive patients into believing otherwise. While some sources in our tradition justify such behavior in the name of buoying up a patient's spirits,[45] deception is generally not the way to do that. Patients usually have a sense of their medical prognosis, and so they do not believe those who tell them otherwise anyway. Moreover, lies can only lead to distrust, anger, and feelings of disrespect and abandonment. The last thing one wants to do is to infantilize patients: they already feel diminished in stature by their illness, and deception makes them feel further diminished, as if they were being treated as children (who, by the way, should also not be misled). Family and friends should clearly not appear at bedside with sullen faces, dwelling on the terrible prognosis. At the same time, they should not pretend that the medical situation is other than what it is.

The patient's spirits can be lifted substantially and appropriately, though, if family and friends concentrate on what can make the remainder of the patient's life meaningful. Some topics that should be raised are practical in nature. Specifically, if patients have not previously filled out a will or a living will, they should be asked to specify their wishes about the distribution of their property and their preferred course of medical treatment, respectively. Even though Jewish law forbids morose talk of death around a seriously patient for fear of undermining the patient's hope for recovery, it permits and even requires that relatives or friends insure that the patient has written a will and even allows saying the final prayer of confession before death (צדוק הדין). One should also be sure that the patient has made funeral and burial arrangements. To preserve the patient's will to live and to fight the disease, Jewish law mandates that one tell the patient that writing a will, making plans for burial, and saying the confessional prayer are being done just in case the patient does not recover, but many people who have done these things have subsequently recovered.[46]

Beyond these practical topics, visitors will buoy the patients' spirits by treating them as adults, respecting them enough to engage in conversation about the same adult topics that previously interested them – and even some that they had not previously explored. One of the most enlightening experiences of my early rabbinic career was teaching a series of classes on Jewish theology to residents of a Jewish nursing home. The group consisted completely of college graduates. Even though none of them had ever studied Jewish theology before, they had specifically asked for these classes

---

[44] B. Berakhot 6a; 7b-8a; J. Berakhot 5:1; cf. M.T. Laws of Prayer 8:1.

[45] Basil F. Herring quotes and discusses those sources in his book, *Jewish Ethics and Halakhah for Our Time* (New York: Ktav, 1984), ch. 2, entitled "Truth and the Dying Patient" (pp. 47-66).

[46] S.A. Yoreh De'ah 335:7; 338:1.

because they were sick of playing Bingo. They had been intellectually active at earlier stages of their lives, and their physical illnesses now did not significantly change their intellectual interests or even their mental capacity – except that I had to speak just a little more slowly than I usually do. The students even read assignments in preparation for the class from specially prepared sheets with enlarged print. I wish my younger students were always as well prepared!

Visitors do not normally discuss Jewish theology, but this example will, I hope, indicate just how seriously I mean to make the point that conversations with patients should be challenging and should cover a wide variety of topics. The very normalcy of such discussions communicates that the illness has not diminished the visitor's respect for the patient's intelligence and humanity, and that the remainder of one's life can still be filled with meaningful conversation.

The Jewish tradition has also provided another mechanism to make the lives of terminal patients meaningful. That is the *ethical will*. In times past, ethical wills were written, but now they can be taped or even videotaped. Patients who know that they have a task to accomplish in leaving their children and (especially) their grandchildren a record of their experiences, values, thoughts, dreams, and hopes will redouble their efforts to live as long as they can so that they can complete this important project.[47]

Moreover, some families can heal troubling relationships that they were not able to resolve earlier in the last stages of the patient's life. The limited term of life remaining for the patient becomes patently clear in such a setting, and that often motivates all concerned to be more forthcoming in their relationships with family and friends than they were previously. Moreover, in positive relationships, the time spent together in a beloved's last days can be the last gift children give their parents or spouses give each other. Thus even though life at this stage may be physically painful, it may be emotionally some of the most significant days the person has lived.[48]

Indeed, the American courts that dealt with assisted suicide addressed what is, in many ways, the wrong question in the first place. We should not be asking whether one may aid another in dying; we should rather explore what prompts people to seek to die in the first place, and then we should remove those motivations through proper pain medication and through attentive care. Those are the most appropriate responses to requests for assisted death.

Medical hopelessness, then, need not and should not amount to psychological hopelessness. People asking for help in dying to overcome the loneliness and the futility of their lives should not be offered aid in dying, but rather assistance in making life meaningful.

Moral

In refusing to allow people to "shuffle off this mortal coil"[49] when and how they wish, we are taking upon ourselves the moral responsibility of imposing our will on them, and why should a society based on individual liberty do that? This last concern, in fact, is precisely the basis of the Ninth Circuit's decision affirming the legality of assisted suicide.

---

[47] For some poignant examples of ethical wills, including many modern ones, see Jack Riemer and Nathaniel Stampfer, eds., *Ethical Wills: A Modern Jewish Treasury* (New York: Schocken, 1983). For some suggestions for preparing an ethical will, see Jack Riemer and Nathaniel Stampfer, eds., *So that your values live on – Ethical Wills and how to prepare them* [capitalized that way] (Woodstock, VT: Jewish Lights Publishing, 1991).

[48] See Elisabeth Kubler-Ross, *Death is of Vital Importance* (Barrytown, NY: Station Hill Press, 1995), for some striking examples of how meaningful and reconciling the last stages of life and death itself can be. I would like to thank my friend and colleague, Rabbi Elie Kaplan Spitz, for alerting me to this book.

[49] The poetic expression comes from Shakespeare, *Hamlet*, Act III, Scene I, line 67.

The liberty argument is not nearly as cogent in Jewish thought as it is in American ideology and law, for Jews are born with duties rather than rights. Even in the American context, though, the government must protect the most vulnerable populations, and the dying are surely among them. Similarly, the Torah's demand, "Do not stand idly by the blood of your brother," was interpreted by the Rabbis as a duty to come to the aid of those at risk.[50]

As indicated above, permitting assisted suicide may at first *look* like an affirmation of the patient's liberty, but it soon transforms into a duty to die. Protecting individuals' liberty, then, is more effectively achieved by making assisted suicide a socially unacceptable option so that individuals need not defend their desire to continue living. The current ban on assisted suicide inevitably infringes on the liberty to gain assistance in dying, but that is a reasonable price to pay in order to preserve the liberty of far more people to continue living without having to justify their choice.

Moreover, until now we have assumed the morally pure situation, where the patient is in pain or in increasing states of degradation (as in Alzheimer's patients), with prospects for only further deterioration, and where the aide is acting out of the sole motive of helping the patient fulfill his or her wishes (stated now or previously) to end life under such circumstances. Real situations, however, are almost never that simple. With regard to the patient, one must ask the hard questions of whether the request to die is a response to a lack of social support, as we have discussed, or a state of psychological depression that can be treated medically, or the patient's worry that further medical care will seriously deplete the estate to be left to the heirs. With regard to the aide, one must ask whether he or she stands to benefit from the end of the person's life, either monetarily or simply by the freedom from taking care of this person any longer. Assisted suicide, in other words, rarely occurs in the morally pure atmosphere usually assumed in arguments about its moral appropriateness, and as soon as one exposes the less noble motives often involved, it seems considerably less honorable.

Another moral issue arises in these cases. As the Ninth and Second Appellate Courts maintained, modern medical advances have made the line between active and passive euthanasia increasingly hard to define. That does not mean, however, that it has disappeared. The distinction between them constitutes the very real moral difference between helping someone live and die in a natural way, on the one hand, and homicide, on the other. Moral sensitivity is precisely the ability to make distinctions, including some hard ones.[51] We have, then, an important moral interest in discerning that line, however difficult it may be to see at times, because nothing less than our character as moral people is at stake.

These theological, social, economic, medical, psychological, and moral factors, then, reinforce the ban embedded in Jewish law on suicide and on assisting a suicide. They also demand that we take a much more active role in ensuring that the dying are not abandoned to physical pain or to social ostracism, that instead we make the mitzvah of ביקור חולים (visiting the sick) a critical part of our mission as Jews. This is especially important as Jews, along with other North Americans, become statistically older, for more and more of us in the time to come will need such care. In attending to the sick, we must assure that their physical needs are met and that their ending time in life is as

---

[50] Lev. 19:16; B. Sanhedrin 73a.

[51] Just as bad as recognizing no distinctions is creating sweeping, unexceptionable categories rather than discerning the fine lines that characterize real moral life. See my response to J. David Bleich in my article, "Moral Distinctions," *Sh'ma: A Journal of Jewish Responsibility*, 21/401 (16 Nov. 1990): 6-8.

psychologically, emotionally, and religiously meaningful as possible. Our compassion, in other words, must be expressed in these demanding ways rather than in acquiescing to a request for assistance in dying, for ultimately the Jewish tradition calls upon us to recognize God's rights of ownership of our bodies and God's exclusive right to take our lives in God's good time.

Conclusion

A Jew may not commit suicide, ask others to help in committing suicide, or assist in the suicide of someone else. Withholding or withdrawing machines or medications from a terminally ill patient, however, does not constitute suicide and is permitted. In my view, but not in Rabbi Reisner's, one may also withhold or withdraw artificial nutrition and hydration from such a patient, for that too falls outside the prohibitions of suicide and assisted suicide.

YD 345.1997b

Statement on Assisted Suicide

This paper was approved by the CJLS on March 12, 1997, by a vote of seventeen in favor, one oppossed, and two abstaining (17-1-2). Voting in favor: Rabbis Kassel Abelson, Ben Zion Bergman, Elliot N. Dorff, Samuel Fraint, Baruch Frydman-Kohl, Nechama D. Goldberg, Arnold M. Goodman, Judah Kogen, Vernon H. Kurtz, Alan B. Lucas, Aaron L. Mackler, Lionel E. Moses, Mayer Rabinowitz, Joel E. Rembaum, Avram Israel Reisner, Joel Roth, and Elie Kaplan Spitz. Voting against: Rabbi Gordon Tucker. Abstaining: Rabbis Shoshana Gelfand and Paul Plotkin.

The Committee on Jewish Law and Standards of the Rabbinical Assembly provides guidance in matters of halakhah for the Conservative movement. The individual rabbi, however, is the authority for the interpretation and application of all matters of halakhah.

Since God infuses each human life with inherent meaning by creating each of us in the divine image, thereby guaranteeing ultimate value regardless of a person's abilities or quality of life; and

Since Judaism views life as sacred and understands human beings to have life on trust from God; and

Since God's creation and ownership of our bodies puts the decision of when life is to end in God's hands; and

Since we nonetheless have both the right and the duty to seek to cure, to relieve pain, and to provide comfort care, including social, emotional, and psychological support to all who are ill; and

Since current efforts to rein in costs for medical care threaten to transform any permission to aid a suicide into a perceived duty to commit suicide, shifting the burden of proof to the one who wants to remain alive;

The Conservative movement's Committee on Jewish Law and Standards has adopted a rabbinic ruling (תשובה) by Rabbi Elliot N. Dorff affirming that:

1. Suicide is a violation of Jewish law and of the sacred trust of our lives given us by God.

2. Assisting a suicide is also a violation of Jewish law and God's sacred trust of life. No human being may take his or her own life, ask others to help them do so, or assist in such an effort.

3. Patients and their care givers nevertheless have the tradition's permission to withhold or withdraw impediments to the natural process of dying, as described in two responsa by Rabbis Elliot N. Dorff and Avram Israel Reisner, previously adopted by the Committee and published in the Spring 1991 edition of the jour-

nal, *Conservative Judaism*, and as applied in the Committee's *Medical Directive for Health Care*, written by Rabbi Aaron L. Mackler on the basis of those responsa.

4. Physicians must assure that patients are given sufficient pain medication as part of their duty to provide medical care, as mandated in Jewish law.

5. In the context of nuclear families, divorce and far-flung families, the mitzvah of ביקור חולים (visiting the sick) becomes all the more imperative in our day that it was in times past to counteract the loneliness that terminally ill patients often face. Individual Jews and synagogues should see this as an important priority of their Jewish commitment.

6. Requests for assistance in suicide are often an expression of the patient's extreme suffering, despair, psychiatric depression and loneliness. The Jewish tradition bids us to express our compassion in ways that effectively respond to the patient's suffering while adhering to our mandate to respect the divine trust of life. Among such options is final care at home with the help of palliative ministrations, including hospice care, to provide the social and emotional support severely sick people need. The approach of death can provide an opportunity for the patient, family and friends to have meaningful closure and final reconciliation.

EDITORS' NOTE: *A "Resolution on Assisted Suicide" reflecting the language of the above statement was adopted by the Ninety-Eighth Rabbinical Assembly Convention in Jerusalem in 1998. See* Proceedings of the Rabbinical Assembly *60 (1998): 290-291 (English), 298-299 (Hebrew).*

YD 345:5.1994

BURIAL OF JEWS PRACTICING CHRISTIANITY

Rabbi Paul Plotkin

This paper was approved on December 14, 1994, by a vote of eighteen in favor and one abstention (18-0-1). Voting in favor: Rabbis Kassel Abelson, Stanley Bramnick, Elliot N. Dorff, Jerome M. Epstein, Samuel Fraint, Susan Grossman, Jan Caryl Kaufman, Judah Kogen, Vernon H. Kurtz, Alan B. Lucas, Aaron L. Mackler, Paul Plotkin, Avram Israel Reisner, Joel E. Rembaum, Joel Roth, Gerald Skolnik, Gordon Tucker, and Gerald Zelizer. Abstaining: Rabbi Ben Zion Bergman.

The Committee on Jewish Law and Standards of the Rabbinical Assembly provides guidance in matters of halakhah for the Conservative movement. The individual rabbi, however, is the authority for the interpretation and application of all matters of halakhah.

שאלה

May a Jew practicing Christianity be buried in a Jewish cemetery?

תשובה

From Rabbi Haim Palagi, in his responsum "Haim B'yad, Siman 99," we see that a מומר (apostate) is seen as falling into the category of הפורשים מדרכי צבור (one who separates from the ways of the community). Of such a person, we are told, אין מתעסקין עמו לכל דבר (we do not deal with him in any manner). This is further defined as not dealing with mourning practices, but there is a significant consensus that Jewish burial is performed.

Indeed, the Hatam Sofer (Responsa, vol. 2, Yoreh De'ah, Siman 341) explains that even for those executed by the Jewish court for idolatry or Sabbath violators, or residents of an עיר הנדחת, there is to be burial. From the context it is certainly in a Jewish cemetery. The apostate must similarly be buried because there still exists the Biblically mandated positive commandment (מצוות עשה) of burial.[1]

The strong historical halakhic consensus is to permit such burial. Yet I would argue against permitting such burial. In this view, I follow the opinion of the late Rabbi Boaz Cohen who wrote Rabbi S. Joshua Kohn of Utica, N.Y. the following letter on October 3, 1939:

---

[1] Deut. 21:23, כי קבור תקברנו.

Dear Joshua Kohn,

In reply to your letter of September 27, I wish to inform you that this young man, since his mother is Jewish, is considered from a legal standpoint a Jew and is entitled to a Jewish burial, even if he had embraced Christianity officially, although in the latter case, it would be necessary to bury him in a special corner of the cemetery.

However, as a matter of general policy, I would urge you strongly to discourage the burial of this young man in a Jewish cemetery in as much as during the lifetime, he externally at least, lived a Christian life even after he reached the age of discretion. I would further advise the mother that it would be manifestly unfair to the father who is a Christian, to have his son buried in a Jewish cemetery, and it would be no more right for her to defer to his wishes.

Back in 1939, when intermarriage was minimal and apostasy significantly less than today, Rabbi Cohen, while affirming the Jewishness of the apostate and his right to burial, still advised not burying the young man in a Jewish cemetery. In today's world with so much intermarriage and proselytizing of Jews, we need to keep the lines of demarcation clear.

According to the Council of Jewish Federations' 1990 National Jewish Population Survey, 210,000 born Jews have changed their religion. Furthermore, 700,000 children under the age of eighteen are being raised in religiously mixed households where they are being raised in a religion other than Judaism.

In the past when we were engaged in a struggle for survival against the emergence of new philosophies or religions, the Rabbis changed or prohibited previously permitted actions so as to clearly differentiate between Jews and sectarians. The fact that we no longer practice the oriental prostration, except on high holidays, is one such example. Rabbi Max Arzt explained that, "Because Christianity had adopted these gestures of adoration — we ceased to practice full prostration."[2]

Similarly the Ten Commandments, once recited in the Temple service, were forbidden to be used in the regular service in order to refute the contention of the heretical sects (מינים) that only the Ten Commandments were divinely given.[3]

So too here, if we accept a position that even an apostate should be allowed full burial in a Jewish cemetery, the current crisis is enough to make us prohibit it. Furthermore, in the literature of the "Jews for Jesus," they do not claim to be Christians, but more insidiously they claim to be "fulfilled Jews." They argue that they are and continue to be Jews but unlike the rest of the Jewish community they surpass us in that we are unfulfilled without Jesus. To allow them to be buried in a Jewish cemetery is to affirm their position and to undermine our defenses.

We must be able in word and in deed to articulate the position that one may be a Jew or a Christian, but one may not be both at the same time.

There is also a sensitivity in the codes that allows for the presumption of duress or mental illness in the apostate that would allow the מרא דאתרא to mitigate the above rul-

---

[2] Rabbi Max Arzt, *Justice and Mercy* (New York: Holt Reinhart and Winston, 1963), p. 182.

[3] B. Berakhot 12a.

ing and allow for burial. There is also a strong concern to allow for last minute תשובה and return to the Jewish fold, even without מקוה, for those who would otherwise require it. It should be left to the מרא דאתרא to examine the possibility that such repentance may have occurred even up to the moment of death, but absent such תשובה, Jewish burial should be denied to an apostate.

Conclusion

Despite the fact that halakhah would allow for Jewish burial of an apostate even while forbidding mourning, we would prohibit such Jewish burial rites to the apostate. Today's environment makes it necessary to prohibit such Jewish rights and privileges including burial in a Jewish cemetery to an apostate. It is hoped that such a public statement would speak loudly to the lie of the "Jews for Jesus" and others, who would advocate the position that one could remain a Jew and practice Christianity at the same time. Thus we hope to establish in the minds of the community, the distinctiveness of Jew and gentile.

YD 345:5.1998

BURY HIM, YES, BURY HIM – A CONCURRING OPINION TO PAUL PLOTKIN'S "BURIAL OF JEWS PRACTICING CHRISTIANITY"

Rabbi Myron S. Geller

This paper was accepted into the record on March 25, 1998, as a concurrence to "Burial of Jews Practicing Christianity," by Rabbi Paul Plotkin. Concurring and dissenting opinions are not official positions of the Committee on Jewish Law and Standards.

The Committee on Jewish Law and Standards of the Rabbinical Assembly provides guidance in matters of halakhah for the Conservative movement. The individual rabbi, however, is the authority for the interpretation and application of all matters of halakhah.

שאלה

May a Jew practicing Christianity be buried in a Jewish cemetery?

תשובה

A Recent Responsum

The שאלה was recently considered by Rabbi Paul Plotkin in a responsum submitted to the Committee on Jewish Law and Standards.[1] This תשובה concurs with Rabbi Plotkin's conclusion but introduces several sources not considered in his paper and makes certain suggestions that the מרא דאתרא, confronted with the difficult task of adjudicating a burial request, may find helpful.

Rabbi Plotkin acknowledges that "the strong historical halakhic consensus is to permit such burial." He cites Biblical and halakhic sources which required burial, presumably in a Jewish cemetery, of criminals executed by the Sanhedrin for idolatry and other transgressions such as murder or sexual violations. Sabbath desecrators, residents of an עיר הנדחת, a wayward city, and apostates. Nevertheless, in our day he bans burial in a Jewish cemetery of an apostate Jew practicing Christianity for several reasons:

---

[1] Above, pp. 400-402.

A) On sociological grounds — the obvious and pervasive problem of intermarriage in American society with the concerns this engenders about apostasy;[2]

B) Jews for Jesus claim to be fulfilled Jews and to allow them to be buried amongst us would affirm their position and undermine our defenses; and,

C) Jewish group identity has been blurred under the impact of intermarriage and the need exists to keep clear the lines of demarcation between Jew and Christian. We must articulate a position that one may be a Jew or a Christian but not both.[3]

Rabbi Plotkin arrives at his conclusion by way of a קל וחומר, an argument from minor to major. He cites a 1939 letter from Rabbi Boaz Cohen urging a colleague to discourage the burial of a young Jewish Christian in a Jewish cemetery. Rabbi Plotkin argues, "Back in 1939 when intermarriage was minimal and apostasy significantly less than today, Rabbi Cohen, while affirming the Jewishness of the apostate and his right to burial, still advised not burying the young man in a Jewish cemetery. In today's world with so much intermarriage and proselytizing of Jews, we need to keep the lines of demarcation clear."[4]

Limits of the Responsum's Precedent

Rabbi Cohen's recommendation was determined by the special circumstances of the case he was considering. It was not based, as is Rabbi Plotkin's conclusion, on a desire to reject apostasy, clarify an individual's blurred identity or provide an educational message to the larger community. The deceased was of mixed parentage and his Jewish mother wanted her son buried in a Jewish cemetery. Rabbi Cohen pointed out that the deceased was raised from childhood as a Christian, and had continued this practice as an adult. "It would be manifestly unfair to the father who is a Christian, to have his son buried in a Jewish cemetery and it would be no more than right for her to defer to his wishes."[5] Even then Rabbi Cohen did not bar the burial, only discouraged it for lack of fairness. It appears from the first part of his letter that, otherwise, he would follow the halakhah which recognizes the apostate as a Jew who is entitled to Jewish burial.

At about the time Rabbi Cohen was writing his advisory, a ruling of the Committee on Jewish Law and Standards, possibly based on the very same case, decided that, "A young man born to a Jewish mother and Christian father who lived all his life as a Christian, should as a matter of general policy, not be buried in a Jewish cemetery. Furthermore, to do so would be manifestly unfair to his Christian father."[6] In suggesting the exclusion from Jewish burial as a matter of general policy, the תשובה intimates that halakhah would dictate otherwise. The CJLS conceded, however, that in the case it was considering, it was appropriate to accommodate halakhah to the wishes and feelings of the Christian father. Neither Rabbi Cohen's letter nor the CJLS ruling speak directly to the case of an apostate Jew whose parents are both Jewish or when the family agrees to seek burial in a Jewish cemetery of an apostate born of a Jewish mother.

---

[2] Above, p. 401.
[3] Plotkin, loc. cit.
[4] Above, p. 401.
[5] Ibid.
[6] *PRA* 7 (1940): 32.

The Apostate in Halakhah

The apostate is neither a newcomer nor a stranger to Judaism. The idolater, that most heinous of apostates, like others condemned by the Bible to capital punishment, was after execution, hanged on a tree as a warning to others. The Torah insists however, לא תלין נבלתו על העץ כי קבור תקברנו ביום ההוא, forbidding the corpse to remain overnight without burial, insisting that the remains be interred that very day.[7] The Mishnah informs us that two cemeteries were maintained for הרוגי בית דין, those executed by the court; one for the decapitated and strangled, the other for the stoned and the burned.[8] It is from this text that the Gemara derives the tradition אין קוברין רשע אצל צדיק, a sinner is not buried next to a saint.[9] This was understood to mean that burial in the same cemetery of saints and sinners was permitted, so long as sinners were located at a remove from saints.

The Shulhan Arukh urges relatives of an apostate not to mourn him when he dies but to dress in white, eating, drinking and celebrating the destruction of an enemy of God.[10] Nevertheless, the burial of an apostate in a Jewish cemetery is obligatory because he is considered to remain a Jew, albeit, one who has sinned.[11]

So too in other areas of halakhah. An apostate's marriage is valid, requiring a גט to dissolve it.[12] חליצה is required from him if his sister-in-law, widowed without children, is to be allowed to remarry.[13] The standard which governs halakhah is the Talmudic principle ישראל אע"פ שחטא ישראל הוא, a Jewish sinner remains a Jew.[14]

Christian Science and Jewish Burial

During the first half of this century an extended discussion took place in the Jewish community over apostasy to the Church of Christian Science.[15] As early as 1912, the Central Conference of American Rabbis had registered concern about Christian Science and its doctrinal appeal to large numbers of Jews. Many Christian Scientists of Jewish birth claimed that they were still Jewish, that they were better Jews for having added Christian Science doctrines to their beliefs and that they wished to be buried amongst their own people in Jewish cemeteries. The CCAR adopted a resolution declaring, "Christian Science in its tenets and beliefs is essentially different from and in fundamental contradiction with Judaism, and that it is impossible for a Jew to accept Christian Science without thereby denying Judaism."[16] Nevertheless, Rabbi Solomon B. Freehof, distinguished halakhist of the Reform movement, concluded that it was necessary to "treat the Christian Scientist of Jewish birth in accordance with the Talmudic dictum: 'Although he has sinned he is still an

---

[7] Deut. 21:23.

[8] B. Sanhedrin 46a.

[9] B. Sanhedrin 47a.

[10] Yoreh De'ah 345:5.

[11] For a fuller discussion of the subject, see Yekutiel Greenwald, כל בו על אבלות, pp. 191-193. Greenwald cites at some length the tradition that the burial of apostates is obligatory within the limits established by halakhah. He then continues, בזמננו שיש לכל כתה וכתה בית קברות מיוחד להן, יקחו את המומר להם. הלא נכנס לאמונתם ומה לנו ולהם. Nevertheless, he acknowledges in conclusion, כן נראה לי, אבל לעת עתה לא מצאתי בשום מקום הערה זו.

[12] Even HaEzer 44:9.

[13] Magid Mishneh, M.T. Hilkhot Yibum, 1:6.

[14] B. Sanhedrin 44a.

[15] Henry L. Feingold, *The Jewish People in America: A Time for Searching: 1920-1945* (Waltham, Mass.: American Jewish Historical Society, 1993), p. 36.

[16] *Yearbook of the Central Conference of American Rabbis* 22: 229.

Israelite' (B. Sanhedrin 44a). We accord him the right of burial in the Jewish cemetery."[17]

Some years later: the Conservative movement also responded to the inroads of Christian Science. In 1920 Rabbi Louis Epstein rendered a report of the Committee on the Interpretation of Jewish Law on behalf of its absent chairman, Professor Louis Ginzberg:

> A congregation affiliated with the United Synagogue had among its membership a woman who was also affiliated with a Christian Science Church and at her death the survivors applies for her burial on the congregation's cemetery. The congregation referred the matter to your Committee on the Interpretation of Jewish Law, and the Chairman with the consent of the other members of the Committee has decided, in view of Jewish Law and as a matter of expediency to check a current evil, that the woman be given the burial rite prescribed by the Law for apostates. Following upon this as a precedent, the Committee feels that congregations affiliated with the United Synagogue shall not tolerate in their membership persons connected with the Christian Science Church or its activities.[18]

The Committee was well aware of the need to confront apostasy to the Christian Science Church and determined that such persons should be excluded from membership in congregations affiliated with the United Synagogue. Still, it followed the halakhah which provides, with restrictions on location, for the burial of apostates in a Jewish cemetery.

Seven years later, however, the exclusion of Christian Scientists from congregational affiliation was expanded to bar their burial in a Jewish cemetery also. Responding to an inquiry from Abraham Neuman, rabbi at Mikveh Israel in Philadelphia, Prof. Ginzberg wrote:

> On the basis of the law referred to in the Mishnah, the Talmud draws the inference that the wicked and the just, the sinful and the pious ought not to be buried in the same cemetery.
>
> 1. The Christian Science Church is undoubtedly a part of the general Christian communion, and any Jew who had become a member of this Church severs his connection with the Synagogue. In an address delivered before the annual convention of the United Synagogue several years ago, I strongly emphasized this fact. I have no copy of my address and doubt whether the United Synagogue has one.
>
> 2. I fully agree with you that the Ethical Culture Society is neither a religious or anti-religious society and, hence, membership in it could not be considered as a break with the Synagogue.
>
> 3. The answer to question three is contained in my general remarks at the beginning of the letter, according to which it is against Jewish Law and practice to bury a person in a Jewish cemetery who had left the Jewish fold.[19]

Two decades would elapse before the CJLS confirmed the ban on the burial of apostates when it ruled "that membership in a Christian Science Church signifies the

---

[17] Solomon B. Freehof, *Reform Jewish Practice*, vol. 1, p. 144.

[18] *United Synagogue of America Annual Reports*, 1920, p. 90.

[19] Eli Ginzberg, *Louis Ginzberg: Keeper of the Law* (Philadelphia: Jewish Publication Society, 1966), p. 228.

adoption of Christianity. Consequently such a person must of necessity be denied burial in a Jewish cemetery."[20]

The halakhah is unequivocal that apostates remain Jews and it is a מצוה דאורייתא to bury a Jewish apostate according to Jewish practice. A number of rulings of the CJLS and from other sources in our movement acknowledge and conform to this halakhic standard. Nevertheless, in response to circumstances that were felt to threaten the community, Prof. Ginzberg and later the CJLS, rejected the burial of apostates in a Jewish cemetery. It is to these rulings that Rabbi Plotkin might turn for precedent.

The Burden of the Mara D'atra

The מרא דאתרא responding to a request for the burial of an apostate in a Jewish cemetery may be confronted with one of a variety of circumstances, including:

(1) An apostate Jew who requests burial in a Jewish cemetery in accordance with Jewish tradition may be expressing a desire for תשובה, a return to the Jewish faith. The מרא דאתרא should make every effort to determine if this has occurred and should respond with the greatest sensitivity and openness to expressions of return or if the individual is already deceased, to testimony of תשובה by family members or others.

(2) As is sometimes the case, the deceased may be brought for burial by Jewish parents or other family members. If burial is refused, great hurt may be inflicted on devoted and caring Jews. The מרא דאתרא should consider the possibility that duress or even mental illness may have driven the deceased from כלל ישראל. If this can be determined, the deceased may be buried in a Jewish cemetery. The historical leniency of halakhah regarding the burial of apostates should always be applied when there is an indication of תשובה, duress, mental illness or other mitigating circumstances.

(3) If the deceased has non-Jewish family members who prefer burial in a Christian cemetery, the concerns expressed by Rabbi Cohen and the CJLS for Christian family members, to whom burial in a Jewish cemetery would be unfair, should be considered.

(4) In the absence of תשובה, duress, mental illness or other mitigating circumstances, the reality of the life of the deceased urges that burial in a Jewish cemetery be barred.

Conclusion

"Despite the fact that halakhah would allow for Jewish burial of an apostate even while forbidding mourning, we would prohibit such burial rites to the apostate. Today's environment makes it necessary to prohibit any Jewish rights and privileges, including burial in a Jewish cemetery, to an apostate. It is hoped that such a public statement would speak loudly to the lie of the 'Jews for Jesus' and others, who would advocate the position that one could remain a Jew and practice Christianity at the same time. Thus, we hope to establish in the minds of the community the distinctiveness of Jews and gentiles.

"There is a sensitivity in the codes that allows for the presumption of duress or mental illness in the apostate that would allow the מרא דאתרא to mitigate the above ruling and allow for burial. There is also a strong concern to allow for last minute תשובה and return to the Jewish fold, even without מקוה, for those who would otherwise require it. It should be left to the מרא דאתרא to examine the possibility that such repentance may have occurred even up to the moment of death, but absent such תשובה, Jewish burial should be denied to an apostate."[21]

---

[20] *PRA* 11 (1947): 62.

[21] Plotkin, above, pp. 401-402, but here changing the order of the last two paragraphs.

YD 352:3.1998

I Shall Sprinkle Pure Water Upon You and You Shall Be Purified: A Question of Taharah

Rabbi Ben Zion Bergman

This paper was approved by the CJLS on March 25, 1998, by a vote of fifteen in favor, two opposed, and two abstaining (15-2-2). Voting in favor: Rabbis Kassel Abelson, Ben Zion Bergman, Elliot N. Dorff, Samuel Fraint, Baruch Frydman-Kohl, Nechama D. Goldberg, Susan Grossman, Vernon H. Kurtz, Alan B. Lucas, Aaron L. Mackler, Joel E. Rembaum, James Rosen, Joel Roth, Gordon Tucker, and Gerald Zelizer. Voting against: Rabbis Myron S. Geller and Judah Kogen. Abstaining: Rabbis Paul Plotkin and Avram Israel Reisner.

The Committee on Jewish Law and Standards of the Rabbinical Assembly provides guidance in matters of halakhah for the Conservative movement. The individual rabbi, however, is the authority for the interpretation and application of all matters of halakhah.

שאלה

It is the practice of a Jewish mortuary in the Los Angeles area that all bodies brought to the mortuary are immediately washed. The rationale for this procedure is hygienic, to ensure the safety of mortuary personnel. The deceased may be carrying infectious bacteria or viruses and the purpose of this initial washing is essentially to provide some measure of disinfection. In recent years, with the proliferation of fatal infection, the mortuary personnel have become even more acutely sensitive to the need for protection.

This initial washing presents two issues which confront Jewish law:

(A) The חברא קדישא personnel have raised the question whether this initial washing preempts, or impacts, in any other way, on the טהרה. In other words, may there be any washing of the body other than the טהרה?

(B) If this initial washing does not conflict with halakhah, can this initial washing be done by anyone regardless of gender? In other words, may a woman be washed by a man and a man by a woman, or must the procedure be done by someone of the same gender as the deceased? In addition to the extra expense of having both male and female personnel available at all times (even in the wee hours of the morning since bodies are brought into the mortuary at any time), the mortuary personnel have raised the issue that to require that the initial washing be done by someone of the same gender impugns their professionalism.

תשובה

A. It should be stated at the outset that every precaution must be taken that nothing be done which would prevent the full טהרה and other ritual laws from being able to be fulfilled. This responsum therefore assumes that all necessary procedures will be followed and limits itself to the questions posed.

In a previous review of this mortuary's procedures, I addressed the question of the legitimacy of the initial washing. I indicated then that the טהרה procedure should be the final process before the deceased is clothed, so that the purification ritual, including the recitation of the expiatory prayers and prescribed Biblical verses, are the last acts preparing the deceased for burial. I then concluded that the initial washing does not preempt nor in any way adversely affect the טהרה.

I come to this conclusion on the basis of several halakhic considerations. The source for the טהרה (ritual purification procedure) of the deceased is to be found in the Mishnah (Shabbat 151a) where it is stated simply that even on the Sabbath:

עושין כל צרכי המת; סכין ומדיחין אותו ובלבד שלא יזיז בו אבר.

> One may perform all that is necessary for the dead viz. rubbing
> with oil, washing with water, but one may not move any limb.

The rubbing with oil, as the commentators indicate, was evidently to facilitate removal of fecal matter and other loathsome substances before the rinsing with water. It is abundantly clear that the motivation for the טהרה procedure in ancient times was respect for the deceased. This is stated explicitly by Nahmanides in *Torat Ha'adam*:

מה ששנו במס׳ שבת, עושין כל צרכי המת סכין ומדיחין וכו, אין זה אלא מפני כבודו.

> What we have learned in Tractate Shabbat that we do all that is
> necessary for the deceased, i.e., rubbing with oil and washing, is
> done only out of respect for him.[1]

The consideration of respect for the deceased was in terms of his or her effect upon others. Thus Rabbi Joseph Karo (Bet Yosef, sec. 352) states:

מדיחין אותו כדי להעביר זוהמתו שלא יקיצו העם בטלטולו.

> We wash the body to remove any filth (possibly fecal matter) so that
> those who carry the body are not nauseated.

Maimonides (Laws of Mourning, ch. 4) also adds the use of aromatic spices to counter offensive odors.

One can cite many other practices motivated by the same consideration. Let me add only one other outstanding example. In the Babylonian Talmud, Tractate Moed Katan 27b it is stated:

בראשונה היו מניחין את המוגמר תחת חולי מעים מתים והיו חולי מעים חיים מתביישין; התקינו שיהו מניחין תחת הכל מפני כבודו של חולי מעים חיים.

> Originally incense would be burned especially beneath the bier of the
> deceased who had intestinal illness. But since this practice of singling
> out this decedent in this way would embarrass living persons with the

---

[1] Cited by Grunwald, *Ach L'tzara*, ch.1, sec. 6a, from *Torat Ha'adam, Sha'ar Hasof*, subsection *Inyan Hak'vura*.

same intestinal problems, they then instituted that incense would be burned under the biers of all deceased, out of consideration for the feelings of the living who suffer from gastro-intestinal diseases.

This example highlights the attitude of Jewish law in its understanding of the respect that must be shown to the deceased. Thus, for example, respect for the dead required speedy burial. Remembering that these laws were formulated in a hot climate with no refrigeration, respect for the dead required burial before putrefaction would set in and render the body loathsome. Yet sometimes, if close family members were in a distant place from which it would take some greater time in order to arrive for the funeral, the burial could be delayed (though not for an excessive amount of time). This is cited in the Talmud Bavli (Sanhedrin 46b, 47a) in the context of a discussion of whether the eulogy is motivated by יקרא דחיי (respect for the living) or יקרא דשכיבא (respect for the dead). While the Gemara finally decides that the eulogy is for יקרא דשכיבא, from the discussion it is clear that both considerations are operative in our dealing with the dead and the two considerations are not antithetical. Specifically, the statement is made:

כל העושה לכבודו של חי, אין בו בזיון למת.

> Whatever is done for the honor of the living is not a dishonor to the deceased.

Rashi specifically points out:

האי דליתייקרו ביה קרוביו לאו בזיון הוא לדידיה.

> That honor accrues to his relatives is not a dishonor to him.

Concern for the living, therefore, is a factor that the halakhah takes into serious consideration, permitting it to affect the burial procedure, as long as it does not cause dishonor to the deceased.

I therefore conclude that the initial washing of the deceased for hygienic purposes is not contrary to Jewish law.

(1) As indicated *supra*, cleansing of the body before the washing with water was part of the procedure. Even as late an authority as Rabbi Solomon Kluger (1785-1869) writes in a volume of responsa (*Ha'elef L'cha Shlomo* No. 305):

לוקחים השמשים אותו מן הארץ, ומקנחין אותו יפה בסדין שלא יהיה עליו שום לכלוך וטינוף ואח"כ יתחילו לרחצו במים חמין מראשו ועד רגלו ואומרים הפסוקים המבוארים בספר מעבר יבק.

> The attendants lift him off of the ground, cleanse him with cloths so that there be no dirt or filth and then they begin to wash him with water from head to foot and recite the verses as specified in the book, *Ma'avar Yabok*.

The rabbinic authorities, therefore permitted removal of the loathsome matter before the טהרה. One can extrapolate from loathsome matter to loathsome bacteria which can cause serious and possibly fatal infection. I am convinced that the same authorities, who urged preliminary cleansing of the body for removal of the hazards that they could see and be aware of, would today urge preliminary cleansing for removal of hazardous substances of which we are now aware.

(2) Additionally, as indicated *supra*, the motivation for the טהרה procedure was respect for the dead. Yet, as also indicated *supra*, יקרא דשכיבא (respect for the dead) and יקרא דחיי

(concern for the living) were both values which the halakhah considered operative in issues of burial procedure. In the present instance, since the initial washing would not be considered disrespectful of the deceased, since it renders the corpse less threatening, certainly יקרא דחיי – concern for the health of the mortuary personnel – should be a major concern.

For these reasons, I reiterate that the initial hygienic cleansing is not inimical to the halakhah and does not impinge upon, preempt, or in any way adversely affect the ritual טהרה.

B. Regarding the issue of the gender of the attendant who does the washing, there is no doubt in my mind that Jewish law would unequivocally require that the washing be done by someone of the same sex as the deceased.

There is a responsum by the author of *T'shurat Shai* (No. 546) which is illustrative. The question concerned a woman who lived in a non-Jewish village who died right before a Jewish holiday and was to be buried on the second day of the holiday. There were no Jewish women in that place to do the טהרה although there were Jewish men, one of whom was learned in Jewish law. There was not sufficient time for Jewish women to arrive there, perform the טהרה on the eve of the holiday and be able to return home before the holiday. The distance from the Jewish village to the non-Jewish village was such that traveling (even on foot) would constitute a violation of the festival. The response was that Jewish women could not violate the law of the holiday and that non-Jewish women should be instructed by the learned Jew and they should perform the טהרה.

Now, the halakhah is clear that טהרה should be performed by Jews. This requirement could have been satisfied by having the טהרה performed by the Jewish men, one of whom was even described as expert and knowledgeable. However, rather than have men take care of a female body, the Rabbinic response was to allow non-Jewish women to perform the necessary ablutions.

This is another case where the halakhah is confronted with a conflict between two disparate values. On the one hand, that only Jews take care of the deceased is a halakhic requirement. (See Responsa of R. David b. Zimri. pt. 2, no. 507.) Rabbi Leopold Greenwald in one of his encyclopedic works on the laws of burial and mourning (*Ach L'tzara*) cites an authority who goes so far as to forbid the deceased to be touched by a non-Jew. It is therefore surprising that the decision was to have non-Jewish women take care of the body. On the other hand, however, there is the Jewish moral value of צניעות (chastity and modest behavior). In all cases, the treatment of the deceased must be in accordance with what the deceased would have wished, were he or she able to express his or her desire. The halakhah will always make the assumption that the deceased would wish that he or she be treated properly and that nothing be done which would, were he or she alive, violate standards of modesty and chaste behavior. Indeed, it is illustrative that in the case cited *supra*, the woman in question is described as not being ritually observant, eating non-kosher food, bread on Passover, etc. Nevertheless, even for her, it was considered inappropriate for men to perform the ritual washing since it would violate the principle of צניעות.

Rabbi Samson Morpurgo (1681-1740), who was Rabbi in Ancona, Italy, in his work *Shemesh Tzedaka* (Book 4, 4:6), raises the question of whether a husband may participate in the טהרה of his wife and clothe her afterwards. Now certainly, for the deceased who was intimate with this man, we cannot impute the same sense of shame and violation of modesty. Nevertheless, after lengthy discussion, he concludes that one should be strict and not allow it rather than take the lenient position.[2]

---

[2] While not affecting the issue upon which the decision was ultimately based, a complicating factor was the fact that the woman had died while in a state of נידה.

Similarly, a modern work, *Death and Bereavement* by Rabbi Abner Weiss, states (page 55): "*Taharah* for deceased Jewish males is performed by Jewish males. If *really* [emphasis in original] necessary, and if a competent rabbi so rules, women may perform *taharah* on men [although not vice-versa]." Evidently, women were assumed to be more chaste and therefore more scrupulously careful in their handling of the male body and less likely to be sexually aroused or engage in lewd or salacious remarks than men might be in the reverse situation. But even then, it was only בשעת הדחק (in a dire emergency). Thus, צניעות was considered an essential value to be safeguarded in our treatment of the deceased.

The requirement that the naked body of the deceased be washed by a person of the same gender should not be construed as, in any way, impugning the professionalism of the mortuary personnel. As professionals, they are able to attend the deceased with complete objectivity and detachment. However, the issue is not the feelings or attitude of the person ministering to the deceased, but the feelings and attitude which the halakhah would presume to be those of the deceased.

The mortuary personnel, in asserting their position, sought to analogize the relationship of the mortician vis-à-vis the deceased to the relationship of doctor or nurse vis-à-vis a patient. However, the analogy is specious. In the doctor-patient relationship, the live patient is making a conscious choice. A patient who is especially modest and embarrassed to be seen naked by someone of the opposite sex will choose a doctor of the same sex. And, as doctors have informed me, should a male patient be embarrassed by being attended by a female nurse, he may request a male nurse and his request would be granted. The same would be true for the female patient who would have the right to reject a male nurse. In the mortician-deceased relationship, however, the deceased cannot make a conscious choice. Jewish law, therefore, must operate with the presumption that every Jew holds to the value of צניעות, presuming therefore that he or she would consider ministrations by someone of the opposite sex as impinging on his or her sense of צניעות. Jewish law would therefore mandate that all ministrations to the naked body of the deceased be done by persons of the same sex.

I repeat that this in no way disparages the professional objectivity of the mortuary personnel. On the contrary, it is reflective of their sensitivity to the values of the deceased.

Conclusion

The initial hygienic cleansing is not inimical to the halakhah and does not impinge upon, preempt, or, in any way, adversely affect the ritual טהרה.

Regarding the issue of the gender of the attendant who does the washing, there is no doubt in my mind that Jewish law would unequivocally require that the washing be done by someone of the same sex as the deceased. In all cases, the treatment of the deceased must be in accordance with what the deceased would have wished, were he or she able to express their desire. The halakhah will always make the assumption that the deceased would wish that he or she be treated properly and that nothing be done which would, were he or she alive, violate standards of modesty and chaste behavior. צניעות is considered an essential value to be safeguarded in our treatment of the deceased. In the mortician-deceased relationship, the deceased cannot make a conscious choice. Jewish law, therefore, must operate with the presumption that every Jew holds to the value of צניעות, presuming therefore that he or she would consider ministrations by someone of the opposite sex as impinging on his or her sense of צניעות. Jewish law would therefore mandate that all ministrations to the naked body of the deceased be done by persons of the same sex.

YD 363.1996

Exhuming the Dead

Rabbi Myron S. Geller

This paper was approved by the CJLS on March 13, 1996, by a vote of eighteen in favor and one opposed (18-1-0). Voting in favor: Rabbis Kassel Abelson, Ben Zion Bergman, Stephanie Dickstein, Elliot N. Dorff, Jerome M. Epstein, Baruch Frydman-Kohl, Shoshana Gelfand, Myron S. Geller, Arnold M. Goodman, Susan Grossman, Judah Kogen, Vernon H. Kurtz, Aaron L. Mackler, Lionel E. Moses, Paul Plotkin, Mayer Rabinowitz, Gerald Skolnik, and Elie Kaplan Spitz. Voting against: Rabbi Gordon Tucker.

The Committee on Jewish Law and Standards of the Rabbinical Assembly provides guidance in matters of halakhah for the Conservative movement. The individual rabbi, however, is the authority for the interpretation and application of all matters of halakhah.

שאלה

As the result of an error by a burial society, an individual was interred, not in the grave site owned by him and his wife, but in a plot owned by an abutter. The abutter claims the occupied site and wants the remains removed from it so that the plot will be available for members of his own family, as he intended when the property was purchased. The family of the deceased refuses to allow the removal of the remains and requests that an additional plot owned by the abutter, adjacent to the deceased, be made available for eventual use by his spouse.

(1) May the remains be disinterred for relocation? Under what circumstances?

(2) If the remains are relocated, may the plot be reused for the burial of the original owner?

תשובה

A General Prohibition

The removal of remains from their place of burial is generally forbidden. The Yerushalmi rules:

אין מפנין את המת ואת העצמות מקבר מכובד למכובד, ולא מבזוי לבזוי,
ולא מבזוי למכובד, ואין צריך לאמר מן המכובד לבזוי.

> Corpses or skeletons may not be removed from an honorable grave to an honorable grave, from one unworthy grave to another, from an unworthy grave to one that is honorable and no need to state, from an honorable grave to one that is unworthy.[1]

---

[1] J. Moed Katan 2:4.

The Bavli makes a similar ruling:

אין מפנין לא את המת ולא את העצמות ממקום ביזוי למקום ביזוי, ולא ממקום מכוער למקום מכוער, ואין צריך לאמר ממקום מכובד למקום בזוי.

> Neither corpses nor skeletons may be removed from an honorable place to an unworthy place, from an ugly place to another ugly place and no need to state, from an honorable place to an unworthy place.[2]

The Tur[3] follows these Talmudic precedents as does the Shulhan Arukh.[4]

Several Reasons for the General Prohibition

(A) The most important reason is cited in the Talmud, in the case of a young man who sold family property shortly before his death. After his burial, the sale was contested by his family, on the grounds that he was a minor. They sought permission to exhume his remains, hoping to show that acceptable marks of puberty could not be found on the body. Rabbi Akiva refused to allow the disinterment because אי אתם רשאים לנוולו, "you are not permitted to humiliate him."[5] In subsequent halakhah, concern about ניוול המת, humiliation of the dead, remains the strongest bar to exhumation.

(B) Another explanation cited is the confusion the dead would suffer if their remains were disturbed while they were experiencing חרדת הדין, trembling at God's judgment.[6] The Scriptural proof text that disturbing the dead causes them confusion is found in the response of Samuel to Saul, when he was brought up from the dead by the woman of En Dor.[7]

(C) Rabbenu Asher makes the additional point that it is a source of בזיון, embarrassment to the dead, to be moved from their burial site before their flesh is consumed from the bones, because in that state, their remains are sickening to the living.[8] However, once the flesh is gone or if the remains are contained in a sealed casket, this reservation does not apply.

Exceptions to the General Prohibition

Despite the general prohibition, under certain circumstances the Rabbis permitted or even required exhumation. The Talmud Yerushalmi permits the removal of remains, even from a worthy to an unworthy place, that they may be buried with אבותיו, the ancestors of the deceased.[9] The Taz understands אבותיו to include not only ancestors but בני משפחתו, one's family in general.[10]

In his code, Rabbi Joseph Karo adds other circumstances when exhumation may be permitted or is required:

A. It is a mitzvah for children to rebury a parent's body in Eretz Yisrael, even if the parent expressed objection during his lifetime to having his remains moved there.

B. When a burial site is unprotected from robbers or natural forces, it is

---

[2] B. Semakhot 13.
[3] Tur Yoreh De'ah 363.
[4] S.A. Yoreh De'ah 363:1.
[5] B. Baba Batra 154a.
[6] Beit Yosef, Tur Yoreh De'ah loc. cit.
[7] 1 Sam. 28:15.
[8] Rosh, Moed Katan 1:13.
[9] Loc. cit.
[10] Yoreh De'ah 363:2.

permissible to remove bodies to locations that are not so compromised.

c. When a stipulation is made at the time of burial about the removal of the body at a later date.

d. When a body is buried in קבר הנמצא, an available site, but without authorization from its owner, the body may be moved.[11]

This last ruling follows the Tosefta which permits the removal of a body from a grave which endangers public safety or which was used without the permission of its owner but bans removal when the owner has granted permission and later changes his mind.[12] When the grave is used without the owner's permission, לא קנה המת מקומו, the deceased has not gained title to the site, and disinterring the remains is proper, in order to return the plot to its rightful owner. Only a מת מצוה, a corpse whose family is unknown and responsibility for whose burial devolves on everyone, acquires title without the owners permission and cannot be disinterred. When the grave is cleared, the place is permitted for use.

The Mitzvah of קבר שלו

Among the traditional requirements for Jewish burial is that which obligates each person to acquire and be interred in קבר שלו, his own burial plot, one which is the property of the deceased. The Talmud quotes Josh. 24:33 about the death of Elazar ben Aharon and his interment at a site owned by his son Pinhas. The Gemara is concerned about the basis of Pinhas' title to the property. Abaye rejects R. Papa's suggestion that Pinhas might have purchased it. Such title, terminating at the יובל, the Jubilee Year, would leave צדיק קבור בקבר שאינו שלו, a saint buried in a grave to which he had not acquired title.[13]

The Talmud understood that a צדיק required קבר שלו, a grave to which he had acquired title; later authorities extended this mandate to all Jews:

> ואם כי בבבא בתרא דף קי״א מצינו "נמצא צדיק קבור בקבר שאינו שלו"
> לא דוקא צדיק אלא כל אחד צריך להיות נקבר בקבר שלו.

> Although Baba Batra 111b speaks of, "a saint buried in a grave to which he has not acquired title," this refers not specifically to a saint but rather to every individual who must be buried in a grave to which he has acquired title.[14]

Rabbi Isaac Elkhanan Spector supplies the rationale for the extension in that each Jew enjoys a חזקה, a presumption, as צדיק to whom the קבר שלו, personal ownership requirement applies. Thus every Jew must be buried in a plot owned in perpetuity by the deceased.[15]

If one is buried in a plot that does not meet this standard but he owns a plot which he has designated for his burial elsewhere, he should be disinterred in order to satisfy the requirement of burial in קבר שלו, a grave to which he has acquired title and in accordance with the wishes of the deceased.[16]

---

[11] S.A. Yoreh De'ah 364:2.

[12] B. Sanhedrin 47b. A distinction is made between קבר הנמצא, a grave in which the deceased has been buried without the owners consent which may be cleared, and קבר הידוע, a grave in which a body was interred with the consent of the owner, which may not be cleared.

[13] B. Baba Batra 111b.

[14] Yekutiel Greenwald, *Kol Bo Al Aveylut*, p. 174.

[15] Ein Yitzhak no. 34.

[16] Maharam Schick, Yoreh De'ah 354.

Justifying Exhumation

When permitting the removal of remains, the Rabbis set aside their concerns about ניוול המת, humiliation of the dead, חרדת הדין, trembling at God's judgment, and בזיון, embarrassment of the dead or found that they did not apply. Maharshal rules that ניוול המת, humiliation of the dead, does not apply when a body is exhumed and reburied in the same cemetery or even in the same city. After the passage of twelve months from the time of death, there is no concern for חרדת הדין, trembling at God's judgment. If the body was buried in a sealed casket, בזיון המת, embarrassment of the dead, is not considered a deterrent to disinterment of the remains. In any case, this category does not apply once the flesh is gone from the bones.[17] Even when these circumstances do not apply, the Rabbis find that the removal of remains to satisfy a halakhic imperative or for the honor of the deceased, overrides reservations about exhumation and reburial.

In the event that an individual is buried in the wrong place because of error or oversight, the remains may be moved at a later time to a family plot and halakhic restrictions on exhumation and the reasons for those restrictions are not applicable.[18]

Reuse of the Empty Grave

A structure built above ground for the burial of the deceased as well as any stones, monuments, markers, articles of clothing or other objects specifically designated for burial with the dead, may not be reused by others. However, the soil of the grave, or the grave, in the event that the site was used without the permission of the owner so that the deceased did not, except in the case of a מת מצוה, a corpse whose family is unknown and responsibility for whose burial devolves on everyone, acquire his place, is permitted to be reused.[19] Rambam takes a stricter view because of his concern for the dignity of the dead but is not followed by most rulings. Greenwald cites the generally accepted view that מותר לקבור מת אחר בקבר שמשם נפנו עצמות מת, it is permissible to bury an individual in a grave from which remains have been disinterred.[20] However, if the grave was prepared for a family member, even if it is permitted to others, it is barred to relatives.[21]

Summary

From the perspective of halakhah, the removal of remains from a grave is generally barred because of concern for the dignity of the dead. Under certain circumstances, remains may be transferred:

  A. to move the remains to a family burial plot;

  B. to move the remains to Eretz Yisrael;

  C. for the security of the remains against vandalism or natural catastrophe;

  D. for public need;[22] or,

  E. if the remains were buried in a plot belonging to someone else.

---

[17] Greenwald, op. cit., p. 234.

[18] Ibid., p. 238.

[19] B. Sanhedrin 47b; S.A. Yoreh De'ah 364.

[20] Ibid., p. 242.

[21] B. Sanhedrin 48a. The burial of another family member in place of the relative for whom the grave was intended is considered a dishonor to the latter.

[22] Public need may include public safety, construction of railroads or highways and other projects involving land taken by governmental authorities. Greenwald argues that property taken by eminent domain is no longer

The grave site from which the body is removed may be used for burial by another person but not by a relative of the person originally interred at the plot.

This תשובה considers only the implications of Jewish law and does not reflect in any way on civil statutes which may override the conclusions stated here. Rabbis should consult with appropriate legal counsel when questions related to exhumation of graves and reburial so require.

Conclusion

The deceased, in our case, had expected to be buried in his own plot, amongst the members of his family. As the result of an error, he was buried in a grave belonging to another person, to which he had no claim and over which he can acquire no title because he is not a מת מצוה, a corpse whose family is unknown and responsibility for whose burial devolves on everyone. Removing his remains to his own plot, would comply with the intention of the deceased when he observed the mitzvah of קבר שלו, acquiring title to his own grave and would bring him to the final resting place he had expected בקברי אבותיו, in his families' burial plot. The continued occupation of the grave by the deceased raises an embarrassing question of unlawful acquisition, from which his family should want to spare him.

There is no question of ניוול המת, humiliation of the dead, חרדת הדין, trembling at God's judgment, or בזיון, embarrassment of the dead. The body would be moved only within the confines of the cemetery, a very short distance, in a casket, more than twelve months after the death occurred.

The reuse or the sale of the plot by the original owners is permitted as long as it is not used by a family member of the individual who was buried there in error.

The leniency of the halakhah to exhume a body under these circumstances in no way compromises the obligation to maintain כבוד המת, the dignity of the deceased, which should be punctiliously respected during disinterment and reburial.[23] There is no need for a ceremony when disinterment and reburial take place, although some words in memory of the deceased may be spoken.[24] The family of the deceased should perform קריעה, the rending of a garment, and observe אבלות, a period of mourning, until evening.[25]

קבר שלו, owned by the deceased. This demands the relocation of remains to a site acceptable to Jewish law. Greenwald cites a ruling of Maharam Schick requiring large-scale disinterment of remains over a sizable area from land taken by the government for the construction of a railroad line. He makes no distinction between the disinterment of individual remains and the relocation of an entire cemetery. Greenwald, op. cit. p. 240.

[23] After this paper was completed, I learned from Rabbi Mayer Rabinowitz that a תשובה on disinterment by Rabbi Jack Segal had been approved unanimously by the CJLS. Rabbi Segal "suggests that every problem of disinterment be presented before a board of three rabbis, and that each case should be judged on its own merits," *PRA* 31 (1967): 208. In my view, the מרא דאתרא should determine if this is called for and may prefer ruling on the matter without recourse to a bet din.

[24] J. Moed Katan, 1.5, states, ליקוטי עצמות אין אומרים עליהן קינים ונהי אין אומרים עליהן לא ברכת אבלים ולא תנחומי אבלים... אבל אומרים עליהם דברים מהו דברים רבנן אמרו קילוסין. See also Division of Religious Activities, National Jewish Welfare Board, *Responsa in War Time*, pp. 61-62.

[25] Greenwald, op. cit., p. 241.

YD 367:1.1991

A Matter of Grave Concern: A Question of Mixed Burial

Rabbi Ben Zion Bergman

This paper was approved by the CJLS on January 30, 1991, by a vote of eight in favor and eight opposed (8-8-0). Voting in favor: Rabbis Kassel Abelson, Ben Zion Bergman, Elliot N. Dorff, Richard L. Eisenberg, Dov Peretz Elkins, Arnold M. Goodman, Howard Handler, and Gordon Tucker. Voting against: Rabbis Stanley Bramnick, David M. Feldman, Samuel Fraint, Lionel E. Moses, Mayer Rabinowitz, Chaim A. Rogoff, Joel Roth, and Morris M. Shapiro.

The Committee on Jewish Law and Standards of the Rabbinical Assembly provides guidance in matters of halakhah for the Conservative movement. The individual rabbi, however, is the authority for the interpretation and application of all matters of halakhah.

שאלה

In an area of Southern California with a growing Jewish population and no local Jewish cemetery, a Christian (or non-denominational) cemetery has offered to set aside a designated section of ground as an exclusively Jewish cemetery.

While proper means of distinct separation from the non-Jewish part of the cemetery will be instituted and maintained, the questioner is concerned that the Jewish section will not really be an exclusively Jewish cemetery, since his Reform colleagues will allow the non-Jewish spouses of their members to be buried there.

His question seeks determination of whether this would vitiate the Jewish character of the cemetery, with the consequence of rendering it halakhically unfit.

תשובה

There is one issue of which the questioner is either unaware or with which he is unconcerned — namely, the legal ownership of the property itself. The issue is twofold: There is the individual's ownership of his or her burial place; and secondly, there is the issue of whether this communal cemetery is קרקע ישראל.

The question of individual ownership arises since in California (and it may also be true in other jurisdictions) the individual purchaser of a cemetery plot does not acquire title to the property. Title remains vested in the non-profit corporation. (Otherwise, the property would become taxable to the purchaser and heirs.) The "purchaser" of a cemetery plot only acquires a license — a right of interment.

While it may not be an absolute halakhic certainty that every Jew must own his or her own burial plot, it was considered improper for a צדיק to be buried in a plot belonging to others. Bava Batra 111b quotes Josh. 24:33 which states: ואלעזר בן אהרן מת ויקברו אותו בגבעת פינחס בנו. The Gemara infers that Elazar apparently had no burial place of his own. This raises the question of how Phineas could have had property other than through inheritance from his father. After hypothesizing that this could have been possible only if Phineas had married a woman of property whose property he inherited upon her death, R. Papa says to Abaye (ibid. 112a), "Perhaps Phineas bought the property." Abaye's response was: פינחס דזבין מיזבן לא מצית אמרת דאם כן נמצאת שדה חוזרת ביובל ונמצא צדיק קבור בקבר שאינו שלו.

While the Talmud specifies צדיק later authorities extended this to all Jews. In *Eyin Yitzhak* (סי׳ ל״ד), Rabbi Isaac Elchanan Spector, dealing with the issue of whether a community may purchase property that would be available as a cemetery only for a limited time, cites this passage and adds:

ואף דאמרו בגמ׳ בלשון צדיק קבור כו׳ עכ״ז הא עלינו החיוב להחזיק לחברו צדיק כמו דמצינו באו״ח סי׳ תקפ״ב סעי׳ ט׳ בהג״ה וט״ז ומג״א שם. ובפרט בעדה שלימה דהם עדת קדושים אין לנו לעשות מעשה ח״ו דיהי׳ נגד מעלת כבודם ויהי גנאי להם ח״ו.

Thus, all Jews are to be considered presumptively צדיקים and, as such, should be buried in graves which belong to them.

Nevertheless, while in our case, title to the property does not become vested in the decedent, the right of interment conferred by contract with the cemetery owners is designated as irrevocable. Indeed, the "purchaser" may sell the right of interment to others, which indicates that to all intents and purposes, even without title in fee simple, he or she exercises dominion over the property. We may therefore maintain that *qua* קבר, the property is קבר שלו/ה.

Since the title to the entire cemetery, including the Jewish section, is vested in the corporation that operates both the Jewish and non-Jewish sections, the Jewish cemetery is not קרקע ישראל. Jewish ownership has been a requirement, and in as late a work as אח לצרה by Rabbi Yehuda Yekutiel Greenwald it is stated:

חוב קדוש הטילן רבותינו על בני ישראל להיות להם בית הקברות מיוחד להם ושיהיה הקרקע שלהם (פרק ג׳ סי׳ י״א).

The issue arose in the early nineteenth century when several municipalities in the Austro-Hungarian Empire established communal cemeteries with sections set aside for the various faiths. At that time, rabbinical authorities insisted that the community attempt to get outright possession of the Jewish section. In the event that that was impossible, then at least control of the Jewish section and the rules governing it were to be in the hands of Jews and proper separation erected between the Jewish and non-Jewish sections.

פתחי תשובה to Yoreh De'ah 363 cites a responsum by R. Moses Sofer in which he declared that it is permitted to disinter bodies from a cemetery owned by non-Jews to be reburied in a cemetery owned by Jews. While exhumation was considered a serious prohibition, evidently the fact that the body was in non-Jewish ground overrode that prohibition. On the other hand, the same passage in the פתחי תשובה cites a responsum by R. Ezekiel Landau to a similar question in which he forbade disinterment. Evidently, to the נודע ביהודה, a cemetery not owned outright by Jews was nevertheless considered a proper cemetery.

In the responsum of R. Isaac Elchanan (cited *supra*), in which he attempts to explain the position of the נודע ביהודה, it is clear that the essential issue is not the matter of title, but rather the assurance that the cemetery will be a Jewish cemetery in perpetuity and that those buried there will not be disturbed. He therefore forbade the purchase (really a lease) of temporary cemetery property since after the fixed period, the bodies will have to be removed. This would be violative of the halakhah for two reasons: חרדת הדין וניוול המת.

In 1959, the issue became a *cause celebre* in the Los Angeles community. Forest Lawn Memorial Park (a non-denominational commercial cemetery operation) established a separate Jewish cemetery called Mt. Sinai Memorial Park. A number of congregations and individuals purchased cemetery property there and the Jewishly-owned cemeteries raised the issue that Mt. Sinai Memorial Park was not קרקע ישראל. The issue was vituperatively debated in the Anglo-Jewish press, leaking over into the general press, with the result that the Jewish Community Relations Committee, seeking to bring the matter to a conclusion, approached the various rabbinic groups and organizations for a statement. Included was the Southern California Board of Rabbis of which I happened to be President at the time. I wrote to the CJLS of the Rabbinical Assembly for guidance. Approximately a year later, I received a response, indicating in essence:

A. Halakhically, there is no איסור to be issued for a cemetery which is owned by non-Jews.

B. However, it would be against the best interests of the Jewish community for control of a Jewish cemetery to be in the hands of non-Jews. Therefore, if possible, congregations, organizations and individuals seeking to acquire cemetery property should ascertain that the ownership is Jewish.

C. Where families or congregations already own plots in cemeteries owned by non-Jews, no aspersion should be cast upon burials there nor should disinterment and reburial in a Jewishly-owned cemetery ever be suggested.

Approximately one year later, Rabbi Joseph Wagner, then President of the local RA Region, wrote to Rabbi Max Routtenberg, then Chairman of the Law Committee, for clarification of the statement. Rabbi Routtenberg's response essentially emphasized the need to safeguard "Jewish legal rules and sensitivities."

בנ״ד — in the present instance — while it is permissible to bury in the Jewish section of the non-Jewish cemetery, the questioner should be alerted to the need to establish that (1) administrative control over the Jewish section should be in the hands of a proper Jewish committee to see that only Jewish rites are performed there, and (2) that the contractual agreements between the cemetery and the purchasers are unconditional, with the non-Jewish cemetery warranting that the Jewish section will remain a Jewish section and never revert to a non-denominational status.

Burial of Non-Jewish Spouses

The questioner's essential concern is that his Reform colleagues will bury the non-Jewish spouses of their members in the Jewish section of the cemetery. Initially, this seems to pose no problem since a baraita cited in Gittin 61a would seem to permit it:

ת״ר מפרנסים עניי נכרים עם עניי ישראל ומבקרים חולי נכרים עם חולי
ישראל וקוברין מתי נכרים עם מתי ישראל מפני דרכי שלום.

Nevertheless, however one may be personally convinced that פשוטו כמשמעו, beginning with Rashi, this was understood by the poskim as not conferring permission to bury Jews and non-Jews together. While the Rif quotes the baraita *ad verbatim*, Rashi comments *ad locum*: לא בקברי ישראל אלא מתעסקין בהם אם מצאום הרוגים עם ישראל.

The Ran quotes Rashi's limitation but differs from him only in that he extends Jewish involvement in non-Jewish burial to isolated instances and not only in the case of a common disaster, which seems to be a possible inference from Rashi. He says: ולישנא לאו דווקא דה"ה כשנמצאו מתי עובדי כוכבים לבד שמתעסקים בהם מפני דרכי שלום.

He substantiates his understanding of the halakhah on the fact that in the Yerushalmi, the parallel baraita appears without the word עם, as follows: וקוברין מתי גויים ומתי ישראל ומנחמין אבילי גויים ואבילי ישראל ומכבסין כלי גויים וכלי ישראל מפני דרכי שלום (ירושלמי גטין פרק ה' ה"ט). The Ran further bases the rational for not burying Jews and non-Jews together on the principle that: אין קוברין רשע אצל צדיק (סנה' מז,א').

Maimonides refers to this halakhah in two places. In הלכות מלכים פ"י סעי' י"ב he states:

וזהו שאמרו חכמים אין כופלין להן שלום בעכו"ם ולא בגר תושב. אפילו העכו"ם צוו חכמים לבקר חוליהם ולקבור מתיהם עם מתי ישראל ולפרנס ענייהם בכלל עניי ישראל מפני דרכי שלום הרי נאמר טוב ה' לכל ורחמיו על כל מעשיו ונאמר דרכיה דרכי נועם וכל נתיבותיה שלום.

Lest you be misled to believe that non-Jews and Jews may be buried together by the words עם מתי ישראל, parallel to בכלל עניי ישראל, the Kesef Mishnah is quick to cite Rashi and the Ran, making sure to point out: ומ"מ לא שיהו קוברים אותם... אצל ישראל... אין קוברין רשע אצל צדיק.

In הלכות אבל פי"ד סעיף י"ב, Maimonides merely states קוברין מתי עכו"ם... מפני דרכי שלום. The Radbaz cites the baraita in Gittin, adding: והא דקתני עם מתי ישראל לאו דוקא אלא שמתעסקין עמהם דהא אין קוברין אותם בקברי ישראל וזהו שהשמיט רבינו מלת עם.

The Meiri, explicating the Mishnah which begins at the bottom of Gittin 59a, incorporates the baraita quoted later in the Gemara, adding: ולא לקברם בבית הקברות של ישראל אלא שאם מצאו ישראלים וגויים מתים משתדלים בקבורתם כדרך שמשתדלים במיתי ישראל.

When the Tur (Yoreh De'ah 367) expressly codifies Rashi's limitation, even citing Rashi explicitly, the Bet Yosef, in commenting on it, adds the statement of the Ran in its entirety. However, when Yosef Karo codified the Shulhan Arukh, he did not include this limitation, saying only: קוברים מתי עכו"ם ומנחמים אביליהם מפני דרכי שלום. By leaving out any reference to עם מתי ישראל or עם אבלי ישראל, the codified halakhah has thus incorporated both Rashi and the Ran.

It is therefore abundantly clear that non-Jews are not to be buried together with Jews. This was so obvious that R. Shlomo Kluger, in שו"ת טוב טעם ודעת סי' רנ"ג, becomes incensed that someone would even address a question to him that implies that he might permit having a Jewish cemetery abut a non-Jewish cemetery without a solid מחיצה. He says:

ע"ד שאלתו אם מותר לערב בית הקברות של ישראל לבית קברות של עכו"ם דהיינו שדופן אחד מן בית הקברות ישראל יהי פרוצה לקברות עכו"ם הנה כועס אני עליו על שאלתו זו כי בודאי עלה על דעתו שאולי אני אהי' המתיר בזה וחשדני בכך ואם הי' יודע בדעתו דבודאי לא אתיר לא היה שואל ממני וגם מה שעלה בלבו ספק כלל בזה אני כועס עליו ולא רציתי להשיב לו כלל: רק מיודעי אמרו לי כי אם לא אשיב כלל אולי יאמר מדשתק אודי אודי לכך נחמתי להשיבו.

He then cites Rashi's comment on the baraita in Gittin and the principle that אין קוברין
רשע אצל צדיק to והבדילה הפרכת לכם בין הקדש ובין קדש הקדשים – He quotes Exod. 26:33. to
show that there must be a physical separation between places of different degrees of sanctity. *A fortiori* there must be a physical separation between הקודש ובין הטומאה אשר מעמידין
על קבריהם צלמים. After further Biblical expositions from Abraham and Ruth, he analogizes
from הלכות עירובין wherein, if there is a breach in the wall of the abutting מקום האסור, then
it is forbidden to carry there, which shows that without a solid barrier:

> נחשב האויר מעורב יחד כן ה"נ מכ"ש דאסור להיות אויר קברות ישראל
> ואויר קברות עכו"ם מעורבין יחד בלי הפסק מחיצה ממש לכך. ח"ו
> להיות כן.

Despite his previous annoyance, he nevertheless signs דברי ידידו.

While it is clear that לכתחילה one must create a physical separation between a Jewish
graveyard and a non-Jewish graveyard, our questioner is asking if the interment of some
non-Jews in the Jewish section invalidates the section for Jewish burial.

R. Moshe Feinstein (*Iggrot Moshe* Yoreh De'ah, vol. 1, siman 160) responds to this
question in a different context. The question addressed to him revolves around the fact
that in the Jewish cemetery in Canton, Ohio there are buried converts who were converted by a Conservative rabbi.

After indicating that there might be some grounds for considering the fact that the
convert did not observe Shabbat and other mitzvot as not necessarily vitiating the conversion, he nevertheless declares it is invalid *ab initio* merely on the basis that it was done by
a Conservative rabbi.

> אבל עכ"פ צריכה לקבל המצות בפני ב"ד, והרבאייס הקאנסערוואטיווע
> מסתמא אין עושין כן דהא אין יודעין דיני גרות. וגם אינם זהירין לקיים
> כדין אף אם היו יודעין וממילא חסר קבלת מצות אף הקבלה הגרועה
> שזה ודאי הוא עיכוב בגרות. וגם הא ב"ד של הקאנסערוואיוון הם
> פסולים לב"ד דהם כופרין בהרבה עיקרי הדת ועוברין על כמה לאוין...
> וגם הוא כודאי שעוברין על כמה איסורין דאורייתא ואף שלא נתקבל
> עדות עלייהו הוא כאנן סהדי שכל מי ששם הבזוי קאנסערוואטיוו עליו
> הוא בחזקת מופקר להרבה איסורין ולכפירה בהרבה עיקרים... ולכן פשוט
> שאין הגרו שעשה הרביי של הקאנסערוואטיוון כלום.

While we would certainly take issue with Rabbi Feinstein's characterization of Conservative
rabbis and of conversions done under Conservative auspices, nevertheless for him the conversion was a nullity and therefore the convert is, for him, still a non-Jew.

Nevertheless, he responds to the question:

> אם מחוייב כתר"ה לצאת במחלוקה גדולה... אני אומר שכיון שמה שאין
> קוברין מתי עכו"ם בקברות של ישראל כדאיתא ברש"י גטין דף ס"א הוא
> מטעם דאין קוברין רשע אצל צדיק כדמפרש שם בר"ן עיי"ש והובא בב"י
> סי' שס"ז ביו"ד עיי"ש לכן החיוב על כתר"ה רק להזהיר את שומרי תורה
> שיצוו שלא יקברום סמוך לגרים כאלו.

Thus, even Rabbi Feinstein does not consider the burial of these converts (who in his
estimation are גויים גמורים) as preventing observant Orthodox Jews from being buried in
the same cemetery.

This is not a case of first impression for the CJLS, although it is difficult to ascertain
with certainty that there is a definitive ruling. In a summary of the decisions of the CJLS
on Mourning and Funerals, one finds, *inter alia*, the following statements:

A. A non-Jew married by a rabbi without conversion may not be buried in a Jewish cemetery (H235).

B. If non-Jewish spouse had attended services and considered themselves (sic) part of the Jewish people, and raised their children as Jews, then they may be buried in a Jewish cemetery. The space of one grave must be left on either side of the non-Jewish grave (K559, W75). (My comment: Must an empty space also be left at head and foot of the interment space?)

C. Non-Jewish wives and children cannot be buried in a Jewish cemetery, although in cases of need certain specific arrangements can be made to have them buried in a Jewish cemetery (N75). (My comment: This is egregiously ambiguous. [A] What about non-Jewish husbands? [B] What could constitute need? [C] What specific arrangements?)

D. A non-Jewish wife may be buried in a Jewish cemetery in the following manner: Her grave is to be partitioned from the Jewish graves by shrubbery or railing or a groove ten טפחים high or deep, or by the space of one empty grave or each side (N287, W75). (My comment: Again the gender distinction exists. Must partition by barrier or empty grave be at both head and foot?)

E. The synagogue constitution, as well as the literature describing cemetery plots, should state clearly that a non-Jewish spouse cannot be buried there (U448). (My comment: This seemingly negates the previous statements allowing burial with empty space on each side.)

F. Some ground contiguous to the cemetery can be set aside for burial of non-Jews who do not object to being buried in such a section of the cemetery (U448). (My comment: The decedent is in no position to voice objection or acceptance. Also, "can be set aside" and "do not object" leaves open the interpretation that if objection is voiced, then they may be buried in the cemetery proper. Is this a correct inference?)

G. It is not advisable to have a non-Jewish spouse buried in a separate section (W6). (My comments: If it were not an oxymoron, one would have to say that this, together with F. above, is clearly ambiguous.)

The confusion rampant in the above only illustrates the difficulty of dealing with the realities of the situation. The reality is that it is inevitable that some non-Jews will be buried in the Jewish section under the mistaken assumption that they are Jewish, or through deception. The reality is that this occurs even in Jewish cemeteries not connected to non-Jewish cemeteries and owned and operated by Jews.

Mt. Sinai Memorial Park referred to above, subsequent to the community furor, was sold to Sinai Temple, a prominent Conservative congregation. Their contract specifically permits burial of non-Jewish spouses. Operators of other Jewish cemeteries in the Los Angeles area who do not make such a specific provision nevertheless maintain, quite correctly, that they are not in a position to be בודק צציות, nor are they the ones to determine who is or who is not Jewish. Their position is that if a rabbi will officiate, they must assume that a Jewish burial is taking place.

It should be pointed out that the problem will not be restricted to non-Jewish spouses. With the adoption of patrilineal descent by the Reform movement, children will also be buried who are halakhically non-Jewish. As time goes on, this will become even more prevalent, as today's "patrilineally Jewish" children become "patrilineally Jewish" adults. There is, therefore, no way to prevent burial of non-Jews in this Jewish cemetery.

There is, of course, one option available to our questioner that affords the maximum assurance that his congregation will not be buried in proximity to the non-Jewish spouses or children of Reform congregants. If the congregation is able to purchase a substantial number of contiguous plots in the cemetery — i.e. an entirely distinct section for the exclusive use of the congregation — the gravesites on the perimeter of the section could be sacrificed and left empty in accordance with CJLS suggestion B. above. (To prevent the empty graves from inadvertently being used, caution would dictate that those gravesites be covered with a hedge or other type of מחיצה. Indeed, I am unaware of the halakhic basis for considering a mere empty grave, without a tangible separation of appropriate size, as constituting a proper מחיצה. In that way, the congregation could control the burials within that section, restricting interment there to Jews who were born of Jewish mother or were converted to Judaism.

However, I would hazard a guess that despite all such precautions, in the course of time, some non-Jewish spouses or children of Jewish fathers only will be interred there. This will occur as a result of ignorance, deception, or negligence. But even if this option were assumed to be fail-safe, I would argue against its necessity and/or its advisability.

The creation of such a distinctly separated section makes a statement about the remainder of the cemetery. If only that section is considered halakhically proper, then, by implication, the rest of the cemetery is פסול. This is then מוציא לעז on the Jews buried there. Furthermore, let us hypothesize the following scenario: The rabbi of this congregation has a member who is married to a non-Jew. Since the non-Jewish spouse cannot be interred in the congregational section, the family purchases plots in the undifferentiated part of the Jewish cemetery because the spouses want to be buried side by side. When the Jewish spouse dies, will the rabbi refuse to officiate at the interment? The questioner's own logic would seem to militate against his participation. In his inquiry to the CJLS he expressed his problem as, "I don't see how this can be considered a Jewish cemetery." Yet can he, both from an ethical and practical standpoint, refuse to officiate? The creation of the distinctly separated section, by virtue of its reflection on the Jewish cemetery of which it is a part, may be counter-productive both for the rabbi and for the congregation.

One can also argue against the necessity from a halakhic standpoint. In the question, there is, as we have noted, the implicit presumption that the interment of some non-Jews, even with Jewish rites, vitiates the Jewish character of the cemetery. But nothing in the sources we have cited indicate this. While it is true that the Jewish section must be separated by a physical barrier from the non-Jewish section, as far as individual graves are concerned, even Rabbi Moshe Feinstein would only caution that שומרי תורה not be buried in adjacent proximity to the non-Jew. But even he does not declare the entire cemetery פסול. If R. Shlomo Kluger can analogize from הלכות עירובין, I can analogize from הלכות מקוואות. As long as there is the requisite amount of מים חיים, the addition of some מים שאובים does not render the מקוה unfit. Similarly, since the vast majority of interments is of halakhically defined Jews, the addition of some non-Jewish bodies does not make the cemetery פסול.

But over and above these arguments, I am motivated by an ethical consideration. As R. Moses Feinstein has indicated in his תשובה (following the Ran), the reason why non-Jews are not to be buried together with Jews is because אין קוברין רשע אצל צדיק. This rationale is presumptively characterizing all non-Jews as רשעים. Whatever may have been the justification for such a presumption in times past, I find such a presumption today ethically offensive. This is particularly so, since the statement in its original context (Sanhedrin 47a) is used to explain why הרוגי ב"ד were buried separately. In other words, in the original context the רשע is an executed criminal. Furthermore, the tradition in saying (חסידי אומות העולם יש להם חלק לעולם הבא (תוספתא סנהדרין פי"ג) recognizes that not all non-Jews are רשעים. Certainly this non-Jewish spouse, who may have contributed service to the synagogue, provided the children with a Jewish education and is not being buried with Christian burial rites or sacraments, should not be presumptively characterized as a רשע.

Conclusion

(A) Although the decedent possesses only a right of interment, and does not own the gravesite, it is still to be considered קבר שלו/ה and we need not be concerned that נמצא צדיק קבור בקבר שאינו שלו.

(B) The agreement with the non-Jewish cemetery operators must vest the Jewish community and its designated representatives with absolute control over the religious administration of the Jewish section. No religious rites other than Jewish may be conducted there, nor may any clergy other than rabbinical be allowed to officiate. The cemetery owners must contractually warranty that the Jewish section will remain an exclusively Jewish cemetery in perpetuity and never revert to Christian or non-denominational status.

(C) While a congregation may, for a variety of reasons, seek to have its own section in the cemetery, it need not establish a barrier separating the section from the rest of the Jewish cemetery. Clearly, the congregation may, in its own wisdom, establish rules of eligibility for interment in the congregational section. Nevertheless, it should not do anything which by inference casts aspersion on the Jewish character of the total Jewish section. The interment of non-Jewish spouses and children by Reform rabbis does not vitiate the Jewish character of the cemetery or its sanctity.

YD 367:1.1994

Peaceful Paths: Burial of Non-Jews in a Jewish Cemetery Following a Common Disaster

Rabbi Myron S. Geller

This paper was approved by the CJLS on October 5, 1994, by a vote of twenty-three in favor (23-0-0). Voting in favor: Rabbis Kassel Abelson, Ben Zion Bergman, Stanley Bramnick, Elliot N. Dorff, Jerome M. Epstein, Samuel Fraint, Myron S. Geller, Arnold M. Goodman, Susan Grossman, Jan Caryl Kaufman, Judah Kogen, Vernon H. Kurtz, Alan B. Lucas, Lionel E. Moses, Paul Plotkin, Mayer Rabinowitz, Avram Israel Reisner, Joel E. Rembaum, Chaim A. Rogoff, Joel Roth, Israel Silverman, Gordon Tucker, and Gerald Zelizer.

The Committee on Jewish Law and Standards of the Rabbinical Assembly provides guidance in matters of halakhah for the Conservative movement. The individual rabbi, however, is the authority for the interpretation and application of all matters of halakhah.

שאלה

The terrorist attack on the Jewish community headquarters building in Buenos Aires, Argentina on Monday, July 25, 1994, killed a large number of Jews and Christians. There are body parts and limbs which are so mangled they cannot be identified for burial. May these limbs and body parts, which could be from both Jews and Christians, be buried together in a mass grave in a Jewish cemetery? Must such burial be restricted to a special section? How shall the gravesite be marked?

תשובה

This responsum will review certain halakhic requirements for a Jewish burial site, the traditional ban on burial together of Jews and non-Jews and special circumstances in which such burial may be permitted.

Requirements for a Jewish Burial Site

Among the traditional requirements for Jewish burial, three which relate to the burial site are:

1. קבר שלו – The plot used for burial should be owned by the deceased. The Talmud quotes Josh. 24:33 about the death of Elazar ben Aharon and his interment at a site owned by his son Pinhas. The Gemara is concerned about the basis of Pinhas' title to the property. Abaye rejects R. Papa's suggestion that Pinhas might have purchased it.

Such title, terminating at the Jubilee year, would leave צדיק קבור בקבר שאינו שלו, a saint buried in a plot which he does not own.[1]

The Talmud understood that a צדיק required קבר שלו, ownership of his burial plot; later authorities extended this mandate to all Jews. "Although Baba Batra 111b states that a צדיק should not be buried in a plot which he does not own, this is not specific to a צדיק, rather every individual must be buried in a plot which he owns!"[2] Rabbi Isaac Elchanan Spector supplies the rationale for the extension in that each Jew enjoys a presumption of sainthood to whom the קבר שלו requirement applies.[3] Thus every Jew must be buried in a plot owned in perpetuity by the deceased.

2. קרקע ישראל – The cemetery in which the individual gravesite is located must be designated exclusively for Jews. "Our rabbis placed a great responsibility on the Jewish community that they have cemeteries designated for their exclusive use and that the land be theirs."[4] Although Jewish ownership of the cemetery is preferred, it is not an absolute requirement of halakhah. קרקע ישראל is not a mandate about title but of exclusive application of "Jewish legal rules and sensitivities," control over the rites to be conducted there and the perpetuity of the designation of the cemetery as Jewish.[5]

3. אין קוברין רשע אצל צדיק – A sinner should not be buried with or near a saint. The Mishnah reports that two cemeteries were maintained for הרוגי בית דין, criminals executed by order of the courts. One was used for the burial of criminals who had been decapitated or strangled, forms of execution which, because they were considered swift and less painful, were imposed for lesser capital offenses. A second cemetery was reserved for those whose violations were so heinous that they were executed by the harsher methods of stoning or burning. In the Mishnah under discussion, the severity of the infraction and subsequent punishment determine in whose proximity violators could be laid to rest. The Gemara explains that a hierarchy of virtue or of sin is applied in determining where people may be buried in a Jewish cemetery.[6]

A Biblical prooftext is provided by R. Aha bar Hanina. He cites 2 Kings 13:21 about the deceased Elisha who resurrected a false prophet rather than allow the sinner to be interred with him. It is noteworthy that Elisha did not use his powers to forestall an attempt to bury the sinner near him. Only when, at the approach of an armed enemy band, the sinner's bones were hastily dumped in Elisha's grave thereby touching those of the saint, did the revival of the sinner occur. Nevertheless, the Rabbis established a principle barring proximate as well as contact burial of sinners and saints.

Burial of Non-Jews with Jews

Later sources, by inference from a minor to a major premise, applied the אין קוברין principle to the burial of non-Jews near Jews, forbidding it in a Jewish cemetery. Thus, in regard to burial in קרקע ישראל, all Jews are presumed to be saints, even executed criminals; all non-Jews, sinners, thereby excluded from burial there.[7]

Although the baraita which states, "Non-Jewish dead may be interred with Jewish dead, מפני דרכי שלום so that we follow peaceful paths," would seem to permit for civil-

---

[1] B. Bava Batra 111b.
[2] Yekutiel Greenwald, *Kol Bo Al Aveylut*, p. 174.
[3] Ein Ytzhak, no. 34.
[4] Greenwald, op. cit., p. 162.
[5] Rabbi Ben Zion Bergman, "A Matter of Grave Concern: A Question of Mixed Burial," above, pp. 418-425.
[6] B. Sanhedrin 47a.
[7] Kesef Mishneh, Hilkhot Melakhim 10:12; S.A. Yoreh De'ah, 367:1.

ity's sake, the burial of non-Jews with Jews in all circumstances, Rashi and others limit its application to a common disaster when non-Jews and Jews are found dead alongside each other.[8] Rashi understands the baraita to refer to a situation in which the identification of the faith group of each of the cadavers is possible and the Rabbis are concerned about the unseemliness of Jews carrying away their own dead for burial while abandoning non-Jewish dead. Only in these circumstances and מפני דרכי שלום, does Rashi acknowledge a Jewish obligation to non-Jewish dead. It is restricted to burial alone, but interment in a Jewish cemetery is not permitted. However, if non-Jewish dead are found without Jewish dead nearby, no obligation falls on Jews to undertake their burial.

Ran reads the baraita text עם מתי ישראל to mean "Non-Jewish dead are buried as are Jewish dead, מפני דרכי שלום." He enlarges the circumstances in which Jews are obligated for the burial of non-Jews to any case when their remains are found, even if no Jewish dead are nearby. He does not, however, question the essential point in Rashi's interpretation of the baraita, that non-Jews may not be buried in Jewish ground and he applies the rationale אין קוברין רשע אצל צדיק.[9]

Even adjacent location of non-Jewish burial ground and קרקע ישראל is restricted in our sources. This view is expressed most forcefully by Rabbi Shlomo Kluger who requires a physical partition between such cemeteries. He cites the use of the פרוכת which separated the קודש from the קודש קדושים, the Holy from the Holy of Holies, to define spaces in the ancient Temple which had different degrees of sanctity. How much more so, he argues, must a physical barrier divide between the sacredness of the Jewish cemetery and the impurity of the Christian.[10] He is particularly exercised about crucifixes in Christian cemeteries which, if no separation and barrier were in place between the two burial grounds, would stand close to the interment site of Jews. Just as crucifixes are barred unequivocally from קרקע ישראל, so too must their shadow be removed from Jewish burial sites by physical separation and partition. Ideally, a space of eight cubits should be left, but if necessary a space of four cubits plus the requisite partition, four cubits in height, may suffice.[11]

Special Circumstances

Despite halakhic imperatives about the exclusivity of Jewish burial ground, circumstances exist which occasionally permit the burial of non-Jews in קרקע ישראל. Thus, the BaH permits Jews and non-Jews found slain together to be buried together in קרקע ישראל and such burial does not render the cemetery unacceptable for further Jewish use. Commenting on permission granted by the baraita cited above to bury non-Jewish dead מפני דרכי שלום, he writes:

> This permission for the burial of non-Jews comes to teach us that in circumstances when they are found slain together with Jews, their dead may be interred בקברי ישראל, in Jewish burial ground. Although there is no doubt that non-Jews may not be buried near Jews since even a Jewish sinner may not be buried

---

[8] B. Gittin 61a.
[9] Ran, Gittin, loc. cit.
[10] Shlomo Kluger, *Tuv Taam Vadaat*, 3:250.
[11] Greenwald, op. cit., p. 163.

near a Jewish saint, nevertheless, non-Jewish dead and Jewish dead may be buried in a single location, מדרכי שלום, when they are found together.[12]

In a more recent though similar case, Rabbi Shlomo Goren reports his perplexity when, following Israel's War of Independence, a large pile of bones assumed to be a mixture of Jewish and non-Jewish remains, the latter in the majority, was found in an area which had formerly been behind enemy lines. Rabbi Goren cites the BaH, but wonders if the BaH would permit burial in קרקע ישראל if the non-Jews involved were "enemies of Israel who fell in their war against us." Rabbi Goren seems to suggest that it is the character and behavior of non-Jews which should determine whether they may be buried, in these special circumstances, in a Jewish cemetery.[13]

Anguished at the prospect of leaving Jewish remains outside a Jewish cemetery, Rabbi Goren turned to the Hazon Ish to resolve his dilemma. The Hazon Ish specifically permitted the burial of all the remains in קרקע ישראל. "This is not a matter of אין קוברין רשע אצל צדיק because we perceive these non-Jewish bones as if they were stones." In this instance, where enemies of Israel were involved, the Hazon Ish did not refer to the דרכי שלום rationale of the baraita. Instead, he introduces a new principle, dehumanizing the non-Jewish remains, treating them as stones and permitting their burial in קרקע ישראל. Based on this ruling, Rabbi Goren had a separate section in the Haifa military cemetery opened where the remains of enemies of the State of Israel and its Jewish defenders were buried together. Rabbi Goren's decision was more stringent than that of the BaH or the Hazon Ish who, under these or similar circumstances, did not require a separate section in a Jewish cemetery for interment together of Jewish and non-Jewish remains to be permitted.

Summary

According to the BaH, non-Jews found slain together with Jews, may be buried in a Jewish cemetery מפני דרכי שלום. In the case under consideration, this would certainly apply to almost all of the non-Jewish body parts and limbs that are available for burial. If remains of the terrorist who caused the tragic loss of life are also present, Rabbi Goren's reservations about burying enemies of the Jewish people together with Jews in a Jewish cemetery may apply here. We may rely upon the precedent established by the Hazon Ish to dehumanize remains of enemies of Israel and view them as nothing more then stones. In our case, common burial for remains of Jews and non-Jews which may include those of the terrorist is permitted in a mass grave.

Since body parts and limbs are not identifiable in our case, the קבר שלו requirement cannot be applied. Halakhic precedent permitting the burial of non-Jews in a Jewish cemetery, under certain circumstances, indicates that doing so does not violate קרקע ישראל and will not bar Jewish burial in adjacent plots in the future. Such burial does not necessitate barriers as might be required between a Jewish and a non-Jewish cemetery. Rabbi Kluger's concern about Jews being buried in the shadow of crucifixes does not apply in a Jewish cemetery where symbols of other faith groups are always to be banned.

It has been noted that non-Jews are identified by tradition, at least in reference to interment in קרקע ישראל, as רשעים. This is the basis for refusing them burial in our

---

[12] Tur, Yoreh De'ah, 151.

[13] Shlomo Goren, Maishiv Milhama, v. 3, p. 407.

cemeteries. When the Hazon Ish introduces a new concept, dehumanizing non-Jewish remains and characterizing them as stones in order to allow their burial in a Jewish cemetery, he refers only to the remains of enemies of Israel in the specific circumstances under discussion and this designation cannot be applied to other non-Jews. However, Rabbi Bergman has already rejected the characterization of all non-Jews as רשעים as ethically offensive in our day. "This is particularly offensive since the statement אין קוברין רשע אצל צדיק in its original context is used to explain why הרוגי בית דין were buried separately. In other words, in the original context the רשע is an executed criminal. Furthermore, the tradition in saying 'The righteous of all nations share in the world to come' recognizes that not all non-Jews are רשעים."[14]

Conclusion

The burial of Jews and non-Jews or their body parts or limbs found together following a common disaster is permitted in a Jewish cemetery. Even when remains of an enemy of Israel may be present, such burial is permitted. Ample precedent exists in ancient and modern sources to allow this course of action. Such burial does not desecrate the final resting place of Jews already interred there and does not prohibit future Jewish burials.

Furthermore, no special section is required for burial. However, the gravesite should be identified as the final resting place of the remains of Jews and non-Jews and a monument should be placed as a memorial to the tragic events which brought them to a common grave.

---

[14] Bergman, above, pp. 424-425, condensed.

YD 374:5.1998

Converts Mourning the Death of Close Relatives

Rabbi Joel E. Rembaum

This paper was approved by the CJLS on June 10, 1998, by a vote of eleven in favor, five opposed, and one abstaining (11-5-1). Voting in favor: Rabbis Kassel Abelson, Ben Zion Bergman, Elliot N. Dorff, Shoshana Gelfand, Arnold M. Goodman, Judah Kogen, Aaron L. Mackler, Mayer Rabinowitz, Joel E. Rembaum, James S. Rosen, and Gerald Zelizer. Voting against: Rabbis Baruch Frydman-Kohl, Lionel E. Moses, Paul Plotkin, Avram Israel Reisner, and Joel Roth. Abstaining: Rabbi Alan B. Lucas.

The Committee on Jewish Law and Standards of the Rabbinical Assembly provides guidance in matters of halakhah for the Conservative movement. The individual rabbi, however, is the authority for the interpretation and application of all matters of halakhah.

שאלה

How should converts to Judaism mourn the death of close relatives who are not Jewish?[1]

תשובה

In recent years Jewish communities have welcomed into their midst ever increasing numbers of גרים, converts to Judaism. Given the demographic trends of American Jewry, there is every reason to assume that this process will continue for the foreseeable future.

Among the halakhic issues that arise as a result of the heightened rate of conversion to Judaism are questions that touch on the relationship between a Jew-by-choice and his or her natural, non-Jewish family. In earlier centuries this matter was at best marginal. The Jewish community was separated physically, emotionally and spiritually from the non-Jewish world. From the third century C.E., conversion to Judaism was an insignificant phenomenon, and when such a conversion did take place a radical separation between the גר, convert to Judaism, and his or her natural family ensued. In many instances in pre-modern times גרים had to flee their original areas of settlement for fear of retribution on the part of the local non-Jewish religious authorities.[2]

---

[1] Many thanks to Rabbi David Golinkin for his source references and, especially, for calling my attention to the paper by Rabbi Etan Shikli, cited in n. 3, below.

[2] See *Encyclopaedia Judaica* (Jerusalem: Keter, 1972), 13:1187-1191.

Relations Between גרים and Their Non-Jewish Relatives

As uncommon as they were, relationships between גרים and their non-Jewish families have been discussed in the halakhic sources for many centuries.[3] From one halakhic point of view גרים ought not to have any legal ties or obligations to their non-Jewish parents because, according to Talmudic tradition, גר שנתגייר כקטן שנולד דמי, "a proselyte who converted is like a new-born infant."[4] This means it is as if גרים are created anew upon conversion, and all links to their natural parents have been severed. The Talmud's discussions in which the principle of גר שנתגייר, a proselyte who converted, is cited revolve around the following questions: May a גר marry close non-Jewish relatives without violating the prohibition against incest? May גרים testify in cases involving their non-Jewish relatives? Does a גר fulfill the obligation of "be fruitful and multiply" through children born to him prior to his conversion? With respect to the laws of primogeniture, does the first Jewish son born to a גר after conversion displace a true first-born son born to the גר prior to conversion? May freed and converted slaves who are brothers marry each other's wives from prior to their conversion?

As Rabbi Etan Shikli has noted,[5] the strong tendency in these cases is to set aside the principle of גר שנתגייר in the face of mitigating circumstances which demand other ethical or rational considerations. Thus, for example, regarding the possibility of permitting what otherwise would be considered incestuous relations between גרים and their non-Jewish relatives, Rav Nahman rules against permitting such relations, שלא יאמרו באין מקדושה חמורה לקדושה קלה, "that it should not be said of the proselytes that they come from a higher degree of sanctity to a lesser degree of sanctity." That is, it should not be said that as non-Jews they would have been forbidden to engage in such unions, while as Jews they would have been permitted.[6]

In the matters of procreation and primogeniture, Resh Lakish applies the principle of גר שנתגייר and concludes that a גר with children from before conversion has not fulfilled the commandment to procreate and the first son born to a גר after conversion can inherit. Rabbi Yohanan disagrees, arguing, דהא הוו [הוה] ליה, "indeed, he had them (him)," meaning that the existential reality is that the גר did have children and does have a first-born son.[7] The law is according to Rabbi Yohanan.[8]

In yet another Talmudic discussion[9] the sages allow a גר to inherit from his non-Jewish father, שמא יחזור לסורו, "lest he return to his waywardness [pagan practices]." The notion of גר שנתגייר is not even raised in this case, and a rational explanation is given to allow the relationship between the גר and his natural father to remain intact.[10]

In sum, it is clear that in certain cases the Rabbis were able to set aside the principle

---

[3] For a review of various halakhic opinions on the matter of the relationship between a convert to Judaism and his or her non-Jewish family see the unpublished paper by Rabbi Etan Shikli in response to the question: "From the perspective of halakhah may a devout Jewish woman ask her husband-to-be who is a convert to Judaism to sever all ties with his gentile family, or is he still obliged to honor his parents and is this obligation contrary to halakhah?" (Hebrew), submitted to Rabbi David Golinkin in Jerusalem, 1 Adar, 5751.

[4] B. Yevamot 22a, 48b, 62a, 97b; Bekhorot 47a.

[5] Shikli, pp. 5-10.

[6] B. Yevamot 22a.

[7] B. Yevamot 62a.

[8] S.A. Even HaEzer, 1:7; Hoshen Mishpat, 277:9.

[9] B. Kiddushin 17b.

[10] Shikli, p. 9.

of גר שנתגייר and look upon the relationships of גרים with non-Jewish family members as if they still were intact.[11]

Similarly, it can be demonstrated that, while a גר is not obligated to fulfill the commandment to honor parents, the overwhelming majority of halakhic authorities who deal with this issue expect גרים to show respect for their non-Jewish parents and desist from demeaning them. Such acts of respect would include visiting them when they are ill. According to certain authorities the reason for this is הכרת טובה, "recognition of goodness" the parents generated for their children.[12] Others simply recognize that common sense dictates that respect be shown by גרים to their non-Jewish parents.[13] Again, the גר-parent relationship is viewed as continuing to be viable.

גרים and Mourning Non-Jewish Relatives

The foregoing analysis serves as a foundation for the primary question to which this paper responds: How should גרים mourn the death of close relatives who are not Jewish? Halakhic opinions on גרים mourning the death of their non-Jewish parents have evolved over time. The Talmud does not address the issue. Based on a Talmudic discussion in B. Yevamot 97b regarding חליצה, removing the sandal, and יבום, levirate marriage, in a case of a woman who converted along with her two sons, the Shulhan Arukh decrees: הגר שנתגייר הוא ובניו... אין מתאבלין זה על זה, "when one converts along with his children...they do not mourn for each other."[14] As the Encyclopedia Talmudit[15] indicates, the reason is גר שנתגייר. From this one can conclude *a fortiori* that a גר should not mourn for a non-Jewish parent. Rabbi Moses Isserles, however, concludes in a subsequent discussion[16] regarding mourners: מי שרוצה להחמיר על עצמו להתאבל על מי שאינו צריך... אין מוחין בידו, "should a person be stringent upon himself and mourn someone whom he is not obligated to mourn...we do not deter him."[17] Were we to follow this approach we would urge the גר not to follow the traditional Jewish mourning procedures, but we might approve of such procedures if the גר were adamant and insisted upon following them.

Approaching the matter from a different perspective, other authorities have been more accepting of a גר grieving for a non-Jewish parent in a traditional Jewish way. Rabbi Aharon Walkin determined that lest גרים say: באנו מקדושה חמורה לקדושה קלה, "we have come from a higher degree of sanctity to a lower degree of sanctity," they are obliged to honor their parents, and, lest they be viewed as demeaning their parents after their death, it may be that they are obligated to say kaddish.[18] As Rabbi Jack Simcha Cohen has noted, Rabbi Walkin also discusses reasons why a גר should not recite kaddish: it is a uniquely Jewish

---

[11] See also David Novak, *Law and Theology in Judaism* (New York: Ktav, 1974), pp. 75-76; *Encyclopedia Talmudit* (Jerusalem: Encyclopedia Talmudit, 1965), 6:259-260 (Hebrew).

[12] Shikli, pp. 10-14.

[13] Shikli, pp. 15-16.

[14] S.A. Yoreh De'ah, 374:5; and see Be'ur Ha-gr'a, ad loc., no. 6.

[15] 6:261.

[16] S.A. Yoreh De'ah, 374:6.

[17] See Hayyim Binyamin Goldberg, *P'nei Barukh – Aveilut Ba-halakhah* (Jerusalem: n. p., 1986), pp. 102, 105; also, *Encyclopedia Talmudit*, 6:261.

[18] Aharon Walkin, *Zekan Aharon, Mahadurah T'nina* (New York: Gilead, 1951), Yoreh De'ah, no. 87; and see n. 6 above.

expression of grief, to be said by Jews for Jews; also, it is intended to elevate the soul of the deceased out of pain to a higher level of bliss, and it can be asked if a non-Jewish soul warrants such a blessing. Rabbi Walkin raises the possibility that the recitation of Psalms by the גר on behalf of the non-Jewish parent would be more appropriate. Rabbi Cohen concludes that while Rabbi Walkin may not consider it mandatory, it is clear that he would hold that the גר definitely may recite kaddish on behalf of his non-Jewish parent.[19] Rabbi Ovadiah Yosef is of the same opinion and notes that it is appropriate to view the kaddish as elevating the soul of the deceased non-Jewish parent to a higher level of bliss.[20] Rabbi Isaac Klein has ruled in a similar fashion, noting that some authorities hold the גר to be obligated to say kaddish. He concludes: "Today, when the bonds of love for family are not severed, there certainly can be no objection."[21]

Rabbi Maurice Lamm has discussed the broader issue of גרים incorporating the full spectrum of Jewish mourning practices when grieving over the loss of non-Jewish parents. In evaluating Rabbi Lamm's opinion, one can see a change in emphasis in his more recent writing where he becomes more supportive of a גר observing the full bereavement ritual. In an earlier work, *The Jewish Way in Death and Mourning*, Rabbi Lamm notes that there is no obligation on גרים to mourn non-Jewish parents in the "prescribed Jewish manner." While גרים are expected to show respect for their parents, they are religiously removed from them. He holds that grief should be expressed in a "Jewish way." While allowing for the possibility that a גר may say kaddish, echoing Rabbi Walkin, he suggests that the recitation of a psalm or the study of a portion of Torah in honor of the non-Jewish parent would be preferable. "The decision to do either rests with the bereaved." In this book Rabbi Lamm believes that a distinction should be made between a Jew and a non-Jew. Likewise, shivah procedures preferably should not be observed fully, as with a Jewish parent. Some may conclude that the parent was indeed a Jew. "The converted Jew should not feel that his emotions of grief must be restrained because of the religious difference. It is only the religious observance which is at issue. Indeed, those mourners who are converts should be shown special kindness during this period."[22]

A decided shift in emphasis can be seen in these selections from Rabbi Lamm's more recent work, *Becoming a Jew*:

> It must be emphasized that the mourning practices should be Jewish observances and decidedly not those of the convert's former religion. Not only respect for parents is important, but also self-respect to express feelings in a way most appropriate to the mourner's life and philosophy. The convert may perform all those mourning observances as do born Jews for their parents. They may serve as pallbearers, bury the dead at their cemetery, fill in their graves, and observe the seven-day (*shivah*) and thirty-day (*sheloshim*) mourning periods. Some authorities, however, say that the full observance of *shivah* and *sheloshim* and the full twelve-month period of mourning is not appropriate.

---

[19] J. Simcha Cohen, *Timely Jewish Questions, Timeless Rabbinic Answers* (Northvale, New Jersey: Jason Aronson, 1991), pp. 5-8.

[20] Ovadiah Yosef, *Sefer Sh'eilot U-t'shuvot Yehaveh Da'at* (Jerusalem, 1983), no. 60, pp. 301-307.

[21] Isaac Klein, *Responsa and Halakhic Studies* (New York: Ktav, 1975), p. 122; *A Guide to Jewish Religious Practice* (New York: Jewish Theological Seminary, 1979), p. 448.

[22] Maurice Lamm, *The Jewish Way in Death and Mourning* (New York: Jonathan David, 1969), pp. 82-83.

As to the question of whether a Jewish mourner should recite the kaddish prayer for gentile parents, former Sephardic Chief Rabbi Ovadiah Yosef urges converts to do so. Whether, in fact, every other rabbi would rule in the same manner is questionable. But there is no doubt that, if the convert mourner wishes to recite the kaddish, he should be encouraged to do so....

However, understandably, the halakhah could not require the convert to respect his parents and formally practice mourning rites. Only the relationship could determine the obligation. Psychological insights available today incline us to encourage the convert to express his mourning. It is a way of living and growing through a situation which, if not handled well, might be postponed for half a lifetime and affect virtually every experience of separation that may occur in the future.[23]

As we have seen, even in earlier periods when relationships between גרים and their natural parents usually were severed, rabbinic authorities did set aside the principle of גר שנתגייר when warranted by special circumstances. Today, when the norm is for גרים to maintain ties to their non-Jewish parents, how much more so should this principle be set aside as we deal with the matter of how גרים are to mourn the loss of their non-Jewish relatives. Today, when a parent or close relative of a גר dies the pain of the grief often is unaffected by the fact that a conversion to Judaism has taken place. The child loves and respects the parent much as he or she did prior to the conversion. Rabbi Yohanan's notion, דהא הוו ליה, "indeed, he had them,"[24] applies here with regard to the existential reality of these feelings. As a consequence, the גר will need a method for managing his or her grief. Inasmuch as the גר is now a Jew, he or she ought to be directed to the full scope of the traditional Jewish way of grieving. To do less would be to deprive the גר of a powerful tool for coping with loss and might suggest that alternate forms of bereavement may be acceptable, including the mourning practices of the religion of the deceased. Hence, the concern שמא יחזור לסורו, "lest he return to his waywardness,"[25] would enter into the picture. All of this would confuse a person whose Jewish identity was still developing and would diminish the significance of Judaism as a meaningfully helpful tradition in the eyes of the גר and his or her Jewish family.

Regarding this last point, consider the words of a גר who lost her non-Jewish father while she was a rabbinical student:

> Now [the time of her father's death] was the time for the halakhah to do what my Episcopalian faith had not been able to do. But it's not there for you as a convert! I felt betrayed — it's all *reshut*, and that's no help. I had to create my own ritual. I wasn't *obligated* to mourn, so I couldn't ask people who didn't really want to do it, to help me. The community doesn't respond to your obligation because you don't have one. And you don't feel you have the right to ask for this on the basis of *reshut*. I didn't get much support from the rabbi of my Shul or from my classmates and faculty either. It was hard to find a minyan to say kaddish....This is the

---

[23] Maurice Lamm, *Becoming a Jew* (Middle Village, NY: Jonathan David, 1991), pp. 249-250.

[24] See n. 7 above.

[25] See n. 9 above.

time when you tend to revert to old motifs and rituals. I needed help in dealing with that. The rabbis and the community weren't aware of this problem, but it's a normal reaction for a mourner. People should expect it, and be aware of it. The community needs to help the convert especially work through this.[26]

At a moment of personal crisis of the magnitude of the death of a loved one, Judaism in the fullness of its capacity to afford comfort, structure and affirmation must be present in the life of a גר. We must keep in mind what Rabbi Isaac Klein has noted with respect to how Judaism manages death and bereavement. He reminds us that two considerations are paramount: יקרא דשכיבא, "the honor due the deceased," and יקרא דחיי, "the honor (concern) due the living," that is, the bereaved.[27] In approaching the needs of the grieving גר we must ensure that he or she is able to express יקרא דשכיבא in mourning the loss of his or her non-Jewish loved ones and is able to benefit from the Jewish expressions of דחיי יקרא generated by family, friends and community. For all these reasons גרים should be considered obligated to mourn their non-Jewish relatives in the same way that born Jews are.

A Case in Point

A member of my congregation who converted to Judaism twenty years ago recently ended her year of mourning for her Catholic father, with whom she remained very close. Upon his death she called me and asked: what do I do? I told her: you are a Jew; you have to mourn your father in the prescribed Jewish way. I was adamant. I did not offer her a choice. I told her that I would make sure that there was a minyan for shivah services at home and would ensure that all her needs as a mourner would be met. She took my counsel seriously. At the funeral, held in a Catholic cemetery, she saw to it that the casket was lowered and earth was placed on it. This was not offensive to her Catholic family, but it did deviate from the norm at Catholic funerals. She sat shivah, a service was held in her home each evening and she came to synagogue regularly throughout the year to recite kaddish. It was clear to her that as a Jew she had to manage her grief in a Jewish way. On the last morning of shivah, as we took the traditional walk, she thanked me for urging her to follow the tradition. She said that it had done its job; she felt comforted. Her Jewish identity was affirmed.

The fact that I strongly believe in the value of the traditional Jewish way of grieving and in the obligation of every Jew, born or converted, to follow this tradition gave me the moral strength to push her and myself to "go the full nine yards." She and I both felt the force of the חיוב, the obligation, as did the community. Were this an option for her, for me and for the community, I doubt if the results would have been the same.

Special Circumstances

There can be no question that situations will arise with regard to a גר mourning the loss of a non-Jewish relative that a born Jew would not encounter with the death of a Jewish relative. In such cases the rabbi of the גר, as מרא דאתרא, will have to evaluate the situation and rule accordingly. Adjustments in the traditional bereavement practices may have to be made, but always within the context of a mandatory structure of mourning. Jewish

---

[26] Quoted in Marion Shulevitz, "Straining the Seams: The Impact of Death and Mourning on Converts, Intermarried Couples and Their Children," *Conservative Judaism* 43 (summer 1991): 58-59.

[27] Isaac Klein, *A Guide to Jewish Religious Practice*, p. 270, citing B. Sanhedrin 46b.

tradition already has built in such adjustments. For example: if a person of modest means will suffer financial loss as a result of sitting shivah for the full seven day period, he or she may go to work on the third day.[28] In this case a pressing need is taken into consideration and a modification in what otherwise is an obligation (sitting shivah for the full seven days) is allowed. Likewise, during the year of formal bereavement following the death of a parent, a mourner may attend a wedding dinner as long as he or she has a responsibility at that dinner that requires his or her presence.[29] Similarly, the rabbi should evaluate the situation of the גר and allow for adjustments in the mourning rituals when necessary.

Here are some examples of the more common questions that can arise regarding special circumstances and some recommended adjustments in the traditional practices that rabbis can make:

(A) What does a גר do regarding preparation for and participation in a non-Jewish funeral? If there are other non-Jewish family members who are assuming responsibility for the funeral arrangements, the גר need not be involved. If appropriate, the גר can ask that the funeral not be delayed too long. The גר may attend the funeral and may give a eulogy or read an appropriate reading (a psalm, for example). The גר may not read any liturgy or text that is taken from the sacred literature of another faith ("The Lord's Prayer," for example) or that expresses the beliefs of another faith or answer "Amen" to any non-Jewish prayers. Similarly, he or she may not participate in a personal way in any non-Jewish ritual (taking communion, for example). If the גר is responsible for the disposition of the remains of a relative, he or she should see to it that the relative is buried in a manner that befits the relative's religious affiliation. The גר may serve as a casket bearer for his or her relative. As in the case study noted above, if the גר can get the family's approval to lower and bury the casket, this should be done. If the family feels strongly that this ought not to be done, however, the גר should not press the issue.

(B) How should a גר observe shivah if he or she is staying with non-Jewish relatives? The גר should return to his or her own home as soon as possible after the funeral to begin traditional shivah observance. If the גר feels obligated to stay with relatives for a period of time after the funeral (to be with a grieving parent, for example), he or she should stay at home and observe all the personal aspects of shivah (not bathing, not wearing leather shoes, not watching television, etc.). If there is a Jewish community nearby and if the family members are not offended, the גר should try to arrange for a minyan at the home. If this is not feasible, the גר should attend services at a synagogue so kaddish can be recited.

Summary

We have seen that the principle, גר שנתגייר כקטן שנולד דמי, was often set aside in Talmudic discussions of the relationship of גרים to their non-Jewish relatives. We have also seen that there are halakhic authorities who would consider the recitation of the kaddish appropriate or even mandatory for a גר who is mourning the death of a non-Jewish parent. Considering these points and Rabbi Maurice Lamm's most recent opinions regarding גרים mourning non-Jewish relatives, the answer to the question, "How should converts to Judaism mourn the death of close relatives who are not Jewish?" should be: Converts to Judaism are required to follow regular Jewish bereavement practices when mourning the death of non-Jewish parents and close relatives, just as born Jews would

---

[28] Klein, *Guide*, pp. 288-289.

[29] Lamm, *Death and Mourning*, p. 182.

for Jewish family members. To do less would be to deny גרים the full benefit of the structured Jewish mourning procedures and would leave converts with the sense that Judaism establishes a double standard in evaluating people's feelings of grief. To do less would encourage גרים to supplement their mourning rituals with customs derived from other religious traditions. Seeing גרים observing modified mourning rituals would reinforce the tendency in born Jews to do less than what is required in grieving over the death of Jewish relatives and the inclination in certain Jews to view גרים as being not fully Jewish. גרים are fully Jewish, and as Jews they should express and manage grief in a full, complete Jewish way, regardless of the religious beliefs of the deceased. In this way גרים will know that Judaism has provided them with the means of showing honor to loved ones and has provided them with the vehicle for finding comfort and reinforcement from community, friends, family and God.

Conclusion

Converts to Judaism are required to follow the prescribed traditional Jewish bereavement practices when mourning the death of non-Jewish parents and close relatives. Should special circumstances arise, a rabbi should be consulted so that appropriate adjustments of these practices can be made.

YD 374:8.1992a

Jewish Ritual Practice Following the Death of an Infant Who Lives Less Than Thirty-One Days

Rabbi Stephanie Dickstein

This paper was approved by the CJLS on June 3, 1992, by a vote of ten in favor, three opposed, and one abstention (10-3-1). Voting in favor: Rabbis Kassel Abelson, Ben Zion Bergman, Stanley Bramnick, Jerome M. Epstein, Samuel Fraint, Arnold M. Goodman, Jan Caryl Kaufman, Mayer Rabinowitz, Avram Israel Reisner, and Gordon Tucker. Voting against: Rabbis David M. Feldman, Howard Handler, and Reuven Kimelman. Abstaining: Rabbi Ezra Finkelstein.

The Committee on Jewish Law and Standards of the Rabbinical Assembly provides guidance in matters of halakhah for the Conservative movement. The individual rabbi, however, is the authority for the interpretation and application of all matters of halakhah.

שאלה

What are the mourning practices and rituals when an infant dies before the thirty-first day of life?

תשובה

The laws and customs relating to mourning developed over thousands of years, yet it often seems as if they had been carefully constructed to meet both the responsibilities of כבוד המת and the complex psychological needs of the mourners. There are specific rules which instruct us how to treat a human body which no longer houses the soul, how to honor the memory of the departed, and how to support the mourners though the various stages of grief, anger, loss and adjustment. Halakhah requires that the community be a part of כבוד המת and comforting the mourners.

One group of mourners has traditionally been denied the comfort of Jewish ritual mourning. These are the parents whose infant lived less than thirty-one days after birth, or whose child is stillborn. In *The Jewish Way in Death and Mourning*, one of the most widely used books on mourning for laypeople, Rabbi Maurice Lamm states the current custom: "A life duration of more than thirty days establishes a human being as a viable person. If a child dies before that time, he is considered not to have lived at all, and no mourning practices are observed, even though the child may have been normal, but was killed accidentally."[1] While

---

[1] Maurice Lamm, *The Jewish Way in Death and Mourning* (New York: Jonathan David Publishers, 1969), p. 83.

the practice described by Rabbi Lamm is not the only halakhic position accepted by the CJLS, nevertheless, it is widely considered by Conservative rabbis and laypeople to be the only halakhic position, and their practice is in accordance with this position (i.e., little or nothing is done).

The Death of an Infant Causes Grief

Our obligation to our community and to halakhah requires that we reevaluate this practice. In the past, infant death was much more common than it is today, although no less painful. In what seems to have been an attempt to be sensitive to the grieving parents, the custom which became accepted in our communities was not to require full mourning of the parents. This custom reflected the general attitude towards infant death. Even twenty years ago, it was common for doctors and others to underestimate the distress of parents whose newborn died. Today, it is no longer the accepted medical practice to ignore the death of an infant, whether it was born alive, or died in the womb. Hospitals have developed protocols to help families face the reality of their loss, and to enable them to mourn.[2] Parents are encouraged to see and touch their child. Pictures may be taken; mementos are preserved. Funerals are recommended, and the parents are encouraged to attend meetings of a support group. All of this is increasingly the established secular, medical procedure. Yet, when the parents approach their rabbi, perhaps to ask him or her to participate in the funeral, the rabbi may not be helpful. At best, he or she does not know what to do or say; at worst, he or she says, "There is no mourning for this נפל." Of course, Jewish tradition does not deny parents the right to grieve privately. However, the strength of Jewish mourning practice is the way in which it meet private grief with specific required rituals and communal involvement. Any death, especially that of an infant, is a theological crisis. Death is a time when religion and ritual can be most powerful, yet our current custom concerning infant death robs us of that power.

The Scope of This Teshuvah

This תשובה will begin by discussing some of the sources which support and contradict the current custom, as well as other sources on issues related to the discussion. It will then summarize the position of the CJLS on these issues. Finally, it will recommend and justify a halakhic position which is different from either custom, or the current position of the CJLS. The subject of this תשובה will be neo-natal death, the death of an infant born alive. However, it is important to note that stillbirth, the death of a potentially viable fetus in utero, is closely related in medical literature, and the parents' experience of that loss is often similar to neo-natal death. The consideration of a Jewish response to stillbirth will be the topic of a separate תשובה.

Past Precedents

Our present custom not to mourn a newborn (note: "mourning" here is used to mean the full range of rituals associated with death) is based on two major halakhic statements. The first is the Rambam in the Mishnah Torah Hilkhot Avel 1:6:

---

[2] Some examples of the material which is available are: "Bereaved Parents Information Packet" from the Childbirth and Parent Education Association of Madison (1978); "Grieving: A Way to Heal" The American College of Obstetricians (1988); "Coping with Perinatal Death" Saheb Sahu, M.D., *Journal of Reproductive Medicine* (Mar. 1981). I would like to thank Dr. Harvey Friedman of Englewood, NJ for sharing these and other materials with me.

> הנפלים אין מתאבלים עליהן וכל שלא שהה שלושים יום... אין מתאבלים
> עליו.
>
> We do not mourn for נפלים (fetuses), and a newborn which does not
> live for thirty days...we do not mourn for it.

The second is the Shulhan Arukh Yoreh De'ah 374:8:

> תינוק כל שלושים יום ויום שלושים בכלל אין מתאבלים עליו.
>
> The infant, for thirty days, even including the full thirtieth day (if
> it dies), we do not mourn for it.

These opinions, in turn, are based on a statement by Rabbi Shimon ben Gamaliel in B. Shabbat 135b:

> תניא רבן שמעון בן גמליאל אומר כל ששהה שלושים יום באדם אינו נפל.
>
> It was taught: "Rabbi Shimon ben Gamaliel said: Anyone who lives
> thirty days is not considered a נפל."

What accounts for the significance of thirty days in considering whether or not an infant is a נפל, and therefore not mourned? R. Shimon b. Gamaliel uses as his proof text Num. 18:16, ופדויו מבן חדש תפדה "and he shall be redeemed from one month." Since thirty days is the age at which we are commanded to redeem the firstborn, this is a reasonable way to define at what age the infant changes status from נפל to human being.

B. Bekhorot 49a has an extended discussion about what happens to the redemption money if a father pays the kohen prior to thirty days, and then the son dies within thirty days of his birth. Tosafot there say that the kohen must return the money, since the Torah commanded the father to pay only from the thirtieth day onward. However, Rashi offers another reason for why the kohen may not keep the money. This issue is not the father's obligation, but that the child was not considered viable since he was less than thirty days old. Therefore, the kohen was not entitled to the money in the first place.

The significance of the viability of the infant is pointed out by both the Kesef Mishnah and the Radbaz on the Rambam referred to above. They comment that up until thirty days, there is doubt (ספק) about whether or not the child will survive. Obligating someone for the full rituals of אבלות is considered to be putting a burden on them. It is a principle of halakhah that in case of ספק in אבלות, we follow the more lenient position. Since up until thirty days is considered to be a ספק whether or not the child will survive, if it does not survive, we are lenient, and do not require the parents to mourn.

Alternative Halakhic Positions

The sources above are the primary statements on which the current custom not to mourn is based. However, this is not the only position found in halakhic literature. There is an opinion that a child which is born alive is mourned even if it dies in the first day of life. This position is first stated in Mishnah Niddah 5:3:

> תינוק בן יום אחד הרי הוא לאביו ולאמו ולכל קרוביו כחתן שלם.
>
> A one-day-old infant, if he dies, is considered to his father and
> mother and all relatives like a full bridegroom.

This opinion is expanded in Talmud Yerushalmi Kiddushin 4:11 where we learn that if a newborn was alive when its head, and the majority of its body emerged from its mother, it is mourned:

> תנאי בן יומו שמת הרי הוא לאביו ולאמו ולכל קרוביו כחתן שלם לא אף
> דבר בן יומו חי אלה אפילו יוצא ראשו ורבו בחיים.

> It was taught: a one-day-old, which dies, it is to its father, and
> mother, and all its relatives like a full bridegroom, and not only if
> it lives a day, but even if it was alive when its head and the major-
> ity of its body emerged.

We find this statement again in Semakhot 3:1. Since the latter two sources are of Palestinian origin, it is possible that in Israel it was customary to mourn for newborn infants, while in Bavel it was not.

However, even in Bavel we find examples of fathers who observed mourning for their newborns. In B. Shabbat 136a we learn that the son of Rav Dimi and Rav Cahana mourned for their newborns who died. In a source from the Middle Ages, *Ma'ase HaGeonim*, we learn that it was a custom in some German communities to mourn for newborns.[3]

Even the Rambam (Hilkhot Avel 1:7) indicates that he also follows the opinion that a newborn who dies prior to the thirty-first day of life, is mourned, if we knew for certain that the infant was carried full-term.

> ואם נודע בודאי שנולד לתשעה חדשים גמורים אפילו מת ביום שנולד
> מתאבלים עליו.

> If a man knows for certain that the child was born after a full nine
> months, even if it dies on the day it is born, we mourn it.

The Shulhan Arukh (Y.D. 374:8) concurs. However, Rashi and others are very strict in defining the meaning of "full-term." We must know for sure that the mother had not had marital relations with her husband for the nine months after the child was conceived. Otherwise, we assume that the child was not full-term. In fact, both of the fathers mentioned in B. Shabbat 136a justify their mourning on the basis of the fact that they knew that their child had been full-term. (Although it is not necessarily by Rashi's criteria קים לי ביה שכלו לו חדשיו).

The question of whether a pregnancy was full-term or not is one of great concern to all of our authorities. Of particular interest is the assumption that a child born after eight months is by definition not viable, although one born after seven months is viable.[4] The classic Talmudic statement of this is B. Shabbat 135a. "An eighth-month child is not handled on Shabbat: the mother bends down to nurse for her own comfort, not for the sake of the child." There is also a discussion about whether an otherwise healthy infant born after eight months can be circumcised on Shabbat. Most of our sources state that we do not mourn for an infant carried only eight months, unless it had been alive for thirty days before dying. B. Niddah 44b claims that Rashbag's statement that we do not mourn an infant who dies before thirty days is made only with regard to an infant who was born after eight months; even Rashbag believes that for a full-term infant, we mourn from the first day of life. It is only when the infant was not known to be full-term that we do not mourn unless the infant survived more than thirty days.

---

[3] *Ma'ase HaGeonim* edited by Avraham Epstein (Israel: M'kitze Nirdamim, 5760), p. 49.

[4] See the gloss on S.A. Yoreh De'ah Hilkhot Avelut 374:8. If a divorced woman marries prior to three months, and we do not know which husband is the father of her dead infant, both husbands have obligations to the child. The first is obligated because it might have been full-term, and the second because the baby might have been born after seven months.

Up until this point, the halakhot we have examined deal only with the gestational and post-natal age of the infant. Does the actual condition or developmental stage of that particular infant affect its status in regard to its parents' obligation to mourn? Does the halakhah make a distinction in mourning between an infant who was born healthy and died as a result of an accident, and one whose hold on life was precarious from the beginning? The Radbaz on the Rambam Avel 1:6 states that even if the infant was eaten by a lion on the thirtieth day, it was, by definition, not considered viable, and we do not mourn it. The Shulhan Arukh (374:8) states that the length of gestation is what determines mourning, and that it does not matter whether or not that particular infant was fully developed.

We have seen that the sources which deal with mourning for an infant who dies on the thirtieth day of life, or prior to that, offer a number of different answers on the question of whether the parents, and other relatives, mourn for that child. Some do not require mourning for any such infant; others do, if the child was know to have been carried full-term, or was potentially viable (i.e., not eighth-month).

Burial Practices

Before we begin to consider our halakhic position, we must examine one other area: burial. The obligation to bury is taken by most scholars to be דאורייתא, and thus in a different category from most other mourning rituals, which are דרבנן. Therefore, while even those who consider the death of the infant to be an issue of ספק, so that with regard to mourning, we are lenient, and do not require it, with regard to burial, we are strict and require burial.[5]

Thus, burial is required for a newborn infant, a stillbirth, and for a fetus miscarried after the fifth month (when it has human form). We find the burial of a newborn described in Talmud Yerushalmi Kiddushin 4:11 and again in Semakhot 3:2:

> יוצא בחיק נקבר באשה אחת ובשני אנשים... אין אומדים עליו בשורה
> ואין אומרים בברכת אבלים עד שיהה בן שלושים יום.
>
> It is taken out in arms and buried by one woman and two men...
> we do not stand in rows, and do not say ברכת אבלים unless it died
> after thirty days.

There is no requirement that those burying the child be relatives, although the Yerushalmi describes the infant being carried by its maternal grandmother. The Rambam Avel 12:10 describes the same type of burial.[6] These, then, are the primary halakhic sources are used as the basis for establishing the halakhah for our community.

---

[5] Isidoro Aizenberg, "Treatment of the Loss of a Fetus through Miscarriage," *PCJLS 86-90*, pp. 255-256.

[6] In the literature on funeral services for children, there is a progression of requirements which depend on the age of the child, as well as his or her social status and intelligence. According to the Rambam (Hilkhot Avel 12:11), the public has no obligation to manifest grief until the child is twelve months old, at which point it is carried on a bier. Semakhot 3:3 says that a child is not carried on a beir until it is three years old. Both the Rambam and the Shulhan Arukh go on to say that whether the public is obligated to attend the funeral depends on whether or not they saw the child go out in public.

According to the Rambam 12:1, the eulogy is intended to honor the dead. However, the criteria which he and the other sources use to define at what age the funeral service is held, and a eulogy spoken, seems to indicate that its purpose is also to comfort the parents. Although the sources disagree about whether that age is three, four, five, six or even thirteen years, they all agree that there is a difference in the funeral depending on whether the parents are poor or rich, young or old. The assumption is that poor or old parents suffer more from the loss of a child than do rich or young parents. Neither Isaac Klein nor Maurice Lamm describe any practical difference in the funeral service for a younger or older child, from that of an adult.

Past CJLS Positions and Discussions

During the past decade, the CJLS has devoted a significant amount of time to the discussion of this issue. In 1987 a תשובה by Rabbi Isidoro Aizenberg on the treatment of loss of a fetus though miscarriage was passed by a vote of 11-0 with one abstention.[7] The תשובה calls for the burial of the fetus after the fifth month, and suggests, if the rabbi deems it desirable, he or she may accompany the parents to the cemetery and can read Psalms and speak words of comfort. A stone with the family name may be put up, but אנינות and אבלות are not observed.

A later paper by Rabbi Aizenberg on infant death distinguishes three different practices.[8] (1) When a full term infant dies within thirty days, there is קריעה, אנינות, burial, shivah and sheloshim; no eulogy is delivered, and the burial is performed by immediate family members. The parents may, if they wish, recite kaddish for thirty days; (2) if the baby was born prematurely, the above customs are followed only if it died more than thirty days after birth; or, (3) if the baby was born prematurely, and died prior to thirty days, it is treated as a fetus. In the case of (2) and (3), the parents may recite kaddish. I do not believe that Rabbi Aizenberg's תשובה is sufficient. Nevertheless, it is far better than the custom, and its lack of widespread dissemination among rabbis and congregants alike is tragic.

A second תשובה, dealing with the entire spectrum of miscarriage, pregnancy loss and infant death, was submitted by Rabbi Amy Eilberg in 1986. She recommended that a flexible range of options, from meditations to full אבלות, should be available to the rabbi to offer the family, based on his or her evaluation of the family's needs. Rabbi Eilberg withdrew the תשובה after it was discussed by the CJLS in 1990.[9]

Rabbi Debra Reed Blank wrote a תשובה, which was adopted in 1991, on the treatment of miscarriage.[10] Her model is primarily one of treating the father and mother under categories related to ביקור חולים, with some additional practices, such as the mother going to the mikveh, and a gathering of family and/or friends for prayers. While this תשובה is an important step, I feel that it is not sufficient in the case of pregnancy loss beyond the point of viability, where the halakhah already requires burial.

I submitted a תשובה on mourning practice following infant death and stillbirth in 1989. That תשובה, in conjunction with Rabbi Eilberg's and Rabbi Blank's תשובות, has been the subject of serious and lengthy discussion by the CJLS. My original תשובה, which, in essence, would have required full mourning for all infants born alive after a certain gestational age, with only some technical differences in the case of a stillbirth, contained elements which troubled many members of the committee. Acting on some of those concerns, I have made some revisions in my original תשובה, including separating neo-natal death from stillbirth.

Mourning Practices in the Case of the Death of a Full Term Infant

I began with the assumption, which is already clearly an option within rabbinic literature, and a position of the CJLS, that in the case of a full-term pregnancy, when any infant dies for any reason, at anytime after birth, its parents and other family members should be obligated for full אנינות, and אבלות just as for any other child. The parents should recite kaddish for thirty days, and should observe the yahrzeit. Since it is likely that most sib-

---

[7] See above, n. 5.

[8] Isidoro Aizenberg, "Mourning for a Newborn," *PCJLS 86-90*, pp. 251-254.

[9] See Amy Eilberg, "Response to Miscarriage: A Dissent," above, pp. 364-366.

[10] Debra Reed Blank, "Response to Miscarriage," above, pp. 357-363.

lings will be very young minors, they have no obligations for kaddish or other mourning rites. Post-bar or bat mitzvah siblings, who will have awareness and feelings about the infant, should be encouraged to use the traditional rituals to work through the many (mixed) feeling they have.

Burial and Funeral Service

The body should be buried in accordance with Jewish practice. The service should contain all elements which are included in our usual burial services. A true eulogy cannot be given, but in its place, the rabbi should speak words of comfort. A selection of prayers and other readings, which would be appropriate for the burial of an infant of any age, has been submitted to the Publications Committee for consideration in the new Rabbi's Manual. The parents should be encouraged to attend the burial of their child. If one or both of the parents feel incapable of attending, then they should be advised to ask another relative or close friend to attend. Grandparents, aunts and uncles and other family and close friends should also be encouraged to attend.

Traditionally, the burial of a נפל could be delayed for any reason. Any other funeral should not be delayed except under exceptional circumstances. One of those circumstances is when the primary mourner cannot get to the cemetery immediately, but could be there within a few days. The funeral of a newborn who dies should be done as soon as possible, but if the mother wants to attend, burial may be delayed until she recovers enough physical strength following the delivery to attend. In conversations with Jewish women of all ages whose infants had died, I found a universal sense of loss that they had not been able to bury their child, and that they had never been told, and did not know they could ask, where exactly the grave was. Attending a funeral is difficult, but it is an essential element in honoring life, acknowledging death, and finding comfort. Rabbis do a kindness to no one when we accept the full responsibility for burying an infant.

Naming

If the infant was not named prior to death, it is usually given a name at the grave. Ways to do this are included in the burial liturgy. The name may be the one the parents intended to use for their child, or they might choose a name like Menachem, or Nechama, indicating a desire for comfort. Jewish folk tradition recommends giving a name so that the parents will be able to later find their child in Gan Eden. Contemporary therapeutic thought is that giving the dead infant a name aids the parents in the healing process, and helps to distinguish that child from any other children of that couple.

Circumcision

Should an uncircumcised boy be circumcised before burial? There is no obligation to do so, since the mitzvot are only obligatory on the living. While the mitzvah of ברית מילה at eight days is the father's, the ברית is between God and the child, who is no longer alive. If מילה is done, either during טהרה or at the grave, there is no ברכה recited, and it need not be done by a *mohel*. Neither the Rambam nor Rabbi Isaac Klein in his *Guide to Jewish Religious Practice* mention the custom at all. The Shulhan Arukh 353:6 says that the infant is circumcised at its grave. Rabbi Lamm states that the custom is to do the circumcision during the טהרה. This is not a custom which we need to perpetuate. However, it the parents request a circumcision, and would be comforted by it, it should be done during or prior to the טהרה.[11]

Autopsy

Jewish law generally opposes autopsies, unless they are required by the law of the land, or would directly save another life. In the case of the death of an infant we should allow, and even encourage, an autopsy if it might be crucial in determining the advisability of future pregnancies for that couple. If an autopsy is done, it should be completed as soon as possible, and with the same restrictions which we put on adult autopsies.

Shivah

My discussion of the area of the community's responsibility to the mourners, primarily in the form of communal responsibilities for shivah, was one which troubled many members of the CJLS. I originally argued for full seven day shivah in all cases. Many members of the committee felt that this was an unreasonable burden on the family and/or the community. They recommended a one or three day shivah, or שבעה בצנעה (private observances, as on Shabbat). Some commented that "we have enough trouble getting a minyan and getting full shivah when an adult has died, how can we expect this for a newborn?" While we cannot put a requirement on the community which it will not observe, that does not, in this case, seem to me to be a relevant argument for not requiring shivah. The reality is that as rabbis, we do our best to be sure that a family has a minyan when they want it, and there is no reason why we should feel an obligation to do more in this case. After all, we are not, please God, talking about a frequent occurrence, so that it would overly burden even a large congregation.

On the contrary, of all of the recommendations in this תשובה, I believe that communal participation in shivah is one of the most important elements. Denial of real loss and isolation are usually two of the most serious impediments to healthy grieving, and eventual resolution. Requiring shivah, with its obligation of communal participation during the shivah period, makes a clear statement that the loss of a human life was real, that the parents and the extended family should be grieving (and not [only] grateful for this blessing in disguise) and that the parents must not be left alone at this time. Family and friends may have already spent time with the baby, and if it was sick, they would have prayed for it. In any event, if things had been different, the community would have been there visiting the new baby and welcoming it with Jewish rituals (in a time frame of one week for a boy). One of the strengths of Judaism is that it requires community for both שמחה and for sorrow. The family whose newborn dies should not also be denied its community.

It is likely that the community will be uncomfortable, and will not know what to say.

---

[11] What is the origin of the custom of circumcising a dead male infant? In B. Sanhedrin 110b, the question is asked, "At what age do infants enter the world to come?" A variety of answers are offered ranging from conception, through birth, through the time that the child can speak, or answer "Amen." R. Nathan b. Isaac says it is from the time of ברית מילה. Since the circumcision is a sign which is always on the body, the boy will be recognized as a Jew, will not be allowed into *Gehinom*, will be reunited with his family and will be resurrected. Saul Lieberman has an interesting discussion of this issue in "Afterlife in Early Rabbinic Literature," (*Harry Austryn Wolfson Jubilee Volume* [AAJR, 1965]). He suggests that although claims are made that this is an ancient rabbinic practice, it may not be that old, or rabbinically sanctioned. Lieberman feels that it is a folk custom which was performed by midwives and others in order to comfort the parents.

It is our responsibility to teach them how to speak with sensitivity to all mourners, these included. But this education will be more likely to take place when we are clearer about what the community is required to do.

Other colleagues have expressed a concern that in requiring full shivah we are placing a burden on a family, and the mother in particular, whose health is delicate. Again, this is not a reason to avoid shivah. Since the funeral of a newborn would have been postponed, or the infant would have lived more than a few days, shivah would most likely not take place until the mother has recovered some physical strength. In most of our communities, the "prime time" of shivah is limited to an hour or so in the evening, and perhaps thirty minutes in the morning, for minyan. Only close friends come by at other times. The first few weeks after coming home without the baby is a time when the house is painfully empty. The presence of comforters in the home will not fill the emptiness, but will "provide a container for it," enabling the parents to begin integrating the emptiness. Additionally, shivah is not only the burden of having visitors, but the חיוב and the permission to do nothing else but mourn. This aspect is particularly important for the father, since it essentially asks him not to return to his employment for a period of time so that he, too, can engage in the work of mourning.

Taking into account these considerations, as well as the inadvisability of advocating anything less than full shivah to our community, we will obligate both the parents and the community for full shivah.

Both Parents as אבלים

Throughout this discussion I have treated the father and mother equally as primary mourners, rather than the mother as a primary mourner, and the father as somewhat outside of that status. Husbands and wives do have different experiences of pregnancy, childbirth, parenthood, and if, God forbid, their infant dies, they do respond differently to that loss. However, the father's loss is no less real than the mother's, for all that its manifestations may be less physical or obvious. Neo-natal death can lead to the isolation of the partners, not only from their community, but also from each other. There is a high rate of marital dissolution associated with such a loss. I strongly believe that requiring halakhic mourning, in which both parents are "equal" mourners, is critical. When the father is treated as a mourner, he is relieved of the burden of "being strong" for his wife. He has a specific set of ritual tasks to do and a specific role, through which he is encouraged to confront the magnitude of his loss in all its dimensions from sadness to rage to helplessness. In addition, family and friends have a responsibility to be present for him, and to care for him as well as for the mother.

Premature Infants

The above is all in the case of a full-term infant who dies after birth. Given our relative medical sophistication, can we continue to make a distinction between an infant who was carried full-term, and one who was not, and should that distinction determine our mourning practices, or lack thereof? It is clear that there is no scientific basis for giving a seventh month newborn more chance of survival that an eighth month infant. On the contrary, it is known that every additional day of pregnancy and every added ounce of weight increases the infant's survival rate. At twenty-seven weeks (the end of the sixth month) a premature child given expert care already has a sixty-six percent chance of survival. By the end of the seventh month (thirty-one weeks) survival rates are at least eighty-five percent. At the end of the eighth month (35-36 weeks) more than ninety-seven percent of infants born alive will live.[12] Since a majority of the infants born alive after twenty-seven weeks of gestation can be expected to survive, we are no longer dealing with the same situation as our predecessors did. For them, premature birth meant that the infant's chance of survival beyond the first few days of life was doubtful. The intention of the halakhah in taking advantage of the principal of leniency in a case of ספק, so that it distinguished between the death of a premature infant, and one who was full term, was to avoid burdening parents repeatedly with the regulations periods of mourning.

Today, we have a different reality. רוב תינוקות, a majority of the infants born alive, even after a gestational period of only twenty-seven weeks, can be expected to survive. By that point in the pregnancy, most parents expect to bring a baby home from the hospital, even if it requires technical assistance at the beginning of its life. When we do not require mourning for an infant who dies after that time, we are not being sensitive to the parents. Our insensitivity contrasts with the sensitivity which we assume on the part of the Rabbis when, confronted by high rates of infant mortality, they sought to avoid burdening the parents. Under present medical conditions, we can no longer justify the leniency of not requiring the parents of a premature infant who dies to observe the rites of mourning as already described above.

Between Premature and Not Gestationally Viable

How premature is too premature, too uncertain, for us to require mourning? This is one point on which I feel that both the CJLS as a Movement-wide halakhic authority, and individual rabbis, must retain some flexibility. The boundaries of medicine's ability to save the lives of tiny infants is constantly being pushed back. Certainly, our limit should not go back beyond the five months at which we begin to require burial. However, between that point, and until about thirty weeks, it seems that a decision concerning mourning, could be made by the rabbi and the parents. There the actual length of the infant's life might become more of a factor than gestational age. In any event, burial is required, and that could serve as a focus of Jewish ritual.

At the moment, this issue of "how premature" remains unresolved. In its discussion, the CJLS apparently approved the opinion that any infant born alive no matter how premature, who remains alive for even the shortest amount of time, is treated כחתן שלם, as a full human being. In a dissenting concurrence, Rabbi Avram Reisner argues that following my primary halakhic reasoning of ספק viability, we should retain the requirement of a certain gestational age (thirty weeks) before implementing full mourning practices as described in this תשובה. A premature infant born prior to that time, who dies before the end of thirty days, would continue to be treated as a נפל.[13]

The Need for Guidance

I will conclude with a comment and a recommendation. The chaos caused by transitional moments requires clear guidance. One function of halakhah is to provide that guidance: "This is what Jews do, this is what they do not do." In practice, we may be flexible within

---

[12] Alan Guttmacher, *Pregnancy, Birth and Family Planning*, revised by Irwin Kaiser (New York: New American Library, 1986), pp. 59-60.

[13] Rabbi Avram Israel Reisner, "Kim Li: A Dissenting Concurrence," below, pp. 450-451. While I agree in essence with Rabbi Reisner, I would prefer the limit to be a few weeks earlier than the 30 weeks gestational age that he recommends. Alternatively, or in addition, thirty days of life seems to me to be too long a period of time to determine whether full mourning should be required. I would be more comfortable with a shorter required time of life. My final position on this may depend on the final decision concerning the ritual response to stillbirth.

certain boundaries, and we recognize that our congregants will do what they want in areas where we rabbis are not the main actors. Nevertheless, there are halakhic positions which govern our actions and advice. I believe that if we are to be helpful as rabbis, with the full force of the power of Judaism, to families who have lost a baby, we must have clear halakhic guidelines. It is not for the rabbi to decide whether each particular family has a חיוב to mourn or not. And yet, as I have listened to rabbinic colleagues, I keep hearing a need for flexibility in addition to halakhic, or even only pastoral, guidelines. While I believe that there will always be a need for some flexibility (and some of those places are mentioned above), I also feel that much of the perceived need for so much flexibility come precisely from our lack of a position.

First, given the well known, although incorrect, statement that there is no mourning for infants, our congregants do not expect a response from us, and may not even call us.

Second, for the same reason, we as rabbis do not seek out these parents, and we do not speak with the authority that makes people do more or less what we say at other life cycle events.

Third, again for the same reasons, the extended families and community, which usually know their roles in Jewish life cycle rituals, do not know their roles here. We are afraid that we cannot count of this essential component of the mourning rituals.

Fourth, we live in a society which is still working out new responses to neo-natal loss. While many hospitals have protocols for dealing with neo-natal death, once the family leaves the hospital, there is still a tendency to ignore and downplay the loss.

Fifth, even experienced colleagues have faced this situation only a few times. So each of us makes our judgment based on the particular needs of the few families we have encountered, as well as on our own ability to deal with this tragedy. For all of these reasons, I believe that if we develop a halakhically supported, and pastorally helpful response, to neo-natal death, (and to stillbirth,) then the perceived need for halakhic flexibility, as opposed to rabbinic sensitivity, will be lessened.

Finally, in our classes on life cycle rituals, and in our conversations with expectant parents, we must discuss the fact that there is a Jewish response to miscarriage, stillbirth and infant death, and we must assure parents that neither we as rabbis, nor the Jewish community, will abandon them if everything does not turn out as they pray that it will.

Conclusion

It is an official position of the CJLS that in the case of neo-natal death — the death of a full-term or premature infant, prior to the completion of the thirtieth day of life — the death is treated in the same manner as we treat the death of someone who lived more than thirty days. That is: the body is treated and prepared as any Jewish body, there is burial and a funeral service (with readings and comments which are sensitive to the situation). The parents, and non-minor siblings, have the obligations of קריעה, אנינות, אבלות, shivah, recite kaddish for thirty days, and observe yahrzeit. The community has all of its obligations for נחום אבלים, including preparing the סעודת הבראה and providing a minyan for shivah and beyond.

YD 374:8.1992b

KIM LI: A DISSENTING CONCURRENCE

Rabbi Avram Israel Reisner

This paper was submitted as a response to "Jewish Ritual Practice Following the Death of an Infant Who Lives Less Than Thirty-One Days," by Rabbi Stephanie Dickstein. Dissenting and concurring opinions are not official positions of the Committee on Jewish Law and Standards.

The Committee on Jewish Law and Standards of the Rabbinical Assembly provides guidance in matters of halakhah for the Conservative movement. The individual rabbi, however, is the authority for the interpretation and application of all matters of halakhah.

The Committee on Jewish Law and Standards passed Rabbi Stephanie Dickstein's paper, "Jewish Ritual Practice Following the Death of an Infant Who Lives Less Than Thirty-One Days," at its meeting on June 3, 1992, by a substantial margin, thus bringing to a conclusion an on-again-off-again debate over the past five years. At issue was the tradition not to require mourning practices for an infant that does not live thirty days.

Rabbi Dickstein pointed out again, as had been noted before, that that tradition substantially misstated the precedents and the early law. Indeed, the Talmud reports that certain Amoraim mourned their infants lost prior to thirty days of age, where they felt them to have been born at full term, and that is the codified law. Nevertheless, over the years there were voices on the Committee who were uncertain whether the old halakhah should be reinstated in the face of an overruling custom. I am pleased that the overwhelming majority of the Committee saw fit to do so. Given modern medicine and hygiene, there is little reason to treat a full-term infant as other than a complete human being.

Rabbi Dickstein went further and argued that, given the state of medical information and technology, it is desirable to treat viable pre-term newborns in the same way we treat full-term infants. In her paper as presented before the CJLS, she was unwilling to determine precisely the point of viability. Effectively, she found thirty weeks to be a point of viability לכל הדעות, requiring אבלות at that point, but, uncertain about ever-shifting and debated medical determinations, she left it to "the rabbi and the parents" to determine if mourning would be applied before then, from five months (twenty-three weeks) until "around thirty weeks."

I strongly support Rabbi Dickstein's view, proposed before her by Rabbi Eilberg, that viability by today's medical standards should affect our understanding of the Amoraic claim, קים לי דכלו לו חדשיו. I challenged in committee, however, the flexible standard. I do not believe halakhah abides flexible standards. Flexible judgment about arriving at the standard, of course, but the rabbinic dictum of לא פלוג argues against such an amorphous ruling. I asked Rabbi Dickstein for a date certain. She was unwilling, on one foot, to offer

450

such and, in what I took to be undue haste, the Committee opted to delete any specific age. To wit, a child, born alive, even much smaller and younger than any reasonable viability standard, is the proper subject of אבלות by this decision. In that one stroke, I believe, the Committee went further than it should have and further, I suspect, than Rabbi Dickstein or most of its members intended.

It was argued, in those last frantic moments before the vote, that the text in Mishnah Niddah (5:3) which refers to a day-old infant as חתן שלם justifies such a ruling. I do not believe that it does. That a fourteen-week fetus barely of human form, born alive but living only a few minutes, should be considered by some sources fully human while others remain unconvinced even of full-term infants until thirty days had elapsed seems to me much broader than the likely Tannaitic debate. Rather, the debate is to be understood, I believe, concerning a fully formed baby (whatever that means precisely — I shall return to this in a moment). Is said infant חתן שלם at birth or only at thirty days? An unformed infant is clearly not שלם.

As I write I wonder whether I should rather have dissented than concurred, but having argued in favor of the major premises of Rabbi Dickstein's paper I felt constrained to concur. Nevertheless, I believe strongly that viability may serve as the equivalent of the claim of קים לי, but simple live birth may not.

How then to determine viability rabbinically? The Report of the Committee on Fetal Extrauterine Survivability of the New York State Task Force on Life and the Law determined in January 1988 "that an anatomic threshold of development occurs around 23-24 weeks of gestation (500 grams). Before this time the fetal organs. . .are not sufficiently developed to permit extrauterine survival," and that that threshold will stand for "the foreseeable future." This is, however, a threshold of potential survivability. At that gestational age an infant will likely succumb, but intervention is warranted since there is at least some chance the child will survive. This is a valuable measure to determine neonatal care, but it has only a very weak claim on the rather certain rabbinic category of קים לי. Similarly, the 26-27 week threshold that many have considered relates to crossing the fifty percent barrier. At that point it is somewhat likelier that the infant will survive (50-60 percent) than that it will not. But again I ask, what is the meaning of ספק if not the 50-50 chance? Why, at all, the wait until thirty days — certainly infant mortality even then was not so high that a preponderant majority of infants did not survive? The measure which our sources attest is one of virtual certainty, קים לי.

I propose that that measure is attained in our day at 31-32 weeks, that is, the end of the seventh month of gestation when survival rates are greater than eighty-five percent according to Rabbi Dickstein's source (1986!), and certainly eighty percent according to the New York State Task Force report. At that point, it seems possible to say קים לי with conviction. Furthermore, this coincides with a rabbinic model. The Rabbis claimed that בן שבע חי, בן שמונה מת. This refers, of course, to the end of the respective months, with בן תשע a full-term infant. I do not know what science stood behind that rabbinic finding or whether it was simply a justification of why some infants live and some die. No matter. Present-day science finds no such correlation. Every passing day enhances a fetus' chance to survive. Yet it is those last two months which are in question, not more. While we perforce abandon בן שמונה מת, we can affirm בן שבע חי.

Let the completion of seven months, rather than the former nine, serve as the grounds for the claim of קים לי. Before that level of development let the old law stand that the child needs to prove viability by living thirty days to be considered a full legal person. That is what I believe we should rule. And that, in any case, is how I propose to follow this ruling. I recommend that others do the same.

YD 400:1.2000

WELCOMING MOURNERS ON SHABBAT

Rabbi Baruch Frydman-Kohl

This paper was approved by the CJLS on September 20, 2000, by a vote of twenty-one in favor (21-0-0). Voting in favor: Rabbis Kassel Abelson, Ben Zion Bergman, Elliot N. Dorff, Paul Drazen, Jerome M. Epstein, Baruch Frydman-Kohl, Nechama D. Goldberg, Arnold M. Goodman, Susan Grossman, Judah Kogen, Aaron L. Mackler, Daniel S. Nevins, Hillel Norry, Stanley Platek, Paul Plotkin, Mayer Rabinowitz, Avram Israel Reisner, Joel E. Rembaum, James S. Rosen, Joel Roth, and Elie Kaplan Spitz.

The Committee on Jewish Law and Standards of the Rabbinical Assembly provides guidance in matters of halakhah for the Conservative movement. The individual rabbi, however, is the authority for the interpretation and application of all matters of halakhah.

שאלה

In many siddurim, greetings for mourners are found following the hymn לכה דודי in the Kabbalat Shabbat service. If services are not held prior to sunset, is it proper to greet mourners who attend late Friday night services or Shabbat morning worship with the words המקום ינחם אתכם בתוך שאר אבלי ציון וירושלים, "May the Ever-present console you along with others who mourn within Zion and Jerusalem"? Would this, or other statements which recognize mourners and offer public consolation to them, cause public mourning on Shabbat?

תשובה

It is a fundamental mitzvah to offer consolation to mourners (נחום אבלים) and it is permitted to do so as individuals or as a congregation on the Shabbat.

The Mitzvah of Consolation

In his commentary to the Mishnah, Rabbi Yom Tov Lipmann Heller (Moravia, 1579-1654) cites the Spanish moralist Rabbenu Yonah ben Avraham of Gerona (c. 1200-1263) and indicates that this mitzvah has Biblical authority, since he views acts of חסד to be specifically mandated by the Torah:

תנחמי אבלים מדאורייתא דבכלל גמילות חסדים הוא שהוא מן התורה.

> Consoling mourners is a Biblical commandment since it is in the general category of acts of loving-kindness which are considered to be of Torah status (Tosafot Yom Tov to Mishnah Berakhot 3:2).

Rabbi Heller establishes this status in relation to the Talmudic discussion about acts of loving-kindness found in Bava Kamma 100a and Bava Metzia 30b. Both sources refer to Exod. 18:20 as the basis for this commandment:

והזהרתה אתהם את־החקים ואת־התורת והודעת להם את־הדרך ילכו בה ואת־המעשה אשר יעשון.

> And enjoin upon them the laws and the teachings and make known to them the way they are to go and the practices they are to follow.

Similarly, Rabbi Israel Lipschutz (Germany, 1782-1860) writes:

תנחמי אבלים ה"ל גמילות חסדים דאורייתא.

> Consoling mourners is [an act of] loving-kindness which is of Torah status (Tiferet Yisrael on Mishnah Berakhot 3:2).

However, Maimonides (Spain and Egypt, 1135-1204) classifies this commandment as one of rabbinic status:

מצות עשה של דבריהם לבקר חולים ולנחם אבלים. אף על פי שכל מצות אלו מדבריהם, הרי הן בכלל "ואהבת לרעך כמוך."

> It is a positive commandment from their words to visit the sick and to console the mourners. Even though all these mitzvot are Rabbinic, they are included in the [Biblical] commandment "You shall love your neighbor as yourself" (M.T. Hilkhot Avel 14:1).

Writing in the Ashkenazi tradition, Rashi (France, 1040-1105) similarly states that, תקנתא דרבנן בעלמא הוא, "Consoling mourners is a general rabbinic enactment," (Sanhedrin 70b, s. v. לאתויי).

Regardless of the juridical classification, it is clear that all authorities regard this as a religious obligation of great importance.

The Period of Consolation

Maimonides indicates that while the initial act of consoling mourners takes place immediately following the burial, "Afterwards, the mourner returns to his home. Every day within the seven days of mourning people should come to console [the mourner]" (Mishneh Torah, Hilkhot Avel 13:1-2). In a similar manner, Rabbi Menahem Meiri (Provence, 1249-1316) defined the formal time framework for consoling mourners:

תנחומי אבלים והוא מה שהיו נכנסים אצל האבל כל שבעה לנחמו.

> Consoling the mourners refers to [people] going in to the mourner throughout the seven days to console him (Moed Katan 24b, ad loc.).

One should make every effort to reach out to the mourner during this period.

The Prohibition Against Public Mourning

However, it is also well established that there is no public mourning on Shabbat. The Talmud (J. Moed Katan 3.5, 82d) interprets Prov. 10.22:

ברכת ה' היא תעשיר ולא־יוסף עצב עמה.

> It is the blessing of the Eternal that enriches, and no sadness/toil can increase it.

"The blessing of the Eternal" is understood to refer to Shabbat, which was blessed by God, while the "sadness" — which is linked to the mourning of King David — is not "increased" on Shabbat. Maimonides codifies this:

אין אבילות בשבת אלא בדברים שבצנעה.... אבל דברים שבגלוי אינו נוהג בהן אבלות.

> There is no mourning on Shabbat except for those things which are in private. . . .But public acts of mourning are not followed (M.T. Hilkhot Avel 10:1).

Mourners change their clothing, sit in their usual way and attend synagogue, but still maintain private mourning practices, such as restrictions on bathing, shaving and sexual relations. Consequently, many have questioned whether it is proper to formally console mourners on the Sabbath, since that is an acknowledgement of their grief which might be linked to a public form of mourning.

Moreover, Rabbi H. Rabinowicz of England (*A Guide to Life* [New York: Ktav, 1964], p. 68, citing Moed Katan 15a and Yoreh De'ah 385.1), notes that during the first three days of shivah, the mourner neither greets nor responds to greetings. This custom is linked to the words האנק דם מתים אבל לא–תעשה, "Moan softly; observe no mourning for the dead" (Ezek. 24:17). One might therefore imagine that formally welcoming mourners at any point during this period would appear to be a form of prohibited greetings. All this would seem to prohibit the offering of consolation on Shabbat if it fell during the first three days of grief.

Greeting Mourners on Shabbat is Allowed

In the Talmud (J. Moed Katan 3.5, 82d) and in the aggadic midrash *Yalqut Shim'oni* (Beresheet 15, s. v. ויכעלו) the case of Rabbi Oshaya the Elder is recounted. He greeted someone on Shabbat with שלום עליכם in accordance with his practice, saying, "I do not know the custom of your place, but שלום עליכם in accordance with the custom in my place." From this we see that it is permissible to greet mourners on Shabbat.

If so, what types of greeting are appropriate? Rabbi Yosef ben Moshe (Bavaria, 1423-1490) composed *Leket Yosher*, which contains halakhic vignettes about and rulings by his teacher, Rabbi Israel Isserlein, (Germany, 1390-1460), the author of *Terumat ha-Deshen*. Rabbi Yosef indicates that the restriction on greeting the mourner refers only to the words שלום עליכם, but not to "Good Shabbat," since such a greeting does not use the word שלום which is a true word of consolation (sec. 1, Orah Hayyim, p. 110, no. 3). Despite the case of Rabbi Oshaya in the Talmud, Rabbi Yosef restricts greetings with the words שלום עליכם and not to more common greetings or salutations. If so, as long as one avoids certain terminology, greeting mourners on Shabbat would be permissible. Moreover, since public forms of mourning are not in effect, one may speak directly to the mourner even during the first three days of אבלות.

However, this linguistic restriction cannot ultimately be sustained. First of all, much depends, as Rav Hai Gaon observed, on the custom of the land (cited by Bet Yosef to Tur Yoreh De'ah 393). Additionally, Maimonides (Mishneh Torah, Hilkhot Avel 10:1) and Rabbi Yosef Karo (Bet Yosef, Tur Yoreh De'ah 400, s.v. ומה שכתב) specifically use the word שלום when they rule that on Shabbat a mourner may offer greetings to all, לכל אחד נותן שלום. Since such actions are visible and public mourning is prohibited on Shabbat, it is permissible to greet the mourner and for the mourner to respond to and initiate greetings.

Consoling Mourners on Shabbat

What about extending condolences? The Talmud tells us of a debate between Bet Shammai and Bet Hillel regarding consoling mourners on Shabbat. Bet Hillel permitted and Bet Shammai prohibited such activity. Ultimately,

> ואמר רבי חנינא בקושי התירו... לנחם אבלים בשבת.
>
> Rabbi Hannina stated that reluctantly they permitted consolation on Shabbat (Shabbat 12b).

Rashi offers the rationale for the reluctance: consolation would cause pain, thus minimizing the joy of Shabbat. Rabbi Alfasi indicates that the reason is that the visitor may join in the cries of pain.

In a responsum dedicated to the question of whether it is permitted to console mourners during Hol Hamoed, Rabbi Tzemach Duran (Algeria, fifteenth century) discussed offering consolation on Shabbat. He cites Rabbi Hai Gaon who differentiated between formal condolences, which would be prohibited, and merely sitting with the mourner to lessen his or her burden. Rabbi Duran indicates that the only concern is the prohibition against speaking about weekday matters on Shabbat:

> ודבר דבר: שלא יהיה דבורך של שבת כדבור של חול.
>
> "Restrain yourself from speaking words": Your speech on Shabbat should not be similar to your speech during the week (*Yachin U-Voaz* 1:117).

Rabbi Duran subsequently indicates that, if local custom would be disturbed by authorizing the consoling of mourners on Shabbat, the rabbi addressing the query may maintain the prohibition. However, basing himself on Maimonides, Rabbi Duran indicates that this restriction is not necessary:

> הדבר ברור שמותר לנחם אבלים בשבת... ואין חוששין שמא יצטער או שמא יצעוק.
>
> The matter is clear: it is permissible to console mourners on Shabbat...and we do not worry that perhaps one will be caused pain or cry out.

In a similar fashion, while recognizing that when visiting mourners it was customary to sit on the ground with them, Rabbi Yosef Karo does not limit this behavior on Shabbat:

> משום שרוב עם לא סגי להו בלאו הכי.
>
> Most people would not feel that they had [provided] sufficient [consolation] without this [sitting on the ground with the mourner] (Bet Yosef Yoreh De'ah 393).

It should be noted that although ordinarily offering consolation is mandatory, Rabbi Karo carefully moderates his language when he writes that such consolation is allowed:

> יכולים לנחם אבלים בשבת... ולא יאמר לו כדרך שאומר לו בחול.

> One may console mourners on Shabbat...but one should not do so
> in the same way that consolation is offered during the week (S.A.
> Orah Hayyim 287:1).

This hesitancy is noted by Rabbi Israel Kagan who contends that it is permitted, but not necessarily appropriate, to console those in grief on Shabbat (Mishnah Berurah 287:1.1). A trend is beginning to appear. Public mourning is prohibited, but greetings are permitted and consolation may be offered. Some linguistic limitations are in order so as to preserve the differences between Shabbat and the week. Personal visits are in order.

Mourning and Consoling are Two Distinct Mitzvot

This emerging position is consolidated by Rabbi Yichya ben Joseph Tzalach (Maharitz) of Sana who was recognized as a halakhic authority throughout Yemen. In his commentary on S.A. Orah Hayyim (Shoshanat HaMelech, 1:52), he contrasts the position of Rabbi Karo that consolation is permissible with the opinion of Rambam that there is no אבלות on Shabbat and, consequently, no consolation. He artfully differentiates between mourning (which is prohibited) and consoling (which is permitted). These constitute two distinct actions of individuals with different obligations. The mourner must not show public signs of grief. Members of the community have an obligation to console. Many years later, Rabbi Maurice Lamm stated: "Visitors do not customarily pay condolence calls on the Sabbath or holidays as these are days when one should not mourn publicly. However, the mourner may receive company and condolences on these days" (*Jewish Way in Death and Mourning*, p. 139).

Rabbi Yehiel Michal Epstein (Arukh Hashulhan Yoreh De'ah 393:10) reviews the matter and notes that the Rosh and the Tur already reiterated the position of Rav Hai Gaon that many mourning customs depend on the local patterns (הכל כמנהג המדינה). For example, in some communities mourners remain at home during shivah; in others they go to synagogue for prayers during the week. In Ashkenaz, the custom became for the mourner to go to synagogue on Shabbat and after prayers to be the first to exit the service. The mourner would then sit in front of the synagogue so that the entire congregation could go to sit with him before he would return home. In some cases, the community would then accompany the mourner home and sit with that person for an hour. Rabbi Epstein cites Rabbi Moshe Isserles (Rema) that now we no longer offer consolation in the same way, although there were some congregations in his day where the *shamash* would announce before Kabbalat Shabbat that the community should go to the mourner. Rabbi Epstein is correct when he states once again: "It is evident that all these matters depend on local custom" (393.12).

Taking Public Notice of Mourners

According to Rabbi Yehiel Michel Tuktsinsky (Gesher HaHayyim, 20:5.2), it is permissible to offer condolences on Shabbat and Yom Tov (based on Moed Katan 20a and Tur Orah Hayyim 385.2). He points out that Sephardim even visit homes on Shabbat, in a way similar to the pattern in Ashkenaz described by Rabbi Epstein. Citing Sofrim (ch. 19, end) and Pirkei d'Rabbi Eliezer (ch. 17), Rabbi Tuktsinsky notes that since גמילות חסד is so important, there were distinct entrances to the Temple in Jerusalem for mourners and the newly married to use on Shabbat. People would gather there between the gates and say to those in mourning, "May the One who dwells in this House comfort you."

Following the destruction of the Temple, it became customary for mourners and wedding celebrants to go to the synagogue. As a consequence, the custom gradually developed to include in the words of consolation a reference to Zion. Still later, it became an Ashkenazic pattern to console mourners during Kabbalat Shabbat, following לכה דודי and before the Shabbat psalm. This also served to indicate the cessation of public mourning on Shabbat (Gesher HaHayyim, 20:5.2-3, p. 209). While Rabbi Tuktsinsky places this Temple custom prior to Shabbat, it is actually clear in Pirkei d'Rabbi Eliezer that these greetings took place on the Shabbat (היו הולכים בשבתות).

Acknowledgement is Not Consolation

Rabbi Moshe Feinstein (*Iggrot Moshe*, Orah Hayyim 5:20) differentiates between public acknowledgement of mourners and actual consolation. When asked whether it is permissible to offer תנחומים on Shabbat, Rabbi Feinstein indicates that the articulation of the words המקום ינחם at the conclusion of לכה דודי does not constitute תנחומים, since the mitzvah of comforting the mourner is to quiet the soul of the person in grief and this can be done only when one sits and converses with the mourner. Public acknowledgement of the mourners does not relieve members of the congregation of their particular and personal obligations to visit the mourner and relieve his or her soul by quiet conversation about the deceased.

Rabbi Feinstein defines a noticeable shift from the initial stages of the rabbinic tradition when a formulaic articulation was considered to be the act of consolation. Now, the formulaic pronouncement is seen as a way of drawing public recognition to those in mourning so that individuals in the community may fulfill their personal obligations to offer consolation. Although Rabbi Feinstein assumes that לכה דודי is chanted prior to the onset of Shabbat, the basic principle would be maintained even in the context of a late Friday night service. We already have seen that some communities had the custom to escort mourners home following evening services on Shabbat and to remain with them for a while. We may extend condolences during Shabbat morning services, for this is comparable to those medieval authorities who permitted personal visitation on Shabbat to offer consolation.

It would seem clear that such communal recognition was not considered to be in violation of the prohibition against public mourning on Shabbat. Moreover, the obligation to offer condolences and to support the mourner remains in effect at all times, even though the mourner may not engage in those public acts which are characteristic of the week of shivah.

Awareness Creates the Opportunity for חסד

In modern congregations, as in some pre-modern communities, many people are not in daily contact with one another. They see each other in synagogue on a weekly basis. A public announcement that an individual is in mourning creates an awareness of a personal loss. This enables other members of the community to seek out the mourner to listen to his or her grief and to offer personal condolence and support. Even the classical formula המקום ינחם need not be considered public consolation on Shabbat, but simply regarded as a statement that a person is in the week-long period mourning. Certainly, other forms of condolences would be permitted.

In our congregational context, such announcements may be made when mourners enter the synagogue following לכה דודי, or at other times during the service, such as if they stand for public acknowledgement before Mourner's Kaddish.

Although such an announcement may cause some pain or weeping, those reactions need not restrict the practice of calling attention to the mourners. Moreover, the avoidance of acknowledgement may be seen as violating the principle of respect for the survivors (יקרא דחיי), just as drawing public attention to the loss may actually be seen as a way of honoring the deceased (יקרא דשכיבא). A simple statement may thus bring a measure of comfort to those in mourning. Such formulaic announcements may be made on Shabbat, since they do not require those in mourning to adopt any of the public practices of shivah. It is already evident that such announcements take place in our congregations and the legitimacy of local custom is particularly *apropos* here.

Conclusion

Accordingly, we have decided that since the community is obligated to offer comfort to mourners even on Shabbat, it is permissible for individuals to greet and welcome mourners during late Friday night services and during Shabbat morning services. As well, it is permissible for individuals and the congregation as a whole to extend condolences to mourners. The language of greeting may include the phrases המקום ינחם or "We extend to you the cup of consolation" since these are formulaic in nature. Such greetings and condolences are not to be considered in violation of the sanctity of Shabbat nor should they be thought to be sufficient to offer true personal consolation. This public acknowledgement of the mourners (as well as information about the location of shivah and the times of מנינים) should be seen as serving the purpose of drawing congregational attention to those in grief and encouraging others to fulfill their individual obligations to pay personal visits to the mourners during the shivah period. Such personal visits may take place on Shabbat, but are more properly carried out during the week days.

Responsa Relating to Even HaEzer
אבן העזר

הלכות פריה ורביה	Marriage and Fertility
הלכות אישות	Interpersonal Relations
הלכות גיטין	Divorce

EH 1:3.1994

Artificial Inseminiation, Egg Donation and Adoption

Rabbi Elliot N. Dorff

This paper was approved by the CJLS on March 16, 1994, by a vote of twenty one in favor and one abstention (21-0-1). Voting in favor: Rabbis Kassel Abelson, Ben Zion Bergman, Stanley Bramnick, Elliot N. Dorff, Samuel Fraint, Myron S. Geller, Arnold M. Goodman, Susan Grossman, Jan Caryl Kaufman, Judah Kogen, Vernon H. Kurtz, Aaron L. Mackler, Herbert Mandl, Lionel E. Moses, Paul Plotkin, Mayer Rabinowitz, Joel E. Rembaum, Chaim A. Rogoff, Joel Roth, Gerald Skolnik and Gordon Tucker. Abstaining: Rabbi Reuven Kimelman.

The Committee on Jewish Law and Standards of the Rabbinical Assembly provides guidance in matters of halakhah for the Conservative movement. The individual rabbi, however, is the authority for the interpretation and application of all matters of halakhah.

שאלה

An infertile Jewish couple has asked the following questions: Which, if any, of the new developments in reproductive technology does Jewish law *require* us to try? Which *may* we try? Which, if any, does Jewish law *forbid* us to try? If we are not able to conceive, how does Jewish law view adoption?

תשובה

These questions can best be treated by dividing those issues that apply to the couple from those that apply to potential donors of sperm or eggs, and by separately delineating the status in Jewish law of the various techniques currently available.

For the Couple

May an infertile Jewish couple use any or all of the following methods to procreate: (1) artificial insemination with the husband's sperm; (2) artificial insemination with a donor's sperm; or, (3) egg donation? *Must* they use one of these methods if they cannot procreate through their own sexual intercourse? (4) Is adoption permissible? (5) Which of these methods for becoming parents, if any, fulfill the commandment to procreate?

For the Donor

May Jews donate their sperm or eggs so that other people who are infertile can have children? If so, are there any restrictions?

(The Subcommittee on Bioethics has agreed to divide the many issues on the beginning of life, and so those connected with in vitro fertilization (IVF), gamete intrafallopian transfer (GIFT), zygote intrafallopian transfer (ZIFT), and surrogate motherhood, while described here, will be treated in a separate responsum.)

Within Jewish sources, children are seen as one of God's chief blessings. Sarah, Rebecca, Rachel, and Hannah have trouble conceiving and bearing them, but that only adds to the preciousness of the children they ultimately have. God's blessings of the Patriarchs promise children as numerous as the stars, and later Deuteronomy and the Psalmist include children prominently in their descriptions of life's chief goods.[1]

Moreover, Jewish law understands propagation not only as a blessing, but a commandment. It is, indeed, the first of the biblical commandments, and its occurrence in the creation story in the opening chapter of the Torah indicates the centrality of children in the Bible's understanding of human life. While both husband and wife are obviously necessary to procreate, for exegetical and, probably, economic and/or physical reasons, the Mishnah later asserts that it is only the man who is subject to the commandment — the reason why Jewish law is more permissive in the use of female contraceptives than male ones — and that to fulfill this biblical demand one must have two children.[2] Here, though,

---

[1] Sarah, Rebecca, Rachel and Hannah have trouble having children: Gen. 15:2-4; 18:1-15; 25:21; 30:1-8, 22-24; 35:16-20; 1 Sam. 1:1-20. God's blessings of the Patriarchs promise numerous children: Gen. 15:5; 17:3-6, 15-21; 18:18; 28:14; 32:13. Children figure prominently in the descriptions of life's chief goods in Deuteronomy (e.g., 7:13-14; 28:4, 11) and in Psalms (e.g., 128:6).

[2] The biblical command to "be fruitful and multiply": Gen. 1:28. The Mishnah's determination that it is only the man who is subject to the commandment: M. Yevamot 6:6 (61b), where the ruling is recorded as the majority opinion (that is, without ascription) and where Rabbi Yohanan ben Beroka immediately objects: "With regard to both of them [i.e., the male and female God first created] the Torah says, 'And God blessed them and said to them... "Be fruitful and multiply."'" The Talmud (B. Yevamot 65b-66a) brings conflicting evidence as to whether or not a woman is legally responsible for procreation and ultimately does not decide the matter. That is left for the later codes; cf. M.T. Laws of Marriage 15:2; S.A. Even HaEzer 1:1, 13. The Talmud there also brings conflicting exegetical grounds for the Mishnah's ruling restricting the command to men, basing it alternatively on "Replenish the earth and subdue it" (Gen. 1:28) or on Gen. 35:11, "I am God Almighty, be fruitful and multiply." There are problems in using both texts, however. The traditional pronunciation of the Hebrew verb in the first verse (Gen. 1:28) is in the plural, making propagation a commandment for both the man and the woman; it is only the written form of the text that is in the masculine singular (and even that can apply, according to the rules of Hebrew grammar, to either men alone or to both men and women). The second verse (Gen. 35:11) is indeed in the masculine singular, but that may be only because God is there talking to Jacob; the fact that Jacob is subject to the commandment proves nothing in regard to whether his wives were.

These problems make it likely that the real reason for limiting the commandment of procreation to men is not exegetical at all, and we have to look elsewhere for what motivated the Rabbis to limit it in that way. I would suggest that that reason is to be found in the economic sphere — specifically, that since men were going to be responsible for supporting their children (although there is some question as to whether they were legally obligated to support their daughters), it was against the man's best economic interests to have children, and so it was precisely the men that had to be commanded. Alternatively, since the man has to offer to have conjugal relations with his wife for procreation to take place, it may be that physical factor that prompted the Rabbis to impose the commandment on men.

The Mishnah's determination that that command is fulfilled with a minimum of two children is also found in M. Yevamot 6:6 (61b). In that Mishnah, the School of Shammai say that one has to have two boys and the School of Hillel say that one must have a boy and a girl. The Talmud understands the School of Shammai's position to be based on the fact that Moses had two sons, Gershom and Eliezer (1 Chron. 23:15); while the Mishnah already states that the School of Hillel's ruling is based on Gen. 1:27, according to which God created the human being, "male and female God created them."

There are several variations on this ruling in the sources. A Tosefta (T. Yevamot 8:3), included in the Talmud (B. Yevamot 62a), asserts that the School of Shammai actually requires two males and two females, while the School of Hillel requires a male and a female. Yet another talmudic tradition (ibid.), in the name of Rabbi Nathan, states that the School of Shammai requires a male and a female, while the School of Hillel requires

as usual, the Mishnah is only specifying the minimum needed to fulfill one's obligation under the law. Jewish practice at that time and throughout the centuries since then, and indeed later Jewish law itself, together make it clear that one was supposed to have as many children as one could, for, as Maimonides says, "whoever adds even one Jewish soul is considered as having created an [entire] world."[3]

As the biblical stories indicate, though, couples cannot always have the children that both they and the Jewish tradition would like. Like the biblical characters, modern couples often experience their inability to have children as frustrating and degrading. Somehow, they think, we should be able to do what our bodies were designed to do and what most other people's bodies enable them to do. Especially when all one's married friends are having children, an infertile couple often feels not only unlucky and deprived, but embarrassed and defensive as they continually feel the need to explain why they do not have children too. Infertility even challenges many people's feeling of adequacy as a man or as a woman – and as a mate. Some marriages fall apart due to the tension engendered by continued, unsuccessful attempts to have children.

The Jewish emphasis on children can actually be an additional source of consternation for infertile couples. Couples who cannot have children are no longer obligated to fulfill the commandment to propagate, for commandments make logical and legal sense only when the one commanded has the ability to obey. Still, Jewish couples who seek to abide by Jewish law – and even those who do not – often *feel* that they are letting down not only each other, but their parents, the Jewish people, and God.

In addition to these legal concerns, there are emotional and theological components of the tradition that add to infertile couples' misery. The tradition, as we have noted, glories in children. So, for example, when the Psalmist wants truly to bless his listener or reader, he says:

> Happy are all who fear the Lord, who follow His ways. . . .Your wife shall be like a fruitful vine within your house; your sons, like olive saplings around your table. So shall the man who fears the Lord be blessed. May the Lord bless you from Zion; may you. . .live to see your children's children. May all be well with Israel![4]

---

either a male or a female. The Jerusalem Talmud (J. Yevamot 6:6 [7c]) records the position of Rabbi Bun (Abun) who takes note of the context of the School of Hillel's ruling right after that of the School of Shammai's ruling requiring two boys. Rabbi Bun therefore reads the School of Hillel as agreeing that two boys would suffice to fulfill the obligation, but "*even* a boy and a girl" would, and thus the School of Hillel is offering a leniency over the School of Shammai's requirement of two boys, in line with the School of Hillel's general reputation. Rabbi Bun also notes that if that were not the case – that is, if the School of Hillel were saying that *only* a boy and a girl would fulfill the obligation – then this ruling should appear in the various lists of the stringencies of the School of Hillel in Chapters 4 and 5 of M. Eduyot, but it does not. Despite these variants, the codes rule that the obligation to propagate is fulfilled only when one has a boy and a girl: M.T. Laws of Marriage 15:4; S.A. Even HaEzer 1:5.

Based on Exod. 21:10, the Rabbis deduced the obligation for a man to offer to have sex with his wife independent of the possibility of propagation. See M. Ketubbot 5:6.

[3] The Talmud (B. Yevamot 62b) encourages couples to have as many children as possible on the basis of Isa. 45:18 ("Not for void did He create the world, but for habitation [לשבת] did He form it") and Eccles. 11:6 ("In the morning, sow your seed, and in the evening [לערב] do not withhold your hand") When codifying this law, Maimonides adds the explanation quoted; see M.T. Laws of Marriage [אשות] 15:16. Maimonides' theme of a whole world being created with the birth of a child is echoed in M. Sanhedrin 4:5, "If anyone keeps a person (according to some manuscripts, "within the people Israel") alive, it is as if he has sustained an entire world," and the converse appears in B. Yevamot 63b: "If someone refrains from propagation, it is as if he commits murder (literally, 'spills blood') and diminishes the image of God."

[4] Ps. 128:1, 3, 4, 5.

As that passage indicates, such positive feelings about children are, at least in part, due to the tradition's conviction that children are an expression of God's blessing of those who abide by the conditions of God's Covenant with Israel. As the Torah says explicitly:

> If you obey these rules and observe them faithfully, the Eternal, your God, will maintain for you the gracious covenant that God made on oath with your forbears. God will love you and bless you and multiply you.... There shall be no sterile male or female among you.[5]

While this sounds warm and loving to those who have children, it has a very different ring to those who do not. As one infertile Jewish woman has written,

> Fertility, it seems, is an integral component of the covenant. Is barrenness, then, next to godlessness? If you who are fertile have received a sacred blessing, have we who are not received a divine curse?[6]

Of course, the people involved in the biblical stories of infertility include no less than our Patriarchs and Matriarchs, who are depicted as being in very good graces with God. Indeed, in later sections of the Torah, the merits of those people and the oath God swore to them are the grounds for forgiving the seriously erring Israelites after the molten calf incident and for God's choosing the people Israel in love.[7] The Torah, therefore, is ambivalent about piety producing fertility and about fertility being the mark of piety, and that should hopefully be of some comfort to infertile Jewish couples.

If the biblical stories of infertility raise internal, theological problems within the Torah, their prevalence should not surprise us at all. In our own time's one in seven couples in the United States is infertile, where "infertile" denotes a couple who is actively trying to have a child over the period of a year and cannot conceive. Since Jews go to college and graduate school in percentages far exceeding the national norm, they generally do not even try to have children until their late twenties or thirties. That compounds the problem yet further for the Jewish people, for infertility increases with age: 13.9 percent of couples where the wife is between thirty and thirty-four are infertile, 24.6 percent where the wife is between thirty-five and thirty-nine, and 27.2 percent where the wife is between forty and forty-four As many as 1.2 million patients are treated annually in the United States for infertility problems, with approximately one billion dollars spent each year in their care. Even so, for as many as one in five infertile couples, a cause is never found, and as many as half the infertile couples seeking treatment are ultimately unsuccessful, despite trying various avenues of treatment.[8]

---

[5] Deut. 7:12-14.

[6] Julie Stockler, "The Longing for Children," *Moment* 18:5 (Oct. 1993): 94.

[7] Exod. 32:13; Deut. 7:6-8.

[8] U.S. Congress, Office of Technology Assessment, *Infertility: Medical and Social Choices*, OTA-BA-358 (Washington, D.C.: U.S. Government Printing Office, May 1988), pp. 1, 3, 4, and 6. According to that report, in 1982, an estimated 8.5 percent of married couples with wives aged fifteen to forty-four were infertile, 38.9 percent were surgically sterile, and 52.6 percent were fertile. As the report notes, however, surgical sterilization masks some couples who were infertile anyway, and so if they are excluded from the population base, the 2.4 million infertile couples account for 13.9 percent of the remaining 17.3 million couples, or roughly one in seven. See also Lori B. Andrews, *New Conceptions* (New York: St. Martin's Press, 1984), p. 160; Paul Lauritzen, "Pursuing Parenthood: Reflections on Donor Insemination," *Second Opinion* (July 1991): 57-58.

In contrast to biblical times, though, scientific methods now exist to enable the other half of these couples to bear children. This provides new hope to such couples, and we certainly rejoice with them when they succeed in having the children they want. Whenever we *can* do something new, though, we must ask the moral and legal question of whether we *should* or do so, and the new methods of achieving conception come with some clear moral, financial, communal, and personal costs that must be acknowledged and balanced against the great good of having children.

Traditional Sources on Non-Sexual Insemination

Artificial insemination is one method used when a couple cannot conceive through sexual intercourse because of sexual dysfunction, insufficient or abnormal sperm, or less than the required mobility of the sperm. There are four sources within the tradition that contemplate insemination of a woman without sexual intercourse, and so even though they do not reflect methods of insemination parallel to modern means, they are commonly invoked in contemporary Jewish discussions of artificial insemination.

The first occurs in the Talmud:

> Ben Zoma was asked: "May a high priest [who, according to Lev. 21:13, must marry a virgin] marry a maiden who has become pregnant [yet who claims she is still a virgin]? Do we take into consideration Samuel's statement, for Samuel said: 'I can have repeated sexual connections without [causing] bleeding [i.e., without the woman losing her virginity],' or is the case of Samuel rare?" He replied: "The case of Samuel is rare, but we do consider [the possibility] that she may have conceived in a bath [into which a male has discharged semen, and therefore she may marry a high priest]."[9]

However implausible conception by these means may seem to moderns, this talmudic source clearly contemplates the possibility of conception without sexual intercourse, and its simple meaning is that artificial insemination neither invokes the prohibitions nor leads to the illegitimacy of adultery or incest through sexual relations. Even some medieval and early modern rabbis, though, had trouble imagining such a situation, let alone using it as a basis for legal decision, and so they interpret the passage metaphorically.[10] Others, however, accept the possibility of such conception and interpret the passage on its face, leading Rabbi Moshe Feinstein, for example, to permit donor insemination.[11]

The second source generally cited is a medieval Midrash regarding Ben Sira, second-century B.C.E. author of a book of the Apocrypha often cited in the Talmud. This legend, first mentioned by Rabbi Jacob Moellin Segal (1365-1427) in his work *Likutei Maharil*, claims that Ben Sira was conceived without sexual intercourse by the prophet Jeremiah's

---

[9] B. Haggigah 14b.

[10] Judah Rozanes, *Mishneh Le-Melekh* on M. Laws of Women (הלכות אשות) 15:4; Moses Schick (Maharam Schick), *Taryag Mitzvot*, ch. 1; Solomon Schick, *Responsa Rashbam*, Even HaEzer, ch. 8.

[11] E.g., Rabbis Hayyim Joseph David Azulai, quoted in Immanuel Jakobovits, "Artificial Insemination, Birth Control, and Abortion," *Ha-Rofeh Ha-Ivri* (1953) 2:169-183 (English) and 114-129 (Hebrew); Rabbi Jonathan Eybeschuetz, *Benei Ahuvah* on M. Laws of Women (הלכות אשות) 15:6; and Rabbi Jacob Ettlinger, *Arukh La-Ner* on B. Yevamot 12b. The sources in this and the previous note are cited in Rosner, "Artificial Insemination," in Fred Rosner and J. David Bleich, *Jewish Bioethics* (New York: Sanhedrin Press, 1979), p. 116, notes 4-7. Rabbi Moshe Feinstein also bases his permission to use donor insemination on this source, noting that it specifically classifies the child as legitimate; see *Iggrot Moshe*, 4 Even HaEzer 1:10, 2:11, 3:11.

daughter in a bath, the father having been Jeremiah himself who, coerced by a group of wicked men, had emitted semen into the water. The Midrash is undoubtedly based on the fact that the Hebrew spellings of "Jeremiah" and "Sira" have the same numerical equivalent (271). The legend subsequently appears in many medieval texts as well as most, if not all, of the rabbinic responsa dealing with artificial insemination.[12] The story is denied, however, by Rabbi David Gans, who notes its absence in the Talmud and the classical collections of Midrash, and who quotes Rabbi Solomon ibn Verga to the effect that Ben Sira was the son of the daughter of Joshua ben Jehozadak, a High Priest mentioned in the Book of Ezra.[13] Be that as it may, this story supports three contentions: that conception without sexual intercourse is possible; that, unlike sexual intercourse, it does not impart the status of illegitimacy (ממזר) as it normally would on a child conceived by a father and daughter; and, since the legend asserts that Ben Sira was the child of Jeremiah, the sperm donor is apparently to be considered the legal, as well as the biological, father of the offspring.

The third source commonly quoted is the comment of Rabbi Perez ben Elijah of Corbeil in his work *Haggahot Semak*, who states:

> A woman may lie on her husband's sheets but should be careful not to lie on sheets upon which another man slept lest she become impregnated from his sperm. Why are we not afraid that she become pregnant from her husband's sperm and the child will be conceived of a menstruating woman [niddah]? The answer is that [we are not concerned about the child being the progeny of a menstruating woman] since there is not forbidden intercourse, [and so] the child is completely legitimate [kasher] even from the sperm of another, just as Ben Sira was legitimate. However, we are concerned about the sperm of another man because the child may eventually marry his sister.[14]

Whether or not a woman can, in fact, be impregnated by sperm on a sheet (presumably shortly after the man left the bed), Rabbi Perez clearly assumes that she can, and thus we have another source within the tradition that contemplates insemination without sexual intercourse. Like the legend cited above, Rabbi Perez assumes that the child so conceived is legitimate, even if the sexual union of the biological parents would have been prohibited – here, because the woman was (or might have been) menstruating. He also mentions a concern that will arise in cases of artificial insemination by a donor (and also in cases of adoption), namely, the worry that the child will later have intercourse with his half-sister or her half-brother, an act that Lev. 18:9 classifies as incest. The people involved would presumably be acting unknowingly, of course, and one then must ask whether the prohibition would apply; but even if it does not, contemporary Jewish law must be concerned with the danger of genetic defects in the children of such a biologically consanguineous relationship.

Finally, Rabbi Moses ben Nahman (Nahmanides), in explaining the verse, "One may not have intercourse with one's neighbor's wife for seed [or sperm]" (Lev. 18:20),

---

[12] J.D. Eisenstein, "Alfa Beta de-Ben Sira," *Otzar Midrashim* (New York: Hebrew Publishing Company, 1928), p. 43; cf. J. Preuss, *Biblical and Talmudic Medicine*, trans. Fred Rosner (New York: Sanhedrin Press, 1978), pp. 463-464; H. Friedenwald, *The Jews and Medicine* (Baltimore: Johns Hopkins Press, 1944), vol. 1, p. 386; Immanuel Jakobovits, *Jewish Medical Ethics* (New York: Bloch, 1959, 1972), pp. 244-250.

[13] David Gans, *Zemah David* (Offenbach, 1968). 1:1:441. p. 14b. S. Verga, *Shevet Yehudah* (Lemberg, 1846).

[14] Quoted by Rabbi Joel Sirkes. *Bayit Hadash* ("*Bah*") on the Tur, Yoreh De'ah 195. Also quoted by Rabbi David ben Samuel Ha-Levi, *Turei Zahav* ("*Taz*"), on S.A. Yoreh De'ah 195:7.

points out that the last two Hebrew words of that verse seem unnecessary. He then raises the possibility that they were included in the text to emphasize one reason for the prohibition of adultery, namely, that society will not know from whom the child is descended. On this basis, Rabbi Yoel Teitelbaum rules that donor insemination is biblically prohibited, for it is like adultery in that the identity of the donor is usually unknown and because D.I. establishes a genetic relationship between the biological father and the child which, had there been intercourse, would have been categorized as an act of adultery. Rabbi Eliezer Waldenberg goes even further: he uses Nahmanides' interpretation as forbidding the very act of injecting a donor's semen into a married woman's womb as an act of adultery, regardless of the absence of sexual contact involved.[15]

Note that the first three sources are all ruling after the fact (בדיעבד) of insemination. Using them for rulings of artificial insemination, then, whether such rulings be stringent or lenient, will require us to ignore this disanalogy.

There is another problem in using them. As a matter of general policy, I maintain that we should use the precedents within our tradition to guide us in our own rulings as much as possible, even when they are scant in number and considerably different in context from the questions we are asking, as long as we keep these disanalogies in mind in assessing the weight we give the precedents and the conclusions we draw from them.[16] Rabbi Teitelbaum, however, already anticipates a problem in using the commentary of Nahmanides, for it is not obvious that biblical commentaries were ever intended to be sources of law.[17] Moreover, the first three sources discussed in this section, the ones that explicitly contemplate the possibility of artificial insemination, are so unlike the contemporary conditions in which the question of the permissibility of artificial insemination arises that one wonders whether they can seriously serve as a legal resource for our questions.

The Range and Costs of Available Infertility Treatments

The methods of insemination described in the sources above, even if physically possible, are happenstance at best. Modern infertility treatments differ from the first three of the above sources in two significant ways. First, when contemporary techniques are used, all parties involved intend for conception to take place; and, second, the probability of that happening is considerably greater than it is in the situations described by the first three sources.

Specifically, in our time, about fifty percent of infertile couples are ultimately treated successfully, and about eighty percent of those are aided in producing children through con-

---

[15] Rabbi Moses ben Nahman, *Commentary to the Torah*, on Lev. 18:20. Rabbi Yoel Teitelbaum, *Divrei Yoel* 110, 140. Rabbi Eliezer Waldenberg, 9 *Tzitz Eliezer* 51:4; see also 3 *Tzitz Eliezer* 27:1, where Rabbi Waldenberg vigorously opposes the ruling of Rabbi Peretz, quoting a number of early decisors who disagree with him on the unqualified legitimacy of a child born without sexual union.

[16] See Elliot N. Dorff, "Toward A Methodology for Jewish Medical Ethics," *Jewish Law Association Studies* 6, B.S. Jackson and S.M. Passamaneck, eds. (Atlanta: Scholars Press, 1992), pp. 35-57; and, more briefly, in "A Jewish Approach to End-Stage Medical Care," *PCJLS 86-90*, pp. 66-77. For other positions that challenge the appropriateness of the legal methodology that I think we should use in making Jewish normative decisions, see Daniel H. Gordis, "Wanted – The Ethical in Jewish Bio-Ethics," *Judaism* 38:1 (winter 1989): 28-40; David Ellenson, "How to Draw Guidance from a Heritage: Jewish Approaches to Mortal Choices," in Barry S. Kogan, ed., *A Time to Be Born and a Time to Die* (New York: de Gruyter, 1990), pp. 219-232; and Louis Newman, "Woodchoppers and Respirators: The Problem of Interpretation in Contemporary Jewish Ethics," *Modern Judaism* 10 (Feb. 1990): 17-42.

[17] Yoel Teitelbaum, 2 *Divrei Yoel*, 110, 140. He claims that biblical commentaries may nevertheless be considered a source of law if they engender a stringency rather than a leniency. For Rabbi Moshe Feinstein's reply, see *Dibbrot Moshe*, Ketubbot 238-239.

ventional medical and surgical therapy. Medical treatment ranges from relatively simple techniques like teaching the couple to pinpoint the time of ovulation for maximum potential for conception to more sophisticated treatments like artificial insemination or drug therapy to stimulate the ovaries to ovulate. Surgical treatments also span a wide spectrum of complexity, ranging from ligation of testicular veins for eliminating varicocele to delicate microsurgical repair of reproductive tract structures in both men and women.

Ovulation induction, surgery, and artificial insemination are the most widespread and the most successful approaches to overcoming infertility. Drug therapy with Clomid for stimulating ovulation and artificial insemination are successful in slightly less than fifty percent of the cases in which they are tried, and they generally cost $300 or $400. (If Pergonol is used instead of Clomid, the cost is considerably greater, amounting to $2,000 to $3,000 per cycle.) Corrective surgery, of course, is also expensive, but where it is appropriate, it holds out the hope for a permanent solution to the couple's infertility problems.

Three more complicated and more expensive reproductive technologies – in vitro fertilization (IVF), gamete intrafallopian transfer (GIFT), and zygote intrafallopian transfer (ZIFT) – account for the other twenty percent of those couples who are successfully treated.[18] In addition, the couple may enlist the help of another woman through "traditional surrogacy" or gestational surrogacy. Since these procedures are not the subject of this responsum, I will not describe them in detail here. Suffice it to say, though, that these procedures are much more costly ($8,000-$10,000 for each try), have a much lower rate of success in producing a baby (approximately ten percent for each attempt), and raise gnarly legal, moral, and psychological problems.[19]

Even the less costly and morally less complicated methods of correcting infertility, though, have financial, legal, moral and psychological costs, and couples thinking about using them must recognize these burdens and plan support mechanisms to deal with them before deciding to employ such aids. Sex on schedule does indeed take much of the joy out of making love. It also makes you think of your body as a machine somehow detached from "you." Since that machine is not working as well as you would like, at least in this one area, you may lose a measure of self-confidence and self-respect. Many feel sad and alone; some cannot talk about this even with their spouse. Indeed, some fear losing their spouse altogether due to the trials of reproductive technology; infertility is already a strain on most marriages, but using reproductive technology focuses attention on children and the couple's inability to have them. If repeated attempts are necessary, repeated failures are

---

[18] The 85-90% and 10-15% breakdown between conventional treatments and the more technologically sophisticated approaches of IVF, GIFT, and ZIFT is found in the report of the Office of Technology Assessment of the U.S. Congress, *Infertility*, p. 7.

[19] Doctor Brenda Fabe, a gynecologist/obstetrician at Kaiser Permanente Hospital in West Los Angeles, supplied these approximate costs for me. See also Elizabeth Royte, "The Stork Market," *Lear's* (Dec. 1992): 52-55, who reports similar prices.

Royte also notes that success rates "were widely overreported in the early 1980s, with clinics reporting take-home baby rates of thirty to thirty-five percent. After an Office of Technology Assessment investigation in 1987, numbers became more realistic, but because the fertility industry isn't yet regulated by law, there are still no reporting standards." As a result, instead of live births, clinics may count pregnancies, and "they may not disclose the number of babies born with congenital diseases or that die within a month of birth." Moreover, "a woman who has triplets may add three births to the clinic's log, though only one mother takes babies home." (All citations from p. 54.)

The American Fertility Society asserts that IVF has a 15.2 percent success rate, and then only counting couples who produce quality eggs, sperm, and embryos (p. 54). That does not count the couples who drop out because they cannot produce such genetic materials. Still, ten years ago, IVF's success rate stood at less than five percent; by 1987 it had doubled (p. 55), and by now it has effectively tripled.

possible, and the couple will need to deal with ever-renewed hopes and oft-recurring disappointments. After all, only half of the couples with infertility problems are ultimately successful in having children of their own through the techniques now available.[20]

None of this is sufficient reason to ban the use of these techniques by Jews, but the psychological costs of seeking to treat infertility in these technological ways, as well as the economic, legal, and moral ones, must be balanced against the emotional costs of not having children or of having them through adoption. Infertile couples are under no Jewish obligation to use modern technology to have children. If they nevertheless choose to do so, they must recognize and take into account all of the factors involved in order to make a reasonable and Jewishly responsible decision.

Let us return to the beginning. Couples having trouble getting pregnant are normally first advised to time their intercourse to coincide with the woman's most fertile time. Rabbis do not object to this since it usually comes at the beginning of the time when the couple is permitted by the laws of family purity (טהרת המשפחה – or, as Rabbi Susan Grossman has suggested, קדושת המשפחה) to have conjugal relations after waiting for the woman's menstrual period to be over.[21]

If timing does not work, physicians commonly do a thorough analysis of both the husband and wife. If corrective surgery can help either or both of them to become fertile, Jewish law would permit taking the risks of surgery for such a purpose, although it would not require it. The life or health of neither of them is threatened by their inability to have a baby, and so the surgery would not be required on those grounds. Furthermore, even though the man has a duty to procreate under Jewish law, he is under no obligation to undertake the risks of surgery to fulfill that duty — although, again, both he and his wife may do so.

Sometimes drug therapy is required to stimulate the woman's ovaries. Even though there is evidence that such drugs increase to some extent the risk of ovarian cancer, high blood pressure, and strokes, the demonstrated risk is not so great that such therapy must be prohibited because of the overriding Jewish concern of Jewish law to preserve the woman's life and health.[22] On the other hand, because the woman's own health is not threatened by her infertility, and because, in any case, she is not subject to the command to procreate, she is not at all required by Jewish law to use such drugs. That is an option she has, an option she can choose to act on or refuse with the full endorsement of Jewish law for either choice.

---

[20] U.S. Government, *Infertility*, p. 9.

[21] Susan Grossman, "Feminism, Midrash, and Mikveh," *Conservative Judaism* 44 (winter 1992): 14. Rabbi Grossman has pointed out to me that sometimes one of the manifestations of a woman's infertility problem, particularly in older women, is that she spots during the middle of her cycle, and that could mean, according to the laws of family purity, that she must refrain from conjugal relations with her husband for three days during her time of ovulation to insure that her menstrual period is indeed over. To make it possible for such women to have conjugal relations during ovulation despite such spotting, traditional women, sometimes with the collusion of Orthodox rabbis, have invented creative ways to circumvent such possibilities, such as wearing dark underwear during that time so that the spots are not noticeable. For those infertile couples in the Conservative community who observe the laws of family purity, we would heartily endorse such creative solutions to this problem of staining, especially since the time about which we are talking is, at worst, during the women's "clean days," which are only rabbinically enacted, while the commandment to have children incumbent upon her husband is biblical.

[22] The general imperative to take steps to maintain our health is, according to Maimonides and Isserles, based on Deut. 4:9 and 4:15, "and you shall guard yourselves." The verses in context speak about guarding ourselves against following other gods, but Maimonides and Isserles applied them to guarding our bodies against illness as well. See M.T. Laws of Ethics (דעות), chs. 3-5; Laws of Murder 11:4-5; S.A. Yoreh De'ah 116:5 (gloss). Because they are reading the verses out of context, there is a debate in later sources as to whether by quoting these verses they mean to make the requirement biblical or whether the verses are merely a supporting text (*asmakhta*) and the command is therefore rabbinic: see the Tumim (27:1), affirming its biblical nature, and the

The next most common method of reproductive therapy is artificial insemination, including artificial insemination by the husband (A.I.H.) or by a donor (A.I.D., or so as not to confuse that with the AIDS virus, the more common abbreviation is now D.I. for donor insemination or, in some discussions, S.D.I. for surrogate donor insemination). This responsum will focus on both these forms of artificial insemination, along with the converse of D.I., egg donation, and the alternative to all such reproductive technologies, adoption. In so doing, hopefully this responsum will lay the groundwork for another, later responsum that will deal with the yet more complicated issues raised by IVF, GIFT, ZIFT, and surrogacy.

Artificial Insemination Using the Husband's Sperm

A. Circumstances in which Artificial Insemination is Used

The practice of artificial insemination has been used and documented in animals since the late eighteenth century, and the first successful case in humans was reported by the Scottish surgeon, Dr. John Hunter, in 1790.[23] This, however, may be long after such success with artificial insemination actually occurred, for whereas IVF, GIFT, and ZIFT require surgery and therefore doctors, hospitals, and anesthesia, and whereas artificial insemination is now usually done in a doctor's office or as an out-patient in a clinic or hospital, women may have performed artificial insemination on their own for some time before this using the "turkey baster method."

In any case, while artificial insemination is only one method used to treat infertility, the process has a much higher national success rate (fifty-seven percent) than other available procedures (estimated as seventeen percent at best), and it is less invasive and less dangerous than some of the alternatives. Moreover, although many people assume that infertility is almost always rooted in a problem in the female, actually close to half of the time the problem resides in the male.[24] Average sperm counts over the past fifty years have declined by fifty percent for reasons that researchers are now investigating.[25] Whatever the cause, the consequent need for artificial insemination has increased dramatically in the last several decades. Thus when it becomes clear that a couple is infertile and cannot be made fertile through timing their intercourse for the woman's most fertile period, through pills to aid ovulation, or through surgery to remove blockages in the testes or fallopian tubes, artificial insemination is usually the first technique attempted. Estimates for the number of children born each year in the United States through donor insemination range from 10,000 to more than 30,000, and many more are born through A.I.H. Dr. Fred Rosner estimated in 1970 that by then some 250,000 Americans were the product of

---

Lehem Mishnah to M.T. De'ot 3:5 and the Meiri, who both consider it to be rabbinic. In any case, saving a life (פקוח נפש) the extreme case of maintaining our health and the issue here, is a well-attested principle in Jewish law, one that the Rabbis deduce from Lev. 18:5, understanding "and you shall live by them [i.e., My commandments]" to mean that you shall not die by them; see B. Shabbat 32b, 129a, 132a, 151b; Yoma 82a-85b; M.T. Hilkhot Yisodei Torah 5:1. The Rabbis also asserted the converse, that we may not unduly put ourselves at risk; see n. 85 below.

[23] Fader, *Sperm Banking: A Reproductive Resource* (Los Angeles: California Cryobank, Inc., 1994), p. 3. Immanuel Jakobovits, *Jewish Medical Ethics*, p. 244, claims that the first successful human insemination was in 1866.

[24] Fader, ibid., pp. 8, 11.

[25] "Health Report," *Time*, 7 June 1993, p. 20. Two researchers claimed recently that the decline is due to men's increased exposure to estrogen in milk from hormone-dosed cows and water supplies contaminated by chemical spills.

artificial insemination, and the U.S. Government's 1987 survey suggested that some 65,000 children are born each year through artificial insemination, almost half through D.I. and the remainder through A.I.H.[26]

About half of all artificial inseminations are done to overcome fertility problems in the husband, and the other half serve to circumvent problems in the wife (or in both partners). If the number of sperm in the husband's semen is too small to generate children, or if it is insufficiently motile (that is, if it is not shaped correctly or energized enough to swim up the vaginal cavity), then if it can be made effective if several ejaculates are combined, the husband's semen, thus enhanced, is used for inseminating his wife.[27] This is Artificial Insemination by the Husband (A.I.H.).

If the husband's sperm is not sufficiently numerous or motile, and if attempts to enhance its number or mobility fail, the couple can ask for donor insemination (D.I.). While it is possible that the sperm of a fertile, male family member can be used, the more common practice is to use the sperm of a donor to a sperm bank whose medical history and often whose occupation and personal characteristics are known to the couple but whose identity is usually not revealed to them.

Semen has proteins that, if injected directly into the woman's uterus, could produce anaphylactic shock in the woman, collapse, and perhaps even death. As a result, in most artificial inseminations, whether using the husband's semen or a donor's, the semen is put at the opening of the cervix so that the mucous membranes in the cervical canal can remove the antigens in the semen, leaving only sperm that reaches the uterus. This, of course, is exactly what happens in normal intercourse, and this form of artificial insemination is the cheapest and most effective way of assisting generation.

Under some conditions, however, this relatively easy method cannot be used, and so more developed and more expensive means of reproductive technology must be invoked — assuming that the couple chooses to do so. Specifically, if concentrating several ejaculates does not work to increase the sperm's mobility or number, the semen may be "washed" or "spun down" with various tissue culture media to separate viable sperm from the other components of the semen. Since this process removes the semen's accompanying antigens, the sperm thus isolated can be injected directly into the uterus,

---

[26] The numbers in this paragraph are from Andrews, *New Conceptions*, p. 160; Lauritzen, "Pursuing Parenthood," pp. 57-58; Fred Rosner, "Artificial Insemination in Jewish Law." *Judaism* (fall 1970) (reprinted in Rosner and Bleich, *Jewish Bioethics*, p. 105); and Fader, *Sperm Banking*, pp. 12-13. The 1987 U.S. Government report was based on a survey conducted by the Office of Technology Assessment, entitled, *Artificial Insemination: Practice in the United States: Summary of a 1987 Survey-Background Paper*, OTA-bp-ba-48 (Washington, D.C.: U.S. Government Printing Office, Aug. 1988). That survey reported only a thirty-seven percent success rate for artificial insemination (instead of fifty-seven percent), and thus 65,000 babies from the 172,000 women inseminated each year. Even so, that is still more than double the highest success rate claimed by those using the more complicated methods — and almost four times as high as the actual ten percent success rate of those procedures.

[27] According to Meredith F. Small ("Sperm Wars," *Discover*, July 1991, p. 50), "Doctors look for a sperm count of at least 20 million per milliliter of semen, but they are more interested in sperm mobility — the speed and swimming direction of individual sperm — because a few fast swimmers are more likely to succeed than millions of sluggards. Reproductive physiologists believe that at least forty percent of the sperm viewed under the microscope must be vigorous, well-aimed swimmers for a couple to have a good chance at conception." Of the 300 million sperm in a typical human ejaculation, within ten minutes of landing at the cervix only thousands speed toward the fallopian tubes at the far end of the uterus, where the egg lies in wait after drifting down from the ovaries, and only two hundred sperm typically make it to the egg. Once one sperm has managed to bore into the egg, the shell of the egg releases enzymes that detach the other sperm. Ibid., pp. 51-52. This article also presents the results of recent research to the effect that sperm counts for ejaculations during intercourse decreased the more time couples spent together and, conversely, increased when the male assumed female infidelity. That is *not* a justification for an infertile couple to try promiscuity as a therapy!

thus ameliorating problems of mobility. Moreover, because washing away the other elements of the semen concentrates the sperm, problems of low sperm count can also be overcome through this method.

Artificial insemination is also used to overcome reproductive problems in the female. If, for example, the woman's cervix is damaged, the man's sperm cannot reach the uterus and must be washed and artificially implanted there. Similarly, if the woman's cervix does not make good mucus naturally, or if the drugs she is taking to stimulate her ovaries spoils the effectiveness of her cervical mucus, the sperm must be washed and implanted into her uterus to avoid shock. In such cases, the husband's sperm is used when it can be, and these constitute other situations when A.I.H. is used. If the husband's sperm cannot be used and if the woman suffers from any of these problems, a donor's sperm may be implanted in her uterus, and this, then, is another set of circumstances in which D.I. is used, in this case to resolve problems in both the male and the female.

B. Rabbinic Responses to A.I.H.

When the semen of a man is united artificially with his wife's ovum, most rabbis who have written on the subject have not objected.[28] Because of Judaism's appreciation of medicine as an aid to God, there is no abhorrence of such means merely because they are artificial.

The only issue is the means by which the husband's sperm is obtained. To insure that there is no "destruction of the seed in vain," some rabbis advocate collecting it from the vaginal cavity after intercourse, but an obstetrician I consulted, one who has many observant Orthodox and Conservative patients — told me that collecting sperm in that way is simply "unrealistic." Moreover, the vaginal pH kills the sperm since it is more acidic than cervical mucus. Consequently, rabbis have permitted using a condom to collect the semen for A.I.H. (clearly one without spermicide). Some of these rabbis insist, though, that the condom have a small hole in it so that there is still some chance of conception through the couple's intercourse. While I have no particular objection to such stringencies, it does seem to me that they are unnecessary, for producing semen for the specific purpose of procreating cannot plausibly be called wasting it — and, indeed, some Orthodox rabbis follow the same line of reasoning and permit a man to masturbate to produce semen for artificial insemination of his wife.[29] We should adopt this latter approach.

In the same spirit, Rabbi Morris Shapiro has argued that where the husband is the donor, he should be credited with fulfilling the mitzvah of procreation, for the mitzvah is to produce two viable children for which both intercourse and artificial insemination are merely preparations.[30] This severs the command to procreate from the method of conception, interpreting the command instead as a matter of the couple's intent to produce children and their success in doing so. Despite this separation of procreation from sexual intercourse and the emotional bonding that commonly accompanies it, I would agree with Rabbi Shapiro for three reasons. (1) The sperm involved is the husband's in

---

[28] See, for example, Immanuel Jakobovits, *Jewish Medical Ethics*, p. 264; J. David Bleich, *Judaism and Healing: Halakhic Perspectives*, (New York: Ktav, 1981), pp. 83-84. Dr. Rosner lists, in addition, Rabbis Feinstein, Schwadron, Walkin, and Zevi Pesah Frank as permitting A.I.H., while Rabbis Tanenbaum and Waldenberg "frown upon it, stating it is permissible only in extreme situations" — but, of course, that is, by hypothesis, always the case. See Rosner, "Artificial Insemination," in Rosner and Bleich, *Jewish Bioethics*, p. 112.

[29] Cf. Bleich. ibid. p. 84, n. 3 for a list of sources on this issue.

[30] Rabbi Morris Shapiro, "Artificial Insemination in Jewish Law," prepared in Aug. 1978 for the Committee on Jewish Law and Standards, p. 3.

any case, and the child is therefore the husband's according to all understandings of Jewish law.[31] (2) The husband, by hypothesis, cannot fulfill the commandment in any other way. By virtue of going through the expense and trouble of artificial insemination, though, he has demonstrated clearly that he wants to obey the commandment, and the Talmud says that God attributes the merit of fulfilling a commandment if one tries to do so but cannot.[32] Finally, (3) the husband generally goes through considerable humiliation, pain, and perhaps depression in coming to terms with his inability to impregnate his wife through sexual intercourse, and therefore we should do all we can to augment his satisfaction with the whole procedure so that he does not forever associate his new child with his own frustration in the process of conceiving him or her — a result that is as important for the child as it is for the man.

Artificial Insemination with a Donor's Sperm: Legal Concerns

When the husband cannot provide sperm capable of impregnating his wife, the matter becomes more complicated. After such infertility is diagnosed, the obligation to procreate ceases to apply to the man, for one cannot be legally obligated to do that which one cannot do. A Jewish couple faced with this situation, then, should pause, seek counseling, and think carefully about whether they want to use donor sperm or engage in costly and often frustrating attempts to have a child through some of the new reproductive technologies.

There is no Jewish obligation to do any of these things. The Jewish tradition would have all people, fertile or infertile, understand that our ability to procreate is not the source of our ultimate, divine worth; that comes from being created in God's image, which is true of each of us from the moment of birth to the moment of death, whether or not we manage to have children in between. (Note that, in contrast to many religions of the ancient past, God in the Bible and in the Talmud and Midrash specifically does *not* engage in sexual union to create us or anything else, and so imitating God does not require procreation through sexual union.) As Jews, we gain additional divine worth through our Covenant with God, which foresees a reward of children "as numerous as the stars above" but which is made with the current generation of Jews just as much as with any past or future one. Moreover, the religious commandment to generate children, which, in any case, traditionally is only incumbent on the male, ceases to apply to those men who cannot have them, and there is no guilt or shame involved in that. That is just the way God created some of our bodies.

On the other hand, as I shall argue below, the couple *may* choose to use at least some of the new procedures. Such a choice, though, should be made only when the couple has understood all the factors involved. In addition to the psychological problems described above that affect the vast majority of couples who have infertility problems, using someone else's sperm (or eggs) engenders some specific problems of its own that

---

[31] Dr. Rosner cites all of the following who claim that the donor is considered the father in Jewish law: Rabbis Moses of Brisk, Samuel ben Uri, Judah Rozanes of Constantinople [a commentator on Maimonides' *Mishneh Torah*], Jacob ben Samuel, Israel Ze'ev Mintzberg, Simeon Zemah Duran, and Jacob Ettlinger. Rabbis Jacob Emden and Moses Schick rule that the child is the son of the donor, but the donor has not fulfilled the commandment of procreation because there has been no sexual act involved. Only Rabbis Hadaya and Moses Aryeh Leib Shapiro on Dr. Rosner's list do not consider the child as that of the donor. See Rosner, "Artificial Insemination," in Rosner and Bleich, *Jewish Bioethics*, p. 111, with the specific sources in notes 30-37 on p. 117.

[32] B. Berakhot 6a; B. Kiddushin 40a; J. Peah 1. But according to B Kiddushin 39b, there is one exception to the converse of this rule. Specifically, in weighing the culpability of a person, God does not ordinarily connect an evil thought to its act (even if not fulfilled), but God does so when one thinks of idolatry.

will be described below. The couple must understand the strains that all these factors are likely to impose on their marriage if they go through with these procedures, and they must make plans to get help in dealing with them. Finally, they should investigate alternatives like adoption before trying such reproductive technology.

If the couple does choose to forge ahead and use donor sperm, may they do so in accordance with Jewish law? Rabbis addressing that question to date have raised several legal and moral objections:

A. Adultery and Illegitimacy

Some rabbis object to donor insemination on grounds of adultery. If artificial insemination is construed as adultery, then its product would be an illegitimate child (ממזר) who himself or herself and whose descendants may not marry a Jew for ten generations according to the Torah.[33] Rabbi Eliezer Waldenberg, for example, takes strong exception to donor insemination on these grounds:

> The very essence of this matter — namely, the placing in the womb of a married woman the seed of another man — is a great abomination of the tent of Jacob, and there is no greater profanation of the family than this in the dwelling places of Israel. This destroys all the sublime concepts of purity and holiness of Jewish family life, for which our people has been so noted since it became a nation.[34]

For me, however, this misstates our concern with preventing adultery. The Torah, of course, prohibits adultery with no special explanation aside from the general rationales it gives for all of its laws regarding prohibited sexual relations, namely, that we should observe those commandments to make us holy and pure as a people. From the context of the Torah, holiness clearly denotes making us different in moral character and action from the ancient Egyptians and Canaanites, and purity entails avoiding pollution of the land of Israel through licentious sexual practices;[35] but these terms can well include other factors as well, factors intrinsic to what we understand holiness and purity in spousal relations to mean. The question, then, is whether artificial insemination violates our understanding of holiness and purity in a marital relationship.

The crucial part of those concepts involved in the prohibition of adultery, it seems to me, is maintaining the trust between husband and wife; it is that trust that is violated when either spouse has an extramarital affair. In standard cases of artificial insemination by a donor, however, the husband not only knows about the insemination, but deeply wants it so that he and his wife can have children.[36] This, of course, is not in and of itself sufficient to make donor insemination acceptable, for even if both partners agreed to each other's adultery, that would not make it permissible. The vast majority of cases of adultery, how-

---

[33] Deut. 23:3.

[34] *Tzitz Eliezer* vol. 9, 51, ch. 5, sec. 1, p. 251.

[35] For the prohibition of adultery see Lev. 18:16 and 20:10. For the rationale that observing this will make us holy and pure, see Lev. 18:24 and 20:8, 26. For separation from the practices of the Egyptians and Canaanites as an explicit component of the meaning of those terms, see Lev. 18:3, 27, 30; 20:23, 24, 26. For avoiding pollution of the land of Israel as another component of the meaning of these terms: Lev. 18:25-29; 20:22.

[36] Rabbi Paul Plotkin has suggested that, biblically at least, the ban of adultery is based not on the breach of trust involved, but on the violation of the husband's acquisition of his wife (קנין). In D.I., though, the husband agrees to the procedure, and so presumably his rights of possession are not violated.

ever, involve a breach of trust, and it is that which explains much of our abhorrence of adultery, for such untrustworthiness undermines the honesty and holiness that we want in marriage. While trust is the critical feature that is lacking in most cases of adultery, it is fully present in most, if not all, cases of donor insemination. Contrary to Rabbi Waldenberg, then, I think that artificial insemination by a donor is not an "abomination" or "profanation" that destroys all Jewish concepts of holiness and purity, but rather is a desperate attempt to have children — an undisputed good in marital relationships for the Jewish tradition — in a context of mutual openness and trust.

On a more technical level, the Talmud, Maimonides, Rabbi David Halevi (the "Taz"), and the majority of recent authorities have already maintained that adultery takes place only when the penis of the man enters the vaginal cavity of the woman.[37] That is clearly not the case when insemination takes place artificially. The lack of contact of the genital organs in donor insemination, then, means that it does not legally constitute adultery, and the child conceived by D.I. is legitimate and does not suffer from the liabilities of an illegitimate child (ממזר).

Not only is the physical contact missing; the intent to have an illicit relationship is also absent. While lack of intent to commit adultery does not excuse an act of sexual intercourse from the requirement to bring a sin offering, it does excuse the couple from the more serious penalties of extirpation (כרת), death at the hands of the court, or lashes.[38] Thus the intent of the couple is an important legal consideration, and it is even a more important moral consideration. In the case of D.I., the couple's intent is the exact opposite of adultery, for they are going through expensive and emotionally taxing procedures in an effort to express their love *for each other* through having and raising a child. Thus D.I. should not be construed as adultery either theologically, legally, or morally.

---

[37] B. Shavuot 18a; cf, M. Yevamot 6:1 (53b), B. Yevamot 54a, and B. Horayot 4a. M.T. Laws of Forbidden Intercourse 1:10-11. This is also the opinion of Rabbi David Halevi (the "Taz") of the seventeenth century, who bases it on the responsa of Rabbi Peretz, an eleventh-century scholar; see *Turai Zahav* in S.A. Even HaEzer 1:8. Rabbi Peretz is quoted there as asserting that "in the absence of sexual intercourse, the child resulting from the mixing of sperm and egg is always legitimate." Rabbi Bleich, who vigorously opposes A.I.D., nevertheless notes the following modern authorities (Aharonim) who require sexual contact for a sexual act to be termed adulterous: Rabbi Shalom Mordecai Schwadron, *Teshuvot Maharsham* (Brezany, 1910). vol. 3, no. 268; Rabbi Aaron Walkin, *Teshuvot Zekan Aharon* (New York, 1951), vol. 2, no. 97; Rabbi Ben Zion Meir Hai Uziel, *Mishpetai Uziel* (Tel Aviv, 1935), Even HaEzer, vol. 1, no. 19; Rabbi Moshe Feinstein, *Iggrot Moshe* (New York, 1961), Even HaEzer, vol. 1, no. 10; and Rabbi Eliyahu Meir Bloch, *Ha-Pardes*, Sivan 5713. On the other hand, he cites the following who do not require sexual contact for the prohibition of adultery to take effect: Rabbi Yehudah Leib Zierlson, *Teshuvot Ma'arekhei Lev*, no. 73 and Rabbi Ovadiah Hadaya, *No'am*, vol. 1 (5718), pp. 130-137, with reference also to Rabbi Eliezer Waldenberg, *Tzitz Eliezer*, vol. 9, no. 51, sec. 4. These latter authorities stress that Lev. 18:20 reads literally, "and to the wife of your fellow you shall not give your intercourse for seed to defile her," which, in their view, would include providing semen even without sexual intercourse. See J. David Bleich, *Judaism and Healing*, p. 84, notes 1 and 2.

In the discussion of this responsum by the Committee on Jewish Law and Standards, Rabbi Paul Plotkin noted that for those who insist on contact of the genital organs to establish adultery, there is a parallel in the Talmud's insistence that the Torah's prohibition against eating blood is violated only when the blood is ingested in the normal way, through the throat. Therefore, contrary to the Jehovah's Witnesses, who interpret the biblical command more broadly, we Jews permit blood transfusions, even when they are precautionary and not clearly essential for the saving of a life. See B. Sanhedrin 63a, and another responsum of mine (Elliot N. Dorff, "A Jewish Approach to End-Stage Medical Care," *PCJLS 86-90*, pp. 101-102), in which I use this precedent along similar lines to permit the withdrawal of artificial nutrition and hydration. While I would agree that this case is parallel to the one at hand — and I want to thank him for calling my attention to that — and while that strengthens the point being made here, we do not need to depend upon it to establish that adultery occurs only where there is genital contact because the Talmud and later authorities already make that point.

[38] See M.T. Laws of Forbidden Intercourse 1:1, 9, 12 (and see the commentary of the Maggid Mishneh there).

B. Unintentional Incest in the Next Generation

If the donor is anonymous, there is also the possibility of unintentional incest in the next generation, for the product of the artificial insemination might happen to marry one of the children whom the donor has with his wife. In that case, the child born through donor insemination would be marrying his or her biological half-brother or half-sister. This issue is resolved in Jewish law if the donor is known and the children avoid his offspring as mates. It is also resolved if it is known that the donor is not Jewish, for Jewish law does not recognize family relationships among non-Jews through the father's line.[39] On that basis, Rabbi Moshe Feinstein permitted D.I. if the donor were not Jewish – although he was later pressured to withdraw his responsum.[40] The pressure notwithstanding, Rabbi Feinstein stood on sound Jewish legal grounds in permitting D.I. from a non-Jewish donor.

Some Orthodox rabbis object to using the sperm of a non-Jewish donor, however, for fear that this will pollute the purity of the Jewish genetic line and will transfer non-Jewish qualities of character (whatever that means) to Jewish offspring. Curiously, physicians report that traditional Jews prefer non-Jewish donors for fear of incest in the next generation, but liberal Jews want Jewish donors. The motivations for that may be many, but undoubtedly for some people insemination by a non-Jew smacks of inter-marriage, and others probably hold an ethnic notion of Jewish identity and want a Jewish donor for reasons not unlike the Orthodox arguments against polluting the Jewish biological line. This line of reasoning is clearly rooted in exclusivist views of Jews and non-Jews, views to which we should not be party. In the case of the Orthodox respondents who hold this view, it is also, as Daniel J. Lasker has shown, the product of kabbalistic affirmations of original sin, a doctrine roundly rejected by the non-mystic sources of Jewish thought – and rightly so.[41]

There is another factor, though, that should prompt us strongly to urge that the identity of the donor, or at least substantial parts of his medical history, be known. In addition to Jewish law's prohibition of sexual intercourse between Jews and non-Jews, there is an independent commandment in Jewish law to maintain health. We therefore must be concerned to prevent progeny with serious genetic defects or diseases due to the consanguinity of the couple This is clearly a concern if we know that the donor is Jewish, but in our own day, with rampant intermarriage, it is even a worry if the donor is not Jewish, for a child born through D.I. may some day marry a non-Jew who is his or her natural half-brother or half-sister – or have intercourse with such a person outside of marriage. This concern is all the more worrisome because sperm banks are largely unregulated and many use the same donors for numerous inseminations.[42] All these factors would argue all the more strongly in the present circumstances of rampant intermarriage that a child born through D.I. should

---

[39] B. Yevamot 98a; cf. Tosafot, B. Yevamot 22a, s.v. ערוה. M.T. Laws of Forbidden Intercourse, 14:13; S.A, Yoreh De'ah 269:3.

[40] Moshe Feinstein, *Iggrot Moshe*, Even HaEzer (New York. 1961), vol. 1, nos. 10 and 71, pp. 12-14, 169-171; Hoshen Mishpat, vol. 2 (New York. 1963), no. 11, pp. 322-324. On the pressure that ultimately caused him to withdraw these responsa, see Zvi Hirsch Friedman, *Sefer Sedeh Hemed* (Brooklyn, 1965/6), p. 34.

[41] Daniel J. Lasker, "Kabbalah, Halakhah, and Modern Medicine," *Modern Judaism* 8:1 (Feb. 1988): 1-14, esp. pp. 7-11.

[42] Currie-Cohen, Lullrel, and Shapiro, "Current Practice of Artificial Insemination by Donor in the United States," 300 *New England Journal of Medicine* 585 (1979). Thirty-one percent of the inseminating doctors surveyed in that study indicated that they use the sperm of several donors within one menstrual cycle, while 51.1 percent reported that they use a single donor, but change donors with each new cycle, and one donor had been used to produce fifty pregnancies; see p. 587. If the subject is a donor for a minority ethnic group in the

know the identity of his or her natural father, whether Jewish or not — or at least enough of his medical history to avoid people with similar medical histories as mates. The same, incidentally, would be true for an adopted child.

In light of much larger numbers of non-Jews than Jews in North America, this concern would not be as great if it were known that the natural father (or, in the case of adoption, the natural parents) were not Jewish, for then the chances of such an unwitting, consanguineous union occurring are much, much smaller. The day is probably not too far off when such unions can be prevented through DNA analysis of the child and his or her potential mate without revealing anything about the identity of the donor.

The strong recommendation of the American Association of Tissue Banks-Reproductive Council, however, and the preference of most donors and sperm recipients are that the parties involved remain unknown to each other. However, in the future a health condition may arise in the child whose proper treatment requires more information from the donor than he provided on the initial questionnaire, or, conversely, a genetic condition might appear in the child that could have health implications for the donor's children or family. Therefore, responsible sperm banks keep donor and patient files and continue to track the whereabouts of donors and patients.

Moreover, while children born through donor insemination currently do not have at age eighteen the same legal rights as adopted children do to trace their biological parents, D.I. children may well gain such rights in the future, especially since the medical and psychological needs that propelled the change in legislation for adopted children are similar in D.I. children. That, then, is another reason for couples using D.I. to make sure that the sperm bank they are using keeps careful and current records of their donors and recipients.[43]

Disclosure of the identities of donors and recipients, then, is still preferable for the physical reasons described above and the psychological reasons delineated below, but the common practice of confidential donor insemination is permissible *if* the sperm bank keeps thorough records on all its donors and recipients and conscientiously updates them as necessary. Furthermore, as much as possible of the donor's medical history must be revealed to the child in order to prevent possible genetic diseases in that child's own offspring.

---

area, the chances of intermarriage by the children become even greater; see p. 589, n. 9. Medical students are the most tapped resource; cf. George Annas, "Fathers Anonymous: Beyond the Best Interests of the Sperm Donor," 14 *Family Law Quarterly* 7 (1980). Apparently one such case actually took place in Tel Aviv, and in another case in the United States incest was avoided only by the intervention of a doctor who knew of the couple's common paternal roots: see Hoffer, "The Legal Limbo of Artificial Insemination by Donor," *Modern Medicine*, 1 Nov. 1979, p. 27.

I was not able to find any definitive study of the practice of sperm banks on this issue after the Cohen study of 1979. On the other hand, while that may have changed, none of the sources I consulted — including a 1993 summary of law regarding artificial insemination published by the American Bar Association — reported any new legislation prohibiting such multiple uses of one donor's sperm. See Julia J. Tate, *Artificial Insemination and Legal Reality* (No city indicated: American Bar Association, Section of Family Law, 1992), 27 pages.

On the contrary, in the booklet published by California Cryobank, Inc. (Fader, *Sperm Banking*, at n. 23 above), the practice is that sperm donors must agree to donate sperm twice a week for a minimum of a year, and preferably two. They have that policy because they freeze the man's sperm for six months while they continue to test him for AIDS and venereal diseases to make sure that his sperm is not infected, and "without the year minimum commitment from donors, this safety measure could not be carried out" (p. 21). They report that "the number of live births from one donor usually ranges between two and ten" (p. 21), and they retire a donor after his sperm has produced ten live births. Nevertheless, they maintain that the chance of offspring from a single donor inadvertently marrying and having children, "although not impossible, . . .is extremely remote," especially because they distribute frozen sperm internationally (pp. 21-22).

[43] See Fader, *Sperm Banking*, pp. 26-27.

C. Identity of the Father

While adoption was applauded in Jewish law, it did not gain the legal power to replace the child's natural parentage. So, for example, if an orphan is the child of a כהן but his adoptive father is a ישראל, the child retains his natural father's status at birth. The same would presumably be true for the child born through D.I. But what if the biological father's status is not known? And what if the donor is a non-Jew — or, at least, is not known to be a Jew?

In addition to these questions of personal status, there are related questions of inheritance. Would the child of D.I. inherit from the sperm donor, the husband (the "social father"), neither, or both?

And then there is the question of the commandment to "be fruitful and multiply." Does a man fulfill that obligation if he consents to have his wife impregnated with the semen of another man? Does he fulfill it if his own semen is artificially implanted in his wife's uterus? What if he himself is a semen donor?

By and large, rabbis have ruled that the provider of the semen is the father. Nevertheless, some rule that a semen donor does not fulfill the obligation to procreate because there is no sexual act involved, and some do not see either the donor or the social father as the father for purposes of Jewish law.[44] These varying positions, of course, would directly affect the answers to the questions raised above regarding personal status (כהן, לוי, or ישראל) and inheritance within Jewish law in addition to the question of the commandment to procreate.

Let us take them one by one. With regard to personal status, if the donor's status as a כהן, לוי, or ישראל is known, the child inherits that. If the donor's status is not known, the child is usually treated as a ישראל as a default status. If it is not certain that the donor of the semen is a Jew, that does not matter with regard to the Jewish identity of the child, for Jewish law determines a person's Jewish identity according to the bearing mother. Her religion can usually be determined, and then, if necessary, the child can be converted to Judaism as an infant. The more complicated questions of personal status regarding the possibility of incest in the next generation have been treated above.

As for inheritance, thirty-one American states have passed laws making the child of a married couple who use D.I. the legal child of the couple. Unlike adoption, no court order or other official action is required for this to be the case, but some states restrict this parentage to cases in which a physician did the procedure, and most (twenty-six) require that the husband's consent to the donor insemination be in writing. Eighteen of these thirty-one states have adopted some form of the Uniform Parentage Act, which defines the donor as *not* being the father with regard to either rights or responsibilities, as long as a physician was involved in the insemination.[45] Donors who want to protect their property, though, may want to remain anonymous in states that have not passed the act, where a physician was not

---

[44] See n. 30 above.

[45] John Yeh and Molly Uline Yeh, *Legal Aspects of Infertility* (Boston: Blackwell Scientific Publications, 1991), pp. 41-48. The Uniform Parentage Act, 9A U.L.A. 592 (1979), drafted in 1973 by the National Conference of Commissioners on Uniform State Laws and approved by the House Delegates of the American Bar Association in 1974, has since been passed in whole or in part by the following states: Alabama, California, Colorado, Delaware, Hawaii, Illinois, Kansas, Minnesota, Missouri, Montana, Nevada, New Jersey, New Mexico, North Dakota, Ohio, Rhode Island, Washington, and Wyoming. Section 5(A) deals with donor insemination.

This acceptance of donor insemination in American law took some time. In 1964, Georgia became the first state to pass a statute legitimizing children conceived by donor insemination, on condition that both the husband and wife consented in writing, and the first American appellate court ruling affirming that stance was in

involved, or where the husband did not provide written consent to the procedure (or the donor has no way of knowing whether the husband did). In any case, since Jewish law does not govern inheritance in the United States or Canada, the implications of D.I. for inheritance within Jewish law need not concern us; it is, after all is said and done, a moot issue for Jewish law, determined by the law of the state.

What Jewish law does determine, though, is whether a Jewish man fulfills the commandment to be fruitful and multiply through agreeing to have his wife impregnated by a donor, and the answer to that has generally been "No."[46] Rabbi Joseph Soloveitchik, however, has said that raising adopted children does fulfill the commandment,[47] and the same reasoning would seem to apply to a child conceived through D.I.

The first point that must be mentioned here is that donor insemination stretches our understanding of fatherhood. We normally assume that the same man who sired a child will be the one who raises him or her. When that does not happen, the legal category of fatherhood and the concept underlying it must be applied to new circumstances, and then we should not be surprised if the attribution of fatherhood does not fit exactly right, no matter which way we rule.

In our case, some factors would lead us to call the semen donor the father for purposes of the commandment of propagation. Unless there has been a formal, legal act of adoption, in American law we call the man who brings up a child but who did not sire it "the foster father" or "the step-father," depending upon the circumstances. That usage, which exists in Rabbinic law as well (*apotropos*), would argue for seeing only the biological father as the one official "father." Moreover, as I shall describe in more detail in the section on adoption below, while the Jewish tradition applauded adoption as a way of providing parental support and education for orphaned children, it never ascribed legal parentage to the adoptive parents but rather saw them as the agents of the child's natural parents. That precedent would seem to apply to the biological and social fathers of a child born through D.I. as well, making the social father the agent of the biological father and not his legal substitute. Underlying both the linguistic usage and the law on adoption is the genetic fact that it is the natural father's DNA that the child inherits, not the social father's. Modern research has made us increasingly aware of the impact of our genes on who we are as people, not only biologically, but in a number of

---

1968 in the California Supreme Court case, *People v. Sorenson*. The court there upheld Mr. Sorenson's criminal conviction for not supporting a D.I. child conceived with his consent during his marriage. The court held that the sperm donor had no more responsibility for the use of his sperm than a blood donor had for the use of his/her blood. This was in sharp contrast to the 1954 ruling of the Supreme Court of Cook County, which held that regardless of the husband's consent, D.I. was "contrary to public policy and good morals, and constituted adultery on the mother's part," so that the child so conceived was the mother's exclusively and "the father has no rights or interest in said child." See Fader, *Sperm Banking*, pp. 4-5. Thus the 1973 recommendation of the Commissioners on Uniform State Laws that children born through D.I. be considered legitimate was, for most jurisdictions, breaking new ground. It has, however, been widely followed: see S. v. S., 440 A.2d 64 (N.J. 1981); In re Adoption of Anonymous, 345 N.Y.S.2d 430 (1973); Noggle v. Arnold, 338 S.E.2d 763 (Ga. 1985); R.S. v. R.S., 670 P.2d 923 (Kan. 1983); Mace v. Webb, 614 P.2d 647 (Utah 1980); In re Custody of D.M.M., 404 N.W.2d 530 (Wis. 1987); L.M.S. v. S.L.S., 312 N.W.2d 853 (Wis. 1981); In re Baby Doe, 353 S.E.2d 877 (S.C. 1987). Thus, the man who consents to the artificial insemination of his wife is now legally obligated to support the resulting children, either on the theory of equitable estoppel (since he, after all, consented to the insemination), or on the theory of adoption, according to which the husband, by his consent, has formally or informally adopted the children.

[46] For example, Bleich, *Judaism and Healing*, p. 30.

[47] Melech Schachter, "Various Aspects of Adoption," *Journal of Halakhah and Contemporary Society* 4 (fall 1982): 107.

character traits as well. That genetic contribution of the semen donor, while shaped by the child's upbringing, is ultimately indelible. It influences the medical history of the child, and it determines the identity of the people whom it is genetically dangerous to marry, lest the children born of that marriage suffer from the diseases rooted in their consanguineous union.

On the other hand, there are other factors that would lead us to classify the social father as the one who fulfills the command to propagate. According to the biblical law of levirate marriage, when a man dies childless, it is the duty of his brother to have conjugal relations with the deceased man's widow so that a child might be born bearing the parentage of the deceased brother. That precedent would argue that the semen donor is not the father.[48] Moreover, one classical Rabbinic source ascribes fatherhood to the man who raises a child, not to the one whose semen gave him birth. It is a homiletical (midrashic) source, and therefore not one that intends to announce law, but it does invoke a parable that places its ruling in a legal context, the writing of a marriage contract, and, contrary to other sources, it specifically proclaims the guardian the father. Based on Isa. 64:7, "But now, O Lord, You are our Father," the Midrash says:

> The Holy One, blessed be He, said: "You have abandoned your ancestors, Abraham, Isaac, and Jacob, and you are calling Me father." They said to Him: "We are recognizing You as [our] father. Parable: An orphaned girl grew up with a guardian [*apotropos*], and he was a good and faithful man who raised her and watched over her as is fitting. He wanted to marry her off, and the scribe came to write her marriage contract. He said to her: "What is your name?" She said: "So-and-so." He said to her: "And what is the name of your father?" She began to be silent. Her guardian said to her: "Why are you silent?" She said to him: "Because I know no father except you," for the one who raises [a child] is called father and not the one who begets. Similarly, these orphans, Israel, for it says, "We were orphans without a father" (Lam. 5:3), their good and faithful Guardian is the Holy One, blessed be He, [and] Israel began to call Him "our Father," as it says, "But now, O Lord, You are our Father" (Isa. 64:7). The Holy One, blessed be He, said: "You have abandoned your ancestors and you call Me 'Our Father'?" as it says, "Look back to Abraham, your father, [and to Sarah who brought you forth]" (Isa. 51:2). They said to Him: "Master of the world, the one who raises [a child] is the father and not the one who begets [him/her]," for it says, "For You are our father, for we have not known Abraham" (Isa. 63:16).[49]

---

[48] Deut. 25:5-10. This law may only refer to inheritance rights, but the language of Deuteronomy seems to indicate a stronger relationship, for the levir is to have a child with his sister-in-law, whom he takes "as his wife," but "The first son that she bears shall be accounted to the dead brother, that his name may not be blotted out in Israel" (Deut. 25:6).

[49] Exodus Rabbah 46:5. In contrast, another, deservedly famous source (B. Sanhedrin 19b) proclaims that "Whoever brings up an orphan in his home, Scripture ascribes it to him *as if* he had begotten him." This source in Exodus Rabbah, however, removes the "as if."

Furthermore, the fact that the semen donor never intended to raise the child makes him somewhat like the gentile who renounces the idolatrous status of a given idol and thereby converts it into a mere statue;[50] similarly — although obviously with no implications whatsoever that a child is an idol! — the donor's explicit intention to have someone else raise the child might, it could be argued, amount to a renunciation of his status of fatherhood and a transfer of it to the social father. Yet another precedent that argues in this direction is that of Jacob, who adopts Ephraim and Menasheh, even though he did not beget them, and their descendants thus become two of the twelve tribes of Israel, along with the descendants of the rest of Jacob's sons.[51]

Aside from these arguments based on facets of Jewish law, a number of contemporary realities would argue in this direction. American law, as we have seen, construes the man who raises the child to be his or her father for all legal purposes. With the exception of the physician who asks for a medical history of the child's family, all of the people who come into the child's life see the social father as the father too. That is right and proper, for the social father, after all, invests a lifetime of energy, love, and substance in the child, while in most cases the donor never even meets the child. Jewish law generally awards privileges only to those who bear concomitant responsibilities, and that would certainly suggest in this case that the man who raises the child, rather than the man who merely ejaculates, should merit the status of fulfilling the commandment of propagation. Such a ruling would accord with both the intentions and the actions of both men involved.

Whichever way we rule, then, some aspects of the ruling will seem counterintuitive, for in some ways the semen donor really is the father, and in some ways the social father is. Seeing exclusively one or the other as the father hides important aspects of the child's being. We need, then, to craft a ruling that recognizes the fatherhood of both men involved in the distinctive ways in which they are the child's father.

For purposes of the commandment of propagation, we must see the semen donor as the father of the child. In part, this is because of the precedents cited at the start of this responsum — although, as I indicated there, those stories are not really on point as analogies for the modern practice of D.I. More substantively, then, it is the ultimate fact that the child's genetic heritage is that of the semen donor that motivates this ruling. That fact is important legally in two ways. First, Jewish law abhors incest, counting it among only three prohibitions which one may never violate, even at the cost of one's life.[52] Aside from this legal and moral factor, we also have a medical concern, for we now know the genetic basis of family diseases imparted through consanguineous unions. For both these reasons, then, we must consider the semen donor to be the father for purposes of the commandment of propagation. As we shall note below, this imposes upon him some duties from which American law makes him exempt, and that must be part of his understanding and undertaking when agreeing to be a semen donor.

---

[50] M. Avodah Zarah 4:4-7; T. Avodah Zarah 6:2; B. Avodah Zarah 43a, 52a-55a; M.T. Laws of Idolatry 8:9-12; S.A. Yoreh De'ah 146:1-12.

[51] Gen. 48:5-6. As Rabbi Reuven Kimmelman has pointed out to me, however, Jacob, while not the biological father of Ephraim and Menasheh, was their biological grandfather, unlike the social father of a D.I. child. Furthermore, biblical terminology often does not discriminate between children and grandchildren, and since Joseph was Jacob's first-born son by Rachel, Ephraim and Menasheh may represent Joseph's double portion through primogeniture — although we do not hear of a similar provision for Reuven, Leah's first-born son. In any case, these factors would argue against using this last example to support the social fathers claim to fulfilling the command to procreate, while the specific language of the verses in Genesis, by which Ephraim and Menasheh are legally taken as Jacob's sons even though they are not biologically his sons, would seem to support his claim.

[52] B. Sanhedrin 74a; M.T. Laws of the Foundations of the Torah 5:1-3; S.A. Yoreh De'ah 157:1.

This is not to deny the critical input of the social father in the raising of the child. The second important point to make here, then, is that the command to procreate, like all other commandments, does not apply to those who cannot fulfill it. "In cases of compulsion (אונס), the All-Merciful One exempts him," the Rabbis say.[53] Thus men who cannot impregnate their wives should not see themselves as thereby failing to obey Jewish law; their inability to procreate frees them of the responsibility to do so. In that way, they are legally in a better status than those men who have had many children, but all of the same gender, for such men presumably could still fulfill the commandment of begetting a boy and a girl but technically have not done so.[54] Even there we would probably be inclined to say that the man is exempt from having any more children after having two, regardless of their gender, because no man can consciously control the gender of his children; how much the more is that man exempt who cannot have any children at all.

Moreover, the social father should be aware that there are more than enough other commandments he can and must fulfill, including many dealing with the children the man has with his wife through D.I. In fact, in some ways, the fact that the social father is not legally the father in Jewish law gives the man who assumes all the obligations of raising the children conceived through D.I. a special status. As the Talmud says,

> "Happy are they who act justly, who do right at all times" (Ps. 106:3). Is it possible to do right at all times?...Rabbi Samuel bar Nahmani said: This refers to a person who brings up an orphan boy or girl in his house and enables them to marry.[55]

Thus while the social father — that is, the one who rears the child — is not the father in the technical sense of being the biological parent and therefore does not fulfill through D.I. the specific commandment to procreate, he is the "real" father in most significant ways for the child and "does right at all times."

I would suggest that we go yet further. According to traditional sources, one who raises another person's biological child does not assume the biblical prohibitions associated with one's own child. Thus intercourse between an adoptive parent and the adopted child is not a violation of the biblical laws of incest,[56] and adopted children raised in the same home may, according to the Talmud, marry each other.[57]

---

[53] The principle is announced in B. Nedarim 27a, B. Bava Kamma 28b, and B. Avodah Zarah 54a. There is some discussion among medieval commentators as to whether in cases of compulsion the obligation continues but the person is not culpable for failing to fulfill it (that is, the exemption applies only to culpability for failure to perform the commanded act), or whether the obligation ceases to apply altogether (that is, the exemption is from the obligation itself). The answer depends on whether the person, although unable to fulfill the obligation now, could fulfill it later, in which case the obligation continues and the principle excludes only culpability at this time; or whether the compulsion will continue indefinitely, in which case the obligation itself ceases. In any case, Tosafot (B. Gittin 41a, s.v לישא) apply the principle directly to the obligation to be fruitful and multiply, claiming that in such an instance the obligation itself ceases. In general on this topic, see *Encyclopedia Talmudit* (Hebrew), "אנס" vol. 1, pp. 346-360, esp. pp. 347 and 360.

[54] See note 2 above.

[55] B. Ketubbot 50a.

[56] S.A. Even HaEzer 15:11.

[57] B. Sotah 43b. One medieval authority, Rabbi Judah ben Samuel, decreed that such marriages may not be performed; cf. Judah ben Samuel of Regensberg (He'Hasid), *Sefer Hasidim*, sec. 829. This decree, however, has not been generally accepted; see Rabbi M. Sofer, *Responsa*, 2 Yoreh De'ah 125. As Michael Broyde notes, however, although legally permitted, few such marriages are performed; see Michael Broyde, "Marital Fraud," *Loyola of Los Angeles International and Comparative Law Journal* 16:1 (Nov. 1993): 98, n. 15. The rabbinic prohibition I am proposing below takes that reluctance one step further by giving it legal form.

Even though there is no biological relationship between the social father and the child adopted or born through D.I., and despite the permissive rulings on adoption cited above, I think that the emotional and educational relationships are sufficiently strong for us to apply the category of secondary relations (שניות) to D.I. children – and also to adopted children. That is, in most cases of D.I., the wife's eggs are used for all of the couple's children, and then sexual relations between two of the children, who are biologically half-brothers and half-sisters, are prohibited according to the Torah itself. But even if a couple has a girl and a boy who were both born using another woman's eggs and another man's sperm, we would see it as incest of the second degree for them to have sexual relations, and consequently we would not marry them. The same would be true for two adopted children, even if their biological parents are four separate people, all different from the social parents. Moreover, we would see intercourse between adoptive parents and their adopted children, or between the social father and the donor-inseminated child he is raising, as prohibited incest of the second degree. That is a stringency over the traditional sources, but one that the close relationship created in raising a child warrants.

In sum, because the child's genetic heritage is not the social father's and because traditional sources define an adoptive parent as the agent of the natural parent, we cannot consider the social father as fulfilling the commandment of propagation when either D.I. or adoption is used. Our marital law, though, must recognize the strong bonds that social parents create between themselves and all the children they raise and among all the children themselves, whether they became the social parents' children through artificial insemination, egg donation, or adoption. Consequently, sexual relations between the parents and children or between the children themselves are prohibited in the second degree.[58] Furthermore, the social father's name may be invoked when the child is being identified by his or her Hebrew name, as, for example, when called to the Torah.[59] Similarly, children of donor insemination should consider themselves obligated to fulfill the Torah's commands to honor one's parents (Exod. 20:12; Deut. 5:16) and to respect them (Lev. 19:3) as applied to the social parents, and conversely, the social parents should consider themselves responsible to fulfill the duties that the Torah and the Jewish tradition impose upon parents *vis-a-vis* their children.[60]

---

[58] I would like to thank Rabbi Gordon Tucker for suggesting this approach in the meeting of the Committee on Jewish Law and Standards on 8 Dec. 1993. The Torah's definition of sex between half-siblings as incest: Lev. 18:9; 20:17. The Rabbinic category of incest in the second degree: B. Yevamot 21a; M.T. Laws of Marriage 1:6; S.A. Even HaEzer 15:1ff. In line with this treatment of adoptive and D.I. relationships on a rabbinic, rather than a biblical level, we would maintain the rabbinic rulings that award the possessions, earnings, and findings of a minor child to the custodial, rather than the natural, parents (B. Bava Metzia 12b; S.A. Hoshen Mishpat 370:2). and, despite the laws prohibiting unmarried and unrelated people from living together (ייחוד), we would permit, for example, an adopted son whose adoptive father has died to continue living alone with his adoptive mother. See Broyde, "Marital Fraud," pp. 98-99.

[59] This has been the ruling of the Committee on Jewish Law and Standards, which validated a responsum in 1988 by Rabbi Avram Reisner to the effect that an adopted child may use the patronymic and matronymic of his/her adoptive parents, and a convert need not use בן/בת אברהם אבינו. The same would apply to children born through D.I. See *PCJLS 86-90*, pp. 168-169.

[60] For a brief description of the obligations of children to parents as defined by Jewish tradition, see my article, "Honoring Aged Mothers and Fathers," *Reconstructionist* 53:2 (Oct.-Nov., 1987): 14-20. For a more extended description, see Gerald Blidstein, *Honor Thy Father and Mother* (New York: Ktav, 1975). For a description of the duties of parents toward their children, see Ben-Zion Schereschewsky, "Parent and Child," *Encyclopaedia Judaica* 13:95-100. Vol. 10 of *The Jewish Law Annual* (Boston: Boston University Institute of Jewish Law, and Philadelphia: Harwood Academic Publishers, 1992) was devoted in its entirety to legal aspects of the relationships between parents and children. While the Talmud and later Jewish law codes do not speak of D.I. children specifically, they do require that children honor and

These rulings, then, openly recognize both the ways in which the semen donor (i.e., the biological father) has a relationship to the child and the ways in which the social father does. Donor insemination has real import for both men involved and for the child, and both men must be seen as the "real" father of the child in the critical, but different, ways in which they both are.

Artificial Insemination with a Donor's Sperm: Moral Concerns

A. Licentiousness

Since these strictly legal concerns can be met, most rabbis who have objected to donor insemination have done so on moral grounds. In my own view, positive law and morality are one undifferentiated web, where each can and should influence the other. That is especially true in a religious legal system like the Jewish one, where a fundamental assumption is that the law must express the will of a moral — indeed, a benevolent — God. Thus the moral concerns that donor insemination raises are not, for me, "merely" moral, but fully legal.[61]

It is especially interesting, though, to see rabbis who usually shun moral arguments in their legal decisions resort to them when they cannot find legal grounds to deny the legitimacy of donor insemination. Thus, Rabbi J. David Bleich, for example, claims that since, according to Jewish law, the provider of the semen is the father, the adoptive father does not fulfill the mitzvah of procreation by consenting to have his wife impregnated by another man's seed, even if he subsequently assumes all of the responsibilities of parenthood. In Rabbi Bleich's view, this reduces artificial insemination by a donor to a matter of personal desire that must be weighed against the potential legal problems of adultery, wasting of seed, and incest in the next generation. Despite this, he hesitantly permits it under certain circumstances.[62]

Others have similarly voiced concern about the morality of using someone else's body or semen in this way, and others worry that artificial insemination will increase the prospects of widespread licentiousness. Rabbi Jakobovits voices these moral concerns in strong language:

> If Jewish law nevertheless opposes A.I.D. [artificial insemination by a donor] without reservation as utterly evil, it is mainly for moral reasons, not because of the intrinsic illegality of the act itself. The principal motives for the revulsion against the practice is the fear of the abuses to which its legalization would lead, however great the benefits may be in individual cases. By reducing human generation to stud-farming methods, A.I.D. severs the link between the procreation of children and marriage, indispensable to the maintenance of the family as the most basic and sacred unit of human

---

respect their stepfather and stepmother (B. Ketubbot 103a; S.A. Yoreh De'ah 240:21), and the same would clearly apply to the social parents of D.I. children.

[61] I have written about this in several contexts: "The Interaction of Jewish Law with Morality," *Judaism* 26:4 (fall 1977), pp. 455-466; "Judaism as a Religious Legal System," *Hastings Law Journal* 29:6 (July, 1978): 1331-1360, esp. pp. 1347-1360; and *A Living Tree: The Roots and Growth of Jewish Law* (with Arthur Rosett) (Albany, NY: State University of New York Press, 1988), pp. 249-257.

[62] Bleich, *Judaism and Healing*, p. 80.

society. It would enable women to satisfy their craving for children without the necessity to have homes or husbands. It would pave the way to a disastrous increase of promiscuity, as a wife, guilty of adultery, could always claim that a pregnancy which her husband did not, or was unable to, cause was brought about by A.I.D., when in fact she had adulterous relations with another man. Altogether, the generation of children would become arbitrary and mechanical, robbed of those mystic and intimately human qualities which make man a partner with God in the creative propagation of the race.[63]

We, however, should take a much more positive attitude toward artificial insemination, even when the wife of an infertile man is being inseminated with a donor's semen. After all, people who want to be licentious will find many ways to do so without artificial insemination. Indeed, artificial insemination is so onerous a mode of illicit sex — if it be that at all — that it is downright implausible that people would go to the trouble and expense of using it for such purposes. Furthermore, the couple is, by hypothesis, using D.I. when they have no other way to achieve a precious goal in Jewish law and thought, the bearing of children. As will be discussed below in greater detail, we should applaud their efforts, both because the Jewish tradition has always valued children, and also because having and raising Jewish children is a demographic imperative for the Jewish community in our time.

B. The Impact on the Marriage and on the Parent-Child Relationship

Rabbi Jakobovits' point about severing the tie between generation and parenting is more complicated. We clearly do not want to transform generation to stud farming, we certainly do want to acknowledge the importance of fathers in the rearing of children, and we do want to preserve the tie between children and loving families.

These concerns should not, however, lead us to prohibit artificial donor insemination. At the very most, they would lead us to restrict our approval of it to married couples who cannot have children in any other way, and it may not even do that. This responsum specifically will not treat the issue of artificial insemination of single women because that would require a much more extensive analysis of our developing understanding of "family" and of the evidence available regarding the well-being of children raised by single, but loving, parents. We shall not undertake that here. The question that led to this responsum, though, asks about artificial insemination in the context of infertile, married couples, and so to weigh the morality of donor insemination in that situation, we must analyze what it does to the relationship between husband and wife and between parents and child.

In a philosophically penetrating article probing the nature of parenthood, Paul Lauritzen, a man whose own wife was artificially inseminated, notes that one need not deny the significance of genetic relationships to affirm that the more important parental relationship to a child is that of caring for it:

---

[63] Jakobovits, *Jewish Medical Ethics*, pp. 248-249. Cf. pp. 244-250 and 272-273 generally. Cf. also Bleich, ibid., pp. 81-84; Alex J. Goldman, *Judaism Confronts Contemporary Issues* (New York: Shengold, 1978), pp. 74-86. This was also the opinion of Rabbi Jacob Breish, who engaged in a vigorous debate with Rabbi Moshe Feinstein, agreeing with him that donor insemination was technically legal, but asserting that it would result in a general decline of moral values, that "from the point of view of our religion these ugly and disgusting things should not be done, for they are similar to the deeds of the land of Canaan and its abominations." 3 *Helkat Ya'akov* 45-51. For the debate with Rabbi Feinstein: *Dibbrot Moshe*, Ketubbot, pp. 232-248.

> Caring for, nurturing, and nourishing a child in the context of an ongoing social, emotional, and loving relationship is more important than physically begetting a child, however ineradicable and significant the physical/biological connection that is created thereby.... While genetic connection may foster relational bonds, it is the bonds that are crucial, not the genetic ties.[64]

Lisa Sowle Cahill has argued against artificial insemination (and adoption) on the ground that biological relation offers children greater moral protection from abandonment than the parental bonds to which individuals freely consent, but, as Lauritzen says, that is not necessarily so:

> While it may be true that biological relation will often, in Cahill's words, "undergird and enhance" the interpersonal relation between parent and child, this biological relation is not necessary to the development of an intense, ongoing social relationship; nor does the existence of biological relation ensure a social commitment to care.... Parental responsibilities are, in a sense, inalienable, but it is not genetic connection that makes them so; rather it is the intense, person-specific nature of the interpersonal bonds constituting the parental relation that makes parental responsibility largely nontransferable.[65]

The real moral problems in donor insemination for Lauritzen, then, are those that threaten the purpose of parenthood and the relationship between husband and wife. Chief among those are secrecy and the genetic asymmetry donor insemination creates in the relationship between each of the parents and the child. In addition, as Jews we must also ask how our moral evaluation of donor insemination should be affected, if at all, by the demographic realities of the low Jewish birthrate and high rates of Jewish intermarriage and assimilation in which this question is being asked in the first place.

1. Secrecy

The secrecy that often surrounds artificial insemination is sometimes justified as a protection for the child, sometimes as protection for the husband, and sometimes as protection for the donor. We shall consider each in turn.

Children, the argument goes, may feel perplexed and odd if they know they were conceived in an unusual way, especially as they approach puberty. Moreover, when they have their inevitable quarrels with their parents, children born through donor insemination, like adopted children, may feel and say that they would not be having such problems if their *real* fathers were there. Secrecy presumably shields children from such feelings and helps them accept their social parents, even in time of tension.

Secrecy about how a child was conceived, though, undermines the trust that must be at the very core of a child's relationship with his or her parents — especially on a subject as critical to a child's identity and self-image as his or her origins. Since secrecy almost definitely will require one or both social parents to lie to the child on a number of occasions, the potential damage is even worse. As Sissela Bok notes in her book, *Lying*, lies are

---

[64] Paul Lauritzen, "Pursuing Parenthood: Reflections on Donor Insemination," *Second Opinion* (July, 1991): 63. I want to thank Rabbi Aaron Mackler for calling my attention to this article and those listed on this topic in n. 68 below.

[65] Ibid., pp. 65-66.

particularly corrosive and contagious within families. "The need to shore up lies, [to] keep them in good repair," she writes, "the anxieties relating to possible discovery, the entanglements and threats to integrity — are greatest in a close relationship where it is rare that one lie will suffice."[66] Indeed, as Lauritzen points out, this is possibly the most egregious case of "living a lie," for when the truth about a child's origins through artificial insemination is kept from the child, everything about the parent-child relationship is based on a presumed or explicit lie. That surely is "incompatible with the commitments that responsible parenthood entails,"[67] not only theoretically, but practically, for it engenders shame and guilt, fear and suspicion.

Secrecy does not protect the husband's ego either. It is perfectly normal for men who cannot impregnate their wives to feel angry, inadequate, ashamed, and even guilty. The only hope of coping with such feelings over the long run is not through denial, but rather through expressing them (literally, pushing them out of himself) through open communication with those who are likely to sympathize and support him.

If he can talk about this with his wife, she can reassure him that she still considers him a manly mate, whatever his sperm count or mobility may be. Furthermore, he will soon discover, if he does not already know, that marriage is not exclusively based on the ability to procreate, that it includes, more importantly, sharing life together. Given the possibilities of artificial insemination and adoption, one can surely include the raising of children, which, after all, takes much more of one's time, energy, and commitment and offers a much more sustained basis for sharing than procreation alone does. If the man is sufficiently self-assured to talk with his male friends about this too, he may well find that he is not alone, that some of his friends may be experiencing the same problems or know of others who are, and that, in any case, they will not abandon him as a friend and will not think less of him as a man.

On the other hand, if the man cannot muster enough self-confidence to have such discussions with his wife and friends, he ironically cuts himself off from the very strengthening he so desperately needs. Secrecy about his wife's donor insemination thus will not help him, but will rather compound the problems in making the necessary adjustments in one's thought, feelings, and plans. As Lauritzen says,

> Unfortunately, to mask a problem is not to resolve it, and the secrecy only serves to delay an acknowledgement of the emotional and psychological effects of sterility. Infertile individuals need to mourn and grieve the children they will not produce; they need to resolve any feelings of inadequacies that sterility may engender, and secrecy is an obstacle to meeting both needs.[68]

Moreover, the secret of a woman's donor insemination can be revealed at any time in an angry moment, and that cannot help but add stress to a marriage. Furthermore, relatives and friends who do not know about the donor insemination will quite inno-

---

[66] Sissela Bok, *Lying: Moral Choice in Public and Private Life* (New York: Vantage Books, 1978), p. 224; cited in Lauritzen, "Pursuing Parenthood," p. 69.

[67] Ibid.

[68] Ibid., p. 69. Cf. Rona Achilles, "Anonymity and Secrecy in Donor Insemination: In Whose Best Interests?" *Sortir la maternite du laboratoire*, Conseil du Statut de la Femme (Montreal: Government of Quebec, 1988), pp. 156-163 (notes on pp. 407-408); and Patricia P. Mahlstedt and Dorothy A. Greenfeld, "Assisted Reproductive Technology with Donor Gametes: The Need for Patient Preparation," *Fertility and Sterility* 52:6 (Dec. 1989): 908-914.

cently add to the man's pain when they talk about whom the child resembles. All of these factors mean that the husband's manliness is much better protected if he does not keep the donor insemination of his wife a secret.

Jewish law also would encourage the husband to avoid secrecy. "Be fruitful and multiply" is certainly a commandment, one that North American Jews, who statistically have a 1.6 or 1.7 reproductive rate, nowadays all too often ignore. As we have noted above, however, if one *cannot* fulfill this commandment, one ceases to be obligated by it. Therefore, an infertile man should not feel any shame or guilt for failing to fulfill this commandment since it does not apply to him. Moreover, procreation is not the only duty we have regarding children. Those who cannot procreate may not be able to fulfill that commandment, but they surely can raise children through artificial insemination or adoption. In so doing, they fulfill many commandments and act with real, ongoing חסד (lovingkindness, fidelity) to the children who are, in most significant ways, their sons or daughters. For both of these reasons, then, an infertile Jewish man whose wife is artificially inseminated or whose children are adopted has nothing to hide – and nothing to gain by secrecy.

That leaves the donor. Secrecy surrounding artificial insemination is most often justified to protect the potential pool of donors, for if the donor's identity were known, it is feared, he might be held financially, morally, and perhaps legally responsible for the care of the child or the mother. This might include not only child support and a claim on the biological father's estate when he dies, but also monetary compensation for any disease or disability that passed through the semen from the donor to the child, especially given the general lack of regulations governing sperm banks.[69] Moreover, according to Yeh and Yeh, "many potential donors would be reluctant to give specimens if they knew that their names would be given out publicly."[70] Conversely, the social parents may want to keep the identity of the donor secret to prevent unwanted intrusions by that man in their lives and in the life of their child on the grounds of his biological connection to the child.

Some of these are real concerns, and some are not. As noted above, since the 1970s, most American states have enacted the Uniform Parentage Act or other legislation that makes the husband, and not the donor, the legal father of the child, with most of these states requiring that the husband agree to the procedure in writing and that there be a physician involved in the insemination. The only legal concerns of donors with regard to inheritance or child support, then, involve donations in those states that did not pass the Uniform Parentage Act or its equivalent and donations where the requirements were not met in the laws of those states that did pass such legislation. The latter situation occurred in a recent case where lesbians used a friend as a sperm donor, and he subsequently won the right in court to be involved in the child's upbringing.[71]

Potential liability for diseases contracted through the insemination is a more serious possibility that might lead potential donors to remain anonymous. Indeed, three recent law review articles argued that legal notions of warranty should be invoked or legislation should

---

[69] Richard Doren has stressed this point in arguing for greater control of sperm donations while yet preserving donor confidentiality; see Richard Doren, "The Need for Regulation of Artificial Insemination by Donor," *San Diego Law Review* 22:1193-1218 (1965).

[70] Yeh and Yeh, *Legal Aspects of Infertility*, p. 48.

[71] *Jhordan C. v. Mary K. and Victoria T.*, 179 Cal. App. 3d 386, 224 Cal. Rptr. 530 (1986).

be passed to prosecute such claims, at least if the donor knowingly hid important genetic information or lied about it.[72] This is especially important in light of the fact that donors are usually paid, and even though the sums are modest (typically, $25 for each donation), the money may encourage donors to be careless or evasive in their answers to questions about their physical histories or perhaps even to lie. Only three states — California, Florida, and Indiana — have enacted legislation going beyond the required testing of sperm donors for the HIV virus, and no state has statutorily imposed regulations sufficient to meet the recommended guidelines of the American Fertility Society.[73] This is undoubtedly because in-depth testing of donors and their sperm could cost recipients an additional $800 to $900.[74] That would make donor insemination much more expensive than the $200 to $500 that it commonly costs now, but, of course, it is nothing in comparison to the costs of caring for a genetically defective or diseased child. No legal action has yet been brought against a donor on these grounds, but one could understand why a donor might want to avoid any chance of that through anonymity.

The social parents may also want to preserve the donor's anonymity in order to keep him out of their lives and the life of the child. Of course, those states that have passed the Uniform Parentage Act or its equivalent have thereby established protection against that since the sperm donor, according to such statutes, is legally not the father in any way; but that applies only when all of the details of the law are carried out, such as written permission of the husband and supervision by a physician, where these are mandated by law. Courts have given donors paternal rights where these aspects of the law have not been fulfilled and where the donor has evidenced through his actions that he wanted to serve as the child's father.[75] Thus, even in those states that have laws governing this, and all the more so in those that do not, the social parents may want to guarantee their freedom from the donor through keeping his identity secret.

It is interesting that Australia, which pioneered open adoptions, has also enacted laws that mandate that donors, donors' spouses (if married), and infertile couples be counseled *not* to preserve anonymity before participating in donor programs. A registry in which donors are identified is open to children at age eighteen, equivalent to the law on adoption.[76]

---

[72] Doren, "The Need for Regulation of Artificial Insemination by Donor," at n. 69 above; L. Thomas Styron, "Artificial Insemination: A New Frontier for Medical Malpractice and Medical Products Liability," *Loyola Law Review* 32:411-446 (1986); Anita M. Hodgson, "The Warranty of Sperm: A Modest Proposal to Increase the Accountability of Sperm Banks and Physicians in the Performance of Artificial Insemination Procedures," *Indiana Law Review* 26:357-386 (1993). Styron, at p. 443, n. 190, records the donor agreement recommended by the American Fertility Society to preserve the donor's anonymity yet making him responsible to notify a designated party "should I contract any contagious or venereal disease."

[73] Hodgson, ibid., p. 359 and n. 10 there. See 1991 Cal. Adv. Legis. Serv. 801 (Deering); FLA. STAT. ch. 381.6105 (1990); IND. CODE, par. 16-8-7.5-6 (1988).

[74] Hodgson, ibid., p. 360 and n. 12 there.

[75] *C.M. v. C.C.*, 377 A.2d 82, 152 N.J.Super 160 (Juvenile and Domestic Relations court, Cumberland County, N.J.), 1977; *Jhordan C. v. Mary K. and Victoria T.*, 224 Cal Rptr 530, 179 Cal. App.3d 386 (1986); *In the Interest of R.C.* 775 P.2d 27, 34 (Colo. 1989). The condition that the donor show interest in serving as the father through his consistent actions is critical, for the U.S. Supreme Court, in ruling that a biological father who had no relationship with the child was not entitled to notice of the child's adoption proceedings, held in *Lehr v. Robertson* 463 U.S. 248, 103 S.Ct 2985, 77 L.Ed.2d 614 (1983) that "the mere existence of a biological link does not merit equivalent constitutional protection" to one who did maintain a relationship with the child.

[76] S. Alias and G.J. Annas, "Social Policy Considerations in Noncoital Reproduction," *Journal of the American Medical Association* 255 (1986): 62, cited in Mahlstedt and Greenfeld (at n. 68), p. 911. These laws also prohibit payment for specimens and mixing of donor and husband sperm.

American states, however, have uniformly protected the identity of the donor, and even those who keep records of the donation only allow them to be opened for "cause" or "good cause," some requiring a court order to do so, and this was the position incorporated into the Uniform Parentage Act as well.[77] Thus American states apparently do not want to go as far as Australia has done in revealing donors, social parents, and children to each other.

Even so, one can protect the *confidentiality* of the donor without keeping the fact of the donation a secret. One can even divulge to the child many facts about the donor without compromising his privacy — an important point given that children often want to know and, one might even say, have the right to know, many genetic characteristics of their biological fathers.

At present, only three states (California, Illinois, and Ohio) require the physician to keep records of the attributes of the donor, and fifteen others require that some state agency have such records.[78] We should encourage registration at least of the donor's medical history and, if possible, of other personal characteristics that the donor would like his progeny to know about him. As Mahlstedt and Greenfeld say, "Considering donors real people with specific interests, skills, and family histories enables the donor children to identify positively with their genetic heritage."[79] Moreover, as we noted above, it enables the children to avoid having incestuous sex, either within or without marriage. That is not only important legally and morally, but also physically, for one wants to avoid the genetic problems that can arise in the progeny of an incestuous relationship. For both psychological and physical reasons, then, if the donor insists on confidentiality, his sperm may be used for insemination within the bounds of Jewish law as we interpret it only if information about his medical history, and preferably tidbits about his character and interests, be made available to both the social parents and to the child.

The above approach to matters of secrecy is based on the best advice available in the psychological literature which, in turn, is based on the experience of many, many people — couples, donors, and children — involved in donor insemination. Still, even with all of this input, some couples may choose to keep the donor insemination a secret from their children, family, and friends — just as they do not reveal other things to anyone else, like, for example, the times they have intercourse — in order to make themselves and their child feel as close to them and as "normal" as possible. We should understand and permit that decision, but only after sharing with parents the advice that has emerged from those who have dealt with donor insemination extensively and the reasons for that advice, as described above.

2. *Asymmetry*

The fact that a child born through donor insemination is the biological descendant of the mother but not that of her husband makes for an asymmetry in their relationship to their child. That can cause problems in their spousal relationship if the husband never works out his feelings of anger, impotence, shame, and perhaps even guilt at not being able to father a child. Every time he sees the child, he may be reminded of his own infertility and, in contrast, his wife's ability to procreate. He may once again resent his predicament and, through psychological transference, his wife. The asymmetry

---

[77] Yeh and Yeh, *Legal Aspects of Infertility* (at n. 45), pp. 45-46.

[78] The Health Department is mandated to keep such records in Alabama, Colorado, Minnesota, Montana, Nevada, New Jersey, and Wisconsin; a local court or the Registrar of Vital Statistics keeps such records in Connecticut, Idaho, Kansas, New Mexico, Oklahoma, Oregon, Washington, and Wyoming. See Yeh and Yeh, *Legal Aspects of Infertility*, pp. 45-46.

[79] Mahlstedt and Greenfeld, "Patient Preparation" (at n. 68), p. 911.

involved in donor insemination also may cause problems in the father-child relationship. In Lauritzen's words:

> When the child is young, there will be the inevitable speculation about whom the child resembles. For the father this is likely to be painful and to frustrate rather than further the parent-child bond. If the child develops in ways or with interests different from the father's, or if the child is particularly close to his mother, the father may well feel left out, an outsider in the family. If the child is told about the conception, he is likely at some point to wield this information to inflict pain. He may shout in anger that he hates his mother, but only to his father will he say that he, the father, is not his real parent. So the absence of genetic relation is likely to be painful and isolating, and in this pain the mother cannot fully share.[80]

Adoption engenders some of the same feelings, and adjusting to them is in some ways easier and in some ways harder than adjusting to donor insemination. On the one hand, neither of the parents can see an adopted child as their biological progeny, and so the problems for the husband-wife relationship caused by the asymmetry of donor insemination would not affect adoption.

On the other hand, though, the parent-child relationship may be more difficult, for in donor insemination the child knows that at least one of the social parents (the mother) is also his or her biological parent, while in adoption both biological parents are unknown. Thus the child's genetic uncertainty and the lure to blame the parents' lack of biological connectedness in moments of tension are doubled. Moreover, many adopted children feel that they have been fundamentally rejected by their genetic parents, leading some to seek the identity of, and a meeting with, their genetic parents as adults. That often produces less than desirable results for all parties concerned: the child may be deeply disappointed in the reality, as against the dream, of the kind of human beings the genetic parents are; the genetic parents may find being discovered by the child after all these years to be most unwelcome, making the child feel rejected yet again; and the social parents feel that somehow they were inadequate as parents, that they never succeeded in overcoming the lack of biological relationship between them and the child despite years of love and effort, if the child now seeks to know and be connected with his or her biological parents.[81]

While these dangers in both donor insemination and adoption should not be minimized, they should not be exaggerated either. We do, after all, have many "blended" families today in which children are raised by a biological parent and by a nonbiological parent. That may not be ideal for the same reasons of asymmetry that artificial insemination is not ideal, and yet we know that committed spousal and parent-child relationships based on honesty, trust, and respect most often overcome the difficulties. One must remember, too, that in marriages in which fertility is not a problem, the families that result from them are not always ideal; each marriage and family has its difficulties that the people involved must overcome, and the asymmetry of artificial insemination is just a pitfall of a specific sort. The couple and child *will* need to talk out the issues fully, perhaps with professional help, but it is certainly not

---

[80] Lauritzen, "Pursuing Parenthood" (at n. 8), p. 71.

[81] For a recent, poignant article about this, see Susan Chira, "Years After Adoption, Adults Find Past, and New Hurdles," *New York Times*, 30 Aug. 1993, pp. A1, C11. I would like to thank Professor Vicki Michel and Rabbi Elie Spitz for calling this to my attention.

impossible for a marriage and family to survive the asymmetry of artificial insemination and even to emerge stronger as those involved join in dealing with its challenges.

The same point applies to grandparents. As Mahlstedt and Greenfeld point out, if grandparents remain distant from grandchildren conceived through artificial insemination, it is generally not in reaction to the means of conception, but it is rather a continuation of the poor relationships that the social parents had with them from the start on other grounds entirely. It is *those* personal problems that must be addressed before the special issues deriving from donor insemination can be successfully confronted.

This is very important for the social parents to recognize, for family support is critical to meeting the challenges that the asymmetry inherent in donor insemination poses. As Mahlstedt and Greenfeld say:

> The social attitudes which concern infertile couples most are *not* those of the church or the law, but those of their families. . . .It is their support that most effectively enables confidence, conviction, and courage to emerge in the couple's experience with donor conception. Couples who receive family love and support reflect less ambivalence about their choice, more comfort in sharing their means of conception with others, and more confidence in their abilities to cope with negative social attitudes.[82]

Thus with grandparents, with other family members, and with friends, as with the social parents themselves, good relations apart from this issue will help everyone deal with it, and bad relations will make that task harder. Within a reasonably strong network of relationships, however, including especially their own, the asymmetry inherent in donor insemination need not become an insurmountable obstacle to a strong marriage and to good parenting, and it therefore should not be prohibited on that moral ground.

3. Demographic Concerns

In addition to these moral issues that presumably affect couples of all faiths involved in donor insemination, there are specific Jewish issues in judging its morality. Rabbi Jakobovits mentioned adultery and diminution of the role of the father as reasons to oppose donor insemination, despite his inability to find legal grounds to do so. For reasons discussed above, I have rejected those contentions of his. There is one important moral factor, though, that, on the contrary, argues for permitting donor insemination. That factor is the demographic context in which this question is being asked.

Jewish families in the past had numerous children. This was in part, no doubt, because so many children died in childbirth or of childhood diseases, and so one might have only a few children survive to adulthood even if one had significantly more than that in the first place. Thus while birth control was known and used when medically necessary for either the mother or the infant she was nursing, it was not even contemplated, as far as we can tell from the sources, for purposes of family planning.[83]

Contemporary Jews generally do not share this ethic. Survival rates to adulthood are much better now, and so Jewish couples need no longer conceive many more children than they ultimately want to have. Moreover, they commonly want to provide substantial educational and material benefits to the children they do have, and that argues for smaller

---

[82] Mahlstedt and Greenfeld, "Patient Preparation," p. 913.

[83] On this topic and on many others relevant to this responsum, see David M. Feldman, *Birth Control in Jewish Law* (New York: New York University Press, 1968), esp. chs. 9–13.

families so that they can afford to do that. Economic necessity and the women's movement have made the dual-career marriage commonplace, and so couples are reluctant to have many children when they know that they will have limited time to care for them. These factors, plus the loss of a third of world Jewry in the Holocaust, plus assimilation and intermarriage, have together produced the serious demographic problems that our contemporary Jewish community has.

This must enter into our moral evaluation of donor insemination because a Jewish examination of any moral issue cannot be adequate to Jewish concerns if it only narrowly considers the specific legal issues involved. Any tradition based on law must grapple with its sources if it is to be true to itself and if it is to reap the many benefits inherent in a legal system,[84] and I have done that in some detail above. The law, though, must be interpreted with full cognizance of the specific context to which it is to be applied, for otherwise it risks two opposite dangers: it could either be ignored and thus dishonored, or else — perhaps the greater danger — it could be obeyed despite the personal, social, and moral havoc it wreaks on the situation it was meant to guide with sensitivity and wisdom. Certainly, Jewish law, which tries to delineate the will of God as we understand it, must now, as it has in the past, pay attention to the welfare of the Jewish community and of the specific people involved as any good God would. Moreover, the Conservative movement, with its commitment to historical analysis, must surely not only recognize the influences of historical circumstances on the legal judgments of the past, but must also take the responsibility to meet the needs of Judaism and the Jewish community in its responsa of the present.

In our case, then, when the demographic statistics are as threatening as they are for the continuity of the Jewish tradition and the Jewish community, any room in the law to enable Jews who are otherwise infertile to have children must be used. The moral scales, in other words, are decisively balanced by these communal scales in favor of donor insemination when the couple cannot have children in any other way.

4. Compassion

These communal considerations stand quite apart from, and in addition to, the compassion one must surely have for couples who have tried to have children and cannot. In such situations, both members of the couple suffer immensely. In addition to the frustration of being unable to have children when they deeply want to do so, they often have feelings of inadequacy as either men or women. Infertility certainly requires couples to alter their understandings of what it means to be a man, a woman, and a couple, for one important part of all of those concepts is no longer true. Thankfully, the greater publicity about infertility in our time, including its frequency, and the availability of support groups and helpful publications, have enabled many couples to overcome the emotional hurdles involved; but more than a few couples have broken apart because of their inability to have children. In addition to our communal concerns mentioned above, then, our attention to the needs of Jews who are trying to fulfill Jewish law and actualize Jewish ideals, and our interest in preventing divorce to the extent that we can, should also prompt us to prefer the permissive lines of reasoning in the sources described above.

Compassion in these cases, though, goes in two directions. Just as we want to be responsive and affirming to the couples who want to use these new techniques to have children, we also want to recognize that some couples will choose not to engage in these

---

[84] I spell out some of the advantages of encasing values in law in my article, "The Interaction of Morality and Jewish Law," *Judaism* 26:4 (fall 1977): 455-466, and in my book, *Knowing God: Jewish Journeys to the Unknowable* (Northvale, NJ: Jason Aronson, 1992), pp. 71-75.

procedures. In some cases, the cost will be a factor. In others, the psychological problems engendered by the asymmetry of donor insemination and egg donation pose too much of a threat to the marriage. For these and other reasons, couples may legitimately refuse to use either donor insemination or egg donation, and we should not make them feel that they have let down the Jewish people, their partner, or potential grandparents. The commandment to procreate does not apply to a couple who cannot have children through their own sexual intercourse, and that recognition will surely be liberating for some couples. There are, after all, many commandments and many opportunities in life to do good deeds, and so, as much as we may individually or collectively support those couples who decide to use D.I. or egg donation, we must also be sensitive to the good reasons that will motivate other couples not to use them.

Using Donated Eggs

A. Balancing the Risks of Egg Donation with the Alternative of Adoption

The parallel phenomenon to donor insemination in the female is egg donation. In cases where a woman cannot produce eggs but can carry a fetus, she may have eggs of a donor woman fertilized in a test tube with either the sperm of her (that is, the infertile woman's) husband or of a donor, and then the zygote is implanted in her uterus for gestation. Moreover, even if a woman over age forty can produce eggs, the success rate of IVF in such women is so dismal that doctors generally recommend the use of a younger woman's eggs instead.

This procedure is much newer than artificial insemination because semen can be obtained through simple ejaculation, while the techniques for harvesting and preserving eggs for donation have been developed only in recent years. Egg donation is also more dangerous to the donor than artificial insemination is. A man who produces sperm for purposes of donation does not thereby entail any physical danger (although there may be psychological or legal risks for him in such donations, as discussed above). The same immunity from physical danger does not apply to the woman who produces eggs for donation. For that procedure to have a better chance of working, and to reduce the number of times the woman must undergo the procedure to harvest the eggs, the woman's ovaries must be stimulated by drugs to produce multiple eggs. As discussed below, there is some evidence that this increases her risk of having ovarian cancer and some other maladies, especially if she does this often. The number of women who are willing to donate eggs is therefore considerably and understandably smaller than the pool of semen donors.

One can understand, though, why the recipients of egg donation want it. Unlike adoption, the woman will go through pregnancy, and many women want to have that experience. Moreover, since Jewish couples find it hard to locate a healthy infant to adopt of their own race, and since some will not adopt any other kind of child, a woman who can bear a child but who cannot produce eggs may seek a woman with characteristics similar to her own to donate eggs so that the offspring will look like her and, assuming that her husband's sperm is used, like her husband as well. The same desires often lead couples who need D.I. to seek a donor similar in characteristics to the husband.

Couples sometimes want children who look like them to maximize their own feelings and those of the child of belonging to each other while simultaneously minimizing the awareness of family, friends, and others that the child became the couple's through any process other than the usual way. This is understandable; after all, for all of us, part of the lure of having children is that they represent one of the ways in which we gain eternity, a piece of us that remains after we die. There is, however, inherent racism involved in refusing to adopt a child of a race different from one's own, and that is both theologically and legally problematic. God, according to our tradition, created all people, with no race inherently more worthy than any other, and membership in a particular race is not a necessary condition for being Jewish — as the plethora of races among Israel's Jews amply attests. Race is not a sufficient condition for being Jewish either, as the many non-Jews of all races demonstrate. Consequently, while such discrimination may be acceptable in the name of enabling the couple and child to overcome some of the problems inherent in egg donation, D.I., or adoption so that the parents and child can bond all the more effectively, rabbis must help couples see that these procedures are both possible and fully valid within Jewish law with donors and children of any race as long as conversion takes place when necessary.

One critical factor that makes egg donation less acceptable than artificial insemination, though, is the extra danger for the donor. Jewish law, after all, does not permit one to endanger oneself unduly: "[The strictures against] endangering oneself are more stringent than [those against violating] a prohibition," says the Talmud.[85] One must not "stand idly by the blood of one's neighbor," according to the Torah, and so some risk is required or at least permitted to save the life of another; but in the case of egg donation we are not talking about saving a life but rather enabling a couple to conceive a new life. Since no physical danger will ensue to the couple if they fail in that project, we cannot justify the danger to the egg donor on that basis. The risks to the donor, though, are not so great as to force us to ban the procedure entirely out of concern for the life or health of the donor. They are significant enough, however, for us to say that egg donation should only be used when the couple has seriously considered all other options for having children, including adoption.

B. Moral and Psychological Issues in Egg Donation

For the infertile couple, most of the moral and psychological issues in egg donation are the same as those we already encountered in artificial insemination. If the sperm used is the husband's, the couple will face the asymmetry mentioned above — although, of course, in the opposite direction, for the husband will be biologically related to the offspring while the wife will not be a provider of the child's gametes. Unlike the case of artificial insemination, though, a woman who carries a child, even if the egg came from another person, has the satisfaction of being the gestational mother, a source of meaning and connection to the child that a man can never experience. If the husband cannot produce sperm with sufficient number or mobility so that the couple must use both donated sperm and eggs, both social parents will not be the biological parents of the child, in which case they must face the problems that adoptive parents encounter. The openness in communication required of all parties involved in artificial insemination must therefore characterize cases of egg donation as well. Finally, the same demographic crisis and the same compassion for the infertile couple that should affect our understanding of artificial insemination should likewise incline us to permit egg donation when the couple cannot have a child in any other way.

Legally, in egg donation as in artificial insemination, contact of the genital organs and intent to have an adulterous relationship are both missing, and so the prohibition against adultery is not relevant. Furthermore, in light of the added expense and the significantly

---

[85] B. Hullin 10a. See B. Berakhot 32b; B, Shabbat 32a; B. Bava Kamma 15b, 80a, 91b; M.T. Laws of Murder and the Guarding of Life 11:4-5; S.A. Orah Hayyim 173:2; Yoreh De'ah 116:5 (gloss).

decreased chances of success over artificial insemination, egg donation is even less plausibly construed as a form of licentiousness.

The paucity of egg donors makes it permissible for a fertile sister to donate eggs to an infertile one. Since donor sperm is readily available and inexpensive, it is generally inadvisable for a fertile brother to donate sperm for the impregnation of his infertile brother's wife, for while that is not technically incest, it *feels* very close to it and raises all kinds of boundary problems for the brothers and the child later on ("Is Uncle Barry really only my uncle, or is he my substitute father when I want him to be?").[86] Since donated eggs are less available and more expensive, though, and since the lack of genital contact means that legally there is no taint of incest, we would allow a fertile sister to donate eggs to her infertile sibling, but only after appropriate counseling and careful consideration of how the sisters are going to handle these boundary questions as the child grows.

c. Identity of the Mother

There is only one source, to my knowledge, that even contemplates anything close to egg donation. Noting that the Torah specifically calls Dinah "the daughter of Leah" (Gen. 30:21) rather than following its more usual practice of identifying the child by her father's name, the Talmud tells a story to explain why the Torah did this. When Jacob already had ten sons, the story goes, Leah became pregnant. She knew that Jacob was to father a total of twelve sons, and she did not want her sister, Rachel, to bear him less than the two sons that each of the maidservants, Bilhah and Zilpah, had already produced. Consequently, Leah prayed that the child she was carrying not be a boy, and ultimately Dinah was born to her. The most common understanding of that story is that in response to Leah's prayers, God changed the gender of the child in utero. (For some reason, the commentators never imagined that Leah could have been carrying a girl in the first place!) The *Targum Jonathan*, however, understands the story to mean that in response to Leah's prayers, God exchanged the female child (Dinah) in Rachel's womb with the male child (Joseph) in Leah's, thus effecting an embryo transfer so that Leah would give birth to a girl and Rachel to her first son. Rabbi Samuel Edels (the "Maharsha," 1555-1631) also claims that this is the correct interpretation of the talmudic story.

The question is whether this interpretation of the story, which is ultimately built on the Torah's identification of Dinah as Leah's daughter, should serve as a precedent for determining the identity of the mother of a child conceived through egg donation. Even if we assume that the story is indeed one of embryo transfer, and even if we ignore the fact that in the story God is the one who effects the embryo transfer rather than human beings, there are real questions as to whether any story should be used for legal rulings, and all the more so one like this that is really only one possible interpretation of what is, in turn, a talmudic tale. Rabbi J. David Bleich, who called attention to the story, himself casts doubt on the use of it for this purpose.[87]

Other grounds, though, support the holding that the bearing mother, rather than the egg donor, should be identified as the mother of the child. Specifically, Jewish law,

---

[86] A brother's sperm was, of course, used in levirate marriages (Deut. 25:5-10), but there the husband had died, and so there is no threat of the complications inherent in the blurring of roles between the brothers. Indeed, in that case it would actually be in the child's best interest if the uncle acted as a substitute father.

[87] The talmudic story: B. Berakhot 60a. The comment of *Targum Yonaton* is on Gen. 30:21. Maharsha's support of that interpretation: B. Niddah 31a. Rabbi J. David Bleich's refusal to use this source to determine the identity of the child's mother on the basis of parturition (along with Rabbi Joshua Feigenbaum) because halakhic principles are not derivable from aggadic sources (quite remarkable, given Rabbi Bleich's usual

in general, defines a child's native religion according to the religion of the birth mother at the time of birth.[88] Therefore, if a woman converts to Judaism during pregnancy, the child is born a Jew.[89] Moreover, for purposes of redemption of the firstborn son, Jewish law defines that child as the one who "opens the womb."[90] All of these precedents, of course, assume that the birth mother provides genetic material as well, but the law clearly focuses not on conception or gestation, but on birth. The only factor, in fact, that would argue against defining the status of the child according to the birth mother is the parallel to fatherhood, for, as we have noted, it is the sperm donor, rather than the social father, who counts as the genetic father in Jewish law. There, however, the social father is never physically involved with the child until after birth, while in the case of egg donation, the birth mother's body nurtures the child throughout gestation. As a result, in accordance with the line of precedents noted above that make the status of the mother at birth the defining factor for determining the religious identity of the child, we hold that a child born to a Jewish woman is Jewish, regardless of the religious status of the ovum donor.[91]

D. The Problem of Selective Abortions

Because the rate of success with IVF, GIFT, and ZIFT is currently so low, the standard practice in North America among infertility specialists is to implant four or five sets of gametes (GIFT) or zygotes (IVF or ZIFT) each cycle in the hope of raising the odds of success to twen-

---

methodology): J. David Bleich, "Maternal Identity," *Tradition* 19:4 (winter 1981): 359-360. See also Fred Rosner, *Modern Medicine and Jewish Ethics*, 2d ed. (Hoboken, NJ: Ktav, and New York: Yeshiva University, 1991), pp. 115-116. I would like to thank Rabbi Aaron Mackler for calling my attention to these materials.

  I think that we not only can use aggadic material as the source of general principles, but commonly do so in halakhic practice. Moreover, I think we should do so, for only then can our beliefs have impact on our actions. We must just be intelligent enough to understand that stories, unlike laws and judicial precedents, are not generally told in a form intended to be examined in legal detail but rather are to be read as articulating general principles, and we must also remember that stories, perhaps even more than legal precedents, may conflict with each other. Furthermore, in the use of stories for legal purposes, we must examine them, as we analyze potential precedents, for the analogies and disanalogies between them and the case at hand. In the case here, though, I would agree with Rabbi Bleich that this story is a very thin reed on which to determine the mother's identity, not so much because it is aggadic, but because it represents only one reading of what is already a fantastic tale designed more to indicate the kindness of Leah and the miracles of God than the way rabbis should rule in cases of egg donation. For the general point about the use of stories within the context of legal reasoning, see my articles, "Methodology in Jewish Medical Ethics," *Jewish Law Association Studies VI: The Jerusalem 1990 Conference Volume*, B.S. Jackson and S.M. Passamaneck, eds. (Atlanta, GA: Scholars Press, 1992), pp. 35-57; and more briefly, "A Jewish Approach to End-Stage Medical Care," *PCJLS 86-90*, pp. 67-70.

[88] M. Kiddushin 3:12; B. Kiddushin 70a, 75b; B. Yevamot 16b, 23a, 44a, 45b; M.T. Laws of Forbidden Intercourse 15:3.

[89] S.A. Yoreh De'ah 268:6.

[90] Exod. 13:2, 12, 15; 34:19; Num. 3:12; 18:15.

[91] When this responsum was approved by the Committee on Jewish Law and Standards, this matter had not yet been determined, and so I maintained then that unless both the ovum donor and the birth donor were Jewish, the child should undergo the rites of conversion. Subsequently, however, the Committee approved the responsum of Rabbi Aaron L. Mackler ("In Vitro Fertilization," below, p. 523), according to which "the woman who gestates [a donated ovum] and gives birth to the child is to be treated as the child's mother for purposes of Jewish law, including the determination of Jewish identity." I have therefore adjusted this printed version of my responsum to reflect that subsequent Committee decision.

  This would mean that in the reverse situation, when a Jewish woman's egg is implanted into a non-Jewish surrogate for gestation and birth the child would not be Jewish by birth and would need to undergo conversion.

ty-five percent or so. The use of multiple eggs in any attempt at impregnation, however, produces the need in some cases selectively to abort one or more fetuses. Women can generally safely carry up to three children, but being able to bear more than three healthy babies without undue threat to the mother's health is rare, and so the common practice is to abort all but three fetuses if more than that successfully implant into the uterus. In most cases, the couple is lucky if even one of the implants "take" — indeed, they are then beating three-to-one odds — but in some instances all four or five attach themselves to the uterus and begin to develop.

The Jewish tradition requires abortion when the mother's life or health is at stake, and it sanctions it when there is a risk to her life or health beyond that of normal pregnancy. Abortion, though, is generally prohibited, and the burden of proof is always on the one who wants to abort. We therefore do not want to create situations where we know ahead of time that we may well have to abort one or more fetuses.

Moreover, abortion often engenders psychological issues, even if it is necessary. Those are likely to be all the more severe for a couple with fertility problems in the first place.[92] Therefore, to avoid the need for selective abortions as much as possible, Jews may only implant two, or at most three, zygotes for IVF or ZIFT and may only use two, or at most three, eggs for GIFT.

E. The Obligation to Procreate

Couples who choose *not* to use egg donation as a means of overcoming their infertility need not feel guilty in doing so. As noted above,[93] even though men clearly cannot have children without women, the Rabbis restricted the commandment to procreate to men. Since women do not fall under that legal obligation, then, infertile women are not failing to fulfill any commandments relevant to them by refusing to be impregnated by donated eggs. Given the potential psychological problems engendered by the asymmetry involved in producing a child with the husband's sperm but another woman's egg, one can understand why some women, at any rate, would refuse to undergo the procedure, and that refusal must be respected.

This will mean, though, that the woman's husband will not be able to procreate with his wife (assuming that his sperm is fit to produce children in the first place), and the Mishnah rules that a man who cannot procreate with his wife after trying for ten years must divorce her and marry another in an attempt to fulfill the commandment to procreate.[94] By the late Middle Ages, though, that rule had largely fallen into disuse, as Rabbi Moses Isserles ultimately codifies:

> Today it is not the custom to force somebody on this issue. Similarly, anybody who has not fulfilled the commandment "be fruitful and multiply" and goes to marry a woman who is not capable of having children because of sterility, age, or youth, because

---

[92] I want to thank Rabbi Judah Kogen for calling my attention to the psychological aspects of this situation.

[93] See n. 2 above.

[94] M. Yevamot 6:6. In mishnaic times, the man legally could have taken a second wife to fulfill the commandment to procreate, but the Mishnah does not mention that possibility, probably because by mishnaic times polygamy, while legal, was already frowned upon. Thus, not one of the more than 2,000 Sages mentioned in the Talmud has a second wife, and a second wife was called a צרה, trouble. See also the story of Rabbi Judah Ha-Nasi's son, who could not have children with his wife. His father told him to divorce her, but he said, "People will say, 'This poor one waited all these years in vain.'" His father said, "Take a second wife," but he answered, "People will say, 'This is his wife, and this is his concubine.'" He therefore prayed for her, and she was able to conceive (B. Ketubbot 62b). In any case, by the Middle Ages, polygamy was outlawed altogether in Ashkenazic communities through the revision of the law (תקנה) accredited to Rabbi Gershom of Mayence (d. 1028).

he loves her or [even] for her wealth, even though by law we should prevent such a marriage, it has not been the practice for many generations for the court to interfere in the affairs of couples. Similarly, if a man marries a woman and waits ten years [without children], we do not force him to divorce her, although he has not fulfilled the commandment "be fruitful and multiply." And the same applies to other matters regarding couples.[95]

Infertile couples who choose not to pursue egg donation, then, need not feel that they are thereby violating Jewish law. Again, they *may* use egg donation as a means to have children, but they *are not required* to do so. Those who opt not to use this method should consider adoption, which will satisfy many of the same needs and will open the couple to the possibility of fulfilling many other commandments associated with children.

Donating One's Sperm or Eggs

Until now, we have considered artificial insemination and egg donation from the point of view of the couple seeking children. What about the donors, though? As we have said above, virtually all halakhic authorities to date have permitted a husband to produce sperm for A.I.H. when he cannot impregnate his wife otherwise. But is it permissible for a Jewish man to donate his sperm for purposes of donor insemination? Conversely, may a Jewish woman donate her eggs for purposes of enabling another woman to become pregnant? If the answers to either or both of these questions is affirmative, are there any restrictions on that permission?

Donor insemination, it will be remembered, constitutes procreation in Jewish law on the part of the donor. This introduces an appropriate note of seriousness to semen donation. It is not, and should not be construed as, simply another job for a college or medical student to earn some spare change. The (typically) young man involved should recognize that he is making it possible for a couple to have a child, with all the positive implications of that for the couple and, if Jews are the recipients, for the Jewish people. He should approach this whole process, in other words, with a sense of mitzvah, duly appreciative of the awesomeness of the human ability to procreate and of his role in helping that happen for an infertile couple.

He should also understand that, like it or not, he will have an important, biological relationship to the offspring. He may want to keep his identity confidential so as not to incur any risk of personal or legal problems with the couple or with the child later on. Since the laws on this are not universal and not totally clear, he may indeed have to retain confidentiality to avoid such consequences, at least as many state laws in the United States are written now.

The donor should recognize, however, that since the child will inherit his genes, he should supply him or her with as much information about his physical and personal characteristics as possible without compromising the confidentiality of his identity. Only then can the child know enough about his or her medical history to take appropriate preventive and curative steps against genetically inherent diseases or susceptibilities to disease, and only then can the child avoid having sex with a genetic relative. Furthermore, as I have said above, the more the donor reveals about his personal characteristics and interests, the more the child can achieve a sense of self-identity, and so the donor should provide at least some of that information to the social parents and, through them, to the child.

---

[95] S.A. Even HaEzer 1:3 (gloss).

The donor should also be concerned about his own future children not unwittingly marrying a genetic relative. This too argues for sharing as much information as possible with the child born of artificial insemination so that at least someone is guarding against such an occurrence. All of these problems disappear, of course, if both he and the social parents decide to reveal their identities to each other and to the child, but that raises other problems, and he must consider those too.

None of these difficulties should make semen donation forbidden; the great good of enabling an infertile couple to have a child outweighs them all. This includes any objections to the masturbation through which the semen will be procured, for the intent to produce a child removes any stigma of "wasting of the seed." The donor, though, must at least understand the complications involved and plan for how he will respond to them.

The same concerns apply to egg donation, but that procedure has the additional concern of the risks involved in harvesting the eggs. Because doctors can now be guided by ultrasound to the ovaries so that they can remove eggs vaginally, surgery is no longer necessary to harvest eggs. To minimize the number of times that a woman must undergo the procedure, though, and to maximize the possibility of pregnancy in the recipient, the woman must be treated with drugs to produce more than one egg. (Eggs cannot yet be frozen.) Recent studies have found, however, that there is some increased risk in egg donors of a number of maladies, including even stroke and heart attack, and that "women who had used fertility drugs had three times the risk of invasive epithelial ovarian cancer compared to women without a history of infertility...[and] four times the risk of ovarian tumors of low malignant potential (borderline tumors) seen among women lacking a history of infertility." On the other hand, as of 1988, 1.9 million women aged fifteen to forty-four years were estimated to have taken fertility drugs, and only a very small percentage of those has contracted ovarian cancer. As a result,

> At present, there is no need to change medical practice regarding use of fertility-enhancing drugs. There is enough cause of concern, however, to slightly alter the physician's approach to counseling patients. We suggest advising patients receiving fertility drugs as to the possible increased risk of ovarian cancer. Especially careful consideration should be given to counseling women who wish to donate eggs, particularly repeat donors, because they derive no reproductive benefit from their fertility drug exposure.[96]

With this state of medical knowledge, then, a Jewish woman *may* take on the risks of egg donation, but not repeatedly, and only if she is assured by physicians after due examination that she personally can do so without much danger to her own life or health, for that clearly takes precedence in Jewish law to the good of enabling an infertile couple to have children, as great a good as that is.

---

[96] Robert Spirtas, Steven C. Kaufman, and Nancy J. Alexander, *Fertility and Sterility* [the journal of the American Fertility Society] 59:2 (Feb. 1993): 291-292. I want to thank my friend, Dr. Michael Grodin, for sharing this article with me. The 1988 Congressional report also reported a number of other possible complications caused by commonly used drugs to stimulate the ovaries, including early pregnancy loss, multiple gestations (fetuses), ectopic pregnancies, headache, hair loss, pleuropulmonary fibrosis, increased blood viscosity and hypotension, stroke, and myocardial infarction; see *Infertility* (at n. 8 above), pp. 128-129. Once again, though, the demonstrated risks are not so great as to make stimulation of the ovaries for egg donation prohibited as a violation of the Jewish command to guard our health, but they are sufficient to demand that caution be taken and that the number of times a woman donates eggs be limited.

Egg donors face some of the same issues of confidentiality as do semen donors, but several of the factors are different. Sperm is not in short supply, but eggs are. Furthermore, no state currently has laws unequivocally declaring the social mother, and not the egg donor, to be the legal mother (perhaps because of the newness of the procedure), and so the legal risks of future obligations are substantially greater for egg donors than they are for semen donors. These elements would argue for a greater measure of acceptance of confidentiality in egg donation than we would be prepared to accept in semen donation. On the other hand, the egg donor, no less than the semen donor, contributes substantially to the child's genetic structure, and so she too should reveal as much as possible of her medical history and personal characteristics for the good of the child.

Adoption

When a couple cannot have children, adoption is an available option. Several passages in the Bible suggest that adoption existed during Biblical times,[97] although the evidence is equivocal and is not specified in any legal source of the Bible. In later Jewish law, adoption is not a defined institution as such, but Rabbinic law provided for the approximate equivalent. The Rabbinic court, "the father of all orphans,"[98] appoints guardians for orphans and children in need, and the guardians have the same responsibilities as natural parents have. They must care for the child's upbringing, education, and physical accommodations, and they must administer the child's property. If the guardian dies, his or her estate is responsible to continue providing for the child's care. The sense of guardianship in Jewish law is so strong that it was once invoked in a New York case to extend the obligations of the adoptive father beyond the demands of civil law.[99]

Contrary to modern, American adoption, however, in Jewish law the adoptive parents do not become the legal parents, but rather function as the agents of the natural parents.[100] Therefore, natural parents continue to have the usual parental obligations to the child, and the

---

[97] For example, Gen. 15:2-3 and 48:5-6 are probably the most plausible cases, but some suggest that all or some of the following passages refer to adoption as well: Gen. 16:2, 30:3, 38:8-9, 50:23; Exod. 2:10; Lev. 18:9; Deut. 25:6; Ps. 77:16; Ruth 4:16-17; Esther 2:7, 15; Ezra 2:61, 10:44; and 1 Chron. 2:35-41, 4:18. The evidence is murky, especially when one tries to differentiate adoption from fosterage and from inheritance rights alone. See Jeffrey Tigay, "Adoption," *Encyclopaedia Judaica* 2:298-301; and Michael Broyde, "Marital Fraud" (at n. 57), p. 97, n. 11.

[98] B. Bava Kamma 37a; Gittin 37a.

[99] *Wener v. Wener* 59 Misc. 2d 959, 301 N.Y. Supp. 2d 237 (Sup. Ct. 1969); and cf. appeal 35 App. Div. 2d 50, 312 N.Y. Supp. 2d 815 (2d Dept. 1970), where the judgment was affirmed but not its religious grounds.

[100] Michael Broyde claims (in his article, "Marital Fraud" [at n. 57], p. 97, n. 11.) that there are four instances in the Bible in which adoptive parents are called natural parents, but, as noted in n. 97 above, all of the biblical instances of possible adoption are unclear. In any case, the Talmud assumes those ascriptions of parentage not to be legal pronouncements, but rather descriptions of the close relationships between the children and adoptive parents: see 1 Chron. 4:18; Ruth 4:17; Ps. 77:16; 2 Sam. 21:8; and B. Sanhedrin 9b.

Broyde (ibid., n. 10) calls attention to the disparate approaches taken by Roman and American law, which severed all previous relationships between the biological parents and the adopted children (to the point that, until recent amendments, the parties to the adoption were to remain anonymous to each other), as against English common law, which rejected the institute of adoption altogether, as against the intermediate position taken by Jewish law, which saw the adopted parents as agents of the biological parents. He cites, among other articles, C.M.A. McLauliff, "The First English Adoption Law and Its American Precursors," 16 *Seton Hall Law Review* 656, 659-660 (1986), and Sanford N. Katz, "Re-writing the Adoption Story," 5 *Family Advocate* 9-13 (1982). Because of the theory underlying American law, most states still ascribe to adoption law the ability to recreate maternal and paternal relationships even if the child, under the new legislation passed in many states, knows the biological parents.

guardian fulfills those obligations on behalf of, but not in legal substitution for, the natural parents. Along the same lines, the personal status of the child in matters of Jewish identity, ritual, and marriage depends upon the status of the natural parents.[101] Therefore, when it is not known that the gestational mother was Jewish, the child must be formally converted.

At the same time, rabbinic sources express immense appreciation for the adoptive parents; taking a child who is, in essence, an orphan into one's home and raising that child is a חסד (an act of faithfulness, of loving kindness) of the first order. Thus the Talmud says that one who does so "is as if he has given birth to him," and, in a source quoted earlier but that bears repeating, notes that the adoptive parents manage to act rightly at all times:

> "Happy are they that act justly, who do right at all times" (Ps. 106:3). Is it possible to do right at all times?...Rabbi Samuel bar Nahmani said: This refers to a person who brings up an orphan boy or girl in his house and enables them to marry.[102]

This appreciation has legal consequences. As we have noted above, the possessions, earnings, and findings of minor, adopted children go to their custodial, rather than their natural, parents; this is probably a matter of equity, for this provision is in partial compensation for the expenses of raising children.[103] Similarly, according to Rabbi Moses Sofer, adopted children do not incur the obligations of mourning upon the death of their natural parents, but they do have such obligations when their adoptive parents die.[104] Moreover, in appreciation of the immensely significant role that adoptive parents have in their children's upbringing, and in recognition of the close bonds that adopted siblings create with each other, we consider adopted children, like children born through donor insemination, to have the status of relatives of the second degree (שניות), and therefore sex or marriage between them is prohibited. Furthermore, as with children born through D.I., the social father's name may be invoked when the child is being identified by his or her Hebrew name, as, for example, when called to the Torah.

Many infertile, Jewish couples cannot find Jewish children to adopt because of the high rate of abortion among Jews. That argues for two things: first, Jews should understand that while Jewish law requires abortion when the life or health of the mother is at stake and permits it when there is a risk to the mother's life or health above that of normal pregnancy, by and large the Jewish tradition *prohibits* abortion. Jews all too often wrongly assume that because Jewish law requires or permits abortion in some cases, it does so in all cases, and so all too many of our people are using abortion as a *post-facto* form of birth control. They need to be disabused of this misconception of Jewish law – and made aware

---

[101] Cf. *Encyclopaedia Judaica*, "Adoption," 2:298-303; "Apotropos," 3:218-222; and "Orphan," 12:1478-1480 for a summary of all of the laws in this and the last paragraph. See especially B. Sanhedrin 19b; S.A. Even HaEzer 15:11. Cf. also Michael Broyde, "Marital Fraud" (at n. 57), pp. 96-100, who points out that in this way Jewish law is in marked contrast to Roman law as well as American law, but in agreement with English common law.

[102] B. Megillah 13a; B. Ketubbot 50a. See also Exodus Rabbah, ch. 4; S.A. Orah Hayyim 139:3; Abraham Gumbiner, *Magen Avraham*, on S.A. Orah Hayyim 156; Moshe Feinstein, *Iggrot Moshe* on Yoreh De'ah 161.

[103] B. Sanhedrin 12b awards such possessions to the child's father; S.A. Hoshen Mishpat 370:2 specifies that this means the child's custodial father; and Rabbi J. Falk, *Meirat Einaim*, on S.A. Hoshen Mishpat 370:2, suggests that this is a matter of equity. Thus, a financially independent minor does not transfer his income to his parents because he is supporting himself; cf. S.A. Hoshen Mishpat 370:2.

[104] M. Sofer, *Responsa*, 1 Orah Hayyim 164. Sofer assumes that mourning is a rabbinic institution, which itself is a matter of dispute: compare S.A. Yoreh De'ah 398:1 with Moses Isserles, Yoreh De'ah 399:13 (gloss). For other examples of rabbinic institutions not strictly applied in the context of custodial parentage, see, generally, S.A. Orah Hayyim 139:3; Abraham Gumbiner, *Magen Avraham*, on S.A. Orah Hayyim 156; Moshe Feinstein, *Iggrot Moshe*, Yoreh De'ah 161.

of the physical and psychological dangers involved in abortion. They also should come to understand that even if they cannot or will not care for the child, there is an abundance of infertile couples who would do so willingly and lovingly, and that makes non-therapeutic abortions even less justifiable.

In addition, though, Jewish couples contemplating adoption need to widen their search to include non-Jewish children, including ones who are not Caucasian. Conversion will be necessary, but for children that is a relatively easy process. Moreover, as noted above, race is not a factor in Jewish identity — or in the joy (and troubles!) of raising children.[105] Similarly, it is not only infants and able-bodied children that a couple should consider for adoption; older children and those with some disability are also God's children — and are more available for couples seeking to adopt. Indeed, Jews should consider the possibility of adoption of such children even when they have already had two or more children through their own sexual intercourse and have thereby fulfilled the demands of Jewish law to procreate.

At the same time, couples need to be aware of some of the special legal and psychological issues which may arise in adoption. The highly publicized Baby Jessica case, in which a two-and-a-half-year-old child was taken in August, 1993, from the adoptive parents who had raised her from birth and returned to her biological parents, indicates the importance of attending to the legal details of adoption — and of changing the laws in many states that make such a case possible. Apart from physical harm to the child, that is undoubtedly the adoptive parents' worst nightmare, and it probably is not in the child's best interests either. Biological parents do have a right and an obligation to care for their children, but if they give up both the rights and obligations of parenthood in a formal, legal way, adoptive parents and children have the right to be secure in their status as a family.

More commonly, adoptive parents must face psychological issues. Family members may say insensitive things — or bend over backwards in avoiding mention of the adoption. Adopted children will be reminded of their special status each time school forms ask for their medical history. During adolescence, when all children need to differentiate themselves from their parents and often feel misunderstood in the process, adopted children may think that their biological parents *would* understand them if they were present. That may be the occasion for some angry and hurtful remarks as the child attacks the adoptive parents where they are most vulnerable. Moreover, adopted children sometimes seek out their biological parents when they reach adulthood, and the adoptive parents need to understand that that does not usually mean that the child is rejecting them as parents. To cope with issues like these, adoptive parents are well advised to get appropriate counseling even before the child comes into their home and should avail themselves of subsequent counseling as needed.

Along the same lines, Jewish men and women who are not able or willing to adopt should seriously consider becoming Jewish Big Brothers and Jewish Big Sisters to enable children who have lost their father or mother through death or divorce to have a close, adult male or female model to balance the gender of their single parent as they grow up. Both adoption and service as a Jewish Big Brother or Big Sister are significant acts of חסד (loyalty and lovingkindness) whose beneficial effects often last throughout the child's life, and thus those who do them should feel religiously as well as personally confirmed and appreciated.

---

[105] Despite the thousands of black children waiting to be adopted, it may not be easy for white people to adopt them, for state and private adoption agencies, often backed by state laws, prohibit such adoption for fear that white parents will undermine the ethnic identity of the child. See Lynn Smith, "Salvation or Last Resort?", *Los Angeles Times*, 3 Nov. 1993, pp. E-1, 3.

In sum, then, adoption is an honored course of action in our tradition. In light of the physical risks of egg donation, and in view of the tradition's overwhelmingly positive attitude toward adoption, we must urge couples to reconsider adoption before engaging in egg donation.

Summary

1. Medical Interventions to Induce Fertility

When couples cannot have children, Jewish law clearly allows that they take advantage of fertility drugs and other techniques that may help them to have children through their own sexual intercourse — as couples undoubtedly prefer as well. Then the emotional values of coitus and reproduction can be preserved, and the medical intervention is solely to aid a natural process.

2. Artificial Insemination

When such interventions do not work, artificial insemination is permissible. Use of the husband's sperm, if possible, is preferable to that of a donor, but even donor insemination is permissible. In the case of A.I.H., the semen may be collected in a condom, but even masturbation to procure the husband's semen is permissible. Since the husband's semen is being used, he fulfills the commandment to procreate through artificial insemination.

In the case of donor insemination, as much about the donor as possible should be revealed to the social parents and, through them, to the child so that the child can have as strong a sense of his or her medical history and personal identity as possible. Secrecy about the artificial insemination should be avoided on all sides and for everyone's benefit — although, for legal reasons and out of respect for a donor's wish for privacy, confidentiality, but not total anonymity, is permissible.

Donor insemination does not constitute licentiousness or adultery, and the child so conceived is fully legitimate. For purposes of priestly status, the child follows the status of the semen donor, if that is known, or else adopts the default status of a ישראל.

While the social father does not fulfill the commandment to procreate through D.I., he does fulfill many other commandments connected to the raising of children, making him the child's father in many important senses even if not in the biological one. Children conceived through D.I. are prohibited to each other by the Torah as sexual partners and as candidates for marriage since they share a mother and are thus half-brother and half-sister. If the eggs are also donated and therefore the children have no biological relationship to each other, the children are nevertheless prohibited to each other for purposes of sex and marriage under the rabbinic category of relatives of the second degree because they grew up in the same home as sister and brother. The masturbation required for donor insemination does not constitute "wasting of the seed." Even if the donation will be to a sperm bank such that it may be used for inseminating a non-Jewish woman, masturbation for this purpose is permissible.

While donor insemination is permissible, infertile couples are *not required* to use it to have children, for, in any case, the husband does not fulfill the obligation to procreate through donor insemination. If the husband cannot procreate, he is exempted from the commandment, and he should feel no guilt on that account. Thus if the psychological problems engendered by the asymmetry of donor insemination pose a significant threat to the marriage or if other concerns make them feel reluctant, a couple may, in full compliance with Jewish law, elect not to use donor insemination to have children. If they wish to raise children, they should think of adoption as an alternative, but even that is not required by Jewish law.

3. Egg Donation

Similar conclusions apply to egg donation. The act is not licentious or adulterous since there is no contact of the genital organs of the egg donor and the husband, and so the child so conceived is fully legitimate. The identity of the mother for purposes of Jewish law follows the bearing mother. The same need for openness about the child's origins within the family, and the same desirability for the child to know as much as possible about the egg donor, apply to egg donation just as they apply to donor insemination. Because of the shortage of donated eggs, a fertile sister may donate eggs to her infertile sibling, despite the potential psychological problems involved, but only after appropriate counseling and only after all concerned determine that, on balance, the advantages of this arrangement outweigh its disadvantages. (We would not extend the same permission to brothers because there is no shortage and little cost in using donor sperm, and thus there is no need to incur the psychological risks involved in a relative's donation.) In order to avoid selective abortions as much as possible, a maximum of three eggs or zygotes may be implanted at any one time.

If the husband's semen is used to fertilize the egg(s) procured through donation, he fulfills the commandment to procreate through his wife's pregnancy by means of egg donation. Even so, a couple in this situation is not required to use egg donation to have children to fulfill the commandment; they may do so, but they also may opt not to do so. That is because the woman is not subject to the commandment, and the man, though obligated by it, is no longer forced to divorce his wife if he cannot have children by her. If a donor's semen is used as well as a donated egg, the husband does not fulfill the commandment to procreate, although here, as with donor insemination generally, he ceases to be obligated by the commandment and may fulfill many other commandments in the raising of the resultant child(ren).

While the risks to the donor inherent in egg donation are not so significant as to ban the procedure out of concern for the life and health of the donor, they are not negligible, and so egg donation should only be done when the couple has considered all other options of having children, including adoption.

4. Permissibility to Donate Sperm or Eggs

Men may donate their sperm to enable an infertile couple to have children, but only after due consideration of the implications of what they are doing and only with due respect and, indeed, awe for the whole procedure. Similarly, women may donate their eggs for the same purpose, but only under the same conditions and, in addition, only when they are assured, with their own medical condition duly examined, that they can undergo the procedure of harvesting eggs from their bodies without much risk to themselves. Recent studies suggest that women cannot safely serve as egg donors many times over because each instance of hyperovulation increases their risk of ovarian cancer. The evidence is not yet sufficient to ban egg donation entirely, but it does argue against undergoing multiple procedures of egg donation.

If semen or egg donors want to keep their identity confidential, they may do so. They do have a duty, however, to share as much of their medical history and personal characteristics with their offspring as they can consistent with that wish.

5. Adoption

Adoption does not fulfill the commandment to procreate, for Jewish law sees the child as the product of the biological parents. Nevertheless, people who adopt children fulfill many other commandments and do a real act of faithfulness and loving-kindness (חסד). As a result, adoption is a time-honored institution in Jewish law. Couples thinking about adopting one or more children should realize, though, that adoption often involves some special psychological problems for the social parents and for the child, especially during adolescence, and so the parents and child should get counseling, if possible, better to be able to cope with those issues.

Jewish law appreciates adoption of older children as much as infants, non-Caucasian ones as much as Caucasian ones, and handicapped children as much as able-bodied ones; indeed, since older, non-Caucasian, and disabled children are the primary populations of children waiting to be adopted, it probably is an even greater חסד to adopt them than it is to adopt a healthy, white infant. In any case, Jews must be educated to the Jewish acceptability of all these options for adoption and to the preferability of adoption over egg donation. They should also be educated to the possibility of adoption in addition to procreating and to the חסד involved in helping children with only one parent through programs like Jewish Big Brothers.

6. The Scope and Tenor of this Responsum

All of the above conclusions concerning artificial insemination and egg donation assume the case of the question asked — i.e., a married couple who cannot have children. This responsum does not treat, and therefore expresses no opinion about, the more complicated case of single women who wish to be inseminated (and, in some cases, also implanted with the egg of another woman), single men who artificially impregnate surrogate mothers, or single men or women who adopt children for purposes of becoming parents.

Jewish law clearly assumes that it is best for children to have both a mother and a father as it describes differing roles for both parents.[106] Furthermore, recent studies reaffirm the importance of fathers in the raising of a child, and a recent movie was

---

[106] Thus in the case of divorce, children below the age of six must be put in the custody of their mother, for they are mainly in need of the physical care and attention that mothers typically give children at that age, and above the age of six boys must be with their father, so that he can carry out his obligation to teach his male children Torah, while girls must be with their mother so that she can instruct them in the ways of modesty: see B. Ketubbot 102b, 103a; M.T. Laws of Marriage (אשות) 21:17; S.A. Even HaEzer 82:7. One talmudic passage even describes differing contributions of each parent in the physical make-up of the child, the mother contributing red matter (probably because menstrual blood is red) and the father contributing white matter (probably because semen is white), while God, each person's third parent according to the Rabbis, breathes life into the child; see B. Niddah 31a. These differing roles lead to differing reactions of the child to each parent, which, according to the Rabbis, explains why the Torah commands us to honor the father before the mother (Exod. 20:12), but to revere the mother before the father (Lev. 19:3): see Mekhilta, "Massekhta deBahodesh" (ed. Horowitz-Rabin), 8, p. 232 and its parallel in B. Kiddushin 30b-31a (although that version lacks the significant phrase, "Where a deficiency exists, He filled it"), and see Sifra "Kedoshim" 1:9 (p. 87a) and Mishnah Keritot, end (trans. H. Danby, p. 572), according to which even the mother must honor the father.

In modern times, we would certainly have a different understanding of what and how each parent contributes to the biological make-up of the child, and we would probably dispute the rigid roles for mothers and fathers delineated in the sources too; but the underlying point that parents of both genders have distinctive roles to play is, I think, still right. This is one instance of my general approach to matters of gender, for I have long affirmed that men and women are equal, but, at least in some significant ways beyond their anatomies, different; see my article, "Equality with Distinction," in "*Male and Female God Created Them*," by Judith Glass and Elliot N. Dorff (Los Angeles: University of Judaism [the *University Papers* series], Mar. 1984), pp. 13-23. More current research — e.g., Deborah Tannen's book, *You Just Don't Understand: Women and Men in Conversation* (New York: Ballantine Books, 1990) — confirms that thesis all the more. This makes it all the more important for children to have caring adults in their lives of both genders.

based on the search for her father by a child born through D.I. to a single mother.[107] An adequate treatment of the use of artificial insemination, egg donation or adoption by singles thus requires a full-fledged analysis of Jewish law and of contemporary psychological and sociological studies to determine how Jewish law should treat these new family configurations.

Such an analysis would also have to take into account the complications raised by American law, for protections against the paternity of the semen donor built into the Uniform Parentage Act and similar legislation have not been applied by recent court decisions to single parents.[108] Moreover, some states do not recognize the right of lesbians or gay men to be parents, even if they are the biological parents.[109]

Adoption by single people on the face of it poses fewer problems since the child is already born and is, by hypothesis, an orphan; but, in contrast to cases of divorce or the death of a spouse, this involves consciously creating a single-parent home. Single parents often do a remarkable job of raising their children, and it is certainly better for a child to have one caring parent than foster parents or no parents at all. Still, if the child could be adopted by two parents, that might well be better for the welfare of the child.

---

[107] For a popular summary of this, see Lee Smith, "The New Wave of Illegitimacy," *Fortune*, 18 Apr. 1994, pp. 81-94. According to Smith:

> Data on thousands of children collected for the Department of Health and Human Services show that:
> - Kids from single-parent families, whether through divorce or illegitimacy, are two to three times as likely to have emotional or behavioral problems, and half again as likely to have learning disabilities, as those who live with both parents.
> - Teenage girls who grow up without their fathers tend to have sex earlier. A 15-year-old who has lived with her mother only, for example, is three times as likely to lose her virginity before her 16th birthday as one who has lived with both parents (p. 82).

Smith also cites David Popenoe, a Rutgers University sociologist, who says that while the social sciences can seldom prove anything in the strict sense of proof, there remains "a strong likelihood that the increase in the number of fatherless children over the past 30 years has been a prominent factor in the growth of violence and juvenile delinquency." Thus more than half of the 14,000 inmates surveyed by the Justice Department in 1991 did not live with both parents while they were growing up (p. 82). The consensus of the experts Smith consulted indicates that "a father shows a child, especially a boy, how to fit into the community. Dr. Frank Pittman, an Atlanta psychiatrist, says in his recent book, *Man Enough*, that a father's role is not to make his sons more aggressive or to show them how to take what is theirs. On the contrary, his function is to define the limits of manhood. A boy doesn't have to be John Wayne. Jimmy Stewart is man enough" (p. 94).

The movie cited is *Made in America* (1993), with Whoopi Goldberg and Ted Danson, in which the daughter presumably born using the sperm Danson's character donated to a sperm bank in his teens seeks him out when she is a senior in high school. The movie bespeaks two worries about D.I. – i.e., that the children will have a deep-seated need to know their biological fathers, and that sperm banks will not keep accurate records.

[108] That was the ruling of the Juvenile and Domestic Relations Court in *C.M. v. C.C.* (1977), the California Court of Appeals in *Jhordan C. v. Mary K. and Victoria T.*, and the Colorado Supreme Court in *In the Interest of R.C.* (1989), (all at n. 75 above), and also the Oregon Court of Appeals in *McIntyre v. Crouch*, 780 P.2d 239, 98 Or. App. 462 (1989).

[109] This was the basis of the recent Virginia ruling that Sharon Bottoms could not retain custody of her daughter, born by artificial insemination. Virginia is one of just four states where legal precedent deems gay parents unfit (Arkansas, Missouri, and North Dakota are the others), and New Hampshire and Florida categorically bar gays as adoptive parents. On the other hand, in the nation's capital, local officials held a seminar this past summer to instruct gays on how to adopt, and New Jersey, Massachusetts and six other states explicitly permit a lesbian to adopt her lover's child and become a second parent. See "Gay Parents: Under Fire and on the Rise," *Time*, 20 Sept. 1993, pp. 66-71. American law in all its diversity, then, is another factor which must be considered in artificial insemination of single women, and the matter is clearly complicated further if the women involved are lesbians.

This responsum, in any case, has not carried out the necessary analysis of these situations.[110] Its task, instead, is to respond to the far more numerous cases of artificial insemination, egg donation, and adoption being used by infertile couples to have children.[111]

As medicine becomes ever more adept at helping infertile couples conceive on their own, donor insemination, while necessary and permissible now, may no longer be necessary. Just recently, Belgian scientists "invented a new treatment for male infertility that they say may allow virtually any man, no matter how few or misshapen or immobile his sperm cells, to father a child" through the direct injection of a single human sperm cell into a human egg in a petri dish.[112] Hopefully, one day egg donation will not be necessary for infertile women either.[113] Then the emotional, moral, and legal problems these procedures raise may resolve themselves.

---

[110] Our colleague, Rabbi David Golinkin, has written a responsum on one aspect of these questions; see his paper, "Artificial Insemination for a Single Woman," *Responsa of the Va'ad Halakhah of the Rabbinical Assembly of Israel* (Jerusalem: The Rabbinical Assembly of Israel and The Masorti Movement, 5748-5749), vol. 3, pp. 83-92. I am sure, though, that his is only the first of many responsa which will deal with what is, for all of us, a very new kind of family. The question is no longer whether such families exist, for a considerable number of women have already been artificially impregnated; the question is rather what Jewish law should say about such procedures, and why.

Newsweek (2 Aug. 1993, Michele Ingrassia et al., "Daughters of Murphy Brown," p. 59) recently reported that,

> The greatest burden of single parenthood falls on the children. As research increasingly shows, children reared in one-parent families tend to have more educational, emotional, and financial difficulties than those who grow up with two parents. Since the problems are often economic, some of the effects may be eased for children of well-educated, middle-class women.
> Psychologist Anna Beth Benningfield argues that children can accept any situation as normal, as long as there's a strong sense of family. Though [single parent Jane] Saks would have preferred a more conventional setup, she believes it makes little difference in an era of sky-high divorce rates. . . .What is critical is how mother responds when her child asks: where's Dad?

In checking with some child psychologists I know, current research indicates that children, on average, do indeed do worse with one parent rather than with two, but only when that single parent is isolated as the only care-giver for the child. If the parent has sufficient funds to hire help, or if, in poor or rich families, there is a strong network of support from family and friends, children do no worse, on average, than they do with two parents. In making these comparisons, one must remember that the criteria for measuring adjustment and well-being are themselves sometimes at issue and that many contemporary families with two parents are themselves dysfunctional. Still, this remains a concern.

The one clear thing is that children born to a Jewish woman through artificial insemination are fully Jewish.

[111] According to the 1987 national survey commissioned by the United States Office of Technology Assessment (see n. 8 above), 11,000 physicians around the county provided artificial insemination services to approximately 172,000 women. Eighty percent of the requests for artificial insemination were prompted by male infertility in the husband of a couple; only four percent (approximately 5,000 women) were cases of single women seeking to become pregnant. On the other hand, The California Cryobank, based on its own records, estimates that approximately twenty-five percent of the women requesting artificial insemination today (1994) are without male partners. That is quite some discrepancy! Still, even with the twenty-five percent figure, the vast majority (seventy-five percent) of artificial inseminations are done for infertile couples, the subject of this responsum. See Fader, *Sperm Banking* (at n. 23), pp. 6, 11.

[112] Gina Kolata, "New Pregnancy Hope: A Single Sperm," *New York Times*, 11 Aug. 1993, p. C11. I would like to thank Rabbi Avram Reisner for drawing my attention to this. Fader, though, maintains that Alan Trounson reported success with microinjection of an individual human sperm into a human egg at the Sixth World Congress on Human Reproduction in Tokyo in 1987; see Fader, *Sperm Banking* (at n. 23), p. 10.

[113] In any case, it appears that the health care reforms planned by the Clinton Administration do not include payment for IVF, and since egg donation requires that, it may become the privilege of only the rich and therefore quite rare. See Edwin Chen and Robert A. Rosenblatt, "Clinton Promises Sweeping Coverage in Health Care Plan," *Los Angeles Times*, 11 Sept. 1993, pp. A1, A16, and the exclusions listed on p. A17.

Conclusion

In the future, as technology develops yet further, we may no longer be faced with some of the specific questions addressed in this responsum. In the meantime, though, artificial insemination, egg donation, and, especially, adoption are Jewishly permissible procedures within the parameters outlined above. Even in those cases where the commandment to procreate is not fulfilled, these techniques enable the social parents to experience the joys and challenges of parenthood, thereby growing themselves, and they add to the numbers of the Jewish people at a time when that is nothing short of critical. Because of the way the commandment to procreate has been interpreted in Jewish sources, because of the physical dangers sometimes incurred, and because of the psychological problems involved in the asymmetry that these methods of having children sometimes create, infertile couples are not required to engage in these procedures to have children. For those who do use them, though, our endorsement of their choice to have children by these methods is not grudging, but enthusiastic. May God grant them the children they seek, and may they raise their children to Torah, the wedding canopy, and to good deeds.[114]

---

[114] I would like to thank the following physicians for helping me with the medical and general ethical aspects of this responsum: Dr. Brenda Fabe, M.D., a gynecologist/obstetrician at Kaiser Permanente Medical Center in West Los Angeles and director of physicians for Camp Ramah in California; Dr. Michael Grodin, M.D., Professor of Medical Ethics at Boston University School of Medicine; and Dr. Cappy Miles Rothman, a male infertility specialist and urologist in Los Angeles. I would also like to thank Professor Vicki Michel, J.D., past Co-Chair of the Los Angeles County Joint Commission on Bioethics of the American Bar Association and the American Medical Association, and Professor Arthur Rosett of UCLA School of Law, both of whom helped me with the sections of this responsum referring to American law and some general ethical concerns as well. In addition, Rabbis Kassel Abelson, David Feldman, Aaron Mackler, Avram Reisner, and Joel Roth, my fellow members of the Subcommittee on Bioethics of the Committee on Jewish Law and Standards, had significant input on many aspects of this responsum, and I am indebted to them. As usual, none of the people mentioned here is responsible for any of the errors or judgments of this responsum, but they have all contributed immensely to my own thinking on these complicated issues, and they have my sincere appreciation as colleagues and as friends.

EH 1:3.1995

IN VITRO FERTILIZATION

Rabbi Aaron L. Mackler

This paper was approved by the CJLS on December 13, 1995, by a vote of twenty in favor and one abstention (20-0-1). Voting in favor: Rabbis Kassel Abelson, Ben Zion Bergman, Stephanie Dickstein, Elliot N. Dorff, Jerome M. Epstein, Baruch Frydman-Kohl, Shoshana Gelfand, Myron S. Geller, Susan Grossman, Judah Kogen, Vernon H. Kurtz, Alan B. Lucas, Aaron L. Mackler, Mayer Rabinowitz, Avram Israel Reisner, Joel E. Rembaum, Gerald Skolnik, Elie Kaplan Spitz, Gordon Tucker, and Gerald Zelizer. Abstaining: Rabbi Paul Plotkin.

The Committee on Jewish Law and Standards of the Rabbinical Assembly provides guidance in matters of halakhah for the Conservative movement. The individual rabbi, however, is the authority for the interpretation and application of all matters of halakhah.

שאלה

In vitro fertilization (IVF) involves the fertilizing of a human ovum (egg cell) by sperm outside the human body. The resulting embryo can be transferred to a woman's uterus for gestation and (when successful) the birth of a child. This technique gives rise to a number of important questions:

1. May an infertile couple utilize IVF, using the husband's sperm and wife's egg, to have a child? What is the status of the offspring?

2. Does halakhah provide any guidance regarding the transfer of embryos to the woman's uterus for gestation?

3. May more embryos be created by IVF than are needed for immediate use? What may be done with extra embryos, including those that are cryopreserved (frozen)?

4. Is IVF using donated sperm and/or ova permitted? What is the status of the offspring?

תשובה

Judaism values children as a blessing for their parents and for the broader community. For those able to do so, having children represents the fulfillment of a mitzvah, one that can be traced back to God's charge to "be fruitful and multiply" (פרו ורבו) in the biblical account of creation.[1] In vitro fertilization, like other reproductive technologies, offers the potential

---

[1] M. Yevamot 6:6 states:

לא יבטל אדם מפריה ורביה אלא אם כן יש לו בנים. בית שמאי אומרים, שני זכרים, ובית הלל אומרים, זכר ונקבה, שנאמר, זכר ונקבה בראם.

One must not abstain from "fruitfulness and increase" unless one has children. The School

to bring a new child into the world. In appropriate cases, this can provide life to a child who otherwise would not have been born, add joy and harmony to the family, and contribute to the strengthening of the Jewish (and human) community.[2] At the same time, reproductive technologies can impose significant personal, financial, and physical costs on the individual or couple using them, and in some cases on children born of the procedure.

More broadly, the use of reproductive technologies can affect communal values and practices concerning children, reproduction, and the family. The United States and other societies have explored these concerns through a variety of means, including examination by professional associations and interdisciplinary commissions, and developments in civil law. In the Jewish tradition, the central means of responding to these concerns is through halakhah, or Jewish law.[3]

In Vitro Fertilization and Embryonic Development

In vitro fertilization (IVF) involves the fertilization of an ovum outside the body; "in vitro," literally meaning "in glass," refers to the petri dish in which sperm and ova are combined. In the first successful use of IVF as a reproductive technology, British researchers Robert Edwards and Patrick Steptoe fertilized an ovum produced by Leslie Brown with sperm produced by her husband and transferred the fertilized ovum to her uterus, leading to the birth of Louise Brown in July 1978.

As typically practiced today, a woman preparing for IVF receives hormones to stimulate the development of several ova. Shortly before ovulation would occur, a physician uses ultrasound to guide a needle through the cervix to the ovaries to gather or "retrieve" developed ova. After inspection and appropriate preparation, the ova are combined with prepared sperm. The resulting embryo is allowed to develop for a time period of up to a few days,

---

of Shammai say: two males. The School of Hillel say: a male and a female, as it is written, 'male and female He created them' [Gen. 1:27].

Jewish law follows Hillel's view, but encourages continuing to engage in procreation even if one already has a son and a daughter. While having children (specifically, a boy and a girl) represents the fulfillment of a mitzvah, those unable to have children are exempt from the obligation. Indeed, Rabbi J. David Bleich argues that the mitzvah of procreation is best understood not as having children, which is beyond one's control, but as continuing one's practice of potentially procreative intercourse with one's spouse at least until a boy and a girl are born (*Judaism and Healing* [New York: Ktav, 1981], p. 113).

Jewish law describes the obligation to procreate as incumbent upon the male. This formulation (exegetically based on the wording of Gen. 1:28) may reflect a sociological background in which men have greater control than women over whether they would marry and procreate; or a view that women should be encouraged but not technically obligated to entail the risks of pregnancy and childbirth. M. Yevamot 6:6; Shulhan Arukh, Even HaEzer 1; David M. Feldman, *Health and Medicine in the Jewish Tradition* (New York: Crossroad, 1986), pp. 69-71; David M. Feldman, *Marital Relations, Birth Control, and Abortion in Jewish Law* (New York: Schocken, 1978), pp. 46-59; Elliot N. Dorff, "Artificial Insemination, Egg Donation, and Adoption," above, pp. 462-465. Unspecified citations of Dorff below refer to this paper.

[2] Dorff; Michael Gold, *And Hannah Wept* (Philadelphia: Jewish Publication Society, 1988); Richard V. Grazi, ed., *Be Fruitful and Multiply* (Jerusalem: Genesis, 1994); Mordechai Halperin, "Applying the Principles of Halakhah to Modern Medicine: In-Vitro Fertilization, Embryo Transfer, and Frozen Embryo," *Proceedings of the Association of Orthodox Jewish Scientists*, vols. 8-9 (New York: Sepher-Hermon, 1987), pp. 198-200. Here and elsewhere I draw on Dorff's recent responsum. Like Dorff, I only address the case of a married couple that seeks to have offspring. While some unmarried women wish to use donated sperm to reproduce, relatively few seek (or require) IVF procedures. In any case, the use of IVF by unmarried women raises concerns beyond the scope of this paper.

[3] See, e.g., Elliot N. Dorff, "A Methodology for Jewish Medical Ethics," in *Contemporary Jewish Ethics and Morality*, ed. Elliot N. Dorff and Louis E. Newman (New York: Oxford University Press, 1995), pp. 161-176.

reaching the stage of 2-8 cells, and is then transferred to a woman's uterus, using a catheter inserted through the cervix. When the procedure is successful, the embryo continues to develop and implants in the uterus, leading to pregnancy and the birth of a child. At the 2-8 cell stage, the embryo could be cryopreserved or "frozen" for transfer at a later time.[4]

In vitro fertilization was originally developed to assist women with damaged or absent fallopian tubes. The fallopian tube, connecting the ovary and uterus, is typically the site of fertilization as well as the path by which the fertilized ovum reaches the uterus. IVF has also been used in response to other female infertility factors such as endometriosis or ovulatory problems, for male factors, and for "unexplained infertility."[5] The Society for Assisted Reproductive Technology and the American Society for Reproductive Medicine report that in 1993 IVF and related procedures were performed for 50,844 cycles, leading to 8,741 deliveries. The most common procedure, IVF using the recipient's ova and without embryo freezing, led to delivery of a child following 18.6% of egg retrievals. An individual's prospects might be significantly higher or lower, depending on personal and medical factors. For example, success rates have been found to be higher when no male factor is involved, and for women under age forty.[6]

The process of fertilization begins with the sperm penetrating the ovum. After about twenty-four hours, the chromosomes of the sperm and egg combine, a process referred to as syngamy. The embryo soon begins a series of cell divisions, but does not yet change in overall size. Within a few days, when the embryo has reached the eight-cell stage, the fusion of genetic material is complete and gene expression (functioning) begins. Transfer of an IVF embryo to a woman's uterus generally occurs between the two-cell and eight-cell stage.[7]

A series of changes takes place between this stage, about day 3 after fertilization, and day 14. Through day 3, each cell has the ability to develop into any type of cell or to divide off and develop into a separate embryo. With increasing differentiation within the embryo, cells begin to lose this ability after day 3, but some such abilities may persist until about day 14. In the uterus, implantation begins at about seven days after fertilization, and is completed by about fourteen days. During this second week of development the embryo begins to gain internal organization of a basic sort, such as the

---

[4] Canada, Report of the Royal Commission on New Reproductive Technologies, *Proceed with Care* (Ottawa, 1993) [cited below as Canada]; Ethics Committee, American Fertility Society, *Ethical Considerations of Assisted Reproductive Technologies, Fertility and Sterility* 62 (1994): 35S [cited below as AFS]. The term "embryo" is used broadly in this paper to refer to the product of fertilization throughout its early development. Because of the rudimentary nature of its development at this stage, many prefer the term "preembryo" (AFS) or "zygote" (Canada).

Similar techniques are employed in two related alternative procedures. In GIFT (gamete intrafallopian transfer), ova and sperm are mixed and placed directly in the fallopian tube. With ZIFT (zygote intrafallopian transfer), the embryo produced in vitro is transferred to the fallopian tube rather than the uterus. Both of these procedures require laparoscopy, a somewhat more invasive procedure than the transcervical procedures used in IVF (Canada; Grazi; AFS, 38S-40S). While this responsum focuses on IVF, its conclusions would in general apply to these procedures as well.

[5] Canada; AFS, 35S-36S.

[6] Society for Assisted Reproductive Technology, American Society for Reproductive Medicine, "Assisted Reproductive Technology in the United States and Canada: 1993 Results Generated from The Society for Reproductive Medicine/Society for Assisted Reproductive Technology Registry," *Fertility and Sterility* 64 (1995): 13-21 [cited below as SART]. For the sake of comparison, the average monthly likelihood of fertilization leading to live birth among sexually active fertile couples not using contraception in the general population is about 20-25%.

[7] Canada, pp. 149-60; AFS, 29S-31S; U.S., National Institutes of Health, "Final Report of the Human Embryo Research Panel," 27 Sept. 1994, 20-36, 57-63; Thomas A. Shannon and Allan B. Wolter, "Reflections on the Moral Status of the Pre-embryo," *Theological Studies* 51 (1990): 606-610.

differentiation of the embryo itself from the placenta. At about day 14, the embryo first exhibits a "primitive streak," a clustering of cells at one end of the embryo. Formation of the neural groove, the rudimentary beginning of the nervous system, occurs in the third week. Current scientific capabilities generally cannot maintain an embryo in vitro beyond about the first week of development. As noted above, transfer of an embryo for reproduction occurs well before this time, at about day 3 of development.[8]

In Vitro Fertilization Using a Couple's Own Ova and Sperm

Most halakhic authorities who have addressed the issue of in vitro fertilization have treated this issue as similar to artificial insemination. Many permit in vitro fertilization using a wife's egg and husband's sperm. Central issues typically include whether the husband violates the prohibition against "wasteful emission of seed," whether the couple can be sure that the embryo transferred to the woman in fact derives from their gametes (sperm and ova), and whether the husband fulfills the mitzvah of procreation. Thus, for example, Rabbi Ovadiah Yosef rules that IVF is permitted when it represents the only way for a couple to have children, and that the child is to be considered the parent's offspring in all regards.[9]

Rabbi Eliezer Yehudah Waldenberg represents an exception to this rule, arguing that IVF is more problematic than artificial insemination on technical grounds, and should be absolutely forbidden.[10] Rabbi Avigdor Nebenzal, writing in response to Waldenberg, raises a number of objections to his position. Prohibiting IVF, even as a last resort, could prevent the husband from fulfilling the mitzvah of procreation, increase the couple's anguish and bitterness of spirit, or lead to divorce. Producing sperm in order to fertilize an egg would not represent "emission of seed in vain," for the husband's intention is procreative. While IVF raises some legitimate concerns, these must be weighed against the "happiness of the couple among the people Israel."[11]

Rabbi J. David Bleich raises two additional concerns with the procedure. First, IVF is objectionable if it entails a risk for the embryo and increases the likelihood of a seriously impaired child. Bleich argues that the uncertainties inherent in the first uses of IVF would represent an unacceptable risk: "it will require the birth and maturation through adolescence into adulthood of a significant number of healthy and normal test-tube babies before the technique may be viewed as morally acceptable." Second, Bleich objects to the possible destruction of embryos that might result if more are created than are to be transferred for implantation. He expresses hope that, in time and given proper safeguards, IVF "can be a welcome means of bestowing the happiness and fulfillment of parenthood upon otherwise childless couples."[12]

---

[8] Ibid.

[9] Cited in Moshe Drori, "Genetic Engineering – Preliminary Discussion of its Legal and Halakhic Aspects," *Tehumin* 1 (1980): 287-288. On "wasteful emission of seed" (הוצאת זרע לבטלה; or "destruction of seed," השחתת לרע), see Feldman, *Marital Relations*, pp. 109-131.

[10] Waldenberg asserts that IVF violates the prohibition against "wasteful emission of seed," for while artificial insemination transfers a husband's sperm to his wife's reproductive system, in IVF sperm remains outside her body. IVF diverges more dramatically from natural reproduction, "upsetting the order of creation" (משנים בזה סדרי בראשית), making it impossible to view the husband or wife as parents of the offspring. Finally, Waldenberg argues that it is much more difficult to be certain that a transferred embryo represents the product of the couple's gametes than it is to ensure that the husband's sperm is used in artificial insemination. *Tzitz Eliezer* vol. 15, siman 45, pp. 115-120. This responsum appears as well in *Assia* no. 33 (1982): 5-13.

[11] "*In Vitro* Fertilization – Comments," *Assia* no. 35 (1983): 5.

[12] "Test-Tube Babies," in *Jewish Bioethics*, eds. Fred Rosner and J. David Bleich (New York: Sanhedrin Press, 1979), pp. 80-85.

Finally, Rabbi David Feldman observes that "with so pronatalist a. . .tradition, the Jewish response has been understandably affirmative to new reproductive techniques, such as in-vitro fertilization." He notes the concerns of some that technological interventions such as IVF interfere with the natural process of reproduction.[13] He nonetheless argues that, given safeguards against abuse, IVF can provide an appropriate way for humans to act as partners with God in improving upon nature, and represents a positive response to the deeply human desire for offspring.[14]

I would agree with Feldman and others that the technological interventions required for IVF do not in themselves rule out the procedure. The Jewish ideal, when it is possible, is for children to be conceived through marital intercourse.[15] In the case of an infertile couple, however, this is not possible. Medical interventions to assist the natural process of reproduction can enable the couple to have a child. The use of IVF in such situations accords with our responsibility to be both reverent and active in our partnership with God. Similarly, I would agree with Rabbi Nebenzal and others that producing sperm for the purpose of reproduction does not violate any prohibition.[16]

Rabbi Bleich's concern about the destruction of embryos will be addressed in the section on embryos not transferred for gestation below. The issue of risk to children born of IVF must be taken seriously by halakhah. Current information, however, suggests that the procedures do not involve prohibitive risks. Studies indicate that children born of IVF do not suffer from congenital anomalies to a greater extent than the general population. IVF as currently practiced is associated with an increased likelihood of multiple pregnancies and births (such as triplets and quadruplets), and multiple births entail an increased risk of low birth weight, which in turn is associated with increased risk of disability. In addition, the risk of perinatal death may be somewhat higher for births following IVF than for other births.[17]

The biomedical community should monitor long-term effects of IVF and continue to work to lessen all risk involved with this procedure. Couples using IVF should do their best to assure that any potential harm to children is minimized. While risks must be considered carefully by the couple in deciding about IVF, as they must be considered in any medical decision, currently available information suggests that they should not preclude the practice. Risks to the couple, specifically the woman, must be taken seriously as well; Jewish law and values prohibit us from endangering our lives or exposing ourselves to

---

[13] As noted above (n. 10), such concerns have been raised by Rabbi Eliezer Waldenberg. They also have been expressed within the context of Christian and secular ethics. See Leon R. Kass, *Toward a More Natural Science* (New York: Macmillan, Free Press), p. 72; Congregation for the Doctrine of the Faith, *Instruction on Respect for Human Life in its Origin and on the Dignity of Procreation: Replies to Certain Questions of the Day* (Washington, DC: United States Catholic Conference, 1987). A somewhat differing Roman Catholic view may be found in Lisa Sowle Cahill, "Moral Traditions, Ethical Language, and Reproductive Technologies," *Journal of Medicine and Philosophy* 14 (1989): 515-516.

[14] Feldman, *Health and Medicine*, pp. 71-72.

[15] As expressed by the medieval *Iggret Hakodesh*: "The union of man with his wife, when it is proper, is the mystery of the foundation of the world and its civilization. Through the act they become partners with God in the act of creation. This is the mystery of what the sages said, 'When a man unites with his wife in holiness, the Shekhinah is between them in the mystery of man and woman.'" *The Holy Letter*, trans. Seymour J. Cohen (Northvale, NJ: Jason Aronson, 1993; reprint of New York: Ktav, 1976), p. 92. This point is nicely expressed in a paper by Rabbi Daniel Schiff of the Reform movement, "Developing Halakhic Attitudes to Sex Preselection," 1995, pp. 21-22 of typescript. [Since published in *The Fetus and Fertility in Jewish Law*, eds. Walter Jacob and Moshe Zemer (Pittsburgh: Rodef Shalom Press, 1995), pp. 91-117.]

[16] Nebenzal, p. 5; Dorff, above, p. 472.

[17] Canada, pp. 527-534; Norma C. Morin et al., "Congenital Malformations and Psychosocial Development in Children Conceived by In Vitro Fertilization," *Journal of Pediatrics* 115 (1989): 222-227.

excessive risk.[18] Currently available information suggests that medical risks of the procedures are not in general prohibitive. Commonly used techniques to retrieve ova and transfer an embryo to the uterus do not require use of general anesthetic, and are fairly non-invasive. Potential harms associated with drugs that promote ovulation should be carefully evaluated by individuals and their physicians, but would not in general rule out the practice.

Couples, in particular women, should be aware of these risks. They should also be aware of the personal and psychological toll that the use of reproductive technologies such as IVF often entails. Financial costs of IVF should be considered as well. Finally, all should be aware that many couples who undergo these procedures do not have a child, and should have a realistic sense of the likelihood of a child in their specific circumstances. Some studies suggest that "the stress of repeated of failures of treatment is particularly difficult for couples to cope with."[19] Both thorough counselling and social support are important for all who consider using IVF or other reproductive technologies.

In light of these factors, it is clear that couples are not required by Jewish law to utilize procedures such as IVF. Given the risks, burdens, and uncertainty involved, the use of reproductive technologies such as IVF is clearly not obligatory, and probably would be ill-advised in some cases. Such interventions should not occur without the fully informed and voluntary consent of those involved, and the decision of a couple or individual not to use these procedures would be fully justifiable and must be respected. As expressed by Rabbi Elliot Dorff, "The Jewish tradition would have all people, fertile or infertile, understand that our ability to procreate is not the source of our ultimate, divine worth; that comes from being created in God's image."[20] Individuals who cannot have children can make other vital contributions to strengthening the Jewish (and human) community.[21] In particular, they should strongly consider adoption, which provides an opportunity to raise a child, strengthen the community, and provide a life-changing benefit for a child who cannot be cared for by biological parents.[22]

Having said this, it is clear that IVF is permissible for those who choose to utilize these procedures. For these couples, technical and other halakhic concerns are outweighed by the great good of a new human life, the addition to the harmony and joy of the family, and the contribution to the strengthening of the Jewish community and humanity.[23] A child born as a result of IVF using a couple's sperm and egg is fully the parents' child in all respects, and causes the mitzvah of "be fruitful and multiply" to be fulfilled.

---

[18] As expressed by the Talmud (Hullin 10a), חמירא סכנתא מאיסורא, that which is dangerous is to be avoided even more stringently than that which is ritually forbidden. The Rabbinic tradition finds this value expressed positively in the verse from Deuteronomy (4:15), ונשמרתם מאד לנפשתיכם, "you should take care of yourselves diligently." See Feldman, *Health and Medicine*, pp. 24-26; Dorff, above, p. 495.

[19] Canada, pp. 532, 527-534. For a popular discussion of the potential frustrations and personal costs of these procedures, see Sharon Begley, "The Baby Myth," *Newsweek*, 4 Sept. 1995, pp. 38-47.

[20] Dorff, above, p. 473. Dorff accordingly states that "infertile couples are under no Jewish obligation to use modern technology to have children. If they nevertheless choose to do so, they must recognize and take account of the factors involved in order to make a reasonable and Jewishly responsible decision." Dorff, above, p. 469.

[21] See above, Dorff, p. 473; Gold. While this paper is addressed in particular to Jews, all humans have intrinsic value as beings created in the image of God and participants in God's covenant with the children of Noah; see Louis Finkelstein, "Human Equality in the Jewish Tradition," in *Aspects of Equality*, ed. Lyman Bryson et al. (New York: Harper and Brothers, 1956), pp. 179-205. The message of Isa. 56:3-5 is relevant as well. God assures those "who have chosen what I desire and hold fast to my covenant — I will give them, in My House and within My walls, a monument and a name better than sons or daughters. I will give them an everlasting name that shall not perish."

[22] See Dorff, above, pp. 501-504.

[23] Cf. Nebenzal.

Transferring In Vitro Embryos for Gestation

A. Preimplantation Genetic Testing

Genetic information about embryos can be obtained through a number of techniques. In one approach, a cell is removed from an embryo at an early stage of development, when the embryo consists of eight cells. While the embryo can continue to develop normally, the DNA (genetic material) of the single cell is amplified to provide a sufficient quantity of material to allow for genetic testing. In research reported in 1992, genetic diagnosis was performed on embryos created from the sperm and ova of couples, both members of which were carriers for the (recessive) disease of cystic fibrosis. For two couples, some embryos were identified that would be affected by the disease and were not transferred, and other embryos (representing carriers or noncarriers) were transferred. One of the women became pregnant, and gave birth to a girl unaffected by the disease.[24]

Asked about genetic testing, Rabbi Y. Zilberstein responded that "one cannot close the door in the face of despondent people who suffer mental anguish in fear of giving birth to sick children, pressure which can drive the mother mad. Therefore, in the case of a serious genetic disease that affects the couple, it is difficult to forbid the suggestion [for genetic testing through IVF]."[25]

Genetic diagnosis and selective transfer of embryos is clearly no more problematic than prenatal diagnosis and abortion of a fetus affected with a severe genetic disease, which has been accepted in the Conservative movement and by some in Orthodoxy.[26] If anything, selective non-transfer of an early in vitro embryo would be preferable to abortion of a more fully developed fetus in utero. The use of IVF for genetic testing faces great practical obstacles, and the risks and uncertainties of IVF will preclude requiring such use for the foreseeable future. For those couples who desire to use IVF and preimplantation genetic testing to avoid having a child with a severe genetic disease, the procedure is certainly fully acceptable.

B. Gender Selection

Similar (and often somewhat simpler) techniques can be used to determine the gender of an embryo. In some cases, a severe genetic disease may be linked to a sex chromosome, and so affect primarily children of only one gender, generally males. For example, if a woman is a carrier for Duchenne's muscular dystrophy, half of her sons but none of her daughters would be likely to be affected by the disease. In such situations, preimplantation sex selection of embryos would represent a form of testing for a severe genetic defect, and would be acceptable.

Sex selection in other situations would be more problematic. The desire for a child of a particular gender would not be enough to justify the risks and other problems associated with

---

[24] Alan H. Handyside et al., "Birth of a Normal Girl After In Vitro Fertilization and Preimplantation Diagnostic Testing for Cystic Fibrosis," *New England Journal of Medicine* 327 (1992): 905-909; Joe Leigh Simpson and Sandra Ann Carson, "Preimplantation Genetic Diagnosis," *New England Journal of Medicine* 327 (1992): 951-953. See also AFS, 64S-66S; William Edward Gibbons et al., "Preimplantation Genetic Diagnosis for Tay-Sachs Disease: Successful Pregnancy after Pre-Embryo Biopsy and Gene Amplification by Polymerase Chain Reaction," *Fertility and Sterility* 63 (1995): 723-728.

[25] Responsum to Richard Grazi, Shevat 5751 (1991), cited in Richard V. Grazi and Joel B. Wolowelsky, "Preimplantation Sex Selection and Genetic Screening in Contemporary Jewish Law and Ethics," *Journal of Assisted Reproduction and Genetics* 9 (1992): 321; this material appears also in Grazi, p. 189.

[26] E.g., Kassel Abelson, "Prenatal Testing and Abortion," *PCJLS 80-85*, pp. 3-10.

IVF. Moreover, sex selection by any means raises important concerns. It is offensive to regard one gender as in general better than or preferable to the other, and it would be wrong to choose the gender of a child or take any other action on the basis of sexist views. Moreover, some studies suggest that couples with a strong preference regarding their child's gender disproportionately would choose boys. If sex selection were to be widely practiced, this might lead to an overabundance of males in society, entailing significant social problems.[27]

Rabbi Bleich observes that classical Rabbinic sources do not object to sex selection, and the Talmud provides advice on increasing the likelihood of a male birth. These sources would be more concerned with legitimacy of the method used for sex selection than with the attempt to influence the gender of one's offspring. Bleich nonetheless argues that, based on demographic concerns, "society would find ample justification in the teachings of Judaism for discouraging widespread sex preselection."[28] Rabbis Y.B. Shafran and Y. Zilberstein have specifically ruled against the use of IVF for sex selection.[29] I would agree that (with the exception of sex-linked disease) IVF should not be used solely for the purpose of sex selection.[30]

c. Number of Embryos Transferred

A question can also be raised with regard to the number of embryos to be transferred to the woman's uterus. A number of embryos are generally transferred together in order to increase the likelihood of at least one implanting. At the same time, transferring a large number of embryos increases the risk of multifetal pregnancies. Multifetal pregnancy, especially when involving more than two or three fetuses, increases risks for the woman and for the fetuses.[31]

A procedure of multifetal pregnancy reduction has been developed to selectively abort some of the fetuses in order to lessen the risk for the woman and/or the other fetuses. If a woman is pregnant with more than two fetuses, multifetal pregnancy reduction would be halakhically acceptable in appropriate cases — certainly in order to protect the woman from a serious threat to her health, and arguably with the independent justification of protecting the remaining fetuses.[32] At the same time, this procedure may itself entail risks for the woman and especially for the remaining fetuses. From the standpoint

---

[27] See Schiff, pp. 18-19, and Owen D. Jones, "Sex Selection: Regulating Technology Enabling the Predetermination of a Child's Gender," in *Harvard Journal of Law and Technology* 6 (fall 1992): 12-17, cited therein. Schiff argues that, assuming that it is not sexist in application, sex preselection is not inherently objectionable; nonetheless, the use of a fully efficient method of sex selection would represent hubris and an inappropriate overreliance on technology. See also AFS, 64S-66S.

[28] "Sex Preselection," *Judaism and Healing*, pp. 110-115.

[29] In Grazi and Wolowelsky, pp. 320-21.

[30] One possible exception would be the case of a couple undergoing IVF for independent reasons who gain knowledge about the sex of embryos. If the couple has only children of one sex, one could argue that they could use available information to choose embryos of the other sex for implantation. This would help them to achieve the classical goal articulated by Hillel of having at least one child of each gender (M. Yevamot 6:6; see n. 1 above). A practice of sex selection limited to this situation would avoid the concerns with sexism and demography noted above.

[31] Canada, pp. 527-530; Fred Rosner, "Pregnancy Reduction in Jewish Law," *Journal of Clinical Ethics* 1 (1990): 181.

[32] Richard V. Grazi and Joel B. Wolowelsky, "Multifetal Pregnancy Reduction and Disposal of Untransplanted Embryos in Contemporary Jewish Law and Ethics," *American Journal of Obstetrics and Gynecology* 165 (1991): 1268-1271; J. David Bleich, "Pregnancy Reduction," *Tradition* 29, no. 3 (1995): 55-63; Yitzchak Mehlman, "Multi-Fetal Pregnancy Reduction," *Journal of Halachah and Contemporary Society* 27 (1994): 35-68; Rosner, pp. 181-86; and numerous sources cited in these articles.

of Judaism, it would be important to take reasonable steps to lessen the likelihood of the need for multifetal pregnancy reduction, as it would be appropriate to lessen the likelihood of recourse to abortion in other circumstances.

Many who have examined the practice of IVF have recommended limiting the number of embryos transferred to no more than three. This limit is found in guidelines of Britain's Human Fertilisation and Embryology Authority, Canada's Royal Commission on New Reproductive Technologies, and the European Society of Human Reproduction. The Canadian Commission, for example, argues that transferring more than three embryos increases the risk of multifetal pregnancy, but does not increase the likelihood of success, and in fact may lessen the likelihood of the live birth of a child.[33] The specific concern of Jewish law and ethics to minimize risk to the woman and fetuses provides additional support for this limit. No more than three embryos should be transferred in a procedure. To the extent possible, transferring only two embryos would be preferable.[34]

Embryos that are Not Transferred for Gestation

While it would be possible to use only one or two ova in an IVF procedure, current IVF practices involve attempts to fertilize all ova retrieved from the woman's ovaries, often five to ten or more. One reason is that fertilization does not always occur, and exposing all available ova to sperm maximizes the chance that the needed number of embryos will be created. In addition, current capabilities allow for the successful cryopreservation or freezing of early-stage embryos, but not of unfertilized ova. "Extra" embryos, beyond the number appropriate for immediate transfer, could be frozen for later use, in case the current transfer does not result in the birth of a child or the couple wishes to have additional children using IVF. Embryos are generally frozen between the one-cell and eight-cell stage. Embryo freezing avoids the need for additional egg retrieval procedures, and may be desirable for other medical or personal reasons.[35]

Creating extra embryos and freezing embryos, as currently practiced, would be halakhically acceptable.[36] These procedures both enhance the likelihood of success and minimize the medical risks and burdens faced by the woman. This permissibility is based on the assumption that cryopreservation of embryos is safe, as appears to be the

---

[33] Canada, pp. 527-30; Great Britain, Human Fertilisation and Embryology Authority, *Manual for Centres* (1990), Code of Practice, 7.i.

[34] This agrees with the position of Dorff, above, pp. 497-498. A group of Belgian researchers found that "limiting the number of embryos transferred to only two did not influence the take home baby rate but eliminated triplet and quadruplet gestations. Moreover, the number of patients with good quality supernumerary [extra] embryos available for cryopreservation increased." Martine Nijs et al., "Prevention of Multiple Pregnancies in an In Vitro Fertilization Program," *Fertility and Sterility* 59 (1993): 1245-1250.

The Ethics Committee of the American Fertility Society (AFS), while expressing similar concerns, has offered a somewhat more complex recommendation. "The goal of this procedure is to maximize pregnancy rates while minimizing multiple gestation rates." Variations among particular cases, however, argue against establishing a standard numerical limit. Rather, "the number of preembryos transferred should be limited... to anticipate that no quadruplet pregnancies will occur and that triplet pregnancies will be minimized to 1% to 2%." I would suggest that this criterion could be used to determine when the number of embryos transferred should be limited to two, and when transferring three would be indicated. Unusual cases in which transferring more than three embryos would be necessary for a reasonable chance of pregnancy, and would be consistent with the AFS guidelines, should be dealt with on a case-by-case basis.

[35] Canada, pp. 507-512, 595-596; AFS 56S-59S. For 1993, 6869 transfers of frozen embryos for gestation were reported, and 9,100 IVF procedures gave rise to frozen embryos. SART, p. 18.

[36] See similarly Halperin, pp. 207-208.

case. While the freezing of embryos is permissible, it poses problems as well, as will be seen below. If it becomes technically possible to freeze and thaw unfertilized ova, this would be preferable.[37]

Freezing embryos with the possibility of future transfer, and maintaining them in the frozen state, also appear to be consistent with any obligations concerning appropriate treatment of the embryos.[38] Other options for frozen or newly created embryos are more problematic (although not necessarily prohibited). These include: 1) thawing a frozen embryo without transferring it (or not transferring a newly created embryo), so that the embryo dies; 2) using the embryo for scientific research; and, 3) donating the embryo for use by another.

Some halakhic authorities have ruled that in vitro embryos, at least those that are not intended to be transferred, have no significant halakhic status, and may be discarded. Rabbi Hayyim David Halevi, for example, holds that "all ova that are fertilized in vitro do not have the legal status of an embryo; one does not violate the Sabbath on their behalf, and it is permissible to discard them if they were not chosen for transfer, since the law of abortion only applies to [an embryo] in the womb....In vitro, there is no prohibition whatsoever."[39] Rabbi Mordechai Eliyahu, while somewhat less categorical, agrees: "Fertilized ova that have been designated for transfer to a woman's uterus should not be destroyed, since a live fetus will develop from them, but fertilized ova that have not been designated for transfer may be discarded."[40]

In contrast, Rabbi Bleich objects that "there are no obvious grounds for assuming that nascent human life may be destroyed simply because it is not sheltered in its natural habitat, i.e., its development takes place outside the mother's womb." He suggests that in vitro embryos that are viable should not be destroyed.[41]

My own view is that the early embryo should be accorded a significant degree of respect and sanctity as a wondrous divine creation and potential human life. It would seem implausible to claim that Jewish restrictions with regard to in utero embryos and fetuses are simply irrelevant because of the embryo's location. At the same time, the fact that the embryo is in vitro does make its potential development more complicated and less likely. Moreover, embryos at the early stage at which freezing occurs are still a

---

[37] See AFS, 54S-55S.

[38] Transfer of the embryo for gestation in most cases would not raise any special concerns. In some cases one member of the couple may oppose transfer of an embryo deriving in part from his or her gametes; this might occur following divorce, or due to other considerations. Given the personal and halakhic concerns involved, and the understanding of the status of the fetus developed in the body of this paper, such opposition should be respected. Those using IVF should be encouraged to indicate at the time of cryopreservation their preferences regarding disposition of embryos under various circumstances that might arise, but should have the right to alter their decision. As a moral matter, an individual should reflect carefully before opposing transfer that accords with a prior decision, or that (e.g., following divorce) would provide important benefits for one spouse without entailing significant difficulties for the other (זה נהנה וזה לא חסר). Still, an individual could have valid personal and halakhic reasons to oppose transfer. Transfer for gestation should not occur over the opposition of either individual.

[39] "Fetal Reduction," *Assia* no. 47-48 (1990): 15.

[40] "Destroying Fertilized Eggs and Fetal Reduction," *Tehumin* 11 (1990-91): 272-273. A *Compendium on Medical Ethics* edited by R. David M. Feldman and Fred Rosner similarly states (p. 51): "A fertilized egg not in the womb, but in the environment – the Petri dish – in which it can never attain viability, does not yet have humanhood. It may be discarded or used for the advancement of scientific knowledge." (6th ed., New York: Federation of Jewish Philanthropies of New York, 1984).

[41] Bleich, "*In Vitro* Fertilization," *Tradition* 25, no. 4 (1991): 97. Unspecified citations of Bleich below refer to this article.

mass of undifferentiated cells which can give rise to two or more embryos.[42]

A non-Jewish ethicist has suggested that frozen embryos should not be destroyed; he argues that freezing the embryo indefinitely would be preferable, and could be defended either on grounds of respect for the embryo's status, or as a symbolic expression of respect for human life generally.[43] Such an approach would accord well with Jewish law and values. Nonetheless, it does not seem to be required halakhically. Thawing a frozen embryo in order to discard it would be halakhically permissible.

The use of embryos for non-therapeutic research, in order to gain scientific knowledge but without the expectation that the embryo would be transferred for gestation, is a topic of current controversy in the United States and other countries. Many have suggested that in vitro embryos that a couple does not wish to implant could be used for research under certain conditions: for example, that the information is important and could not be gained in any other way, that the experiment has been appropriately reviewed, and that embryos are not maintained beyond the fourteenth day of development.[44]

A full analysis of the issue of embryo research is beyond the scope of this paper. Allowing an embryo to be observed for scientific research does not seem intrinsically more objectionable than simply discarding the embryo. On the other hand, using an embryo for research becomes more troubling as the embryo reaches further points of development. A *Compendium on Medical Ethics*, edited by Rabbi David Feldman and Dr. Fred Rosner, allows the use of "a fertilized egg not in the womb. . .for the advancement of scientific knowledge."[45] The rationale for this position, and guidance for its application, require further examination beyond the scope of this paper.

The donation of embryos is discussed in the next section.

Donor Sperm, Eggs, and Embryos

A. Using Donor Gametes and Embryos

Some couples are unable to have children using their own sperm and eggs, even with the assistance of procedures such as IVF. These cases raise the difficult question of whether

---

[42] This fits relatively well with the legal category of "mere fluid" (מיא בעלמא) found in the Talmud in connection with the early fetus. Yevamot 69b; see Feldman, *Marital Relations*, p. 266. Given the current state of scientific knowledge, it may be less plausible to see as "mere fluid" later stages of embryonic and fetal development, especially beyond the fourteenth day. None of the CJLS papers on abortion rely on this view of the embryo or fetus, and none distinguishes between abortion before or after the fortieth day of development.

On this issue, my position would be similar to those of the AFS Ethics Committee; Shannon and Wolter, "Reflections on the Moral Status of the Pre-embryo;" and Richard McCormick, "Who or What is the Preembryo?", *Kennedy Institute of Ethics Journal* 1 (1991): 1-15. These contrast with the Vatican's position that "the human being must be respected – as a person – from the very first instant of his existence," i.e., the moment of conception. Congregation for the Doctrine of the Faith, *Instruction on Respect for Human Life in Its Origin and on the Dignity of Procreation* (Washington, DC: United States Catholic Conference, 1987), p. 12.

[43] David T. Ozar, "The Case Against Thawing Unused Frozen Embryos," *Hastings Center Report* 15, no. 4 (1985): 7-12.

[44] AFS, 78S-80S; NIH. Yet additional concerns would be raised by the creation of an embryo specifically for purposes of research, a prospect beyond the scope of this paper. Non-therapeutic research discussed in the body of the paper is distinct from therapeutic research, in which IVF procedures take place within the context of a research protocol, intended to increase the likelihood of success and benefit the couple and/or the fetus. Like other therapeutic research, this would not be inherently problematic, provided that the couple is aware of the research protocol and consents to participation, and risks and benefits are appropriately weighed.

[45] Feldman and Rosner, p. 51.

sperm, eggs, or embryos, donated by another person may be used by a couple to have a child.[46] This question has been addressed at length by Rabbi Dorff. Dorff acknowledges that the use of donated gametes raises significant concerns in Jewish law, including the possibility of incest in future generations, and ambiguity with regard to the identity of the child's parents. Even more significantly, the use of donor gametes entails personal and psychological difficulties for all involved; it has the potential to add strain to the marriage, and complicate the relationship of the child to his or her (social) parents.[47]

Nonetheless, motivated largely (but not exclusively) by compassion for couples who desire the procedure, Dorff deems the use of donor gametes permissible, providing that certain guidelines are met. The couple should seriously investigate alternatives, including adoption. They should be aware of all that the use of donor gametes involves, including the likely strain entailed. As well, they should receive thorough counselling and plan for the best ways to meet these challenges. Couples who use donor gametes should not keep this use secret, especially within the family. Based on the experience of many families who have used reproductive technologies, an open approach promotes the ability of family members to receive needed support, and contributes to the family's harmony and the psychological health of all involved.[48]

I would concur with Dorff's position with regard to the use of sperm in IVF, including the guidelines and restrictions that accompany his permission for the use of donor gametes, and extend this position to the use of donated eggs and embryos.[49] I would emphasize that no couple or individual should use donated gametes without careful reflection and a fully informed and voluntary decision. A decision by either member of the couple not to make use of these procedures must be fully respected, and would be strongly supported by ethical and halakhic considerations.

B. Maternal Identity

In the case of sperm donation, as Dorff argues, the sperm donor is the genetic father, and should be viewed as the father both with regard to technical issues of Jewish identity and in order to prohibit marriage (or sexual relations) with genetic relatives. At the same time, the social father of a child conceived using donor insemination, like the social father of an adopted child, is "the 'real' father in most significant ways," and is accorded by Jewish tradition the special status of one who "does right at all times."[50]

Paternal identity is complicated by the use of donor sperm in that two men might be

---

[46] Reporting on procedures conducted in 1993, the Society for Assisted Reproductive Technology notes 2,766 IVF procedures using donated eggs, leading to 716 deliveries, and an additional 625 procedures using donated embryos, leading to 108 deliveries. (The paper also reports 246 procedures involving gestational surrogacy, resulting in seventy-eight deliveries. A halakhic analysis of surrogate motherhood is beyond the scope of this paper.) SART, pp. 17-18.

[47] Dorff, above, pp. 474-494. On the psychological challenges posed by the use of donor gametes, see also Patricia P. Mahlstedt and Dorothy A. Greenfeld, "Assisted Reproductive Technology with Donor Gametes: The Need for Patient Preparation," *Fertility and Sterility* 52 (1989): 908-914. Most Orthodox sources either do not address the issue of donated sperm, eggs, or embryos, or argue against these practices; see, e.g., Halperin, pp. 203-207. For a somewhat differing view, see Richard V. Grazi and Joel B. Wolowelsky, "Donor Gametes for Assisted Reproduction in Contemporary Jewish Law and Ethics," *Assisted Reproduction Reviews* 2 (1992): 154-160.

[48] Ibid. Couples should also be aware that in many states legal issues concerning the use of donor eggs and embryos have been less clearly addressed in legislation than have corresponding issues in the use of donor sperm, although this difference seems unlikely to have any practical effect. AFS, 47S-49S.

[49] Dorff (above, pp. 474-475) notes, and rejects, the argument of some authorities that donor insemination constitutes (or is akin to) adultery in introducing another man's sperm into a woman's reproductive system. This concern is even less significant with IVF, in which an embryo, and not sperm, is placed in a woman's uterus.

[50] Dorff, above, p. 482, citing Ketubbot 50a.

seen as fathers: the genetic father and the social father. The use of donated eggs complicates maternal identity to an even greater extent, for not two but three factors are relevant. The donor of the eggs could be seen as the genetic mother; the woman who is pregnant with and gives birth to the child could be seen as the gestational or birth mother; and the woman who raises the child could be seen as the social mother.

A number of halakhic authorities have addressed the issue of maternal identity in such cases. Many of these statements have been summarized in a review article by Rabbi Bleich.[51] These sources suggest that maternal identity is to be determined primarily by gestation and birth.

A central precedent in the discussion is the case of a pregnant woman who converts: conception is by a non-Jew, from an ovum from a non-Jew; the fetus is gestated by a non-Jew and then by a Jew; and a woman who is Jewish gives birth. Orthodox sources debate whether the child requires immersion, and the rationale for the requirement or lack of requirement. The Conservative position, however, is clear. Following the Shulhan Arukh, Rabbi Isaac Klein rules: "If a woman converts while pregnant, the child does not require conversion, even if it was conceived before conversion, because at the time of its birth its mother was already Jewish."[52] The woman's status at the time of birth determines the child's identity. By extension, the status of the birth mother determines the child's identity for IVF. While this argument provides the central basis for a Conservative position on maternal identity, this position may be supported by additional considerations as well.[53]

---

[51] Bleich, pp. 82-102.

[52] Klein, *A Guide to Jewish Religious Practice* (New York: Jewish Theological Seminary of America, 1979), p. 446. The Shulhan Arukh (Yoreh De'ah 268:6) states this conclusion, but does not offer a rationale: כותית שנתגיירה והיא מעוברת בנה אין צריך טבילה. The Talmudic source of this ruling, Yevamot 78a, is not in itself decisive on the issue of maternal identity. Bleich argues that Yevamot 97b, discussing the status of twins born to a woman who converts while pregnant, supports the identification of the birth mother as halakhic mother.

[53] Among the supporting arguments:

A. Halakhah views the status of a fetus as subservient to that of the woman. As the Talmudic phrase, עובר ירך אמו, (Hullin 58a) is explicated by Rabbi David Feldman: "The fetus is deemed a 'part of the mother' rather than an independent entity." David M. Feldman, "Abortion: The Jewish View," in *PCJLS 80-85*, p. 11. This phrase is also cited in the teshuvot of Rabbi Robert Gordis ("Abortion: Major Wrong or Basic Right," *PCJLS 80-85*, p. 22) and Rabbi Isaac Klein ("A Teshuvah on Abortion," *PCJLS 80-85*, p. 33). Accordingly, the status of the gestating woman determines the status of the fetus, and the status of the birth mother determines the status of the child.

B. The above argument is strengthened by the fact that embryo transfer takes place well within the first days of development of the embryo, when the Talmudic designation of the embryo/fetus as "mere fluid" (מיא בעלמא, Yevamot 69b) most clearly applies. See n. 42 above, and Bleich, pp. 93-94, who rejects this view in part because of his belief that "the developing fetus is a 'person' in its own right."

C. Halakhic identification of a firstborn son as one who "opens the womb" supports defining the birth mother as the child's mother. See Exodus 13, and Dorff, above, p. 497.

D. Some have suggested that one reason for basing Jewish identity on matrilineal descent is that the child's mother can always be identified; see, e.g., Walter Jacob, ed., *Contemporary American Reform Responsa* (New York: Central Conference of American Rabbis, 1987), p. 63; Shaye J.D. Cohen, "The Origins of the Matrilineal Principle in Rabbinic Law," *AJS Review* 10 (1985): 40-41, who reports but argues against this view. This consideration would support determining the child's status on the basis of the birth mother.

E. Targum Yonatan (Gen. 30:21) and Rabbi Samuel Edels (Maharsha, commenting on Niddah 31a) relate that, prior to the birth of Joseph and Dinah, Leah was pregnant with a male, and Rachel with a female. Leah prayed that Rachel would give birth to the male, and God switched the embryos. Dinah, conceived by Rachel but born to Leah, is considered Leah's child; Joseph, conceived by Leah but born to Rachel, is considered Rachel's child. Thus, the status of the birth mother determines the child's identity. See Bleich, p. 84; Dorff, above, p. 496.

F. As discussed below, identifying the birth mother but not the genetic mother as the halakhic mother facilitates the use of donated eggs and embryos, and enables Jews to donate eggs and embryos. This policy/ethical concern, while not necessarily decisive, represents an important halakhic consideration that minimally serves to reinforce the above arguments.

[See also, "Maternal Identity and the Religious Status of Children Born to a Surrogate Mother," above, pp. 137-145.]

Accordingly, the woman who gestates and gives birth to the child is to be treated as the child's mother for purposes of Jewish law, including the determination of Jewish identity. If a Jewish woman gives birth to a child, that child should be considered Jewish, whether the egg came from a Jewish or non-Jewish woman. If a non-Jewish woman gives birth to a child, that child would not be Jewish (and so would require conversion in order to be recognized as a Jew), whether the egg came from a Jewish or non-Jewish woman.

A less satisfactory alternative position to identifying the birth mother as mother, which might also be compatible with halakhic precedent, would be to recognize *both* the genetic and birth mothers as having maternal status: even if birth is the primary determinant of maternal identity, the genetic mother would be treated as mother because of doubt, or to follow a more stringent position. This alternative is in some ways attractive at the theoretical level, for it would formally recognize the contributions of both women to the child's birth. At the practical level, however, it would impose unnecessary complications for the use of donated ova.[54] If an anonymously donated egg were used, the presumption (outside of Israel) would be that the donor is not Jewish; accordingly, the child (born to a Jewish mother) would require conversion in order to be fully Jewish. Moreover, the child would have obligations of honoring her or his (genetic) mother (כיבוד אב ואם) that likely would be unfulfilled.

Furthermore, eggs from a known or designated donor are used in about a quarter of ovum donation procedures in the United States and Canada,[55] in part because donating ova is more invasive and entails greater risks than donating sperm, and ova are accordingly less readily available (and more expensive). Accordingly, I agree with Rabbi Dorff that a fertile sister (or other relative) may donate eggs to an infertile woman, provided that all involved receive appropriate counselling and consider ways in which they would deal with "boundary questions" ("Is my aunt also my mother?" "Is my niece also my child?")[56] In such a case, officially recognizing the genetic mother as mother would complicate this enterprise by answering these boundary questions in the affirmative: my aunt is indeed my mother (in addition to my birth/social mother). Such a halakhic stance would be likely to undermine family harmony and the psychological well-being of all involved.

While the genetic mother should not be viewed as mother halakhically, genetic siblings should not marry (or engage in sexual relations with) one another. The most basic reason for this prohibition is that offspring of a consanguineous union face a high risk of genetically-based disease; this concern alone would suffice to support a rabbinic prohibition. Combining this ruling with those found in Rabbi Dorff's paper, one comes to the unsurprising conclusion that one should not marry (or engage in sexual relations with) children of one's genetic, gestational, or social parents. Technically, the prohibition would be Toraitic with regard to children of one's genetic father and birth mother, and would reflect the category of secondary relations (שניות) for children of other parents.[57]

Based on the reasoning allowing a couple to use donor sperm or eggs in order to have a child, couples could use both donor sperm and eggs in IVF when necessary to have a

---

[54] Some analogous complications are accepted in the use of donor sperm (Dorff). However, because Jewish identity (for those who do not convert to Judaism) is based on the mother's status, egg donation would entail additional problems. More importantly, the complications do not seem to be avoidable with sperm donation, and may be avoided here simply by following the position most clearly suggested by halakhic precedent.

[55] In 599 out of 2,766 cycles; SART, p. 17.

[56] Dorff, above, p. 496.

[57] See Dorff, above, pp. 482-483; Shulhan Arukh, Even HaEzer 15. A child born from IVF who unknowingly engaged in sexual relations with a genetic sibling would not be culpable. Children born of these procedures should in no way be stigmatized.

child. Similarly, a couple could use a donated embryo. This might be required in an unusual case in which the husband had a medical indication for donor sperm and the wife had an indication for donor eggs, but was able to gestate and give birth to a child. It might also be suggested if the couple had indications for a donated egg, and donor embryos but no donor eggs were available.[58]

c. Donating Embryos

A final and difficult issue concerns whether a couple may donate extra embryos formed from their gametes. Here my inclination is to follow, and expand upon, Rabbi Dorff's permission for Jews to donate sperm and eggs in order to enable another couple to have a child. I would emphasize that such donation is not required, and may be done "only after due consideration of the implications of what they are doing and only with due respect and, indeed, awe for the whole procedure."[59]

Rabbi Dorff notes that donating sperm or eggs entails a biological connection with resulting children that may have great personal significance, and that has importance in halakhah. Thus, for example, a sperm donor should take steps to ensure that no marriages or sexual relations occur among genetic offspring arising from donated sperm and genetic offspring within the man's own family. An egg donor would face similar responsibilities (even though they would be rabbinic rather than Toraitic in their basis.) Other responsibilities for one's genetic children, as well as any medical risks, must be faced as well.[60]

An additional concern raised by the donation of eggs or embryos must be addressed, but can be readily dealt with on the basis of the position developed above. If (disagreeing with my position) the genetic mother were to be considered the child's mother, then a child born of an embryo that develops from a Jewish woman's egg, or a child born from an egg donated by a Jewish woman, would be Jewish. I can see no way that halakhah would permit a Jewish woman or couple to make donations that would lead to a Jewish child who would be raised as a non-Jew. If this alternative position were followed, either Jews would not be able to donate eggs or embryos, or they would be able to do so only if the clinic could guarantee that these would be used to help infertile Jews but not non-Jews. Such a position would be highly problematic, to say the least.[61]

As argued above, however, the birth mother is the sole halakhically recognized mother, and so a child born to a non-Jew from an egg or embryo donated by Jews would not be Jewish. Accordingly, Jews can donate eggs and embryos, within the guidelines developed above and in Rabbi Dorff's paper. This position accords with the traditional mandates of תיקון העולם, improving the world and maintaining social order, and דרכי שלום, the ways of peace.

---

[58] AFS, 50S. Donated embryos generally are not created for the purpose of donation, but represent "extra" embryos that another couple does not wish to use. Accordingly, genetic screening may be less complete than is usually the case for donated sperm or ova.

[59] Dorff, above, p. 505.

[60] Dorff, above, pp. 499-501; AFS, 47S-49S. While the ovum donor is not halakhically considered the child's parent, her responsibilities for the welfare of the child as another human being are similar to those faced by the sperm donor.

[61] A similar concern is raised by Bleich, pp. 94-95, although my response to this issue differs markedly from his. In discussing the permissibility of autopsies, R. Yehudah Leib Graubart argues that to discriminate against non-Jews, so as to appear to care little for the life and health of non-Jews, would represent a desecration of God's name. He argues that concern to avoid such desecration not only would support ruling in accord with a lenient position (as in this paper), but could suffice to allow that which otherwise would be prohibited. *Responsa Havalim Ban'inim*, vol. 3, sec. 64 (Jerusalem: Feldheim, 1975, reprint); cited in part in Isaac Klein, *Responsa and Halachic Studies* (New York: Ktav, 1975), p. 41. I am grateful to Rabbi Elliot N. Dorff for alerting me to this reference.

If Jews are willing to accept donated embryos, then allowing Jews to donate embryos as well helps to maintain the system, fulfilling one sense of תיקון העולם, as well as contributing to the improvement of the world, fulfilling another sense. This permission promotes harmonious relations between Jews and non-Jews, fulfilling one sense of דרכי שלום, as well as promoting the value of harmony and peace.

"Great is peace (שלום), for all blessings are contained within it."[62] We hope that in vitro fertilization and other reproductive technologies, used responsibly in accord with the guidance of halakhah, will contribute to wholeness and healing (שלמות) for infertile couples who choose to use these procedures, harmony (שלום בית) in their families, and healthy new life that will add to the peace of Israel and the world.[63]

Conclusions

1. An infertile couple may utilize IVF, using the husband's sperm and wife's egg, to have a child. They are under no obligation to do so. Before undergoing IVF procedures, the couple should consider medical risks as well as the personal and psychological toll that IVF often entails. A child born as a result of such an IVF procedure is fully the parents' child in all respects, and causes the mitzvah of "be fruitful and multiply" to be fulfilled.

2. Couples who wish to use IVF and preimplantation genetic testing to avoid having a child with a severe genetic disease may do so.

3. IVF should not be used solely for the purpose of gender selection. If used to avoid having a child with a severe disease that is gender-linked, however, preimplantation testing would represent a form of genetic testing, and would be acceptable.

4. In order to avoid risks to the mother and child, and decrease the likelihood of abortion, no more than three embryos should be transferred in an IVF procedure. To the extent possible, transferring only two embryos would be preferable.

5. Creating extra embryos and freezing embryos are halakhically acceptable. Embryos may be maintained as frozen indefinitely, but thawing a frozen embryo that the couple does not wish to implant, in order to discard it, would be halakhically permissible.

6. Couples considering the use of donated sperm, ova, or embryos should consider the halakhic and personal concerns involved, receive thorough counselling, and seriously investigate alternatives, including adoption. Those wishing to use donated sperm, ova, or embryos may do so.

7. The woman who gestates and gives birth to a child is to be treated as the child's mother for purposes of Jewish law, including the determination of Jewish identity. One should not marry or engage in sexual relationships with the offspring of one's birth, genetic, or social parents.

8. After careful consideration of the implications of their actions, a couple may donate an embryo formed from their sperm and egg to enable another couple to have a child.

---

[62] Leviticus Rabbah 9:9.

[63] For their suggestions and thoughtful insights which have contributed greatly to this paper, I would like to thank Dr. David Kelly, Lorraine Newman Mackler, and members of the Committee on Jewish Law and Standards, including my fellow members of the Subcommittee on Biomedical Ethics: Rabbis Kassel Abelson, Elliot N. Dorff, David M. Feldman, Shoshana Gelfand, Avram Israel Reisner, Joel Roth and Elie Kaplan Spitz.

EH 1:3.1997a

ON THE USE OF BIRTH SURROGATES

Rabbis Aaron L. Mackler and Elie Kaplan Spitz

This paper was approved by the CJLS on September 17, 1997, by a vote of fifteen in favor and two abstentions (15-0-2). Voting in favor: Rabbis Kassel Abelson, Ben Zion Bergman, Elliot N. Dorff, Baruch Frydman-Kohl, Shoshana Gelfand, Nechama D. Goldberg, Judah Kogen, Aaron L. Mackler, Paul Plotkin, Avram Israel Reisner, Joel E. Rembaum, James S. Rosen, Joel Roth, Elie Kaplan Spitz and Gerald Zelizer. Abstaining: Rabbis Lionel E. Moses and Gordon Tucker.

The Committee on Jewish Law and Standards of the Rabbinical Assembly provides guidance in matters of halakhah for the Conservative movement. The individual rabbi, however, is the authority for the interpretation and application of all matters of halakhah.

The practice of surrogacy involves powerful and sometimes conflicting Jewish concerns, including the value of procreation, respect for persons (כבוד הבריות), and concern for the well being of all of the vulnerable people involved. The Rabbinical Assembly Committee on Jewish Law and Standards has approved two different papers on this sensitive subject, by Rabbis Aaron L. Mackler and Elie Kaplan Spitz. Both agree that, on the one hand, traditional Jewish law does not mandate an absolute prohibition of surrogacy in all cases. On the other hand, surrogacy entails serious potential problems which would make it inappropriate in at least some cases. The two papers differ, however, both in their general evaluation of surrogacy and on some more particular points.

General Evaluation

For Rabbi Spitz, the great benefit of providing a child to an infertile couple is decisive. Concerns with avoiding exploitation of the surrogate, and harm to children born of the procedure, are real but manageable. These must be addressed by couples considering surrogacy, and ideally would be dealt with at the policy level by civil legislation. At the same time, the data of the last fifteen years indicate that problems as a result of these risks occur only in a small number of cases, and that the vast majority of surrogacies have resulted in offering the couple the joy of parenthood without harming or exploiting the surrogate or others. "From a Jewish perspective, it would be wrong to outlaw a procedure that has the potential to help so many couples overcome infertility and which works smoothly in the overwhelming majority of cases."

Rabbi Mackler expresses greater concern with potential harms and exploitation. There is a danger of treating people as commodities, and in some extreme cases, contracting/intended parents have sought to refuse custody of a child born with birth defects or of the undesired gender. When the surrogate has other children, those children face the potential psychological harm of seeing their mother go through pregnancy and give birth to a child who is given to others. The risk of exploitation (עושק) of surrogates is real as well. While such harms have been documented in some cases, their extent is debated and difficult to ascertain precisely. Still, these have been enough to lead secular groups such as the Ethics Committee of the American Fertility Society, which generally supports reproductive technologies, to express "serious ethical reservations," and "not to recommend widespread clinical application of clinical surrogate motherhood at this time." From a Jewish perspective, "surrogacy cannot be halakhically recommended, and in at least most cases would be forbidden by Jewish law and ethics."

Particular Guidelines

Whether surrogacy agreements might be appropriate in most cases or only in exceptional cases, both rabbis agree on some important guidelines:

1. Couples contemplating the use of a surrogate should consider the halakhic and personal concerns involved, receive thorough counseling, and seriously investigate alternatives including adoption. Either member of the couple would be fully justified in a decision not to proceed with surrogacy, and such refusal must be fully respected.

2. The surrogate should be protected from pressure to continue pregnancy when she judges abortion to be required to avoid serious threat to her health, and conversely she should be protected from pressure to abort.

3. In the formulation of surrogacy agreements, and all actions taken with regard to surrogacy, greatest concern must be given to the well-being and rights of the child to be born of the procedure, as well as any other children who might be affected. Concern must be given to avoid exploitation of other vulnerable parties, including the surrogate, as well.

4. Both Rabbi Spitz and Rabbi Mackler agree that a surrogate may receive reimbursement for her expenses and that any money the surrogate receives cannot be contingent on her giving up custody of the child. For Rabbi Spitz, it is appropriate that a surrogate be paid a reasonable sum for her services, which is separate and distinct from payment for a child. This payment is compensation for time engaged in the medical, psychological, and legal procedures; physical restrictions due to pregnancy; medical risk; and the use of her womb. The permissibility of payment is rooted in the reality that not everyone has a volunteer family member or friend to assist in the much wanted blessing of a child. For Rabbi Mackler, any payment to a surrogate mother beyond reimbursement of expenses would be discouraged as dangerously close to babyselling, or minimally the selling and purchase of parental relationships, which are inconsistent with halakhah.

5. Both Rabbi Spitz and Rabbi Mackler address the possibility of a dispute arising over the custody of the child, and each discusses the response he views as most consonant with Jewish law and ethics. For Rabbi Spitz, during the pregnancy a surrogate has the right to withdraw from the agreement, an extension of her freedom of choice. Upon birth to a gestational surrogate the surrogate should have no right to challenge custody. In contrast, an ovum surrogate may assert her maternal rights, but the burden of proof is on her to show cause why the original intent should not be honored. For Rabbi Mackler, the surrogate mother, as gestational and birth mother, is halakhically recognized as mother, and should have the right to contest the assumption of custody by the intended parents (one of whom would be halakhically recognized as the child's father). This right would be held by both "ovum surrogates" and gestational surrogates. Custody of the

child, in these as in other cases, should be determined on the basis of the child's best interest, as required by Jewish ethical values as well as halakhic precedent. The views of Rabbi Spitz and Rabbi Mackler on this matter are not necessarily offered as decisive halakhic rulings, however, and both rabbis recognize that in practice custody likely would be determined by general civil law.

6. The sole position approved by the Committee on Jewish Law and Standards is that the religious status of a child follows that of the gestational/birth mother, in cases involving surrogacy as in all other cases. Children born to a non-Jewish surrogate (whether a gestational or ovum surrogate) would require conversion to be halakhically recognized as Jewish. Rabbis should display personal and pastoral sensitivity in such cases.

Any individuals considering surrogacy, as well as other interested readers, are strongly advised to read the full papers.

EDITORS' NOTE: *The full responsa by Rabbis Spitz and Mackler can be found below, pp. 529-550 and 551-557, respectively.*

EH 1:3.1997b

ON THE USE OF BIRTH SURROGATES

Rabbi Elie Kaplan Spitz

This paper was approved by the CJLS on June 4, 1997, by a vote of six in favor, six opposed and eight abstaining (6-6-8). Voting in favor: Rabbis Kassel Abelson, Elliot N. Dorff, Alan B. Lucas, Mayer Rabinowitz, Joel Roth, and Elie Kaplan Spitz. Voting against: Rabbis Samuel Fraint, Arnold M. Goodman, Aaron L. Mackler, Paul Plotkin, Avram Israel Reisner, and James S. Rosen. Abstaining: Rabbis Ben Zion Bergman, Jerome M. Epstein, Shoshana Gelfand, Myron S. Geller, Susan Grossman, Judah Kogen, Vernon H. Kurtz, and Joel E. Rembaum.

The Committee on Jewish Law and Standards of the Rabbinical Assembly provides guidance in matters of halakhah for the Conservative movement. The individual rabbi, however, is the authority for the interpretation and application of all matters of halakhah.

שאלה

Is an infertile couple's use of a surrogate mother acceptable? Specifically, is it permissible to:
1. Use an ovum surrogate?
2. Pay her for her services?
3. Employ a gestational surrogate?
4. Is the mitzvah of procreation met through a surrogate birth?

תשובה

Surrogates: Some Background

The Rabbinical Assembly Committee on Jewish Law and Standards dealt with the permissibility of ovum surrogacy in 1988. In that opinion, authored by Rabbi David Lincoln, the committee concluded: "The mitzvah of having children is so great, we should not deny couples this opportunity." That opinion was written while there was still relatively little experience with ovum surrogacy. Gestational surrogacy had not yet taken place. In order to evaluate the increased data of the last decade and to analyze in greater detail the ramifications of surrogacy this paper is presented.

Jewish law lacks direct precedent for surrogate birth. Much of the rabbinic debate that has taken place has focused on theoretical risks.[1] Halakhic authorities are in agreement

---

[1] Noam Zohar of Jerusalem, writes, "Regarding surrogacy the rejection is almost universal." "Artificial Insemination and Surrogate Motherhood: A Halakhic Perspective," *S'vara*, vol. 2, no. 1 (1991): 13-19.

Little in fact has even been written. To quote Pinhas Shifman of Hebrew University in Jerusalem, "Rabbinic opinion has not yet addressed itself to religious problems created by surrogate motherhood." "The Right to

that a couple has no duty to resort to surrogacy to fulfill the mitzvah of procreation. The difference of opinion is whether an infertile couple may choose to do so. Before an analysis of the ethics of surrogacy, let us clarify terms and examine the data which encompass the experience of the last fifteen years.

What is a Surrogate?

There are two categories of surrogate motherhood, based on the surrogate's genetic relationship to the child. Currently in the majority of cases the surrogate is an ovum surrogate: both her ovum and womb are used. She is impregnated by artificial insemination with the sperm of the intended father and agrees to give the newborn over to him and his wife.[2] The first acknowledged paid surrogacy arrangement occurred in 1980.[3] As many as 4,000 children were born to surrogates[4] since then, and the present

---

Parenthood and the Best Interests of the Child: A perspective on Surrogate Motherhood in Jewish and Israeli Law," 4 *Human Rights Annual* 555, 560 (1987).

Among the Orthodox rabbis, I have not found a rabbi in favor of ovum surrogacy; among the non-Orthodox rabbinate opinions are divided. A selection of rabbinic views to date follows:

- Immanuel Jakobovits: "To use another woman as an incubator...for a fee...[is a] revolting degradation of maternity and an affront to human dignity." *Jewish Medical Ethics* (New York: Bloch, 1959, 1975), pp. 264-265.
- Moshe Tendler, opposed to both ovum and gestational surrogacy as undermining a woman's dignity, "If the surrogate is a married woman...this is not a curative modality. It substitutes illness for illness, pathology involving many for the pathology of one woman." "Infertility Management: Cure or Ill," *Sh'ma* 17 (15 May 1987), pp. 109-110.
- Daniel H. Gordis: "Jewish women should not serves as surrogates for pay, nor should Jewish couples seek to hire such women. Our commitment to human dignity and social good and our desire to forge a link between halakhah and morality requires a stance no less inflexible than this." "Give Me Progeny...: Jewish Ethics and the Economics of Surrogate Motherhood," *University of Judaism Papers* 8, no. 1 (Los Angeles: University of Judaism, 1988), p. 21.
- Marc Gellman: "The sanctity of family life requires a single husband and wife." "The Ethics of Surrogate Motherhood," *Sh'ma*, pp. 105, 107.
- David M. Feldman: ovum-surrogacy contract is unenforceable as a matter of public policy; courts should determine custody based on best interests of the child. *Sh'ma*, pp. 108-109. In *Health and Medicine in the Jewish Tradition* (New York: Crossroads, 1986), pp. 71-75, supports gestational surrogacy as a last resort.
- Rabbinical Assembly Committee of Law and Standards voted in favor of surrogacy (5 June 1985): responsa by Rabbi David Lincoln — anything that helps overcome low Jewish birthrate is welcome. *PCJLS 86-90*, pp. 3-6.
- Walter Jacobs on behalf of the Central Conference of American Rabbis, *American Reform Responsa* (New York: CCAR, 1983), cautiously permits surrogacy due to importance of procreation.
- Seymour Siegel: "Our society rests on the expectation that contracts made in good faith will be honored." Surrogacy contract is moral and hence should be enforced. "The Ethics of Baby M's Custody." *Sh'ma*, at pp. 108-109.
- Michael Gold: accepts surrogacy as a last resort response to infertility, although prefers adoption and sees need for surrogacy legislation. *And Hannah Wept* (Philadelphia: JPS, 1988), pp. 120-127.
- Fred Rosner permits gestational surrogacy as a last resort. *Modern Medicine and Jewish Ethics*, (New York: Ktav, 2d ed., 1991), p. 114.

[2] Overwhelmingly today the initiating couple is a husband and wife. Beyond the scope of this paper are the possibilities of single and gay parents and the anonymous donation of the sperm and/or the ovum.

[3] Lori B. Andrews and Lisa Douglass, "Alternative Reproduction," 65 *Southern California Law Review*, pp. 623, 637 (1991).

[4] No official statistics are maintained by any agency and the 4,000 figure is only an estimate, but it is widely cited. Minority Report of the Advisory Panel to the Joint Legislative Committee on Surrogate Parenting,

pace is estimated at 1,000 new agreements a year.⁵

A gestational surrogate, the second category, essentially serves as an incubator. Referred to as a "tummy mummy," the gestational surrogate is impregnated through in vitro fertilization with a fertilized ovum of the intended parents.⁶ In vitro ("in glass") fertilization produced a child for the first time in 1978.⁷ The first birth of an infant carried by a gestational surrogate was in 1986.⁸ Yet gestational surrogacy is increasing quickly and may soon outnumber "traditional surrogacy" activity.⁹

Dollars and Sense: What are Some of the Conditions and Costs of a Surrogate Agreement?

Surrogacy arrangements usually involve pay and a written agreement. This is not always the case. There are moving stories of family members using the technology to facilitate birth.¹⁰ A well-publicized example is the case of Arlette Schweitzer, who was the gestational surrogate for her daughter, who lacked a uterus. Mrs. Schweitzer gave birth to her granddaughter!¹¹

Yet, most couples lack the family member or friend who will incur the inconvenience and run the risks of pregnancy as a gift. In the 1970s, surrogacy couples often found their own surrogates for pay and entered into private contracts. Today people overwhelmingly use an established center which includes the guidance of an attorney, well-drafted agreements, and a psychologist. To date, sixty percent of surrogacy births were arranged through such a surrogacy center.¹²

A couple who contracts with a paid ovum surrogate will spend approximately $42,000; of that amount, the surrogate will typically receive $12,000.¹³ For the couple, the most uncertain variable in cost is the expense of medical procedures, particularly for gestational surrogacy. Each in vitro attempt, which commonly uses three fertilized eggs, has less than a one out of six success rate. The average medical cost for a successful in vitro fertilization is $22,000.¹⁴

California Legislature (1991), p. M8 (hereinafter Minority Report); Andrews and Douglass, p. 670; Susan Edmiston, "Whose Child is This," *Glamour* 89 (Nov. 1991): 234, 276; Estimate of New York Health Department cited in *Center for Surrogate Parenting Inc. Newsletter*, vol. 1 (spring 1993): 1.

⁵ Edmiston, p. 236.

⁶ In this procedure an egg is removed from a ripe follicle and fertilized by a sperm cell outside the human body. The fertilized egg is allowed to divide in a protected environment for about two days and then is inserted into the uterus of the gestational surrogate.

⁷ Louise Brown was born in England in 1978. Andrews and Douglass, p. 625.

⁸ Andrews and Douglass, p. 670, citing Wulf H. Utian et al., "Preliminary Experience with In Vitro Fertilization – Surrogate Gestational Surrogacy Pregnancy," *Fertility and Sterility* 52 (1989): 633.

⁹ Minority report, p. M9, writes: ". . .the Center [for Surrogate Parenting] reports that approximately 50% of current surrogate activities involving their professional program involve gestational arrangements."

¹⁰ See Deborah Diamond, "Labor of Love," *Ladies Home Journal* (Sept. 1994): 173. The touching story of sister carrying child for sister, who, until that point had been unsuccessful getting pregnant but as it turned out, simultaneously got pregnant with twins by in vitro fertilization. Consequently, the once infertile couple began parenthood with three children.

¹¹ "Miraculous Babies – The Woman Who Bore Her Own Grandchild," *Life*, Dec. 1993, pp. 78-79; *Time*, 19 Aug. 1991, p. 58.

¹² Andrews and Douglass, p. 671, n. 236.

¹³ Sums supplied by Center for Surrogate Parenting, Beverly Hills, CA (1994). Other costs include approximately $5,000 for medical costs; $13,600 for administrative costs; $4,000 for psychological costs, $3,000 to retain legal counsel; $4,000 for miscellaneous costs.

¹⁴ Andrews and Douglass, p. 635, citing Office of Technology Assessment, 100th Congress, 2d Session, *Infertility: Medicine and Social Choices* (Washington, D.C.: U.S. Government Printing Office, 1988), p. 50.

Surrogacy contracts serve to protect the surrogate's interests and to assure clear expectations for all parties involved.[15] Among the items often contained in an agreement are:

- Complete freedom of choice for the surrogate prior to conception, including the right to withdraw from the agreement.
- Payment for the surrogate of all medical costs, psychological counselling, attorney fees, and living expenses or pay (not to exceed a reasonable amount); to be paid on a monthly, installment basis.
- A commitment of the intended parents to accept the newborn, regardless of the child's physical condition, and the surrogate's agreement to turn the newborn over to the intended parents upon birth.
- A guarantee of the surrogates' right over her body during pregnancy, which includes the right to operations to protect her health and abortion (which would effect payment). In addition, the surrogate agrees not to abuse her body, including the use of illicit drugs, which if violated to the detriment of the fetus allows for compensatory damages.

Who Agrees to be a Surrogate?

At least eight Ph.D. dissertations and other professional level studies have been conducted to ascertain the emotional, psychological and financial profiles of surrogates.[16] The American Bar Foundation, consistent with the other research, found that the typical surrogate mother was twenty-eight years old, married with two children, employed full-time, and had thirteen years of education. Her husband was supportive of her decision to serve as a surrogate. Most were Caucasian, middle-range in income bracket, in good health, and had positive experiences in past pregnancies.[17] While money was a factor in choosing to become a surrogate, it rated consistently lower than the desire to help another couple.[18]

Why Hire a Surrogate?

Surrogacy is a last resort solution for female infertility. Infertility is defined as the inability to achieve a pregnancy after one year of regular, unprotected sexual relations or the inability of the woman to carry a pregnancy to live birth. Close to one out of seven couples will experience some degree of infertility.[19] In forty percent of those cases the infertility is directly linked to the woman.[20]

---

[15] William Handel of the Center for Surrogate Parenting (8383 Wilshire Boulevard, Suite 750, Beverly Hills, California 90211; [213] 655-1974) is the most accomplished attorney in the area of surrogacy agreement drafting.

[16] Minority Report, p. 16, n. 9, contains a list of the studies, which includes: "Surrogate Mother Demographics" by H. Daniel and K. Linkins (Harvard Medical School), which concludes that the primary motivation of surrogates is altruism; "Psychiatric Evaluation of Women in the Surrogate Mother Process," American Journal of Psychiatry (Oct. 1981), which is a favorable evaluation of surrogate mother candidates; Hilary Hanafin, Ph.D., "Surrogate Parenting: Reassessing Human Bonding," concludes no evidence of regret by surrogates; open contact between parties was an important variable.

[17] Minority Report, p. 16; Lisa Douglass, "Empirical Studies of Surrogate Mothers and Their Children."

[18] Not one surrogate in Hanafin's study said that money was the deciding factor for participation. Cited in Andrews and Douglass, pp. 673-674.

[19] Andrews and Douglass, p. 626, citing Office of Technology Assessment (1988).

[20] In forty percent of the couples the trouble is traced to the man, in another forty percent it is traced to the woman, and in the rest of the couples the source of the problem cannot by identified. "Miraculous Babies," Life, supra, p. 76; Andrews and Douglass, p. 634.

Not so long ago biology was destiny. Only recently have doctors learned to manipulate the mechanics of pregnancy and birth. There are many interventions short of surrogacy. Today medical intervention may open closed passageways, concentrate the sperm of a man with a low sperm count, or circumvent absent or dysfunctional tubes through in vitro fertilization. In addition to using refined medical technology couples often utilize new social arrangements. The American Fertility Society esti-mates that as many as fifty thousand couples each year use a third-party to have a child.[21] A third party participates either as a sperm-donor, ovum-donor, or as a surrogate.

Donor insemination, which overcomes the inability of a man to produce healthy sperm, is the most widely practiced third party intervention. Since the 1950s, donor insemination is responsible for as many as three hundred thousand births.[22] Donor insemination is conception in a doctor's office: the donor produces the sperm by masturbating and that semen is then injected with a syringe into the woman's vagina. Surrogacy, which addresses a woman's infertility, is the female equivalent of donor insemination.

In the case of the ovum surrogate, the wife either lacks healthy ovaries or the ability to produce ova for retrieval and is unable to carry a baby to term. Gestational surrogacy is a solution for women with one of a variety of fertility problems: a malformed or absent uterus; a medical condition which would make pregnancy dangerous for her, such as severe hypertension, diabetes, or lupus; or, a condition that would endanger the fetus, such as phenylketonuria.[23]

An infertile couple approaching an adoption agency is likely to encounter a long wait and complex selection process before succeeding in adopting a child.[24] The advantage in using a third-party, either through artificial insemination by a donor or surrogacy, is that the offspring is genetically linked to one, or in the case of gestational surrogacy to both, of the prospective parents. The genetic link meets the psychological need for continuity of a genetic chain, provides the gratification of a child who looks and may act like one of the parents, and may allow for more than one child that is genetically linked to his or her siblings.

There are serious potential problems entailed by surrogacy, too, it involves a third-party who may change her mind and assert her maternity of the child. For the future child there is the potential stigma of having been born to a woman who is not part of the child's life. There is also an ethical concern in barring access of a genetic mother to her child. Additionally, in contrast to adoption, in surrogacy arrangements parents accept responsibility for a future child who may turn out to be impaired.

To better assess the nature of these risks it is important to examine the legal data from the past two decades.

---

[21] Edmiston, p. 236.

[22] Minority Report, *supra* p. 7, citing at n. 2; Donovan, "New Reproductive Technologies: Some Legal Dilemmas," *Family Planning Perspectives* 18, no. 2 (Mar./Apr. 1986).

[23] Andrews and Douglass, p. 670; phenylketonuria is a genetic defect that may lead to mental retardation unless identified very early on in the child's life.

[24] Avi Katz, "Surrogate Motherhood and the Baby-Selling Laws," *Columbia Journal of Law and Social Problems* 20 (1986): 1, 4 at n. 12: "While there is an abundance of older, handicapped, or minority children waiting for adoption, healthy white infants are in scarce supply."

Surrogate Lawsuits

In recent years failed surrogacy arrangements have led to highly publicized, painful lawsuits. The most infamous of the surrogacy cases and among the first was the Matter of Baby M,[25] in which Mary Beth Whitehead, a twenty-nine year old surrogate, reneged on a contract to surrender the baby she bore for a childless couple. William Stern had supplied the sperm for the artificial insemination of Mary Beth Whitehead, and had paid her $10,000 to carry the fetus to term. In 1988 the New Jersey court held that the agreement between Whitehead, the surrogate, and the Sterns, the intended parents, was not binding because it violated the rule against payment for an adoption. The judge treated the matter as a custody case and awarded the child to her biological father, William Stern.

Most of the lawsuits filed to date are products of the surrogate changing her mind and wishing to keep the newborn. A recent example is the Marriage of Moschetta case[26] in which the ovum surrogate asserted her maternal rights when she learned that the intended couple had separated. The surrogate said that she had implicitly agreed to give the child only to a stable, married couple. The judge ruled that the contract was not binding and dealt with the case as one of custody. The biological father and surrogate were given joint custody and the intended mother – who lacked a biological link – was denied any privileges.

Although the emotional costs of failed surrogacy arrangements are high, surrogacy overwhelmingly succeeds. According to the Health Department of the State of New York, from an estimated four thousand children born to surrogates from the late 1970s to the early 1990s, only twelve surrogacy-related cases had been filed in the U.S. courts, and in every case except one, custody was awarded to the intended parents.[27]

Only one gestational surrogate case has wound up in court. In Anna Johnson v. Mark and Crispina Calvert,[28] the paid surrogate, Anna Johnson, asserted a maternal right to the child. The California Supreme Court upheld the lower courts and ruled that the contract between the parties for turning over the child was binding. Moreover, the court held that the intended mother, who was also the biological mother, was "the natural mother under California law." Currently in California it is only the genetic-intended mother's name that appears on the birth certificate of child born by a gestational surrogate.

Legal cases reveal only some of the complications entailed by surrogacy. There is little psychological data on the emotional costs of surrogacy to the surrogates family who see their wife or mother turn over a child she has borne. The long term feelings of surrogates concerning the process is still unclear due to the limited number of years that surrogacy has taken place and warrants ongoing evaluation.

To date the rabbis who have written on surrogacy have done so from a theoretical vantage point and have largely concluded that surrogacy is unacceptable. Jewish law is worth reexamining in light of the positive track record of surrogacy to date, the growing use of surrogacy, and the fact that surrogacy has successfully allowed for the blessing of children.

---

[25] 537 A2d 1227 (NJ, 1988)

[26] 25 Cal. App. 4th 1218, 30 Cal. Rptr. 893 (1994), the appellate court has redirected the trial court to examine the criteria of custody, but has also held that the surrogacy agreement was in no way binding. See the trial court opinion at LA Super CT., NO D324348; featured on CBS's *48 Hours*, 23 Nov. 1991.

[27] *Center for Surrogate Parenting Inc. Newsletter* (spring 1993) 1; Edmiston puts the number at fifteen, Edmiston, *supra*; Minority Report cites only ten lawsuits; an editorial in *USA Today*, 26 Sept. 1990, says, "Of the 1,000 babies born in the past decade, only a handful have wound up in court" (p. 126).

[28] 5 Cal. 4th 84, 19 *California Reporter*, p. 494 (1993).

Values Implicit in Jewish Law

Jewish law has no direct precedent for modern surrogacy. Until recently the possibility of gestational surrogacy was restricted to the realm of science fiction.[29] Similarly, ovum surrogacy in a monogamous context did not take place.

Early rabbis, however, possessed a prescient imagination and were able to envision embryo transfer. Targum Yonaton says that Dinah was conceived by Rachel and transferred to the womb of Leah, and Joseph was conceived by Leah and transferred to the womb of Rachel.[30] Such speculation, however, has no legal significance since the commentator derived no legal lesson from this legend and, in the Rabbis' account, neither mother intended nor even knew that the embryo transfer had occurred.

Surrogacy is a matter of legal first impression in Jewish law, as in American law. The analysis of jurists to date, both in the U.S. Courts and in the writing of the rabbis, has largely tried to analyze it within previously existing categories. Yet, ovum surrogacy is something new, a constellation of five factors: artificial insemination; payment of fees to a biological mother; agreement by a biological mother to relinquish rights; legitimation by a biological father; adoption by his wife.[31] Gestational surrogacy, in which the birth mother has no genetic link to the newborn is totally new. To define surrogacy with partial analogies to existing laws is a distortion and a disservice to halakhah.

Whether surrogacy is worthy of halakhic support comes down to a balancing test of moral, financial, communal, and personal costs coupled with the gains to the intended parents. Since there is no direct legal precedent for surrogacy in Jewish law, a place to begin such an analysis is with underlying values found in Judaism which touch on surrogacy.

Procreation

Children are among God's chief blessings. Indeed, procreation is the first command in the Torah: פרו ורבו ומלאו את הארץ, "Be fruitful and multiply and fill up the earth."[32] So important are offspring that the Mishnah contains a debate between Hillel and Shammai as to the number — they each say two — and genders of children — males for Shammai, one of each for Hillel — needed to fulfill the Biblical mandate.[33] Nonetheless, the Tosafot criticizes those who fulfill only the minimum requirement.[34]

Abundance of offspring is a recurring promise to the patriarchs: your descendants

---

[29] Surrogacy has been mentioned in futuristic literature, including George Orwell's *1984* (1949), p. 66, reference to totalitarian "Junior Anti-Sex League" which advocated all reproduction by artificial insemination or "artsem;" Aldous Huxley's *Brave New World* (1932), pp. 1-14, description of hatcheries used for human reproduction in totalitarian world; Margaret Atwood, *The Handmaid's Tale* (1986). These citations are noted by the California appellate court in Anna J. v. Mark C., 91 *Daily Journal* D.A.R. 12433, n. 7.

[30] Berakhot 60a, discussed in Fred Rosner, *Modern Medicine*, p. 122. The background on the legend is the story that knowing that Jacob would become the father of a total of twelve sons and not wishing her sister Rachel to bear fewer sons than the maidservants, Bilhah and Zilpah, Leah prayed that her already conceived fetus be born a female. In Berakhot, her prayer is answered by a sex-change. However, Targum Yonaton, on Gen. 30:2, suggests that an embryo transfer occurred to solve the problem. Bleich cites the talmudic commentary of Rabbi Samuel Edels as supporting the embryo transfer idea as a way to understand Berakhot 60a.

[31] Andrea E. Stumpf, "Redefining Mother: A Legal Matrix for New Reproductive Technologies," 96 *Yale Law Journal* 187, pp. 191-192 (1986).

[32] Gen. 1:28.

[33] Yevamot 6:6, Shammai sees Adam's two sons as the model; Hillel looks to Adam and Eve.

[34] Tosafot to Bava Batra 60b. s.v. דין.

shall be "like the stars in the heavens and sands of the sea."[35] The promise, however, required parental effort — hence the statement in the Midrash: there are three partners to creation — the father, mother, and God.[36] Rabbi Eleazar ben Azariah is quoted in a midrash as saying, "he who does not engage in procreation is as if he diminished the Divine image," for without human descendants there is no one to embody God's image.[37] In light of the importance of procreation, permission was given to even sell a Torah scroll to enable a marriage where procreation had yet to be fulfilled.[38] For in the words of Isaiah: "The world was created to be inhabited."[39]

Despite God's promise of progeny, each of the patriarchs had wives who confronted infertility.[40] Reflective of the pain of these couples are Rachel's words to Jacob: "Give me children lest I die!" In response, "Jacob was incensed at Rachel, and said, 'Can I take the place of God who has denied you fruit of the womb?'"[41] Jacob's anger reveals both his frustration and limitation. There was no medical knowledge in his day that could have solved Rachel or Jacob's infertility. An infertile couple only had prayer and the possibility of the aid of a third party — which we will see was Rachel's solution.

Third-Party Intervention

In response to infertility the Torah provides for third party intervention. Interestingly, there is such a possibility for both female and male infertility, the categories of שפחה and יבום. These two responses of last resort are not the direct equivalent of modern day surrogacy or artificial insemination by a donor, but are worth examining closely to uncover underlying values.

שפחה[42]

Unable to conceive, Rachel says to Jacob:

הנה אמתי בלהה בא אליה ותלד על ברכי ואבנה גם אנכי ממנה.

Here is my handmaid Bilhah, come unto her, and she shall give birth on my knees and I will be built up through her.[43]

Rachel's use of Bilhah her שפחה, Hebrew for handmaid, as her surrogate had precedent both among the patriarchs and the society in which she lives.

Sarah, too, resorts to a שפחה. "Look, the Lord has kept me from bearing," Sarah says to Abraham. "Consort with my handmaid, Hagar; perhaps I shall have a child

---

[35] Gen. 15:5; 22:17; 26:4; Exod. 32:13; Deut. 1:10; 10:22; 28:62.

[36] Niddah 31a.

[37] Genesis Rabbah 34:14 and is incorporated by Joseph Karo, Shulhan Arukh, Even HaEzer 1:1; even stronger were the words of Eliezer ben Hyrcanus, "Who brings no children into the world is like a murderer," Yevamot 63b.

[38] Megillah 27a.

[39] Isa. 45:18.

[40] A description of Sarai offering Avram her handmaid Hagar in order to have children through her is Genesis, chapter sixteen. In regard to Rebecca, the Torah records: "And Isaac entreated the Lord for his wife, because she was barren, and the Lord was entreated of him, and Rebecca his wife conceived" (Gen. 25:21).

[41] Gen. 30:1-2.

[42] שפחה and אמה are used interchangeably in the Torah to describe a slave of the patriarch's wife, who, as property of the patriarch, was also a member of the extended family (see Gen. 16:1 and 30:3,9). פלגש, concubine, was one of a harem of freeborn or freed women belonging directly to the patriarch as a secondary wife. See L. Epstein, *Marriage Laws in the Bible and Talmud* (1942), pp. 34-62.

[43] Gen. 30:3.

through her."⁴⁴ Abraham consents and Hagar gives birth to Yishmael. Later on when Leah (Rachel's sister) is unable to continue to bear children, she asks Jacob to consort with her handmaid, Zilpah.⁴⁵

The handmaids are subservient to the matriarchs. Their rights are limited. Hence, when Sarah is displeased with Hagar, who at this point is pregnant by Abraham, Abraham says to Sarah: הנה שפחתך בידך עשי לה הטוב בעיניך "Behold, your שפחה is in your hands, do with her that which is good in your hands."⁴⁶ Subsequently, Sarah is so harsh with Hagar that she runs away.⁴⁷

Consistent with the matriarchs' primacy in the marriage, when children are born to Bilhah and Zilpah, it is Rachel and Leah who give the children their names.⁴⁸ When Rachel says, "she shall give birth on my knees," she uses language similarly found as a formal act of adoption in contemporaneous Hittite documents.⁴⁹ The children born to the handmaids are considered Jacob's sons and are included among the twelve tribes along with the natural sons of Leah and Rachel.

Parallel to the Biblical שפחה are legal accounts found in ancient Near East documents. The Code of Hammurabi warns expressly that a slave girl elevated by her mistress could not claim equality.⁵⁰ A nuzi marriage document stipulates: "If Gillimninu bears children, Shennima shall not take another wife. But if Gillimninu fails to bear children, she shall get for him a slave girl as concubine. In that case, Gillimninu herself shall have authority over the offspring."⁵¹ Despite the second class status of the שפחה in the Torah, she also has certain privileges which are absent in modern surrogacy arrangements. The שפחה is part of the patriarch's family and apparently helps to raise her own children.

Some critics of surrogacy have pointed to the case of Hagar as a warning. To quote Arlene Agus: "Despite many circumstances — the status and rights offered Hagar, the absence of payment, the shared custody arrangement — the arrangement failed. Perhaps there is a lesson to be learned here."⁵² But, holding out Hagar and Sarah's relationship as typical overlooks the apparent success of Rachel and Leah with their handmaids.⁵³ Moreover, modern surrogacy offers the advantage of simplifying the family arrangement so that two women do not need to compete for the affection of the same man.

Indeed, the most obvious difference between the שפחה and the modern day surrogate is that the שפחה existed in a polygamous context. Then it was socially acceptable for a man to impregnate a woman in addition to his primary wife. With Rabbenu Gershon's mandate

---

⁴⁴ Gen. 16:2.

⁴⁵ Gen. 30:9.

⁴⁶ Gen. 16:6.

⁴⁷ Gen. 15:6.

⁴⁸ Rachel, Gen. 30:6 (Dan), 30:8 (Naftali); Leah, Gen. 30:10 (Gad), 30:3 (Asher).

⁴⁹ Sarna says that the origin of placing a child on knees as an act of adoption is in the idea of the knee as the seat of generative power. Indeed in Akkadian knee is *birku* which is used as a euphemism for sexual parts. This act of adoption is also found in ancient Greece and Rome. Sarna, *Genesis* (Philadelphia: JPS, 1989) (hereinafter JPS), p. 207.

⁵⁰ Pritchard, *ANET*, Code of Hammurabi 146, p. 172, cited in *The Torah: A Modern Commentary*, Gunther Plaut, ed, UAHC (hereinafter UAHC).

⁵¹ Quoted by Speiser, *Genesis* (Garden City, NJ: Doubleday, 1964), p. 120, cited in UAHC, p. 111.

⁵² Arlene Agus, *Lillith* (spring 1988): 31.

⁵³ Yishmael, Hagar's son, is only one of five children born to a Biblical surrogate. The other four are treated as the full sons of Jacob and no problems for their mothers are reported. In addition, when Hagar leaves the surrogate arrangement she does so with her son.

in the tenth century monogamy was required, a restriction which some critics construe as a prohibition of surrogacy today.[54]

Yet, there is a fundamental difference between procreation in the past and today. In the ancient world the only way a man had children with a woman was through sexual intercourse. Today, children may be born without violating the sacred sexual intimacy of marriage. In that light, artificial insemination by a donor is not considered an act of adultery across a broad spectrum of halakhic authorities.[55] Because of the division between sex and procreation, and even between gestation and providing the ovum, modern surrogacy is not easily dismissed by reference to the category of monogamy alone.

Despite some differences between the שפחה and the contemporary surrogate, there are significant shared values to glean from the Bible's acceptance of a third party to procreation. First, the use of a third party is a permitted last resort to assure genetic continuity for the husband. Although the patriarchs and matriarchs could have adopted a child, a legal category in the ancient world too, they chose the option of using a שפחה. Second, although children were born to the שפחה, the Torah recognized the maternal role of the "intended mother" and gave her rights. The offspring were adopted by the matriarchs and named by them. Third, although the שפחה was not recognized as a "wife," her offspring were treated as a descendant of the patriarch, which entailed full inheritance rights.

יבום

A second Biblical category of third-party intervention, יבום, offered a form of artificial insemination. An analysis of יבום demonstrates the Bible's willingness to redraft familial lines to overcome infertility. Moreover, the history of the category of יבום reveals that the halakhah evolves and responds to changing social mores.

When a man died childless, his next of kin was commanded to procreate with the widow in order to perpetuate the deceased's name and memory. This duty, called יבום, is present in Genesis. When Tamar's husband, Er, died without issue, her father-in-law, Judah, said to his second son, Onan: "Join with your brother's wife and do your duty by her as a brother-in-law and provide offspring for your brother — ויבם אותה."[56] Onan was an intended surrogate for his deceased brother. This form of artificial insemination required sexual intercourse, the only conceivable way to fertilize a woman in the ancient world.

The law of יבום, levirate marriage, is codified in Deuteronomy as follows:

> When brothers dwell together and one of them dies and leaves no son, the wife of the deceased shall not be married to a stranger, outside the family. Her husband's brother shall unite with her: take her as his wife and perform the levir's duty. And the firstborn she bears shall succeed in the name of his brother that is dead, that his name not be blotted out of Israel.[57]

Normally marriage between a man and his brother's former wife was forbidden.[58] יבום was

---

[54] Marc Gellman, *supra*.

[55] Only a small number of the authorities permit artificial insemination by a donor, because of concerns with potential incest. Rabbi Elliot N. Dorff, in his responsa for the CJLS, above, pp. 473-477, has permitted the use of donor insemination and in response to the concern of incest encourages as much information as possible to be shared with the prospective parents and for them to share it with their child. In addition, Rabbi Dorff notes Rabbi Feinstein's position that incest is a limited concern when the donor is not Jewish.

[56] Gen. 32:8.

[57] Deut. 25:5-6.

[58] Lev. 18:16 and 20:21.

the exception to the rule. Apparently, familial continuity and having a child was so great a value that it overrode the societal norm of familial boundaries.

Deuteronomy did, however, provide a brother-in-law with a way out of the levirate duty too. The man could publicly refuse to perform יבום. The widow had to agree, which was marked by a public ritual, called חליצה ("removal"), whereby she removed her brother-in-law's shoe, spit toward his face, and declared, "This is what shall be done to the man who will not build up a family for his brother."[59]

Recent scholarship documents that יבום was not unique to the Bible. It was part of a legislative pattern of the ancient Near East. A fragmentary text from the Middle Assyrian Empire's compendium of laws (fifteenth and fourteenth centuries B.C.E.) requires a widow who has no son to be married off by the father-in-law to the son of his choice.[60] In the Hittite laws, approximately from Abraham's lifetime, is the statement that if a married man dies, "his brother shall take his wife, then (if he dies) his father shall take her."[61] These laws offered financial and physical protection for a widow, and they also treated the woman as the property of the clan.

יבום in Jewish law evolved in response to changing societal mores. As Judaism moved away from polygamy, the Rabbis of the Talmud interpreted the Torah to make חליצה easier. יבום was restricted to the case of a brother who died without any issue,[62] instead of the previous gloss of a male child, and the brother-in-law could fulfill the command only if his motives were pure.[63] Therefore, if he was drawn to the widow by her attractiveness, he was barred from having sex with her. The Rabbis also made it easier for the widow to release her brother-in-law. Rather than spitting in his face she was permitted to symbolically spit on the ground in front of her brother-in-law.[64]

Although the Biblical law's interpretation evolved, the Rabbis of the Talmudic and subsequent and even later halakhic authorities remained divided over the preference of חליצה to יבום.[65] The difference in opinion correlates with whether the rabbis lived in a polygamous or monogamous society.[66] Only in 1950 did the two chief rabbis of Israel, a state which prohibited polygamy, issue an edict (a תקנה) which prohibited יבום. They explained that in modern society, most levirs do not undergo levirate marriage for the sake of fulfilling a mitzvah, and that there is a need to maintain a norm of monogamy to protect society's stability.[67]

יבום and שפחה are two biblical examples of third-party intervention in the context of

---

[59] Deut. 25:8-9.

[60] A, par. 33, cited in Sarna, JPS, p. 266, n. 8.

[61] Par. 193, cited in Sarna, ibid.

[62] M. Yevamot 2:5 and B. Yevamot 22b; M. Nedarim 5:3.

[63] M. Bekhorot 1:7 and Rashi there (Bekhorot 13a); also T. Yevamot 6:9, where Abba Saul said, "I am inclined to think that the child of such a union is a ממזר."

[64] Yevamot 12:6; Yad, Yibum 4:1-23; S.A., Even HaEzer 169.

[65] In the third generation of tannaim, levirate marriage was customarily upheld (Yevamot 8:4). Although the majority of Babylonian amoraim left the choice between marriage and חליצה to the levir (Yevamot 39a-b), the Palestinian amoraim held that חליצה took priority. This summary is from *Encyclopaedia Judaica (E.J.)*, "Levirate Marriage and Halitzah," vol. 11, pp. 125-126.

[66] In the medieval rabbinic period, Sephardic rabbis gave priority to levirate marriage — see Alfasi to Yevamot 39b; Maimonides, Yad, Yibum 1:2; and Joseph Karo, S.A., Even HaEzer 165:1; the rabbis of northern France and Germany held that חליצה took priority over יבום — see Rashi and Rabbenu Tam; Asher b. Yehiel, Tur, Even HaEzer 165; and Moses Isserles, Rema, Even HaEzer 165:1.

[67] Cited in *E.J.*, 11:129.

polygamy. Each was a last resort. Although significantly different from contemporary surrogacy, we may learn the following values and lessons from these precedents:

- Social norms are dynamic and halakhah responds to evolving societal mores.
- Extraordinary effort and even crossing familial lines is accepted as a last resort in assuring genetic continuity.
- Recognition is warranted for the investment made by an initiating mother and her role in shaping the identity of her adopted child.

In contrast to the days of the patriarchs, sex is no longer needed for procreation. Hence polygamy and monogamy may no longer define reproductive boundaries. There are two distinct questions which emerge in assessing the novelty of contemporary surrogacy: Does Judaism accept scientific intervention to overcome infertility? And is it moral for a couple in our day to use a third party to enable procreation?

Science as Blessing and Mandate

When the Torah commands "be fruitful and multiply," it continues, "and conquer it (the earth) – וכבשוה."[68] The phrase "and conquer it" is interpreted as a mandate to serve as God's partner in maintaining and assisting nature.[69] In that light, Rabbi Seymour Siegel writes:

> We are called upon to care for nature and to preserve it — but not to worship it. We are also called upon to use our ingenuity, our imagination, and intelligence to improve nature when human happiness and well being [are] thwarted. This is the basis for the whole medical enterprise.[70]

Physicians, in the Jewish tradition, help fashion creation. Their role is beautifully illustrated in the following midrash of a pair of leading Rabbis in second-century Palestine:

> Once Rabbi Yishmael and Rabbi Akiva were strolling in the streets of Jerusalem along with another man. They met a sick person who said to them, "Masters, tell me how I can be healed." They quickly advised him to take a certain medicine until he felt better.
>
> The man with them turned to them and said, "Who made this man sick?"
>
> "The Holy One, Source of Blessing," they replied.
>
> "And do you presume to interfere in an area that is not yours? He afflicted and you heal?!"
>
> "What is your occupation?" they asked the man.
>
> "I'm a tiller of the soil," he answered, "as you can see from the sickle I carry."
>
> "Who created the field and the vineyard?"

---

[68] Gen. 1:28.

[69] An important essay on this theme is Joseph Soloveichik's "The Lonely Man of Faith," *Tradition* 7 (1965): 1-67.

[70] Seymour Siegel, unpublished responsum prepared for the Committee of Jewish Law and Standards of the Rabbinical Assembly (1978), quoted in Gold, p. 83.

> "The Holy One, Source of Blessing."
>
> "And you dare to move in an area that is not yours? God created these and you eat their fruit?"
>
> "Don't you see the sickle in my hand?" the man said. "If I did not go out and plow the field, cover it, fertilize it, weed it, nothing would grow."
>
> "Fool," the Rabbis said, "just as a tree does not grow if it is not fertilized, plowed and weeded — and even if it already grew, but then is not watered it dies. So the body is like a tree: the medicine is the fertilizer and the doctor is the farmer."[71]

Medicine, in this account, is seen as a way to actualize God's blessing. Rabbis Akiva and Yishmael's words are a compelling response to those, like the Catholic Church,[72] which speak of natural law and greatly restrict the use of technology to overcome infertility. The imagery of the two Rabbis — speaking of seed, field, and fruit — is well-suited to the area of medical intervention and procreation.

Rabbis universally accept the use of medical technology, but may question the ethical implications of the process. Hence, Rabbi Jakobovits, the former chief rabbi of England and among the first to write on the ethics of reproductive technology, said in 1975:

> Artificial insemination utilizing an outside donor (AID) is, however, considered to pose grave moral problems. Such operations, even if they may not technically constitute adultery, would completely disrupt the family relationship. Moreover, a child so conceived would be denied its birth-right to have a father and other relations who can be identified. Altogether, to reduce human generation to "stud-farming" methods would be a debasement of human life, utterly repugnant to Jewish ideals and traditions. . . .
>
> Hardly less offensive to moral susceptibilities is the proposal to abort a mother's naturally fertilized egg and to reimplant it into a "host-mother" as a convenience for women who seek the gift of a child without the encumbrance and disfigurement of pregnancy. To use another person as an "incubator" and then take from her the child she carried and delivered for a fee is a revolting degradation of maternity and an affront to human dignity.[73]

Rabbi Jakobovits' words are a sample of the alarm generated by the new tools of medical reproductive intervention. It is not the use of the tools which is objectionable, but the social and ethical implications. Regrettably, the concerns have rarely encompassed the data of the last two decades and instead have focused on theoretical scenarios, often of the most extreme kind. Surrogacy is something fundamentally new which warrants a balancing test of the gains and risks and must be seen as a new composite of legal concerns.

---

[71] Midrash Samuel 4:1; Midrash Temurah as cited in *Otzar Midrashim*, J.D. Eisenstein, ed. (New York, 1915), vol. 2, pp. 580-581.

[72] "Instruction on Respect for Human Life in Its Origin and on the Dignity of Procreation," *Origins*, vol. 16, no. 40 (19 Mar. 1987): 700. Cited by Gold, at ch. 5, n. 3: Prohibition of procreation by non-natural means.

[73] Immanuel Jakobovits, at pp. 264-265.

Ethical and Legal Objections to the New Social Arrangements

A private arrangement like that of the Sterns and Mary Beth Whitehead would not bind a court, according to Jewish law, because traditionally parents do not have the right to independently determine the status of their children. In all such matters of parental responsibility and rights, including custody, it is the court who makes an authoritative determination based on the best interests of the child.[74]

Whether surrogacy is in the best interests of children and a societal good is a widely debated question. If these novel social arrangements are ethical, enhance family, and serve to protect the child, then the courts might choose to oversee and validate such agreements. The following analysis of the ethical and legal concerns which stem from surrogacy affirms the needs of the child as the priority.

Baby-Selling

Baby-selling is repugnant to the Jewish tradition and illegal in all fifty states. Hence, a mother in the United States may not receive payment for her child when she turns her offspring over to another couple for adoption. Nonetheless, most surrogate birth arrangements involve pay. Is the pay to a surrogate mother the equivalent of baby selling?

When the California Legislature's Subcommittee gave their findings on surrogates in 1991, the majority equated surrogacy with adoption and wrote: Paid surrogacy arrangements would "treat the child as a commodity and would set up a distinction between ordinary adoptions and surrogacy adoptions that would be neither defensible or practically enforceable."[75] The recommendation of the California Legislative Committee was to permit surrogacy for free, but to make it a criminal offense to participate on any level in enabling surrogacy for pay. While the California legislature is still debating the question, four states have made it outright illegal to receive payment as a surrogate.[76]

There are, however, some critical differences between adoption and surrogacy. First, the intended father — in either ovum or gestational surrogacy — is the genetic and intended father of the child.[77] Second, the intended parents accept responsibility from the moment of conception. The interests of the child to enter a secure home where he or she is wanted is therefore protected. Third, there is limited duress on the woman agreeing to give up the child, because she makes her decision even before conception.

Distinctions between the typical surrogate and adoption-giving mother further demonstrate that surrogacy and adoption are dissimilar. The profile of a typical adoption mother is an unmarried teenager who lacks financial security and is giving birth for the first time. The adoption-oriented mother has usually gotten pregnant unintentionally, which both she and the biological father regret. She is vulnerable to the manipulation of baby-brokers who may offer her a small monetary fee and care during pregnancy in exchange for the child.[78] Adoption law seeks to protect a vulnerable pregnant mother and

---

[74] See "Parent and Child," in *E.J.*, vol. 13, p. 99, citing *Piskei Din shel Batei HaDin HaRabanim B'Yisrael* 2:3, 171-177; 5:171, 173.

[75] *Advisory Panel Report, Joint Committee on Surrogate Parenting*, Sunny Mojonnier, chair, California, Legislature (1991) p. 15.

[76] Arizona, Kentucky, Michigan and Utah. Five more states ban payment but have the caveat of allowing "expenses" — Florida, New Hampshire, New York, Virginia and Washington.

[77] A father has a duty to maintain his minor children (M.T. Ishut 13:6; S.A., Even HaEzer 73:6, 7), and is responsible whether or not he is married to the woman, e.g., born out of wedlock — Resp. Ribash no. 41; Resp. Rosh 17:7 — cited in *E.J.*, "Parent and Child," 13:96.

[78] Katz, p. 8.

to facilitate giving up an unwanted child, rather than to orchestrate a child's conception.[79]

The chances of an adoptive mother changing her mind about giving up a child are also significant, commonly put at between five to fifteen percent.[80] In one study adoption specialist Carol Wolfe, MFCC, interviewed 250 birth mothers who had agreed to place their children with prospective adoptive parents. In ninety-five of these cases (thirty-eight percent), one or the other party withdrew from the agreement prior to or following the birth.[81]

In contrast, surrogate mothers make a decision prior to conception — usually with the aid of an attorney and therapist — to give the child to parents who very much want to establish a family. Because of the time frame there is no need for hurried decisions, no rival bidding, and no unwanted pregnancy. The studies on surrogates consistently show that surrogates are usually married, have already borne at least one child, and are financially and psychologically stable.[82]

An ovum surrogate mother, let alone a gestational surrogate, does not experience the stress of an unplanned pregnancy. Nor is she likely to feel guilty about giving away her child if she views herself as performing a good deed for the natural father and his wife.[83] The fact that less than one percent of surrogate arrangements have ended up in the courts is strong evidence that surrogacy is different from adoption after birth.

Critics of paid surrogacy say that the payment to the surrogate is for the child because that is what the intended parents really want and that such payments demean human life. Sharon Huddle, who founded the National Coalition Against Surrogacy argues: "The ultimate victims are children. Their very existence was pre-negotiated, pre-designed, and contracted for just like any other commercial transaction."[84]

While it is tempting (and rhetorically effective) to characterize the money that changes hands as a payment for a commodity (the child), it is unclear that this is true. Pregnancy entails lost time, medical risk, and pain, all of which warrant remuneration.[85] In addition, payments to an ovum surrogate may be viewed as the biological father's attempt to protect the welfare of his child by insuring that the mother is provided with proper care.[86]

If payment is banned, then there is the need to pressure a friend or relative to serve as an unpaid surrogate, an act of persuasion which may be even more coercive and problematic than remuneration. It is unrealistic to expect that couples who wish to have a child through a surrogate will be able to find one without participating in the cost, including living costs, entailed by pregnancy. To ban paid surrogacy is to encourage a "surrogacy underground," because the law will not eliminate a strong desire to utilize medical technology to have one's own children through a third party.

---

[79] Margaret D. Townsend, "Surrogate Mother Agreements: Contemporary Aspects of a Biblical Notion," *University of Richmond Law Review*, 16 (1982): 406.

[80] *Center for Surrogacy Parenting Newsletter*, vol. 1, no. 4 (spring 1993): 1.

[81] Ibid.

[82] Andrews and Douglass, pp. 673-674.

[83] Katz, p. 8.

[84] Cited in Andrews, "Surrogacy Wars," *California Law* 12 (Oct. 1992): 47.

[85] In the Talmud there are parallel categories of compensation for willful injury: נזק — loss or damage; צער — pain and suffering; רפוי — medical expenses; שבת — loss of earnings; בושת — humiliation. See B. Bava Kamma, ch. 8; Hoshen Mishpat 420.

[86] Carmel Shalev, *Birth Power: The Case for Surrogacy* (New Haven, Ct.: Yale University Press, 1989), p. 159. She points out that giving life a monetary value took place in the nineteenth century with respect to life insurance, which was thought to represent a form of trafficking in human lives. Shalev wrote the book as her doctoral dissertation at Yale Law School and currently practices law in Jerusalem.

Money linked to pregnancy does not mean that the resulting child is any less loved or is reduced to a mere commodity. Currently, a billion dollars a year are spent in medical clinics to assist procreation. The money does not detract from the uniqueness of the child; it only underscores that a child is a much-wanted blessing.

The best interests of a child are served if the child is loved, cared for, and nurtured, which has little to do with the manner of conception and gestation. Payment compensates the surrogate for the hardship of pregnancy and helps assure that the intended child is properly taken care of beginning with conception. Surrogacy is not baby-selling, unless there is exploitation.

עושק – *Exploitation*

עושק, which translates as exploitation, is condemned in Jewish law. The prohibition stems from the biblical injunction, לא תעשק את רעיך "Thou shall not oppress your neighbor."[87] Technically, this mandate is identified by its Biblical context and in later Jewish law as the wrongful withholding of funds, usually that of wages.[88] Nonetheless, עושק may also be understood more broadly as a moral condemnation of taking advantage of the distress, weakness or inexperience of another person.[89] If there was exploitation, a Jewish court might disregard an agreement, as it does with gambling contracts.[90] Marc Gellman, among others, argues that עושק is inherently present in surrogacy arrangements.[91] He goes on to cite the statement in the Talmud that it is better to do a little good with what is yours than to do much good by exploiting that which belongs to others.[92]

The charge that surrogacy is exploitative is rooted in a variety of concerns: abuse of poor women by the rich; insensitivity to the birth mother's sacrifice in surrendering a child; frivolous avoidance of natural childbirth by fertile women; and undue risk with devaluing and commodifying the body. Put succinctly by Professor George Annas: "The core reality of surrogate motherhood is that it is both classist and sexist: a method to obtain children genetically related to white males by exploiting poor women."[93]

On the other side is the argument articulated by Carmel Shalev that "the exclusion of domestic reproduction labor from the public economy is the ultimate manifestation of a patriarchal double standard."[94] Shalev says that it is the historical failure to value the domestic work of mothers and housewives that has contributed to the sense that gestation has no value as a form of productive labor. She argues that women may exercise reason with respect to reproduction and may responsibly share birth power with those less fortunate.[95] As men get paid for their muscles, Shalev says, women should get reimbursed for their wombs.

Much of the debate to date has taken place in the theoretical realm. For instance, there is no evidence that women have used surrogates to avoid the hardship of pregnancy, as Rabbi Jakobovits had feared. Indeed, looking at the actual data on exploitation and surrogacy, Judge Parnelli in Anna Johnson v. Calvert wrote for the California Supreme Court:

---

[87] Lev. 19:13 – לא תעשק את רעיך.
[88] See Rashi to Lev. 19:3; Yad, Gezelah va-Avedah 1:4; and "Oppression," *E.J.*, 12:1435-1436.
[89] Bava Metzia 59b, also note Rashi there.
[90] Sanhedrin 25b; M.T. Gezelah 6:6-16.
[91] Gellman, p. 106.
[92] Sukkah 29b, cited by Gellman as an argument against ovum surrogacy.
[93] George Annas, "Fairy Tales Surrogate Mothers Tell," *Law, Medicine and Health Care* 16 (1988): 27.
[94] Shalev, p. 164.
[95] Shalev, p. 142.

> Although common sense suggests that women of lesser means serve as surrogate mothers more often than do wealthy women, there has been no proof that surrogacy contracts exploit poor women to any greater degree than economic necessity in general exploits them to accept lower-paid or otherwise undesirable employment.[96]

The service as a surrogate is not to be equated with slavery, which some have done. The woman makes the choice in a free-willed manner and is given the right to withdraw at any point. She is not giving up her womb permanently, but using it for a specific purpose which is inherently time-bound.

In reference to the ovum surrogate, who is giving up a child which is genetically her own, a larger perspective is helpful. We as a committee have approved the donation of sperm and ovum. An ovum surrogate is essentially donating her ovum. Rather than it being placed in another woman, she is donating the ovum and serving as the gestational surrogate for that donated egg.

Another challenge to surrogacy, as articulated by Andrea Dworkin among others,[97] is that surrogacy is a form of prostitution. There are, however, fundamental differences between surrogacy and prostitution, as well. The goal of prostitution is a fleeting moment of carnal pleasure. In contrast, surrogacy enables a profound societal gain — the creation of a child. Second, prostitutes are easily and often exploited. Those who use their services usually have little regard for the prostitutes' well-being. In contrast, intended parents are committed to a surrogate during the extended time frame of conception and gestation. They are concerned for the surrogate's lifestyle, home life, emotional and psychological stability, physical health, and a myriad of other factors that could affect the baby's health. It is hard to imagine an employer who cares more for his or her workers than do intended parents for a surrogate. Last, the use of a surrogate, as in the case of artificial insemination, does not violate the marital bond, as would adultery. A third party who assists procreation does not harm a marriage, but strengthens it.

Exploitation is of critical concern and warrants monitoring by the courts and legislators, but is not inherent to surrogacy. If pay for the use of a womb is accepted as legitimate, then surrogacy for pay is defensible. If we recognize women as responsible and accountable for their decisions, then we should acknowledge that surrogacy provides women the opportunity to give the blessing of a child to a couple in need and allows the surrogate to get paid legitimately for her efforts.

Unjustified Risk

God commands: "Guard your lives carefully."[98] This charge led the codifiers of Jewish law to say that a person should not unreasonably risk his or her life.[99] No doubt giving birth entails risk. As one obstetrician (Dr. Jay Masserman) said to me, the day a woman gives birth is generally the most dangerous of her life. Rabbi Marc Gellman has challenged surrogacy on this basis, saying that a surrogate cannot justify self-endangerment, because she has no חיוב, legal obligation, to give birth for another couple.[100] However,

---

[96] 5 Cal. 4th, p. 97; 9 *California Reporter*, 2d, p. 503.

[97] Andrea Dworkin, *Right-Wing Women: The Politics of Domesticated Females* (New York: Coward, McCann, 1983), pp. 181-183, cited in Andrews and Douglass, and in Shalev, p. 148.

[98] Deut. 4:15 – ונשמרתם מאד לנפשתיכם.

[99] Hullin 10a; see Berakhot 32b; Shabbat 32a; Bava Kamma 15b, 80a, 91b; M.T. Hilkhot Rozeach 11:4-5; Orah Hayyim 173:2; Rema to Yoreh De'ah 116:5.

[100] Gellman, p. 106.

in the technical sense of חיוב, a woman is never obligated to procreate. The command is only binding on men.[101]

Yet, the rabbis have seen pregnancy as worthy of risk-taking by women. As a wife undertakes a risk to allow her husband to fulfill a mitzvah, so does the surrogate. As a woman derives joy from giving birth to her own child, so may a woman gain fulfillment in enabling another couple to be blessed with a child. The exception to self-endangerment can be read more broadly than Gellman's definition of חיוב and may be understood as a risk which provides a substantial good.

In that light, Rabbi Elliot N. Dorff permits ovum donation despite medical risks, and notes that the risks are smaller than kidney donation from a live donor, who only has two kidneys to start with, and which is permitted.[102] Moreover, the Sages permitted the performance of paid tasks, like sailing, which in their day entailed substantial risks to safety. And today we would allow a Jew to serve as an astronaut despite the risks and with only theoretical gains. In the case of surrogacy it is technically a mitzvah for the man in the couple to have a child, and it benefits family life. To enable a couple to have a child justifies risk.

A woman who is at greater risk than most during pregnancy should not serve as a surrogate because of the prohibition of self-endangerment. Fortunately, the risks of pregnancy and childbirth have declined in recent decades due to improved monitoring of the pregnant woman and the fetus and safer c-section techniques. Nonetheless, when a woman and her husband consider her serving as a surrogate they must take risk into account and be sure that her health is sound.

אסמכתא – *Finality of Conditions*

Another contractual concept which is discussed as a challenge to surrogacy agreements is that of אסמכתא,[103] which literally means "lean-on," and means that a contract is binding only if we can reasonably presume that the intentions of both parties are serious, deliberate, and final.[104] Maimonides goes so far as to void all contracts which are bound by an "if" clause, because the condition precedent implies that the contract only takes effect in the future.[105]

Yet, Maimonides and later poskim did accept commercial futures contracts when written with the language of "from now" (מעכשו), clarifying that the parties were bound from the moment of entering the agreement.[106] The symbolic act of acquisition (קנין), often marked by the exchange of a handkerchief, served to show that the parties had made up their minds to enter into an immediately binding transaction. Consequently, social agreements of future marriage, when properly composed, were enforced with penalties for breach of promise.[107] Nonetheless, the moral question remains whether a woman can in

---

[101] Yevamot 6:6. The majority holds that only men are required; a dissenting opinion is voiced by Rabbi Yohanan ben Berokah, who would obligate both men and women. Feldman, *Health and Medicine*, supra p. 71, shares this law and explains it as based on possibility of man engaging in polygamy and with the gloss of Rabbi Meir Simchah of Dvinsk (d. 1927) that since the pain and risk of childbearing is upon the woman, the Torah could not in fairness command a woman to undergo that pain and risk.

[102] Rabbi Elliot N. Dorff, "Artificial Insemination, Egg Donation and Adoption," above, p. 500.

[103] Gold, p. 122.

[104] Bava Metzia 48b, 66a-b, 109a-b; Bava Batra 168a.

[105] Yad, Mekhira 11:2,6.

[106] Yad, Mekhira 11. See discussion by A. Zvi Ehrman, "*Asmakhta*," in Menachem Elon, ed., *Principles of Jewish Law* (Jerusalem: Keter, 1974), pp. 171-174.

fact make a final decision to relinquish a yet unborn child.[108]

In response to such concerns, Carmel Shalev is vehement in her objection to the "insinuation that it is unreasonable to expect a woman to keep her promise because her faculty of reason is suspended by the emotional facets of her biological constituency."[109] Shalev says that as an artist may grow attached to a work of art, he or she is still bound by the agreement to part with the work. Likewise, Rabbi Seymour Siegel argued that a woman has the capacity to make a decision and should be bound by her word.[110] On a contract level the response to אסמכתא is that surrogacy is an agreement for services which binds the parties from the moment they enter into the agreement.

During the pregnancy a surrogate should have the right to withdraw from the agreement — an extension of her freedom of choice. But once the child is born it should be assumed that it goes to the intended parents. After all, it is their responsibility to accept the child from the moment of birth regardless of birth defects. After birth an ovum surrogate may assert her maternal rights, but the burden of proof is on her to show cause why the original intent should not be honored. אסמכתא is a legal concern in Jewish law to assure predictability of outcomes, which the court should protect in a surrogacy case as well, unless there is a violation of the best interests of the child.

דבר שלא בא לעולם – *Futures*

Another contractual concern related to אסמכתא is the prohibition against contracts for "something which is not yet in existence" – דבר שלא בא לעולם.[111] Parties could not technically give title to that which did not yet exist. Yet, here too the problem was overcome with language which shifted the focus to the parties themselves, who did exist, and their obligation to act in a certain way.[112] Hence, the concern is moot when a surrogate agreement is understood as a contract for services of pregnancy which binds the conduct of the respective parties, rather than determination of the status of the future child.

Family Integrity

Surrogacy is challenged in broad terms as contrary to a public policy of preserving family life. Some of the objections are as follows:

- "Frivolous motivations [for surrogacy] soon become socially acceptable."[113]
- "To use another person as an 'incubator' and then take from her the child she carried and delivered for a fee is a revolting degradation of maternity."[114]

---

[107] Ehrman, "*Asmakhta*," Tos. to Bava Metzia 66a; Sanhedrin 24b-25a and Shulhan Arukh, Hoshen Mishpat 207:16, although, Ashkenazic authorities widely argue that the penalty was not a matter of contract law, but compensation for damage and insult.

[108] This question is raised by Michael Gold, p. 122, who doesn't answer it, but goes on to emphasize that a woman who makes such an agreement still has a moral duty to fulfill it, quoting the Sages: "He who exacted punishment from the generations of the Flood and from the generations of the Tower of Babel will also exact punishment from one who does not abide by his word" (Bava Metzia 4:2).

[109] Shalev, p. 121.

[110] Siegel, pp. 107-108.

[111] Tosefta, Nedarim 6:7; also see Bava Metzia, *hamafkid* (ch. 3).

[112] Bava Batra 157a; Tur and Shulhan Arukh, Hoshen Mishpat 60:6.

[113] Tendler.

Jewish tradition values family integrity, which includes the ability to define who is in the family; forging secure family bonds; fashioning personal identity; and preserving the sanctity of marriage.[115] It is precisely the value of family which motivates an advocacy of surrogacy. For such arrangements allow for much-wanted children who enhance and create families. Infertility imposes a great strain on a marriage which for the couple with an infertile woman may find a solution in the benign assistance of another woman.

There is currently no evidence of harm to a family unit which has had a child through surrogacy, such as the jealousy of the non-genetic parent or half-siblings of either family. If anything, the stories to date are overwhelmingly of the joy of gaining a child. No doubt there are risks worthy of monitoring through careful consideration and counselling before entering such an agreement. But, most persuasively is the fact that with thousands of children born to surrogates – thousands of children who otherwise would not have been born – only a minuscule percentage have resulted in litigation or reported problems. Surrogacy, evidenced anecdotally by the successes, strengthens family.

Conclusion: A Path for Surrogacy

The novelty of a woman carrying a child for another couple will take time to gain social acceptance. Comfort with surrogacy will properly increase and theoretical fears will dissipate as the data builds an unimpeachable case of happy families who successfully overcame the infertility of the female spouse.

Jewish law contains many examples of the power of the courts to redefine family relationships and rights. Such change comes slowly and is a response to shifting societal norms and new variables. Moreover, the legislation of the state, as in the case of adoption, may give Jewish courts authority to foster entirely new social arrangements. Yet, the reality is that Jewish courts, particularly in our Movement, refrain from monitoring social arrangements and adjudicating disputes. Largely, our בתי דין concern themselves with matters of marriage and divorce.

In Jewish law there is the principle of דינא דמלכותא דינא, the law of the land is the law. This principle, originally enunciated by Samuel in the Talmud in reference to civil matters,[116] would apply on a broader basis to any practice in violation of local law. Consequently, if legislatures prohibit surrogacy then Jewish courts and lawyers would need to abide by that holding.[117] If we believe in the benefits of surrogacy than we need to encourage our legislators to pass supportive legislation. We need to caution our members that if the law of their state prohibits surrogacy they must not violate the law, including the participation in writing "illegal" contracts.

Although surrogacy is a potentially positive use of new technology, controls are needed to protect against abuses and to oversee the best interests of the child. Without effective legislation there is the threat of reproductive anarchy. Recent alleged unauthorized use of ova by fertility physicians at the University of California at Irvine demonstrates the potential havoc created by an abuse of consent. Legislation must assure that the expectations of all the parties involved are clearly defined in an agreement and that there is mon-

---

[114] Jakobovits.

[115] Concerns cited by Agus, "Surrogacy."

[116] Nedarim 28a; Gittin 10b; Bava Kamma 113a; Bava Batra 54b, 55a.

[117] There is no state in the Union which has legislated surrogacy contracts as legal and enforceable. Only nineteen states have any laws on the subject as of the end of 1993 and most placed limits, some even made it a crime to engage in surrogacy for profit (editorial in *USA Today*, 19 Nov. 1993, p. 12A). State Legislatures are actively considering legislation. In 1992, there were fifteen states with legislation; the most common – applicable in eleven states – is to void paid surrogacy contracts. Lori B. Andrews, "Surrogacy Wars," p. 50.

itoring of the professionals.[118]

Wise legislation would require that even prior to conception parties would appear before a state court and request permission to enter into a surrogacy agreement. The judge would confirm the surrogate's physical health, emotional stability, informed consent, prior experience with pregnancy, and if she was married, confirm her husband's approval. The court would also determine that the initiating couple would make good parents and that their motive was infertility. The court would oversee fair compensation to any involved parties, including agencies or professionals and require that insemination be done by a licensed physician. The court would also ascertain that there was professional counselling and psychological preparedness for all parties prior to entering the agreement.

Guidelines for surrogacy agreements coupled with court monitoring would offer the following necessary ingredients for the child's security: certainty, efficiency and finality. Such legislation is a means for making workable that which might otherwise create social disorder. There is a need for such control to avoid underground, unscrupulous practices. Indeed, legislatures could make it a crime to enter a surrogacy agreement absent court approval and thereby put teeth into a law which would limit abuse of a potential blessing.

Couples should consider surrogacy as a last option to overcome infertility due to its great financial and emotional costs. Among the substantial emotional costs are the uncertainty of success — which may entail great psychological stress — and the possibility of a change in mind by the surrogate, which might entail a lawsuit or simply great disappointment. In addition, there remain ongoing ethical concerns which warrant ongoing evaluation, such as the impact of surrogacy on the family of the surrogate. Nonetheless, when a couple is aware of these risks the Rabbinical Assembly Committee of Law and Standards should affirm in light of the current evidence that surrogacy is permitted by halakhah.

Does Surrogacy Allow for Fulfilling the Mitzvah of "Be Fruitful and Multiply"?

Yes. A man, according to Jewish law, is considered the natural father of the offspring of his sperm. Hence, with the aid of a surrogate, a man would fulfill the mitzvah of procreation, which is incumbent only on the man. In the same vein, whether the child was a Kohen, Levite, or Israelite would be determined by the biological father.[119]

Must an Infertile Couple Hire a Surrogate to Fulfill the Mitzvah?

No. Surrogacy is an extraordinary method to conceive and gestate a child. A couple is only obligated to use natural means to fulfill the procreative mandate.[120]

Summary

Surrogacy — both ovum and gestational — is a new legal construct. Jewish law has no precedent for child-making without sex, let alone the splitting of biology and gestation. This is a time to acknowledge that new variables provide a need to craft law. To determine whether Jewish law should support surrogacy is to balance the gains of surrogacy over its potential damage.

---

[118] Examples of model legislation are Uniform Status of Children of Assisted Conception Act, National Conference of Commissioners of Uniform State Laws, 1988; analyzed and supported in Paul J. Greco, "Parental Guidance Suggested: A Proposal for Regulating Surrogacy," *Columbia Journal of Law and Social Problems* 22 (1989): 115; favorable legislation was drafted by California State Senator Watson, Senate bill 2635 (1988), and passed by the California legislature, but vetoed by Governor Pete Wilson.

[119] Dorff similarly holds according to the link to the biological father that the tribal identity follows the source of the sperm, above, pp. 478, 504.

[120] Dorff similarly writes in reference to the use of donor insemination, above, pp. 504-505.

Adoption is to be encouraged, but there are couples who will prefer a genetic link to the father (artificial insemination, ovum donation, or ovum surrogacy) or to the mother (gestational surrogacy). At first impression there may be a visceral discomfort with these relatively new modes of reproduction, specifically the transfer of genetic material or the use of a womb for another couple. Yet, when we examine this new technology in the context of its outcome, we find the blessing of children to couples who want them very much. The bigger picture, which includes the intended result, makes surrogacy more acceptable upon reexamination.

A contemporary surrogate is not the equivalent of the שפחה, because the surrogate may have a husband and children of her own and she is not involved in raising the intended child. Yet, the new medical technology allows the surrogate to help an infertile couple without violating her own sexual, marital commitment to her husband. And the intended child is given a home by parents who are genetically linked to the intended child and accept responsibility for the newborn from the point of conception.

The precedents of שפחה and יבום evidence that such constructs evolve in response to changing variables, including shifting social mores. Surrogacy has grown dramatically over the past two decades, because it meets the needs of many couples. As a new social construct, related to but different from שפחה, it warrants an open-minded examination. It is not ostensibly forbidden by Jewish law, and, if anything, the past constructs suggest the possibility of new social forms as a last resort solution to female infertility. There are potential abuses in surrogacy, and some cases have already led to lawsuits. Before a couple opts to use a surrogate they should explore all their reproductive options and be aware of the serious costs and risks entailed by depending on a third party to their child's birth.

Legislation would help overcome potential abuses, such as exploitation of surrogates. The test of a new social construct is not whether it can thrive in the absence of legislation, but whether legislation can control abuse.[121] In the context of surrogacy the success of the surrogacy centers in screening potential surrogates and writing contracts with clearly stated expectations reveals the potential of the courts to make surrogacy workable for all parties. To ban a technique based on potential psychological harm may cause even greater psychological harm by its absence. Jewish ethical concerns including baby-selling, exploitation, family integrity, and contractual needs for a meeting of the mind are each balanced in favor of surrogacy upon close examination.

From a Jewish perspective, it would be wrong to outlaw a procedure that has the potential to help so many couples overcome infertility and which works smoothly in the overwhelming majority of cases. On balance, surrogacy offers the joy of parenthood, a profound benefit to society. Judaism, we see in this analysis, affirms couples who say as did the matriarch Sarah: "Through her I too shall bear a child."[122]

Conclusion

It is permissible to employ a surrogate, whether gestational or ovum, to overcome infertility and to serve as a surrogate. A man fulfills the mandate of procreation in having a child with a surrogate.

---

[121] Greco, p. 180.
[122] Gen. 16:2.

EH 1:3.1997c

SURROGATE PARENTING

Rabbi Aaron L. Mackler

This paper was approved by the CJLS on June 4, 1997, by a vote of six in favor, seven opposed, and seven abstentions (6-7-7). Voting in favor: Rabbis Arnold Goodman, Susan Grossman, Judah Kogen, Aaron L. Mackler, Paul Plotkin and James S. Rosen. Voting against: Rabbis Kassel Abelson, Elliot N. Dorff, Samuel Fraint, Shoshana Gelfand, Mayer Rabinowitz, Joel Roth, and Elie Kaplan Spitz. Abstaining: Rabbis Ben Zion Bergman, Jerome M. Epstein, Myron S. Geller, Vernon H. Kurtz, Alan B. Lucas, Avram Israel Reisner, and Joel E. Rembaum.

The Committee on Jewish Law and Standards of the Rabbinical Assembly provides guidance in matters of halakhah for the Conservative movement. The individual rabbi, however, is the authority for the interpretation and application of all matters of halakhah.

שאלה

May an infertile couple use a surrogate mother to gestate and give birth to a child? Does halakhah provide guidance regarding such cases?

תשובה

The practice of surrogate parenting touches on powerful and sometimes conflicting ethical values, and has the potential to dramatically affect the lives of all involved in cases in which it occurs. In the United States over the past decades the practice has been the topic of vigorous ethical, legislative and popular debate.[1] Sharply differing and powerfully expressed views may be found among Jewish thinkers as well.[2] In the Jewish context, central values include

---

[1] See, e.g. Rosemarie Tong, "Reproductive Technologies: Surrogacy," in *The Encyclopedia of Bioethics*, revised ed., ed. Warren T. Reich (New York: Macmillan, 1995), 4: pp. 2225-2229; American Fertility Society Ethics Committee, "Ethical Considerations of Assisted Reproductive Technologies," *Fertility and Sterility* 62 (1994): 67S-77S; New York State Task Force on Life and the Law, *Surrogate Parenting* (New York: New York State Task Force on Life and the Law, 1988); Larry Gostin, ed., *Surrogate Motherhood: Politics and Privacy* (Bloomington: Indiana University Press, 1990).

[2] See, for example, David M. Feldman, "The Case of Baby M," in *Jewish Values in Health and Medicine*, ed. Levi Meier (Lanham, MD: University Press of America, 1991), pp. 163-69; Fred Rosner, *Modern Medicine and Jewish Ethics*, 2d ed. (Hoboken, NJ: Ktav, 1991), pp. 113-16. Most authors do not develop an extensive halakhic argument about the practice of surrogacy; while many express misgivings, some suggest that the practice is halakhically permitted, and others that it should not occur. Immanuel Jakobovits, for example, argues: "To use another person as an 'incubator' and then take from her the child she carried and delivered for a fee is a revolting degradation of maternity and an affront to human dignity" (*Jewish Medical Ethics*, 2d ed. [New York: Bloch, 1975], p. 265). In a brief paper written for the Committee on Jewish Law and Standards in 1984, Rabbi David H. Lincoln states that "we should not deny couples this opportunity" of

those of procreation and raising children, respect for persons (כבוד הבריות), and appreciation for the human role as active but reverent partners with God in improving the world.[3]

In an extensive, thoughtful, and eloquent paper, "On the Use of Birth Surrogates," Rabbi Elie Kaplan Spitz argues in favor of surrogacy.[4] For Rabbi Spitz, the great benefit of providing a child to an infertile couple is decisive. Concerns with avoiding exploitation of the surrogate, and harm to children born of the procedure, are real but manageable. In my judgment, a different halakhic conclusion is required. I appreciate Rabbi Spitz's careful work and sincere intentions, and hope that my disagreements with him will be part of a מחלוקת לשם שמים, helping to clarify the best direction for development of halakhah.

I would agree with Rabbi Spitz that the real life experience of an infertile couple, for whom surrogacy could provide a child, bears great weight. I have argued elsewhere that such concerns, together with the Jewish tradition's valuing of procreation, would suffice to justify the use of in vitro fertilization in a variety of cases. Objections by some that reproductive technologies are artificial, as well as additional concerns, would be outweighed by the great good of enabling the birth of the child. In that paper I emphasized as well that the members of the couple are in no way required to use reproductive technologies, and that their value as persons does not depend on their ability to have a child, but rather is intrinsic, stemming from the creation of all humans in God's image (בצלם אלוקים).[5] In the case of surrogate parenting, however, precisely this value of respect for persons and human dignity is at risk. The real life experiences of all of the vulnerable persons involved, including the surrogate and especially her children, are weighty and must be considered. In light of these concerns, I argue, surrogacy cannot be recommended by halakhah and would be ill-advised in most cases.

My paper will focus on three particular concerns: a Jewish understanding of gestation and birth; the risk of harm and exploitation (עושק) and the appropriate halakhic response; and more specific questions raised by surrogacy agreements. A companion paper, "Maternal Identity and the Religious Status of Children Born to a Surrogate Mother," addresses that issue.

The Significance of Gestation and Birth

Gestation and birth are profoundly significant for halakhah, both on the basis of traditional halakhic texts, and because of broader ethical and theological concerns that I believe are important factors in the halakhic process. Appreciation of this significance is not necessarily decisive in determining the acceptability of surrogacy and related issues, but it is likely to influence both the articulation of halakhic guidelines and the application of these guidelines in particular cases.

---

using a surrogate, though he does not explicitly address halakhic issues other than those of artificial insemination. At the same time, he expresses significant concerns. "Are we not degrading her [the surrogate], however noble her intentions? Can we really allow a single woman to become pregnant? If married, there is something very distasteful in carrying another man's baby even if technically she has not committed adultery." In light of psychological and legal concerns, "great caution must therefore be exercised" (David Lincoln, "Surrogate Motherhood," *PCJLS 86-90*, pp. 3-6). The ensuing decade-and-a-half has provided more extensive experience with surrogacy and discussion of the issues involved, most prominently in connection with the Baby M trial. These developments now allow for a more extensive evaluation of surrogacy.

[3] See Aaron L. Mackler, "An Expanded Partnership with God? In Vitro Fertilization in Jewish Ethics," *Journal of Religious Ethics* 25 (1997): 79-81.

[4] Elie Spitz, "On the Use of Birth Surrogates," above, pp. 529-550.

[5] Mackler, "In Vitro Fertilization," above, pp 510-525.

As I argue elsewhere, halakhic sources indicate that maternal identity is determined primarily by gestation and birth. A woman who gives birth to a child is identified as that child's mother. Indeed, this represents the sole position authorized by the Committee on Jewish Law and Standards with regard to maternal identity.[6]

More generally, gestation and birth represent powerful experiences of intimacy and nurturing that have great significance. Parents' feelings of attachment at the birth of their children reflect not only awareness of genetic linkage, but also the lived experience of months of physical changes, observations, and care-giving, as well as the intense and miraculous event of birth. The mother's experience has included unique connections of biology combined with the conscious acceptance of risks and burdens, and emotional and intellectual responses of often surprising power. Perhaps for this reason, the Hebrew word for intense and other-regarding love, רחמים, is linked to the word for womb, רחם.

Accordingly, Jewish law and ethics would not agree that a "gestational surrogate" who gestates and gives birth to a child "essentially serves as an incubator," as Rabbi Spitz at one point suggests, nor would it agree to refer to her as a "tummy mummy."[7] It is not her tummy, but her womb, and with it her experience of biological connection and intense other-regarding care, that need to be acknowledged. According to halakhah, she simply is the mother of the child.

Such acknowledgment of the importance of gestation and birth has been reflected by non-Jewish as well as Jewish writers. Lawyer George Annas, for example, argues that in cases of dispute the relationship of gestational mother to the child should be recognized as primary, in part because of the extent of her biological and psychological investment in the child.[8] Rosemarie Tong notes a feminist objection to surrogacy, that "such arrangements privilege a possible relationship over an actual one, an abstract intention over concrete experience." Concerns are also expressed with treating persons and relationships as commodities.[9] As Rabbi Spitz notes, not all feminists agree in rejecting surrogacy, but Tong's feminist claims focusing on relationships and responsibilities resonate importantly with general Jewish values. While some thinkers have speculated that a woman's role of gestation and birth might be replaced by an artificial womb, others have speculated that with developments in genetic engineering, the role of sperm and eggs in conveying genetic information might be replaced, strengthening the claims of gestation as primary. Both sets of claims are speculative; the important point is to avoid an unwarranted assumption that genetics are somehow essential and gestation and birth somehow accidental to parental identity.[10]

---

[6] Mackler, "Maternal Identity and the Religious Status of Children Born to a Surrogate Mother," above, pp. 137-145; Mackler, "In Vitro Fertilization," above, pp. 510-525. There is no reason to speculate that the identification of the birth mother as mother in earlier sources is based on an assumption of a genetic link, unless one simply assumes or has established on other grounds that genetics should be primary. In fact, the few cases that reflect a divergence of gestation/birth and genetics support gestation and birth as primary. A central precedent is the case of a pregnant woman who converts: the child is Jewish because, while the ovum was originally from the woman when she was not Jewish, the woman's status at the time of birth determines maternity.

[7] Spitz, above, p. 531.

[8] George J. Annas, "Death Without Dignity for Commercial Surrogacy: The Case of Baby M," *Hastings Center Report* 18, no. 2 (1988): 23-24.

[9] Rosemarie Tong, "The Overdue Death of a Feminist Chameleon: Taking a Stand on Surrogacy Arrangements" in *The Ethics of Reproductive Technology*, ed. Kenneth D. Alpern (New York: Oxford University Press, 1992), pp. 285, 289, 291.

[10] Intuitively it might seem to some that gestation is a relatively straightforward process that science likely will develop ways to replace artificially, while the genetic material of the human genome is hopelessly complex and will elude scientists. On the other hand, the understanding of human genetics and the ability to synthe-

Potential Harms and Exploitation

While appreciation of the significance of birth and gestation will affect judgments on surrogacy, the central issues are the assessment of risks of harm and exploitation, and the proper halakhic response. Here my greatest concern is for children affected by the procedures, although concern to avoid harm for any of the vulnerable people who might be involved is warranted. There is a danger of treating children as commodities; in some extreme cases contracting/intended parents have sought to refuse custody of a child born with birth defects or of the undesired gender. The risk of this occurring, and less extreme dangers, are present in a broader range of cases.[11]

Another type of concern arises when the surrogate has other children, as in the case of the "typical" surrogate who is married and has two other children.[12] The potential for psychological harm for these children, as they see their mother go through pregnancy and give birth to a child who is given to others, is very real.[13] Another ethical concern to which halakhah would be sensitive is the interference of surrogacy with the

---

size genetic material have been progressing rapidly and at accelerating rates, while the capacity to nurture the developing human are only very slowly, if at all, moving later than the first week of embryonic development in vitro, and earlier than about week 23-24 of development for extremely premature infants (New York State Task Force on Life and the Law, *Fetal Extrauterine Survivability* [New York: New York State Task Force on Life and The Law, 1988]). More generally, speculation on future scientific progress is uncertain at best. Writing in 1957, Isaac Asimov was able to envision a world of interstellar space travel and human-like robots, in which most of the process of gestation and human development could be managed artificially, but in vitro fertilization remained elusive and fertilization itself could only take place in the body (*The Naked Sun* [New York: Doubleday, 1957]). Within a few decades, this apparently elusive element had in fact been achieved, while other developments remained distant.

[11] See, for example, the discussion of the Malahoff case, "Parenting Through Contract When No One Wants the Child," in Alpern, pp. 335-337; Angela R. Holder, "Surrogate Motherhood and the Best Interests of the Child," in Gostin, p. 79. In a Michigan surrogacy case, Patty Nowakowski unexpectedly became pregnant with twins. The contracting couple told her that they would not accept responsibility for a boy, and when a girl and a boy were born, they only took the girl home (New York State Department of Health, *The Business of Surrogate Parenting* [Albany: New York State Department of Health, 1992], p. 8). As Holder (p. 79) observes:

> In the usual situation of babies born with unexpected handicaps, parents may be shocked but they do not attempt to solve their problems by displacing custody onto anyone else. In the surrogate situation, however, the mother has doubtless attempted not to think of herself as the baby's "mother" or to become too attached, since she plans to surrender it for adoption. Thus it is certainly not surprising that, if a problem occurs, her response is, "Here, take it. I did what I was supposed to do, so give me my money." The father-by-contract, as well, having thought of the arrangement as placing an order for a baby, not surprisingly takes the position that there has been some sort of breach of warranty of quality and doesn't want the baby either. Regardless of obligation to support, the situation does not bode well for love and acceptance of the handicapped child.

[12] Spitz, above, p. 532.

[13] Evidence regarding this harm remains largely anecdotal, as does evidence about the benefits and harms of surrogacy in general. One example is provided by a surrogate mother named Sally, responding to Phyllis Chesler's question as to whether Sally's (other) children ask about Jason, the child in the surrogacy arrangement (Phyllis Chesler, *Sacred Bond: The Legacy of Baby M* [New York: Vintage, Random House, 1988], pp. 66-67).

> Yes. Quite often. My daughter Rebekah says that if she has a baby she'll never give it away. She's been asking me, "Did you really have to give Jason away?" It's on her mind a lot. It's on my son Matthew's mind, too, but he tries not to talk about it. I've begun to encourage them to talk about it.

Similarly, Kathleen King agreed to serve as a surrogate but came to feel attached to the child during pregnancy. She reports that after she surrendered the child one of her other children asked, "I heard you are giving my brother away. Are you going to give me away?" (New York State Department of Health, p. 7). While careful counseling would likely lessen the harm to the surrogate's other children, these children still would be exposed to the risk of significant harm, without their consent.

sexual relations of a (married) surrogate and her husband, and the potentially negative effect on their relationship more broadly.[14]

Additional concerns involve the potential of harm to and exploitation of the surrogate. One type of exploitation is that of coercion or unfair treatment by intended parents or surrogacy agencies. While relatively few surrogates have brought lawsuits, this says little either way about the existence of עושק. Victims of עושק are precisely those who are least likely to sue. Think, for example, of recent immigrants working in sweatshops, or oppressed agricultural workers. Victims of עושק not only lack financial resources, but tend to feel intimidated and unsure of their own self worth, and are unlikely to assert themselves against those whom they correctly perceive as more powerful. On the basis of available information, it is difficult to determine how many surrogates are satisfied, and how many suffer in silence.[15]

Other concerns are of the type that would be more prominent in Jewish law and ethics than in U.S. law, for example. An important precedent for Rabbi Spitz is the case of Sarah, who said of Hagar, "Through her I too shall bear a child." Appeals are also made more to general halakhic precedents of שפחה (handmaid/concubine) and יבום (levirate marriage).[16] All of these precedents are problematic for contemporary Jewish law and ethics. Over the centuries, Judaism has become increasingly sensitive to the demand not to use people. This stems from a number of factors, including the unfolding in Oral Torah of the significance of humans being created בצלם אלוקים, and the influence of Kantian ethics. Largely in response to these ethical concerns, halakhah has abolished (at least *de facto*) the institutions of שפחה and יבום, replacing the latter with חליצה. In light of such developments, Sarah's intention to have her child through another woman is troubling. Similarly, as Robert Gordis observes, the elimination of יבום represents "the dual process of extending the rights of women, on the one hand, and limiting the powers of men on the other."[17] Whatever the acceptability or excusability of these practices in the past, the development of halakhah reflects an understanding that it would be wrong for a person to use someone else in these ways in order to have a child. While Rabbi Spitz notes distinctions between יבום/שפחה and surrogacy, he appeals to these precedents precisely because of important common features, and these commonalities raise ethical problems.

As Rabbi Spitz rightly notes, the extent of harm and exploitation is unproven and uncertain. The difficult question then is how halakhah should respond to plausible but uncertain harms and exploitation, what might be termed ספק עושק. ספק עושק does not carry the same decisive power as ספק פקוח נפש (possible saving of or danger to life), but cannot be ignored. One instructive model is offered by the Ethics Committee of the American Fertility Society. This committee is composed of scientists and health care professionals involved in developing and providing assisted reproductive technologies, as well as others sympathetic with such practices. For this committee, however, the potential harms of surrogacy mandate great caution, if not rejection:

---

[14] I am grateful to Rabbi Susan Grossman for this observation.

[15] See Chesler for interviews with surrogates and accompanying discussion.

[16] Spitz, above, pp. 536-540, 550.

[17] Robert Gordis, *The Dynamics of Jewish Law* (Bloomington: Indiana University Press, 1990), pp. 150-53. Other developments in halakhah have increasingly supported the practice of adoption, and have in at least many aspects recognized adopting parents as the child's parents for halakhic purposes. See Rabbi Elliot N. Dorff, "Artificial Insemination, Egg Donation and Adoption," above, pp. 501-504; Rabbi Avram Israel Reisner, "On the Conversion of Adopted and Patrilineal Children," *PCJLS 86-90*, pp. 157-183.

The Committee continues not to recommend widespread clinical application of clinical surrogate motherhood at this time. Because of the legal risks, ethical concerns, and potential physical and psychological effects of surrogate motherhood, it would seem to be more problematic than most of the other reproductive technologies. . . .The Committee recommends that if surrogate motherhood is pursued, a number of unresolved issues need to be addressed in the research, [including] the psychological effects of the procedure on the surrogates, the couples, and the resulting children; the effects, if any, of bonding between the surrogate and the fetus in utero; . . .the effects on the surrogate's own family due to her participation in the process. . . .The Committee has serious ethical reservations about surrogacy that cannot be fully resolved until appropriate data are available for assessment of the risks and possible benefits of this alternative. In light of these reservations, some members of the Committee judged that surrogacy could not be ethically recommended. Others concluded that it could be cautiously recommended while research on the key issues continued.[18]

Deciding About Surrogacy and Surrogacy Agreements

Minimally, halakhah would share the "serious reservations" expressed by the American Fertility Society Ethics Committee and others. It also would be concerned with broader if less tangible dangers of the commodification of human persons and relationships. Surrogacy cannot be recommended by halakhah, and would be ill-advised in most cases.

In light of Rabbi Spitz's paper, however, I must admit that the question of whether the reservations are strong enough to support an absolute prohibition on surrogacy in all cases is less clear. If grounds to permit surrogacy are found in a particular case, at a minimum certain requirements would be clearly mandated by halakhah to protect the well-being, rights, and dignity of any children affected, and all other vulnerable persons, including the surrogate.

1. Couples contemplating the use of a surrogate mother should consider the halakhic and personal concerns involved, receive thorough counseling, and seriously investigate alternatives, including adoption. Either member of the couple would be fully justified in a decision not to proceed with surrogacy, and such refusal must be respected.

2. The surrogate mother, as gestational and birth mother, is halakhically recognized as the child's mother. She should have the right to contest the assumption of custody by the intended parents (one of whom would be halakhically recognized as the child's father). This right would be held whether the ovum originally came from the surrogate, the intended/social mother, or another woman. The exact parameters of this right are beyond the scope of this paper, and in practice would be determined by general civil law. Custody of the child, in these as in other cases, should be determined on the basis of the child's best interest, as required by Jewish ethical values as well as halakhic precedent.[19]

---

[18] American Fertility Society Ethics Committee, 76S-77S.

[19] See S.A. Even HaEzer 82:7, where Karo states that in case of divorce a child should stay with the mother until age six, and Isserles adds that this should only be the case when it serves the best interests of the child, which should be decisive. George Annas (23) supports the ruling of the New Jersey Supreme Court in the Baby M case that custody of children in surrogacy disputes should be decided according to the best interests

3. The gestational/birth mother should be protected from pressure to continue pregnancy when she judges abortion to be required to avoid serious threat to her health, and from pressure to abort when she judges continuation of the pregnancy to be consistent with her physical and psychological health.

4. Halakhah would discourage, if not prohibit, payments to a surrogate mother beyond reimbursement of expenses. Any money the surrogate receives cannot be contingent on her giving up custody of the child. For the surrogate to receive money if she gives over custody of the child would represent baby-selling, or minimally the selling and purchase of parental relationships, which are inconsistent with halakhah.

5. In the formulation of surrogacy agreements, and all actions taken with regard to surrogacy, greatest concern must be given to the well-being and rights of the child to be born of the procedure, as well as any other children who might be affected. Concern must be given to avoid exploitation of other vulnerable parties, including the surrogate, as well.

While these provisions represent the minimal requirement of Jewish law and ethics, they would be difficult to implement in commercial surrogacy. If these provisions are followed, surrogacy would likely be limited to cases in which all parties are well-intentioned and trust one another. Such a limitation would itself be appropriate.

A final note concerns the acceptability of a woman serving as surrogate mother, gestating and giving birth to a child to be raised by another couple. Minimally, all of the above requirements would apply. In addition, if a Jewish woman gives birth to a child, the child would be Jewish. As argued in this paper and my accompanying paper, and authorized by the Committee on Jewish Law and Standards, the birth mother's status would define the child's in all cases. Accordingly, allowing Jewish women to serve as surrogates entails either the birth of Jewish children who will be raised as non-Jews, or the surrogate's willingness to serve only for Jewish couples. Either option would be highly problematic. Unless this problem is explicitly and satisfactorily addressed, I do not see how halakhah can authorize Jewish women to serve as surrogates.[20] If this is the case, this provides an additional consideration against halakhically supporting surrogacy. To authorize Jews to use others as surrogates but not serve as surrogates would itself be problematic, as reflected in the Jewish tradition's commitment to דרכי שלום, the paths of peace.

Conclusion

Surrogacy cannot be halakhically recommended, and in at least most cases would be forbidden by Jewish law and ethics. Any exceptional cases in which surrogacy is accepted would need to meet specific requirements safeguarding the well-being, rights, and dignity of any children affected, and all other vulnerable persons, including the surrogate.[21]

---

of the child, and that the child should remain with the mother until permanent custody can be determined. In at least some situations, the surrogate mother's seeking of custody would be a morally appropriate course of action. David M. Feldman (163) comments that in the Baby M case, the judge should have thanked Mary Beth Whitehead "for reminding us of the special bond of attachment that a mother forms with her child; and he should have gratefully acknowledged her message that surrogacy as an option ought to be discouraged."

[20] While Rabbi Spitz, in earlier drafts of his paper, approved Jews serving as surrogates, his final draft as approved by the CJLS does not offer this permission.

[21] For their suggestions and thoughtful insights which have contributed greatly to this paper, I would like to thank Lorraine Newman Mackler, and members of the Committee on Jewish Law and Standards, including my fellow members of the Subcommittee on Bioethics: Rabbis Kassel Abelson, Elliot N. Dorff, Shoshana Gelfand, Avram Israel Reisner, Joel Roth, and Elie Kaplan Spitz.

EH 4.2000a

Mamzerut

Rabbi Elie Kaplan Spitz

This paper was approved by the CJLS on March 8, 2000, by a vote of fifteen in favor, three opposed and two abstaining (15-3-2). Voting in favor: Rabbis Kassel Abelson, Elliot N. Dorff, Paul Drazen, Jerome M. Epstein, Nechama D. Goldberg, Arnold M. Goodman, Susan Grossman, Judah Kogen, Aaron L. Mackler, Daniel S. Nevins, Paul Plotkin, Joel E. Rembaum, James S. Rosen, Elie Kaplan Spitz, and Gordon Tucker. Voting against: Rabbis Samuel Fraint, Mayer Rabinowitz and Joel Roth. Abstaining: Rabbis Vernon H. Kurtz and Avram Israel Reisner.

The Committee on Jewish Law and Standards of the Rabbinical Assembly provides guidance in matters of halakhah for the Conservative movement. The individual rabbi, however, is the authority for the interpretation and application of all matters of halakhah.

שאלה

Is mamzerut operative in our community?

תשובה

Why is this תשובה necessary? At first impression, the issue of mamzerut in the Conservative movement is settled. The Rabbinical Assembly Committee on Law and Standards has held on two occasions that "the institution of mamzerut is inoperative." This halakhically pivotal holding is contained in the minutes of the meeting of June 23, 1970, and was reaffirmed by the smaller Steering Committee on February 14, 1977. There is no record of the votes and only a sparse written discussion. No responsa on mamzerut were ever submitted. The lack of written analysis conformed to the workings of an earlier era of the Committee on Jewish Law and Standards.

Since 1985, a responsum is written prior to a CJLS vote. Responsa provide legal analysis and focal points of discussion. Such a written record serves to explain our rationale to our colleagues and to educate our larger constituency. The reasoning and decisions of the CJLS define who we are as a halakhic movement. There is a need to revisit mamzerut with a thorough analysis because this halakhic question goes to the core of how we as Conservative Jews address the clash between a Torah precept and moral sensibilities. The purpose of this responsum is to decide anew and to provide the underlying halakhic reasoning of our movement's stand on mamzerut.

Who is a Mamzer and What are the Consequences?

Torah Origins
Deut. 23:3 condemns the mamzer:

לא יבוא ממזר בקהל ה׳ גם דור עשירי לא יבא לו בקהל ה׳.

> A mamzer shall not enter into the congregation of the Lord; none of his descendants, even in the tenth generation, shall be admitted into the congregation of the Lord.

This is the only place in the Torah in which the term mamzer is used. Many of the concepts in this verse are unclear, eliciting a variety of questions: Who is a mamzer? What does it mean to be prohibited "from entering the community?" Is the ostracizing literally for ten generations? And why is the punishment for the mamzer so severe?

The Ambiguity of the Term "Mamzer"
The word mamzer appears in only one other place in the Tanakh, Zechariah (9:6):

וישב ממזר באשדוד והכרתי גאון פלישתים.

> And a mamzer shall dwell in Ashdod, and I will cut off the pride of the Philistines.

The obscurity of the term led to a variety of interpretations. The Septuagint translated mamzer as "offspring of a harlot."[1] Abraham Geiger attributed the origin of the word to מעם זר, "belonging to a foreign nation," which he understood as a condemnation of progeny of a non-Jewish father and a Jewish mother.[2] Both the Jerusalem and Babylonian Talmuds contain Rabbi Abahu's definition of mamzer as a conjugation of מום זר, a "strange blemish," suggesting a defect in a newborn's pedigree.[3]

The Rabbinic Definition
By the first half of the second century there was a consensus that a mamzer was the offspring of a forbidden union, but the Rabbis disagreed in defining the nature of the forbidden union. The Mishnah of Yevamot 4:13 reads:

> Who is a mamzer? "[The offspring of] any union of near relationship to which the term 'he shall not come' applies." These are the words of R. Akiva. Simeon of Teman says, "[the offspring of] any union for which the penalty is excision at the hand of Heaven (כרת)." And the halakhah is in accord with his words. R. Joshua says, "[the offspring of] any union for which the penalty is death at the hand of the Court." Said R. Simeon b. Azzai: "I found a family register in Jerusalem, in which it was recorded: 'So-and-so

---

[1] The reading is a result of changing the final ר into a ן. Louis Jacob's "The Problem of the Mamzer," in *A Tree of Life* (Oxford, England: Alden Press, 1984), p. 257.

[2] *Urschrift and Übersetzungen der Bibel* (Breslau, 1857), pp. 54-55, cited in David Novak's "The Conflict between Halakhah and Ethics: The Case of Mamzerut," *Halakhah in a Theological Dimension* (Chico, CA: Scholar's Press, 1985), p. 13. Novak relates that this early definition of mamzerut changed with Ezra's promulgation of a shift to the mother as the source of religious identity.

[3] J. Kiddushin 3:12, 64c, attributed to Abahu. The same idea is presented anonymously in Yevamot 76b.

is a mamzer, because he is the offspring of a married woman,' which confirms the words of R. Joshua."[4]

The Mishnah states that the halakhah follows the opinion of Simeon of Teman. His criteria of sexual acts prohibited by כרת became the accepted definition of mamzer in the post-Mishnaic period and the rule is treated as a given in an anonymous mishnah.[5] In addition, Rabbi Joshua's holding that the offspring of sexual acts that warrant the death penalty also became accepted law. By the third century,[6] a mamzer was defined as the issue of a couple whose sexual relationship is forbidden according to the Torah and is punishable by כרת or death. Consequently, the definition of mamzer as contained in the Codes[7] encompasses the following three scenarios:

1. A child born as a result of incest, namely where the union is prohibited by Jewish law (עריות) subject to the punishment of excision כרת or the death penalty;[8]

2. A child born of the sexual intercourse of a married woman with a man other than her lawful husband;[9] and,

3. The child of a woman who, acting on the assumption that her husband had died, remarried and had a child from the second husband. When her first husband is proved to be alive, the child from the second marriage is a mamzer.

The Rabbis applied the Biblical verse to both men and women.[10] Although Simeon of Teman defined mamzer as the offspring of any union punishable by כרת, which would include sex with a menstruant woman, the Gemara exempted such a child as belonging to the category of mamzerut.[11] Finally, a mamzer is not properly translated as a "bastard," which in English is an illegitimate child, a category that does not exist in rabbinic Judaism.

What Does it Mean to be Kept Out of the "Assembly Of The Lord"?

On the surface, the Biblical phrase might restrict access to the Temple,[12] but the Rabbis understood the phrase more broadly due to the context of the surrounding verses.[13] The Rabbis interpreted to be "kept out of the assembly of the Lord" as prohibiting the marriage between a mamzer and an Israelite. A mamzer could thereby only marry another

---

[4] The content of this mishnah is presented in an expanded form in Sifre Deuteronomy 248.

[5] Kiddushin 3:12.

[6] In Yevamot 45a, the third century Amora, Rabbi Dimi speaks in the names of Rabbi Isaac ben Aboudimi and Yehudah HaNasi as saying that "if an idolator or slave had intercourse with the daughter of an Israelite, the child born of such a union is a mamzer."

[7] S.A. Even HaEzer 4:13.

[8] Kiddushin 3:12; Yevamot 4:13. The categories of incest are listed in Lev. 18:6-18, 20.

[9] Yevamot 45b; Maimonides, M.T. Issurei Bi'ah 15:1; Tur and Beit Yosef, Even HaEzer 4; S.A. Even HaEzer 4:13.

[10] Yevamot 4:13; Sifre Deuteronomy 248.

[11] Yevamot 49a-b.

[12] As used in the following Biblical parallelism in Lam. 1:10 – כי ראתה גוים באו מקדשה אשר צויתה לא יבאו בקהל לך – "for she has seen that heathen nations invade her sanctuary, those whom you did forbid to enter into your congregation."

[13] Kiddushin 4:1; also see Yevamot 8:2, 76a, 78a; Kiddushin 72b.

mamzer,[14] a convert or a freed slave,[15] or a non-Jew.[16] If a mamzer married an ordinary Jew, the penalty was lashes and immediate divorce,[17] and their offspring were mamzerim.[18]

Except for the prohibitions of marriage, a mamzer was considered a full member of the Jewish community and was required to carry out all religious duties, including procreation. A mamzer was deemed a son and brother in respect to rules of inheritance, levirate marriage, and conduct towards parents.[19] His birth released his father's wife from the obligation of levirate marriage and חליצה. The mamzer was eligible to hold any public office, including service as a civil judge[20] and even theoretically becoming a king.[21] The Sages comment that a mamzer could achieve the status of a scholar, who took precedence over an ignorant High Priest.[22]

And yet, there was also ambivalence as to the full participation of mamzerim in communal life. The Mishnah in Soferim (1:13) says that some hold that a Torah scroll written by a mamzer is unfit for use in the synagogue.[23] Rabbi Moses Sofer (1762-1839) wrote that although a mamzer may receive ordination as a rabbi, a community should not appoint a mamzer as its rabbi.[24] Even more amazing and cruel is the ruling of Ismael ha-Kohen of Modena (Italy, 1723-1811), who permitted the branding of a child's forehead with the word mamzer, despite the rabbinic prohibition of tattoos, in order to prevent a violation of the biblical prohibition of marrying a mamzer. The twentieth century Munkacser Rav, Zevi Hirsch Shapira of Czechoslovakia, mentioned in a responsum the extreme measure of tattooing the mamzer's forehead and approved of it in theory.[25]

What Does the Torah Mean by an Exclusion for "Ten Generations?"

The Talmud understands "ten generations" as meaning forever.[26] Although the child of a mamzer and another Jew is considered a mamzer,[27] the rule allows for a loophole. The child

---

[14] Yevamot 45b; Kiddushin 69a; 74a; Maimonides, M.T. Issurei Bi'ah 15:33; S.A. Even HaEzer 4:24.

[15] Kiddushin 73a, note Rashi there; Maimonides, M.T. Issurei Bi'ah 15:7; S.A. Even HaEzer 4:22.

[16] "Although it is generally prohibited for a freeman [even a freeman who is prohibited from marrying into the congregation] to cohabit with a Canaanite slavewoman, a mamzer is permitted to do so; see Kiddushin 69a. See Tosaphos below 79a ד"ה ונתינים for a reason as to why a mamzer is different in this regard." B. Yevamot 78a, the Schottenstein Edition (New York: Artscroll/Mesorah, 1999), n. 30.

[17] The Talmud records that the penalty for falsely calling someone a mamzer is lashes (Kiddushin 28a). The Tosafot comments, the penalty for the false accusation is commensurate with the penalty for a mamzer marrying a Jew. This rule gets codified in Isserles' S.A. Hoshen Mishpat 7:2. The requirement of an immediate divorce is stated in S.A. Even HaEzer 4:18; 22:24; 154:20.

[18] J. Kiddushin 3:12, 64a; Yevamot 78b.

[19] Yevamot 22a; Maimonides, M.T. Nahalot 1:7; S.A. Hoshen Mishpat 276:6.

[20] Sanhedrin 32b; Kiddushin 76a. Maimonides holds that this applies even if all three judges were mamzerim – M.T. Sanhedrin 2:9; also S.A. Hoshen Mishpat 7:2.

[21] Tosafot to Yevamot 45b comments that a mamzer remains "thy brother," which satisfies the requirement of Deut. 17:15 – "From among your brethren shall you set a king over you."

[22] Horayot 3:8; 13a. Neither the Mishnah, nor the Talmud's explication, define the term "takes precedence" in this specific case. The preceding Mishnah used the term "take precedence" to signify that the person would be saved first from danger; it is used in other mishnayot to refer to which has priority in terms of recognition.

[23] See S.A. Yoreh De'ah 281:4.

[24] Hatam Sofer, Even HaEzer pt. 2, no. 94.

[25] *Darkhey Teshuvah* 190:1, cited in Jacobs, "The Problem of the Mamzer," p. 265.

[26] Yevamot 8:3. This understanding is based on a גזרה שווה, an association of like words here and in the laws against Amonites and Moabites – Sifre Deuteronomy, Ki Tetze, sec. 249.

[27] Kiddushin 67a.

of a male mamzer and a non-Jew is born a non-Jew, who is therefore not a mamzer[28] and may convert to Judaism.

The Ethical Problem

A child is born a marital pariah due to no fault of his or her own, but rather for the sins of his or her parent. The unfair anguish inflicted by this halakhah is already voiced in Midrash Vayikra Rabbah as follows:

> "And I returned and considered all the oppressions that were done under the sun; and behold the tears of those that were oppressed, and they had no comforter; and on the side of their oppressor there was power, but they had no comforter (Eccles. 4:1)."
>
> Daniel (Hanina) the Tailor interpreted this verse: "all the oppressions," these are the mamzerim. . . .Their mothers committed a sin and these humiliated ones are removed?! This one's father had illicit sexual relations — What did he [the child] do? Why should it make a difference for him?
>
> "They had no comforter," but "from the hand of their persecutors there is strength," this is the Great Assembly of Israel which comes against them with the power of the Torah and removes them based on "no mamzer shall enter the congregation of the Lord (Deut. 23:3)." Thus, God says, "I have to comfort them," because in this world they are refuse (פסולת), but in the Messianic Age (לעתיד לבוא). . .they are pure gold.[29]

Daniel the Tailor's sympathy for the mamzer is reflected in a legal debate over whether the mamzer will be purified in the Messianic era and be permitted to marry freely. Rabbi Meir said no and Rabbi Jose said yes.[30] The Jerusalem and Babylonian Talmuds are split as to whose opinion is correct. The former holds by Rabbi Meir and the latter by Rabbi Jose, with both citing the same Rabbi Joseph for concurrence![31] This debate reflects an ongoing split between those who interpreted scripture as literal and eternally binding regardless of an apparent moral grievance and those who were troubled by the moral implications and were willing to consider a promise of change, even if it had to wait for the Messianic era.

Daniel the Tailor's sympathy for the mamzer is linked to a Torah value emphasized by the prophets. The Torah says, "The fathers shall not be put to death for the [sins of their] children, nor children for [the sins of their parents]; every person shall be put to death for his [or her] sin."[32] At the same time there is a second strand in Torah, at least on the literal level, which deals harshly with innocent children. We are told that God remembers wrongdoing until the third or fourth generation.[33] The Moabites, the Torah declares, can never enter the people of Israel.[34] We are commanded to wipe out the Amalekites in every

---

[28] Kiddushin 3:12.

[29] Midrash Vayikrah Rabbah 32:8; and in a shorter version, Ecclesiastes Rabbah 4:1.

[30] T. Kiddushin 5:4, ed. Zuckermandel, p. 342 — cited by Louis Jacobs, "The Problem of the Mamzer," p. 267.

[31] J. Kiddushin 313m, 64d and B. Kiddushin 72b.

[32] Deut. 24:16.

[33] Exod. 20:5 and 34:7; Num. 14:18.

[34] Deut. 23:4-8; Neh. 13:1.

generation, because of what their ancestors did to us.[35] And there is the law of mamzerut, which would keep the child of an illicit relationship outside the community.[36]

In the later Biblical writings the idea of protecting innocent children from the sins of their parents is emphasized. In the words of Ezekiel (18: 1-4; 18-19):

> The word of the Lord came to me: What do you mean by quoting this proverb upon the soil of Israel, "Parents eat sour grapes and their children's teeth are blunted"?[37] As I live — declares the Lord God — this proverb shall no longer be current among you in Israel. Consider all lives are Mine; the life of the parent and the life of the child are both Mine. The person who sins, only he shall die. . . .To be sure, his father, because he practiced fraud, robbed his brother, and acted wickedly among his kin, did die for his iniquity; and now you ask, 'Why has not the son shared the burden of his father's guilt?' But the son has done what is right and just, and has carefully kept all My laws: he shall live!

In Ketuvim we find a softening of the literal reading of the prohibition of future generations of Moab marrying an Israelite.[38] Ruth, the Moabitess, marries Boaz, an Israelite.[39] Even more remarkable, we read in the postscript to Ruth that her husband's ancestor Peretz was born from the union of Judah and Tamar. Peretz is ostensibly a mamzer, because Tamar was betrothed to Judah's third son, Shelah, according to the mandate of levirate marriage. Tamar's bethrothed status explains Judah's initial outraged response on hearing of Tamar's pregnancy.[40] He condemned her to death by burning. Nonetheless, not only are the offsprings of Peretz, and Tamar and Boaz, not barred from the people of Israel, among their descendants is King David, and his descendant is none other than the Messiah![41]

Protecting children from suffering due to no fault of their own seems to conflict with the thrice-repeated Biblical statement that God remembers the sins of fathers for three or four generations.[42] Once again, rabbis in the Talmud,[43] midrash,[44] and many classic commentators,[45] rejected the literal reading of the verses and, like Ezekiel, stated that God only punishes children if they acted wrongfully themselves, thereby imitating their sinful parents.

The rule of mamzerut conflicts with the evolving moral challenge that each person is to be punished for his or her own acts. In the words of Louis Jacobs, "Even though the law does not necessarily see it as a penalty, the fact remains that it is a disability of the most

---

[35] Exod. 17:14; Deut. 25:19.

[36] Deut. 23:3.

[37] This folk expression is also condemned in Jer. 31:29 and Ezek. 18:2.

[38] Deut. 23:4-8; Neh. 13:1.

[39] The mishnah and Talmud parse the Torah prohibition as a restriction only on the marriage of male Moabites; see Yevamot 76b-77a.

[40] Gen. 39:24.

[41] Ruth 4:18-22.

[42] Exod. 20:5 and 34:7; Num. 14:18.

[43] Sanhedrin 27b.

[44] Mekhilta BaHodesh 6: "This only applies to those sons who themselves are wicked like their fathers." Also see Tosefta Yoma 5:13 on Exod. 34:7, ed. Zuckermandel: "A person sins once, twice, three times and is forgiven, as it says, 'forgiving iniquity, transgression, and sin' — three times, but thereafter God no longer remits punishment."

[45] Rashi, Sforno, and Ramban.

serious nature, intolerable within a legal system that prides itself on its passion for justice."[46] There is an additional moral problem with mamzerut as understood by the Rabbis. It deprecates the status of converts by permitting a mamzer to marry a convert, but not a native born Jew.[47] This conflicts with the moral value stated in the Talmud that a person is not to be reminded that he or she is a convert, lest it cause embarrassment (אונאת הגר).[48]

In recent years, the numbers of people who qualify as mamzerim have proliferated. In America, there are many who are married by a rabbi, receive a civil divorce but no *get*, and remarry a Jew — either with a Justice of the Peace or a Reform or Reconstructionist rabbi. The children of the subsequent marriage are technically mamzerim, although rarely was it the intent of the parents to knowingly violate the religious law.

In response to the halakhic problem of many Jews remarrying without a *get*, Rabbi Moshe Feinstein ruled that non-Orthodox weddings were not binding.[49] This solved the mamzerut question for the Orthodox. It only underscores our problem as a Conservative movement. We recognize as religiously binding the marriages between Jews when performed according to halakhic standards regardless of our colleagues' denomination. When those marriages end in civil divorce and no *get* is issued, a subsequent marriage poses the problem of mamzerut.

In light of the State of Israel's ingathering of Jews, there is an increased array of potential mamzerim. Rabbi Seymour Siegel was prescient when he wrote close to twenty years ago:

> The imposition of this norm causes untold difficulties, especially in the absorption of groups of Jews who have been removed from the main body of Israel, such as [India's] Bene Israel and the [Ethiopian] Falashas. As these groups have not been instructed in the specifics of religious divorce laws, they are presumed to include mamzerim within their numbers. The problem of mamzerut is bound to be exacerbated when large scale immigration occurs from the communist-bloc countries. Many women, it is to be assumed, married without religious divorces and therefore technically gave birth to mamzerim.[50]

Consequently, in the words of Rabbi Louis Jacobs, "There is a frightening proliferation of technical mamzerim on a scale that is completely unknown or even imagined in the classical period of the halakhah. In addition, there is the creation of a caste of untouchables, which further divide the Jewish community."[51] The risks are more than theoretical. The following are two cases from recent decades.

The Oshry Case

Rabbi Ephraim Oshry, a leading posek on the Holocaust and its aftermath, records in his collection of responsa the following case:[52] A young rabbi came to him for halakhic guid-

---

[46] Jacobs, p. 265.

[47] Kiddushin 73a and see Rashi there; Maimonides, M.T. Issurei Bi'ah 15:7; S.A. Even HaEzer 4:22.

[48] Bava Metziah 58b.

[49] משה פינשטיין, "בקידושי רעפאמער," ספר אגרות משה, אבן העזר, חלק ג, סימן כה, דף תמז (1970). Although this תשובה is written about the halakhically inoperative quality of Reform weddings, Orthodox rabbis have also applied the holding to Conservative rabbis.

[50] Seymour Siegel's "Ethics and the Halakhah," *Conservative Judaism and Jewish Law* (New York: Rabbinical Assembly, 1977), p. 129.

[51] Jacobs at p. 271.

[52] אפרים אשרי, שאלות ותשובות ממעקים, חלק ג, סימן ט, דף עג (Brooklyn, NY: Modern Linotype, 1959). An English translation, "The Case of the Mamzer Rabbi," is found in Ephraim Oshry's *Responsa from the Holocaust* (New York: Judaica Press, 1989), pp. 190-193.

ance. The young man's mother had married before the Holocaust. Her husband was taken away by the Nazis and did not return after the war. She remarried and had a son, who became a rabbi. Decades after the war, the woman's first husband found "his wife." He was outraged that she had remarried and in anger, he publicized that her son, the rabbi, was a mamzer. The son, who lived in Australia and was married with several children, wrote the famous posek for guidance.

Rabbi Oshry examined the responsa literature and with a confession of pain concluded that the young man was, unfortunately, a mamzer. He advised that the man should cease to be a rabbi so as not to profane the Divine Name (חילול ה') and implied that, as a mamzer, he should not be married to a Jewess.

Goren's Langer Case

The most publicized case of mamzerut in recent decades was the predicament of the Langer children.[53] The background was as follows. In August, 1951, Avraham Borokovsky, a convert, appeared with his wife Chava Borokovsky-Langer, before a bet din in Tel Aviv and applied for a religious divorce. Although the couple had lived in Israel for close to twenty years, they had not lived together for many years. The religious court learned that in the intervening years, Chava had married a second man, Otto Langer, and had done so by lying about her marriage status to the rabbi who performed the second marriage. Chava and Otto Langer had two children, Chanoch and Miriam. The bet din of Tel Aviv granted Avraham and Chava Borkovsky a divorce in November, 1955 and declared that Chanoch and Miriam Langer were mamzerim.

In May, 1966, Chanoch Langer applied to marry, which began a series of hearings and remands. The bet din of Petach Tikvah in 1967 held that Chanoch's status as a mamzer remained unchanged and he could not marry his Jewish fiancee. The Supreme Religious Court affirmed the decree in 1970. The case received a great deal of coverage in the Israeli and Jewish press. It was decried as a travesty of justice that a native Israeli, a man who had a bar mitzvah and had served in the Israeli army, should be prohibited from marrying a Jew, because of the misdeed of his mother.

On November 19, 1972, then-chief Ashkenazic rabbi Shlomo Goren issued a ruling in his own name and in the name of eight other rabbis, whose names he refused to reveal, permitting the Langers to marry. He justified his reversal of the earlier courts on the basis of new evidence that Avraham Borokovsky was an insincere convert, which meant that his Jewish marriage was nullified *ab initio* and hence the children were in no way tainted.

Jewish legal authorities protested Goren's finding because of his violation of normal halakhic procedure. Among the irregularities were the following:

- A. Goren failed to give Borokovsky the opportunity to refute the charge that he had renounced his conversion to Judaism by having reverted to Christianity. In fact, there was much evidence that he had conducted himself as a practicing Jew.
- B. When there is "new evidence," the normal procedure is to remand the case to the original bet din, which was not done here.
- C. Goren refused to reveal the names of the other rabbis who issued the decree removing the stigma of mamzerut from the Langer children.

---

[53] An analysis of the Langer case is presented in J. David Bleich's *Contemporary Halakhic Problems* (New York: Ktav, 1977), pp. 167-176.

The Langer case reveals that there are many rabbis who feel bound by the law of mamzerut and are willing to enforce it. Regrettably, the court system in Israel continues to keep lists of people who are labeled mamzerim. Moshe Zemer, a prominent Israeli legal scholar writes: "The Israel religious councils and official rabbinate use a central computer bank to trace the descendants of persons accused of alleged adultery or incest a generation ago or more."[54] There are many Jews in our day who are technically mamzerim and for some there are real consequences. Before discussing how this injustice can be corrected let us look at the reasons offered for the law and the attempts to ameliorate its impact.

The Rationales of Mamzerut

There are two reasons offered for the law of mamzerut: deterrence against illicit sex and the need to maintain the purity of Israel.

Deterrence Against Promiscuity

Jewish tradition emphasizes the sanctity of the marriage bond. Adultery is the seventh of the Ten Commandments[55] and the penalty for violation of this command is death.[56] The following midrash emphasizes that marital faithfulness preserved the Israelites:

> "A closed garden":[57] Rabbi Pineas said in the name of Rabbi Hiyya bar Abba that because Israel protected themselves in Egypt from sexual immorality (מן הערוה), they were redeemed from Egypt... because there was none among them who was promiscuous (פרוץ ערוה), except, you should know, one woman, and Scripture publicized her, that is, "Shlomit bat Dibry of the tribe of Dan...,"[58] "bat Dibry" — R. Isaac said that she brought pestilence on her son.[59]

Two things are learned of the Rabbis' perception of the generation who received Torah: adultery was rare, and when it occurred there were severe consequences for the children. The threat of punishment on children was viewed as a powerful and successful deterrent against sexual violations. In a later generation, Maimonides (Spain-Egypt, 1135-1204) wrote:

> Why is a mamzer penalized because of the immoral behavior of his parents? This was meant to be a deterrent against immoral behavior. In other words, the man and woman who have illicit relations should realize that because of their immorality their children will be penalized by society and severely limited in their choice of a mate.[60]

In the times of the Torah, the Talmudic period, and even the Middle Ages, mamzerut may have served as a check against improper sexual relations. In those times people lived in a closed society, and the only form of marriage was religious. In our open society, mamzerut is no longer a deterrent.

---

[54] Moshe Zemer, "Purifying Mamzerim," *Jewish Law Journal* 10 (1992): 99.
[55] Exod. 20:13; Deut. 5:17.
[56] Lev. 20:10.
[57] Song of Songs 4:12.
[58] Lev. 24:10.
[59] Vayikra Rabbah 32:5; also see J. Kiddushin 1:4; Sifra, Kedoshim, 90d; Yevamot 37b.
[60] Maimonides, *Sefer HaMitzvot*, lo ta'aseh 354; see also M.T. Issurei Bi'ah, ch. 15.

Although the original intent of mamzerut may have been to limit adultery, the Rabbis, acting out of sympathy for the innocent victims, almost eliminated its application to infidelity. The Talmud says that a child of a married woman, whose husband was absent during the gestation, is presumed to be the lawful father.[61] Toward that end, Rabbi Tosfaah, a seventh-generation Babylonian Amora, held that a woman, whose husband was away on travel, was able to carry a fetus for a full twelve months.[62] This ruling, a clear violation of medical experience, was maintained by later codes, including Maimonides' Mishneh Torah.[63]

An accuser had the burden of proof of mamzerut,[64] which required two witnesses to substantiate the charge. Even if adultery was demonstrated, the presumption remained that the lawful husband had conceived the child. On the general principle that a person's confession of his or her turpitude is not admissible as legal testimony the wife and mother could not by her assertion alone classify her child as a mamzer. It was and is the rare case of a husband willing and able to demonstrate with witnesses that his wife's offspring are not his own. In our time the mother's husband might even demonstrate the absence of paternity for purposes of mamzerut by DNA testing, a possibility that has not yet been addressed in the responsa literature.

In our day, mamzerim are overwhelmingly created as a result of Jewish ignorance or apathy, and not promiscuity. Mamzerim are technically produced when a woman has children with a subsequent husband, having failed to obtain a *get* after her first marriage. In contrast to an earlier day, couples in our time are married civilly by a Justice of the Peace or by rabbis who are self-defined as non-halakhic. Rather than flaunting immorality, such couples are making a commitment to monogamy. If the rationale of mamzerut was to prevent promiscuity, it no longer does so, and, if anything, simply punishes the children of the ignorant who are committed to marriage.

Communal Purity

Communal purity is not mentioned in the Talmud as a justification for mamzerut, but it is advanced among medieval and even contemporary commentators. The clearest expression is found in *Sefer HaHinukh* (anonymous, sixteenth century):

> The very conception of the mamzer is exceedingly evil, having been brought about in impurity, abominable intention, and counsel of sin, and there is no doubt that the nature of the parent is concealed in the child [כי טבע האב צפון בבן]. Consequently, God, in His love, has kept the holy people away from him [the mamzer] just as He has separated us and kept us far away from all that is evil.[65]

---

[61] Sotah 27a.

[62] Yevamot 80b.

[63] M.T. Issurei Bi'ah 15:19 – Maimonides adds that the period is not longer than twelve months. Halakhot Gedolot does not accept the twelve month limitation. The S.A. (Even HaEzer 4:14) records both the twelve month limitation and its rejection and holds that since the authorities differ, a child born more than twelve months after the husband's departure from his wife is considered a "doubtful mamzer." Louis Jacobs cites a mystical, magical explanation for how a woman could get pregnant with her husband's child during her husband's apparent absence. The medieval explanation is that the man could have returned swiftly and secretly through the use of the "divine name." Louis Jacobs, pp. 263-264, citing Rosh to Kiddushin, beginning of ch. 4 and Tosafot to Kiddushin 73a, s.v. מאי איכא.

[64] Kiddushin 76b; see also Bava Kamma 35b.

[65] *Sefer HaHinukh*, mitzvah 560.

Ben Zion Uziel, a prominent, contemporary Israeli rabbi, asserts that the concept of communal purity is the underpinning of mamzerut. He writes, "A mamzer's base status should not be seen as a punishment for the sin of his parents, but is rather quasi-physical."[66] Leading medieval rabbis express a link between mamzerut and communal purity. Although Maimonides (Spain-Egypt, 1135-1204) explains the reason for mamzerut as deterrence, he also writes, "The noble people of Israel has to be protected from any adulteration of its purity."[67] Nahmanides (Spain-Israel, 1194-1270) develops this idea:

> The Jew attaches great importance to the strength of the family unit. It is inconceivable to him that an element which might reduce the strength of this valuable asset be admitted into the family. No chances must be taken because too much is at stake.[68]

"Communal purity" rings false in our day. We are not a "pure people." Although Jews may share a greater likelihood of certain genes, such as Tay-Sachs, there is no gene unique to Jews. In regard to breeding, we do not possess a record of pedigree, referred to in some classical sources as *Megillat Yehusin*. In fact, mamzerim have mixed into the community for generations. Already, the Talmud records, "A family that has assimilated [into the community] may remain assimilated."[69] Similarly, Rabbi Eliezer ben Hyrcanus (Palestine, 40-120 C.E.), who is normally known for his stringency, states in the Talmud that if he were asked to rule on the genealogy of a third generation female mamzer, he would declare her pure.[70] The principle of refraining from identifying mamzerim in the community was codified and explained by Moses Isserles (Poland, d. 1572) in his gloss to the Shulhan Arukh:

> It is forbidden to reveal the blemish of a family that is not public knowledge. If the family has been assimilated, it should be left with its presumption of validity, for all families are valid in the Messianic age.[71]

In sum, we, as a people, are mixed with mamzerim. We cannot justify punishing people for the sins of their parents because of the false assertion of purity. Due to the hardship imposed by the label mamzer, rabbis of previous generations sought to narrow the category.

Partial Solutions

The following are a variety of proposed solutions to mamzerut, each of which is fundamentally incomplete. Implicit in all these attempts is the desire to remove the stigma of mamzerut. The survey demonstrates that past generations were stymied by the challenge of changing this Biblical law.

---

[66] Mishpetei Uziel 4, Even HaEzer, no. 3.

[67] Maimonides, *Guide for the Perplexed* 3:49.

[68] Nahmanides' commentary to Deut. 23:3.

[69] Kiddushin 71a-b.

[70] Yevamot 78b. A justification for not examining a person's lineage for mamzerut was the claim in the Talmud Yerushalmi that a mamzer does not live for more than thirty days, which meant that mamzerim were not available for marriage. A variation of this assertion is debated in the Babylonian Talmud, which distinguished between a "completely unknown" mamzer, who some say does not survive at all, and a "somewhat known" mamzer, whose taint is allowed to continue for only three generations, attributed to Rabbi Eliezer (Yevamot 78b).

[71] S.A. Even HaEzer 2:5.

Purification – Rabbi Tarfon's Approach

The Talmud offers a legal loophole to give at least a male mamzer's children entry back into community:

> Rabbi Tarfon says that male mamzerim can be purified. How? A mamzer marries a non-Jewish slave woman (שפחה) and the child born of this union will thus have the status of a slave. Let him then free him (שחררו) and his son will have the status of a free Jew (בן חורין). Rabbi Eliezer says that he will have the status of a slave who is a mamzer.[72]

Both Talmuds and the codes hold according to Rabbi Tarfon.[73] Simultaneously, there is a debate in the Talmud whether such a marriage is permitted at the outset (לכתחילה) or only after the fact (בדיעבד). Maimonides rules that such marriages should be permitted at the outset, because of the need to rectify the status of the children.[74]

Whether Rabbi Tarfon's solution is applicable in our own day is largely a theoretical question, because we live in a monogamous society and we do not have a legal category of concubines. In a Yeshiva law-review-like article written in 1994, Rabbi David Katz examines the contemporary value of Rabbi Tarfon's proposal as a solution to mamzerut.[75] Katz ruled out intermarriage as a Jewish option and focused instead on whether a woman in our day could become a concubine (שפחה). After thirty-one pages of analysis, he concluded that it is "a tenuous option for our day." The major obstacle, he said, was that our society does not permit any forms of slavery.[76] As Conservative Jews, we also reject the category of concubine relationships and the demotion of a woman to such a lower status.

Rabbi Tarfon's "solution" fails to resolve the mamzerut dilemma for another reason, too. Tarfon's recommendation only purifies the offspring of a mamzer (man) and not a mamzeret (woman). He encourages a man to marry a non-Jew, because the children of a non-Jewish woman are non-Jews, who may then convert and be considered as Jews, untainted by their father's status. This "remedy" fails for a mamzeret, because her child is Jewish and therefore a mamzer. In addition, his approach would restrict Jews to non-Jews, a particularly troublesome alternative for our day when the greatest challenge to the Jewish community is intermarriage.

Nullification by the Maharsham's Legal Loophole

There is another legal loophole that in theory enables nullification of marriages that were performed legally, which would provide a possible solution for a child of an illegitimate second marriage. This theoretical construct begins with a husband's right, as described in the Talmud,[77] to appoint a proxy to deliver a *get*. The husband would remain married if he annulled the proxy at any point prior to the delivery of the *get*. Rabban Gamaliel feared that the proxy might unknowingly give an invalid *get* to an

---

[72] Kiddushin 3:13.

[73] Kiddushin 67a and J. Kiddushin 3.15/64d/bottom, which quotes Rabbi Yehudah in the name of Shmuel holding that the law is according to the opinion of Rabbi Tarfon. Also, see Rashi on Kiddushin 67a; Maimonides, M.T. Issurei Bi'ah 15:3; Tur and Beit Yosef Even HaEzer 4; S.A. Even HaEzer 4:20.

[74] M.T. Hilkhot Issurei Be'ah 15:4; also see Karo's S.A. 4:20.

[75] David Katz, "The Mamzer and the Shifcha," *The Journal of Halacha and Contemporary Society* 28 (1994): 73-104.

[76] Moreover, for a Jew to marry a slave he must first sell himself into slavery.

[77] Gittin 32a.

unsuspecting woman, which could lead to the proliferation of mamzerim. Consequently, he prohibited a man from canceling the proxy unless the proxy was physically present. To enforce Rabban Gamaliel's decree, the Talmud held that a bet din could annul a marriage retroactively if the husband cancelled the proxy prior to the delivery of the *get*. The Tosafot noted that Rabban Gamliel's decree could in theory legitimize acts of adultery, with the cooperation of the husband, thereby exempting an adulterer and adulteress from punishment.

The Maharsham, Rabbi Shalom Mordecai Schwadron (Galicia, 1835-1911) quotes the Tosafot in response to a question on mamzerut.[78] The case was as follows: A man from Odessa went abroad. After twelve years and no communication with his wife, his family notified her that her husband was dead. Her brother-in-law performed חליצה and she later remarried with permission of the bet din. During her pregnancy, she received word that her first husband was still alive and that he had lent his passport to another man who had died and was mistakenly identified as her husband.

The rabbi of Odessa asked the Maharsham for a determination of the fate of the woman and her child. The Maharsham concluded that she needed a divorce from both her husbands and that her child was a mamzer. In the Maharsham's discussion he noted a theoretical solution to remedy the status of the child. The first husband could have divorced his wife with a proxy and then cancelled the proxy privately, which would have given the bet din grounds to annul the first marriage. Unfortunately, the Maharsham conceded that his elegant solution of rectifying the child's status was inapplicable because the first husband had already divorced his wife.

Justice Moshe Silberg proposed using the power of annulment as a solution to mamzerut.[79] Rabbi David Novak supports Silberg's proposal as a remedy when the status of the child cannot be ignored. Novak writes:

> The main argument against this solution, as we saw before, was that the Tosafists feared it would lead to sexual immorality since any violated marriage could be annulled retroactively. However, the answer to this objection today is threefold: (1) In today's atmosphere of unprecedented ignorance and apathy among the majority of the Jewish people, fear of the consequence of mamzerut is no longer operative in their sexual decision making; (2) Improperly initiated second marriages, which can easily be performed under either secular or non-halakhic Jewish auspices, are not considered "fornication" by the majority of the Jewish people; and, (3) Any situation which could lead a segment of the Jewish people to believe that intermarriage is the only solution to their personal and familial dilemma must be rectified since intermarriage and its attendant assimilation pose today's greatest threat to the survival of both the Jewish people and Judaism. As the mishnah noted in a famous passage, changes in the law are called for when worse results will emerge from staying with the status quo, "'It is time to act for the

---

[78] Teshuvot Maharsham, vol. 1, no. 9, cited and discussed in J. David Bleich's *Contemporary Halakhic Problems* (New York: Ktav, 1977), pp. 162-167.

[79] "ביטול החוק למען קיימו," *Panim el Panim* 705 (12 Jan. 1973): 14ff. Cited by David Novak, "The Conflict between Halakhah and Ethics: The Case of Mamzerut," *Halakhah in a Theological Dimension* (Chino, CA: Scholars' Press, 1985), p. 28.

Lord; they have violated your Torah.' (Ps. 119:126). R. Nathan said,[80] 'violate the Torah because it is time to act for the Lord!'"[81]

Although Novak makes a strong case for taking dramatic action in response to mamzerut, his annulment approach fails as a general solution, for the following reasons:

- A. If a child was born of an adulterous relationship prior to the retroactive annulment of the marriage the children are mamzerim.[82]
- B. It would require the full cooperation of the first husband, which is difficult to count on.
- C. If a woman obtained a *get* from her husband after the birth of the illicit child, the husband cannot give her a second *get*, as in Maharsham's actual case.
- D. The annulment process requires the cooperation of the wife, a cooperation that we cannot always rely on.

Beyond theoretical problems, there is the ethical rub. Novak acknowledges that even with annulment the children would remain with an informal social stigma as being children of *de jure* "fornication," which, he adds, would "prevent some others from marrying them."[83] In sum, Novak's annulment solution may not cover all cases, is unwieldy in many cases, and leaves the child with a "social stigma." Novak acknowledges that until now the annulment approach was only theoretical because of fear of abuse, but is worth implementing due to the exigency of the situation. Yet, Novak stops short of using the same legal construct of "It is time to act for the Lord" to uproot the concept of mamzerut. He refrains from this more complete change because, he writes, "The authority of any legal system cannot tolerate picking and choosing which institutions are to be upheld and which are to be dropped."[84]

Silberg's Civil Marriage Solution

Professor Moshe Silberg, formerly a justice of the Israeli Supreme Court, advocates a system of civil marriages for mamzerim.[85] He does so in response to a close reading of Maimonides. Silberg points out that Maimonides, in the Mishneh Torah, only prohibits the marriage of a mamzer and a Jew,[86] which Silberg asserts leaves open the possibility of concubines or civil marriage.

Rabbi Judah Dick writes that Silberg's analysis of Maimonides is mistaken.[87] Although Maimonides is silent on concubines in the paragraph on mamzerut, Dick writes, "Maimonides is explicit on limiting concubines to kings,"[88] and prohibiting sex

---

[80] M. Berakhot 9:5.

[81] Novak, p. 28.

[82] Nahmanides, Shitah Mekubezet, and Meiri to Ketubbot 3a, cited in Bleich, p. 164.

[83] Novak, p. 28.

[84] Ibid., p. 27.

[85] Moshe Zemer, "Purifying Mamzerim," *Jewish Law Annual* 10 (1992): 99-113.

[86] Maimonides, M.T. Hilkhot Issurei Bi'ah 15:2.

[87] See Judah Dick in *HaPardes* (Tishri 5732), cited in Bleich, pp. 160-161.

[88] M.T. Hilkhot Issurei Bi'ah 15:2; Louis Jacobs in "The Problem of the Mamzer" (pp. 271-272) notes that Silberg would respond to critics that Maimonides would allow non-royalty to have sexual relations with a concubine. But, Jacobs counters, even so, it would not help a mamzer who is prohibited by Maimonides from a Jewish concubine.

outside of marriage.[89] Even if Silberg's reading of Maimonides is correct, his solution permits a "marriage," but the offspring are mamzerim. Moreover, a "solution" which would deny a Jew a traditional marriage under the huppah and would perpetuate the exclusion of the mamzer from normal Jewish life is not a solution.

Nullification of the First Marriage

The most common approach to "solving a mamzerut" case is to find a way to nullify the first marriage on a case-by-case basis. This is precisely what Rabbi Goren did in the Langer case by his holding that the first husband was not Jewish, due to later acts which demonstrated fraud at the time of "conversion," and hence no Jewish marriage had taken place. On a broader level, Rabbi Moshe Feinstein addressed the widespread, contemporary problem of mamzerut by holding that the weddings of non-Orthodox rabbis were invalid.[90] Since the non-Orthodox marriages were not binding, there was no need for a *get* and children of the marriages were untainted.

Nullification does not work for Conservative rabbis unless there is an actual defect in the original marriage. It is inadequate as a general approach, because not all marriages are performed improperly. Unlike Rabbi Feinstein, we accept the marriages conducted by Reform and Reconstructionist colleagues who have complied with halakhic standards.

Circumvention through Narrow Rules of Evidence

Many post-Talmudic rabbis circumvented mamzerut through applying narrow rules of evidence. Rabbi Louis Jacobs provides the following examples:[91]

A. When a mother confessed that her son was not her husband's, Benjamin Zeev of Arta (sixteenth century) did not accept the confession.[92]

B. Rabbi Moses Sofer (eighteenth century) would not conclude that a child born years after a man had left his wife was a mamzer.[93]

C. Rabbi Moshe Feinstein (twentieth century) ruled that a mother is not believed when she declares that she had been previously married and that her son from her second husband is a mamzer.[94]

Each of these examples reveals a desire to avoid the label of mamzerut and is explained by the rules of evidence as presented in the Shulhan Arukh. Regarding the case of Benjamin Zeev of Arta, a mother's confession is not acceptable testimony to impugn the status of her son.[95] Moses Isserles explains in his gloss that for a married woman, a presumption exists that any offspring are those of her husband. In the matter before Rabbi Moses Sofer, the rabbis were prepared to engage in medical (and mystical) fictions to explain how a legitimate child could have been conceived despite the apparent absence of

---

[89] M.T. Hilkhot Ishut 1:1.

[90] משה פינשטיין. "בקידושי רעפאמער," ספר אגרות משה, אבן העזר, חלק ג, סימן כה, דף תמז (1970).

[91] Jacobs, p. 270.

[92] Responsa, Binyamin Ze'ev, vol. 1, Even HaEzer, no. 136.

[93] Hatam Sofer, Even HaEzer, no. 10.

[94] Moshe Feinstein, *Iggrot Moshe*, Even HaEzer, pt. 3, no. 8, pp. 424-425.

[95] Even HaEzer 4:29. Moses Isserles adds that although there is a presumption that a married woman's offspring are those of her legal husband, there are those who hold that the presumption does not hold for an engaged woman (ארוסה).

the husband. Rabbi Moshe Feinstein could rely on the Talmudic principle that a person should not be believed to impugn him or herself (אין אדם משים עצמו רשע).

Yet, there are other evidentiary circumstances that are not reflected in these cases, where statements provide *prima facie* proof of mamzerut according to the Shulhan Arukh. If a man said, "This is not my fetus or my son," he is believed.[96] If a person says, "I am a mamzer," his testimony is accepted and his son is also classified as a mamzer.[97] The man is believed, because his confession does not impugn his own guilt. He is addressing the conduct of his wife or his parents and his claim is accepted. This was precisely the predicament that Rabbi Oshry faced; a man said that his wife's son was a mamzer, and the rules of evidence made that a compelling and binding claim on the judge. Hence, there are limits to a judge's ability to circumvent mamzerut through evidentiary rules alone.

Implicitly Ignoring Mamzerut

There was a consistent effort in the past to narrow the application of mamzerut by restricting the types of evidence that were admissible to prove adultery. Many rabbis went even a step further and ignored evidence of mamzerut. In the words of Rabbi Louis Jacobs:

> Since the majority of Jews who wish to marry are not mamzerim, the rule of probability can and should be relied upon. There are even rumors, quite persistent, that in prewar days some Orthodox Rabbis would drop broad hints to known mamzerim that they should emigrate to a community where they were not known and marry there.[98] . . .Nevertheless, a very good case can be made out for at least avoiding any investigation the purpose of which is to uncover the identity of mamzerim. This is certainly the norm among the Orthodox in most parts of the United States where cases of mamzerut rarely occur because the Orthodox rabbis are intentionally perfunctory in their investigation.[99]

In the aftermath of the Holocaust, for instance, it is remarkable how few cases of mamzerut arose. The Langer and Oshry cases are exceptions that prove the rule. The rabbis in Israel and America actively ignored the issues of mamzerut, which we may surmise occurred in many cases in the shadow of those horrific years.

We too may choose to ignore the category of mamzerut, but halakhic integrity demands that we justify our action. We need to give guidance to colleagues and congregants on this vexing problem when it arises. A clear statement as a halakhic movement is all the more urgent in the context of rabbis in Israel who keep the category of mamzerut alive, including the maintenance of computer records on mamzerut suspects. We need to address mamzerut precisely because it raises the question whether we will enforce a Torah law that strikes us as unconscionable in light of other Torah values. Mamzerut is a real problem for which only incomplete answers have been offered. In the words of Professor Ze'ev Falk, former rector of the Seminary's Beit Midrash in Jerusalem:

---

[96] Even HaEzer 4:29.

[97] Even HaEzer 4:30.

[98] A precedent for rabbis encouraging suspected mamzerim to go where they are not recognized is in Yevamot 45a, in which both Rav Yehudah and Rava tell men to go where they are unknown. But, in those cases, as Rashi points out, the respective rabbis did not agree with the definition of mamzerut that was applied to the men, namely that a mamzer was the product of relations between an idolator or slave and a Jewish woman.

[99] Jacobs, p. 275.

Injustice was felt, but there was not enough courage to change the law. Although doubts had been raised long ago as to the purity of pedigree of most people, the rules of impediments were nevertheless applied against those who were unfortunate enough to be known as mamzerim.[100]

Morality and Halakhah

Although mamzerut is morally reprehensible, it has remained operative in Jewish law because of systemic fears. The fear is that to make a change on moral grounds is to impugn God, which would unravel the system. Dr. David Weiss Halivni, Professor of Talmud at Columbia University, has stated that contemporary morality is not the basis for change in halakhah. In his article, "Can a Religious Law be Immoral," Weiss wrote:

> Even when the Rabbis altered a law, they never abrogated it. They retained the integrity of the law. By integrity I mean partial applicability. They did not totally eliminate the law. It still remained valid and pertinent to an extreme and rare situation. That was necessary in order not to impugn the Lawgiver with a lack of moral sensitivity which may undermine not only this law, but laws in general. Once one has formulated, as in the case of bastardy, mamzerut, the need for changing the law because of moral exigency, any subsequent change will be interpreted as an admission that initially there was no moral sensitivity, imputing to the Lawgiver a defective moral awareness. The Rabbis instinctively shied away from such a formulation.[101]

When Rabbi David Novak examined the problem of the mamzer, he acknowledged a moral problem, but only looked for a case-by-case solution. Maharsham's annulment strategy, which Novak presented as the best solution, fails to resolve all mamzerut cases. Novak hesitated to change the law on explicitly moral grounds because of the fear that it might lead to the unravelling of halakhah. In his words: "Once it is posited that a Toraitic institution does not exist one cannot talk about a normative process at all any more. The authority of any legal system cannot tolerate picking and choosing which institutions are to be held and which are to be dropped."[102]

It is true that the rabbis in the past did not explicitly use morality as the basis for change or interpretation of a law. In explaining the Torah's statement "an eye for an eye, a tooth for a tooth,"[103] for example, the Rabbis of the Talmud offer ten separate hermeneutic proofs that the verse calls for compensation and not mutilation.[104] Each of the proofs is indirect and tenuous, which explains why so many "proofs" are offered. Underlying the ingenious arguments is an implicit matter of conscience regarding the taking of body parts. In the words of Rabbi Eliezer Berkovits, "The reference to the

---

[100] Ze'ev Falk, *Religious Law and Ethics* (Jerusalem: Mesharim Publications, 1991), p. 147.

[101] David Weiss HaLivni, "Can a Religious Law be Immoral?", *Perspectives on Jews and Judaism: Essays in Honor of Wolfe Kelman* (New York: Rabbinical Assembly, 1978), pp. 165-167.

[102] Novak, p. 26.

[103] Lev. 24:20; Exod. 21:23-25.

[104] Bava Kamma 82b-84a.

overruling ethical principle is not always explicit in halakhic decisions. It is, however, obvious that it plays a decisive role in the final conclusion."[105]

A reliance on hermeneutic rules of interpretation and legal loopholes emerges from the view that Torah embodies an all encompassing, eternal wisdom. There is a price paid, however, for only looking inwardly for the justification of change. The hermeneutic rules may fail to provide a comprehensive solution, as in the case of mamzerut. Preserving the system may begin to look more important than acting justly and halakhah may begin to look more like a chess game than a system of religious striving. In the words of Rabbi Gordon Tucker: "Halakhah is a theological legal system. Separating law from moral principle in such a system, as positivists would be wont to do, is to separate moral principles from God, and that is theologically untenable."[106]

While Conservative Judaism would affirm that the Torah is Divine in its origin, the revelation at Sinai is seen as the beginning of a relationship and not the final word. Interpretation is understood as our communal attempt to understand the will of a compassionate Divine partner. As we mature we are able to understand God's will for us more clearly. If a law appears unconscionable, we would say that the shortcoming is either our previous understanding or that circumstances have so changed that the rule no longer meets its intended result. In the words of Rabbi Elliot N. Dorff:

> The Orthodox would not consider modern ethical sensitivities as sufficient grounds to change the law: for them, the law as it has been formulated over the centuries must be binding. The Conservative movement maintains that the purpose of the law in the first place is largely to concretize moral values, and so the specific form of the law can and should be changed if it is not effectively doing that. In other words, the aggadah should control the halakhah.[107]

When asked if a law of the Torah can be immoral we would respond, no! It is precisely because we see God as the source of morality that we cannot accept that a Jewish law would lead us away from morality. In that light, we say in our collective statement of principles, *Emet ve-Emunah*:

> In some cases changes are necessary to prevent or remove injustice, while in others they constitute a positive program to enhance the quality of Jewish life by elevating its moral standards or deepening its piety. . . .We affirm that the halakhic process has striven to embody the highest moral principles.[108]

---

[105] Eliezer Berkovits, *Not in Heaven: The Nature and Function of Halakha*, (NY: Ktav, 1983), p. 20.

[106] Gordon Tucker, "God, the Good, and Halakhah," *Judaism* 38 (summer 1989): 371.

[107] Elliot N. Dorff, *Conservative Judaism: Our Ancestors to our Descendants* (NY: United Synagogue, 1977; revised 2d ed., 1996), p. 160 of 1st ed. The same point is made in Elliot N. Dorff's "The Interaction of Jewish Law with Morality," *Judaism* 38 (summer 1989): 455-466; Gordon Tucker, "God, the Good, and Halakhah," *Judaism* 38 (summer 1989): 365-376; Bradley Shavit Artson, "Halakhah and Ethics: The Holy and the Good," *Conservative Judaism* 46 (spring 1994): 70-88; Siegel, "Ethics and the Halakhah," p. 128, in which the author writes: "The law must be revised in light of the ethical values. . . .We have a responsibility toward the historic norms which we have inherited, but this responsibility does not extend so far that we must accept them when they result in unethical situations."

[108] *Emet ve-Emunah: Statement of Principles of Conservative Judaism* (New York: JTS/RA/United Synagogue, 1988), p. 24.

Mamzerut poses a moral problem. It punishes an innocent child for the sins of his or her parent. We are concerned for the plight of innocent children because of the teachings of Tanakh and our rabbinic predecessors. Our generation is part of a chain that expresses grave concern over implementing the rule of mamzerut. Daniel the Tailor, in a relatively late midrash, described God shedding tears for the mamzer and promising a cleansing in the Messianic era. The Rabbis narrowed the rules of evidence and posited medical absurdities. Many solutions were offered, but none sufficiently narrowed the category of mamzerut.

We remain with halakhic dilemmas. When we know that a congregant obtained a civil divorce and did not obtain a *get* and the child of the second marriage stands before us ready to get married, what do we do? When we are confronted with a father who says, "This child is not mine!", what do we do? Do we hold that these children are mamzerim and refuse to marry them? We are left with the challenge posited by Rabbi Seymour Siegel: "Let us do now what the *Kadosh Barukh Hu* is to do in the future."[109]

To choose not to implement mamzerut requires humility, both in deference to Torah and to the generations of rabbis who struggled with the moral implications of mamzerut. And yet, mamzerut challenges us to speak with courage and clarity about how Judaism unfolds and how laws do change. Mamzerut is an opportunity to make explicit what was until now implicit, that morality is at the center of the halakhic process.

Toolbox of Halakhic Change

Throughout the generations, the implementation of the Torah's commands has evolved. There are many examples and the following provides a sampling:

(A) Leviticus omits explicit permission for a kohen to bury his wife,[110] which the rabbis read into the text as a requirement.[111]

(B) Numbers offers an actual case of a gatherer of sticks on Shabbat who was publicly stoned for the offense.[112] There are no anecdotes of such a severe penalty for Shabbat violation in the Talmud.[113]

(C) Deuteronomy states that one cannot exempt oneself from a vow,[114] yet the Rabbis allow for rabbinic annulment of unwise vows.[115]

(D) Despite the strong language compelling the death penalty for murder,[116] the Rabbis avoided it through crafting high procedural hurdles, such as: confessions were inadmissi-

---

[109] Siegel, p. 130.

[110] Lev. 21:3 states regarding death and the priest: "None shall defile himself for any [dead] person among his kin, except for the relatives that are closer to him: his mother, his father, his son, his daughter, and his brother, and also for his virgin sister. . . ." Rabbi ben Meir, a 12th century explicator of the literal meaning (פשט) commented: "No husband from among the kinship [of the priesthood] may defile himself for his wife."

[111] The Sifra comments that "except for the relatives that are closer to him" refers to his wife, a position that is also held by Rashi and Abraham ibn Ezra. This idea is codified in Maimonides' M.T., "As regards the wife of the priest, one must render himself impure, even against his will. . . .The Scribes gave her the status of a 'dead person' whom he is commanded to bury."

[112] Num. 15:32-34.

[113] The law is codified in M. Sanhedrin 7:4, "These are they that are to be stoned. . .he who profanes the Sabbath," but no cases are provided in any of the lengthy Shabbat discussions of any such execution.

[114] Deut. 23:24, "That which goes out of your mouth you shall observe and do."

[115] Sanhedrin 68a; M. Haggigah 1:8, "Release from vows hovers in the air and they have nothing on which to lean."

[116] Gen. 9:6, "Whoever shed the blood of man, by man shall his blood be shed, for in God's image did God make man." Num. 35:33, "You shall not pollute the land in which you live; for blood pollutes the land, and the land can have no expiation for blood that is shed upon it except by the blood of him who shed it."

ble; the defendant needed a warning prior to the commission of the crime; and, two trustworthy eyewitnesses were required.[117] These tough procedural requirements gave context to the statement of Rabbis Tarfon and Akiva: "Had we been in the Sanhedrin, no one would ever have been put to death."[118]

There are a variety of halakhic tools that have shaped the Jewish understanding of Torah and have enabled the changing of a halakhic practice.

Interpretation

Interpretation is the major tool for implementing a law differently than its literal reading. In the words of Rabbi Joel Roth, "The meaning of the Torah is determined by the sages and... their interpretations alone are normative."[119] There are three cases in the Talmud in which Torah commands are interpreted as only theoretical in their origins. The three cases are the rebellious child (בן סורר ומורה), the idolatrous city (עיר הנדחת), and צרעת of a house (לבית צרעת) – a kind of fungal infestation, all of which are addressed in Sanhedrin 71a. Regarding each law there is a description of practical impediments barring implementation, followed by a baraita that states, concerning the law:

לא היה ולא עתיד להיות ולמה נכתב דרוש וקבל שכר.

> It never was and never will be. And why is it written? Learn it and you will receive a reward.

And for each law there is a statement made by a Rabbi that he knows of an actual case in which the law was administered. A closer look at these three cases is warranted, because it is tempting to add mamzerut to the list of hypothetical laws.

The Mishnah in Sanhedrin debates the requirements to qualify as a "rebellious son," (בן סורר ומורה) for which the Torah's penalty is death by stoning.[120] The Talmud requires a finding that the child would unquestionably grow to lead a life of crime. To demonstrate fearless, easily repeated, moral depravity, a child needs to steal from his father and consume large quantities of meat and wine in a stranger's domain. The Talmud goes one step further by closely examining the language of the Biblical law. Not only must both parents bring their son to the elders at the gates and agree with the desired outcome, but neither the mother nor father can have any physical handicap and both parents must have a similar voice and physical appearance.

The Talmud quotes the baraita acknowledging that the requirements for "a rebellious son" will never be met. We may infer that the motive in crafting such impossible standards was that the Rabbis found it morally unacceptable that a child would get the death penalty, let alone that his parents would choose to have their child executed. They are willing to see the Torah as providing laws that are only theoretical. At the same time, there are those who prefer to read the Torah more literally, such as Rebbi Yonatan who dissents and is quoted in a baraita saying, "I saw a [rebellious son], and I sat on his grave."[121]

---

[117] M. Sanhedrin 5:1-2; regarding inadmissibility of confessions see Sanhedrin 9b.

[118] M. Makkot 1:10. And yet, there is also a dissent expressed by Rabban Gamaliel.

[119] Joel Roth, *The Halakhic Process: A Systemic Analysis* (New York: Jewish Theological Seminary, 1986), p. 153.

[120] Deut. 21:18-21.

[121] There are two practical problems with this attribution. First, it is improper to sit on a grave. Secondly, Rabbi Yonatan was a kohen, which would have prevented him from going into a cemetery.

To qualify as an "idolatrous city" (עיר הנדחת) the majority of the residents of a town in the land of Israel must worship idols. As a penalty the Torah states that the guilty parties must be killed, and the buildings in the city and the property of all the residents is burned, and the town may never be rebuilt.[122] A baraita asserts that there never was such a town. The statement is attributed to Rabbi Eliezer who said that even one mezuzzah in town barred its classification as an "idolatrous city," and that there never was a town in Israel that failed to have at least one mezuzzah. Again, Rebbi Yonatan is quoted as disagreeing by saying, "I saw [an idolatrous city] and I sat on its rubble."

Leviticus details the laws of a house that contracts a צרעת, discoloration of its walls.[123] The house becomes an object of ritual impurity, which conveys impurity to people or objects within it, and must be destroyed.[124] A baraita declares that there never was such a צרעת-inflicted house. It is attributed to Rabbi Elazer the son of Rabbi Shimon, who declared that the צרעת must be found on all four walls and the discoloration must meet at the corner. He makes this claim based on an interpretation of the relevant verses. In rebuttal there are two Rabbis who testify to each having seen a ruin of a house in Israel – one in Gaza and the other in the Galilee – that were identified by local residents as a צרעת-inflicted house.

Each of these Biblical laws teaches a foundational lesson. "The rebellious child" underscores that disrespect for one's parents is tantamount to blasphemy and likewise warrants the death penalty. The law of the "idolatrous city" conveys that a person, particularly in Israel, is responsible for the faithfulness of his or her neighbors, because their idolatry could lead to destruction of the entire city. The "צרעת house" is more obscure, both in terms of the nature of the tainted growth and the value lesson. Nonetheless, the Rabbis understand צרעת as a product of speaking ill of others (לשון הרע), as shown by Miriam's צרעת after she spoke critically of her brother Moses.[125] Hence, the law of the "צרעת house" teaches that hurtful speech may even lead to destruction of your familial home.[126] At the same time, the actual administration of these laws could lead to unconscionable results, such as the capital punishment of a child, the destruction of an entire town, including the possessions and community of innocent people, and the demolition of a family's home as a result of wrongful speech.

Apparently prompted by moral concerns, most Rabbis understood that these laws were only hypotheticals. The Talmud justifies this outcome by presenting practical impediments, which are tenuously derived from the original Torah verses. There is unquestionably a "picking and choosing" of both how to interpret these verses and the holding that these verses were never meant to be implemented. At the same time, there are dissents, illustrated by "actual cases" of administration of the law that offer a literal reading and make no moral judgment.

In dealing with mamzerut, most Rabbis sought, on a case-by-case basis, to ingeniously avoid labeling a person as a marital pariah. As with the three "hypothetical" laws, evidentiary hurdles were crafted that made the application of mamzerut far more cumbersome than expected from a literal reading of the text. Yet, the Rabbis did not go as far as to say that "the law never was and never will be." The Rabbis failed to assert a decisive, practical impediment that would have consistently barred application of the law. Perhaps the Rabbis felt that there was merit in keeping the law alive, even in a weakened state, due to social efficacy. A second

---

[122] Deut. 13:13-19.

[123] Lev. 14:33-57.

[124] Lev. 14:33-53.

[125] Num. 12:1-15.

[126] Arakhin 15b, also cited as a rationale by Maimonides, Nahmanides, and Sforno.

lesson from the above debate is that there have always been dissenters regarding morally problematic laws who choose to apply the Biblical law in a literal fashion.

It would solve a lot of practical problems to classify mamzerut as a "hypothetical law." We regrettably have a long history of application of the law that does not allow us to say, "the law was never implemented." The most important idea to come out of the survey of Sanhedrin 71a is that there is justification for having a law on the books as a value lesson, even when the law is not administered. When and if we utilize a halakhic tool to bar application of mamzerut, it does not mean that the law is meaningless. In addition, we may anticipate a dissenting opinion in a debate over mamzerut, a dissent that says that the law is in the Torah and therefore must be implemented. To change the precedent of the past, which saw mamzerut as operative, we must look to halakhic tools other than reinterpretation alone.

Communal Legislation – The Takannah

The Torah provides the sages with authority to administer the Law: "You shall act in accordance with the instructions given you and the ruling handed down to you; you must not deviate from the verdict that they announce to you either to the right or to the left."[127] The sages understood this verse as giving them the responsibility to interpret the law and to engage in legislative change.[128] As Rabbi Joel Roth has written: "In the final analysis, the decision of an authority to exercise his legislative function is itself judicial, not legislative."[129]

The methodology and nomenclature for legislative-type change has evolved. Among the Tannaim (Rabbis of the 1st to 3rd centuries, CE), there is no discussion as to the extent and guidelines of legislative action.[130] Changes were made with undefined, broad categories, such as the following:

עת לעשות לאדני הפירו תורתך – "It is time to act for the Lord; they have violated Your Torah" (Ps. 119:126).

A sampling of changes justified with this Biblical verse include:

(A) In response to sectarians who denied a "world to come," the conclusion of a ברכה recited in the Temple was changed from "forever" (מן העולם) to "forever and ever" (מן העולם ועד עולם).[131]

(B) Although only a priest was permitted to wear the formal priestly garb, Shimon the Righteous dressed as the priest to meet with Alexander the Great in order to seek his reversal of a decree giving the Samaritans permission to destroy the Temple.[132]

(C) Although the Rabbis understood the Torah as mandating that "things intended to be oral may not be transmitted in writing,"[133] Rabbi Yohanan and Resh Lakish put the Aggadah into writing to prevent it being forgotten.[134]

---

[127] Deut. 17:11.

[128] Rashba relies on Deut. 17:11 to say that it is a mitzvah to obey the Sages' changes of Torah – Rosh Hashana 16a, s.v. למה.

[129] Joel Roth, p. 155. Also see Menachem Elon, *Jewish Law: History, Sources, Principles* (Philadelphia: Jewish Publication Society, 1994), pp. 497-499.

[130] Elon, *Jewish Law*, p. 504.

[131] M. Berakhot 9:5.

[132] Yoma 69a.

[133] Gittin 60b.

[134] Gittin 60a.

מוטב תעקור אות מן התורה – "It is better to uproot one letter from the Torah."

This phrase is often coupled with the goal of the "sanctification of God's name." It was employed to justify specific acts by Israelite royalty that violated Torah precepts, such as:

(A) King David's turning over seven of Saul's sons for punishment to the Gibeonites[135] in violation of the Torah standard that "sons should not die for the sins of their fathers."[136]

(B) Saul's concubine delaying the burial of a person who was executed[137] in violation of the Torah precept that a person was not to be left hanging after nightfall, "but must bury him the same day."[138]

פעמים שבטולה של תורה זהו יסודה – "Sometimes the cancellation of Torah is its foundation."

This principle was used by Resh Lekesh to justify Moses' shattering of the first set of tablets. Although not the violation of an explicit halakhah, Moses' act is an example of abrogating God's apparent initial intent.[139]

These three broad phrases were largely used to justify, after the fact, one time, exigent acts. Nonetheless, the general category of legislation was also used to support an ongoing change that was felt necessary to preserve the Jewish tradition as a whole. "It is time to act for the Lord; They have violated your Torah," was employed in connection with preserving the Aggadah, the oral explanations of the Biblical narrative, despite a Torah prohibition to do so. Afterwards, the Rabbis continued to write down Aggadah and it constituted a precedent that enabled Rabbi Yehudah HaNasi (Palestine, second to third century C.E.) to compose the Mishnah, a record of the "oral law."

It is tempting to sweep aside mamzerut with the use of a broad phrase acknowledging that there is an exigent need to act. Yet, there is reason to pause and explore if there is a more precise category to justify overturning a Biblical law. It is always best to use no more force than necessary to make a change. Like the drilling of a hole, the skilled carpenter tries to find the bit size that most accurately matches the need. In fact, as the halakhah developed the broad categories were narrowed into more precise rubrics, which warrant a close look.

During the period of the Amoraim, the Rabbis of the third through fifth centuries, the Sages crystallized a number of basic principles that more clearly defined the scope and authority of their legislative activity. For purposes of our discussion there are two relevant categories of "uprooting a Biblical law" (עקירה):

(A) שב ואל תעשה – "Sit and don't do." This principle was largely used to refrain from the communal performance of a mitzvah due to changed circumstances and a countervailing Torah precept. Hence, in order to protect against the violation of carrying from the private to the public domain on Shabbat, the Rabbis prohibited the following activities on Shabbat: the blowing of shofar, shaking of the lulav, and reading of the Megillah of Esther.[140] In addition, the Rabbis said that it was no longer necessary to

---

[135] 2 Sam. 21.
[136] Deut. 24:16; Yevamot 79a.
[137] 2 Sam. 21:10.
[138] Deut. 21:23; Yevamot 79a.
[139] Menahot 99a on Exod. 34:1.
[140] Sanhedrin 19a.

place a blue thread (תכלת) on the four corners of one's garments.[141] Consequently, talitot for the past eighteen hundred years have customarily had white threads only.[142] The reason for this social legislation is unclear, but seems to have arisen at a time when the Romans made it illegal or prohibitively expensive to acquire the blue dye. It led to both hardship in fulfilling a mitzvah and encouraged the sale of counterfeit dyes. The Rabbis' ability to override a clear Torah command, recited in the daily recitation of the Shema, demonstrates once again the Rabbis' authority to alter how a Torah law is implemented in response to changing conditions.

(B) קום ועשה – "Get up and do" [despite it being a violation of the Torah]. The right of the court to permit action in outright violation of the Torah was debated among the Amoraim. Rabbah held that such action was beyond the scope of rabbinic authority and Rav Hisdah said that it was permitted.[143] Nonetheless, in the Talmud's discussion of Elijah's active violation of the law by setting up an altar on Mount Carmel, the prophet's behavior is justified as a response to the exigencies of the moment (שעה הוראת), the need to turn the people away from idolatry by a dramatic act.[144] Later poskim justified the use of "get up and do" in response to a "crisis," even when the implications of the change were ongoing,[145] such as believing a woman when she said that her husband had died[146] and the rabbi's authority to release a person from an oath.[147]

עקירה, "uprooting," was rarely employed, and when used, there was a preference for the less radical, "sit and don't do." The hesitancy to use "communal legislation" was out of respect for precedent and the belief that the laws of the Torah were given by God. עקירה was only justified in the context of a countervailing principle at stake (פנים וטעם בדבר) and an urgent need (הוראת שעה). In 1997, in response to the issues of "Solemnizing the Marriage between a Kohen and a Divorcee," presented by Rabbi Arnold M. Goodman, we of the CJLS permitted the "uprooting" of the Torah law as an act of קום ועשה – "get up and do," based on "the exigencies of the hour," specifically, our concern for Jews marrying Jews (endogamy). Our setting aside a דאורייתא law affirmed our confidence as a bet din in the face of the changed circumstances of our day.

Mamzerut poses dramatic challenges, too, that at first impression warrant a bold response. Due to relatively new opportunities for an array of non-halakhic wedding ceremonies, many Jews are being remarried without a *get*. There is a proliferation of mamzerim, who are largely the products of ignorance or apathy rather than promiscuity. In addition, there are rare cases where Jews are having children in defiance of the law and if mamzerut is enforced, their children would be left to suffer as marital pariahs. Punishment of children for the sins of their parents conflicts with a countervailing Torah principle as important as the need to preserve Shabbat, which overrode other Biblical laws. In our day,

---

[141] Num. 15:37-41; Menahot 4:1; 38a.

[142] Menahot 43b. Rabbi Meir held that the omission of a white thread was an even more serious transgression than blue, because white was readily available.

[143] Yevamot 89a-90b.

[144] Yevamot 90b.

[145] HaMeiri (Rabbi Menahem ben Solomon ha-Meiri, 1249-1316), Beit ha-Behira to Yevamot 89b, 90b; Ritba (Rabbi Yom Tov ben Avraham Ishbili, 1250-1330) to Yevamot 90b, s.v. ונגמר; Rambam (Rabbi Moshe ben Maimon, 1135-1204), M.T. Hilkhot Mamrim 2:4. Maimonides justifies dramatic halakhic action by analogy to an amputation needed to save a human life.

[146] Tosafot to Nazir 43b, s.v. והאי מת. Additional citations in Tosafot that affirm the rabbinic power of עקירה: Yevamot 24b, s.v. אמר; Yevamot 110a, s.v. לפיכך; Ketubbot 11a, s.v. מבטילין; Bava Batra 48b, s.v. תינח.

[147] Maimonides, M.T. Hilkhot Nedarim 3:9.

mamzerut fails to achieve an objective of deterrence against forbidden sexual relationships and it cannot be justified on the basis of "communal purity." As with the marriage between a kohen and a divorcee, we are committed to enabling the solemnization of marriages between Jews. There are grounds for the תקנה of uprooting the law of mamzerut, but there is a narrower category of halakhic change that is better suited. It is wise to operate in a halakhic realm in a way that meets our objectives and causes the least challenge to the larger system. In addition, this final category of halakhic change, the barring of a law through a procedural mechanism, has a history that is closely tied to concerns with evolving social and moral concerns.

A Procedurally Inoperative Law

There are several examples cited in the Talmud of a Biblical law that was made inoperative due to a procedural decision. In each of the cases, a rationale for the change is offered but no express claim is made that the ruling is an uprooting of a Biblical law. Yet, the impact is the same. The following are three examples of judicial discretion that prevented implementation of a Biblical law:

Avodah Zarah 8b states that "Forty years prior to the destruction of the Temple, the Sanhedrin abandoned [their normal place for hearing cases] and held its sittings in Hanuth" [a non-dedicated space for judicial use, also located on the Temple grounds]. Rabbi Nahman ben Isaac says the Sanhedrin's decision resulted in the cessation of capital cases:

> Why? Because when the Sanhedrin saw that murderers were so prevalent that they could not be properly dealt with judicially, they said, 'Rather let us be exiled from place to place than pronounce them guilty [of capital offenses], for it is written (Deut. 12:10), "You shall carry out the verdict that is announced to you from that place that the Lord chose," implying that it is the place that matters.

When the Rabbis stopped considering capital punishment, they did so despite the repeated Torah directive that execution was the just sentence for an array of crimes. They made the change with a procedural act. As they understood the law, a court could only impose capital punishment when the twenty-three-person Sanhedrin held its seat on the Temple grounds, לשכת הגזית, a place that straddled the sanctity of the inner space of the Temple and the courtyard.[148] The Sanhedrin decided to move from its place of authority, thereby barring the hearing of capital cases. The Sanhedrin's motive for making the law inoperative was, to quote the Talmud, because "murderers were so prevalent that they could not be properly dealt with judicially."[149]

There are three possible explanations of their stated concern: capital punishment no longer served as a deterrent, or that the large number of cases could have led to incomplete examination of testimony and consequently unjust verdicts, or that the large case load could have led to unequal administration of who was tried for a capital crime. There is also a historical context to the Rabbis' action: the Romans had officially taken away their authority to hear criminal matters. Regardless of which explanation or combination is chosen the bottom line remains the same: The Rabbis explained their suspension of a Biblical directive on ethical grounds.

---

[148] Tosafot on Avodah Zarah 8b, s.v. מלמד שהמקום גורם.

[149] Avodah Zarah 8b.

Moral concerns also prompted the Rabbis to refrain from administering the Torah mandated laws of "breaking the neck of the heifer" and the sotah-water test. These changes are presented in Mishnah Sotah 9:9:

> When murderers increased in number, the rite of breaking the heifer's neck was abolished. . . .When adulterers increased in number, the application of the waters of jealousy ceased; and Rabbi Yohanan ben Zakkai abolished them as it is said, "I will not punish your daughters when they commit harlotry nor your daughters-in-law when they commit adultery, for they themselves [their husbands, commit adultery, too]" (Hos. 4:14).[150]

The law of "breaking the neck of the heifer" is stated in Deut. 21:1-9 as follows:

> If, in the land that the Lord your God is assigning you to possess, someone slain is found in the open, the identity of the slayer not being known, your elders and magistrates shall go out and measure the distances from the corpse to the nearby towns. The elders of the town nearest to the corpse shall then take a heifer which has never been worked, which has never pulled in a yoke; and the elders of that town shall bring the heifer down to an everflowing wadi, which is not tilled or sown. There, in the wadi, they shall break the heifer's neck. The priests, sons of Levi, shall come forward; for the Lord your God has chosen them to minister to Him and to pronounce blessing in the name of the Lord, and every lawsuit and case of assault is subject to their ruling. Then all the elders of the town nearest to the corpse shall wash their hands over the heifer whose neck was broken in the wadi. And they shall make this declaration: "Our hands did not shed this blood, nor did our eyes see it done. Absolve, O Lord, Your people Israel whom You redeemed, and do not let guilt for the blood of the innocent remain among Your people Israel." And they will be absolved of bloodguilt for the blood of the innocent, for you will be doing what is right in the sight of the Lord.

Despite the clarity of the Biblical mandate, the Rabbis decided not to administer the law "when murderers increased." Although the exact reasoning is unstated, it appears that the increase in murders meant that the dramatic ritual and public disavowal of responsibility no longer had social efficacy. Their decision to stop administering the law of the "breaking of the neck of the heifer" has meant that the law is inoperative down to our own time.

The sotah-water ordeal, named sotah for the tractate of the Mishnah that deals with the topic, is described in Num. 5:11-31.[151] When a husband accused his wife of adultery and she denied it, the priests were directed to administer a lie-detector test. The priest prepared a potion of sacral water and earth from the floor of the tabernacle in an earthen vessel. The priest declared before the accused woman that if she spoke the truth no harm

---

[150] This is the prevalent understanding of the reason that the sotah-water proved ineffective. See the commentaries of Maimonides and Chanoch Albeck. Albeck also cites the explanation of the Tosefta that the test proved ineffective because the adultery was public rather than secretive, see Albeck, M. Sotah 9:9 (תל אביב: מוסד ביאליק-דביר, תשל"ח).

[151] For an analysis of the topic, see Julian Morgenstern, *HUCA* 2 (1925): 113-143.

would come to her when she drank of the holy potion, but if she were lying then the waters would cause her belly to distend and her thigh to sag and she would be cursed among the people of Israel. She was bid to answer "Amen, amen" to the priest's description of the potential curse. The priest's words were written down and then rubbed off into the water of bitterness, including the name of God, and the priest gave the mixture to the woman to drink. This test served to strengthen marital bonds as a deterrent to a woman's secret unfaithfulness and as a remedy against a man's unjustified jealousy.

The priests' refusal to administer this Biblically mandated law testifies to their sense of confidence and responsibility. The Mishnah explains that they stopped utilizing this ritual when "adulterers increased in number." Again, the exact reasoning is left to speculation. Some later poskim wrote that the test itself became ineffective when the husbands were hypocrites, having committed adultery as well. In this explanation, the priests had no choice but to stop using the test since it no longer worked. In light of the other cases of Rabbinic discretion, such as regarding capital punishment and the breaking of the neck of the red heifer, there is reason to believe that the priests made a unilateral decision based on moral and social concerns. The sotah-water test was only administered to women. When marital infidelity increased, it likely struck them as unfair to only put women through such an ordeal and as pointless, since the test no longer served as a societal deterrent against promiscuity. The suspension of the sotah-water ordeal demonstrated the priests' willingness to set aside a Biblical law when it no longer served to meet its intended result and when its administration led to injustice.

As members of our community's law-making body, we are asked to reconsider whether or not mamzerut should have legal efficacy. Our predecessors on the CJLS held that the Biblical law was "inoperative," but they did not offer a halakhic explanation. The length of this תשובה demonstrates the complexity of the matter. Yet, the bottom line remains the same. It is within our authority to refrain from using certain procedures which effectively make the Biblical law inoperative. We have the precedents of Rabbis and priests who refused to hear capital cases, who chose to no longer administer the sotah-test, and who ceased to perform the ritual of breaking the heifer's neck. In each of these cases, the prerogative of making a law inoperative was explained as a response to a change in the social situation that made the Biblical mandate ethically unacceptable or ineffective as a social mechanism.

In our day, mamzerut is both unconscionable and ineffective as a deterrent against sexual misdeeds. When we say that children should not suffer for the sins of their parents, it is not a morality of the hour, but an ethical perspective firmly rooted in our tradition. Admittedly, there are poskim who choose to read the Torah as calling on punishment of innocent children — whether the offspring of former neighboring nations or the children of illicit sexual relations. They are able to point to verses that said that God remembers the sins of parents on their children for generations. Yet, there is another strand in the rabbinic tradition that interprets the Bible to say that God only punishes children when they behave the same way as their parents. Rabbis throughout the generations have sought on a case-by-case basis to undermine the clear intent of the mamzerut law and effectively undermined its implementation in most cases. Yet, they did not solve the problem entirely.

In our day, we have witnessed a proliferation of mamzerut cases, most commonly as a result of ignorance rather than defiance of Jewish tradition. Branding a child as a marital outcast regardless of the parent's intent troubles us. We have made a commitment in the past to enable Jews to marry other Jews even in the face of Biblical prohibitions. To disregard the behavior of parents in our decision to perform the marriage of a Jewish child is not a radical act, but simply an affirmation of our ruling close to thirty years ago.

Our decision, then and now, is to refuse to consider evidence of mamzerut, because the law in our day does not serve as a deterrent to sexual misconduct and instead undermines respect for Torah.

We have a found a way to make mamzerut functionally inoperative. By refusing to entertain evidence of mamzerut, a choice that is our judicial prerogative, we have created an impediment to holding that a person is a mamzer.[152] Consequently, if a person comes to us and says, "My Jewish mother thought my father was dead or divorced without a *get*, remarried, and then had me. What is my status?" We must answer, "I did not hear and will not hear anything that you say regarding your possible status as a mamzer. You are a full Jew. In the Conservative movement, we do not consider the category of mamzerut as operative, because we are committed to judging each person on his or her own merits as a result of the moral teachings of our tradition." Even if we know that a woman in our community divorced without a *get*, remarried, and had a child, we do not consider the status of the child as other than as a Jew.

When we read the verse in Deuteronomy that describes mamzerut, there is still an opportunity to teach a moral lesson. The law of mamzerut conveys the profound seriousness with which the Torah presented the laws of sexual misconduct. Parents were warned with the most frightening threat: If you violate the norms of sexual behavior, your children will suffer. Nothing scares a parent more than harm to his or her child.[153] The importance of sexual restraint remains a lesson implicit in mamzerut, even when choosing not to implement the law. Mamzerut becomes a theoretical teaching, parallel to the laws of the rebellious child, צערת of a house, or the idolatrous city. Unlike those precedents, we cannot say that the rabbinic tradition never enforced this law, but we may say that we no longer do so.

As a Movement we are committed to the Torah being our moral guide, precisely because we take its Divine origins seriously. We cannot conceive of God sanctioning undeserved suffering. At the same time, we approach the halakhic system with respect and a desire to make changes in as small increments as necessary to meet our halakhic goals. As shapers of a life of Torah we are more ready to trim Torah's branches than to cut at her roots unless necessary. Through the procedural mechanism of making mamzerut inoperative we effectively prune a dangerous thorn. We are prompted to act due to a need to harmonize the moral teachings of Torah with her laws.

When we place the Torah in the ark we sing עץ חיים היא למחזיקים בה – "It is a tree of life to those who hold fast to it."[154] The image conveys that the Torah offers spiritual nutrition and comfort in times of need. Torah is also rooted and grounded and thereby defines our distinctive place in the world. Yet, the image conveys that, like a tree, Torah is also alive and growing. We are Torah's gardeners. It is our duty to prune and shape the branches,

---

[152] Another common example of judicial discretion is the widespread refusal of rabbis to consider the evidence of intentional suicide regarding burial. The law in the Talmud and the codes is that an intentional suicide is to be denied the honors of the dead, which was later understood to include burial in the Jewish cemetery (Semahot 2:1; M.T. Hilkhot Avel 1:11; S.A. Yoreh De'ah 345:1). This harsh punishment was rooted in the conviction that intentional suicide denied God's sovereignty. Yet, a presumption was forged that a suicide lacked premeditation (Semahot 2:3; M.T. Sanhedrin 18:6). So far as minors are concerned the presumption was irrebuttable (Semahot 2:4-5; Yoreh De'ah 345:3). In practice rabbis have not sought to rebut the presumption for adults either, in part for concern that the finding would cause distress for the mourners.

[153] Similarly, we find in the Kitzur Shulhan Arukh a related threat concerning masturbation: "Occasionally, as a punishment for this sin, children die when young, God forbid, or grow up to be delinquent, while the sinner himself is reduced to poverty."

[154] Prov. 3:18. I am indebted to Rabbi Bradley Shavit Artson for drawing this analogy to my attention.

which allows it to remain healthy and fruitful. Our prayer continues: דרכיה דרכי נועם – "Her ways are the ways of pleasantness."[155]

When a law of Torah conflicts with morality, when the law is "unpleasant," we are committed to find a way to address the problem. As a halakhic movement we look to precedent to find the tools with which to shape Torah. For the most part, we rely on the strategies of old. At the same time, we are willing to do explicitly what was largely implicit in the past, namely, to make changes when needed on moral grounds. It is our desire to strengthen Torah that forces us to recognize explicitly the overriding importance of morality, a morality which we learn from the larger, unfolding narrative of our tradition. We affirm the holding of the CJLS of the past that mamzerut is inoperative in our time. We affirm that when mamzerut is applied in our day it fails to meet a goal of deterrence and at that same time leads to an unconscionable hardship on innocent people. We affirm that we will not entertain any evidence of mamzerut and instead judge each Jew who stands before us as a person who is only responsible for his or her own wrong-doings.

Conclusion – פסק דין

We render mamzerut inoperative, because we will not consider evidence of mamzerut. We will give permission to any Jew to marry and will perform the marriage of a Jew regardless of the possible sins of his or her parent.

---

[155] Prov. 3:17. The word נועם, translated as "pleasantness," is consistently used in the Tanakh in the context of relationships.

EH 4.2000b

A Concurring Opinion Regarding Mamzerut

Rabbi Daniel S. Nevins

This paper was submitted as a concurrence to "Mamzerut" by Rabbi Elie Kaplan Spitz. Concurring and dissenting opinions are not official positions of the Committee on Jewish Law and Standards.

The Committee on Jewish Law and Standards of the Rabbinical Assembly provides guidance in matters of halakhah for the Conservative movement. The individual rabbi, however, is the authority for the interpretation and application of all matters of halakhah.

I concur with the conclusions drawn by Rabbi Elie Kaplan Spitz in his sensitive and thorough responsum circumscribing mamzerut, the declaration that the offspring of certain forbidden unions are forever unmarriageable by Jewish law.[1] Rabbi Spitz has already reviewed many of the sources and rationales offered for this biblical commandment. He has also demonstrated the classical rabbinic discomfort with this rule, which punishes children for the sins of their parents, a notion usually disavowed in biblical and rabbinic statements.[2]

As Rabbi Spitz notes, poskim have, over the course of two millennia, generally sought to limit the application of this rule, even as they have refrained from declaring it to be inoperative.[3] After considering the possibility of asking the CJLS to validate a motion to uproot this category from the Torah, Rabbi Spitz concludes that it is better to declare that we shall no longer accept any evidence of mamzerut, thereby depriving the rule of its power even as it is retained *de jure*.

My goal is to strengthen the case for keeping this difficult rule on the books while exploring the established methods available for preventing its application. There are both ideological and practical benefits for respecting this rule in theory even as we act to deprive it of practical power. Although this position may be more explicit than that of earlier poskim, it is consistent with their application of narrow rules of evidence that

---

[1] על פי הכתוב, דברים פרק כג פסוק ג, "לא יבא ממזר בקהל ה' גם דור עשירי לא יבא לו בקהל ה':" ובתלמוד בבלי, מסכת יבמות מט, ע"א וכו'.

[2] לדוגמה, במלכים ב פרק יד, פסוק ו, "ואת בני המכים לא המית ככתוב בספר תורת משה צוה ה' לאמר לא יומתו אבות על בנים ובנים לא יומתו על אבות כי אם איש בחטאו ומת יומת:" (וכן במקביל בדברי הימים ב, פרק כה, פסוק ד), ובגמרא סנהדרין כז ע"ב.

[3] Rabbi Spitz also shows that some medieval and even modern sources have vigorously supported strict application of the mamzer rule, reflecting concern for טהרת ישראל, a quasi-racial definition of Jewish identity.

protected innocent children from the mistakes of their parents. It is also worth detailing some of the interpretive methods that are available for rejecting what might otherwise appear to be compelling evidence of mamzerut.[4]

The Ideological Limits of Rabbinic Power

On an ideological level, the law of the mamzer reminds us that we are not the authors of our tradition, but only the latest generation of its devoted interpreters. Indeed, the mamzer law has long fulfilled this function, as Rabbi David Hartman has shown in his book, *The Living Covenant*.[5] There he describes a dialectic of power and powerlessness of our covenanted people vis-à-vis God. Going back to Avraham Avinu, who argued valiantly in defense of the cities of Sodom and Gomorra, but was silent on his own son's behalf, and extending to rabbinic stories such as *tanur shel Achnai*,[6] our predecessors have alternated postures of vigorous assertion and humble submission before God. The law of the mamzer is a statute which the rabbis have, generation after generation, sought to circumscribe without presuming to eliminate altogether. Hartman cites the same Vayikra Rabbah text[7] quoted by Rabbi Spitz as an example of the Rabbis' frustration with this law but their ultimate submission to the authority of the Torah. Hartman concludes that, "It was bold of the rabbis to protest against a law that they saw as fundamentally unjust. Nevertheless, they accepted it with the proviso that in the world to come, God will correct the injustice."[8]

While we modern rabbis may be less comfortable deferring the justice of a wronged individual to the next world, we should acknowledge that God's law is beyond our authority simply to eliminate. Indeed, the interpretive method is far better established and more compelling than the legislative options listed by Rabbi Spitz. Professor Judith Hauptman has argued in her book, *Rereading the Rabbis*, that a similar dynamic obtained in other cases such as the sotah, which the Rabbis supported in theory, but severely circumscribed in practice.[9] She writes:

> On the surface, this tractate appears to endorse and develop the ritual of the bitter waters as set down by the Torah, but in reality, in all of its elaborate expansion, the rabbis eliminate this ancient ritual, paragraph by paragraph, until, almost anticlimactically, at the end of the volume, they supply a historical note that the waters were, in fact, abolished by R. Yohanan b. Zaccai.

---

[4] My focus here is on remarriage without a *get* rather than on cases of incest.

[5] David Hartman, *A Living Covenant: The Innovative Spirit in Traditional Judaism* (New York: The Free Press, 1985), especially ch. 2, "Assertion Versus Submission: The Tension Within Judaism."

[6] בבא מציעא נט ע"ב.

[7] ויקרא רבה (מרגליות) פרשה לב ד"ה [ח] ושבתי אני. (גירסת 7.0 מפרוייקט השו"ת של בר-אילן)

[ח] ושבתי אני וראאה את כל העשוקים (קהלת ד,א). חנינא חייטא פתר קרייה בממזרים. ושבתי אני וראאה את כל העשוקים, אילו הממזרים. והנה דמעת העשוקים (שם/קהלת ד/,א/), אימותיהן שלאילו עברו עבירה ואילין עליביא מרחקין להון. אביו שלזה בא על ערוה זה מה עשה וזה מה איכפת לו. ואין להם מנחם אלא מיד עושקיהם כוח (שם/קהלת ד/,א/), זה סנהדרין גדולה שלישראל/של ישראל/שהיא באה עליהן בכוח התורה ומרחקן, על שם לא יבא ממזר בקהל י"י (דברים כג,ג). ואין להם מנחם (שם/ דברים כ"ג, ג,"/), אמ' הקב"ה עלי לנחמן. לפי שבעולם הזה יש בהן פסולת אבל לעתיד לבוא אמ' זכריה אנא חמיתיה אולוכורוסון דדהב נקי.

[8] Hartman, p. 59.

[9] Judith Hauptman, *Rereading the Rabbis: A Woman's Voice* (Boulder, CO: WestviewPress, 1998), p. 28.

There is ample reason to adopt a similar approach in the case of mamzerut. While it might be more emotionally satisfying to make declarations of our heightened moral sensitivity, such statements are unlikely to convince others who are committed to halakhic process that our conclusions are justified.

Practical Reasons to Retain the Category of Mamzerut

As Rabbi Spitz shows, in antiquity the mamzer law functioned as a limit upon promiscuity and incest, since the lawless couple would have to face the tragic implications of their forbidden union. Rabbi Spitz argues that this practical benefit of mamzerut is no longer relevant, but I am not so sure. Moreover, I believe that mamzerut is part of the foundation for our steadfast insistence on *gittin* in cases of civil divorce. Based on conversations with colleagues in the Reform rabbinate, I believe that our concern over mamzerut motivates some of them to mention and even advocate for the "option" of obtaining a *get* before remarrying a divorced man or woman. Were we to declare the entire category of mamzerut to be inoperative, it could become more difficult to convince remarrying couples to obtain *gittin* prior to their new marriage. Of course, Conservative rabbis would still be forbidden to officiate at such a marriage, but the couple would have one less motivation to comply with the halakhah.

Were we to declare this entire category to be inoperative in our Movement rather than content ourselves to restricting it radically as has been done before, there would be yet another challenge for marriages between Conservative and Orthodox Jews. Moreover, our responsa should not be written only for Conservative Jews, but should be thoroughly grounded in the same sources and methodologies used by other halakhically committed Jews. Interpretation and the restriction of evidence are the established tools for dealing with mamzerut.

Rabbi Spitz includes a substantial section entitled "Toolbox of Halakhic Change" which gives an overview of various methods – some interpretive, some legislative – used by the Rabbis to develop Jewish law. What seems more urgent in our case is a toolbox of halakhic methods for disqualifying evidence of mamzerut, should it be presented to a rabbi. Before proceeding to describe such a toolbox, it is worthwhile to study an actual case and see how a contemporary posek nullified evidence of mamzerut.

Available Options: A Case Study from Rabbi Ovadiah Yosef

A responsum sent by Rabbi Ovadiah Yosef to Rabbi Grubner in Detroit is striking for its factual clarity, which would apparently necessitate application of the law of the mamzer:[10]

> א) והנה גופא דעובדא אודות אשה שלפי דבריה נישאת לבעלה הראשון בחופה וקידושין כדמו"י על ידי רב חרדי, וילדה לו שלשה בנים, ולאחר מכן נפרדו בגירושין אזרחיים על ידי הערכאות, ולא קבלה ממנו גט, ושלשת הבנים נשארו אצלה להחזיקתה, באופן שהבעל ישלם לה דמי מזונותיהם. והבעל הזה התנצר ונשא לו אשה נכריה. ואף היא הלכה ונישאת ע"י הערכאות לאיש אחר וילדה לו בנים ובת אחת אשר זכתה להתחנך "בבית יעקב" החרדי, ומתנהגת למופת בצניעות ובכשרות ככל בנות ישראל הכשרות, ועתה כשהגיע פרקה להנשא לבחור ירא שמים, קמה וגם נצבה השאלה אם מותר לה לבוא בקהל ה', מאחר שלפי דברי אם הנערה שלא קבלה גט כדת מבעלה הראשון כל בניה מהבעל השני פסולים לבא בקהל.

---

[10] שו"ת יביע אומר (חלק ז–אה"ע סימן ו ד"ה א) והנה.

The matter in its essence presented with a woman who, according to her words, was married to her first husband with huppah and kiddushin according to the laws of Moses and Israel by a Haredi rabbi, and she gave birth to three children. Afterwards, she separated from him by civil divorce arranged by the courts, but she did not receive a *get* from him. The three children remained with her, with the father paying child support. The husband then apostatized and married a non-Jewish woman. She too went and remarried by the civil authorities and had sons and a daughter who managed to be educated at the Haredi *Beit Yaakov*. She [the daughter] is distinguished by modest and proper behavior as any proper daughter of Israel. Now that the time has come for her to marry a God-fearing young man, the question of whether she can enter the Lord's congregation has arisen, since by the mother's account, she had not received a religious *get* from her first husband, and thus all of her children from the second husband are unfit to enter the Lord's congregation.

On the face of it, we have here clear evidence of mamzerut. After all, the young woman has presented the question of her status, and her mother admits that she was married the first time by a Haredi rabbi, and that this daughter was born after a second, secular marriage, with no *get* in the interim. This is the type of case that Rabbi Spitz has accurately identified as increasingly common in modern times.

Rabbi Yosef never indicates discomfort with the category of mamzer per se, but he goes to extraordinary lengths to prevent its application in this case. The mother's testimony is immediately disqualified, based upon the Shulhan Arukh.[11] While the father's testimony would be accepted in certain circumstances, the Shulhan Arukh gives numerous reasons to exclude his testimony, especially if there are complicating factors such as grandchildren.[12] In this case, the local court failed to get the father's testimony, apparently after one adversarial phone conversation with his non-Jewish wife. Although the original wedding was performed בחופה וקידושין by a Haredi rabbi whose signature is present on the civil marriage license, his testimony is likewise rejected as עד אחד, an unconfirmed witness. Rabbi Yosef states that even if he were alive and testified before the court, the Haredi rabbi's words would not be accepted without the ketubbah, which has somehow been lost. There is no description of a search to locate this document. Thus we have a legal doubt whether the first couple was even married.

Later in the responsum, Rabbi Yosef relates that the girl's mother testified to the bet din that her first husband continued to visit, and even to be intimate with her, after their civil divorce and her civil remarriage. This is enough to introduce doubt whether the girl's father is indeed the second man.

Rabbi Yosef's presumption is buttressed by various Talmudic statements. In Yevamot 80b, Rabba declared kosher a baby born to a woman whose husband had been abroad for twelve months prior to the birth, on the assumption that the pregnancy may have been prolonged up to three months.[13] In Sotah 27a it is asserted that even if a woman were known to carry on extra-marital sexual liaisons, any child can be presumed to be from her

---

[11] אבן העזר סימן ד סעיף כט. "אשת איש שאומרת על העובר שאינו מבעלה, אינה נאמנת לפוסלו." ועיין ברמב"ם, הל' איסורי ביאה, פ' טו, הלכות יד–טו.

[12] שם. "אבל האב שאומר על העובר שאינו ממנו, או על אחד מבניו שאינו בנו, נאמן לפוסלו והוא ממזר ודאי. ואם יש בנים לבן, אינו נאמן אף על הבן. ואם היא אומרת: מעובד כוכבים או העבד נתעברתי, הולד כשר כשאין הבעל יכול להכחישה בזה."

[13] ועיין בשו"ת אגרות משה חלק אה"ע ד,סימן יז ד"ה והנה מפורש

husband, for most of her sexual unions are presumed to be lawful.[14] The Talmud indicates that even if the lawful husband was observed abroad when his wife conceived, we must still allow for the possibility that a "speedy camel"[15] could have brought him into the proximity of his wife at the time of conception. Presumably the advent of jet planes has further buttressed this consideration.

In this case, even though the mother was civilly divorced from her halakhic husband and living with her civil-marriage second husband, her subsequent children are not assumed by Rabbi Yosef to be mamzerim.[16] Rabbi Yosef is aware that the woman's exonerating testimony of continued intimacy with her first husband is suspicious[17] – and that similar testimony had been discounted by an earlier responsum of the גנת ורדים.[18] Nevertheless, he finds support for believing the mother. Thus he has established doubt whether the girl's social father is also her biological father.

In summary, here is a case in which all parties admit that the mother was married to her Jewish husband by a Haredi rabbi, and that after a civil divorce and remarriage to another man she had more children who were raised as the children of her second (civil marriage) husband. But in the absence of legally sufficient evidence of the first marriage, and in the presence of continued contact between the mother and her first husband, there is a double doubt, ספק ספיקא, about the child's status, and the daughter is allowed to marry.[19] The responsum is full of many other arguments which are worthy of study.

Confronting Possible Evidence of Mamzerut

As Rabbi Spitz has written, there are many such cases in which poskim used narrow rules of interpretation to clear a person of the status of mamzer. Responsa have generally been applications of general principles and relevant precedents to specific cases, rather than sweeping new codifications of the law. Rabbi Yosef would probably not list his methods as a general protocol for pulpit rabbis. He has, however, shown that there are many methods available to protect a person from פסול – the damaging identification as a mamzer.

Does such an array of defenses increase the likelihood that a true mamzer will indeed enter קהל ה' through marriage, and thereby lead to violation of the biblical command? Or, do we say that unless a person has exhausted all possible defenses against the evidence of mamzerut, that he or she is not essentially a mamzer, and should be welcomed under the huppah by the rabbi with a full heart? The latter perspective is more in keeping with

---

[14] "אשת מזנה – בניה כשרין, רוב בעילות אחר הבעל."

[15] "גמלא פרחא," ראה במכות ה/א.

[16] Rabbi Yosef does not discuss the possibility of DNA paternity testing in this undated responsum. It is possible that even such scientific proof would be discounted since it does not meet the standard of שני עדים המעידים בפני הבית דין. Rabbi Yosef also does not recognize that in this case, רוב בעילות אחר הבעל would likely apply to her current (civil) husband, and not to the man whom she divorced, who himself remarried, but who is still halakhically her husband.

[17] One wonders if the bet din somehow suggested to the mother that she might have had some physical contact with her first husband during his periodic visits to pay child support and have visitation with their children.

[18] האה"ע כלל ד ס"ס כט.

[19] In his conclusion, Rabbi Ovadiah Yosef writes:

> ועכ"פ אפילו אי יהבינן שלא יצא הדבר מידי ספק, הרי יש כאן ספק ספיקא, וכמו שביארנו לעיל, שמא נישואיה לבעל הראשוני לא היו בחופה וקידושין כדת, ואת"ל שהיו בחופה וקידושין שמא הבת היא מבעלה הראשון, וגם אפשר שנתגרשה ג' בגט כדמו"י, ואין האשה נאמנת לפסול את בתה, בטענה שנתקדשה ולא נתגרשה כדת. וכבר כתבו הפוסקים להתיר פסולי קהל בספק ספיקא.

halakhic method, and with that in mind, I shall summarize some of the exclusionary techniques available to the rabbi faced with evidence of mamzerut:

A. *Was the possible mamzer's mother really married to a man other than his/her father at the time of his/her conception?*

1. The possible mamzer is not qualified to testify that his or her mother was previously married to a man other than his father.[20]
2. The mother and her first husband are not themselves qualified to testify to the legitimacy of their wedding ceremony, and thereby to doom her offspring from a subsequent man to the status of mamzer.
3. The rabbi who officiated at the first couple's wedding is not qualified to testify that it was a proper wedding, and thereby to doom her offspring from another man to the status of mamzer.
4. Damning evidence such as a ketubbah need not be sought out.
5. Marriages performed by reputable rabbis may be assumed to be valid until a question of mamzerut for the offspring is introduced.

B. *Is it legally certain that the halakhic husband is not the real father?*

1. Geographic separation is not determinative.
2. The mother may be believed to testify on behalf of the child's halakhic legitimacy, but not against it.
3. Scientific paternity tests such as DNA matching need not be sought out, and may be inadmissible as evidence for פסול.

C. *Whose business is it anyway?*

1. Neighbors, civil servants and other interested parties are not allowed to investigate the ancestry of a possible mamzer. This is a rank form of רכילות, or forbidden gossip. Unwarranted בדיקה is a form of אונאה, as it impugns the eligibility for marriage of a Jew.
2. It takes two legitimate witnesses, who can testify to the halakhic marriage of the first couple, *and* to the mother's certain conception of this child by another man, before mamzerut proceedings can even be *initiated*. These witnesses obviously cannot be related to the potential mamzer or to any of the family, and must meet all of the other stringent criteria of Jewish witnesses.

Summary

The law of mamzerut is Biblical and should not be abrogated by the CJLS. Indeed, Conservative rabbis should use their powers of persuasion to encourage non-halakhic rabbis to obtain a *get* prior to performing a remarriage. However, there is ample precedent for restricting the evidence of mamzerut to the point that it would be next to impossible for a rabbi to conclude that a man or woman is inadmissible to קהל ה׳ by means of נשואוין כדת משה וישראל, a proper Jewish marriage. Rabbis are encouraged to use the above list (and other exonerating factors) to set aside evidence of mamzerut. We should further discourage rabbinical authorities such as the Israeli Rabbanut from assembling data bases to expand the number of Jews impugned as mamzerim.

וכך נלע״ד.

---

[20] The codes do allow a person to testify that he is himself a mamzer (S.A. Even HaEzer 4:30; M.T. Isurei Biah 15:16), despite the general principle of אינו נפסל עד שיהיו שם שני עדים שאין אדם משים את עצמו רשע (M.T. Edut 12:2). This testimony is not, however, sufficient to impugn his children as mamzerim. Moreover, it is not evident how a child can testify to the validity of his mother's marriage since he was not yet born!

EH 6:1.1996

SOLEMNIZING THE MARRIAGE BETWEEN A KOHEN AND A DIVORCEE

Rabbi Arnold M. Goodman

This paper was approved by the CJLS on March 12, 1996, by a vote of twelve in favor, four opposed, and two abstentions (12-4-2). Voting in favor: Rabbis Kassel Abelson, Ben Zion Bergman, Stephanie Dickstein, Elliot N. Dorff, Jerome M. Epstein, Shoshana Gelfand, Myron S. Geller, Arnold M. Goodman, Mayer Rabinowitz, Elie Kaplan Spitz, Gordon Tucker, and Gerald Zelizer. Voting against: Rabbis Judah Kogen, Vernon H. Kurtz, Paul Plotkin, and Avram Israel Reisner. Abstaining: Rabbis Baruch Frydman-Kohl and Lionel E. Moses.

The Committee on Jewish Law and Standards of the Rabbinical Assembly provides guidance in matters of halakhah for the Conservative movement. The individual rabbi, however, is the authority for the interpretation and application of all matters of halakhah.

שאלה

May a member of the RA officiate at the marriage between a Kohen and a divorcee?

תשובה

In 1952 the CJLS adopted a responsum authored by Rabbi Ben Zion Bokser[1] permitting RA members to solemnize such a marriage. This היתר has been widely accepted by the overwhelming majority of the RA although his recommendation, that "where such marriage is to take place, the rabbi seek to persuade the couple to refrain from a large public wedding,"[2] has not been widely observed. Rabbi Aaron Blumenthal, in a concurring opinion, differed with Rabbi Bokser, and argued that such marriages be treated no differently than any other. I return to this responsum not because I disagree with Rabbi Bokser, but because his paper fails to offer a satisfactory rationale for overturning a clear Biblical prohibition.

In his responsum, Rabbi Bokser reviewed the sources clearly forbidding such marriages but concluded, "A rabbi who officiates at such a marriage has not acted in a manner inconsistent with his Judaism."[3] His paper was written during a period in which the role of the Kohen was, if not dismissed, then certainly significantly reduced. Rabbi Bokser reflected this sentiment in his contention in 1951 that "the very few prerogatives left to the Kohen stand

---

[1] *PRA* 18 (1954): 55-61.
[2] Ibid., p. 61.
[3] Ibid., p. 58.

as a vital reminder of the immense progress made in the democratization of Judaism."[4] While the role of the Kohen continues to be marginal in most of our congregations, there has been a revival of interest in the institution of the כהונה and its place within our movement. Not surprisingly, issues focusing on the status of the Kohen have come before the CJLS.

In 1990, Rabbi Mayer Rabinowitz concluded, "Where a Rabbi feels that a congregation or service would be better served calling people up to the Torah as rishon, sheni, shlishi, it is entirely permissible to do so. This system allows any congregant who may normally be granted an aliyah at that service to be honored with any of the עליות during the service."[5]

In response to this paper which was overwhelmingly approved by the Committee, Rabbi Herbert Mandl wrote what was a limited dissent. Distinguishing between חול and Shabbat/Yom Tov, he permitted flexibility during the former services but argued for maintaining the practice of giving the first aliyah to the Kohen at the latter services. Yet even on Shabbat and Yom Tov, the Kohen might be bypassed, "provided it does not become a habitual practice Sabbath after Sabbath without reserving at least some special occasions and circumstances when a Kohen will be honored."[6] Rabbi Mandl is clear that his reading of the sources does permit the Kohen to waive his right to the first aliyah, and that this be made clear when a non-Kohen is called up first. His paper was also overwhelmingly approved.

The central issue in the above papers and in the CJLS debates was whether a Kohen had special status by virtue of the historic and traditional interpretation of וקדשתו (Lev. 21:8). The flexibility shown by Rabbi Rabinowitz in permitting congregations to do away with giving the first aliyah to a Kohen was based on the assumption that the practice was מדרבנן. Had his research concluded that it was מדאורייתא, his conclusion may have been otherwise.

The prohibition of a Kohen marrying a divorcee is clearly מדאורייתא. The text in Leviticus clearly forbids a marriage with a divorcee. Rabbi Bokser begins his paper by recognizing that "there is no question that Jewish law objects to such marriage. It is Biblically forbidden. The Talmud reaffirms this prohibition."[7] He develops his argument by showing that where such a marriage does take place, the Talmud ruled קדושין תופסין.[8] To be sure, the children of such marriage are חללים and disqualified from priestly functions, but in the event that they do perform a function it is valid בדיעבד.

The rest of the תשובה is a discussion of the rationale behind the prohibition, the less jaundiced view we have today of a divorcee, the diminished role of the Kohen in our times and the fact that "great numbers of Kohanim today are not conscious of any special status."[9] He observes that "finding of a suitable mate is difficult," and "we must accept the fact that an unequivocal condemnation of such a marriage and an unwillingness to officiate may present Judaism as arbitrary and indifferent to personal happiness and as placing legal formalisms above human values, with the result that such people would feel driven to leave the synagogue and Jewish observances generally."[10]

---

[4] Ibid., p. 56.

[5] Rabbi Mayer Rabinowitz, "Rishon or Kohen," *PCJLS 86-90*, p. 442.

[6] Rabbi Herbert Mandl, "May a Non-Kohen Be Called Up First to the Torah?", above, p. 20.

[7] Bokser, op. cit., p. 56.

[8] B. Kiddushin 67a.

[9] Bokser, op. cit., p. 56.

[10] Ibid., p. 57.

It is always dangerous to impute a rationale to a Biblical commandment, but the very term גרושה (from the root גרש, "to chase away") underscores the tendency to lay the cause of divorce at the feet of the woman. Was the גרושה regarded as a "discard" and hence not fit for a Kohen who was to embody perfection? This point can certainly be argued.

Divorce is viewed differently today. It is often an opportunity for a second chance, and our continued embrace of the Biblical prohibition of the marriage between a Kohen and a גרושה could reinforce the ancient prejudice against a divorced woman. Even if we are willing, however, to extend a welcoming hand to a גרושה, the Biblical prohibition is clear, and the CJLS, reflecting our Movement's commitment to halakhah, must root its decision in appropriate halakhic principles.

The authority to overturn a Biblical prohibition is debated by Rabbi Hisda and Rabbah in a famous sugya in Yevamot.[11] The issue is האם בית דין מתנין לעקור דבר מן התורה?

On Uprooting a Biblical Prohibition

R. Hisda's carefully marshaled arguments are challenged by Rabbah, but there is no question that R. Hisda has articulated a principle that resonates within the Talmud. The Rabbis, in fact, granted a bet din authority "to uproot" in three instances.

1. בשב ואל תעשה. There are instances where the Rabbis ruled that a mitzvah not be performed. Specific examples of this principle are not blowing shofar on Shabbat or blessing lulav and etrog on Shabbat out of concern that the Shabbat ban on carrying in public be violated.

2. בקום ועשה. When there is הוראת שעה, the demands of the moment, it is permitted to violate a specific prohibition, in order to prevent erosions from commitment to the Tradition. The example cited is Elijah offering a sacrifice on Mt. Carmel in order to turn the people back from idolatry.

3. בדבר שבממון. The principle of הפקר בית דין הפקר gives a bet din the right to declare money or articles ownerless.

The Talmud in Nazir 43a permits a Kohen, in clear violation of Biblical law, to involve himself in the burial of his minor wife whose father was dead. In a famous tosafot, Rabbi Yitzhak explains that by Biblical law, she is not a מת מצוה because she has other family. Yet since her relatives and family may have abandoned her, the Rabbis regarded her as a מת מצוה, and even though a bet din does not have the authority to uproot a Biblical prohibition, *"in an instance where there is פנים וטעם בדבר, it is universally accepted that there is authority to uproot."*[12]

Later authorities were reluctant to assume such unilateral authority. Yitzhak Gilat's review of the later literature demonstrates the dual concern that later-day authorities did not have the requisite knowledge, piety, etc., of their Talmudic forbearers and the fear that invoking this principle would create the proverbial slippery slope, thereby weakening the entire halakhic structure. Later authorities thus imposed severe limitations on the conditions and situations where it would be appropriate and necessary "to uproot."[13]

Thus the statement in the Yerushalmi, "when we can fulfill both their [the Sages'] word and the Torah's, you fulfill them. Where you cannot fulfill the words of both, you

---

[11] B. Yevamot 89a-90b.

[12] B. Nazir 43b, Tosafot, s.v. והאי מת מצוה.

[13] Yitzhak Gilat, *P'rakim B'Hishtal'shut HaHalacha*, pp. 191-204.

negate their words and fulfill the words of the Torah."[14] Or in the words of the Bavli, "The Torah comes and negates the Rabbis."[15]

Yet the right "to uproot" was never completely prohibited. There was often the need for an escape hatch, and the right of Rabbinic authorities to do so was articulated by the Rashba as follows: "It was not a matter of the sages deciding on their own to uproot a matter of the Torah, but it is one of the mitzvot in the Torah to obey the 'judges in your day' and anything they see necessary to permit is permissible from the Torah."[16]

The high intermarriage rate is of deep concern. In an instance when two Jews express their desire to marry one another, are we not beholden to remove barriers to their relationship? The high divorce rate is a reality. All too often second marriages of a divorcee are to a non-Jew, and these women are often single mothers with minor children. Exposing them to a home with a non-Jewish stepfather who introduces into their lives a host of non-Jewish relatives is not in the best interests of the Jewish people.

When a גרושה is prepared to marry a Jew, albeit a Kohen, is it appropriate for us, in this day and age, to refuse to solemnize the marriage? Even a strategy of seeking to counsel the couple against marriage because of their respective statuses and agreeing to officiate בדיעבד casts aspersions upon their relationship. A ringing endorsement of their intended union will affirm the importance our Movement attaches to endogamous marriages.

We also regard divorce differently than did our Biblical and Rabbinic forbearers. We no longer perceive the divorced woman as being guilty of ערות דבר (an unsavory act). To exclude a Jewish woman who is divorced from marrying the man with whom she is in love, affirms the negative status of the divorcee. This is inconsistent with our view of divorce or of our assessment of the character of a woman who happens to be a גרושה.

One could defend the decision permitting such marriages by arguing that every Kohen is a ספק, but such an approach creates its own problems. Would we then be honest in our attempts to reintroduce *duhaning* into our Services and to repopularize the פדיון הבן ceremony? To be sure, we can argue that the קדושה of the Kohen should lead to restrictions and regard marriage with a גרושה (or a גיורת) as being the price paid for special status. Those to whom the כהונה is a privilege may well accept this and other limitations. The vast majority of Kohanim in our congregations do not perceive themselves as enjoying a unique status nor will they accept any limitations on their behavior because of their כהונה. Hence, most Kohanim do not *duhan*, they will visit cemeteries and have probably never officiated at a פדיון הבן.

There are those who contend that a Kohen in our day has lesser holiness because there is no longer a בית מקדש where Kohanim offered קרבנות. Are we prepared to say that even if the Temple were to be rebuilt and sacrifices restored that we would still wish to regard a גרושה as an inappropriate bride for a Kohen? While but a rhetorical question at this juncture of history, it touches upon our willingness to reinterpret the status of the גרושה.

The hard fact confronting us is that the Torah is clear that a Kohen is not to marry a divorcee. Nothing in that verse speaks of the level of the קדושה of the Kohen. Even after Temple times, וקדשתו was interpreted to vest the Kohen with certain prerogatives in terms of the synagogue service and the פדיון הבן. The contention in this paper is that despite the קדושה of the Kohen, he may marry a divorcee for the two reasons cited above. The

---

[14] J. Ketubbot 10:2.

[15] B. Shabbat 128b.

[16] *Hidushei Rashba*, Nedarim, p. 90a.

large number of divorcees make it highly probable that a Kohen will find his intended among the divorced women an our community. This high divorce rate together with the high intermarriage rate mandate that we do not place a barrier to such a marriage. This is a הוראת שעה justifying uprooting the Biblical prohibition of Lev. 21:7. Our willingness to do this is further supported by our view that a divorcee is not of a lesser status than her non-divorced sister.

הוראת שעה speaks of crisis. Should the current rate of intermarriage be reversed, a future Law Committee may well decide to review this issue. At this time, however, we face a crisis of such proportion that we dare not, in good conscience, stand between the marriage of two Jews whose union is forbidden by virtue of his being a Kohen and she a divorcee.

Our steadfast refusal to solemnize their marriage, or even to agree to do this only after seeking to dissuade them, may well lead the couple to be married either in a civil ceremony or in a ceremony without full חופה and קדושין. The couple, knowing of our disapproval of our relationship, will find little comfort within our movement and its Synagogues.

Arguing for עקירה of Lev. 21:7 in effect removes it as a prohibition. While the Talmud, accepting the reality of such marriages in its day, ruled קדושין תופסין, the children were חללים and denied all privileges of כהונה, while their father sacrificed his special status only as long as he continued in the marriage. Our decision to negate the prohibitions reaffirms the status of both father and child. Congregations which reserve the first aliyah for Kohanim, which have *duhaning* and which encourage פדיון הבן, are to regard such fathers and sons as acceptable Kohanim.

New times bring new issues and concerns, and affirming the argument of the Rashba, it is the Biblically ordained right and duty of the judges or leaders to rule in the best interests of the people and the Torah. For the Conservative movement, the CJLS is the body vested with the judicial and legislative authority to adapt halakhah in light of contemporary reality and modern concerns.

The decision to uproot Biblical prohibitions and Rabbinic tradition can never be treated lightly. Rashba reminds us that halakhic authorities have been granted the power, either through outright legislation or through midrashic interpretation, to abandon even a Biblical prohibition. The caveat before us is well stated by our colleague, Rabbi Joel Roth who reminds us that "יראת שמים is a *sine qua non* of halakhic authorities. It is the characteristic that guarantees, to the extent anything can, that what motivates halakhic authorities in their commitment to the integrity of the system they govern. יראת שמים on the part of the systemic authorities assures that their actions are taken לשם שמים."[17]

Rashba's principle of granting authority to "the judges in your day" is the rationale permitting uprooting, albeit only after a careful analysis of contemporary needs. We are challenged not to be timid in advocating changes which we, in good conscience, believe are demanded by the shifting circumstances in which we now find ourselves.

Conclusions

1. The prohibition of a Kohen marrying a divorcee is clearly Biblical. The reality is that very few Kohanim who turn to us for marriage are concerned about their status as Kohanim. Our refusal to solemnize their marriage would only lead them to be married either in a civil ceremony or in a ceremony without full חופה and קדושין.

---

[17] Joel Roth, *The Halakhic Process: A Systemic Analysis* (New York: Jewish Theological Seminary, 1986), p.

2. While we regret the dissolution of a marriage, divorce in our day offers men and women an opportunity for a second chance to develop a successful marital relationship. We also no longer perceive a divorcee as a woman who has been discarded by her former husband and hence not suitable as a spouse for a Kohen.

3. The principle that בית דין מתנין לעקור דבר מן התורה is applied only when faced with extreme situations, and we regard the contemporary intermarriage crisis as such a situation. We also note the high rate of intermarriage of divorced women who are often single mothers with minor children.

4. We, therefore, support the decision of two Jews to marry even when he is a Kohen and she is a גרושה, and a member of the Rabbinical Assembly may solemnize such marriage.

5. With the negating of the prohibition in Lev. 21:7, children born of marriages between a Kohen and a גרושה are not חללים, and the Kohen is no longer disqualified to serve as a Kohen in our services or rituals.

6. Such marriages may be properly celebrated in a public manner. *Our goal continues to be to assure that such celebrations be kosher.*

EH 6.8:1996

SOLEMNIZING THE MARRIAGE BETWEEN A KOHEN AND A CONVERT

Rabbi Arnold M. Goodman

This paper was approved by the CJLS on March 12, 1996, by a vote of fifteen in favor and three abstaining (15-0-3). Voting in favor: Rabbis Kassel Abelson, Ben Zion Bergman, Stephanie Dickstein, Elliot N. Dorff, Jerome M. Epstein, Shoshana Gelfand, Myron S. Geller, Arnold M. Goodman, Vernon H. Kurtz, Lionel E. Moses, Mayer Rabinowitz, Avram Israel Reisner, Elie Kaplan Spitz, Gordon Tucker, and Gerald Zelizer. Abstaining: Rabbis Baruch Frydman-Kohl, Judah Kogen and Paul Plotkin.

The Committee on Jewish Law and Standards of the Rabbinical Assembly provides guidance in matters of halakhah for the Conservative movement. The individual rabbi, however, is the authority for the interpretation and application of all matters of halakhah.

שאלה

May a member of the RA officiate at the marriage between a Kohen and a convert?

תשובה

In 1967, the CJLS adopted a teshuvah by Rabbi Isaac Klein permitting RA members to solemnize such marriages.[1] His paper, like Rabbi Bokser's on the marriage between a Kohen and a divorcee, was written during a period in which the role of the Kohen was, if not dismissed, then significantly reduced.[2]

While Rabbi Klein does not deal with the increasing irrelevance of כהונה, he concludes, "In these cases we should also take into consideration the opinion that the status of all Kohanim today is in doubt," which he supports with a brief quotation from the Magen Avraham, "שאין מחזיק אותו ככהן ודאי."[3] Rabbi Klein bases his approval of a rabbi officiating at the marriage between a Kohen and a convert on the grounds that Lev. 21:7 does not specifically mention a convert but a זונה, a word which the Talmud expanded to include all women whose moral purity was impugned. This Rabbinic interpretation is reinforced by a verse in Ezekiel that limits a Kohen to marry a woman "מזרע בית ישראל."[4] Following a review of the later authorities, Rabbi Klein can only

---

[1] *PRA* 32 (1968): 219-223.
[2] *PRA* 18 (1954): 55-61.
[3] *PRA* 32 (1968): 223.
[4] Ezek. 44:22.

conclude, "the accepted law has been that a Kohen may not marry a גיורת."⁵

Rabbi Klein then refutes the assumption that whoever is not a בת ישראל is בחזקת זונה. He reminds us that the proselyte is "most worthy of love, appreciation and endearment. Again and again the Talmud stresses that the proselyte is equal in every respect to an Israelite from birth. The case of a Kohen is practically the only exception."⁶ For him, a new factor to be considered is חילול השם. Basing his argument on two responsa, the first by Rabbi David Hoffman⁷ and the second by Rabbi Yehudah Leib Zirelson,⁸ Rabbi Klein concluded, "There could be no greater חילול השם than for us to declare that such a marriage is forbidden because female proselytes are considered as having the status of זונות because their people are *shtufim b'zimah*."⁹

While Rabbi Klein does not refer to Rabbi Bokser's concern that upholding such prohibitions would present Judaism as being arbitrary and indifferent to human happiness, it is obvious that those who accept this caveat with regard to marriage with a divorcee would apply it also in the case of a convert. Rabbi Klein concludes, "in view of all the foregoing, it is our considered opinion that we permit a Kohen to marry a גיורת.¹⁰

As noted above, prohibition of a Kohen-convert marriage is rooted in the interpretation of the word זונה in Leviticus and in the verse in Ezekiel that the woman be of the seed of the house of Israel. While the Rabbinic interpretation of זונה is deemed to create a Biblical prohibition, the reality today is that a non-Jewish woman is not *ipso facto* a זונה. In fact to embrace this position can lead to a חילול השם, demeaning the Torah not only in the eyes of the non-Jews, but in the eyes of Jews who view the non-Jewish world differently than did our Talmudic ancestors and subsequent generations until this era.

Given the large number of non-Jews who have become Jews-by-choice, any ruling that even alludes to a non-Jewish woman as being a זונה would also make a mockery of the efforts of our colleagues to bring converts into our midst and to commit them to a life of mitzvah. It would also convey a negative message to thousands upon thousands of the children of converts and their families.

The Torah does not explicitly prohibit a Kohen from marrying a גיורת. The prohibition derives from the Rabbinic interpretation of the term זונה in Lev. 21:7. By rejecting the Rabbinic principle that non-Jewish women are בחזקת זנות, there is no need to invoke the principle of לעקור דבר מן התורה. It is not the Biblical prohibition which is the focus of our concern but its Rabbinic interpretation which does not conform either to our moral sense or to the sad reality that the sexual morality of Jewish women – and men – does not differ to any major degree with what prevails throughout our society. The high incidence of Jewish men and women living together prior to marriage concerns us, but this merely indicates that Jewish and non-Jewish women have embraced similar values when it comes to sexual behavior.

Since a convert is regarded as part of the House of Israel, Ezekiel's insistence that a Kohen marry the seed of the House of Israel is realized. The Talmud instructs us that bringing up the ancestry of a גר violates the Biblical prescription of לא תונו, you shall not oppress (with words). The view we espouse is that a גר is to be wholeheartedly embraced,

---

⁵ Klein, p. 221.

⁶ Ibid, p. 7.

⁷ Rabbi David Hoffman, *Melamed L'Ho'il*, vol. 3, p. 8.

⁸ Ma'archay Leib no. 72.

⁹ *PRA* 32 (1968): 222.

¹⁰ Ibid., p. 223.

as reflected in Maimonides' famous response to Obadiah, a convert, who queried whether he could recite the words, "Our God and God of our Fathers." Maimonides replied: "Abraham, our father, peace be with him, is the father of his pious posterity who keep his way and the father of his disciples and of all the proselytes who adopt Judaism. Therefore you shall pray, Our God and God of our fathers, because Abraham, peace be unto him, is your father."[11]

Conclusion

Given our ongoing commitment to accepting converts and the fact of modern life that Jews and non-Jews often develop relationships leading to marriage, we affirm Rabbi Klein's conclusion that — following conversion of the non-Jew — a marriage between a Kohen and a גיורת is not a prohibited marriage and may be solemnized by a member of the Rabbinical Assembly.

---

[11] Franz Kobler, *A Treasury of Jewish Letters*, "Letter of Maimonides," pp. 194ff.

EH 16.1993

THE ROLE OF THE NON-JEWISH PARENT IN BLESSINGS FOR BAR/BAT MITZVAH

Rabbi Jerome M. Epstein

This paper was approved by the CJLS on December 5, 1993, by a vote of six in favor, eight opposed and two abstaining (6-8-2). Voting in favor: Rabbis Ben Zion Bergman, Elliot N. Dorff, Jerome M. Epstein, Susan Grossman, Reuven Kimelman, and Joel E. Rembaum. Voting against: Rabbis Kassel Abelson, Samuel Fraint, Arnold M. Goodman, Jan Caryl Kaufman, Vernon H. Kurtz, Lionel E. Moses, Paul Plotkin and Avram Israel Reisner. Abstaining: Rabbis Ezra Finkelstein and Mayer Rabinowitz.

The Committee on Jewish Law and Standards of the Rabbinical Assembly provides guidance in matters of halakhah for the Conservative movement. The individual rabbi, however, is the authority for the interpretation and application of all matters of halakhah.

שאלה

May a parent who is not Jewish participate in the recitation of a blessing as part of the service in which his or her child becomes a Bar or Bat Mitzvah?

תשובה

In considering this question, a number of issues must be taken into consideration. If the b'rakhah in question is intended to be an integral part of the religious service, the individual reciting the b'rakhah must be able to do it in such a way as to be able to exempt members of the congregation from the need to recite the b'rakhah on their own. The Talmud teaches that an individual may perform a mitzvah as another's agent only if the individual serving as the agent has at least the same obligation as the individual for whom it is being performed.[1]

In the case of an individual reciting a b'rakhah as part of the service — if the b'rakhah is an integral part of that service — that individual must be in a position to exempt those who will hear that recitation. Clearly, a non-Jew is not "obligated" to recite any b'rakhah. Since a non-Jew has no obligation for תפילה, that non-Jew may not lead Jews in obligatory prayer.

A potential problem also exists with the nature of the b'rakhah. The nature of many b'rakhot is such that they are appropriate for recitation only by Jews. For example, for a

---

[1] M. Rosh Hashanah 3:8, Berakhot 20b.

non-Jew to recite אשר בחר בנו or שעשני ישראל is to render the b'rakhah trivial. (Indeed, were a Jew to recite a b'rakhah for a mitzvah for which she/he were not obligated, it would be considered a ברכה לבטלה.)

Thirdly, depending on the religious belief and/or practice of the non-Jew, the recitation of certain b'rakhot and prayers may be theologically meaningless, or may create a situation in which the statements are a mockery.

It is based upon these positions that the Committee on Jewish Law and Standards has a long standing tradition of limiting the ways in which a non-Jew may participate in a religious service. In 1976, Mayer Rabinowitz wrote, "A non-Jew may not be given an aliyah. He may not serve as a שליח ציבור and may not be a member of the choir. However it may be permissible for the non-Jew to read a responsive reading or to address the congregation."[2]

On various occasions, the Law Committee considered the involvement of non-Jews in the religious service. In 1954, the CJLS determined that it was "the unanimous opinion of the Committee that the practice of having non-Jews in synagogue choirs is not in keeping with Jewish standards."[3]

In 1958, Philip Sigal wrote, "Choirs are regarded as extensions of the cantor's voice and it is deemed therefore, incorrect to use non-Jewish singers. By the same token, gentile choir leaders *at services* are deemed contrary to the spirit of the Jewish tradition and practice."[4] The Committee reaffirmed this position in 1978, when in response to a question as to whether it was permissible for a synagogue to hire non-Jews to sing in their choir during services, the Committee "unanimously agreed that such a practice is against the basic tenets of Jewish tradition."[5] It is interesting to note that the rationale of the Steering Committee was that the choir is an extension of the שליח ציבור, and thus, it would not be appropriate for an individual who is not Jewish to participate within that choir.

In these cases, the response of prohibiting the non-Jew from taking particular roles within the religious service was because it could be assumed that the individual may be reciting prayers that were inappropriate either because of content or because that individual would perforce be reciting prayers which traditionally require a שליח ציבור – a role that this individual cannot fulfill because the individual is not Jewish.

In 1979, Seymour Siegel, Chairman of the Committee on Jewish Law and Standards, wrote to Loel Weiss in response to a question regarding non-Jewish participation in a Bar mitzvah ritual that "A non-Jew can participate in a service as long as there is no חיוב involved. He can not have an aliyah, for example. But he might offer a prayer for the government or read a psalm." In this situation, the non-Jew does not take on a role which creates a problem with the religions integrity of the service. By carefully selecting the reading and referring to it as a "reading," the religious value is not compromised.

The significant increase in the rate of intermarriage will ensure that the frequency of congregations confronting this question will grow. Thus, besides considering the legal permissibility of this question and the desire to meet the needs of the family, the policy implications must be considered. As distinctions between Jews and non-Jews are

---

[2] Letter from Mayer Rabinowitz to Louis Kaplan, 15 Sept. 1976.
[3] CJLS minutes, 31 Aug. 1954.
[4] Letter from Philip Sigal to Tzvi Porath, 3 June 1958.
[5] CJLS Steering Committee minutes, 6 July 1978.

blended by the synagogue community, distinctions may be less discernible to those who might consider intermarriage. It is important that we not imply that the non-Jewish parent is a member of the Jewish community. Efforts should be made to find ways to give the non-Jewish parent recognition at the service without demonstrating Jewish communal membership.

Conclusion

Based on the above analysis and considerations, a parent who is not Jewish may not recite a b'rakhah as part of the service in which his or her child becomes a Bar or Bat Mitzvah. There must be distinctive roles for Jewish parents. Each synagogue will have to determine those roles, based upon its service, structure and ritual. Additional readings may be selected or created for the non-Jew outside of the formal liturgy. Extant roles and rituals usually designated and filled by Jews should not be considered. It is advised that these "created" or "selected" readings be utilized only when a non-Jew participates in the service and be instituted at a unique point in the service so that the non-Jew has an appropriate role without, at the same time, signifying, symbolizing or professing his/her membership in the Jewish community.

EH 16.1995

Participation of Non-Jewish Parents or Grandparents in Home Religious Ceremonies

Rabbi Jerome M. Epstein

This paper was approved by the CJLS on June 14, 1995, by a vote of seventeen in favor, two opposed, and two abstaining (17-2-2). Voting in favor: Rabbis Kassel Abelson, Ben Zion Bergman, Stephanie Dickstein, Elliot N. Dorff, Jerome M. Epstein, Myron S. Geller, Arnold M. Goodman, Judah Kogen, Alan B. Lucas, Aaron L. Mackler, Lionel E. Moses, Mayer Rabinowitz, Avram Israel Reisner, Joel E. Rembaum, Joel Roth, Gordon Tucker, and Gerald Zelizer. Voting against: Rabbis Samuel Fraint and Gerald Skolnik. Abstaining: Rabbis Susan Grossman and Paul Plotkin.

The Committee on Jewish Law and Standards of the Rabbinical Assembly provides guidance in matters of halakhah for the Conservative movement. The individual rabbi, however, is the authority for the interpretation and application of all matters of halakhah.

שאלה

What role, if any, may a parent or grandparent who is not Jewish assume in the ברית מילה, שמחת בת, or פדיון הבן for their children or grandchildren when the ceremony takes place in the home?

תשובה

The Committee on Jewish Law and Standards has previously dealt with the issue of the role of non-Jewish parents in ceremonies for their children. Several responsa were adopted by the CJLS at a meeting on March 10, 1982. Responsa by Rabbi Kassel Abelson and Rabbis Joel Roth and Daniel Gordis specifically considered these concerns in the context of קירוב and intermarried families.

Over the past several years, the role of non-Jewish parents in various aspects of Jewish life has been further considered and, at times, reevaluated by the Committee on Jewish Law and Standards because of the significant rise in the rate of intermarriage and the concomitant reactions by the Jewish community.

Most of the recent responsa, including two by this author (CJLS 1989 and 1993), urged that the synagogue consider both policy issue implications and integrity of ideology in addition to halakhah in determining the role of the non-Jewish parent in various aspects of synagogue life. Although there are occasions when halakhah may permit (or may not forbid) certain behaviors, it does not necessarily mean that the actions would be appropriate from a policy perspective.

One issue that must be raised in connection with this שאלה is whether we should draw a distinction between that which is done in the synagogue and that which is done in the home in which the particular celebration is taking place. While a rationale for such a distinction between synagogue and home practice could be (and has been) advanced by those wishing to advocate a more liberal approach to non-Jewish parents, every attempt to do so creates its own problems. Those who maintain that one is communal and one is private will find the issue complicated by small functions in the chapel of a synagogue being more private than large home functions. Those who argue that the presence of clergy is the determinant will find the issue complicated by the fact that clergy often are present as officiants and guests whether the ceremony is at the synagogue or the home. Those who argue that the presence of the "congregation" is the determinant will find the issue clouded in that at many celebrations a significant percentage of the congregants, including leadership, may be present at a home ceremony and in a particular synagogue ceremony where the edifice is being used for convenience, there may be a paucity of congregants. Thus, there is a strong rationale to call for a consistent policy between "mitzvah fulfillment" in the synagogue and "mitzvah fulfillment" in the home. The religious guidelines that govern the one should govern the other. We must maintain our integrity as a Movement based on halakhah.

ברית מילה

The role of the father in the ברית מילה is "to bring his son into the covenant of Abraham." Since a non-Jewish father has not entered "this covenant" himself, it is not appropriate in the instance of a בן ישראלית for him to "bring his son into the covenant." It is also improper for him to recite any of the b'rakhot. Since the recitation of a b'rakhah by a non-Jew does not reflect reality, such recitation would trivialize and distract from the solemnity of the ceremony and, indeed, Judaism itself. Similarly, because of the symbolism attached to it, it would be inappropriate for anyone but a Jew to serve as סנדק (also referred to as בעל ברית) because his role is to hold the baby and thus assist the מוהל. Having not entered the covenant himself, it is difficult to conceive that he can fully appreciate the symbolism of this event. The סנדק is more than a functionary. The Kitzur Shulhan Arukh states, "ויש לאדם לחזור אחר מוהל וסנדק היותר טוב וצדיק "The father should be careful to choose a מוהל and סנדק who are the best and most righteous available" (163:1). However, on the condition that the father has agreed that the child will be raised as a Jew and permits him to enter the covenant, the father may have some ancillary, peripheral and non-halakhic role in the ceremony. While the ברית מילה does have great significance, it has also come to be perceived as a "birth ritual." Thus, to entirely exclude a parent who wishes involvement in this ceremony seems unnecessarily harsh. Some role may be given. Perhaps, the recitation of a personal prayer, a relevant selection from the תנ"ך or a suitable reading might provide an appropriate role. Such a prayer, selection or reading would neither be part of the formal liturgy of the ברית מילה itself nor imply in any way that the parent is Jewish. On the other hand, this recitation may have significance to any parent and may serve the function of helping the parent feel part of this important ceremony. As an alternative, the father or grandfather might explain the significance of the names which the child is given.

(ברית בנות) שמחת בת

The prevalence of the שמחת בת ceremony has grown in the past number of years. In many cases, this ceremony takes place in the home and provides an opportunity for parents and grandparents to celebrate the female birth in a manner similar to the way in which a ברית מילה has become an occasion for celebration of a male birth. While there are no traditional sources to govern parental roles in such a ceremony, specific roles may be found for non-Jewish parents and grandparents. These roles should *not* include the recitation of a b'rakhah. They may, however include appropriate readings, selections from the תנ"ך, recitation of a personal prayer or an explanation of the significance of the names which the child is given. The caveats expressed above regarding the ברית מילה obtain with equal force here as well. The absence of traditional sources should not be perceived as a license for איש כל הישר בעיניו יעשה.

פדיון הבן

Although there is ample evidence that "where the natural father does not take part in the pidyon haben...that the child should not have a pidyon haben, until he attains majority and redeems himself" (Rabbi Joel Roth and Rabbi Daniel Gordis, CJLS 1982), there are a significant number of instances today when a pidyon haben does take place although the natural father is not Jewish. In such instances, it is precluded that the father, himself, redeem the child. Although it is inappropriate for the non-Jewish father to recite a b'rakhah, provide the "redemption sum" or transmit it, he may, however, be offered a role and participate by reciting a personal prayer, selection from the תנ"ך or suitable reading outside of the formal liturgy of the ceremony.

Conclusion

The parent who is not Jewish may not assume a role in the prescribed religious framework or liturgy of the ceremony relating to the birth of his or her children. It is important, however, that appropriate avenues should be sought for suitable roles for involvement in the ceremony should the parent so desire. These roles should affirm the individual's vital position as parent, but must not misleadingly convey any sense that the person is Jewish. While it may be argued that such a position will not entirely satisfy the non-Jew nor enhance our קירוב endeavors, it will clearly demonstrate the concern of Judaism to recognize the importance of parenthood, while affirming the spiritual and theological integrity of the religious ceremony.

With this in mind, there should be no distinction in the role of a non-Jewish parent in a religious ceremony relating to the birth of his or her children, whether that ceremony is in the home, the synagogue or elsewhere.

EH 16.1997

Issues Regarding Employment of an Intermarried Jew by a Synagogue or Solomon Schechter Day School

Rabbi Jerome M. Epstein

This paper was approved by the CJLS on September 17, 1997, by a vote of seventeen in favor and one abstaining (17-0-1). Voting in favor: Rabbis Kassel Abelson, Ben Zion Bergman, Elliot N. Dorff, Jerome M. Epstein, Samuel Fraint, Baruch Frydman-Kohl, Shoshana Gelfand, Nechama D. Goldberg, Judah Kogen, Vernon S. Kurtz, Aaron L. Mackler, Lionel E. Moses, Joel E. Rembaum, James S. Rosen, Joel Roth, Elie Kaplan Spitz and Gordon Tucker. Abstaining: Rabbi Avram Israel Reisner.

The Committee on Jewish Law and Standards of the Rabbinical Assembly provides guidance in matters of halakhah for the Conservative movement. The individual rabbi, however, is the authority for the interpretation and application of all matters of halakhah.

שאלה

May an intermarried Jew who has the potential of being perceived as a Jewish role model be employed or engaged by a synagogue or a Solomon Schechter Day School?

תשובה

Judaism has, from its earliest roots, been concerned about the issue of intermarriage. Statements found in early sources were unequivocal in their prohibition of intermarriage. The rabbinic reading of the Book of Deuteronomy voiced this prohibition by interpreting the traditional text (Deut. 7:3-4) as follows: "You shall not marry with your non-Jewish neighbors; your daughters shall not be given to their sons, nor shall you take their daughters for your sons. For intermarriage will turn your children away from Judaism, and they will end up serving other religions."
    Rabbinic leadership went to great lengths to establish boundaries in order to prevent intermarriage: drinking the wine of non-Jews was prohibited because of the possibility that it would lead to potential romance and ultimately intermarriage (Avodah Zarah 36b). Bread made by non-Jews was similarly prohibited as part of a social precaution because of concerns relating to intermarriage (S.A. Yoreh De'ah 112). There was a concern that an individual who bought bread baked non-commercially by non-Jews might share a meal with non-Jews, develop social relationships and ultimately intermarry with them — causing a rupture in Jewish living. Even though many of these

laws were designed to prevent marriage with idol worshipers, the value inherent in the law was that marriage outside of Judaism would break the chain of Jewish life.

Judaism and Jewish life have been linked to the family. Indeed, the home is considered a מקדש מעט – a miniature sanctuary. It is in the family that the Jew celebrates most of Jewish living. Thus rabbinic leadership throughout the generations established clear laws and customs to foster inmarriage and thus, preserve the integrity of the Jewish family.

In considering the issues of employment of intermarried Jews, it is useful to review the literature and various historical precedents considered by the Committee on Jewish Law and Standards. While the sociological conditions may have changed from the time of the earlier statements, the values concerning intermarriage inherent in those statements and underlying them remain.

From early discussions of intermarriage, the Committee on Jewish Law and Standards understood the communal impact of intermarriage. It affected the individual, but it also affected the community. It was the position of the Committee "that it would be highly improper for a synagogue to accept a Jew who married a Gentile woman as a member of the congregation. Admission of such a person to membership involves tacit approval of his conduct. Marrying outside of the faith is considered tantamount to a rupture with the Jewish community, since the offspring of mixed marriages are usually weaned away from the Jewish religion" (CJLS Report, *Proceedings of the Rabbinical Assembly* 8 [1941-1944]: 142-143). This particular statement was written at a time in which it was generally assumed that when intermarriage occurred, it was between a Jewish man and a non-Jewish woman. Certainly, today when intermarriages occur between Jewish women and non-Jewish men and Jewish men and non-Jewish women, the principle would apply to both men and women.

But, a break in the Jewish community was not the only reason for this widely held position. Arriving at the same conclusion previously expressed, Boaz Cohen, in the name of the Committee on Jewish Law and Standards, postulated another reason when he wrote, "The admission into membership of the congregation of a Jew living with a Gentile wife who refuses to embrace Judaism is a seeming sanction of a flagrant violation of Jewish law and may encourage others who are so inclined, to intermarry inasmuch as they may do so with complete impunity" (letter from B. Cohen to H. Halperin, June 12, 1941).

In 1963, Max J. Routtenberg authored a paper adopted by the Committee as the "majority opinion" noting that "the intermarried Jew, while admitted to membership in the congregation, shall not be entitled to hold any office or to serve as chairman of any committee, nor shall he be singled out for any special honors" (Max J. Routtenberg, "The Jew Who Has Intermarried," *Proceedings of the Rabbinical Assembly* 28 [1964]: 247).

The implications of intermarriage on the community were considered far more serious than the impact on the community of individuals ignoring other halakhot. The Committee on Jewish Law and Standards – reflecting values of the Conservative movement adopted in various responsa – utilized language that would clearly articulate its concern about the increasing prevalence of intermarriage. *As noted previously, intermarriage was considered an act that had communal ramifications.* If an individual intermarriage were ignored, there was a likelihood that it – consciously or unconsciously – would affect the attitudes and behaviors of the community.

As noted, the Committee on Jewish Law and Standards posited that there were congregational/communal "privileges" that should be denied to those Jews who chose to intermarry. When a question was raised by the World Council of Synagogues in 1959, the CJLS acknowledged that "The synagogue cannot deny any rights to a Jew who has married out of his faith. However, *membership in a congregation is to be considered a privilege*, and privileges need not be extended to such a Jew" (CJLS Minutes, April 13 and 14, 1959, p. 3 [emphasis added]). This was merely a reflection of positions of the CJLS in 1947 and 1954 prohibiting Jews who "married outside of the faith" from "privileges of the congregation, including membership and such honors as aliyot" (CJLS Minutes, March 23, 1954, p. 2).

While the CJLS did not believe it was appropriate to "read Jews out" of the community, it was emphasized that the major issue regarding intermarriage was "a consideration of the best and highest interests of the Jewish people. We must clearly state our position on intermarriage in general. Our intentions should not be misunderstood. We affirm our unqualified opposition to the marriage of a Jew to a non-Jew, for a variety of reasons. We regard it as the sacred task of responsible Jewish leadership to combat intermarriage and to counteract forces and influences which lead to such marriages. Our communal agencies and institutions must help by every means at their command, educational, religious, social and recreational, to deepen Jewish loyalties, develop pride in Judaism, and provide the milieu in which young Jews, of both sexes, shall have opportunities for social intermingling" (Routtenberg, "The Jew Who Has Intermarried," *Proceedings of the Rabbinical Assembly* 28 [1964]: 245-246).

Accordingly, for the CJLS, intermarriage was viewed as an inevitable influence in modeling behavior and Jewish responses to various situations. Great strides were taken to make certain that intermarriage *would not* provide a negative model.

Concomitantly, the Law Committee regarded the potential modeling of synagogue leadership as significant. The rabbi was considered more than an officiant. The clergy is a source of significant influence and, therefore, based upon a paper by I. Lubliner, the CJLS adopted a position that a "Conservative rabbi may not embrace by his presence either during or immediately before, or immediately after, the ceremony or reception of any celebration of a marriage in which a partner is non-Jewish without any type of conversion" (CJLS Minutes, January 20, 1972, p. 2). Broadening that position, the CJLS determined that this decision applied to rabbis participating in civil ceremonies and applied to cantors as well (CJLS memorandum, February 24, 1972).

It is evident, then, that those who maintain professional roles in synagogues, are viewed, most frequently, as having responsibilities that go far beyond their particular assigned tasks. *Rabbis, cantors, educators, teachers of all age groups and subjects, youth workers and executive directors are among those viewed as Jewish models.* They assume positions of (and exercise) influence. And, they view themselves as individuals with influence. The Codes of Personnel Practices developed by The United Synagogue of Conservative Judaism, and the respective professional associations for each of the above mentioned categories, delineate the specific role for each position in a fashion that makes it clear that the professional is a model. Representing themselves to the community as a whole, professional organizations describe functions and roles in the realms of both the technical and the influential.

Indeed, the Conservative movement has specifically affirmed the responsibility of employees to model appropriate behavior and action whether or not the individual is directly "a contact person" with youngsters. In 1991, the United Synagogue Commission/Department of Education in guiding both the Solomon Schechter Day Schools and the synagogue schools of our Movement adopted a statement reflecting "that our schools are not permitted to employ individuals as educators *in either administrative or teaching positions* who are intermarried. While as a movement we are ready to reach out to the non-Jew who has married a Jew, we have never been prepared to accept intermarriage as desirable. We should not permit anyone who has intermarried to hold educational positions and thus serve as negative models for our children" (United Synagogue Commission on Jewish Education, Minutes, October 28, 1991).

Highlighting this point, Rabbis Joel Roth and Daniel Gordis (in one of a series of teshuvot on intermarriage and קרוב) point out that intermarried Jews should not serve as elected officials in synagogues because "they are more than passive members of a halakhically improper marriage — they made an active decision to enter into that relationship, a relationship which we consider of paramount danger to the Jewish community. That they should understand the fact that their marriage must affect their status in the Jewish community is not unfair or unethical; it is obligatory and desirable" (Roth and Gordis, "קרוב" and the Status of Intermarried Families," *Proceedings of the Committee on Jewish Law and Standards 1980-1985*, p. 152).

The basic concern of the previously cited material accentuates the potential consequences of contact between representatives of the congregation, and its congregants and families. Anyone who represents the congregation — on any level, coming into contact in a regular and significant fashion with a member — will inevitably impact on that individual. It is clearly assumed that the average member may not make "differentiations" between gradations of title or role. It is natural to assume that those who represent the congregation may be perceived as synonymous with the congregation.

The Talmud makes a point of noting that deference was to be given to an אדם חשוב, an important man. But, at the same time, the Talmud indicates that an אדם חשוב had to be stricter in his behavior because of his status or position in the community (see Shabbat 51a and Moed Katan 11b). That which might be ignored or overlooked in the behavior of most people could not be disregarded in an אדם חשוב. For, people might look to that individual as a "standard" of acceptable behavior. In our society most representatives of our congregations in professional and teaching roles should be considered "important people." Thus, it is important that anyone — irrespective of role or title — who represents the congregation, serve as an exemplar of the congregational norms.

The issue of intermarriage increasingly affects Conservative congregations. Thus, there is a unique challenge in trying to determine an appropriate policy. As articulated in previous responsa of the Committee on Jewish Law and Standards, "sensitivity, sanction, compassion, synagogue affiliation, intermarriage prevention and קרוב must all be weighed, evaluated and balanced. Any policy of the Conservative movement must also consider the issue of integrity. The Conservative movement has determined that intermarriage is destructive to the fabric of that which we hold dear, that which we value. Further, the movement has consistently reaffirmed that an intermarriage has no authenticity in Jewish law" (Rabbi Jerome M. Epstein, 1989).

Ideally, congregations and day schools should only engage individuals for a position in which they will serve as role models if they reflect the institution's value system. Mitzvot such as שבת, כשרות, תפילה, צדקה and personal ethics — as well as in marriage — are important as they are embraced by the value system. Yet, as indicated earlier, the Rabbinical Assembly (as well as other Jewish organizations in North America) has come to the conclusion that the issue of inmarriage is so vital for Jewish survival, that it must be given special emphasis. It is a unique value, for Jewish life is usually influenced to the greatest extent by the family. This in no way implies the slightest denigration or diminution of other mitzvot. Rather, it should be viewed as an opportunity to promote Jewish renaissance.

Conclusion

Congregations and Solomon Schechter Day Schools may not engage or employ any individual who is intermarried for a position in which he/she may serve as a Jewish role model. This specifically includes, but is not limited to, rabbis, cantors, educators, teachers of all age groups and subjects, youth workers and executive directors.

EH 24.1992a

CONSENSUS STATEMENT ON HOMOSEXUALITY

This paper was approved by the CJLS on March 25, 1992, by a vote of nineteen in favor, three opposed, and one abstaining (19-3-1). Voting in favor: Rabbis Kassel Abelson, Stanley Bramnick, Elliot N. Dorff, Richard L. Eisenberg, David Feldman, Samuel Fraint, Arnold M. Goodman, Jan Caryl Kaufman, Reuven Kimelman, Aaron L. Mackler, Herbert Mandl, Lionel E. Moses, Mayer Rabinowitz, Avram Israel Reisner, Joel E. Rembaum, Chaim A. Rogoff, Joel Roth, Morris Shapiro, and Gerald Skolnik. Voting against: Rabbis Dov Peretz Elkins, Howard Handler and Gordon Tucker. Abstaining: Rabbi Ben Zion Bergman.

The Committee on Jewish Law and Standards of the Rabbinical Assembly provides guidance in matters of halakhah for the Conservative movement. The individual rabbi, however, is the authority for the interpretation and application of all matters of halakhah.

The Committee on Jewish Law and Standards of The Rabbinical Assembly affirms the following policies:

(A) We will not perform commitment ceremonies for gays or lesbians.

(B) We will not knowingly admit avowed homosexuals to our rabbinical or cantorial schools or to the Rabbinical Assembly or the Cantors' Assembly. At the same time, we will not instigate witch hunts against those who are already members or students.

(C) Whether homosexuals may function as teachers or youth leaders in our congregations and schools will be left to the rabbi authorized to make halakhic decisions for a given institution within the Conservative Movement. Presumably, in this as in all other matters, the rabbi will make such decisions taking into account the sensitivities of the people of his or her particular congregation or school. The rabbi's own reading of Jewish law on these issues, informed by the responsa written for the Committee on Jewish Law and Standards to date, will also be a determinative factor in these decisions.

(D) Similarly, the rabbi of each Conservative institution, in consultation with its lay leaders, will be entrusted to formulate policies regarding the eligibility of homosexuals for honors within worship and for lay leadership positions.

(E) In any case, in accordance with The Rabbinical Assembly and United Synagogue resolutions, we hereby affirm gays and lesbians are welcome in our congregations, youth groups, camps, and schools.

EDITORS' NOTE: *The following papers from the CJLS deliberations on homosexuality, completed on March 25, 1992, were written mainly in reaction to a paper submitted by Rabbi Bradley Shavit Artson. Rabbi Artson's paper is not included in this collection since it was not adopted by the Committee.*

EH 24.1992b

HOMOSEXUALITY

Rabbi Joel Roth

This paper was approved by the CJLS on March 25, 1992, by a vote of fourteen in favor, seven opposed, and three abstaining (14-7-3). Voting in favor: Rabbis Stanley Bramnick, Jerome M. Epstein, David M. Feldman, Samuel Fraint, Arnold M. Goodman, Reuven Kimelman, Aaron L. Mackler, Herbert Mandl, Lionel E. Moses, Avram Israel Reisner, Chaim A. Rogoff, Joel Roth, Morris Shapiro, and Gerald Skolnik. Voting against: Rabbis Ben Zion Bergman, Elliot N. Dorff, Richard L. Eisenberg, Dov Peretz Elkins, Howard Handler, Joel Rembaum, and Gordon Tucker. Abstaining: Rabbis Kassel Abelson, Jan Caryl Kaufman, and Mayer Rabinowitz.

The Committee on Jewish Law and Standards of the Rabbinical Assembly provides guidance in matters of halakhah for the Conservative movement. The individual rabbi, however, is the authority for the interpretation and application of all matters of halakhah.

Part I

Few topics evoke the type of visceral response that homosexuality does. Responses are often quick and definitive on both ends of the spectrum. I have been cornered by some who wonder how the question could even be on the agenda of the Law Committee. "What is there to say about the subject from a halakhic point of view", they ask? "Putting it on the agenda validates a question which, in fact, has no validity," they claim.

At the other end of the spectrum, I have been contacted by some homosexuals whose claim is equally definitive. "Halakhah has no option but to validate homosexuality as a lifestyle co-equal with heterosexuality. If it does not do so, it has lost any and all influence on the lives of Jewish homosexuals, it has excised the Jewish homosexual from the community, and it has reinforced the homophobia of the American society at large."

To the first group we must assert that there is no question which cannot be on the agenda of the Law Committee. Each age may have its lists of questions which seem unlikely ever to require serious discussion, yet subsequent ages may find it necessary to discuss those very questions. Answers which may have seemed a foregone conclusion years ago, may no longer be self-evidently true. However, willingness to discuss a question in no way predetermines what the answer will be. It is as possible to discuss a question and reaffirm a longstanding precedent as it is to discuss it and abrogate that precedent.[1]

When a longstanding precedent is questioned by a significant number of people who cannot be dismissed as "fringe lunatics," it may no longer be sufficient merely to assert that the precedent stands because it is the precedent. Surely precedent will stand unless

---

[1] When the CJLS took up the question of patrilineal descent there were some who asserted that placing it on the agenda would validate the question and predetermine the answer. In fact, though, the CJLS reaffirmed the longstanding precedent, and that decision was then promulgated as a Standard of Rabbinic Practice.

there is compelling reason for it not to stand. But it must be remembered that those who are questioning the precedent are offering what they believe to be compelling reason for overturning it. One who wishes to reaffirm the precedent must now respond to the claim that there is compelling reason to overturn it. If there is evidence that the "compelling reason" is not as compelling as those who assert it claim, the precedent should stand. If one can offer equally compelling reason why the precedent should stand, then surely the precedent should stand. And if, in the course of discussion and analysis, one comes to the conclusion that there is, indeed, compelling reason to overturn the precedent, one should support overturning the precedent. It is dangerous for halakhah to refuse to discuss a question for fear that legitimate discussion will result in the "wrong" answer.

At the other end of the spectrum there are also things that ought to be said. Halakhists are duty-bound to listen carefully and attentively to the claims and contentions of those who address questions to them. They are also duty-bound, however, to listen with equal attentiveness and care to the claims and contentions of those who may not have addressed questions to them, but who do have something to say on the issue under discussion.

Halakhists are the guardian of a legal system they hold very dear. They ought not to be expected to violate their commitment to that legal system because members of their constituency are unhappy with their decisions. Halakhists can be sensitive, understanding, and caring — and still disagree with the claim of the constituent. It is easy to contend that the halakhist did not really understand because if he had, he could never had have decided as he did. The ease of the contention does not necessarily make it true.

It is possible to reject the claim of a constituent without expelling the constituent from the halakhist's constituency. There are many issues concerning which certain constituents have very strong feelings. They, too, often turn to halakhists for recognition and validation of their views as "the Jewish view." They, too, expect the halakhists to listen carefully and attentively, and to decide the issue as they believe halakhah demands. When the decision is consonant with the claim of the questioner, the questioner is clearly pleased. But when the decision is not as the questioner might have wished, the questioner ought not to feel himself chastised by the answer. The questioner ought not to feel that he has been expelled from the community or excised from the constituency.

We must assert from the outset that the question of homosexuality cannot be excluded from halakhic discourse on the grounds that halakhah stops at the bedroom door. While it may be possible to claim that a secular legal system should say nothing about the legality or morality of private acts between consenting adults, that could hardly be a tenable claim for a religious legal system. Not only are there myriad areas where halakhah does already have something to say about what goes on between consenting adults and behind closed doors, it seems unthinkable to claim that private behavior could or should be of no concern to God.

It seems most reasonable to begin halakhic analysis with statements of the Torah itself. There are two verses that clearly posit some type of prohibition against homosexuality. Lev. 18:22 reads: ואת זכר לא תשכב משכבי אשה תועבה היא – "Do not lie with a man as one lies with a woman: it is an abhorrence." The context of the verse is a list of forbidden sexual unions – עריות.[2] The term תועבה is applied specifically only in verse 22, though verses 26, 29, and 30 apply the term תועבה to all of the forbidden relationships.

Lev. 20:13 reads: ואיש אשר ישכב את זכר משכבי אשה תועבה עשו שניהם מות יומתו דמיהם בם – "If a man lies with a male as one lies with a woman, the two of them have

---

[2] Though the term ערוה does not appear in verse 22, Maimonides lists homosexuality as an ערוה in הלכות מלכים ט:ה.

done an abhorrent thing; they shall be put to death – their bloodguilt is upon them." The context of this verse is similar to the context of the first verse. It appears in a list which basically repeats the prohibitions of Leviticus 18, adding the appropriate punishment for each offense. Lev. 20:13 clearly calls homosexuality a תועבה and stipulates death as the punishment for both of the parties involved.

Referring to an act as תועבה surely is a term of opprobrium. It impels us to look at the term itself to see whether it can shed light. Therefore, a few comments on the term תועבה seem appropriate. These comments will be confined to the term as it appears in the Torah alone.

The term, as it appears in Leviticus 18 and 20, seems to connote some universally recognized inherent quality called תועבה. That is, it could be read to imply that anyone who looks at the acts described in those chapters would recognize them as acts of תועבה, even if they had not been called תועבה by the Torah. In other words, the Torah calls them תועבה because they are inherently תועבה.

Upon closer analysis, however, it seems to me that the opposite is the case. The term תועבה in the Torah does not refer to an inherent quality of an act. Acts are תועבה because the Torah calls them תועבה. "Abhorrence" is not as inherent quality of the act, it is an attributed quality.

The most telling evidence that תועבה is an attributed, rather than an inherent, quality can be found in Genesis and Exodus. The term appears twice in the Joseph cycle. In Gen. 43:32 the Torah says לא יוכלון המצרים לאכל את העברים לחם כי תועבה היא למצרים "The Egyptians could not dine with the Hebrews, since that would be abhorrent to the Egyptians." Mixed eating is not inherently abhorrent. It is not objectively abhorrent. It is abhorrent to Egyptians for whatever reason they consider it abhorrent. It is תועבה למצרים – not inherently. The same analysis could be given for Gen. 46:34: כי תועבת מצרים כל רעה צאן. Similarly, the verse in Exod. 8:22 – כי תועבת מצרים נזבח לה' אלקינו הן נזבח את תועבת מצרים לעיניהם ולא יסקלנו recognizes that תועבה is an attributed quality, not an inherent one.

The Torah recognizes תועבה as an attributed quality for matters that are abhorrent to Jews, too. It is not contending that foreigners might mistakenly think certain things to be abhorrent, while Jews consider abhorrent only those things that are inherently abhorrent. There are four cases that make this abundantly clear, in my opinion. Regarding the sacrifice of a blemished animal the Torah[3] says: כי תועבת ה' אלקיך הוא. Regarding cross-dressing it says:[4] כי תועבת ה' אלקיך כל עשה אלה. Regarding the prohibition to be מחזיר גרושתו the Torah says[5] כי תועבה היא לפני ה' and regarding the use of unjust weights and measures the Torah says:[6] כי תועבת ה' אלקיך כל עשה אלה כל עשה עול. We consider these acts abhorrent because the Torah informs us that God considers them abhorrent, not because they are inherently or objectively abhorrent.[7]

The greatest number of occurrences of the term תועבה in the Torah appears in contexts of the discussion of idolatry. In seven of eleven occurrences the term is linked to תועבת ה'.[8]

---

[3] Deut. 17:1.

[4] Deut. 22:5.

[5] Deut. 24:4.

[6] Deut. 25:16.

[7] The case of Deut. 25:16 will seem the most problematic. Some will claim that dishonesty is inherently abhorrent. I think we must be careful, however. The Torah is full of prohibitions against matters that we recognize as inherently dishonest or immoral – moving boundaries, murders, robbery – yet none of these is called תועבה. In Deut. 25:16, the clause כל עשה עול seems to explain why God considers unjust weights abhorrent, but is not claiming that every act of dishonesty is תועבה.

[8] The seven are Deut. 7:25-26, 12:31, 18:9, 18:12, 23:19, and 27:15.

Two of the remaining four[9] deal with the עיר הנדחת and the יחיד העובד עבודה זרה. In these the behavior of Jews in enticing other Jews to idolatry or themselves engaging in idolatry is defined as תועבה without any further modifier. These verses seem to me to be claiming that these acts are abhorrent because the Torah has already defined idolatry as abhorrent. Their abhorrence is contingent upon idolatry's having been so defined. Similarly, the third of these four[10] – למען אשר לא ילמדו אתכם לעשות ככל תועבתם אשר עשו לאלהיהם – stipulates as abhorrent only those acts which have been previously defined as abhorrent. And the final verse of the four[11] appears in a poetic context and is inappropriate as a source for the meaning of words in legal contexts.

In theory, though, one might wish to claim that the verses in Leviticus about homosexuality are different. They do not say תועבת ה' and are not linked to acts which have been previously defined as abhorrence. Perhaps homosexuality is abhorrent not by attribution, but inherently. I think not.

The final appearance of the term תועבה in the Torah, I think, proves my point. Deut. 14:3 reads: לא תאכל כל תועבה and appears in the Deuteronomic recap of the laws of kashrut. Nowhere in Leviticus 11 are nonkosher animals defined as תועבה. Thus, Deut. 14:3 cannot be alluding to a תועבה which has been previously defined as such. Since one would be very hard pressed to posit that nonkosher animals are inherently abhorrent rather than abhorrent by attribution, it follows that the תועבה of Deut. 14:3 should be understood as we have understood all the other occurrences of the word in the remainder of the Torah. And if that is the case, there seems to be no defensible grounds for asserting that תועבה in the context of homosexuality refers to inherent abhorrence rather than to attributed abhorrence.

Legally speaking, the Torah defines homosexuality as תועבה. It does not define why it is to be considered תועבה. It is quite conceivable that later commentators might attempt to define why it ought to be considered תועבה. But, it should be borne in mind that demonstrating deficiencies in the attempts of the commentators to explain why it ought to be considered תועבה does not remove it legally from the category of תועבה.

There are no other explicit references to homosexuality in the Bible. Gen. 19:5 in the Lot/Sodom incident – הוציאם אלינו ונדעה אתם – is, however, widely interpreted to refer to homosexuality.[12] Similarly, in Judges 19, the פלגש בגבעה also has an apparent reference to homosexuality.[13] Finally, either Rav or Samuel claims that Ham's violation of Noah[14] was an act of homosexuality,[15] and Rav understands Gen. 39:1 – ויקנהו פוטיפר סריס פרעה – to imply a homosexual intent on the part of Potiphar.[16]

The two explicit biblical verses refer to male homosexuality, not to female homosexuality. They cannot be understood legally to refer to female homosexuality even by extension

---

[9] Deut. 13:15, 17:4.

[10] Deut. 20:18.

[11] Deut. 32:16, though see *Sifrei Deuteronomy*, 318 (Finkelstein ed., p. 364), which interprets the תועבה of this verse as homosexuality, based on a גזירה שוה with Lev. 18:22.

[12] Genesis Rabbah 50:5 (Theodor-Albeck ed., p. 522) comments succinctly לתשמיש – וונדעה אותם. Medieval commentators like Rashi, Rashbam, and Ibn Ezra also interpret it thus. Indeed, even the new JPS takes it the same way. It is interesting, however, that Ezek. 16:49, 50 does not include homosexuality in its litany of Sodomite offenses.

[13] Verse 22 reads: ויאמרו אל האיש... לאמר הוצא את האיש אשר בא אל ביתך ונדענו.

[14] Gen. 9:29-35.

[15] Sanhedrin 70a.

[16] Sotah 13b.

(i.e., איש והוא הדין אשה) because of the term משכבי אשה. That term seems to imply some type of penetration by the genital. Since that is impossible in an act of lesbianism, it cannot legally be included under the Torah's prohibition.[17]

The Sages, however, have forbidden female homosexuality. At bottom line, then, the primary difference between male and female homosexuality in halakhah is that one is אסור דאורייתא and the other is אסור דרבנן. Female homosexuality is no less forbidden by the law than male homosexuality. It is the classification of the prohibitions that distinguishes them from one another.

I think it is important, furthermore, to make clear why lesbianism is forbidden דרבנן rather than דאורייתא from a legal point of view. Let us, therefore, look first to a baraita in the Sifra:[18]

"כמעשה ארץ מצרים... וכמעשה ארץ כנען לא תעשו" (ויק' יח:ג) – יכול לא יבנו בניות ולא יטעו נטיעות כמותם? ת"ל "ובחוקותיהם לא תלכו" (שם), לא אמרתי אלא בחוקים החקוקים להם ולאבותיהם ולאבות אבותיהם. ומה היו עושים? האיש נושא לאיש והאשה לאשה. האיש נושא אשה ובתה והאשה ניסת לשנים – לכך נאמר "ובחוקותיהם לא תלכו."

"You should not follow the acts of the land of Egypt...or the acts of the land of Canaan (Lev. 18:3)" — Is it conceivable that [the Israelites] should not built buildings or plant plantings as they [i.e., the Egyptians and Canaanites] do? The Torah states: "You should not follow their practices (id.)" — [implying:] "I [God] have declared prohibited only the practices which they and their ancestors established." And what did they do? A man would marry a man and a woman [marry] a woman, a man would marry a woman and her daughter, and a woman would be married to two men. Regarding these it is said: "You shall not follow their practices."

Among the practices mentioned in the Sifra as intended by Lev. 18:3 is lesbianism. The prohibition is grounded in כמעשה ארץ כנען לא תעשו. According to this baraita lesbianism is forbidden by implication of the Torah itself. If so, why is the claim always made that female homosexuality is forbidden only מדרבנן? Maimonides' wording of the law provides an accurate answer:[19]

נשים המסוללות זו בזו אסור ומעשה מצרים הוא שהוזהרנו עליו... אע"פ שמעשה זה אסור, אין מלקין עליו שאין לו לאו מיוחד. והרי – אין שם ביאה כלל וראוי להכותן מכת מרדות הואיל ועשו אסור.

Lesbianism is forbidden, being "a practice of Egypt" about which the Torah has warned....And even though the act is forbidden, lashes [i.e., the normal legal punishment for a negative commandment] are not given because [the offense] has no unique prohibiting verse[20] and there is no actual intercourse involved.[21] . . . But it

---

[17] Its exclusion also results in a leniency in terms of the punishment prescribed by the law. Only male homosexuality could ever legally entail the death penalty. But see below.

[18] אחרי מות. פרשה ט. ה (הוצאת וייס דף פה, ד).

[19] איסורי ביאה כא:ח.

[20] I.e., there is no specific verse listing the offense explicitly. Rather, the prohibition is general, deduced from the prohibition against "practices of Egypt."

[21] And, therefore, ואת זכר לא תשכב משכבי אשה cannot be generalized by an extension like והוא הדין אשה.

is appropriate that [lesbians] be whipped under the category of מכת מרדות since they have acted in a forbidden manner.

According to Maimonides, therefore, the baraita in the Sifra posits lesbianism as forbidden דאורייתא though not punishable as דאורייתא norms. Since there is no actual intercourse involved, and since there is no *specific* mention of lesbianism in the Torah's prohibition מכות דאורייתא cannot be invoked. Nonetheless, lesbianism is itself אסור דאורייתא and we refer to it as דרבנן only in terms of the applicable punishment – מכת מרדות.

Given what we have just said, it should be clear that the passage in Yevamot 76a which refers to lesbianism as פריצותא בעלמא – "simple lewdness" – has been popularly misunderstood. Understanding that passage to imply that lesbianism is merely some petty offense ignores its context. The question being addressed is whether having engaged in an act of lesbianism renders a woman unfit to marry a priest, because of זנות. If that question were answered in the affirmative, it would imply that an act of lesbianism is intercourse. That was the opinion of Rav Huna. Rava, however, claims that such a woman could not be in the legal category of a זונה because intercourse is not involved. From the perspective of the woman's eligibility to marry a priest, the act was פריצותא בעלמא, i.e., not intercourse. This passage in Yevamot does not contradict the clear statement of the baraita. Both male and female homosexuality are forbidden. Male homosexuality is forbidden by a specific prohibition of the Torah, female homosexuality by implication of the Torah. Both are equally forbidden, though not equally punishable.

Commenting on the Mishnah[22] – הבא על הזכור – the Gemara[23] asserts:

ת"ר: "איש" (ויק' כ: יג), פרט לקטן. "אשר ישכב את זכר" (שם) בין גדול בין קטן... נאמר כאן "דמיהם בם" (שם) ונאמר באוב וידעוני "דמיהם בם" (ויק' כ:כז) מה להלן בסקילה אף כאן בסקילה. עונש שמענו, אזהרה מנין? ת"ל "ואת זכר לא תשכב משכבי אשה תועבה היא" (ויק' י:כב). למדינו אזהרה לשוכב, אזהרה לנשכב מנין, ת"ל "לא יהיה קדש בישראל" (דב' כג:יח) ואמר "וגם קדש היה בארץ עשו ככל התועבות הגויים אשר הוריש וגו'" (מלכ' א' יד:כד) דברי ר' ישמעאל. רבי עקיבא אומר אינו צריך. הרי הוא אומר "ואת זכר לא תשכב משכבי אשה", קרי בה "לא תישכב."

Our sages taught: [The word] "Man" (Lev. 20:13) excludes a minor.[24] [The phrase] "Who lies with a male" [implies] either one who has attained majority or one who is a minor.[25] [How do we know that the punishment is stoning?] It says here (20:13) "Their blood is upon them" and it says regarding the ghost and familiar spirit (Lev. 20:27) "Their blood is upon them." [From this it fol-

---

[22] Sanhedrin 7:4.

[23] Sanhedrin 54a.

[24] I.e., a minor is not culpable if he is the active partner.

[25] I.e., if the active partner is an adult, he is culpable whether the passive partner is an adult or a minor. Sanhedrin 54b, end, indicates a disagreement between Rav and Samuel regarding the lower age terminus for a minor. A baraita is quoted in support of Rav, exempting from punishment if the minor is under nine. That is based on the common premise (Niddah 45a) that an act of intercourse by a male under the age of nine is not legally intercourse. Apparently, Rav agrees with the view of R. Akiva (see below) regarding the derivation of culpability for the passive partner. Since both are derived from לא תשכב, any minor who could not legally be the active partner because his intercourse is not intercourse, cannot cause an adult to incur liability even when the minor is the passive partner. See Rashi to Sanhedrin 54b, end, and Maimonides' codification in איסורי ביאה א:יד.

lows that] just as the latter is punished by stoning,[26] so too is the former punished by stoning. This teaches us the punishment, but what is the source of the prohibition (warning)? The Torah says:[27] "Do not lie with a male as one lies with a woman, it is abhorrent." This verse indicates the source for the prohibition to be the active partner. Where is the source for the prohibition to be the passive partner? The Torah says:[28] "No Israelite man shall be a cult prostitute," and [furthermore Scripture] says:[29] "There were also male prostitutes in the land. [Judah] imitated all the abhorrent practices of nations that the Lord had dispossessed before the Israelites," according to Rabbi Yishmael.[30] Rabbi Akiva says that his proof is unnecessary. [Rather,] read the verb תשכב of the verse ואת זכר לא תשכב משכבי אשה also as תישכב.[31]

What follows clearly from this passage is: (1) that the Talmud understands the Torah to forbid any sexual intercourse between adult males, either as the active partner or as the passive partner;[32] (2) that an adult male is liable as the active partner even if the passive partner is a minor; and, (3) that the legal liability about which the Torah speaks is incurred by the act of intercourse, not by any thought or fantasy of homosexual intercourse.

Moshe Halevi Spero attempted to argue[33] that homoerotic fantasies and homosexual preference are themselves forbidden in halakhah. His basic textual proof comes from the prohibitions of the codes against things which lead to עריות. He provides a list of sources[34] which he claims support his position. It is not necessary of refute his understanding of each of his sources. I shall suffice with demonstrating that he misinterprets the two sources that come closest to supporting his thesis.

Spero refers to Maimonides, הלכות איסורי ביאה 21:1 as one of his proofs. Maimonides

---

[26] The verse says באבן ירגמו אותם דמיהם בם.

[27] Lev. 18:22.

[28] Deut. 23:18.

[29] 1 Kings 14:24.

[30] The derivation of Rabbi Yishmael is somewhat cryptic. Apparently he takes Deut. 23:18 to refer to any passive male partner, not just a male cult prostitute. How does he know that the verse refers to the passive partner? He derives that from the verse in Kings which refers to the act as תועבה and deduces that just as Kings calls קדש a תועבה, so Deuteronomy implies that קדש is a תועבה. And, since Lev. 20:13 applies the term תועבה to both active partner and passive partner, and Lev. 18:22 already implies warning for the active partner, Deut. 23:18 must refer to the passive partner. In addition, the Yad Ramah adds that Deut. 23:18 must be understood to refer to the passive partner because the beginning of the verse (לא תהיה קדשה מבנות ישראל) refers to the passive partner — the woman.

The derivation of Rabbi Yishmael rejects understanding קדש as referring only to cult prostitutes. That is not the פשט of the verse, and Rabbi Yishmael's exegesis may be unclear, but his intent is clear. The fact that his exegesis is not פשט is halakhically irrelevant.

[31] I.e., in the נפעל (passive) voice — "Do not be lain with by a male. . . ." Rabbi Akiva's exegesis is also not פשט, and, as with Rabbi Yishmael, that fact is halakhically irrelevant.

[32] The parallel passage in Yerushalmi Sanhedrin 7:7, 24d-25a says it succinctly: תועבה עשו שניהם שניהם בסקילה, שניהם באזהרה, שניהם בהכרת. The Yerushalmi also provides proofs for the punishment of כרת for both active and passive partners when the full liability for the death penalty is impossible, as, for example, where there was no warning given to the men before the act was committed.

[33] *Tradition*, vol. 17, no. 4 (spring 1979): 57.

[34] In n. 17, ibid.

כל הבא על ערוה מן העריות דרך איברים או שחבק ונשק דרך תאוה ונהנה בקרוב בשר הרי זה says
לוקה מן התורה שנאמר (ויק' יח:ל) לבלתי עשות מחקות התועבות... ונאמר (שם, ו) לא – תקרבו
לגלות ערוה. כלומר לא תקרבו לדברים המביאים לידי גלוי עריות – "One who has non-genital intercourse with any of the forbidden relationships, or hugs and kisses them lustfully, or engages in close bodily contact is liable for lashes by law of the Torah, as it says (Lev. 18:30), 'That you not engage in the abhorrent practices'. . .and it says (Lev. 18:6), 'You shall not come near to uncover nakedness'. . .that is to say, do not approach even those things that might result in forbidden relationships."

Only by the wildest stretch of the imagination can this statement of Maimonides be assumed to render either homosexual fantasies or attraction forbidden. Rather, the passage must be understood to mean that homosexuals must refrain not only from actual homosexual intercourse, but also from other sexual behavior which is not intercourse. The source from Maimonides is surely not forbidding either fantasies or attractions, which are far less controllable than behaviors are.

Spero also refers to Maimonides, הלכות איסורי ביאה 21:9, which reads: אשתו של
אדם מותרת היא לו, לפיכך כל מה שאדם רוצה לעשות באשתו עושה... ואף על פי כן מדת חסידות
שלא יקל אדם את ראשו לכך ושיקדש עצמו בשעת תשמיש... ולא יסור מדרך העולם ומנהגו, שאין
דבר זה אלא כדי לפרות ולרבות – "A man's wife is permitted to him. Therefore, he may behave with her [sexually] as he wishes. Nonetheless it is righteous for a man not be overly frivolous in this regard. Rather, he should sanctify himself at the time of intercourse. . .and not deviate from common behavior in this regard, since the sole purpose of the act of intercourse is procreation."

This passage is obviously a plea by Maimonides for what he considers to be a sexually proper attitude when engaged in sexual behavior. It is a plea not to allow even permissible behavior to blind one to the greater purpose of intercourse. The passage does not forbid fantasizing the acts which it forbids. Maimonides and the Talmud were far too wise to forbid thoughts. It is impossible to forbid them, and any attempt to do so only increases the feelings of guilt of those who have thoughts and cannot control them. Controlling behavior is hard enough. Legislating that thoughts or attractions are forbidden is not only unreasonable, it is foolish.

These are the two of Spero's sources that come closest to reflecting what he contends, and they are very far from convincing. The fact that fantasies and attractions cannot be forbidden legally does not mean that the tradition has nothing to say about them. They are in the category of הרהורי עבירה and should be avoided, if possible.[35] Their power and potency is clearly recognized. The Gemara[36] affirms הרהורי עבירה קשו מעבירה, but that must not be confused with a legal statement. It does not mean that the thoughts are more illegal than the acts. It means they are more burdensome, more difficult to control, more difficult to will out of existence. The sages surely recognized that הרהורים can have undesired consequences. As Rabbi Pinhas ben Ya'ir put it,[37] אל יהרהר אדם ביום ויבא לידי טומאה בלילה.

The issue of הרהור is deserving of its own treatment, but that is not the purpose of this paper. What is important to note is that the avoidance of הרהור is a desideratum, not

---

[35] See Berakhot 12b and *Encyclopedia Talmudit* entry הרהור. The principle of הרהור is the source of many rabbinic statements advocating behavior intended to prevent certain thoughts — e.g., not watching animals mate, not watching women doing laundry at the shore.

[36] Yoma 29a., quoted by Spero, id., p. 62

[37] Ketubbot 46a, and cf. Avodah Zarah 20b.

a legal requirement. One must attempt to avoid הרהור, but is not legally liable for failure. Indeed, the sages clearly recognized the pervasiveness of הרהור. They said:[38] שלש עבירות אין אדם ניצול מהן בכל יום: הרהור עבירה ועיון תפלה ולשון הרע, that הרהור עבירה is one of the three things which humans cannot avoid even for one day. All of the rabbinic dicta about הרהור עבירה must be understood in the light of this statement. As undesirable as הרהור עבירה may be, it is the lot and fate of humans to be subject to it. They can try to avoid it and to control it,[39] but they cannot be free of it. Homosexuals can no more be free of their הרהורים by a simple act of will than heterosexuals can be free of theirs. Indeed, the vast majority of the rabbinic statements about הרהור עבירה are heterosexually oriented.

Let us now note that the verses in Leviticus which prohibit homosexuality are blanket statements of prohibition. They do not stipulate that homosexuals of type X who engage in intercourse are not liable. Anyone who wishes to make such a claim is obligated to provide convincing proof that the distinction he wishes to read into the law is really there.

Our colleague, Rabbi Bradley Artson, has written a paper on the subject of homosexuality which he has presented to the CJLS. It is not my intention to respond to everything he has written, point by point. I must, however, demonstrate in detail why the central core of his argument does not provide the convincing proof that would be required to allow his conclusions to be supported.

Rabbi Artson argues that the Torah's prohibition against homosexuality does not apply to constitutional homosexuals. The Torah does not know of such people, and cannot be forbidding what it does not know about.

It is true that the Sodom episode and the פלגש בגבעה episode reflect homosexual violence, not homosexual love. Nonetheless, it would be erroneous to conclude that only such homosexuality is forbidden. I have demonstrated above that the Torah does not prohibit homosexual attraction – orientation, if you will. The silence of the Torah concerning any distinction between homosexual acts and homosexual orientation is because the Torah does not forbid the latter, only the former. But, the former is forbidden even for one whose orientation is homosexual.

And even if Rabbi Artson is correct about the Torah itself, he himself tacitly recognizes that what is really critical is whether the Sages were able to conceive of such a loving homosexual relationship. If they were, and if they considered it forbidden under the law, that would be determinative.

Rabbi Artson quotes three passages which he interprets to support his claim. I think he misinterprets all three, and will treat them *seriatim*.

The Gemara in Hullin[40] reads: עולא אמר (על הפסוק בזכריה יא:יב – וישקלו את שכרי שלשים כסף): אלו שלשים מצות שקבלו עליהם בני נח ואין מקיימין אלא שלשה: אחת שאין כותבין כתובה לזכר – Ulla said (concerning the verse in Zachariah 11:12 – "They weighed out my wages, thirty shekels of silver"), "[The thirty shekels] refer to the thirty commandments which the Noahides accepted upon themselves, though they comply with only three: One, that they do not write a ketubbah for a male. . . ." Rashi comments on this passage: אע״פ דחשודין למשכב זכור ומייחדין להם זכר לתשמישן, אין נוהגים קלות ראש במצוה זו כל כך שיכתבו להם כתובה – Even though they are suspect to engage in homosexual

---

[38] Bava Batra 164b.

[39] See Kiddushin, 30b – איסורי ביאה כא:יט – אם יבוא לו הרהור יסיע לבו ממשכהו לבית המדרש and Maimonides, מדברי הבאי לדברי תורה.

[40] 92a-b.

behavior and designate[41] a male as their partner, they do not make so light of this mitzvah that they write a ketubbah for their partner.

Polygamy is permitted by biblical and talmudic law, and is not considered either immoral or incapable of being loving, committed, permanent, and sacred. No interpretation of this passage, therefore, can work from the premise that such relationships are necessarily loveless or involve only lustful intercourse, or are like a series of affairs.

Rashi interprets Ulla to be praising the non-Jews for their recognition that no matter how committed, permanent or sacred they might wish their relationship with their homosexual partner-to-be, it cannot be legalized by a marriage contract. The ketubbah provides both a potent symbol and legal protection for the partner. It is the indicator of an acceptable, valid and legal relationship. It is the unacceptability of such a relationship that the passage intimates. Not only, claims Ulla, do Jews recognize that such a relationship – even if loving and permanent – is religiously unacceptable, even non-Jews do not attempt to legitimate what cannot be legitimated. Even if it is a permanent relationship, a loving relationship, a relationship of commitment, it cannot be legitimated. Such a relationship can be conceived of, it cannot be legitimated.

The second passage comes from Genesis Rabbah[42] and reads: ר' הונא בשם ר' יוסף: דור המבול לא נמחו מן העולם עד שכתבו גמומסיות לזכור ולבהמה – Rabbi Huna in the name of Rabbi Joseph [said]: "The generation of the flood was not obliterated from the world until they wrote marriage contracts from males and beasts."

I have translated the term גמומסיות as "marriage contracts" on the basis of both Theodor-Albeck and Mordecai Margulies. It clearly comes from the Greek *gamikon*, which means marriage. It is possible that it is a shortened form of *gamikoi humnoi*, in which case it would refer to "wedding songs."[43] In either case, the term is a positive one. What the passage says, therefore, is that the generation of the flood was not destroyed until they legitimated homosexual behavior, sanctifying it with marriage contracts or marriage hymns, lending to such unions an aura of legitimacy and permanence. The passage clearly recognizes the possibility of such a union and such a relationship, and denies its acceptability. It is so unacceptable that the attempt to validate it brings on the destruction of the flood.[44] It is not that such a relationship cannot be conceived of. It can be conceived of. It cannot, however, be legitimated.

---

[41] Rabbi Artson translates this word as "sequester," which, of course, supports the way he wishes to read the passage. His translations supposes that the word in the original is מתייחדין, not מייחדין. The former implies an illicit being together, while the latter intimates the designation of a single individual as a mate or partner.

[42] 26:5, on Gen. 6:2, Theodor-Albeck ed., p. 248. See also the parallel in Leviticus Rabbah 23:9, on Lev. 18:3, Margulies ed., p. 539; and *Midrash ha-Gadol*, Genesis, 6:11, Margulies ed., p. 153.

[43] Rabbi Artson's translation, "coupling songs," comes from Jastrow, it seems to me. That translation carries a very negative connotation essential to Rabbi Artson's understanding, but not really present in the original. Jastrow may be asserting that the presence of the word מום in the term גמומסיות is the sages derisive perversion of the Greek term. Theodor-Albeck, Margulies, *Sefer he-Arukh* (s.v. גמס), modern translations of Midrash Rabbah and the variants in both Genesis and Leviticus Rabbah argue against his understanding.

[44] Rabbi Artson makes much of the positioning of the passage in Genesis Rabbah, after "כי טובות הנה" – טבת כתיב משהיו מתיבין אותה לבעלה היה גדול נכנס ובועלה תחילה... "ויקחו להם נשים" – אלו נשואות. "מכל אשר בחרו" – זה זכור ובהמה.

He argues that as these do not refer to ongoing love relationships, so, too, the statement of Rabbi Huna does not. Two things argue against Rabbi Artson's claim: (1) the appearance of Rabbi Huna's statement in parallel passages without this context; and (2) the fact that the passage as it stands is a literary crescendo. To wit: the בני האלהים were perverse. They exercised the *jus primus noctus*, they forcibly raped virgins, and they seized the wives of other men. But even these acts of violence did not compel God to wipe out His creation. That happened only when they attempted to legitimate homosexual unions as if they were marriages.

Finally, Rabbi Artson finds the linkage of זכור ובהמה telling and important. Regrettably, he demonstrates a

The final passage has already been referred to earlier.[45] We quote again the part of the passage relevant to this point in the discussion: לא אמרתי (שאסורים משום "ובחוקותיהם לא תלכו") אלא החוקים החקוקים להם ולאבותיהם ולאבות אבותיהם. ומה היו עושים? – האיש נושא לאיש והאשה לאשה, האיש נושא אשה ובתה והאשה ניסת לשנים – "I have forbidden only those practices which they and their ancestors have established. And what did they do? A man would marry a man and a woman marry a woman, a man would marry a woman and her daughter, and a woman would be married to two men."

There is no way to read this passage as implying only lustful, non-supportive, loveless relationships. There is not even a hint of such a thing in this passage. The Torah forbids the marriage of a woman and her daughter.[46] But there is no greater reason to believe that such a marriage would be loveless and non-supportive than would be any other polygamous marriage. Surely the Torah does not assert that polygamous marriages are lustful and loveless by definition. The Torah forbids polyandry, but societies which permit it would find such marriages no less supportive and loving potentially than polygamous marriages in the societies which permit them. It forces the meaning of the words of the Sifra beyond credulity to assert that this passage passes judgment on the nature of the marriages which it lists. No such judgment is passed. These types of marriages are forbidden, not because they are by definition non-permanent, lustful, loveless, or whatever. They are forbidden because the Torah forbids them. Among them are listed homosexual unions of both males and females.

Part one of this paper is at a close. In dealing with the texts of the Bible and the Talmud we have demonstrated that homosexuality is called תועבה by the Torah, but that the term denotes an attributed characteristic, not an inherent one. We have demonstrated that both male and female homosexuality are forbidden in Jewish law, and that it is erroneous to claim that female homosexuality is prohibited by the sages only because of lewdness. We have demonstrated that both the active and the passive partners are liable at law under usual circumstances. We have demonstrated that the prohibitions of the Torah are against sexual relations between homosexuals, not against fantasies, attractions, or orientations. And we have demonstrated that the prohibition of the Torah (דאורייתא) makes no distinction between supportive, loving, permanent relationships and lustful, transient, and non-supportive relationships. Same gender sexual relations of both types are forbidden by the Torah.

Part II

We must now turn our attention to interpretations of the term תועבה. As we do so, we must also remember that if they are found wanting, that proves only that the interpretations are inadequate, not that homosexuality is not תועבה according to the Torah.[47]

Since the Torah itself does not define *why* homosexuality is תועבה, just *that* it is, it seems most logical to begin this quest for an explanation in the Talmud. And, indeed, there is a passage in the Talmud that provides a start for this discussion. In Nedarim 51a, Bar Kappara offers an explanation of the meaning of the term תועבה.

---

bias in his understanding which is not reflected in the text. The text implies that the generation of the flood attempted to legalize and legitimate ongoing and permanent relationships with animals. The linkage implies that as relationships with animals are unacceptable – no matter how permanent or legalized – so, too, are relationships between males – no matter how permanent or legalized.

[45] Sifra, Aharei Mot 9:8, Weiss ed. 85d; see above, p. 617.
[46] Lev. 18:17.
[47] See above, p. 616.

We will subject Bar Kappara's explanation to analysis, but preface the analysis by pointing out the context. The interchange between Bar Kappara and Rebbe, during which Bar Kappara defined the meaning of תועבה, took place at the wedding of Rebbe's son, Rabbi Shimon. Previously, Bar Kappara had promised Rebbe's daughter that he would drink wine while her father danced and her mother sang. At the wedding, Bar Kappara asked Rebbe: מאי תועבה? Whatever explanation Rebbe offered, Bar Kappara refuted. Finally, Rebbe said: פרשיה את – "You explain it!" Bar Kappara told Rebbe to have his wife pour him a drink, and insisted that Rebbe himself get up and dance before him as preconditions to his explaining. Rebbe did both things. Then Bar Kappara said: הכי אמר רחמנא: "תועבה" – תועה אתה בה – "Thus did the Merciful One say: 'To-evah' — You go astray on account of it (or, her)."

This is immediately followed in the gemara by two further episodes that took place at the wedding. Bar Kappara repeated his demands on Rebbe as preconditions to his explaining the terms תבל[48] and זמה.[49] The former he defines as תבלין יש בה? and the latter as זו מה היא.

We refer to the continuation of the passage which contains the definition of תועבה in order to indicate that Bar Kappara himself might not have intended his definitions quite as seriously as we will be taking them. Furthermore, it is quite clear that all three definitions are plays on the words. Having said this, we return to a careful analysis of תועה אתה בה, understanding it as very seriously intended by Bar Kappara.[50]

First we note that תועה אתה בה is clearly a *notarikon*, i.e., תוע (ה אתה) בה. Secondly, we note how difficult it is to translate it into English because of the unclear referent of the pronoun בה. Bar Kappara asked מאי תועבה. He did not specify a particular verse as the locus of the term. On the one hand, therefore, we would like his answer to refer to verses in which the term *as stated*, namely, תועבה, actually appears. If that is his intent, he refers either to Lev. 18:22 or 20:13, for only in those two verses does the term תועבה actually appear. In such a case, the בה must refer to homosexuality, i.e., "you go astray because of it." Bar Kappara's phrase obviously requires בה or the *notarikon* does not work. However, it is very difficult. To what does the בה refer? If its antecedent is a term like משכב זכר, the pronoun should be בו, not בה. The only real possibility is that the בה refers to the noun תועבה, i.e., you go astray because of the abomination. That is not smooth either, because it requires using the term being defined as part of the definition itself.

There is another grammatical possibility. If Bar Kappara's question used תועבה as a general term, rather than with reference to a specific occurrence of the word, his answer need not even be about homosexuality. Bear in mind that all of the sexual offenses are referred to as תועבות in Lev. 18:26, 27, and 29. If Bar Kappara was asking what the meaning of תועבה was in general, as opposed to in regard to homosexuality in particular, the pronoun בה is far less problematic. Since most of the עריות – all of which are תועבות – are women, תועה אתה בה means: "You go astray on account of her." If this explanation is correct, Bar Kappara is referring primarily to the other עריות, not to homosexuality, and we can probably learn nothing from what he says that will shed light on why homosexuality is a תועבה. The advantage to this explanation is that we clearly

---

[48] Lev. 18:23 concerning bestiality.
[49] Lev. 18:17 concerning ערות אשה ובתה. In Yevamot 37b, the same explanation of זמה is given by Rava with reference to Lev. 19:29, ומלאה הארץ זמה.
[50] Let it be clear that if his explanation is dismissed as a joke told at a wedding, when he may even have been less than completely sober, we would have to say that the Talmud gives no guidance as to the meaning of תועבה. We could not conclude that homosexuality is not תועבה on the grounds that Bar Kappara did not mean his explanation seriously. It is for this reason that we will analyze his explanation as if we knew for certain that he meant it with utmost seriousness.

understand the antecedent of the pronoun בה. The weakness of this explanation is that it leaves unexplained the very verses in which the term תועבה actually appears with reference to a specific sexual offense.

There are at least two classical commentators who understand Bar Kappara in this latter way. The מיוחס לרש״י[51] explains Bar Kappara: כלומר, שמניח את אשתו של היתר ותפס זו של זנות – ["You go astray because of her."] That is to say, he abandons his wife who is permissible to him in favor of one with whom relationships are in the category of זנות.

In a similar vein, the בעלי התוספות על התורה[52] explain: מה אל פנית שלא בה אתה תועה – "You go astray on account of her" שכתוב במשלי (ה:טו) שתה מים מבורך ונוזלים מתוך בארך because you paid no heed to what is recorded in Proverbs (5:15). "Drink water from your own cistern and flowing water from your own well." That is, by ignoring the wisdom of Proverbs which indicates that you should stay with a wife who is not עריות, you go astray.

The מיוחס לרש״י and the בעלי התוספות, therefore, opt for clarity of the antecedent of בה, even though, for them, Bar Kappara sheds no light on the specific behavior which is called תועבה by the Torah.

All others, to the best of my knowledge, understand Bar Kappara to be referring to homosexuality, and offering an explanation of why God considers it to be תועבה. Tosafot, the Rosh and the Ran all offer a similar explanation.[53] Indeed, the language of Tosafot and the Rosh is identical: שמניחין נשותיהם והולכין אחר משכב זכר, and that of the Ran very close: שמניח משכבי אשה והלך אצל זכר. The "going astray" according to these three lies in the fact that a man abandons his wife to pursue a homosexual relation.

Let us first assume that the Tosafot et al. correctly understand Bar Kappara. If so, the model of homosexuality to which Bar Kappara refers is the Greek model.[54] In the Greek model it makes perfectly good sense to speak about homosexuality drawing one away from one's wife. The classical Greek model of homosexuality is an older man (about twenty-five), usually married, and a young man (about fifteen). Indeed, when the young man gets married he is expected to have regular heterosexual relations with his wife, and probably take a young male lover.

The pederastic relationship is viewed by the Greeks as a type of role model relationship in which the older man feels a strong attraction to his young lover, while the young man is expected to admire his lover, but not be attracted to him sexually. The pederastic model was supposed to transmit virtues from the old to the younger man.[55] In this model it is quite possible to speak at least of the older man as being מניח אשתו והולך אחר משכב זכר.

While this model is probably very infrequent in our day, there is no question that many men who have been married and have decided in the present climate to "come out of the closet" have also abandoned their wives for homosexual relations, and may have been doing so all along, although not openly.

This proves *only* that the reason of the Tosafot et al. is still applicable. It does not prove that it ought to be applied, or that it is what Bar Kappara meant. Even if it is not

---

[51] Nedarim 51a, s.v. תועה.

[52] End of parashat אחרי מות in vol. 6 (New York: Shulsinger Bros., 1950), p. 49b.

[53] All at Nedarim 51a, s.v. תועה.

[54] That Bar Kappara may well have known and understood the Greek model is possible. He was, we know, a lover of things Greek, especially Greek ideas of beauty and Greek language. See Bereshit Rabbah 36:8. Theodor-Albeck ed., p. 342, and J. Megillah 1:9 71b.

[55] See Michael Ruse, *Homosexuality* (New York: Basil Blackwell, Inc., 1988) pp. 176-182; and Arno Karlen, "Homosexuality in History," in Judd Marmor, ed., *Homosexual Behavior: A Modern Reappraisal* (New York: Basic Books, 1980), pp. 78-80.

what Bar Kappara meant, it seems most plausible that it is what the Tosafot, the Rosh and the Ran meant.

It is most likely that moderns would wish to expand the concern embodied in the statement of Tosafot et al., and analyze its relevance to the issue at hand. Perhaps מניחין נשותיהן וכו' is the way that the Rishonim intimate that homosexuality is disruptive to family life. They would not be the first to make such a claim. Rabbi Akiva, commenting on the verse in Gen. 2:24 says: ודבק – על כן יעזב איש את אביו ואת אמו ודבק באשתו והיו לבשר אחד – ולא בזכר "'He shall cleave' – [implies a union with a woman] and not with a man." It is through union with his lost rib that the man becomes whole again, and a union with a man does not result in such wholeness.

Clearly one might argue that if society would recognize the equal validity of homosexuality with heterosexuality, thereby eliminating the impetus for homosexuals to even consider or attempt heterosexual family arrangements, the disruption would disappear. The disruption occurs when a homosexual finds himself in so unhappy a relationship with a spouse of the opposite sex that he has extramarital affairs with men, or divorces his wife. Either way is disruptive.

That argument, however, is much too restrictive and restricted. The issue need not be only about the disruption of pre-existing heterosexual family structures. The issue could well be couched in terms of the desirability, willingness, and ability of society as a whole to accept multiple familial structures. The claim might be that homosexuality as a recognized, validated, co-equal option is itself disruptive to the family structure. The question is not whether a specific homosexual relationship disrupts a specific family, but whether homosexuality in general is disruptive to families in general.

The issue cannot be entirely separated from the question of procreation, to which we shall come in due course. For the time being, however, the emphasis is on the structure of the family *per se*, without concern for ancillary issues.

Surely one could make a very strong case that there is only one family model in both the Biblical and rabbinic literature. And one could surely claim that the model is intended not merely as a description of the real, but of the ideal.

When God says in Gen. 2:18 לא טוב היות האדם לבדו, אעשה לו עזר כנגדו and that עזר is a woman, does this not posit a heterosexual family as the ideal?[56] From the perspective of the biblical author, God chooses a woman as Adam's helpmate and companion. And notice, too, that the primary purpose of the creation of this first family is for companionship and עזר, not procreation. Even the later contention,[57] והיו לבשר אחד, refers not to procreation *per se*, but to marital intimacy. Surely one could cogently argue that the Bible reflects an ideal, and that it could have posited a homosexual family structure at least in addition to a heterosexual one if it deemed it co-equal or even acceptable. As everyone must admit, a homosexual family can be a source of mutual help, companionship and intimacy. Why is there no mention of such a structure, no hint of it anywhere? Surely one could argue that the reason is because the Bible refuses to see a homosexual family unit as an acceptable structure.

The Rabbis, too, are as clear as one can be on this subject. We need not belabor the issue too much. A couple of examples will suffice. לא איש בלא אשה ולא אשה בלא איש

---

[56] It again becomes important to remind ourselves of the material above, pp. 621ff, in which we demonstrated that the Rabbis *could* conceive of a loving, non-violent homosexual union. That is important again now in order to forestall the contention that Genesis and the Rabbis posited heterosexual families only because they could not conceive of homosexual ones.

[57] Gen. 2:24.

כל אדם שאין לו אשה שרוי בלא שמחה בלא, said the Rabbis.[58] And, ולא שניהם בלא שכינה ברכה בלא טובה, they claimed.[59] Surely a loving homosexual family unit would not be described by its members as בלא שמחה בלא ברכה, בלא טובה, or בלא שכינה. If, as we have claimed above,[60] the Rabbis were able to conceive of a loving homosexual relationship, these statements made by them must be understood to reflect the unacceptability of such unions. The heterosexual family unit is the only one in which the rabbinic tradition can see the presence of God, and the presence of joy, blessing and good. It is not that a homosexual family is inconceivable, but that it is unacceptable.

If these are defensible arguments, or stronger, the explanation of תועה אתה בה as disruptive to family structure stands as a defensible argument in favor of the precedent. That precedent disallows homosexual behavior as co-equal with heterosexual behavior, and, therefore, does not recognize a homosexual family structure as co-equal with a heterosexual family structure.

Thus far, then, we have demonstrated that there is an inherent ambiguity in the words of Bar Kappara. They might not even be about homosexuality. Further, we have dealt with one of the explanations of his words according to those who do take them to be about homosexuality. That is the explanation of the Tosafot, the Rosh, and the Ran, who understand Bar Kappara to refer to the disruption of the family as the "going astray." Even if that is not the original intent of Bar Kappara, it remains, we have demonstrated a clearly defensible interpretation of what תועה אתה בה can legitimately be understood to mean. If for no other reason, then, the weight of precedent does not yet seem to be overridden.

We turn our attention now to the second explanation of the words of Bar Kappara among classical commentators. The פסיקתא זוטרתא on Lev. 18:22 reads: "תועבה היא" תועה בה, שהרי אין לו ממנו זרע אנשים. The quotation of Bar Kappara's words, תועה בה, clearly indicates that the Pesikta is explaining תועבה in terms of Bar Kappara's explanation of it. His comment is interpreted to mean that the "going astray" of homosexuality lies in the fact of its being non-procreative.

The Pesikta is not alone in that claim among classical commentators. Nahmanides, in his comments to the same verse says: וטעם הזכר והבהמה מפורסם כי הוא דבר נתעב ואיננו בקיום המינים. כי האדם והבהמה לא יולידו – "The reason behind the prohibition of homosexuality and bestiality is well-known, being an abhorrent thing because it does not allow for procreation, since a male [with another male, and a male with an] animal cannot procreate." Similarly, ספר החינוך[61] claims: משרשי המצוה לפי שהשי"ת חפץ בישוב עולמו אשר ברא ולכן יצוום לבל ישחיתו זרעם במשכבי – הזכרים כי הוא באמת השחתה שאין בדבר תועלת פרי ולא מצות עונה. "Among the underpinnings of the commandment is that God wishes the world that He created to be populated and He therefore commanded against wasting one's seed in homosexual relations for that is truly wasteful since it is not procreative and not the fulfillment of the mitzvah of conjugal relations." We shall return to the last part of the statement in due course. For the moment, however, the main point is to see that the *Sefer ha-Hinukh* also considers the non-procreative element of homosexuality as a reason for its being תועבה.

Finally, let us note the comment of the תורה תמימה who writes:[62] נראה הכוונה שתועה מדרכי יסודות הבריאה לשכב עם זכר. ובפסיקתא זוטרתא מפרש תועה בה שהרי אין לך ממנו

---

[58] Genesis Rabbah 8:9, Theodor-Albeck p. 63.
[59] Yevamot 62b. See there, in general, for paens of praise to the heterosexual family unit.
[60] Pp. 621ff.
[61] Mitzvah 209.
[62] Lev. 18:22 letter עין.

זרע אנשים והכוונה אחת היא – "The implication [of Bar Kappara's statement] seems to be that one deviates from nature by having relations with a male. And in the פסיקתא זוטרתא [the author] explains that 'You go astray because of it' since you cannot procreate with a male. And the essence of both explanations is the same."

We have left this comment of the תורה תמימה for the last both because of chronological reasons and because he explicitly links the category of unnaturalness with non-procreativity. Since many of the issues raised today also link the two, or equate the two, or consider non-procreativity as a subcategory of unnaturalness, we shall discuss these elements as one unit.

On a most literal and technical level, one might claim that this explanation for the תועבה nature of homosexuality would be untenable if there is homosexuality among lower species. That is, one might claim that if there are instances of homosexuality in nature, then it cannot be called unnatural. Obviously, this point is generally raised because those who raise it can point to evidence of homosexual behavior in nature.[63] The point that there is some behavior among animals that is homosexual need not be contested. Herders and husbandmen have known about it for years.

The question that can be asked against this thesis is whether animal behavior should be used as a criterion for the determination of what is natural for humans. Surely, on one level the answer is "yes," but that may be inadequate. Do not humans commonly claim that it is unnatural for them to go around without clothes, even though animals do? Do humans really think of their acts of intercourse as the same as those of animals? Do humans posit such things as love and attraction as elements of animal copulation? Are not the differences we perceive between ourselves and animals in regard to sexual behavior and intimacy sufficient to warrant the claim that what may be natural for animals is not natural for humans?[64] Surely it is at least defensible, and perhaps far stronger than merely defensible, to claim that "natural" means "natural for human beings," and is not contingent at all on evidence from other animals. An act which may appear in nature among animals may be unnatural for human beings. There are species of animals which eat their young. Would that fact make it natural for human beings to do so? A literalist definition of the term natural is too restrictive, and not very useful toward an evaluation of whether or not homosexuality may be considered natural for human beings.

There is another element to the natural argument which is heard with sufficient frequency that it should be dealt with. Some argue that homosexuality is unnatural because of biological fit. That is, a penis fits comfortably in a vagina from a physiological perspective, whereas it does not fit so elsewhere: and the male organ in the female organ has a biological function (here again the linkage between "natural" and "procreative"), whereas it does not have such a function elsewhere.

The response to these claims contends that physiological fit is hardly a criterion for naturalness for several reasons: (1) Homosexuals have no trouble making their organs fit in orifices that are not vaginas, and (2) there is a long history of the acceptability among heterosexuals of sexual intimacies in which the penis is not inserted into the vagina, but

---

[63] See the chapter by R.H. Denniston in Marmor, op. cit., pp. 25-40. Note, however, that the chapter is entitled "Ambisexuality in Animals," not "Homosexuality in Animals." Denniston reports no instances of exclusively homosexual behavior among lower species. See also, "Is Homosexuality Biologically Natural" by J.D. Weinrich, in W. Paul, J.D. Weinrich, J.C. Gonsiorek and M.E. Hatvedt, eds., *Homosexuality: Social, Psychological, and Biological Issues* (Beverly Hills: Sage, 1982), pp. 197-208.

[64] In Part III of this paper we will deal with the possibility that human homosexuality is natural because it is caused by hormonal imbalances.

elsewhere. If these are not unnatural when carried out by heterosexuals, why should they be considered unnatural when done by homosexuals?

On one level, these claims are absolutely accurate and incontestable. There is a long rabbinic history of recognition of non-vaginal intercourse. Indeed, the very concept of non-vaginal heterosexual intercourse is derived by the Rabbis from the biblical verses which deal with homosexuality. Both Lev. 18:22 and 20:13 refer to משכבי אשה. In its comment to Lev. 20:13, the Sifra reads:[65] "משכבי אשה" – מגיד הכתוב ששתי משכבות באשה. There is mention throughout rabbinic literature of ביאה שלא כדרכה, which is the second type of ביאה implied by the words משכבי אשה. And ביאה שלא כדרכה is most widely understood to mean, or at least include, שלא במקום זרע, i.e., non-vaginal intercourse. On this level, then, there is clear rabbinic recognition of non-vaginal intercourse. Furthermore, the Sages clearly recognize non-vaginal intercourse as intercourse,[66] with all the legal implications thereof.[67]

Nonetheless, the claims in the paragraph above could be cogently argued to be insufficient to warrant the conclusions which some wish to draw from them. First of all, regarding the physiological fit claim, the issue is not whether the fit is possible. No one denies that it is possible. The issue is whether the physiological structures seem designed for that purpose.[68] Is there a biologically natural lubricant which eases penetration and movement both in ביאה כדרכה and שלא כדרכה? Is the threat of abnormal stretching or damaging of tissues the same in both types of intercourse? Is the occurrence of pain as frequent and likely in both types of intercourse? Clearly the answers to these questions might lead one to posit that vaginal intercourse is more natural, the physiological structures themselves being more appropriately designed for vaginal intercourse than for anal intercourse.[69]

Understood as above, the claim that homosexual relations are considered תועבה by the Torah because they are unnatural is not an untenable claim. The term יסודות הבריאה, as used by the *Torah Temimah*, need not (indeed, probably should not) be understood to imply physiological impossibility, but to imply (at least partially) physiological fit. Indeed, one might argue that it is precisely because such relations *can* occur in nature, however poor the physiological fit, that the Torah sees fit to attribute to them the attribute of תועבה as a sign of its rejection of such use of the physiological structures.

This brings us, then, to a discussion of the second element of the "natural argument," namely, that homosexual relations are unnatural because they are not procreative. To this claim, too, there are responses now regularly proffered, generally, two. First, because of technological advances, homosexuals need not be prevented from procreating. They can procreate even without engaging in heterosexual behavior. The male's sperm can be used to impregnate a woman artificially. That woman can then carry and bear the child, which

---

[65] Perek 9, 14 Weiss ed., p. 92b. Cf. Sanh 54a.

[66] E.g., Rashi to Yevamot 34b, s.v. שלא. But see David Feldman, *Birth Control in Jewish Law* (New York: New York University Press, 1968), pp. 155ff, for indications of rabbinic hesitancy in condoning anal intercourse between male and female without reservations.

[67] See Horayot 4a regarding הראה שלא כדרכה as legally הראה; San. 95a for ביאה שלא כדרכה being sufficient for liability for bestiality; Yev. 54a for ביאה שלא כדרכה being קונה ביבמה (and cf. M. Yev. 6:1, 53b. with Rashi and Tosafot ad loc.); and, Kid. 9b for ביאה שלא כדרכה being קונה באשה.

[68] The phrase "designed for that purpose" does *not* mean "designed *exclusively* for that purpose." The fact that something may have a second purpose does not negate that it also has a first purpose.

[69] None of these contentions is meant to deny that aberrations might occur in individual males or females – either physiological or psychological or both – that make some acts of vaginal intercourse seem less "natural" than in general. But, no argument from nature was ever meant to imply that there could be no exceptional cases. Nobody is claiming that nature is always perfect. The fact that there are imperfections in nature, however, hardly justifies calling something natural which is generally unnatural.

can then be raised by the male whose sperm fathered the child. Conversely, a lesbian woman can be artificially impregnated with a man's sperm and bear a child whom she will then raise. Thus, homosexuals, both male and female, can be involved in the procreative process, can have families of their own, and the fact that their sexual relations are with members of the same sex becomes irrelevant.[70] Indeed, one might imagine the sperm of one male homosexual partner being used to impregnate two female lesbian partners, with one of the children becoming the child of the male couple, and the other the child of the female couple. Such children could even have "siblings" who are known to them, and with whom they might relate as "family."

Second, if procreativity is a *sine qua non* for illicit sexual behavior, there are many heterosexual unions which are equally forbidden. All heterosexual acts of non-vaginal intercourse would be forbidden, because they are non-procreative. Sexual intercourse with a post-menopausal woman, an infertile woman, a woman who has had a tubal ligation, becomes forbidden for a man; intercourse with an infertile man becomes forbidden for a woman. Since halakhah clearly does not forbid sexual relations in these circumstances, it must imply that procreativity is *not* a *sine qua non* for licit sexual behavior. Therefore, the non-procreative nature of intercourse is not a grounds on which it should be considered forbidden.

As with most arguments we have thus far discussed, these also have a level of truth to them, the second even more persuasive than the first. But, they are not without their shortcomings.

Among animals, the purpose of sex is entirely for procreation. Copulation is almost always during the females' period of fertility. Even among those species which appear to be "monogamous," sexuality is not a function of love, attraction, or caring. Among humans alone is this not the case. Jewish tradition has long recognized that there are purposes to human sexual intercourse beyond the merely procreative, and it is unnecessary for us to prove its acceptability.[71] But, as permissible as non-procreative sex is, the linkage between intercourse and procreation is not severed entirely. Once intercourse becomes permissible for purposes other than procreation, there is no reason to forbid even non-vaginal intercourse. But it is the inescapable linkage between intercourse and procreation that gives rise to the hesitancy that the Sages expressed about some types of ביאה שלא כדרכה.[72]

How and where should the line be drawn between legitimate non-procreative sex and sex as a means of reproduction? It seems more than merely reasonable to posit the mitzvah of עונה as the characteristic which makes non-procreative sex permissible.[73] Since it is in the nature of human beings to engage in sexual intercourse for purposes other than procreation, such intercourse shall be considered sanctioned (i.e., natural) when it fulfills the other primary purpose of intercourse recognized by the law, namely, the mitzvah of עונה.[74] Since עונה is a mitzvah which applies only between a husband and wife, any act of intercourse between

---

[70] Our discussion of this claim will ignore entirely all of the halakhic questions involved in artificial insemination and the type of surrogacy arrangement implied by this claim. These issues are of only secondary importance in this matter, for the present at any rate.

[71] See Feldman, op cit., pp. 65ff.

[72] See above, n. 66.

[73] The Ravad, in *Ba-alei ha-Nefesh, Sha-ar ha Kedushah*, also lists the benefits accruing to a pregnant woman and her fetus as justification for intercourse. See Feldman, p. 69 and p. 182. This issue need not concern us for the purposes of this paper.

[74] See ch. 4 of Feldman's book for a thorough discussion of the mitzvah itself and the related issues of the quality of עונה and Chapter Five for his discussion of pleasure and wellbeing as motives for intercourse.

a man and someone not his wife cannot be called עונה. One may engage in ביאה שלא כדרכה with one's wife because the mitzvah of עונה can be fulfilled that way. But any ביאה whatsoever with one to whom the category of עונה is inapplicable is not justifiable. The fact that ביאה שלא כדרכה is permissible, natural, as a form of עונה with one's wife does not render it permissible, natural, in a different context, such as homosexual union.

We referred above[75] to the passage from *Sefer ha-Hinukh*. The author stated that homosexual relations were forbidden because they were non-procreative, and added: ולא מצות עונה. Not only do homosexual relationships fail to meet the justification of legitimacy that would be possible if they were procreative, they also fail to meet the other criterion of legitimacy — the mitzvah of עונה. All homosexual sex must be ביאה שלא כדרכה. Such ביאה is permissible only as an act of עונה. The naturalness of ביאה שלא כדרכה is determined not by the substance of the act, but by the legitimacy of the actors so engaged.

Apparently the earliest utilization of the argument from nature came from Plato, and he gives very conflicting messages as to what he meant by it. On the one hand, there are passages which intimate the most literal understanding of the argument. Thus for example Plato writes:[76]

> Our citizens ought not to fall below the nature of birds and beasts in general, who are born in great multitudes, and yet remain until the age for procreation virgin and unmarried, but when they have reached the proper time of life are coupled, male and female. . . surely, we will say to them (i.e., our citizens), you should be better than the animals.

Or, in a similar vein:[77] "If anyone. . .denounces these lusts as contrary to nature, adducing the animals as a proof that such unions were monstrous, he might prove his point."

On the other hand, though, Plato also writes:[78]

> I think that the pleasure is to be deemed natural which arises out of the intercourse between men and women: but that the intercourse between men with men, or of women with women, is contrary to nature.

In this passage it is the phrase *para phusin* which is translated as "contrary to nature." John Boswell has pointed out[79] that Plato probably meant by it "unrelated to birth," "non-procreative" rather than "unnatural" in the sense of being a violation of some moral or physical law. Though this might not have been understood by Plato's intended audience — indeed, Plato seemed to enjoy puns and double meanings — this nuance would surely have been present, and perhaps even primary. If so, Plato, too, may have made the link between "natural" and "procreative." Indeed, he may well have used the word "natural" to mean "procreative."

---

[75] P. 627.

[76] *The Laws*, 840d-e translation B. Jowett in *The Dialogues of Plato* (New York: Random House, 1937), vol. 2, p. 589.

[77] Ibid., 836c, p. 586.

[78] Ibid., 636b-c, p. 418.

[79] *Christianity, Social Tolerance and Homosexuality* (Chicago and London: The University of Chicago Press, 1980), pp. 13-14, n. 22. See also David Greenberg, *The Construction of Homosexuality* (Chicago and London: The University of Chicago Press, 1988), pp. 207ff.

Kant also used the concept of "natural" to mean "non-procreative," and reject homosexuality on those grounds. He wrote:[80]

> A second *crimen carnis contra naturam* is intercourse between *seux homogenii*, in which the object of sexual impulse is a human being but there is homogeneity instead of heterogeneity of sex, as when a woman satisfies her desire on a woman or a man on a man. This practice too is contrary to the ends of humanity: for the end of humanity in respect of sexuality is to preserve the species without debasing the person: but in this instance the species is not being preserved.

Clearly, then, there is a long history, both within Judaism and outside of it, of explaining the prohibition against homosexuality in terms of its non-procreativity, and meaning that by the term unnatural. Could the non-procreative nature of homosexuality and the impossibility of fulfilling the mitzvah of עונה with a sex partner of the same gender be reasonable grounds for the Torah's evaluation of it as תועבה? Surely even those who would prefer a different answer must admit that the answer could be "yes." The preference for a different answer might impel one to interpret the argument from nature very literally, but such a literal interpretation is neither the only one possible, nor, perhaps, even the most probable.

There are two other arguments often offered against the claim that homosexuality is unnatural. These arguments are statistical and cross-cultural. Let us look at each of these, in turn.

In 1948, Kinsey and his associates W.B. Pomeroy and C.E. Martin, published a study[81] based on 6,000 American males from which they concluded that thirty-seven percent of the male population had some homosexual contact after adolescence, that thirteen percent had been more homosexual than heterosexual for at least three years between adolescence and age fifty-five, and that four percent were exclusively homosexual after adolescence. For the purposes of these figures, homosexuality was defined as having achieved orgasm through a homosexual experience. If one included homosexual yearnings that might not have led to an orgasm, the figure for males reached fifty percent. The findings of Kinsey have been subsequently confirmed in published studies.[82]

In 1953 Kinsey and his associates published their findings regarding women.[83] The following paragraph summarizes the findings for women, as compared to the findings for men:[84]

---

[80] *Lectures on Ethics*, translated by L. Infield (New York: Harper & Row, 1963), p. 170, quoted by Ruse, op. cit., p. 186.

[81] *Sexual Behavior in the Human Male* (Philadelphia: W.B. Saunders, 1948).

[82] See, for example, R.W. Ramsay et al., "A case study: homosexuality in the Netherlands," in J.A. Loraine, ed., *Understanding Homosexuality: Its Biological and Psychological Bases* (New York: American Elsevier, 1974), pp. 14-40; and F. Whitam, *Archives of Sexual Behavior*, 12 (1983): 207-226.

Rabbi Samuel Dresner has written an extensive monograph on the subject of homosexuality, as yet unpublished. On p. 37f Dresner writes: "Kinsey's statement...has been under heavy attack...He withheld the fact that a high percentage of subjects were 'prisoners, ex-prisoners, or sex offenders,' and that eighty percent were 'lapsed Protestants'...An associate of the Kinsey Institute, who had broken with its founder, said that 'Kinsey's real activity has generally been misunderstood, owing to a cloud of statistical hokum...[His] not-very-secret-intention was to respectabilize homosexuality and certain sexual perversions...."

I am in no position to judge the conflicting claims concerning Kinsey's statistics. But, for the purposes of this paper, I am prepared to accept them as accurate. Obviously, if they are grossly overstated, their usefulness as an objection to the "unnatural" claim is greatly reduced.

[83] *Sexual Behavior in the Human Female* (Philadelphia: W.B. Saunders, 1953).

[84] Ibid., p. 475.

Among the females, the accumulative incidence of homosexual responses had ultimately reached twenty-eight percent; they had reached over fifty percent in the males. The accumulative incidences of overt contacts to the point of orgasm among the females had reached thirteen percent. . . .Among males they had reached thirty-seven percent. This means that homosexual responses had occurred in about half as many females as males, and contacts which had proceeded to orgasm had occurred in about a third as many females as males. Moreover, compared with the males, there were only about a half to a third as many of the females who were, in any age period, primarily or exclusively homosexual.

The substance of the argument offered from these statistics is that the frequency of homosexuality they reflect makes it untenable to refer to homosexuality as unnatural. Surely, the high incidence of homosexual behavior makes that behavior normal, and behavior which is normal is natural. Thus, the term natural is to be equated with normal.

Again, it must be clear that there is a level of truth to the claim. But again, it must be stated that the argument could well be an oversimplification. The terms "normal" and "abnormal" do not carry with them any denotation of morality or choice. Thus, to call obesity abnormal makes neither a moral judgement nor a claim that the person who is obese is somehow at fault for being obese. The obese person *may* be at fault, or may not be. But the term "abnormal" does not imply either one or the other.

Nor are the terms contingent on numbers, except perhaps in the extreme. Would we not call obesity abnormal even if the percentage of people who struggled with it for a period of at least three years was as high as thirteen percent? If four percent of all adults were perpetually obese throughout adulthood, would we not still call obesity abnormal?[85]

It is even conceivable that very high percentages of incidence might not change our view of what should be called normal or abnormal. Might we not reasonably claim that keeping kosher or observing Shabbat are normal for Conservative Jews, even if the percentage of those who do not is very high? In that context, "normal" means "posited as normative behavior." In a similar vein, if one said that homosexuality is abnormal, one would mean by it that homosexuality is posited as being non-normative behavior. Indeed, it need not make a claim about the desirability or the consequences of the abnormality. Such claims may be made, but they are not inherent to the claim of naturalness or normalcy.

Thus it is surely possible from a halakhic perspective to call homosexuality unnatural and mean by it "posited as non-normative behavior." That sense of the word is not unusual, and is not contingent upon the numbers of people who engage in the non-normative behavior. Furthermore, if a group feels strongly enough about the non-normativeness of a certain behavior, it might even call such a behavior תועבה. If one were to say, "Nudity is unnatural and abhorrent," one could be contending, "Our group feels that nudity is a non-normative behavior pattern, and we feel so strongly about it that we call it abhorrent." This sentence would *not* explain *why* we feel so strongly about nudity that we call it abhorrent. In other words, it is defensible to say that the Torah calls homosexuality תועבה because it feels so strongly that it is a non-normative (i.e., unnatural) behavior pattern that it attributes to it the characteristic of being abhorrent. Why the Torah feels that strongly must be accounted for by some other reason.

---

[85] Obviously if ninety-five percent of all adults were obese throughout adulthood, we might change our definition of normalcy. That is what I meant by the phrase "except perhaps in the extreme" in the first sentence of this paragraph.

Related to the arguments from numbers is the argument from cross-cultural evidence. Since we find homosexuality in virtually every society from antiquity to modernity, both in societies that were permissive of it and in societies that were repressive of it, we are surely mistaken to call it unnatural.

The contention that homosexuality is found in every culture is not really subject to doubt.[86] Even that claim, however, may not really lead to the conclusion many wish to draw from it. That conclusion, after all, seeks ultimately to validate homosexuality as a co-equal lifestyle with heterosexuality, even when (indeed, for some, solely when) homosexuality is the exclusive lifestyle, and points to cross-cultural evidence for support of its naturalness. Yet, note the following contention by J.M. Carrier:[87]

> Heterosexual intercourse, marriage and the creation of a family are culturally established as primary objectives for adults living in all of the societies discussed above. Ford and Beach (in their book, *Patterns of Sexual Behavior* [New York: Harper & Row, 1951] – J.R.) concluded from their cross-cultural survey that "all known cultures are strongly biased in favor of copulation between males and females as contrasted with alternative avenues of sexual expression." . . .Exclusive homosexuality, however, because of the cultural dictums concerning marriage and the family, appears to be generally excluded as a sexual option even in those societies where homosexual behavior is generally approved.

If the argument from cross-cultural and transhistorical evidence were intended to demonstrate that homosexuality is not inherently abhorrent – or else it would be difficult to fathom how it could have such a long history – it might prove its point. But the claim of תועבה is not a claim of inherent abhorrence, but of attributed abhorrence.[88] Cross-cultural and transhistorical evidence can provide no counterclaim to an attribution of abhorrence by a given culture. Indeed, it might even be possible to assert that a given culture attributed abhorrence to homosexuality as a purposeful response to societies that did not do so.[89]

We are all aware, at least intuitively, that terms like "natural" and "unnatural" are, on one level, sociological and cultural terms, rather than biological or objective terms. We would call the consumption of human flesh unnatural, though that is merely our cultural bias. Westerners think that having one day off a week is natural, though that is only a cultural perception. We would probably consider binding the feet of infants unnatural, though there have been societies in which it was very natural.

For a religious tradition to call a type of behavior unnatural may well reflect its biases and values. But, then, is that not part of what religious traditions are supposed to do? To say that homosexuality is unnatural from a Jewish religious perspective is defensible even if all

---

[86] David Greenberg's book, *The Construction of Homosexuality* (see above, n. 79), is a superb and thorough and cross-cultural transhistorical study of homosexuality. At this point in time it is probably the best available resource on the subject. A very readable, and more concise summary of findings can be found in Arno Karlen's chapter, "Homosexuality in History," and J.M. Carrier's chapter, "Homosexual Behavior in Cross-cultural Perspective," in Marmor, op. cit., pp. 75-122.

[87] In Marmor, op. cit., p.118.

[88] See above, pp. 615-616.

[89] That, precisely, is a significant part of the claim of Dennis Prager in the Special Edition of *Ultimate Issues* which he devoted to the issue of homosexuality.

it means is that Jewish religious values and biases favor heterosexuality as the sole legitimate avenues for sexual expression.

Nobody summarizes what we have been claiming about either the argument from numbers or from cross-cultural studies more aptly than David Zvi Hoffman. In his commentary to Lev. 20:13 Hoffman writes:[90] "תועבה" מציין מעשה שה' מגנה אותו אף אם היה דבר נפוץ בין עמים נאורים – "[The term] תועבה denotes an act which God denounces, even if it was widespread among enlightened peoples."

A summary of the road we have been treading since our last summary[91] is now in order. We have been analyzing the second explanation of the classical commentators of the words of Bar Kappara, namely, that homosexuality is called תועבה because it is non-procreative and unnatural. After noting the commentators who make this claim, we analyzed counter-claims to the argument of unnaturalness. We asserted that the argument from the evidence of homosexual behavior in lower animals is unconvincing because it is doubtful that animal behavior should be considered the sole criterion for what is natural in humans. We claimed, further, that the argument from physiological fit is defensible or better because the argument is really from design, not physiological impossibility of exclusiveness. Our discussion of non-procreativity as the basis of the claim of unnaturalness led us to the conclusion that only the mitzvah of עונה legitimates non-procreative intercourse. Intercourse which is neither potentially procreative nor עונה can be called unnatural. We found, in fact, that there were early links between "unnatural" and "non-procreative," dating even from Plato, and later from Kant. Then, we rejected the argument from numbers because "natural" is used to mean "normal," and "normal-abnormal" is not primarily a function of numbers, except perhaps at the extremes. And, finally, we rejected the evidence from cross-cultural and transhistorical studies because the term "natural" is, in some measure, a sociological term, not a scientific or objective one.

In sum, then, we have seen that both explanations of the classical commentators are surely defensible and, in significant parts, much stronger than merely defensible. The arguments against them have points of validity, but they are far from convincing enough to seek to overturn precedent because of them. Even if they were so strong as to force us to reject them, or to reject Bar Kappara's explanation itself, we would have succeeded only in proving that earlier explanations of why homosexuality might be תועבה are insufficient. Even the rejection of Bar Kappara would not lead to the conclusion that the *Torah* is incorrect or insensible in calling homosexuality תועבה.

Part III

Section A

The author of this responsum does not merely concede or acknowledge that knowledge unavailable to earlier ages has potential halakhic relevance today, he affirms it enthusiastically.[92] That being the case, the previous two sections of this paper are insufficient. We must proceed with some analysis of modern theories of homosexuality, and determine whether these theories should have actual halakhic significance.

---

[90] דוד צבי הופמן, ספר ויקרא (ירושלים: מוסד הרב קוק, תשי"ג), כרך ב' עמ. נד.

[91] Above, p. 627.

[92] See, in particular, chs. 9-11 of my book, *The Halakhic Process* (New York: The Jewish Theological Seminary, 1986).

In order to do so usefully, the broad outlines of the theories will be summarized. The summaries will not be in great depth, nor will they be in very technical language. Michael Ruse, in his book *Homosexuality: A Philosophical Inquiry*, has done this superbly, and much of the summary material is culled from the relevant chapters of his book[93] and will not be extensively footnoted in this responsum.

The first theory is the psychological, primarily psychoanalytic, theory first proposed by Freud in *Three Essays on the Theory of Sexuality* (1905). For Freud, every human being is bisexual, and at various stages of our development we go through phases that are appropriate to different sexes. Indeed, even in adulthood we have bisexual elements. Also, as is well known, Freud posited the idea of the libido. That is so well known that it is unnecessary to say more about it.

The first stage that an infant males goes through is called the oral stage. During this stage, the infant is totally dependent on his mother. The child's libidinal energies, are therefore, directed entirely toward his mother (i.e. heterosexual). At about a year and a half, the libidinal energies become directed toward the child's own body as he discovers his ability to produce feces. This is the onset of the anal stage, during which the homosexual nature predominates because his libidinal energies are directed toward himself and his body.

When the child reaches the age of three or four, his attention moves from his anus to his genitals. This is the beginning of the phallic stage. In addition to becoming aware of his own penis, the boy also becomes aware that girls do not have a penis. His sexual energy is turned back in this stage to the most significant female in his life, his mother, and his heterosexual side again predominates. It is during this stage that the child begins to work out the Oedipus complex.

The child enters the period of latency next, as other (non-sexual) elements of his growth continue to take place. The latency period continues until puberty, when the final stage of his psychosexual development takes place. During this stage, the child realizes that his love for his mother is not acceptable, since fulfilling it through consummation would violate a universal taboo against incest. His "successful" resolution of the Oedipus complex results when he transfers his heterosexual attraction from his mother to other females.

The process described above is the conventional (i.e. average, i.e. normal) path leading to heterosexual maturity. For Freud, there are two kinds of abnormalities: neuroses and perversions. A neurosis results from overly great repression of some stage of one's normal growth. Thus, for example, if a child is overly repressed during the anal stage by rigorous toilet training that represses the normal libidinal energies which are concentrated on the feces during this stage, the child must find alternative methods of releasing those libidinal energies. He may do so by developing other avenues of control — keeping things in — as a displacement for the normal libidinal energies which he is not being allowed to express. This example might result in the anal retentive personality. In sum, then, a neurosis is the result of overly great repression of libidinal energies.

Perversions, on the other hand, are not the result of repression, but a lack of proper control. Remember that part of normal growth involves learning to control urges, and that control, when appropriate, leads to the next stage of development, until maturity is reached. Perversion, therefore, is an instance of arrested development. Homosexuals' development is arrested at some point, and they cannot develop to the point that their libidinal energies are directed toward females. For Freud, then, homosexuality is a perversion, not a neurosis.

---

[93] Mainly chs. 2, 3, 5 and 6. See above, n. 55, for publication information.

What might trigger such arrested development? It could happen during the anal stage, which is a homosexual stage for Freud. At a crucial juncture, the development arrests at the perception of male genitals being the norm, and they remain the norm for the rest of the child's life.

A second possibility would be for the arrested development to take place sometime during the phallic stage. The following possible scenario will sound familiar to most moderns. The young boy discovers that females do not have penises, and is frightened by that discovery. He thinks of women as castrated men, and he fears being castrated. If the boy cannot resolve this castration complex successfully enough to allow him to proceed to the next stage of normal heterosexual development, he remains homosexual – i.e., with his development arrested at this point. Female genitals trigger such fear and anxiety in him because of the castration they embody that he cannot develop to the next stage of releasing his sexual energies heterosexually.

A final possibility will also sound very familiar. Indeed, it will sound the most familiar of all. During his teens, the boy is supposed to resolve the Oedipus complex successfully. He must develop from his heterosexual attraction to his own mother to heterosexual attractions to other females (with whom he could consummate his energies). But if he is just too close to his mother because she constantly smothers him with attention, and even more, if at the same time his father is often absent or hostile, the boy's development may be arrested. He cannot transfer his desires from his mother to other women, so he must turn for release of his sexual energies to objects that do not place him in rivalry with his father, and which can be consummated – namely, other men. This scenario reflects homosexuality as a result of the unsuccessful resolution of the Oedipus complex.

The essence of Freudian therapeutic technique is probing into the subconscious. The probing takes place in a host of ways, but emphasis on things like verbal slips and dreams play a central role. The purpose of the therapy is to bring to consciousness repressions of which we were unaware on a conscious level. The very act of bringing them to consciousness helps the patient see that they are there, and allows the patient to rectify the repressions by allowing the libidinal energy now to be released in normal manners, rather than in the abnormal manners that were imposed because of repressions.

Freudian therapy, therefore, is directed toward the successful resolution of neuroses. It does not, however work very much on perversions, since they are not caused by repressions, but by an absence of control. The oft-quoted letter of Freud to an American mother[94] will now make sense:

> By asking me if I can help, you mean, I suppose, if I can abolish homosexuality and make normal heterosexuality take its place. The answer is, in a general way, we cannot promise to achieve it. In a certain number of cases we succeed in developing the blighted germs of heterosexual tendencies which are present in every homosexual, in the majority of cases it is no more possible.

Since homosexuality is not a neurosis, but a perversion, the essence of Freudian therapy is not particularly effective. The most that can be hoped for is the reawakening of the heterosexual tendencies that are part of every person's makeup (since every person is bisexual), but that is not too likely in most cases. What the therapist *can* proba-

---

[94] Ernest Jones, *The Life and Work of Sigmund Freud* (New York: Basic Books, 1955), pp. 208-09. The letter is dated 9 Apr. 1935, and is quoted by Ruse, p. 27.

bly accomplish is helping the homosexual live with and accept his homosexuality.[95]

There are many psychoanalysts, heavily indebted to Freud who have nonetheless broken with him on several issues which have direct bearing on our subject. These people are called "adaptationalists," for reasons that will soon become clear. Without going into great detail, let us refer to the two major differences between the adaptionalists and Freud.

The adaptionalists deny that all human beings are bisexual, in the sense that Freud meant that term. That is, they deny that adult humans have components within them of the male and the female. Just because humans may go through physical stages in their very early development that might lead them to develop either way, that does not prove either that such bisexuality is present in the adult, nor that the physiological reality has a psychological counterpart.[96] In order to call a person bisexual, we must be able to say about the person that he can reproduce both as a male and as a female. Bisexuality must be judged by the character of the person as a whole.

They also criticize Freud's theory of the libido, claiming it to be tautological, perhaps meaningless, and surely not supported by neural activity. We quote from A. Kardiner:[97]

> For example, suppose we observe an infant's relation to its mother. We can say from this clinical observation: The infant is intensely interested in the mother, who is the source of all his gratifications. This is an inference based on observation with which we can all agree, and it tells us something about the mother-child relationship. Suppose now we make use of the energetic hypothesis and say: The infant intensely cathects the mother with libidinal energy. This statement does not add anything to our knowledge about the relationship between the mother and the child. We have merely restated the original observation in hypothetical energic terms. Hence, the tautology.

Using the libidinal hypothesis leads one to believe that the various evolutionary stages of development reflect fixed patterns that are not all dependent upon environment or education. What is needed more is a theory which focuses not on hypothetical concepts, but on how children respond to the external environment.

Normally, a child will develop into a heterosexual adult. However, if something happens in the course of his maturation, he must respond — adapt — in order to survive. What might happen to trigger homosexuality as an adaptation? Something in the child's environment might lead to a fear of women, or of their genitals. As a response and adaptation to this fear, the child might switch from the normal path of development to homosexuality. And what might lead to such a fear on the part of the child? The child's failure to successfully resolve the Oedipus complex could be the most common cause.

Now of course, we are once again on familiar ground, and see the influence of Freud on the adaptationalists, even though they deny two of his major premises: human bisexu-

---

[95] Richard Isay, author of *Being Homosexual: Gay Men and Their Development* (New York: Farrar, Straus and Giroux 1989), argues this position very forcefully, though not necessarily from a Freudian perspective. See also S. Fisher and R. Greenberg, *The Scientific Credibility of Freud's Theories and Therapy* (New York: Basic Books, 1977).

[96] See Sandor Rado, "A Critical Examination of the Concept of Bisexuality," *Psychosomatic Medicine* 2 (1940): 459-467; and Lionel Ovesey, "The Homosexual Conflict: An Adaptational Analysis," *Psychiatry* 17 (1954): 243-50, for example.

[97] "A Methodological Study of Freudian Theory: II, The Libido Theory," *Journal of Nervous and Mental Disease* 129 (1959): 137, quoted by Ruse, p. 47.

ality and the libidinal theory. For them, however, human beings never go through a natural homosexual phase. If a human becomes homosexual it must be because something deflects him from the natural development into heterosexual maturity. Something must force the child to repress his natural evolution into heterosexual maturity.

This, then, leads us to the primary reason for our summary of the view of the adaptationalists. For Freud, homosexuality is a case of arrested development, a perversion as opposed to a neurosis, and not subject to effective treatment by analysis which seeks to alleviate the results of repressions. For the adaptationalists, on the other hand, homosexuality is precisely a neurosis, caused by a repression along the normal path of heterosexual development. As a result, the adaptationalists affirm that homosexuals can be brought over to heterosexuality through analysis, by bringing to consciousness the fears and anxieties that brought about the neurosis.

This ought not be oversimplified to imply that adaptationalists believe that every homosexual can be transformed into a heterosexual. There are factors that make success more likely and the absence of which make failure more likely. For example: being fairly young, having some heterosexual urges, having strong desire to become heterosexual.[98]

Freud is not nearly as clear about female homosexuality as he is about male homosexuality. In brief, though, the following would summarize his views on lesbianism. Through the oral and the anal stage, the development of a girl is the same as the development of a boy, with the primary erotic figure in their lives being their mothers. When the girl reaches her period which is parallel to the phallic stage, she, too, discovers her clitoris, as a boy discovers his penis. Later during this period, the girl discovers that she is castrated, because she has no penis. Her mother, too, she discovers, is similarly castrated.

The discovery that she lacks a penis begins to evoke in the girl a desire for one, and she envies anyone who does have one, and denigrates those who do not. The girl begins to turn against her mother — for it is she, after all, who has brought her into this world so woefully inadequately equipped — and turns toward her father as the other side of the female Oedipus complex. There follows the girl's latent period until puberty. At that point, the normal girl will transfer her sexual feelings for her father to other men, and the focus of her sexual pleasure will move from the clitoris to the vagina.

Freud is not very clear or explicit about the causes of lesbianism, but seems to hold that just as parents playing "abnormal" roles might cause homosexuality in men, so might it cause lesbianism in women. It might also be caused by female fear of male genitals.[99]

Our summary of the psychoanalytic theory of the etiology of homosexuality is at an end. Now we must remind ourselves why we are dealing with the subject in the first place. Our interest is as halakhists, not as psychoanalysts. That is, it is not our obligation to determine whether Freud is right or wrong, but to analyze whether conclusive evidence in either direction would constitute sufficient grounds for us *as halakhists* to seek to overturn the halakhic precedent against homosexuality. Only if we discover that such evidence would impel us to seek to overturn the precedent would it become necessary for us to make some judgment about whether the evidence is valid or invalid. And if we are forced to make such a judgment, we must remember that our conclusion might well be that a definitive judgment is impossible. Then, of course, we would have to determine the effect of a תיקון on

---

[98] See, especially, the work of Irving Bieber et al., *Homosexuality* (New York: Basic Books, 1962).

[99] This parallels the adaptationalist view of one of the causes of homosexuality in males, i.e., male fear of female genitals. This reason of Freud's for the cause of female homosexuality is generally adopted by adaptationalists. See Lionel Ovesey, "Masculine Aspirations in Women: An Adaptational Analysis," *Psychiatry* 10 (1956): 341-351.

the precedent. Bearing these facts in mind will help to clarify why we will discuss some matters at length, and virtually ignore others (even though discussion of them might be both fascinating and interesting, and even though many [whose purpose is not the same as ours] might well discuss them at great length).

For the purpose of our analysis we shall consider the Freudian position and the adaptationalist position together, except when the differences between them become relevant to the analysis. When that happens, the distinction will clearly be made.

Let us suppose, first, that the psychoanalytic position were conclusively demonstrable as false. That is, suppose we had incontrovertible evidence that no homosexuals came from family constellations (except insofar as such a constellation might be attributable to pure chance) that psychoanalytic theory would lead us to believe should be frequent. What would the halakhic consequence be of such a finding? The finding would have no halakhic significance whatsoever. Since, at most, the halakhic sources may indicate reasons why homosexuality is to be considered תועבה, and those reasons are not linked in any way to the etiology of homosexuality, proving that the psychoanalytic theory is absolutely incorrect would leave us exactly where we began. Homosexuality would still be considered תועבה, and the tradition would still offer defensible (or stronger) reasons to explain why it should be considered so. And finally, those reasons would be independent of the etiology of homosexuality.

Now let us suppose the opposite. That is, let us suppose that the psychoanalytic theory could be conclusively demonstrated to be correct. For the sake of simplicity, let us even assume that the evidence proved that there was only one etiology of homosexuality, namely, an overprotective mother and a hostile or absent father. And, let us assume even further that the evidence proved that that constellation was not only sufficient, but necessary. Anyone with an overprotective mother and a hostile or absent father became homosexual, and no heterosexual had an overprotective mother and a hostile or absent father.

Would these facts, unknown to the Torah or the Sages, impel us to seek a change in the precedent? I think not, but let us proceed a step at a time. If the facts as laid out in the preceding paragraph were true, and we accepted any or all of the traditional explanations of why the characteristic of תועבה is attributed to homosexuality by the Torah, those explanations would not cease to be acceptable because we can now understand the etiology of homosexuality.

And if the facts were true, and we rejected even all of the traditional explanations of why homosexuality is called תועבה, where would that leave us? It would leave us with the given that the Torah attributes the characteristic of תועבה to homosexuality, with no adequate explanation of the reason for its doing so, and a set of facts that is irrelevant to either concern. It is the last clause of the sentence that needs clarification. It seems unlikely that we would succeed in claiming that homosexuality is called תועבה *because* it is caused by overprotective mothers and hostile fathers. That is, there does not seem to be a defensible argument to lead one to that conclusion. Yet, it seems equally implausible to argue that our knowledge of the etiology of homosexuality proves that there is *no* reason for attributing to it the quality of תועבה.[100]

---

[100] An analogy might help. Assume that the Torah calls stealing תועבה, and that one traditional explanation of why it is so called is that stealing is an antisocial behavior. Assume furthermore that some theory now proves conclusively that the etiology of stealing is always a lack of parental attention. Surely we would not claim that stealing is תועבה because it is caused by inattentive parents. Nor, however, would we claim that knowledge of its etiology removes it from the category of antisocial behavior. It remains תועבה – in this instance, an antisocial behavior – even though we now know its etiology.

Thus, if we knew that the psychoanalytic theory was absolutely correct, there would still be no reason to seek overturning the precedent, whether or not we accept the classical explanations of why the Torah calls homosexuality תועבה. How much more is this the case when we consider the reality that the psychoanalytic theory is not proved conclusively either right or wrong, and when we consider the reality that the theory itself allows for more than one etiology of homosexuality. If we would not find reason to overturn precedent if the theory were a ודאי (either positive or negative), how much more so if it is a ספק!

There is, however, one argument that might be made to impel us to seek to overturn the precedent. One might argue that the Torah not only did not know the etiology of homosexuality when it declared it to be תועבה, the Torah assumed its etiology to be something entirely other than what our new knowledge now recognizes it to be. The Torah assumed homosexuality to be a free choice on the part of the individual, a choice totally under the individual's control and one which the individual makes without any other factors predisposing him (or literally causing him) to make that choice. Given our new knowledge, the argument would go, we must seek to overturn the precedent because the moral God would not demand the avoidance of a behavior of one whose attraction to that behavior was not a matter of pure volition. This argument, notice, does not deny that the traditional explanations for why the Torah called homosexuality תועבה might, in fact, be defensible or stronger. It argues that even if they are, there are other grounds to supersede the precedent.

The argument is a complex one, and it must either be answered or accepted. It cannot be ignored. He who raises such an argument must be reminded that it is based on premises and assertions that are presumed to be true, though not proved to be true. Therefore, the rabbinic principle of המוציא מחבירו עליו הראיה must be applied. The Torah makes a blanket statement of prohibition, as we have demonstrated in Part I of this paper. One who wishes to argue that such a blanket statement is predicated on a certain assumption must prove himself correct. Mere assertion is not legally sufficient. In the absence of compelling evidence to the contrary, one ought to assume that a blanket prohibition is just that, and independent of etiology.

But even if one were to concede for the sake of argument that the Torah assumed homosexuality to be entirely voluntary, overturning the precedent would be considered only if there were no way to retain the precedent (particularly because the reasons for it are not denied by the argument), even in the face of the new knowledge. Put differently, if knowledge of the etiology holds out the possibility that one who is homosexual can be changed from homosexuality to heterosexuality, the precedent can and ought to be retained, and therapy urged.

Many who are demanding recognition of homosexuality as a co-equal lifestyle tacitly recognize this, because the success rate of therapy for homosexuality is often raised by them. The claim is that since homosexuality cannot be reversed, and is not chosen freely by those who are homosexual, therapy is not the answer to the rectification of the perceived immoral demand made upon them.

As poskim, we must realize that the claim is anything but objective. The adaptionalists, even if not the classical Freudians, assert that change from homosexuality to heterosexuality is possible. Some, such as Irving Bieber,[101] claim reasonable rates of success in therapy. Even such a liberal on homosexual issues as Judd Marmor wrote:[102]

---

[101] See above, n. 98.
[102] Op. cit. (above, n. 55), pp. 276-77.

Some homosexuals, however, are unhappy with their sexual orientation. . . .[I]f their motivation to change is sincere and strong, I believe they deserve an opportunity to try to accomplish their goal. . . .Not that this is always possible. Even the most optimistic psychotherapists rarely report more than a 50 percent success in changing a homosexual orientation to a heterosexual one. On the other hand, the general view in the gay community that treatment is *never* successful is without foundation. The fact that most homosexual preferences are probably learned and not inborn means that, in the presence of strong motivation to change, they are open to modification, and clinical experience confirms this. The kernel of truth in the gay point of view, however, is that once a major pathway to sexual gratification has been established and reinforced by repeated experiences, the tracks of that pathway can never be totally obliterated. Thus although it is possible for successfully treated homosexuals to change their overt behavior from homosexual to heterosexual, the tendency toward erotic arousal by the same sex is probably never totally lost.

For a Jew concerned with obedience to the will of God as expressed in halakhah, that very concern constitutes a strong and sincere motivation to change. When that motivation is coupled with the knowledge that halakhah forbids only overt behavior, as we have demonstrated above,[103] not erotic arousal by the same sex or even homosexual fantasies, the chances for halakhically acceptable change seem to be enhanced.

Change from homosexuality to heterosexuality, *measured by the only criterion the halakhah forbids, namely, overt behavior*, can take place in some relatively significant percentage according to many therapists.[104] If so, as poskim we must favor the precedent over the desire to overturn it. The counterclaim that all therapy is ineffective has hardly been proved sufficiently to warrant using it as grounds for arguing in favor of the overturning of established precedent.[105]

Rabbis would be well advised to remember how hard change for homosexuals is to accomplish. But this knowledge should move them to greater awareness of what has a chance of increasing the effectiveness of therapy,[106] and not move them to assert that the difficulty of therapy constitutes grounds for overturning the precedent.

But what, the question at the next stage of our investigation will be asked, about the homosexual who has tried therapy without success, or who is in one of the categories (such as obligatory homosexuals who trace their homosexual feelings and arousals to very early ages) that are poor therapeutic prospects? Would not our new knowledge of the etiology of homosexuality, as against the Torah's assumption that homosexuality is an act of pure and simple volition, lead us to advocate overturning the prohibition at least for them?

---

[103] Pp. 619-621.

[104] We have restricted our analysis to the psychoanalytic approach. As poskim we ought not ignore as a datum of our decision-making the views of other approaches. See ch. 21 of Marmor's book by Lee Birk. Birk is a behaviorist, and he reports remarkable rates of success in therapy.

[105] This is especially true when the legal prohibition is דאורייתא as in the case of homosexuality. To the extent that דאורייתא norms can be overturned at all — see ch. 7 of my book — doing so on the basis of such inconclusive evidence is surely not defensible.

[106] Marmor, ibid., p. 277 lists several factors: (1) Youth. Therapy is more effective when initiated before the age of thirty-five. (2) Previous heterosexual experience. (3) Recency of onset of homosexual activity. And, (4) "masculine" looking and acting men tend to succeed in therapy more than "effeminate" ones. Cf. above, p. 639.

At this point, our answer begins to be expressed with great anguish, but must be given nonetheless. Firstly, there is the matter of the principle of לא פלוג. Even if we were to come to the conclusion that the precedent should be overturned for such people, making legal distinctions between homosexuals of category A and homosexuals of category B is legally very difficult, probably impossible. The very positing of the distinction as having legal consequences would push many homosexuals to define themselves as members of the second category. The very impetus for the strong motivation to change would be removed even for those for whom it would be an effective start to change. We quote again the words of Marmor:[107] "The fact that most homosexual preferences are probably learned and not inborn meant that, in the presence of strong motivation to change, they are open to modification." When we posit a class of homosexuals to whom the prohibition no longer applies because therapy does not work for them, we remove the strong motivation for therapy to work from many for whom it probably could work. Therapy is difficult even for those for whom it can work. When we permit the claim that therapy does not work to exempt one from the prohibition, most will take the path of least resistance. The very motivation to succeed in therapy will be undercut by the knowledge that dispensation will be granted if therapy fails. Of course, therefore, therapy – hard, long and expensive – will fail. That which we might posit as a possible last resort will become, in fact, a quick and first resort.

But there is even more to say, and it, too, is said with heavy heart for those who must bear the burden of its message. We have asserted above[108] that even if the Torah misperceived the etiology of homosexuality, that "argument does not deny that the traditional explanations for why the Torah called homosexuality תואבה might, in fact, be defensible or stronger. It argues that even if they are, there are other grounds to supersede the precedent." Now we must deal with the implied question: Are the "other grounds" sufficient to supersede the precedent when the traditional explanations are at least defensible, and perhaps stronger?

Put forthrightly, the question can be restated thus: Would a moral God ever demand that people who are as they are through no choice of their own nonetheless behave in a way that suppresses an essential element of what they are in order to reflect and embody values and principles that for most others do not entail suppression of essential elements of what they are? Refraining from homosexual behavior embodies values and principles which we have enunciated in both classical and modern terms in Part II of this paper. For the heterosexual population, compliance with the prohibition does not entail suppressing their essential sexuality. For the homosexual population that might be successfully changed from homosexuality to heterosexuality, the moral God might well demand that they comply with the prohibition – even if they choose not to try to change. Since change might be possible, one cannot say that homosexuality constitutes an essential part of what they are. Therefore, suppression of homosexual behavior does not constitute a suppression of an essential element of what they are. But for obligatory homosexuals and for those for whom therapy has truly failed, homosexuality can probably be called an essential part of what they are. For such as these, then, demanding compliance with the prohibition against homosexual relations entails suppressing an essential element of what they are. Would God demand such a thing? That is the question.

One must admit from the outset that few things compare with sexuality, and that perfect analogies are hard find. I do, however, think we can offer one close analogy, at least for the open-minded. I would imagine that for a kohen, particularly in days when the priestly establishment functioned more or less as ordained by Jewish law, being a priest

---

[107] Ibid., p. 276.
[108] P. 641f.

was part of the essential psychological make-up of kohanim. The priesthood was an essential part of what they were. It was an essential part of how they saw themselves and how others saw them.

Jewish law mandated certain behaviors for priests, and given their psychological make-ups, it does not seem at all unreasonable that these behaviors were an essential part of who and what they were. Let us posit serving at the altar and blessing the people as two examples.

Jewish law also mandated both that certain genealogical imperfections and certain physical imperfections disqualified the kohanim so affected from serving in these functions. Surely, too, the imperfections were not their own choice, and they could not be changed. If we assume, as we both must and will for the purposes of this analysis, that there are defensible reasons for the laws which forbid imperfect priests from engaging in these behaviors, the analogy is complete.

The position of the law must be understood as follows: The desirable values and principles embodied in the mandate which prohibits imperfect kohanim from serving at the altar and from blessing the people are so important to God that He asks His devoted kohanim to suppress that essential element of what they are for the greater good of embodying the principles which the mandate reflects. He asks of them an act of great sacrifice as part of their service to Him. It is a hard act He demands of them, and its difficulty is made even greater by the fact that their need to suppress an element of their essential character arose through no act of will on their own part. But, in the final analysis, one would have to admit that Jewish law recognizes that an act of personal suppression of an element of one's character is not an inherently immoral demand. The fact that the demand is difficult and may even fill one with both anguish and anger does not make the demand immoral.

The idea that one might be called upon to suppress a behavior because the behavior violates a principle or a value which we mandate is not so unusual, in general. We expect people to suppress the behavior called stealing, even if they are poverty stricken and are stealing food to satisfy their hunger, because we feel that the value embodied by the prohibition against stealing is not superceded even by the hunger which results from poverty. It is true that we try to provide an alternative to allow the hunger to be alleviated, like soup kitchens, charity, welfare, etc., but the principle is still the same.

We may be able to understand when one cannot fulfill the mandate that the law imposes, but that does not lead us to the conclusion that the mandate was itself immoral. So, too, we must conclude that it is not inherently immoral to esteem the values and principles embodied in the prohibition against homosexuality so greatly that we recognize the morality of the mandate even in the hardest of cases — the obligatory homosexual or the homosexual for whom therapy has failed. We may understand when one cannot fulfill the mandate that the law imposes, but that does not lead us to the conclusion that the mandate was itself immoral.

We asked whether a moral God could prohibit homosexual behavior even in the hardest of cases. We have answered that He could, and did. As a result, we are led to the virtually inescapable conclusion that the knowledge gained from psychoanalytic theory does not provide compelling reason to advocate overturning the established precedent against homosexuality, even in the hardest cases, קל וחמר in the less hard cases.

One more issue is raised so often that I feel it necessary to add a postscript to this part of the paper, even though the answers to the issues have been implied already. Many point to the decision of the American Psychiatric Association (APA) removing homosexuality from its list of mental disorders. They see in that decision corroboration of their contention that homosexuality should be recognized as a co-equal lifestyle with heterosexuality. If the mental health professionals recognize homosexuality as nonpathological, so should the rest of the community. And if it is nonpathological, there is no reason it should not be equally acceptable with heterosexuality.

First the facts, quoted from Marmor:[109]

> Early in 1972 the members of the Massachusetts District Branch, a component society of the American Psychiatric Association, acting entirely on their own, passed a resolution expressing their conviction that homosexual behavior in and of itself was not a mental illness and requesting the APA to remove it from the DSM-II [second edition of the APA *Diagnostic and Statistical Manual for Mental Disorders* — J.R.]. This resolution was sent through normal channels to the Reference Committee. . . .The Reference Committee, following normal procedure, referred the resolution to the Council on Research and Development, which in turn sent the matter to one of its component committees, the Committee on Nomenclature. . .recommended to the Council on Research and Development that it be removed from DSM-II. This decision was approved by the Reference Committee and brought to the Board of Trustees of the APA in December for a final decision. The Board ratified the recommendation. . . .Under normal circumstances a decision of the Board of Trustees does not have to be ratified by the membership. Opponents of the decision, however, quickly marshaled the necessary two hundred signatures to compel a referendum of the entire membership of the APA. . . .The decision of the Board of Trustees was upheld by a substantial majority, with 5,854 (fifty-eight percent) in favor and 3,810 (37.8 percent) opposed; 367 (3.6 percent) abstained.

One of the things that these final figures do not tell us is what the number of eligible voters was. Those who voted numbered slightly over 10,000, but the total number of eligible voters numbered 18,000.[110] Those who voted in favor equal only 32.5 percent of the total eligible. I do not know at all how those 8,000 who did not vote felt. On an issue which was probably a very "hot" one in the APA, it is unlikely that many failed to vote because they were uninterested in the issue and had no feelings on the subject. At a minimum, the statistics are sufficiently ambiguous that they do not warrant the conclusion drawn from them except on the most technical level.[111] There is certainly a different flavor to the claim that fifty-eight percent voted to remove homosexuality from the list of mental illness than there is to claim that thirty-three percent so voted.

Far more crucially, however, reference to the vote of the APA as part of halakhic discourse is erroneous on two counts. First, when the figures of the APA vote are used to justify a claim that homosexuality should be recognized as halakhically co-equal with heterosexuality, outside experts are being allowed to determine halakhah. Outside ex-

---

[109] Ibid., pp. 392-93.

[110] See the letter from Dr. Mortimer Ostow in *Conservative Judaism* 40 (fall 1987): 105.

[111] I am reminded of the Seminary faculty's vote on the ordination of women. Though I have forgotten (or suppressed) the exact figures, I recall enough to know that anyone who gauged the sentiment of the faculty as a whole solely on the basis of the percentages of the votes, and totally ignored the members of the faculty who simply did not vote as a protest, would have gotten a very skewed picture.

perts can provide data for the consideration of halakhists, but they cannot decide halakhah.[112] And most importantly, arguing on the basis of the decision of the APA works only if one believes that the Torah called homosexuality תועבה because it was pathological, or that תועבה means pathological. Then it might make sense to argue that since moderns no longer consider it pathological we should no longer consider it תועבה.[113] But, we have demonstrated right from the beginning of Part I that the term תועבה refers to an attributed characteristic, and bears no hint of meaning pathological. Homosexuality may or may not be pathological. I shall let mental health professionals argue about that. But that homosexuality is תועבה has nothing to do with whether or not it is pathological.

In the final analysis, recourse to the decision of the APA is misleading at best and, at worst, a vitiation of legitimate halakhic process.

Section B

We turn our attention now to the second theory of the etiology of homosexuality, the biochemical, or hormonal theory.[114] As was the case in our discussion of the psychoanalytic theory, here, too, an introduction is required.

Any organ that separates certain elements from the blood and secretes those elements for the body to use (as, for example, adrenaline) or to discard (as for example, urine) is called a gland. There are two types of glands. One type has special passages called ducts, which carry the secreted element directly to the place where it is needed by the body. A good example of such a gland is the salivary gland, which has ducts which carry the saliva directly to the mouth. The second type of gland has no special ducts which carry the secreted element to the needed location. Instead, these ductless glands secrete their products directly into the blood stream, by which the products are carried throughout the whole body. Ductless glands are called endocrine glands, and their products are called hormones.[115] A partial list of the endocrine glands would include the pituitary, thyroid, adrenal, kidney, pancreas, and ovary (in females) and testes (in males).

Some endocrine glands work very directly. That is, where the concentration in the blood of the product of that gland is low, the gland works actively to separate and secrete more of the product. When the concentration is high, the gland is not as active. Other glands, however, do not work so directly. They produce a hormone which then acts on another gland, which is then stimulated into action or inaction. Hormones which act primarily on other glands are called tropic hormones.

Another example will clarify the interrelated functioning of the hormonal system. In a woman's cycle, the pituitary begins by producing a hormone called FSH (follicle stimulating hormone). The FSH is a tropic hormone, which acts on the ovary. There are two effects of the action of FSH on the ovary. First, a layer of cells (follicle cells) gathers around the immature ovum, and second, the ovary releases a female sex hormone (estrogen) into the blood stream. The released estrogen hormones cause the wall of the uterus to build up so that the uterus can hold the egg if it becomes fertilized.

---

[112] See pp. 231-33 of my book, *The Halakhic Process*.

[113] Note, of course, that such a claim would be immediately subject to the first objection, just raised.

[114] The author has even less expertise in this theory than he does in psychoanalytic theory. A reiteration of indebtedness to Ruse for a comprehensible explanation in lay terms is therefore greatly in order.

[115] Ruse suggests *Hormone: A Delicate Balance* (New York: Pegasus, 1972) by R. Le Baron as an excellent, non-technical presentation of the subject.

When the estrogen level reaches a certain point, it triggers in the pituitary a change from the production of FSH to the production of LH (lutenizing hormone). The LH releases the ovum from the follicle, and causes the release of another ovarian sex hormone, progesterone. The progesterone, in turn, causes a continued build up of the uterine wall, which collapses in a flush of blood if fertilization does not take place.

In males, the pituitary releases FSH which acts on the testes to cause the production of sperm, and LH acts on them to cause production of the male sex hormones, called androgens. The principle androgen is called testosterone.

Hormones are crucial in the development of human sexuality. In order to understand their importance we must back up for a moment. Of the twenty-three pairs of chromosomes, one pair is the sex chromosomes, crucial in determining whether the child is a boy or a girl. Each parent contributes one sex chromosome to the zygote. The mother always contributes an X chromosome, and the father may contribute either another X chromosome or a Y chromosome. Under normal circumstances, the XX combination result in a female child and the XY combination will result in a male child.

During the first trimester of pregnancy there is no sex differentiation in the fetus. That is, whatever the chromosome combination, all fetuses have rudimentary male organs – Wolffian ducts – and rudimentary female organs – Mullerian ducts. Sex differentiation takes place subsequently, and the key factor in the differentiation is the male sex hormone.

It is not the presence of the Y chromosome that *itself* produces a boy. Rather, the Y chromosome somehow triggers the production in the fetal testes of two hormones – androgen and Mullerian-inhibiting substance. This latter hormone acts on the Mullerian ducts, causing them to regress and shrink rather than develop into a uterus and Fallopian tubes. At the same time, the androgen acts on the Wolffian ducts causing them to develop into male internal organs and external genitalia.

While the fetal testes produce hormones, fetal ovaries do not. What is needed in order to get a male child is the hormones of the fetal testes that inhibit the development of the Mullerian ducts and enhance the development of the Wolffian ducts. If the androgen is not produced and secreted, or if the androgen cannot be effective for some reason, the fetus will not become a boy. Without androgen, the fetus will develop morphologically into a female.[116]

Sex hormones do not play much of a part in a child's life, either male or female, between birth and puberty. At about that time, however, the hypothalamus triggers the pituitary to produce the tropic hormones which then produce an effect on the sex glands. The estrogens in the female lead to the development of such characteristics as breasts and broad hips. The androgens in males lead to such development as the growth spurt, the growth of pubic hair, enlargement of the penis and deepening of the voice.

The effects of sex hormones is well known, and, in part, was well known before modern scientific understanding. Castration of males before puberty prevents the development of the characteristics of mature adult males because it prevents the production of androgens by the testes. Females whose gonads are either missing or non-functioning will not develop as sexually mature women because the ovaries do not produce estrogens. When either males or females with missing or non functioning sex hormones are treated

---

[116] There are people who suffer from a disorder known as androgen-insensitivity syndrome. These people have the XY chromosome combination, but are morphologically female. When they reach puberty they develop as mature women. However, the effects of the Mullerian-inhibiting hormone secreted by the fetal testes early on in pregnancy have made the female organs ineffective. Therefore, these people – chromosomal males and morphological females – cannot bear children.

with the missing hormones, they mature in a normal way.[117]

Conversely, when mature adults are either missing the appropriate sex hormone or have the inappropriate sex hormone, in males[118]

> The visible effects are enlargement of breasts: a tendency of feminine deposition of subcutaneous fat: reduced oiliness of the skin: reduced facial acne, if present: and an arrest of masculine balding, if it has begun. Beard and body hair do not disappear, but the hairs tend to be less wiry, and more slow growing.

In addition, the penis and testicles shrink somewhat, the male becomes unable to achieve and maintain an erection and the production of sperm and seminal fluid ceases. In females, doses of androgens produce more body hair and more oily skin, deepen the voice, suppress the menstruation and may enlarge the clitoris. There is no possibility, however, of hormones during adulthood undoing the effects of hormones in early life, making a man into a woman or vice versa.

Most will immediately recognize that there is a link between physiology and sexual attitudes and behavior. Hormones clearly play an important role in that linkage. The ancients knew this too, even if they did not have the scientific terminology. Eunuchs are boys castrated before puberty. Since the production of male sex hormones begins at that time, castration before puberty prevents the production of androgens. Eunuchs were purposely used to attend to the harem because the castration of the young boy also inhibited or eliminated entirely sexual desire. But it is also true that male castrates who are given long term treatment of androgen replacement therapy beginning at about the normal time of puberty mature physiologically in a normal fashion, and demonstrate sexual drives and desires.

If one begins with the assumption that homosexual inclinations are by definition inclinations appropriate to the opposite sex — homosexual males showing "female" inclinations and homosexual females showing "male" inclinations — certain conclusions seem to follow. Since we know that both sexes produce both androgens and estrogens, male homosexuals would probably be men with high levels of estrogens and female homosexuals would be women with high levels of androgens. We quote now directly from Ruse:[119]

> I think it is true to say that all hormonal explanations of human homosexuality have some variant on this conclusion at their core — after all, it is difficult to see how they could avoid it. However, intensive studies on humans and animals have shown that whatever else may be the case, *the relationship between hormones and homosexuality is not a simple one of cause and effect.* It is just not true that in any straightforward crude sense male homosexuals have an excess of female hormones and lesbians have an excess of male hormones. If this were so, then correcting the imbalance ought to be a relatively simple matter and ought to be followed by clear-cut, not to say dramatic, results. In particular, dosing homosexuals with the appropriate hormones ought to pro-

---

[117] See J. Money and A. Ehrhardt, *Man and Woman, Boy and Girl: The Differentiation and Dimorphism of Gender Identity from Conception to Maturity* (Baltimore: Johns Hopkins University Press, 1972), p. 214.

[118] Ibid., p. 208, quoted by Ruse, p. 95.

[119] P. 97. Emphasis added.

duce heterosexuals, and, (as a kind of control) dosing heterosexuals with appropriate hormones ought to produce homosexuals. But none of these results obtain. If male homosexuals are given androgens, their sexual drive if anything goes up; but it is just as fixedly or even more directly homosexual. Conversely, if heterosexuals are given oestrogens (as is sometimes done in the treatment of certain forms of cancer, particularly that of the prostate), they do not become homosexual. It is true that the drive and the ability of such heterosexuals is reduced, but this is a fact that they regret bitterly, for their heterosexual orientation is just as fixed as ever.

Still, it appears so eminently logical that there should be some relationship or linkage between sex hormones and sexuality, that research has proceeded along other lines of inquiry. The first line seeks to discover whether there are any differences between homosexuals and heterosexuals to be deduced from long term hormonal imbalance, as opposed to massive doses of hormones after sexual orientation has already been established. Again we quote from Ruse.[120]

> Early attempts to find significant differences between the pertinent hormonal levels of adult heterosexuals and homosexuals met with little or no success. However, in recent years more sophisticated and accurate methods of hormone concentration measurement have been developed, and there have been renewed interests in comparing adult heterosexual and homosexuals hormonally. Unfortunately, the flood of studies has come up with entirely contradictory results. Some few studies have produced results suggesting that male homosexuals have depressed testosterone levels. Other studies found absolutely no significant differences between testosterone levels of homosexuals and heterosexual controls, nor did they find any connection between testosterone level and intensity of homosexual orientation (as measured by the Kinsey scale). And there are yet other studies suggesting that male homosexuals may have testosterone levels above those of heterosexuals! . . .The findings for women also fail to establish any direct connection between lesbianism and high adult androgen levels. . . .The conclusion to be drawn from all of this is surely not that there are absolutely no hormonal differences between homosexuals and heterosexuals. What is clear, however, is that today one would be naive, not to say presumptuous, to claim definitively that there are such differences.

The second line of inquiry focuses on people who have experienced hormonal deficiencies or excesses, primarily before birth, that is, fetal hormonal deficiencies or excesses. The primary researcher in this area is John Money of Johns Hopkins, and it is to his work that we now turn.

People who have no sex hormones at all during fetal development because they have non-functioning or missing gonads, are born looking female and are raised as girls. The evidence is that they identify unequivocally as females and have a strong desire to fulfill female roles — heterosexual romance, marriage, babies, etc.

---

[120] P. 98f.

People with no functioning androgen (including people who produce androgen but are insensitive to it), but some estrogen, are born looking female even if they are genetically male (XY). They do not, however, have female internal organs.[121] Obviously they will be raised as females, and because they do produce some estrogen, they will mature as females. Such people tend to be heterosexual in their attractions, i.e., attracted to males.

The third category is genetic males who are partially insensitive to androgen.[122] Because there is some androgen sensitivity, there is usually some development of male external genitalia. At birth, the child will appear hermaphroditic and might be assigned designation either as a boy or a girl. Money studied a group of ten such people.[123] Of the ten, eight were raised as males and two as females.

Money found that the children raised as boys showed some marked differences from fully androgenized boys. Specifically, they tended to be less aggressive, less competitive in sports, less socially assertive. These are the types of behavior often referred to as "sissy boy syndrome." All of the children[124] felt themselves to be unequivocally part of the sex to which they had been assigned, and all were heterosexually oriented in their attitudes (daydreams, etc.), and behavior.

The next category consists of girls who are over androgenized.[125] Money found these girls to be consistently more tomboyish than most girls, even when they had been raised unequivocally as females, had any physical problems surgically corrected and had treatment to suppress excess androgen.

Regarding adult sexual orientation, early reports favored the view that even if the tomboyism persisted into adulthood, androgenized women were as likely to turn out heterosexual as non-androgenized women were. More recent reports, however, are beginning to indicate that a greater percentage of such girls than would be the case randomly are either homosexual or bisexual.

Boys with greater amounts of prenatal androgen tend to become aggressive and competitive, but show no distinctive sexual orientation.[126] Boys who received larger than normal amounts of estrogen before birth were less athletic and less assertive, but there was no report on their sexual orientation.[127]

We quote again from Ruse:[128]

> Summing up the results of his (and like) studies, Money therefore sees a picture where prenatal hormones can play an important role in future gender identity (including presumably sexual orientation), but where the environment in the form of the child's upbringing can play

---

[121] Their bodies have produced the Mullerian-inhibiting substance which acts on the Mullerian ducts to prevent formation of female internal organs.

[122] This is Reifenstein's Syndrome.

[123] J. Money and C. Ogunro, "Behavioral Sexology: Ten cases of genetic male intersexuality with impaired prenatal and pubertal androgenization," *Archives of Sexual Behavior* (1974): 181-205.

[124] Except for one of the "girls" who was raised in an atmosphere of ambiguity about her sex.

[125] There are two usual causes. First, it may be a side effect of treatment of the mother to prevent miscarriage: second, it may be the result of AGS (andrenogenital syndrome), a genetic defect causing the production of too much androgen.

[126] A. Ehrhardt, "Prenatal androgenization and human psychosexual behavior," in J. Money and H. Musaph, eds., *Handbook of Sexology* (New York: Elsevier, 1977), p. 251.

[127] Ibid., p. 252.

[128] P. 102.

just as important a role — indeed, probably more important.... Adult sexual orientation can therefore be influenced by prenatal hormones, although there is certainly no absolute link of cause and effect.

In a sense, these words say it all. Nobody questions that hormones influence development in many ways. It is logical to assume that sex hormones influence sexual maturation and even sexual orientation. But there is not any evidence that allows a jump from high androgenization or low estrogenization to lesbianism or from low androgenization or high estrogenization to male homosexuality. It is not clear that such factors are even sufficient, let alone necessary conditions for homosexuality.

None of this is to deny why the hormonal theory has a great deal of appeal to many homosexuals and to the families of homosexuals. If homosexuality is directly attributable to hormonal imbalance, there can be no more valid a value judgement about homosexuality than there can be a value judgement about dwarfism or giantism. When parents of homosexuals speak of the atypical behaviors of their children as youngsters, either sissyboys or tomboys, they may be overexaggerating the relationship between those syndromes and hormonal imbalance. That is surely understandable because it alleviates guilt feelings on the part of the families. If it is possible to posit a cause and effect relationship between prenatal hormonal imbalance (over which the parents surely have no control) and subsequent atypical syndromes (which might be taken to prove that the prenatal imbalance must have been present), and between those syndromes and homosexuality, all feelings of guilt or inadequacy disappear. Neither the family nor the homosexual bears any responsibility for the homosexual's homosexuality. Environment becomes totally irrelevant. The homosexuality of the individual was hormonally predetermined.

Our description of the second common theory of the etiology of homosexuality is at an end. We must now turn our attention to the relevance of the hormonal theory halakhically, just as we did after our description of the psychoanalytic theory.

Let us suppose, first, that the hormonal theory is conclusively proved to be false.[129] That is, science is finally able to prove beyond question that the sex hormones effect sexual differentiation prenatally, and affect sexual maturation and sexual desire at puberty and thereafter, but have nothing to do with the object of one's sexual desires. To the extent that statistics seem to indicate a greater than random incidence of homosexuality in a certain group, the incidence is to be definitively accounted for by some other reason.[130] The halakhic consequence of such a finding would be identical to what we concluded above[131] regarding a similar hypothesis concerning the psychoanalytic theory. Namely, the conclusive disproof of the hormonal theory would have no halakhic significance whatsoever. Homosexuality would still be considered תועבה, the tradition would still offer defensible or stronger reasons why it is to be so considered, and those reasons would still be independent of the etiology of homosexuality.

---

[129] Remember, the hormonal theory is predicated on an assumption that male homosexuals are showing female emotions and female homosexuals are showing male emotions. That is a faith claim, not a scientific one.

[130] We reported above on boys who received more than normal doses of estrogen prenatally. The study (which did not say anything about the sexual orientation of the subjects) was based on the sons of severely diabetic mothers. (That, indeed, is why the children were exposed to the extra estrogen in the first place, because their mothers received hormone shots.) If there had been found a greater than random incidence of subsequent homosexuality among the boys, it could be attributable to the tendency of sick mothers to be overly protective of their children. I am, of course, not claiming this as fact. However, it is as reasonable an hypothesis to account for the increased incidence as the hormonal hypothesis.

[131] P. 640.

Now let us suppose the opposite, that the hormonal theory could be conclusively demonstrated to be correct. Let us even suppose that the theory could be made sufficiently precise to allow the attribution of actual straightforward cause and effect between some hormonal cause (or causes) X and homosexuality. We would ask again as we asked above: Would these facts, unknown to the Torah or the Sages, impel us to seek a change in the precedent?

If we still affirmed the defensibility and strength of the classical explanations of the reasons why homosexuality is called תועבה by the Torah, those reasons would continue to be acceptable even though we might now know the etiology of homosexuality. And, if we rejected the classical explanations for why the Torah calls homosexuality תועבה, we would still find ourselves in the position of affirming that homosexuality is תועבה because the Torah attributes that quality to it, and we would still not know why the Torah does so. But, whatever the reason for such attribution by the Torah, knowledge of the etiology of homosexuality would not render it false or unacceptable.

More importantly, if we could get to the point where hormonal theory is proved to be correct, the hope for hormonal therapy to bring about heterosexual development is enhanced. The possibility of prenatal testing at the appropriate time for the secretion of the appropriate hormones in the appropriate amounts is not out of the question. Though it may not yet be possible, some medical achievements of our age would have been considered impossible dreams even half a generation ago. If the reasons the halakhah forbids homosexuality continue to obtain, why would one seek to overturn the precedent when the discovery of the actual etiology holds out great hope for the eventual ability to control against it?

We have thus far presented the strongest case scenarios, by positing the hormonal theory as proven either conclusively incorrect or conclusively correct. If in either of these cases there does not seem to be grounds for overturning the established precedent, how much more is that the case when the evidence for the theory is itself so "iffy," inconclusive and tentative.

As above[132] however, we must raise again the issue of whether or not we would seek to overturn precedent if it were clear to us that the Torah not only did not know the etiology of homosexuality, but assumed it to be something entirely different from what our current knowledge teaches us. Having raised the question again of whether a moral God could demand the avoidance of behavior of one whose attraction to that behavior is entirely non-volitional, we refer again to what we have already written in response to that question on pages 643-644. Here too, then, we conclude that the knowledge gained from biochemical theories does not provide compelling reason to advocate overturning the established precedent against homosexuality.

As there was a postscript to Section A of Part III, so too, there is one to Section B. It deals with the category of אנס.

Rabbi Hershel J. Matt was, to the best of my knowledge, the first one who seriously proposed using the category of אנס regarding homosexuals.[133] The essence of his claim is that moderns recognize homosexuality to be more than an overt act of choice. Rather, it is an entire orientation which the person did not choose in any conventional sense and which is not usually subject to change. For Matt, however, homosexuality does not become a co-equal lifestyle. Modern knowledge requires, for him, that we not be quick

---

[132] P. 641.

[133] Hershel J. Matt, "Sin, Crime, Sickness or Alternative Lifestyle?: A Jewish Approach to Homosexuality," *Judaism* 27:1 (winter 1978): 13-24, esp. pp. 16-17.

to judge homosexuals, that we have deep compassion for their plight in our society, that we demonstrate those feelings of compassion and do all within out power to move our communities to greater understanding of homosexuals so that they will also demonstrate the compassion which the Torah mandates, and that we oppose legal penalties for homosexuality. Yet, "such a stance would maintain the traditional view of heterosexuality as the God-intended norm and yet would incorporate the contemporary recognition of homosexuality as, clinically speaking, a sexual deviance, malfunctioning, or abnormality — usually unavoidable and often irremediable."[134] Thus, even this most liberal view falls far short of validating homosexuality as a co-equal lifestyle.[135]

Rabbi Norman Lamm had raised the subject earlier.[136] He rejected the possibility that אנס could be used halakhically as a grounds for permitting homosexuality. What he did claim, however, was that with restrictions and some reservations, the category can be used to define homosexuality as an illness rather than a crime. If it is an illness, the category of אנס which applies to constitutional homosexuals "lays upon us the obligation of pastoral compassion, psychological understanding and social sympathy. . . .[T]he objective crime remains a *ma'aseh averah*, whereas the person who transgresses is considered innocent on the grounds of *ones*. . . .Under no circumstances can Judaism suffer homosexuality to become respectable."[137] Lamm uses the category of אנס only to exonerate from legal culpability, not to give any imprimatur of acceptability to homosexual behavior. Whether or not specific reference to the category of אנס is made, those who use the non-choice nature and the generally irremediable status of homosexuality as Jewish arguments for leniency are, in fact, arguing from the אנס category. Therefore, we must look at the category briefly.

We intend to offer specific halakhic recommendations about homosexuals in Part IV of this paper. Until that point it will suffice to affirm Lamm's contention that the claim of אנס does not *permit* any behavior, it merely *exonerates* from legal liability. The operative phrase is אנס רחמנא פטריה[138] — "The Merciful exempts with regard to one who acts under duress (compulsion)." The critical word is פטריה, which almost always means פטור אבל אסור — "Exempt from liability, though the act remains forbidden."

We have asserted above[139] that the Torah does not prohibit attractions or orientations. It prohibits only behaviors. The category of אנס does not ever apply to thoughts or fantasies

---

[134] Ibid., p. 20.

[135] In the annotated bibliography in Christie Balka and Andy Rose, eds., *Twice Blessed: On Being Lesbian, Gay and Jewish* (Boston: Beacon Press, 1989), p. 296, Matt's *Judaism* (1978) piece is described as follows: "For many years this essay was considered the authoritative liberal Jewish statement on homosexuality." The annotators assert, furthermore, that "[h]e calls for a marriage ceremony or similar affirmation for gay and lesbian Jews." That is hardly true. On p. 22 of his article, Rabbi Matt wrote, "Even if the flexibility and resourcefulness of the halakhah were renewed and increased. . .it is hardly conceivable that a homosexual departure from the Torah's heterosexual norm would ever be accepted by halakhically faithful Jews or ever be recognized as *k'dat moshe v'yisrael*." On pp. 22-24, Matt formulates a response to this which he puts into the mouths of homosexuals. The article ends with the end of their response. It does not contain Matt's resolution. Perhaps the annotators are correct, but the article seems to me to end with a תיקו. Even Rabbi Matt's article, "Homosexual Rabbis?", *Conservative Judaism* 39:3 (spring 1987): 29-33, does not validate homosexuality as a co-equal lifestyle.

[136] Norman Lamm, "Judaism and the Modern Attitude to Homosexuality," in *Encyclopaedia Judaica Yearbook, 1974* (Jerusalem: Keter Publishing House, 1974), pp. 194-205, reprinted in Menachem Marc Kellner, ed., *Contemporary Jewish Ethics* (New York: Sanhedrin Press, 1978), pp. 375-399.

[137] Ibid., pp. 202-203; Kellner, pp. 394-395.

[138] Bava Kama 28b, Nedarim 27a, and Avodah Zarah 54a.

[139] Pp. 619-621. See, too, the succinct comment of Rabbi Walter Wurzburger in *Judaism* 32:4 (fall 1983): 425.

or attractions as an exculpatory factor. There can be no exculpation for a matter for which there could never have been liability in the first place.

Furthermore, the category can apply in sexual matters only to the passive party, in a rape case, for example. In the first place, the source of the principle אנס רחמנא פטריה is the case of the נערה המאורסה, about whom the Torah says:[140] ולנערה לא תעשה דבר, and the נערה was the passive and forced party. And secondly, Rava claims (and his view is the normative halakhic position)[141] that אין אנס לעריות לפי שאין קישוי אלא לדעת אלא בישן — "The category of אנס is inapplicable to [the active parties in] forbidden sexual relationships because there are no unwilling erections except during sleep."

Whether or not there can really be an involuntary erection other than during sleep is not particularly relevant. What Rava means is that one who is *unwilling* to engage in an act of intercourse can not be forced against his will to achieve an erection that would allow him to do so.

The issue is not whether one might or might not find oneself sexually aroused by someone without having chosen to be aroused by that person. The question is whether one can be forced against his will to engage in the act of intercourse with any person.[142] The arousal which is the result of sexual attraction does not compel anyone to engage in an act of intercourse against his will.

While it is not difficult to understand why one might wish to apply the category of אנס to homosexuals, particularly constitutional homosexuals, it is halakhically indefensible, as we have shown.

Section C

The third (and newest) attempt to explain the etiology of homosexuality is the genetic, or sociobiological theory. This theory, too, requires an introduction.

Sociobiology is defined as "the systematic study of the biological basis of all social behavior."[143] Sociobiological explanations of homosexuality will understand it as a social phenomenon — i.e., involving interaction between people — governed by the Darwinian evolutionary model which understands life as a process of natural selection (survival of the fittest). The essence of the natural selection process is response to struggles for existence and reproduction, which are necessary for survival.

Before we begin our presentation of the theory itself we owe it to ourselves to be conscious of several points. We humans pride ourselves on our having transcended nature in many ways. The development of human culture, with language, science, and religion often both seems to and does, in fact, elevate us above pure biological determinism. On the other hand, human culture is comparatively young from an evolutionary perspective. For the vast part of the history of life (not restricted to human life) on earth, evolution has been the primary factor. It is the epitome of human hubris to assume that we have so far transcended our own biology that evolution is now an irrelevant factor. The extent to which human social realities are themselves the result of the evolutionary process is a

---

[140] Deut. 22:26.

[141] Yevamot 53b, and see Maimonides, M.T. Issurei Bi-ah 1:9 and Sanhedrin 20:3.

[142] The exotic cases dealt with by the Rishonim, like the status of one who has already achieved erection for permissible intercourse and is then compelled to engage in intercourse with an ערוה, are not relevant to this discussion.

[143] E.O. Wilson, *Sociobiology: The New Synthesis* (Cambridge, Mass.: Harvard University Press, 1975), p. 2, quoted by Ruse, p. 130.

matter of considerable debate, as one might imagine. For the purposes of our inquiry, however, we will not reject the possibility that even our human social behaviors are more controlled by evolution than we might like or be willing to admit.[144]

Also, we affirm that the discipline of sociobiology is justifiably concerned with the phenomenon of homosexuality. It is not correct to assert that psychoanalysis and endocrinology are within their disciplines to be concerned with homosexuality, but sociobiology is not. From the perspective of Darwinian evolutionary theory, human nature is directed towards reproduction. From that perspective, physical characteristics, mental properties and social activities are all directed toward that ultimate goal. Surely, therefore, it must be a legitimate concern of the sociogiologists to attempt to understand how and why a social phenomenon which is not geared to reproduction exists within their theoretical framework. And, so long as we are not prepared to reject evolution entirely, we must see whether any light that sociobiologists may shed on the subject impinges on our halakhic stance.

Acknowledging yet again my indebtedness to Michael Ruse for his clear and thorough presentation,[145] we begin the presentation of the three suggestions for the etiology of homosexuality proposed by sociobiologists.

The first theory is called the balanced superior heterozygote fitness theory. Genes, the unit through which heredity is passed on from generation to generation, are located on the chromosomes. Chromosomes come in pairs. Therefore, each gene has a mate on the complementary chromosome. When both alleles (gene forms) are identical, the lifeform of which they are a part is a homozygote with regard to the characteristic which those genes govern. If the alleles are not identical, the lifeform is a heterozygote.

If a certain homozygote (let us call it $A_1 A_1$) is more beneficial to the survival and reproduction of an organism than homozygote $A_2 A_2$ or than heterozygote $A_1 A_2$, then homozygote $A_1 A_1$ will become the genetic norm (since it is the "fittest"), and $A_2 A_2$ and $A_1 A_2$ will disappear.

If, on the other hand, the "fittest" allele is $A_1 A_2$, neither of the homozygotes can disappear. Why? Since survival and reproduction are best with the heterozygote, and since there is no way for the organism to have such a combination without getting one of each type of gene from the parents, both homozygotes must continue to exist in some 'balanced' situation. Furthermore, the homozygotes must continue to exist even if they are totally unfit (i.e., entirely non-reproductive).[146]

The first sociobiological explanation of homosexuality would, therefore, be as follows: Homosexuality is the direct result of a homozygote $H_1 H_1$. The second homozygote, $H_2 H_2$, reproduces averagely. But the superior reproducer is the heterozygote $H_1 H_2$, because it has a natural immunity to some disease. In order for the heterozygote to exist,

---

[144] Ruse, on p. 132, points out that there may be biologically determined factors that underlie areas of human social behavior, even where there is wide variation in the behavior between one society and another. With all of the diversity in marriage norms, for example, polyandry is still exceptionally rare. Given the different biological natures of men and women, it is almost never in the reproductive interest of a society for husbands to share one wife since that would limit rather than expand reproduction. Therefore, a polyandrous adaptation would be counterproductive to the procreative push of evolution. Only in a group where men must band together tightly to eke out a subsistence living might polyandry be reproductively adaptational, since long-term survival depends on reducing reproduction.

[145] See ch. 6 of his book.

[146] From Ruse, p. 134: "The best attested case of this phenomenon in humans is that centering on sickle cell anemia. Procession of one sickling allele (heterozygously) gives a natural immunity to malaria, a highly adaptive feature in various parts of the world. Procession of two sickling alleles (homozygously) produces severe anæmia and death in childhood. The disease persists, because the threat of malaria is so strong."

there must be in each generation some balanced number of existing homozygotes. Consequently, homosexuality must exist in every generation in order to guarantee the survival of the fittest allele group, $H_1 H_2$, which is the most adaptive.

The balanced superior heterozygote fitness theory is the most straightforward of the sociobiological theories we will discuss. Of course, the specific homosexual-orientation-producing homozygote allele has not been identified, nor has anybody yet defined what makes the heterozygote allele most adaptive. Furthermore, it has two greater weaknesses. First, there is evidence that male homosexuality runs in families,[147] and that would be very unlikely according to this theory. Second, if the mere procession of the homozygote allele results in homosexuality as a biological inevitability, there should be no sets of identical twins (whose genetic structure is absolutely identical of necessity) in which one is homosexual and the other is heterosexual. Regarding this fact Ruse writes:[148]

> Although there are some reports that identical twins do tend to share orientation, and some of these reports are better than others (Heston and Shields), there are some very strong and very careful findings of identical twins, one of whom is heterosexual, and one of whom is homosexual (Rainer et al.; Green).

The claim of the balanced superior heterozygote fitness theory is so inconclusively proved at this point in time that a posek who relied upon it as the grounds for overturning an established precedent (one of which is דאורייתא, at that) would be on extremely thin ice, at best. Even if it were conclusively proved to be correct, it would provide the posek with potentially significant extra-legal data. Even then, though, it would still be the posek who would have to decide whether it was actually significant halakhically. We will return to that consideration when we consider the sociobiological theories in general.

The second genetic or sociobiological theory is the kin selection theory. From the Darwinian perspective, what counts most biologically is reproducing one's own genes, i.e., making copies of one's own genes through reproduction. But, since what is critical is the copies of one's genes, it might not make any significant difference where the copy came from, so long as it is a good copy. Insofar as one's relatives produce relatively similar copies of one's own genes, one's reproductive drive can be biologically fulfilled through the reproduction of one's close relatives.

Usually, one would choose to reproduce oneself, since, after all, nobody else is as closely related to one as oneself. But there could be exceptions. Among the hymenoptera (wasps, bees and ants), kin selection has resulted in some females caring for their siblings rather than reproducing themselves, because that results in the production of more copies of their genes than if they reproduced themselves. The non-reproducing hymenoptera are sterile. The process of natural selection has brought this about. The non-reproducing females do not need to reproduce in order to fulfill the biological function of propagating, so the natural selection process has done away with that ability in them.

---

[147] See J.D. Rainer, "Genetics and Homosexuality," in A. Kaplan, ed., *Human Behaviour Genetics* (Springfield: Thomas, 1976), pp. 301-316; and R.C. Pillard and J.R. Weinrich, "Evidence of Familial Nature of Male Homosexuality," *Archives of General Psychiatry* 43 (1986): 808-812.

[148] P. 145. The studies listed in the parentheses refer to L.L. Heston and J. Shields, "Homosexuality in Twins: A Family Study and a Registry Study," *Archives of General Psychiatry* 18:2 (1968): 149-160; J.D. Rainer et al., "Homosexuality and Heterosexuality in Identical Twins," *Psychosomatic Medicine* 22 (1960): 251-258; and R. Green, *Sexual Identity Conflict in Children and Adults* (New York: Basic Books, 1974).

If one equates the lack of human reproduction with sterility, the analogy to homosexuality in humans becomes apparent. The process of kin selection results in some becoming homosexual because they fulfill the biological drive toward reproducing copies of one's genes through helping their relatives reproduce, usually by their ability to bring the benefits of society to their reproducing relatives. The natural selection process helps them along by giving them a sexual orientation that releases them from trying to have their own children, which, for them, would be maladaptive. It is homosexuality that is adaptive under these circumstances.

Why would one move in that direction rather than making copies of his or her genes him or herself? Either because the person would be an inefficient reproducer personally (i.e., a poor quality heterosexual), or because the person would be exceptionally good at helping relatives fulfill the biological drive — or both.[149]

We will describe the third genetic theory before we discuss the last two theories together. The third theory is the parental manipulation theory. At its core lies the realization that since the biological task of every individual is to reproduce his or her own genes, there is room for competition even within a family, with one member trying to force another to further his or her own biological mandate. Since parents tend to be stronger than their children, parental manipulation may be a factor from a sociobiological point of view.

How does the parental manipulation theory work to produce homosexuals? The parents who may already have passed on their genes to their own children are nonetheless driven to increase the number of genes even for succeeding generations. For the parents it does not matter whether the genes are reproduced by each child reproducing or by some children reproducing significantly more. If the parents see that they can enhance the total number of reproductions by suppressing the reproduction of one child so that that child becomes an enabler and helper to that child's siblings, the parents might do just that. From the parents' perspective, the biological drive to increase the number of gene copies as much as possible is best fulfilled by manipulating one child into a homosexual path.

There is much in common between the kin selection theory and the parental manipulation theory. In both we would be looking for some kind of evidence that the homosexual is aiding relatives in some way. But the major difference between them is that in the kin selection theory, the homosexual's orientation serves his or her own needs; and in the parental manipulation theory, the orientation of the homosexual serves the needs of others, primarily the parents of the homosexual.

There are difficulties with both the kin selection and the parental manipulation theories that we must point out explicitly. First of all, note that these last two theories are not genetic in the same way that the balanced superior heterozygote fitness theory is. According to the latter, there is a specific configuration of genes that results in homosexuality. According to the kin selection and parental manipulation theories, there is nothing in the genes *per se* that results in homosexuality. With the right environmental push, the genetic impulse to reproduce might push one along a homosexual path. The type of genetic

---

[149] The kin selection theory can probably account for the greater number of male homosexuals than female homosexuals. Men, by their physiological nature, can reproduce an almost infinite number of times. The normal process of natural selection provides all males with the sex drive to go out and reproduce. With their enormous reproductive potential, men are in competition with all other men to find avenues to fulfill their drive. If anything goes wrong with a male he will be unable to meet the competition, i.e., he will be an inefficient heterosexual. Therefore, men are subject to greater pressure to switch to homosexuality.

Women on the other hand, are far less likely to be inefficient heterosexuals because they can only have a very small number of offspring (in comparison to men). The chances of their being losers in the biological stakes are much lower, and there is, therefore, much less reason for them to seek the homosexual alternative.

inevitability that the balanced superior heterozygote fitness theory implies is totally missing in the other two.

In the kin selection model, we seek evidence of its defensibility by looking for indications that something in the childhood of homosexuals might have made them ineffective reproducers and we seek indications that homosexuals are able to aid in the reproductive struggle by bringing the good of society to their families. Surely there is no well-known evidence of childhood traumas that might move those children onto the homosexual path because they perceive that they would be ineffective heterosexuals. And, particularly in our society, it is extremely doubtful that homosexuals are any more effective at bringing the blessings of the good of society to their families than heterosexuals.[150] Indeed, the opposite seems to be the case in many instances. Is homosexuality, therefore, a maladaptive turn in our society which is still just holding on as a legacy of the past, and which will be obliterated by the natural selection process itself because it is maladaptive?

These same objections apply also to the parental manipulation theory. There, too, the parents turn their child toward homosexuality because it can increase their reproduction through the good that the children can bring to their siblings. What's more, the turning that the parents do must be reflected by some evidence of trauma or something else during childhood which can be used to deflect the child from reproducing by him or herself.

Unlike our treatment of the psychoanalytic and the hormonal theories, the author finds it important at this point of Section c to deal briefly with a couple of the objections that might be raised against the entire sociobiological enterprise, particularly as it affects homosexuality.

First and foremost, some might be inclined to reject it out of hand because of the nature of its language. The way sociobiologists talk and write contains frequent reference to people "choosing" a specific reproductive strategy, or to the genes "choosing" to do something or other. The orientation of the homosexual is directed toward some certain end, like aiding siblings in reproduction by bringing the benefits of society to them, or people are in "conflict" with each other, especially within families in which there can easily be "conflicts of interest." None of these terms are themselves offensive. However, some might object to their use regarding genes, or actions which cannot be called "chosen" or even conscious. Problems of verification might impel some to reject the enterprise out of hand. Let us quote Ruse's response:[151]

> Again, the critic has a good point; but again, it is not definitive. There is no doubt that sociobiologists do use their language loosely. . .metaphorical language is what they surely use when they speak of the mechanisms for producing homosexuals. There is no literal manipulation, nor is it supposed that actual relationships are calculated and acted upon. . . .[I]n using the language of intention or purpose or design, sociobiologists are doing no more than is done by any Darwinian evolutionist. They are dealing with adaptations (or maladaptations), trying to see what ends they serve in the struggle to reproduce. The language of conscious purpose comes naturally here. . . .If one thinks of nature consciously trying to further its biological ends, and that natural selection "designs" features to aid in this task, one can follow

---

[150] Perhaps there are such indications in those societies where homosexuals function as shamans or priests because they are thought to have magical or religious powers.

[151] P. 139.

through pertinent causal chains. . . . The aim is primarily that of finding out what people are up to, without so much worrying about what people think they are up to.

The second objection that some might raise that would lead them to reject the entire enterprise is the sociobiologist's definition of homosexuality as something akin to eye color, that is, "above culture, and preserved in splendid, eternal isolation."[152] The sociobiologists tend to give homosexuality a real existence, and then link it to the genes. If by that linkage they mean that all homosexuality is identical, as all blue eyes are identical — that the features and activities that are common to homosexuals in our culture have been common to all homosexuals in all cultures and times — then they are probably wrong. But, in truth, that is probably not what they are claiming. "[T]here are threads linking homosexuals. Culture may be crucial for homosexual identity. It is a lot less obvious that it is crucial for homosexual orientation. There is good reason to think that this is a transcultural phenomenon and as such (at least) plausibly a candidate for a biological explanation."[153]

By affirming that the sociobiological enterprise should not be rejected out of hand, we have now gotten to the point where we must discuss whether the knowledge gleaned from it about the etiology of homosexuality ought to have actual significance halakhically.

On the one hand, the answer can be given with great brevity. No. The knowledge gained from the sociobiological theories is more in the category of ספק than the knowledge gained from psychoanalysis and endocrinology, though they were ספק enough. As we stated above regarding the balanced superior heterozygote fitness theory, a posek who relies on such theories to overturn established precedent, especially דאורייתא precedent, could be doing so only at the cost of responsible halakhic decision-making.

On the other hand, though, the issue deserves a more theoretical answer, similar to the answers we offered regarding the same question as applied to psychoanalytic and hormonal theories. It deserves such treatment for two reasons:

(1) Who can say what future research will find? What if scientists are able to find significant corroborative evidence of those matters we indicated above still require such evidence? Would that evidence then imply that the data have become halakhically significant?

(2) Scientific evidence favoring the sociobiological theories would probably be more difficult for a posek to grapple with than evidence favoring the other theories. Neither psychological nor biochemical theories can be called "natural" in the way that sociobiological theories can be. For Freud, homosexuality is a perversion, and for the adptationalists it is a neurosis — but for neither is it "normal." For the biochemists, homosexuality may be the result of hormonal imbalances, excesses or deficiencies. To the extent that hormones are "natural," so, then, would homosexuality be "natural." Normally, there are neither excesses nor deficiencies. For the psychologists and the biochemists, then, homosexuality is abnormal (a term which is descriptive and carries no necessary implications as to whether the abnormality is illness or pathology, or neither).

For the sociobiologists, however, the situation is different. Homosexuality is genetically inevitable according to the balanced superior heterozygote fitness theory, and it is not a genetic aberration or mistake. The homozygote that results in homosexuality must exist for the sake of the general good that is derived from the heterozygote of which one of the genes of the homosexual homozygote is a necessary part. Homosexuality is not an aberration, an excess, a deficiency, but a necessary ingredient for the natural selection process.

---

[152] Ibid., p. 138.
[153] Ibid.

For the kin selection and parental manipulation theories the push to homosexuality (whether it comes from the homosexual or from family manipulation) serves an important natural and desirable function, aiding in reproduction. Homosexuality is not abnormal or aberrational, it is part of the natural selection process of evolution. It is not some type of error in God's creation (as hormonal imbalance might be), it is an integral part of the evolutionary process. And, for a believing Jew, evolution is not free and independent from God's providence.

For these reasons, the question must be addressed with the same seriousness we addressed it at the ends of Section A and Section B of this part. To rely on the newness of the theories, or the paucity of evidence to support them as the total reason for rejecting their halakhic significance would be inadequate. So, we turn to the same hypothesis we turned to at the end of the previous sections of this part.

If the sociobiological theories were conclusively proven to be false, we would be at a position already familiar to us from our analysis of the psychoanalytic and the biochemical theories. The Torah would still have called homosexuality תועבה and the reasons for that attribution would still be defensible or better. The characteristic of being תועבה would be true irrespective of the etiology of homosexuality. The conclusive disproof of the sociobiological theories would leave the precedent intact.

For the purposes of our analysis of the opposite hypothesis, that sociobiological explanations are proved to be correct, we can deal with the kin selection theory and the parental manipulation theory at the same time. Since both are essentially the same except for the "detail" of who does the pushing along the homosexual path, we can deal with the essence of both of them.

In what many might find an unusual twist at first blush, the proof of either of these theories would serve to reinforce at least one of the classical explanations of the reason for the prohibition against homosexuality. The person who becomes homosexual is pushed along that path in order to enhance and further propagation of the family, primarily by bringing to bear upon it the benefits of society which allow for greater propagation. The family and procreation stand at the core of these sociobiological theories, just as these two factors (and in the relationship between them) were central explanations of the reason homosexuality is called תועבה by the Torah.[154]

Validating homosexuality as a co-equal lifestyle would have the effect of undermining the reason for its very existence according to these sociobiological theories. Co-equal validation is usually understood to imply the setting up of homosexual families structured along the same basic lines as heterosexual families, except that the two mainstays of the family are of the same sex. Doing that absolutely undermines the genetic intent of the selection process. When homosexuals set up nuclear family structures that are other than the families into which they were born, i.e., their parents and siblings, their attention will become directed to the new family structure. That very fact undermines the purpose for which the homosexuals were pushed along the homosexual path in the first place. Once the lifestyle receives co-equal validation, the efforts of the homosexuals will not be directed toward the greater propagation of the families into which they were born. Furthermore, whatever benefits of society the homosexuals are uniquely competent to bring their families, they will bring to their "new" families, not to their birth families. And, again, the intent of the selection process will be subverted by the very people whose orientation was intended to have the opposite effect.

---

[154] See above, pp. 626ff.

The orientation was intended to free them from the very things that validation of co-equality would impose. The validation would change the entire "purpose" of homosexuality according to these sociobiological theories, and change it in such a way as to be counterproductive. So, if anything, the kin selection and parental manipulation theories, if either were proved to be absolutely correct, would argue against the validation of homosexuality as a co-equal lifestyle.

Furthermore, if these theories are correct, they can even be helpful in explaining the notorious promiscuity of homosexual males. Heterosexual intercourse is, in essence, a compromise between the male and the female. The male could further the reproduction of the copy of his genes innumerable times, by copulating constantly with many, many partners. The female, however, who has to go through considerable difficulty to reproduce copies of her genes (pregnancy, labor, delivery), and who can really only reproduce a limited number of times (particularly in comparison to males), finds it in her best interests to be very selective in choosing partners with whom to copulate. Heterosexual intercourse, therefore, becomes a compromise between a male and female. Once the need for compromise is removed from the male because the process of natural selection has turned him to the homosexual path, restraint disappears as well. Hence, homosexual men tend to have a large number of sexual partners.[155]

The validation of homosexuality as a co-equal lifestyle creates the impetus to impose a pattern of behavior on homosexuals (particularly males) that the very reason for their homosexuality subverts. It seeks to impose patterns of behavior on them that their very genetic make-up makes it unlikely that they can live up to. And, if they do live up to them, it subverts the natural selection process entirely by diverting the homosexuals from their role as enablers.

The kin selection and parental manipulation theories, if proved correct, argue against the validation of homosexuality as a co-equal lifestyle.[156] The orientation has a natural purpose. The validation of that orientation as similar to heterosexuality except for the object of one's desires is counterproductive from a sociobiological perspective.

The responsible halakhist, therefore, would be ill advised to utilize such theories as grounds for seeking abrogation of the precedent. The theory itself argues against the conclusion of co-equal validation, and using it to advocate a conclusion which is contraindicated by it would be halakhically irresponsible and indefensible.

We come now to our discussion of the halakhic significance of the balanced superior heterozygote theory. Remember that we posited that the homozygote $H_1 H_1$ results in homosexuality, the homozygote $H_2 H_2$ reproduces in an average way, and that the most fit reproducer is heterozygote $H_1 H_2$.

---

[155] See Donald Symons, *The Evolution of Human Sexuality* (New York: Oxford University Press, 1979), esp. p. 286. Cf. Ruse, p. 137.

[156] Do these theories argue for validation of homosexual intercourse, even without validation of the co-equality of the homosexual lifestyle with the heterosexual lifestyle? From a halakhic perspective the answer is surely "no." Validation of co-equality of lifestyle would imply that the intercourse between members of the same sex could be fulfillment of עונה, even if not procreative. However, non-procreative עונה is linked to the physiological possibility for the act, under general and normal circumstances to be procreative. Therefore, since there could never be procreative intercourse between members of the same sex, nonprocreative עונה is impossible. Since the only sexual relations allowed by halakhah must be either procreative or the fulfillment of עונה, halakhists could not reasonably conclude that kin selection and parental manipulation lead to an halakhic category that allows intercourse outside of the context of procreation or עונה. The only thing that might be argued is that homosexuals who do act on their orientation by engaging in homosexual intercourse are in the category of אנס. On that subject, see above, pp. 652-654.

From the perspective of the natural selection process, the people who possess *either* of the homozygote alleles have been called upon to make some "sacrifice" for the greater good of the majority. Both of the homozygotes have been dealt less than the most fit genes, and neither can account for why he is "chosen" to maintain the balance in order to insure that the majority will be heterozygotes.

The quest for co-equal validation constitutes an attempt to claim that both sets of genes are equally fit, that the $II_1 II_1$ allele is not less fit than the $II_1 II_2$ allele. From the standpoint of the sociobiologist it is an unacceptable (probably absurd) claim. To utilize a claim based on false scientific premise as the scientific grounds to overturn established precedent is halakhically irresponsible. It is not irresponsible to point out that according to this theory homosexuality is genetically inevitable in homosexuals. It is an untenable jump however, to claim that genetic inevitability makes the result adaptive or equal to the superior heterozygote. The scientific data themselves do not lead to a conclusion of co-equality, and could not be used halakhically to support such a conclusion.[157]

What would be correct for halakhists to emphasize, if the balanced superior heterozygote fitness theory were ultimately proved to be absolutely correct, is that heterosexuals should recognize the sacrifice the natural selection process has imposed upon homosexuals for the heterosexual's benefit. Not only does Providence deal them a less fit set of genes, God calls upon them to refrain from the behavior which the genetically inevitable orientation seems to foist upon them. But homosexuals, by the same token, should also recognize that the sacrifice is a sacrifice. They may have become what they are in orientation through no choice of their own, but that reality does not negate the reasons why acting on that orientation remains halakhically unacceptable.

In sum, then, we have looked at each of the three sociobiological theories and concluded that even if they were ultimately proved correct, they would not result in defensible halakhic arguments for overturning the established precedent forbidding homosexual behavior.

With this we conclude our analysis of the three regnant hypotheses concerning the etiology of homosexuality – the psychological, the hormonal and the genetic. We find none of them sufficient to warrant our utilizing it to overturn precedent at this time; and none of them sufficient to warrant utilizing it to seek to overturn the precedent even when we posit that all elements of ספק are removed from it and it is proved either absolutely incorrect or absolutely correct.

Let us summarize our findings to this point. In Part I of this responsum we have found:

(1) That the Torah attributes to homosexuality the characteristic of תועבה, which is not an inherent quality, but an attributed one.

(2) That both male and female homosexuality are forbidden.

(3) That both the active and the passive partner are liable at law, under normal circumstances.

(4) That the prohibition is against sexual relations between members of the same sex, not against fantasies, attractions, or orientation.

(5) That the prohibition applies not only to lustful, transient and non-supportive homosexual relations, but also to supportive loving and permanent homosexual relations.

In Part II of this responsum we analyzed the statement of Bar Kappara that תועבה signifies תועה אתה בה and we have found:

---

[157] See preceding note regarding whether these data would lead poskim to conclude that homosexual intercourse is permissible, even if homosexuality is not deemed co-equal.

(1) That Bar Kappara might not have been referring to homosexuality at all, but to עריות in general.

(2) That the first classical interpretation of his words as implying the disruption of the heterosexual family ideal and model is clearly defensible and applicable.

(3) That the second classical explanation of his words as implying the non-procreative and unnatural aspects of homosexuality is clearly defensible and applicable.

In Part III of this responsum we have analyzed the three most prevalent modern theories of the etiology of homosexuality, the psychoanalytic, the biological (hormonal), and the sociobiological (genetic). We have found that none of these theories, even if assumed to be absolutely correct with no hint of ספק, negates the applicability of the reasons for which homosexuality is called תועבה. Furthermore, we have found that even if we assume that the Torah misunderstood the etiology of homosexuality to be something other than we know, there would still not be any cogent and compelling reason to seek to overturn the precedent against homosexuality on the basis of our current knowledge.

In sum, then, it is the clear obligation of responsible halakhists to reaffirm precedent with all vigor, there being at a minimum no compelling reason to overturn it and, at best, many cogent reasons to continue to affirm it.

Part IV

In the final analysis, a responsum such as this cannot end with הלכה עיונית alone. We must turn, then, to הלכה למעשה, actual answers to practical questions that arise. After all, the CJLS is discussing this issue because it has been asked real questions by individuals and organizations that normally turn to it for guidance.

It is not without some significant trepidation that one begins addressing the specific questions that need to be answered. Since not all questions can be directly answered, and since differences in situations often necessitate different responses, we can hope to give sufficient guidance only if we also offer principles which will enable decision-makers to render decisions consonant with the intent and spirit of this responsum.

Furthermore, halakhic conclusions often sound dispassionate. They often do not openly reflect the anguish of the decisor in having to reach them, or the decisor's recognition of the difficulty and *angst* they might cause those who are bound by them. I shall do my best to address these concerns both in this section of the paper and in Part V.

In the opinion of this author, the clarity of the halakhic position on homosexual behavior is not open to any real doubt. The biblical and rabbinic sources do not really lend themselves to permissive interpretations. Furthermore, that being the case, we have also summarized and analyzed the current knowledge on the etiology of homosexuality in Part III. That section began with the premise that modern knowledge might well have an impact upon halakhic decision-making by providing data which might impel poskim to reinterpret or overturn accepted precedents and norms, even ones which are דאורייתא.[158] Our conclusion, however, was that modern knowledge – even if we assumed it to be definitively proved – does not, *in this case*, offer any compelling reasons to overturn the normative halakhic precedents. Part III did not presuppose its own conclusion: it was an attempt to lay out the arguments and reasoning which led to its conclusion.

---

[158] Those who are familiar with my paper on the ordination of women are aware of my willingness to advocate just such steps.

As a first principle to guide decision-making, therefore, we should assert that the halakhically committed Jewish community, *qua* community and acting through its communal institution, ought not take any act which can reasonably be understood to imply the halakhic co-equality, validation, or acceptability of a homosexual lifestyle.

The halakhic community recognizes the legitimacy of the ongoing union of a couple through the institution of marriage. Where there can be no halakhic legitimacy to the union, no matter how loving and caring, there can be no marriage. The halakhic community, therefore, should not legitimate such unions by performing or recognizing affirmation ceremonies. In this we are acting in consonance with the same principle regarding intermarriage. There, too, we claim that there is no halakhic validation possible for an intermarriage. As a result, we do not perform or recognize intermarriage as legitimate. We understand that they can be loving and caring, we reach out to the intermarried, we do our best to make the intermarried feel comfortable in our midst — but all of us draw the line at performing the marriages or recognizing them as halakhically valid. Here, too, that must be our approach. We do understand that homosexual couples can be loving and caring, we must reach out to them, and we must do our best to make them feel comfortable in our midst — but the line must be drawn at performing the marriages or recognizing them as halakhically valid.

As we have seen in the case of intermarriage, where outreach ends and validation begins is not always clear. Such ambiguity will inevitably exist regarding homosexual couples too. The clarity of our commitment to the basic principle will not obviate differences of opinion on certain specific questions. As we have been able to live with those ambiguities regarding intermarriage, so we will be able to live with them regarding homosexual couples. But, the basic principle should remain clear.

It is one thing to speak about communal validation of homosexuality as halakhically co-equal, but quite another thing to speak of individual homosexuals. As a prelude to doing just that, then, permit me to posit what seems to me to be a fundamental difference between the various views expressed before the Law Committee in the course of its deliberation.

In its resolution of 1990,[159] the Rabbinical Assembly affirmed "our tradition's prescription for heterosexuality." The term "prescription" is not the same as the term "preference." "Prescription" is a term which is clearly stronger and more authoritative than "preference." At a minimum, though, "prescription" includes "preference."

I must say that I do not know that many persons come to Conservative rabbis for advice on sexual preference and behavior. What faces us in this committee is a situation in which the behavior is a given, and we are asked to consider its consequences. If, however, a person were to consult a rabbi on this matter, one might conjure up a scene in which a young man might say, "Rabbi, I am deeply confused, I am having trouble sorting out my sexual identity and my sexual behavior. I need help. It is clear to me that most of my arousals are homosexual, though some are heterosexual. That would probably put me, for example, if we try to look at it with some objectivity, around a 4 or a 5 on the Kinsey scale. I can't even tell if my heterosexual arousals are more than incidental, Kinsey's 4, or really just incidental, Kinsey's 5. Can you possibly tell me what Jewish law would have me do? I know that you will be concerned that you may tell me something that will offend me, or that I will not be willing or able to do what you tell me Jewish law would require, or that I may need counseling to reconcile myself to your answer, but let's try to set all of that aside for the moment and just give me an answer as to what you think that Jewish law would have me do." There seems to me little ambiguity what the resolution of the RA would have

---

[159] *PRA* 52 (1990): 275, quoted below, p. 673-674.

the rabbi answer. Since, at the minimum, the resolution implies a clear preference for heterosexuality, it bids us to answer the questioner by telling him that Jewish law would have him act on his heterosexual urges, and not on his homosexual urges. For anyone between a 3 and a 5 on the Kinsey scale, the preference for heterosexuality bids us urge that he refrain from acting on whatever homosexual urges he feels. It seems to me that we would probably all agree that the RA resolution means at least this.[160]

Imagine the same question addressed to a rabbi, but in place of defining oneself as a 4 or 5, the questioner defined himself as a 6 — exclusively homosexual. At bottom line, then, the question is, "What would Jewish law have me do if my arousals and attractions are exclusively homosexual?" I am convinced both that the halakhic analysis of this question and the wording of the RA resolution require that the rabbi answer, "Jewish law would have you be celibate." Prescribing heterosexuality means proscribing all other types of sexual expression. Inability to abide by the heterosexual prescription does not validate violating the homosexual proscription.

Nobody should misunderstand the dispassionate sound of the answer as an absence of feeling on the part of the posek who gives it. It is given with anguish, tears, and a heavy heart. It is given only after being convinced that the values implied by the prohibition are of such importance that they warrant asking an individual to suppress acting on his or her sexuality. It is given with the hope that the Jew committed to halakhah will find that that very commitment will provide the "strong motivation to change"[161] that will make the questioner "open to modification. . .to change [his] overt behavior from homosexual to heterosexual, [even though] the tendency toward erotic arousal by the same sex is probably never lost."[162] It is given with the prayer of the rabbi that someone will be able to counsel the questioner in a way that will allow him or her to accept the celibacy if modification continues to prove impossible. It is given coupled with a clear understanding of just how difficult the requirement is, and the implications of that difficulty for the life of the person. But, in the final analysis, it is, I think, the answer both of the halakhah and of the Rabbinical Assembly resolution.

The Rabbis may not have had a term for "role model," but the concept was hardly foreign to them. Statements like כל תלמיד,[163] and כל תלמיד חכם שאין תוכו כברו אינו תלמיד חכם, בזמן שהרועה תועה הצאן and,[164] בתר רישא גופא אזיל,[165] and חכם שנמצא רבב על בגדו חייב מיתה, תועין אחריו[166] attest to their understanding of the concept. Leaders are role models whether they like it or not. Religious leaders are, therefore, religious role models. A religious leader in a Movement committed to halakhah serves as a role model of what that commitment means.

It is important to note that the role modeling I refer to, as it pertains to homosexuality, has nothing to do with whether people learn homosexuality from role models.[167] Rather, I refer to role modeling of what is halakhically acceptable.

---

[160] I do recognize the possibility that some might place 5s in a category with 6s (no heterosexual urges) as opposed to placing them in a category with 3s and 4s. If so, 5s should be dealt with as a part of what follows immediately.

[161] Above, p. 642, quoted from Judd Marmor.

[162] Ibid.

[163] Yoma 72b, in the name of Rava.

[164] Shabbat 114a, in the name of Rabbi Yohanan. And, note the words of Rashi: ד"ה שממאסין - משניאי עצמן בעיני הבריות אומרים אוי להם ללומדי תורה שהם מאוסים ומגונים. נמצה זה משניא את התורה.

[165] Eruvin 41a.

[166] Pirkei de-Rabbi Eliezer, ch. 40.

[167] Poskim would be well-advised to stand clear of that dispute among "experts," and not be too quick to decide that one group of experts is correct and the other is wrong.

As we look at various leadership roles within the Jewish community, we must act carefully. The more it is clear that a given leadership role in the Jewish community provides a role model for halakhic acceptability, the less ambiguity there will be in our stand. The less it is clear that a given leadership role in the Jewish community provides a role model for halakhic acceptability, the more ambiguity there will be in our stand.

This much, though, seems very clear. Clergy in the Conservative movement are perceived almost universally as role models for halakhic acceptability. Therefore, persons who live an openly homosexual lifestyle could not reasonably be accepted as rabbis or cantors precisely because their lifestyle suggests that homosexuality is halakhically acceptable. I shall not attempt to define with absolute precision how "living an openly homosexual lifestyle" should be defined. I will say, however, that it does not invite or condone invasive investigations into the private lives of candidates for the rabbinate or the cantorate.

Other categories of religious leadership are not as clear, because there is not nearly the unanimity of agreement whether they function as role models, or to what degree. Besides that, there is a widespread tolerance within our Movement for leaders in these categories to behave openly in other ways that suggest halakhic acceptability for behaviors which we do not really consider halakhically acceptable, as for example, שמירת שבת and kashrut. This reality puts us on the horns of a dilemma. Though we have never posited this reality as our goal or model, it is just that in the eyes of many. It is, in a sense, precisely this reality that creates the chasm that generally exists between the clergy of the Movement and the vast majority of its laity in terms of halakhic observance and halakhic expectation.

Since our primary concern here is with the role modeling influence of avowed and open homosexuals on the communal perception of halakhic acceptability, that influence should be judged in the same way as the role modeling influence of open מחללי שבת or אוכלי טריפות is judged. How that judgement is made about them varies from community to community, from institution to institution, from school to school. The guiding principle should be that openly homosexual behavior should be a factor for non-clergy religious leadership positions, professional and lay, in the same measure that other unacceptable halakhic behaviors are a factor. Only the authorized governing individuals or boards of the community organizations, institutions and schools are competent to make this judgment because they are the ones most familiar with the actual facts and situations. But those boards must remember that our concern here is not with openly homosexual behavior *per se*, but with it as a reflection of halakhically unacceptable role modeling. On this premise, open חלול שבת or אכילת טריפות and open homosexual behavior are equal — to be considered or ignored equally.

I reiterate that the stress on *openly* homosexual behavior as the sole criterion of potential consideration precludes any right of any institution, organization or school to engage in invasive investigations of the *private* lives of individuals. Private behavior that is not halakhically acceptable but which does not flout communal standards publicly is simply not a factor, because it bears no role modeling influence.

The issue of intimating halakhic acceptability to what we consider halakhically unacceptable is also involved in such matters as synagogue honors. Here, too, the waters are very muddy. Intermarriage is again a good example. Because we wish to make clear that we, as a community, stand against the validation of intermarriage as a co-equal halakhic option, we take certain steps almost universally and other possible steps are taken in some communities and not taken in others. Regarding other halakahically unacceptable behaviors, such as חלול שבת and kashrut, however almost no community within our Movement takes any steps to restrict honors from those who engage in those unacceptable behaviors.

I see no reasonable option but to leave to the local מרא דאתרא to determine for (and possibly with) his or her community which category open homosexual behaviors fall into, the intermarriage category or the חלול שבת category. In either case, though, the essential point is that we are treating openly homosexual behavior as a halakhically unacceptable behavior, just as we treat intermarriage and חלול שבת as halakhically unacceptable behaviors. Our exclusive focus is on the behavior, not on the individuals who engage in the behavior. We disapprove of the behaviors, not of the people.

We have asserted that halakhah does not prohibit homosexual attractions or arousals. Its exclusive concern is with homosexual behavior, primarily homosexual intercourse. As a result, it follows that one who is of homosexual orientation, but affirms that the lifestyle that usually accompanies that orientation is halakhically unacceptable and therefore chooses to live a celibate life, suffers no halakhic restriction of any kind whatsoever. Such a person could serve in any position of religious leadership, professional or lay, including the rabbinate and the cantorate. Such people are, in fact, serving as role models of what is halakhically acceptable.

In this claim I agree in large measure with Dr. Mortimer Ostow who wrote:[168] "I recommend to Chancellor Cohen that only those homosexual applicants be accepted for rabbinic training who abstain completely from homosexual indulgence, who agree that homosexual behavior is halakhically unacceptable."

If Ostow had stopped there, I would be in total agreement with him. However, he added two other conditions which I reject. He wrote: ". . .who acknowledge the perverse nature of their homosexual inclination and who undertake intensive psychotherapy in the hope of overcoming it." Since I have asserted throughout that homosexuality is called תועבה for reasons that are independent of whether it is a perversion, I see no reason to insist that a homosexual concede that it is a perversion. Finally, while I might well urge such individuals to seek some type of therapy, I cannot go as far as Ostow. I cannot agree to any restrictions on a celibate homosexual who believes that his or her inclinations are not subject to psychotherapy at all (and therefore refuses psychotherapy) because they are genetically or biochemically caused. Nor would I consider psychotherapy with some goal other than "overcoming it" insufficient. The goal of the psychotherapy *might* be to come to grips with the anger or frustration the homosexual feels at the restriction on behavior his or her commitment to celibacy for solely halakhic reasons imposes upon him or her.

In attempting to anticipate the reaction that some might have to what I have written למעשה in this section of the paper, I suspect that certain circles will understand my words as an invitation (or perhaps demand) to homosexuals that they remain "in the closet." While I can understand what might lead one to make such a claim, I wish to make it absolutely clear that that is not my intention.

I understand the phrase "remain in the closet" to mean "remain silent and discrete about the practice of one's homosexuality." That, of course, has not been my recommendation at all. I have said that people of homosexual orientation who remain celibate incur no halakhic disability. I have urged halakhically concerned homosexuals to refrain entirely from homosexual practice by remaining celibate if necessary. That is not the same as practicing homosexuality with silence and discretion. I have invited persons committed to halakhah to refrain from prohibited behavior, not to circumvent the prohibition by violating it in silence and with discretion.

Finally, I wish to make as clear as I possibly can that nothing I have written in this section of this responsum can or should be construed to intimate any restriction what-

---

[168] *Conservative Judaism* 40 (fall 1987): 104.

soever on the academic freedom of anyone. Nothing I have written forbids or discourages anyone from arguing that in his or her opinion homosexuality ought to be halakhically permissible. Nothing I have have written forbids or discourages anyone from offering interpretations of the legal texts of the halakhic system to support the conclusion opposite from mine. Nothing I have written forbids or discourages anyone from invoking extralegal factors and arguing that they permit or even compel what I do not think they permit.

If more than one paper is adopted by the CJLS on this subject, the papers adopted become valid options for all members of the Rabbinical Assembly. If only one paper is adopted, however, it is reasonable to anticipate that virtually all rabbis would govern their own *behavior* by the guidelines set forth in the paper which is approved, though even that would not be enforceable unless that paper were recommended by the CJLS as a Standard of Rabbinic Practice and approved as such by the Convention of the RA.

Part V

To the heterosexual community

Throughout this paper I have assiduously avoided using words, phrases and terminology which are much in vogue these days. I have refused to use words like "gay," "straight," and "homophobia" because their very use is intended to carry implications that I have been unwilling to imply. Instead, I have chosen to use terminology which is more dispassionate and which has been used in scientific discourse until very recent times. The purpose of this choice on my part has been to avoid as much as possible the value overtones usually understood to be implied by the use of the terminology currently in vogue.[169]

Rejection of the terminology, however, should not be confused with rejection of all of the claims of the group that uses that terminology. There are, indeed, many elements of truth to the complaints of the homosexual community against the heterosexual community and it is the obligation of the heterosexual community to give them careful consideration – even though we have concluded that halakhah cannot condone homosexual behavior.

Much of the heterosexual community reacts to homosexuality as if it were inherently ugly, inherently immoral and inherently repulsive. None of these claims is true. Homosexuality, from a halakahic perspective, is תועבה, but it is the Jewish legal tradition that attributes that characteristic to it. We have spent much time in this paper attempting to understand why the law attributes the quality of abhorrence to homosexuality. We have concluded that the reasons for it remain more than merely defensible. They are cogent and compelling, and they buttress our reaffirmation of the normative proscriptive precedent. But the abhorrence remains attributed, not inherent.

What difference does it make whether the halakhic abhorrence of homosexuality is inherent or attributed? It seems to me that the difference lies primarily in the reaction of the heterosexual community to it.

If homosexuality is inherently immoral, ugly and repulsive, the heterosexual community feels a type of justification in vilifying people who are homosexual. How can they engage in such repulsive behavior? Only pure and unadulterated רשעות could prompt one

---

[169] I am aware, of course, that once the usage of terms like "gay" becomes widespread, the usage of the term "homosexual" is also perceived to bear implications. Regrettably, that is unavoidable even when unintended.

to engage willingly in behavior which even he must know and feel is inherently ugly. What greater immorality can there be for one who is not mentally deranged than to behave in a manner that is inherently abhorrent?

If, however, homosexuality is neither inherently immoral, ugly, or repulsive, the perceived justification for the vilification of the class of homosexuals no longer exists. There are good reasons for homosexual behavior to be illegal, but those reasons do not include any judgments about the inherent ugliness, repulsiveness, or immorality of the behavior. Homosexual behavior is to homosexuals as heterosexual behavior is to heterosexuals. Just as the latter engage in intercourse because they find it beautiful, fulfilling, rewarding and meaningful, so, too, do the former. Homosexual love for homosexuals is as potentially beautiful, fulfilling, rewarding and meaningful for homosexuals as heterosexual love is for heterosexuals. Halakhah prohibits homosexual behavior for reasons it deems sufficient, but not because the behavior is inherently רשעות.

At the core of the unwarranted reaction of too much of the heterosexual community lies its conviction that homosexuality is somehow chosen by homosexuals. The heterosexual community must understand that homosexual orientation is almost never chosen by homosexuals in any conventional sense.[170] The passions, attractions and fantasies felt and experienced by homosexuals are no more often of their own making than the passions, attractions and fantasies of heterosexuals. A heterosexual rarely blames him or herself for feeling an attraction to the spouse of someone else, even though acting on that attraction is illegal. The heterosexual does not castigate him or herself as inherently ugly or repulsive because of the attraction or the fantasy. In the same way, heterosexuals may not blame homosexuals for their attractions and fantasies, as if they arose from an act of pure will. Homosexuals are no more evil and subject to vilification because they fantasize an illegal relation than are heterosexuals who do the same thing.

That, of course, brings us to the next issue, namely, what type of reaction by the Jewish community is warranted and responsible toward homosexuals who behave in the manner which halakhah forbids? I find it unacceptable for the community to be more severe and intolerant in its reactions to the illegal act of homosexual behavior (which is not chosen in any conventional sense) than it is to the illegal acts of חלול שבת or intermarriage (which are freely chosen). Yet, by and large, that is exactly what usually happens.

The Conservative Jewish community bends over backwards to be understanding and tolerant of those who flout its commitments regarding Shabbat observance and intermarriage and a host of other illegal acts that each of us could list. "שמירת שבת is so hard for those unaccustomed to it." "The economic and social costs to the שומר שבת are sometimes greater than many of our constituents can undertake." "We must reach out to the intermarried lest we lose them entirely." "All of our efforts must be geared toward effectuating the conversion of the non-Jewish spouse and we cannot accomplish that by ostracizing the intermarried."

Homosexuals are no less members of the Jewish community though they may flout its commitments than are מחללי שבת or the intermarried who also flout its commitments. If קירוב is the order of the day for our constituents who behave in halakhically unacceptable ways, it is also the order of the day for our constituents who behave in the halakhically unacceptable way called homosexual behavior. As we never give up on

---

[170] Even if there are "choice points" in a person's life, the person rarely is aware that he or she is standing before a choice point. It is not like a person who consciously knows that he or she is about to choose between two different model cars and can just as easily opt for one model as for the other.

the possibility of leading the intermarried to a commitment to our laws and resulting in the conversion of the non-Jew, so, too, must we never give up on the possibility of leading the homosexual to a commitment to our laws and resulting in his or her adoption of celibacy.

Part IV of this paper was devoted in large part to the halakhic task of drawing the line between actions that would undermine our values and commitments by actually validating what is illegal and actions that would not. We cannot validate illegal acts, but neither can we treat those who engage in those illegal acts any more severely or intolerantly than we treat those who engage in other equally halakhically unacceptable acts.

We cannot forbid the formation of separate synagogues predicated on the premise of the co-equality of homosexuality with heterosexuality and yet make homosexuals so uncomfortable and unwanted in our synagogues that we actually push them to form their own synagogues. We can adamantly forbid public acts that impart an imprimatur of halakhic acceptability to homosexual behavior, but cannot also ostracize and push away those homosexuals who refrain from those public acts.

It is conceivable that the establishment institutions of the halakhic Jewish community might someday be forced into decisions that are undesired because the homosexual community of Jews will accept continued membership in the larger Jewish community only if homosexuality is validated as an acceptable halakhic option. But, unless and until such a time arrives, the institutions of the normative halakhic community may not turn away from and reject homosexuals any more than they turn away from and reject other groups who engage in halakhically illegal acts.

More than anything else, the heterosexual community must remember that the halakhic demand being made upon homosexuals – celibacy – is far more severe and difficult a demand than any that is made by halakhah on heterosexuals. Homosexuals must observe all of the same mitzvot as heterosexuals, and are denied the pleasure and fulfillment of sexual relations. If the heterosexual community is able to be embracing to those who backslide regarding halakhic demands less onerous than celibacy, surely it can be at least no less embracing to those who backslide regarding this most onerous halakhic demand. To embrace does not mean to condone. It means never to be מתיאש מן התשובה.

To the homosexual community

There is a fundamental difference between the primary premise of the halakhic system and the primary premise of the American legal system. "Obligation" is the operative term which characterizes halakhah, while "rights" is that term for American law. In Jewish law, the category of individual rights does not hold the virtually sacrosanct status that it does in the United States. In the American system, there is always tremendous opposition to any legislation that impinges on the presumed broad rights of individuals to act as they wish, especially when their actions do not impinge on others or when they result from consensual agreement.[171]

Jewish law is a religious legal system. In the final analysis, it seeks to determine what God wishes. God's wishes clearly impinge with great frequency on the behavior of individuals, even when that behavior does not impinge on others, or when that behavior might be engaged in with the consent of another. Jewish law dictates what one may eat,

---

[171] Consider, for example, the opposition voiced against seatbelt laws and helmet laws for cyclists. Purely paternalistic legislation is almost impossible to pass in the United States.

drink, and wear; it posits restrictions and obligations on the relationship between a person and the person's spouse, and most of those restrictions and obligations cannot be superseded by the consent of the two spouses. The law obligates Jews and they are expected to submit themselves to its authority, even when it mandates or forbids actions that are wholly personal or consensual.

The homosexual Jewish community must recognize that if it seeks halakhic validation of the homosexual lifestyle as co-equal with heterosexuality, that validation cannot be predicated on the claim that homosexual relationships are consensual. The degree to which a homosexual relationship is loving, caring and supportive is non-determinative in deciding whether it is legal.

Members of the homosexual community must recognize that saying no to a request for halakhic validation of homosexuality does not imply rejection of homosexuals or their exclusion from the greater community. Rather, the halakhic community is more than merely entitled to stand by its commitment to the authority of halakhah, it is obligated to do so. And when the best possible halakhic thinking leads to the conclusion that the halakhic precedent ought to stand, it is unfair of anyone to assert that the conclusion is possible only for decisors who do not understand, who do not empathize, who are insensitive, who do not care for all of the elements of their community, who harbor an irrational and unwarranted fear of a segment of the community.

It is possible for a decisor to be understanding, empathic, sensitive, caring and without irrational fears and yet conclude that the halakhic precedents are defensible, warranted and compelling. The decisor and the halakhic community are then entitled to turn to the segment of the community whose question has been answered negatively for its understanding. The halakhically concerned community of Jewish homosexuals must demonstrate its understanding of "obligation" rather than "rights" as the core value of halakhah. That community must recognize that the demand of halakhah upon it reflects the common halakhic demand to put one's commitment to the values which the precedents embody above one's personal feelings, to submit one's personal feelings and behavior to the authority of the law, even though one wishes that the law might be different.

The demand of halakhah vis-à-vis the homosexual reflects a difference of degree rather than a difference of kind, and the homosexual community must understand that the decisors of the halakhic community can and do understand this. When a decisor is forced to declare an animal nonkosher, at a great cost, inconvenience and pain to the family which presented it for inspection, the decisor *does* feel the family's pain and is himself pained. But the cogent and compelling reasons for obedience to the norms of kashrut supersede both his pain and that of the affected family. When a decisor must declare that two people who wish to be married may not be married because their union is a halakhically consanguineous marriage, the decisor *does* feel the couple's pain and is himself pained. But the cogent and compelling reasons for obedience to the norms of forbidden marital unions supersede both his pain and that of the affected couple. That is precisely what is meant by submission to the halakhic system.

Castigating the halakhic community and its decisors as insensitive and unfeeling because they have given a negative answer is unwarranted. When a decisor has investigated all possible avenues to permit an agunah to be remarried and has concluded that it cannot be done without sacrificing the ideals and values which the norms embody, he reaches his conclusion with heavy heart and tearful eyes. That heavy heartedness and tearfulness are caused precisely *because* the decisor knows and feels the pain and anguish his decision will inevitably cause. There is no glee in the mind of the decisor when he reaches a decision that imposes any hardship of any kind on any individual. Nonetheless, the values and ideals of the law — the community's best understanding of God's will — sometimes make the imposition of such a hardship unavoidable.[172] והמבין יבין.

Part VI

Postscript

It has been the purpose of this paper to deal with homosexuality as an halakhic issue. That purpose has been completed. Nonetheless, I consider it critical to make a few additional comments that are not technically part of an halakhic analysis, but are, in my opinion, crucially important.

I asserted briefly from the outset[173] that the issue of homosexuality could not be excluded from halakhic discourse by the claim that halakhah must stop at the bedroom door. For a religious legal system, that claim is simply untenable. The United States legal system, however, is not a religious legal system. It behooves us, therefore, to reflect briefly on the practical consequences of the difference between a religious and a secular legal system vis-à-vis the issue of homosexuality. Since these remarks constitute a postscript to the essence of this paper, they are not intended to be an in-depth analysis, but rather more in the category of ראשי פרקים.

We have claimed that the classical explanations of why the Torah has chosen to attribute to homosexuality the attribute of תועבה remain defensible, at a minimum and arguably, convincing and compelling to this day. Those reasons — disruptive to family structure and life, unnatural, nonprocreative — justify the prohibition against homosexual behavior which the halakhah mandates. The reasons are of legitimate concern to a religious legal system.

It is far harder to argue that those same reasons are of legitimate concern to a secular legal system. Indeed, one would be very hard pressed to defend that claim at all. If "rights" is the primary category of significance in the United States legal system, rather than "obligation," the rights should be virtually unrestricted. They are legitimately restricted by the state only if the unrestricted exercise of individual rights by members of the society presents some kind of danger or threat to the legitimate interests of the state itself or to its citizens.

I am unable to offer any cogent argument to demonstrate why the private sexual acts of consenting adults should present any danger or threat to the legitimate interests of the state itself or to its citizens, under common circumstances. Therefore, I can see no justification for civil legislation proscribing such acts. The fact that those acts may be unnatural

---

[172] I leave a final point for a footnote. The ideological commitment of the Conservative movement to halakhah and its authority is, in large measure, independent of whether or not the constituency recognizes that ideological commitment or acts on it. Therefore, it would be untenable to argue that since a large percentage of the Movement does not take halakhah seriously, the Movement need not take halakhah seriously. The Movement could not possibly justify anything as halakhically acceptable on the grounds that halakhah does not matter to the constituents, nor could it reasonably declare that for a certain issue it suspends its commitment to halakhah. It follows, therefore, that if the homosexual community seeks validation within Conservative Judaism, it must seek halakhic validation. Only that could validate it authentically. Furthermore, if halakhic validation is found to be unwarranted or impossible, the homosexual community cannot demand validation within Conservative Judaism extra-halakhically. Such validation could come only at the cost of a gross violation of one of the very characteristics of the Movement that impel the homosexual community to seek its validation in the first place.

[173] Above, p. 614.

and non-procreative in the sense we have defined[174] presents no danger to the state or to its citizens,[175] and therefore, should not be the subject of civil legislation.[176]

There is no inconsistency whatsoever in making the halakhic claims made in this paper, on the one hand, and asserting absolute opposition to any infringement of the civil rights of homosexuals on the other. The halakhic tradition has every right to make judgements about the acceptability of the private acts of consenting adults, the secular American legal system does not; the halakhic tradition has every right to restrict from leadership positions persons whose behavior implies an imprimatur of halakhic acceptability, the secular American legal system does not.

Neither the halakhic tradition not the American legal system can justify civil discrimination, violence or the threat of violence, official or unofficial prejudice against homosexuals.

Jews who are halakhically committed must tread a fine line between their very defensible halakhic/religious conclusions and their legal and moral responsibilities within the secular state. Treading that line is not always easy and usually requires considerably explanatory effort. That careful treading is beautifully reflected in a resolution of the Rabbinical Assembly, passed at the 1990 Convention:[177]

> WHEREAS Judaism affirms that the Divine image reflected in every human being must always be cherished and affirmed, and
>
> WHEREAS Jews have always been sensitive to the impact of official and unofficial prejudice and discrimination, wherever directed, and
>
> WHEREAS gay and lesbian Jews have experienced not only the constant threats of physical violence and homophobic rejection, but also the pains of anti-Semitism known to all Jews and additionally, a sense of painful alienation from our own religious institutions, and
>
> WHEREAS the extended families of gay and lesbian Jews are often members of our congregations who live with concern for the safety, health and well-being of their children, and
>
> WHEREAS the AIDS crisis has deeply exacerbated the anxiety and

---

[174] Above, pp. 627-630.

[175] Of course, if all of the citizens of the state chose to engage exclusively in nonprocreative sex, that could be understood to be a threat to the survival of the state itself. As a practical matter, though, the issue need not concern us.

[176] While *I* am not convinced, I admit that one might make a defensible argument that a homosexual family structure presents a danger to the very fabric of the state and that it is therefore within the legitimate interests of the state to forbid the family structure which presents the danger. It the state adopted such a position, it might refuse to recognize homosexual marriages as marriages and, therefore, refuse to such unions the legal standing that accompanies being defined as a family. It could, however serve no compelling purpose to the state to forbid consenting adults to engage in nonprocreative or unnatural intercourse — provided the adults do not seek recognition of their union as having family status.

Similarly I recognize that one might make a defensible argument that the presence of homosexuals in some clearly definable subgroups within society (e.g., the army, the police, the firefighters) might have consequences that could pose a danger or threat to the state or to its citizens. But even in these cases, it is not the unnaturalness or the nonprocreativity of the homosexual behavior that provides the state with its compelling interest. Rightly or wrongly, those who make these claims assert that it is the social consequences of these relationships on such matters as discipline and trust that validate the state's interest in the behavior of the homosexuals involved. The state has no legitimate interest in the behavior *per se*. Its interest is solely in the threatening or dangerous consequences of the behavior to the state or its citizens. ואכמ״ל.

[177] *PRA* 52 (1990): 275.

suffering of this community of Jews who need in their lives the compassionate concern and support mandated by Jewish tradition,

THEREFORE BE IT RESOLVED that we, The Rabbinical Assembly, while affirming our tradition's prescription for heterosexuality,

1) Support full civil equality for gays and lesbians in our national life, and

2) Deplore the violence against gays and lesbians in our society, and

3) Reiterate that, as are all Jews, gay men and lesbians are welcome as members in our congregations, and

4) Call upon our synagogue and the arms of our movement to increase our awareness, understanding and concern for our fellow Jews who are gay and lesbian.

Epilogue

It has no doubt been noted that until the term AIDS appeared in the quotation of the resolution of the Rabbinical Assembly directly above, the term had not appeared in this entire responsum. To many, that fact must seem strange. This Epilogue is devoted to a brief explanation of this strange fact.

There are, indeed, many halakhic issues that must be addressed as a result of the AIDS crisis. Those issues include some very difficult and complicated matters. Among others, issues include טהרה of the bodies of victims of AIDS, the dilemma of privacy vs. disclosure, what constitute appropriate actions for the protection of the unaffected vs. unwarranted actions that reflect unjustified ostracism of those affected by AIDS. A paper on the halakhic questions that have arisen as a result of the AIDS crisis is currently being written for the consideration of the Law Committee.

The subject of this paper, however, was the questions of the halakhic status of homosexual behavior and that question is not related to AIDS in any way, in my opinion. My opinion is predicated on two premises, which, when spelled out, will clarify why AIDS has not been mentioned.

I reject categorically that AIDS can be viewed as God's punishment of homosexuals. Were it possible to view it that way, AIDS would have to have been mentioned as a support for the prohibition against homosexuality, for surely God does not punish people for behavior which is approved as halakhic.

This is not the place for a lengthy discourse on why I reject the premise that AIDS is Divine punishment for homosexuality. A brief statement will suffice.

I see no evidence of God's direct intervention as a punishment for such violations of Jewish law. There is no indication either in the Torah or in Rabbinic literature that the violation of the prohibition against homosexuality is any more heinous than the violation of any of the other prohibitions which are legally punishable in the same way as homosexuality is. The list of such offenses[178] includes, *inter alia*, blasphemers, Sabbath desecraters and those who curse their parents. Since there is no halakhic justification for singling out homosexuals from the entire list of offenders who are technically liable for stoning and since Sabbath desecrators (to pick one category) do not seem to be suffering from AIDS in

---

[178] M. Sanhedrin 7:4.

any significant percentage to warrant the conclusion that God is using AIDS as a punishment for those who are liable for stoning.¹⁷⁹ I reject categorically any such claim. Once rejected, any reference to AIDS as support for the proscriptive precedent is not only unwarranted, it is outrageous.

That, of course, leaves the other side of the possible equation, namely, that the AIDS crisis constitutes some type of grounds for validating homosexuality halakhically. I reject that possibility with equal adamance. Those who suffer from AIDS have legitimate halakhic claims toward the rest of the Jewish community. Those claims stem from halakhic requirements for treatment of the sick and suffering and care for the families of the sick and suffering. Victims of AIDS have legitimate halakhic claims that stem from halakhic requirements concerning הלוית המת. But none of the legitimate halakhic claims of sufferers and victims of AIDS has anything to do with the question this responsum addressed. The anguish, torment and cruelty that AIDS inflicts upon those who suffer from it, upon their families, upon their communities, upon the entire Jewish community have no bearing whatsoever on the halakhic question of the halakhic status of the homosexual behavior itself. All suffering is a tragedy. Great suffering is a great tragedy. But neither suffering nor tragedy, in and by themselves, constitute grounds for the grant of a היתר to what is אסור.

יהי רצון מלפניך ה' אלקי שלא יארע דבר תקלה על ידי ולא אכשל בדבר הלכה וישמחו בי חברי ולא אמר על טמא טהור ועל טהור טמא ולא יכשלו חברי בדבר הלכה ואשמח בהם.¹⁸⁰

---

¹⁷⁹ What's more, even if one were willing to accept the claim that God does punish those who would be liable at law for offenses for which they cannot now be punished by judicial procedures because we are no longer entitled to try דיני נפשות, AIDS is not the appropriate punishment. After all, the Gemara (Sanhedrin 37b) which asserts that theological premise demands that the God-inflicted punishment be recognizable as approximating the actual punishment for which the person would be liable. For חייבי סקילה, the Gemara posits או נופל מן הגג או חיה דורסתו, paralleling the punishment of being thrown off a cliff onto rocks. AIDS hardly qualifies to be viewed as a replacement for סקילה.

¹⁸⁰ Berakhot 28b.

EH 24.1992c

HOMOSEXUALITY AND THE POLICY DECISIONS OF THE CJLS

Rabbi Reuven Kimelman

This paper was approved by the CJLS on March 25, 1992, by a vote of eleven in favor, seven opposed, and five abstentions (11-7-5). Voting in favor: Rabbis Kassel Abelson, David Feldman, Samuel Fraint, Arnold M. Goodman, Reuven Kimelman, Herbert Mandl, Mayer Rabinowitz, Chaim A. Rogoff, Joel Roth, Morris Shapiro, and Gerald Skolnik. Voting against: Rabbis Elliot N. Dorff, Richard L. Eisenberg, Dov Peretz Elkins, Howard Handler, Jan Caryl Kaufman, Joel E. Rembaum, and Gordon Tucker. Abstaining: Rabbis Ben Zion Bergman, Stanley Bramnick, Aaron L. Mackler, Lionel E. Moses and Avram Israel Reisner.

The Committee on Jewish Law and Standards of the Rabbinical Assembly provides guidance in matters of halakhah for the Conservative movement. The individual rabbi, however, is the authority for the interpretation and application of all matters of halakhah.

Whereas the halakhic issues regarding homosexuality have already been dealt with in other responsa, this response deals with the public policy issues.

Many of the issues that I raise with regard to Rabbi Artson's thesis have already been dealt with considerable acumen by its author. He is aware of the dangers of the slippery slope and believes that the necessary precautions have been taken. Accordingly, he strives to build a wall between a permissive position on "monogamous" homosexuality and a prohibitive one on intermarriage. He is also quite aware that the sole use of the criterion of compassion would undermine any overall standards, for any standard can shown to be lacking compassion in a specific case. It is well known that hard cases make poor laws. Laws command respect by working most of the time. Extra-legal compassion often consists of responding to particular cases as opposed to a class of cases. Any assessment of the resolution has to weigh the chances of avoiding the slippery slope based on compassion alone.

The author is also fully aware that whether the prohibition of homosexuality in the Torah is of attributed or of intrinsic status is a red herring. He writes as follows:

> The argument about whether תועבה is an attributed or an intrinsic status becomes irrelevant when it is recognized that all values in the Torah are understood to be attributed — by God. The Torah doesn't distinguish between what we would call morality and ritual. Rather the biblical standard is one of obedience, of making God's will one's own. God may designate something as a תועבה for Jews but not so for non-Jews, or may label a practice abhorrent for all humankind. In either case, attribution of a status is a

reflection of a (perceived) divine evaluation not an independent human asessment.

In actuality, the move from attributed to instrinsic status is part of the process of providing rationales for the mitzvot. It is not unusual to have something in the Bible of attributed status to assume metaphysical status in medieval literature, especially in Kabbalah. For example, things in the Bible which defile (Lev. 11:43) can in the Talmud desensitize (B. Yoma 39a) and in Kabbalah render the soul defective. A good example of this is the history of the explanation of nonkosher food.[1] Such explanations seek to demonstrate the convergence between human experience and divine evaluation.

Finally, Rabbi Artson is also aware of the recent research that has severed the connection between the terms קדש/קדשה and the cult thereby weakening the link between harlotry or homosexuality with that of idolatry. The fact that Deuteronomy's diatribe against all forms of idolatry does not include homosexuality and that the prohibition against קדש and קדשה (Deut. 23:18) appears in a list of moral wrongs indicates that homosexuality is understood in the context of immoral sexuality, not idolatry.

My remarks therefore focus on those beliefs that inform Rabbi Artson's resolution. These include the belief that:

1. Loving stable homosexuality can be a good.
2. It should be sanctified through Jewish ritual, because "a willingness to perform a commitment ceremony for monogamous homosexuals strengthens Judaism."
3. "Encouraging sexual responsibility and stability among homosexuals can only strengthen family values and traditional communities for all."
4. "We must find a way to draw these people into the fabric of Jewish community, with the goal of bringing them to a life of Torah and mitzvot."

Just because many will resolve the issue on straight halakhic considerations does not mean that these arguments should not receive their due. It is no small matter to claim that a single resolution will strengthen Judaism, strengthen family values, and bring people to a life of Torah and mitzvot. Indeed were this resolution to achieve all this it would be quite remarkable. After all, how many of our Movements' resolutions have in fact strengthened Judaism, family values, and brought many to a life of Torah and mitzvot?

The question for anyone willing to vote for this resolution, regardless of its halakhic validity, is the likelihood of the prognosis. This century does not suffer from a shortage of resolutions calling for the abrogation of Jewish law for the greater good of Judaism.

In periods of ethical relativism such as ours, ethical issues tend to be reduced to other categories. A powerful tactic in the arsenal of ethical relativism is the displacement of the language of ethics by the language of medicine and aesthetics. In a universe of discourse circumscribed by medicine and aesthetics, evil becomes unhealthy and wrong becomes distasteful. The ultimate in the relativizing or trivializing of the ethical is its psychologization. The reductionism which follows in its wake is the categorization of ethical issues as health ones and ethical objections as phobias. The triumph of the therapeutic is the victory of good feelings over bad deeds. In such an atmosphere, negative behavior can be legitimated by positive feelings. All that is needed is a nice-sounding therapeutic term for a morally condemnable act. When the aversion against murder is dubbed "androphobia" or "phobiocide" and cannibalism dubbed "carniphobia," the victory of the medical-psychological over the religio-ethical will be complete. This terminological shift from the moral to the medical is

---

[1] Compare *The Letter of Aristeas*, 142-151, with Isaac Arama, *Akedat Yitsak*, Eighth Gate, end of ch. 60, or with Elijah Vidah, *Reshit Hokhmah*, Gate of Holiness 15:1.

not that far off. Just consider how the slope that runs from the condemnation of "murder" down to the purported neutrality of "euthanasia" becomes slippery when greased by mediating expressions such as "killing," "mercy-killing," and "putting him out of his misery."

The phenomena of the slippery slope pinpoints the dilemma in the transfer of objections from the ethical to any of its alternatives. The latter cannot provide clear demarcations between the permitted and the prohibited. The result is that the relaxation of one standard induces the relaxation of another until the very idea of standards gets called into question. In the absence of standards, ethical issues become matters of taste. Issues of taste are rarely subject to debate and when debatable are rarely resolvable. Since whether something is healthy or unhealthy, beautiful or ugly, is insufficient to determine whether it is right or wrong, neither the language of aesthetics nor that of health is adequate for the formulation of a religious policy analysis.

Social science is also not our salvation. It cannot be relied upon to resolve our problem as there is almost always available an alternative reading of the data. This is so not just because value-free research is rare or non-existent, but rather because values are built into the way research questions are formulated. Indeed, values frequently determine what is considered data. Othertimes, research itself is driven by values. Facts do not speak for themselves. Contexts give them both voice and meaning. It is rare that a context is not generated by perspectives charged with values. There is hence hardly a field of human consequence in which researchers of different values do not produce different conclusions. Since values have consequences, the consequences that we seek to promote should be driven by religious values. We cannot abdicate our obligation to make value judgments

This obligation is especially pertinent in the light of contemporary approaches of seeking to understand even sexuality, that most-biologically rooted of human phenomena, in terms of social construction. Social constructionists believe that we only experience the world in terms of the shared meanings that we have collectively built. It is through these shared meanings that we interpret one another's words and actions. All understanding takes place within these shared meanings or perspectives. Since assessments can only be made from within a perspective, there is no perspective-free understanding from which other perspectives can be judged. This way of understanding the human construal of reality means that nobody sees things as they really are. Indeed there is no such thing; there is only the way things appear from a perspective. By exposing the absence of any unmediated facts or neutral perception, the point is made that everything we know or see is known and seen as a function of some perspective or paradigm. It is not unusual for those who adhere to this mode of argumentation to go on and claim that all perspectives are beclouded by interests, indeed that all arguments over principle are really arguments over interests, as there is no disinterested way of understanding.

Those who apply this epistemology to sexuality argue that all sexual norms are a result of a perspective and thus no one perspective has a right, in the absence of any foundational perspective, to dictate to another perspective. Those who advocate this position, and their number is legion as their intellectual pedigree is long, frequently do so in order to argue for a change in policy. The difficulty is that once the argument has been made for undermining the ultimate validity of any one perspective, the basis for arguing for a change dissipates. One cannot, with any degree of methodological consistency, argue for a change in sexual perspective while undermining the foundation of all sexual perspectives. Once the anchors are lifted, all perspectives become free-floating.

On the contrary, those who argue for the social construction of sexuality deprive themselves of any basis for change. They cannot argue for any fundamental right of sexual expression believing as they do that all such arguments are rooted in a particular perspective and are solely a function of the interests of the advocate.

Indeed, by the very nature of their argument social constructionists would have to concede a community's right to promote its interests. If one cannot advocate a policy because of its rootedness in reality, then one can only advocate it because of one's interests. It is not past reality but future results that are decisive. Removing metaphysical considerations from policy analysis paves the way for pure consequentialism. On those grounds, religious public policy has only to ask itself about the consequences of its policies. Authorized to promote those policies that will sustain and enhance its chances for continuity, the argument for the social construction of reality provides yet another reason for the religious community to implement policies based on its value-judgments.

From the perspective of framing the issue of homosexuality in terms of public policy rather than private morality means asking whether there is a Gresham law of sexuality. That is to say, that as bad coinage drives out good coinage, so bad sex drives out good sex. This applies all the more so were the bad sex a norm rather than an exception. Ascertaining whether valorizing homosexuality is at all detrimental to family-producing sexuality is at the heart of public policy analysis. If it is, then the approval of *a priori* non-procreative marriages as a class could tend to devalue the type of sexuality that leads to procreation.

The devaluation of procreative sex is not inconsequential. Without commitments of time, money, and emotions, there will be no family to speak of. The creation of families is a major investment. Because of the toil, anguish, and expense of raising children, societies concerned with their biological future extend special inducements for the assumption of such responsibility. Economically, these inducements can come in the form of tax deductions, tax-supported public education, tax write-offs, tax deductions for interest on mortgage loans, and so on. Religiously, the inducements include the reward of doing a commandment, genetic and cultural continuity, family and social expectations, and that joy of raising children properly.

The religious meaning of marriage is not exhausted by human intimacy. By contributing to an ethos that sees the relationship as the sole end of marriage, we undermine efforts to persuade couples to assume their responsibility for the type of investment in the future that childbearing entails. Our credibility is compromised when we promote child-bearing families while sanctifying relationships which are inherently childless. The religious community has a vested interest in getting people to deal with their sexuality in a manner that is supportive of family and children. Indeed, the strength of the community is dependent upon persuading its members to define their self-interest in terms of responsibility for others, starting with spouse and children. In order for such a family-centered message to be received unambiguously, there is a need to filter out any messages that could relativize the social and moral status of heterosexuality and the family.

Modern Jewish life is already marked by too many couples declining to invest in the future by replenishing themselves. We have little control over that. We are responsible, however, for that which we affect. The performing of homosexual "marriages" abets that trend. It is difficult to maintain credibility advocating the importance of child-bearing families while sanctifying marriages which in their essence are not reproductive. By contributing to an ethos that sees the relationship as the sole end of marriage, we undermine efforts to persuade couples to assume their responsibility for the type of investment in the future that childbearing entails. Our cause is not helped by delivering mixed messages.

Childless marriages are different from those with children in their impact on the parents and on society. It is the birth of a child that most fully validates sexual partnership as a means of continuity. As the Talmud (Yevamot 64a) notes, a childless marriage brings about a withdrawal of the divine presence from Israel, as it says, "to be a God to you and to your seed after you" (Gen. 17:7) — "Whenever your seed is after you, the divine presence dwells, [whenever] there is no seed after you, upon whom will the divine presence dwell, on wood and stones?" Apparently, there is a special divine concern for those who invest in progeny. Rabbis are acutely aware of the impact of children from their involvements in divorce cases. When there are children the sense of tragedy is qualitatively different. The presence of children intensifies the feeling that marriage break-up frays the social fabric of community. There is of course a considerable difference in having compassion for a couple who cannot have children as opposed to one for which it was never biologically intended.

Contemporary technology and mores have widened the gap between sex and love as well as between childbearing and parenting. In cases where medical intervention is needed to induce pregnancy, this may accrue to the benefit of all involved. Sundering these links for a whole class of people, however, undermines the centrality of the family for the locus of love, sex, childbearing, and parenting. Judaism would be false to its own best insights were it to become a partner to the dissolution of its major contribution to the civilization of humanity — the family..

The building blocks of family are male and female. A man without a wife, according to the Midrash (Genesis Rabbah 17:2 and parallels), lacks blessing, bliss, well-being, protection, and atonement. There is even the opinion there that a single male, unable to realize his full humanity, cannot be called אדם. Male-female interaction contributes to the stabilizing of gender identity along with the flowering of masculinity and femininity. Although they share much, the differences between the two should not be underestimated. Male and female love are not identical. Besides the obvious differences, female love possesses a futurity that cannot easily be duplicated by male love. Anatomically and psychologically, feminine love is more bound up in creating a future than its masculine counterpart. When male love is female-centered, it thinks beyond itself. Without the female pull toward the future, male love can become exclusively focused on the present.

It is through commitment to the female that male sexuality lays claim to the future. As George Guilder writes in his book *Sexual Suicide*, a man's "participation in the chain of nature, his access to social immortality, the very meaning of his potency, of his life energy, are all profoundly" bound up with a woman's durable love. Traditionally, women have leveraged the male sexual drive into domestication. Without channeling the sexual drive into family making, we could become totally enmeshed in "nowness" with little thought of the future. It is precisely the link with the future inherent in heterosexual relations that allows glimmers of the transcendent to be refracted through human sexuality. When the Midrash (Genesis Rabbah 9:7) notes that "were it not for the evil impulse, a man would not build a house, marry a wife, and produce children," it is expressing appreciation for the divine cunning in the use of our physical sensations to enhance our concerns for building a better tomorrow.

It is no wonder that the talmudic Rabbis saw in a loving husband-wife relationship a fitting dwelling place for the divine presence. The Kabbalah went one step further by picturing the husband-wife relationship as capable of completing the circuit of divine electricity, as it were, that charges all of life. Since the unity of husband and wife is a source of special blessing, there is a linkage with the divine made possible through marriage. Indeed, it is precisely in the complementarity of husband and wife that humanity realizes the fullness of the divine image. Kabbalistically-speaking, marriage makes possible a certain plugging into the Infinite. As such, it entitles one to don the mantle of infinity – a טלית. This understanding may lie behind the traditional requirement of a married cantor for the High Holy Days.

Over the years, family in Judaism has come to serve the ideal of monogamy. Since in nature the male of the species is rarely monogamous, it is unlikely that most men are naturally monogamous. Those who are have so committed themselves to marriage that they have appropriated their wives psychic predisposition toward monogamy. The multiple encirclings of the groom by the bride under the marriage huppah can be understood as seeking to weld man's polymorphic sexuality to his wife. For civilization to succeed, male sexual impulses and psychology need to be subordinated to the long-term horizons of female psychology and biology. Through love of wife, husbands can achieve a futurity that many women are graced with biologically. This helps explain the fact that so many happily married men deep down believe, however loath they may be to admit it, that marriage has had a domesticating, indeed civilizing, effect on them. We males frequently become nurturers through our wives and in return extend their nurturing capabilities. Just contrast the statistics of the leisure activities and acts of violence of single men with their married counterparts. It is no wonder that Judaism has found no better civilizers than the life of Torah and a good family.

Despite the fragility of the contemporary husband-wife bond, it remains surprisingly stable in comparison with other chosen, nonbiological relationships. Such stability is undoubtedly anchored in a profound biological and psychological basis.

Marriage involves more than the ratification of love between two people. It is the transformation of love into a biological and social continuity that transcends the participants to become the basis of human community. Married love is an investment of faith in the future of the family, society, and humanity. A couple's love for their children properly nurtured can lead to care for the community that supports them and to a willingness to work for a future to house them.

Family involvement leads to the expansion of both horizontal and vertical horizons. Horizontally, concern for family can lead to concern for community and ultimately for the extended human family. The mutual helpfulness that takes place within the family can set the pattern for such throughout society. Having a family reinforces the sense of an interdependent humanity. This understanding may lie behind the talmudic exclusion of a childless judge from adjudicatng cases of capital punishment. Vertically, continuity is epitomized through having children. Anybody who has counselled a barren couple knows how much the absence of children can undermine the professed motives of marriage. Marriage both institutionalizes the desire for continuity and spurs it on.

At least since the first paschal offering upon the redemption from Egypt, biblical religion has invested in the family as its central vehicle of education and continuity. Ever since, this holiday of redemption has become the quintessential family holiday. It is clear that a religion committed to a multi-generational covenant to bring about the redemption will be inclined to invest in that agency that is intrinsically multi-generational. As no other biological community can so easily becomes a historical community as the family, so no other institution has the wherewithal to stretch from the first to the final redemption.

The two themes of redemption and family are linked, according to the Talmud (Shabbat 31a), on the day of judgment. At that time, we are asked about trying to have children right before we are asked about awaiting the redemption. The sequence and juxtaposition of the two highlights their relationship and commonality. Both attest to long-term commitments. Indeed, the extended vision produced through having children can enhance the capacity for the long-term envisioning required for redemption. A perspective that limits itself to the self and its indulgences will tend to exclude both. Family, for its part, forces us to see ourselves in a larger context of meaning both within a generation of humanity and throughout the generations. Any effort that serves to undermine, whether intentionally or not, the primacy of the family is *eo ipso* inimical to the interests of religion and its vision of redemption. This may explain why the Talmud (Pesahim 88b) cites the verse from Isaiah, "He did not create it a waste, but formed it for habitation," in support of the idea of תיקון עולם. This weave of family, religion, and redemption also stands behind the proclamation of the psalmist:

> He established a testimony in Jacob and appointed a law in Israel which He commanded our fathers to teach to their children; that the next generation might know them, the children yet unborn, and arise to tell them to their children, so that they should set their hope in God (Ps. 78:4-7).

The sense of family as expressed in biblical law and narrative underscores both marital and filial bonds. Much of the prohibited sexual activity serves to maintain and enhance these bonds by focusing on the exclusivity of these relationships. Besides undermining the primacy of the family, same sex activity has the potential of undermining the whole idea of sexual prohibitions. The legitimation of loving homosexual relations easily slides into the legitimation of "loving" incestuous, pedephiliac, and adulterous relationships. Such is the slippery slope in today's sexual climate as it was apparently in antiquity. Accordingly, Rabbi Akiba in Talmud Sanhedrin (58a) derives the prohibition of incest, homosexuality, adultery, and bestiality all from different parts of the same verse of Gen. 2:24.

To note that Torah is a reflection of culture without underscoring how often it was and remains a protest against the ethos of the day is to do a disservice to the biblical impact on civilization. In the same vein, Jewish political thought from Albo to Luzzatto opposed utopian schemes of social organization from Plato to Thomas Moore precisely on the issue of the inviolability of the family unit. The biblical sexual ethos with all its prohibitions is but the flip side of its commitment to the sanctity of the family unit.

Sociologically speaking, deviations from the norm come in clusters. One could easily imagine somebody contending that he is sexually functional only with other married women or with his daughters. Once a dysfunctionality becomes respectable it tends to attract others. There are now support groups called NAMBLA for men with sexual appetites for children, of course only consenting [sic] children. Once feelings are accepted as the criterion for overturning a prohibition, every leak in the dam threatens to become a flood. Moreover, if there is a market for promoting incestuous relations and the like, there will always be some health expert ready to publish a book on how loving, stable, incestuous relations are healthy for the participants. They are already appearing on TV talk shows. Books that tout the benefits of extra-marital relations for "healthy" marriages are readily available. Capitalistic cultures are most effective in producing suppliers for demands.

Those who advocate an abdication of the norms of the Torah frequently do so on the assumption that the prohibition against homosexuality was based on health considerations and its voluntary nature, both of which they claim no longer obtain. Whatever the health status of homosexuality or its etiology, it bears little on the issue of maintaining the privileged position of the normative family in Jewish life. Its impact is independent of its origin. Moreover, we lack the evidence to assess whether health considerations played any role in the Torah's prohibition. Those who claim to know have already made up their mind on the validity of the prohibition as those who ruled against the validity of kashrut, a century ago, had made up their mind on the Torah's assessment of health factors.

There is also no evidence to suggest that homosexual behavior was condemned on the basis of choice. Indeed, both Talmuds (B. Sanhedrin 75a; J. Shabbat 14:4, 14d) roundly prohibit even for curative purposes a sexually sick man from having relations with a woman otherwise prohibited to him (see Maimonides, M.T. Hilkhot Yesodei Ha-Torah 5:9). Note that it is not the sexual orientation, which may or may not be of one's choosing, that is subject to opprobrium, but its expression in behavior. It is precisely the chosenness of the behavior that argues against any analogy with the mamzer (i.e., a child of a biblically prohibited relationship).

The subject of choice is important for the understanding of the nature of love. Despite the fact that love is the quintessential expression of human choice, many claim to be its victim as if love were a condition. This sense is reinforced by the metaphor "falling in love." Nothing creates the sense of helplessness more than the feeling of falling. Although this sense of helplessness may characterize the feelings of teenage love, it rarely characterizes mature adult love. As M. Scott Peck's notes in his chapter "Love is Not a Feeling," in his book *The Road Less Traveled*, the misconception that love is a feeling results from confusing the process by which an object become important to us with actual loving. Mature love, according to him, is less a feeling than a commitment and the exercise of wisdom, since love is, "the will to extend oneself for the purpose of nurturing one's own or another's spiritual growth." Love cannot be reduced to a happening, nor is it effortless. On the contrary, love is a process that demands considerable investment of resources, material and spiritual. It is at least as much volitional as it is emotional. In this sense, true love is not the feeling of being overwhelmed, but a purposeful thoughtful decision. Thus a better metaphor than "falling in love" is that of "a labor of love." Indeed, without labor there may be no love, for no love will long last without laboring at it.

The biblical expression "Love your neighbor as yourself" reads literally "Love to your neighbor....," meaning, "Act lovingly to your neighbor as you would have your neighbor act lovingly to you." The point is that love is as love does. Precisely because love is as love does, one cannot claim to love while one is abusing. How often have abusive husbands excused their behavior while protesting their love. Describing love as "falling" promotes the belief that one has no control over whom one loves. From here to believing that one can love while mistreating is not a big step.

The belief that being in love is being passive or being out of control engenders the belief that one is a victim of love. Such expressions facilitate the refusal to take responsibility for one's acts. As long as I am allowed to perceive love as an external force operating on me, I do not have to own up to the attendant commitments of a relationship. In fact, whereas teenagers fall in love, adults commit to love. Loving is correlated with the will to love. Adopting teenage love as the model of love results in still another case where the claim to victimization can be exploited to avoid moral accountability.

The result of teenage love becoming the model of human love has also had a destabilizing impact on married love as a long-term relationship. How often have we heard of people justifying their divorce on the claim that they do not feel the same way as when they were married. The assumption is that love is static. Static love can easily ooze into stagnant love. No adult loves their spouse thirty years after marriage the same way they did upon marriage. Mature love assumes growth. The difference is more of quality than quantity. While teenage love is oftentimes a losing of oneself in the other, adult love is just as often a gaining of self. In the former, people live off each other; in the latter, they nurture each other. So often teenage love claims that it cannot live without the other, whereas adult love is more often a living for each other. This accounts for the intensity of teenage love being swallowed up in the present as if there were no tomorrow, while adult love is so future oriented. When love is felt as a losing of self or as being swallowed up, it evidences total emotional dependency. As such, its dissolution can lead to the contemplation of taking one's own life or even the other's. In the former, the rejected despairs over a life no longer felt worth living; in the latter, he figures that if he cannot have her nobody can. In either case, such responses to unrequited love show how much the love involved a feeding off of each other. This is quite visible evidence to how much the gap between teenage and adult love is comparable to the gap between symbiotic love and synergetic love.

The difference is most evident when viewing the beloved not only as a mate but also as a parent of one's children. Where there is no commitment to the welfare of the other, there is no commitment to the future. In such cases, it is as easy to fall out of love as it is to fall in. In neither case is there any residue of responsibility. When marriages, which never got beyond teenage love, end in divorce, they tend to produce deadbeat dads who refuse to meet their obligations to wife and child. Conceiving and experiencing love as a losing of a sense of self paves the way for a losing of a sense of responsibility.

Once love is understood as a choice and not as a falling, it becomes subject to the standards of adult accountability. Adults choose to love, choose whom to love, and choose how to love. In so far as love is expressed in behavior it is a product of choice. This applies whether it be heterosexual or homosexual behavior. It is precisely the chosenness of such behavior that argues against any analogy with the mamzer. A mamzer is a product of parental behavior, not one's own. If an analogy is in order, kleptomania may, however poor, be an instructive one. Feeling that what is their own cannot have much worth, kleptomaniacs take things precisely because they belong to others. Notwithstanding our compassion for the low esteem that generates the characterological problem of kleptomania, we still cannot condone the stealing. In both cases, compassion for a person's orientation however involuntary does not entail approval of behavior. Moreover, even if judgments are to be mitigated because of duress, psychological pressure is still not the mitigating factor that physical coercion is.

Whatever the truth of the genetic origin of homosexuality, it is evident that social conditions enhance its expression especially for borderline cases. Even the advocates of a neurobiological etiology are unable to identify those genes which carry, as it were, a homosexual code. The most that can be affirmed is that it is polygenic. Even those who argue for a neurobiological base realize that it is only part, however great, of the case. It is simply not possible to achieve total correlation between genes or chromozones and behavior in healthy people. Were it otherwise, the spiritual dignity of humankind would be seriously compromised, for human beings would be nothing more than automatons of the body. A total correlation between chromosomes and behavior would reduce human behavior to instinct and undermine any claim to human freedom. In actuality, there is hardly any human behavior that is not a product of both biology and choice. It is precisely the distinctive combination between the two that makes humans unique in the animal kingdom. Since no single factor accounts for sexual identity all the more so for its existence, it is clear that expressions of homosexuality as that of heterosexuality are multifactorial.

Gender distinctions are not absolute. Male and female represent the neurobiological and psychological poles of a continuum. Whereas moving from one pole to the other is rare, sliding along the continuum is not, especially among the young when gender identity is still in formation. Such sliding may be a product of nurture as much as nature. Much of the content of sexual roles results from observation and imitation of others. If neural correlates are as plastic as some researchers claim, then clearly some neural links are reinforced by repeated behavior. In any case, certain environments encourage the expression of one predisposition over another. Latent tendencies properly cultivated become overt. Frequently, all that is needed are role-models and supportive surroundings. While it is theoretically possible to distinguish between biological gender and gender identity and to make a further distinction between them and sexual orientation, those concerned with the stability of family life have a vested interest in maximizing the convergence between the three so that gender, identity, and orientation follow normative lines. It is precisely because we understand our social codes to be the result of nature and design, human and divine, that we are so concerned that Jewish life foster environments which encourage optimal Jewish behavior.

Jewish public policy is responsible for the health of the Jewish community. As such its primary, though not exclusive, concern is with those trying to raise wholesome Jewish families. While it is admirable to reach out and to "enfranchise" a group of Jews into the community, it is important to realize that outreach always has an impact on the cohesiveness of any community. Frequently, it is a price worth paying, but not at the expense of those whose life-style reflects a long term commitment to the continuity of the community. From the point of view of market strategy, it is unwise to risk the loyalty of an already committed population for the possibility of securing that of a questionable one, especially one unable to perform the basic function of continuity.

Some people have considered leaving more liberal movements for more conservative ones when the former legitimate homosexuality. To call this "homophobia" sheds no more light on the phenomenon than calling its opposite "heterophobia." People tend to join synagogues in search of a community of shared values in order to provide themselves and their children with a haven from the corrosive impact of popular culture. Common values are predicated on shared convictions about what is right and what is wrong, what is decent, and what is obscene. Otherwise, there is no communal bonding. For a religious community to bond, it must not only share a sense of what is noble and what is base, but also what is sacred and what is profane.

There are those who would preclude rabbinic involvement in commitment ceremonies for homosexuals, but allow for their presence. Rabbinic presence at alternative lifestyle ceremonies, however, can serve to validate the lifestyle. The nonverbal message could be that one lifestyle is as good as another. Since the implication of the term "lifestyle" itself is that choice is the basis of validity, it would border on naïveté to discount the symbolic meaning of rabbinic presence Regardless of what is said to the contrary, words rarely erase visual perceptions. What we do speaks so loudly, it is difficult to hear what we say to the contrary. Prohibiting rabbis from the performance of such ceremonies while permitting their presence *qua* rabbis is disingenuous. To make public distinctions the significance of which is not comprehendible by the public is poor policy. In the public mind, rabbinic presence is understood as condonation if not approval.

In sum, religious legitimation of extra-normative sexual relationships threatens to undermine the privileged position of normative marriage. Such legitimation tends to equalize the status of the two especially in the eyes of children. Instead of being a social ideal, family-centered marriage would become simply another alternative. Reduced to an option for some, it would lose its status as social ideal. Already a besieged institution, it is questionable whether its protective walls can withstand much more battering.

What should be done? I move that: We affirm the privileged position of the family as the key to Jewish life and continuity; we express our concern for the humanity and the plight of the homosexual; we ban all homosexual activity for candidates and members of the rabbinate and cantorate, thereby setting standards for the Conservative movement as a whole; we not ordain self-declared homosexuals nor accept them into our professional organizations; and, we prohibit any involvement with ceremonies which serve to confirm Jewishly homosexual relationships.

EH 24.1992d

ON HOMOSEXUALITY

Rabbi Mayer Rabinowitz

This paper was approved by the CJLS on March 25, 1992, by a vote of eight in favor, five opposed, and ten abstaining (8-5-10). Voting in favor: Rabbis Kassel Abelson, Arnold M. Goodman, Aaron L. Mackler, Mayer Rabinowitz, Avram Israel Reisner, Chaim A. Rogoff, Morris Shapiro, and Gerald Skolnik. Voting against: Rabbis Richard L. Eisenberg, Dov Peretz Elkins, Howard Handler, Joel E. Rembaum, and Gordon Tucker. Abstaining: Rabbis Ben Zion Bergman, Stanley Bramnick, Elliot N. Dorff, David M. Feldman, Samuel Fraint, Jan Caryl Kaufman, Reuven Kimelman, Herbert Mandl, Lionel E. Moses, and Joel Roth.

The Committee on Jewish Law and Standards of the Rabbinical Assembly provides guidance in matters of halakhah for the Conservative movement. The individual rabbi, however, is the authority for the interpretation and application of all matters of halakhah.

For those of us who consider ourselves halakhic Jews, it is sometimes difficult and challenging to reconcile our dedication to the halakhic process with our concern for the needs of the individual. One of the most challenging such issues is homosexuality.

While the halakhah itself may not always change to suit the purposes or conditions of individual Jews, the halakhic community must concern itself with both "halakhah" and "community."

Both Rabbi Artson[1] and Rabbi Roth[2] have written detailed תשובות representing two diametrically opposed points of view. Rabbi Artson would sanctify a monogamous homosexual relationship, while Rabbi Roth upholds the traditional halakhic view that prohibits homosexual acts. Both reach their conclusions based upon detailed analysis of the relevant texts — biblical and rabbinic — as well as information gathered from psychiatrists, psychologists, sociologists and anthropologists.

However I find that both papers have missed some very important elements in this issue, and neither represents a consensus of the CJLS.

It is very clear that the prohibition against homosexuality is biblical.[3] Nowhere does the Torah explain the reason why homosexuality is prohibited. While the Torah uses the term תועבה to describe homosexuality, the Torah does not explain why it is a תועבה.

Rabbi Artson's attempt to separate a loving monogamous homosexual relationship from the term תועבה falls short. He attributes reasons and conditions to the text which are simply not there. Rabbi Roth's analysis of whether תועבה is an inherent or attributed qual-

---

[1] "Gay and Lesbian Jews: A Teshuvah," presented to the CJLS.
[2] Joel Roth, "Homosexuality," above, pp. 613-675.
[3] Lev. 18:22 and 20:13.

ity also misses the point. Since we do not know the reason why it is a תועבה, it makes no difference whether the quality is attributed or inherent. Therefore, any attempt to change the law on the basis of reasons is impossible.

In order to define a halakhic position on homosexuality, we must deal with the prohibition itself, and not with the variety of reasons or interpretations offered.[4] The very fact that there are many interpretations proves that we do not know why homosexuality is prohibited.

A biblical law may be changed by either reinterpretation or abrogation. The verses in Vayikra leave no room for interpretation; they are clear, specific and the intention is directly stated.[5] We are left, therefore, with the possibility of utilizing the method of לעקור דבר מן התורה, of abrogating biblical law. In order to determine if this method is applicable to the issue of homosexuality we must understand this concept of abrogation and its application.

The rabbis have the power to abrogate biblical law.[6] This right was exercised infrequently, as a last resort, and only when the Rabbis were convinced there was sufficient cause and compelling reason to do so. At the same time, they were convinced that it had to be done for the betterment of the Jewish people as a whole, not simply for the benefit of a minority of the people. An examination of the precedents for the abrogation of biblical law indicates that this process was applied only for such compelling reasons as preserving family life,[7] maintaining a livelihood,[8] and protecting against the erosion of halakhah.[9]

Both Rabbis Artson and Roth have discussed the etiology of homosexuality. Many others have done so as well. What is clear is that there is no agreement in the literature as to the cause, manifestation and treatment of homosexuality. Therefore, it is impossible at this time to "prove" that there are as yet grounds for abrogating biblical law. Even if we were to be presented with absolute proof that homosexuality is genetic, the burden of proof would be on those wishing to abrogate the law to show that it is necessary and beneficial for the majority of the Jewish people.

The first commandment given by God in the Torah is the commandment to procreate.[10] The biblical premise is that of heterosexuality.[11] There is no doubt that heterosexuality is the world view of the Torah and the Rabbis. This is how Judaism understands the will of God. The fact that procreation may be possible through new techniques such as artificial insemination and surrogate motherhood, as well as adoption, does not negate the premise of heterosexuality that Judaism adheres to as the will of God. Therefore these techniques do not present sufficient reason to abrogate the law.

All legal systems aim to incorporate the needs and requirements of the largest number of members of the group for the benefit of the group as a whole. However, there is

---

[4] Some examples of rabbinic interpretations are: *Sefer HaHinukh*, 209; Torah Temimah, Lev. 18:22; Tosafot and Rosh, B. Nedarim 51a, s.v. תועה אתה בה; Rabbi David Hoffman in his commentary to Lev. 18:22.

[5] To argue, as Rabbi Artson does, that the prohibition refers only to certain types of homosexual relationships is wrong. משכב זכר in the verse is contrasted to משכב אשה. To claim a restriction on one would require the same to be said about the other. In fact, a loving monogamous heterosexual relationship for men was not known or prescribed in the Torah.

[6] B. Yevamot 89b-90b. See also Tosafot Nazir 43b, s.v. והאי.

[7] M. Eduyot 6:1.

[8] B. Sanhedrin 2b-3a; B. Gittin 36a-36b.

[9] B. Berakhot 54a; 63a.

[10] Gen. 1:28.

[11] Gen. 2:18ff.

no legal system that does not impose some restrictions upon a minority of the group. These restrictions are imposed because the law gives the greater value to the overwhelming majority. Not everyone is given the same opportunity or protection. There is no legal system that can take into consideration the needs of each individual in the group. Consideration of חוששין למיעוטא[12] — of whether we take into account the needs of the minority of cases — is rejected for practical reasons, because it would be impossible to maintain a system if every minority or exception were incorporated into the law.

In addition, even if we are willing to take into consideration the new techniques of procreation, the needs of a minority, and a definite knowledge of the etiology of homosexuality, there still remains the question of whether abrogating the law is for the betterment of the majority. There is no doubt that the abrogation will benefit the homosexual community. However, we must be convinced that this abrogation will definitely benefit the non-homosexual community as well. המוציא מחברו עליו הראיה,[13] the burden of proof is upon those advocating the change.

The approach of the Torah and rabbinic Judaism's understanding of God's will concerning the issue of homosexuality should not have to be defended. The burden of proof is on those who wish to change the law. The majority, and not the minority, is the basis upon which the question should be decided.

The halakhic community has always tried to accommodate individuals who may violate religious injunctions. Norms have been maintained, while those who do not or cannot observe the norms were and are still part of the community. This is done out of a concern for the survival of Judaism, and sensitivity to the situations of human beings and the realities of life. An example of this is the way the CJLS dealt with the various issues concerning Shabbat in the 1950s.[14] A similar approach must be used in the case of homosexuality. We must differentiate between the norm and the individuals who violate it. The burden is upon those who observe the norm to make those who do not observe it feel part of the community.

However, we must draw a distinction between those Jews who do not observe the prohibitions against homosexuality, and those who openly advocate homosexuality as a viable, alternate Jewish lifestyle. The Jewish community must be educated to understand and accept homosexuals, many of whom are committed Jews. They must be welcomed in our synagogues and organizations, and we must make them feel a part of our community.

Therefore, we declare that it is a prohibition for synagogues, individuals and organizations to discriminate against gays and lesbians. By prohibiting this type of behavior, and by educating the community, we can succeed in eliminating within our organizations and synagogues the unfair use of homosexuality as a weapon.

Private sexual practices should not be a criterion for office or for leadership. When such a preference does become known, but not advocated as a viable alternate Jewish lifestyle, it should be treated in the same manner as we treat our other violators of halakhic norms.

Each of us makes choices as to what we will or will not observe; then we resolve for ourselves the conflicts that our choice creates. The community does not judge us on the basis of these conflicts, nor should it judge the homosexual on the basis of his or her homosexuality alone. The community, rather, must be a support and a haven for any Jew

---

[12] B. Yevamot 119a.

[13] B. Yoma 9a; Bava Kamma 6b.

[14] Mordecai Waxman, ed., *Tradition and Change*, pp. 327-407.

in conflict, and should, through acceptance and compassion, help the Jew come closer to resolving those conflicts.

However, the homosexual who openly advocates homosexuality as a totally acceptable alternate Jewish lifestyle represents a very different problem to the Jewish community. In maintaining his or her position, the "advocate" openly and clearly promotes a position which is contrary to halakhah, the ideals and norms of Judaism. It is, therefore, unfair and inappropriate that such "advocates" hold positions of honor or leadership within congregations, communities and schools committed to halakhah. We would not extend those privileges, for example, to those who would claim that non-שמירת שבת is an acceptable alternate Jewish lifestyle. A position of leadership or honor requires a commitment to the norms of halakhah.

The creation of synagogues or other religious institutions specifically for a group that advocates a position that is contrary to halakhah is inconsistent with a commitment to halakhah. Each institution has sub-groups within the membership that share common interests and needs. There is no need to develop new institutions for each sub-group. In fact, it is the responsibility of our institutions and synagogues to welcome homosexuals as members, and to offer them all the privileges available with membership. However, any organized action or program that would advocate homosexuality as an acceptable viable Jewish lifestyle would be prohibited.

Membership categories should reflect the traditional heterosexual premise of Judaism, that is to say, family membership in a category that applies to people who are blood relatives, or whose status as a family is recognized and sanctified by Judaism.

Jews who wish to enter the rabbinate, cantorate or the field of Jewish education as leaders of the community must abide by the halakhic norms that the community accepts and sets. Therefore, those who "advocate" homosexuality as an acceptable alternate Jewish lifestyle would not and may not be accepted. It is understood that religious leaders commit themselves to leading halakhic lives that uphold the norms of Judaism. All Jewish religious leaders face conflicts between their personal practice and commitments to halakhah, or between their needs and adherence to halakhah. Nevertheless it is expected that when one's personal needs or practice are no longer consistent with the accepted norms of halakhah, such leaders will resign their positions. This is a choice all of us face, and these choices dictate where and how we live and in what profession we work.

Halakhah does not guarantee the right for everyone to become a rabbi or cantor or Jewish leader. Theoretically, it does provide the opportunity to do so if certain requirements are met. The advocacy of a position that is opposed to a norm, such as homosexuality, would and does disqualify such a person. It is not a matter of fairness or "rights." It is a matter of "obligation" – חיוב – and how one settles personal conflicts with halakhah.

Conclusions

1. Judaism's view of the will of God as expressed in the Torah and by the Rabbis is that of heterosexuality.

2. The only way to change the halakhah concerning homosexuality is by means of abrogating biblical law – לעקור דבר מן התורה. In order to do so, the needs of the majority of the community must prevail, and it must be shown that such abrogation is for the overall good of the Jewish community.

3. We hereby declare that it is an איסור – a prohibition – to discriminate against gays or lesbians in all areas of life.

4. We hereby declare that it is an איסור – a prohibition – to discriminate against gay and lesbian individuals in synagogue membership.

5. Homosexuals who advocate homosexuality as an acceptable alternate Jewish lifestyle are prohibited from holding positions of leadership in our synagogues, institutions and schools.

6. It is a חיוב – an obligation – for our synagogues, institutions and schools to welcome homosexuals (non-advocates), and to offer them the same privileges offered to all other members, many of whom have conflicts between their personal lives and needs, and their commitment to halakhah.

EH 24.1992e

JEWISH NORMS FOR SEXUAL BEHAVIOR: A RESPONSUM EMBODYING A PROPOSAL

Rabbi Elliot N. Dorff

This paper was approved by the CJLS on March 25, 1992, by a vote of eight in favor, eight opposed, and seven abstaining (8-8-7). Voting in favor: Rabbis Ben Zion Bergman, Elliot N. Dorff, Richard L. Eisenberg, Dov Peretz Elkins, Howard Handler, Jan Caryl Kaufman, Joel E. Rembaum, and Gordon Tucker. Voting against: Rabbis Stanley Bramnick, Samuel Fraint, Arnold M. Goodman, Reuven Kimelman, Herbert Mandl, Avram Israel Reisner, Joel Roth, and Morris Shapiro. Abstaining: Rabbis Kassel Abelson, David M. Feldman, Aaron L. Mackler, Lionel E. Moses, Mayer Rabinowitz, Chaim A. Rogoff, and Gerald Skolnik.

The Committee on Jewish Law and Standards of the Rabbinical Assembly provides guidance in matters of halakhah for the Conservative movement. The individual rabbi, however, is the authority for the interpretation and application of all matters of halakhah.

Rabbi Roth and Rabbi Artson have each written well-researched and passionate תשובות on homosexuality. Each of them, though, assumes that we know much more about the relevant facts concerning homosexuality than we actually know. I understand fully the desire to come to definitive decisions about this matter, for it affects many lives and arises inevitably and perhaps often in a rabbi's service. Moreover, human beings often manifest what Dewey called a "quest for certainty" – for psychological, if not for philosophical or social, reasons. We like to have things neat and clean. It gives us a sense of security and order. It also confirms our sense of self. The world in which we live, however, is, as Dewey noted, not static or easily defined, and so that quest is not only misguided, but potentially dangerous.

Law that comes out of the need for certainty when none can legitimately be had is always bad law. The same is true for ethics. As Aristotle said, "Our discussion will be adequate if its degree of clarity fits the subject-matter; for we should not seek the same degree of exactness in all sorts of arguments alike, any more than in the products of different crafts."[1]

For reasons that I shall delineate below, we do not know enough now to make a definitive decision on homosexuality. In that situation, adopting either Rabbi Roth's or Rabbi Artson's responsum is, at least at this time, a "no-win" situation for us, and adopting both is worse. Still, I can provide somewhat more detail than I previously supplied as to the nature of the study I propose and the interim policies I am suggesting. I am,

---

[1] Aristotle, *Nicomachean Ethics*, ch. 3; cf. ch. 7.

therefore, writing now to summarize and supplement the arguments I have presented at our last two meetings for my three-pronged proposal — namely, that,

(1) We, as the Committee on Jewish Law and Standards, affirm the 1990 Rabbinical Assembly resolution on gay and lesbian Jews and the similar 1991 resolution of the United Synagogue of Conservative Judaism.[2]

(2) We ask the President of the Rabbinical Assembly, the Chancellor of the Jewish Theological Seminary of America, and the President of the United Synagogue of Conservative Judaism — the three leaders whose appointments we bear — to constitute a commission that would spearhead a movement-wide study of both heterosexual and homosexual norms. The study should examine all relevant halakhic precedents, guided by responsa already submitted to the CJLS and any other material written for it; solicit germane expert scientific testimony; investigate pertinent sociological realities; and address the theological and moral concerns involved in these issues as it seeks to make a judgment as to good social policies for the Conservative movement on sexuality. The commission should include rabbinic and lay members, men and women, heterosexuals and homosexuals, and a cross-section of ages. The educational arms of the Movement should be engaged in creating appropriate educational materials and programs on these issues for teenagers and adults as part of the process of this Movement-wide study. The commission should be asked to report its findings to the three leaders who constituted it and to the Committee on Jewish Law and Standards as soon as possible, but hopefully no later than three years from the adoption of this proposal.

(3) In the meantime, as according to our usual procedures, the status quo norms will remain in effect. Specifically,

(A) We will not perform commitment ceremonies for gays or lesbians.

(B) We will not knowingly admit avowed homosexuals to our rabbinical or cantorial schools or to the Rabbinical Assembly or the Cantors' Assembly. At the same time, we

---

[2] The Rabbinical Assembly resolution (*Proceedings of the Rabbinical Assembly* 52 [1990]: 275) is as follows:

GAY AND LESBIAN JEWS

WHEREAS Judaism affirms that the Divine image reflected by every human being must always be cherished and affirmed, and

WHEREAS Jews have always been sensitive to the impact of official and unofficial prejudice and discrimination, wherever directed, and

WHEREAS gay and lesbian Jews have experienced not only the constant threats of physical violence and homophobic rejection, but also the pains of anti-Semitism known to all Jews and, additionally, a sense of painful alienation from our own religious institutions, and

WHEREAS the extended families of gay and lesbian Jews are often members of our congregations who live with concern for the safety, health and well-being of their children, siblings and other relatives, and

WHEREAS the AIDS crisis has deeply exacerbated the anxiety and suffering of this community of Jews who need in their lives the compassionate concern and support mandated by Jewish tradition,

THEREFORE BE IT RESOLVED that we, The Rabbinical Assembly, while affirming our tradition's prescription for heterosexuality,

1) Support full civil equality for gays and lesbians in our national life, and

2) Deplore the violence against gays and lesbians in our society, and

3) Reiterate that, as are all Jews, gay men and lesbians are welcome as members in our congregations, and

4) Call upon our synagogues and the arms of our movement to increase our awareness, understanding and concern for our fellow Jews who are gay and lesbian.

The Nov. 1991 resolution of the United Synagogue was identical, except that it omits the "Whereas" clause on AIDS and the fourth resolution.

will not instigate witch hunts against those who are already members or students.

(c) Whether homosexuals may function as teachers or youth leaders in our congregations and schools will be left to the rabbi authorized to make halakhic decisions for a given institution within the Conservative movement. Presumably, in this as in all other matters, the rabbi will make such decisions taking into account the sensitivities of the people of his or her particular congregation or school. The rabbi's own reading of Jewish law on these issues, informed by the responsa written for the Committee on Jewish Law and Standards to date, will also be a determinative factor in these decisions.

(d) Similarly, the rabbi of each Conservative institution, in consultation with its lay leaders, will be entrusted to formulate policies regarding the eligibility of homosexuals for honors within worship and for lay leadership positions.

(e) In any case, in accordance with the Rabbinical Assembly and United Synagogue resolutions we are hereby affirming, gays and lesbians are welcome in our congregations, youth groups, camps, and schools, and appropriate steps must be taken to insure that this welcome is not empty rhetoric.

I make this proposal for three reasons. First, on the merits of the case, I do not agree with either Rabbi Roth's or Rabbi Artson's reading of the Jewish tradition on this issue for reasons that I shall explain below. Second, even if I did concur with either of them, I do not think that the Conservative movement is ready for either one of the two תשובות before us — again, for reasons that I shall explain below. Finally, I do think that this is a golden opportunity for the Conservative movement to study something together and to say something important about how Judaism should affect a significant area of our lives in contemporary times, and it would be a terrible shame if this opening were lost.

The Impact of Historical Consciousness on Legal Method

First, then, to the merits of the case. Rabbi Roth asks us to see gay sex[3] as a תועבה. He reads the texts of our tradition in a highly formalistic way. As evidenced by his book on halakhic process, that kind of reading pervades his philosophy of Jewish law generally. His formalism is not of the most extreme sort, for he does acknowledge "extra-legal" factors as potential sources for influencing decisions. Nevertheless, his view is formalistic in that the legal process is seen as logical deduction from previous texts of the law. Even in his modified brand of formalism, a very heavy burden of proof must be borne in order to invoke any non-textual factor to alter what the decisor takes to be the meaning of the texts because authority ultimately rests in them.

Rabbi Roth's responsum heavily depends upon his method. Since Leviticus calls homosexuality an abomination (תועבה), the responsum begins with an analysis of what that means. There is no problem in this; indeed, other methods might begin the same way. Where other methods would differ from his, however, is in what comes next. The text, for Rabbi Roth, is so powerful a determinant of the outcome of the law that even interpretations as to *why* the text calls gay sex an abomination cannot be used to challenge the law. Indeed, he tells us that if any or all of the interpretations are "found wanting" — that is, if they do not convince us to maintain the law as stated in the text — "that

---

[3] I am aware that the words describing sexual orientations have taken on political meanings for some people. Let me say at the outset, then, that I intend no such political connotations. As evidence of that, and simply for variety of style, I shall use words like "homosexual," "gay," "lesbian," "heterosexual," and "straight" in roughly equal proportions. That will hopefully enable me to discuss the issues involved without any position preconceived or indicated in the language I use.

proves only that the interpretations are inadequate, not that homosexuality is not תועבה according to the Torah."[4]

Of course, the Torah does call a man's "lying with a man as one would lie with a woman" an abomination, and so in the exclusively textual sense he is obviously correct; the text says what he says it does. The issue, though, is not that, but whether we rabbis should now determine the law in line with that text or not, and it is *that* decision that Rabbi Roth wants to determine on strictly textual grounds. If interpretations of the rationales of the text cannot count for Rabbi Roth against the text itself, factors completely outside the text (like historical context, science, morality, theology) have in his method an even more tenuous hold on the law. They do have some bearing on the law, and in this Rabbi Roth's formalism is of a modified sort. In his terminology, however, such factors are "extra-legal" — outside the law — precisely because he identifies the law with the texts in the first place. Given that assumption, such "extra-legal" factors must understandably have truly overwhelming force to justify any change in the law. It is not surprising, then, that Rabbi Roth concludes thus: "We have found that none of these [scientific] theories, even if assumed to be absolutely correct with no hint of ספק [doubt], negates the applicability of the reasons for which homosexuality is called תועבה [abomination]"[5] — let alone, as Rabbi Roth's specific rulings on homosexuality make clear, the ultimate judgment that it is an abomination.

I think that formalism, even of this modified type, is an erroneous way to understand any legal system, certainly one that has undergone all of the historical vicissitudes of Jewish law. One simply cannot pretend that the texts of our tradition existed in some pristine metaphysical realm in which the only issue was the logical relationships tying one to another. As Supreme Court Justice and legal philosopher Oliver Wendell Holmes Jr. noted almost a century ago, proper legal reasoning is not simply a matter of deductive reasoning from previous texts. It is not a form of mathematics, where one must worry exclusively about doing one's sums correctly; it requires attention to historical context and conscious recognition of the moral judgments each judicial decision involves:

> I once heard a very eminent judge say that he never let a decision go until he was absolutely sure that it was right. So judicial dissent often is blamed, as if it meant simply that one side or the other were not doing their sums right, and, if they would take more trouble, agreement inevitably would come.
>
> This mode of thinking is entirely natural. The training of lawyers is a training in logic. The processes of analogy, discrimination, and deduction are those in which they are most at home. The language of judicial decision is mainly the language of logic. And the logical method and form flatter that longing for certainty and for repose which is in every human mind.
>
> But certainty generally is illusion, and repose is not the destiny of man. Behind the logical form lies a judgment as to the relative worth and importance of competing legislative grounds, often an inarticulate and unconscious judgment it is true, and yet the very root and nerve of the whole proceeding. You can give any conclu-

---

[4] Joel Roth, "Homosexuality," above, p. 623.

[5] Above, p. 663.

sion a logical form. You always can imply a condition in a contract. But why do you imply it? It is because of some belief as to the practice of the community or of a class, or because of some opinion as to policy, or, in short, because of some attitude of yours upon a matter not capable of exact quantitative measurement, and therefore of founding exact logical conclusions. Such matters really are battle grounds where the means do not exist for determinations that shall be good for all time, and where the decision can do no more than embody the preference of a given body in a given time and place.[6]

If the historical method, to which we are committed as the Conservative movement, means anything, it requires us to consider the historical realities behind the relevant texts on any given issue and to apply them with as clear a vision of their historical context as we can muster. We then must compare that context to our own to see if the same norms should apply.

The historical method also, as Holmes rightly states, requires us to recognize that the way in which we choose to interpret and apply received texts depends on an antecedent moral judgment that we make. Historical awareness affects not only our understanding of the past, but of the present and future as well. One who has such awareness must acknowledge that jurists choose *which* of many possible texts to interpret and which to ignore, and they choose *how* to interpret and apply the texts they have selected to examine. In making that choice, their moral convictions inevitably, and often consciously, play an important role, in some cases even a determinative one.

In a religious legal system like Jewish law, concepts of God, humanity, and nature must also affect the jurist's decisions, for in articulating what Jews believe *is* the case, such beliefs set the ideational framework for determining what *ought to be*. In other words, as I see it, moral, theological, social, and historical factors are all part and parcel of the law along with the texts that try to keep up in articulating the law's ongoing development. Consequently, these extra-textual (but not extra-legal) factors can and should have a strong affect on the law without meeting nearly as heavy a burden as Rabbi Roth's methodology would impose.

In theological terms, then, we must *now* determine what we think God now wants of us. In making that decision, traditional texts definitely do play an important role, for they link us to our ancestors and to our heritage, they articulate our tradition's understanding of God, humanity, and the world, and they specify the practices by which Jews have acted on their conceptions throughout history. Moreover, in contrast to Reform positions, we believe that a burden of proof must be borne to deviate from established law — whether that is expressed in the texts of our tradition, in its underlying values and concepts, or in the practices of the observant Jewish community — and we must make such decisions as a community, not as individuals. In the process of our deliberations, however, citing texts is not sufficient and not necessarily the most cogent kind of proof, for we must evaluate traditional texts in light of all that we believe and know. Not for naught did the Talmud warn the judge in every generation to judge "according to what he sees with his own eyes."[7]

---

[6] Oliver Wendell Holmes, Jr., "The Path of the Law," *Harvard Law Review* 10 (1897): 457.

[7] B. Bava Batra 131a. Holmes' philosophy of law was only one of the first alternatives to legal formalism; it is surely not the only one. The precise nature of the interaction between legal texts and the law as lived in the community has been vigorously debated in the twentieth century, most recently by people like Robert Cover, ז״ל, Ronald Dworkin, and Michael Moore. This is not the place to discuss their various approaches and to evaluate the applicability of their theories to Conservative Jewish law. Instead, what I have written in this section is only meant to demonstrate the limitations of the kind of formalism Rabbi Roth espouses, and I leave it to another time to develop some of the positive theses of recent philosophy of law.

The Critical Factor: The Lack of Choice

Rabbi Roth's legal formalism is bad enough intellectually, but here the results of that method lead him — and, I fear, too many of us — to unbelievably cruel results. All who know Rabbi Roth, myself certainly included, know that he is anything but a cruel man. His method of interpreting Jewish law, however, has led him, in this instance, to results that are unquestionably cruel. Since the vast majority of psychological literature on the subject attests, as Rabbi Roth admits himself, that psychological techniques are incapable of changing a homosexual person into a heterosexual one, Rabbi Roth is effectively — indeed, explicitly — asking gays and lesbians to refrain from sexual expression all their lives. That result is downright cruel.

Moreover, it is not halakhically necessary and not ultimately Jewish. On the latter point, I, for one, cannot believe that the God who created us all created ten percent of us to have sexual drives that cannot be legally expressed under any circumstances. That is simply mind-boggling — and, frankly, un-Jewish. Jewish sources see human beings as having conflicting urges that can be controlled and directed by obedience to the wise laws of the Torah; it is Christian to see human beings as endowed with urges that should ideally be forever suppressed. It makes of God a cruel director in this drama we call life, and our tradition knew better. It called God not only merciful, but good. God's law, then, must surely be interpreted to take those root beliefs of our tradition into account.[8]

In the case at hand, the simple fact is that all of the organizations of our time that embody relevant expertise on these issues have officially said that homosexuality is not a sickness and that, in any case, it is not reversible.[9] Of course there are individual psychologists or psychiatrists who hold some other view, but to cite them, as Rabbis Roth and Norman Lamm do, is to choose what are by now isolated opinions in the world of psychology to buttress their weak scientific case. It is just like quoting some of our Conservative rabbinic colleagues who think that we should accept patrilineal descent and then pretending that that is the policy of the Conservative movement. Like it or

---

[8] Along these lines, of all the arguments I have heard over the last six months on this issue, Rabbi Morris Shapiro's is clearly the most intriguing. After our February meeting, he told me that after the Holocaust he no longer can believe in a good God. He therefore sees the commandments of God as decrees that bind us with no pretension of their being good in any of the usual senses of that word. For him, then, the Torah's prohibitions of homosexual sex acts fall under the general rubric of God's inscrutable commands. As he emphasized during our March meeting, we can challenge God's morality, but we must do so out of a sense of humility and, in any case, our challenges do not give us grounds to change the law. We simply cannot understand God but must obey His laws nonetheless.

Rabbi Shapiro has the courage of his convictions, and I sincerely and deeply admire that. My own view on the Holocaust and its implications for our faith, expressed some years ago ("God and the Holocaust," *Judaism* 26 [winter 1977]: 27-34), posits, as Rabbi Shapiro does, that God was indeed involved in the Holocaust. I, however, still maintain the traditional faith that, even with that unfathomable fact, God is ultimately good. It is possible that the differences between us are generational; born in 1943, I, after all, did not experience the Holocaust as an adult, as he did. Instead, I was shaped by the frankly comfortable American environment in which I grew up, and my theology undoubtedly reflects that — although I hope it is not insensitive to human suffering, as evidenced most especially in the Holocaust. In any case, I believe, along with the Jewish tradition, that God, however inscrutable at times, is ultimately good, and that fundamental belief must enter into how I and all who share that belief interpret Jewish law.

[9] The American Psychiatric Association deleted homosexuality from its list of mental disorders in 1974, and similar decisions were made by the American Psychological Association in 1975 and by the National Association of Social Workers in 1977. Although political factors may have influenced those decisions in part, that stance remains the considered opinion of the mental health professions, now with even more evidence. See the *American Psychiatric Association Diagnostic and Statistical Manual of Mental Disorders*, 3d ed., revised (DSM IIIR), 1974, 1986.

not, the clear evidence of the psychological community — clearer now than when they took their respective actions in the mid-1970s — is that homosexuality is not an illness and that it is not reversible.

That, for me, is the critical factor that must lead us to rethink our position on this whole issue halakhically. I am impressed by the massive historical data that Rabbi Artson has brought to our attention about the nature of homosexuality in the past, and it may be, as he contends, that cultic, promiscuous, or abusive homosexual relations are the only ones our ancestors could possibly have meant to condemn since those are the only kinds they knew. We all, though, have read Jewish texts on this issue for so long to prohibit all forms of homosexuality that it is jolting to read them in his way. For me, the jury is not yet in on the issue, especially given two texts: the one in the Sifra[10] that describes the marriages of men to each other or women to each other as one of the practices of the Egyptians and the Canaanites; and the one in the Talmud,[11] which, at least as Rashi understands it, praises non-Jews for at least not writing marriage contracts for people of the same gender who were having sex together, presumably in an ongoing and stable relationship.

What *is* clear, though, is that all the traditional Jewish texts assume that homosexuality is a violation of the law because the homosexual could *choose* to be heterosexual. That, we have found, is definitely *not* the case. Three new studies raise the possibility that homosexuality is genetically and/or neurologically determined — or, at least, that genetic and neurological factors over which the person has no control are major factors in making him or her homosexual.[12]

These, however, are only preliminary results. Moreover, even if we assume that these studies are correct, one can, at least at this point, raise "the chicken and the egg problem" — i.e., do these physical factors, which are different in homosexuals, cause homosexuality, or is it homosexual behavior that engenders these physical features of a person? Further research may someday soon resolve these questions.

What is therefore more cogent for me now is the testimony of gays and lesbians themselves. Constitutional gays and lesbians — that is, those who cannot meet their physical and emotional needs in heterosexual romantic relationships (i.e., those in category six and many of those in category five of Kinsey's delineation) — attest that being gay is not something they chose. In fact, because of the widespread discrimination against gays and lesbians in our society, such people usually denied their homosexual orientation for many years and actively tried to fight off their homosexual tendencies.

Jewish law takes such evidence very seriously. Although according to all of the relevant professional organizations, homosexuality is not an illness, it is a feature of a person that that person is likely to know better than anyone else. In that sense, it is akin (although *not* equivalent) to the circumstances under which Jewish law recognizes a patient's need for food on Yom Kippur: "Wherever the person says, 'I need it,' even if a hundred [physicians] say that he does not need it, we listen to him, as Scripture says, 'The heart knows its own bitterness.'"[13] Thus even if the compulsion is culturally generated rather than biologically so, and even if some people would then claim that the culture must be changed in some way to avoid homo-

---

[10] Sifra, "Aharei Mot," Parashah 9:8.

[11] B. Hullin 92a-92b.

[12] *Newsweek* just recently ran a cover-page article discussing this and other research on the matter. See "Is This Child Gay? Born or Bred: The Origins of Homosexuality," *Newsweek*, 24 Feb. 1992, pp. 46-53. See also "What Causes People to be Homosexual?" *Newsweek*, 9 Sept. 1991, p. 52; and "Survey of Identical Twins Links Biological Factors with Being Gay," *Los Angeles Times*, 15 Dec. 1991, p. A43.

[13] B. Yoma 83a; M.T. Hilkhot Shevitat Asor 2:8; S.A. Orah Hayyim 618:1.

sexuality, for the individual homosexual that compulsion is already a fact of his or her existence — one for which the homosexual himself or herself provides the most reliable evidence and one which, on the best of authority, cannot be altered.

The combination of these sources of evidence, it seems to me, necessitates a rethinking and recasting of the law, *for if anything is clear about the tradition, it is that it assumed that gay behavior is a matter of choice*. Otherwise, a commandment forbidding it would logically make no sense — any more than would a commandment prohibiting breathing for any but the shortest periods of time.

Now, of course, it is logically possible to say to gays and lesbians, as Rabbi Roth does, that if they cannot change their homosexual orientation, they should remain celibate all their lives. As I said before, that flies in the face of some very deeply rooted theological assertions of Judaism. Moreover, it seems to me that that is not halakhically required. If gays and lesbians are right in asserting that they have no choice in being homosexual — and, given the widespread discrimination in our society against them, I have no reason to doubt them in this claim and, indeed, every reason to believe them — then they are as forced to be gay as straights are forced to be straight. That is, gay men can no more extirpate their sexual or emotional attractions to other men and cultivate sexual and emotional attractions of a romantic sort toward women than straight men can expunge their sexual or emotional attractions to women and create them toward men — and, of course, the same thing, *mutatis mutandis*, is true for lesbians and straight women. We are all equally "forced" (אונס) in our sexual orientations.

In discounting this line of reasoning, Rabbi Roth cited the comment by Rava[14] that אונס does not apply to a male's sexual arousal, that having an erection is always voluntary. There are, of course, some problems with this assumption strictly on a factual level. Rava himself recognizes that nocturnal emissions cannot be called voluntary since they occur during the unconsciousness of sleep. Involuntary erections, though, are not restricted to sleep. Males (especially teenagers) often have erections in embarrassing situations where they definitely do not want their penises to be erect. Even if we interpret Rava to be referring exclusively to the context of sexual intercourse, where his remark is more plausible, *his legal ruling would only say that having an erection is always construed to be voluntary; the object which arouses that desire may well not be* — and, indeed, the existence of erections in embarrassing circumstances would argue that it is not.

Indeed, Jewish law seems to acknowledge this differentiation between the voluntarism that produces an erection in a man and the compulsion of the situation or person that may lead the man to produce it. The Talmud specifically includes incest and adultery (עריות גילוי) among the three prohibitions that one must obey even at the cost of one's life.[15] What happens, though, if a person acquiesced to the forbidden sexual act under these circumstances? The Torah already exempts a woman who does this — indeed, that case becomes one of the paradigms for other cases of compulsion. There is general agreement among later Jewish legists that this biblical exemption remains valid even in cases of incest or adultery despite the fact that later rabbinic law specifically provides in such cases that she is supposed to give up her life, if she can, to prevent the illegitimate sex act.[16]

What about a man, though, who has illegitimate sex to save his life? In line with the talmudic assumption that male erections are voluntary, most rabbis do not exempt such

---

[14] B. Yevamot 53b; cf. M.T. Laws of Forbidden Intercourse 1:9; Laws of Courts (Sanhedrin) 20:3. Rabbi Roth cites this point of law above, p. 654.

[15] B. Sanhedrin 74a.

[16] Deut. 22:26-27. Cf. M.T. Laws of the Foundations of the Torah 5:4; Sanhedrin 20:2.

men from the death penalty for such offenses, *but some do!*[17] Even those who make the man liable for capital punishment do so on the explicit assumption that a man can be *coerced to want* to have an erection;[18] he is thus held liable for wanting to engage in the sex act — even though he was being forced into it at the threat of losing his life and even though women so threatened were exempted. I find this latter understanding of his desires implausible and the ruling unfair, but for our purposes the important thing is not that; it is rather to note that even those who take the latter position recognize that a man can have erections in response to people and situations in which he is forced to "want" to participate. This is hardly the level of voluntarism for which we would normally make a person responsible. Most importantly, rabbis *on both sides of this debate* did not automatically assume that the men to whom the talmudic law applied must be passive recipients of the aggressor's sexual advances but rather could be the active partner in the forbidden sex act. This indicates clearly that all of these rabbis knew that male erections were not all voluntary, that sexual intercourse, even for a man, could be coerced.

Thus Jewish law recognizes the fact that we know from experience, i.e., males can be coerced into sex, even as the active partner. אונס — compulsion, that is — can apply to males engaged in sex. That is not what we usually expect in cases of incest, adultery, or rape, and Rava's statement may therefore properly be the judicial standard in assessing culpability in most such cases. The case of engaging in sex to save one's life, however, makes clear that Rava bespeaks a general policy, not an inviolable rule. If his statement is to be consistent with the rest of Jewish law, it cannot plausibly be construed entirely to rule out coercion as an excuse for illegitimate sex for either females or males, even when the latter produce erections in the process.

The Legal Implications of Compulsion

What are the legal consequences if one is compelled to do that which is against the law? Normally, the judgment in Jewish law for such acts is that the person is exempted from any punishment even though the act itself remains forbidden (פטור אבל אסור).[19] Thus, if at some future time this person or any other adult Jew engages in the act *without* being compelled to do so, he or she would be totally liable at law for the infraction. On the theological level, such a person will have committed a sin — that is, a violation of God's will and hence a rift in one's relationship with God. The person who sins willingly must suffer the attendant consequences delineated in Jewish law and must seek to make amends to those he or she has wronged and to God through the process of return (תשובה). The previous occurrence of a situation in which the person was compelled is no excuse for any future time when he or she is not.

The category in Jewish law of פטור אבל אסור, however, normally applies to cases in which the compulsion is *temporary*. The classical case in the Mishnah is that of the person who vows to eat with his friend but is prevented from doing so because the friend or his child became ill or because a rising river prevented the one who vowed from reaching his

---

[17] R. Solomon ibn Adret (Rashba) on B. Yevamot 53b; Responsa of Rabbi Yitzhak bar Sheshet Barfat (the Rivash), nos. 4, 11, and 387; Magid Mishnah on M.T. Laws of Forbidden Intercourse 1:9, in the name of "There are those who say." See also Tosafot to B. Yevamot 53b, s.v. שאנסתהו and s.v. אין.

[18] Kesef Mishnah to M.T. Sanhedrin 20:3. In general on this topic, see *Encyclopedia Talmudit*, s.v. אונס, vol. 1, pp. 346-360, esp. pp. 348-9 (N.B. notes 20-24) and p. 358 (N.B. n. 148) (Hebrew).

[19] B. Bava Kamma 28b et al. See also Sifra on Lev. 20:3; Sifra, "Tzav," end of ch. 14; M.T. Laws of the Foundations of the Torah 5:4; Tosafot on B. Yevamot 54a.

friend's residence. As Rabbenu Nissim explains the passage, the Mishnah's cases are specifically cases in which there is *not* full compulsion *and yet* the person is automatically freed of his vow without the need to go to a sage for release from it, for, as Rabbenu Nissim says, "it never occurred to the one exacting the vow that it would apply if something happened such that one could not fulfill it."[20] The word used to describe what happens to the vow in the first Mishnah of that chapter, in fact, is התירו, "they unfastened (released) it," the verb form of מותר (permitted), a considerably more accepting evaluation of the failure to fulfill the vow than פטור אבל אסור (freed of liability but still prohibited). The Talmud, though, does not go that far. "When a person is compelled," explains Rava, even in these temporary ways, "the All Merciful One frees him [from any punishment] (אונס רחמנא פטריה)."[21] (Notice the theological language embedded in the law on this issue.)

What would happen, however, if the person could never fulfill the commandment because he or she is *always compelled?* The closest parallels to such a situation are those in which our human bodies compel us to do something. That is true, for example, of our needs to eat, to eliminate waste, and to have sex. In each case, Jewish law assumes that we cannot, and indeed should not, refrain from these actions altogether. It regulates, however, the circumstances in which these compulsions may be legitimately met. It says, for example, that we may only eat according to the dietary laws and with proper blessings before and after meals; that we must cover our feces; and that we must restrict sex to marriage. This channeling of our natural energies into a specific path for their satisfaction is one way God makes us holy.

These analogues in Jewish law, then, suggest that if homosexuality proves to be an orientation over which the individual has no choice, then the proper reading of Jewish law should be that homosexual acts, like heterosexual ones, should be regulated such that some of them are sanctified and others delegitimated — or perhaps even vilified as abominations. Putting the matter theologically, as the texts on compulsion do, if human beings can never reasonably require that which a person cannot do, one would surely expect that to be even more true of God, who, presumably, knows the nature of each of us and therefore the commandments appropriate to the various groups of us.

The Remaining Questions Regarding Homosexuality

Why, then, is there any question on this issue? That is, why am I *not now* suggesting that we conceive of homosexual sex as being halakhically on a par with heterosexual sex?

In part, it is because the biological information on which I have based my reasoning above is all very new. In fact, as I have said above, at this point I am more convinced by the testimony of gays and lesbians themselves as to the involuntary nature of their homosexuality than I am by the three recent scientific studies that suggest this view of the matter. Another important piece of evidence is the position taken by all the professional organizations of those having psychological expertise that a homosexual orientation is not a disease and that, in any case, it is not subject to change by the techniques known to them.

Taken together, these data are sufficient for me to affirm confidently that we should no longer see homosexuality as a moral abomination. The tradition, in saying that it was, clearly assumed that sexual attraction to, and sexual intercourse with, people of

---

[20] Rabbenu Nissim's comment is printed on the page of the standard editions of the Babylonian Talmud, B. Nedarim 27a. That the vow is canceled automatically follows from M. Nedarim 3:1, of which this Mishnah is the explanation.

[21] M. Nedarim 3:3 (27a); B. Nedarim 27a; M.T. Laws of Sanhedrin 7:10; Laws of Selling 11:13, 14; Tur and S.A. Hoshen Mishpat, ch. 21; 54:5; and 207:15.

the same gender were totally voluntary. We certainly know enough by now to assert that that is a factual error.

I hesitate, though, to overturn a long history of Jewish norms on this subject by fully equating the moral status of homosexuality with heterosexuality on the basis of the firm knowledge we now have. As disconcerting and frustrating as this may be, to the extent that law is based on scientific information, it must take account of the tentative nature of new findings in an area and be flexible enough to respond to what we know now, recognizing always that more information may make further changes in any of a variety of directions advisable.

Moreover, even if homosexuality were proven beyond a shadow of a doubt to be involuntary, that would still not force a halakhic conclusion. Here Rabbi Roth's point in philosophy of law is absolutely correct: scientific information should inform the legist's decision, but it does not determine it. The decisor must take a whole host of factors into consideration — scientific, moral, social, historical, economic, educational, and theological — and integrate them all into his or her decision.

What are the other relevant considerations in this case?

Of the issues discussed by Rabbi Roth, it is not, for me, the description of heterosexuality as "natural" or "normal" — and, conversely, of homosexuality as "unnatural" or "abnormal." It is rather matters of propagation and parenting.

"Natural" and "Normal"

Rabbi Roth and others denigrate homosexual acts as "unnatural" and/or "abnormal." These terms, indeed, often accompany some of the most passionate anti-gay rhetoric. They express, at least, the feelings of the speaker that homosexual sex acts are revolting, that they do not fit the speaker's understandings of what is right and proper.

When one examines the usage of these terms in arguments against homosexuality, however, one finds that the speakers all too easily slip from using their descriptive meaning to articulating a prescriptive judgment (G.E. Moore's "naturalistic fallacy"). Rabbi Roth's discussion of this matter (above, pp. 628-630) is an example of this danger. He, among others, also wrongly identifies homosexual sex with anal sex.

It certainly is the case, for example, that the vagina excretes fluids that make penetration by the penis easier and less painful for both the man and woman involved in heterosexual intercourse, while the anus has no such feature. That is a descriptive fact of nature. That fact imposes a norm, however, only if one believes that everything natural, in this descriptive sense, is good. That, though, we Jews surely do not believe. We engage in medical treatments, after all, precisely to alter what is the natural course of a disease.

In general, Moore's point is that we cannot deduce values from facts. Facts certainly influence our value judgments, but one needs to invoke and apply a value system and its attendant perspective on life to proclaim some actions good and some bad. It is precisely that value judgment, however, that is in question with regard to homosexuality. Thus calling anal sex acts "unnatural" in a prescriptive sense does not resolve, but rather begs, the question of what our value stance *should* be with regard to such acts.

Moreover, homosexual sex is not the same as anal sex. Lesbians, after all, cannot engage in anal sex; only some gay men do, and some heterosexuals do, too. As a result, anal sex is *not* the equivalent of homosexuality or even of homosexual sex. There is, in other words, a basic confusion of definition here. Homosexuality is an orientation, probably best defined as "the attraction to, and the capacity romantically to love, members of the same sex." This orientation, like a heterosexual orientation, involves sex acts, but it is not restricted to them, for emotional components of romantic love and the many non-sexual expressions of the commitment involved in such love play a critical role in defining the orientation. Both a homosexual orientation and homosexual acts are to be distinguished from anal sex acts, which are practiced by no lesbians, some gay men, and some heterosexuals.[22] As a result, if anal sex is judged as abnormal in either a descriptive or prescriptive sense, it is *that* which we should discuss, not homosexuality or homosexual sex acts *per se*.

Our tradition had an ambivalent attitude toward heterosexual anal sex.[23] Although some sources oppose it on grounds of being "unnatural," that, I am afraid, is deducing norms from facts (Moore's naturalistic fallacy again). Some people — perhaps many — simply do not like it aesthetically. That is good reason for such people not to engage in it, but not a basis for the many disqualifications imposed on homosexuals by contemporary society or by Jewish tradition. The substantive issue regarding anal sex, it seems to me, is the impossibility of procreating that way, and I shall address the important matter of procreation below; but then procreation is the issue, not homosexuality or heterosexuality.

The term "normal" is even more ambiguous and hence even more problematic. Does it mean what the statistical norm of people do? If we understand it in that *descriptive* sense, why should we assume that "normal" behavior, so understood, is necessarily right or good? We surely can think of many cases in which we would say that the majority engage in downright immoral actions — even abominations.

Does "normal" instead mean normative? If it does — and it certainly seems to denote this in some of Rabbi Roth's material — then ascribing normalcy to some acts and abnormalcy to others requires a moral judgment about the acts. But how we should judge homosexuality is precisely the point at issue. It cannot be decided simply by calling it "normal" (in the *prescriptive* meaning of that term) or "abnormal"; that would be begging the question.

Propagation and Parenting

Two other issues, however, seem to me to be more cogently related to our contemporaneous judgment of homosexuality. Propagation by homosexuals may be possible through the new techniques of artificial insemination and surrogate motherhood, but the former, and especially the latter, involve halakhic problems even in the context of heterosexual marriage and, all the more so, outside it. Adoption is, of course, a possibility and, indeed, an honored one in our tradition; but people seeking to adopt a child these days are experiencing immense difficulty in finding one — at least if they want a healthy infant. Consequently, the interest of the Jewish tradition in propagation cannot be met as easily — physically or morally — in homosexual unions as Rabbi Artson suggests.

Rabbi Kimelman and I — and, I would imagine, all of the rest of the Conservative rabbinate — share the Jewish tradition's concern for procreative marriages. It is important to recognize, though, that gays and lesbians increasingly have the same desires. Two decades ago, when we were in the midst of the "Me generation" and when propagation was, in any case, all but impossible for homosexuals, even those who wanted to have children had to resign themselves to the impossibility of doing so. Now, in the 1990s, both factors have

---

[22] I am indebted to Mr. David Bianco for clarifying this for me.//
[23] See David M. Feldman, *Birth Control in Jewish Law* (New York: New York University Press, 1968), pp. 155ff. for a discussion of the ambivalent attitudes rabbis over the ages had toward anal sex. Rabbi Roth discusses this; see above, pp. 628ff.

changed. Marriage and families are "in," and medicine has now provided lesbians and even gay men with the potential for having children. Consequently, it will no longer do, if it ever could, to object to homosexuality on the grounds that homosexuals cannot and, in any case, do not want to, procreate. They can and do — and so the only question is whether the means by which they can and do, namely, artificial insemination and surrogate motherhood, pose any inherent problems in themselves or specifically in the context of unmarried people.

The Jewish emphasis on having and educating children raises an anomaly in Rabbi Roth's position. He is willing to accept gays and lesbians to rabbinical school and to allow them honors in our congregation only on the condition that they remain celibate. That is precisely the stance of the Catholic Church. For Catholics, however, all priests and nuns must be celibate, and so their policy with regard to gays and lesbians is simply a consistent extension of their policy toward heterosexuals training for the clergy. Similarly, the Catholic Church prohibits "artificial" means of propagation (or birth control) precisely because they are artificial, whether used by heterosexuals or homosexuals. Within Judaism, however, neither of those conditions applies: we expect rabbis to marry and procreate — to the point that we even look somewhat askance at those who can but do not; and we not only permit, but encourage, couples who are having difficulty conceiving to use whatever methods medicine can provide to help them have children — with the exception, according to most opinions, of surrogate motherhood. A demand for celibacy of candidates for professional or lay leadership, then, seems to be altogether strange within a Jewish context, even granted our residual problems with some of the new procreative methods.

Beyond these matters of propagation, there is the issue of parenting. One should expect the result that recent studies suggest — namely, that two people raising one or more children do better, on average, than one, if only because two people have twice the time and energy to deal with the children that one person has. These factors of time and energy remain the same whether the two people involved are of opposite genders or of the same gender. This finding obviously does not mean that single parents will necessary fail or that two parents will necessarily succeed, but the availability and skills of two people can reasonably be expected to be a net advantage over one. Moreover, another recent study has given us preliminary information, at least, that children who grow up with homosexual parents are no more likely to be homosexual themselves than children who grew up in a heterosexual environment.[24] It is, of course, also true, as Rabbi Artson notes, that *some* single parents or homosexual couples may actually do a better job of loving and supporting their children (however obtained) than some heterosexual couples do.

As a matter of general policy, though, it is still better, I believe, for children to have both a male and female parent as influences in their lives rather than one parent or two parents of the same gender. That certainly has been the experience of Jewish Big Brothers, which now provides male models on at least an occasional basis for both boys and girls growing up exclusively with their mothers. A Jewish Big Brother helps to some degree to fill in for the absence of the father, but it surely is not ideal. The more we learn about males and females, the more we discover that men and women differ from each other in immensely significant ways. Deborah Tannen's recent bestseller, *You Just Don't Understand*, demonstrates that males and females even talk in gender-specific, distinctive ways, and that betrays much deeper differences in male and female patterns of thought, feeling, and action, as other recent

---

[24] *New York Times*, 21 Jan. 1987, p. C16; Samuel Guze, "Children in Lesbian Homes," *Psychiatric Capsule & Comments*, 6, 4:1-2.

studies have proven. All individuals are unique, but we apparently do share some far-ranging characteristics with the other members of our gender that go well beyond the ways we eliminate bodily waste and our physical roles in sexual intercourse. That means that, all else being equal (which, of course, it seldom is), we should, as a matter of policy, prefer heterosexual parenting over that of single parents or homosexual couples.

Please note: I am not now claiming that these factors — the moral and physical problems involved in homosexual propagation and the psychological advantages of having both a mother and a father — bear sufficient weight to justify prohibiting homosexual relations or to restrict the positions homosexuals should be permitted to assume within the Jewish community. Whether they do or not is a judgment that we as the Committee on Jewish Law and Standards must make in consultation with the Conservative community. Of the various factors that Rabbi Roth and others mention as grounds for their opposition to condoning homosexuals functioning in public roles, these are the ones that I take to have *some* substance. Whether it is enough to justify exclusionary policies of any type toward homosexuals within our Movement is something that we need to discuss openly as a movement.

In the meantime, to sustain both the letter and the spirit of the resolutions of the Rabbinical Assembly and the United Synagogue, we need to do everything in our power to make people and families of all configurations — married, divorced, single parents, singles, heterosexuals and homosexuals — welcome within our midst. We dare not make them feel shunned or alienated by our synagogues or educational institutions — as all too many unmarried adults do. After all is said and done, what we really want is to increase the number of homes in which we can say that each is a בית נאמן בישראל, a faithful home amongst the people Israel. Since such homes come to be only with the education and spiritual sustenance that synagogues and schools provide, our only hope of achieving that goal depends upon taking positive steps to make sure that the welcome that our Movement's resolutions articulate is expressed in our actions as well as our words. Our tradition has depicted ideals of family life, and we may make some decisions about leadership roles with those in mind; but with well over half of adult American Jews finding themselves outside the context of heterosexual, child-bearing marriages, we as a Jewish community had better adjust our institutions and programs fast if we are going to survive as a people. Moreover, as children of God and members of our people, Jews of all sorts deserve no less.

The Readiness of the Conservative Movement for Any Decision on Homosexuality

Having discussed the case on its merits, let me now turn my attention to the community for whom our deliberations are intended. The Talmud, after all, asserts that rabbis may not decree rulings that the community cannot tolerate.[25] While we usually think of that statement as a limit on the court's authority to enact stringencies, it should be understood to apply to leniencies as well. In both cases, the community's readiness for a judicial action must be a factor given consideration. Law does not exist in a vacuum; it can be effective only if it fits its audience. The law should guide and not just condone, but to provide effective direction it must know the sensitivities and practices of the people who are supposed to live by it. Judges in any legal system must be good educators, and that is all the more true for rabbis whose legal decisions are only one aspect of their educational roles.

---

[25] B. Avodah Zarah 36a et al.; M.T. Mamrim 2:5.

Gender identity goes to the very root of who we are as human beings. As a result, even raising the issues surrounding homosexuality threatens many people's understanding of themselves and the way they want others to see them. Fear and apprehension pervade the atmosphere. Part of the fear, no doubt, stems from the threat homosexuality poses to many heterosexuals' fundamental beliefs as to what is right and proper in sexual behavior. Another part of the fear may come from an insecurity in one's own gender identity. The roots of this are very understandable, for human sexuality does *not* come in two, well-defined, exclusive packages, but rather ranges over a spectrum. For most of us, in fact, there is a blend of homoerotic and heteroerotic urges, based, in part, on the estrogen and testosterone that the pituitary glands of every one of us produce.[26]

Our people, even if not Jewishly sophisticated, are predominantly college-educated, bright, and current in their thinking. The vast majority of them, I suspect — especially the younger element, for whom sexual urges are all the more pressing — not only know the new findings of science and psychology regarding homosexuality, but also know that these results require rethinking the whole issue of gender identity and appropriate morals for sex. This is part of what is behind the fact that about half the states of the United States now permit consensual sex among adults regardless of gender.[27] Except for those who are too afraid of this whole issue to talk about it, then, our people know enough, and have been sensitized to this issue enough, to know that a blanket prohibition of homosexuality simply does not accord with scientific facts as we know them now, for it places an undue burden of suppression on those who cannot choose a heterosexual form of expression for their sexual and emotional needs.

They also know and appreciate that gays and lesbians cannot be shunted off to the Reform or Reconstructionist movements, for many homosexuals want to take an active role in the more traditional form of Judaism we embody, especially those who grew up in our own synagogues or in Orthodox synagogues. Some want to be rabbis, cantors, teachers, or youth leaders in our Movement, for they are committed to Conservative Judaism and want to act in a professional role to see it prosper. And so the Conservative laity, I think, is not ready for Rabbi Roth's paper.

On the other hand, most of our laypeople, I think, are not ready for Rabbi Artson's paper either. The new knowledge about the etiology and history of homosexuality has shown us many things, but it is all very new for the vast majority of us. Indeed, it is only my interests in bioethics and the phenomenon of AIDS that introduced me to this whole area earlier than most (the early 1980s), and I personally am still having trouble thinking about, and emotionally adjusting to, the moral and halakhic implications of what we have learned so far.

I am convinced that, with all sorts of exceptions, the reaction of people to homosexuality generally follows generational lines. People currently in their teens, twenties, and thirties by and large react more liberally to homosexuality than do people in their forties, fifties, and sixties. There is a simple explanation for this. As one of my graduate students told me, even if you are a straight who finds the very imagination of homosexual sex acts disgusting, if people you know and love have discovered themselves to be gay, you can no longer think of the phenomenon as something strange and threatening. I have no doubt that the percentage of gays when I went to high school and college in the late 1950s and

---

[26] The relationship between these hormones and sexual orientation, however, is anything but simple. Some studies have found that when given testosterone gay men become more same-sex oriented, not less.

[27] Richard D. Mohr, "Gay Basics: Some Questions, Facts, and Values," in James P. Sterba, ed., *Morality in Practice*, 3d ed. (Belmont, CA: Wadsworth Publishing Co., 1991), p. 406.

early 1960s was no smaller than it is today, but I never knew that any of my friends was gay (although I discovered at the twenty-fifth reunion of my college graduating class that one of my former roommates was). Older people may now know a number of younger people who are gay, but that is not the same thing as growing up knowing such people. Consequently, even if Rabbi Artson is totally correct — and I am not convinced he is — it will take some time, particularly for those of us beyond forty years of age, to see that he is. The same, I think, would be true of my analysis based on biological compulsion.

This need for time for thought and emotional adjustment is true for many of us individually, but it is also true for the Conservative movement as a whole. In the last two decades, after all, we have instituted major changes with regard to the legal status of women within Judaism. We had been preparing for those changes, though, over a long period of time and in many varied arenas. The men and women of our movement have been sitting together for prayer and studying together from early in this century, if not before. The first Bat Mitzvah occurred in 1922, but it was not until the 1960s or 1970s that many synagogue had boys and girls do equivalent things in celebration of reaching the age of mitzvot. Changes in the Jewish marriage contract (כתובה) to insure that divorced women can remarry began in the 1950s. Women were permitted to be called to recite the blessings over the reading of the Torah in 1954, but, again, most synagogues did not begin doing that until the 1970s. Counting women as part of a minyan only became widespread in the 1980s, and only now are Conservative synagogues beginning to hire female rabbis or cantors. The history of this line of development was certainly not always smooth, and we are still feeling the reverberations of these changes. I, for one, am very much in favor of these modifications in Jewish practice to include women, but I recognize that they have taken a toll on our sense of cohesiveness and identity as a movement. We are still smarting from the rancor that some of these changes produced.

We have not had anything like that preparation or time to absorb the new knowledge about homosexuality and the new sensitivity toward gays and lesbians. Quite apart from the merits of the case, then, I frankly doubt that the Conservative movement is ready now to make the kinds of changes that Rabbi Artson wants us to make — and certainly not without a major effort in the Movement to study sexual norms on both the lay and rabbinic levels. The recent, fractious experience of mainline Protestant churches on this issue has been anything but encouraging.[28]

But it is not just a matter of time and education; there are also some hard questions that must be answered before the Jewish community can be expected to adopt anything like Rabbi Artson's position. For example, what would family values be like under such a construction? What is, or should be, the halakhic and moral status of artificial insemination and surrogate motherhood, and does it make any difference if the couple involved is straight or gay?

What, if any, are the implications for children being exposed to the sexual models of all sorts that they are in fact now seeing in their teachers and youth leaders? After all, even those who maintain that there is a biological basis for homosexuality acknowledge that that is only part of the picture and that other factors influence the formation of one's sexual orientation. What does that mean, if anything, regarding openly gay teachers and youth leaders? Or is it a matter of the age of the children or the discretion of the teacher or youth leader, whether straight or gay?

---

[28] See, for example, "Homosexuality Issue Threatens National Council of Churches," *Los Angeles Times*, 7 Dec. 1991, p. B-4.

What, if any, are the ramifications of gay parenting? Are the preliminary results correct — namely, that there are no significant differences in the results vis-à-vis the emotional security and interpersonal skills of the child when cared for by either a heterosexual and homosexual couple? Are the current studies also correct in stating that the instance of homosexuality in children is no greater when raised by gays than by straights? Does that matter?

What shall we say about bisexuals? Do we urge them to act only on their heterosexual tendencies? Is a homosexual "putting a stumbling block before the blind"[29] in engaging in a relationship with a bisexual in the first place?

These questions are precisely that — questions, not veiled assertions. They bespeak deeply felt concerns of our community, though, including this member of it. Thus, even if Rabbi Artson is right, I do not think that affirming his position at this time would be understandable to many in our Movement, and it would undoubtedly lead to derision on the part of those who object to it on halakhic or other grounds.

We are, then, precisely in the situation we should expect when new information has come to light: we know enough to know that old standards must be altered, but not enough to know how. It is this intermediate and tentative position, with all of its ambiguities and frustrations, that, I think, is at the heart of the 1990 resolution of the Rabbinical Assembly that Rabbi Roth quotes and the similar 1991 resolution of the United Synagogue of Conservative Judaism.[30] The very fact that the Rabbinical Assembly and the United Synagogue went out of their way in those resolutions to make sure that gay and lesbian Jews understand that they are welcome within the Conservative movement indicates, I think, that the Conservative rabbinate and laity do *not* want simply to reaffirm that gay relations are an abomination. Why, after all, would we extend ourselves officially to invite into our midst people who openly practice acts so odious as to merit the description "abominations" (not just "sins")? That would make no sense. I think, therefore, that my reading of the tradition on this matter, as indicated above, is a much more faithful rendering of these resolutions than is Rabbi Roth's.

On the other hand, the resolutions' reassertion of heterosexuality, while consistent with Rabbi Artson's position, was intended, I think, to say that we cherish Jewish family values and do not yet know how they can be preserved in the context of a homosexual union. Consequently, I dare to think that my proposal is also more in line with the resolution than is Rabbi Artson's.

I recognize fully that "justice delayed is justice denied," and so homosexuals, in particular, will justifiably feel frustrated by the delay in action on this issue that I am proposing. I also recognize that there is a basic inconsistency in my position: on the one hand, I want us to work to eliminate licentiousness in both heterosexual and homosexual relationships; but, on the other hand, I am not, at least at this time, advocating that we perform commitment ceremonies for gays or lesbians. Needless to say, I am not happy about these results.

The Talmud, though, was wise in requiring rabbis to take community receptivity into account in their legal findings. That does not mean that the law should simply condone whatever the community is doing; on the contrary, religious law can and should be normative, even to the extent of asking the community to stretch in its moral aspirations to become a holy people. There is a point, though, when the elasticity of the community

---

[29] Lev. 19:14, which is interpreted by the Rabbis to prohibit not only a physical stumbling block, but also an intellectual and, especially, a moral one. Examples of this verse being interpreted to prohibit a physical stumbling block: B. Moed Katan 5a. An intellectual one: Sifra, "Kedoshim," on Lev. 19:14; B. Nedarim 62b. A moral one: B. Pesahim 22b; B. Moed Katan 17a; B. Kiddushin 32a; B. Bava Metzia 75b.

[30] See above, p. 692, n. 2. Rabbi Roth cites it above, pp. 673-674. It is drawn from *PRA* 52 (1990): 275.

approaches the breaking point, and rabbis have the responsibility to recognize that point and to frame their decisions accordingly. Otherwise the law may be pristine in its purity and logically correct in its sums — whether in maintaining past views or in legislating new ones — but simultaneously be the source of derision, abandonment, or, worse still, the breakup of the community it was meant to guide and govern in the first place.

If I am correct, then, we do not, as a movement, have at this time a definitive position on homosexuality. That does not mean, however, that we have made no decisions whatsoever. Based, I think, largely on the new information we have about the involuntary nature of homosexuality, we have, through the Rabbinical Assembly and United Synagogue resolutions, rejected the classification of all homosexual relations as an abomination — although some forms of gay sex clearly are an abomination, just as some forms of straight sex are. If we had not done that, the resolution would make no sense. We have not, however, thought through all of the implications of this new knowledge, especially how we should reconcile it with the traditional Jewish family values we cherish. Both resolutions, by juxtaposing our openness to gay and lesbian Jews with our commitment to Jewish family values, ask us, separately and together, to carry out the process of thinking through these two convictions.

The Challenge – and Opportunity – Before Us

The case of homosexuality begs for legal reconsideration precisely for the reason that Rabbi Roth demonstrates — namely, that the word תועבה (abomination), which the Torah ascribes to homosexual sex, does not describe a fact of nature but rather assigns a moral and legal assessment to a given act. Since we now have new knowledge about it, we rabbis have the clear obligation to see homosexual sex anew "with our own eyes" in light of that knowledge. In these cases, even if in none other, Holmes is certainly right: when new facts present themselves, law certainly cannot be a matter of doing one's sums using the previous texts — as if it ever can be.

I am arguing for as open and broad a process of reconsideration as possible. Only if we discuss sexual norms openly with our community can our discussion be informed and legally effective. Only if we frankly and honestly discuss heterosexual norms of sexual conduct before we address homosexual norms can straights have any credibility with gays on this issue. For that matter, when we come to homosexuality, gays and lesbians must be included in the discussion. This whole process may be painful, for if the statistics on heterosexual activity in our society are right, seventy-two percent of high school seniors have had sexual intercourse, almost all while unmarried, and by the senior year of college it is undoubtedly closer to eighty-five or ninety percent.[31] The percentages only go higher as people age further. Rabbis across the continent have confirmed my experience that couples coming to be married during the last ten years or so overwhelmingly list the same address and are no longer even embarrassed about that. Given these realities, traditional norms restricting legitimate sexual intercourse to marriage almost definitely will need to be adjusted — or remain ignored.

I, for one, believe that restricting sexual intercourse to marriage should remain the ideal; with all the sexual license of our society, I still believe strongly in the institution of

---

[31] That seventy-two percent of high school seniors have engaged in sexual intercourse is disclosed in the report of the federal government's Centers for Disease Control, as reported in "54% of High School Youth Have Had Sex, Report Says," *Los Angeles Times*, 4 Jan. 1992, p. A-2. (While I guessed that eighty-five to ninety percent of college seniors have engaged in sexual intercourse when I wrote this responsum, subsequently a definitive study confirmed that guess: Robert T. Michael, John H. Gagnon, Edward O. Laumann, and Gina Kolata, *Sex in America: A Definitive Survey* [Boston: Little, Brown, and Company, 1994], p. 91.)

marriage, in חופה and קדושין, and the reservation of sexual intercourse until then. Contemporary rabbis, though, like those of the mishnaic period, must recognize that not everyone will abide by that ideal.[32] *This, however, should not mean that Judaism then has nothing to say about sexual norms to those who are not achieving the ideal in this area; it should not be "all or nothing."* Judaism, I think, would still have much to say to couples who are not abiding by the ideal. Jewish values relevant to such a situation would include the following, among others: modesty in dress and speech and privacy in sexual expression; honesty and openness in determining the nature of the relationship and its planned duration ("truth in advertising"); compassion and fairness in dissolving the relationship (if that happens) and in dividing the formerly shared property; the Jewish concern for health in communicating honestly about one's susceptibility to AIDS and to other venereal diseases and in protecting each other from them to the extent that that is possible; responsibility in planning for the possibility of children — and for custody of them if the arrangement is dissolved; etc. The process of determining how Jewish values can still instruct an unmarried couple living together may disturb us rabbis and others devoted to the tradition, but it is absolutely necessary if Judaism is going to have any effect whatsoever on Jews' sexual lives.

In view of my interest in an open discussion of these matters, one other thing must be said. As much as I object to the cruelty of Rabbi Roth's ultimate judgments, I object even more to the suggestion he made in the first draft of his paper that his opinion be adopted as the sole opinion that any Conservative rabbi may follow, on pain of expulsion.[33] Our new knowledge about homosexuality is enough *at least* to say that nobody can speak with one definitive voice on the etiology of the phenomenon or on what standards are best for Judaism and for Jews with regard to it. Rabbi Roth's suggestion of invoking precedents of זקן ממרא smacks of witch hunts and inquisitions — and, frankly, of the utter fear many of our Orthodox colleagues have of voicing their honest opinions on many issues and of acting on them. No matter what our various positions on homosexuality may be, we must clearly and definitively reject such a move in order to preserve one of the real assets of Conservative Judaism, its recognition of the dynamism of Jewish history and the consequent wisdom of openness and pluralism in dealing with issues where old certainties are no longer so certain.

My proposal suffers from a procedural problem: a move to table requires a majority, while acceptance as a validated option within the Conservative movement requires six. If the CJLS in its wisdom, then, refuses to table this matter and adopt the plan I am proposing, I will submit my paper as a responsum requiring six votes. Rabbi Roth has softened the application of his position somewhat since our February meeting, and, at bottom, that puts his rulings not far from mine, at least for the present. I, however, would leave it to individual rabbis to determine the status of homosexuals within their synagogues, saving only the prohibition against commitment ceremonies for the interim, while he would be more restrictive. More importantly, he and I disagree on the status of homosexual sex acts for the constitutional homosexual. He sees them as an abomination to be avoided by celibacy; I see them as the only way some of God's creatures can fulfill their sexual and emotional needs and therefore not an abomination *per se*. Clearly, some

---

[32] M. Ketubbot 1:5, its explanation and expansion in B. Ketubbot 12a, and M. Yevamot 4:10 all testify to the fact that in Judea (in contrast to the Galilee) the custom was that a man lived with the family of the woman he intended to marry during the year between betrothal and marriage. Consequently, he was barred from claiming that she was not a virgin at marriage since we assume that he may well be the one who made that so.

[33] For the final version, see above, p. 668.

homosexual sex acts are an abomination, just as some heterosexual sex acts are, and we need to define the spectrum of sex acts, from abominations to sanctified relationships, for both heterosexuals and homosexuals. We need, in other words, to explore both heterosexuality and homosexuality to devise norms that reflect Jewish beliefs and values and that will be taken seriously in our time.

Opening the issue of homosexuality emphatically does *not* entail overturning all the other prohibitions in Leviticus 18 or 20. That is the worst sort of use of the domino theory. As with most applications of that theory, it ignores relevant differences among the various members of the group, differences that fully account for why, contrary to the theory, laws and people do not fall like dominos. In our case, the whole point of this paper is that homosexuality is different from all other sex acts in that list in that current evidence indicates that the homosexual has no choice in being homosexual. It is that piece of new information that underlies a rethinking of the status of homosexual sex acts. This clearly does *not* apply to any of the other acts prohibited in Leviticus. Heterosexuals may surely be tempted to have sex with forbidden human partners or even with animals, but they can, and by law must, choose to channel their sexual energies within the bounds of marital sex.

One last matter: Rabbi Fraint asked whether the number of people we are talking about makes any difference. Yes and no. Yes, if only one or two per Jewish community were involved, I might say we should just shove the issue aside halakhically and deal with the matter solely on the basis of counselling. It takes considerable time, energy, and emotional investment, after all, to rethink patterns of thought and action that we have pursued for centuries, especially when they are embodied in Jewish law. But no, that is not the case. *At the very lowest estimate,* four percent of the human community is homosexual. If the American Jewish community numbers approximately six million, that means that 240,000 Jews are homosexual – almost as many, according to the *American Jewish Yearbook*, as there are in Rabbi Fraint's home town of greater Chicago. If the more commonly accepted estimate of ten percent is used, we are talking about 600,000 – a number equivalent to all the Jews in Chicago, Philadelphia, and Boston put together. Because of the high social and economic cost entailed in acknowledging homosexuality, even on a supposedly anonymous survey, the estimates are, if anything, low.

As I said during the December meeting, I think it would be a disaster for the Movement if the Committee on Jewish Law and Standards approved opposing papers on a topic as central to people's lives as their sexuality is; it would mean that we are totally incoherent. I think it would be even worse, though, if only Rabbi Roth's position were validated. We would then not only be ignored, especially by most of our younger members, straight as well as gay; we would be seen as austere, alienating, and cruel.

This, however, brings me back to the beginning. I strongly recommend that we table action on Rabbi Roth's and Rabbi Artson's תשובות and engender a Movement-wide discussion of appropriate Jewish standards of sexuality for our age. I am convinced that it would not take all that long to devise such standards – maybe two or three years – and that whatever time, money, and energy it would take would be more than worth it. We would be addressing something that, in some form, is part of literally everyone's life, and we would be doing it openly, Jewishly, and, hopefully, intelligently.

I have no special wisdom as to the most effective format for this discussion; that is a matter we should discuss among ourselves and with the educational arms of the Movement. The tasks would be two-fold, probably accomplished in different ways and by different people: (1) to establish Jewish sexual standards for our time, recognizing in that process the values of the tradition, the social realities of modern life, and the new knowledge we have of the дляmation of sexual orientations; and, (2) to educate our constituency as to the product of our deliberations so that they will at least know that Judaism, in this area as in all others, continues to have something important to say to them even if one is not fully complying with its ideal norms. Lay leaders of various ages should be involved on both levels to give us rabbis some input as to both the practices and views of those not as involved with the tradition as we are. Moreover, given that at some point we will want to apply the tradition to homosexual sex, gays should be specifically included in the discussion.

If the CJLS were to initiate such a process, we would be acting as rabbis for our community in a very powerful sense of the title "rabbi," for we would be bringing the values and laws of the Jewish tradition to bear on an important part of the real lives of our people. What we need now is creative vision and cooperative discussion, not a premature lashing out at the "other." We have a golden opportunity in our hands to generate some real intellectual and moral movement in our Movement; we should not miss it.[34]

---

[34] I would like to thank Mr. David Bianco and Rabbi Daniel Gordis, both of whom did me the favor of providing detailed and constructive critiques of earlier drafts of this paper. I would also like to thank the members of the Committee of Jewish Law and Standards, many of whose comments at the three meetings at which this subject was discussed also led to rethinking and revision. That is how we all learn!

EH 24.1992f

THE STATUS OF HOMOSEXUALS IN THE SYNAGOGUE: A CONCURRING OPINION

Rabbi Kassel Abelson

This paper was submitted as a concurrence to the CJLS "Consensus Statement on Homosexuality" and the papers by Rabbis Roth, Kimelman, Rabinowitz, and Dorff. Concurring and dissenting opinions are not official positions of the Committee on Jewish Law and Standards.

The Committee on Jewish Law and Standards of the Rabbinical Assembly provides guidance in matters of halakhah for the Conservative movement. The individual rabbi, however, is the authority for the interpretation and application of all matters of halakhah.

שאלה

Has the time come for the Conservative synagogue to change its attitude towards homosexuality and lesbianism and accord gay couples full recognition as alternative family units, sanctifying marriages and arranging divorces?

תשובה

The question as formulated above seems to be the real question that the CJLS should be dealing with. To my mind, neither Rabbi Roth's nor Rabbi Artson's paper deals directly with this question, though both have mustered much learning and given deep thought to their papers. However I think that there are weaknesses in both papers that make them difficult to accept as the approach of the Conservative movement to this difficult problem.

Rabbi Roth bases his case on the term תועבה. And he points out that "the Torah recognizes תועבה as an attributed quality for matters that are abhorrent to Jews, too." He brilliantly analyses the context in which the word תועבה is found in the Torah, and succinctly summarizes the traditional approach to sex and procreation. His summary of the present-day approaches to the causes of homosexuality is masterful, but superfluous in view of his conviction: "And, if we rejected the classical explanations for why the Torah calls homosexuality תועבה, we would still find ourselves in the position of affirming that homosexuality is תועבה because the Torah attributes that quality to it, and we would still not know why the Torah does so. But, whatever the reason for such attribution by the Torah, knowledge of the etiology of homosexuality would not render it false or unacceptable."

If it is true, as he states that תועבה is an "attributed quality," then the answer turns on who is doing the "attributing." If it is God, then the question is the difficult theological one,

"Does God ever change His mind?" This leaves us with an easy way to avoid grappling with difficult questions — and not only the question of homosexuality, but with most every difficult question where change from an accepted practice is involved, whether it is Toraitic or Rabbinic. However, if the answer is that homosexuality is "abhorrent to Jews" then the question is a sociological one, and answered best by פוק וחזי, by acknowledging that the Torah reflected the abhorrence for homosexuality by the Jews of its day, and it is up to us to determine what Conservative Jews think and feel today — and then to determine, as responsible halakhists, whether this is the direction that we should be endorsing or discouraging.

Rabbi Artson's paper is a fascinating re-creation of a past that may never have existed. "The idea of two men or two women loving each other, living together, nurturing each other — and in that context making love — became a possible self identity only with modernity. The Torah did not prohibit what it did not know." The past did know of close relationships between individuals of the same sex: Damon and Pythias in Greek culture, and David and Jonathan in Hebrew culture. If such close loving friendships existed, why suppose that the existence of such loving steadfast devotion did not also exist in homosexual relationships of the time? If we assume that such relationships did not then exist, if they had existed, why should we assume that the Torah, and later the Rabbis, would have sanctified them? The objections of the later commentaries that homosexual relationships would preclude procreation and lead to family instability would have applied even at the earlier period. In any event, the argument from the imagined past does not point to what we should do today in our communities.

I would agree with Rabbi Dorff that we do not have sufficent information on what our community thinks, feels and is doing in the area of sexuallty in general and in the area of homosexuality in particular. We do need more information and a systematic process of collecting such information should be undertaken. The information should then be fully evaluated in the light of the values of the tradition, before we issue definitive responsa on the subject. In the interim there is a need for guidance for our congregations and our congregants. What follows is an outline of recommendations which should be helpful in dealing with situations which arise in our congregations.

Conclusion

1. Our rabbis and our congregations should not accord new status to homosexual/lesbian relationships.

2. Our rabbis should not be involved in affirmation nor separation ceremonies for gay couples.

3. Synagogue facilities should not be made available for gay ceremonies.

4. Gay individuals should be accepted as members of our congregations. Two individuals living in the same household should be eligible to join the synagogue with seperate membership.

5. If gay couples raise children, the children may be named in the synagogue, become bar/bat mitzvah, or be confirmed, for they are Jews in their own right. Special ceremonies for the acting parents will have to be worked out, acknowledging their roles in the lives of the children, while avoiding any hint of sanctifying their relationship to one another.

6. Individuals who become active in congregations should be allowed to be elected to office and to head committees, but it should be mabe clear that their significant other will not be given special recognition.

7. Gay individuals who openly profess their homosexuality should not be admitted to rabbinical or cantorial school, for rabbis and cantors serve as exemplars of the Jewish way of life.

EH 24.1992g

ON HOMOSEXUALITY AND BIBLICAL IMPERATIVES: A CONCURRENCE

Rabbi Avram Israel Reisner

This paper was submitted as a concurrence to the CJLS "Consensus Statement on Homosexuality" and the papers by Rabbis Roth, Kimelman, Rabinowitz, and Dorff. Concurring and dissenting opinions are not official positions of the Committee on Jewish Law and Standards.

The Committee on Jewish Law and Standards of the Rabbinical Assembly provides guidance in matters of halakhah for the Conservative movement. The individual rabbi, however, is the authority for the interpretation and application of all matters of halakhah.

I was heartened to see that the Committee affirmed the traditional prohibition of homosexuality. I did not feel another resolution was tenable. I wanted to enter into the record the reasons why and offer a text which I found persuasive which is not represented in the other papers appended here.

Our Torah and tradition bear a very difficult message for modern interpreters; a counterintuitive one that I feel strongly is essential. Against rigid orthodoxy, we correctly claim the grant of אין לדיין אלא מה שעיניו רואות (the judge must rely on his own insight). But God's commands are not infinitely malleable and the דיין must as well train his eyes to the Torah and tradition. For the Torah's premise, that of the concept of revelation, is that God gave specific instructions to Israel and that thus, in some sense, it is His word that we are instructed to follow and are always struggling to find. In our tradition, antiquity, that is proximity to Sinai and the events of revelation, is a *prima facie* argument in favor of a practice, rather than its indictment as superannuated, antediluvian, passé.

When, then, can we rely on our own insights, and when do we follow what we have received? I have always held there to be three gradations in the mutability of halakhic prescriptions, roughly as set forth by Maimonides in his introduction to the Mishneh Torah. That which is of recent or popular vintage is most susceptible to our inclinations and by that I mean, effectively, all that is post-Talmudic. Those rulings have their provenance during our own halakhic epoch. Within this category, it is true, we might be differentially more respectful of a Rishonic precedent than one of Aharonic vintage but it is a matter of degree, not of kind.

Worthy of a higher degree of respect are classic rabbinic rulings from the period of Mishnah and Talmud. Ours is a rabbinic Judaism. Many of the institutions which create and inform Judaism as we know it were expounded or created by the men (such they were) of that age. But we too are rabbis equally, both men and women. As Rabbi Solomon Luria writes in his elegant argument for academic freedom in the Introduction to his ים של שלמה (Hullin):

אני אמרתי אלהים אתם ובני עליון כלכם אכן כאדם תדרושון.

> I have said: You are as gods, all heavenly progeny, but you teach
> only as humans.

Our allegiance to rabbinic structures and rulings is profound, they are subject to our faith, but also, ultimately, subject to our best judgement.

The third category, however, is beyond us. It is the category of Torah. Now as to the Sinaitic provenance of any single command many will argue. But we insist that that form of command and response, נעשה ונשמע, a faithful and total commitment, was true of Sinai, and that we are no less committed to a covenant of observance today than we were then. In effect, the text of the Torah, though we understand that it, too, is the product of generations, represents that original covenant. It serves as our constitution and cause, the heart of our exegesis, the font of our nation's self-understanding. In this area, it is not sufficient to claim authority, though as Drs. Roth and Rabinowitz indicate, authority exists to change even the prescriptions of Torah. In this area the standard is much stricter. To abrogate Torah one needs to argue compelling national need, the requirements of Israel's survival. Then, indeed, Torah may succumb — provisionally, at least. Let God or Elijah eventually set the record straight.

In this matter of homosexuality we find ourselves squarely questioning the propriety of a clear Biblical prohibition. While Rabbi Artson tried artfully to dodge that bullet, it was the overwhelming consensus of the Committee that that could not be done. What we debated, in fact, was what I presume to have been the source of Rabbi Artson's involvement — to wit, whether the dislocation and pain felt by homosexuals today was sufficient ground to overturn the Torah's prohibition. Here, I feel, we were led astray by the term תועבה, "an abomination." That term and our profound feeling that it was inappropriate caused much consternation even among those inclined to be most cautious about the Torah's text. It bears stating clearly and repeating that we did not need to and did not, in fact, debate whether homosexuality must now and ever be considered an abomination. We needed only to consider the prohibition. Without further argument, I think the burden of overturning Torah's text, that we act for the survival of Israel, was not met by the private anguish that we heard. I was dismayed, however, by the cavalier dismissal of the voice of Vayikra that was heard in some of our discussions. Others can brand Vayikra as a product of "excessive priestly zeal." We consider it Torah. We choose, as our tradition would have it, to read this very prohibition on Yom Kippur. To disregard this level of commandment is to set every other commandment at risk. We do so at our peril.

Withal, we might consider waiving the Torah's prohibition if we were certain of our grounds. But scientific evidence with regard to the origin and unambiguous nature of homosexuality is unclear. The Biblical and rabbinic creation traditions, on the other hand, are not ambiguous at all. Gen. 2:18ff. reflects the creation of humankind and commands:

על כן יעזב איש את אביו ואת אמו ודבק באשתו והיו לבשר אחד.

> Therefore a man shall leave his father and his mother and cling to
> his wife, and they shall be one (Gen. 2:24).

All creatures were considered, all possibilities were open. A clone of Adam (עצם מעצמי, bone of my bones) would be male. But the result, the fit mate, is woman. We do not need Bavli Sanhedrin (58a, Bereishit Rabbah 18:5) to interpret for us:

ודבק באשתו – ולא באשת חברו, ולא בזכור, ולא בבהמה.

"And cling to his wife" – and not to his neighbor's wife, and not to a male, and not to an animal.

The Midrash, in its response to the anthropomorphic and polytheistic threat implied in the words בצלמנו כדמותנו resolves them thus:

לא איש בלא אשה ולא אשה בלא איש ולא שניהם בלא שכינה.

No man without a woman, no woman without a man, and neither without God's presence (Sanhedrin 38a, Bereishit Rabbah 8.9).

The very fact of procreation, the very first official commandment, argues persuasively the Torah's premise and expectation of heterosexuality.

Now, I understand that this is myth. But it is constitutive myth. It is fundamental to our perception of the world. It makes the Jewish people who they are. If we were to abandon this we could as well abandon the tale of the Exodus or challenge the notions of creation or revelation. Extreme claims, they are not about homosexuality, which in and of itself is not as threatening. They are about Torah and the notion of covenant and allegiance to our received traditions.

Indeed, even in the Torah one can discern clear emphasis on certain bodies of laws, among them chapter 18 in Vayikra wherein the prohibition of homosexuality is found. The exhortation to "do and observe" the "ordinances and statutes" of the Lord (and not those of the nations) is repeated three times to begin the chapter and again three times to end the chapter. Similarly the Rabbis note that the sexual offenses listed must be unusually significant because this chapter begins and ends with the words אני ה' אלהיכם – "I am the Lord your God." The classic Tannaitic exegesis to this chapter speaks volumes, and it is that text that finally convinces me that there is no room to overturn this particular regulation.

We read selections from Sifra, Aharei Mot, *ad locum* (Perek 13):

דבר אל בני ישראל ואמרת עליהם: אני ה׳ אלהיכם. רשב״י אומר: אני ה׳ שקבלתם מלכותי עליכם במצרים? אמרו לו: הין והין. קבלתם מלכותי. קבלו גזירותי! אני הוא שקבלתם מלכותי בסיני? אמרו לו: הין והין. קבלתם מלכותי. קבלו גזירותי!

"Speak to the children of Israel and say to them: I am the Lord your God." R Shimon bar Yohai says: "Am I the Lord Whose sovereignty you accepted in Egypt?" And they said: "Yes. Oh, yes." "You accepted My sovereignty. Accept My decrees!" "Am I He Whose sovereignty you accepted at Sinai?" And they said: "Yes. Oh, yes." "You accepted My sovereignty. Accept My decrees!"

ר׳ אומר: גלוי היה לפני מי שאמר והיה העולם שסופן לינתק בעריות לכך בא עליהן בגזירה, אני ה׳ אלקיכם, דעו מי הגוזר עליכם.

R. says: It was self-evident to He Who spoke and the world came to be, that [Israel's] fate was to be torn apart over sexual mores.[1] Therefore He came to them with a decree, "I am the Lord your God. Know Who it is Who issues you (these) decrees."

---

[1] The Hebrew is not perfectly clear. This might refer to Israel's detachment from its land on account of its transgression, but this interpretation is suggested by the reference to this Midrash on Yoma 75a.

את משפטי תעשו ואת חקתי תשמרו ללכת בהם אני ה' אלקיכם. עדיין יש תקוה ליצר הרע להרהר ולומר שלהם נאים משלנו. תלמוד לומר ושמרתם ועשיתם כי היא חכמתכם ובינתכם.

"My ordinances you shall do and My statutes you shall keep; I am the Lord your God." The evil inclination may yet hope to cause hesitation, saying: "Their ways are better than ours." Therefore the Torah teaches (Deut. 4:6): "Observe and do, for this is your wisdom and insight (in the eyes of the nations who shall hear all these statutes and say: 'Surely this great nation is a sage and insightful people')."

את משפטי תעשו – אלה הדברים הכתובים בתורה שאילו לא נכתב בדין היה לכתבן. ואת חקתי תשמרו – אלו שיצר הרע משיב עליהן ועכו"ם משיבין עליהן... תלמוד לומר אני ה' חקקתים. אין אתה רשאי להשיב עליהן.

"My ordinances you shall do" – these are those matters written in the Torah which, were they left unwritten, would need to be written. "And My statutes you shall keep" – these are those matters that the evil inclination argues against or that non-Jews argue against...therefore the Torah teaches "I am the Lord" – I, the Lord, enacted them; you are not free to retort to them.

ללכת בהם – אינך רשאי ליפטר מתוכן.

"To walk by them" – You may not exempt yourself from them.

ושמרתם את משמרתי – להזהיר בית דין על כך.

"And you shall keep My charge" – a warning to the bet din (to be mindful) of these matters.

Rarely do the words of our Sages speak to us so directly. It is in that light that a judge can do only that which he or she sees. I am satisfied that we did so.

EH 24.1992h

In the Image of God: A Dissent in Favor of the Full Equality of Gay and Lesbian Jews into the Community of Conservative Judaism

Rabbi Howard Handler

This paper was submitted as a dissent to the CJLS "Consensus Statement on Homosexuality" and the papers by Rabbis Roth, Kimelman, Rabinowitz, and Dorff. Concurring and dissenting opinions are not official positions of the Committee on Jewish Law and Standards.

The Committee on Jewish Law and Standards of the Rabbinical Assembly provides guidance in matters of halakhah for the Conservative movement. The individual rabbi, however, is the authority for the interpretation and application of all matters of halakhah.

The policies recently passed by the Rabbinical Assembly Committee on Jewish Law and Standards directly contradict the resolution passed by the Rabbinical Assembly convention in May 1990. The Rabbinical Assembly Convention Resolution:

> . . .affirms that the Divine image reflected by every human being must always be cherished and affirmed, and
>
> WHEREAS Jews have always been sensitive to the impact of official and unofficial prejudice and discrimination, wherever directed, and
>
> WHEREAS gay and lesbian Jews have experienced not only the constant threats of physical violence and homophobic rejection, but also the pains of anti-Semitism known to all Jews and, additionally, a sense of painful alienation from our own religious institutions, . . .
>
> THEREFORE BE IT RESOLVED that we. . .
>
> Reiterate that, as are all Jews, gay men and lesbians are welcome as members in our congregations, and
>
> Call upon our synagogues and the arms of our movement to increase our awareness, understanding and concern for our fellow Jews who are gay and lesbian.

However, the policies affirmed on March 25, 1992, by the Committee on Jewish Law and Standards prohibit rabbis from performing commitment ceremonies for gays or lesbians, and they prohibit avowed homosexuals' admittance to our rabbinical and cantorial schools or to the Rabbinical Assembly or the Cantors' Assembly. In addition, individual rabbis may with full support of the CJLS deny to gay or lesbian Jews the opportunity to be teachers, youth leaders, the recipients of honors in worship and lay leaders.

The CJLS has made gay and lesbian Jews second-class citizens or, even worse, a tolerated minority. Gays and lesbians will not feel welcomed by these recent policies of the CJLS. The policies are discriminatory at best and profoundly oppressive in any event. There is no reason for us to hesitate in accepting gays and lesbians into our community with complete equality. If a gay man or lesbian is qualified to serve as a rabbi or cantor, we should encourage them. If a gay or lesbian couple want to mark the holiness of their committed relationships to each other, we must assist them and celebrate with them.

During the deliberations of the CJLS some colleagues raised two primary arguments against this full acceptance of gays and lesbians. Some feel that gays and lesbians are by their very nature either licentious or inimical to the institution of family. Rabbi Elliot N. Dorff pointed out that it is foolish to think that gays and lesbians have cornered the market on sexual licentiousness. Does any rabbi serve a congregation where the sex lives of his or her congregants are completely pure? That gays and lesbians are more prone to loose sexual mores has never been proven, and even if this were to be, it is very likely a direct result of society's unwillingness to recognize and support gay and lesbian relationships.

Statistics prove that gays and lesbians are increasingly involved in family living. The gay and lesbian synagogue in San Francisco runs a Hebrew school for the children of its members. Recently the gay and lesbian synagogue in New York held a Hanukkah party for members and friends with children. The gay and lesbian community is currently enjoying a baby boom. Many Jews are involved in this phenomenon. Moreover, social researchers have documented that one third of all families have a gay or lesbian member.

During the Committee meetings, Rabbi Gordon Tucker protested that this extreme and rigid iconization of the nuclear family is a distortion of Jewish tradition. Singles of all sorts and lifestyles are and have always been part of God, Torah and Israel. In fact we, the Conservative movement, are often the only family that many single people have. Each and every synagogue is a large family composed of smaller families. Our Movement is an even larger family made up of these extended families. There is room in our Movement for gay and lesbian synagogues. It is sad to note that when the gay and lesbian synagogue in New York City asked to affiliate with our Movement and when the congregation asked to interview Conservative rabbis for the position of Rabbi in their congregation, they received no assistance or support from the Rabbinical Assembly and a negative response from United Synagogue. We rejected a congregation of some 1,100 Jews whose style of worship and Jewish values reflect our own.

Gays and lesbians are very much part of the world of families and many gay and lesbian Jews are part of Conservative Jewish families. We gain nothing by alienating them with offers of second class status. If we were to truly welcome them into our community, we would add many enthusiastic members to the ranks of our Movement.

Members of the CJLS also argued against acceptance of gays and lesbians because a single verse in Lev. (18:22) forbids sex between two men and the Rabbis added to this Torah prohibition a prohibition against lesbian sex. This is not an ethical issue, since there is nothing unethical about two people pursuing their sexual orientation in a loving and committed way. As a ritual prohibition we can preserve or transform it as the Rabbis have done with so many other issues. Our willingness to override the traditional prohibitions associated with homosexuality depends on the degree to which we accept sexual orientation as a given and not a matter of choice. We should conclude as have many others that:

1. Homosexuality occurs in nature;

2. Homosexuality is not a disease or an illness;

3. Sexual orientation is a primary component of personal identity, rather than a description of a sexual act;

4. A significant percentage of all people are gay or lesbian in orientation;

5. The origins of sexual orientation, heterosexual and homosexual are unclear and are to be found in a complex of issues which may include biological as well as psychobiological and social factors; and,

6. Children are no more or less likely to become heterosexual or gay or lesbian due to sexual orientation of public role models.[1]

Having reached these conclusions, it becomes imperative to prevent the unethical and unjust treatment of gays and lesbians. The mechanisms to change the tradition are neither new nor extreme. Rabbi Morris Shapiro pointed out that the mechanism offered to us by Yevamot 89a-90b, בית דין מתנין לעקור דבר מן התורה (a court may make a condition uprooting a matter of Torah law through active abrogation), was restricted by the later generations to the "passive abrogation" of Torah law.[2] Even so, in the spirit of tradition and change, the Rabbis were never at a loss for ways to transform or circumvent a biblical institution when later on it came to be viewed as ethically unjustifiable.

We read in the Torah (Deut. 21:18-21):

> If a man has a wayward and defiant son, who does not heed his father or mother and does not obey them even after they discipline him, his father and mother shall take hold of him and bring him out to the elders of his town at the public place of his community. They shall say to the elders of his town, "This son of ours is disloyal and defiant; he does not heed us. He is a glutton and a drunkard." Thereupon the men of his town shall stone him to death, thus you will sweep out evil from your midst: all Israel will hear and be afraid.

This institution was unendurable and so the Tannaim circumvented the Torah's command as follows:

> בן סורר ומורה לא היה ולא עתיד להיות ולמה נכתב לומר דרוש וקבל שכר.
>
> There never has been a stubborn and rebellious son and never will be. Why was the law written? That you may study it and receive reward (Tosefta Sanhedrin 11:6; Talmud Sanhedrin 71a).

Rabbi Joel Roth has noted that in this case, the Rabbis abrogated a Torah law because of ethical concerns.[3] This is precisely what we must do here. Just as the Tannaim circum-

---

[1] *Homosexuality and Judaism: The Reconstructionist Position*, Report of the Reconstructionist Commission on Homosexuality (Wyncote, PA: 1992).

[2] The importance of this passage has been discussed in many places by modern scholars of Jewish law. See Joel Roth, *The Halakhic Process* (New York: Jewish Theological Seminary, 1986), pp. 190ff.

[3] Joel Roth, *The Halakhic Process*, pp. 154, 303.

vented the Torah's command to stone our rebellious children to death, so must we circumvent the Torah's command to discriminate against gays and lesbians. The verse in the Torah forbidding sex between men and the rabbinic prohibitions against gay and lesbian sex in general can be studied for their historic value but in no way determine or limit our ability to welcome gays and lesbians wholeheartedly into the Conservative movement.

Any and every rabbi may justifiably feel that Jewish tradition offers us the opportunity to welcome gays and lesbians into the Conservative community and to encourage them to participate in the adventure of Jewish civilization to the fullest extent of their capabilities.

I therefore conclude that Conservative rabbis and the Conservative movement through all of its branches, basing themselves on sources from our tradition, can and should:

(1) Welcome gays and lesbians into our synagogues by reaching out to them with offers to participate in our services to the fullest extent of their capabilities.

(2) Encourage gays and lesbians to assume lay leadership roles for which they are qualified, i.e. board member, youth leader, Hebrew school teacher, synagogue executive director et al.

(3) Admit qualified candidates who are gay or lesbian to the rabbinical and cantorial schools of the Jewish Theological Seminary of America.

(4) Acknowledge the importance and holiness of committed gay and lesbian relationships by performing commitment ceremonies for gay and lesbian couples.

EH 24.1993a

PLACING HOMOSEXUAL RABBIS IN CONGREGATIONS

Rabbi Kassel Abelson

This paper was approved by the CJLS on May 19, 1993, by a vote of thirteen in favor and eight opposed (13-8-0). Voting in favor: Rabbis Kassel Abelson, Stanley Bramnick, Jerome M. Epstein, Samuel Fraint, Reuven Kimelman, Vernon H. Kurtz, Lionel E. Moses, Paul Plotkin, Mayer Rabinowitz, Avram Israel Reisner, Chaim A. Rogoff, Joel Roth, and Gerald Skolnik. Voting against: Rabbis Ben Zion Bergman, Elliot N. Dorff, Myron S. Geller, Arnold M. Goodman, Susan Grossman, Jan Caryl Kaufman, Aaron L. Mackler, and Gordon Tucker.

The Committee on Jewish Law and Standards of the Rabbinical Assembly provides guidance in matters of halakhah for the Conservative movement. The individual rabbi, however, is the authority for the interpretation and application of all matters of halakhah.

שאלה

An avowed homosexual who is a member of the Rabbinical Assembly has asked that his name be sent by the Joint Placement Commission for rabbinic placement to congregations. May the Joint Placement Commission place such a rabbi in a congregation?

תשובה

On March 25, 1992, the Committee on Jewish Law and Standards adopted a consensus statement by a vote of nineteen in favor, three opposed and one abstaining. There were five provisions in this consensus statement only one of which applies to the question. It states:

> We will not knowingly admit avowed homosexuals to our rabbinical or cantorial schools or to the Rabbinical Assembly or to the Cantors' Assembly. At the same time, we will not instigate witch hunts against those who are already members or students.

An obvious intent of this consensus statement was not to permit the ordination of gay rabbis and cantors and their admission to the professional organizations, so as to avoid placement of gay rabbis and cantors in congregations. There is also the proviso that "we will not instigate witch hunts against those who are already members or students," which points to a policy of not searching to see if one is a homosexual, or in any way penalizing those who are not "avowed homosexuals." The consensus statement does not, however, deal explicitly with a policy for present members of the Rabbinical Assembly who openly avow their homosexuality. In such cases, it would seem that the first half of the statement would then apply, and we should not place "avowed homosexuals" in congregations. If we were to make exceptions for present members of the Rabbinical Assembly, we would be contradicting the intent of the policy barring admission to the rabbinical and cantorial schools and to the Rabbinical Assembly and the Cantors' Assembly.

Conclusion

In accord with the apparent intent of the consensus statement, the Joint Placement Commission should not recommend "avowed homosexuals" for placement in congregations.

EH 24.1993b

PLACING HOMOSEXUAL RABBIS IN CONGREGATIONS

Rabbi Arnold M. Goodman

This paper was approved by the CJLS on May 19, 1993, by a vote of seven in favor and fourteen opposed (7-14-0). Voting in favor: Rabbis Elliot N. Dorff, Myron S. Geller, Arnold M. Goodman, Susan Grossman, Jan Caryl Kaufman, Aaron L. Mackler, and Gordon Tucker. Voting against: Rabbis Kassel Abelson, Ben Zion Bergman, Stanley Bramnick, Jerome M. Epstein, Samuel Fraint, Reuven Kimelman, Vernon H. Kurtz, Lionel E. Moses, Paul Plotkin, Mayer Rabinowitz, Avram Israel Reisner, Chaim A. Rogoff, Joel Roth, and Gerald Skolnik.

The Committee on Jewish Law and Standards of the Rabbinical Assembly provides guidance in matters of halakhah for the Conservative movement. The individual rabbi, however, is the authority for the interpretation and application of all matters of halakhah.

שאלה

An avowed homosexual who is a member of the Rabbinical Assembly has asked that his name be sent by the Joint Placement Commission for rabbinic placement to congregations. May the Joint Placement Commission place such a rabbi in a congregation?

תשובה

The consensus statement passed by the CJLS on March 25, 1992, states:

1. We will not knowingly admit avowed homosexuals to our rabbinical or cantorial schools or to the Rabbinical Assembly or to the Cantors' Assembly.

2. At the same time we will not instigate witch hunts against those who are already members or students.

The first part of the statement makes it clear that avowed homosexuals are not to be trained as rabbis or cantors or admitted into the RA/CA.

The second sentence makes it clear that we are not to engage in a witch hunt to uncover the sexual preferences of any colleague. It leaves unsaid what, if any action, is to be undertaken if knowledge of homosexuality comes to the attention of the RA either through a colleague's public avowal of his or her homosexuality or through a revelation made public by a third party in the process commonly referred to as "outing." Do we grandfather such colleagues and allow them to continue in our Assembly, or do we request their resignation?

The thrust of the Roth paper is clear that a homosexual should not be permitted to serve as a rabbi or cantor. The tone of the paper would lead one to posit that the halakhic ban of homosexuality would take precedence over the "grandfather" principle, and the colleague would no longer be allowed to continue in the RA.

I am not at all certain that this was the intent of the majority of the CJLS. Certainly in many cases, justice would have us refrain from stripping a colleague from membership in the RA, and one such case should be in the case before us now: a colleague, having been "outed," has avowed his homosexuality.

We can argue that a "closet" homosexual who accepted ordination from the Seminary and/or joined the RA following the 1992 CJLS statement may be charged with entering under false pretenses and perhaps not deserve the protection of the "grandfather" principle. Colleagues "on board" prior to the 1992 statement, however, should be "grandfathered" and allowed to continue as full fledged members of the RA.

The privileges of RA membership are many: *hevruta*, programming material, sermonic material, participation in convention, guidance when faced with job tensions or family tensions. For colleagues who desire to change their pulpits or who must change their pulpits, the most important RA privilege is placement. It is no accident that gross violation of placement procedure is grounds for expulsion from the RA.

For us to interpret the 1992 statement as grounds to refuse full placement privileges, on the grounds of homosexuality, to a colleague who entered the RA prior to 1992, will ultimately become the bases for challenging his or her right to remain in the RA. Denying placement is a grave injustice; to have this become the slippery slope which would ultimately become a precedent to justify expulsion would be an even graver injustice.

Conclusion

Given the silence of the 1992 statement on the question of placement of homosexual colleagues and give the importance of placement privileges, the Joint Placement Commission should recommend to congregations "avowed homosexuals" who were members prior to 1992.

EH 24.1993c

A Concurring Opinion to Arnold M. Goodman's "Placing Homosexual Rabbis in Congregations"

Rabbi Aaron L. Mackler

This paper was submitted as a concurrence to "Placing Homosexual Rabbis in Congregations," by Rabbi Arnold M. Goodman. Concurring and dissenting opinions are not official positions of the Committee on Jewish Law and Standards.

The Committee on Jewish Law and Standards of the Rabbinical Assembly provides guidance in matters of halakhah for the Conservative movement. The individual rabbi, however, is the authority for the interpretation and application of all matters of halakhah.

The issue of homosexuality confronts us with a real and painful dilemma, in which important Jewish norms and values conflict. I believe that given the current state of our scientific knowledge, of the development of halakhic arguments, and of our insight into God's will, the traditional prohibition of homosexual activity must be maintained. At the same time, individuals violating this norm cannot be penalized to a greater extent than those comparably violating other halakhic prohibitions. In Rabbi Joel Roth's words ("Homosexuality," above, p. 669), "I find it unacceptable for the community to be more severe and intolerant in its reactions to the [halakhically] illegal act of homosexual behavior (which is not chosen in any conventional sense) than it is to the illegal acts of חלול שבת or intermarriage (which are freely chosen)." (I understand that Rabbi Roth and I differ regarding some of the implications of this statement.)

I believe that this approach must guide enforcement related to the prohibition on homosexual behavior. In rabbinic placement, infractions of this halakhic norm should be dealt with in a manner similar to other infractions of halakhah. I was impressed by Rabbi Joel Meyers' description of the way in which the Rabbinical Assembly deals with violations of halakhah or other normative standards. Individual cases are considered by the Vaad Hakavod and other bodies such as the Joint Placement Commission, with sensitive judgments made on a case by case basis. In particular cases, a rabbi might be denied use of placement services, or be subject to other penalties or restrictions.

While I understand the attraction of a simple policy regarding placement of avowed homosexuals, the complexities of the issue and variation among particular cases demand prudent judgments on a case by case basis. A rabbi who seeks to publicize his practice of homosexual behavior, and proclaims homosexuality as an equally legitimate Jewish lifestyle, would represent one type of "avowed homosexual." A rabbi who is "outed" against his will, and when pressed reluctantly acknowledges his behavior, would represent another. Other factors would need to be considered as well.

I would have preferred that the CJLS had not been asked to endorse a blanket policy with regard to the placement of an avowed homosexual. I believe that Rabbi Kassel Abelson's paper represents an overly blunt prohibition. I would have greater sympathy for a general policy that the Joint Placement Commission should not recommend for placement those who avowedly violate halakhah, although my sense is that this position is currently approximated in practice to an appropriate degree. Such a general formulation would provide a vital context for both the application and the perception of the policy. To articulate a policy banning placement for the entire class of avowed homosexuals, and not for other avowed violators of Jewish law, would be to be more severe with regard to the halakhically illegal act of homosexual behavior than with regard to other halakhic infractions such as חלול שבת. It certainly would appear as more severe to some in the movement, deepening their sense of hurt and alienation, and might be cited by others to justify practices that discriminate against open homosexuals relative to open violators of Shabbat, for example.

My vote for Rabbi Arnold M. Goodman's paper is reluctant, for I believe that it expresses an overly broad acceptance of the placement of avowed homosexuals. At a theoretical level, I am uncomfortable with his paper as well as Rabbi Abelson's. In practice, though, I believe that Rabbi Goodman's position would somewhat more readily allow for the approach that I judge most proper: treating violations of the halakhic prohibition of homosexuality similarly to other halakhic violations. Those whom blunt policy excludes from placement are out of the system. Those who can be placed remain subject to the standards and procedures of the Rabbinical Assembly, including the Vaad Hakavod, and the prudential wisdom of the Joint Placement Commission.

It is conceivable that a situation might arise in which an argument could be made for singling out the class of avowed homosexuals, or avowed violators of another specific Jewish norm, as forfeiting access to the placement system. Such an argument would need to be very powerful to overcome the costs involved in being more severe with this halakhic prohibition than other comparable prohibitions. Both the compelling reasons for the blanket denial of placement, and the failure of any alternative to achieve the desired result, would need to be set forth with great care. In my judgment, the case for a specific policy against placement for avowed violators of the halakhic prohibition of homosexual behavior in particular has not been adequately made.

EH 24.1993d

THE GAY PLACEMENT QUESTION

Rabbi Ben Zion Bergman

This paper was submitted as a dissenting opinion to Rabbi Kassel Abelson's "Placing Homosexual Rabbis in Congregations." Dissenting and concurring opinions are not official positions of the Committee on Jewish Law and Standards.

The Committee on Jewish Law and Standards of the Rabbinical Assembly provides guidance in matters of halakhah for the Conservative movement. The individual rabbi, however, is the authority for the interpretation and application of all matters of halakhah.

Rabbi Abelson, in denying the avowed homosexual the services of the Placement Commission, relies for the most part on the wording of the "consensus" resolution of the CJLS in which avowed homosexuals and lesbians were not to be admitted to the Seminary Rabbinical School. The resolution also states, however, that no investigation, witch hunt, or oath of non-homosexuality will be required of candidates for admission to the Rabbinical School. Rabbi Abelson argues that to be consistent with that resolution which denies the avowed homosexual admission to the Rabbinical School, we must also deny the avowed homosexual member the services of the Placement Commission. The argument is flawed on several grounds.

First of all, the analogy does not hold. On the one hand, I believe that the resolution is silent on the matter of the rabbinical student whose homosexuality is discovered after admission as a student. Now, one can argue that the implication of the resolution denying admission indicates the present stance of the Seminary not to ordain homosexuals. Therefore, a student who is found to be homosexual will be expelled or, if allowed to continue his or her studies, would not be on an "ordination track." This is a reasonable inference. However, the analogy to the situation under consideration would require the expulsion of the homosexual member from the Rabbinical Assembly, which is not being contemplated at this time.

Secondly, the resolution must be seen within the context of all other relevant resolutions and pronouncements. Simultaneously with the "consensus" resolution, there was also passed a resolution calling for the establishment of a commission to study the issue. One can reasonably infer, from that fact, that the "consensus" resolution only reflected the status quo, which might be subject to change. Otherwise, why establish a commission mandated to study the question and to report to the CJLS in three years? The CJLS, at that point, no matter what the recommendation of the Study Commission might be, could reaffirm the present position or reject or amend it. The "consensus" resolution, therefore, only reflects a present and not necessarily unalterable position. Had the Seminary and United Synagogue gone along to participate in the Study Commission, one might have made the argument that the purpose of the Commission was to study the issue from a theological, moral, ethical, philosophical and sociological standpoint without necessarily having implications for הלכה למעשה. Once it is the CJLS alone that is undertaking the study and to whom the Commission makes regular reports, the implication becomes all the stronger that the purpose of the study is to have possible effect on הלכה למעשה. Therefore, one can argue that the resolution only reflects the status quo, and if analogy to the Rabbinical Assembly membership is in order, the status quo obtains there as well.

Thirdly, denial of the services of the Placement Commission to a member of the Rabbinical Assembly is curiously inconsistent with the resolution on the treatment of homosexuals passed several years ago by the RA in convention assembled. That resolution called for an end to discrimination against homosexuals precisely, in addition to other areas, in employment. Denying the services of the Placement Commission to an RA member who is homosexual is precisely discriminating in the area of employment.

Which is precisely what brings me to the fourth and possibly most cogent argument, which I present as a member of the California Bar. Denying the services of the Placement Commission to a member of the RA, who has paid his or her dues faithfully, and who is retained as a member in good standing, would make the RA vulnerable to a very grievous lawsuit.

Without stating my own personal views, let it be said that the alternative could be the expulsion of the avowed homosexual from membership in the RA. That, however, is not the prerogative of the CJLS and, besides prejudging and preempting the result of the Study Commission, has serious policy and public relations implications. Failing that step, however, the RA cannot deny the avowed homosexual member access to any of its services which are available to every other member.

EH 126:1.1996

Mix and Match: The Use of Aramaic Phrases in Legal Documents Written in Hebrew

Rabbi Lionel E. Moses

This paper was approved by the CJLS on March 12, 1996, by a vote of fifteen in favor, one opposed, and one abstaining (15-1-1). Voting in favor: Rabbis Kassel Abelson, Ben Zion Bergman, Stephanie Dickstein, Elliot N. Dorff, Baruch Frydman-Kohl, Shoshana Gelfand, Myron S. Geller, Arnold M. Goodman, Judah Kogen, Vernon H. Kurtz, Lionel E. Moses, Paul Plotkin, Mayer Rabinowitz, Elie Kaplan Spitz, and Gerald Zelizer. Voting against: Rabbi Avram Israel Reisner. Abstaining: Rabbi Jerome M. Epstein.

The Committee on Jewish Law and Standards of the Rabbinical Assembly provides guidance in matters of halakhah for the Conservative movement. The individual rabbi, however, is the authority for the interpretation and application of all matters of halakhah.

שאלה

Is it halakhically necessary for official documents that are published by the Rabbinical Assembly and that certify that a procedure was a מעשה בית דין to use the phrase במותב תלתא בי דינא כחדא הוינא in order for the document to have legal status?

Abstract

This brief paper seeks to demonstrate that while it is halakhically acceptable for a legal document that certifies that an event was a מעשה בית דין not to use the phrase במותב תלתא בי דינא כחדא הוינא at all, under specific circumstances, it is preferable for the phrase to be included. The paper will furthermore urge the use of the Aramaic phrase within the context of a primarily Hebrew document because of the long history of mixing of Aramaic expressions in Hebrew texts in general, and in rabbinic legal documents in particular, even though it is halakhically valid to translate the phrase into Hebrew.

תשובה

The phrase במותב תלתא בי דינא כחדא הוינא has its roots in the Babylonian Talmud in two discussions about certification of documents (קיום שטרות). The Mishnah (Sanhedrin 1:1) establishes the rule that monetary matters (דיני ממונות) are the jurisdiction of a rabbinic court of three judges. The judges for monetary matters need not be experts (מומחים), but may, in fact, be non-professionals (הדיוטות), a leniency enacted in order to ensure that loans will be easily accessible to the poor.

The discussion in B. Ketubbot 22a centers on a hypothetical situation in which three judges gathered to authenticate a loan (שטר חוב) and before all three had signed the document, one of the members of the bet din died:

אמר רב זעירא הא מילתא מרבי אבא שמיע לי, ואי לאו רבי אבא דמן עכו שכחתה. שלשה שישבו לקיים את השטר, ומת אחד מהם, צריכין למיכתב: במותב תלתא הוינא וחד ליתוהי.

Rabbi Zeira taught: "I heard this matter [regarding the certification of documents] from Rabbi Abba, and if I had not heard Rabbi Abba of Akko teach [this law], I would have forgotten it. If three [judges] sat down to certify a document [such as a loan, which requires the action of certification of a bet din] and one of the judges died [before he signed], it is necessary for the [remaining] judges to write [into the document]: 'We sat down [in judgment] as three [judges] and one is no longer present.'"

From this brief section of the Gemara we learn a number of things:

1. The phrase במותב תלתא הוינא was apparently not a required phrase in all documents which were official acts of a bet din.

2. The expression was included in such official documents only where one of the judges died before signing and its inclusion was a teaching of Rabbi Abba of Akko, who considered its inclusion halakhically mandatory in order to certify the document.

3. Despite the fact that Rabbi Zeira cites the case in rabbinic Hebrew, שלשה שישבו ומת אחד מהם, nonetheless, the legal formulation is stated in Aramaic במותב תלתא...ליתוהי, providing an indication that the Aramaic was perhaps the traditional formulation of the expression and that the rabbis of Babylonia had no qualms about mixing and matching Aramaic and Hebrew in the same text.

The question that devolves from this statement of Rabbi Zeira is, why was it halakhically necessary to include the phrase במותב תלתא הוינא וחד ליתוהי specifically in the certification of a document where one of the judges died before signing? The answer is patently simple. In a document, where all three judges signed, the phrase was redundant and superfluous. This conclusion can best be seen from the continuation of the text in the Gemara:

אמר רב נחמן בר יצחק: ואי כתב ביה: "שטרא דנן נפק לקדמנא בי דינא," תו לא צריך. ודילמא בית דין חצוף הוא? וכדשמואל, דאמר שמואל: "שנים שדנו – דיניהם דין אלא שנקרא בית דין חצוף." דכתיב ביה: "בי דינא דרבנא אשי." ודלמא דרבנן דבי רבי אשי כדשמואל סבירא להו? דכתיב ביה: "ואמר לנא רבנא אשי."

Rav Nahman bar Yitzhak taught: "If he wrote [in the document certifying the loan], 'This document went out from us, a bet din,' he does not have to write anything else [even if one of the judges died before signing the document]."

[The Gemara now raises an objection to the opinion of Rav Nahman bar Yitzhak who claims a document can be certified with the signatures of only two judges, when the third died before signing, simply by stating that a bet din saw the document and certified it, without specifying that the original bet din had three judges.]

"[If we accept the halakhic legality of the opinion of Rabbi Nahman bar Yitzhak, the Gemara objects, might the unsuspecting reader of the document mistakenly conclude that] the bet din [that certified the document] was [what is called] an arrogant court (בית דין חצוף) and that [this certifying bet din] accepted the opinion of Samuel [who taught], "If two sat in judgement, their decision is valid, but [such a court] is called an arrogant court!"

[The Gemara responds to its objection by stating that] [a court would never certify a document merely by stating that the document went out from a bet din followed by two signatures, but rather in the document] what was written was "The court of our teacher, Rav Ashi."

[Again the Gemara raises the same objection as it did to the teaching of Rav Nahman bar Yitzhak.] "Perhaps the students of Rav Ashi accepted the opinion of Samuel [that a document certified by only two judges was valid even though such a court is considered an arrogant court]."

[The Gemara responds to this last objection by saying that] what was written [in the document] was "Rav Ashi said to us."

This final conclusion of the Gemara is obscure and vague. Rashi gives two possible explanations. The first, which Rashi himself considers more probable, is that by mentioning Rav Ashi by name, the judges are telling us that the original court that sat in deliberation was a court of three judges, even though only two signatures appear, because Rav Ashi would only accept the legitimacy of a court of three judges. Alternately, albeit less likely, by mentioning Rav Ashi by name, the judges were implying that Rav Ashi himself was the third judge, since the word לנא is plural, implying the presence of at least two other judges.

What does this section of the Gemara add to what we have already learned from Rabbi Zeira?

1. According to Rabbi Nahman bar Yitzhak, it is only necessary to state that a document was certified by a bet din without specifying that three judges sat in judgement, even if one of the judges died before signing.

2. Although Rav Nahman bar Yitzhak's formulation is rejected because it leaves open the potentially mistaken conclusion that the document was certified by an arrogant court of only two judges, it is still possible to certify a document with only two signatures by stating that the document was issued by a court under the jurisdiction of an eminent rabbi like Rav Ashi, because he would not brook any compromise on the minimum number of judges certifying a document, even if only two of the judges remained alive to sign it.

3. Finally, and most significantly, it appears that the expression במותב תלתא הוינא is included in the document first, because one of the judges had died before signing, and second, to remove all suspicion that the document was certified by a court with fewer than three judges. If, however, the signatures of all three judges appeared, the phrase במותב תלתא הוינא is superfluous and redundant and may be omitted without impugning the validity of the document.

These tentative conclusions based on the Gemara alone are confirmed in the codes. We begin, out of chronological order, with the Tur. In the Tur, Hoshen Mishpat, chapter 46, in a section dealing with the laws concerning lending and loans, Rabbi Yaakov ben Asher writes about the procedure for certifying loan documents (the so-called שטר חוב):

> וכיצד הוא הקיום? באים עדי השטר ומעידים לפני שלשה, ואפילו הם הדיוטות, "זאת היא חתימתנו." וכותבין למטה, "במותב תלתא כחדא הוינא, ואתא פלוני ופלוני ואסהידו קדמנא אחתימות ידייהו, ומדאיתבר, לנא דהא הוא חתימת ידייהו, אשרנוהו וקיימנוהו כדחזי." וחותמין למטה.

What is the procedure for certifying [a loan document]? The witnesses to the document come [to the court] and testify before three [judges], even [three] who are not professional or expert judges, [and they say,] "These are our signatures." [And the judges] write below [the signatures], "Sitting [as a court of] three [judges] and we were of one opinion, there came [before us] so-and-so and so-and-so and they testified in our presence regarding their signatures. And when it became clear to us that these were indeed their signatures, we settled the case and certified the documents, as is fit." [Then, the judges] signed below [their statement].

The text of the Tur makes three things clear:

1. In the community of the Tur and undoubtedly elsewhere, it was customary to add the apparently redundant phrase במותה תלתא כחדא הוינא to documents that required the action of a court (מעשה בית דין), even if all three judicial signatures were present.

2. The formula of certification in the community of the Tur was written entirely in Aramaic.

3. The expression for describing the operations of the bet din was במותה תלתא כחדא הוינא, without the words בי דינא. Thus, either the words בי דינא were understood as being implied or במותב תלתא was the linguistic equivalent of בי דינא, making the latter words redundant and superfluous.

None of the commentaries to the Tur make any mention of the language in which the certification is formulated. This might appear to imply that commentators like the Beit Yosef (Rabbi Yosef Karo) and the Darkhei Moshe (Rabbi Moses Isserles) took for granted that the language of certification would be Aramaic, since otherwise, they might have stated וכך הם כותבים בכל לשון, "Thus the judges write (the certification) in any language." This conclusion, however, is by no means necessary, as we shall see below from the formulation of Maimonides. Thus, the gloss of the Beit Yosef on the phrase במותב תלתא simply states the obvious: three judges are needed to certify a document and if only two judges sign the document, Karo follows the opinion of the Nimukei Yosef, who says such certification is worthless (הוא ודאי אינו כלום). In a similar vein, the Darkhei Moshe quotes the Mordechai to Gittin (Perek HaShole'ah, paragraph 368) that if a *get* (whose authenticity requires the action of a bet din) is certified by only two judges, the *get* is invalid (אינו גט).

Maimonides, in the sixth chapter of Hilkhot Edut, describes the juridical procedures for certifying a document in the presence of a bet din. After listing five possible procedures for certifying a document in paragraph 2, Maimonides writes the following information in paragraph 4:

בית דין שכתבו: במושב שלשה היינו, ונתקיים שטר זה בפנינו, הרי זה
מקוים, אף על פי שלא פירשו באיזה דרך מן החמשה דרכים נתקיים.

> A bet din which wrote [on a document it was certifying], "We were sitting [as a court of] three when this document was brought before us for certification," such a document is certified, even though they [the members of the bet din] did not specify by which of the five methods the document was certified.

The most obvious feature to note in Maimonides is that not only is the formulation by which the document is certified written in Hebrew, but even the Talmudic expression במותב תלתא הוינא is translated into Hebrew. While it is true that Maimonides wrote the Mishneh Torah in rabbinic Hebrew in general, where the custom is universal to write a document in Aramaic, such as a ketubbah or *get*, Maimonides retains the Aramaic. Thus, his rendering of במותב תלתא הוינא into Hebrew is not merely stylistic consistency, but rather an indication that Maimonides sees no halakhic objection to rendering an Aramaic phrase from the Talmud into Hebrew.

This last conclusion is strengthened and validated when we consider the sixth paragraph in chapter 6 of Hilkhot Edut, where Maimonides deals with the hypothetical situation presented in the Talmud, with which we began our discussion (B. Ketubbot 22a):

שלשה שישבו לקיים את השטר, ומת אחד מהם, צריכין לכתוב: "במושב
שלשה היינו, ואחד איננו." שמא אמר הרואה: "בית דין בשנים קימוהו."

> Three judges who sat [in judgment] to certify a document and one of the judges died [before signing], [the remaining judges] must write, "We were sitting [in judgment] as three [judges] and one [of us] is no longer here [that is, he died]," lest the person who sees the document might [mistakenly] conclude, "This document was certified by a court of [only] two [judges]."

In this halakhah, Maimonides intentionally translates an Aramaic quotation from the Gemara, indeed an attributed statement of Rabbi Abba of Akko (במותב תלתא הוינא וחד ליתוהי), into Hebrew. The only conclusion to be drawn is that, at least for Maimonides, the language of the juridical certification bears no halakhic status. The bet din can write their certifying document either in Hebrew or Aramaic, even going as far as translating an attributed statement from Aramaic to Hebrew.

To this point, we have reached the following halakhic conclusions based on the Tur and Maimonides:

1. Certification of a document such as a loan requires judicial action (מעשה בית דין) and that such judicial action requires a bet din of three judges who can be non-professionals (הדיוטות).

2. In certifying a document, the Tur uses the formula במותב תלתא כחדא הוינא in Aramaic, followed by the signatures of the three judges.

3. In certifying a document, Maimonides uses the expression במותב שלשה היינו, a Hebrew translation of במותב תלתא כחדא הוינא.

4. In certifying a document when one of the judges has died before signing, Maimonides actually translates an attributed quotation from the Talmud from Aramaic to Hebrew.

One question remains open, namely, is the phrase במותב תלתא בי דינא כחדא הוינא, whether in Hebrew of Aramaic, necessary altogether, if the document is signed by all three judges? For a clear answer to this question, we turn to the Shulhan Arukh, Hoshen Mishpat 46:29:

ג' שישבו לקיים את השטר ומת אחד מהם, צריכין לכתוב: "במותב תלתא הוינא וחד ליתוהי," כדי שלא יאמר הרואה שבית דין של שנים קיימוהו. אפילו היה כתובו "בבית דין יאמר," שמא דימו ששנים בית דין הם. ואם יש בו משמעות שהיו שלשה, לא צריך. ויש אומרים שאם לא כתבו "וחד ליתוהי," כשר. ומכל מקום, לכולי עלמא אם כתבו "בי דינא ובמותב תלתא," תו לא צריך, וחותמים שנים מהם ודיו.

[The Shulhan Arukh is once again concerned with the hypothetical situation of a court that is certifying a document and one of the three judges dies before signing the document.]

"When three [judges] sat in judgment to certify a document and one of the judges died [before he signed the document], it is necessary to write, 'We sat [in judgment] as three [judges] and one is no longer here.' [This expression is included] so that when a person subsequently sees [the document with only two signatures], he/she will not conclude that a bet din of [only] two judges certified [the document].

"Even if the document included the words 'by a bet din' (but not the words "We sat in judgment as three judges and one of them is no longer here"), such wording is not sufficient, lest one might conclude that it was a bet din of only two judges.

"However, if there is some clear indication that the bet din originally had three judges (even though there are only two signatures), nothing more needs to be written.

"There are those who say that even if the text omits the words 'and one of them is no longer here' (וחד ליתוהי) the document is fit for use and legitimate.

"In any case, if he wrote the words 'a court with three judges sitting in judgment,' nothing else needs to be written and the two remaining judges sign and that is sufficient."

In this paragraph, Karo appears particularly loquacious, even to the point of redundancy, but each statement further specifies and delimits the law. Once again, it is clear that the codified law is concerned with appearances and with removing all doubt or suspicion that a court of two judges was sufficient to certify the document.

Most important, however, for the resolution of our question, is the third statement of the Shulhan Arukh, namely, if there is a clear indication that the bet din was composed of three judges, it is unnecessary for the document to specify verbally that three judges sat together in judgement. It is the Rema, Rabbi Moses Isserles, who clarifies what might be considered "a clear indication" that the court, in fact, had three judges:

ואם כל שלשה חותמים, אין צריך לכתוב, "במותב תלתא היונא."

If all three judges sign (the document) it is unnecessary to write the words במותב תלתא היונא.

While the gloss of the Rema may appear to be self-evident, what is significant is that the Rema states that a document is validly certified even without the words במותב

תלתא חיונא. All that is necessary is the signatures of all three judges to indicate that the certification was a judicial action (מעשה בית דין).

The Use of Aramaic Expressions in a Hebrew Document

We have seen through the discussion above that the expression במותב תלתא בי דינא כחדא הוינא is essentially superfluous if there is *prima facie* evidence that the court which certified a document as legally valid was a court with three judges. This *prima facie* evidence is provided by the signatures of the three presiding judges. The question that remains, however, is if the superfluous phrase is used, is it preferable to use the Aramaic formulation or to be linguistically consistent and translate the expression into Hebrew.

The literary tradition of retaining Aramaic phrases within the context of Hebrew documents has very early antecedents. The stylists of the Bible saw no difficulty in mixing pure Aramaic phrases into Biblical Hebrew contexts. Thus, Gen. 31:44-51 relates the story of the covenant established between Jacob and Laban, before Jacob crosses the Jabbok River to return to Canaan. As a sign of the covenant, Jacob and Laban establish a mound of stones as a boundary between their respective territories. In verse 47, Laban names the boundary marker יגר שהדותא; Jacob, however, gives it the Hebrew name גלעד, a name repeated by Laban in verse 48. Notwithstanding the difficulties and the obvious doublets in the verses, Martin Noth,[1] followed by A.F. Campbell,[2] attributes both verses 47 and 48 to the Yahwist, although Noth does suggest that verse 47, which includes the Aramaic phrase, is a later addition.

This mixture of pure Aramaic in a Hebrew context continues sporadically in later biblical literature. Thus, in Jer. 10:11, we encounter an entire verse in Aramaic:

כדנה תאמרון להום, אלהיא די שמיא וארקא לא עבדו, יאבדו מארעא ומן תחות שמיא אלה.

Thus you shall say to them: "Let the gods who did not make the heaven and the earth perish from it, the earth, and from under these heavens."

Whatever the exegetical explanation, this verse is addressed to the "House of Israel," who, throughout the balance of the chapter, is addressed in Hebrew.

The same mixture of Aramaic and Hebrew occurs in both the books of Ezra and Daniel. Ezra 4:8-6:19 is written entirely in Aramaic, not surprisingly since Reichsaramaisch was the official state language of the Persian Empire and the passage includes official correspondence to and from the Persian court. Nonetheless, Ezra 5:1-5:5 is the report of a prophecy of Haggai and Zechariah to the Jews in Judea and Jerusalem and it, too, is written in Aramaic. Finally, fully half of Daniel (2:2-7:28) is written in Aramaic, the balance written in Hebrew.

This responsum is not the appropriate occasion for an exhaustive survey of the use of Aramaic in Hebrew texts. Such a mixture of language does, however, occur both in liturgical texts and in the Talmud. Thus, one of the earliest prayers, according to the prevailing scholarly opinion, is the Kaddish, which unabashedly switches back and forth between Hebrew and Aramaic. Similarly, two late prayers, written long after Aramaic ceased to be the *lingua franca* of the Near East, namely יקום פורקן and בריך שמה דמרא עלמא are both

---

[1] Martin Noth, *A History of Pentateuchal Traditions*, trans. Bernard W. Anderson (Englewood Cliffs, NJ: Prentice Hall, 1972), p. 29.

[2] Anthony F. Campbell and Mark A. O'Brien, *Sources of the Pentateuch* (Minneapolis, MN: Fortress Press, 1993), p. 116.

written in Aramaic. The mixture of Hebrew and Aramaic in the Babylonian Talmud is regular and even the passage quoted above from Ketubbot 22a is a mixed-language text.

The Use of Aramaic Phrases in Rabbinic Documents

Documents serve in a legal system to define the terms of an agreement and to attest to the validity and authenticity of that agreement. Contemporary rabbinic documents are used primarily to attest to life-cycle events in the life of the person or persons named in the document. Such documents today include, but are not limited to, baby-naming certificates for daughters, Brit Milah certificates for sons, Bar and Bat Mitzvah certificates, ketubbot, gittin and the documents associated with their delivery (הרשאות, פטורים) and certificates of conversion. Some of these, like ketubbot and gittin, are well attested from classical times and are referred to in Hebrew as שטרות. Others, such as baby-naming certificates and Bar and Bat Mitzvah certificates, are contemporary inventions and are simply called תעודות. Since these תעודות do not require the signature of qualified witnesses, they bear little or no legal status. Finally, there are documents related to conversion to Judaism. Although these documents are generally referred to as תעודות (certificates), a word that usually refers to documents that bear little or no legal status, conversion documents, in fact, bear significant legal status and invariably require action of a bet din in order to be certified as authentic.

Contemporary rabbinic documents represent only a small selection of documents that were used by rabbis or rabbinic courts in the past. Documents such as שטר חוב, שטר מכירה, תנאים, and a שטר מתנה are only a few of the nearly forty different document types that are recorded in a work called the *Nahalat Shivah* (נחלת שבעה) by Rabbi Samuel ben David Halevi. It is worthwhile to review the style of a number of the documents recorded by the *Nahalat Shivah* for the following reasons: (1) to determine whether the classical formulations of rabbinic documents were written in Hebrew or Aramaic; and, (2) to ascertain if those documents that were formulated in Hebrew also included phrases or expressions in Aramaic.

Having already concluded that there is no halakhic impediment to translating standard Aramaic phrases into Hebrew and having already observed that there is a long history of inserting Aramaic expressions into Hebrew literary texts, the question remains whether that tendency to insert Aramaic expressions into Hebrew texts also applies to rabbinic documents written primarily in Hebrew.

The answers to these questions, as we might expect, are quite self-evident. First, certain document types were traditionally written in Aramaic and others were typically written in Hebrew. Thus, for example, the ketubbah was typically written in Aramaic, but as we well know, there is ample evidence of ketubbot written in other languages as well. Similarly, the *get* was written in Aramaic and because of the serious implications of improperly written *gittin*, extreme care was taken in standardizing the text of the *get*. On the other hand, documents traditionally written primarily in Hebrew include the שטר מכירת חמץ and the תנאים that are written for a bride and groom before the wedding.

When we look at those documents written primarily in Hebrew, we see that some contain no Aramaic expressions at all, while others contain a few well-known Aramaic expressions. Even though it would have been halakhically legitimate to translate these expressions into Hebrew, they are so familiar and standard in their Aramaic formulation that had these phrases been translated into Hebrew, the tone of authenticity might have been lost.

Certainly the two most familiar Aramaic phrases that appear repeatedly in Hebrew documents are וקנינא מן פלוני לפלוני על כל מא דכתוב and דלא כאסמכתא ודלא כטופסי דשטרי ומפורש לעיל במנא דכשר למקניא ביה. In the collection of documents edited by the *Nahalat*

Shivah, the first phrase occurs in the document used to extend the date for the fulfillment of marriage conditions (שטר הרחבת זמן על תנאים)[3] in the document used to amend a ketubbah (the so-called תוספת כתובה),[4] the document in which a husband releases his wife from taking an oath regarding her ketubbah (שטר מחילה על הכתובה),[5] the document in which a woman attests that her ketubbah has been paid to her (שובר על הכתובה)[6] and the document attesting to a loan made by a daughter to her father from her assets (שטר חצי זכר).[7]

In the same collection of documents, the second phrase (beginning וקנינא), is used in the document that pre-arranges the conditions of marriage (the so-called תנאים),[8] in the document used to extend the date for the fulfillment of the marriage conditions (שטר הרחבת זמן על תנאים),[9] in the document used to amend the ketubbah (the so-called תוספת כתובה),[10] in the document in which a husband gives up his rights to his wife's property (שטר סילוק איש מנכסי אשתו)[11] and in the document attesting to a loan made by a daughter to her father from her assets (שטר חצי זכר).[12]

While there are other less frequently attested Aramaic expressions used in the context of legal documents written primarily in Hebrew as recorded by the *Nahalat Shivah*, we need to consider the use of the expression במותב תלתא בי דינא כחדא הוינא as it appears in the documents recorded in the *Nahalat Shivah*. First, it is important to note that with only one exception, the document in which a woman takes an oath that she has not renounced her ketubbah,[13] all documents in which this expression occurs are written entirely in Aramaic. Only the document in which the woman swears that she is not renouncing her ketubbah and holds her husband and his heirs responsible for its payment includes this Aramaic expression in the context of a Hebrew document.[14] Second, it is important to note that in the versions of documents recorded by the *Nahalat Shivah* that attest to an action of a bet din, virtually all the documents are written entirely in Aramaic. Finally, in one document that attests to the action of a court, a document called by the Nahalat Shivah שטר ביכורין,[15] a Hebrew alternative to the Aramaic expression is used, namely:

נחנו בעלי דינין חתומי מטה מודים ומעידים בחתימת ידינו דלמטה והיא תעיד עלינו במאה עדים כשרים ונאמנים שאנחנו חתומי מטה בררנו יחד שני דיינים מוהר״ר פב״פ ומוהר״ר פב״פ.

Documents of the Rabbinical Assembly

Over the past four decades, the Rabbinical Assembly has published a number of documents that may be used by its rabbis to attest to certain life-cycle events. These documents include

---

[3] HaLevi, Samuel ben David, *Nahalat Shivah* (B'nei Brak), p. 46.
[4] Ibid., p. 93.
[5] Ibid., p. 101.
[6] Ibid., p. 102.
[7] Ibid., p. 107.
[8] Ibid., p. 34.
[9] Ibid., p. 46.
[10] Ibid., p. 93.
[11] Ibid., p. 104.
[12] Ibid., p. 107.
[13] Ibid., p. 96.
[14] Ibid.
[15] Ibid., p. 129.

a Brit Milah certificate, a baby-naming certificate for girls, ketubbot, and a general document for use at conversions. The Brit Milah certificate, the baby-naming certificate and the Conversion Document are all written in Hebrew. On the other hand, following a long history of tradition, most Rabbinical Assembly ketubbot are written in Aramaic, although the Committee on Jewish Law and Standards has authorized a version of the ketubbah that is written entirely in Hebrew.

Over the last three years, the Publications Committee of the Rabbinical Assembly has been preparing a new edition of the *Rabbi's Manual*. Among its many features, this manual plans to introduce standardized texts for conversion documents not only for adult converts, but also for adopted children and for children converted by a bet din because their mother was not Jewish at the time of their birth. Since the act of conversion is a judicial action (מעשה בית דין), it is important to reach an opinion on the formulation of such conversion documents. Inherent in publishing such documents is whether it is necessary or advisable to incorporate the Aramaic phrase במותב תלתא בי דינא כחדא הוינא. This question becomes more pressing because like their more generic predecessors, these conversion documents are written in Hebrew, with the exception of the phrase תלתא בי דינא כחדא הוינא במותב.

From the above discussion, we may safely draw the following conclusions:

1. There is a long history of the use of Aramaic phrases embedded in primarily Hebrew texts. This is not only true for biblical, liturgical and rabbinic texts, but equally true for legal documents used by rabbis.

2. There is no halakhic objection to rendering these Aramaic expressions into Hebrew.

3. The specific phrase במותב תלתא בי דינא כחדא הוינא is typically used in texts that are exclusively written in Aramaic, although it is attested in a document written primarily in Hebrew as well.

4. The phrase במותב תלתא בי דינא כחדא הוינא has been shown to be redundant and unnecessary if the document is signed by three rabbinic judges; for that reason, Rabbi Moses Isserles has ruled that if all three judges sign the document, the phrase may be omitted altogether without any halakhic ramifications.

Conclusions

This conclusion comes as a recommendation for הלכה למעשה, the practical application of Halakhah. Despite the observation that there are no negative ramifications if the phrase במותב תלתא בי דינא כחדא הוינא is omitted altogether or rendered into Hebrew, it is recommended that the Aramaic formulation be retained in all Rabbinical Assembly documents in which it would be appropriate, for the following reasons:

1. The phrase has a long history with roots in the Talmud itself and appears consistently in documents that attest to the action of a bet din. Tradition should have a strong vote, if not a veto, unless there is a pressing reason to change tradition.

2. Consistency in language, that is, using only Hebrew in Rabbinical Assembly documents written primarily in Hebrew, is a legitimate position, but slavish adherence to consistency in language depletes the richness and coloration of rabbinic documents and unnecessarily ends a lengthy stylistic tradition.

3. The use of phrases such as במותב תלתא בי דינא, as well as the other two phrases discussed in the body of this text, adds a tone of authenticity to the document, which is not so much substantive as it is subliminal.

4. Since all our Hebrew documents are accompanied by a parallel English translation, there can be no objection that the bearer of the document will not understand the text

because he or she does not know Aramaic. The Hebrew documents exist for the dual purpose of promoting and maintaining the Hebrew language, but also to provide a document that will be universally understood by colleagues throughout the world. The presence of Aramaic expressions in a primarily Hebrew document, not only does not detract from this last purpose, but in fact, helps give the document a ring of familiarity.

5. Finally, the Hebrew language style used in Rabbinical Assembly documents is itself a formal, classical style. The use of standard Aramaic phrases in such a Hebrew document appears consistent with this classical style.

EH 140:3.2000

ON RESTORING THE SHALIAH L'KABALAH

Rabbi Ben Zion Bergman

This paper was approved by the CJLS on March 7, 2000, by a vote of twenty in favor and one opposed (20-1-0). Voting in favor: Rabbis Kassel Abelson, Ben Zion Bergman, Elliot N. Dorff, Paul Drazen, Jerome M. Epstein, Samuel Fraint, Baruch Frydman-Kohl, Myron S. Geller, Nechama D. Goldberg, Arnold M. Goodman, Susan Grossman, Judah Kogen, Alan B. Lucas, Aaron L. Mackler, Daniel S. Nevins, Avram Israel Reisner, Joel E. Rembaum, James S. Rosen, Elie Kaplan Spitz, and Gordon Tucker. Voting against: Rabbi Joel Roth.

The Committee on Jewish Law and Standards of the Rabbinical Assembly provides guidance in matters of halakhah for the Conservative movement. The individual rabbi, however, is the authority for the interpretation and application of all matters of halakhah.

שאלה

Jewish law permits the appointment of a שליח (agent) to act on a person's behalf and the action of the שליח is considered as effective and as binding as if done by the principal. Thus, a man, for his convenience or for any other reason, may designate agents to write and deliver a *get* (writ of divorce) to his wife and the marriage is dissolved when the *get* is delivered to her possession. In Talmudic times it was equally possible for the wife to appoint a שליח to accept the *get* from her husband and thus not be required to be personally present for the delivery to her, with the *get* becoming effective upon delivery to her שליח.

In the Middle Ages, Ashkenazic Jews, while retaining the capability of the husband to appoint a שליח to act on his behalf in the divorce procedure, began to deny that capability to the wife. The rule denying the wife the privilege of appointing a שליח לקבלה (an agent to accept the *get* on her behalf) is attributed to Rabbenu Peretz. The general custom now prevalent among Ashkenazic Jews is that the wife may not appoint a שליח to act on her behalf in the ritual acceptance of the *get*.

Inasmuch as in modern times, the wife may possibly be as involved in economic and social activities as the husband, requiring her personal involvement in the procedure can be as burdensome for her as it is for the husband. Therefore, for moral and ethical reasons, should the CJLS rescind the discriminatory practice now prevalent and reinstate the ability of the wife to appoint a שליח to represent her in the *get* procedure?

תשובה

There is no question that, halakhically, a woman may appoint a שליח לקבלה (an agent to accept the *get* for her). This is derived from a baraita which states:

"ושלח" מלמד שהוא עושה שליח: "ושלחה" מלמד שהיא עושה שליח:
"ושלח ושלחה" מלמד שהשליח עושה שליח (קדושין מ״א:).

ושלח implies that he may appoint an agent; ושלחה implies that she may appoint an agent; ושלח ושלחה implies that the agent may appoint an agent (Kiddushin 41b).

The Mishnah (Gittin 6:1,2) specifically deals with the effectiveness of a woman to appoint a שליח לקבלה. In Mishnah 1 it is clear that if the woman instructs her שליח with the language: התקבל לי גטי, "Accept my *get* for me," once the husband has given it to the שליח, the husband can no longer retract. As Rashi explains:

כיון דאיהי שויחיה שליח הרי הוא כידה ונתגרשה מיד בקבלתו של זה.

Since she has made him her שליח, he is the equivalent of her hand and she is divorced immediately upon his acceptance of it.

R. Shimon ben Gamaliel adds that the language of agency appointment does not have to be specifically התקבל לי גטי ("Accept my *get* for me") but even טול לי גטי ("Take my *get* for me") would have the same effect. The Gemara (63b) cites a baraita that expands it even further by adding שא לי ויהי לי בידך, "Pick up for me, let it be mine in your hand," as valid language of agency appointment.[1] Mishnah 2 only delineates the proof required for her to establish her status as a divorcee since, as the Gemara notes (64a), בשעת גזרה שנו: "This was taught at a time of foreign oppression," meaning that it was dangerous to keep גטין and they were destroyed immediately upon delivery to the שליח — a further indication of the effectiveness of the שליח לקבלה as finalizing the procedure.[2]

Both the Shulhan Arukh and the Rambam codify this in no uncertain terms. In Even HaEzer 140:3 it states:

האשה עושה שליח לקבלה והיא מגורשת בקבלתו מיד כשיגיע הגט לידו ודינו כדין האשה לכל דבר לענין אם זרק גט לחצרו.

The wife may appoint a שליח לקבלה and she is divorced immediately upon his acceptance when the *get* was thrown into his courtyard.

In 140:4 the precise language of agency appointment is specified, אמרה לו התקבל לי גיטי או טול לי גיטי כולן לשון קבלה הן: "If she said 'Accept my *get* for me', or 'Take my *get*', these are both valid expressions for agency appointment," with the Rema (Rabbi Moses Isserles) adding ויש אומרים דה״ה שא לי: "And there are those who say that the same is true if she said, 'Pick up for me,'" clearly based on the baraita cited *supra*.[3]

It should be pointed out that the Rema — who, in the sections of the Even HaEzer cited above, voices no objection to the institution of a שליח לקבלה — in Sec. 141:29, which describes the procedure of delivery to the שליח לקבלה, adds the following gloss:

וכל זה מדינא, אבל י״א שנכון להחמיר שלא לגרש ע״י שליח לקבלה כלל. וכן נוהגין.

---

[1] The גירסא of the Rif leaves out שא לי.

[2] The requirement of proof by witnesses of delivery by the husband and receipt by the שליח לקבלה as necessary only when the *get* itself is unavailable is clearly stated by the Rambam in Hilkhot Gerushin 6:2: בשאבד הגט או נקרע אבל אם היה הגט יוצא מתחת ידי שליח קבלה אינו צריך עדים במד״א. See also Even HaEzer 101:10.

[3] The Shulhan Arukh evidently follows the גירסת הרי״ף with the רמ״א adding שא לי which is found in our texts, as a יש אומרים.

This is entirely in accordance with the law, but there are some who say that it is proper to be more strict and not divorce through a שליח לקבלה at all, and that is our practice.

The permissibility of a שליח לקבלה is expressed by the Rambam in Hilkhot Gerushin 6:1:

השליח שעושה האשה לקבל לה גט מיד בעלה הוא הנקרא שליח קבלה ומשיגיע הגט ליד שלוחה תתגרש כאילו הגיע לידה.

The שליח that the wife appoints to accept her *get* for her from the hand of her husband is called שליח לקבלה and when the *get* reaches his hand she is divorced as if it had come directly to her hand.

Despite this clear mandate, it has nevertheless become customary not to allow a שליח לקבלה. When this became the general rule is not easily ascertained since, as we have already seen, the Shulhan Arukh permits it and even indicates the procedure for such an agency appointment (Even HaEzer 101:8). Also, as late an authority as the נודע ביהודה (Rabbi Ezekiel Landau 1713-1793) permits it, only raising questions as to the specificity of the appointment language. Similarly, an even later source, the קב נקי (Kav Naki), delineates the procedure (סדר שליח לקבלה סעיף ב'), differing from the Even HaEzer only by requiring that it be before a bet din and not only in the presence of two witnesses, as the Even HaEzer requires.[4]

There are two reasons usually advanced for the disallowal of a שליח לקבלה. One reason given is that it is a בזיון לבעל (disrespectful of the husband). Yet this rationale is applied in the Gemara only to the case of שליח to שליח. There is a dispute between Rav and R. Hanina (Gittin 63b), with Rav saying אין האשה עושה שליח לקבל לה גיטה מיד שליח בעלה (the wife may not appoint a שליח to accept her *get* for her from her husband's שליח), and R. Hanina maintaining אשה עושה שליח לקבל לה גיטה מיד שליח בעלה (the wife may appoint a שליח to accept her *get* for her from her husband's שליח). When the Gemara asks מ"ט דרב, "What is Rav's rationale?" they give two possible rationales: איבעית אימא משום בזיון דבעל, אב"א משום חצרה הבא לאחר מכן ("if you wish, I can say that his reason is disrespect of the husband, or if you wish, I can say his reason is on account of the possibility of her courtyard being acquired later"). The latter rationale statement means that while it is true that the *get* must be acquired by her, it can be acquired by חצרה (her courtyard) as an extension of ידה (her hand): חצר איתרבאי משום ידו, "A courtyard has been included as subsumed under his hand" (Bava Metzia 12a). However, if she acquired the courtyard after the *get* was placed there, the acquisition is ineffective since the *get* must be transferred to her, either into her hand or into her courtyard as an extension of her hand, and at the time of transfer, the courtyard was not hers. Rashi then explains that permitting a שליח לקבלה to accept it from the husband's שליח could create a false analogy with the courtyard by denoting the courtyard as the husband's שליח and then by her acquiring the courtyard it becomes her שליח לקבלה.

In any event, whatever the rationale of Rav, his view is apparently rejected by most of the major poskim. That a woman may appoint a שליח לקבלה to accept the *get* on her behalf from her husband's שליח is stated in Even HaEzer 141:1, where the Rema, like the נודע ביהודה (Noda Biyhudah – Rabbi Ezekiel Landau), only raises the question of the specificity of language required. In the Rambam (Hilkhot Gerushin 6:9) it states quite clearly: ויש לאשה לעשות שליח קבלה לקבל לה גיטה מיד שלוחו של הבעל, "A wife may appoint a שליח לקבלה to receive her *get* for her from her husband's שליח." The מגיד משנה (Magid Mishnah

---

[4] The Kav Naki attributes the rule to Rabbenu Peretz. He cites later authorities who found many objections to the rule. He cites the only reason for their reluctance to reinstitute the שליח לקבלה – שלא לפגוע בכבודו של רבנו פרץ וחבריו – "Not to offend the honor of Rabbenu Peretz and his colleagues."

ad locum) quotes the view of Rav in the Gemara from Gittin cited *supra* but adds, citing the Halakhot Gedolot and R. Hai Gaon, that הלכה כר׳ חנינא — "the law is in accordance with R. Hanina." He sees this as also the view of the Rambam, R. Tam and the Rashba, adding וזה עיקר — i.e., the predominant position. His statement also reflects the view of the Rif (Rabbi Isaac Alfasi) who says clearly that הלכה כר׳ חנינא — "the law is in accordance with R. Hanina" — and who also cited R. Hai Gaon.

Nevertheless, the Shulhan Arukh, op. cit., adds:

וי״א שאין האשה יכולה לעשות שליח לקבל מיד שליה בעלה.

There are those who say that a wife may not appoint an שליח to accept from her husband's שליח.

The Bet Shmuel *ad locum* cites the rationales ascribed to Rav in the Gemara adding that if we accept the rationale of בזיון לבעל (disrespect to the husband) this would create a חשש דאורייתא (a concern regarding the validity of the *get* under Torah law), since the husband might not be transferring the *get* with full and unconditional volition. Parenthetically, he quotes a responsum of the Rashba (Rabbi Solomon b. Adret) stating that similarly the husband cannot appoint a שליח to give the *get* to the wife's shaliah, משום בזיון דהאשה (because of disrespect to the wife). He goes on to state that if we accept the second rationale משום דדומה לחצרה הבאה אח״כ (because it is similar to a courtyard acquired later by her) then there is only a חשש דרבנן (a concern only vis-à-vis rabbinic law). He then further elaborates:

ואם היא עשתה שלוחה בתחילה אז משום חצירה הבאה אח״כ ליכא ומשום בזיון איכא אע״ג דהיא עשתה שלוחה קודם לכן ואם היא היתה טרודה בעת שהביא לה גט ומחמת טרדה עשתה שליח לקבלה י״א בכה״ג ליכא משום בזיון הבעל והר״ן כתב אף בכה״ג איכא משום בזיון דהבעל וכתב בתשו׳ ריב״ש סי׳ נ״ה דהעיקר הוא דהאשה יכולה לעשות שליח לכן היכא דאיכא שום חשש איסור אם ישלח ע״י שליח לידה עדיף טפי שתעשה היא ש״ק לקבל מיד שלוחו.

If she appointed her שליח first, then the rationale regarding the later-acquired courtyard would not apply but the rationale regarding disrespect of the husband would still be applicable even if she appointed her שליח first. But if she was occupied at the time that he [her husband's שליח] brought her the *get* and because of her preoccupation she appointed a שליח לקבלה, there are those who say that in that case there is no disrespect of the husband. But the Ran (Rabbenu Nissim) wrote that even in those circumstances there is disrespect of the husband. But in the Responsa of Rabbi Isaac b. Sheshet, No. 55, it is written that the basic principle is that a wife may appoint a שליח. Therefore where there is any concern regarding forbidden relations when the *get* is sent via a שליח it is preferable that she appoint a שליח לקבלה to receive it from the husband's שליח.

However, the פתחי תשובה quotes ספר גט מקושר who disagrees with the last point.

One is prompted to ask what constitutes בזיון הבעל (disrespect of the husband). In other words, in what way is the husband humiliated or offended by her appointment of a שליח לקבלה to accept the *get* from his שליח להולכה (delivery שליח)? The statement of the Ran cited by Bet Shmuel, *supra*, is instructive. Rabbenu Nissim takes issue with the conclusion of the Rif that הילכך הלכה כר״ח — "Therefore the law is in accordance with R. Hanina." The Rif comes to that conclusion based upon the case cited by the Gemara in connection with the dispute between Rav and R. Hanina wherein the husband's שליח found the wife while she was kneading, and rather than interrupt her kneading, she responded to the שליח by saying להוי פקדון בידך (גרסת הריף: להוי פקדון בידך) – "Let it be in your hand" (the reading of the Rif, "Let it be a bailment in your hand"). Since the subsequent discussion of the case and its determination focused only on the fact that in that case לא חזרה שליחות אצל הבעל (agency had not returned to the husband), and when there was a separate שליח לקבלה that issue would not arise, the Rif said, הלכך הלכה כר״ח – "Therefore the law is in accordance with R. Hanina." Rabbenu Nissim, however does not necessarily accept the inference drawn by the Rif and R. Hai Gaon. He states as follows:

> זהו דעתם ז״ל ואחרים דוחין דליכא למפשט מהא דקי״ל כרבי חנינא אלא היכא דוקא דליכא בזיון דבעל כי הכא כיון דקא לשה ליכא בזיון אבל היכא דאיכא למיחש לבזיון דבעל אפשר דלא קיי״ל כוותיה ולא נהירא דבכי האי גוונא נמי איכא בזיון כיון שלא הפסיקה לישתה לקבל גיטה... ומשכחת לה אפילו אליבא דרב כגון דבעל לא קפיד וליכא משום בזיון דידיה וקדמה איהי ושויה שליחא וליכא למיחש משום חצרה הבאה לאחר מכן.

This is their opinion but "others" reject it, for one cannot infer from this that it establishes that the law is in accordance with the view of R. Hanina except where there is specifically no humiliation of the husband as in this case; since she was kneading there was no disrespect. But where there is concern for humiliation of the husband, perhaps the law would not be established in accordance with his [R. Hanina's] view. But this is not understandable for also in this case there is humiliation, since she did not cease her kneading to accept her *get*. But it [her ability to appoint a שליח לקבלה] could occur even in consonance with the view of Rav, in a case where the husband would not take umbrage and he would not consider it disrespectful; and if she appointed her שליח first there would not be concern regarding the later-acquired courtyard issue.

In other words, the בזיון הבעל (the husband's humiliation) seems to consist of seeing her appointment of a שליח לקבלה after the husband has gone to the trouble and expense of writing the *get* and sending it by a שליח, as cavalier and disdainful on her part. But even the אחרים (the "others"), who reject the conclusion of the Rif, would seem to accept that there is no humiliation in those cases where the personal acceptance of the *get* by the wife would be burdensome to her – even as trivial a burden as temporarily interrupting her kneading. And even the Ran, who would not accept that as vitiating any בזיון דבעל (disrespect of the husband), would also accept that there is no humiliation where the husband does not care (כגון דבעל לא קפיד). In all other cases however, the Ran, rejecting the conclusion of the Rif, goes on to state the more stringent position:

> חיישינן לדרב ואין האשה עושה שליח לקבל את גיטה מיד שליח בעלה ואם עשאתו חולצת ולא מתייבמת.

We pay heed to the view of Rav and the wife may not appoint a שליח to accept her *get* from the hand of her husband's שליח and if she does so [in specific circumstances] she requires חליצה and there can be no levirate marriage.

In any event, the factor of בזיון הבעל (disrespect of the husband) as disallowing a שליח לקבלה was a consideration only where the שליח לקבלה was accepting the *get* from the husband's שליח. Evidently, at some point that factor was transferred as a vitiating factor in the case of the husband's direct delivery.[5] It is perhaps understandable that, in earlier times, the wife's reluctance to accept the *get* directly from her husband was viewed as cavalier and disdainful behavior on her part and therefore, an appointment of a שליח לקבלה was a humiliation for the husband, having to deal through a third party. (Parenthetically, it should be noted that requiring the wife to accept the *get* through a third party — i.e., the husband's שליח — was not considered a בזיון דהאשה [humiliation of the wife], a factor which the Rashba evidently would take into consideration. See *supra*.)

But, דיו לבא מן הדין להיות כנידון — "A law deduced from another law cannot be more stringent than the one from which it is derived." Even if there is some legitimacy in transferring a reluctance to accept a שליח לקבלה from the case of שליח to שליח to the case of husband to שליח, it should not be dealt with more stringently than in its original setting. This would mean that:

A. According to the Rif and R. Hai Gaon, הלכה כר׳ חנינא: "The law is in accordance with view of R. Hanina," there is no consideration at all to be given to בזיון דבעל (husband's humiliation), and if that factor is not operative in the case of שליח to שליח, it cannot be transferred to the case of husband to שליח;

B. אליבא דאחרים דוחין: "According to the 'others' who reject the Rif's conclusion (that the law is according to R. Hanina)," that factor should not be invoked to forbid a שליח לקבלה, if the wife's personal acceptance would be burdensome to her; and,

C. Even אליבא דר״ן: "According to Rabbi Nissim," the factor is not operative where the husband does not consider her appointment of a שליח לקבלה as a humiliation, which, I submit, would be true in the overwhelming majority of cases today.

The other reason advanced for the withdrawal of the wife's prerogative of appointing a שליח לקבלה to accept the *get* on her behalf from the husband, is the difficulty of conclusive evidence of the authenticity of the agency appointment. However, it is difficult to understand why that should be a greater issue in the case of the woman's appointment of a שליח to accept the *get* than it is in the case of a man's appointment of a שליח to deliver the *get*.

In any event, we have already alluded to a difference between the Even HaEzer and the Kav Naki regarding the appointment procedure. It is clear that both are concerned with evidentiary issues. It must be remembered that they were both dealing with a situation in which the wife would appoint the שליח *verbally*. First of all, she may not have been able to write, or even read, the text of the מינוי שליחות (agency appointment). Consequently, you needed some evidence that she had made this appointment. Therefore, she made the appointment in the presence of two witnesses who signed the מינוי שליחות, attesting to her oral appointment. That the issue was evidentiary is implicit in the words of the Kav Naki who requires a bet din, by the added stipulation that the signatures of the members of the bet din should be recognized at the place where the husband is to deliver the *get* to the wife's שליח. That stipulation indicates why the Kav Naki requires a bet din. The signatures of two witnesses who are ordinary laymen might not be recognized and the מינוי שליחות might be suspect of being fraudulent. A bet din in one city, however, would probably have had previous correspondence with the bet din where the *get* is to be delivered and there is greater likelihood

---

[5] See n. 4.

that the signature of the judges would be recognized and their authenticity confirmed. That's probably why the Kav Naki prefers a bet din over merely two witnesses.

The Shulhan Arukh, on the other hand, is content with two witnesses, possibly relying on the fact that in his day, just as there were professional scribes, there may have been professional witnesses who signed many documents and therefore their signatures could be authenticated by the recognizability of the signatures or by comparison with another previously authenticated bearing their signatures (כתב ידם יוצא ממקום אחר).

However, I would argue that if the issue is evidentiary, we now have a better way to evidence the wife's appointment of her שליח לקבלה – namely, by her own signature on a document that she reads and understands. The function of the witnesses, in that case, would not be to evidence that she had made the agency appointment; that is evidenced by her signature. The witnesses' function would be to authenticate that she is who she claims to be – namely, Mrs. X, the wife of Mr. X – essentially the function performed today by a notary.

Additionally, today, with the technology available of telephone, fax, e-mail, etc. it is relatively easy for a bet din in one place to communicate with the rabbinical authorities in the other place to ascertain the legitimacy of the procedure, the signatures, and the identity of all of the parties.

Incidentally, the same reasoning applies to the husband's appointment of a שליח. In Even HaEzer 100:11, where both parties admit to the agency appointment, there is no need for witnesses. If witnesses are required, as Rema (Rabbi Moses Isserles) does require, it is only to obviate any problems in case משלח כופר (the principal denies making the appointment).

Consequently, to reinstitute the שליח לקבלה, the wife's appointment of her שליח לקבלה should be evidenced by a form, signed by her, and her signature attested to by two witnesses.

The Alternatives – שילוש הגט *and* גט זיכוי

In those instances where the cooperation of the wife is not forthcoming, either through her unavailability or her intransigence, and she will not personally accept the *get*, it has become the practice to issue a גט זיכוי, in which the husband, in the presence of a bet din and/or witnesses, delivers the *get* to some individual with the formula: זכה בגט זה לאשתי פב"פ... – "Acquire this *get* on behalf of my wife. . . ." The halakhic legitimacy of this practice is supported by the principle that זכין לאדם שלא בפניו ואין חבין לאדם שלא בפניו – "One may act for another's advantage even without his or her presence [or knowledge] but one may not act to the disadvantage of others without their presence [or knowledge]." This can be invoked only if there is a presumption that the *get* is a זכות (an advantage) for the wife and not a disadvantage.

In law, presumptions upon which legal decisions are based are characterized either as absolute presumptions or as rebuttable presumptions. The presumption that the *get* is זכות (an advantage) was clearly considered a rebuttable presumption in the halakhah.

In Yebamot 108b the question is asked:

המזכה גט לאשתו במקום יבם מהו? כיון דסניא ליה זכות הוא וזכין לאדם שלא בפניו או דילמא כיון דזימנין דרחמא ליה חוב הוא לה ואין חבין לאדם שלא בפניו.

What is the law regarding one [who is childless] who has another acquire the *get* on behalf of his wife [so that upon his death she is not bound to the levir]? Since she dislikes him [the brother-in-law] it is advantageous for her, and one may act for another's advantage without the other's knowledge; or perhaps, there are times when she loves her brother-in-law and this would be disadvantageous [since she could not marry him, coming under the prohibition of "brother's wife"], and one may not act to another's disadvantage without the other's knowledge.

The answer of R. Nachman was חוששין לדבריה וחלצת ולא מתייחמת: "We are concerned with her statement and she requires חליצה, and may not enter a levirate marriage" – which means that the presumption that a *get* is an advantage is rebuttable. When Ravina (ibid.) raises the question of whether the *get* is an advantage in the case of a couple who are constantly quarreling (במקום קטטה), the Gemara cites another presumption (evidently considered an absolute presumption at that time), טב למיתב טנדו מלמיתב ארמלו: "It is better to be married [under any circumstances] than to dwell in lonely widowhood." Clearly, the presumption that a *get* is זכות (an advantage) was a rebuttable presumption in Talmudic times. However, in today's world where a woman can be socially and economically independent, we would not presume that marriage under any circumstances would always be better than being single. Furthermore, since there has been a civil divorce, it is clearly an advantage that she also be divorced under Jewish law so that she may remarry in accordance with Jewish law. Therefore, today there can be no question of the legitimacy of a גט זיכוי.

However, a different problem is presented by a גט זיכוי. With a גט זיכוי, the husband is essentially appointing a שליח לקבלה for the wife. Quite correctly, the Tosafot on Ketubbot 11a (ד"ה מטבילין אותו על דעת ב"ד משום דזכות הוא) makes the point that זכייה שלא בפניו הוי מטעם שליחות, "Any act on behalf of another is contingent upon agency" – meaning that any זכיה שלא בפניו (act without the other's knowledge) presumes that were one able to communicate with the other party (the principal), since the proposed action is presumed to be totally advantageous to him (or her), the principal would certainly appoint the one proposing to do the act as his or her שליח. On the other hand, if there is even the slightest disadvantage to the principal (קצת חובה), one cannot make this presumption. The Tosafot cites the example, based on Bava Metzia 71b, of תרומה (Terumah – the portion of the produce that must be given to a kohen). The Torah does not define the amount that must be given as Terumah, although the Talmud designates the norms as either ⅟₆₀, ⅟₅₀, or ⅟₄₀, depending on the generosity of the farmer. Yet even if someone were to propose giving the lowest normal amount in order to make the grain consumable, to the advantage of the absent owner, he cannot presume to act on the owner's behalf since he (the owner) might have wanted to rely on the principle that מדאורייתא חטה אחת פוטרת את הכרי, "By the law of the Torah, one kernel exempts the entire bin," or, conversely, he may have wanted to give more.

What is even more egregiously anomalous is that in a גט זיכוי, we are actually allowing the husband to appoint a שליח for his wife, where the law might not allow a presumptive שליח. On the passage in Yebamot cited *supra*, Rashi defines the question המזכה גט לאשתו מהו – "What is the law [regarding] one who has another acquire the *get* on behalf of his wife?" – as שעשה שליח לקבלה וזיכה לה גט ע"י שליח שתתגרש מעכשיו, "He appointed a שליח לקבלה and had her acquire the *get* by this שליח in order that she may be divorced from that moment."

The conclusion of the Gemara that a שליח לקבלה cannot be appointed by the husband is codified by the poskim. In Even HaEzer 140:4:

אבל האיש אינו יכול לעשות שליח קבלה שאינו יכול לעשות שליח לחובתה שלא מדעתה ואפי' היתה אשת מוכה שחין או שהיתה קטטה ביניהם ותובעת להתגרש ויש מי שאומר בזו שהיא ספק מגורשת.

However, the husband cannot appoint a שליח לקבלה for he cannot appoint a שליח to act to her disadvantage without her consent, and even if she were married to one afflicted with loathsome sores or there was constant strife between them and she requests to be divorced; but there are those who say that in those circumstances she is a "questionable divorcee."

That this would prohibit a גט זיכוי, even in the case of the one married to the husband with the loathsome sores, is explained by the Turei Zahav ad locum: טב למיתב טנדו מלמיתב ארמלו, "It is better for her to be married [under any circumstances] than to dwell in spinsterhood." The Rema (Rabbi Moses Isserles) cites exceptions in the case where (A) the husband is a מומר (heretic); (B) the יבם (brother-in-law) is a מומר; (C) she is נאסרת על בעלה (forbidden to her husband); or, (D) she is a מומרת, but notes that even on this point there are more stringent authorities. The Taz (Turei Zahav) identifies the stringent authority as Rabbenu Nissim.

It seems to be abundantly clear that the practice of גט זיכוי was not as easily halakhically justifiable as the use of a שליח לקבלה. However, as I pointed out above, the change in societal conditions and the institution of civil divorce have changed the circumstances to the point that a גט זיכוי is certainly justifiable today. Therefore, there should be no aspersions cast on the use of the גט זיכוי. On the contrary, the גט זיכוי is a useful instrument. Just as הפקעת קידושין (annulment) is a remedy for the wife in the case of the recalcitrant or unlocatable husband, so the גט זיכוי provides a remedy in the case of the recalcitrant or unlocatable wife. However, it more than borders on the outrageous that we allow a גט זיכוי, wherein the husband designates a שליח לקבלה for the wife and do not permit her to appoint her own שליח לקבלה. Therefore, in the modern world, wherein women have rightfully attained independent and equal status, allowing the wife to appoint a שליח לקבלה is much preferable to the use of a גט זיכוי, reserving use of the גט זיכוי to the case of the unjustifiably recalcitrant wife.

The other alternative used by some is שילוש הגט, wherein the husband hands the גט to a שליש (a trustee) who is to keep it in trust for the wife, should she change her mind and decide to accept it. The husband is then given a document indicating that he is permitted to remarry. In this procedure, there has been no final severance of the marital relationship. Until the wife comes to accept the get from the שליש, they are still married under Jewish law. Allowing the husband to remarry is essentially a violation of the חרם דרבנו גרשום (the ban on polygamy).

To my mind, this alternative is egregiously inferior to the alternative of גט זיכוי, even with all of its problematics. Although Rabbenu Gershom's ban also included the impermissibility of divorcing a wife without her knowledge and consent, and the use of a שליש avoids that, between the two clauses of Rabbenu Gershom's ban, the ban on polygamy was the most compelling. The גט זיכוי, on the other hand, does sever the marital relationship and the couple is divorced. Although it does effect a divorce without the consent of the wife, it can be justified on the basis of זכין לאדם שלא בפניו, "One may act on behalf of others for their advantage, even without their consent and knowledge." And the get is advantageous for the wife, whether she believes it to be or not. It allows her to remarry in accordance with Jewish law. Furthermore, it prevents her subsequent marriage to another from being an adulterous union.

Summary

I would therefore argue that, in keeping with the halakhah, we should reinstitute the appointment of a שליח לקבלה by the wife, and that such is to be preferred to a גט זיכוי or שילוש הגט. It is not only more acceptable halakhically but is also more ethically acceptable. The fact that the practice has been suspended for some time is not a sufficient rationale, particularly from the standpoint of Conservative Judaism which seeks to give ethical, equitable and egalitarian considerations their due weight in the determination of halakhic practices. It should be pointed out that in the Conservative movement we have reinstituted הפקעת קידושין (annulment) which was certainly suspended for an even greater length of time — if, indeed, it was ever an actual procedure. Even the Rema, who indicates that in his day the practice was to disallow a שליח לקבלה, acknowledges that the use of a שליח לקבלה was entirely within the law. Whatever conditions at the time of the Rema may have justified the practice current in his day, our contemporary conditions motivate and militate for the reinstitution of the שליח לקבלה.

In today's societal and economic circumstances, women are in ever greater measure involved in the professions, or in entrepreneurial affairs, heading large business organizations, or otherwise gainfully employed in the corporate structure. The wife's personal appearance to accept the *get* may be as burdensome to her as the husband's personal appearance before the bet din may be to him. It is therefore ethically unacceptable to allow him to evade the personal appearance by appointment of a שליח and to deny her the same right. Additionally, considering the contemporary mind-set, one is hard pressed to imagine that her appearance by attorney (שליח) would be considered a בזיון דבעל (disrespectful of the husband) who is not likely to take umbrage. Furthermore, the evidentiary issues encountered in previous centuries, can now be rendered moot by the use of a form for the agency appointment that is understandable to the woman and signed by her personally, her signature attested to by witnesses, and by the availability of modern technology which renders any evidentiary problems easily soluble. There is therefore no valid rationale in our times for not allowing a שליח לקבלה.

The use of the גט זיכוי should be retained to provide a remedy for the husband in those cases where the wife's cooperation is unattainable because of her unjustified recalcitrance or her inaccessibility.

Conclusion

A proper form for the appointment of a שליח לקבלה should be created and all מסדרי גטין (rabbis certified to issue *gittin*) should be informed that they may now elect to have the wife appoint a שליח לקבלה in those cases where the wife will not appear personally for the delivery of the *get*. The גט זיכוי should be retained for use in the case of a recalcitrant or unavailable wife.

EH 150:4.1999a

Renewal of Marriages for Couples Without Get

Rabbis Kassel Abelson and Mayer Rabinowitz

This paper was approved by the CJLS on December 1, 1999, by a vote of nineteen in favor and one opposed (19-1-0). Voting in favor: Rabbis Kassel Abelson, Elliot N. Dorff, Paul Drazen, Samuel Fraint, Baruch Frydman-Kohl, Myron S. Geller, Arnold M. Goodman, Vernon H. Kurtz, Alan B. Lucas, Aaron L. Mackler, Daniel S. Nevins, Paul Plotkin, Mayer Rabinowitz, Avram Israel Reisner, Joel E. Rembaum, James S. Rosen, Joel Roth, Elie Kaplan Spitz, and Gordon Tucker. Voting against: Rabbi Judah Kogen.

The Committee on Jewish Law and Standards of the Rabbinical Assembly provides guidance in matters of halakhah for the Conservative movement. The individual rabbi, however, is the authority for the interpretation and application of all matters of halakhah.

שאלה

A couple has been divorced by the civil court for several years. They never obtained a גט. They have not married other people during this period. They would like to "remarry." If they may, is there a special ceremony in such a case? May a rabbi perform the ceremony?

תשובה

Civil Divorce

The classical sources do not deal with civil divorce and remarriage. However the Rambam touches on a related issue in a discussion of a doubtful divorce, or a defective *get*:

> אם גרש את אשתו בגט פסול או שהיתה ספק מגורשת ורצה להחזירה הרי זו מותרת לבעלה ואינו צריך לחדש הנשואין ולברך שבע ברכות ולכתוב כתובה עד שתתגרש גרושין גמורין.

> If he divorced his wife with a defective *get* or there was a doubtful divorce and he wants to take his wife back, she is permitted to her husband. He does not need to renew the marriage (נשואין), and to recite the Seven Blessings (שבע ברכות), and to write a new ketubbah, until there is a full divorce.[1]

---

[1] Rambam, Hilkhot Gerushin 10:3.

Similarly, the Even HaEzer discusses a case where a husband had issued a rabbinically defective *get* and would like to reaffirm the marriage ties instead of issuing a kosher *get*:

מי שגירש את אשתו בגט שיש בו פסול מדבריהם או שהיתה ספק מגורשת ורצה להחזירה צריך לקדשה אבל אינו צריך לברך ז' ברכות ולא לכתוב לה כתובה אחרת.

Someone who has divorced his wife with a rabbinically (but not Biblically) defective *get*, or if there is a doubt if she is divorced and he wishes to take his wife back he must betroth her. However, he does not have to recite the שבע ברכות or to write for her a new ketubbah.[2]

The requirement of the Even HaEzer that צריכה לקדשה, "he must betroth her," is in a case where there was a *get* but some defect was found in it, or where there is a doubt about the divorce. In our case there was no *get* or doubtful divorce. She is still married to him. Hence no קדושין would be required.

The Rambam states that there is no need to לחדש נשואין, to renew the marriage. The Magid Mishnah *ad locum* says that if there is a doubtful divorce then the Rambam requires new קדושין. But once again our case does not require or permit new קדושין.

The original ketubbah implies that if she is freed to marry another man then she is entitled to collect what is due her. Since she is not allowed to marry another, due to the fact that she is still married, the original ketubbah is still in effect. Therefore a new ketubbah is not required. In fact the Rambam states:

שהמגרש את אשתו והחזירה סתם על כתובתה הראשונה החזירה.

If a man divorces his wife and remarries her, he does so based on the original ketubbah.[3]

A contemporary posek, Rabbi Moshe Feinstein, deals with a case of a couple that had been divorced in a civil court two years before and are now reconciled and wish to be remarried. They require a civil ceremony, but do not want to go to a judge lest they be mistaken for non-observant Jews and would like a rabbi to "remarry" them. Rabbi Feinstein advises against a ceremony, even without ברכות, lest it mislead people into believing that a civil divorce has standing in Jewish law.

However, there is a change in the situation of the couple. The husband will be taking her anew to his home, as was the case in the beginning of the marriage. Rabbi Feinstein advises the rabbi to sign the civil license and have it witnessed. This would also avoid the need for the couple to have to resort to a judge for the civil license, which would also be misleading, albeit in a different way.[4] It is interesting to note that Rabbi Feinstein approves of a rabbi acting solely in a civic capacity, even where there is no specific Jewish religious role for the rabbi.

A Religious, Psychological and Civil Need

A civil divorce is not recognized as a divorce by Jewish law. Hence the couple is still married, according to Jewish law. We concur with Rabbi Feinstein that there is a role for the rabbi in the renewal of their marriage relationship. But we would not limit the rabbi's role to filling out the civil license, though this is important.

---

[2] Even HaEzer, Hilkhot Gittin 150:4.

[3] Rambam, Hilkhot Ishut 16:30.

[4] R. Moshe Feinstein, *Iggrot Moshe*, Yoreh De'ah, B, siman 44.

The civil divorce has left its mark on everyone who is involved. The man and woman have lived their lives as divorced for years. If there are children, the children know that their parents were divorced by the civil courts, and they need a symbolic reunion of their parents. In the eyes of society they are divorced. And, there needs to be a civil marriage ceremony to reestablish a legal relationship.

Of utmost importance the couple has chosen not to go to a judge to perform a civil ceremony. They have come to a rabbi, for they are looking for a religious renewal of their relationship. They are part of our community, and we should be responsive to their need.

Our community, too, is not Rabbi Feinstein's community. He knows his community and its needs, when he advises the rabbi not to give legitimacy to a civil divorce, by not having a Jewish ceremony. The primary need of our community, however, is for a Jewish and religious affirmation of what is a renewal of a relationship that had been estranged. The miracle of such a reconciliation, and the ability to bridge disruptive differences in a relationship, needs to be celebrated.

Not a Marriage but a Renewal

Rabbi Feinstein's concern about according legitimacy to civil divorce, and weakening the felt need for a Jewish divorce, can be handled in a different way. The rabbi in an interview should explain that, according to Jewish law, a civil divorce does not end a Jewish marriage. A Jewish divorce is required. Hence the ceremony that will be performed is not a Jewish marriage, but a renewal of their previous marriage, a celebration of the end of their estrangement. The term "renewal ceremony" should be used by the rabbi in all discussions with the couple. The rabbi should encourage the couple to use the term "renewal ceremony" with their family and friends, and if invitations are sent out, the invitations, too, should use the term "renewal ceremony" and not "remarriage." This also should be emphasized in the rabbi's remarks during the ceremony, so that those attending will not be misled.

Renewal Ceremony

The renewal ceremony should pay heed to the cautions of both the Rambam and the Even HaEzer and not use a new ketubbah, though the original ketubbah, when identified as such, may be read again. If the original ketubbah is no longer available, a כתובה דאירכסא (replacement) should be provided and identified as such. The ברכות ארוסין and the שבע ברכות are not to be recited, to avoid ברכות לבטלה (mention of God's name in vain).

The rabbi will have to develop a ceremony which, while it should not be a marriage ceremony, may utilize some parallel elements. The *Moreh Derekh* has a section on anniversary ceremonies (vol. 1, pp. C68-70) containing material which, with a little modification, can be used in a renewal service.

Keep in Mind

1. While the Rabbinical Assembly has a policy forbidding its members to participate in a purely civil ceremony, this renewal ceremony also has religious overtones. Note that a civil marriage license is required, and should be filled out and witnessed before the ceremony.

2. A new ketubbah should not be filled out. If the old ketubbah is used it should be described as the same one used at the first wedding. If a כתובה דאירכסא (replacement) is used it must be identified as such (reading aloud the part which indicates it is a replacement). However if the couple wants to write תנאים, the rules that will be the basis of their old/new rela-

tionship, they should be encouraged to do so. It should be signed before the ceremony. If this document is used at the ceremony, it should not be designated as the ketubbah.

3. Since a huppah symbolizes the home, it may be used during the ceremony. However, reference should be made to the fact that "once before you stood under the huppah to establish a Jewish home, and now you are renewing your relationship and are re-establishing your home, affirming your determination to once again make a life together."

4. If rings are used, it is preferable to use the original wedding rings. If they are no longer available, new rings may be used. However, it is prohibited to use the הרי את מקודשת לי formula. Substitute, for the husband, וארשתיך לי לעולם....For the wife, it is appropriate to say דודי לי ואני לו.

5. The ברכות ארוסין should not be used. The שבע ברכות should not be recited with שם and מלכות. An abbreviated version may be used (see p. C69, vol. 1 of *Moreh Derekh*). The blessing over wine should be recited, and both drink from the wine, followed by שהחינו.

6. The rabbi, in his or her remarks, should refer to the fact that this is not a marriage, but the renewal of a relationship that had been broken and is once again made whole (שלם).

Conclusion

A couple that has been divorced in the civil courts, but has not gotten a Jewish divorce, is still considered to be married by Jewish law. Neither party has remarried in the interim. If they decide to reconcile, they do not require a Jewish marriage ceremony. However a renewal ceremony which celebrates their reconciliation is strongly recommended. A rabbi should compose an appropriate ceremony and perform it. However, a new ketubbah should not be written, nor should the traditional שבע ברכות be recited.

Appendix: Sample Ceremony of Renewal

(Based on the Anniversary service found in the RA *Moreh Derekh*.)[5]

Rabbi's words of introduction:

[NUMBER] years ago, in the presence of family and friends you consecrated your love for each other. The challenges of marriage and the difficulties you experienced in your relationship brought you to a parting of the ways. Today you are renewing your marriage and consecrating your life together, promising one another to share the joys and sorrows, the tasks and responsibilities of family life. May God bless you and strengthen your resolve in the years ahead.

Ring Ceremony:

[GROOM], will you now take the ring and place it once again on [BRIDE]'s finger, affirming וארשתיך לי לעולם, "I will betroth thee to me forever."

[BRIDE], will you now take the ring and place it on [GROOM]'s finger, affirming דודי לי ואני לו, "My beloved is mine, and I am his."

The original ketubbah or תנאים *may be read.*

[GROOM] and [BRIDE], [NUMBER] years ago you stood under the huppah and heard the שבע ברכות, the Seven Benedictions, recited. I will now repeat a version of these blessings, following which you will sip from the same cup of wine, symbolizing your renewed determination to share all that life brings, both its joys and its sorrows.

Blessing over wine, followed by שהחינו.

---

[5] See *Moreh Derekh*, Rabbinical Assembly, section on Anniversary celebrations.

EH 150:4.1999b

Renewal of Marriages for Couples Without Get: A Dissenting Opinion

Rabbi Judah Kogen

This paper was submitted as a dissent to "Renewal of Marriage for Couples Without Get" by Rabbis Kassel Abelson and Mayer E. Rabinowitz. Dissenting and concurring opinions are not official positions of the Committee on Jewish Law and Standards.

The Committee on Jewish Law and Standards of the Rabbinical Assembly provides guidance in matters of halakhah for the Conservative movement. The individual rabbi, however, is the authority for the interpretation and application of all matters of halakhah.

If a couple who had been married under Jewish law is divorced under civil law without terminating the marriage under Jewish law, and now wishes to restore their marital union, we all agree that: (A) They do not require a new Jewish marriage ceremony; (B) they may not have a new Jewish marriage ceremony; (C) they must have a new civil marriage ceremony; and, (D) a public re-affirmation of their marriage is desirable (though not required.) Rabbis Abelson and Rabinowitz call for the rabbi who conducts the public re-affirmation of their marriage to also — at the same time — officiate at their *civil* marriage ceremony.

Most, if not all jurisdictions in North America allow clergy to perform marriages on the same basis as civil officiants. Thus, a rabbi may be permitted *by the state* to solemnize the marriage of couple not eligible to be married under Jewish law. We have always discouraged rabbis from doing so. It is the policy of the Rabbinical Assembly that a rabbi may not officiate at a wedding which is a civil marriage but not in conformance with Jewish law. The Rabbinical Assembly has, in fact, imposed sanctions on rabbis who have done so. In the most extreme cases, the halakhic consideration would be that the officiating rabbi is labeled a מומר לאותו דבר and would be banned from solemnizing any marriages at all.

The fact that the state may permit us to do something does not mean we should permit ourselves to do it. We, as a rule, expect that a rabbi will solemnize only marriages which take place under Jewish law. While the couple in this case must be remarried under civil law, the fact that the rabbi conducts the ceremony allows all concerned to conclude that Jewish law recognizes their civil ceremony as binding. It makes it appear as if a new religious ceremony is required and also makes it appear as if couples divorced under civil law may remarry under the auspices of a rabbi.

We would be much better advised to have the couple remarry in a civil ceremony conducted by a Justice of the Peace and reaffirm their marriage publicly in a separate religious ceremony such as the one proposed by Rabbis Abelson and Rabinowitz. Similarly, a couple who choose to be reunited after a lengthy separation who were never divorced under either legal system, may opt for the same re-affirmation ceremony which presupposes that the couple has always been married and is now restoring their family life. By the same token, a situation may arise in which a couple which had been divorced under civil law but not Jewish law chooses to re-marry (under civil law) and opts to forego the reaffirmation ceremony suggested by the authors of this responsum. In that case, it should be clear that a rabbi should not conduct the civil wedding ceremony under any circumstances.

Responsa Relating to Hoshen Mishpat
חושן משפט

הלכות דיינים   Jurisprudence

הלכות חובל בחבירו   Harming Others

HM 2.1993

A Principled Defense of the Current Structure and Status of the CJLS

Rabbi Gordon Tucker

This paper was discussed and accepted into the record of the CJLS on February 17, 1993, without being voted upon.

The Committee on Jewish Law and Standards of the Rabbinical Assembly provides guidance in matters of halakhah for the Conservative movement. The individual rabbi, however, is the authority for the interpretation and application of all matters of halakhah.

Introduction

Every so often in the history of the Rabbinical Assembly, concerns are raised about the structure of the Committee on Jewish Law and Standards (henceforth: CJLS), and whether it adequately serves both the ideology of the movement and the needs of the RA's members. Such discussions surrounded its creation in 1927, its restructuring in 1948, and various changes in its by-laws. Indeed, my own earliest, and still most vivid memory of a spirited exchange on the floor of the RA Convention, was the heated debate at the 1976 Convention, during which members presented a resolution which stated, among other things, that the CJLS, as then structured, "weakens the authority of all rabbis, whether the individual rabbi agrees or disagrees with the majority decision of the Committee. . . .In this way, the Mara D'atra becomes less and less his own congregation's interpreter of the classical sources of the Jewish tradition."[1] The resolution called for the CJLS to be dissolved, and to be replaced by a "Panel on Jewish Law", which would have had the authority to respond only to individual rabbis who had sent in queries, and which would not have produced published, authoritative responsa. Although the resolution was defeated, it did enjoy some significant, and vocal support. It is perhaps worth remembering that the opposition to the central authority of the CJLS in that instance, and in other similar ones, came from members dissatisfied with what they considered liberalizing decisions of the Committee. To them, the authority of the מרא מאתרא meant not legal atomism and chaos, but their right to issue פסקי הלכה in accordance with their own consciences and religious convictions, taking the histories and needs of their communities into account.[2] There was then, and I believe still is, a strong majority in the RA that believes in the

---

[1] *PRA* 38 (1976): 318.

[2] The 1976 episode, and a host of other important details of CJLS history through 1980, is described thoroughly in

importance of a central Law Committee with significant scholarly and moral authority in the Movement, and which simultaneously is committed to a certain inalienable authority that each local rabbi has in the area of halakhah. There is surely a tension here, and the rules of the CJLS have, in their fluctuation over the years, reflected that tension. But the argument of this paper will be not only that the CJLS structure accurately mirrors the political and professional dynamics of the Conservative rabbinate, but that it also conforms best to our religious convictions, and indeed to corresponding tensions evident in many, diverse classical sources on halakhic authority.

To be more specific, it is this conception of the role and the authority of the CJLS that I will be defending here:

> The CJLS is the central body in the Conservative movement for halakhic discussion and decision making. Its authority derives from the assent of the members of the Rabbinical Assembly that there should be a central body composed of members who have significant expertise in Jewish law, and who are willing and able to devote a significant amount of time to researching, discussing, and debating halakhic matters that affect Conservative Rabbis and the movement generally. The CJLS thus brings a much-needed consolidation and focusing of legal opinion to what otherwise would be an overly decentralized and chaotic field. For this reason, the CJLS can be said to be the halakhic voice of the movement as a whole, and it is thus undesirable and inconsistent with Rabbinical Assembly aims for there to be other law committees or panels that publicly issue responsa in the name of Conservative Judaism. (An exception to this observation is the authority explicitly granted to the Masorti movement's panel to issue responsa on דברים התלוים בארץ.) Because it is a body that seeks to coalesce judgment around particular halakhic opinions, and not simply to give voice to individually held positions, it is right and proper that six members of the CJLS be required to define an authoritative opinion. Because it is a body that is ultimately here to provide service and guidance to Rabbinical Assembly members, it is also right and proper that authoritative opinions not be categorized by the number of votes that they received, and that they not be binding on Rabbinical Assembly members in a coercive sense, but rather only in the sense that we are bound by our covenant to one another to give extraordinary weight to CJLS responsa in reaching our own legal decisions. Should a Rabbinical Assembly member choose, upon study and consideration, not to follow any CJLS position on a given matter, he or she would thus be unable to claim any authority or backing for that position from the CJLS, a "sanction" which in some circumstances could be substantial, in others not. Some constituencies of the movement, such as the United Synagogue, can choose and have chosen to bind themselves to follow only authoritative CJLS opinions. And finally, the CJLS may, as a legislative initiator, propose to the Convention a Standard of Rabbinic Practice, which would coercively

---

the unpublished paper, "The Clearing House: A History of the Committee on Jewish Law and Standards," by George Nudell.

apply to all Rabbinical Assembly members. The plenum of the Convention actually enacts the Standard. Thus, it could be said fairly that halakhic authority in our movement is shared. It ultimately resides with the Mara D'atra, though by covenant the CJLS in practice serves as the authoritative guide for legal decision, and by Rabbinical Assembly rules, the CJLS and the plenum share the legislative power to enact the Standards that define, in part, our legal boundaries.

And now to the defense.

Majoritarianism and Authoritarianism

The CJLS operates on what I shall call a "modified majoritarian principle" for which there is, apparently, no real precedent in pre-modern Jewish life. It is a "modified" majoritarianism because, as is well known, we do not have "majority" and "minority" opinions as such, and even positions that do not enjoy a majority, or even a plurality, on the CJLS can be authoritative Committee pronouncements. Yet it is majoritarian in the sense that votes are taken, and CJLS rules define a threshold (six votes) below which opinions are יחידים דעות and are denied Committee sanction. We will turn our attention to the CJLS's characteristic modifications of majoritarianism a bit later. For now, we must focus on majoritarianism in any form as a Jewish religious construct.

The adherence in Rabbinic Judaism to the majoritarian principle is among its most basic postulates. It is classically formulated in any number of texts, and for our present purposes two of these will illustrate the point sufficiently:

1. ולמה מזכירין דברי היחיד בין המרובין הואיל ואין הלכה אלא כדברי המרובין.³

2. רבנן פליגי עילווך ויחיד ורבים הלכה כרבים או דילמא רבנן כוותך סבירי להו.⁴

Both of these texts incidentally make it quite clear that the issue of majoritarianism is inseparable in Rabbinic Judaism from the equally important matter of the authority of the rabbinic court. For the text in עדויות goes on to restrict severely the circumstances under which a court's rulings may be overturned, and the text in ברכות implies that Rabban Gamaliel's sons would have disregarded their father's ruling (on the latest hour for reciting the evening שמע) had a majority of his contemporaries ruled differently. We shall return to this connection presently. For now, it is clear that the Rabbinic view of the law allowed for it to be determined by a majority vote, and that was quite a stunning departure from the biblical view that God's law is mediated through prophets or oracular devices, which are assumed to be unambiguous and with respect to which majority views are irrelevant. The Rabbis knew they were doing something quite different from what prophets had done, and that in some sense their own enterprise was incompatible with prophecy and the direct divine authority it claimed. Consider this passage from the Sifra:

אלה המצות: אין נביא רשאי לחדש עוד דבר מעתה.⁵

---

³ משנה עדויות א׳: ה׳.

⁴ בבלי ברכות ט.

⁵ ספרא בחקתי י״ג:ז׳.

which retroactively nullified the innovative power of any prophet after Moses, in apparent flat contradiction of the plain intent of Deuteronomy 18.[6] Even more to the point, Maimonides, in the introduction to his commentary on the Mishnah, states what he believes to be the fundamental difference between rabbinic activity and the activity of all prophets other than Moses (who is referred to here as הנביא):

> ומי שלא שמע בו פירוש מפי הנביא ע"ה... הוציא דינים בסברות במדות
> השלש עשרה... שהתורה נדרשת בהם... וכשהיתה נופלת המחלוקת היו
> הולכים אחרי הרוב כמו שנאמר אחרי רבים להטות. ודע שהנבואה אינה
> מועילה בפירושי התורה ובהוצאת ענפי המצות בשלש עשרה מדות אבל
> מה שיעשה יהושע ופנחס בענין העיון ובסברא הוא שיעשה רבינא ורב
> אשי.[7]

In fact, not only is prophecy obsolete, one may not even legitimately think of reviving it:

> וכן... שאמר בדין מדיני התורה שה' צוה לו שהדין כך הוא והלכה כדברי
> פלוני, הרי זה נביא השקר ויחנק – אע"פ שעשה אות – שהרי בא להכחיש
> התורה שאמרה לא בשמים היא.[8]

And yet, despite the ideology that saw prophecy as a dead institution of the past, some Rabbis, certainly, saw themselves as the *successors* of the prophets:

> אמר רבי אבדימי דמן חיפה מיום שחרב בית המקדש ניטלה נבואה מן
> הנביאים וניתנה לחכמים. אטו חכם לאו נביא הוא? הכי קאמר אע"פ שניטלה
> מן הנביאים מן החכמים לא ניטלה. אמר אמימר וחכם עדיף מנביא.[9]

These are strong and bold statements attributed in this text to two different אמוראים of different places and different generations. And indeed, it has many echoes in talmudic and later rabbinic literature. This has important implications. Among other things, it means that the negation of prophecy did not necessarily mean that the rabbinic court would forego the authority that the prophets enjoyed. Rabban Gamaliel claimed precisely that kind of authority on a number of famous occasions, and although he attributed what some viewed as his high-handedness to utilitarian social/political motives,[10] others after him went beyond utilitarianism to make stronger claims about the majoritarianism of the rabbinic court. Nahmanides, for example, in his comment on Deut. 17:11 – לא תסור מן הדבר אשר יגידו לך ימין ושמאל – began with Rabban Gamaliel's utilitarian justification for the domination of the majority, but then went on to a more metaphysical claim:

> כי על דעת שלהם הוא נותן לנו התורה אפילו יהיה בעיניך כמחליף הימין
> בשמאל וכל שכן שיש לך לחשוב שהם אומרים על ימין שהוא ימין כי רוח

---

[6] Verses 14-22 of that chapter set forth the obligation to heed the teachings of a prophet who has been granted a revelation by God, and who correctly predicts a wondrous event. The need for a "sign" obviously presumes some new, innovative, perhaps even startling statement by the prophet. Indeed, the context of this section is equally clear that Israel is being singled out from the nations in the following sense: the other nations rely on "readings," of the stars, or other phenomena or forces of nature. Israel is not to "read" that which is there, but is to be granted continually renewed revelations from God, through a prophet.

[7] רמב"ם, הקדמה לפירוש המשניות.

[8] רמב"ם, *משנה תורה*, "הלכות יסודי התורה" ט"ו:ד'. Again, the contradiction of Deut. 18:14-22 is noteworthy.

[9] בבלי בבא בתרא י"ב.

[10] רשב"ע, גלוי וידוע לפניך שלא לכבודי עשיתי ולא לכבוד בית אבא עשיתי אלא לכבודך שלא ירבו מחלוקות בישראל – בבא מציעא נ"ט:

השם על משרתי מקדשו ולא יעזוב את חסידיו לעולם נשמרו מן הטעות ומן המכשול.[11]

Here we have the claim that there is a Divine Providence which warrants that the majority of the court will invariably be right, and thus a justification for the court taking on the authority of the prophet, to the point of the most severe sanctions against those who would defy its rulings.

The point of the texts brought in the previous paragraph is that it would be a mistake to celebrate the Rabbis' majoritarianism as a clear triumph of democracy or decentralization of religious authority; on the contrary, their majoritarianism operated within a clearly defined elite circle, and the court constituted by that circle was endowed with the authority of the priest or the prophet, in that failure to submit to the discipline of its rulings was punishable by death.[12] The Rabbis may have opened up the univocal and uncompromising biblical כה אמר ה' into a process of debate and vote, but they still operated under a very authoritarian rubric. Once the debate and the vote were over, dissent was, at least theoretically, to be suppressed. Whatever "democratization" was inherent in the move from prophet to published text was all but nullified by the rigid authority claimed by the majority on the basis of the Deuteronomic לא תסור.[13]

Such, at least, was the theory. A closer consideration of the issue, and examination of some of the relevant texts, reveals, however, that majoritarianism was not necessarily and inexorably bound up with the authoritarianism symbolized by Rabban Gamaliel. For some in the Rabbinic world, the break with prophecy was more complete and more fundamental.

To understand this other mind set, I think it important to reflect on at least one aspect of the history of the verse in Exod. 23:2: לא תהיה אחרי רבים לרעות ולא תענה על ריב לנטות אחרי רבים להטת. Biblically, the meaning of the verse is, after all, fairly clear: "don't follow a majority when it is wrong." And certainly, the biblical view was that although a majority may have rejected, e.g., Jeremiah's instructions condemning the formation of alliances against Babylonia, Judeans loyal to God were expected to follow the prophet's "minority" view. A referendum, even if conducted solely among the prophetic elite, would have been irrelevant to the biblical mind.

Rabbinically, however, something unusual and striking happens to this very clear verse. In Mishnah Sanhedrin 1:6, for example, it is taken for granted that אחרי רבים להטת means "follow the majority," the exact opposite of its plain meaning. The understanding of the phrase לא בשמים היא, attributed to רב ירמיה (oh, the irony of the name here!) in בבא מציעא נ"ט: goes so far as to say that the majoritarian view is a constitutional principle by which God is, therefore, also bound. Now, why in biblical Judaism was it so clear that a majority should not necessarily be followed, and why, in Rabbinic Judaism was it so clear that a majority must be followed? The reason, I believe, is this: from the point of view of biblical Judaism, there is a truth, quite independent of the majority, that can be

---

[11] רמב״ן, פירוש התורה, דברים י״ז:י״א.

The ספר החינוך (ע״ח) formulates this in its own way:

...רבוי הדעות יסכימו לעולם אל האמת יותר מן המעוט. ובין שיסכימו לאמת או לא יסכימו לפי דעת השומע, הדין נותן שלא נסור מדרך הרוב.

[12] This, of course, is the law of the זקן ממרא, which the Rabbis transferred to their courts from Deut. 17:12, where it applies to the authority of the כהן. The analogous authority of the biblical prophet is stated in Deut. 18:19, where the death penalty is not explicitly stated, but the ominously threatening sanction אנכי אדרש מעמו gives the imagination clear direction.

[13] Deut. 17:11. We shall have occasion to return to this verse and its exegesis a bit later.

gotten through a prophet, or perhaps through the priestly אורים ותמים. From the point of view of Rabbinic Judaism, however, the statement כה אמר ה' is constitutionally forbidden, as much as would be a law that outlawed political dissent in Massachusetts. Rabbinic Judaism, in this understanding, is about the notion that we can't get religious truth directly. The majoritarianism of the Rabbis thus can be understood as flowing from an epistemological agnosticism, a conviction that what David Hartman has called the "immediacy" of the biblical period[14] is forever gone. And thus, the new reading and use of אחרי רבים להטות and such well-worn phrases as אלו ואלו דברי אלקים חיים must be seen for what they are: dramatic changes in the very definition of religious truth.

From this point of view, majoritarianism is not a matter of גזרת הכתוב, a new form of quasi-prophetic authority, but is rather born of a coming to terms with what truth means in the post-biblical and pre-messianic condition of epistemological indeterminism. It is our best tool for getting at religious truth, and thus the debates that precede the vote, and even the dissents that follow it, are integral parts of that quest for truth. This is no mere speculation; it is, in fact, reflected in a variety of rabbinic texts that decidedly do not see majoritarianism as being inevitably wedded to authoritarianism. One such text will suffice for the moment. It appears in the Palestinian Talmud, Tractate Sanhedrin, as a comment on the Mishnah which states the general principle that in both monetary and capital cases, the majority is to be followed:

אמר רבי ינאי אילו ניתנה התורה חתוכה לא היתה לרגל עמידה מה טעם
וידבר ה' אל משה אמר לפניו רבונו של עולם הודיעיני היאך היא ההלכה
אמר לו אחרי רבים להטות רבו המזכין זכו רבו המחייבין חייבו כדי שתהיה
התורה נדרשת מ"ט פנים טמא ומ"ט פנים טהור.[15]

Were it not for the last phrase, this text might also have been interpreted in such a way that the majoritarian principle was one dictated by גזרת הכתוב, and thus consistent with a Rabban Gamaliel-type exercise of coercive power. But כדי שתהיה התורה נדרשת seems to say more than that, and its significance was picked up by Moses Margoliot in his commentary on the Yerushalmi:

הודיעיני היאך ההלכה: שלא יהיה בה ספק. א"ל זה אי אפשר, אלא אחרי
רבים להטות וכו' מפני שהתורה צריכה שתהיה נדרשת במ"ט פנים לכאן
ולכאן ואם אני מגלה לך ההלכה שוב לא תהיה נדרשת בהרבה פנים.[16]

The פני משה is making the following point: If there is any גזרת הכתוב operative here at all, it inheres only in God's decision not to allow religious truth to be unambiguous and univocal. But given that decision (which is, like all of God's decisions, ultimately inscrutable), the majority enjoys no providential guarantee, nor any special metaphysical status. It is simply that the way, the best way, to approximate religious truth ever more closely is to foster the debates out of which a majority emerges. The way in which the פני משה here draws out the language of the ירושלמי makes it further clear that diversity in debate, and even a certain indeterminacy, is "good" for Torah — it is the way in which Torah should be pursued. And the truly remarkable thing about the ירושלמי here is that it retrojects this all the way back to Mount Sinai. Unlike the ספרא and the רמב"ם at which we looked earlier,[17] Moses himself

---

[14] See David Hartman, *Conflicting Visions* (New York: Schocken, 1990), pp. 19-30 ("Joy and Responsibility").

[15] ירושלמי סנהדרין ד':ב' (כ"ב).

[16] פני משה, ירושלמי סנהדרין ד':ב'.

[17] See n. 5 and n. 7 above.

(whom רמב״ם had called הנביא) is, according to this text, already in the post-prophetic age!

We have thus seen that there are two possible readings to the majoritarianism by which the decisions of the rabbinic courts have always been characterized. One of these is that the "procedures" changed, as it were, in post-biblical times. That is, the prophetic revelation was replaced with the sittings and votings of rabbinic courts, but the metaphysical and epistemological status of the pronouncements remained essentially the same. Religious truth was determinate, and it was determined by the court's majority. From that view followed the sanctions invoked by Rabban Gamaliel and all of his intellectual successors.[18] But there is another reading of the rabbinic majoritarianism, which we have begun to see emerge. That is the interpretation under which majority decisions are a best approximation to a truth which God has decided to leave indeterminate to humans, and are thus both the culminations of rounds of debate and dissension, and the preludes to further such rounds. We shall now spell this alternative view out just a bit more.

Majoritarianism without Authoritarianism

The theory under which all associated with the Rabbinic community owed unquestioning allegiance and obedience to the majority decisions of the court certainly did not operate unexceptionally. It was not just pivotal figures of the early period, such as Rabbis Eliezer and Yehoshua, who registered dissents and were said to have paid prices for those dissents. It seems from other texts, about later Sages, that the habits of asserting independence from majority decisions persisted. Consider an account given in the ירושלמי: The Mishnah states that:

אין נוטעין ואין מבריכין ואין מרכיבין[19] ערב שביעית פחות מל׳ יום לפני
ראש השנה ואם נטע או הבריך אי הרכיב יעקור.

Now the ירושלמי tells the following story:

לא עקר פירותיו מה הן? רבי בא רבי לא הוון יתבין בצור אתא עובדא
קומיהון. הורי רבי לא ישפכו פירותיו. א״ר בא אני לא נמניתי עמהן
בעלייה.[20]

The context makes it clear that a vote had been taken to add the additional and extraordinary sanction that if one (A) had violated what was a protective injunction pertaining to ערב שביעית, and (B) had also neglected to obey the sanction that required uprooting the sapling planted during the extended protective period, that one also (C) had to dispose of the fruit of such a tree when it was matured. But the text also makes it clear that רבי בא, not having been part of the voting body, would not agree to such a prolif-

---

[18] I am referring here, at least, to the interpretation on such sanctions given by רמב״ן (see note 11 above), whose understanding is by no means idiosyncratic and isolated, nor even original to him. As we've seen, however, the text in בבא מציעא נ״ט: attributes to Rabban Gamaliel a prudential/utilitarian, rather than a metaphysical/epistemological motive (שלא ירבו מחלוקות בישראל). I shall take up the utilitarian point of view explicitly only briefly in this paper, long enough to illustrate that once the metaphysical point of view is countered with a plausible alternative, the conditions of Jewish modernity to which we have become accustomed present, in addition, a ready counter to the utilitarian argument for attaching nearly inviolate authority to majority decisions.

[19] The reference here is, of course, to grafting part of a tree onto another tree of the same species. Grafting across species is forbidden whether or not it is the sabbatical year.

[20] ירושלמי שביעית ב׳:ו׳ (ל״ג:).

eration of גזרות, and felt free to rule on his own, as he saw fit.[21]

What makes the behavior attributed to רבי בא and others so striking to us is the fact that the juridical authority claimed by the Rabbis under לא תסור seems so strong.[22] Let us be specific about what a majoritarianism without authoritarianism must overcome, in terms of the textual tradition. One of the most famous of all the authoritarian texts is the one from the ספרי, constituting a comment on Deut. 17:11:

לא תסור מן הדבר אשר יגידו לך ימין ושמאל – אפילו מראים בעיניך על שמאל שהיא ימין ועל ימין שהיא שמאל שמע להם.[23]

The impact of this comment is potentially enormous, and it seems unequivocally to support the idea that the decisions of the rabbinic court have been endowed with a special status that transcends human reason, and therefore commands human assent.[24] What complicates the situation, and opens up alternative understandings, is an apparently diametrically opposed baraita which appears in the ירושלמי. It reads as follows:

יכול אם יאמרו לך על ימין שהוא שמאל ועל שמאל שהוא ימין תשמע להם? ת"ל ללכת ימין ושמאל – שיאמרו לך על ימין שהוא ימין ועל שמאל שהוא שמאל.[25]

Many efforts have been made to harmonize and reconcile the baraitot in the ספרי and the ירושלמי. The one that will be of most interest to us here, not only because of its persuasiveness, but also because it comes from a rabbi of the modern era, is that of David Zvi Hoffmann. Hoffmann notes that there are two verses in Deuteronomy that give a command with the words לא תסור – in 17:11 (the one we have looked at already), and in 28:14 – ולא תסור מכל הדברים אשר אנכי מצוה אתכם היום ימין ושמאל. In 28:14, the word אנכי is spoken by God, and therefore Hoffmann claims that we have here two potentially conflicting commands. One commands unswerving obedience to the rabbinic court (at least as the Rabbis understood 17:11), and the other commands unswerving obedience to God. That Hoffmann recognizes these as a potential conflict already demonstrates that he rejects the metaphysical view of the authority of a rabbinic majority (for the metaphysical view identifies that majority with the unitary will of God). Moreover, Hoffmann says that according to 17:11 (and thus the ספרי), one who wishes to follow the court without doing any study or investigation of one's own is fulfilling religious obligations fully. Indeed, Deuteronomy and the ספרי state the imperative so strongly in order to give

---

[21] Essentially the same story is told, with some different names (though רבי בא is still the main character) in ירושלמי מעשר שני א':א' (נ"ב:). A different story which also illustrates an ambivalence about the authority attached by some to court majorities is found in תוספתא אהילות י"ח:ח.

[22] Since רבי בא explicitly said אני לא נמניתי עמהן, this is not a claim that he was somehow flouting the law of ממרא זקן, which was not taken to apply to non-members of the voting court. Rather, it is a claim that the general, but unmistakable spirit of so many texts that the rabbinic court was to be the legal authority seems to be violated by the kind of cavalier statement attributed to רבי בא and others. See what follows in the main text of the paper.

[23] ספרי דברים קנ"ד.

[24] It won't do to argue, as some have tried, that the words מראים בעיניך in themselves allow us to conclude that this rule applies only when one only "suspects" that the court has made a mistake, but not when one "knows" it, since there are parallels to the ספרי passage in which the text reads simply מראין (which should probably be understood as מורין) and יאמרו לך. See David Zvi Hoffmann, *The Highest Court*, trans. Paul Forchheimer (New York: Maurosho Publications, 1977), pp. 111-112.

[25] ירושלמי הוריות א':א' (מ"ה:::). An interesting question here is just what the proof text appealed to by the ירושלמי is, if any. The problem is that consultation with a concordance confirms that there is no such verse as ללכת ימין ושמאל!

lenient decisions of the court greater authority: "The לא תסור had to be pronounced absolutely for the High Court as, otherwise, it would not have any validity, as many an individual would have denied recognition to a decision that rendered things easier out of scruples of conscience."[26] However, one who chooses to investigate and study further, and who comes to the conclusion that the majority of the court is mistaken, must reckon with the לא תסור of Deut. 28:14, which commands unswerving obedience to the commands of God. The court has no unbreakable monopoly on legal competence. Here are Hoffmann's strong and far-reaching words: "But on the other hand, so says the Baraita of the Yerushalmi, the second לא תסור has been pronounced for the word of God with all the more emphasis and absolutely. *For the Torah has been given as an inheritance directly to the whole community of Jacob, and no edict of the authority is able to delete even one word from the Torah....* In this case there is thus a conflict between the two לא תסור and the individual has to decide for one of them."[27] For Hoffmann, the issue was clear. The majoritarianism of Rabbinic law is not a גזרת הכתוב, which every individual, no matter who he or she is, is obligated to submit to. It is rather a divinely sanctioned accommodation to the indeterminacy of religious truth (also divinely ordained, according to the ירושלמי סנהדרין and the פני משה cited above, n. 15 and n. 16). The court's majority provides for the promulgation of the best consensus (of the community which looks to the court) as to what God's commands are. Once promulgated, those decisions are all that members of the community need follow to remain in good standing and good conscience. They do not, however, forbid or prevent individuals who can investigate on their own, and who can study, understand, and critique those very decisions, from coming to their own conclusions, following their reasons and their consciences.[28]

Here we have a persuasive justification for the majoritarianism without authoritarianism that we seek — and that characterizes the relationship between the CJLS and the individuals and institutions of our Movement. It is significant that this defense can not only be extracted from the classical texts (both normative and narrative), but is also explicitly and forcefully given in the writings of a traditional halakhist of the modern era — one who understood well what the forces of emancipation had irrevocably done to make a rigid, centralized, halakhic authoritarianism unwise. Indeed, it was not just Hoffmann in Germany who articulated this. For roughly at the same time that

---

[26] David Zvi Hoffmann, *The Highest Court* (see n. 24 above), p. 116. One cannot help being reminded here of the dissatisfactions voiced in the past against what were viewed as overly liberal majority decisions of the CJLS, and the desire of those who identified themselves as liberals to defend the central authority of the CJLS. See, again, the Nudell paper (cited above in n. 2) and the 1976 *Proceedings of the Rabbinical Assembly*.

[27] David Zvi Hoffmann, op. cit., pp. 116-117 (emphasis mine). Hoffmann is primarily speaking of occasions on which the individual scholar, acting as local jurist, would follow what his competent understanding told him was the will of God, rather than accept an overly lenient decision of the court. The substance of Hoffmann's argument, however, is equally valid for, and can be easily extended to, other cases in which the individual who is competent in halakhic texts would feel compelled to diverge, in teaching and practice, from the majority of the central court. Such occasions might include judgments that an overriding ethical imperative underlying the halakhic system itself had been neglected by the court's majority.

[28] These last two sentences correspond rather closely to two of the characteristics of the status of the CJLS set forth at the beginning of this paper. Specifically, it is perfectly in order and normative for individuals (lay or rabbinic) in the Movement, and indeed, for entire institutions such as the United Synagogue, to accept only authoritative decisions of the CJLS as their halakhic imperatives. At the same time, it is also normative and proper for rabbis, particularly those who are charged with making halakhic decisions for congregations, to study CJLS opinions and to come to their own decisions, even if they do not coincide with any CJLS opinions. That is the point of the ירושלמי in הוריות (see n. 25 above), and indeed, the בבלי as well (see: ב: הוריות, the section ending with the words דטעו במצוה לשמוע דברי חכמים).

Hoffmann made his argument cited above, a similar interpretation of the baraita in the ספרי was given in Eastern Europe by Naphtali Zvi Yehudah Berlin, the נצי"ב of Volozhin. The נצי"ב understands a comment in the שאילתות דרב אחאי גאון to be a reaction to a peculiarity in the text of Deut. 17:10. In that verse we are told: ועשית על פי התורה; and in 17:11 we are told: פי הדבר אשר יגידו לך מן המקום ההוא אשר יבחר ה'. אשר יורוך... תעשה לא תסור מן הדבר אשר יגידו לך ימין ושמאל. Here is the נצי"ב's commentary:

> ומקרא דעל פי התורה וגו' מיותר שהרי כבר אמר ועשית על פי הדבר וגו'
> ותו מאי הוא על פי הדבר ומאי הוא על פי התורה? משום הכי מפרש דאמר
> משה לפני המקום יתברך בזמן שלא יהיה המקום אשר יבחר ה' קיים
> מה יעשו? וא"ל על פי התורה וגו'. נמצא דבזמן שבהמ"ק קיים מה שיאמרו
> הסנהדרין אפילו שלא בהוכחה מכללי התורה ישמעו, אבל בזמן שאין
> בהמ"ק קיים דוקא על פי התורה.[29]

That is, a metaphysical aura may have surrounded the court at the time when the Temple stood, but that is all (safely?) in the past now. For the נצי"ב, normal rabbinic practice demanded that reasons be given for rulings of the court (for he understands the otherwise superfluous word תורה as "reasoned teaching" rather than as "pronouncement"). For those who had the competence to evaluate the court's proceedings, the court's authority extended no further than the persuasiveness of its arguments. The נצי"ב underscored this even more vividly in his commentary on the Torah:

> אבל בזמן שאין בהמ"ק קיים אזי דוקא על פי התורה אשר יורוך... וכל
> הדרשות אמת והתורה כפטיש יפוצץ סלע.[30]

We need no better summary of this position than that.

In order to conclude this section, a few words should be said about the utilitarian argument (attributed, as we've seen, to Rabban Gamaliel himself) that, irrespective of what one believes about the metaphysical significance of the rabbinic court, obedience to central authority serves to prevent undesirable fragmentation and sectarianism in the community. It has already been noted above that Hoffmann's and Berlin's endorsements of the right of the individual to diverge from the court's rulings on the basis of conscientious study and consideration are significant in the light of the fact that they are both nineteenth century, post-emancipation halakhists. Indeed, the contemporary Jewish world is marked not only by an irrevocable religious decentralization, but also by theological views which would seem to make the disutility of strongly sanctioned religious authority outweigh whatever gain might be expected from the point of view of promoting halakhic uniformity. Now a structure marked by a central interpretive body which is paralleled, and in some sense rivaled, by the halakhic authority of each individual מרא דאתרא is not unlike other familiar structures with parallel or overlapping jurisdictions. The late Robert Cover gave a principled defense of the jurisdictional complexities, redundancies, and rivalries in the American federal system against those who have argued for the desirability of a more uniform, linear flow of legal authority. It is an instructive defense for our purposes. For like those who have criticized the Conservative movement's legal structure (with local decisors somewhat beholden to, but still independent of, the CJLS) as incoherent and haphazard, there have always been those who have looked at concurrent and overlapping jurisdictions in the United

---

[29] העמק שאלה, על שאילתא נ"ח (משפטים), אות ל"ז.

[30] העמק דבר, על דברים י"ז:י"א (emphasis mine).

States as "an accident of history and a...malformed jurisdictional anomaly that we have endured, but not loved, for so long."[31]

But there is another way to view such complexities, argued Cover; not as a "dysfunctional relic," but rather as a product of a coherent evolution, which persists because of its strong functionality. He gave a number of interesting and compelling defenses of the maintenance of rival jurisdictions, but perhaps the most intriguing one — and one we would do well to heed — concerns the benefits of legal innovation that jurisdictional complexity and decentralization opens up:

> There may be with respect to many matters a potential for a unitary national norm....However, more typically we rely upon a regime of polycentric norm articulation in which state organs and lower federal courts enjoy a great deal of legislative autonomy. This multiplicity of norm articulation sources provides opportunities for norm application over a limited domain without risking losses throughout the nation. This proliferation of norm-generating centers also makes it more likely that at least one such center will attempt any given, plausible innovation....The multiplicity of centers means an innovation is more likely to be tried and correspondingly less likely to be wholly embraced. The two effects dampen both momentum and inertia.[32]

Stated in our terms, this argument means that, in addition to all the principled reasons we have given for maintaining the distinctive and delicate balance between the CJLS and the מרא דאתרא, our Movement's structure allows for religious and halakhic creativity locally, where the need for it first arises, and where its authenticity can best be evaluated. This is a precious resource indeed, and it should not be lightly dismissed for the sake of an elusive "uniformity" which will disappoint tomorrow those whom it satisfies today.

The analogy to a federal system should not be thought strange here. Indeed, we have not only theoretical statements on local autonomy from such sources, ancient and modern, as have been cited above, but historical precedents as well. H.H. Ben-Sasson, for example, characterized the status of the well-known ועד ארבע ארצות as follows:

> The Council of the Lands of the Polish Crown originated from the rabbinical court at the fairs held in Lublin. It acquired the status of a central bet din because of its activity during the meetings of merchants and heads of the communities and because famous rabbis participated in its deliberations....Even at the zenith of the activities of the councils, the autonomy of the individual community, which had its own independent boroughs, was undiminished...the bet din was competent to adjudge disputes among the constituents of the council, or between the council and its constituents.[33]

The ועד functioned for over 200 years, and served a crucially important centralizing

---

[31] Robert Cover, "The Uses of Jurisdictional Redundancy: Interest, Ideology, and Innovation," in *William and Mary Law Review* 22 (1981): 640.

[32] Ibid, pp. 673-674.

[33] H.H. Ben-Sasson, "Councils of the Lands," *Encyclopaedia Judaica* (Jerusalem: Keter Publishing House, 1972), vol. 5, pp. 995-996.

function. But it did not supplant local juridical competence, unless issues affecting the polity as a whole came before it.³⁴

Hundreds of years earlier, Rabbenu Gershom (early eleventh century) had already put together a similar kind of "federal system," at least as it is described by Finkelstein:

> [T]he traditional unity of the Jewish people had at last been disrupted. . . .Whereas previously the Jews throughout the world had looked to some central authority to guide them in matters of religious observance, each community now had its own traditions. . . .Rabbenu Gershom undertook no less a task than that of bringing all these scattered communities into a federation. . . .[T]he idea of a democratic federation had never been fully developed in Israel. There had been obedience to constituted authority but this authority was always based on that of past ages. Rabbenu Gershom proposed to establish a voluntary constitution among the communities that would claim its authority solely from those whom it governed.³⁵

Menahem Elon, in fact, understands the era of Rabbenu Gershom and its aftermath to have been a sort of watershed in Jewish jurisprudential history. It was, he tells us, at that time that central courts, like those of the Babylonian Geonim, ceased to function as master "receivers" to which all questions of consequence were transmitted. Local halakhah began to make its existence felt:

> כאשר אנו מציינים, שעיקרה של חליפת השאלות ותשובות מתקופה זו ואילך היתה בתוך כל מרכז ומרכז, אין כוונת הדברים לומר, שמכאן ואילך נותקו קשרי השאלות ותשובות בין המרכזים השונים. מתחילתה של תקופה זו, ובמשך כל הזמן שלאחר מכן, מצויות בידינו ידיעות רבות על שאלות ותשובות, שנשלחו ממרכז אחד למשנהו... ההבדל העקרוני, שחל מבחינה זו בין השו"ת בתקופת הגאונים לשו"ת שבתקופות שלאחר מכן, היה אפוא בכך, שבתקופת הגאונים עיקרן ורובן של השאלות באו למרכז שבבבל, ולאחר מכאן היתה חליפת השאלות ותשובות העיקרית בתוך אותו מרכז ורק חלק ממנה התנהל גם בין המרכזים השונים.³⁶

The local halakhah that was developing became prominent enough to have moved Rabbenu Tam, in the twelfth century, to make a sweeping statement (which was, admittedly, close to a דעת יחיד, but noteworthy nonetheless). He claimed that a majority can enforce its will on the minority only if the latter explicitly agreed to that majority's

---

³⁴ No exact analogy between the ועד and the CJLS is being claimed here. The sole point is that the co-existence of a central body with agreed-upon judicial powers and local centers of authority has good precedents in Jewish life. Nevertheless, the CJLS's role in initiating Standards of Rabbinic Practice can perhaps be seen as analogous to the handling of such polity-wide issues by central organs of authority in the past. Indeed, Standards are small in number, and are generally confined to such issues as conversion, Jewish status, etc. in which the crossing of jurisdictional lines makes reliance on each מרא דאתרא either impractical or nonsensical.

³⁵ Louis Finkelstein, *Jewish Self-Government in the Middle Ages* (New York: Philipp Feldheim, 1964), pp. 21-23. Finkelstein's work included as well, on pp. 257-264, the enactments of the Frankfurt Synod of 1603. That Synod had to "beg of every Rabbi who is not a member of this council to agree to these decisions. . ." (Section 9). Again, we see the balance between the central body with legislative power ceded and recognized by the communities, and the local rabbis who, like רבי בא centuries earlier, seemed to be able to say אני לא נמניתי עמהן בעלייה.

³⁶ מנחם אלון, *המשפט העברי* (ירושלים: הוצאת מגנס, תשל"ח), כרך ב', עמ' 1232–1233.

authority in advance.[37] If such points of view existed concerning the legislative power of central courts (i.e., concerning תקנות), about which there was always greater utilitarian concern about community harmony, how much more so would local autonomy be accepted with respect to interpretive, or judicial functions.

These several precedents are illustrative of how our judicial and community history often knew delicate balances between central authority and local autonomy. They should quell fears with respect to our own particular version of non-authoritarian majoritarianism as embodied in the CJLS. There is, indeed, not only nothing to fear, but perhaps blessing as well. As Cover put it:

> It seems unfashionable to seek out a messy and indeterminate end to conflicts which may be tied neatly together by a single authoritative verdict. . . .I, ultimately, do not want to deny that there is value in repose and order. But the inner logic of "our federalism" seems to me to point more insistently to the social value of institutions in conflict with one another. It is a daring system that permits the tensions and conflicts of the social order to be displayed in the very jurisdictional structure of its courts.[38]

The creation and maintenance of the central authority of the CJLS witnesses to the value all Rabbinical Assembly members place on "repose and order." But we, too, are a kind of federalism, with local rabbis playing the role, if we may say so, of lower, local tribunals. The tensions between the CJLS and the מרא דאתרא, which we have lived with since 1927, witnesses to our readiness to be "daring," and to uphold a structure which reminds the Jewish world, and ourselves, of theological principles that we recognize in our classical sources, and in which we deeply believe.

Conclusion

This paper has been a principled defense of, not a realistic resignation to, the current structure and status of the CJLS. That is, the previous sections have reviewed the textual and theological bases for the authority traditionally vested in the majoritarian procedures of rabbinic courts. We have seen that two alternative views (at least) are possible with respect to this matter: the first has been seen to flow from metaphysical beliefs about the divinely bestowed authority of the court's majority decisions, and the second has been seen to result from a theological conviction about epistemological indeterminacy in the post-prophetic age. Each one of these views carries with it implications concerning the rights of minorities and of individuals not on the court, implications which sharply diverge one from the other. While each view can consistently be maintained, it has been argued here that the second view is most in keeping with the history and theology of the Conservative movement, appropriate for the decentralized condition of the modern Jewish community, and amply supported by halakhic sources, ancient and modern. Indeed, the CJLS already operates under procedures quite different from traditional rabbinic majoritarianism. It has, since 1967, not even designated its opinions as "majority" or "minority" opinions, and it has done so out of a conviction that the majority of the court should not be granted a

---

[37] Elon (see previous note), vol. 1, p. 581. Also see Elon's discussion in vol. 1, pp. 549-550, concerning the tendency, after the time of Rabbenu Gershom, for there to be ordinances and rulings of a local nature that were not expected to be adopted by all Jews.

[38] Cover, op. cit., p. 682.

monopoly on legal competence and authority. What we have argued for, to wit a "majoritarianism without authoritarianism," thus applies with even greater force to the CJLS, with its already modified majoritarianism. Reaffirming the responsibility of each מרא דאתרא to study and consider CJLS opinions, and reaffirming the right of that מרא דאתרא to choose even a halakhic path not chosen by the Committee (except, of course, in cases where a Standard has been promulgated by the CJLS and the Convention), should be seen not as a challenge to the legal and moral suasion which the CJLS will always wield. Nor should it be spoken of apologetically as a haphazard quirk of the Movement, made necessary by political contingencies. Rather, it should be understood as an extension of the very logic that has created the CJLS and its internal rules, and as our faithfulness to obligations to God and to community that, as David Zvi Hoffmann observed, will sometimes live in tension. It is hoped that this paper may facilitate not only a new understanding of the current structure and status of the CJLS, but a new pride in it as well.

HM 424.1995

Family Violence

Rabbi Elliot N. Dorff

Part I: The Legal Status of Abuse

This paper was approved by the CJLS on September 13, 1995, by a vote of sixteen in favor and one opposed (16-1-0). Voting in favor: Rabbis Kassel Abelson, Ben Zion Bergman, Stephanie Dickstein, Elliot N. Dorff, Shoshana Gelfand, Myron S. Geller, Arnold M. Goodman, Susan Grossman, Judah Kogen, Vernon H. Kurtz, Aaron L. Mackler, Paul Plotkin, Mayer Rabinowitz, Joel E. Rembaum, Gerald Skolnik, and Elie Kaplan Spitz. Voting against: Rabbi Gerald Zelizer.

The Committee on Jewish Law and Standards of the Rabbinical Assembly provides guidance in matters of halakhah for the Conservative movement. The individual rabbi, however, is the authority for the interpretation and application of all matters of halakhah.

שאלה

1. *Beating:* According to Jewish law as interpreted by the Conservative movement, under what circumstance, if any, may:

    A) husbands beat their wives, or wives their husbands?

    B) parents beat their children?

    C) adult children of either gender beat their elderly parents?

2. *Sexual abuse:* What constitutes prohibited sexual abuse of a family member?

3. *Verbal abuse:* What constitutes prohibited verbal abuse of a family member?

תשובה

The Importance of the Conservative Legal Method to These Issues[1]

In some ways, it would seem absolutely obvious that Judaism would not allow individuals to beat others, especially a family member. After all, right up front, in its opening

---

[1] I would like to express my sincere thanks to the members of the Committee on Jewish Law and Standards for their helpful suggestions for improving an earlier draft of this responsum. In addition, I would like to thank Rabbi Debra Orenstein for her extensive comments on that earlier draft; Professor Judith Hauptman for sharing her work on wife-beating with me and for pointing me to the article by Abraham Grossman on that subject; Naomi Graetz, who has written a book-length manuscript soon to be published on wife-beating

chapters, the Torah tells us that we are all created in the image of God.² That fundamental tenet would seem to require that, at a very minimum, we do not physically abuse others. The classical Rabbis of the Jewish tradition, those who wrote the Mishnah, the Talmud, and the Midrash, certainly understood that to be the case, for rabbinic law assumes that we do not have the right to strike others and thus specifies five sorts of compensation for personal injuries. Specifically, assailants must pay their victims for their lost capital value, their time lost from work, their pain and suffering, their medical expenses, and the embarrassment they suffered.³ Courts may impose lashes for trespasses of the law, but due care had to be taken in the process to preserve the dignity of God and God's human creature, and even courts now refrain from such punishment.⁴ Indeed, the Rabbis took the notion of the integrity of the individual so far as to say that those who slander others (let alone cause them physical injury) are as though they had denied the existence of God.⁵ Conversely, Rabbi Eliezer said, "Let your fellow's honor be as dear to you as your own."⁶

Given these underlying principles, one would expect that any family violence that occurred within the Jewish community would be based on misinformation about our tradition, neglect of it, or simply the foibles of individuals. Unfortunately, when we probe the sources, we find some that permit forms of family violence, and some that actually encourage it. Consequently, before we delve into this subject, it is critical to indicate that the very method that we Conservative Jews use to interpret and apply the Jewish tradition requires us to see sources within their historical context and to make judgments appropriate to ours.

The Jewish tradition, after all, has spanned many centuries. During that time, it has not remained the same. Sometimes its development has been an internal unfolding of its inherent commitments in thought and in practice, and sometimes the example of other peoples among whom Jews lived produced changes within Judaism. Moreover, not all of the tradition is of an everlasting and compelling quality, and so generations of Jews have reinterpreted some parts of the tradition, all but ignored some, added other elements, and

---

and who was kind enough to share the results of her research with me and to offer constructive criticism of an earlier draft; Ms. Benay Lappe for giving me some materials on the definitions of the various forms of abuse from the psychological literature; Dr. Ian Russ for supplying me with a bibliography on sexual abuse of children (see n. 57 and n. 63 below) and for giving me important suggestions regarding the psychological aspects of this responsum; and Mr. Mark Rotenberg for sending me information on false reports of abuse.

This responsum is based on an essay I wrote for a joint project of the University of Judaism and the Jewish Family Service of Los Angeles. The book in which it originally appeared is *Shalom Bayit: A Jewish Response to Child Abuse and Domestic Violence*, Ian Russ, Sally Weber, and Ellen Ledley, eds. (Los Angeles: The Shalom Bayit Committee, 1992), pp. 48-57, 64-66. That book can be procured from The Family Violence Project, Jewish Family Service of Los Angeles, 22622 Vanowen Street, West Hills, CA 91207, phone (818) 587-3322.

² Gen. 1:26-27; 9:6.

³ M. Bava Kamma 8:1 and the Talmud thereon.

⁴ Thus the Torah (Deut. 21:22-23) demands that even someone executed on court order for cause be buried the same day to preserve a degree of respect for God's creation ("for an impaled body is an affront to God"), and the Torah (Deut. 25:3) similarly restricts the number of lashes a court may inflict to forty, "lest being flogged further, to excess, your brother be degraded before your eyes." The Rabbis, in fact, diminished the number further on these grounds; cf. M. Makkot 3:10-11; B. Makkot 22a; M.T. Sanhedrin, ch. 17. For a summary of the use and restrictions of flogging as a penalty, see "Flogging," *Encyclopaedia Judaica* 6:1348-51. Such flogging, though, was restricted to courts and was not, one would expect, given to individuals to impose on others. Since the Enlightenment, Jewish courts in the Diaspora no longer have had the authority to inflict lashes, and the Israeli system of justice does not include such a penalty either.

⁵ J. Pe'ah 1:1.

⁶ M. Avot 2:15.

have even taken steps to make some portions of the tradition effectively inoperative. These changes have sometimes occurred through conscious, judicial decisions and sometimes through the changing customs of the people Israel in many times and climes.

That historical understanding of Judaism is critical for identifying its contemporary message on any subject, and the topic of family violence is no exception. We look to the tradition for enlightenment and guidance, and we often find it in a simple, straightforward manner. Sometimes, however, traditional sources say things that we find obsolete or even offensive. When that occurs, we have not only the right, but the duty to exercise judgment. We must determine whether such a mode of thinking or acting recorded in the tradition is an historical remnant that must be altered because contemporary circumstances or moral sensitivities have changed, or whether the tradition as it stands is, instead, an indictment of our own way of doing things and a challenge for us to change. Thus, to accomplish our expectation to be taught by the tradition, we must be aware of the twin duties we have as its heirs: we must learn it and preserve it, and, at the same time, evaluate it and reinterpret it when necessary. Only then can it continue to speak to us with wisdom and power.

One other factor must be mentioned at the outset. This responsum is written in answer to Jews asking about the status of family violence in Jewish law. Jews expect their tradition to give them guidance beyond the demands of civil law, for we aspire to holiness. We certainly cannot interpret Jewish law to allow us to be less moral than what civil law requires.[7] Since civil law in most areas of the Western world now prohibits most forms of family violence, Jews must eschew it for that reason in addition to the grounds afforded by the Jewish tradition.

Acknowledging Family Violence Within Our Community

Family violence is not only an unpleasant memory from sources of the past; it afflicts our own Jewish families as well. That has not been part of our self-image; the contemporary Jewish community, in fact, is only now openly admitting that family violence occurs within its midst. Somehow we were supposed to be immune from such behavior; that was, our sources assure us, what non-Jews did, not how Jews behave. To take just one element of this problem, each of the past several years in the United States there have been over 400,000 reports of verifiable sexual assaults against children filed with authorities by teachers and doctors who deal with obviously battered and traumatized youngsters, and

---

[7] One might argue that Jews must avoid family violence because we are bound by civil law under the dictum, "the law of the land is the law" (דינא דמלכותא דינא). That may well be true, but it is not as clear as one might think, for that dictum was usually restricted to commercial matters. Even during the Middle Ages, though, Jews were forced by the government under which they lived to abide by its laws, and rabbis generally saw that as a Jewish obligation as well as a civil one — at least to protect the Jewish community from expulsion or governmental interference. Certainly, when Jews began living as full citizens under governments shaped by the philosophy of the Enlightenment, they saw themselves both legally and morally bound to abide by the government's laws, and that continues to this day. The operative principle, then, is not so much "the law of the land is the law" as it is the need to avoid the חילול השם (desecration of God's name) involved in Jews breaking just civil law and the requirement in Jewish law that Jews see themselves bound by moral standards beyond those of other nations.

For a discussion of the scope and rationales of "the law of the land is the law," see Elliot N. Dorff and Arthur Rosett, *A Living Tree: Roots and Growth of Jewish Law* (Albany: State University Press of New York, 1988), pp. 515-23. For a discussion of sanctification of God's name (and avoiding desecration of God's name) and holiness as reasons to obey Jewish law, see Elliot N. Dorff, *Mitzvah Means Commandment* (New York: United Synagogue, 1989), pp. 113-134. For the demand that Jews be at least as moral as non-Jews, see, for example, David Novak, *The Image of the Non-Jew in Judaism* (New York: Edwin Mellon, 1983), pp. 90-93, and "Kiddush Ha-Shem," *Encyclopaedia Judaica* 10:979-80.

studies indicate that at least one out of every three girls and one out of every five boys is sexually abused before age eighteen. Moreover, the number of cases of battered children reported to state agencies per year has grown from roughly two million in 1986 to three million in 1994, and some two thousand children, most of them under age four, die each year at the hands of parents or caretakers.[8] It is too early to know whether we Jews engage in these and other forms of family violence to the same degree as do other groups within the general population, but our community surely suffers from all modes of this malady.

Moreover, family violence occurs among the Orthodox at least as much as it does among Conservative, Reconstructionist, and Reform Jews. Devotion to tradition has not, unfortunately, prevented violent behavior within the family. Nobody, though, has the right to brag; family violence is all too common throughout our community. I have been a member of the Board of Directors of the Jewish Family Service of Los Angeles for about a decade now, with special interest in its Family Violence Project, and I have consequently been informed of the woeful extent to which this plague infests our community. Similar projects are now in place or in the planning stages in New York, Chicago, and other cities as Jewish communities throughout North America, Israel, and indeed the world finally acknowledge the problem and then take steps to deal with it.[9]

Beating Wives or Husbands

In this area of family violence as in all the areas to follow, we must be careful to distinguish acceptable forms of physical contact from abuse. Affectionate or supportive forms of such contact between spouses are certainly not included in the category of abuse; they are easily differentiated from objectionable behavior by their motive, the willingness of the partner to be touched in that way, and the lack of physical and emotional wounds that normally result. Even a one-time slap in anger, while not pleasant or ideal, does not constitute abuse. When I speak in this section of beating a spouse, then, I am referring to repetitive blows, delivered out of anger, a desire to control, or some other motive inimical to the welfare of the victim, that ultimately inflict bleeding or a bruise, even a temporary one.

Naomi Graetz has written a book-length manuscript on rabbinic responsa regarding wife-beating.[10] She divides the responsa into five categories:

---

[8] The 400,000 figure: Christine Gorman, "Memory on Trial," *Time*, 17 Apr. 1995, p. 55. The estimate of one out of every three girls and one out of every five boys: J. Crewdson, *By Silence Betrayed: Sexual Abuse of Children in America* (New York: Harper and Row, 1988). The figures for battered children in 1986 and 1994: *U.S. News and World Report*, 8 May 1995, p. 14, based on statistics from the National Committee to Prevent Child Abuse. That 2,000 children died through parental neglect or abuse: *U.S. News and World Report*, 8 May 1995, p. 14, based on statistics from "A Nation's Shame: Fatal Child Abuse and Neglect in the United States," a 248-page report of the U.S. Advisory Board on Child Abuse and Neglect.

[9] I would like to thank Rabbis Vernon Kurtz and Gerald Skolnik for alerting me to the current efforts and plans of the Chicago and New York Jewish communities, respectively, on these matters, and Ms. Anita Altman, Director of Resource Development for the New York UJA Federation, for sending me a fact-sheet on the services currently provided by New York area Jewish agencies to counteract family violence and the grant proposal that was just funded to coordinate their efforts. For a summary of some Conservative movement efforts on this, see Bette Fried, "Responding to Domestic Violence: A Progress Report," *United Synagogue Review* 47:2 (spring 1995): 15-16, 23.

[10] Some of her research can be found in her article "Rejection: A Rabbinic Response to Wife Beating," in Tamar Rudavsky, ed., *Gender and Judaism: The Transformation of Tradition* (New York: New York University Press, 1995), pp. 13-23. I want to thank her for sharing this article with me before it was published together with another as yet unpublished article that summarizes her research and that spells out this typology together with parts of her book-length manuscript on this subject. I also want to thank Professor Judith Hauptman for sharing her article-in-progress on this subject with me; it is now tentatively entitled, "Traditional Jewish

1. *Acceptance* — i.e., those rabbis who know that some Jewish husbands beat their wives and permit it. Such rabbis justify it either as a means for the husband to educate his wife in proper behavior, or as a way to obtain domestic harmony (שלום בית). Rabbis who permit husbands to beat their wives when they fail to perform the duties required of them by law or when they violate prohibitions in the law include Rabbi Yehudai Gaon (eighth century, Babylonia), Rabbi Shmuel Hanagid (936-1056, Spain), "the Gaon" reported by Rabbenu Nissim, and Maimonides, who writes that, "A wife who refuses to perform any kind of work that she is obligated to do may be compelled to perform it, even by scourging her with a rod."[11] Later Rabbi Israel Isserlein (1390-1460, Germany/Austria) permitted a husband to beat his wife if she cursed her own parents "in order to keep her away from this strict prohibition."[12]

A variation on this approach permitted a husband to beat his wife if she had hurt him, presumably so that after he vents his anger in this way, domestic harmony would return. That is how R. Shelomo ben Adret ("Rashba," c. 1235-c. 1310, Spain) rules,[13] and so does R. Moses Isserles ("Rema," c. 1525-1572, Poland), who condones wife-beating as a response to taunting or degradation. Thus R. Isserles rules that when the beating is rooted in the husband's aggression, it is not acceptable, and the court should compel him either to desist or to divorce his wife:

> A man who strikes his wife commits a sin, just as if he were to strike anyone else. If he does this often, the court may punish him, excommunicate him, and flog him using every manner of punishment and force. The court may also make him swear that he will no longer do it. If he does not obey the court's decree, there are some authorities who say that we force him to divorce her, if he has been warned once or twice, because it is not the way of Jews to strike their wives; that is a non-Jewish form of behavior.[14]

However, when the beating is caused by her antagonistic behavior, then the husband is subjected to no such penalties:

> But if she is the cause of it — for example, if she curses him or denigrates his father and mother — and he scolds her calmly at first but it does not help, then it is obvious that he is permitted to beat her and castigate her. And if it is not known who is the cause, the hus-

---

Texts, Wife Beating, and the Patriarchal Construction of Jewish Marriage." Naomi Graetz argues the same thesis — namely, that wife-beating stems at least in part from the inherent inequality in Jewish marriage — but from a metaphoric rather than a legal ground in her article, "The Haftorah Tradition and the Metaphoric Battering of Hosea's Wife," " *Conservative Judaism* 45:1 (fall 1992): 29-42. [NOTE: Graetz's book, subsequently published, is *Silence is Deadly: Judaism Confronts Wifebeating* (Northvale, NJ: Jason Aronson, 1998).]

[11] M.T. Laws of Marriage 21:10; cf. 21:3. The Mishnah (M. Ketubbot 5:5) requires a wife to "grind (flour), bake (bread), wash (clothes), cook food, nurse her child, make his [her husband's] bed, and work in wool." In M.T. Laws of Injury and Damage 4:16, however, Maimonides makes the husband who beats his wife liable for the usual remedies of assault, and in M.T. Laws of Marriage 15:19 he says that a man should honor his wife more than his body and love her as his body. For Rabbi Yehudai Gaon's position, see Otzar Ha-Geonim to Ketubbot, pp. 169-70. Rabbenu Nissim refers to "the Gaon of blessed memory" who allows a husband to whip (or to refuse to sustain) his wife if she refuses to do the chores delineated for her by law; see Rabbenu Nissim on Ketubbot 63b. For Rabbi Shmuel Hanaggid's position, see his Ben Mishlei, S. Abramson, ed. (Tel Aviv, 1948), p. 117, sec. 419.

[12] Terumat Hadeshen, sec. 218.

[13] Rashba, Responsa, pt. 4, sec. 113; pt. 5, sec. 264; and pt. 7, sec. 477.

[14] S.A. Even HaEzer 154:3 (gloss).

band is not considered a reliable source when he says that she is the cause and portrays her as a harlot, for all women are presumed to be law-abiding (כשרות).[15]

2. *Denial* — i.e., those rabbis who deny that Jewish husbands beat their wives. We have already seen in R. Isserles' comment that wife-beating "is a non-Jewish form of behavior" — even though he then condones it for Jews under specific circumstances.[16] R. Abraham ben David of Posquieres ("Rabad," c. 1125-1198, Provence) is more consistent. In commenting on the passage in which Maimonides permits a husband to beat his wife if she refuses to do the housework required of her by law, he expresses great surprise and says, "I have never heard of women being scourged with a rod."

3. *Apologetic* — i.e., those rabbis who seek to defend the honor of the Jewish community by whitewashing the facts. This usually involves a heavy dose of denial. When the facts cannot be ignored, though, apologists seek to marginalize the phenomenon, stating that Jews who engage in wife-beating do so less frequently and less violently than non-Jewish batterers; or to justify such behavior, maintaining that Jews who actually engage in such behavior do not really hurt their wives or do so for a good reason; or to displace the blame by shifting it to the surrounding culture. Often, even while acknowledging some of the evidence of wife-beating, apologists ignore other pieces of it that do not fit their thesis. Naomi Graetz points to Rabbi Joseph Hertz as an example of such an apologist.[17]

4. *Rejection* — i.e., declaring that wife-beating is unconditionally unacceptable. This is the strain of rabbinic rulings that is most in keeping with our own point of view. The three medieval rabbis who were most articulate on this issue were R. Simhah b. Samuel of Speyer (second half of the twelfth and the beginning of the thirteenth centuries, Germany), Rabbi Meir b. Barukh of Rothenburg ("Maharam," c. 1215-1293, Germany), and R. Perez b. Elijah of Corbeil (died c. 1295, France). R. Simhah, the earliest of these three, condemns wife-beating in the strongest of terms. He sees wife-beating as more serious an offense than assaulting any other person because a husband takes on a specific obligation to honor his wife in the marriage contract (ketubbah) beyond the normal obligations we all have to respect the integrity of other creatures of God. Consequently, Rabbi Simhah decrees penalties for wife-beating that are considerably more severe than the five remedies for general assault. He says:

> Therefore penalize him severely, whether physically or financially, for what has happened. Great repentance is necessary, and deal severely with him in the future as you see fit.[18]

Rabbi Joseph Karo records Rabbi Simhah's opinion more fully:

> I found in a responsum of Rabbenu Simhah that "it is an accepted view that we have to treat a man who beats his wife more severely than we treat a man who beats another man, since he is not obligated to honor the other man but is obligated to honor his wife, more, in fact, than himself. And a man who beats his wife should be

---

[15] S.A. Even HaEzer 154:3 (gloss). See also Moses Isserles, Darkhei Moshe to the Tur, Ever HaEzer 154:15.

[16] A note found in Isserles there (S.A. Even HaEzer 154:3) says that this was said several centuries earlier by R. Mordecai ben Hillel in his commentary on the fourth chapter (Na'ara) of Ketubbot, but I was not able to find it there.

[17] Joseph Hertz, *The Pentateuch and Haftorahs* (London: Soncino, 1938), p. 935.

[18] R. Simha in Or Zarua, Piskei Bava Kamma, sec. 161.

put under a ban and excommunicated and flogged and punished with various forms of torment; one should even cut off his hand if he is accustomed to it (wife-beating). And if he wants to divorce her, let him divorce her and give her the ketubbah payment."

Further on he writes:

You should impose peace between them, and if the husband does not fulfill his part in maintaining the peace but rather continues to beat her and denigrate her, let him be excommunicated, and let him be forced by non-Jewish (authorities) to give her a writ of divorce."[19]

(In traditional Jewish law, only a man can initiate a divorce, but under specific circumstances a court will coerce him to grant his wife a writ of divorce (a *get*) "until he says, 'I want to!'"[20] Such coercion has historically included everything from gentle persuasion to defaming him to his friends and employer to lashes, depending upon the degree of the husband's recalcitrance and the remedies available to the Jewish court. In modern times, the State of Israel has gone as far as imprisoning men who have refused to grant their wives a writ of divorce at the command of the court, but Jewish courts in the Diaspora lack that power and have instead used other tactics up to, and including, dissolution of the marriage through annulment.)[21]

Rabbi Meir of Rothenburg follows R. Simhah's lead. He too rules that "a man who beats his wife...is compelled (by the court) to give her a divorce."[22] Moreover, he says that, "The batterer must be boycotted and excommunicated, beaten and punished with all sorts of beatings, and his hand should be cut off if it used to beat her."[23]

Finally, in proposed legislation (תקנה), R. Perez b. Elijah of Corbeil, notes that, "The cry of the daughters of our people has been heard concerning the sons of Israel who raise their hands to strike their wives. Is it not rather forbidden to strike any person in Israel?" Citing the authority of the Tosafists, R. Samuel, R. Jacob Tam, and R. Isaac, sons of R. Meir, R. Perez then decrees that one who beats his wife must, on complaint of his wife, or one of her relatives, "undertake on pain of excommunication not to beat his wife in anger or cruelty or so as to disgrace her, for that is against Jewish practice." Furthermore, if the husband disobeys, the Court will assign the wife alimony as if the husband were away on a journey.[24]

5. *Evasiveness* — i.e., evasion of responsibility by the rabbis of the time, or "the wringing hands syndrome." The rabbis recognize that wife-beating is wrong, but they maintain

---

[19] Joseph Karo, Bet Yosef to the Tur, Even HaEzer 154:15.

[20] Kiddushin 50a; Yevamot 106a.

[21] For a discussion of how the Conservative, Orthodox, and Reform movements have dealt with this issue, and the legal theory behind each approach, see Dorff and Rosett, *A Living Tree* (at n. 7), pp. 523-45.

[22] Quoted in Moses Isserles' commentary on the Tur: Darkhei Moshe, Even HaEzer 154:11. However, another source (Responsa of Binyamin Ze'ev — first half of the sixteenth century, Greece — no. 88) cites Rabbi Meir of Rothenburg as one of those who permit physical punishment to chastise a wife. On this entire subject, see Samuel Morell, "An Equal or a Ward: How Independent Is a Married Woman According to Rabbinic Law?", *Jewish Social Studies* 44, nos. 3-4 (summer-fall 1982), pp. 190-201; and Rachel Biale, *Women and Jewish Law* (New York: Schocken, 1984), pp. 92-96.

[23] Maharam, Responsa of the Maharam (Prague edition), sec. 81. See also what he wrote in the Cremona edition, sec. 291, which is a later answer.

[24] Louis Finkelstein, *Jewish Self-Government in the Middle Ages* (New York: Jewish Theological Seminary of America, 1924), pp. 216-7. On the topic of those who reject wife-beating altogether see Graetz, "Rejection: A Rabbinic Response to Wife Beating" (at n. 10).

that they are powerless to do anything about it. So, for example, R. Solomon b. Abraham Adret ("Rashba," 1235-1310, Barcelona, Spain) says:

> A question was asked of him: What is the ruling for a husband who regularly beats his wife, so that she has to leave his home and return to her father's home?
>
> The answer is: The husband should not beat his wife. She was given to him for life, not for sorrow. He should honor her more than his own body. The court investigates to determine who is responsible. If he beats her, she is allowed to run away, for a person does not have to live with a snake. But if she curses him for no reason, the law is with him, for the woman who curses her husband leaves without collecting the money promised in her marriage contract (ketubbah). At any rate, I do not see that the court can do more than tell him in strong language not to beat her and warn him that if he beats her not according to law, he will have to divorce her and give her the money of her marriage contract.[25]

Similarly, R. David b. Solomon ibn Avi Zimra ("Radbaz," 1479-1573, Spain, Egypt), affirms the right of a husband to beat his wife "if she behaves improperly, according to our Torah, in order to bring her back to the right path, for she is under his jurisdiction." He adds the condition, though, that there must be witnesses to the wife's violation of the law, and he asserts that "he is not allowed to beat her for matters that pertain to him personally, for she is not his servant." Moreover, "if he habitually beats her, he should be punished." In a clear reference to R. Simha, however, he says, "There is one who exaggerated in his teaching and said that we can force him to divorce her, even by use of non-Jewish courts." In another responsum, Radbaz goes so far as to say that if the court does force the husband to divorce his wife on this ground, her children by a second marriage would be illegitimate (mamzerim).[26] In other words, the husband's actions may be wrong, and the court may even punish him for that, but it cannot free the woman to marry someone else on that ground. This Naomi Graetz rightly classifies as evasion of responsibility on the part of the court.

In sum, then, the sources are not as unified in their stance against wife-beating as we probably would have expected and certainly would have hoped. In general, rabbis living in Muslim countries were the most permissive of wife-beating, those in France less so, and those in Germany not at all. According to Avraham Grossman, wife-beating among Jews in Muslim countries was frequent, especially among the lower social strata and particularly when economic times were hard. Moreover, the phenomenon of early marriage for girls contributed to this, for the older men who were their husbands may have assumed that they were not only partners, but substitute parents for their wives. Undoubtedly, rabbis in Muslim countries were also influenced by Muslim practices, for the Quran calls upon the husband to beat his wife if he suspects that she is behaving immodestly or disobeying him.[27] Even so, Grossman asserts, "the situation of Jewish women in Muslim countries was better than that of the Muslim women." Conversely, in Germany in the eleventh to thirteenth centuries, women enjoyed high social status: the legislation of Rabbenu Gershon prohibited

---

[25] Rashba, Responsa, pt. 7, no. 477.

[26] Radbaz, Responsa, pt. 3, no. 447; pt. 4, no. 157.

[27] Quran, ch. 4, v. 38. See J. Schacht, *An Introduction to Islamic Law* (Oxford, 1964), pp. 161-168.

polygamy, restricted divorce against the will of the woman, and fixed a high sum in the woman's marriage contract, and women played a significant role in supporting the family. In addition, the Ashkenazic Hasidim made any insult or shame caused to a person, including wife-beating, not only a crime, but a sin, where repentance was inflicted measure for measure. This attitude clearly influenced those outside the community of Hasidim as well.[28]

In addition to these historical factors, there is an important legal institution underlying whatever permission exists in some sources for a husband to beat his wife, namely, that Jewish law assumes that the husband owns his wife. The Mishnah and Talmud went very far to protect the rights of the woman, but, after all is said and done, the very language for betrothal is that a man "acquires" (קונה) his wife.[29] It is precisely this that Naomi Graetz, Judith Hauptman, and others suggest we change to uproot the underlying legal context that sets the stage for the permission of wife-beating.

Even if one does not want to go that far in changing institutions from the past, we can certainly say that we no longer think of marriage as the acquisition of the husband, even if we still use that terminology (קנין). Husbands in our day have no more right to discipline their wives than wives have to discipline their husbands. In our times, then, the opinions of Maimonides and Isserles on this issue, among others, must be set aside as no longer applicable. Instead, relying on opinions like those of R. Simhah, R. Meir of Rothenburg, and R. Perez b. Elijah of Corbeil, as well as our own judgment, *we declare wife-beating is prohibited by Jewish law*. Indeed, those of us who want to retain the language of קנין for marriage would point out that, in traditional Jewish marital law, when a husband "acquires" his wife, he thereby takes on a number of binding legal and moral obligations to her, and, as we Conservative rabbis interpret those obligations, wife-beating is not only inconsistent with, but contrary to, those obligations.

Moreover, in cases where wife-beating occurs and cannot be corrected through therapy for the husband, we will do all in our power to help the woman free herself from the marriage. That includes counseling to help her make the decision to extricate herself from the abusive situation, referrals to Jewish Family Service or other such agencies that can facilitate that process and show her how to protect herself (and her children) from further harassment, guidance (if necessary) in obtaining legal help to dissolve the marriage in civil law, and then appropriate actions within Jewish law to dissolve the marriage by a formal Jewish writ of divorce (*get*), if possible, or by an annulment (הפקעת קידושין), if necessary. A commitment to the life and health of the woman demands no less.

The same is true in the opposite direction. While there is not, to my knowledge, any source within our tradition that ever allowed the wife to beat her husband, it does occur. Indeed, if instances of wife-beating are underreported because of worries about shame, slander, and economic support, instances of husband-beating are probably even more underreported because men are too embarrassed to admit that they have been battered by a woman; since childhood, after all, boys are taught that they are supposed to be the physically stronger gender.[30] Con-

---

[28] Avraham Grossman, "Medieval Rabbinic Views on Wife-Beating, 800-1300," *Jewish History* 5:1 (spring 1991): 53-62, especially pp. 57 and 59-60. I want to thank professor Judith Hauptman for calling my attention to this article.

[29] M. Kiddushin 1:1.

[30] As I was writing this, I happened to come across a "Dear Abby" column in the morning paper just on this topic. Abigail Van Buren states that "the number of men who have been battered by women would shock most people. This crime is underreported because many men are too embarrassed to admit that they have been battered by a woman." She then cites a letter from a man who "was raised never to hit a woman – even in self-defense" – another contributing factor to this phenomenon – but "many times my ex-wife

sequently, it is worthwhile to mention here that it is also the case that *husband-beating is also prohibited by Jewish law*[31] and is equally as reprehensible. In such cases as well we will do all in our power to help the man free himself from the abusive situation in ways similar to those delineated above for a wife suffering abuse.

The Rabbinical Assembly's recently-issued *Rabbinic Letter on Intimate Relations* applies this line of thinking to sexual areas as well. The Letter specifically prohibits coercive sex, and it recommends divorce, rather than passive acceptance, if the marital bond includes abuse by either party. This responsum specifically endorses those stands.

Child Beating

If a man's wife was construed as his possession in the past, all the more so were his children — a tenet that is shared by American law and that only recently has been challenged in the court case of Gregory K. "'Portable property' was Emerson's term for children, and most people believe kids do belong to their parents, body and soul. As a practical matter, the courts have tended to uphold that view."[32]

Similarly, if discipline was the major justification for Maimonides for beating a wife, that rationale applies all the more for children — at least in some Jewish sources. "Spare the rod and spoil the child" has firm roots in the biblical Book of Proverbs:

> Do not withhold discipline from a child; if you beat him with a rod he will not die. Beat him with a rod and you will save him from the grave.[33]

This applied to mothers as well as fathers:

> Rod and reproof produce wisdom, but a lad out of control is a disgrace to his mother.[34]

Along these lines, the Rabbis specifically exempt parents and teachers from the monetary damages usually imposed on those who commit assault on the theory that beating a child is sometimes necessary to carry out the parental duty of teaching the child Torah

---

would throw things at me and come at me with her fingernails, drawing blood from the scratches she would inflict on my face and neck. She even broke my arm and ribs when she threw a heavy chair at me." When he finally sued for divorce, she retaliated by filing charges that he had sexually molested their child. He had to "endure humiliating questions," and it cost him $10,000 in legal fees to prove his innocence — and that his ex-wife was clinically psychotic and paranoid with multiple personality disorders. "Meanwhile, the accusations were devastating." Aside from documenting one case of husband-abuse, this illustrates another point that will be discussed in Part IV, below — namely, the need to take careful steps in determining just who is at fault when there is alleged abuse. Abigail Van Buren, "Not All Spouse Abusers Are Men," *Los Angeles Times*, 28 May 1995, p. E2.

[31] M.T. Laws of Injury and Defense 4:18; S.A. Hoshen Mishpat 424:10. After this responsum was submitted and approved by the Committee on Jewish Law and Standards, Naomi Graetz pointed out to me that it should take note as well of the fact that some gay and lesbian partners abuse each other in patterns similar to wife-beating. While it would not be fair to the Committee to insert this in the body of the responsum after their vote, let me at least mention what is clearly in the spirit, if not the letter, of the responsum that the Committee approved — namely, that the same condemnation of abuse would apply to gay or lesbian partners, and the same aid to the abused party to extricate him/herself from the abusive situation must be extended.

[32] Pat Wingert and Eloise Salholz, "Irreconcilable Differences," *Newsweek*, 21 Sept. 1992, pp. 84-90. The citation appears on p. 84.

[33] Prov. 23:13-14; cf. Prov. 3:11-12, 13:24, 19:18, 20:30, 29:17.

[34] Prov. 29:15.

in its widest sense, including the difference between right and wrong.[35] (The teacher is, in the Rabbis' view, simply an agent to enable the parents to fulfill this responsibility of theirs.) Deuteronomy, the fifth book of the Torah, goes even further: it states that parents may bring a "wayward and defiant son, who does not heed his father and mother and does not obey them even after they discipline him" to the town elders to be stoned.[36] In the latter case, of course, the physical damage to the child is to be inflicted by public authorities and not the parents, and that is a significant difference, but the parents are still the instigators of this procedure.

One must immediately distinguish, though, between discipline of a child and child abuse. It is arguable whether striking a child is ever a good way to discipline a child, but if it is, that constitutes one end of a spectrum. Presumably, at that end the parent would hit the child only when the child's behavior was so unusually vile that, in the estimation of the parent, milder forms of reprimand would not work.

At the other end of the spectrum is child abuse, wherein the parent's striking of the child is frequent, uncontrollable, unprovoked, and excessively severe. Hitting the child is not responsive to the child's behavior or needs, but rather acting out the parent's frustration. This occurs especially when the parent either does not understand the needs of the developing child or has expectations of behavior that do not match the child's capabilities. Parents also abuse children when they do not know alternative, effective methods of discipline. Striking the child, then, is the parent's misdirected attempt to calm his or her own inner anxiety and is either not responsive at all, or is not properly responsive, to the child's behavior in his or her social and developmental context.

In between those extremes are cases in which the line between legitimate discipline and child abuse is harder to discern. Even granted such ambiguities in the middle of the spectrum, though, we surely have a problem in our society when ten to twenty percent of university students retrospectively report that as they were growing up, both they and other family members were beaten to the point of producing, at a minimum, bruises or bleeding.[37]

At most, then, verses like the ones from Proverbs cited above legitimate striking a child only for reasons of discipline, and then only when no milder form has been effective in correcting the child's behavior. We moderns, though, no longer think of children as the parents' property to do with as they will, but rather as the parents' blessings and the parents' responsibility to raise into moral, informed, caring, and productive adults. Moveover, we also now recognize that hitting a child is usually not the best way to accomplish those ends. Consequently, while we Conservative rabbis would acquiesce to a light smack on the buttocks (a "potch") or even striking the child elsewhere on the body with an open hand (but not punching or pummeling with a fist), only those types of contact

---

[35] M. Makkot 2:2; B. Makkot 8a-b. For a collection of rabbinic statements concerning corporal punishment, see Zvi Elimelekh Bloom, *Hanhaaot Ha-Hinukh* (Jerusalem, 5741), pp. 140-158. See also Gerald Blidstein, *Honor Thy Father and Mother: Filial Responsibility in Jewish Law and Ethics* (New York: Ktav, 1975), pp. 123-6, 208-9.

[36] Deut. 21:18-21. "Wayward and defiant" is the rendering of the new translation published by the Jewish Publication Society of America; other translations render "stubborn and rebellious." Verse 20 adds that, "He is a glutton and a drunkard."

[37] John N. Briere, *Child Abuse Trauma* (Newbury Park, CA: Sage, 1992), pp. 7-8. I would like to thank Ms. Benay Lappe for calling my attention to this book and for lending it to me. Others, however, maintain that the degree of physical injury is not what makes an action abusive; it is rather the use of physical force in an unwanted and intimidating way. ("Unwanted" must be part of that definition because people who voluntarily play football are certainly expecting to be subjected to physical force and even intimidating force, but since they see that as part of the fun of the game and since they voluntarily play, football in and of itself does not constitute "abuse.")

that do not produce bleeding or a bruise would be permissible. In contrast to the verses cited above from the Book of Proverbs and to the practice permitted in times past, however, *we forbid striking a child with a rod, belt, or instrument of any kind.* We also hereby declare that, as we interpret and apply the Jewish tradition in our day, it clearly and emphatically prohibits a parent's use of corporal punishment to the point of abuse — i.e., where the child is seriously harmed or where the punishment is clearly excessive as a response to the child's misdeed.[38]

After all is said and done, though, the use of corporal punishment, even within permissible parameters, is questionable. That same biblical Book of Proverbs that advocates the use of physical force in raising children also says, "Educate a child according to his own way."[39] The Talmud understands this to mean that parents should make age-appropriate demands so as not to put their children into a situation in which corporal punishment would be called for. In other words, parents have a duty to set reasonable standards for their children so as to avoid even being tempted to use physical forms of discipline. They must not put a stumbling block in the way of their children fulfilling the commandment of honoring them.[40]

Even in the worst of cases — the kind described by Deuteronomy — the Talmud could not accept anything like the death penalty. The Rabbis therefore legislated evidentiary procedures that made it impossible ever to attain a capital conviction in such a case. Once having created these barriers, they themselves said, "A wayward and defiant son [subject to execution according to Deut. 21:18-21] never was and never will be."[41] If the Rabbis insisted that even courts not go to the limit available to them under biblical law in physically punishing children, parents should certainly limit the physical punishment they inflict — or, even better, refrain from it altogether. After all, if the parents' duty is to teach the child proper behavior, they should not, in the process of doing so, do to the child exactly what they do not want the child to do to others. Educationally and pragmatically, then, as well as Jewishly, the best policy is not to use physical punishment at all.

One especially troubling aspect of this picture occurs in instances where parents beat retarded children. While there is minimal justification for beating a normally intelligent child for purposes of discipline, retarded children often cannot even understand why they are being subjected to blows, and so the abuse loses much of its justificatory cover. One

---

[38] M.T. Laws of Assault and Injury 5:1; Laws of Study (Talmud Torah) 2:2; S.A. Yoreh De'ah 240:10, 450:1; Kitzur Shulhan Arukh 165:7. Cf. M. Semahot, 2:4-6, B. Sotah 47a, and B. Sanhedrin 107b.

[39] Prov. 22:6. The context of the verse — especially the second line of the couplet — requires that the first part of the verse be rendered as the new translation of The Jewish Publication Society of America does: "Train a lad in the way he ought to go; he will not swerve from it even in old age." The Hebrew of the first part of the verse, however, is hard to read that way, and the Rabbis understood its words according to their usual meaning, as translated and developed here.

[40] B. Kiddushin 30a, and see Rashi there. Cf. also B. Mo'ed Katan 17a. Maimonides, following the Talmud, speaks of this restriction as applying to a "big child," which presumably means an older child (twenty-two or twenty-four years old, according to Rashi on B. Kiddushin 30a, s.v. משיתסר; see also S.A. Yoreh De'ah 240:20), or one married (even at a younger age), and perhaps even one financially independent of the parents, whatever his or her age. Maimonides, though, in the law immediately previous to this one, states that even though inordinate demands are included in the commandments of honoring and respecting one's parents, parents (presumably of younger children too) should not make harsh demands on their children lest they thereby create an obstacle to the child's ability to fulfill the commandments demanding their honor and respect; indeed, one who does so is to be excommunicated for violating the commandment in Lev. 19:14 of not producing such an obstacle! See M.T. Laws of Rebels 6:8-9. (Lev. 19:14 is interpreted by the Rabbis to prohibit putting a stumbling block not only before the physically blind, but also before those who are intellectually or morally blind; see Sifra on that passage, B. Pesahim 22b, and B. Mo'ed Katan 17a, which explicitly uses that verse to prohibit striking one's grown child.)

[41] B. Sanhedrin 71a.

can understand the extra measure of frustration that parents might feel in raising a retarded child, and one can certainly appreciate the additional demands that that entails over those involved in rearing a child of normal intelligence, but parents of retarded children need to get help so that they can respond to those aspects of parenting their special-needs child in appropriate, non-violent ways.[42]

The same rules that apply to the discipline of children — but with even less endorsement for striking the child — apply to family-like situations outside the family where adults are in charge of children. Thus teachers, youth group leaders, counselors, coaches, and the like may, at the very most, give a light slap on the buttocks to children to get them out of bed or going to the next activity. They may not strike the child in any form of corporal punishment.

None of the above, of course, is intended to prohibit hugging a child so as to comfort him or her or putting an arm around the child's shoulders as an expression of congratulations in, for example, a ball game. On the contrary, parents who refuse to hug their children or kiss them thereby deprive them of some of the most effective and needed forms of love. All of the above strictures, then, are with reference to acts of violence against the child, differentiated from acts of love or friendship by both the intention and context of the parties and the form and energy of the physical contact.[43]

Beating Parents

Abuse of elderly or infirm parents is, unfortunately, a growing phenomenon in our society, especially as people live longer and suffer from the mental and physical disabilities of old age. The Jewish tradition has no room for maltreatment of parents. Parents, of course, are human beings and are therefore protected under the general rules against assault and the monetary remedies entailed therein. The Torah, though, makes parents special. It specifically prohibits striking one's father or mother, and it prescribes the death penalty for one who does so.[44] That, I take it, leaves little room for doubt about the Torah's view of striking parents.

---

[42] I want to thank Naomi Graetz for pointing out to me the importance of noting this special class of cases of child abuse.

[43] When I returned home after the meeting of the Committee on Jewish Law and Standards during which this responsum was approved, I found an article in the *Los Angeles Times* describing the efforts of some Latino parents to save their children from America's world of drugs, sex, and violent gangs by returning them to live with relatives in Latin America, which "offers more rigid school discipline and law enforcement, and encourages stiff corporal punishment — a welcome contrast, they say, to America's softer legal and social systems." The article depicts a mother who "is still bothered by the fact that when school officials here saw the bruises from the beating she had given Maria, they warned her that she could go to prison. . . .It galled her when Maria began to threaten to call 911 to avoid physical punishment, while De La Cruz was required to enroll in parenting classes to avoid criminal charges for beating the girl. When she sent Maria to live for seven months with an aunt in Guadalajara, De La Cruz told the aunt to beat Maria if necessary. . . .Maria, afraid that her aunt would hit her, did not misbehave. She said she found out that 'in Mexico, that's your child and no one else's business. The police don't care.' In Los Angeles, De La Cruz had wanted to make her daughter get a full-time job after school to keep her off the streets. That was something else American law did not allow children to do. . . .Today, Maria has replaced gang parties with the LAPD (Los Angeles Police Department) Explorer Academy. A ninth-grader, she has made finishing high school her highest priority." I am not citing this article to justify child abuse, but simply to indicate the other side of the story that we so often — and rightly — hear, namely, that while corporal punishment should in most cases be avoided, as I have maintained here, discipline of children is definitely necessary, and in some circumstances even corporal punishment short of child abuse may be appropriate. Jose Cardenas, "Unruly Teens Packed Off to Mexico," *Los Angeles Times*, 12 Dec. 1995, pp. B1 and B6.

[44] Exod. 21:15. Cf. B. Sanhedrin 84b. If the child did not cause a bruise while striking his or her parents, however, the child is liable for the damages of assault rather than for the death penalty; cf. M. Bava Kamma 8:3.

If any more grounding is sought for prohibiting parental abuse, it would come from the Torah's positive commandments to honor and respect one's parents. The biblical commands specifically mention that mothers as well as fathers are to be revered and honored, and the Rabbis construed these commands to be demanded of daughters as well as sons. The Rabbis understood "respect" to require that children not harm parents and "honor" to insist that they actively provide for them:

> What is "honor" (כבוד) and what is "respect" (מורא)? Respect means that he (the son) must neither stand in his (the father's) place nor sit in his place, nor contradict his words, nor tip the scales against him (in an argument with others). Honor means that he must give him food and drink, clothe and cover him, and lead him in and out.[45]

So, for example, if the child has food and the parent does not, the law permits forcing the child to provide food for the parent, and a midrash gives a trenchant justification:

> "Honor your father and mother.... You shall not murder." Why are these two laws juxtaposed (in Exod. 20:12-13)? To teach you: If a man has food in his house and does not share it with his father and mother, even when they are young and most certainly when they are old, then he is considered as if he were an habitual murderer. Therefore the verses "Honor (your father and mother)" and "You shall not murder" stand next to one another.[46]

The Talmud, on the one hand, sets limits to these obligations, so that, for example, one may provide for one's parents out of their assets rather than from one's own.[47] On the other hand, stories in the Talmud recount instances in which specific people went to extraordinary lengths to honor and respect their parents, and these are taken as models for us all.[48] With this as a background, one can understand that the tradition, which prized honor and respect of parents so much, would in no way countenance parental abuse.

These laws stand on their own, independent of any assessment of the quality of parenting that one's own parents provided. There are at least two rationales in Jewish sources to justify a duty to honor even bad parents. One is that the parents, along with God, are the three partners in the creation of their children. Children owe their very existence to their parents, and for that reason alone parents have a call on the children's time, their effort, their honor, and their respect. Moreover, the divine partnership in the creation of a person along with the parents means, for the Talmud, that "if people honor their father and mother, God says, 'I reckon it to them as if I dwelled among them and as if they honored Me.'"[49]

---

[45] The biblical command to honor parents: Exod. 20:12; Deut. 5:16. The command to respect parents: Lev. 19:3. That daughters as well as sons are commanded to honor and respect their parents: M. Kiddushin 1:7; B. Kiddushin 29a. The Rabbinic exposition of those commands: Kiddushin 31b, from which this citation comes; M.T. Laws of Rebels (Mamrim) 6:3; S.A. Yoreh De'ah 240:2, 4; cf. also 228:11. For further development of these commandments, see my article, "Honoring Aged Fathers and Mothers," Reconstructionist 53:2 (Oct.-Nov. 1987): 14-20.

[46] Tanna d'bei Eliyahu 26. Cf. M.T. Laws of Rebels 6:3 and S.A. Yoreh De'ah 240:5 for forcing the child to provide food.

[47] B. Kiddushin 31b-32a; M.T. Laws of Rebels 6:3; S.A. Yoreh De'ah 240:5. Using one's own resources is, however, preferred: cf. Kesef Mishneh to M.T. Laws of Rebels 6:7.

[48] B. Kiddushin 31b-32a; J. Kiddushin 1:7 (67b); J. Pe'ah 1:1 (15c-d); Deuteronomy Rabbah 1:15.

[49] B. Kiddushin 30b.

Secondly, parents are commanded to teach their children how to behave according to the dictates of the Torah. While some parents fail miserably in this task, to the extent that they carry out this obligation, they fulfill a God-like role and are to be respected as such. Philo, a first century Jewish thinker from Alexandria, put this point well. The tradition understands the first five of the Ten Commandments as those governing the relationships between human beings and God, while the second group of five shape the relationships among human beings. Noting that the command to honor parents is placed as the fifth of the Ten Commandments and thus the last of the first set, even though parents and children are clearly human beings, Philo says:

> After dealing with the seventh day (the Fourth of the Ten Commandments), He gives the Fifth Commandment on the honor due to parents. This commandment He placed on the borderline between the two sets of five: it is the last of the first set, in which the most sacred injunctions, those relating to God, are given, and it adjoins the second set, which contain the duties of human beings to each other. The reason, I think, is this: we see that parents by their nature stand on the borderline between the mortal and the immortal sides of existence — the mortal, because of their kinship with people and other animals through the perishableness of the body; the immortal, because the act of generation makes them similar to God, the progenitor of everything. . . .
>
> Some bolder spirits, glorifying the name of parenthood, say that a father and mother are in fact gods revealed to sight, who copy the Uncreated in His work as the Framer of life. He, they say, is the God or Maker of the world; they (the parents) only of those whom they have begotten. How can reverence be rendered to the invisible God by those who show irreverence to the gods who are near at hand and seen by the eye?[50]

Thus abuse of parents is even more specifically and severely denounced in the Jewish tradition than abuse of other people or even other family members.[51] The positive obligations to honor and respect one's parents add yet more strength to the general obligation to respect the divine element in each one of us. Since respect of a person would certainly preclude abuse, we are doubly warned in the case of parents against beating them.

Not all parents, of course, are model human beings or paradigm parents; some are nasty or even abusive. According to some Jewish sources, one is required to love them nevertheless, either as a corollary of honoring them or as an instantiation of the command, "Love your neighbor as yourself."[52] Maimonides, however, does not require love of parents:

---

[50] Philo, *Treatise on the Decalogue*, Loeb Classical Library edition, trans. F.H. Colson, vol. 7 (1939), pp. 61, 67, 69.

[51] This does not mean that one must continue to administer life-support systems to parents in failing health beyond all hope of cure. Quite the contrary, doing so might arguably be construed as abuse! On such medical issues at the end of life, see my "A Jewish Approach to End-Stage Medical Care," *PCJLS 86-90*, pp. 65-126; and Avram Israel Reisner, "A Halakhic Ethic of Care for the Terminally Ill," *PCJLS 86-90*, pp. 13-64.

[52] The command to love your neighbor as yourself: Lev. 19:18. Rashi, on B. Kiddushin 32a, s.v. פודין and ומאכילין; R. Elazar Azkari, *Sefer Haredim* (Warsaw: 1879), p. 31; R. Abraham Danzig, *Hayyei Adam* (1810) 67:1. These sources are cited and discussed in Blidstein, *Honor Thy Father and Mother* (at n. 35 above), pp. 56-57.

> Know that the Torah has placed us under a heavy obligation in regard
> to the proselyte. We were commanded to honor and revere our parents, and to obey the prophets. Now it is possible for a person to
> honor and revere and obey those whom she or he does not love. But
> with the proselyte there is a command to love him or her with a great,
> heartfelt love...much as we are commanded to love God Himself.[53]

Moreover, one may certainly disagree with one's parents — although not in a way that they are publicly shamed, as the rabbinic definition of "respect" cited above specifies.

When parents have abused their children or violated the law, a number of Ashkenazic sources (Rashi, Rabbenu Tam, R. Moses Isserles) assert that the Torah's commands to honor and respect them no longer apply. Sephardic sources, however, generally assert that the commands to honor and respect parents continue even in the face of abuse or other illegality. This is true for R. Alfas, Maimonides, and R. Karo.[54]

This dispute has an effect not only on whether one must provide for formerly abusive parents, but how. Ideally, the children should tend to their parents' needs themselves, for, as the Talmud notes, part of the honor of parents comes from their child's personal care for them.

> You are My children, and I am your Father....It is an honor for
> children to dwell with their father, and it is an honor for the father
> to dwell with his children....Make, therefore, a house for the
> Father in which He can dwell with his children.[55]

When the relationship between parents and children makes that emotionally impossible, however, children may use the services of others to fulfill their filial obligations.[56] For that matter, even when the relationships between parents and children are good, people may choose to use nursing homes and similar facilities when that proves to be best for all concerned. In those cases, however, children continue to have the obligation to visit their parents as often as possible, by telephone if not in person. The need we all have for family ties does not diminish in old age; if anything, it may get stronger as we cope with illness and our ultimate demise. The Talmud's insistence on personal care is thus as important today as it was in the past.

While one may, if necessary, delegate the care of one's parents to others rather than performing the duty oneself, beating parents is another matter. The former is failing to do one's duty in the optimal way; the latter is violating an explicit interdiction — actually, a

---

[53] Maimonides, *Responsa*, ed. J. Blau, vol. 2, no. 448, p. 728. Cited in Blidstein, *Honor* (at n. 35), p. 55.

[54] Rashi: B. Sanhedrin 47a, s.v. על; B. Berakhot 10b, s.v. גירר. Rabbenu Tam: Tosafot to B. Yevamot 22b, s.v. כשעשה; Mordecai to Yevamot, sec. 13. R. Alfas: B. Yevamot 22b. Maimonides: M.T. Laws of Rebels (Mamrim) 5:12; see also 6:11. Karo and Isserles: S.A. Yoreh De'ah 240:18 (with gloss). On this generally, see Blidstein, *Honor* (at n. 35), pp. 130-6; and Benay Lappe, "Does a Child Who Has Been Sexually Abused by a Parent Have the Obligation to Say Kaddish for That Parent: A Teshuvah," an M.H.L. thesis at the University of Judaism, Los Angeles, 1993.

[55] Exodus Rabbah 34:3. Note also that one version of the story of the death of Rabbi Judah, president of the Sanhedrin, has it that as he was dying he specifically asked for his children to be in attendance; see B. Ketubbot 103a. The ideal of giving personal care, however, did not become a legal requirement recorded in the codes — although those legal texts probably assume such care; cf. Blidstein, *Honor* (at n. 35), pp. 113-115.

[56] *Sefer Hasidim*, P. Margaliot, ed. (Jerusalem: 1957), sec. 564, p. 371; cf. sec. 343, p. 257. R. Eliezer Pappo, *Pele Yo'etz*, pt. 1, "Kaph," pp. 170-172; cited in Blidstein, *Honor* (at n. 25), p. 115. The entire Autumn 1994 issue of *The Melton Journal* was devoted to the treatment of the elderly in the Jewish tradition and in modern contexts. It is all worthwhile, but for our purposes I want to call special attention to the article by Eliezer Diamond, "'Do Not Cast Us Away in Our Old Age': Adult Children and Their Aging Parents," pp. 12, 13, 20.

host of them. The specific prohibitions of the Torah against parental abuse and the concepts and laws of reverence and honor for parents add to the general laws punishing assault in Judaism's unequivocal condemnation of parental abuse.

In sum, then, one may not love one's parents, either for cause or just as a function of the personalities involved, and if the cause is severe enough, one may even be released from the commands to honor and respect them. One may also arrange for care for one's parents at the hands of others, assuming that personal caring is either physically or emotionally impossible or practically less desirable and that arrangements are nevertheless made for visiting and calling often. At no time, though, do children have the right to assault their parents.

Sexual Abuse

"Sexual abuse," as applied to children, is defined in psychological literature as "sexual contact, ranging from fondling to intercourse, between a child in mid-adolescence or younger and a person at least five years older." When defined that way, "at least twenty percent of American women and five to ten percent of American men experienced some form of sexual abuse as children."[57] Among adults, sexual abuse is usually understood to be any nonconsensual sexual act or behavior. This definition assumes that we fully acknowledge the well-known ambiguities of some expressions of agreement or refusal, but it asserts that such ambiguity does not affect all or even most expressions of one's desires. For either age group, sexual abuse demeans and humiliates, making one feel shameful and exposed, particularly with regard to one's sexuality.

Some forms of sexual molestation of either women or men leave wounds, including permanent ones that preclude the victim's future ability to procreate. Even those attacks that do not leave such wounds fall under the category of physical abuse, for they represent unwanted and often violent invasions of one's body. Consequently, all of the objections described above to beating a family member would also apply to sexual assault.

Sexual violation, however, is objectionable on other grounds as well. The Torah states unequivocally, "None of you shall come near anyone of his own flesh to uncover nakedness: I am the Lord." After a long list of such forbidden relationships, it then states that such were the abhorrent practices of the nations that occupied the Promised Land before the Israelites. The land thus became defiled and is now spewing them out — almost as if the land had gotten an upset stomach from toxic food. The Israelites themselves may remain in the holy land only if they eschew such practices and act as a holy people. Furthermore,

> All who do any of those abhorrent things shall be cut off from their people. You shall keep My charge not to engage in any of the abhorrent practices that were carried on before you, and you shall not defile yourselves through them: I the Lord am your God.[58]

Sexual contact with members of one's own family, then, is seen in Judaism as abhorrent and as a violation of the holiness of the people Israel and its land. Put another way, part

---

[57] David Finkelhor, "Current Information on the Scope and Nature of Child Abuse," in *The Future of Children*, vol. 4, no. 12 (Los Altos, CA: The Center for the Future of Children, The David and Lucille Packard Foundation, 1994), pp. 21-53. Briere, *Child Abuse Trauma* (at n. 37 above), p. 4, reports higher figures (twenty to thirty percent for females, ten to twenty percent for males), but that undoubtedly includes acts short of physical contact like voyeurism and being the subject of unwelcome sexual advances. A by-now classic study of one aspect of this subject is *Father-Daughter Incest* by Judith Lewis Herman, with Lisa Hirschman (Cambridge, MA: Harvard, 1981).

[58] The two cited verses are Lev. 18:6 and 18:29-30.

of what it means to be a people chosen by God as a model for others is that Jews must not engage in incest or sexual abuse. To do so violates the standards by which a holy people covenanted to God should live and warrants excommunication from the people Israel. Jews are expected to behave better than that.

Why does the Torah speak of incest and sexual abuse as "defilement" and "abomination" in addition to its usual language of transgression? In part, it is because the Promised Land was itself seen as alive and violated by such conduct, but surely the words refer to the human beings involved too. One's bodily integrity is compromised when one is sexually abused. That is experienced not only as an assault upon one's body, but also — and usually more devastatingly — as an onslaught upon one's person. One has lost one's integrity — not only in body, but in soul. One no longer feels safe in the world; at any moment, one can be invaded in the most intimate of ways. The abuse is thus indeed a defilement: what was sacred and whole now is desecrated and broken.[59]

Sexual abuse is also the source of much embarrassment. The Torah makes this exceedingly clear: "If two men get into a fight with each other, and the wife of one comes up to save her husband from his antagonist and puts out her hand and seizes him by his genitals, you shall cut off her hand; show no pity."[60] Despite the special justification the woman had for shaming her husband's assailant, the Torah demands drastic steps in retribution for the degradation she caused — although the Rabbis transformed this to a monetary payment that she must pay.[61] (Incidentally, note that, as the Torah recognized, feelings of shame and embarrassment are experienced by men who are sexually abused just as much as they are by women.) The Talmud, when determining the payment to be exacted for the shame involved whenever one person assaults another, uses this case as the paradigm for what embarrassment means. We are humiliated when we are sexually abused — even just touched in our private parts against our will — for we feel that our sense of self has been invaded, that our honor has been compromised in the most fundamental way possible.

When children are sexually abused, the damage is even worse. Children depend upon the adults in their lives — parents, other family members and friends, teachers, clergy, coaches — to help them master the skills of living. Their psychological well-being depends upon their ability to trust such people to act for their welfare, for that is the only way that children can learn to trust themselves and others. Thus, when an adult sexually abuses a child, the child may not at first experience it as an assault; for young children, it may even be just an interesting, pleasurable game. Whether immediately or gradually, however, children come to recognize sexual activity with adults as an abuse of their bodies and their wills, and they feel not only violated, but betrayed. This often leads to difficulty later on in forming relationships with others, especially sexual ones, and, in some cases it even undermines the person's ability to trust the world enough to go out into it for any productive activity.

This kind of frontal assault on not only the body, but the psyche of the child is clearly prohibited by all the Jewish laws mentioned above prohibiting assault, sexual contact with one's family members, sexual contact outside marriage, and embarrassment of others.

---

[59] I think that we would all agree that the Torah's use of the words "abomination" and "defilement" aptly apply to the kind of sexual abuse of which we are speaking. Whether we should also endorse this biblical language with regard to its prohibition against homosexuality is, to put it mildly, a matter of dispute. Even those who would permit homosexual relations, though, would definitely apply that language to coercive sex (be it homosexual or heterosexual), and that is the subject here.

[60] Deut. 25:11-12.

[61] Sifre on Deut. 25:12; cf. M. Bava Kamma 8.1, B. Bava Kamma 83a, 86a-b, 28a, etc.

The Jewish tradition understands the Torah to ban not only sexual penetration, but any form of illicit fondling or inappropriate behavior for the purpose of gratifying sexual desire.[62] Indeed, in light of the extensive damage it causes to the future ability of the child to cope with life, without too much exaggeration I would say that, in the case of children, sexual abuse is akin to murder.[63]

Verbal Abuse

Verbal abuse of either one's spouse or one's children is not treated in Jewish sources as an offense special and apart from the offense of verbally abusing any other person, but it certainly is included within the latter, more general prohibition. By "verbal abuse" we commonly mean comments that degrade a person, especially if they are said constantly. "You never get it right," "You are simply stupid," and "How could anyone like you?" are examples of such abuse. Overly harsh criticism, name-calling, and intimidating speech are also included in the category of verbal abuse. (Sexual harassment, when verbal, is a specific form of such abuse that raises problems beyond those that I am discussing here.)

Some call this "emotional abuse" or "psychological abuse," and psychological literature includes definitions that point to a number of identifying dysfunctions.[64] While I have no doubt that such abuse happens and that this phenomenon needs further study and refining, both as to identification and cure, I hesitate to use either of those terms now for fear that some will understand them to include anytime that one person makes another feel bad. When one does that as part of justified and constructive criticism, however, that may actually be a good thing to do, although even then it should be done as tactfully as possible. Generally, making others feel bad is something one should strive to avoid, but it does not rise to the level of abuse for which another is responsible unless that other person does specific things that cause the feelings. Consequently, to make the offense as clearly identifiable as possible, I shall retain the phrase "verbal abuse," insisting that there be objectively recognizable behavior that makes the culprit guilty of an offense.

One must first distinguish justifiable rebuke for errors from verbal abuse. That distinction follows more or less along the same lines as the one between reasonable discipline and physical abuse. Specifically, verbal abuse is constant, uncontrolled, and unprovoked, while a warranted reprimand occurs only when an error is made and when the reproach is proportionate to the error. At their best, negative evaluations are also constructive, with suggestions for change, a factor that is always absent in cases of verbal abuse. While verbal abuse is often perpetrated by one who has power over the other, it can occur among equals as well, as, for instance, when "friends" insult each other, not in jest or good humor but in an effort to embarrass, humiliate, or harm the recipient in some other way.

---

[62] B. Shabbat 13a; M.T. Laws of Forbidden Intercourse 21:1; Maimonides, *Sefer Ha-Mitzvot*, Prohibition no. 353; *Sefer Ha-Hinukh* no. 188; S.A. Even HaEzer 20:1. Some, however, maintain that intimacy without penetration is not biblically, but rabbinically prohibited. See, for example, Nahmanides on B. Shabbat 13a and on *Sefer Ha-Mitzvot*, ibid.; the Gaon of Vilna, Biur ha-Gra on S.A. Even HaEzer 20:1.

[63] Dr. Ian Russ, a child psychologist active in the Conservative movement and a good friend, has suggested the following as the best literature on the long-term, serious effects of the sexual abuse of children: John Briere, *Therapy for Adults Molested as Children: Beyond Survival* (New York: Springer Publishing, 1989); John Briere and Diana Elliott, "Immediate and Long-Term Impacts of Child Sexual Abuse," in *The Future of Children* (see n. 57 above), pp. 54-69; Christine Courtois, *Healing the Incest Wound* (New York: W.W. Norton, 1988); and D. Everstine and L. Everstine, *Sexual Trauma in Children and Adolescents: Dynamics of Treatment* (New York: Brunner/Mazel, 1989). I would like to thank Dr. Russ for supplying this bibliography for our use.

[64] See Briere, *Child Abuse Trauma* (at n. 37 above), pp. 8-12.

Verbal abuse of anyone is forbidden by the Jewish tradition under the biblical command, "and you shall not wrong one another" (Lev. 25:17).[65] This prohibition includes verbal abuse of minors as well as adults,[66] an important point especially for teachers and parents.

In addition to these general interdictions of verbal abuse, Jewish sources tell a man to be especially careful not to abuse his wife verbally "for since she cries easily, it is all too easy to oppress her."[67] Similarly, the Talmud says that a man's wife is given to him so that he might realize life's plan together with her; she is not the man's to vex or grieve: "Vex her not, for God notes her tears."[68] These commands are derived, in part, from the promise that the man is required to make in the wedding contract to honor his wife. Indeed, "He who loves his wife as himself and honors her more than himself is granted the Scriptural promise, 'You shall know that your tent is in peace.'"[69] Contemporary readers may be offended by the sexism of some of these remarks, but that sensitivity should lead one to argue that wives as well as husbands are duty-bound to avoid verbally abusing their spouses, for husbands, too, can and do feel hurt by such shaming.[70]

In any case, the sexism in some of these rabbinic comments should not blind us to the power that they gain from the theological basis they explicitly invoke: verbal abuse violates not only the relationship among the human beings involved, but also that between the individual and God. Therefore, even though, to my knowledge, verbal abuse of one's spouse is never categorized as an independent violation of the law with its own distinctive legal remedies, it partakes of another form of sanction available to a specifically religious legal system, namely the disapproval of one's tradition and of God. One honors God and the Jewish people when one honors others; conversely, one dishonors God and desecrates God's people (חילול השם) when one verbally abuses a human being created in the divine image.

There is a related, more general category, though, that is framed in a combination of legal and theological terms. That category is אונאת דברים, oppression by means of words. Since one biblical command not to oppress one's fellow already covers the financial areas of life, the Rabbis applied the second verse prohibiting oppression of one's neighbor to verbal abuse.[71] As illustrations of that, they say that one may not remind repentant sinners of their past sins, or converts of their previous, non-Jewish lives. Similarly, one may not call people by an opprobrious nickname, even if they say they do not mind, and one may not taunt people about their illnesses or the loss of their children.

In that same section, the Talmud points out that verbal abuse is more serious an offense than financial deception is. The latter, after all, affects one's money, while the former affects one's person. Moreover, financial misappropriation can be returned, while verbal abuse can

---

[65] See Me'irat Einayim to S.A. Hoshen Mishpat 420:49.

[66] B. Bava Kamma 90a; M.T. Laws of Assault and Injury 3:5; S.A. Hoshen Mishpat 420:38.

[67] Bava Mezia 59a. Literally, "for since her tears are common, her oppression is near." Rav, whose comment this is, does not limit his remark to verbal abuse, but the context is discussing the prohibition of oppressing people by means of words.

[68] Ketubbot 61a.

[69] Yevamot 62b; the verse cited is Job 5:24.

[70] Robert Bly is perhaps most well-known for making this point in a number of his books, from *Iron John* on. Whether due to nature or nurture or both, boys and men are, in his analysis, particularly sensitive to shaming, especially when it is done by someone close to the particular male involved and even more when it is done in public.

[71] The Rabbis in Bava Mezia 58b apply Lev. 25:14 to monetary oppression and Lev. 25:17 to verbal oppression.

never be recompensed. The Torah itself reflects this increased severity of verbal abuse over monetary crimes, for it specifically warns us to fear God with respect to the former but does not include that admonition with regard to the latter. None of this, of course, justifies monetary cheating in any way, but it does underscore the importance that the Rabbis attached to the avoidance of verbal abuse.

As violations of a negative, biblical command, acts of verbal abuse would make a person subject to lashes inflicted by the court in addition to the opprobrium of the community and of God. It would not justify victims striking back with physical blows or with verbal abuse of one's own — although one may and should defend oneself from such abuse by either telling the abuser off or by removing oneself, if possible, from the context of the abuse. Thus, even though verbal abuse of one's spouse and children is never developed as an independent violation of the law, it is certainly included in the more general prohibition proscribing verbal oppression of any member of the community.

Parents, again, occupy a special place in these matters. The Talmud tells a remarkable story to illustrate offensive verbal abuse against parents:

> A man may feed his father on fattened chickens and inherit hell (as his reward), and another may put his father to work in a mill and inherit paradise.
>
> How is it possible that a man might feed his father fattened chickens and inherit hell? It once happened that a man used to feed his father fattened chickens. Once his father said to him: "My son, where did you get these?" He answered: "Old man, old man, eat and be silent, just as dogs eat and are silent." In such an instance, he feeds his father fattened chickens, but he inherits hell.
>
> How is it possible that man might put his father to work in a mill and inherit paradise? It once happened that a man was working in a mill. The king decreed that millers should be brought to work for him. The son said to the father: "Father, go and work in the mill in my place[, and I will go to work for the king]. For it may be [that the king's workers will be] ill-treated, in which case let me be ill-treated instead of you. And it may be [that the king's workers will be] beaten, in which case let me be beaten instead of you." In such an instance, he puts his father to work in a mill, but he inherits paradise.[72]

Thus verbal abuse of parents, aside from sharing in the more general prohibition of oppressive speech (אונאת דברים), involves the added violation of disrespect for parents.

Conclusions of the Response to Part I

1. Beating wives, husbands, or anyone else, and other forms of physical abuse, such as sexual abuse, are absolutely forbidden by Jewish law as we Conservative rabbis understand it.

2. Parents are obligated to discipline their children but should use means that do not in and of themselves teach children that physical assault is a right of parents or anyone in authority. For most people, that means *no use of any form of hitting at all*. For those who do use spanking or other forms of physical beating as a mode of discipline, it is difficult to

---

[72] J. Peah 1:1 (15c); see B. Kiddushin 31a-31b; S.A. Yoreh De'ah 240:4.

draw definitive lines as to what is permissible and what is prohibited, but some guidelines can be stipulated. Specifically, a light smack on the buttocks (a "potch") or a slap with an open hand is permissible, but any strike that causes bleeding or bruises, or blows administered with a rod, belt, or other weapon are forbidden. All the more so, any assault that causes severe, permanent damage to the child is clearly and emphatically forbidden. In addition, since discipline of the child is the only acceptable justification, random or unbridled beating or any beating unrelated to discipline of the child in a very specific way would also be forbidden. In general, discipline is better done without beating of any kind.

The same rules — but with even less endorsement for striking the child — apply to family-like situations outside the family where adults are in charge of children. Thus teachers, youth group leaders, counselors, coaches, and the like may, at the very most, give a light slap on the buttocks to children to get them out of bed or going to the next activity. They may not strike the child in any form of corporal punishment.

None of the above is intended to prohibit either a parent or a parent-substitute (counselor, coach, etc.) from hugging a child so as to comfort him or her or putting an arm around the child's shoulders as an expression of congratulations in, for example, a ball game. All or the above strictures are with reference to acts of violence against the child, differentiated from acts of love or friendship by both the intention and context of the parties and the form and energy of the physical contact.

3. Children may not beat their parents, even when parents were formerly abusive themselves. Adult children may designate others to care for their parents if the emotional or physical conditions make that necessary, but separation is one thing, abuse another.

4. Verbal abuse is also forbidden. One may and should criticize others, including one's family members, when criticism is called for, but that must be done constructively and, if possible, in private.

Part II: Witnesses to the Act or Results of Abuse

This paper was approved by the CJLS on September 13, 1995, by a vote of seventeen in favor (17-0-0). Voting in favor: Rabbis Kassel Abelson, Ben Zion Bergman, Stephanie Dickstein, Elliot N. Dorff, Shoshana Gelfand, Myron S. Geller, Arnold M. Goodman, Susan Grossman, Judah Kogen, Vernon H. Kurtz, Aaron L. Mackler, Paul Plotkin, Mayer Rabinowitz, Joel E. Rembaum, Gerald Skolnik, Elie Kaplan Spitz, and Gerald Zelizer.

The Committee on Jewish Law and Standards of the Rabbinical Assembly provides guidance in matters of halakhah for the Conservative movement. The individual rabbi, however, is the authority for the interpretation and application of all matters of halakhah.

שאלה

1. Do the prohibitions of לשון הרע (defamatory speech about a person), causing shame to a person (בושת), or desecrating God (חילול השם) make it wrong for a witness to the act or results of abuse to make the abuse public?

2. Do any of these duties or the traditional prohibition against handing Jews over to non-Jews for prosecution (מסירה) make it wrong for a Jewish witness to report abuse inflicted by a Jew to civil authorities?

3. Conversely, is there a positive obligation to intervene to halt the abuse by making it public and by contacting civil authorities?

4. In the case of a child, do parents' obligations to teach their children and the prerogatives that issue from that command supersede the duty to try to prevent harm to the child by reporting the abuse and, if necessary and appropriate, testifying against the parents?

תשובה

Two commands within Judaism are sometimes misinterpreted to prevent someone from making one's way out of an abusive situation. One is the prohibition against "evil speech" (לשון הרע), and the other is the Jewish imperative to avoid shame.

The Jewish tradition forbids several kinds of speech that are related, but different. These include lies (שקר); truths that it is nobody's business to know (רכילות, or gossip); and truths that, for all their truth, are defamatory (לשון הרע). It is this last type that some people invoke to claim that Judaism prohibits an abused wife or child from publicly declaring the abuse in an effort to get help. Since complaints about the abuse, the argument goes, will inevitably defame the abuser, the abused may not describe what is going on to others.

Defamatory speech is an important thing to avoid as much as possible, but there are some very clear exceptions to the prohibition. One exception occurs when failure to defame the person will result in harm to someone else. If you are asked to be a reference for someone applying for a job, for example, and if your report will be generally negative, you are duty-bound either to refuse to write a letter of reference in the first place or to tell the truth, however negative it may be. Similarly, when failure to disclose the abuse to the proper authorities will result in continued abuse, the abused person, and, for that matter, anyone who notices the abuse, is obliged to reveal the abusive facts: even though that will inevitably defame the abuser, that is not only permissible, but mandatory when it is done in an effort to prevent harm to another.[73] As Maimonides writes,

> Anyone who can save [someone's life] and does not do so transgresses "You shall not stand idly by the blood of your neighbor" (Lev. 19:16). Similarly, if one sees his brother drowning in the sea, accosted by robbers, or attacked by wild animals and can save him personally or can hire others to save him, and does not save him, or he heard non-Jews or informers plotting evil or attempting to entrap another and he does not inform him. . .transgresses "You shall not stand idly by the blood of your neighbor."[74]

Indeed, if one person (A) is attacking another (B), any third party (C) has not only the right, but the obligation to stop A — even at the cost of A's life if that is necessary. This is the law of the pursuer (רודף).[75] Unlike the law in many American states, Jewish law would

---

[73] B. Bava Kamma 56a; S.A. Hoshen Mishpat 28:1 (gloss). In B. Pesahim 113b, Rav Papa has a man named Zigud punished for testifying alone against another man named Tuvya on the ground that the testimony of a single witness is inadmissible and so Zigud, knowing that he was the only witness, was effectively spreading defamatory information (מוציא שם רע) about Tuvya. That, however, was when the act had already occurred; the requirement in Bava Kamma and in the comment of Isserles to testify even singly in all cases in which there is a benefit, including preventing another person from sinning, refers to a future gain.

[74] M.T. Laws of Murder 1:14. In 1:15, Maimonides adds both affirmative and negative injunctions to this obligation based on Deut. 25:12, "And you shall cut off her hand (being applied here to the abuser); your eye shall have no pity." See also Rashi, B. Sanhedrin 73a, s.v. לא תעמוד.

[75] M. Sanhedrin 8:7; B. Sanhedrin 73a.

thus justify C in even killing an abusive spouse or parent if that were the only way to stop constant assaults on B, but only when there is imminent danger of the death or rape of B. In other words, Jewish law allows a third party (C) to do what B him/herself could legally do according to both legal systems as an act of self-defense.[76]

The law of the pursuer is based on a broader principle in Jewish law, that of פיקוח נפש (saving a life). Specifically, the Torah proclaims the command to follow God's commands and to live by them (Lev. 18:5). The Rabbis interpreted this to mean that we must live by them and not die by them. Toward that end, the Rabbis determined that we not only may, but must, violate all but three of the commandments if that is necessary to save a life. The three exceptions that we may not violate even to save a life are murder, incest/adultery, and idolatry. The first of those exceptions, however, applies only when we would be murdering an innocent person to save our own or someone else's life; if, instead, the person in question is threatening oneself, we both may and must seek to kill him or her first, and if the person in question is pursuing another, we must intervene, even to the point of killing the pursuer, as the law of רודף demands.[77]

Now, of course, these are extreme cases. They demonstrate, however, exactly how far Jewish law was willing to go in order to stop assaults. Civil law is not as supportive of those who murder family members to stop assaults, and even Jewish law would permit homicide in such cases only when the pursuer's murder or rape of another is imminent and unavoidable by any other means. People thus clearly need to extricate themselves from such situations before they ever come to this. Nevertheless, if Jewish law justifies even homicide to prevent assault, it certainly expects third parties to intervene in less violent ways to free abused people from the situations of their abuse, such as reporting cases of abuse to legal authorities. "One may not stand idly by the blood of one's neighbor," the Torah enjoins.[78] One who has information to report and fails to do so is in violation of that commandment and of Lev. 5:1, "If he does not come forth with his information, then he shall be subject to punishment."[79] While in monetary affairs the witness may wait until summoned, in other matters, such as abuse, the witness must come forward voluntarily in order to "destroy the evil from your midst."[80]

This is true whether the abuser is a parent, a teacher, or anyone else. Abusive teachers must be removed from classrooms. The leaders of schools, camps, and youth groups must, of course, investigate the claim before taking such action, and the usual presumption of innocence applies. I shall discuss that aspect of the matter at some length in Part IV of this responsum. If the charges prove true, however, Jewish institutions have a clear duty to protect their students from verbal, physical, and sexual abuse.

---

[76] Tosafot, B. Sanhedrin 72b, s.v. כאן באב על הבן, make this explicit with regard to children's right (obligation?) to defend themselves against abusive parents.

[77] B. Yoma 85a-b; B. Sanhedrin 72a, 74a. On these principles generally, cf. Immanuel Jakobovits, *Jewish Medical Ethics* (New York: Bloch, 1959, 1975), chs. 3-7.

[78] Lev. 19:16. The new translation of the Jewish Publication Society reads, "Do not profit by the blood of your fellow," interpreting this phrase, whose meaning is uncertain, as the note there says, in the context of the civil legislation in the verse immediately before this one. The rabbinic tradition, however, interpreted and applied Lev. 19:16 to establish a positive obligation to come to the aid of those in danger: cf. M. Sanhedrin 8:7; B. Sanhedrin 73a.

[79] M.T. Laws of Testimony 1:1.

[80] Kesef Mishneh to M.T. Laws of Testimony 1:1; Rosh to Makkot, ch. 1, no. 11. "Destroy the evil from your midst" occurs a number of times in the Torah as a general purpose of the law: Deut. 13:6, 17:7, 19:19, 21:21, 22:21, and 24:7; cf. also 17:12 and 22:22.

This raises one complication that inheres in cases of child abuse. Typically, the teacher or friend who reports the abuse is doing so on the testimony of the child together with supportive evidence in the form of bruises on the child's body. One rabbi who specialized in the laws of defamation, the Hafetz Hayyim, ruled that any information that would cause harm to the accused must only be revealed if it could be legitimately introduced into a Jewish court of law.[81] Since the testimony of minors is usually inadmissible,[82] this would preclude many interventions to redeem a child from an abusive situation. As I will spell out later in this responsum, recent evidence indicates that minors — and, for that matter, adults remembering childhood events — are prone to remember them as others suggest they were, and that should prompt us to be even more skeptical of children's testimony.

Some Jewish authorities, however, accept the testimony of minors if supported by other evidence,[83] and that should be our stance. Children, after all, are not to be presumed untruthful, especially in matters as painful and personal as this, and the corroborating, external evidence can alleviate any doubt we might otherwise have. In any case, the report that must be given to civil authorities generally remains confidential and goes only to the governmental agencies responsible for child welfare, which must investigate further. Consequently, even if one takes the ruling of the Hafetz Hayyim as being authoritative, this should not prevent adults who hear of child abuse from children and see evidence thereof from taking steps to have the complaint examined and, if it proves accurate, acted upon.

The Scope of the Laws of Shaming Another

Similar remarks apply to the issue of shame. Judaism certainly prohibits embarrassing someone else publicly. Indeed, rabbinic statements compare public shaming of a person to killing him or her. Moreover, as we have seen, an assailant must pay for the embarrassment caused to the victim and his or her family as part of the remedies for causing a personal injury. The Talmud, in fact, engages in a sophisticated discussion of the nature of shame, asking whether it is the degradation in the public's esteem or in the victim's own sense of self-worth that is at the heart of the phenomenon of shame.[84] These sources within the tradition that proscribe shaming others are all corollaries to the underlying theological principle of Judaism that human beings are worthy of respect as creatures of God created in the Divine image.

Some things, though, take priority over this prohibition. Specifically, as in the case of defamatory speech, when shaming another is not done out of meanness or indifference but is rather an outgrowth of a practical or moral necessity, it is justified, and, in some cases, required. For example, if someone is committing fraud, a person who discovers this is not only allowed, but duty-bound to expose the fraud. Even though that will inevitably embarrass the perpetrator, the overriding need is to enable his or her innocent victims to recover what they can and to protect all of his or her future victims.

---

[81] Hafetz Hayyim, *Be'er Mayyim Hayyim*, Laws of Slander 9:20.

[82] M.T. Laws of Testimony 9:1; S.A. Hoshen Mishpat 35:1.

[83] S.A. Hoshen Mishpat 35:14, gloss. Isserles there accepts children as עדי בירור (witnesses of explanation) based on the enactments (*takkanot*) of either Rabbenu Tam or Rabbenu Gershom.

[84] The comparison of publicly embarrassing a person to killing him or her, which appears in Bava Metzia 58b, is aided by a play on words: the Hebrew expression for "embarrassing" a person (מלבין פני חבירו ברבים) literally means to make the person's face white, and that occurs also when one dies. The legal remedy in personal injury cases for embarrassment is discussed in the Mishnah Bava Kamma 8:1 and 8:6 and in the Talmud at Bava Kamma 86a-b, where the discussion of the essence of shame also appears.

If such monetary concerns supersede the concern of shaming another, preventing bodily injury or even death does so all the more. As in the case of defamatory speech, we may not stand idly by but must rather expose the abuser so as to stop the abuse and get help for his or her victims. This is demanded, as explained above, both under the laws of רודף (the pursuer) and also under its legal root, the requirement to violate all but three of the commandments of the Torah in order to save the life of another (פיקוח נפש). Identifying an abuser will inevitably cause him or her shame, and we should not do that any more than necessary. The Torah, after all, demands that we respect even the executed body of a murderer by not letting it remain unburied overnight.[85] But we are not only permitted, but required to override our concern for embarrassing the perpetrator to stop the abuse and to get help for the victims.

Informing Civil Authorities: The Issues of Mesirah and Hillul Ha-Shem

Traditional Jewish law forbids מסירה, turning Jews over to non-Jewish courts for judgment.[86] This prohibition undoubtedly arose out of two concerns. First, rampant discrimination against Jews in society generally made it unlikely that Jewish litigants would get a fair hearing. On the contrary, a dispute among Jews aired in a gentile court might supply the occasion for punishing both Jewish litigants and perhaps the entire Jewish community. Better that we not call attention to ourselves altogether.

Moreover, rabbis over the generations wanted to make sure that the authority of Jewish law was not undermined any more than necessary through the use of non-Jewish courts by Jews. In civil matters there was often no choice, and so Samuel in the third century already announces the principle of דינא דמלכותא דינא, the law of the land is the law. That was restricted, though, to civil matters, and until the Enlightenment, Jews did, in fact, use Jewish courts to adjudicate even their civil disputes, although often by the generally accepted, non-Jewish laws of commerce in force at the time. How, then, can a Jew in good conscience inform civil authorities about a Jew who is apparently abusing his or her family member?

Since the advent of the Enlightenment, a number of rabbis have ruled that the laws of מסירה no longer apply. Some, like the Arukh Ha-Shulhan, have maintained that using non-Jewish courts was prohibited only when they were unfair to Jews (and perhaps to others as well), and when the prosecution of a Jew in a non-Jewish court would be the occasion for persecution of the entire Jewish community. Since neither of these factors characterizes courts in Western democracies nowadays, Jews may use non-Jewish courts.[87]

Even if one maintains that the prohibition of using non-Jewish courts still holds, it would not apply to criminal matters, where Jewish courts have no jurisdiction or power to punish. Thus Rabbi Moses Isserles, who lived in a pre-Enlightenment society (sixteenth-century Poland), cites others who lived even earlier who hold that "if a person is struck by

---

[85] Deut. 21:23.

[86] B. Gittin 88b; M.T. Laws of Courts (Sanhedrin) 26:7. See Dorff and Rosett, *A Living Tree* (at n. 7 above), pp. 320-324 and 515-539. See also Herschel Schachter, "Dina deMalchusa Dina," *Journal of Halacha and Contemporary Society* 1:1, and Simcha Krauss, "Litigation in Secular Courts," *Journal of Halacha and Contemporary Society* 11:1. I am indebted for much of the material of this section to the article by Rabbi Mark Dratch, "The Physical, Sexual and Emotional Abuse of Children," in *Shalom Bayit: A Jewish Response to Child Abuse and Domestic Violence*, Ian Russ, Sally Weber, and Ellen Ledley, eds. (Los Angeles: University of Judaism and the Jewish Family Service of Los Angeles, 1994, the edition for the Orthodox community), pp. 1-8, 59-62.

[87] Arukh Ha-Shulhan, Hoshen Mishpat 388:7.

another, he may go to complain before the non-Jewish court even though he will thereby cause great harm to the injurer."[88] Since Jewish courts in our day have even less power and authority to handle such matters than they did in pre-Enlightenment times, Ashkenazi Jews, those whose ancestors came from Central and Eastern Europe, can rely on that ruling.

Sephardic Jews generally follow Rabbi Joseph Karo, author of the Shulhan Arukh on which Rabbi Isserles commented. Rabbi Karo asserts that the prohibition of מסירה continues to his day, making it illegal for a Jew who is being harassed to report that to the civil authorities. Even Karo, though, maintained that when there is a מצער הציבור, a menace to the community as a whole, מסירה is permissible.[89] He was probably talking about non-Jews attacking the Jewish community as a whole for the reprehensible action of one of its members. Legal authorities in Western democracies are unlikely to inflict penalties on the Jewish community as a group on the excuse that there are some Jews who are batterers; the government is much more likely to prosecute such people as individuals, just as they would any other citizen who violated the law.

In our time, though, abuse of spouses, elderly parents, and especially children has unfortunately reached the extent of a מצער הציבור in three other senses — namely, those who abuse others constitute a physical threat not just to the ones they have already abused, but to all potential, future victims as well and therefore to the entire community; secondly, abusers pose a threat to the sense of well-being of the community as a whole by making it an unsafe place to live; and, thirdly, abusers within our community defame us as a community and God whom we worship, and the desecration of the divine Name (חילול השם) involved is also a source of pain and suffering for the community. Consequently, it is certainly within the spirit of these precedents, if not their letter, to assert that for both Sephardic as well as Ashkenazi Jews, victims of abuse and witnesses to abuse may, and indeed should, enlist the help of governmental agencies. In any case, we in our time, as the Conservative movement's Committee on Jewish Law and Standards, hereby rule that, according to Jewish law as we interpret it, victims of abuse should inform the police and avail themselves of the remedies and protections that civil law affords.

Rabbis present a special case in this because American law recognizes a clergy-client (usually called "priest-penitent") privilege. Thus if a Jew in the course of counseling with his or her rabbi disclosed that he or she had engaged in spousal or child abuse, American law would protect the confidentiality of that disclosure unless the counselee waived that right or indicated his or her intention to engage in future abuse of the same kind. Absent either of those conditions, the rabbi might be successfully sued as a breach of privacy for reporting the past abuse to civil authorities — although some states interpret the immunity of clergy to the child abuse reporting laws very narrowly.[90] For purposes of this responsum, then, suffice it to

---

[88] S.A. Hoshen Mishpat 388:7, gloss, and see comment no. 45 of the Shakh on that passage. Shakh there (on 338:12), in comment no. 60, understands Isserles to be saying categorically that "if someone is accustomed to strike others, it is permissible to hand him over (to gentile authorities) for one's protection so that he will not strike people any longer." See also glosses of Isserles to Hoshen Mishpat 388:9 and 26:4 and his commentary Darkhei Moshe to the Tur, Hoshen Mishpat 338, comment no. 14. The earlier sources he cites are the Teshuvot Maimoniot of Maimonides (1140-1204, Spain and Egypt), Nezikin, Responsum no. 66; the Mordecai (Mordecai ben Hillel Ha-Kohen, 1240?-1298, Germany), R. Jacob ben Judah Weil (Germany, d. 1456), and Maharam of Riszburg (possibly R. Menahem of Merseburg, first half of the fourteenth century, Saxony, Germany).

[89] S.A. Hoshen Mishpat 388:12, according to the text quoted by Shakh at that place, comment no. 59, and by the Gaon of Vilna (Gra), no. 71.

[90] The exception to the clergy/client privilege was established in the case of *Tarasoff vs. Board of Regents of the University of California* 529 P. 2d 553 (Cal. 1974); modified 551 P. 2d 334 (Cal. 1976), which also affirmed the general privilege itself. The California Evidence Code, Article 8, Section 1033, states: "Subject to Section 912, a

say that the provisions in Jewish law demanding that we save life and limb would require those who know about an abusive situation to report it to the civil authorities so that it might end, and, from the perspective of Jewish law, that would apply to rabbis no less than to any other Jew. Rabbis who become aware of an abusive situation in a counseling setting, however, should consult with an attorney to determine whether civil law grants them the right to report the matter in the specific case before them and, if not, they should seek to end the abusive situation in some other way.[91]

---

penitent, whether or not a party (i.e., litigant in the case before the court), has a privilege to refuse to disclose, and to prevent another from disclosing, a penitential communication if he claims the privilege;" and Section 1034 states: "Subject to Section 912, a clergyman, whether or not a party, has a privilege to refuse to disclose a penitential communication if he claims the privilege." The parallel Arkansas statute reads: "No minister of the gospel or priest of any denomination shall be compelled to testify in relation to any confession made to him in his professional character, in the course of discipline by the rule of practice of such denomination." New York and Michigan, like California, substitute "allowed" for "compelled," thus giving the penitent the right to prevent the clergyperson from revealing the confession made to him/her in his/her capacity as a member of the clergy. This "seal of the confessional" has been generally recognized by the civil courts even in those states that do not have such a privilege written into their evidence codes, even though by the old common law confessions were not considered privileged. New York is possibly the first of all English-speaking states from the time of the Reformation to grant this protection, for it is documented in a decision of De Witt Clinton made in June, 1813. See Louisell, Kaplan, and Waltz, *Cases and Materials on Evidence*, 3d ed. (Mineola, NY: Foundation Press, 1976), pp. 666-667. I would like to thank Rabbi Ben Zion Bergman for these references.

[91] It is important as well to determine whether the clergy member's immunity from the legal responsibility to report abuse is narrowly or broadly construed in the state in which it takes place. Thus although California has written that privilege into its laws of evidence, Dr. Ian Russ has shared with me an official opinion of the state's Office of the Attorney General according to which a clergy member's immunity from being a mandated reporter of child abuse only exists in the "priest-penitent" relationship and not when the rabbi is serving as a teacher, camp counselor, or educational director. Under this interpretation, the privilege would never apply to those professionals or rabbis acting in those capacities; it probably would not even apply to a cantor, for even though cantors are construed as clergypersons in California for the purposes of performing weddings, they are not regularly called upon to engage in confidential counseling, and their job description rarely includes that. Moreover, even for rabbis, the privilege may be very narrowly construed, for, as the definition of priest-penitent privilege in the third paragraph of this opinion and in the last paragraph of it indicate, it exists only when the religion itself affirms it, but Judaism prefers saving life and limb to privacy.

The Attorney General's office opinion states the following:

RESPONSIBILITY OF THE CLERGY UNDER THE CHILD ABUSE REPORTING LAW
(Penal Code Sections 11165-11174)

Participation of the clergy in reporting a case of suspected child abuse is entirely voluntary. Priests, ministers, rabbis and other clergy are not included in any of the categories of professionals required to report child abuse...(See Stats. 1980, ch. 1071, nos. 1-4)....

It must be remembered, however, that insofar as a member of the clergy is also practicing a profession or vocation which is included in one of the categories of mandated reporters, he or she must report suspected child abuse discovered while acting in that capacity. For instance, clergy who are teachers, school administrators, marriage, family and child counselors, or social workers are required to report....In no event, however, may clergy be required to reveal "penitential communications," for these communications are protected by the penitent-clergyperson privilege.

A "'penitential communication' is a communication made in confidence, in the presence of no third person so far as the penitent is aware, to a clergyperson who, in the course of the discipline or practice of his or her church, denomination, or organization, is authorized or accustomed to hear such communications and, under the discipline or tenets of his or her church, denomination, or organization, has a duty to keep such communications secret."

This penitent-clergy privilege, when coupled with the Right to Privacy guaranteed by the California Constitution, may serve to limit voluntary reports of child abuse by the clergy. The privilege can be effectively waived only by the penitent, for even if a clergy member wishes to waive the privilege and disclose a penitential communication, the penitent may nonetheless invoke the privilege to bar disclosure.

Another concern that sometimes inhibits people from reporting abuse to the civil authorities is the prohibition of חילול השם, defaming the reputation of God and God's chosen people. The worry is that public acknowledgement that some Jews abuse their family members through reporting such abuse to the authorities will reflect poorly on the entire Jewish community and perhaps even become the excuse for acts of anti-Semitism.

חילול השם, though, cuts both ways. Not reporting or testifying about such abuse will undoubtedly redound to the detriment of the Jewish community, for, as the Mishnah reminds us, attempting to sequester a חילול השם will always be unsuccessful: "Whoever desecrates the name of Heaven in private will ultimately be punished in public; whether the desecration was committed unintentionally or intentionally, it is all the same when God's name is profaned."[92] That is especially so when civil law requires reporting abuse, for then the Jews involved in trying to hide the abuse will be correctly perceived as engaged in illegal activities as well as unwise and uncaring conduct. This, too, would be a threat to the welfare of the community (מצער הציבור).

The Jewish community is not perfect. Jews cannot expect that of themselves, and non-Jews must be taught not to expect that either. We ultimately do more for our own reputation as a community and for the Name of God, our covenanted partner, if we own up to the problems in our communities and try honestly to deal with them. חילול השם, then, far from prompting us to try to hide the abuse that is going on among us, should motivate us instead to confront it and to root it out.

The Scope of Parental Prerogatives

"And you shall teach your children diligently" (Deut. 6:7), a part of the first paragraph of the Shema, is an obligation that Jews know well. To fulfill that duty, parents may enlist the aid of teachers, but ultimately the responsibility rests with the parents. Consequently, Jewish law assumes that children would ordinarily reside with their parents so that the latter could fulfill this duty — in addition, of course, to the emotional bonding that is so vital to the well-being of the child.

Custody of children, however, is not automatically a parental right in Jewish law. It depends upon the welfare of the child. Thus in divorce proceedings, for example, there is a presumption in the law that children are served best when they are living

---

The clergy member and the penitent are joint holders of the privilege. That means that the clergy member has the right to invoke the privilege on his or her own behalf, or the penitent has the additional right to prevent the clergy member from disclosing a penitential communication. Thus, the intent of the law to afford maximum personal privacy to penitents is manifest. Accordingly, it appears that a clergy member may not report, even voluntarily, child abuse learned of in the course of receiving a penitential communication unless the penitent himself or herself waives the privilege afforded that communication.

Remember, however, that the legal limitations on disclosure of information received in confidence apply only to those communications that in every aspect meet the definition of a "penitential cnmziunication" as noted above. Thus, it appears that suspected child abuse learned of through other "confidential" communications received by clergy in the course of performing pastoral functions may be reported under the Child Abuse Reporting Law. Whether or not a clergy member should do so is a matter of personal conscience and integrity measured in the light of the moral and religious obligations of the clergy member's own religious affiliate.

MARGARET E. GARNAND
Deputy Attorney General, Sacramento

[92] M. Avot (Ethics of the Fathers) 4:5.

with the parent of the same gender.⁹³ That presumption is based on the social setting of times past in which it was only fathers who knew enough to teach their sons a profession and possibly Torah (most fathers had little formal training in Judaica themselves), and it was only mothers who knew enough about household skills to teach them to their daughters. The social situation in modern times has changed considerably, and that in itself may call this presumption into question with regard to contemporary custody decisions. The important thing for our purposes here, though, is that even in traditional Jewish law the presumption is rebuttable.⁹⁴ In particular, the welfare of the child and, as a corollary, the need to maintain close ties among all of the children can and often do override these gender-based assumptions.⁹⁵ A parent's right to have custody of his or her children, then, applies only when the welfare of the child is served by that arrangement.

In our case, if the child is in any danger of physical or sexual abuse, the welfare of the child would certainly supersede any parental claim to custody. Even if removal from the parental home would lead to the child's placement in a foster home or a non-Jewish institution, that must be done to save the life of the child. פיקוח נפש takes precedence over the positive obligation to teach one's children Torah and the negative command prohibiting the placing of a stumbling block before the blind (Lev. 19:14), which was interpreted to include the educationally and morally blind.⁹⁶ Moreover, the one who reports the apparent abuse does not know that the child will be raised by non-Jews: the court may determine that abuse did not, in fact, take place, or, if it did, the court may (and probably will) place the child with other family members or other Jews. The Jewish community should certainly see it as an obligation to offer such Jewish facilities for children and adults who need them, as Jewish Family Service of Los Angeles, for example, does through Vista Del Mar (for children) and Gramercy Place (for abused wives and their children). Even in the extreme case, however, where the child is ultimately taken from his or her parents and raised by non-Jews, one who reports such abuse to the authorities is correctly preferring the saving of the child's life over the other commandments mentioned above.

---

⁹³ B. Eruvin 82a; B. Ketubbot 65b, 122b-123a. For these and other relevant sources and a discussion about them, see Basil Herring, "Child Custody," in *Jewish Ethics and Halakhah for Our Times*, vol. 2 (New York: Yeshiva and Ktav, 1989), pp. 177ff.

⁹⁴ See, for example, S.A. Even HaEzer 82:7.

⁹⁵ See Eliav Schochetman, "On the Nature of the Rules Governing Custody of Children in Jewish Law," *The Jewish Law Annual*, vol. 10 (Philadelphia: Harwood Academic Publishers, 1992), pp. 115-158; Michael J. Broyde, "Child Custody in Jewish Law: A Pure Law Analysis," *Jewish Law Association Studies VII: The Paris Conference Volume*, S.M. Passamaneck and M. Finley, eds. (Atlanta: Scholars Press, 1994), pp. 1-20.

⁹⁶ Sifra on Lev. 19:14; B. Pesahim 22b; B. Mo'ed Katan 17a; B. Kiddushin 32a; B. Nedarim 62b; B. Bava Mezia 75b. Abaye sets a limit to this concern — namely, that we must concern ourselves with what the person with whom we are dealing will do and not with others with whom she or he will come into contact (B. Avodah Zarah 14a), but R. Barukh Halevi Epstein argues that that only applies to a non-Jew, and with regard to Jews we must be concerned not to mislead even those who may be lead astray by the ones with whom we are now interacting; cf. his Torah Temimah on Lev. 19:14, comment no. 93.

In any case, in the situation we are dealing with here, the concern is that placing a child in a non-Jewish home will lead him/her to be ignorant of Judaism and even to convert out of the faith. As serious as that concern is, it must be set aside to save the life of the child. As Rabbi Lionel Moses has pointed out, however, it is not clear that פיקוח נפש would justify such action to save a child from verbal abuse. In such cases, all involved with the case must take special care to make sure that removing the child from the custody of one or both parents is warranted and that the new home for the child is Jewish — which, we would hope, is the normal procedure in cases of physical and sexual abuse too.

Conclusions to the Response to Part II

1. It is not a violation of Jewish laws prohibiting defamatory speech (לשון הרע) or shaming another (בושת) for an abused party, or, for that matter, for anyone who witnesses the abuse, to report it to civil authorities. On the contrary, the requirement that one preserve not only oneself (פיקוח נפש) but others as well, demanded by the laws of the pursuer (רודף) and of not standing idly by when another is in danger (לא תעמוד על דם רעך), not only permit, but require others who discover spousal, filial, or parental abuse to help the victim report the abuse and take steps to prevent repetition of it.

2. It is not a violation of Jewish law to hand over Jews suspected of abusing others to civil authorities for trial and, if found guilty, for punishment. On the contrary, because Jewish courts have no power to invoke civil and criminal penalties, and because courts in Western countries can be assumed to be fair in treating individual Jews and not punish the entire Jewish community for their transgressions, and because most, if not all, civil jurisdictions now require that such abuse be reported (at least when it is done to children), it is the Jewish, and often the civil, duty of Jews to report abusers to governmental authorities.

3. Parents' duties to educate their children do not justify abusing them. Consequently, Jews who suspect that children are being abused must report such abuse to the civil authorities, even if that may mean that the child will be taken from the custody of one or both parents and even if, in the extreme, it will mean that the child will be raised by non-Jews. Saving a life takes precedence over the presumption that parental custody is usually best for the child and even over the duty to raise the child as a Jew.

Part III: The Abused Party

This paper was approved by the CJLS on September 13, 1995, by a vote of seventeen in favor (17-0-0). Voting in favor: Rabbis Kassel Abelson, Ben Zion Bergman, Stephanie Dickstein, Elliot N. Dorff, Shoshana Gelfand, Myron S. Geller, Arnold M. Goodman, Susan Grossman, Judah Kogen, Vernon H. Kurtz, Aaron L. Mackler, Paul Plotkin, Mayer Rabinowitz, Joel Rembaum, Gerald Skolnik, Elie Kaplan Spitz, and Gerald Zelizer.

The Committee on Jewish Law and Standards of the Rabbinical Assembly provides guidance in matters of halakhah for the Conservative movement. The individual rabbi, however, is the authority for the interpretation and application of all matters of halakhah.

שאלה

1. Do the laws of לשון הרע or those that forbid causing shame (בושת) to someone else forbid the abused party from making the abuse public? From seeking help from outside sources, including the police? From seeking to end the relationship on the grounds of the abuse?

2. Is there a positive obligation in Jewish law for victims of abuse to take such steps?

Response to Part III

In the case of the abused party, the duty to disclose is even stronger than it is for other people. "Avoiding danger is a stronger obligation than any prohibition," the Talmud says, and saving a life supersedes all commandments save the prohibitions against murder, idolatry, and incest or adultery. Furthermore, saving your own life takes precedence over saving the lives of others.[97]

This applies even to cases where the victim's life is not at stake through physical or sexual abuse, but even where the victim is constantly subjected to verbal abuse. Thus if a parent becomes insane and continuously hurls insults at her or his adult child, the Talmud and codes even permit the child to distance him or herself from ths verbally abusive parent as long as the child fulfills the command to honor one's parents by providing for the parent's care at the hands of another.[98] Contemporary circumstances involving Alzheimer's patients come immediately to mind, for this precedent makes it clear that one may, and probably should, place a parent in the advanced stages of that disease in a facility designed for that purpose so that the parent can be continuously protected against harming her or himself and, where applicable, so that the child need not suffer the parent's verbal abuse.

These Jewish legal principles together mean that abused adults have a positive obligation to ignore the issues of defamation of the abuser since that is necessary to save their lives, and their duty to report an abuser in the context of saving their own lives is even greater than their responsibility to disclose abusers of others. Abused minor children, like all children, cannot be made legally responsible for this or anything else, but they certainly have the sanction of the tradition to reveal parental abuse to those who can help them, despite the defamation involved.

The other Jewish value that sometimes stymies abused people from seeking help is the need to maintain the family's honor and to avoid causing it shame. Since disclosure of an abusive spouse or parent is certainly an embarrassment to all concerned, some abused people feel that it would be better to continue suffering the abuse than to endure the shame of publicly identifying the family's abuser. Sometimes abused people mistakenly feel that the abuse is at least partly their fault, and this adds to the reticence to "come out of the closet" with regard to the abuse.

As discussed above, the Jewish tradition was keenly aware of the offense involved in publicly embarrassing a person. The injury involved is all the worse when it affects a family member. Thus it is not surprising that the Talmud uses a family situation to illustrate both the intensity of shame when one family member abuses another and the broad scope of the command to honor parents. Specifically, it tells a story in which an elderly woman publicly shames her adult son and yet the son continues to honor her. In approving the son's actions, the Talmud was not sanctioning public degradation of children; quite the contrary, the story can make its point only if the hearer or reader assumes that normally parents should not publicly humiliate their children.[99] Thus avoiding shame within a family is definitely a concern of the tradition, even more than it is within the public arena.

The concern for honor, though, may not get in the way of preserving one's life and health. It may be painful to "air your dirty laundry in public," but when someone's life or health is at stake, one must endure the dishonor — and all the more when the life at

---

[97] Hullin 10a; see S.A. Orah Hayyim 173:2, Yoreh De'ah 116:5 (gloss). The three exceptions are specified in Sanhedrin 74a. That saving your own life takes precedence over saving the lives of others is established in B. Bava Mezia 62a.

[98] B. Kiddushin 31b; M.T. Laws of Rebels 6:10. Radbaz on that passage points out that this may be best for the parent, for the child is forbidden from striking the parent, but others may do so if that is in the parent's best interests, "for there are incidents every day" in which striking a person can retrieve him or her from his or her insanity (or, presumably, at least from the behavioral effects of it).

[99] B. Kiddushin 31a.

stake is your own. Consequently, abused adults must muster the courage to disclose the abuse to those who can help them out of the abusive circumstances in which they live, however much shame they initially feel in doing so. Abused minor children, while not legally liable in Jewish law for doing this, are encouraged to do so. Both children and adults caught in this painful situation can take heart in the fact that ultimately such bravery will not only restore whatever dignity they lost in the process, but actually increase their self-respect and honor as they escape the cycle of abuse and mistaken self-blame in which so many are unfortunately enmeshed.

Conclusions of the Response to Part III

1. It is not a violation of Jewish law prohibiting defamatory speech or shaming another for the victim of abuse to seek help to stop the abuse or to extricate oneself from the abusive relationship altogether. Those whom one seeks out could be agencies within the Jewish community and/or governmental authorities.

2. On the contrary, it is a positive obligation of the most authoritative sort for victims to contact others to help them save their own lives by freeing them from the context and the relationships in which the abuse is taking place.

Part IV: The Abuser

This paper was approved by the CJLS on December 13, 1995 by a vote of twenty in favor (20-0-0). Voting in favor: Rabbis Kassel Abelson, Ben Zion Bergman, Stephanie Dickstein, Elliot N. Dorff, Jerome M. Epstein, Baruch Frydman-Kohl, Myron S. Geller, Arnold M. Goodman, Susan Grossman, Judah Kogen, Vernon S. Kurtz, Alan B. Lucas, Aaron L. Mackler, Paul Plotkin, Mayer Rabinowitz, Avram Israel Reisner, Joel E. Rembaum, Gerald Skolnik, Elie Kaplan Spitz, and Gerald Zelizer.

The Committee on Jewish Law and Standards of the Rabbinical Assembly provides guidance in matters of halakhah for the Conservative movement. The individual rabbi, however, is the authority for the interpretation and application of all matters of halakhah.

שאלה

1. What precautions must we take to ensure that people are not falsely accused of being abusers?

2. When it is confirmed that someone is an abuser, what steps does Jewish law impose on her or him to make amends for the abuse? What may (must) the community do in response to such amends?

3. What steps can rabbis and educators take to prevent future abuse and to alleviate the effects of past abuse?

Response to Part IV

Until now, we have assumed that it is clear that a given person has abused another. While the combination of physical evidence and admission by the culprit make that so in many cases, it is not always an undisputed claim. After all, multiple bruises attest to abuse, but they do not identify who inflicted it, and the accused may deny that she or he caused the harm. In some cases of alleged physical or sexual abuse, there may be no physical evidence at all. In recent, highly-publicized cases before the American courts, the incidents happened years, if not decades, ago. What steps, then, must we take to confirm the abuse and the identity of the abuser?

In Jewish law, even more than in American law, a person is innocent until proven guilty. Moreover, while self-incrimination is "like a hundred witnesses" in civil matters,[100] it is not accepted as a ground for court action in criminal matters.[101] Indeed, long before we get to the standards of evidence required in Jewish legal actions, we have the overarching principle that we may not slander people (מוציא שם רע), let alone deprive them of their jobs or their freedom on the basis of such slander. While the Torah explicitly prohibits talebearing,[102] the Talmud hesitates to impose legal remedies for slander due to its general principle that legal redress can be exacted only if damage is done to another directly.[103] Nevertheless, later courts decreed severe legal remedies for slander, basing themselves on the Talmud's granting of power to inflict sanctions beyond the letter of the law if it is for the benefit of society.[104] Thus R. Asher b. Jehiel (d. 1327) states that it is the custom of the courts everywhere to impose fines on "those who put others to shame with their words" and to assess the damages according to the social status of the offender and the victim,[105] and Rabbis Karo and Isserles go further yet:

> If a man spits on his neighbor, he is liable to pay damages, but he should not pay if he only spits on his neighbor's garments or if he shames him verbally. But the courts everywhere and at all times should introduce legislation for this matter as they see fit. Some say that he is to be placed under a ban of excommunication until he pacifies the victim of his insult. [Gloss] And some say that he is to be flogged.[106]

Legal procedures exist, of course, to identify and punish those who commit wrongs. Mere suspicion of wrongdoing, however, does not constitute guilt, and slandering a person to make others incorrectly think that she or he committed an offense — or that it is confirmed that s/he did when that has not yet been determined — is thus itself a punishable crime.

Nowadays, we do not have the authority to impose fines or lashes, but a person who accuses another of abuse knowing that the accusation is false and solely for purposes of slandering or otherwise harming the accused or for gaining sympathy for oneself should be subjected to appropriate sanctions. The falsely accused person can, of course, and should avail him/herself of any and all remedies prescribed in civil law. In addition, though, he or she has a right to expect the Jewish community to demonstrate its disgust at such behavior and its unwillingness to tolerate it. In the process of dealing with such an instance, the relevant laws prohibiting defamation (מוציא שם רע, Num. 12:1-6; Deut. 22:13-19), lying (שקר, Lev. 19:11), and even the related law about plotting witnesses (עדים

---

[100] B. Kiddushin 65b; Bava Metzia 3b; etc.

[101] B. Sanhedrin 9b, 10a, 25a; B. Ketubbot 18b; B. Yevamot 25b. See also T. Sanhedrin 11:1; B. Ketubbot 27a; B. Bava Kamma 72b. Cf. Aaron Kirschenbaum, *Self-Incrimination in Jewish Law* (New York: Burning Bush Press, 1970); and "confession," *Encyclopaedia Judaica* 5:877-8.

[102] Lev. 19:16; cf. Jer. 9:2-4; Ps. 34:13-15.

[103] B. Bava Kamma 91a.

[104] B. Bava Kamma 46a.

[105] R. Asher b. Jehiel ("ROSH"), Responsa, no. 101.

[106] S.A. Hoshen Mishpat 420:38.

זוממים, Deut. 19:15-21) should be taught, along with their rabbinic developments. In addition, sanctions appropriate to the situation should be employed. Depending upon the situation, that might include dismissal from a job in the Jewish community (on grounds of moral turpitude), expulsion from the camp, school, or synagogue in which the incident took place, and, minimally, a demand for a public apology before the entire congregation or in the synagogue bulletin.

All such sanctions, of course, apply only to cases where there clearly was no abuse and where the accuser knew that and nevertheless lodged the complaint; they would not be appropriate in cases where there is reasonable question as to whether the defendant's actions constitute abuse or not. In such cases, the accuser, in lodging the complaint, acted out of an honest, even if mistaken, understanding of the situation, and is blameless for doing so. The defendant can then dispute that understanding in a judicial tribunal if she or he thinks that the accuser misconstrued the situation, and the judges can decide.

The presumption of innocence built into Jewish law is even more critical in light of some evidence that false reports of abuse occur more often than one might expect and in light of the disputable evidence that has recently been adduced in some such cases. Specifically, the incidence of false rape reports has been variously computed in research studies as being between two and fifty percent (the latter figure based on police reports of two large Midwestern universities). That discrepancy is much too large to feel confident in any of the results, and, as David Marcus, a student of CJLS member Mark Rotenberg, has suggested in an unpublished research paper on this subject, the numbers depend crucially on the definition used by various police agencies and researchers of "false" and "unfounded" reports.[107] Nevertheless, even if the incidence is at the very lowest percentage reported, Jewish legal and moral norms regarding slander would require that we be extremely cautious in reporting, let alone acting upon, such allegations, and similar concerns would apply to charges of domestic abuse and violence.

The other phenomenon that would make one uneasy about accusing people too quickly and too confidently is the recent use of recovered memory in American court cases regarding sexual abuse of children, sometimes decades after it is alleged to have happened, and even abuse of teenagers or adults remembered years later. As Christine Goritan notes:

> In recent years, thousands of Americans, many with the help of psychotherapy, claim to have recovered bad memories. They have recalled being raped, being sexually abused or even seeing someone killed. And in most cases, they did not remember the events for decades after the crimes were supposed to have taken place. A large number of juries have believed these stories — enough to convict two men of murder and award millions of dollars in damages to victims. But some scientists have challenged the validity of repressed memories, arguing that many of these recollections

---

[107] David Marcus, "False Rape Reports," unpublished paper written at the School of Law of the University of Minnesota. Marcus cites, among other statistics, the FBI *Uniform Crime Reports* (1992), pp. 23-4, according to which eight percent of forcible rape complaints were "unfounded," meaning that they were "determined through investigation to be false;" Morrison Torrey, "When Will We Be Believed? Rape Myths and the Idea of a Fair Trial in Rape Prosecutions," 24 U.C. Davis L. Rev. 1013, 1028 (1991); Susan Brownmiller, *Against Our Will* (1975), p. 387; and Sedelle Katz and Mary Ann Mazur, *Understanding the Rape Victim* (1979), p. 209, all report that about two percent of rape accusations prove to be false. On the other end of the spectrum, Eugene J. Kanin, "False Rape Allegations," *Archives of Sexual Behavior* 23:1 (1994), p. 84, reports that forty-one percent were false in his study of rape allegations in a small Midwestern city, and in the police records of two large Midwestern state universities that he examined, exactly half (fifty percent) were false (Kanin, p. 90).

are false creations, born of patients' suggestibility and their therapists' leading questions.[108]

Elizabeth Loftus, a professor of psychology at the University of Washington, has shown just how easy it is to create a false memory. She asked older relatives of twenty-four people to make up a story about the younger person being lost at the mall between the ages of four and six. Eighteen of twenty-four insisted that the incident never happened, but six not only believed the story but also developed their own memories of the fictitious event. Without corroborating evidence, Loftus says, an accurate memory cannot be distinguished from an imagined one.[109]

On the other hand, other elements of Jewish law create a real tension with these concerns. As much as we are commanded by our tradition to assume the innocence of the accused, we are also commanded not to stand idly by while the life or safety of others is threatened and, indeed, to take steps to save them. Child and spousal abuse, after all, are real. Nobody is disputing that. Indeed, family violence of all types is an enormous problem in our society, and it clearly must stop. In the process of rooting it out, however, we must be diligent in preserving the presumption of innocence firmly embedded in the Jewish tradition while we also take steps to protect those who may have been harmed and may be hurt again.

I personally know of a case in which a youngster at Camp Ramah accused his teacher of hitting him. There were no witnesses, there was no bruise, and the teacher denied it altogether. Even though the camper had been in trouble with other staff members on other occasions, and even though the teacher had had an unblemished record in these matters, the camp authorities chose to remove the teacher from his position for fear of a lawsuit. I certainly understand that fear, especially given today's litigious society, but Jewish law would not countenance that action. In our zeal to protect our students and families from abuse, we must not ride roughshod over the reputations, the livelihoods, and the very lives of the accused simply because they are accused.

In all of these matters, it would be well for us to remember both sides of Sir Mathew Hale's famous eighteenth-century dictum to a jury: rape "is an accusation easily to be made and once made, hard to be proved, and harder to be defended by the party accused, tho [sic] never so innocent."[110] We must, on the one hand, not dismiss out of hand the accusations of children and adults of physical, sexual, or verbal abuse. On the other hand, though, we must remember that, in the many cases where there are no witnesses or physical evidence, the credibility of such accusations must be weighed against a strong presumption of the innocence of the accused until and unless a finding of guilt is reached by an appropriate tribunal.

Making Amends

When a fair hearing determines that there is sufficient evidence that a given person has abused another, in addition to whatever civil or criminal penalties apply, Jewish families and communities need to take steps to avoid any further abuse. This may mean, for a family, moving out of the quarters occupied by the abuser or forcing him or her to move out

---

[108] Christine Gorman, "Memory on Trial," *Time*, 17 Apr. 1995, p. 54.

[109] Ibid., p. 55.

[110] Cited by Marcus (at n. 107 above), p. 1, n. 1, and in Katz and Mazur (at n. 107 above), pp. 205-6. This quotation is discussed in the modern context of our concern for paying more attention to the testimony of women alleging rape (and children alleging abuse) by Brownmiller (at n. 107 above), p. 369.

of theirs, and it may mean, for a Jewish school, youth group, or camp, relieving the person of her or his job and perhaps even ostracizing the abuser from the community.

At the same time, the Jewish tradition puts great faith in the ability of those who do wrong to make amends and correct their behavior. It never expects us to be perfect: Jewish liturgy, after all, has us say three times each day, "Forgive us, our Father, for we have sinned," and every Yom Kippur evening we know full well that next year we will be back trying to cleanse our souls once again. The date is already scheduled! That does not mean, however, that efforts to improve oneself are fruitless and that we therefore have no duty to try. Quite the contrary, Judaism imposes a positive obligation on us to do teshuvah, to take steps to return to the proper path, and it assumes that we can do it if we really try.

What are those steps? They include: (1) acknowledgement of the wrong; (2) remorse; (3) public confession; (4) asking for forgiveness from the aggrieved party; (5) restitution to the extent that that is possible; and, (6) refraining from committing the wrongful act the next time the opportunity arises.[111] The famous twelve-step programs used to help people with addictions of various sorts have strong echoes with these traditional steps in Judaism, and Jewish forms of those programs have therefore quite naturally emerged. They offer one form of changing abusive behavior that has proven effective for many people. It should be said, then, that in addition to the famous programs of this sort for alcoholics, drug abusers, and overeaters, there also exist Parents Anonymous for those who physically abuse their children and Parents United for those who sexually abuse their children.

Going through such a program, of course, is anything but easy, for it seeks to change long-standing behavior. Indeed, unless successful therapy has intervened through programs such as the ones mentioned above, people who were themselves abused as children are more likely than the general population to abuse their own children. At the same time, though, most people who have been abused do not abuse others, and usually that is because they have found a caring community who confirm their own self-worth despite the degradation they suffered from previous abuse. That makes it all the more imperative for synagogues to sponsor groups such as Parents Anonymous and Parents United or at least to refer those of their members who abuse family members to such groups, and it also makes it critical that synagogues accept such steps as indications of teshuvah, making the person worthy of reinstatement into the community as a whole. Teshuvah, after all, is very difficult, especially when it involves deeply-rooted behavior patterns such as the ones we are discussing. No wonder, then, that the Talmud says that fully righteous people (צדיקים) cannot stand in the same place as those who have repented, for the strength needed to repent is much greater than the strength needed to be good in the first place.[112]

If one succeeds in reversing a history of abuse, one attains the status of a person who has returned (בעל תשובה). American law makes felons who have served their sentence indicate their criminal past on all sorts of documents, and such people often continue to be denied voting privileges, the right to apply for a government job, etc. Jewish law requires us to trust the process of return (teshuvah) much more strongly. It mandates that Jews not even mention the person's past violations, let alone bar him or her from full participation in society. Such recounting of the person's wrongful deeds is categorized as verbal abuse (אונאת דברים) itself. Moreover, it puts obstacles in the way of those who try to do better, a violation of the

---

[111] For a good summary of these steps as required by rabbinic sources, see Maimonides, Laws of Repentance (Teshuvah), especially 2:1-2.

[112] Sanhedrin 99a, and see Rashi's comment there. See Graetz, "The Haftorah Tradition" (at n. 10), for further discussion of when and how the safety of the synagogue can be helpful for airing matters of human intimacy, including areas of vulnerability such as being a victim or perpetrator of abuse.

biblical command, "Before a blind person you may not put an obstacle."[113] Thus the Jewish tradition strongly encourages abusers to seek help to control their abusive drives, promising full restitution in legal, social, and theological status if they succeed.

The abuser, however, must go through all these steps to be accorded the renewed status of being in good standing within the community. Being punished by the civil authorities is not sufficient. So, for example, in one of our congregations a man who for years was head of the synagogue's Cub Scout troop was later accused by a number of his former charges of sexual abuse. On the strength of the testimony of a number of these teenagers, he was sent to prison. When he was released, he wanted to join the synagogue once again. He refused, however, to admit that he had ever done anything wrong. That does not constitute teshuvah, despite the time he had spent in prison, and so the congregation was right in refusing to readmit him to membership.

If the man in this example (which actually occurred) had fulfilled the requirements of teshuvah, the congregation would be duty-bound to readmit him to membership but would not be obligated to reinstate him as its Cub Scout leader. While one may not routinely remind the offender or anyone else of his or her past offense, one may, and probably should, invoke that information in making decisions regarding the ways in which that person is permitted to interact with others. People may do full teshuvah and yet continue to be sorely tempted to repeat their offense if the opportunity arises. For such people, it is a favor neither to the offender nor to the people she or he may harm to put the culprit in the position where such temptation exists; that would be "putting an obstacle before the blind."[114] The past offense is enough of a ground to suspect that the offender may remain weak-willed in this area and likely to harm others once again. This is especially true for child abusers, whose behavior is so deeply rooted in their psyche that it is often impossible to undo. The only way to prevent future abuse, then, and the very therapy which they need is for the perpetrators to avoid situations in that they will be tempted to engage in such acts.

Therefore, even though we may not gratuitously mention the offense or bar the person from activities irrelevant to the offense, we may, and probably should use that knowledge to help the offender avoid tempting situations and to protect others at the same time.[115] We need to support people in their efforts to return to proper behavior, but we are not obligated to give such people opportunities to test their new resolve, especially when the welfare of others is at stake.

---

[113] One of the specific examples of אונאת דברים given in Bava Mezia 58a is reminding a person of past violations of the law. The verse forbidding putting a stumbling block before the blind (Lev. 19:14) is probably talking in its plain meaning about physically blind people and physical stumbling blocks, but the classical Rabbis applied it also – indeed, more often – to intellectual and characterological stumbling blocks put before those who are blind in those areas. See n. 40 above.

[114] See n. 40 and n. 113 above for the meaning of this expression in Jewish law.

[115] As Rabbi Mayer Rabinowitz has pointed out, if the process of teshuvah works to its fullest extent, the abuser should not even be tempted to abuse others when confronted with situations similar to the ones that led him or her to abuse people in the past. In a similar situation, we do not tell recovering alcoholics to avoid going to a Kiddush after worship services altogether; we ask them, instead, to participate in the Kiddush and to take grape juice instead of wine. On this model, abusers who have gone through full teshuvah might be trusted, at least under supervision, to resume their former tasks with children.

While I can understand this line of reasoning, and while I can imagine situations in which that may be appropriate, I hesitate to recommend it because in cases of abuse, more than in cases of alcoholism, the welfare of others is directly affected. Moreover, a significant percentage of alcoholics have managed to achieve and sustain a state of recovery, but pedophiles have much greater difficulty overcoming their addiction. It is therefore better for all concerned for them simply to avoid situations in which they may be tempted. We must trust the process of teshuvah while being realistic of its limits – and of the need to protect those who would be victims if it fails.

As a result, it may well be that, for such people, full teshuvah may not be possible. For its own protection and for the sake of the abuser too, the community may not afford the abuser the opportunity to complete the last stage of teshuvah, where the sinner confronts the same situation in which she or he previously sinned and acts differently. In such cases, the community, recognizing that that is the case not because of a failure in the abuser's resolve to do teshuvah but rather because of their own decision, may reinstate the abuser into the community, despite his or her failure to complete the process of teshuvah, for all purposes except for functioning in situations where she or he was previously abusive. The process of teshuvah, as described in the sources, may not be possible or appropriate for all cases, and the community's norms must respond accordingly.[116]

The Role of Rabbis and Educators in Preventing Abuse and in Repairing its Consequences

While rabbis and Jewish educators may agree wholeheartedly with the thrust of this responsum, many would probably ask what they can and should do to prevent abuse, where possible, or at least to alleviate its consequences. The Clergy Advisory Board of the California Department of Social Services has produced a brief pamphlet that was distributed to all members of the Board of Rabbis of Southern California as well as members of the clergy of all religions throughout the state.[117] It focuses on child abuse, but its recommendations can easily be adapted to spousal or parental abuse as well. In the paragraphs below, I will paraphrase and embellish upon the pamphlet's instructions, generalizing them to apply to spousal abuse as well as child abuse, to jurisdictions outside California, and to specifically Jewish concerns and contexts:

1. *Learn to recognize abuse.* If you fail to recognize the signs of abuse in your congregation, school, camp, or youth group, the abuse will undoubtedly continue. The opportunity to protect people from future abuse is often lost due to ignorance, denial, or fear of interference. Our professional schools and organizations should provide training for their students and members in how to discern potentially abusive situations, take family histories that include instances of abuse, provide religious counseling for abusers and their victims, and know which other professionals within the community should be called upon to help in both preventive and curative actions.

2. *Do not assume that you can handle the situation alone.* While clergy can be critical in helping victims and perpetrators of abuse, as explained below, they should not try to do this alone. If abuse is going to be stopped and its effects ameliorated, professionals of various sorts must be called upon. One clergy member is quoted in the pamphlet as saying this:

> A father divulged to me that he was molesting his daughter. He was repentant. I prayed with him, but did not seek further help to protect the victim. She later made a serious attempt on her life because, even after repentance and prayer, the father had continued to molest. It shook me.

---

[116] I would like to thank Rabbi Joel Rembaum for pointing out this aspect of the situation and its implications for the process of teshuvah.

[117] *Protecting Our Children: Information for Clergy Members about Abuse and Neglect*, a publication of the Clergy Advisory Board of the California Consortium to prevent Child Abuse, in collaboration with the Office of Child Abuse Prevention of the California Department of Social Services, 1600 Sacramento Inn Way, Suite 123, Sacramento, CA 95815. Copies can be ordered by calling (800) 405-KIDS.

3. *Know and obey your government's requirements to report abuse to legal authorities.* Many states, provinces, and cities have enacted laws that require clergy and teachers, as well as physicians, to report abuse to legal authorities. Exactly what must be reported, and to whom, varies. California, for instance, wants rabbis and teachers to err on the side of over-reporting abuse rather than underreporting it: California law specifies that educational and religious professionals must report suspicions of abuse and leave it to legal authorities to determine whether those suspicions are founded. The laws in other places may be different, going further in the direction of protecting the accused. In cases of spousal abuse, reports are generally made to the police, and in some locations that is true for child abuse as well; in other places instances of child abuse are to be reported to the Office of Children's Protective Services (or the equivalent agency of state or local government, whatever its title).

Sometimes clergy or teachers become aware of abuse through the confession of a congregant in a private counseling setting, and that raises questions of confidentiality. California law, though, specifically requires professionals to break professional-client confidentiality when the safety or physical welfare of a child or adult is involved, and it protects professionals from lawsuits complaining of such a breach of confidentiality. I would imagine that the laws and/or judicial rulings in most other locations follow suit.

In any case, rabbis and teachers everywhere have a legal responsibility to be on the alert for instances of family violence and to report such cases to legal authorities when civil law requires it. Failure to do so may subject rabbis or teachers personally, as well as the religious or educational institution for which they work, to both civil and criminal prosecution. Insurance companies are increasingly restricting their coverage so that they can avoid liability, for such suits, thus making the rabbis and educators and their institutions all the more legally exposed.

4. *Protect your congregation or school from potential abusers.* People who prey on children often seek positions that will give them access to, and authority over, children. Potential molesters cannot, of course, be identified by appearance alone. Synagogues, schools, youth groups, and camps, though, should, as part of their hiring policies and procedures, take measures to screen out those likely to molest the children under their care. This is important not only for the institutions and its charges, but also for the molester, for we are mandated not to "put a stumbling block before the blind" (Lev. 19:14) – in this case, the morally blind who would be tempted to use their position of authority to abuse those in their care.[118]

This, of course, is easier said than done, for as much as institutions must prevent molesters from being part of their staff, they also must avoid making unfair and unwarranted judgments of applicants. They certainly must not base their decisions on prejudices – say, against males, or against homosexuals (the overwhelming majority of convicted child molesters are heterosexual). At the same time, though, background checks should include attention to this aspect of a person's history.

5. *The abuser may be a colleague.* The recent, highly-publicized cases of child abuse perpetrated by a small number of Catholic priests illustrate that religious or educational professionals are unfortunately not beyond suspicion in these matters. As indicated above, due process must be applied in any investigation of such allegations, and the presumption of innocence must be preserved. If child or spousal abuse by a rabbi or educator is confirmed, however, other Jewish professionals on the staff and in the vicinity must be prepared to respond to the scandal and the public outrage. As the California pamphlet puts it, "While the needs of the victim are primary, compassion needs to be extended to the injured religious community and the perpetrator as well." We would undoubtedly add

---

[118] See n. 40 and n. 113 above for the meaning of this expression.

that steps must be taken to heal the community, help it avoid such incidents in the future, and bring the perpetrator both to justice and to the process of teshuvah.

6. *Clergy and educators can take specific steps to prevent and alleviate this problem.* In addition to the steps described above, the California booklet mentions the following:

(A) *Provide child and spousal abuse services and support other communal efforts to do the same.* To quote the California booklet, with additions for the case of spousal abuse,

> Anything that your community of faith does to strengthen families is child abuse [and spousal abuse] prevention. For some at-risk families, participation in religious services is their only real support system. You can reach out to families in isolation and turmoil by addressing parenting [and spousal] issues through sermons, study groups, or by sponsoring public forums.

Such discussions may well center on our new *Rabbinic Letter on Intimate Relations* because that provides a safe forum for opening up on all issues of human intimacy, including these troubling ones, and it does so in the context of Jewish conceptions, laws, and values. In addition, Mother's Day or Father's Day, or the story of the binding of Isaac read on Rosh Hashanah or during the year, may be used as the occasion for a worship service, forum, sermon, or readings on these subjects.

In addition, synagogues and Jewish federations should support efforts, typically by Jewish Family Service agencies, to establish safe houses with kosher facilities for victims of abuse. As a joint effort of synagogues and Jewish Family Service, synagogue services should be made available to residents in such facilities, and, conversely, experts in this area from Jewish Family Service should be called upon for preventive and educational programs within our synagogues and educational institutions.

(B) *Use the power of the religion and the community to deter abuse.* Rabbi Simhah, cited above, speaks of excommunicating a wife-beater from the congregation, and, in the case of the child abuser who wanted to rejoin a Conservative synagogue without doing full teshuvah, that congregation did just that — and rightly so. Where there is a reasonable expectation that continued membership within the community will more likely bring a change in behavior, the synagogue can and should still express its disgust for such behavior by, for example, refusing to give honors or positions of leadership to those known to physically or verbally abuse others. Rabbis should not hesitate to use theological language in explaining to abusers that such behavior is not only a violation of a Jewish communal norm, but a transgression of God's will as embedded in Jewish law and lore.

(C) *Counsel adult survivors of abuse.* Adults who abuse others were often abused themselves as children. If they are going to be able to break the cycle of abuse, they will need considerable counseling, instruction in good patterns of family interactions (since, by hypothesis, they never saw first-hand while growing up how families can handle their tensions in a healthy way), and reenforcement in acting differently from how their abusive parents did. Synagogues can, for example, form support groups for adult children of abuse, with opportunities to express their rage and to learn how to create a healthy family life; Jewish Family Service may be of aid in establishing and staffing such groups.

(D) *Address the spiritual aspect of healing.* We rabbis all too often underestimate the role of religious conviction in aiding the healing process. Virtually all of the Twelve-Step programs place heavy reliance on faith in God, not only because historically such programs emerged from Christian faith communities, but also because they have found that healing is assisted greatly when a person feels that she or he is being aided both by others who have the same problem and by God. We need to cease to be embarrassed by such religious language. We should unselfconsciously invoke the religious tenets of our tradition to help people who have been abused to heal the wounds of the past and to reconstruct and redirect their lives.[119]

Conclusions of the Response to Part IV

1. Jewish institutions, and Jews individually, must take every precaution from jumping to conclusions of guilt merely because someone is accused of perpetrating abuse. Jewish law ascribes a strong presumption of innocence to each person, and so the burden of proof is on the accuser. Furthermore, any and all evidence must be carefully weighed by communal authorities and a formal determination of guilt must be reached before any action against an alleged abuser is taken. Allegations alone are not sufficient to justify that.

2. The process of return (teshuvah) described in our sources for other offenders is open to a person engaged in family violence too, but it must be complete to warrant reinstatement in the community. Where full teshuvah does occur, Jews are not permitted even to mention the former abuse in general conversation, but they may use that information in making practical decisions about what may tempt the abuser and/or pose a danger to others.

3. Where full teshuvah does not occur, synagogues may deem it appropriate to use the religious and communal power at their disposal to express their disgust at the abusive behavior and to motivate the abuser to change his or her ways. This may include suspension or refusal of membership and denial of honors in worship and in leadership. The rabbi may also use theological as well as communal language in explaining to the abuser why her or his behavior is unacceptable. The specific sanctions should be tailored by the rabbi and lay leaders in charge to the particular situation with the goals of preventing future abuse and of motivating the abuser to make amends and to change his or her ways. In some cases, full teshuvah may be impossible for the abuser because of the community's decision to protect itself from future abuse of the same nature by the perpetrator; in such circumstances, the community should reinstate the abuser, even absent full teshuvah, once she or he has completed all of the steps of teshuvah that the community will allow him or her to do.

4. Jewish professionals and institutions can prevent and ameliorate cases of abuse by:

   A. Learning to recognize the signs of abuse;

   B. Bringing in other professionals within the community who have expertise in this area to help the institution take steps to avoid abuse, identify likely instances of abuse, and heal it when it occurs;

   C. Knowing and obeying the relevant civil laws requiring reports of abuse or suspicions of abuse to civil authorities;

   D. Taking steps to avoid hiring individuals with abusive behavior in their backgrounds, especially vis-à-vis the population whom the person now seeks to serve, while simultaneously avoiding prejudice about groups of people whom one thinks are likely to abuse;

---

[119] The entire Fall 1994 issue of *Religious Education* (vol. 89, no. 4) was devoted to the cover topic, "Religious Education and Child Abuse." That issue includes important articles on how religious educators (and presumably rabbis and cantors among them) can recognize child abuse when it happens, help victims to extricate themselves from the abuse, and help to prevent child abuse in the first place. Marian Wright Edelman of the Children's Defense Fund, James Fowler, and Nel Noddings are among the writers.

E. Understanding that professionals and laypeople entrusted with positions of leadership within the synagogue or educational program are not automatically above suspicion in these matters and, where abuse is confirmed, by immediately removing the abuser from the position, pulling the community together to heal its pain and wounds, and taking steps to avoid abuse in the future;

F. Including multifaceted efforts to strengthen the family in addition to programs that directly discuss the unacceptability of family violence and the alternative ways to deal with tensions within the family; and,

G. Unselfconsciously and forthrightly using the religious, as well as the communal, bases of authority available to religious institutions to teach people the Jewish imperative to recognize and avoid abuse and to prod abusers to change their behavior.

Reconnecting with God's Image Within Us

While questions can sometimes arise about the legitimate use of corporal punishment as a form of discipline, most cases of abuse cannot be justified in any way as rooted in a concern for discipline. They are, instead, bald exercises of physical might for purposes of exerting power over someone and/or of expressing one's own aggressions on innocent victims. Judaism unequivocally sees these as forbidden. Jewish law specifies punishments for those who strike others and demands that the objects of such attacks do everything in their power to escape such situations, even if it means defaming the assailant or embarrassing oneself. Judaism also prohibits verbal abuse of all kinds, claiming that in significant ways it is worse than monetary fraud.

It is important to recognize that such an attitude on Judaism's part is deeply rooted in its theology, its overarching conception of the human being. In secular systems of thought, abuse is problematic because it violates the Golden Rule and more generous, humanitarian concerns. When the topic is abuse within the family, further matters arise, including the resultant inability of the family to provide the safety, warmth, and education on which society depends and the inherent violation of the sanctity of the family. Judaism shares all of these concerns, but it has more, for abuse of another represents a denial of God's image in every human being.

In conceiving of the situation in that way, Judaism also can provide a real source of strength for abused people struggling to escape from their situation and to rebuild their lives. No matter how much someone else has diminished your self-image, Judaism is telling us, you must recognize that ultimately you are created in the image of God. Among other things, that means that like God, you have inherent worth, regardless of what anyone else says or does. That divine value represents a challenge to us, for we must each strive throughout our lives to realize the divine within us. It is a challenge, though, that gives life meaning and hope.

The following High Holy Day Message of the Jewish Theological Seminary of America for 1992, published in *Newsweek*, the *New York Times*, and the *Wall Street Journal*,[120] summarizes these themes nicely:

---

[120] Published in *Newsweek*, 28 Sept. 1992, in selected regions; and in the *New York Times*, 1 Oct. 1992, and the *Wall Street Journal* on the same date. The bold print indicated here is as it appeared in the published message.

"Know whom you put to shame, for in the likeness of God is (s)he made" (Genesis Rabbah 24:8).

Some people who are reading this were beaten yesterday, or terrorized, or kept in isolation. Some who tormented them are reading this now. And they are not strangers to each other; they are family. Intimates. People like us. Us.

Home should be a haven, the place where you can count on being valued and protected. If instead it is a place where the people closest to you beat you up, or keep you on edge with threats, or isolate and demean you – then what is safe?

Violence in the family is not love; it is not discipline; it is not deserved. It is an abuse of power, and it is wrong – because decent people don't behave that way; because it is against the law, and for one more reason: we are all made in the image of God. To lash out in violence – especially against someone whose life is linked with yours – is to violate a likeness of God, and to degrade that likeness in yourself.

Are you being hurt or humiliated by the person you are closest to? Believe that you do not deserve the abuse. No one has the right to tell you that you are worthless: your worth comes from God.

Have you been taking out your anger and frustration against the people who depend on you? Know that you are better than that; you are made in the image of God. You have the power to stop hurting and belittling them. God gives it to you.

To all who read this, we ask:

- Look at yourself, at your partner, at your elderly parents, at your children, as images of God. Treat each of them with the respect which that demands.

- Make your home a haven. Instead of raising your hand or your voice, raise your own dignity and the self-esteem of the people who turn to you for love. You may not be able to perfect the world, but this much you can do.

- Help your religious community to face the fact of domestic violence and to offer active support to those who have been enduring abuse, threats, and humiliation. A house of God should be a place for teaching restraint, decency, and reverence; make yours that place.

- Behave as though God made you worthy: it is true. Behave as though the world depends on your humanity and decency. It does.

". . .for the sin which we have committed before Thee, openly and in secret. . ." (High Holy Day Liturgy)

Contributors

Rabbi Kassel Abelson, ordained at the Jewish Theological Seminary in 1948, is Rabbi Emeritus of Beth El Synagogue, Minneapolis, Minnesota, Past President of the Rabbinical Assembly, and Chairman of the Committee on Jewish Law and Standards.

Rabbi Ben Zion Bergman, ordained at the Jewish Theological Seminary in 1948, is Familian Adjunct Professor of Rabbinic Literature at the University of Judaism.

Rabbi Debra Reed Blank, ordained at the Jewish Theological Seminary in 1989, is Assistant Professor of Jewish Liturgy at the Jewish Theological Seminary.

Rabbi Stanley Bramnick, ordained at the Jewish Theological Seminary in 1956, is former National Business Administrator for the National Ramah Commission and former Business Administrator for Camp Ramah in Nyack.

Rabbi Stephanie Dickstein, ordained at the Jewish Theological Seminary in 1989, is Assistant Dean and Director of Admissions at the Rabbinical School at the Jewish Theological Seminary.

Rabbi Elliot N. Dorff, ordained at the Jewish Theological Seminary in 1970, is Rector and Sol & Anne Dorff Distinguished Professor of Philosophy at the University of Judaism, and Vice Chairman of the Committee on Jewish Law and Standards.

Rabbi Amy Eilberg, ordained at the Jewish Theological Seminary in 1985, is a pastoral counselor in private practice in Palo Alto, California.

Rabbi Jerome M. Epstein, ordained at the Jewish Theological Seminary in 1970, is Executive Vice President of the United Synagogue of Conservative Judaism.

Rabbi David J. Fine, ordained at the Jewish Theological Seminary in 1999, is Secretary to the Committee on Jewish Law and Standards.

Rabbi Baruch Frydman-Kohl, ordained at the Jewish Theological Seminary in 1977, is Rabbi of Beth Tzedec Congregation, Toronto, Ontario.

Rabbi Shoshana Gelfand, ordained at the Jewish Theological Seminary in 1993, is Director of Programs at the Wexner Heritage Foundation.

Rabbi Myron S. Geller, ordained at Torah Vadaath in 1959, is Rabbi of Temple Ahavat Achim, Gloucester, Massachusetts.

Rabbi Nechama D. Goldberg, ordained at the Jewish Theological Seminary in 1993, is Director of Administration and Finance at Hebrew College.

Rabbi Arnold M. Goodman, ordained at the Jewish Theological Seminary in 1952, is Rabbi of Congregation Ahavath Achim, Atlanta, Georgia, and Past President of the Rabbinical Assembly.

Rabbi Howard Handler was ordained at the Jewish Theological Seminary in 1983.

Rabbi Reuven Kimelman, ordained at the Jewish Theological Seminary in 1970, is Associate Professor of Near Eastern and Judaic Studies at Brandeis University.

Rabbi Judah Kogen, ordained at the Jewish Theological Seminary in 1974, is Rabbi of Congregation B'nai Sholom, Newington, Connecticut.

Judge Norman M. Krivosha, formerly Chief Justice of Nebraska, practices law with the firm Kutak Rock in Lincoln, Nebraska.

Rabbi Vernon H. Kurtz, ordained at the Jewish Theological Seminary in 1976, is Rabbi of North Suburban Synagogue Beth El, Highland Park, Illinois, and President of the Rabbinical Assembly.

Rabbi Alan B. Lucas, ordained at the Jewish Theological Seminary in 1978, is Rabbi of Temple Beth Sholom, Roslyn Heights, New York.

Rabbi Aaron L. Mackler, ordained at the Jewish Theological Seminary in 1985, is Associate Professor of Theology at Duquesne University.

Rabbi Herbert J. Mandl, ordained at the Jewish Theological Seminary in 1969, is Rabbi of Kehilath Israel Synagogue, Overland Park, Kansas.

Rabbi Lionel E. Moses, ordained at the Jewish Theological Seminary in 1977, is Rabbi of Shaare Zion Congregation, Montreal, Quebec.

Rabbi Daniel S. Nevins, ordained at the Jewish Theological Seminary in 1994, is Rabbi of Adat Shalom Synagogue, Farmington Hills, Michigan.

Rabbi Paul Plotkin, ordained at the Jewish Theological Seminary in 1976, is Rabbi of Temple Beth Am, Margate, Florida.

Rabbi Joseph H. Prouser, ordained at the Jewish Theological Seminary in 1988, is Rabbi of Little Neck Jewish Center, Little Neck, New York.

Rabbi Mayer Rabinowitz, ordained at the Jewish Theological Seminary in 1967, is Librarian and Associate Professor of Talmud at the Jewish Theological Seminary.

Rabbi Joel E. Rembaum, ordained at the Jewish Theological Seminary in 1970, is Rabbi of Temple Beth Am, Los Angeles, California.

Rabbi Avram Israel Reisner, ordained at the Jewish Theological Seminary in 1977, is Adjunct Professor at Baltimore Hebrew University.

Rabbi James S. Rosen, ordained at the Jewish Theological Seminary in 1982, is Rabbi of Beth El Temple of West Hartford, Connecticut.

Rabbi Joel Roth, ordained at the Jewish Theological Seminary in 1968, is Louis Finkelstein Professor of Talmud and Jewish Law at the Jewish Theological Seminary, and Rosh Yeshivah of the Conservative Yeshivah, Jerusalem, Israel.

Rabbi Gerald C. Skolnik, ordained at the Jewish Theological Seminary in 1981, is Rabbi of Forest Hills Jewish Center, Forest Hills, New York.

Rabbi Elie Kaplan Spitz, ordained at the Jewish Theological Seminary in 1988, is Rabbi of Congregation B'nai Israel, Tustin, California.

Rabbi Gordon Tucker, ordained at the Jewish Theological Seminary in 1975, is Rabbi of Temple Israel Center in White Plains, New York, and Adjunct Assistant Professor of Jewish Philosophy at the Jewish Theological Seminary.

Rabbi Gerald L. Zelizer, ordained at the Jewish Theological Seminary in 1964, is Rabbi of Neve Shalom, Metuchen, New Jersey, and Past President of the Rabbinical Assembly.

Source Index

Books of the Bible are arranged according to the *Tanakh*. The *midrashim* are arranged the same way through the *megilot* and then alphabetically. The Mishnah and Talmud sections are arranged according to tractates.

The Bible

Genesis
1:21	105
1:26, 28	208, 462n2, 535n32
1:26-27	511n1, 774n2
1:28	540n68, 687n10
2:18	626, 687n11, 715
2:24	626, 682, 715-716
6:2	622n42
9:2	208
9:5	381n5
9:6	576n116, 774n2
9:29-35	616n14
14:19, 22	380n3
15:2-3, 4	462n1, 501n97
15:5	462n1, 536n35
15:6	537n47
16:1	536n42
16:2	501n97, 537n44, 550n122
16:6	537n46
17:3-6, 15-21	462n1
17:7	680
18:1-15	462n1
18:18	462n1
19:5	616
22:17	536n35
24:47	118n17
25:21	462n1, 536n40
26:4	536n35
27:1	335
28:14	462n1
30:1-2	536n41
30:1-8	462n1, 537n48
30:3	501n97, 536nn42-43, 537n48
30:6, 9, 10	536n42, 537n45, n48
30:21	142
30:22-24	462n1
31:44-51	736
32:8	538
32:13	462n1
34:7	563n44
35:11	462n2
35:16-20	462n1
38:8-9	501n97
39:1	616
39:24	563n40
43:32	615
46:34	615
48:5-6	481, 481n51, 501n97
50:23	501n97

Exodus
2:10	501n97
4:10, 11-12	342, 343
8:22	615
12	165
12:17	167
13	142n16, 165, 522n53
13:1-2	163, 497n90
13:12, 15	497n90
15:26	321n2
17:14	563n35
18:20	226, 227, 453
19:5	380n3
20:5	562n33, 563n42
20:10	66
20:11	380n3
20:12-13	483, 506n106, 566n55, 786, 786n45
21:6	118n15
21:10	463n2
21:15	785n44
21:19	389n35
21:19-20	321
21:22	250n189
21:23-25	288, 574n103

23:2	763	25:36	258, 259n223
26:33	422	26:16	321n2
32:2	118n18	*Numbers*	
32:13	464n7, 536n35	3:11-13	163
34:1	580n139	3:12	497n90
34:7	562n33, 563n44	3:48	10n7
34:19	172-173	5:11-31	583-584
35:22	118n19	6	14
Leviticus		6:22-27	9n1, 10n5, 13n1
5:1	796	12:1-6	806
5:23-24	217n85	12:1-15	578n126
11	109, 616	14:18	562n33, 563n42
11:43	677	15:32-34	576n112
12:2-3	126	15:37-41	581n141
18	615, 710, 716	15:38	6
18:3	474n35, 617, 622nn42-43	18:15	497n90
18:5	260, 470n22, 796	18:15-16	163, 164, 166, 441
18:6	620, 789	19:2	105n12
18:6-18	560n8	31:50	118n19
18:9	466, 483n58, 501n97	35:3	276-277
18:16	474n35, 538n58	35:33	576n116
18:17	623n46, 624n49	*Deuteronomy*	
18:20	466, 475n37, 560n8	1:10	536n35
18:22	614, 616n11, 619n27, n30, 624, 627, 629, 686n3, 693, 715, 719	4:6	717
		4:9	381n5, 469n22
18:23	624n48	4:15	108, 469n22, 515n18, 545
18:24, 25-29	474n35	4:35, 39	380n3
18:26, 29, 30	614, 624	5:16	483, 786n45
18:27, 30	474n35, 620, 624	5:17	566n55
18:29-30	789	6:7	801
19:3	190n103, 483, 506n106, 786n45	6:18	142
19:11	806	7:3	128
19:13	217n85, 544	7:3-4	608
19:14	343, 383, 383n15, 707n29, 784n40, 796n78, 802, 810n113, 812	7:6-8	464n7
		7:12, 13, 14	462n1, 464n5
19:15	335n51	7:25-26	615n8
19:16	175n2, 219, 219n97, 220, 284, 321, 344, 345, 396, 795, 796n78, 806n102	10:14	380n3
		10:22	536n35
19:18	322n7, 787n52	12:3-4	151
19:19	104	12:12	795n74
19:22	14n9	12:31	615n8
19:28	115n1	13:5	321
19:29	624n49	13:6	796n80
20	615, 705	13:7	383n16
20:8, 10	474n35, 566n56	13:9	383n16
20:13	614-615, 618, 619n30, 624, 629, 635, 686n3	13:15	616n9
		14:3	616
20:17	483n58	15:4	300
20:21	538n58	15:7	218n91
20:22-24, 26	474n35	15:8	324
20:27	618	15:10	217-218
21:3	576n110	15:19	173
21:7	597, 598, 600	17:1	615n3
21:8	10n4, 14, 219n94, 594	17:4	616n9
21:17-21	342	17:7	796n80
24:10	566n58, n59	17:10	768
24:20	574	17:11	579n128, 762, 763n13, 766, 768
25:14	792n71	17:12	763n12, 796n80
25:17	792, 792n71	17:15	561n21
25:23, 42, 55	380n3	18:9,12	615n8
25:35-36	345		

18:14-22	762, 762n6, n8	17:23	381n8
18:19	763n12	21	580n135
19:15	807	21:8	501n100
19:19	796n80	21:10	580n137
20:19-20	387n29	*1 Kings*	
20:21	538, 539n58	14:24	619n29, n30
21:1-9	583	17	204n36
21:15	173	*2 Kings*	
21:18-21	577n120, 720, 783n36, 784	4	204n37
21:21	796n80	4:6	587n2
21:22-23	774n4	25:6-7	342
21:23	400n1, 580n138	*Isaiah*	
22:1	176n4	3:21	118n19
22:2	220, 267, 300n350, 321, 405	19:22	321n2
22:5	615n4	44:5	116, 116n7
22:9-11	104	45:18	463n3, 536n39, 682
22:13-19	806	49:16	116n8
22:21, 22	796n80	51:2	480
22:26, 27	654n140, 698n16	56:3-5	515n21
23:3	474n33, 559, 562, 563n36, 587n1	57:18-19	321n2
23:4-8	562n34, 563n38	63:16	480
23:18	619n28, n30, 677	64:7	480
23:19	615n8	*Jeremiah*	
23:24	576n114	9:2-4	806n102
24:1	314n393	10:11	736
24:4	462n1, 615n5	29:7	335n50
24:7	796n80	30:17	321n2
24:11	462n1	31:29	563n37
24:16	562n32, 580n136	33:6	321n2
25:3	774n4	*Ezekiel*	
25:5-10	480n48, 496n86	16:11	118n19
25:6	480n48, 501n97, 538	16:49, 50	616n12
25:8-9	539n59	18:2	563n37
25:11-12	790n60	18:1-4, 18-19	563
25:16	615nn6-7	24:17	454
25:19	563n35	44:22	599n4
27:15	615n8	*Hosea*	
28:14	766-767	4:14	583
28:22	321n2	6:1	321n2
28:59-60	321n2	*Zechariah*	
28:62	536n35	9:6	559
32:3	23n5	11:12	621
32:6	380n3	*Psalms*	
32:16	616n11	24:1	380n3
32:39	321n2	34:4	23n5
Joshua		34:13-15	806n102
1:8	44	50:23	308n378, n379
7	147	77:16	501n97, n100
Judges		78:4-7	682
8:24	118n19	103:2-3	321n2
16:21	342	104:24	380n3
19:22	616	106:3	482, 502
24:33	415, 426	107:20	321n2
1 Samuel		119:126	571, 579
1:1-20	462n1	128:1, 3-5	463n4
28:15	414n7	128:6	462n1
31:3-5	381		
2 Samuel			
6:8	47		

Proverbs
2:20	225
3:11-12	782n33, 783, 784
3:17	288, 586n155
3:18	585n154
5:15	625
10:22	453-454
13:24	782n33
19:18	782n33
20:30	782n33
22:6	784n39
23:13-14	782n33
29:15	782n34, 783
29:17	782n33
29:19	235

Job
5:18	321n2
5:24	792n69
37:7	116n9

Song of Songs
4:12	566n57

Ruth
4:16-17	501n97, n100
4:18-22	563n41

Lamentations
1:10	560n12
5:3	480

Ecclesiastes
4:1	562
8:5	135
11:6	463n3

Esther
2:7, 15	501n97

Daniel
2:2-7:28	736

Ezra
2:61	501n97
4:8-6:19	736
5:1-5	736
10:44	501n97

Nehemiah
13:1	562n34, 563n38

1 Chronicles
2:35-41	501n97
4:18	501n97, n100
23:15	462n2

2 Chronicles
25:4	587n2

Bible Commentaries and Translations

Ba'alei haTosafot
Leviticus
Aharei Mot	625

Ha-Emek D'var
Deuteronomy
17:11	768n30

Ibn Ezra
Genesis
19:5	616n12

Leviticus
21:3	576n111

Klei Hemdah
Numbers
Pinhas	275-276

Meshekh Hokhmah
Exodus
4:19	275n274

Pesikta Zutrata
Leviticus
18:22	627, 628

Ramban
Genesis
1:26	208

Exodus
34:7	563n44

Leviticus
18:20	466-467
18:22	627
19	105
19:14	343, 343n21

Numbers
12:1-15	578n126

Deuteronomy
17:11	762-763, 765n18
23:3	568

Rashbam
Genesis
19:5	616n12

Rashi
Genesis
19:5	616n12

Exodus
34:7	563n44

Leviticus
19	105-106
19:3	190n103, 544n88
21:3	576n111

Deuteronomy
15:4	300

Zechariah
11:12	621-622

Sforno
Exodus
34:7	563n44

Numbers
12:1-15	578n126

823

Targum Jonathan
Genesis
30:2   535n30
30:21   142, 496, 496n87, 522n53

Torah Temimah
Leviticus
18:22, no. 70   627-628, 629
19:14, no. 93   802n96
19:16, no. 110 284
Numbers
18:22   687n4

Midrashim

Midrashei Halakhah

Mekhilta Derabbi Yishmael
Bo
16   29n10
17   173n3
Beshalah
6   278n285
Mekhilta deBahodesh
6   563n44
8   506n106

Sifra
Shemini
1   11n10
Aharei Mot
9:5   617, 617n18, 618
9:8   623n45, 697
9:14   629n65
13   716-717
Kedoshim
1:9   506n106
4:17   105
19:14   383n15, 707n29, 784n40, 802n96
90d   566n59
Emor
20:3   699n19
21:3   576n111
21:8   219n94
Behar
5:3   259n223
Tzav
14   699n19
Behukotai
13:7   761-762, 764

Sifre
Bamidbar
43   11n11
154   766, 766nn23-24, 767
248   560n4, n10
249   561n26
286   250n190
318   616n11

Devarim
25:12   790n61

Sifrei Zuta
27   11, 11n12

Midrashei Aggadah

Genesis Rabbah
6:18   43-44, 44n3
8:9   627n58, 716
9:7   680
17:2   680
18:5   715
24:8   816
26:5   622n42
33:1   385n22
34:13   381n5
34:14   536n37
36:8   625n54
50:5   616n12

Exodus Rabbah
1:12   165
4   502n102
19:1, 5   105n12
19:6, 8   106n12
34:3   788n55
46:5   480n49

Leviticus Rabbah
9:9   525
23:9   622n42
32:5   566n59, 588n7
32:8   562n29
34:3   381n4

Deuteronomy Rabbah
1:15   786n48

Kohelet Rabbah
1:38   210n64
4:1   562n29

Midrash Ha-Gadol
Genesis
6:11   622n42

Midrash Samuel
4:1   541n71

Pesikta de Rav Kahana
14   154n6

Pirkei d' Rabbi Eliezer
17   456, 457
40   665n166

Yalkut Shimoni
Genesis
15   454
Ecclesiastes
978   385n22

Mishnah

Berakhot
4:1	50
5:5	65n3
9:5	571n80, 579n131

Kilayim
9:5	129

Shabbat
6:6	119, 119n20, n24

Rosh Hashanah
3:8	602n1

Megillah
3	14n3
3:1	26
4:1	39, 39n9
4:2	37, 37n2, 39, 39n8

Hagigah
1:8	576n115

Yevamot
2:5	539n62
4:2, 9, 12	236n149
4:10	709n32
4:13	559-560, 560n8, n9
6:1	475n37, 629n67
6:6	462n2, 482, 482n54, 498n94, 510n1, 511n1, 517n30, 535n33, 546n101
8:2	560n13
8:4	539n65
9:3	236n149
12:6	539n64
13:12, 13	236n149
14:1, 8, 9	236n149

Ketubbot
1:5	709n32
4:9	326n22, 326n23
5:5	777n11
5:6	463n2
7	236n149

Nedarim
3:1	700n20
3:3	700n21
5:3	539n62

Sotah
3:4	289
9:9	583, 583n150, 584

Gittin
5:8	334n48
6:1, 2	742
7:8	202, 202n26

Kiddushin
1:1	781n29
1:7	786n45
3:12	497n88, 560n5, n7, 562n28
4:4	320n1

Bava Kamma
6:5	241n163
8:1	774n3, 790n61, 797n84
8:3	785n44
8:6	246, 381n5, 797n84
8:7	384n20

Bava Metzia
2	225
2:11	300n352
4:2	547n108

Bava Batra
2:4	339-340

Sanhedrin
1:1	730
1:6	763
4:5	463n3
5:1-2	577n117
7:4, 10	383n16, 576n113, 618n22, 674
8:7	795n75, 796n78

Makkot
1:10	577n118
2:2	783n35
2:7	273-274
3:6	116, 116nn2-3
3:10-11	774n4

Eduyot
1:5	761n3
4, 5	463n2
6:1	687n7

Avot
2:15	774n6
2:16	385n22
4:5	801n92

Horayot
3:7-8	299
3:8	561n22

Menahot
4:1	581n141

Bekhorot
1:7	539n63
8:2	172

Keritot 506n106

Ohalot
7:6	348, 352n16

Niddah
3:2	352-353
5:3	349n7, 371, 441, 442, 451

Mishnah Commentaries

Maimonides
Perush ha-Mishnayot
Introduction	762n7

Nedarim
4:4	220, 220n105

9:5 253n199
Sotah
9:9 583n150
Tamid
7:2 13n2
8:2 11n14

Tiferet Yisrael
Berakhot
3:2 453
Makkot
2:8 274

Tosafot Yom Tov
Berakhot
3:2 452-453

Tosefta

Berakhot
6:15 28n10
Pe'ah
4 345n33
Kilayim
2:15 108n18
Terumot
1:3 340n14
Shabbat
2:15 107n17
15:5-7 350n11
15:7 348n2, 351n13
Yoma
5:13 563n44
Megillah
3:20 23n2
Yevamot
6:9 539n63
8:3 462n2
Nedarim
6:7 547n111
Sotah
9:9 583n150
Kiddushin
5:4 562n30
Sanhedrin
11:6 720
13 425
Bava Kamma
9:11 381n5
Bava Metzia
3 547n111
11:33 278n285, 282n301

Oholot
18:18 766n21

Tosefta Commentaries

Tosefta Kifshutah (Lieberman)
Berakhot
6:15 28n10
7:1 28n10
Kilayim
1:6 106n14
2:15 108n18
Shabbat 351n14
Megillah
3:20 23n2
Bava Metzia
11:33-37 276n279, 282n301

Babylonian Talmud

Berakhot
4a 385n22
5b 385n23
6a 394n44, 473n32
7a 222n108
7b-8a 394n45
8a 154n4
9 761n4
10b 788n54
12a 401n3
12b 620n35
20b 602n1
21a 24n5, 29n10
27a 50
28b 675
32a 495n85
32b 545n99
33a 284, 304
45a 24n5
45b 222n108
48b 29n10
54a 687n9
55a 267n249
58b 388n33
60a 496n87, 535n30
63a 687n9

Shabbat
11b 119, 119n21
12b 455
13a 791n62
22a 128, 129
29b 128n1
31a 681
32a 545n99
32b 470n22
41b 128n1
51a 611
67b 149, 149n10
68b 149, 149n11
75a 129, 385n25

111b	129	*Megillah*	
114a	665n164	7b	201n24
128a	215n82	13a	502n102
128b	95n3, 596n15	21a-b	22-23, 24, 29n10, 37, 37n3
129a	470n22	21b	33
129b	249	22a	154n6
132a	470n22	23a	26
135a	126, 350n11, 442	26b	155n8
135b	349n7, 350n12, 441	27a	536n38
136a	351n13, 442		
151a	409	*Mo'ed Katan*	
151b	181n46, 349n6, 470n22	5a	308n379, 383n15, 707n29
		11b	611
Eruvin		15a	454
14b	279n292	17a	383n15, 707n29, 784n40, 802n96
19a	385n22	20a	456
41a	665n165	27b	409-410
46b	279	28b	14n6
51a	279n292		
82a	802n93	*Hagigah*	
		3b	340
Pesahim		10b	65n3
22b	383n15, 707n29, 784n40, 802n96	14b	465
54a	109-110	15a	351n14
76b	112n1, 113n3		
88b	682	*Yevamot*	235
101a	129	16b	497n88
113b	795n73	21a	483n58
		22a	432n4, 561n19
Yoma		22b	539n62
9a	688n13	23a	497n88
29a	620n36	25b	806n101
37a	24n5	37b	566n59, 624n49
69a	579n132	39a-b	539n65
70a	24n6	44a	497n88
72b	665n163	45a	560n6, 573n98
75a	716	45b	497n88, 560n9
82a	176n10, 177n12, 331n39, 345	46a-b	132-133
82a-85b	470n22	47b	147
83a	697n13	48b	432n4
85a, 85b	183n61, 260n225, 279, 304, 389n36, 796n77	49a-b	560n11, 587n1
		53b	654n141, 698n14
86	387	54a	475n37, 629n67
		62a	432n4, n7, 462n2
Sukkah		62b	463n3, 627n59, 792n69
29b	544n92	63b	463n3, 536n37
49b	345n33	65b-66a	462n2
		69b	142, 522n53
Beitza		76a	560n13, 618
23b	128	76b	559n3, 563n39
		77a	563n39
Rosh Hashanah		78a	139, 522n52, 561n16
27a	22	78b	560n13, 561n18, 568n70
34b	82, 82n2, 87n13	79a	580n136, n138
		80b	567n62, 590
Ta'anit		88b	219, 219n94
11a	385n22	89a-90b	581n143, 595n11, 720
20b	284n308	89b-90b	687n6
21a	284n308	90b	581n144
21b	209n62	97b	139, 432n4, 433, 522n52
23b	252n198	98a	476n39
24b	284	106a	779n20
25a	284n308	108b	747-748
26b-27a	12n15		

119a	203, 203nn32-33, 688n12	63b	742, 743, 744
		64a	742
Ketubbot		67a	279n292
5b	128n1		
6a-b	129	*Kiddushin*	
12a	709n32	9b	629n67
18b	806n101	17b	432n9
19b	157, 157n13	21b	118n16
22a	731, 734, 737	28a	561n17
27a	806n101	29a	786n45
46a	620n37	29b	284n308
49b	217n88, 237-238	30a	784n40
50a	235, 240, 482, 502n102, 521n50	30b	621n39, 786n49
61a	792n68	31a	804n99
61a-b	283	31a-b	793n72
62b	204, 204n38, n41, 498n94	31b	786n45, 804n98
65b	802n93	31b-32a	786n47, n48
67b	324n13	32a	707n29, 802n96
69b	520n42	39b	395n22, 473n32
77a	235n146	40a	473n32
97a	222	41b	65n3, 742
102b	506n106	50a	106n20
103a	484n60, 788n55	65b	806n100
122b-123a	802n93	67a	561n27, 569n73, 594n8
		69a	561n16
Nedarim 278		70a	497n88
22a	383n17	71a-b	568n69
27a	482n53, 653n138, 700nn20-21	72b	560n13, 562n31
28a	68n6, 548n116	73a	564n47, 567n63
37a	65n1	75b	497n88
39b-40a	393	76b	567n64
42b	383n15	82b	208-209
51a	623-624		
62b	707n29, 802n96	*Bava Kamma*	
80b	276, 280, 282, 283, 304	6b	688n13
81a	276, 304	8	543n85
		15b	495n85, 545n99
Nazir		24a	279n292
38a	215n80	28a	790n61
42a	129	28b	482n53, 653n138, 699n19
43a	595	35b	567n64
		37a	501n98
Sotah		46a	806n104
13b	616n16	47b	384n19
14a	321, 344	55a-56a	241, 383n16, 384n19
21b	289	56a	795n73
27a	567n61, 590-591	72b	806n101
38a-b	14n9	80a	495n85, 545n99
38b	10n2	82b-84a	574n104
43b	482n57	83a	790n61
47a	784n38	84a	287
		85a	253nn205, 207, 321, 328n32
Gittin		86a-b	790n61, 797n83
10b	68n6, 548n116	90a	792n66
32a	569n77	91a	246-247, 806n103
36a-36b	687n8	91b	247n172, 381n5, 495n85, 545n99
37a	501n98	92a, 93a	387n29
45a	325n20, 332n43	99b	222-223
57b	381n9	100a	453
59a	421	113a	68n6, 548n116
59b	16n1, 17	118a	226-227
60a-b	579nn133-134		
61a	334n48, 383n17, 420-421		

Bava Metzia
3a	806n100
12a	743
12b	483n58
24b	224, 231n138
30a	224n112
30b	223, 226, 453
32a-32b	95n3, 190n103
33a	300, 308
38a	62
48b	546n104
58a	65n1, 810n113
58b	564n48, 792n71, 797n84
59a	792n67
59b	544n89, 588n6, 762n10, 763, 765n18
62a	258, 804n97
66a-b	546n104, 547n107
75b	383n15, 707n29, 802n96
77b	67n4
82a	304
83a	225
96a	65n3
109a-b	546n104

Bava Batra
2b	340n13
12a	762n9
22a	384n18
22b	340n12
54b-55a	68n6, 548n116
111b	415, 419, 427
112a	419
131a	695n7
154a	414n5
157a	547n112
164b	621n38
168a	546n104

Sanhedrin
2b-3a	687n8
9b	501n100, 577n117, 806n101
10a	806n101
12b	502n103
17b	322, 344
19a	580n140
19b	480n49, 502n101
24b-25a	547n107, 806n101
25b	544n90
27b	563n43, 587n2
29a	383n16
32b	561n20
37b	675n179
38a	716
44a	147, 147n3, 405n14, 406
46a	405n8
46b	436n27
46b-47a	410
47a	405n9, 425, 427n6
47b	415n12, 416n19, n20
48a	416n21
54a	287n311, 618-618, 629n65
54b	618n25
56a-b	104n9
58a	682, 715
60a	104n9
63a	475n37
68a	576n115
70a	616n15
70b	453
71a	577, 579, 720, 784n41
72a	796n77
73a	176n3, n8, 220n104, 257, 267-268, 283, 287n311, 293, 300, 304, 321, 396n50
74a	176n10, 287n311, 381n6, 382n10, 389n36, 481n52, 698n15, 796n77, 804n97
74b	274n272, 382n10, 389n36
75a	683
84a	270n257
84b	785n44
85a	250n190
91b	376n12
95a	629n67
99a	809n112
107b	784n38
110b	446n11

Makkot
5a	591n15
8a-b	783n35
11b	275n276
22a	774n4

Shevu'ot
8a	247n177
18a	475n37
35a-b	151

Avodah Zarah
8b	582
14a	802n96
18a	381n7
20b	620n37
28b	285
36a	704
36b	608
54a	482n53, 653n138
55b	383n17

Horayot
4a	475n37, 629n67
13a	299, 299nn348-349

Menahot
18b	12n15, 15n10
38a	581n141
41b	128
42a-b	3-4, 5
43b	581n142
60a	106n14
99a	580n139

Hullin
10a	112, 495n85, 515n18, 545n99, 804n97

11b	178n23	*Ma'aser Sheni*	
58a	142, 522n53	1:1 (52c)	766n21
72a	215n80	*Shabbat*	
92a-b	621, 697n11	6:1 (7d)	253n199
110b	217n90	14:4 (14d)	683
132b-133a	15n10		
		Megillah	
Bekhorot		1:9 (71b)	625n54
30b	147	4:1	28n10, 33n17
37a	119n24	4:1 (77d)	38nn5-6
47a	432n4	4:5	23n2, 24
47b	172	4 (75a)	37-38, 38n4
49a	441		
		Moed Katan	
Arakhin		1:13	414n8
15b	578n126	1:5	417n24
		2:4	413
Niddah		3:5 (82d)	453, 454
23b-24a	353n20		
31a	496n87, 506n106, 536n36	*Yevamot*	135, 203
38b	351n13	4:2	350n11
44b	442	6:6 (7c)	463n2
45a	618n25	9:4 (10b)	236-237, 236n151
61a	265, 266, 267, 304		
61b	181n46	*Ketubbot*	
		10:2	595-596, 596n14

Minor Tractates

		Sotah	
Soferim		3:4 (19a)	289n318
1:13	561		
13	32n17	*Gittin*	
19	456	5:9 (61a)	421
		7:3 (48d, 40a)	202, 202n27
Semahot		7:8 (76b)	202
2:1	585n152		
2:1-5	381n5	*Kiddushin*	
2:3, 4-5	585n152	1:4	566n59
2:4-6	784n38	1:7 (67b)	786n48
3:1	442	3:12 (64a, c)	559n3, 561n18
3:2	443	3:13 (64d)	562n31, 569n72
3:3	443n6	3:15 (64d)	569n73
13	414	4:11	371, 441-442, 443

Palestinian Talmud

		Sanhedrin	
Berakhot		4:2 (22a)	764n15, 767
5:1	394n44	7:7 (24d-25a)	619n32
5:3	23, 23n2,n3, 32n17, 33		
7:1	28n10-29n10, 33n17	*Horayot*	
		1:1 (45d)	766n25

Talmud Commentaries

Pe'ah	
1	473n32
1:1 (15c-d)	774n5, 786n48, 793n72
1:5	345n33

Maharsha
Niddah 31a 142, 522n53

Kilayim	
1:7	105, 106n14

Maharshal on
Bava Kamma
6 siman 6 242-243
8 siman 59 249

Shevi'it	
2:6 (33d)	765n20

Meiri on
Moed Katan
24b 453

Terumot 278	
8:4 (32b, 46b)	262-263, 264, 304

Yevamot
89b, 90b   581n145
Ketubbot 3a 571n82
Gittin 59a   421

P'nei Moshe on
Yerushalmi
Sanhedrin 4:2 764, 767

Sefer Ha-Aggudah on
Bava Metzia 230n132

Sefer Hafla'ah
Ketubbot
49b   218, 218n92

Ramban
Shabbat
6a   409
13a   791n62
Ketubbot 3a 571n82
on
Sefer HaMitzvot
353   791n62

Ran on
Yevamot 22a 432, 432n6
Ketubbot 63b 777n11
Nedarim
8a   248n182
51a   625, 626, 627
Gittin
61a   421, 428n9
63b   744-745
Sanhedrin
73a   269, 269n256, 270-271
47a   421
Shevu'ot 11a 248n181
Hullin 132b 216, 216n84, 217

Rashba on
Rosh Hashana
16a   579n128
Yevamot 53b 699n17
Ketubbot 50a 238n156
Nedarim
90a   596n16
Gittin
63b   744, 746
Bava Metzia
59b   762n10

Rashi on
Shabbat
11b   119, 119n22
12b   455
114a   665n164
129a   359n6
136a   442

Sukkah
33b   385n25
Hagigah
3b   340n15
Yevamot
39b   539n66
45a   573n98
53b   629n67
108b   748
Ketubbot
22a   732
33a   250n190
50a   238, 240
86a   216
Nedarim
40a   359n10
Gittin
61a   421, 422, 428n8
62b   742
Kiddushin
30a   784n40
32a   787n52
67a   569n73
73a   561n15, 564n47
82b   320n1
Bava Kamma
85a   389n35
Bava Metzia
12a   743
32a   190n103
59b   544n89
77a   67n4
Sanhedrin
44a   147, 147n3
46b-47a   410
47a   788n54
54b   618n25
70b   453
73a   176n10, 795nn74-75
99a   809n112
Menahot
27a   106
Hullin
132b   216n83
Bekhorot
13a   539n63
47b   172n2
49a   441, 442
Niddah
23b   353n22
61a   265
Nedarim 51a 625

Ritba on
Yevamot
47b   133
90b   581n145

Ketubbot 50a	238n155
Gittin 59a-b	20
Menahot 60a	106n14

Rosh on
Megillah	
3:3	25
Moed Katan	
1:13	414n8
Nedarim	
51a	625, 626, 627, 687n4
Kiddushin 3	567n63
Bava Kamma	
8:13	247n175
Bava Metzia	
2:7	228, 228n127, 229
Makkot	
1:11	796n80
Avodah Zarah	
1:25	65n1

Shita Mekubbetzet on
Ketubbot	
3a	571n82
50a	238n156

Tosafot on
Eruvin	
46b	279n290
83b	279n290
Ta'anit 28a	279n291
Yevamot	
22a	476n39
22b	788n54
39b	539n66
47b	133
49b	561n21
53b	629n67, 699n17
54a	699n19
79a	561n16
110a	581n146
Ketubbot	
5b	128n1
11a	581n146, 748
49b	217-218
50a	235, 238, 240
70a	236-237, 237n152
Nedarim	
51a	625, 626, 627, 687n4
Nazir	
43b	581n146, 595n12, 687n6
Sotah 21b	289n318
Gittin	
20b	117n11
41a	482n53
45b	4, 4n4, 6, 6n7, 7
57b	382n11
63b	744

Kiddushin	
28a	561n17
73a	567n63
Bava Kamma	
55a-56a	241-242
85a	389n35
91b	249
Bava Metzia	
24b	226
66a	547n107
71b	748
Bava Batra	
22a	384n18
48b	581n146
60b	535n34
Sanhedrin	
72b	796n76
73a	269, 269n256, 270
Avodah Zarah	
8b	582n148
11a	209n59
18a	382n11
Menahot	
42a-b	4-5
60a	106n14
Niddah	
61a	265-266, 266n247

RIF
on
Shabbat 12b 455
Gittin	
61a	421
63b	742n1, 744-745
Yevamot	
22b	788n54
39b	539n66
Bava Kamma	
32a	247n175

RIF COMMENTARIES

Nimukei Yosef on
Yevamot 47b 133

MAIMONIDES, MOSES

Mishneh Torah
Hilkhot Yesodei haTorah	
5	382n10
5:1	470n22
5:1-3	481n52
5:4	698n16, 699n19
5:9	683
5:11	228n128
6:1-2	151
9:4	762n8, 764
Hilkhot De'ot	
1:5	228n128

3-5	381n4, 469n22	15:4	569n74
3:3	388-389	15:7	561n14, 564n47
4:1	325, 389n34	15:14-15	590n11

Hilkhot Talmud Torah
2:2   784n38

Hilkhot Avodah Zarah
10:5   334n48

Hilkhot Avodat Kokhavim
12:11   116nn4-5

Hilkhot Teshuvah
2:1-2   809n111

Hilkhot Tefilah
3:1   51n4
8:9-10   84n6
12:1   36-37, 37n1
12:6   24-25
14-15   14n3
15:1, 6, 12   10nn2-3, n6

Hilkhot Sefer Torah
7-10   153n1
10:1   154n7

Hilkhot Tzitzit 5n5

Hilkhot Berakhot
8:1   394n44
10:12   388n33
11:2   17

Hilkhot Shevitat Asor
2:8   697n13

Hilkhot Ishut
1:1   572n89
1:6   483n58
13:6   542n77
15:2, 4 462n2
15:16   463n3
15:19   777n11
16:30   752n3
21:3,10 777n11
21:11   280-281
21:17   506n106

Hilkhot Gerushin
6:1   743
6:2   742n2
6:9   743
9:11   202n29
10:3   751

Hilkhot Yebum and Halitzah
1:2   539n66
4:1-23   539n64

Hilkhot Issurei Biah
1:1, 12 475n38
1:9   475n38, 654n141, 698n14
1:10-11 475n37
1:14   618n25
10:11   353n21
14:13   476n39
15   566n60
15:1   560n9
15:2   571n86, n88
15:3   497n88, 569n73

15:16   592n20
15:19   567n63
15:33   561n14
20:13   12n16
21:1   619-620, 791n62
21:8,9   617-618, 620
21:19   621n39

Hilkhot Shevu'ot
5:17   247n174
6:9   253n204

Hilkhot Nedarim
3:9   581n147

Hilkhot Matnot Aniyim
7:3   324n14
7:7   334n48
7:10   326n25
7:13   334n47
8:10   325
8:15-18 299n347

Hilkhot Bikurim
1:10   10n8

Hilkhot Kilayim
1:6, 7   107, 107n16
3:5   109

Hilkhot Sh'gagot
7:2   149n12

Hilkhot Gezeilah va-Aveidah
1:4   544n88
6:6-16   544n90
11:7   225n115

Hilkhot Hovel u'Mazik
3:5   792n66
4:16   777n11
4:18   782n31
5:1   247n173, 250n189, 381n5, 784n38
5:5   387n29
5:11   384n20

Hilkhot Rotzeah u'Shmirat Nefesh
         273
1:6   176n7
1:14   176n6, 256-257, 257n214, 292-293, 344, 795, 795n74
1:15   795n74
2:3   381n5
7:8   274
11:4-5   381n5, 469n22, 495n85, 545n99
13:4   224n113, 228n128
13:13   95n3

Hilkhot Mekhira
11   546n106
11:2,6   546n105
11:13,14 700n21
29:5   341

Hilkhot Sekhirah
9:4   67n4

Hilkhot Nahalot
1:7   561n19
2:11   173

Hilkhot Sanhedrin
7:10   700n21
17   774n4
18:6   381n5, 585n152
20:2, 3 654n141, 698n14, n16

Hilkhot Edut
1:1   796n79
6:2, 4, 6   733-734
9:1   797n82
9:10   340-341
12:2   592n20

Hilkhot Mamrim
2:4   581n145
2:5   704n25
5:12   788n54
6:3   786nn45-47
6:8-9   784n40
6:10   804n98
6:11   788n54

Hilkhot Avel
1:6, 7 440-441, 442
1:11   381n8, 585n152
3   409
10:1   454
12:1   443n6
12:10, 11   443, 443n6
13:1-2 453
14   361n15
14:1   453
14:4   362n20
14:12   345, 421

Hilkhot Melakhim
9   106n14
9:5   614n2
10:6   106n14
10:12   421

Sefer HaMitzvot
26   10n2
297, 9 260nn227-228, 263
353   791n62
354   566n60

Teshuvot 82-83
2:448   788n53
66   799n88

Guide for the Perplexed
3:45   342n20
3:49   106n13, 568n67
3:16-23 385n22

COMMENTARIES ON THE MISHNEH TORAH

Kesef Mishneh on
Hilkhot Rotzeah u'Shmirat Nefesh
1:14   257
Hilkhot Sanhedrin
20:3   699n18

Hilkhot Edut
1:1   796n80
9:9   341n16

Hilkhot Mamrim
6:7   786n47

Hilkhot Avel
1:6   441

Hilkhot Melakhim
10:6   106n14
10:12   427n7

Hagahot Maimoniot on
Hilkhot Tzitzit
1:12   5n6
Hilkhot Gezeilah va-Aveidah
11:3   227, 228
11:17   228n128
Hilkhot Rotzeah u'Shmirat Nefesh
1:14   257, 257n214

Lehem Mishneh on
Hilkhot De'ot
3:1   381n5
3:5   470n22
Hilkhot Melakhim
10:6   106n14

Maggid Mishneh on
Hilkhot Gerushin
6:9   743
10:3   752
Hilkhot Yibum
1:6   405n13
Hilkhot Issurei Biah
1:1, 12 475n38
1:9   475n38, 699n17

Mishneh LaMelekh on
Hilkhot Ishut
15:4   465n10
Hilkhot Kilayim
1:6   106n14

Rabad on
Hilkhot Ishut
21:10   778

Radbaz on
Hilkhot Tefilah
8:9-10 84-85, 85nn7-8
Hilkhot Shevu'ot
6:9   253n204
Hilkhot Kilayim
1:6, 7 106n14, 107, 107n16
Hilkhot Mamrim
6:10   804n98
Hilkhot Avel
1:6   441, 443

Codes and Commentaries

BaH on
Tur
Yoreh De'ah
151   428-429
195   466n14
Hoshen Mishpat
426   272

Beit Yosef on
Tur
Even HaEzer
1   343n24
3   560n9
Orah Hayyim
179   45, 45n6
243   65n1
Yoreh De'ah
352   409
363   414n6
367   421
393   454, 455
400   454-455
Even HaEzer
154   779n19
Hoshen Mishpat
12   228, 228n126, 234
46   733
420   247, 247n177
426   284

Darkhei Moshe on
on
Tur
Even HaEzer
154   778nn15-16, 779n22
Hoshen Mishpat
46   733
338   799n88

Drisha on
Tur
Yoreh De'ah
297   107n17

Levushei Mordecai on
Orah Hayyim
128:39   14, 14n7
669   27n8
Hoshen Mishpat
39   331n39

Mordecai on
Yevamot
13   788n54
Ketubbot
4   778n16
194   237, 237n153
204   237, 237n153, 240

Gittin
368   733
Bava Metzia
2:257   227n122, 228, 229-230, 231n137, 232, 234, 236, 239-240

Tur
Orah Hayyim
128-130   14n3
385   456
Yoreh De'ah
363   414n3
367   421
393   456
Even HaEzer
4   560n9
165   539n66
Hoshen Mishpat
21   700n21
46   733, 734
54   700n21
207   700n21
420   247n176
426   257n215

Minor Codes

Hayei Adam
67:1   787n52

Hokhmat Adam
68:1   113

Kitsur Shulhan Arukh
28:12   153n3
163:1   606
165:7   784n38

Or Zarua
Piskei Bava Kamma
161   778n18

She'eltot
58   768
129   263n237, 265-266
147   259n224, 277-278

Shulhan Arukh

Orah Hayyim
8:5   28n10
14:1   6, 6n8
110:3   454
124:2   85, 85n9, 86n12
128:1   10n6
128:39   14n5
135:8, 10   25
139:3   502n102, n104
139:4   23n4
139:11   45n7
140   24
141   38n7
141:2   23, 23n4

141:6	34	268:12	147-148, 148n6
154:5	155nn8-9	269:3	476n39
173:2	495n85, 545n99, 804n97	269:4	139
199:10	341	279	156, 156n12
219:1	360n12	281:4	561n23
219:8	360n12	282:10	155n8
233:1	50n1	295:7	107
235:8	51n3	297:4, 5	103n5, 106-107
244:1	65n2	305:11	166-167, 168
244:5	67n4	305:24	174
252:2, 3	65n2, 67n4	335	323n8, 361n15
282	32n17	335:4-5, 6	361n18
284	32, 32n17	335:7	394n46
284:4	34n21	335:8	361n19
287:1	456	336	328n28, 333n44
307:20	107n16	336:1	321-322
318:1	107n16	338:1	394n46
328:2, 17	177n13, 190n107, 287n314	339:1	381n7
329:4	182n51	345:1	381n5, n8, 585n152
330:5	350n11	345:3	585n152
431:1	72n3	345:5	405n10
470:1	71n2	353:6	445
546	167	363:1	414n4
576:3	209n62	364	416n19
618:1	697n13	364:2	415
666:4	30n11	367	421
		367:1	427n7
Yoreh De'ah		374:5, 6	433, 433n14, n16
98	102n4	374:8	441, 442, 442n4, 443
98:1	76n2	385:1	454
99:5	76n3	393:10	456
112	608	450:1	784n38
116:1, 2, 3	112, 113		
116:5	469n22, 495n85, 804n97	*Even HaEzer*	
137:1	176n9	1:1	462n2, 511n1, 536n37
157:1	382n10, 481n52	1:5	463n2
180:2, 3	117, 117nn12-13	1:7	432n8
194:2, 3	353, 360n14	1:13	462n2
228:11	786n45	2:5	568n71
240:2, 4	786n45, 793n72	4:13	560n7
240:5	786n46, n47	4:14	567n63
240:10	784n38	4:18	560n17
240:15	190n103	4:20	569n73, n74
240:18	788n54	4:22	560n15, 564n47
240:20, 21	484n60, 784n40	4:24	560n14
245:7	324n17	4:29	572n95, 573n96, 590nn11-12, 591n18
248:1, 2	323n11, 326n25	4:30	573n97, 592n20
249:1	323n12	5:14	209n60
249:16	323n8, 324n17	15	523n57
250:1	324n15, 330n34, 345	15:1	483n58
251:3	334n47	15:11	482n56, 502n101
251:9	299n347	22:24	561n17
252:1, 4	325nn19-20, 327, 332n43, 333n44	44:9	146, 146n1, 405n12
252:6	332n42	73:6, 7	542n77
252:5-12	326n25	78, 79	326nn22-23
252:8	299n347	80:12	280
252:10	326n23	82:7	506n106, 556n19
252:11, 12	325, 326n24	101:8	743
255:2	327	101:10	742n2
263:1	177n12	101:11	747
266:10	126	121:3	341n17
268:6	139, 497n89, 522n52	140.3	742

140:4	742, 742n3, 748-749
141:1	744
144:3	202n29
150:4	752n2
154:3	777n14, 778n15
154:20	561n17
165:1	539n66
169	539n64

Hoshen Mishpat

7:2	561n20
21	700n21
28:1	795n73
35:1	797n82
35:14	797n83
46:29	734-735
54:5	700n21
60:6	547n112
207:15, 16	547n107, 700n21
250:5	359n6
259:5	230n134, 233n143
272:9	95n3
276:6	561n19
277:9	432n8
325	359n6
333:5	67n4
370:2	483n58, 502n103
388:7	799n88
420	543n85
420:1, 31	247n178, 381n5, 387n29
420:38	792n66, 806n106
421:12	384n20
424:8	343n25
424:10	782n31
426	284
427:9	112
427:10	381n5

REMA

Orah Hayyim

14:1	6, 6n9
124:2	86, 86n10
128:44	14n3, n4
135	39, 39n11
135:1	26
135:10	25
199:10	341
219:8	360n12
235:8	51
282:2-3	26
284:5	26n7
669	26

Yoreh De'ah

1:3	498-499
99:6	104n8
116:2	113n3
116:5	112-113, 469n22, 545n99
240:18	788n54
248:15	299n347
250:1	324

268:12	148
270-278	153n1
279	156, 156n12
282	153n2
393:12	456
399:13	502n104

Even HaEzer

1:6	343n24
4:29	572n95
82:7	556n19, 802n94
101:11	747
140:4	742n3, 749
141:1	743
141:29	742-743
165:1	539n66

Hoshen Mishpat

7:2	561n17
12:2,4	232-234, 235
26:4	799n88
28:1	795n73
35:14	797n83
46:29	735-736
259:5	230n134, 233n143
388:9	799n88

SHULHAN ARUKH COMMENTARIES

Arukh Hashulhan on

Orah Hayyim

8:11	28n10, 33
139:15	47, 47n10
233:1	51n2
233:10	51n5
235:8	51n3
669:2	27

Yoreh De'ah

84:36	103
121:27	79, 79n3
251:4	334n47
279:1	157, 157n13
305:44	167
393:10, 12	456

Hoshen Mishpat

27:3	151
426:4	308

Be'er Heiteiv on

Orah Hayyim

1	32n17
4	86n11

Bet Shmuel on

Even HaEzer

80:12	281-282
141:1	744

Beur ha-Gra on

Yoreh De'ah

6: 374:5	433n14

837

Even HaEzer
20:1   791n62
Hoshen Mishpat
71   799n89

Birkhei Yosef on
Even HaEzer
17:1   201n25

Dagul Merevavah on
Yoreh De'ah
268:6   139, 139n8

Darkhei Teshuvah
190:1   561n25

Eliyahu Rabbah on
Orah Hayyim
12:669   33n18
329:8   261

Hatam Sofer on
Orah Hayyim
25   18
2:113   79, 79n1
Yoreh De'ah
2:341   400
245   135
Even HaEzer
2:94   561n24
10   572n93

Helkat Mehokek
Even HaEzer
80:15   281n297

Kaf HaHayyim
135   18

Kereti u'Feleti on
Yoreh De'ah
40:5, 4   197n10

Knesset HaGedolah on
Yoreh De'ah
157   302n358
Even HaEzer
17:2   204n35
Hoshen Mishpat
425:10   261-262
426   296n339
and
Hagahot Beit Yosef
1   296n339
35   302n358

Magen Avraham on
Orah Hayyim
14:1   7, 7n11
44:5   153n3
128:457   12n16
135:1   26

141   23n4
156   502n102, n104
173:2   113n2
282:2-3   26
3:284:4   34n21
328:2   190n107
330:16   351n14
568:10   168
669   23n5

Mishnah Berurah on
Orah Hayyim
7-8   34n21
8:13   28n10, 31n13
10   34n21, 53, 54
12   27, 27n8
14:1   7n10
36   25, 26
199:10   341
243:1   53-54, 65n1
245   54
284:8   34n20
287:1   456
329:4   343n23
as
Be'ur HaHalakhah on
Orah Hayyim
128:39   17

Pithei T'shuvah
Orah Hayyim
1:164   502n104
Yoreh De'ah
2:125   482n57
157:15   291n324
194:5   354n25
276:9   151
363   419
Even HaEzer
141:1   744

Sefer Meirat Einayim (Sema) on
Hoshen Mishpat
370:2   502n103
420:49   792n65
426:2   261

Sha'arei Teshuvah on
Orah Hayyim
8:7   28n10
197:8   103n8
219:8   360n12
344   52n6

Shakh on
Yoreh De'ah
99:6, 21   104n8
157:15, 3   291
252:10   299n349
297:3   106n14
179:8   151
180:3   117n3

Hoshen Mishpat
45: 388:7 799n88
59: 388:12 799n89
60: 338:12 799n88

Shoshanat HaMelekh on
Orah Hayyim
1:52 456

Shulhan Arukh ha-Rav
8:5, 4 251n194
on
Orah Hayyim
329:8 262
Hoshen Mishpat
7 262

Taz on
Orah Hayyim
128:44 14n4
135:3,sub 3 17
219:8 360n12
Yoreh De'ah
116:3 113
195:7 466n14
363:2 414n10
Even HaEzer
1:8 475n37
140:4 749

Urim ve-Tumim on
Hoshen Mishpat
12:4 234-235
27:1 469n22

Further Commentaries and Responsa

Abudraham 45, 45n5

Akedat Yitsak
Eighth Gate
60 677n1

Amudei Or
96:3 266n247

Arugot HaBosem on
Orah Hayyim
19 316, 316n399

Arukh La-ner on
Yevamot
12b 465n11
Sanhedrin
73a 268, 268n251, 271n262

Aszod, Yehuda
45 19-20
on
Yoreh De'ah
265 168

Ben Mishlei
419 777n11

B'Or haTorah
8 355n25

B'samim Rosh
345 382n12

Be'er Mayyim Hayyim
9:20 797n81

Benei Ahuvah
Hilkhot Ishut
15:6 465n11

Binyamin Ze'ev on
Even HaEzer
88 779n22
1:136 572n92

Binyan Tsion on
Orah Hayyim
97 158, 158nn14-17
1:108 209n61

Dikdukei Soferim on
Eruvin 46b 279n290

Divrei Menahem on
Hoshen Mishpat
3: 27 198, 198nn14-17, 19n18

Divrei Yoel
2:110,140 467n15,n17

Ein Yitzhak
34 415n15, 419-420, 427n3

Ha'elef l'cha Shlomo
305 410

Haim B'yad
99 400

Hakham Zevi
nos. 74,76,77 197n8

HaManhig on
Hilkhot Shabbat
56 43n2, 44-45

Hashmatot on
Hilkhot Sefer Torah
18n3

Hatam Sofer
83 341n18

Havalim Ban'imim
3:64 524n61

Havvat Yair see also Subject Index
146 257-258

Hazon Ish on
Hilkhot Kilayim
1   106n13
2:16   108n19
Yoreh De'ah
4:14   197n11
155:4   351n15

Helkat Yaakov
1:30   209n61
3:45-51   485n63

Hemdat Yisrael
310   381n5

Heshiv Mosheh
48   227n121

Iggrot Moshe on
Orah Hayyim
1   73n4
1:102   34n22
2:88   341n18
4:90   60nn1-2
5:20   457
Yoreh De'ah
1:36   196n6
1:223   363n22
1:145   282
1:160   422
1:161   502n102, n104
2:44   754
2:118, 191 168-169, 170
2: 174:4   291n323
3: 120:5   103n6
3: 140   185n72
Even HaEzer
1:10   465n11, 475n37, 476n40
1:71   476n40
2:11   465n11
3:8   572n94
3:11   465n11
3:25   564n49, 572n90
4:17   590n13
65   331n39, 345
Hoshen Mishpat
1:3   251n192
1:103   249-250
2:11   476n40

Imrei Yosher
2:22   313n392
2:140,3   122n4

Kav Naki
Even HaEzer
101:8   743, 743n4, 746

Kitvei HaRamban
2:43   322

Kol Bo Al Aveilut
            181n45, 189n96, 382n12, 405n11, 409n1, 415n14, 416nn17-18, 427n2, n4

Korban Netanel on
Megillah
no. 60   25

Kuzari
3:49   211n65, n66

Lev Aryeh
2:36   205-206, 205n46
2:38   291n323

Ma'arkhei Lev
72   600n8
73   475n37

Maharam
81   779n23
291   779n23

Maharam Schick
on
Orah Hayyim
59   18
60   19
238   79, 79n2
Yoreh De'ah
155   268, 268n250
354   415n16
in
Taryag Mitzvot
1   465n10
238   296n340

Maharil on
Orah Hayyim
139:4   23n4

Maharik
9   17

Maharsham
1:9   570n78
1:214   18
3:268   475n37

Mateh Yehonaton on
Yoreh De'ah
116:1   113

Mekor Hayyim
Yerushalmi
3:96   155n9

Melamed Leho'il
2:86   132
3:8   600

Migdal Oz
Even Bochan
1:3   267n249
1:65   303n362
1:78   303, 303n361

Mima'akim
2:1	122n7
2:10	177, 177n17
3:9	564-565

Mi-ma-yanei ha-Yesua
32	24n6, 40, 40n12

Minhat Hinnukh
48	251nn193-194

Minhat Yitzhak
1:115	331n39
4:123	350n11
5:121	233
5:7, 13	272n264
6:103	292n327

Mintz responsa
85	46n9

Mishneh Halakhot
4:245	248n183, 253
6:324	264n239, 269n253, 279n287, 290n322, 302n356, 304n363

Mishpetei Uziel
Even HaEzer
1:19	475n37
4:3	568n66

Mor Uktziyah
135	18

Nishal David on
Even HaEzer
6	283

Nishmat Avraham on
Hilkhot Aveilut
349:2, 3	250-251
349:3, 2	213n75
349, 264	296n336
Hilkhot Avodah Zarah
157:5	267n249
on
Hoshen Mishpat
4:420:1	309, 309n384, 310-311
4:420:2	313,392
in
Mahadurah Tanina
Even HaEzer
Hilkhot Ketubbot
80:1	267n249

Noda B'Yehuda on
Orah Hayyim
2, 5:19	44, 44n4
9	157, 158, 158n14
Yoreh De'ah
9	120n25
210	213n74
310	178n23

Even HaEzer
101:8	743
141:1	743

Otsar HaGeonim
Ketubbot	777n11

Pe'at Sadekha
155	228-229, 228n129

Pele Yo'etz
1:20	788n56

Piskei Ricanati
470	285n310

Pri ha-Aretz on
Yoreh De'ah
2	331n39

Radbaz responsa
2:507	411
3:447	780n26
3:627 (52)	285-288, 305
4:157	780n26
4:1139 (67)	289n319
1165	84-85, 85nn7-8
5:582	292-296, 305

Rashi responsa
173	147n2

Rashba responsa
4:113	777n13
5:264	777n13
7:477	777n13, 780n25
no. 763	381n8

Reshit Hokhmah
Gate of Holiness
15:1	677n1

Ribash responsa
4	699n17
11	699n17
36	26n7
41	542n77
55	744
387	699n17

Rosh responsa
17:7	542n77
101	806n105

Seder Hadorot
2:200	302n359

Sefer HaHinnukh
Mitzvot
78	763n11
188	791n62
209	627, 631, 687n4
392	170
529	387n29
560	567

Sefer Haredim 787n52
on
Orah Hayyim
669   23n5

Sefer Hasidim on
Sanhedrin
340   316n397
674, 73a   269, 301-302
698   301
343   788n56
564   788n56

Sefer Issur ve'Heter
59: 36   209nn58-59
59:38   261-262

Sefer Mitzvot haGadol (Semag)
Asin (pos. mitzvah)
74, 46d   279n291

Sefer Ra'avia
Megillah
579   279n291

Sefer Ra'avan on
Bava Metzia
24b   230n131
Ketubbot
49b   230n131

Seridei Esh
2:102   134-135
3:6   123, 123n8
3:7   209n61

Shaarei Ephraim
3:6   34n20
8:56   27n8
9:8, 30   27n8

Sha'arei HaT'filah
19   18n2

She'elat Moshe
50   255n211

Shemesh Tzedaka
4:4, 6   411

Shevut Yaakov
1:168   239-240
3:71   209n61

Shevet Mi Y'hudah
1:1:21   103n8
1:1:54   177n16
1:1:60   179n24
1:1:61   185n72
1:1:368   177n16

Shevet Yehudah
14b   466n13

T'shurat Shai
546   411

Teshuvah Me'Ahavah on
Yoreh De'ah
53   354n25
336   328n30

Tuv Ta'am Vada'at
3:250   421-422, 428, 428n10

Trumat haDeshen
105   209, 209n56
218   777n12

Tzitz Eliezer
3:27, 1   467n15
6:36   34n22
9:45, 5   264n242
9:45, 6, 9, 11 269n253, 284-285, 289n320, 290
9:51, 3   348n4
9:51, 4   467n15, 475n37
9:51, 5, 1   474, 474n34
10:25, 7a-b   273n266, 302
10:25, 7, 5   289n320
10:25:21   103n8
10:25, 28   295-296
13:88   352
13:102, 1, 3, 5 348n4, 349, 349n6, 350n9
14:68   209n61
15:43   348n4
15:45   513n10
17:23   215n79
17:24   204-205, 204n42
17:64   205
24:31   330n35, n36

Va-Yeshev Moshe
1:84   220n99
93:2   252n198
94:246a   252n196, 254-255

Yabia Omer
5:22   122n2
on
Yoreh De'ah
2:25, 2   168, 168n1
Even HaEzer
6:5, 1   589-590, 591n19

Yachin u-Voaz
1:117   455

Yad Eliyahu
43   299n345
43:48a-50b   258n220, 299, 300-301

Yehaveh Da'at
3:84:284   296n337
60:301-7   434n20

Zachor Yitzchok
Yevamot
46a   132-133

Zekan Aharon
Yoreh De'ah
2:97   475n37
87: 374:6   433, 433n18

Zemah David
1:1441   466n13

Zemah Zedek
89   231

Zer Zahav
21 on
Sefer Issur ve'Heter
59:38   280, 280n293

Zocher HaBrit
179:14   167, 168

SUBJECT INDEX

For legal, medical, and secular references see within individual topics; those footnotes are not indexed exhaustively. Also, passing mentions of Jewish law concepts are not included. Finally, this index is to be used together with the Source Index when searching for rabbinic, toraitic and talmudic references.

Aaron, 9, 10, 11, 13, 14, 15n10, 342
Abahu, Rabbi, 559
Abaye, 129, 275n276, 415, 419, 426, 802n96
Abba (R'Ba), 328, 329, 731, 765-766, 766nn21-22, 770n35
Abba bar Hanina, 393
Abba bar Zabda, 147
Abba Hilkiah, 252
Abba Mari, 29n10
Abba of Akko, 731, 734
Abba Saul, 539n63
Abelson, Kassel
  abortion, 516n26
  generally, 145n28, 509n114, 525n63, 557n21, 605
  get and marriage renewals, 751-754, 755, 756
  God and Torah, 151-152, 153-162
  homosexuality, 712-713, 722-723, 727, 728
  kashrut, 78-80, 91-92, 98-100, 100n6
  liturgy, 81-88
  Shabbat and holidays, 36-42, 71-74
Abortion, 163, 348, 350n10, 356, 358n5, 366, 368, 378, 497-498
  Jewish attitude towards, 142n14, 144nn23-24, 352n16, 502-503, 516, 520n42, 522n53
  late term and, 350n10, 375-376
Abraham, Abraham S., 185n72
Abulafia, Meir ha-Levi. SEE *Ramah*
Abuse. SEE Family violence
Adam (and Eve), 106, 110, 535n33, 626
Adoption, 163, 483n59, 550
  in artificial insemination issues, 469, 478-479, 483, 489, 491, 494-495, 505
  and Jewish tradition, 501-504, 515, 537n49, 540, 555n17
  baby-selling, 533n24, 542-543
  procreation *mitzvah*, 482, 488, 506
Adret, Solomon ben Abraham. SEE Rashba

Adultery, 538, 545, 566-567, 570, 584, 698
  and artificial insemination, 467, 474-475, 475n37, 521n49
Aggadah, 284, 496, 497n87, 575, 579, 580
Agudat Ezov, 265-266, 267, 268, 307-308
Agunah, 671
Agus, Arlene, 537, 548n115
Ahai Gaon, 768
Aharonim, 17-18, 54, 264, 269, 284, 714
AIDS, 673, 674-675, 709
Aizenberg, Isidoro, 368, 436n5, 437
Akiva, Rabbi, 165, 253n199, 322, 393, 540, 559, 577
  attitude on homosexuality, 618n25, 619n31, 626, 682
  and ben Peturah debate, 258-260, 268n250
  on self-injury and sacrifice, 246-247, 247n111, 301-302, 302n358
Albeck, Hanokh (and Theodor-), 320n1, 583n150, 616n12, 622n43
Alcoholism, 810n115
Alfasi, Isaac. SEE *Rif*
Aliyah, aliyot, 44, 49, 483
  b'rakha l'vatala. SEE Blessings
  customs and practice, 17, 18, 20, 39
    mehilat kohen, 18-19, 20
    minhag hamakom, 30, 41, 42
  halakhah on, 16n1,17-18, 19-20
  maftir, 21, 32, 33, 34n21, 35
  number of, 25-26, 28, 37, 39, 42
  and *hosafot*, 30, 32n16, 33, 35
  obligatory *aliyot*, 16n1, 18-19, 20, 22, 25, 30, 32n16, 39
  reading of haftarah, 21, 26, 32, 33, 33n17, 34n21, 38
  responsa
    conclusions and votes, 16, 20, 21, 29, 35, 36, 42
    on joint *aliyot*, 21-35, 36-42
    on non-*kohen* as first *aliyah* in presence of *kohen*, 16-20

844

Shabbat and holidays, 17, 18, 25-26, 39
Simhat Torah, 17, 22n1, 26-27, 27n8, 28, 29, 33, 39-40, 41, 42
trei kolei la mishtamei, 21, 22-24, 33, 35
women, 22, 30, 31n15
SEE ALSO Blessing; *Kohen, kohanim*; Torah, reading of
Alliance for Bio-Integrity, 105, 108-109
Altman, Anita, 776n9
Ambulance, 177
America, 64, 65, 66-67, 768
  abortion, 350, 378
  adoption, 501n100, 503
  in artificial insemination and IVF cases, 477-479, 488-490, 499, 523, 533n22
  infertility, 464, 470-472, 507-508
  in use of birth surrogates, 145n27, 526-527, 534, 542, 544-545, 548-549, 555-556
  in assisted suicide cases, 380, 382, 386-387, 388, 389-391
  and euthanesia, 395-397
  blood donations, 216
  clergy/client privilege, 799, 799n90, 800
  death and organ donations, 183n64, 190nn102-103, 308
  family abuse, 775-776, 781n30, 782, 783n37, 785n43, 789, 809
  Good Samaritan laws, 389n36
  health care in, 320, 329n33, 333, 335, 391-393
  homosexuality, 670, 672, 682
  kashrut and, 91, 92, 94-96
  mamzerut, 564, 573
  and mental disabilities, 337-339, 385-386, 395
American Medical Association, 390
American Psychiatric Association (APA), 644-646, 696n9
Ami, Rabbi, 17, 262-263, 264, 266, 295, 301
Amidah. SEE *Kohen, kohanim*; High Holy Days; Liturgy
Amoraim, 37, 41, 129, 580, 581. SEE ALSO INDIVIDUALS BY NAME
Amputation, 581n145. SEE ALSO IN RELATED TOPICS
Ana, 110
Anesthesia, 213, 214. SEE ALSO Circumcision
Animals, 93-97, 101-102
Annas, George, 138, 142, 544, 553, 556n19
Annulment. SEE Divorce; Get; *Mamzerut*
Anti-Semitism, 334, 673
Antoninus, 376n12
Apochrypha, 465
Apostasy
  Christian Science, 405-406
  halakhah on, 146, 147-148, 148n9, 401, 404-405, 407
  intermarriage concern, 401, 404
  Jews for Jesus, 401, 402, 404, 407
  responsa
    on burial of, 400-402
      concurring opinion, 403-407
    on children of, 146-150
      and Jewish marriages, 146-148, 149
      ritual requirements, 148-149
      and Christian upbringing, 148-150
      conclusions and votes, 146, 150, 400, 402

statistics, 401
teshuvah (repentance), 402, 407
SEE ALSO Burial; Christianity
Arabs. SEE Moslem
Arama, Isaac, 677n1
Aramaic language, 730-731, 732, 736, 736-738, 739
Arik, Meir ben Aaron Judah, 122, 122n4
Arik, Mordecai, 313n392
Aristotle, 686
Aron ha Kodesh, 150, 153, 154, 156, 157, 158, 161
Artificial insemination, 108, 511-513
  adoption. SEE Adoption
  adultery question. SEE Adultery
  community behavior, 493-494, 503
    Jewish demographic concerns, 486, 492-493
  conversion, 497n91, 505
  determination of parents' Jewish identity, 478, 479-484, 521-524, 528, 549n119, 496, 497n91
  genetics, 479-480, 499-500, 501, 516-517
  race, 495, 503, 506
  donor insemination, 474, 475, 483-485, 488, 490-492, 504-505, 538, 549n120
  husband as donor, 470-472, 473, 473n31, 478-479, 504
  sperm banks, 476, 476n42, 477 SEE ALSO UNDER egg donation
  egg donation, 470, 494-497, 498, 499-501, 504, 505-506, 520-525
  embryos, 512n4, 517-520
  halakhah on artificial insemination, 465-467, 472-473, 478, 484
    on donors, 521-524, 524n60, 525
    on embryos, 518-519, 520
      fetus and human life issue, 519, 520nn42-44, 522n53
    in vitro fertilization, 513-515
    on wasting one's seed, 513n9
  incest, 476-477, 481, 482, 483, 483n58, 496, 504, 545
  infertility and treatments of, 464, 464n8, 467, 468-470, 508
  mitzvah of procreation and children, 462, 462n2, 463-465, 472-473, 482, 483, 485, 488, 498
  monetary issues, 515, 515n19
  obligation, 462, 463, 473, 478, 479, 482n53, 498-499, 511n1, 515n20
  relationship problems, 463-464, 468-469, 473-474, 485-486, 487, 630n70
    asymmetrical views toward child, 490-492, 495-496
  responsa
    on artificial insemination, egg donation, and adoption, 461-509
    on in vitro fertilization, 497n91, 510-525
    conclusions and votes, 461, 509, 510, 525
  risks, 500, 500n96, 514-516, 518
  secrecy and its ramifications, 486-490
  summary and scope of responsa, 504-508, 511n2
  surrogates for births, 526-528, 541, 529-550, 551-557
  SEE ALSO Abortion; Adoption; America; Incest; Surrogacy
Artson, Bradley Shavit
  generally, 585n154, 705, 706

845

homosexuality, 612, 691, 693, 702
  interpretation of, 621-622, 622n41-44, 676-677, 686-687, 687n5, 697, 713
  as parents, 702, 703
  writings, 575n107
Arukh Hashulkhan, 47, 103, 151, 167, 308, 334n47, 456
Arzt, Max, 102n4, 401n2
Asher b. Jehiel. SEE Rosh
Ashkenazi, Jonah (*Tosafot Avodah Zarah*), 209, 209n58
Ashkenazi, Zevi. SEE *Hakham Zevi*
Ashkenazim, 18, 230, 245, 378, 539n66, 547n107, 741
  and family violence, 780-781, 788, 799
  and mourning practices, 453, 456
  Torah customs, 46, 48-49
Assimilation, 486
Astor, Carl, 388n33
Aszod, Yehuda, 19-20
Atkins, Gary, 171
Auerbach, Shlomo Zalman, 103n6, 206, 213-214, 252, 253, 311, 313n392
Aufruf, 22, 25-26, 30, 36, 41
Australia, 489
Autopsy. SEE UNDER Death
Azkari, Elazar, 787n52
Azulai, Hayyim Joseph David. SEE *Hida*

Babad, Joseph. SEE *Minhat Hinukh*
Babies
  autopsy, 446
  burial practices. SEE mourning practices
  circumcision, 445-446, 446n11
  CJLS positions, 444, 451
  fetus (*nafal*). SEE Fetus
  medical terms. SEE WITHIN RESPONSA
  mourning practices, 356, 440-441, 442-443, 444-445, 446-447, 449, 450-451
    halakhic precedents, 440-443, 443n6, 449
  pregnancy loss and duration, 365-366, 442-443
  prematurity, 355, 356, 447-448, 450
  responsa
    conclusions and votes, 347, 356, 439, 449
    on neonates, newborns and limiting medical treatment, 347-356
      genetic abnormalities of, 352-355, 375
      medical definition, 348n2
    on ritual practice of infant death less than 31 days, 439-449
      dissenting concurrence, 450-451
      kim li, 349n7, 370n3, 448, 448n13, 450-451
    status of newborns, 350-352, 352nn16-17, 355
    stillbirth, 439, 443
    surrogates for births, 526-528
  SEE Miscarriage AND UNDER OTHER RELATED TOPICS
Baby-naming, 30, 36, 373, 377-378, 445, 483, 737, 739
Bacharach, Ya'ir Haim. SEE *Havvat Ya'ir*
BaH, 429, 466n14
  on *aliyot* and Torah reading, 25, 28, 30, 33, 41
  and *lifnim meshurat ha-din*, 230, 232-233, 235, 236, 239, 240, 244, 247n177
Bakshi-Doron, Eliahu, 313n392
Bar Kappara, 623-624, 625-626, 627, 628, 635, 662-663
Bar/Bat Mitzvah, 16, 166, 341, 701, 737
  aliyot for *b'nai mitzvah*, 21, 32-34, 34nn20-22, 35, 36, 41, 42
  responsum on role of non-Jewish parent in blessings, 602-604
    conclusion and vote, 602, 604
    non-obligation, 602, 603
    previous CJLS decisions, 603
Barnard, Christiaan, 182
Baron, A.L., 122, 122n5
Bedikat/be-ur hametz. SEE *Pesah*
Beit Yosef, 228, 229, 230, 239, 240, 244, 245
Ben-Sassoon, H.H., 769
Ben Meir, Rabbi, 576n110
Ben Peturah, 258-260, 268n250
Ben Sira, 465-466
Ben Zoma, 465
Bene Israel. SEE *Mamzerut*
Benjamin of Tudela, 48
Benjamin Ze'ev, of Arta, 572
Benveniste, Hayyim. SEE *K'nesset haG'dolah*
Bergman, Ben Zion
  burials and preparation, 408-412, 418-425, 427n5, 430
  conversion, 127-131
  generally, 383n17, 800n90
  get, 741-750
  homosexuality, 728-729
  Shabbat and business, 58-63, 64, 65-66, 67-68, 69
  stillbirths, 377-378
Berkovits, Eliezer, 574-575
Berlin, Naftali Zevi. SEE *Netziv*
Berman, Martin, 30n12
Bet din, 148, 149, 417n23, 595, 717, 746-747
  and conversion, 131, 134
  and *mamzerut*, 565, 566, 570, 590
  SEE ALSO Rabbinical Assembly
Bet Knesset, 46n8
Bet Yosef. SEE Karo, Joseph
Biale, Rachel, 779n22
Bianco, David, 702n22, 711
Bieber, Irving, 639n98, 641
Bio-ethics. SEE UNDER RELATED TOPICS
Birkhei Yosef. SEE Azulai, Hayyim Joseph David
Birth. SEE UNDER RELATED TOPICS
Blank, Debra Reed, 357-363, 364, 365, 366, 368, 371, 444
Blecher, Lou, 75n1
Bleich, J. David, 140, 396n51, 565n53
  artificial insemination, 465n11, 475n37, 479n46, 496-497n87
  donating blood, 215, 220
  heart (and other) transplants, 199, 201, 203-204, 205, 307
  human life, 175n1, 176n5, 185n72, 354n25
  procreation, 484, 485n63, 511n1, 513, 517, 519, 522
  self-sacrifice and danger, 264, 290n321
  writings, 108n21, 139n6, 154n5, 328n28
Blessings, 343, 372, 579, 601, 752
  and *aliyot*, 27, 29n10, 30-31, 39. SEE ALSO *b'rakha l'vatala*

birkat kohanim, 9-12, 14, 147n5
birkat hamazon. SEE Grace after meals; *Kohen, kohanim*
b'rakha l'vatala, 21, 24n6, 28, 33, 35, 37-38, 40, 41, 157, 753
gomel, 360, 361
procreation, 462n2. SEE ALSO RELATED TOPICS
sheva berakhot, 754
and women, 11, 165, 462n2
Blidstein, Gerald, 483n60, 783n35, 787n52
Bloch, Eliyahu Meir, 475n37
Blood
bloodletting, 215, 249, 250
blood transfusions, 306n369, 475n37
burial of. SEE Burial
danger of blood loss, 286-287, 294
donations of, 178, 215n80, 216. SEE ALSO Organ donations
heart transplants, 205-206
as if shedding blood, 177, 393, 463n3, 576n116
in health care, 322, 326n25, 327, 333, 336
as if sweeter than another's. SEE Danger; Jewish law concepts: *lo ta'amod*
and *kashrut*, 97, 103
Bloom, Zvi Elimelech, 783n35
Blumenthal, Aaron, 593
B'nai Noah, 104, 105n12, 106n14, 616
Noahide laws, 135, 136, 621
Body piercing. SEE UNDER Tattooing
Bok, Sissela, 486-487
Bokser, Ben Zion, 593-594, 599, 600
Boorse, Christopher, 331n37
Bone marrow transplants. SEE UNDER Organ donations
Borowitz, Eugene B., 335, 335n49
Boswell, John, 631
Bramnick, Stanley, 13-15
Braun, Abraham (*Zer Zahav*), 280
Breisch, Jacob, 485n63
Brit bat. SEE Women
Brit kodesh program, 123n12
Brit milah. SEE Circumcision
Broyde, Michael, 110n24, 482n57, 501n97, n100, 502n101, 802n95
Bun, Rabbi, 463n2
Burial, 177, 178, 367, 381, 382
karka yisrael, 419, 420, 427, 428, 429
mehitzah, 423, 424
ownership of plot, cemetary property, 418-419, 420, 427, 429
patrilineal issue, 424, 425
question of cemetary as Jewish, 419-420, 424, 425
requirements of Jewish burial site, 426-427
responsa
on mixed burials, 418-425
on non-Jews and burial in a disaster, 426-430
burial of non-Jewish spouses, 420-425
CJLS decisions, 422-423, 424
conclusions and votes, 418, 425, 426, 430
sinners and saints, 421, 424-425, 427, 428, 429-430
SEE ALSO Apostasy; Babies; Death; Intermarriage; Tattooing
Business. SEE *Shabbat*

CCAR. SEE Reform movement
Cahill, Lisa Sowle, 486, 514n13
Campbell, Anthony F., 736
Camps. SEE Conservative Judaism
Canada, 512nn4-7, 514n17, 515n19, 518, 523
Cantors' Assembly, 612, 692, 722-723, 724-725
Castration, 107n17
Celibacy. SEE Homosexuality
Cemetery. SEE Burial
Chavel, Bernard, 322n7
Cheese. SEE *Kashrut*
Children, 381, 585
abuse, 782-785
aliyot, 26, 27
babies, 280-281, 282
caesarean birth, 126, 142n16, 164, 171-174, 177n17, 350n10
conversion, 133, 478, 528
custody, 801-802
funeral services for children, 443n6
honoring parents, 484n60, 785-786. SEE ALSO Parent and child
neo-natology. SEE Babies
rights of, 315-316
tattoos, 117-118
SEE ALSO RELATED TOPICS; Family violence
Choirs, 603
Christianity
views, 148n8, 384, 405-406, 514n13, 520n42, 541, 696, 703
SEE ALSO Apostasy; Non-Jews
Church. SEE Apostasy; Christianity
Circumcision (*brit milah*), 16, 253, 350, 372, 606, 737, 739
before infant burials, 445-446
kavvanah, 123
pain and suffering, 122, 123
postponement of, 164, 167
question of older males, 121, 123
responsa
on anesthesia and, 121-124
on induction of birth on *Shabbat* and, 125-126
on medical complications. SEE under Conversion
conclusions and votes, 121, 124, 125, 126
scheduling births and, 125-126, 176
on *Shabbat*, 442
SEE ALSO Apostasy; Conversion
Cities of refuge. SEE Murder
Coercion. SEE *Mitzvot*; Organ donations
Cohen, A., 376n12
Cohen, Boaz, 136, 139n7, 148, 400-401, 404, 407, 609
Cohen, David Ber, 354n25
Cohen, Diane, 372n6
Cohen, Eugene J., 168
Cohen, Gerson D., 667
Cohen, Jack Simcha, 433-434, 434n19
Cohen, Seymour J., 515n15
Cohen, Shaye J.D., 142n17, 522n53
Cohn, Haim, 185, 185n71
Colon, Joseph. SEE *Maharik*
Committee on Jewish Law and Standards (CJLS)

847

generally, 117
previous decisions. SEE WITHIN INDIVIDUAL RESPONSA
and abortion, 348, 520n42
process and rules of procedure, x
rabbinic standards, xi, 190n107, 760-761, 770n34
responsa
  on structure and status of CJLS, 759-772
    conclusion and vote, 759, 771-772
    evolution of Jewish law, 761-771
    history of, 759, 759n2
    mara d'atra, 759, 760, 768, 769, 771, 772
    role and authority of, 760-761, 767, 768-769, 770n34, 771
  statements
    on assisted suicide, 382, 398-399
    on homosexuality, 612
  sub-committee on biomedical ethics, 145n28, 354n24, 462, 509n114, 525n63, 557n21
  terminal illness, 385, 475n37
  women, 3, 31n15
SEE ALSO INDIVIDUAL RESPONSA AND SUBJECT HEADINGS
Community, 401, 753
  concerning health care, 319-320, 322, 333-335
  and family violence, 775, 775n7, 776n9, 801, 806-809, 812-813, 815
  and homosexuality, 668-670, 685, 687-689, 704, 726
  regarding *mamzerut*, 581, 587n3
  SEE ALSO *K'lal Yisrael*
Conservative Judaism, 9, 121, 164
  and halakhic historical method, 493, 597, 693-695, 739, 750, 759-760
  in family violence, 773-775, 776n9, 779n21, 783-784
  mamzerut, 558, 564, 569, 572, 585-586, 589, 592
  matrilineal descent, 522, 522n53, 528
  mental retardation, 342n19, 345
  Orthodoxy's opinion of, 422, 564n49, 572
  taharat hamishpaha, 469n21
  tumat acu'um, 141
  views on
    abortion, 142, 516
    burials, 106n18
    ceremonies, 121, 164, 166, 169, 342n19, 753-754
    conversion, 150
    egalitarianism, 7
    and employment of intermarrieds. SEE WITHIN RESPONSUM
    expression of God's name, 152
    family violence, 808, 815-816
    homosexuality, 672n172. SEE ALSO Homosexuality
    Torah and revelation, 575, 585
  SEE ALSO WITHIN EACH INDIVIDUAL RESPONSUM
Conversion
  burials of, 422
  generally, 207n51, 739
  keruv, 130, 669
  mamzerut, 561, 564, 569
  naming after, 483n59
  previous CJLS decision, 127-128, 130, 599-601
  responsa
    on circumcision and, 132-136
      hatafat dam brit, 134, 136, 148, 150

      medical complications, 133, 134-135
      requirements of, 133-136
    conclusions and votes, 127, 131, 132, 136, 431, 438
    on converts' mourning close relatives, 431-438
      of children, 432-433
      and *halakhah* regarding non-Jewish relatives, 431, 432-433
      ritual practices for mourning, 434-435, 436-437
    on marriage to a *kohen*. SEE *Kohen, kohanim*
    on one spouse only converting, 127-131
  surrogacy, 523, 523n54, 528
  SEE ALSO Tattooing
Contracts, 144, 546-547, 548, 730-740. SEE ALSO *Get*; *Ketubbah*; *Shabbat*; Surrogacy agreements
Cooking. SEE Food
Councils of the Lands, 769-770, 770n34
Covenant, 736. SEE ALSO Circumcision; God
Cover, Robert, 695n7, 768-769, 771
Cowley, A., 117n10
Creation, 105, 106n15, 109, 110n24, 208-209, 335, 513n10
Cross-breeding. SEE Genetic engineering
Cytron, Barry D., 387n29

Danger, 108-109, 112-113, 113n2, 114, 176-177
  blood donations, 215, 220
  nursing mother, 280-282, 283
  in organ donations or transplants, 195, 196, 212-213, 291, 304, 317, 553
  putting oneself in jeopardy, 268-269, 295-296, 495, 500n96, 545-546, 803
    ben Peturah dispute. SEE UNDER Ben Peturah
    to benefit someone else, 256-258, 258n218, 264-266, 273
    cities of refuge, 275-276
    drowning, 269-272
    hasid shoteh (foolish saint). SEE *Hasid shoteh*
    hiring someone to help, 268, 270-272
    sages' lives versus others, 276-280, 282, 299-300, 303-304
  and *Shabbat*, 260, 285-288, 289, 291
  summary of sources on self-endangerment, 304-305
  SEE ALSO Organ donations; *Pikuah nefesh*
Daniel (Hanina) the tailor, 562, 576
Daniels, Norman, 331n37
Danzig, Abraham, 787n52
Darkhei Moshe, 733
Daughters. SEE *Kohen, kohanim*; Women
David ben Joseph (*Abudraham*), 45
Deafness, 340, 341
Death
  autopsy, 15, 177n16, 178nn21-23, 179, 524n61
  brain death, 182-183, 183nn56-57, n60, 184n70, 185, 186n78, 196n7, 354n25
  with dignity, 14, 183-185
  "eye for an eye" quotation, 288
  for *kiddush HaShem* (sake of God), 381
  responsa
    conclusions and votes, 408, 412, 413, 417
    on exhumation, 413-417
      exceptions to prohibition, 414-415, 416n22

848

halakhah and removal of remains, 413-414, 415, 417n23
  mourning rituals, 417
  ownership of plot, 415, 417
  relocation and reuse of graves, 414-415, 416
  on *taharah* and mortuary preparation, 408-412
    hevra kadisha and *taharah*, 408, 409-411
    hygiene, 408, 410
    met mitzvah, 415, 416, 417
    mortuary handling, 409, 410, 411, 412
    respect or humiliation for deceased, 410-411, 412, 414, 416, 417
    trembling at God's judgment, 414, 416, 417
  and resurrection, 201-202, 202n28, 203-204
  selling body parts, 313, 313n392
  SEE ALSO Babies; Burial; Organ donations; Suicide
Deceit. SEE Conversion
Demsky, Aaron, 116-117
Deuteronomy, 44
Dialysis. SEE Medicine
Diamond, Eliezer, 788n56
Diaspora, 14nn3-4, 37
Dichowsky, Shlomo, 326n25
Dick, Judah, 571
Dickstein, Stephanie, 348n2, 349n7, 350n10, 367-376, 377, 378, 439-449, 450, 451
Dimi, Rabbi, 393, 442, 560n6
Disability, 342-343, 388. SEE ALSO Group homes
Discipline, 782-785. SEE Family violence; Punishment
Divorce, 129, 506n106, 519n38, 581, 683
  coercion and duty-bound to, 235, 236-237
  and family violence, 777, 779, 781
  and *mamzerut*, 561n17, 780
  and procreation, 498n94, 499
  and remarriage, 201, 202, 314n393
  SEE ALSO Apostasy; *Get*; Kohen, *kohanim*; *Mamzerut*
DNA, 101, 103n5, 567, 591n16
Doctors and physicians, 253n207, 351, 540-541
  and commerce in transplants, 313
  duty to heal, 321, 329, 329n33, 389n35
  and pain and suffering, 391, 399
  SEE ALSO INDIVIDUAL TOPICS; Health care
Domb, Cyril, 323n12
Dorff, Elliot N.
  on artificial insemination, IVF, and surrogacy, 461-509, 511nn1-2, 514n16, 515, 515nn20-22, 518n34, 521, 521nn47-50, 523, 524nn60-61, 538n55, 546, 459nn119-120, 555n17
  on assisted suicide, 379-397
  on family violence, 773-816
  generally, 68nn5-6, 145n28, 183, 344, 352n17, 525n63, 557n21
  on homosexuality, 691-711, 719
  medical care, 319-336, 475n37
  other responsa, 47-48, 64-70, 93-97, 102n4, 145n26
  writings of, 92, 141n11, 143, 143n21, 184n67, 192, 331n39, 385n24, 389n37, 467n16, 483n60, 484n61, 493n84, 497n87, 506n106, 511n3, 575n107, 696n8, 774n1, 775n7, 779n21, 787n51
Douglas, Mary, 105n10
Dresner, Samuel, 632n82

Drori, Moshe, 513n9
Drowning, 256, 270, 289, 293, 297. SEE ALSO *Hasid shoteh*
Drucker, Steven, 104n8
Drugs, 196, 206
Druk, Zalman, 18
Dubose, Edwin R., 384n21
Dukhaning. SEE Kohen, *kohanim*
Dunn, C.S., 93n1
Duran, Simeon ben Zemach, 473n31
Duran, Zemach ben Solomon (*Yachin U-voaz*), 455
Dworkin, Andrea, 545
Dworkin, Ronald, 695n7

Ear piercing. SEE UNDER Tattooing
Earthenware. SEE *Kashrut*
Edels, Samuel. SEE *Maharsha*
Eastern Europe, 121. SEE ALSO *Ashkenazim*
Edwards, Robert, 511
Education, 7-8, 150, 324n17
Egalitarianism. SEE Conservative Judaism; Women
Egypt, 165, 616, 617, 681
Eilberg, Amy, 364-366, 373n7, 444
Eisenberg, Richard, 22n1, 47-48, 48n11
Eisenstadt, Avraham Tzvi Hirsch (*Pithei Teshuvah*), 151
Eisenstein, J.D., 30n11, 466n12, 541n71
Elazar ben Aharon, 415, 419, 426
Elazar ben Shimon, 578
Elazar ha-Kappar, 247, 247n177
Elderly, 788, 788n56, 794. SEE ALSO Family violence
Eleazar, Rabbi, 385
Eleazar ben Azariah, 536
Elephantine, 117
Eliezer, Rabbi, 105, 132-133, 578, 765, 774
Eliezer ben Hyrcanus, 536n37, 568, 568n70, 569
Elijah, 200n23, 204, 581
Elisha, 200n23, 204
Eliyahu ben Samuel, of Lublin. SEE *Yad Eliahu*
Eliyah, Mordecai, 519
Elyashev, Yosef Shalom, 315, 317
Elkins, Herschel T., 92
Ellenson, David, 467n16
Elon, Menahem, 546n106, 547n107, 770, 771n37
Embarrassment, 792n70, 797, 797n84, 798, 804. SEE ALSO Family violence
Emden, Jacob (*Migdal Oz*), 267n249, 303, 303n361, 305, 318, 473n31
Emet ve-Emunah, 575
Encyclopedia Talmudit, 340n12, 359n6, 381n5, 482n53, 699n18
  converts and mourning obligations, 433n11, n17
  non-Jews and *Shabbat*, 54, 65n1
  self-injury, 381n5
England, 95-96
Enzymes. SEE *Kashrut*
Epstein, Avraham, 442, 442n3
Epstein, Baruch ha-Levi (*Torah Temimah*), 284, 802n96
Epstein, Jehiel Michal HaLevi. SEE *Arukh Hashulkhan*
Epstein, Jerome, 602-604, 605-607, 608-611
Epstein, Louis, 406, 543n42
Esther, 274, 274n272, 275, 276n277, 580

Ethical wills, 395, 395n47
Ettlinger, Jacob (*Binyan Tsion*), 158, 158nn15-17, 268, 465n11, 473n31
Eulogy. SEE Mourning
Euthanasia, 384-385, 386-389, 392, 396
Evil, 473n32, 567
Evolution. SEE God
Eybeschuetz, Jonathan, 465n11
  on heart transplants, 197, 198, 199, 201, 203, 205
  and *lifnim meshurat ha-din*, 235-236, 237, 238, 239, 244-245
Eye banks. SEE Organ donations
Ezra, 36, 466, 559n2

Fabe, Brenda, 509n114
Falashas (Ethiopians). SEE *Mamzerut*
Falk, Joshua, 107n17, 261, 502n103
Falk, Ze'ev, 573-574
Families. SEE RELATED TOPICS
Family purity, 360-361, 372, 469, 469n21
Family violence
  Conservative halakhic method, 773-775
  God's image within us, 774, 815-816
  halakhah, tradition, and abuse, 774-775, 777-782
  Jewish community, 775, 775n7, 776
  kinyan, 781
  responsum on, 773-816
    on abuser and abused party, 803-805, 805-816
      spouses and children, 776-782, 782-785, 785n43, 797, 802, 802n96
      retarded children, 784-785
      parents or elderly, 785-789, 793
      sexually, 782, 789-791
      verbally, 791-793
    conclusions and votes, 773, 793-794, 803, 805, 814-815
    on legal status of abuse, 773-794
    on witnesses to act or results of abuse, 794-803
    lashon ha-ra. SEE UNDER HALAKHIC CONCEPTS
    scope of parental prerogatives, 801-802
    shame (*boshet*), 781, 792n70, 797-798, 803
  role of the rabbi and educators, 811-814
Fasting, 153, 316, 316n398
Federation. SEE Community; Organizations
Federation of Jewish Men's Clubs, 169n2
Feeding, 103, 385, 397, 475n37
Feigenbaum, Joshua, 496n87
Feingold, Henry L., 405n15
Feinstein, Moshe, 341n18, 345, 363n22, 564, 572, 573
  artificial insemination, 465n11, 467n17, 476, 485n63, 538n55
  b'nai mitzvah, 34n22
  burial, 422, 424-425
  giving blood, 249-250, 251n192, 253
  life and death, 183n60, 282, 291-292, 292n326
  marriage renewal ceremonies, 752-753
  Pesah, 73
  Shabbat and business, 59, 60, 61, 62, 63
Felder, Aaron, 375n10
Felder Gedaliah, 33n17, 34n20, 34nn22-23
Feldman, David M., 331n39, 359n7, 363n23

abortion, 142nn14-15, 348n3, 522n53
anal sex, 629n66, 630nn71-74, 702n23
birth control and procreation, 492n83, 511n1, 513n9
  generally, 509n114, 525n63
  on IVF, 514, 519n40, 520, 520n42
  on surrogacy, 530n1, 546n101, 551n2, 557n19
Felik, Yehuda, 104n9
Fetus, 440, 441, 445, 448
  halakhah on viability of fetus and life, 358, 367, 522n53
  change in halakhic attitude on viability, 370-371
  child as full human being, 166, 350-351, 351n13, 352-354, 354n25, 355n27
  status and viability, 142, 348-350
  SEE ALSO Babies
Finkelstein, Louis, 159-160, 333n46, 515n21, 770, 770n35, 779n24
Fish. SEE Food
Fisher, S., 638n95
Fleischman, Alan, 354n24
Flekeles, Eleazar, 328, 330, 354-355n25
Flood, 622
Food, 334. SEE ALSO *Kashrut*; *Pesah*
  responsum on mixing fish and meat, 112-114
    conclusion and vote, 112, 114
    cooking or eating together, 113
    and danger to life, 112-113, 114
Fraint, Samuel, 705
France, 43, 44, 45
Frank, Aaron, 93, 93n1, 95, 96
Frank, Adam, 93, 95, 96
Frank, Zevi Pesah, 472n28
Fraud. SEE Conversion
Freehof, Solomon B., 405-406, 406n17
Freud, Sigmund, 636-640
Fried, Bette, 776n9
Friedenwald, H., 466n12
Friedlander, Israel, 82n4, 83n5
Friedman, Harvey, 440n2
Friedman, Theodore, 177-178, 178n18, 188
Friedman, Zvi Hirsch, 476n40
Frydman-Kohl, Baruch, 385n22, 452-458

Gans, David (*Zemach David*), 466
Geiger, Abraham, 559
Gelatin. SEE *Kashrut*
Gelfand, Shoshana, 3-8, 145n28, 525n63, 557n21
Geller, Myron S., 387n30, 413-417, 426-430
Gellman, Marc, 530n1, 538n54, 544n91, 545
Genetic engineering
  kosher and non-kosher ingredients, 102-104
  kilayim, 104-108, 109-110
  plants and animals, 104, 105-106, 107-108, 110
  responsum on *kashrut* and, 101-111
  conclusion and vote, 101, 110-111
Genetics, 104n8, 105, 533, 568, 684, 765n19
  and artificial insemination, 479-480, 486, 533
  SEE ALSO Homosexuality
Genizah, 154, 155, 156-159, 161
Genomes, 138n5
Gentiles. SEE *B'nai Noah*; Non-Jews; *Shabbat*

Gerondi, Jonah, 261n230
Gershom of Mayence, 498n94
Gershuni, Judah, 197-198, 198n13, 199
  Sefer Kol Tzofekh, 197n12
Get, 341n17, 779, 781
  and apostasy, 146, 149, 405
  as certified documents, 733, 734, 737, 738
  concerning *mamzerut*, 564, 569-570, 576, 581, 589, 590
  get zikui, 747-749
  R.A. policy, 753, 755
    role of rabbi, 752-753, 755, 756
  responsa
    conclusions and votes, 741, 750, 751, 754
    on renewal of marriages without a *get*, 751-754
      appendix and summary, 750, 754
        renewal ceremony, 753-754
      civil divorce issue, 751-753
      dissenting opinion, 755-756
    on *shaliah l'kabalah* (agent to accept), 741-750
      annulment, 749
      bet din, 746-747
      bizyon l'ba'al (disrespect to the husband), 743-746, 750
      discontinuation of, 743-747
      halakhah on permissibility of *shaliah l'kabalah*, 741-743
      proof of *shaliah*'s appointment, 743, 746-747
      shilush ha-get, 749-750
  and resurrection, 200, 202
Gilat, Yitzhak, 595
Gillman, Neil, 169n2
Ginsburg, Marvell, 155n10
Ginzberg, Eli, 406n19
Ginzberg, Louis, 406, 407
Glass, Judith, 506n106
God
  b'tzelem elokim, 815-816. SEE ALSO Jewish law concepts
  and blessing, 11, 47, 462
  and children, 462n2, 464, 535-536
    as *mamzerim*, 562-563, 576, 585
    procreation, 473n32, 485, 514, 515n21, 540-541. SEE ALSO Circumcision
  and creation, 105, 110n24
    disabled people, 342-343
    healing, 321n2, n4, 327, 384-385, 389n35, 540 and *Shabbat*, 286
    resurrection, 200, 204
    suicide, 380-381, 387n29, 388-389, 398
  and *halakhah*, 414, 574-575, 763
    service to, 333n46, 763, 766-767, 772
  and homosexuality, 615-616, 627-628, 641, 643, 644, 653, 660, 676, 688, 689, 696, 696n8, 700
    punishment of, 674-675, 675n179
  as parent, 376, 506n106, 786-787
  and *lifnim meshurat ha-din*, 222n108
  responsum on English rendition of, 151-152
    conclusion and vote, 151, 152
    name of, 116, 151, 567n63
  in revelation, 581, 714, 716-717, 762n6, 764-765

SEE ALSO IN INDIVIDUAL RESPONSA; *Hillul HaShem*; *Kiddush HaShem*; *Pidyon HaBen*
Gold, Michael, 511n2, 515n21, 530n1, 540n70, 541n72, 546n103, 547n108
Goldberg, Hayyim Binyamin, 433n17
Goldberg, Zalman Nehemiah, 140n9, 141, 141n13
Golding, Martin, 326n25, 331n40
Goldman, Alex J., 485n63
Goldman, Nechama D., 43-49
Golinkin, David, 183, 183n59, 184, 184n69, 189n96, 192, 431n1, 432n3, 508n110
Golinkin, Noah, 71n1
Gombiner, Abraham. SEE *Magen Avraham*
Goodman, Arnold, 126, 126n1, 581, 593-598, 599-601, 724-725, 727
Gordis, Daniel H., 467n16, 530n1, 605, 607, 610-611, 711
Gordis, David, 1
Gordis, Robert, 142n14, 522n53, 555, 555n17
Goren, Shlomo, 210, 429, 565-566, 572
Goritan, Christine, 807-808
Goses, 354n25
Gossip, 592. SEE ALSO Jewish law concepts: *lashon ha-ra*
Grace after meals (*birkat hamazon*), 12, 28-29n10, 73, 341
Graetz, Naomi, 776-777, 778-780, 781, 782n31, 785n42
  writings, 773n1, 777n10, 779n24, 809n112
Grandin, Temple, 93, 93n1, 95, 96
Graubart, Yehudah Leib, 524n61
Grazi, Richard V., 516n25, 517n29, n32, 521n47
Greary, Dennis, 339n7
Greenbaum, Dorothy, 123n13
Greenberg, Simon, 3n1, 335n49
Greenfeld, Dorothy A., 487n68, 490, 492, 521n47
Greenwald, J.J. SEE Grunwald, Judah
Greenwald, Yekutiel Yehuda (Leopold), 405n11, 409n1, 411, 415n14, 416-417n22, 417n25, 419
Grodin, Michael, 500n96, 509n114
Grossman, Abraham, 773n1, 780
Grossman, Susan, 469, 469n21, 555n14
Grossnass, Aryeh Leib (*Lev Aryeh*), 205-206, 291n323, 295
Group homes
  responsum on homes in one's back yard, 337-346
    conclusion and vote, 337, 346
    disability in the Torah and rabbinic literature, 342-343
    environmental issues, 337-338
    halakhah regarding support, 344-345
    laws regarding mental health institutions, 338-339
    mental health categories, 338
    "N.I.M.B.Y.", 339-340
    shoteh, peti, and halakhic definitions, 340, 341, 341n18, 342, 343
    United States demographics, 337-339
    websites, 337n1, 338n3, 338n6, 339n10
Grunwald, Asher Anshel, 167, 168
Grunwald, Judah, 103n8
Guilder, George, 680
Gutal, Neria, 351n13

Hadaya, Ovadiah, 473n51, 475n37
Hafetz Hayyim (Israel Meir Ha-Kohen), 25, 27, 27n8, 53-54, 63
Haftarot. SEE UNDER Aliyot; Torah, reading of
Hagahot Maimoniot, 230, 235n147, 244, 295
  self-jeopardy, 257, 261-265, 266, 271, 274, 278, 283
  SEE ALSO Meir HaKohen
Hagar. SEE Matriarchs
Haggai, Rabbi, 202
Hai Gaon, 454, 455, 744, 745, 746
Hahillukim. . .MizrahUvnei Eretz Yisrael, 48
Hakham Zevi, 197n8, 198, 199, 201, 205, 217, 219
Hakhomim, 51, 52
HaKohen, Aaron ben Jacob (HaManhig), 44, 45
Halakhah. SEE Jewish law
Halakhot Gedolot, 567n63, 744
Ha-Levi, David ben Samuel. SEE Taz
Ha-Levi, Hayyim David (Mekor Hayyim), 155n9, 273, 519
Ha-Levi, Samuel ben David (Nahalat Shivah), 737-738
Ha-Levi, Yehudah, 211, 211n66
Halitzah, 139-140, 405, 433, 745, 748
  historical view towards, 539n63, nn65-66, 555
  and mamzerut, 561, 570
  SEE ALSO Marriage; Yibum
Hallel. SEE Liturgy
Halperin, Harry, 609
Halperin, Mordecai, 312n388, 511n2, 518, 521n47
Hamel, Ronald P., 384n21
Hametz, 60-61, 72, 73, 76, 77, 737
Hammer, Reuven, 341-342, 342n19
Hammurabi Code, 544
Hanafin, Hilary, 532n16, n18
Hanagid, Shmuel, 777
Handel, William, 532n15
Handler, Howard, 171-174, 718-721
Hanina, Rabbi, 237-238, 455, 743, 744-745, 746
Hanina ben Dosa, 284-285
Hanina ben Hakhinai, 204
Hanina ben Teradyon, 381
Hannah, 462, 462n2
Harlow, Jules, 171n1, 321n4
Hartman, David, 588, 764
Hasid shoteh (foolish saint), 288, 289, 290, 290n321, 292, 296-297, 298, 305, 308
  SEE ALSO Organ donations
Hasidim, 781
Hatafat dam brit. SEE Circumcision; Conversion
Hatam Sofer, 47, 218, 341, 341n18
Hauptman, Judith, 588, 773n1m 776n10-777n10, 781, 781n28
Havla-ah (overall lease), 54, 63
Havvat Ya'ir, 257-258, 259, 259n221, 260, 260n228, 261, 304
HaYarhi, Abraham ben Nathan, 43-44
Hazak, hazak, v'nithazak. SEE UNDER Torah, reading of
Hazzan, 83, 681, 800n91. SEE ALSO Shaliach Tzibur
Hazon Ish. SEE Abraham Karelitz
Health. SEE Health care; Life
Health care, 103, 381n4
  responsibility of
    community, 324n18, 326-327, 328, 330, 331n37, 332-336
    costs to, 325, 327, 335
    federations, 334, 336
    limits on, 331, 332-333
    prevention, 322, 331n41, 332, 333, 336
    talmudic requirements for, 322, 324, 331n37, 332, 335
    doctors, 320n1, 321, 328-330, 331, 333, 334, 336
    individual's responsibility, 320-322, 325-327, 328, 329, 333-334, 336
    duty to wife and family, 325-326, 326n23
    insurance, 331, 332
    precedents and analogies, 323-325
      bikkur holim, 323. SEE ALSO Mitzvot
      captivity and pidyon shevuyim, 323, 324-325, 325n20, 327, 330, 332
      individual's responsibility in, 325-326, 332, 333
      tzedakah and the poor, 323nn8-11, 326n23, 327, 328, 334
        basic requirement of, 324, 330n34, 333
    responsum on responsibilities for providing, 319-336
      conclusions and vote, 319, 327, 330, 335-336
      introduction, 319-320
  SEE ALSO Organ donations
Hebrew language, 10. SEE ALSO Rabbinical Assembly
Heilprin, Yehiel ben Solomon, 302n359
Helbo, Rabbi, 393
Heller, Haim (Ha'amek She'elah)
  and ben Peturah dispute, 260, 261
  and self-jeopardy, 260n228, 264n240, 265, 266-267, 271, 283n303
Heller, Yehiel, 266n247
Heller, Yom Tov Lipmann, 452-453
Herring, Basil, 394n45, 802n93
Hershler, Moshe, 200, 200nn21-23, 201, 204, 206, 207n49, 296-297
Hertz, Joseph, 778
Herzbrun, Michael, 121-122
Heschel, Abraham Joshua, 335n51
Heschel, Susannah, 335n51
Hevra kadisha, 184. SEE ALSO Death
Hida, 201-204, 465n11
High Holy Days, 681
  responsum on omission of silent amidah, 81-88
    analysis, 81, 82-86
    conclusion and vote, 81, 88
    Conservative practices, 86-87, 88
    heikha kedushah, 88
    repetition, 82-83
    shortening length of services, 87-88
Hila, Rabbi, 105
Hillel, 17, 381n4, 455, 462n2, 463n2, 511n1, 517n30, 535, 535n33
Hillul HaShem, 88, 96, 135, 524n61, 565, 600, 775n7, 792, 794, 799-801
Hirschhorn, Joshua, 24n6, 27-28, 28-29n10, 31n13, 39-40, 41
Hiya bar Abba, 133, 226-227, 385, 566
Hiyya, Rabbi, 134, 223
Hafetz Hayyim, 456, 797

Hoffman, David Zvi (*Melamed Leho'il*), 19, 132, 136, 600, 635, 766-768, 772
Holidays, 48, 201. SEE ALSO UNDER INDIVIDUAL HOLIDAYS
Holmes, Jr., Oliver Wendell, 694-695, 695n7
Holocaust, 117, 121, 381n8, 382-383, 564-565, 696n8
Home. SEE Non-Jews
Homosexuality
  AIDS, 673, 674-675, 709
  attitudes, 668-672, 688, 690, 705-706, 709-710, 721
  celibacy, 698, 703, 709
  ceremonies, 685, 707, 709, 713, 719, 721. SEE ALSO Marriage
  children, 618nn24-25, 636-639, 647, 650, 658, 719, 720. SEE ALSO Families
  ethical issues on, 677-678
  etiology
    as a choice, 641, 644, 663, 696-700
    as part of nature, 628-629, 629n69, 631, 633, 642-643, 701-702, 720
    theories on, 636-642, 646-651, 654-662, 687
  fantasies (*hirhur*), 620-621, 623, 669
  gender identity, 705-706
  halakhah analysis, 656, 659, 663-668, 689
    on etiology
      as overt behavior, 642-645
        lo plug, 643
        oneis, 652-654, 661n156, 698, 699-700
        to'evah, 640-641, 643, 646, 651-652, 660, 663, 667, 668
      and abuse, 789-790, 790n59
      interpretation of term, 623-632, 633, 634, 635, 676-677, 686-687, 707, 715
      historical method of, 693-695, 697. SEE ALSO RESPONSA HEREIN
    majority vs. minority, 687-688, 689
    outline of, 614-623, 662-663
    sources on, 614-617, 696, 708, 712
      puk v'hazei, 713
      la-akor davar min haTorah (abrogating Torah law). SEE UNDER Jewish law concepts
  lesbianism. SEE Lesbianism
  relationships, 625, 629-630, 634, 661, 673n176
    abusive, 782n31, 790n59
    as families, 507n109, 530n2, 626-627, 640, 660, 679-682, 685, 702-704, 707, 709, 719
    in monogamous homosexuality, 676, 677, 679, 686, 687n5
  statistics, 708, 710
  responsa
    on CJLS decisions and, 676-685
      conclusion and vote, 676, 685
      Conservative movement's process, 706-707, 709, 710, 712, 719
      and public policy and social construction, 678-679, 685
    on homosexuality, 613-675
      consensus statement, 612, 722, 724, 728-729
      epilogue, 674-675
      postscript and vote, 612, 672-674
      R.A. resolution on, 673-674, 692, 692n2, 693, 704, 707, 708, 718

on issue of, 686-690
  conclusion and vote, 686, 689-690
  leadership and clergy, 666, 688-689, 705, 713, 721
on placement of homosexual rabbis, 722-723, 724-725
  conclusion and vote, 722, 723, 724, 725
  concurring opinion, 726-727
and proposal on Jewish norms for sexual behavior, 691-711
  conclusion and vote, 691, 708-711
  concurring opinion on biblical imperatives, 714-717
  concurring opinion on status in synagogues, 712-713
  dissenting opinion, 718-721, 728-729
Horowitz, Pinhas ha-Levi, 282
Horowitz, Zevi Hersh ha-Levi (*Sefer Hafla'ah*), 218, 219
Hospice care, 390-391, 399
Huddle, Sharon, 543
Humiliation. SEE UNDER Family violence
Hunter, John, 470
Hunting, 120

Ibn Verga, Solomon, 466, 466n13
Idolatry, 116, 383nn15-16, 400, 403, 473n32, 481, 578, 581, 585, 616. SEE ALSO Tattooing
Iggeret Hakodesh. SEE Cohen, Seymour J.
Ila'a, Rabbi, 237
Illness. SEE Health care
Immersion (*tevila*). SEE Apostasy; Conversion
Impurity, 577-578, 620-621
In vitro fertilization (IVF). SEE Artificial insemination; Surrogacy
Incest, 350, 521, 588n4, 698. SEE ALSO Artificial insemination
Infertility. SEE Artificial insemination
Injury. SEE Danger; Self-injury
Intermarriage, 476, 477n42, 486, 569, 664, 666, 676, 726
  attitude towards, 131, 596, 597, 598
  and *bimah* (pulpit) privileges, 34, 602-604
  responsum on employment by a synagogue/day school, 608-611
    conclusion and vote, 608, 611
    previous CJLS decisions, 609-611
    role model, 610-611
  SEE ALSO Conversion
Internet, 118n14, 211n67, 337n1, 338n3, 338n6
Isaac, Rabbi, 566, 779
Isaac ben Aboudimi, 560n6
Ishmael. SEE Matriarchs
Ishmael, Rabbi, 223-224, 547, 619, 619nn30-31
Ishmael ha-Kohen, 561
Isserles, Moses ben Israel. SEE Rema
Isserlein, Israel. SEE *Trumat HaDeshen*
Israel, 216, 429, 474, 474n35, 564
  Israel Medical Association, 136n1
  Rabbinic court decisions, 232-233, 244, 565-566, 570-572, 573, 779
  Sabbatical year, 765, 765n19

Jacob. SEE Patriarchs
Jacob, Walter, 142n17, 161n20, 522n53, 530n1
Jacob ben Asher. SEE *Tur*
Jacob ben Samuel, 473n31
Jacobs, Louis, 559n1, 561n25, 563-564, 567n63, 571n88, 572, 573
Jakobovits, Immanuel, 796n77
  abortion and artificial insemination, 465n11, 466n12, 470n23, 472n28, 484-485, 485n63
  babies and treatment, 352, 354n25
  health care, 323n8, 328n31
  life and death, 176, 176n11
  organ transplants and donations, 183, 188, 188n89, n94
  difference between *mitzvah* and *hovah*, 180nn39-40
  surrogacy, 529n2, 530n1, 541, 548n114
Jastrow, Marcus, 622n43
Jellinek, Aaron, 302n359
Jeremiah, 335, 465-466, 763
Jerusalem, 226
Jewish Big Brothers/Big Sisters, 503, 703
Jewish Community Relations Committee (JCRC). SEE Organizations
Jewish ethics, 144
Jewish identity, 522n53
Jewish law
  adoption, 501-504
  artificial insemination, 467n16, 484, 493
  coercion/mandate to perform *mitzvot*. SEE *Mitzvot*
  as Conservative Jewish law
    and CJLS, 771-772
    concerning family violence, 781, 793
    on *get*, 741-750
    on homosexuality, 691-693, 704, 707-708
      commitment to *halakhah*, 672n172
    regarding the fetus, 141, 142, 368
  conversion, 128-130
  generally, 103
  halakhah l'ma'aseh, 663, 667, 729, 739
  on homosexuality, 613-614, 693-694,
    toraitic or rabbinic, 714-715, 716-717
  mamzerut, 574-575
  principles, 107, 128-129, 301, 368, 641
    apostasy, 149
    hukah, 105n12, 106-108, 110
    kal va'homer, 269, 285-287, 644. SEE ALSO WITHIN INDIVIDUAL RESPONSA
    lo plug, 643
    mesirah, 794, 798-801
    self-jeopardy, 112-113, 271, 285-286
      toraitic or rabbinic, 247-249, 288-289, 300-301
  procreation. SEE UNDER *Mitzvot*
  rabbinic Judaism
    interpretation of law, 577-579, 579n128, 580-582, 763-764
    evolution of, 761-766
    majority vs. minority, 687-688, 761-764, 765, 766, 767, 768, 770-771
    toraitic law made inoperative, 581, 582-586, 587-592
      la-akor d'var min haTorah. SEE UNDER Jewish

law concepts
  suicide, 380-383
  FOR FULLER DISCUSSIONS SEE WITHIN INDIVIDUAL RESPONSA
Jewish law concepts
  la-akor davar min haTorah (abrogating Torah law)
    categories of, 580-581, 595-596, 597
    on homosexuality, 687, 689, 715, 720-721
  aris, 54
  asmakhta, 553-554
  ba'al tashhit, 387n29
  b'tzelem Elohim, 117-119, 120, 184, 332, 344, 388
    and artificial insemination and IVF, 463n3, 473, 515n21
    and family violence, 774, 792, 797, 815-816
    and organ donations, 314, 317
    and surrogacy, 536, 552, 555
  batul bashishim, 76, 77, 98, 102, 103, 104n8
  bayit ne'eman bi-yisrael, 704
  deiyo leba min ha-din l'hiyot k'niydon, 746
  d'var shelo ba l'olam, 547
  dine dimalkhuta dine, 68, 190n103, 309, 548, 775n7
  eilu v'eilu divrei elokim hayyim, 764
  eyno b'livisha eyno b'aseya, 4
  harei at mekudeshet li, 754
  hasid shoteh. SEE *Hasid shoteh*
  hevra kadish and *tahara*, 178n19, 408-412
  hiyyuv. SEE Obligation
    b'dinei shamayim, 240-241, 242-243
    differences with *mitzvah*, 180nn39-40
  holeh lifneinu. SEE Organ Donations
  kinyan, 781
  lifnim meshurat ha-din, analysis and discussion of, 222-246, 255
    sources on, 222-225, 227n121, 228-235, 244-245
  lo ba-shamayim hi, 763
  lashon ha-ra, 794, 795, 797, 803, 806, 808
  lo ta'amod al dam rai-ekha, 344, 345, 495, 795, 796
    blood and marrow donations, 216-217, 222, 245-246
    coercion for, 219, 220, 255
    and health care, 321, 335n51, 396
    organ donations, 175-176
    regarding heart transplants, 291
    self-jeopardy and, 256-257, 262, 267-270, 272, 284, 292-294, 300-301
  mipnei darkhei shalom, 143, 334, 421, 427, 428, 429, 524-525, 557
  motzi shem ra, 795n73, 806
  mumar, 749, 755
  na'aseh ve-nishmah, 715, 716, 717
  olam ha-ba, 333n46, 381, 385, 425, 579, 588
  ona'at devarim, 792, 793, 809, 810n113
  mi'd'oraita hitah ahat poteret et ha-kri, 748
  patur aval asur, 699-700
  pidyon shevuyim, 323, 324-325, 325n20, 327, 330, 332, 333
  pikuah nefesh. SEE *Pikuah nefesh*
  puk ve-hazei, 713
  quotations
    "eye for an eye" quotation, 288
    "love your neighbor as yourself", 683

"putting a stumbling block before the blind", 707, 784n40, 802, 810, 810nn113-115, 812
"saving a life is as if saving a world", 163, 163n3, 257, 308, 316
rodef, 269-270, 796, 798
shalom bayit, 777
shvut, 60, 65
taharat hamishpaha. SEE Family purity
takkanah, 84-85, 238, 498n94, 539, 579-582, 779, 797n83
 and *gezeirah*, 275, 312n388, 314, 318
tikun olam, 332, 524-525, 683
tirkhe di-tzibura, 87. SEE ALSO High Holy Days
to'evah, oneis. SEE UNDER Homosexuality
tzaar baalei hayyim, 93, 95, 97, 208, 209, 354n25
tzniyut, 119, 120
va-aristikh li l'olam, 754
v'hai ahikha imkha, 258, 259
v'hai bahem, 260
v'rapo y'rapei, 309n383, 389n35
yirat shamayim, 597
zaken mamre, 667, 168, 709, 763n12, 766n22

Jewish Theological Seminary, 14n4, 120, 136, 159, 185n71, 645n111, 687, 721, 729, 815-816
Jewish Welfare Board, 417n24
Jews by Choice. SEE Conversion
Jews for Jesus. SEE Apostasy
Joint Placement Commission. SEE Rabbinical Assembly
Jonah, Rabbi, 261n230
Joseph, Rabbi, 562, 622
Josephus, 110
Joshua, 44
Joshua, Rabbi, 133, 559, 560, 765
Jubilee year, 415, 427
Judah, Rabbi, 376n12
Judah ben Samuel, He-Hasid of Regensburg. SEE *Sefer Hasidim*
Judah Loew ben Bezalel. SEE *Maharal miPrague*
Judges. SEE *Bet din*; Rabbinical Assembly

Kabbalah, 677n1, 680-681
Kaddish, 52, 736
Kagan, Israel. SEE *Hafetz Hayyim*
Kagan, Richard, 188-189
Kant, 632, 635
Kaplan, Louis, 603n2
Karas, Phyllis Klasky, 93n1
Kardiner, A., 638
Karelitz, Abraham (*Hazon Ish*), 106n13, 107-108, 197n11, 351, 429-430
Karo, Joseph, 23n4, 45, 113, 168, 409, 455, 733
 on danger and self-jeopardy, 257, 261, 269
 and family violence, 778-779
  mesirah, 799
 lifnim meshurat ha-din, 234
 and *mitzvot*, 273
Kasher, Menahem M., 198-199, 199n18
Kashrut, 109, 616, 666
 American law on, 91-92, 94-96
 batul ba-shishim, 98
 d'var hadash, 100

responsa
 conclusions and votes, 78, 79-80, 91, 92, 93, 97, 98, 100
 on K as symbol, 91-92
 on microbial enzymes (rennin, rennet), 98-100
  manufacture of cheese, 99, 100, 103
  previous CJLS decisions, 98-99, 100, 100nn5-6
  status as food, 99
 on shackling and hoisting animals, 93-97
  shekhita, 94-95
  tza-ar baalei hayyim, 93, 95, 97
 on teflon type utensils, 78-80
  halakhah, 78-79
  teflon process, 78
 SEE ALSO Food; Genetic engineering; *Pesah*
Katz, David, 569
Katz, Jacob, 67n4, 147, 147nn4-5
Katz, Morris H., 99n3
Kav Naki, 743, 743n4, 746
Kavvanah, 123. SEE ALSO Liturgy; Prayer
Kellner, Menahem Marc, 653n136
Kelly, David, 525n63
Kereti u'Peleti, 197, 197n10, 199, 205
Kesef Mishneh, 421. SEE ALSO Karo, Joseph
Ketubbah, 68, 622, 706, 733, 734, 737, 738, 752, 753-754
Kevorkian, Jack, 389
Kiddush HaShem, 381, 580, 775n7
Kiddushin. SEE Marriage
Kidneys. SEE Organ donations
Kilav, Avraham Yitzhak Halevi, 140, 140n10
Kilayim. SEE Genetic engineering
Kill. SEE Murder
Kimelman, Reuven, 481n51, 676-685, 702
Kinsey, Alfred, 632nn81-82, 633, 697
Kirschenbaum, Aaron, 806n101
K'lal Yisrael, 407, 464, 559n2, 716, 775-776, 789-790
Klein, Isaac, 79n4, 82n3, 123n14, 190n106, 191, 382n12, 443n6, 445
 autopsies, 177n15, 178n23, 524n61
 on converts, 434n21, 436n27, 437n28, 522nn52-53, 599-601
 kashrut of cheese, 98-99, 100n5
 status of child, 139, 139n7, 140, 141, 142, 142n14
 Torah scroll, 153n3
Klein, Menashe, 247n179, 248-249, 251n192, 264n239, 295
Kluger, Solomon ben Judah Aaron. SEE *Maharshak*
Knaus, William, 392
K'nesset, 178n23
K'nesset haG'dolah, 204, 261-262, 296, 302n358
Kobler, Franz, 601n11
Kogan, Barry S., 467n16
Kogen, Judah, 13-15, 14n4, 87n14, 498n92, 755-756
Kohen, kohanim
 and *birkat hamazon*, 12, 644
 and death, 576nn110-111, 577n121
 halakhah on, 9-11, 12, 13, 594-595
  akirah, 595-597
 kedusha status of a *kohen*, 342, 579, 594, 643-644, 764

associative or lineal, 10, 11, 14, 31n15, 32, 42, 763n12
  rights of daughters, 10, 11n10, 12, 14, 31n15
  and *pidyon haBen*, 10, 12, 14, 171, 352n16, 596
  responsa
    on *aliyot*, 16-20
      conclusion and vote, 16, 20
      first *aliyah*, 12, 14, 31n15, 32n16, 39, 594
      and leaving sanctuary. SEE *Aliyot*
    on gender for *birkat kohanim*, 9-12, 13-15
      conclusions and votes, 9, 12, 13, 15
      requirements of, 14nn3-4, 17, 147n5
    on *kohen* and marriage, 618
      children, 594, 597
      conclusions and votes, 593, 597-598, 599, 601
      with a convert, 599-601
      with a divorcee, 581, 582, 593-598
      previous CJLS decisions, 11n9, 14n8, 31nn14-15, 42, 593-594, 599-600, 601
Kohn, Ingrid, 374n8
Kohn, S. Joshua, 400-401
Kol Nidre. SEE *Yom Kippur*
Kook, Abraham Isaac, 135-136
Korban Netanel (Weil, Nathanel), 25, 33
Kraemer, David, 144, 144nn23-24
Krivosha, Norman, Judge,
  generally, 58, 59, 61, 62, 63, 64, 65, 67, 68
  responsa, 53, 55-57
Krochmal, Menahem Mendel (*Zemah Zedek*), 231, 232, 240, 244
K'tivah. SEE UNDER *Shabbat*
Kubler-Ross, Elisabeth, 395n48
Kurtz, Vernon H., 121-124, 125-126, 166-170, 776n9

Lamm, Maurice, 178n19, 184n66, 367n1, 456
  converts' mourning practices, 434-435, 437
  mourning infants, 439-440, 443n6, 445-446
Lamm, Norman, 653, 696
Landau, Ezekiel ben Judah. SEE *Noda b'Yehudah*
Landlord and tenant. SEE *Shabbat*
Lappe, Benay, 774n1, 783n37, 788n54
Lasker, Daniel J., 476
Lau, Israel Meir, 313, 314n394
Lauritzen, Paul, 464n4, 471n26, 485-486, 487, 487nn66-68, 491
Lauterbach, Jacob Z., 119, 173n3
Lawrence, Frederick, 382
Lease. SEE *Shabbat*
Ledley, Ellen, 774n1
Leprosy, 112, 112n1, 114, 114n4, 577, 578, 585
Lesbianism, 144, 616-618, 623, 630, 633, 651, 701, 702-703. SEE ALSO Homosexuality
Letter of Aristeas, 677n1
Levi'im. SEE *Kohen, kohanim*
Lieberman, Saul, 14n4, 276n279, 282, 282n301, 446n11, 451
Life, 292, 293, 297, 311, 333
  categories to save, 305
  lives of teachers, 299-300
  healing, 389n35
  of prisoners, 317
  SEE ALSO Babies; Danger; Organ donations; *Pikuah nefesh*
Life support systems, 787n51
Lifnim meshurat ha-din. SEE UNDER Jewish law; Organ donations
Lima, Moses (*Helkat Mehokek*), 281
Lincoln, David H., 58-59, 60, 529, 530n1, 551n2, 552n2
Lipschutz, Israel (*Tiferet Israel*), 453
Liturgy, 33, 87
  Aramaic formulations, 736-737
  for funeral of stillborn, 373
  prostration, 401
  Siddur Sim Shalom, 321n4
  SEE ALSO Synagogue
Living will, 189, 189n100
Loewy, Robert H., 358n2
Loftus, Elizabeth, 808
Love, 683-684. SEE ALSO IN RELATED TOPICS
Lubliner, Immanuel, 610
Lubow, Akiba, 148n9
Lucas, Alan B., 115-120
Lulav, 4, 580
Luria, Solomon. SEE *Marharshal*

Ma'ariv. SEE Synagogue
Mackler, Aaron
  concerning assisted suicide, 383n14, 387n27, 399
  generally, 137n1, 138n2, 486n64, 497n87, 509n114
  responsa, 726-727
    health care, 319-336, 344
    in vitro fertilization, 497n91, 552n3, 553n6
    surrogacy, 137-145, 526-528, 551-557
  writings, 143n20, 323n10
Mackler, Lorraine Newman, 145n28, 525n63, 557n21
Magen Avraham, 51, 599
Maharal miPrague, 110n24
Maharam Schick, 18, 19, 177n16, 268n250, 296, 417n22, 465n10, 473n31
Maharik, 17, 18
Maharil, 23n4, 465-466
Maharsha, 142, 496, 496n87, 522n53, 535n30
Maharshak, 18, 410, 421-422, 424, 428
Maharshal, 242-244, 245, 249, 416, 715
Maharsham, 18, 472n28, 475n37, 569-570, 574
Mahlstedt, Patricia P., 487n68, 490, 492, 521n47
Mahzor, 86, 87
Maibaum, Matthew, 388n32
Maimon, Judah Leib, 260n229, 282n298
Maimonides, Moses, 113, 156, 332, 445, 455, 601
  aliyot, 25
  divorce, 202
  doctor, 220-221, 220n105
  doing damage or danger to self or others, 247, 271-272, 272n264, 273, 274-275, 276, 279n291, 282, 283
  educational purposes, 161
  High Holy Days *amidah* and *takkanah*, 82-84, 85, 88
  homosexuality and lesbianism, 617-618
  family violence, 777, 781, 782, 784n40
  kohen, kohanim, 10, 19
  legal reasoning, 714, 733, 762n7
  mamzerut, 566, 567n63, 568, 571, 571n88, 572

oaths, 253, 253n206
obligation (*hiyyuv*), 227-228, 230, 232, 244, 245, 271-272, 787-788
saving life, 292-293, 295
self-injury, 249, 250, 251, 251n192, 305
Torah service, 36-37
tzitzit, 5-6
SEE ALSO *Mitzvot*
Mamzerut, 343, 466, 475, 546n63, 683, 780
  responsum on *mamzerut*, 558-586
    children, 559-560, 561-563, 565-566, 569, 576, 581, 584, 588, 684
    conclusion and vote, 558, 586
    concurring opinion, 587-592
    definition and consequences (*karet*), 559-562, 564
    ethical problem, 562-564
    halakhic sources, 559-566, 576-577
      interpretation of, 577-579, 580-582
    Israel, 565-566, 573, 592
    marriage, 569-560, 564, 569, 584, 589-591
    previous CJLS decisions, 558
    reasons for law of *mamzerut*, 566-568
    solutions, 568-574, 584-585, 590-591, 592
    takkanah, 579-582
    toraitic law made inoperative, 582-586, 589
Mandl, Herbert, 16-20, 132-136, 594
Manslaughter. SEE Murder
Mara d'atra, xi, 88, 312n388, 355, 436, 449
  apostasy, 148, 148n8, 149, 150, 401-402, 407
  authority, 759, 768
  burials and cemeteries, 417n23, 424
  homosexuality, 612, 664-667, 685, 693, 709, 711
  miscarriage, 360-361, 362
Marat ayin, 54, 109
Margolioth, Ephraim Zalman, 27n8, 31n13, 33n17
Margoliot, Moses (*P'nei Moshe*), 764
Margulies, Mordecai, 622n43
Marmor, Judd, 625n55, 634n87, 641-642, 643, 645, 665n161
Marriage, 324, 738
  ceremonies
    as commitment, 612, 623, 664, 685, 682. SEE Homosexuality
    for renewal, 751-754, 755-756
  death, resurrection and, 201-205
    regarding organ donations, 315
  and disabilities, 341n17
  family violence, 776-782
  halitzah and levirate marriage. SEE *Halitzah*; *Yibum*
  intermarriage. SEE Conversion
  kohanim, 10, 581, 593-598, 599-601
  mamzerut, 563-564, 584, 586, 589-591
  monogamy, 681-682. SEE ALSO Homosexuality; Polygamy
  procreation, 536
    and adopted/genetic siblings, 482n57, 523
  sexual behavior
    norms of, 701-702, 710-711
    pre-marital sexual relations, 708-709
  taharat haMishpaha, 360-361
SEE ALSO Apostasy; Divorce

Martin, C.E., 632
Martyrdom. SEE *Kiddush HaShem*; Suicide
Masorti movement, 760
Masturbation, 585n153
Matriarchs
  embryo transfer, 496, 522n53, 535n30
  infertility, 462n2, 464, 481n51
  shifhah, 536, 536n40, 537-538, 550, 555, 569
Matt, Hershel, 652-653, 653n135
Mattathias of Chinon, 227, 227n124
Matzah. SEE *Pesah*
Meat. SEE Food
Medicine, 321
  treatments, 117, 323, 354n25
  SEE ALSO Circumcision; Health care; Organ transplants
Megilat Yehusin, 568
Mehlman, Yitzchak, 517n32
Meier, Levi, 551n2
Meir, Rabbi, 107n17, 203, 562, 581n142, 779
Meir b. Barukh, of Rotenburg, (*Maharam*), 778, 779, 779n22, 781
Meir ha-Kohen, of Rothenberg
  coercion and *mitzvot*, 230, 235n147, 244
  self-jeopardy, 261-265, 266, 271, 274, 278, 283
  SEE ALSO *Hagahot Maimoniyot*
Meir Simha of Dvinsk (*Or Sameah*), 274, 274n272, 275, 276, 276n277, 546n101
Meiri, Menahem ben Solomon, 247-248, 249, 269n254, 470n22, 581n145
Meiselman, Moshe, 220, 297, 307
Menahem of Merseburg, 799n88
Mental retardation. SEE Group homes
Messiah and Messianic age, 562, 568
Meyers, Joel, 728
Mezuzot, 4, 578
Michel, Vicki, 491n81, 509n114
Middle Ages, customs of, 119. SEE ALSO *Ashkenazim*
Midrash, 248
  Genesis Rabbah, 45, 47. SEE ALSO SOURCE INDEX
Midrash Temurah, 541n71
Mikveh, 135, 139, 148, 149, 150, 360-362, 363, 402, 424
  SEE ALSO Conversion; Family purity; AND RELATED TOPICS
Milk. SEE *Pesah*
Minhah. SEE Synagogue
Minhat Hinukh, 251
Minhat Yitzhak, 233, 244, 272n264, 273, 292, 295, 350n11
Mintz, Moses ben Isaac, 46
Mintzberg, Israel Ze'ev, 473n31
Minyan, 113, 154, 701
Miracles, 284-285
Miriam, 578
Miscarriage and stillbirth
  medical determination of viability, 371
    definition of fetus and miscarriage, 354n24, 356, 357, 358, 365, 366
    mental stress, 359-360, 362, 364, 365
    mourning practices, 357-358, 362, 370-375, 376
    pregnancy loss, 365-366, 369-370, 374n8

857

woman as *holeh*, 359-360, 365, 372, 376
 bikkur holim for, 359-363, 365
 community response towards, 360-361, 362, 363
 mikveh, 360-362, 363
 yahrzeit/yom nihum, 374-375, 376
 responsa
  on miscarriage, 357-363
   conclusion and vote, 357, 363
   dissenting opinion, 364-366
  on stillbirth, 367-376, 377-378
   burial and funeral of stillbirth, 370, 372-374, 376
    naming of, 373, 377
   conclusion and vote, 367, 376
   dissenting concurrence, 370-371, 375, 377-378
   halakhic background, 367-368, 369
   definition of, 348-350, 353n20, 368, 370-371
   obligation (*hiyyuv*), 368, 370, 375
   soul of, 376n12
 SEE ALSO Babies; Women
Mishnah editions, 320n1. SEE ALSO Albeck, Hanokh
Mishneh Torah, 7. SEE ALSO Maimonides
Mitzvot
 "be fruitful and multiply"
  and artificial insemination, 472-473, 479, 482n53, 484, 487, 488
  and homosexuality, 687, 702-703
  and in vitro fertilization 510n1, 513, 515, 525
  surrogacy, 540, 549
  and infertility, 462n2, 463-465
  onah. SEE Homosexuality
 bikkur holim, 323, 393-394, 396, 399
  for miscarriages and stillbirths, 359-363, 364, 365, 372
 compensation for, 253, 256, 310-311, 312-313, 313n392, 314
 greeting mourners, 452-458
 hidur mitzvah, 7
 honoring parents, 506n106, 785-786, 786nn45-47, 787-788
  and teachers, 299-300, 301, 302nn358-359, 303n361. SEE ALSO Parent and child; Children
 mentally disabled and, 340, 341, 341n18, 342
 positive and negative ones, 802, 803-804
  coercion, 215, 216-219
  self-injury, 248, 251n192, 274-275
  and *lo ta'amod*, 256-257, 271-272, 273, 291-292, 795
  time-bound, 3
 tzedakah, 218, 323-324, 326n23, 327, 328, 330n34, 333-334, 345
 SEE ALSO UNDER INDIVIDUAL TOPICS
Mizrahi, Israel Meir, 331n39
Mohel. SEE Circumcision; *Shabbat*
Moellin, Jacob ben Moses. SEE *Maharil*
Money, John, 648n117, 649-650
Monogamy. SEE Homosexuality; Marriage
Moore, G. F., 701-702
Moore, Michael, 695n7
Mor Uktziyah (Jacob Emden), 18
Mordechai, 4, 235, 235n147, 244, 245, 778n16, 788n54, 799n88

SEE ALSO SOURCE INDEX
Moreh Derekh (Rabbi's Manual), 445, 739, 753, 754
Morgenstern, Julius, 583n151
Morrell, Samuel, 779n22
Morpurgo, Samson, 411
Morreim, Haavi, 329n33
Moses, 9, 13, 36-37, 122, 275, 462n2, 578, 580, 762, 764-765
Moses, Lionel E., 48, 48n12, 730-740, 802n96
Moses of Brisk (Brisker Rav), 219n95, 473n31
Moslems, 83, 780
Moss, Lisa Braver, 122, 123
Mourning
 babies and stillbirths, 356, 366, 367
 organ donations, 187
 responsum on practices for non-Jewish relatives, 431-438
  conclusion and vote, 431, 438
 shivah, 154, 200
 SEE ALSO Babies; Conversion; Miscarriage; *Shabbat*
Munk, Samuel David, 228-229, 230, 240, 244, 245
Murder, 305n365, 463n3, 796
 assisted suicide, 384
 case of the *rodef*, 269-270
 cities of refuge, 274-275, 275n276
 embarrassment same as, 797n84
 halakhic changes for, 576-577, 482
 heart transplants, 196, 197-198, 199n18, 203-206
 self-sacrifice and, 301-302
 withholding medical care, 329, 354n25
 SEE ALSO Suicide
Music. SEE UNDER *Shabbat*
Mutilation, 184. SEE ALSO Tattooing

Nahalat Shivah. SEE Ha-Levi, Samuel ben David
Nahman, Rabbi, 748
Nahman ben Isaac, 582
Nahmanides (Ramban), 134, 135, 322, 331n39, 359n10, 432, 466-467, 568
 views on *kilaim* and creation, 105, 106n15, 109
Naming. SEE IN RELATED TOPICS
Nathan, Rabbi, 462n2
National Jewish population survey, 401
Nazarali, Shemin, 123n11
Nebenzal, Avigdor, 219n95, 513, 514, 515n23
Nefesh. SEE Soul
Neonates. SEE Babies
Nesiyat kapayim. SEE *Kohen, kohanim*
Netziv, 259-260, 261, 263, 266, 267, 280, 768
Neuman, Abraham, 406
Neuwirth, Joshua Isaiah, 177n14, 182n51, 255n211, 304, 305
Nevins, Daniel S., 587-592
Newman, Louis, 467n16
Niddah (menstruation), 411n2, 466
Nimukei Yosef, 733
Nishmat Avraham
 artificial hearts, 195n4, 206
 blood and bone marrow donations, 213-215, 250-253, 267n249, 304
 kidney donations, 309-311

monetary compensation, 313n392
self-jeopardy, 276n278, 296
Noda B'Yehuda, 139n8, 140n9, 177n16, 419
Non-Jews, 272, 345, 481, 557, 569, 676
  burials, 405-406, 420-425
  family violence, 775, 775n7, 776, 777, 778
    mesirah, 794, 798-801, 802n96
  organ donations, 252n196
  as parents of *bar/bat mitzvah*, 602-604
  responsum on home ceremonies and relatives, 605-607
    brit milah, *pidyon haBen*, and *simhat bat*, 606-607
    conclusion and vote, 605, 607
    previous CJLS decisions, 605-606
  SEE ALSO Conversion; *Mamzerut*; *Shabbat*; Surrogacy
Noth, Martin, 736
Novak, David, 12n16, 17, 183n62, 433n11, 559n2, 570-571, 574, 775n7
Nudell, George, 760n2

Obadiah, 601
Oberlander, Gedalya ben Yehiel, 168, 169n3
Obligation (*hiyyuv*)
  and coercion
    in divorce, 236, 237
    in *hiyyuv be-dinai shamayim*, 240-243, 244, 245, 766-767
    verbally, 238-240, 243-244
  and homosexuality, 670-672
  and mandatory obligation, 175-177, 224-225, 226-227, 234, 271n260, 279
    mitzvah versus obligation, 180nn39-40, 181, 215-216, 310-311
    and miscarriages and stillbirth, 368, 370
    and saving scholars, 299-300
    in organ donations, 291-292, 296-297, 315-316, 317, 318
    self-jeopardy, 263-265, 275, 286-288, 293, 294, 296, 795-796, 304-305. SEE ALSO UNDER Jewish law concepts: *lifnim meshurat ha-din; lo ta'amod*
  and negative *mitzvot*, 217, 218, 219, 228, 230nn131-134, 231-232, 235
    in organ donations, 215-222, 230, 245-246, 318
  and procreation, 462-463n2, 478, 545-546
  SEE ALSO *Pikuah nefesh*
Olam haBa. SEE UNDER Jewish law concepts
Oppenheim, David, 283
Orenstein, Debra, 373n7, 773n1
Organ and tissue donations
  autopsies. SEE Death
  candidates for, 179-181, 186-187, 191
  determination of death. SEE Death
  emotional/psychological considerations, 180, 181, 184, 185-187, 219
  experimental procedures, 195-196, 207, 214
  and issues of danger. SEE ALSO Danger
    ben Peturah dispute. SEE UNDER ben Peturah
    to donor, 212-213, 215, 220, 307-308, 311, 315, 317. SEE ALSO monetary compensation
    halakhah on self-injury, 246-249, 250-254, 256-257, 290n321, 309

    summary of sources on, 304-305
    halakhic analysis on. SEE UNDER Radbaz
    to patient, 195, 196
  lifnim meshurat ha-din, discussion of, 222-246, 255
    sources on. SEE UNDER Jewish law concepts
  lo ta'amod al dam rai-ekha. SEE UNDER Jewish law concepts
  money or compensation, 249-250, 252-255, 256, 288, 309, 310, 312nn386-388, 313-314
  need issues, 213-214, 215, 252-253, 256, 308
  obligation. SEE Obligation
  pain, 213, 249, 250-251, 254, 267n249, 303n361
  pikuah nefesh. SEE *Pikuah nefesh*
  prisoners, 317-318
  responsa
    on obligation to preserve life and post-mortem donations, 175-190
    burial of organs, 178
    conclusion and vote, 175, 189-190, 191
    donation card format and pamphlet, 191-193
    kevod hamet, 177-178, 183-185, 190, 191, 192
    objections to obligation requirement, 177-179, 181-182
    post-mortem transplants, 103-104, 178n20, 179, 181-182
    specific procedures, 188-189
  on organ donations, 194-318
    Animal organs, use of, 208-211
      conclusion and vote, 208, 211
      experimental procedures, 208, 211n68, 317
      heart transplants, 210-211
      porcine parts, 209, 209n62, 211, 211n66
      primacy of human life, 208-209
      tsaar baale hayyim, 208, 209
      websites, 211n67
      xenografts, 211
    Artificial limbs, use of, 194-207
      conclusion and vote, 194, 207
      heart transplants, 195-201, 203, 204, 205-207
      porcine parts, 195n2
      resurrections, 199-200, 201, 202n28, 203, 204
      types, 195
    Blood and bone marrow, use of, 212-256
      conclusion and vote, 212, 255-256. SEE ALSO Blood banks and storage, 215, 215n80, 246, 248-249, 252-253, 255, 309
    Kidneys and livers, use of, 256-318
      conclusion and vote, 256, 318
      transplants and donations, 212, 220, 221n107, 254, 306-307, 309n381, 310-312, 314, 315
      dialysis. SEE experimental procedures
      ovaries and sperm, 212n69
  Shabbat and, 254-255, 256, 271, 271n260, 279, 285-288, 289, 291
Organizations, 333-334, 420. SEE ALSO Community; *K'lal Yisrael*
Orthodoxy, 183, 469n21, 522, 564, 575, 709, 779n21
  abortion, 516
  artificial insemination, 472, 476
  in vitro fertilization, 521n47
  surrogacy, 530n1

mamzerut, 564, 572, 573, 589
  SEE UNDER INDIVIDUAL RESPONSA
Oshaya the Elder, 454
Oshry, Ephraim, 122-123, 177, 382-383, 383n14, 564-565, 573
Ostow, Mortimer, 645n110, 667

P'sukei di-zimra. SEE Liturgy
Pain and suffering, 213n72
  community health care and, 327, 399
  danger and self-jeopardy, 267, 267n249, 282, 303n361
  nursing mother, 280-281
  and suicide, 382, 383, 399
  terminal illness, 385, 386, 391
  SEE ALSO Circumcision; Euthanasia
Palagi, Haim, 400
Paley, Charles, 348n2, 350n10, 371n5, 375n11
Pappo, Eliezer (*Pele Yo'etz*), 788n56
Parent and child, 414, 485-486, 585
  and family violence, 782-789, 804
  and homosexuality, 658, 660, 684
  honoring parents, 316n398, 484n60, 506n106, 577-578, 720, 785-788, 804
  in-law, 238, 251, 501, 501n100, 502, 507
  obligations towards, 303, 483nn59-60, 542n77, 784, 787
  and organ donations, 315-316
  SEE ALSO Children; Family violence
Passover. SEE *Pesah*
Patients, 323, 327
  terminally ill, 385-386, 391, 392-395, 396, 399
  SEE ALSO Health care; Suicide
Patriarchs, 122, 736
  and children's lineage, 480, 481n51
  and procreation, 462n2, 464, 496, 535-536, 538
  and surrogacy, 536n40, n42, 537n53
Patrilineage, 613n1, 691
Payer, Lynn, 391n39
Peck, M. Scott, 683
Perez ben Elijah of Corbeil, 466, 778, 779, 781
Peretz, Rabbi, 467n15, 475n37
Peri Hadash (Hezekiah Da Silva), 46
Persecutions, 176n9
Pesah, 51, 80, 99, 100, 167, 216, 217
  responsa
    conclusions and votes, 71, 74, 75, 77
    on canned tuna fish, 75-77
      batul ba-shishim, 76, 77
      kashrut concerns, 76-77
      process and regulations, 75-76
    on starting on Saturday night, 71-74
      customs and practices, 72, 73-74
      matzah or *hallah*, 72, 73-74
      previous CJLS decisions, 71n1
      Shabbat meals, 72-73, 74
      siyyum bekhor and *seudah*, 71
      synagogue preparations, 72
Philo, 787
Phoebus, Samuel (Bet Shmuel), 281-282
Pichnik, Aron, 18-19, 20
Pidyon HaBen, 163-164, 165, 369, 607

responsa on caesarean births and delay of, 166-170, 171-174
  birth type (*peter rehem*), 142n16, 164, 172-173, 174
  as a business arrangement, 167
  conclusions and votes, 166, 169-170, 171, 174
  Shabbat and *Yom Tov*, 167-168, 169
  time factors, 166-169
  SEE ALSO *Kohen, kohanim*
Pidyon HaBen k'Hilkhato. SEE Oberlander, Gedalya
Pikuah nefesh
  and *hasid shoteh*, 289-290
  and infertility, 470n22
  mitzvah versus obligation, 181-182, 214, 220-221
  and organ donations, 309, 344
  post-mortem donations as, 181-182, 188, 189-190
  precedence over other obligations, 175-178, 178n23, 180n40, 192, 252n196, 274-275, 555, 802n96, 803
    exceptions to, 796, 798
    over clergy/privacy privilege, 800n91
  in self-jeopardy, 271, 274-275, 282
  and *Shabbat*, 255, 256, 260, 279, 285-288, 343, 349
  SEE ALSO Danger; Organ donations
Pineas, Rabbi, 566
Pinhas ben Elazar, 415, 419, 426
Pinhas ben Ya'ir, 620
Pithei T'shuvah, 419, 482n57, 502n104, 561, 572-573
Plants. SEE Genetic engineering
Plato, 631, 635
Plaut, Gunther, 537n50
Plotkin, Paul, 112-114, 400-402, 403-404, 407, 474n36, 475n37
Plotzki, Meir Dan (*Klei Hemdah*), 275-276, 276n278
P'nei Moshe, 32-33n17, 262
Polygamy, 498n94, 537-538, 539-540, 546n101, 622, 623, 749, 781
Pomeroy, W.B., 632
Porath, Tzvi, 603n4
Posner, Raphael, 81n1
Prager, Dennis, 634n89
Prayer, 24n5, 360, 361, 362, 394, 602-603
  SEE ALSO Liturgy; Miscarriage; Synagogue
Pregnancy. SEE RELATED TOPICS
Preuss, J., 466n12
Prisoners, 317-318
Pritchard, James, 537n50
Prohibitions. SEE Homosexuality
Prophets, 761-762, 762n6, 763, 763n12, 764
Prostitution. SEE Surrogacy
Prouser, Joseph H., 175-190, 191, 192, 344
Punishment, 287, 774n4
  in family violence issues, 778-779, 780, 782-785
  and homosexuality, 617n17, n20, 618, 618n25, 619

Ra'avan, 230n131, n132, 231, 244
Ra'avia, 227, 227nn124-125, 230, 230nn131-132, 231, 232
Raba of Parzikia, 113n3
Rabbah, 129, 201, 581,590
Rabbah bar bar Hannah, 225-226, 228, 229
Rabban Gamaliel, 82, 348n2, 569-570, 577n118, 761, 762, 765, 768

Rabban Simeon ben Gamaliel (*Rashbag*), 110, 349n7, 350-352, 352n16, 356, 441-442, 742
Rabbenu Geshom (*M'Or Hagolah*), 147n5, 537-538, 749-750
  and family violence, 770, 780-781, 797n83
Rabbenu Hananel, 236-237, 245
Rabbenu Nissim of Gerondi (*Ran*), 25, 700, 777
  and burials, 421, 424
  and divorce, 744-745, 746, 749
  and performance of *mitzvot*, 216-217, 219
  on self-injury and self-endangerment, 248, 270-271
Rabbenu Peretz, 741, 743n4
Rabbenu Tam, 4, 5, 6, 238, 539n66, 744, 770-771, 779, 788n54, 797n83
Rabbenu Yehuda, 5, 6
Rabbenu Yeruham, 228, 229, 230, 234, 244
Rabbenu Yonah ben Avraham of Gerona, 452
Rabbinical Assembly
  civil marriages, 753-754, 755
  intermarriage, 611
  proceedings of. SEE IN INDIVIDUAL RESPONSA
  rabbinic letter on human intimacy, 782
  resolutions
    on homosexuality, 612, 664-665, 668, 673-674, 692n2, 693, 704, 707, 708, 718
    on organ and tissue donation, 190n107
  responsa
    on artificial insemination, 508n110
    on homosexuality and placement, 719, 722-723, 724-725, 726-727, 728-729
    violations of *halakhah* and standards, 726
    on legal document language requirements, 730-740
      Aramaic required phrases. SEE UNDER Aramaic language
      bet din, 730-732, 733-735, 737, 738, 739
      and certification, 730-731, 733-736
      conclusion and vote, 730, 739-740
      Conservative legal documents, 738-739
      types of rabbinic documents, 737-738
  SEE ALSO Committee on Jewish Law and Standards; Conservative Judaism
Rabbis
  clergy/client privilege, 799-800, 811-814
  SEE ALSO Mara d'atra
Rabinovitch, Isaac Jacob (Ponivicher Iluy), 132-133, 134, 136
Rabinowicz, H., 454
Rabinowitz, Mayer E., 603n2, 810n115
  generally, 385n26, 417n23
  responsa
    on homosexuality, 686-690
    on *kashrut*, 75-77, 95n2, 100n6
    on *kohanim*, 9-12, 31n14, 42, 594
    on marriage renewal ceremonies, 751-754, 755, 756
Radbaz (David ibn Zimra), 84-85, 88, 780
  responsa on danger, 285-289, 290, 290n321, 291, 292-296, 297, 298, 299, 305
RaH. SEE Rav Kahana
Ramah, 247, 247n179, 249, 252
Ran. SEE Rabbenu Nissim
Rape, 350, 807-808. SEE ALSO Family violence

Rashba, 381n8, 596, 694n17, 744, 746, 777, 780
Rashbam (Samuel ben Meir), 11, 465n10, 744
Rashi, 10, 106n15, 140, 147n5, 320n1
  on burials, 421, 422
  performance of *mitzvot*, 216n83, 225
Raskas, Bernard, 156n11
Rav, 3, 4, 129, 149, 225-226, 228, 300, 616, 618n25, 743, 744, 745, 792n67
Rav Ashi, 4, 113n3, 241-242, 243, 283n303, 732
Rav Assi, 17, 126
Rav Hisda, 581, 595
Rav Huna, 17, 340, 618, 622
Rav Gidal, 353n20
Rav Kahana, 105, 237, 393, 442
Rav Nahman, 231, 232
Rav Nahman bar Yitzhak, 731-732
Rav Nathan bar Ami, 217, 218
Rav Papa, 222, 415, 419, 426, 795n73
Rav Yehuda, 3-4, 224, 230, 231, 232, 573n98
Rav Yochanan, 340
Rav Yosef, 226, 227
Rava, 353n20, 573n98, 654
  on homosexuality, 618, 624n49, 654, 665n163, 698, 699
  and performance of *mitzvot*, 217, 218, 231, 232
Ravad (Abraham ben David), 630n73
Ravina, 748
Recanati, Menahem, 285-286, 287, 291, 305
Reconstructionist movement, 564, 572, 700, 720n1
Red heifer, 105n12, 583, 584
Redemption, 163, 164, 166, 167, 171-172
  SEE ALSO Jewish law concepts: captivity; *Pidyon HaBen*
Reform movement, 405, 424, 425, 564, 572, 589, 705, 779n21
  responsa, 119n23, 142n17, 161n20, 388n32, 406n17, 514n15, 530n1, 695
Regenstein, Carrie, 100n7
Regenstein, Joe, 93n1, 94, 96, 100n7, 103n7
Reicher, Jacob (*Shevut Ya'akov*), 239-240, 245
Reisner, Avram Israel
  on *aliyot*, 21-35, 40-41
  on births and babies, 347-356, 370-371, 448n13, 450-451
  on conversion and children, 145n26, 483n59, 555n17
  generally, 12n16, 144n25, 145n28, 508n112, 509n114, 525n63, 557n21
  on *kashrut*, 101-111
  regarding care of terminally ill, 183n58, 352n17, 385n25, 397, 398-399, 787n51
  regarding homosexuality, 714-717
Relationships. SEE Homosexuality; Marriage
Rema (Moses Isserles), 6-7, 245, 433, 456, 568, 572n95, 750
  aliyot, 24, 41
  family violence, 777, 781
  fish and meat, 112, 113, 113n3
  hazak hazak, 45, 46
  language in legal documents, 733, 739
Rembaum, Joel E., 431-438, 811n116
Repentance. SEE Sin
Resh Lakish, 24n6, 432, 579, 580

danger and self-jeopardy, 262-263, 264-265, 271, 291
  hiyyuv or piety, 237, 278, 279, 283, 301
Resurrection. SEE UNDER Organ donations
Reuven ben Strobilus, 301-302, 302nn358-359
Revelation, 575, 716. SEE ALSO God
Ri (Isaac ben Samuel of Dampierre), 5, 237n152, 249, 250, 279n291
Ribash (Isaac ben Sheshet Perfet), 26, 26n7, 33n17, 542n77, 699n17, 744
Riemer, Jack, 187n84, 395n47
Rif, 257, 261, 744, 746. SEE ALSO SOURCE INDEX
Rishonim, 5, 41, 263, 264, 626, 654n142, 714
Ritba (*Yom Tov* ben Avraham Ishbili), 581n145
Rose, Andy, 653n135
Rosen, James S., 337-346
Rosenbaum, Irving J., 381n8, 382n13
Rosett, Arthur, 66, 67, 68, 68nn5-6, 509n114, 775n7, 779n21
Rosh (Rabbenu Asher), 10, 18, 51, 257, 261, 267, 295, 539n66
  burial, 382n12, 414, 456
  lifnim meshurat ha-din, 228-229, 230-232, 234, 239-240, 244-245
  pidyon haBen, 167, 168
Rosh Hodesh. SEE Torah, reading of
Rosner, Fred, 103n6, 108n21, 183n60
  artificial insemination and fertilization, 465n11, 470, 471n26, 472n28, 473n31, 497n87, 517n31-32, 519n40, 520
  health care and obligation, 326n25, 328n28
  surrogacy, 530n1, 535n30, 551n2
Rotenberg, Mark, 774n1
Roth, Joel, 3n1, 68, 127-128, 148n9
  generally, 145n28, 158n14, 509n114, 525n63, 557n21
  on halakhic process, 577, 579, 597, 635n92, 646n112, 695, 695n7, 696, 720
  on homosexuality, 613-675
    references to views on, 686-687, 691, 693-694, 696, 698n14, 701, 702, 708, 710, 712, 726
    in the Conservative movement, 703, 704, 705, 707, 709, 725
  on intermarriage and ritual ceremonies, 605, 607, 610-611
  on *kashrut*, 93-97
  on *kohen*, kohanim, 10, 14n8, 31n15, 32, 42
  on organ donations and transplants, 194-207, 208-211, 212-318
  on *Shabbat*, 53-54, 62, 63
Routtenberg, Max, 420, 609, 610
Rozanes, Judah (*Mishneh Le-Melech*), 465n10, 473n31
Rudavsky, Tamar, 776n10
Ruse, Michael, 625n55, 632n80, 636, 646nn114-115, 648-649, 650-651, 655nn144-146, 656n148, 658-659
Russ, Ian, 774n1, 791n63
Russell, Louise, 331n41
Russia, 121

Sa'adia Gaon, 385n22
Sacks, Andy, 123n13
Sacrifice. SEE Temple

Samuel, 129, 149, 465, 548, 569n73, 732, 779
  danger and self-jeopardy, 260, 276, 277, 279
  divorce, 236n151
  homosexuality, 616, 618n25
  lifnim meshurat ha-din, 224, 230, 231, 232
Samuel bar Avudma, 29n10
Samuel bar Nahmani, 29n10, 482
Samuel ben Uri, 473n31
Samuel, Mar. SEE Samuel
Sanhedrin, 403, 582
Sarna, Nahum, 537n49
Sasso, Sandy Eisenberg, 373n7
Schachter, Melech, 479n47
Schereschewsky, Ben-Zion, 483n60
Schick, Moses. SEE Maharam Schick
Schick, Solomon, 465n10
Schiff, Daniel, 514n15, 517n27
Schochetman, Eliav, 802n95
Schwadron, Shalom Mordecai. SEE *Maharsham*
Schwartz, Earl, 387n29
Scott, Russell, 178nn21-22
Sebert, Laurence, 165
Sefer Hasidim, 301-302, 302n360, 303, 305, 314n393, 316, 482n57
Sefer Ra'avan (*Zofenat Pa'ane'ah*), 230n131, 242n167
Sefer Shmirat Shabbat k'Hilkhatah. SEE Neuwirth, J.I.
Sefer Mitzvot Hagadol (*Semag*), 279n291
Segal, Jacob Moellin. SEE *Maharil*
Segal, Jack, 417n23
Self-injury, 246-250, 251, 252, 253, 254, 381, 381n5, 543n85. SEE ALSO Danger; Organ donations; Suicide
Sephardim, 84-85, 169n3, 378, 539nn65-66
  and family violence, 780, 788, 799
  mourning customs of, 453, 455, 456
  Torah customs of, 43, 44, 45, 48-49
Septuagint, 559
Sereifa, 14
Sermons, 87
Sex. SEE WITHIN INTERRRELATED SUBJECT HEADINGS
Shabbat, 709
  and *aliyot*. SEE *Aliyot*
  behavior on, 128-129, 149, 184, 400, 403, 442, 576, 580, 581, 666-667, 726, 727
  and *birkat kohanim*, 14, 14n4
  and *brit milah*. SEE Circumcision
  and cooking, 107n17
  and driving, 177
  and *pikuah nefesh*, 343, 349, 349n6, 350, 355n25.
    SEE ALSO Organ donations
  responsa
    on greeting mourners on *Shabbat*, 452-458
      conclusion and vote, 452, 458
      differences between mourning and greeting, 455-456
      greeting mourners, 454-457
      mitzvah on consoling, 452-453, 456-457
      public mourning on *Shabbat*, 453-454
      time during service, 452, 458
    on leasing businesses for *Shabbat*
      addendum, 62-63
      as closed corporation, 61, 63

862

conclusions and votes, 53, 54, 58, 61-62, 64
concurring opinion, 64-70
kablanut (hiring a non-Jew), 54, 67, 67n4
loss of income, 54, 58
previous responsa, 58-59
Shabbat lease forms and analysis, 55-57, 59-61, 62-63, 66-67, 69-70
stock ownership and, 61
work and non-Jew, 54, 60, 61, 62-63, 64, 67, 68
and *Yom Tov*, 53-54, 58-63, 64-70
Shafran, Y.B., 517
Shakh (Shabbetai b. Meir ha-Kohen), 104n8, 151
Shalev, Carmel, 543n86, 544, 547
Shaliah tzibur, 11, 14, 38, 82, 83, 84-85, 88, 603. SEE ALSO *Hazzan*
Shame. SEE UNDER Family violence
Shammai, 455, 462n2, 463n2, 511n1, 535, 535n33
Shannon, Thomas A., 512n7, 520n42
Shapira, Eliyahu (Eliya Rabbah), 261, 261n232
Shapira, Zevi Hirsch, of Munkacz, 561
Shapiro, Morris, 472, 472n30, 478n44, 696n8, 720
Shapiro, Moses Aryeh Leib, 473n31
Shatnez. SEE Genetic engineering
Shema, 14n3, 81, 150, 581, 761, 801
Shemini Atzeret, 48
Shikli, Etan, 431n1, 432, 433nn12-13
Shimon ben Elazar, 209
Shimon ben Lakish. SEE Resh Lakish
Shimon bar Yochai, 44, 716
Shimon the Righteous, 579
Shivah. SEE UNDER RELATED TOPICS; Mourning
Shneur Zalman of Lyady, 262
Shoah. SEE Holocaust
Shofar, 87, 88, 580
Shomer, 62
Shulevitz, Marion, 435-436, 436n436
Shulkhan Arukh, 7, 18, 51, 257, 282
Siegel, Seymour, 108n22, 183, 530n1, 603
and birth surrogates, 540n70, 547n110
mamzerut, 564, 575n107, 576
Sifra, 617, 618
Siftei Kohen. SEE *Shakh*
Sigal, Philip, 603
Silberg, Moshe, 570, 571-572
Silver, Eric, 123n13
Simeon, Rabbi, 116, 128, 129, 172
Simeon ben Azzai, 559-560
Simeon ben Judah, 116
Simeon ben Teman, 559, 560
Simha b. Samuel (*Or Zaruah*), 778, 779, 780, 781, 813
Simhat bat. SEE UNDER Women
Simhat Torah, 17, 22n1, 26-27, 47, 48, 158
Simons, Marlise, 108
Sin and repentance, 147, 147n5, 321, 402, 405, 694
in assisted suicide cases, 383-384
in family violence issues, 777, 808-810, 813, 814
Sinai. SEE Revelation
Sirillo, Solomon, 32-33n17
Sirkes, Joel. SEE *Bah*
Skin disease, 276, 277
Skin grafting. SEE Organ donations

Skolnik, Gerald, 30n12, 163-165, 776n9
Slander. SEE Jewish law concepts: *lashon ha-ra*
Slavery, 118, 139, 432, 545, 560n6, 569n76
mamzerut, 560n6, 561nn15-16
shifhah. SEE UNDER Matriarchs
Slutz, Meir, 271, 271nn260-262
Small, Meredith F., 471n27
Smith, Lee, 507n107
Smoking, 108, 108n22
Society. SEE Community
Sodom and Gomorrah. SEE Homosexuality
Sofer-Abraham, Abraham. SEE *Nishmat Avraham*
Sofer, Moses. SEE *Pithei T'shuvah*
Solomon ben Isaac. SEE Rashi
Solomon Schechter Day Schools, 608-611
Soloveitchik, Joseph B., 187n84, 479, 540n69
Soloveitchik, Moses, 141, 141n12
Sotah, 583, 583n150, 584
Soul, 184, 185, 215, 376n12, 387
Spector, Isaac Elkhanan, 115, 419
Speiser, Ephraim A., 537n51
Spero, Moshe Halevi, 385n26, 617n17, 619-620, 620n36
Spiegel, Yaakov S., 43n1
Spirituality, 7-8, 87-88, 813-814
Spitz, Elie Kaplan
generally, 145n28, 395n48, 491n81, 525n63, 557n21
mamzerut, 558-586, 587, 587n3, 588, 589, 591
surrogacy, 137n1, 138, 143-145, 526-528, 529-550, 552-553, 554n12, 556, 557n20
Stampfer, Nathaniel, 395n47
Starzl, Thomas, 179-180
Steinberg, Abraham
on heart and organ transplants, 194n1, 196, 220, 213n71, 313
newborn babies, 351n13, n15, 352n17, 355n25, n27
Steptoe, Patrick, 511
Sternbuch, Moshe, 141n11, 143, 254, 311n385, 312, 315-317
Stiller, Calvin, 185n74, 186, 187n86, 190n103, n105
Stillbirth. SEE UNDER Miscarriage
Stock ownership. SEE *Shabbat*
Stockler, Julie, 464, 464n6
Suffering. SEE Pain and suffering; AND RELATED TOPICS
Suicide, 327, 684
responsum on assisted suicide, 379-397
aides and assisting, 382, 383-386
burial of, 381, 381n8, 382, 382n12, 383, 585n152
CJLS statement and resolution on, 398-399
conclusion and vote, 379, 397
euthanasia, 384-385, 386-389, 392, 396
halakhah and 380-385, 385n25, 386-387
martyrdom and conversion, 381-383
medical and legal background, 379-380, 385, 386-387, 387n27, 390-393
pain and suffering, 382, 383, 385, 386, 391, 391n40, 396
society demographics, 389-391, 395-396, 399
SEE ALSO Murder; Patients
Surrogacy
background information, 529-533

863

ethics and morality of, 533, 540, 542-544
  custody question, 527-528
  family integrity, 547-548
genetics, 533, 540, 542
halakhah on, 139-143, 530n1, 535-539, 551-552n2, 556
  obligation to procreate, 545-546
responsa on birth surrogates, 526-528, 529-550
  gestation and birth, 138, 139, 142-143, 531, 542, 552-553, 553-554n10
responsa on children's religious status and, 137-145, 551-557
  analysis and guidelines of, 527-528
  CJLS previous decisions, 529-530
  conclusions and votes, 137, 145, 526, 529, 548-549, 550, 551, 557
  Jewish identity of child, 553n6, 556, 557
  maternal identity, 137-145, 553, 556, 559n2
    conversion of, 139-140, 141
  tumat ac'um, 141
  risks and exploitation, 533, 542-546, 554n13, 555-557
  science as God's partner, 540-541
  statistics, 530-531, 532n20, 533
  surrogacy agreements, 531-532, 534, 537n53, 538-540, 543n86, 546-547, 554n11, 556-557, 630n70
    monetary issues, 527, 530, 531, 531n13, 532, 542-544, 554n11, 557
  SEE ALSO Adoption; America; Matriarchs; *Yibum*
Synagogue
  programs, 809-810, 812, 813
  responsa on times of *Minhah* and *Ma'ariv*, 50-52
    conclusion and vote, 50, 52
    time frames, 51
    types of *minhah*, 51-52
  concurring opinion on homosexuals in synagogues, 612, 688, 689, 690, 693, 707, 713-714
  SEE ALSO Burial; Intermarriage; Liturgy; Torah, reading of; *Yom Kippur*

Ta-Shma, Israel M., 47
Tabernacle, 171
Taharat ha-mishpaha. SEE Family purity
Takkanah. SEE UNDER Jewish law
Talitot, 3, 5, 581, 681. SEE ALSO *Tzitzit*
Talmud
  Babylonian (*Bavli*), 24, 203n33, 221, 245
  El-Am, 154n6
  Palestinian (*Yerushalmi*) 23n4,n5, 29n10, 30, 41, 202, 257, 260, 260n228, 264, 264n239, 266, 291, 293, 295, 301, 305, 764
  differences between *Bavli* and *Yerushalmi*, 203, 258, 258n219, 259, 261, 265, 268, 271, 272-273, 274, 279, 282, 283-284, 285, 304, 442, 562
Tam, Jacob ben Meir. SEE Rabbenu Tam
Tannaim, 579
Tannen, Deborah, 506n106, 698-699
Tarfon, Rabbi, 265-266, 569, 577
Tattooing, 561
  responsum on tattooing and body piercing, 115-120
  b'tzelem elokim. SEE Jewish law concepts
  body and ear piercing, 118-120

children's decorations, hand stamps, 117-118
conclusion and vote, 115, 120
halakhah on, 115-117
on Torah scrolls, 155, 15n10
Tay-Sachs disease, 516n24
Taz, 17, 466n14, 475
Tefilin, 3, 4
Teitelbaum, Moses, 227n121
Teitelbaum, Yoel, 467, 467n15, n17
Temple, destruction of, 10, 11, 13, 428, 456, 579, 582
  rituals, 11-12, 13, 14-15, 15n10, 149, 560, 596
Ten Commandments, 143, 401, 566, 580, 787
Tendler, Moshe, 123n13, 182n49, 190n104, 530n1, 547n113
  on brain death, 183, 183nn60-61, 184, 184n70
Terumah, 31n15, 748
Teshuvah. SEE Sin and repentance
Tigay, Jeffrey, 501n97
To-evah. SEE Homosexuality
Toledano, Jacob Moses, 46
Toledano, Pinehas Barukh, 273n268, 276n278, 283, 295
Tong, Rosemarie, 138, 553
Torah teachings, 716-717, 790, 790n59
  Conservative Judaism's view on, 575, 585-586
  SEE ALSO UNDER INDIVIDUAL TOPICS
Torah, reading of, 36, 156
  aliyot. SEE *Aliyot*
  haftarot in, 21. SEE ALSO UNDER *Aliyot*
  holidays. SEE ALSO *Simhat Torah*
  honor to the Torah, 24, 28, 29n10, 37, 153-154
  institution of Torah reader, 23n4, 37-38, 41, 43-44, 45
  kohen aliyah. SEE Kohen, *kohanim*
  origins of, 36-37
  triennial cycle, 22n1, 47
    responsum on *hazak hazak v'nithazak*, 43-49
    conclusion and vote, 43, 49
Torah scrolls, 387, 536
  responsa on displaying pasul torah, 153-162
    conclusion and vote, 153, 161-162
    as exhibit in museums, 159-160, 161
    Holocaust scrolls, 155-156, 156n11, 160, 161
    kavod to a Torah, 153-154, 160, 161
    Memorial Scrolls Trust, 155-156, 156n11
    moving of, 154, 154n6
    ownership or selling of, 154, 159
    pasul torahs, 154-155, 156, 157-158, 160, 161, 162
    practice of the people, 160
Tosafot, tosalists, 4, 10, 242-243, 267, 570, 779
  and coercion, 218n92
  and viability of newborn life, 352n16
Tosfaa, Rabbi, 567
Treif, 79, 80
Treifah, 178n23, 197, 197n11, 354n25
Triennial cycle. SEE Torah, reading of
Tucazinsky, Jehiel (Gesher Ha-Hayyim), 185n72, 359n8, n10, 361nn15-17, 382n12, 387-388, 456-457
Tuchinski, Jehiel. SEE Tucazinsky, Jehiel
Tucker, Gordon, 385n25, 483n58, 575, 575n107, 719
  responsa on CJLS, 759-772
Tuna fish. SEE UNDER *Pesah*

Tur (Jacob ben Asher), 18, 24, 25, 261, 272, 272n264, 295, 733
Turei Zahav. SEE Taz
Trumat HaDeshen, 209, 261n230, 454, 777
Truman, Harry S., 159, 159nn18-19
Tzalach, Yichya ben Joseph, of Sana (Maharitz), 456
Tzitz Eliezer. SEE Waldenberg, Eliezer
Tzitzit, 581
   responsum on women and making tzitzit knots, 3-8
      conclusion and vote, 3, 8
      non-Jews, 3-4, 5
      programs on, 7-8

Ulla, 32-33n17, 33, 621, 622
Union of Concerned Scientists, 108
United Network of Organ Sharing (UNOS). SEE Organ donations
United States. SEE America
United Synagogue of America, 406n18, 610, 612, 704, 707, 719, 729, 760
Untermann, Isser Yehudah, 103, 177, 178-179, 181, 182, 184, 185
Urim ve-Tumim. SEE Eyebeschuetz, Jonathan
Usha, 238
Uziel, Ben Zion Meir Hai (Mishpetai Uziel), 178n23, 475n37, 568

Va'ad Hakavod. SEE Rabbinical Assembly
Veltman, Larry, 123n12
Vida, Elijah, 677n1
Vows, 576, 576nn114-115. SEE ALSO IN RELATED TOPICS

Wagner, Joseph, 420
Waldenberg, Eliezer
   artificial insemination, 467n15, 472n28, 475, 475n37
   babies, 355n25
   blood and organ donations, 214-215, 219, 221, 222
   hasid shoteh, 289n320, 290, 313n392
   health care, 330
   in vitro fertilization, 513, 513n10, 514n13
   self-endangerment, 284-285, 302n360, 303
Walkin, Aharon, 433n18, 434, 472n28, 475n37
War, 255
Warhaftig, Itamar, 317n401, 318
Wasserman, Moshe, 255n211
Waxman, Mordecai, 688n14
Weber, Sally, 774n1
Weil, Jacob ben Judah, 799n88
Weinberg, Jehiel Jacob, 123n8, 134-135, 264-265, 266n247, 273
Weiss, Abner, 412
Weiss, Isaac Jacob. SEE Minhat Yitzhak
Weiss, Loel, 603
Weiss-Halivni, David, 120, 574
Weizmann, Chaim, 159
Weizmann Institute, 111
Welner, Moshe Dov, 219n95
Wines, 102n4
Winkler, Mordekhai, 331n39
Wolfe, Carol, 543
Wolff, Eliezer, 102n4

Wolowelsky, Joel B., 516n25, 517n29,n32, 521n47
Women, 246, 269, 411, 620n35, 645n111, 698, 706
   and conversion, 133, 432n3
   and divorce, 201-202, 202n28, 235, 236-237, 442n4, 748
   as a holeh in miscarriages, 359-360
   infertility, 462-465, 536, 536nn60-62, 537-538. SEE Artificial insemination
   nursing mother, 280-283
   and physiology of, 646-647, 657n149, 701
   responsa
      on bat kohen and priestly blessing, 9-12. SEE ALSO Kohen, kohanim
      on making tzitzit knots, 3-8
      talit and tefilin. SEE tzitzit
      on simhat bat for first-born girls, 163-165, 607
         conclusion and vote, 163, 164, 165
   SEE ALSO Family violence; Homosexuality; Mamzerut; Marriage
World Council of Synagogues, 609-610
World Health Organization, 337n2
Worship. SEE Kohen, kohanim; Liturgy; Synagogue
Wozner, Samuel ha-Levi (Shevet ha-Levi), 219-220
Wurzburger, Walter, 653n139

Ya'avetz, Moshe Ze'ev. SEE Agudat Ezov
Yad Eliahu, 318
   on ben Peturah dispute, 258-259, 259n221, 260, 261
   danger and self-jeopardy for saving another, 265-268, 298-299, 305
   on self-endangerment in general, 262, 263, 302-304
Yad Ramah, 619n30
Yaffe, Mordecai, 27n8
Yahrzeit, 16, 52, 374-375
Yeh, John and Molly Uline, 488
Yehuda haNasi, 460n6, 580
Yehudah, Rabbi, 51, 52, 107n17, 128, 134, 569n73
Yehudah ben Baba, 302n359
Yehudai Gaon, 777
Yibum (levirate marriage), 139-140, 352n16, 405, 433, 561, 748
   and artificial insemination, 496n86, 538, 539nn65-66, 539-540
   and death, 202, 203n33
   and procreation, 480, 480n48
   and surrogacy, 550, 555
Yihud (living together), 483n58
Yisraeli, Shaul, 221n107, 222, 244, 245, 273n268, 297n344, 313
Yochanan, Rabbi, 134, 353n20, 385, 432, 435, 579, 665n164
   lifnim meshurat ha-din, 226, 228, 237-238, 239
Yochanan ben Beroka, 462n2, 546n101
Yochanan ben Zakkai, 105n12, 583, 588
Yochanan haSandlar, 107n17
Yom Hashoah. SEE Holocaust
Yom Kippur, 39, 84, 103, 159, 176, 697, 715
   SEE ALSO High Holy Days
Yom Tov. SEE Holidays; Shabbat; Torah, reading of
Yonah, 105
Yonatan, Rabbi, 29n10, 262-263, 264, 577-578

Yosef ben Moshe (*Leket Yosher*), 454
Yosef, Ovadiah, 108n22, 122, 123, 296, 435, 513, 589-591
   danger and self-jeopardy, 264, 271, 279n291, 283, 284
Yosi, Rabbi, 29n10, 105, 110, 134, 223, 562
   danger and self-jeopardy, 276, 277, 278, 279, 280, 282
   death and resurrection, 202-203, 203n33, 204

Zeira, Rabbi, 23n5, 24n6, 26, 28, 29n10, 30, 41, 201, 731
Zelizer, Gerald L., 146-150
Zemah Zedek. SEE Krochmal, Menahem Mendel
Zemer, Moshe, 566, 571n85
Zevin, Shlomo Yosef, 251n194, 276n278
Zierlson, Yehudah Leib (*Ma'arekhei Lev*), 475n37, 600
Zilberstein, Isaac, 309, 315, 316n400, 352n16, 355n25, 516n25, 517n29
Zofenat Pa'ane'ah. SEE *Sefer Ra'avan*
Zohar, Noam, 536n1
Zorger, Moshe Ze'ev, 220, 252, 253, 254-255, 311n385, 312
Zutra, Mar, 283n304